ISSN 0749-064X

Contemporary Theatre, Film and Television

A Biographical Guide Featuring Performers,
Directors, Writers, Producers, Designers, Managers,
Choreographers, Technicians, Composers, Executives,
Dancers, and Critics in the United States, Canada,
Great Britain and the World

Thomas Riggs, Editor

Volume 104

GALE
CENGAGE Learning™

Detroit • New York • San Francisco • New Haven, Conn • Waterville, Maine • London

Contemporary Theatre, Film & Television, Vol. 104

Editor: Thomas Riggs

CTFT Staff: Mariko Fujinaka, Annette Petrusso, Susan Risland, Jacob Schmitt, Lisa Sherwin, Arlene True, Andrea Votava, Pam Zuber

Project Editors: Laura Avery, Tracie Ratiner

Editorial Support Services: Natasha Mikheyeva

Composition and Electronic Capture: Gary Oudersluys

Manufacturing: Drew Kalasky

For product information and technology assistance, contact us at
Gale Customer Support, 1-800-877-4253.
For permission to use material from this text or product,
submit all requests online at **www.cengage.com/permissions.**
Further permissions questions can be emailed to
permissionrequest@cengage.com

While every effort has been made to ensure the reliability of the information presented in this publication, Gale, a part of Cengage Learning, does not guarantee the accuracy of the data contained herein. Gale accepts no payment for listing; and inclusion in the publication of any organization, agency, institution, publication, service, or individual does not imply endorsement of the editors or publisher. Errors brought to the attention of the publisher and verified to the satisfaction of the publisher will be corrected in future editions.

EDITORIAL DATA PRIVACY POLICY. Does this publication contain information about you as an individual? If so, for more information about our editorial data privacy policies, please see our Privacy Statement at www.gale.cengage.com.

Gale
27500 Drake Rd.
Farmington Hills, MI 48331-3535

LIBRARY OF CONGRESS CATALOG CARD NUMBER 84-649371

ISBN-13: 978-1-4144-4616-5
ISBN-10: 1-4144-4616-0

ISSN: 0749-064X

This title is also available as an e-book.
ISBN-13: 978-1-4144-5724-6
ISBN-10: 1-4144-5724-3
Contact your Gale sales representative for ordering information.

Printed in the United States of America
1 2 3 4 5 6 7 14 13 12 11 10

Contents

Preface

Provides Broad, Single-Source Coverage in the Entertainment Field

Contemporary Theatre, Film and Television (CTFT) is a biographical reference series designed to provide students, educators, researchers, librarians, and general readers with information on a wide range of entertainment figures. Unlike single-volume reference works that focus on a limited number of artists or on a specific segment of the entertainment field, *CTFT* is an ongoing publication that includes entries on individuals active in the theatre, film, and television industries. Before the publication of *CTFT*, information-seekers had no choice but to consult several different sources in order to locate the in-depth biographical and credit data that makes *CTFT*'s one-stop coverage the most comprehensive available about the lives and work of performing arts professionals.

Scope

CTFT covers not only performers, directors, writers, and producers, but also behind-the-scenes specialists such as designers, managers, choreographers, technicians, composers, executives, dancers, and critics from the United States, Canada, Great Britain, and the world. With 191 entries in *CTFT 104*, the series now provides biographies on approximately 27,452 people involved in all aspects of theatre, film, and television.

CTFT gives primary emphasis to people who are currently active. New entries are prepared on major stars as well as those who are just beginning to win acclaim for their work. *CTFT* also includes entries on personalities who have died but whose work commands lasting interest.

Compilation Methods

CTFT editors identify candidates for inclusion in the series by consulting biographical dictionaries, industry directories, entertainment annuals, trade and general interest periodicals, newspapers, and online databases. Additionally, the editors of *CTFT* maintain regular contact with industry advisors and professionals who routinely suggest new candidates for inclusion in the series. Entries are compiled from published biographical sources which are believed to be reliable, but have not been verified for this edition by the listee or their agents.

Revised Entries

To ensure *CTFT*'s timeliness and comprehensiveness, entries from previous volumes, as well as from Gale's *Who's Who in the Theatre*, are updated for individuals who have been active enough to require revision of their earlier biographies. Such individuals will merit revised entries as often as there is substantial new information to provide. Obituary notices for deceased entertainment personalities already listed in *CTFT* are also published.

Accessible Format Makes Data Easy to Locate

CTFT entries, modeled after those in Gale's highly regarded *Contemporary Authors* series, are written in a clear, readable style designed to help users focus quickly on specific facts. The following is a summary of the information found in *CTFT* sketches:

- *ENTRY HEADING:* the form of the name by which the listee is best known.

- *PERSONAL:* full or original name; dates and places of birth and death; family data; colleges attended, degrees earned, and professional training; political and religious affiliations when known; avocational interests.

- *ADDRESSES:* home, office, agent, publicist and/or manager addresses.

- *CAREER:* tagline indicating principal areas of entertainment work; resume of career positions and other vocational achievements; military service.

- *MEMBER:* memberships and offices held in professional, union, civic, and social organizations.

- *AWARDS, HONORS:* theatre, film, and television awards and nominations; literary and civic awards; honorary degrees.

- *CREDITS:* comprehensive title-by-title listings of theatre, film, and television appearance and work credits, including roles and production data as well as debut and genre information.

- *RECORDINGS:* album, single song, video, and taped reading releases; recording labels and dates when available.

- *WRITINGS:* title-by-title listing of plays, screenplays, scripts, and musical compositions along with production information; books, including autobiographies, and other publications.

- *ADAPTATIONS:* a list of films, plays, and other media which have been adapted from the listee's work.

- *SIDELIGHTS:* favorite roles; portions of agent-prepared biographies or personal statements from the listee when available.

- *OTHER SOURCES:* books, periodicals, and internet sites where interviews or feature stories can be found.

Access Thousands of Entries Using *CTFT*'s Cumulative Index

Each volume of *CTFT* contains a cumulative index to the entire series. As an added feature, this index also includes references to all seventeen editions of *Who's Who in the Theatre* and to the four-volume compilation *Who Was Who in the Theatre.*

Available in Electronic Format

Online. Recent volumes of *CTFT* are available online as part of the Gale Biographies (GALBIO) database accessible through LEXIS-NEXIS. For more information, contact LEXIS-NEXIS, P.O. Box 933, Dayton, OH 45401-0933; phone (937) 865-6800, toll-free: 800-543-6862.

Suggestions Are Welcome

Contemporary Theatre, Film and Television is intended to serve as a useful reference tool for a wide audience, so comments about any aspect of this work are encouraged. Suggestions of entertainment professionals to include in future volumes are also welcome. Send comments and suggestions to: The Editor, *Contemporary Theatre, Film and Television,* Gale, 27500 Drake Rd., Farmington Hills, MI 48331-3535; or call toll-free at 1-800-877-GALE.

Contemporary Theatre, Film and Television

ACORD, Lance 1964–

PERSONAL

Born September 9, 1964, in Fresno County, CA. *Education:* Attended San Francisco Arts Institute.

Addresses: *Agent*—Dattner Dispoto and Associates, 10635 Santa Monica Blvd., Suite 165, Los Angeles, CA 90025; Creative Artists Agency, 2000 Avenue of the Stars, Los Angeles, CA 90067.

Career: Cinematographer. Park Pictures (production company), owner. Director of photography for numerous television commercials, including "Rucker Park" for Nike, "Long Run" for Adidas, and "Crazy Legs" for Levi's, "Free Throw" for ESPN.

Member: American Society of Cinematographers.

Awards, Honors: MTV Video Music Award, best cinematography, 2001, for "Weapon of Choice"; Chlotrudis Award nomination, best cinematography, Chicago Film Critics Association Award, best cinematography, and Film Award nomination, best cinematography, British Academy of Film and Television Arts, all 2004, all for *Lost in Translation;* Directors Guild of America Award nomination, outstanding directorial achievement in commercials, 2004.

CREDITS

Film Cinematographer:
Billy Nayer (animated short film), BNS Productions, 1992.
Gentle Giants (short film), Zeitgeist Films, 1995.
RoadMovie (documentary; also known as *R.E.M.: Road Movie*), Warner Bros. Records, 1996.

How They Get There (short film), Palm Pictures, 1998.
Buffalo '66, Lions Gate Films, 1998.
Free Tibet (documentary), Shooting Gallery, 1998.
Being John Malkovich, USA Films, 1999.
Eventual Wife (short film), Cinemax, 2000.
Chop Suey (documentary), Zeitgeist Films, 2001.
(And camera operator) *Southlander: Diary of a Desperate Musician* (also known as *Southlander*), Propaganda Films, 2001.
The Dangerous Lives of Altar Boys, THINKFilm, 2002.
Adaption, Sony Pictures, 2002.
(16mm film unit) *Jackass: The Movie* (also known as *Jackass*), Paramount, 2002.
(And camera operator) *Lost in Translation,* Focus Features, 2003.
Marie Antoinette, Columbia, 2006.
Where the Wild Things Are (also known as *Where the Wild Things: The IMAX Experience*), Warner Bros., 2009.
Wild in the Streets (documentary), Ocule Films, 2009.

Film Work:
Director, *Tesla: Tripping the Light Electric* (documentary), 2000.
Executive producer, *The New Tenants* (short film), Park Pictures, 2009.

Film Appearances:
(Uncredited) Himself, *Adaption,* Sony Pictures, 2002.
Collaborators (short documentary), Field Recordings, 2009.

Television Cinematographer; Specials:
Lick the Star (short film), Independent Film Channel, 1998.

Television Appearances; Episodic:
"Where the Wild Things Are," *HBO First Look,* HBO, 2009.

Also appeared in "The Dangerous Lives of Altar Boys," *Anatomy of a Scene,* Sundance Channel.

RECORDINGS

Videos; Appearances:
Lost on Location: Behind the Scenes of "Lost in Translation" (short documentary; also known as *Lost on Location*), Universal Studios Home Video, 2004.
The Difference (short documentary), Eastman Kodak Company, 2004.
The Making of "Marie Antoinette" (short film), Sony Pictures, 2007.

Videos; Work:
Cinematographer, "It's Oh So Quiet," *Bjork: Volumen* (also known as *Bjork: Greatest Hits—Volumen 1993–2003*), Warner Home Video, 1999.
Cinematographer, "Bachelorette" and "Let Forever Be," *The Work of Director Michel Gondry* (documentary), Palm Pictures, 2003.
Director, "A Change Would Do You Good," *The Very Best of Sheryl Crow: The Videos,* Universal Music & Video Distribution, 2004.
Cinematographer, "Seven Seconds," *The Work of Director Stephane Sednaoui* (documentary), Universal Music & Video Distribution, 2005.

Also director of photography for numerous music videos, including "Seven Seconds" by Neneh Cherry and Yossou N'Dour, 1994; "Crush with Eyeliner" by R.E.M., 1994; "Red Umbrella" by Kostars, 1995; "It's Oh So Quiet" by Bjork, 1995; "Car Song" by Elastica, 1995; "La, La, La" by Tranquility Bass, 1997; "Let Forever Be" by Chemical Brothers, 1999; "Weapon of Choice" by Fatboy Slim, 2001.

ALAN, Lori 1966–
    (Lori Allen)

PERSONAL

Original name, Lori Alan Denniberg; born July 18, 1966, in Potomac, MD; father, an advertising executive, actor, and voice artist; mother, an actress and voice artist. *Education:* Attended Emerson College and New York University; trained at Circle in the Square, New York City, and with Chicago City Limits, Who's on First, and Gotham City Improv; studied acting, voice, comedy, and other disciplines.

Addresses: *Agent*—Atlas Talent Agency, Inc., 15 East 32nd St., New York, NY 10016; AKA Talent Agency, 6310 San Vicente Blvd., Los Angeles, CA 90048; (voice work) Jeff Danis, Danis Panaro Nist, 9201 West Olympic Blvd., Beverly Hills, CA 90212. *Manager*—Polaris Entertainment, 9171 Wilshire Blvd., Suite 441, Beverly Hills, CA 90210.

Career: Actress, voice artist, and writer. Stand–up comedienne at Gotham City Improv (also known as Groundlings East), New York City, and other venues; performed as a solo storyteller; provided voice work for several television and radio commercials.

Member: American Federation of Television and Radio Artists (member of the board of directors of the Los Angeles chapter, beginning 2002).

Awards, Honors: Ovation Award, best ensemble performance (with others), LA Stage Alliance, 1999, for *Reefer Madness!.*

CREDITS

Television Appearances; Animated Series:
Voice of Lieutenant Felina Feral, *Swat Kats: The Radical Squadron* (also known as *Swat Kats*), syndicated, c. 1993–95.
Voice of Susan Storm "Sue" Richards/the Invisible Woman and other characters, *Fantastic Four* (also known as *Marvel Action Hour: Fantastic Four*), syndicated, 1994–96.
Voice of Brooke Lloyd and other characters, *Hey Arnold!* (also known as *Hey, Arnold!*), Nickelodeon, between 1997 and 2001.
Voice of Nurse Pitts, *The Kids from Room 402* (also known as *La classe en delire*), TeleToon and Fox, c. 1999–2001.
Voice of Diane Simmons and other characters, *Family Guy* (also known as *Padre de familia* and *Padre del familia*), Fox, 1999–2003, 2005—.
Voice of Pearl Krabs and other characters, *SpongeBob SquarePants* (also known as *SpongeBob, Spongeboy Squarepants,* and *Toon Jam*), Nickelodeon, beginning 1999.
Voice of Felicity and other characters, *3–South,* MTV, 2002–2003.
Voice of Dixie, Ivory, and other characters, *Rick & Steve the Happiest Gay Couple in All the World,* Logo, beginning 2007.

Television Appearances; Live Action Movies:
Karen Kupfer, *The Rockford Files: I Still Love L.A.,* CBS, 1994.
Estelle, "Buford's Got a Gun," *The Showtime 30–Minute Movie* (also known as *30–Minute Movie*), Showtime, 1995.

Television Appearances; Specials:
Provided the voice of Diane Simmons and other characters for animated programs related to *Family Guy.*

Television Appearances; Animated Episodes:
Voice of Cindy and loudspeaker, "Larry & Steve," *What a Cartoon!* (also known as *The Cartoon Cartoon*

Show, What a Cartoon: Larry & Steve, The What a Cartoon Show, World Premiere Toons, and *World Premiere Toons: Larry & Steve*), Cartoon Network, 1996.

Voice of Lareece and Winney, "Chicken's First Kiss/Squirt the Daisies/I. M. Weasel: I Am Ambassador," *Cow and Chicken,* Cartoon Network, 1997.

Voice of porcupine and skunk, "Enter the Daggett/Bugaboo," *The Angry Beavers,* Nickelodeon, 1997.

Voice of judge and second woman, "Me an' My Dog/Cow's Dream Catcher/I. M. Weasel: Desert Island," *Cow and Chicken,* Cartoon Network, 1998.

Voice of Sharon Stone, "Hurray for North Hollywood: Parts 1 & 2," *Animaniacs* (also known as *Animania* and *Steven Spielberg Presents "Animaniacs"*), The WB, 1998.

Voice of production assistant and robot, "Karma Krisis/A Star Is Bruised/The Prince and the Pinhead," *Johnny Bravo,* Cartoon Network, 1999.

Voice of district attorney, "The Tick vs. Justice," *The Tick,* Fox, 2002.

Voice of game, "Sim Sammy/Otto Hangs 11," *Rocket Power,* Nickelodeon, 2002.

Voice of Grandma, reporter, and woman, "Ninja Worrier (aka Chopping Spree)," *Stroker and Hoop,* Cartoon Network, 2005.

Voice of Leslie, Henna St. Chloe–Butz, and coed, "XXX Wife (aka Stroke Her and Boob)," *Stroker and Hoop,* Cartoon Network, 2005.

Voice of librarian, Rosella, and second girl, "Duck/Aren't You Chupacabra to See Me?," *Grim & Evil* (also known as *The Grim Adventures of Billy & Mandy*), Cartoon Network, 2005.

Voice of Sunshine, Porsche, and tour guide, "Just Voodoo It," *Stroker and Hoop,* Cartoon Network, 2005.

Voice of Brenda, "U Is for Undivided," *W.I.T.C.H.,* ABC Family, 2006.

Voice of various ladies, "The Party Cruise/Won Ton Bombs," *Chowder,* Cartoon Network, 2009.

Also provided the voice of Susan Storm "Sue" Richards/the Invisible Woman for "Down to Earth: Parts 1–3," *Silver Surfer,* Fox and TeleToon.

Television Appearances; Live Action Episodes:
Martha, "Kiss the Girls and Make Them Die," *Law & Order* (also known as *Law & Order Prime*), NBC, 1990.

Beverley, "Answered Prayers," *Phenom,* ABC, 1993.

"Family Membership," *Dave's World,* CBS, 1994.

(As Lori Allen) Theresa, "Reality Check," *Ned & Stacey* (also known as *Ned and Stacey*), Fox, 1995.

Liz, "Boyd Gets Shrunk," *Boston Common* (also known as *Boston College*), NBC, 1996.

Liz, "Out, Out, Damn Jack!," *Boston Common* (also known as *Boston College*), NBC, 1996.

Liz, "Virginia Reeling," *Boston Common* (also known as *Boston College*), NBC, 1996.

Rachel Carson, "Into the Light," *Touched by an Angel,* CBS, 1996.

Jean, "Coffee & Commitment," *Will & Grace,* NBC, 2001.

Cynthia, "Lost and Bound," *Charmed,* The WB, 2002.

Voice of Sabrina's car, "Driving Mr. Goodman," *Sabrina, the Teenage Witch* (also known as *Sabrina* and *Sabrina Goes to College*), The WB, 2002.

Loretta, "Mutt and Jake," *Good Morning, Miami,* NBC, 2003.

Macy's salesperson, "The Eye Inside," *Six Feet Under,* HBO, 2003.

Sonya, "The One Where Monica Sings," *Friends* (also known as *Across the Hall, Friends Like Us, Insomnia Cafe,* and *Six of One*), NBC, 2003.

Receptionist, "Color and Light," *Desperate Housewives* (also known as *Beautes desesperees, Desperate housewives—I segreti di Wisteria Lane, Desupareto na tsuma tachi, Esposas desesperadas, Frustrerte fruer, Gotowe na wszystko, Kucanice, Meeleheitel koduperenaised, Mujeres desesperadas, Noikokyres se apognosi, Szueletett felesegek,* and *Taeydelliset naiset*), ABC, 2005.

Valerie Esposito, "Still Life," *CSI: Crime Scene Investigation* (also known as *C.S.I., CSI, CSI: Las Vegas, CSI: Weekends,* and *Les experts*), CBS, 2005.

Ms. Flowers, "Just Desserts," *Cory in the House,* The Disney Channel, 2007.

Ms. Flowers, "Mall of Confusion," *Cory in the House,* The Disney Channel, 2007.

Ms. Flowers, "Rock the Vote," *Cory in the House,* The Disney Channel, 2007.

Ms. Flowers, "We Don't Have Chemistry," *Cory in the House,* The Disney Channel, 2008.

Patron in Java Cafe, *Days of Our Lives* (also known as *Cruise of Deception: Days of Our Lives, Days, DOOL, Tropical Temptation, Tropical Temptation: Days of Our Lives, Des jours et des vies, Hortonsagaen, I gode og onde dager, Los dias de nuestras vidas, Meres agapis, Paeivien viemaeae, Vaara baesta aar, Zeit der Sehnsucht,* and *Zile din viata noastra*), NBC, 2008.

District attorney Deborah Janowitz, "Derailed," *Southland* (also known as *LAPD*), NBC, 2009.

District attorney Deborah Janowitz, "Mozambique," *Southland* (also known as *LAPD*), NBC, 2009.

District attorney Deborah Janowitz, "Westside," *Southland* (also known as *LAPD*), NBC, 2009.

Judy Roberts, "Chuck versus the First Kill," *Chuck,* NBC, 2009.

Kathy Weber, "Strike Three," *The Closer* (also known as *L.A.: Enquetes prioritaires* and *Se apostasi anapnois*), TNT, 2009.

Appeared in other programs, including *Just Shoot Me!* (also known as *Blush, Shooting Stars, Voila!, Ai, que vida!, Ammu van!, Dame un respiro, Den xereis ti sou ginetai,* and *Just Shoot Me—Redaktion durchgeknipst*), NBC.

Television Appearances; Animated Pilots:

(As Lori Allen) Voice of Susan Storm "Sue" Richards/the Invisible Woman, "The Origin of the Fantastic Four: Parts 1 & 2," *Fantastic Four* (also known as *Marvel Action Hour: Fantastic Four*), syndicated, 1994.

Voice of Diane Simmons, "Death Has a Shadow," *Family Guy* (also known as *Padre de familia* and *Padre del familia*), Fox, 1999.

Television Appearances; Live Action Pilots:

Ellen, *Those Two,* CBS, 1993.

Linda, *The Hard Times of RJ Berger* (also known as *Hard Times* and *The Hard Times of R. J. Berger*), MTV, 2010.

Television Work; Animated Series:

Additional voices, *What-a-Mess* (also known as *What a Mess*), ABC, 1995–96.

Animated Film Appearances:

Voice of Auntie Scraps, *Virtual Oz,* Paramount/Educational Film Exchanges, 1996.

Voice of mother and wife, *Toto Lost in New York,* Paramount/Educational Film Exchanges, 1996.

Voice of Pearl Krabs, *The SpongeBob SquarePants Movie* (animated and live action; also known as *SpongeBob SquarePants* and *Sponge Bob: Square Pants*), Paramount, 2004.

Voice of Diane Simmons, *Family Guy Presents Stewie Griffin: The Untold Story* (also known as *Family Guy: The Movie*), Twentieth Century–Fox Home Entertainment, 2005.

Live Action Film Appearances:

Cleopatra, *Holy Matrimony* (also known as *Holy Days*), Buena Vista, 1994.

Girl with an attitude, *Boys on the Side* (also known as *Avec ou sans hommes*), Warner Bros., 1995.

Mrs. Habib, *Father of the Bride Part II,* Buena Vista, 1995.

Gwen, *Garage Sale* (short film), 1996.

Harmony, *The Fluffer,* First Run, 2001.

Anita Levine, *Comic Book: The Movie,* Miramax Home Entertainment, 2004.

Attractive woman, *Divorce Sale* (short film), 2009.

Animated Film Additional Voices:

Tokyo Mater (animated short film; also known as *Tokyo Martin*), Walt Disney Motion Pictures Group, 2008.

WALL*E (also known as *WALL–E* and *Wall-E*), Walt Disney Studios, 2008.

Cloudy with a Chance of Meatballs (also known as *Cloudy with a Chance of Meatballs: An IMAX Experience*), Columbia, 2009.

Toy Story 3 (also known as *Toy Story 3: An IMAX 3D Experience*), Walt Disney Studios, 2010.

Stage Appearances:

Ronnie, *Trudy & Paul Come to the Rescue* (one–act play), Manhattan Punchline (comedy club), New York City, c. 1992.

Mae, *Reefer Madness!* (musical), Hudson Backstage Theatre, Los Angeles, 1999.

Hanna and Queen Celia, *SnEauX! The SINsational Gothic Figure Skating Musical* (also known as *SnEauX! The Musical*), Matrix Theatre Company, Los Angeles, 2003.

Reader, Novel Beginnings I program, *WordTheatre,* M Bar and Restaurant, Los Angeles, 2006.

The Hungry & Horny Show (sketches, stand–up comedy, and talk show; also known as *The Hungry and Horny Show*), Whitefire Theatre, Sherman Oaks, CA, and Lyric Theatre, Los Angeles, both 2007, Hayworth Theatre, Los Angeles, c. 2007, and the Court Theatre, c. 2007.

Lori Alan the Musical! (solo show), M Bar and Restaurant, c. 2007.

Reader, "Viva Las Vegas," PEN Emerging Voices program, *WordTheatre,* M Bar and Restaurant, 2008.

What a Pair (benefit concert), Orpheum Theatre, Los Angeles, 2008.

The Silverlake Rant!, Bootleg Theater, Los Angeles, 2008, M Bar and Restaurant, 2009.

Voice of Chairry, Magic Screen, Ginger the Horse, the Flowers, and the Fish, *The Pee–wee Herman Show,* Club Nokia @ LA Live, Los Angeles, 2010.

Appeared in other productions, including an appearance as the first Alice, *A … My Name Is Alice,* Soho Theatre; as Ruth, *Mary Had a Little Cult,* Theatre/Theater, Los Angeles; as Ruth, *The Pirates of Penzance* (comic opera), Brimmer Street Theatre; in *It Takes All Kinds,* Hudson Theatre, Los Angeles; and in *The Trial of Persephone* (reading of musical), evidEnce room, Los Angeles area. Worked as a stand–up comic and performed in improvisational productions.

Internet Appearances:

Appeared in clips broadcast on *Funny or Die,* http://www.funnyordie.com, including providing the voice of Chairry for *Pee-wee Gets an iPad.*

RECORDINGS

Video Games:

Voice of the boss, *Metal Gear Solid 3: Snake Eater* (also known as *Metal Gear Solid 3* and *MGS3*), Konami, 2004.

(As Lori Allen) Voices, *Area 51,* Midway Manufacturing Corporation, 2005.

Voice of the boss and Rosemary, *Metal Gear Solid 3: Subsistence,* Konami, 2005.

(From archive footage) Voice of the boss, *Metal Gear Ac!d2,* originally released in Japan, 2005, Konami, 2006.

Voice of Diane Simmons, *Family Guy,* 2k Games, 2006.

Voice of Amy Yablans, Olivia Moretti, and Eloise Stanwick–Lourdes, *CSI: NY* (also known as *CSI: NY–The Game*), CBS/Ubisoft/Legacy Interactive, 2008.

Voice of newscaster, *Marvel: Ultimate Alliance 2* (also known as *Marvel Ultimate Alliance 2: Fusion*), Savage Entertainment, 2009.

Albums; with Others:

Reefer Madness: The Movie Musical/Reefer Madness: The Original Los Angeles Cast (cast recordings of television movie and stage production), Ghostlight, 2008.

WRITINGS

Writings for the Stage:

(With others) *The Hungry & Horny Show* (sketches, stand–up comedy, and talk show; also known as *The Hungry and Horny Show*), Whitefire Theatre, Sherman Oaks, CA, and Lyric Theatre, Los Angeles, both 2007, Hayworth Theatre, Los Angeles, c. 2007, and the Court Theatre, c. 2007.

Lori Alan the Musical! (solo show), M Bar and Restaurant, Los Angeles, c. 2007.

(With others) *The Silverlake Rant!,* Bootleg Theater, Los Angeles, 2008, M Bar and Restaurant, 2009.

With Andrew Shaifer, wrote *It Takes All Kinds,* Hudson Theatre, Los Angeles. Also wrote material for stand–up performances, contributed to improvisational productions, and worked on other productions.

OTHER SOURCES

Electronic:

Lori Alan Official Site, http://www.lorialan.com, January 11, 2010.

ALLEN, Kim 1982–

PERSONAL

Born February 22, 1982, in MA. *Education:* New York University, B.F.A., drama, with minors in biology and anthropology.

Career: Actress.

CREDITS

Film Appearances:

Bartender, *Cosa Bella* (short film), Wolfe Releasing, 2006.

Lauren, *8 Easy Steps* (short film), Shorts International, 2009.

Claire, *Sonnet for a Towncar* (short film), 2010.

Salome, *Violet Tendencies,* 2010.

Television Appearances; Series:

Amanda Holden, *Army Wives,* Lifetime, 2007–2008.

Lara Fasano, *The Guiding Light* (also known as *Guiding Light*), CBS, 2009.

Television Appearances; Pilots:

Leading woman, *Lipstick Jungle,* NBC, 2008.

Rachelle, *The Beautiful Life: TBL* (also known as *The Beautiful Life*), The CW, 2009.

Television Appearances; Episodic:

Raven, "Tell Me No Secrets," *The Bedford Diaries,* The WB, 2006.

Avery Hubert, "Betrayed," *Law & Order: Criminal Intent* (also known as *Law & Order: CI*), NBC, 2008.

ALLEN, Lori
    See ALAN, Lori

AMTER, Alice

PERSONAL

Born in the United Kingdom. *Education:* B.A., modern languages and international relations.

Addresses: *Agent*—Michael Zanuck Agency, 28035 Dorothy Dr., Suite 120, Agoura Hills, CA 91301.

Career: Actress.

CREDITS

Film Appearances:

Countess St. Croix, *Mirror, Mirror IV: Reflection* (also known as *Mirror, Mirror 4: Reflection*), Worldwide Entertainment Corporation, 2000.

Bar wench, *Sinbad: Beyond the Veil of Mists,* Phaedra Cinema, 2000.

Space chick, *Pacino Is Missing,* 2002.

Big haired woman, *The Good Girl,* Fox Searchlight, 2002.

Donna, *Bad Boy* (also known as *Dawg*), Dawg LLC, 2002.

Hooker, *Hunting of Man,* 2003.

Marta, *A Man Apart* (also known as *Extreme Rage*), New Line Cinema, 2003.

Katherine Miller, *Exorcism,* York Entertainment, 2003.

Boob babe, *Rent–a–Person* (short film), 2004.

Palm reader, *Pit Fighter,* Regent Entertainment, 2005.

Alcemena, *Prometheus and the Butcher* (short film), Kingsapo Productions, 2006.

Esperanza McNunn, *American Zombie,* Cinema Libre Studio, 2007.

Mrs. Koothrappali, *The Big Bang Theory* (short film), 2007.

Layla Jesrani, *The Drucker Files* (short film), NBC Universal, 2007.

Eve, *Penance,* 2009.

Hospital attendant, *Infection: The Invasion Begins,* Moving Pictures Film and Television, 2010.

Television Appearances; Series:

Amira, *Presidio Med,* CBS, 2002–2003.

Mrs. Kootharappali, *The Big Bang Theory,* CBS, 2007–2009.

Television Appearances; Pilots:

Captain Berava Gree, *The Privateers,* 2000.

Gypsy woman, *Skip Tracer,* CBS, 2008.

Television Appearances; Episodic:

Dr. Miriam Nagarvala, "Suffer the Little Children," *ER,* NBC, 1998.

Dr. Miriam Nagarvala, "A Hole in the Heart," *ER,* NBC, 1998.

Mey Said, "Second Opinion," *Strong Medicine,* Lifetime, 2000.

Philida Bosco, "8 1/2 Narrow," *Judging Amy,* CBS, 2001.

Flower lady, "The Italian Affair," *'Til Death,* Fox, 2007.

Anjali Patel, "The Projectionist," *The Cleaner,* Arts and Entertainment, 2009.

Also appeared as Chloe, "Real Unreal," *Frat Ratz,* Digital Entertainment Network.

Stage Appearances:

Appeared in *The Insect Trainer;* as Vampira, *Plan 9 from Outer Space,* Los Angeles; Hyppolyta, *A Midsummer Night's Dream,* Stella Adler Theatre, Los Angeles.

ARMSTRONG, Alun 1946–

PERSONAL

Born July 17, 1946, in Annfield Plain, County Durham, England; children: Joe (an actor).

Addresses: *Agent*—Julian House, Markham, and Froggatt, 4 Windmill St., London W1P 1HF, England.

Career: Actor.

Awards, Honors: Laurence Olivier Award, best actor in a musical, Society of West End Theatre, 1994, for *Sweeney Todd;* Royal Television Society Award nomination, best actor, 2001, for *This Is Personal: The Hunt for the Yorkshire Ripper;* Dallas Out Takes Award, best actor in a feature film, 2005, for *When I'm Sixty–Four.*

CREDITS

Film Appearances:

Keith, *Get Carter,* Metro–Goldwyn–Mayer, 1971.

Tommy, *The Wild Bunch* (also known as *Existence* and *The 14*), 1973.

(As Alan Armstrong) George, *The Sex Victims,* 1973.

Milkman, *The Likely Lads,* 1976.

Corporal Davies, *A Bridge Too Far,* United Artists, 1977.

Lacourbe, *The Duellists,* Paramount, 1977.

Grimes, *The French Lieutenant's Woman,* United Artists, 1981.

Torquil, *Krull* (also known as *Dragons of Krull, Dungeons and Dragons, The Dungeons of Krull,* and *Krull: Invaders of the Black Fortress*), Columbia, 1983.

Zemba, *Djavolji raj* (also known as *That Summer of White Roses*), 1989.

Stefano, *The Child Eater,* 1989.

Ralph Lockhart, *White Hunter, Black Heart,* Warner Bros., 1990.

Dr. Victor Weeks, *American Friends,* Castle Hill, 1991.

John Stone, *London Kills Me,* Fine Line, 1991.

Osgood, *Blue Ice,* Classico Entertainment, 1992.

Sergeant Owens, *Patriot Games,* Universal, 1992.

Thrasher, *Split Second,* Interstar Releasing, 1992.

Dad, *My Little Eye,* 1992.

Reuben Smith, *Black Beauty,* Warner Bros., 1994.

Mornay, *Braveheart,* Paramount, 1995.

Uncle Vernon, *An Awfully Big Adventure,* Fine Line, 1995.

Inspector Teal, *The Saint,* Paramount, 1997.

High constable, *Sleepy Hollow* (also known as *Sleepy Hollow—Koepfe werden rollen*), Paramount, 1999.

Sammy, *With or Without You,* Miramax, 1999.

Uncle Henry, *G:MT Greenwich Mean Time* (also known as *G:mt*), Icon, 1999.

Zaretsky, *Onegin*, Samuel Goldwyn, 1999.

Samuel Brubeck, *Harrison's Flowers* (also known as *Les fleurs d'Harrison*), Universal, 2000.

Wyatt, *Proof of Life*, Warner Bros., 2000.

Curator Baltus Hafez, *The Mummy Returns*, Universal, 2001.

Bill, *Strictly Sinatra*, USA Films, 2001.

Pissaro, *Paradise Found*, Lions Gate Films, 2001.

David, *It's All about Love*, Strand Releasing, 2004.

Cardinal Jinette, *Van Helsing*, Universal, 2004.

St. Peter, *Millions*, Fox Searchlight, 2004.

Magistrate Fang, *Oliver Twist*, TriStar, 2005.

Dad, *A Ticket Too Far* (short film), Chimera Pictures, 2006.

Uncle Garrow, *Eragon*, Fox 2000, 2006.

Television Appearances; Series:

Neil Henshaw, a recurring role, *Bedtime*, BBC1, 2002.

Brian Lane, *New Tricks*, BBC, 2003–2009.

Television Appearances; Miniseries:

Billy Shepherd, *Days of Hope*, 1975.

Joe Gowlan, *The Stars Look Down*, 1975.

Weaver, *Romance*, 1977.

Neville Keaton, *Get Lost!*, Yorkshire Television, 1981.

Mr. Wackford Squeers and Mr. Wagstaff, *The Life and Adventures of Nicholas Nickleby* (broadcast of stage performance; also known as *Nicholas Nickleby*), Channel 4, 1982, then The Disney Channel, 1983.

Sergeant McGing, *Murder in Eden*, BBC, 1991.

Rufus Hilton, *Stanley and the Women*, 1991.

Gerald Faulkner (Goggle Eyes), *Goggle Eyes*, 1992.

Roy Grade, *Goodbye Cruel World*, 1992.

Uncle Teddy, *The Life and Times of Henry Pratt*, 1992.

Austin Donohue, *Our Friends in the North*, 1996.

Teddy Middlemass, *Underworld*, 1997.

Detective Chief Inspector Frank Jefferson, *In the Red*, BBC, 1998.

Daniel Peggotty, *David Copperfield*, PBS, 1999.

Henry Fox, *Aristocrats*, PBS, 1999.

Mr. Fleming, "Oliver Twist," *Masterpiece Theatre*, PBS, 1999.

Assistant Chief Constable George Oldfield, *This Is Personal: The Hunt for the Yorkshire Ripper*, 2000.

George Mole, *Adrian Mole: The Cappuccino Years*, 2001.

Narrator, *Extinct*, 2001.

Charlie Macintyre, *Messiah 2: Vengeance Is Mine* (also known as *Messiah Part II: Vengeance Is Mine*), BBC, 2002.

Richard Bolton, *Sparkhouse*, BBC, 2002, Showtime, 2003.

Peter Delany, *Between the Sheets*, ITV, 2003.

Inspector Bucket, *Bleak House*, BBC1, 2005.

Jeremiah Flintwinch and Ephraim Flintwinch, *Little Dorrit*, PBS, 2008.

Southouse, *Garrow's Law*, 2009.

Television Appearances; Movies:

Mike, "The Eyes Have It," *Thriller*, ABC, 1973.

Brodovich, "Shooting the Chandelier," *BBC2 Play of the Week*, BBC2, 1977.

Sergeant, *Number One*, 1984.

Mr. Smeth, *The House*, 1984.

Maxwell Randall, *Billy the Kid and the Green Baize Vampire* (also known as *Billy and the Vampire*), ITV, 1985.

Murray Lester, *Number 27*, BBC, 1988.

Frank Burroughs, "Nineteen 96," *Screen One*, 1989.

Willy, "A Night on the Tyne," *Screen Play*, 1989.

Evans, "Sticky Wickets," *Screen One*, 1990.

Dad, *The Widowmaker*, 1990.

Capshaw, *MacGyver: Trail to Doomsday*, ABC, 1994.

Charlie Foster, *Doggin' Around*, BBC, 1994.

(Uncredited) The butler, *The Haunting of Helen Walker* (also known as *The Turn of the Screw*), 1995.

Mikey, *Sorry about Last Night*, 1995.

Jimmy Hardcastle, *Brazen Hussies*, BBC, 1996.

Pastor Harold Poelchau, *Witness against Hitler*, 1996.

Mick Ross, *Breaking the Code*, PBS, 1996.

George, *Score*, 2000.

Martin, *Inquisition*, 2002.

Mr. Samuel Evans, *Carrie's War*, PBS, 2004.

Jim, *When I'm Sixty–Four* (also known as *When I'm 64*), BBC2, 2004.

Bob Jenkins, *The Girls Who Came to Stay* (also known as *The Girls from Belarus*), 2006.

Jim, *The Dinner Party*, 2007.

Ernest Whitehouse, *Filth: The Mary Whitehouse Story*, PBS, 2008.

Television Appearances; Specials:

Michael Biddle, "Only Make Believe," *Play for Today*, BBC, 1973.

First docker, "Easy Go," *Play for Today*, BBC, 1974.

"Chester Mystery Cycle," *BBC Play of the Month*, BBC, 1976.

Richard Clewes, "Risking It," *Centre Play*, 1977.

Mr. Briggs, "Our Day Out," *Play for Today*, BBC, 1978.

Provost, "Measure for Measure," *The Complete Dramatic Works of William Shakespeare*, PBS, 1979.

Dad, "All Day on the Sands," *Six Plays by Alan Bennett*, 1979.

(Uncredited) *Animating Shakespeare*, 1992.

Thenardier, "'Les Miserables' in Concert," *Great Performances*, PBS, 1996.

Himself, *The Making of "Aristocrats,"* PBS, 1999.

Narrator, *Challenger: Go for Launch*, 2000.

Narrator, *7Up*, 2000.

Television Appearances; Episodic:

Ray Davies, "The Wrong 'un," *New Scotland Yard*, 1972.

Tel, "George," *Villains,* 1972.

Glazier, "Ross Evan's Story," *Armchair 30,* 1973.

David Miller, "A Quiet Man," *Softly Softly* (also known as *Softly, Softly: Task Force*), BBC, 1973.

Truckdriver, "Discretion," *Hunter's Walk,* ATV, 1973.

Scaife, "Conduct Unbecoming," *Whatever Happened to the Likely Lads?,* 1974.

Bob Graham, "It's Always a Gamble," *Justice,* 1974.

Joe, "The Hammer of God," *Father Brown,* 1974.

Peter Jenner, "Stay Lucky, Eh?" *The Sweeney,* Thames, 1975.

Vince Gregson, "The Fatted Calf," *Public Eye,* Thames, 1975.

Jim, "The Favourite," *The Squirrels,* 1975.

Private George Harris, "Dirtier by the Dozen," *The New Avengers* (also known as *The New Avengers in Canada* and *Chapeau melon et bottes de cuir*), 1976.

Sweeney, "Shoulder to Shoulder," *The Squirrels,* 1977.

Spraggon, "A Test of Character," *Porridge,* BBC, 1977.

"Seven Year Itch," *A Sharp Intake of Breath,* 1978.

Detective Superintendent Boley, "Pressure," *Z Cars,* BBC, 1978.

Louis Mendoza, "Officers of the Law," *Enemy at the Door,* 1978.

"Freedom of the Dig," *Premiere,* 1978.

Trahearne, "Fear of God," *Armchair Thriller,* 1980.

Presenter, *The Book Tower,* 1984.

Detective Superintendent Figg, "Death of a Hitman," *Bulman,* Granada, 1985.

Councillor Stennalling, "Not a Pretty Site," *This Is David Lander,* 1988.

Voice of Troll, "The True Bride," *The Storyteller* (also known as *Jim Henson's "The Storyteller"*), Channel 4, 1988.

Superintendent Holdsby, "Happy Families," *Inspector Morse,* Central, 1992, then PBS, 1994.

Trevor, "England Show I," *Married ... with Children,* Fox, 1992.

Trevor, "England Show II: Wastin' the Company's Money," *Married ... with Children,* Fox, 1992.

Trevor, "England Show III: We're Spending As Fast As We Can," *Married ... with Children,* Fox, 1992.

Voice of Caliban, "The Tempest," *Shakespeare: The Animated Tales,* HBO, 1992.

"Confession," *Tales from the Crypt* (also known as *HBO's "Tales from the Crypt"*), HBO, 1996.

Alas Smith & Jones (also known as *Smith & Jones*), BBC2, 1998.

GMTV, ITV, 2004.

Stage Appearances:

The Changing Room, Royal Court Theatre, London, 1971.

Azdak, merchant, musician, and stable man, *The Caucasian Chalk Circle,* Royal Shakespeare Company, Warehouse Theatre, London, 1980.

Alun, *Bastard Angel,* Royal Shakespeare Company, Warehouse Theatre, 1980.

Dogberry, *Much Ado about Nothing,* Royal Shakespeare Company, Warehouse Theatre, 1980.

Harry Baker, Lionel Frontage, and Norman Leathers, *The Loud Boy's Life,* Royal Shakespeare Company, Warehouse Theatre, 1980.

Mr. Wackford Squeers, Mr. Wagstaff, and other roles, *The Life and Adventures of Nicholas Nickleby,* Royal Shakespeare Company, Aldwych Theatre, London, 1980, then Plymouth Theatre, New York City, 1981–82.

Trinculo, *The Tempest,* Royal Shakespeare Company, Royal Shakespeare Theatre, 1982, then Theatre Royal, Newcastle–upon–Tyne, England, 1983.

Petruchio and a player, *The Taming of the Shrew,* Royal Shakespeare Company, Royal Shakespeare Theatre, Stratford–upon–Avon, England, 1982, then Theatre Royal, Newcastle–upon–Tyne, and Barbican Theatre, London, both 1983.

Reflections, Royal Shakespeare Company, Gulbenkian Studio, Newcastle–upon Tyne, 1983.

Ralph Trapdoor, *The Roaring Girl,* Royal Shakespeare Company, Royal Shakespeare Theatre, then Barbican Theatre, both 1983.

John Proctor, *The Crucible,* Royal Shakespeare Company, Theatre at Christ Church Spitalfields, London, 1984.

Leontes, *The Winter's Tale,* Royal Shakespeare Company, Theatre at Christ Church Spitalfields, 1984.

Thenardier and member of chain gang, *Les Miserables* (musical), Royal Shakespeare Theatre, Barbican Theatre, then Palace Theatre, London, both 1985.

Thersites, *Troilus and Cressida,* Royal Shakespeare Company, Royal Shakespeare Theatre, 1985, then Barbican Theatre, 1986.

Stuart Clarke, *Fashion,* Royal Shakespeare Company, Other Place Theatre, Stratford–upon–Avon, 1987, then Pit Theatre, London, 1988.

Barabas, *The Jew of Malta,* Royal Shakespeare Company, Swan Theatre, Stratford–upon–Avon, 1987, then People's Theatre, Newcastle–upon–Tyne, and Barbican Theatre, both 1988.

Sweeney Todd (musical), Royal National Theatre, London, 1993.

Willy Loman, *Death of a Salesman,* Royal National Theatre, 1997.

Jack, *Mappa Mundi,* Royal National Theatre, Cottesloe Theatre, London, 2002.

Pizarro, *The Royal Hunt of the Sun,* Royal National Theatre, 2006.

Major Tours:

Azdak, merchant, musician, and stable man, *The Caucasian Chalk Circle,* Royal Shakespeare Company, 1979.

Dogberry, *Much Ado about Nothing,* Royal Shakespeare Company, 1979.

John Proctor, *The Crucible,* Royal Shakespeare Company, 1984, 1985.

Leontes, *The Winter's Tale,* Royal Shakespeare Company, 1984, 1985.

RECORDINGS

Videos:

(Uncredited) Voice of Baltus Hafez, *Spotlight on Location: The Mummy Returns,* 2001.

Voice of Cardinal Jinette, *Van Helsing: The London Assignment* (also known as *Van Helsing Animated*), Universal Home Video, 2004.

Voice of Cardinal Jinette, *Van Helsing* (video game), Vivendi Universal Games, 2004.

Little Dorrit: An Insight, Warner Home Video, 2009.

OTHER SOURCES

Periodicals:

Radio Times, August 24, 2002, p. 49; November 5, 2005, p. 40.

B

BAKER, Joan 1960–

PERSONAL

Full name, Joan Marie Baker; born October 14, 1960, in San Francisco, CA; daughter of James P. Baker; married Rudy Gaskins, October 24, 1998. *Education:* Studied dance at Alvin Ailey American Dance Center.

Addresses: *Agent*—Innovative Artists, 235 Park Ave. South, New York, NY 10003; Push Creative, 244 West 49th St., Suite 400, New York, NY 10019.

Career: Actress and voice artist. Appeared in television commercials, including Medicare, 2005; provided voice work for television, radio, and film for such clients as ABC News, American Express, King World, ESPN, Bloomberg TV and radio, Showtime, HBO, NBA Entertainment, Court TV, *Imus in the Morning,* Sony Music, JP Morgan Chase, Costco, and *New York Times* classified; provided voice for six public service announcements for the Muhammad Ali Center, 2004; narrated a documentary about the founding of the William Jefferson Clinton Library, 2004 (now on permanent display); served as the voice of the NCAA basketball tournament, CBS Sports, 2008; provided live voice announcements for Promax TV conferences, NAMIC, and the Vision Awards; national spokeswoman and voice artist for Neumann USA. Creator and seminar leader for "Make Millions with Your Voice," Learning Annex; creator of Voices Remember (Broadway benefit).

Member: American Federation of Television and Radio Artists, Actors Equity Association, Screen Actors Guild.

Awards, Honors: Off Off Broadway Award, best actress in a play, 1998, for *The Marriage Proposal.*

CREDITS

Film Appearances:

Voice of Vaiya, *M.D. Geist* (animated) 1996.

Voice of Vaiya, *M.D. Geist II* (animated), Central Park Media Corp., 1997.

Talk show host, *Personals* (also known as *Hook'd Up*), Unapix Entertainment, 1999.

Uncle John Shaft's girlfriend, *Shaft* (also known as *Shaft—Noch Fragen?*), Paramount, 2000.

Narrator, *A Life of Consequence* (short documentary), 2009.

Also appeared as narrator, *Causing the Miraculous* (short documentary).

Film Work:

(Uncredited) Automated dialogue replacement (ADR), *Cold Mountain,* Miramax, 2003.

ADR, *Dear John,* Screen Gems, 2010.

Television Appearances; Specials:

Show announcer, *Moving Image Salutes Will Smith* (documentary), Bravo, 2007.

Television Appearances; Episodic:

Dancer, "Rosie O'Donnell/James Taylor," *Saturday Night Live* (also known as *SNL*), NBC, 1993.

Hermes clerk, "Coulda, Woulda, Shoulda," *Sex and the City* (also known as *S.A.T.C.*), HBO, 2001.

Courtroom stenographer, *The Guiding Light* (also known as *Guiding Light*), CBS, 2004–2006.

Stage Appearances:

Appeared in *The Marriage Proposal.*

RECORDINGS

Video Games:

Voice of Vice City TV reporter, *Grand Theft Auto: Vice City Stories* (also known as *GTA: Vice City Stories*), Take Two Interactive Software, 2006.

Voice of Alison Maybury, *Grand Theft Auto IV* (also known as *GTA IV*), Take Two Interactive Software, 2008.

WRITINGS

Nonfiction:

(With others) *Secrets of Voice–Over Success: Top Voice–Over Actors Reveal How They Did It,* 2005.

(With others) *Daughters of Men: Portraits of African–American Women and Their Fathers,* 2007.

(With others) *The Career Clinic: 8 Simple Rules for Finding Work You Love,* 2008.

(With others) *Put Your Dreams First: Handle Your [entertainment] Business,* Hachette Books Group/ Grand Central Publishing, 2009.

OTHER SOURCES

Electronic:

Joan Baker Official Site, http://www.joanthevoice.com/, February 10, 2010.

BARUCH, Steven 1938–

PERSONAL

Born 1938.

Career: Producer and executive. Baruch, Frankel, Viertel Group (stage production company); also known as Viertel, Baruch, Frankel Group, Frankel, Viertel, Baruch Group, Frankel, Baruch, Viertel, Routh Group, Baruch, Viertel, Routh, Frankel Group, and R/F/B/V Group), New York City, partner and producer, 1985—.

Awards, Honors: Drama Desk Award nomination, outstanding new play, and Lucille Lortel Award, outstanding play, League of Off–Broadway Theatres and Producers, both 1989, for *The Cocktail Hour;* Drama Desk Award, outstanding new play, and Outer Critics Circle Award, best off–Broadway play, both 1992, for *Marvin's Room;* two Drama Desk Award nominations, outstanding new play, 1993, for *Jeffrey* and *Oleanna;* Antoinette Perry Award nomination, best musical, 1995, for *Smokey Joe's Cafe;* Antoinette Perry Award nomination, best revival of a musical, 1998, for *The Sound of Music;* Drama Desk Award nomination, outstanding new musical, 1998, for *Forever Tango;* Lucille Lortel Award and Outer Critics Circle Award nomination, both outstanding revival, 1999, for *The Mystery of Irma Vep;* Antoinette Perry Award nomination, best musical, and Drama Desk Award nomination, best new musical, both 2000, for *Swing!;* Drama Desk Award and Lucille Lortel Award, both unique theatrical experience, 2001, for *Mnemonic;* Antoinette Perry Award nomination and Drama Desk Award, both best revival of a musical, 2006, for *Sweeney Todd;* Antoinette Perry Award and Drama Desk Award, both best revival of a musical, 2007, for *Company;* Drama Desk Award nomination, unique theatrical experience, 2007, for *Mayumana's Be;* Antoinette Perry Award and Drama Desk Award, best revival of a play, both 2009, for the trilogy *The Norman Conquests.*

CREDITS

Stage Producer:

Sills & Company, Lamb's Theatre, New York City, 1986.

Frankie and Johnny in the Clair de Lune, Manhattan Theatre Club, Westside Theatre Upstairs, New York City, 1987–89.

Penn & Teller, Ritz Theatre (now Walter Kerr Theatre), New York City, 1987–88.

The Cocktail Hour, Promenade Theatre, New York City, 1988–89.

Love Letters, Promenade Theatre, then Edison Theatre, New York City, 1989–90.

Penn & Teller: The Refrigerator Tour, Eugene O'Neill Theatre, New York City, 1991.

Song of Singapore (musical), Song of Singapore Theatre, New York City, 1991.

Penn & Teller Rot in Hell, John Houseman Theatre, New York City, 1991–92.

Marvin's Room, Playwrights Horizons Theatre, Minetta Lane Theatre, New York City, 1992.

Oleanna, Orpheum Theatre, New York City, 1992–94.

Jeffrey, Workshop of the Players Art, Minetta Lane Theatre, 1993–94.

Later Life, Playwrights Horizons Theatre, 1993–94.

Das Barbecu (musical), Minetta Lane Theatre, 1994.

Smokey Joe's Cafe (musical), Virginia Theatre, New York City, 1995–2000.

Three–for–All, Union Square Theatre, New York City, 1997.

Forever Tango (dance special), Walter Kerr Theatre, 1997–98, then Marquis Theatre, New York City, 1998.

The Sound of Music (musical), Martin Beck Theatre, New York City, 1998–99.

The Mystery of Irma Vep, Westside Theatre Downstairs, New York City, 1998–99.

The Weir, Walter Kerr Theatre, 1999.

Swing! (musical revue), St. James Theatre, New York City, 1999–2001.

Mnemonic, Theatre de Complicite, John Jay College of Criminal Justice of the City University of New York, New York City, 2001.

My Old Lady, Promenade Theatre, 2002.

The Water Coolers, Dillon's Theatre, New York City, 2002.

Little Shop of Horrors (puppet musical), Virginia Theatre, 2003–2004.

Sweeney Todd (musical), Eugene O'Neill Theatre, 2005–2006.

The Fantasticks (musical), Jerry Orbach Theatre, Snapple Theatre Center, New York City, beginning 2006.

Company (musical), Ethel Barrymore Theatre, New York City, 2006–2007.

Mayumana's Be, Union Square Theatre, New York City, 2007.

A Little Night Music (musical), Walter Kerr Theatre, 2009.

The Norman Conquests: Round and Round the Garden, Circle in the Square, New York City, 2009.

The Norman Conquests: Table Manners, Circle in the Square, 2009.

The Norman Conquests: Living Together, Circle in the Square, 2009.

Burn the Floor (dance special), Longacre Theatre, New York City, 2009–10.

Baruch's production company presented numerous other stage plays, with other partners at the helm.

Major Tours:
Coproducer, *Penn & Teller,* U.S. cities, 1985.

Also coproduced tours of *Smokey Joe's Cafe, Stomp,* and *Tap Dogs.*

ADAPTATIONS

A performance of the stage production of *Frankie and Johnny in the Clair de Lune* was filmed as *Frankie and Johnny,* released by Paramount in 1991. A performance of the stage production *Smokey Joe's Cafe* was televised by Broadway Television Network and also offered as a pay–per–view selection in 2000. A performance of the stage production *Company* was televised as *Company: A Musical Comedy,* and broadcast by PBS in 2007.

BELLISARIO, David

PERSONAL

Son of Donald (a writer, producer, and director) and Margaret (maiden name, Schaffran) Bellisario; brother of Julia B. Watson (a producer); stepbrother of Michael Bellisario (an actor), Troian Avery Bellisario (an actress), and Sean Murray (an actor).

Career: Producer.

Awards, Honors: Emmy Award nomination (with others), outstanding drama series, 1992, for *Quantum Leap.*

CREDITS

Television Work; Series:
Associate producer, *Magnum, P.I.,* CBS, 1984–87.
Associate producer, *Quantum Leap,* NBC, 1989–90.
Coordinating producer, *Quantum Leap,* NBC, 1991–93.
Associate producer, *JAG* (also known as *JAG: Judge Advocate General*), NBC, 1995–96, then CBS, 1997–98.
Coproducer, *JAG* (also known as *JAG: Judge Advocate General*), CBS, 1998 2000.
Producer, *JAG* (also known as *JAG: Judge Advocate General*), CBS, 2000–2005.
Producer, *Navy NCIS: Naval Criminal Investigative Service* (also known as *NCIS* and *NCIS: Naval Criminal Investigative Service*), CBS, 2003–2009.
Producer, *NCIS: Los Angeles,* CBS, 2009—.

Television Work; Other:
Coproducer, *Crowfoot* (movie), CBS, 1995.
Coordinating producer, *JAG* (pilot; also known as *JAG: Judge Advocate General*), NBC, 1995.

Television Work; Episodic:
Coordinating producer, "War Cries," *JAG* (also known as *JAG: Judge Advocate General*), NBC, 1995.

BELLISARIO, Michael 1980–
(Michael Angelo Bellisario, Michaelangelo Bellisario)

PERSONAL

Full name, Michael Angelo Bellisario; born April 7, 1980, in Los Angeles County, CA; son of Donald P. Bellisario (a writer, producer, and director) and Lynn Halpern.

Addresses: *Agent*—Paradigm, 360 North Crescent Dr., North Building, Beverly Hills, CA 90210.

Career: Actor.

CREDITS

Film Appearances:
(As Michaelangelo Bellisario) Nuzo's son, *Last Rites,* Metro–Goldwyn–Mayer, 1988.
(Uncredited) *Beanstalk,* Paramount Home Video, 1994.

Johnny Z, *Four Deadly Reasons,* 2002.
Jared, *Kush,* Endurance Pictures, 2007.
James Vane, *The Picture of Dorian Gray,* 2007.

Film Work:
Automated dialogue replacement (ADR), *Grandma's Boy,* Twentieth Century–Fox, 2006.

Television Appearances; Series:
Midshipman Mike "Mikey" Roberts, *JAG* (also known as *JAG: Judge Advocate General*), CBS, 1998–2005.
Charles "Chip" Sterling, *Navy NCIS: Naval Criminal Investigative Service* (also known as *NCIS* and *NCIS: Naval Criminal Investigative Service*), CBS, 2005.

Television Appearances; Movies:
Jock, *The Other Me,* The Disney Channel, 2000.

Television Appearances; Pilots:
Antonio, *JAG* (also known as *JAG: Judge Advocate General*), NBC, 1995.

Television Appearances; Episodic:
(As Michael Angelo Bellisario) Son, "A Distant Shout of Thunder," *Tales of the Gold Monkey,* ABC, 1983.
Little boy, "Camikazi Kid—June 6, 1961," *Quantum Leap,* NBC, 1989.
Billy the bat boy, "Play Ball—August 6, 1961," *Quantum Leap,* NBC, 1991.
Martin, Jr., "A Tale of Two Sweeties—February 25, 1958," *Quantum Leap,* NBC, 1993.
Kid number two, "Mirror Image—August 8, 1953," *Quantum Leap,* NBC, 1993.
(Uncredited) Pizza boy, "Ghost Ship," *JAG* (also known as *JAG: Judge Advocate General*), CBS, 1997.
Rowdy fan, *Kevin Hill,* UPN, 2004.

BELLISARIO, Troian Avery 1985–
   (Troian Bellisario)

PERSONAL

Born October 28, 1985, in Los Angeles County, CA; daughter of Donald P. Bellisario (a writer, producer, and director) and Deborah Pratt (an actress).

Addresses: *Agent*—Don Buchwald and Associates, 6500 Wilshire Blvd., Suite 2200, Los Angeles, CA 90048.

Career: Actress.

CREDITS

Film Appearances:
Nuzo's daughter, *Last Rites,* Metro–Goldwyn–Mayer, 1988.
Kristen, *Billboard Dad,* Warner Bros., 1998.
Jani, *Unspoken* (short film), Alluvial Filmworks, 2006.
Tatum, *Archer House* (short film), University of Southern California School of Cinema and Television, 2007.
Victoria, *Intersect* (short film), 2009.
P.A., *Peep World,* 2010.

Television Appearances; Pilots:
Spencer Hastings, *Pretty Little Liars,* ABC Family, 2010.

Television Appearances; Episodic:
Teresa, "Another Mother—September 30, 1981," *Quantum Leap,* NBC, 1990.
Teresa Garcia, "The Rose Cadillac," *Tequila and Bonetti,* CBS, 1992.
(As Troian Bellisario) Erin Terry, "Tiger, Tiger," *JAG* (also known as *JAG: Judge Advocate General*), CBS, 1998.
(As Troian Bellisario) Kimberly Baron, "Dangerous Words," *First Monday,* CBS, 2002.
(As Troian Bellisario) Kimberly Baron, "Strip Search," *First Monday,* CBS, 2002.
(As Troian Bellisario) Sarah McGee, "Red Cell," *Navy NCIS: Naval Criminal Investigative Service* (also known as *NCIS* and *NCIS: Naval Criminal Investigative Service*), CBS, 2005.
(As Troian Bellisario) Sarah McGee, "Twisted Sister," *Navy NCIS: Naval Criminal Investigative Service* (also known as *NCIS* and *NCIS: Naval Criminal Investigative Service*), CBS, 2005.

BLACKWELL, Blanche
   See ESTERMAN, Laura

BLADE, Jake
   See SHAW, Scott

BOWIE, John Ross 1971–
   (Jon Ross Bowie)

PERSONAL

Born May 30, 1971, in New York, NY; married Jamie Denbo (an actress), June 5, 2004. *Education:* Ithaca College, bachelor's degree, English, and teaching certificate.

Addresses: *Agent*—TalentWorks, 3500 West Olive Ave., Suite 1400, Burbank, CA 91505. *Manager*—Principato, Young Management, 9465 Wilshire Blvd., Suite 880, Beverly Hills, CA 90212.

Career: Actor and writer. Appeared in television commercials, including T.G.I. Friday's restaurants, Keystone light beer, 21st Century Auto Insurance, Jack in the Box restaurants, Pep Boys Auto stores, Progressive Auto Insurance, and DiGiorno pizza; appeared in blogs for Target's online employee benefits. Naked Babies (a sketch comedy troupe), member. Former member of Egghead (a pop–punk band).

CREDITS

Film Appearances:
Ewan Piggott–Smith, *Banall to the Bone: Portrait of an Artist* (short film; also known as *Picasso by Proxy*), 2000.
Waiter, *Road Trip,* DreamWorks, 2000.
Daniel Benjamin, *Blackballed: The Bobby Dukes Story* (also known as *Blackballed*), The 7th Floor, 2004.
Elliot, *What the #$*! Do We (K)now!?* (also known as *What the Bleep Do We Know!?*), Samuel Goldwyn, 2004.
Bert, *Life of the Party,* Warner Bros., 2005.
Elliot, *What the Bleep!?: Down the Rabbit Hole,* Samuel Goldwyn, 2006.
Horowitz—"Small World," *The Great Sketch Experiment* (short film), 2006.
Rory, *The Santa Clause 3: The Escape Clause* (also known as *Pretender*), Buena Vista, 2006.
Cute food spewing guy, *Because I Said So,* Universal, 2007.
Priest, *Wild Girls Gone,* 2007.
Dr. Clark Teddescoe, *Sex Drive* (also known as *Sexdrive*), Summit Distribution, 2008.
Dan the Wiccan, *He's Just Not That Into You* (also known as *Er steht einfach nicht auf dich!*), New Line Cinema, 2009.
Richard, *Fully Loaded,* 2009.

Television Appearances; Series:
Walter "Wally" Berman, *A.U.S.A.,* NBC, 2003.
Barry Kripke, *The Big Bang Theory,* CBS, 2009.

Television Appearances; Movies:
Bob, *Nadine in Date Land,* Oxygen, 2005.

Television Appearances; Pilots:
IFC executive, *Fur on the Asphalt: The "Greg the Bunny" Reunion Show,* Independent Film Channel, 2005.
Dr. Max Von Sydow, *Children's Hospital,* Cartoon Network, 2010.

Television Appearances; Episodic:
Japa–Noi businessman, "Mogomra vs. the Fart Monster," *Upright Citizens Brigade,* Comedy Central, 1999.
Man with binoculars, "Small Town," *Upright Citizens Brigade,* Comedy Central, 2000.
Cyber–flex user, "Virtual Reality," *Upright Citizens Brigade,* Comedy Central, 2000.
CocoNate, "The Juicer," *Happy Family,* NBC, 2004.
Mr. Campbell, "Do the Math," *Joan of Arcadia,* CBS, 2004.
Lester Jaynem, "American Dreamers," *CSI: NY* (also known as *CSI: New York*), CBS, 2004.
Marcus, "Once in a Blue Moon," *Charmed,* The WB, 2004.
Wayne Ellis, "Making the Grade," *Kevin Hill,* UPN, 2004.
Patrick, *The Bad Girl's Guide,* UPN, 2005.
(Uncredited) Spa employee, "Ready, Aim, Marry Me," *Arrested Development,* Fox, 2005.
Adam Clemo, "Hit Me!," *Las Vegas,* NBC, 2005.
(As Jon Ross Bowie) Pageant dad, "The Prefect of Wanganui," *Reno 911!,* Comedy Central, 2005.
George Cheslow, "Weekend Warriors," *Psych,* USA Network, 2006.
Attorney, "Chapter Twelve 'Godsend,'" *Heroes,* NBC, 2007.
Peter Ellis, "A La Cart," *CSI: Crime Scene Investigation* (also known as *CSI: Las Vegas, C.S.I.,* and *Les experts*), CBS, 2007.
Ren Faire guy, "Ex–wife and Her New Husband," *Reno 911!,* Comedy Central, 2007.
Ren Faire guy, "Dangle's Wedding," *Reno 911!,* Comedy Central, 2007.
Pageant father, "Did Garcia Steal Dangle's Husband," *Reno 911!,* Comedy Central, 2008.
Pageant father, "Baghdad 911," *Reno 911!,* Comedy Central, 2008.
Tom Donovan, "Mr. Monk Joins a Cult," *Monk,* USA Network, 2008.
Voice of Integritone number two, "Artificial Unintelligence/We Got the Bee," *The Mighty B!* (animated), Nickelodeon, 2008.
Voice of Integritone 2, "Dopplefinger/Little Womyn," *The Mighty B!* (animated), Nickelodeon, 2008.
Rob, "The Apartment," *Worst Week,* CBS, 2008.
Voice, *Family Guy* (animated), Fox, 2008.
Simon, "Fairy Tale," *Wizards of Waverly Place,* The Disney Channel, 2009.
"Way Beyond the Call," *Trust Me,* TNT, 2009.
John Fowler, "Denise Handicapped," *Curb Your Enthusiasm,* HBO, 2009.
Dennis, "Mattress," *Glee,* Fox, 2009.

Internet Appearances; Episodic:
Appeared as himself, "John Ross Bowie," *The Real Cool Club* (a web series), www.thestream.tv.

WRITINGS

Television Episodes:
"We Got the Bee," *The Mighty B!* (animated), Nickelodeon, 2008.
"L'il Orphan Happy," *The Mighty B!* (animated), Nickelodeon, 2008.

BOWLBY, April 1980–

PERSONAL

Full name, April Michelle Bowlby; born July 30, 1980, in Vallejo, CA. *Education:* Studied ballet, French, and marine biology at Moorpark College; studied drama with Ivanna Chubbuck.

Addresses: *Agent*—WME Entertainment, One William Morris Pl., Beverly Hills, CA 90212.

Career: Actress.

CREDITS

Film Appearances:
Natasha, *All Roads Lead Home,* Waldo West Productions, 2008.
Mia, *The Slammin' Salmon,* Anchor Bay Films, 2009.

Television Appearances; Series:
Kandi, *Two and a Half Men,* CBS, 2005–2007.
Meg, *How I Met Your Mother* (also known as *H.I.M.Y.M.*), CBS, 2007–2009.
Stacy Barrett, *Drop Dead Diva,* Lifetime, beginning 2009.

Television Appearances; Movies:
Heather, *Sands of Oblivion,* Sci–Fi Channel, 2007.

Television Appearances; Pilots:
Stacy Barrett, *Drop Dead Diva,* Lifetime, 2009.

Television Appearances; Episodic:
Kaitlin Rackish, "What's Eating Gilbert Grissom?," *CSI: Crime Scene Investigation* (also known as *CSI: Las Vegas, C.S.I.,* and *Les experts*), CBS, 2004.
Jenny Lee, "Crime and Misdemeanor," *CSI: NY* (also known as *CSI: New York*), CBS, 2005.
Jasmine, "The Ex–Appeal," *Stacked,* Fox, 2005.
Sydney, "Rich Man, Poor Girl," *Freddie,* ABC, 2005.

Princess Gugulfa, "Princess," *Out of Jimmy's Head,* Cartoon Network, 2008.
Ashley, "Bachelorette," *Kath & Kim* (also known as *Kath & Kim: The American Series*), NBC, 2009.
Hot groupie/Marta Petrovich, "Unshockable," *CSI: Crime Scene Investigation* (also known as *CSI: Las Vegas, C.S.I.,* and *Les experts*), CBS, 2010.

BROOKS, Mel 1926–
(Melvin Brooks)

PERSONAL

Original name, Melvin Kaminsky; born June 28, 1926, in Brooklyn, NY; son of Max (a process server) and Kate (a garment worker; maiden name, Brookman) Kaminsky; married Florence Baum (a dancer), 1952 (divorced, 1959); married Anne Bancroft (an actress), August 5, 1964 (died, June 6, 2005); children: (first marriage) Stefanie, Nicholas, Edward; (second marriage) Maximilian. *Education:* Attended Virginia Military Institute, 1944.

Addresses: *Office*—Brooksfilms, 9336 West Washington Blvd., Culver City, CA 90232. *Agent*—Trident Media Group, 41 Madison Ave., New York, NY 10010.

Career: Actor, director, screenwriter, producer, and song composer. Worked variously as a jazz drummer, stand–up comedian, handyman, and social director of Grossinger's Resort in the Catskills, NY, after World War II; sketchwriter for Sid Caesar, collaborating on television shows, 1949–58; Crossbow Productions (a production company), founder and president, 1961–1981; Brooksfilms, Limited (a production company), founder and president, beginning 1981. Appeared in television commercials, including Big Pens, 1970. *Military service:* U.S. Army, combat engineer, 1944–46; served in Europe and North Africa.

Member: Directors Guild of America, Writers Guild of America, Screen Actors Guild.

Awards, Honors: Emmy Award nominations, best comedy writing, 1955, outstanding writing achievement in comedy, 1956, 1957, all for *Caesar's Hour;* Grammy Award nomination (with Carl Reiner), best spoken word comedy, National Academy of Recording Arts and Sciences, 1960, for *2,000 Years;* Grammy Award nomination (with Reiner), best comedy performance, 1961, for *2,000 and One Years;* Grammy Award nomination (with Reiner), best comedy performance, 1963, for *At the Cannes Film Festival;* Academy Award, best short subject, 1964, for *The Critic;* Emmy

Award nomination (with Buck Henry), best writing achievement in comedy, 1965, for "Mr. Big," *Get Smart!;* Emmy Award, outstanding writing achievement in a variety comedy, 1967, for *The Sid Caesar, Imogene Coca, Carl Reiner, Howard Morris Special;* Academy Award, best story and screenplay written directly for the screen, 1968, Golden Globe Award nomination, best screenplay, Writers Guild of America Screen Award, best written American screenplay, Writers Guild of America Screen Award, best written American comedy, 1969, all for *The Producers;* Writers Guild of America Screen Award nomination, best comedy adapted from another medium, 1971, for *The Twelve Chairs;* Academy Award nomination (with Gene Wilder), best screenplay adapted from another medium, 1974, Nebula Award (with Wilder and Mary Wollstonecraft Shelley), best dramatic presentation, Writers Guild of America Screen Award nomination, best comedy adapted from another medium, 1975, Golden Scroll Award, best director, Academy of Science Fiction, Fantasy, and Horror Films, 1976, all for *Young Frankenstein;* Academy Award nomination (with John Morris), best song, Academy Award nomination (with Wilder), best writing—screenplay adapted from other material, 1974, Film Award nomination (with others), best screenplay, British Academy of Film and Television Arts, Writers Guild of America Screen Award, best comedy written directly for the screen, 1975, all for *Blazing Saddles;* Writers Guild of America Screen Award nomination (with others), best comedy written directly for the screen, Golden Globe Award nomination, best motion picture actor—musical/comedy, 1977, both for *Silent Movie;* Golden Globe Award nomination, best motion picture actor—musical/comedy, 1978, for *High Anxiety;* Grammy Award nomination, best comedy recording, National Association of Recording Arts and Sciences, 1981, for "The Inquisition," *History of the World, Part I;* Grammy Award nomination (with Steve Barri), best comedy recording, 1981, for *History of the World, Part I;* Academy Award nomination, best picture, 1981, for *The Elephant Man;* American Comedy Awards Lifetime Achievement Award, 1987; Emmy Awards, outstanding guest actor in a comedy series, 1997, 1998, 1999, American Comedy Award, funniest male guest appearance in a television series, 1997, 2000, all for *Mad about You;* Grammy Award, best spoken comedy, 1999, for *Carl Reiner & Mel Brooks: The 2000 Year Old Man in the Year 2000: The Album;* Antoinette Perry Awards, best musical, best book of a musical, and best original score (music and lyrics), Drama Desk Award, best book and best lyrics, 2001, Laurence Olivier Award (with Thomas Meehan Brooks), best new musical, Society of London Theatre, 2005, all for *The Producers;* Laurel Award Screen Writing Achievement, Writers Guild of America, 2003; Daytime Emmy Award nomination, outstanding performer in an animated program, 2005, for *Jakers! The Adventures of Piggley Winks;* Golden Globe Award nomination, best original song—motion picture, 2006, for *The Producers;* Drama Desk Award nomination, outstanding lyrics, 2008, for *Young Frankenstein;*

Kennedy Center Honors, 2009; Honorary Award, Ernst Lubitsch Award, 2009.

CREDITS

Film Appearances:

Voice of old man from Russia, *The Critic* (animated short film), Pintoff–Crossbow Productions, 1963.

(Uncredited) Singer in "Springtime for Hitler," *The Producers,* 1968.

Tikon, *The Twelve Chairs,* UMC Pictures, 1970.

Governor Lepetomane, Indian Chief, and World War I aviator, *Blazing Saddles* (also known as *Mel Brooks' "Blazing Saddles or Never Give a Saga an Even Break"*), Warner Bros., 1974.

(Uncredited) Voice of hurt cat, *Young Frankenstein,* 1974.

Mel Funn, *Silent Movie,* Twentieth Century–Fox, 1976.

Dr. Richard Thorndyke, *High Anxiety,* Twentieth Century–Fox, 1977.

Professor Max Krassman, *The Muppet Movie,* Associated Film, 1979.

Moses, Comicus, Torquemada, Jacques, King Louis XVI, and other characters, *History of the World: Part I* (also known as *Mel Brooks' "History of the World: Part I"*), Twentieth Century–Fox, 1981.

Frederick Bronski, *To Be or Not to Be,* Twentieth Century–Fox, 1983.

Himself, *Sunset People,* 1984.

President Skroob and Yogurt, *Spaceballs* (also known as *"Spaceballs": the Video*), Metro–Goldwyn–Mayer/United Artists, 1987.

Voice of Mr. Toilet Man, *Look Who's Talking Too,* TriStar, 1990.

Goddard "Pepto" Bolt, *Life Stinks* (also known as *Life Sucks*), Metro–Goldwyn–Mayer–Pathe, 1991.

Rabbi Tuckman, *Robin Hood: Men in Tights* (also known as *Sacre Robin des bois*), Twentieth Century–Fox, 1993.

(Uncredited) Guest checking out, *Silence of the Hams* (also known as *Il silenzio dei prosciutti*), Summit Group, 1994.

Mr. Welling, *The Little Rascals,* United International Pictures, 1994.

Dr. Abraham Van Helsing, *Dracula: Dead and Loving It* (also known as *Dracula mort et heureaux de l'etre*), Columbia, 1995.

Jake Gordon, *Svitati* (also known as *Screwloose*), Medusa, 1999.

Stressed old man, *Sex, loenger, and videovaald,* 2000.

Himself, *The Sid Caesar Collection: The Magic of Life TV,* Creative Light Worldwide, 2000.

Himself, *The Sid Caesar Collection: Inside the Writer's Room,* Creative Light Worldwide, 2000.

Himself, *The Sid Caesar Collection: Creating the Comedy,* Creative Light Worldwide, 2000.

Himself, *The Sid Caesar Collection: The Fan Favorites—The Professor and Other Clowns,* Creative Light Worldwide, 2001.

Himself, *The Side Caesar Collection: The Fan Favorites—Love & Laughter,* Creative Light Worldwide, 2001.

Himself, *The Sid Caesar Collection: The Fan Favorites—The Dream Team of Comedy,* Creative Light Worldwide, 2001.

Himself, *Hail Sid Caesar! The Golden Age of Comedy,* 2001.

Himself, *Back in the Saddle,* 2001.

Himself, *The Terrible Elephant Man Revealed* (also known as *The Elephant Man Revealed*), 2001.

Himself, *The Making of "The Producers,"* 2002.

Himself, *Sid Caesar Collection: Buried Treasures—Shining Stars,* Creative Light Entertainment, 2003.

Himself, *Sid Caesar Collection: Buried Treasures—The Legend of Sid Caesar,* Creative Light Entertainment, 2003.

Himself, *Sid Caesar Collection: Buried Treasures—The Impact of Sid Caesar,* Creative Light Entertainment, 2003.

Voice of Bigweld, *Robots* (animated; also known as *"Robots": The IMAX Experience*), Twentieth Century–Fox, 2005.

Voice of Hilda the Pigeon and Tom the Cat, *The Producers,* Universal, 2005.

Himself, *The Making of "Robots,"* 2005.

Himself, *"Spaceballs": The Documentary* (short documentary), Metro–Goldwyn–Mayer, 2005.

Film Director:

The Critic (animated short film), Pintoff–Crossbow Productions, 1963.

The Producers (also known as *Springtime for Hitler*), Embassy, 1968.

The Twelve Chairs, UMC Pictures, 1970.

Blazing Saddles (also known as *Mel Brooks' "Blazing Saddles or Never Give a Saga an Even Break"*), Warner Bros., 1974.

Young Frankenstein (also known as *Frankenstein Jr.*), Twentieth Century–Fox, 1974.

Silent Movie, Twentieth Century–Fox, 1976.

High Anxiety, Twentieth Century–Fox, 1977.

History of the World: Part I (also known as *Mel Brooks "History of the World: Part 1"*), Twentieth Century–Fox, 1981.

Spaceballs (also known as *"Spaceballs": The Video*), Metro–Goldwyn–Mayer/United Artists, 1987.

Life Stinks (also known as *Life Sucks*), Metro–Goldwyn–Mayer–Pathe, 1991.

Robin Hood: Men in Tights (also known as *Sacre Robin des bois*), Twentieth Century–Fox, 1993.

Dracula: Dead and Loving It (also known as *Dracula mort et hereux de l'etre*), Columbia, 1995.

Film Executive Producer:

(Uncredited) *The Elephant Man,* Paramount, 1980.

(Uncredited) *Frances,* EMI, 1982.

(Uncredited) *My Favorite Year* (also known as *My Favourite Year*), Metro–Goldwyn–Mayer, 1982.

The Doctor and the Devils, Twentieth Century–Fox, 1985.

The Fly, Twentieth Century–Fox, 1986.

Solarbabies (also known as *Solar Warriors*), Metro–Goldwyn–Mayer/United Artists, 1986.

84 Charing Cross Road, Columbia, 1986.

(Uncredited) *The Fly II,* Twentieth Century–Fox, 1989.

The Vagrant (also known as *Psychose meutriere*), 1992.

Film Producer:

High Anxiety, Twentieth Century–Fox, 1977.

History of the World: Part I (also known as *Mel Brooks "History of the World: Part 1"*), Twentieth Century–Fox, 1981.

To Be or Not to Be, Twentieth Century–Fox, 1983.

Spaceballs (also known as *"Spaceballs": The Video*), Metro–Goldwyn–Mayer/United Artists, 1987.

Life Stinks (also known as *Life Sucks*), Metro–Goldwyn–Mayer–Pathe, 1991.

Robin Hood: Men in Tights (also known as *Sacre Robin des bois*), Twentieth Century–Fox, 1993.

Dracula: Dead and Loving It (also known as *Dracula mort et heureux de l'etreu*), Columbia, 1995.

The Producers, Universal, 2005.

Film Work; Additional Voices:

(Uncredited) *The Prince of Egypt* (animated), Dream-Works, 1998.

Film Creator:

The Critic (animated short film), Pintoff–Crossbow Productions, 1963.

Film Consultant:

Get Smart, Warner Bros., 2008.

Television Appearances; Series:

Your Show of Shows, NBC, 1950–54.

Voice of blond–haired cartoon man, *The Electric Company,* PBS, 1971–77.

Voice of Wiley the Sheep, *Jakers! The Adventures of Piggley Winks* (animated), PBS, 2003–2006.

Himself, *Curb Your Enthusiasm,* HBO, 2004.

Voice of President Skroob and Yogurt, *Spaceballs: The Animated Series* (animated; also known as *Mel Brooks' "Spaceballs: The Animated Series"*), G4, 2008.

Television Appearances; Movies:

Voice of Snowman, *It's a Very Merry Muppet Christmas Movie,* NBC, 2002.

The Roman Spring of Mrs. Stone, Showtime, 2002.

Television Appearances; Specials:

The All–Star Comedy Show, ABC, 1962.

The 41st Annual Academy Awards, 1969.

Annie, the Woman in the Life of a Man, 1970.

Annie and the Hoods, ABC, 1974.

Voice of baby boy in nursery, *Marlo Thomas and Friends in Free to Be ... You and Me* (also known as *Free to Be ... You and Me*), ABC, 1974.

Title role, *The 2,000 Year Old Man,* CBS, 1975.

(Uncredited) *The Muppets Go Hollywood,* 1979.

The American Film Institute Salute to Alfred Hitchcock, 1979.

Dom DeLuise and Friends, ABC, 1983.

An Audience with Mel Brooks, 1983.

The 5th Annual American Comedy Awards, ABC, 1991.

Naked Hollywood, Arts and Entertainment, 1991.

More of the Best of the Hollywood Palace, ABC, 1993.

Hal Roach: Hollywood's King of Laughter, The Disney Channel, 1994.

Host, *Frankenstein: The True Story* (also known as *It's Alive: The True Story of Frankenstein*), 1994.

Sid Caesar: Television's Comedy Genius, 1994.

Caesar's Writers, PBS, 1996.

American Dreamers, TNT, 1996.

I Am Your Child (also known as *From Zero to Three* and *Johnson & Johnson Presents: I Am Your Child*), ABC, 1997.

Pretty as a Picture: The Art of David Lynch, 1997.

Presenter, *The 49th Annual Primetime Emmy Awards,* 1997.

The 50th Emmy Awards, NBC, 1998.

"M*A*S*H," Tootsie & God: A Tribute to Larry Gelbart, PBS, 1998.

AFI's 100 Years ... 100 Movies, CBS, 1998.

Bravo Profiles: The Entertainment Business, Bravo, 1998.

The Television Academy Hall of Fame, UPN, 1999.

Neil Simon: The People's Playwright, Arts and Entertainment, 1999.

AFI's 100 Years, 100 Laughs: America's Funniest Movies, CBS, 2000.

Intimate Portrait: Madeline Kahn, Lifetime, 2000.

Mark Twain Prize—Celebrating the Humor of Carl Reiner, PBS, 2001.

Hail Sid Caesar: The Golden Age of Comedy, Showtime, 2001.

The First Ten Awards: Tony 2001, PBS, 2001.

Artists and Entertainers, Cable News Network, 2001.

The 55th Annual Tony Awards, CBS and PBS, 2001.

Inside TV Land: "Get Smart," TV Land, 2001.

Recording "The Producers": A Musical Romp with Mel Brooks, PBS, 2001.

100 Years of Hope and Humor, NBC, 2003.

10 Most Excellent Things: "The Producers," 2005.

Assembling "Robots": The Magic, the Music & the Comedy (short documentary), Fox, 2005.

Forbes Celebrity 100: Who Made Bank?, E! Entertainment Television, 2006.

The Dick Cavett Show with Mel Brooks, TCM, 2006.

AFI's 100 Years ... 100 Movies: 10th Anniversary Edition, CBS, 2007.

A Night at the Movies: The Suspenseful World of Thrillers (documentary), TCM, 2009.

Himself, The Kennedy Center Honors: A Celebration of the Performing Arts (also known as *The 32nd Annual Kennedy Center*), CBS, 2009.

Television Appearances; Pilots:

The Colgate Comedy Hour, NBC, 1967.

Television Appearances; Episodic:

2000–year–old man, *The New Steve Allen Show,* 1961.

"Strictly for Laughs," *Open End* (also known as *The David Susskind Show*), 1964.

Comedian, *The Hollywood Palace,* 1964, 1965, 1966, 1967.

The Celebrity Game, 1965.

Guest panelist, *The Hollywood Squares,* 1967, 1968, 1969, 1972, 1975, 1978.

Cameo, "Episode #35," *Rowan & Martin's "Laugh–In"* (also known as *Laugh–In*), 1969.

"The Were Wolf of London/The Plainsman," *Don Adam's Screen Test,* syndicated, 1975.

Les rendez–vous du dimanche, 1976.

Lordagshjornet (also known as *Julehiornet, Nytarshjornet,* and *The Saturday Corner*), 1978.

"Mickey's 50," *The Wonderful World of Disney,* 1978.

Aspel & Company, 1985.

Cinema 3 (also known as *Informatiu cinema*), 1987, 1996.

Bernard "Buzz" Schlanger, "Due Diligence," *The Tracey Ullman Show,* Fox, 1990.

La palmera, 1991.

Showbiz Today, Cable News Network, 1991, 1993, 1995, 1997.

Voice of Tom, "Miracle on Third or Fourth Street," *Frasier,* NBC, 1993.

"Sid Caesar: Television's Comedy Genius," *Biography,* Arts and Entertainment, 1994.

Voice of himself, "Homer vs. Patty and Selma," *The Simpsons* (animated), Fox, 1995.

"Carl Reiner: Still Laughing," *Biography,* Arts and Entertainment, 1995.

"The Peter Sellers Story," *Arena,* 1995.

"Mel Brooks, Rudiger Hoffmann," *RTL Samstag Nacht,* 1996.

Tal como somos, 1996.

Uncle Phil, "The Grant," *Mad about You,* NBC, 1996.

Uncle Phil, "The Penis," *Mad about You,* NBC, 1997.

Uncle Phil, "Uncle Phil and the Coupons," *Mad about You,* NBC, 1997.

Uncle Phil, "Uncle Phil Goes Back to High School," *Mad about You,* NBC, 1999.

"Gene Wilder," *Bravo Profiles,* Bravo, 2001.

"Mel Brooks/Jason Alexander," *Primetime Glick,* Comedy Central, 2003.

"The Films of David Lynch," *The Directors,* Encore, 2003.

Voice of Santa Claus, "Holly Jolly Jimmy," *The Adventures of Jimmy Neutron: Boy Genius* (animated), Nickelodeon, 2003.

"Syncopated city: 1919–1933," *Broadway: The American Musical*, PBS, 2004.
"Putting It Together: 1980–Present," *Broadway: The American Musical*, PBS, 2004.
Channel 4 News (also known as *ITN Channel 4*), Channel 4, 2004.
"Robots," *HBO First Look*, HBO, 2005.
Dateline NBC (also known as *Dateline*), NBC, 2005.
Film 2005 (also known as *The Film Programme*), BBC, 2005.
Go' aften Danmark, 2006.
"The Homecoming Meet & Greet/Peter and Jerry at 2nd Stage/*Young Frankenstein* Opening," *Broadway Beat,* 2007.

Also appeared as himself, "Frank Sinatra: The Voice of the Century," *Biography,* Arts and Entertainment.

Television Talk Show Guest Appearances; Episodic:

Toast of the Town (also known as *The Ed Sullivan Show*), 1961.
The Tonight Show Starring Johnny Carson, NBC, 1962, 1975, 1980, 1991, 1992.
The Andy Williams Show, 1966.
The Mike Douglas Show, 1967, 1968.
The Woody Woodbury Show, 1968.
The Dick Cavett Show, 1970, 1972.
The Late Show, Fox, 1986.
The Last Resort with Jonathan Ross (also known as *The Last Resort*), 1987.
Saturday Night Clive, 1989, 1991.
Clive Anderson Talks Back, 1993.
The Tonight Show with Jay Leno, NBC, 1993.
Gottschalk Late Night, 1993.
Larry King Live, Cable News Network, 1993, 1998.
Corazon, corazon, 1996.
The Rosie O'Donnell Show, syndicated, 1997.
Late Show with David Letterman, NBC, 2000.
The Martin Short Show, 2000.
Rove Live, Ten Network, 2003.
Enough Rope with Andrew Denton, Australian Broadcasting Corporation, 2004.
Parkinson, BBC, 2004.
Corazon de ..., 2006.

Television Work; Series:

(With Buck Henry) Creator, *Get Smart!,* NBC, 1965.
Creator and executive producer, *When Things Were Rotten,* ABC, 1975.
Executive producer, *The Nutt House,* NBC, 1989.
Executive producer, *Spaceballs: The Animated Series* (animated; also known as *Mel Brooks' "Spaceballs: The Animated Series"*), G4, 2008.
Creator and producer, *Spaceballs: The Animated Series* (animated; also known as *Mel Brooks' "Spaceballs: The Animated Series"*), G4, 2008.

Television Work; Specials:

An Audience with Mel Brooks, 1983.

Television Director; Episodic:

Spaceballs: The Animated Series (animated; also known as *Mel Brooks' "Spaceballs: The Animated Series"*), 2008.

Stage Producer:

All–American (musical; based on the novel *Professor Fodorski* by Robert Lewis Taylor), Winter Garden Theatre, New York City, 1962.
The Producers, St. James Theatre, New York City, 2001–2007.
Young Frankenstein, Hilton Theatre, New York City, 2007–2009.

Stage Appearances:

Made debut in *Separate Rooms,* Red Bank, NJ.

RECORDINGS

Albums:

(With Carl Reiner) *2,000 Years,* Capitol, 1960.
(With Reiner) *2,000 and One Years,* Capitol, 1961.
(With Reiner) *At the Cannes Film Festival,* Capitol, 1961.
(With Reiner) *2,000 and Thirteen,* Warner Bros., 1973.
Contributor, *High Anxiety* (soundtrack), Elektra, 1977.
(With Steve Barri) *History of the World: Part I* (includes "The Inquisition"), Warner Bros., 1981.
(With Reiner) *The 2000 Year Old Man in the Year 2000,* Rhino, 1997.

Author and performer (with Reiner), *The Incomplete Works of Carl Reiner and Mel Brooks* (contains *2,000 Years, 2,000 and One Years,* and *At the Cannes Film Festival*).

WRITINGS

Screenplays:

(With others) *New Faces* (based on Broadway revue *New Faces of 1952*), National Pictures/Twentieth Century–Fox, 1954.
(Uncredited) *The Ladies Man,* 1961.
The Critic (animated short film), Pintoff–Crossbow Productions, 1963.
The Producers, Embassy, 1968.
The Twelve Chairs (based on a novel by Ilya Arnoldovich Ilf and Evgeni Petrov), UMC Pictures, 1970.
Shinbone Alley, 1971.
10 From Your Show of Shows, 1973.

(With Andrew Bergman, Richard Pryor, Norman Steinberg, and Alan Uger) *Blazing Saddles* (based on a story by Bergman; also known as *Mel Brooks' "Blazing Saddles or Never Give a Saga an Even Break"*), Warner Bros., 1974.

(With Gene Wilder) *Young Frankenstein* (based on characters created by Mary Wollstonecraft Shelley), Twentieth Century–Fox, 1974.

(With Ron Clark, Rudy De Luca, and Barry Levinson) *Silent Movie*, Twentieth Century–Fox, 1976.

(With Clark, De Luca, and Levinson) *High Anxiety*, Twentieth Century–Fox, 1977.

History of the World, Part I (also known as *Mel Brooks "History of the World: Part 1"*), Twentieth Century–Fox, 1981.

(With Meehan and Graham) *Spaceballs* (also known as *"Spaceballs": The Video*), Metro–Goldwyn–Mayer/United Artists, 1987.

(With De Luca and Steve Haberman) *Life Stinks* (also known as *Life Sucks*), Metro–Goldwyn–Mayer–Pathe, 1991.

(With J. David Shapiro and Evan Chandler) *Robin Hood: Men in Tights* (also known as *Sacre Robin des bois*), Twentieth Century–Fox, 1993.

Dracula: Dead and Loving It (also known as *Dracula mort et heureux de l'etre*), Columbia, 1995.

Svitati, Medusa, 1999.

Film Songs:

The Producers (also known as *Springtime for Hitler*), Embassy, 1968.

The Twelve Chairs, UMC Pictures, 1970.

Blazing Saddles (also known as *Mel Brooks' "Blazing Saddles or Never Give a Saga an Even Break"*), Warner Bros., 1974.

High Anxiety, Twentieth Century–Fox, 1977.

History of the World: Part 1 (also known as *Mel Brooks History of the World: Part 1*), Twentieth Century–Fox, 1981.

To Be or Not to Be, 1983.

Spaceballs, Metro–Goldwyn–Mayer/United Artists, 1987.

Robin Hood: Men in Tights (also known as *Sacre Robin des bois*), 1993.

Television Specials:

Accent on Love, 1959.

The Man in the Moon, 1960.

Inside Danny Baker, 1963.

(With others) *The Sid Caesar, Imogene Coca, Carl Reiner, Howard Morris Special*, CBS, 1966.

(With Carl Reiner) *The 2,000 Year Old Man*, CBS, 1975.

Television Pilots:

Black Bart, CBS, 1975.

(With Alan Spencer) *The Nutt House*, NBC, 1989.

Television Episodes:

(With others) *Broadway Review* (also known as *The Admiral Broadway Revue*), NBC, 1949–50.

(With others) *Your Show of Shows* (also known as *Sid Caesar's "Show of Shows"*), NBC, 1950–54, 1976.

(With others) *Caesar's Hour*, NBC, 1954–57.

(With others) *Sid Caesar Invites You*, ABC, 1957–58.

"Archy and Mehitabel," *Play of the Week*, 1960.

Get Smart!, NBC, 1965.

When Things Were Rotten, ABC, 1975.

Spaceballs: The Animated Series (animated; also known as *Mel Brooks' "Spaceballs: The Animated Series"*), G4, 2008.

Television Theme Music; Series:

Spaceballs: The Animated Series (animated; also known as *Mel Brooks' "Spaceballs: The Animated Series"*), G4, 2008.

Television Scores; Specials:

Recording "The Producers": A Musical Romp with Mel Brooks, PBS, 2001.

Stage Writing:

(With others) *New Faces of 1952* (Broadway revue), Royale Theatre, New York City, 1952–53.

(Author of book with Joe Darion) *Shinbone Alley* (musical; based on the "Archy and Mehitabel" stories by Don Marquis), Broadway Theatre, New York City, 1957.

(Author of book) *All–American* (musical; based on the novel *Professor Fodorski* by Robert Lewis Taylor), Winter Garden Theatre, New York City, 1962.

The Producers, St. James Theatre, New York City, 2001–2007.

Young Frankenstein, Hilton Theatre, New York City, 2007–2009.

Nonfiction:

(With Carl Reiner) *The 2000 Year Old Man in the Year 2000*, Cliff Street Books/HarperCollins, 1997.

(With Thomas Meehan) *The Producers: The Book, the Lyrics, and the Story Behind the Biggest Hit in Broadway History: How We Did It*, Talk Miramax Books/Hyperion, 2001.

OTHER SOURCES

Books:

Adler, Bill, and Jeffrey Fineman, *Mel Brooks: The Irreverent Funnyman*, Playboy Press, 1976.

Crick, Robert Alan, *The Big Screen Comedies of Mel Brooks*, McFarland & Company, 2002.

Dictionary of Literary Biography, Volume 26: *American Screenwriters*, Gale, 1984.

Holtzman, William, *Seesaw: A Dual Biography of Anne Bancroft and Mel Brooks*, Doubleday, 1979.

Parish, James Robert, *It's Good to Be the King: The Seriously Funny Life of Mel Brooks*, John Wiley & Sons, 2007.

Sinyard, Neil, *The Films of Mel Brooks,* 1988.
St. James Encyclopedia of Popular Culture, St. James Press, 2000.
Yacowar, Maurice, *Method in Madness: The Comic Art of Mel Brooks,* St. Martin's, 1981.

Periodicals:
Billboard, December 10, 2005, p. 23.
Daily Mail (London), December 26, 2005, p. 15.
Entertainment Weekly, June 28, 1996, p. 116; December 6, 2002, p. 76.
New Yorker, November 19, 2007, p. 88.
People Weekly, July 20, 1987, pp. 39–41; November 3, 1997, p. 37; December 31, 2001, p. 100.
U.S. News and World Report, July 7, 1997, p. 81.
St. Paul Magazine, August, 1998, pp. 25–27.
USA Today, September 28, 2007, p. 1E.

BROSNAN, Pierce 1953–

PERSONAL

Full name, Pierce Brendan Brosnan; born May 16, 1953, in Navan, County Meath, Ireland; son of Thomas Brosnan (a carpenter) and May Carmichael (a nurse); married Cassandra Harris (an actress), December 27, 1977 (died December 28, 1991); married Keely Shaye Smith (a journalist), August 4, 2001; children: (first marriage) Sean William, Charlotte, Christopher; (second marriage) Dylan Thomas, Paris Beckett. *Education:* Trained for the stage at the Drama Centre, London, 1973–76.

Addresses: *Office*—Irish Dreamtime, 3000 Olympic Blvd., Bldg. 3, Suite 2332, Santa Monica, CA 90404. *Agent*—Special Artists Agency, 9465 Wilshire Blvd., Suite 470, Beverly Hills, CA 90212; Creative Artists Agency, 2000 Avenue of the Stars, Los Angeles, CA 90067; Independent Talent Group, Oxford House, 76 Oxford St., London W1D 1BS, England. *Publicist*—PMK–BNC, 700 San Vicente Blvd., Suite G910, West Hollywood, CA 90069.

Career: Actor and producer. Theatre Spiel (a street theatre company), founder, 1971; Oval House Theatre Company, founder, 1971; Irish DreamTime (a production company), founder, partner, and producer. Appeared in television commercials, including Diet Coke, Maidenform lingerie, MasterCard, Ferrero Rocher chocolates, Dannon yogurts, Visa, Friexnet sparkling wines, Sagres beers, and L'Oreal products; appeared in print advertisements, including Cuervo Gold Tequila, Maidenform lingerie, Omega watches, Ericsson Mobile, Forest Stewardship Council, Ford Thunderbird, 2002, Galaxy suits, Aquascutum menswear, and Vistula Clothing. Previously worked as a fire eater with the circus, commercial illustrator, and assistant stage manager, York Theatre Royal, York, England.

Awards, Honors: Golden Globe Award nomination, best performance by an actor in a supporting role, 1985, for *Nancy Astor;* MTV Movie Award nomination (with Famke Janssen), best fight, Saturn Award nomination, best actor, Academy of Science Fiction, Fantasy, and Horror Films, 1996, both for *GoldenEye;* star on the Hollywood Walk of Fame, 1997; European Film Award nomination, outstanding European achievement in world cinema, Saturn Award, best actor, Academy of Science Fiction, Horror, and Fantasy Films, 1998, both for *Tomorrow Never Dies;* Blockbuster Entertainment Award, favorite actor—drama/romance, 2000, for *The Thomas Crown Affair;* Empire Award, best actor, Blockbuster Entertainment Award, favorite actor—action, 2000, both for *The World Is Not Enough;* Humanitarian Award (with Keely Shaye Smith), Women in Film Crystal Awards, 2001; Career Achievement Award, Chicago International Film Festival, 2002; Honorary Order of the British Empire, 2003; Saturn Award nomination, best actor, Academy of Science Fiction, Fantasy, and Horror Films, 2003, for *Die Another Day;* Audience Award nomination, best actor in a film, Irish Film and Television Awards, 2003; Glow Award, best voice performance—male, G–Phoria Awards, 2004, for *James Bond 007: Everything or Nothing;* Outstanding Irish Contribution to Cinema Award, Irish Film and Television Awards, 2004; Achievement in the Arts Award, Malibu Film Festival, 2005; Role Model Award, Young Hollywood Awards, 2005; Golden Globe Award nomination, best performance by an actor in a motion picture—musical or comedy, Saturn Award nomination, best actor, Academy of Science Fiction, Fantasy, and Horror Films, 2006, Irish Film and Television Award nomination, best actor in a lead role in a feature film, 2007, all for *Matador;* National Movie Award nomination, best performance—male, 2008, People's Choice Award nomination (with others), favorite cast, 2009, for *Mamma Mia!.*

CREDITS

Film Appearances:
Resting Rough, 1979.
(Uncredited) Actor playing "Jamie," *The Mirror Crack'd,* Associated Film Distributors, 1980.
First Irishman, *The Long, Good Friday,* Embassy, 1980.
Jean Charles Pommier, *Nomads,* Atlantic, 1985.
Major Valeri Petrofsky, *The Fourth Protocol,* Rank, 1987.
Captain/Colonel William Savage, *The Deceivers,* Cinecom, 1988.
Mark Taffin, *Taffin,* Metro–Goldwyn–Mayer/United Artists, 1988.

Narrator, *The Seven Wonders of the Ancient World,* 1990.

Harry Rudbeck, *Mister Johnson,* Avenue Entertainment, 1991.

Dr. Lawrence Angelo, *Stephen King's "The Lawnmower Man"* (also known as *Lawnmower Man* and *Virtual Wars*), New Line Cinema, 1992.

Stuart "Stu" Dunmeyer, *Mrs. Doubtfire,* Twentieth Century–Fox, 1993.

Garavan, *Entangled* (also known as *Les veufs* and *Fatal Attack*), CineTel Films, 1993.

Ken Allen, *Love Affair,* 1994.

James Bond, *GoldenEye,* Metro–Goldwyn–Mayer/ United Artists, 1995.

Himself, *The "Goldfinger" Phenomenon* (short documentary), 1995.

Title role, *Daniel Defoe's "Robinson Crusoe"* (also known as *Robinson Crusoe*), 1996.

Himself, *The Disappearance of Kevin Johnson,* 1996.

Alex, *The Mirror Has Two Faces,* TriStar/Sony, 1996.

Professor Donald Kessler, *Mars Attacks!,* Warner Bros., 1996.

Himself, *James Bond 007: Yesterday and Today* (short documentary), 1996.

Harry Dalton, *Dante's Peak,* Universal, 1997.

James Bond, *Tomorrow Never Dies* (also known as *TND*), Metro–Goldwyn–Mayer/United Artists, 1997.

Himself, *Highly Classified: The World of 007* (documentary), 1997.

Himself, *Sammy the Screenplay,* 1997.

Voice of King Arthur, *The Magic Sword: Quest for Camelot* (animated; also known as *The Magic Sword: Quest for Camelot*), Warner Bros., 1998.

Joe Brady, *The Nephew,* 1998.

Himself, *Gray Magic: The Plight of San Ignacio Lagoon,* 1998.

James Bond, *The World Is Not Enough* (also known as *Bond 19, Bond 2000, Death Waits for No Man, T.W.I.N.E., Twine,* and *Fire and Ice*), 1999.

Title role, *Grey Owl,* 1999.

Title role, *The Thomas Crown Affair,* Metro–Goldwyn–Mayer, 1999.

John MacGhee, *The Match* (also known as *The Beautiful Game*), United International, 1999.

Himself, *The Making of "The World Is Not Enough"* (short documentary), Herzog, 1999.

Narrator, *Dolphins,* MacGillivray Freeman, 2000.

Himself, *Ian Fleming: 007's Creator* (short documentary), 2000.

Himself, *Inside Q's Laboratory* (short documentary), 2000.

Himself, *Inside "The Living Daylights"* (short documentary), 2000.

Andrew "Andy" Osnard, *The Tailor of Panama,* Columbia, 2001.

The Perfect Fit (short documentary; also known as *A Conversation with Pierce Brosnan and Geoffrey Rush*), Columbia TriStar, 2001.

Desmond Doyle, *Evelyn* (also known as *Ein Vater kampft um seine kinder*), United Artists, 2002.

James Bond, *Die Another Day* (also known as *D.A.D.*), Twentieth Century–Fox, 2002.

Cameo, *Austin Powers in Goldmember,* New Line Cinema, 2002.

Himself and James Bond, *Shaken and Stirred on Ice* (short documentary), 2002.

Laws of Attraction, Dreamtime, 2003.

(English version) Narrator, *Deep Blue* (documentary), Miramax, 2003.

Himself, *Deadly Sounds in the Silent World* (short documentary), 2003.

Daniel Rafferty, *Laws of Attraction,* New Line Cinema, 2004.

Max Burdett, *After the Sunset,* New Line Cinema, 2004.

Julian Noble, *The Matador* (also known as *Mord und margaritas*), Miramax, 2005.

Himself, *Deadly Sounds in the Silent World II,* 2005.

Gideon, *Seraphim Falls,* Destination Films, 2006.

Himself, *Whaledreamers* (documentary), 2006.

Himself, *Creating an Icon* (short documentary), 2006.

Himself, *The Return of Bond: The Start of Production Press Event* (short documentary), 2006.

Himself, *The Hong Kong Press Conference* (short documentary), 2006.

Himself, *Directing Bond: The Martin Chronicles* (short documentary; also known as *The Martin Chronicles*), 2006.

Himself, *"GoldenEye": Building a Better Bond* (short documentary; also known as *Building a Better Bond*), Sony Pictures Home Entertainment, 2006.

Himself, *Driven to Bond: Remy Julienne* (short documentary; also known as *Anatomy of a Car Chase: Remy Julienne*), Metro–Goldwyn–Mayer Home Entertainment, 2006.

Himself, *The British Touch: Bond Arrives in London* (short documentary), Sony Pictures Home Entertainment, 2006.

Narrator, *The Official Film of the 2006 FIFA World Cup* (documentary), Sony, 2006.

Tom Ryan, *Butterfly on a Wheel* (also known as *Shattered, Desperate Hours,* and *The Butterfly*), Lions Gate Films, 2007.

Richard Langley, *Married Life* (also known as *Pour le meilleur et pour le pire*), Sony Pictures Classics, 2007.

Himself, *Behind the Scenes of "Seraphim Falls"* (short documentary), Sony Pictures Home Entertainment, 2007.

Sam, *Mama Mia!* (also known as *Mamma Mia! The Movie* and *Mamma Mia!*), Universal, 2008.

Narrator, *Thomas & Friends: The Great Discovery—The Movie,* Kidtoon Films, 2008.

Allen Brewer, *The Greatest,* Paladin, 2009.

Mr. Brunner/Chiron, *Percy Jackson & the Olympians: The Lightning Thief* (also known as *Percy Jackson and the Lightning Thief*), Twentieth Century–Fox, 2010.

Adam Lang, *The Ghost Writer* (also known as *Der Ghostwriter* and *L'homme de l'ombre*), Summit Entertainment, 2010.

Charles, *Remember Me,* Summit Entertainment, 2010.

Film Producer:

The Nephew, 1998.

The Thomas Crown Affair, Metro–Goldwyn–Mayer, 1999.

Evelyn (also known as *Ein Vater kampft um seine kinder*), United Artists, 2002.

The Matador (also known as *Mord und margatritas*), Miramax, 2005.

Butterfly on a Wheel (also known as *Shattered, Desperate Hours,* and *The Butterfly*), Lions Gate Films, 2007.

Film Executive Producer:

The Match (also known as *The Beautiful Game*), United International, 1999.

Laws of Attraction, Dreamtime, 2004.

The Greatest, Twentieth Century–Fox, 2009.

Television Appearances; Series:

Title role, *Remington Steele,* NBC, 1982–87.

Television Appearances; Miniseries:

Rory O'Manion, *The Manions of America,* ABC, 1981.

Robert Gould Shaw, "Nancy Astor," *Masterpiece Theatre,* PBS, 1984.

Ian Dunross, *James Clavell's "Noble House"* (also known as *Noble House*), NBC, 1988.

Phineas Fogg, *Around the World in 80 Days* (also known as *Il giro del mondo in 80 giorni* and *In 80 tagen um die welt*), NBC, 1989.

Television Appearances; Movies:

Edward O'Grady, *Murphy's Stroke,* 1979.

Title role, *Remington Steele: The Steele That Wouldn't Die,* 1987.

Neal Skinner, *The Heist* (also known as *The Hei$t*), HBO, 1989.

Professor Charles Lattimore, *Murder 101,* USA Network, 1991.

Paul Tomlinson, *Victim of Love* (also known as *Raw Heat*), CBS, 1991.

Danny O'Neill, *Live Wire,* HBO, 1992.

Mike Graham, *Alistair MacLean's "Death Train"* (also known as *Death Train* and *Detonator*), USA Network, 1993.

Sir William Johnson, *The Broken Chain,* TNT, 1993.

Patrick Brody, *Don't Talk to Strangers* (also known as *Dangerous Pursuit*), 1994.

Mike Graham, *Alistair MacLean's "Night Watch"* (also known as *Night Watch, Detonator II: Night Watch,* and *Detonator 2: Night Watch*), USA Network, 1995.

Television Appearances; Specials:

The NBC All Star Hour, NBC, 1983.

The Night of 100 Stars II, ABC, 1985.

NBC 60th Anniversary Celebration, NBC, 1986.

Happy Birthday Bugs!: 50 Looney Years, CBS, 1990.

Host and narrator, *Robin Hood: The Myth, the Man, the Movie,* CBS, 1991.

The World of James Bond (also known as *The World of 007*), Fox, 1995.

Himself (as James Bond 5), *In Search of James Bond with Jonathan Ross,* 1995.

Telemaraton, 1995.

"GoldenEye": The Secret Files, 1995.

"Star Trek": 30 Years and Beyond, UPN, 1996.

The American Film Institute Salute to Clint Eastwood, 1996.

Lights, Camera, Action! A Century of the Cinema: A Star is Born, 1996.

The Secrets of 007: The James Bond Files, CBS, 1997.

Host, *Voices of Hope—Finding the Cures for Breast and Ovarian Cancer,* Lifetime, 1997.

James Bond: Shaken and Stirred, 1997.

Bravo Profiles: The Entertainment Business, 1998.

The Bond Cocktail, 1999.

And the Word Was Bond (also known as *And Then There Was Bond, The Word Is Bond,* and *The Word Was Bond*), 1999.

The BBC and the BAFTA Lifetime Achievement Tribute to Richard Attenborough, 1999.

The James Bond Story (documentary; also known as *007: The James Bond Story*), AMC, 2000.

Narrator, *Building the Impossible: The Seven Wonders of the Ancient World* (documentary; also known as *The Seven Wonders of the Ancient World*), The Discovery Channel, 2000.

Now Pay Attention 007! (also known as *Now Pay Attention 007!—A Tribute to Desmond Llewellyn*), 2000.

James Bond Down River (also known as *Bond Down River*), 2000.

Host, *Heroes for the Planet A Tribute to National Geographic,* National Geographic Channel, Fox News Channel, and CNBC, 2001.

"Beauty" and "Fame," *The Human Face* (documentary; also known as *The Human Face with John Cleese*), The Learning Channel, 2001.

Judi Dench: A BAFTA Tribute, BBC, 2002.

Best Ever Bond, ITV, 2002.

James Bond: A BAFTA Tribute, BBC, 2002.

The Bond Girls: The E! True Hollywood Story, E! Entertainment Television, 2002.

Premiere Bond: "Die Another Day," 2002.

Best Ever Bond, 2002.

MTV Movie Special: "Die Another Day," MTV, 2002.

Happy Birthday Mr. Bond, 2002.

Host, *AFI's "100 Years ... 100 Movie Quotes: America's Quips, Comebacks and Catchphrases,"* CBS, 2005.

AFI Life Achievement Award: A Tribute to Sean Connery, USA Network, 2006.

Just Another Day, 2006.

Boffo! Tinseltown's Bombs and Blockbusters (documentary), HBO, 2006.

Remington Steele, America's Top Sleuths (documentary), Sleuth Channel, 2006.

Happy Birthday, Elton! From Madison Square Garden, New York (also known as *Elton 60: Live at Madison Square Garden*), My Network TV, 2007.

The 2009 Golden Globe Awards Red Carpet Special, NBC, 2009.

Presenter, *The 3rd Annual CNN Heroes: An All–Star Tribute* (also known as *CNN Heroes: An All–Star Tribute*), Cable News Network, 2009.

Participant, *Hope for Haiti Now: A Global Benefit for Earthquake Relief,* ABC, The CW, NBC, PBS, Fox, and CBS, 2010.

Television Appearances; Awards Presentations:

The 37th Annual Primetime Emmy Awards, NBC, 1985.

The … Annual People's Choice Awards, CBS, 1988, 1996.

Host, *The 49th Annual Golden Globe Awards,* TBS, 1992.

Primer plano, 1995.

The Blockbuster Entertainment Awards, UPN, 1996, Fox, 2000.

The 68th Annual Academy Awards, ABC, 1996.

The 1998 Genesis Awards, Animal Planet, 1998.

Presenter, *… MTV Europe Music Awards,* MTV, 1999, 2002.

The 5th Annual GQ Men of the Year Awards (also known as *GQ's 2000 Men of the Year Awards*), Fox, 2000.

VH1 Big in 2002 Awards, VH1, 2002.

The 2002 MTV Movie Awards, MTV, 2002.

The 2002 ABC World Stunt Awards, 2002.

Presenter *The … Annual Screen Actors Guild Awards,* TNT, 2003, 2006.

Presenter, *The … Annual Academy Awards,* ABC, 2004, 2005.

… Irish Film and Television Awards, IFTN, 2004, 2007.

The British Comedy Awards 2004, ITV, 2004.

Presenter, *The … Annual Golden Globe Awards,* NBC, 2004, 2005, 2009.

The Orange British Academy Film Awards, 2005, BBC, 2006.

Presenter, *The 3rd Annual Film and Television Awards,* 2005.

Television Appearances; Pilots:

Wilde, *Running Wilde,* 1992.

Television Appearances; Episodic:

Radio Man, "Blood Sports," *The Professionals,* 1980.

Jogger, "Carpathian Eagle," *Hammer House of Horror,* 1980.

Dennis, "The Silly Season," *Play for Today,* 1982.

Remington Steele, "The Straight Poop," *Moonlighting,* ABC, 1987.

"Filmen *Mrs. Doubtfire* svensk premiar," *Nyhetsmorgon,* 1994.

"Filmen *Golden Eye,*" *Nyhetsmorgon,* 1995.

"Desmond Llewellyn," *This Is Your Life,* 1995.

"The Best of Muppets Tonight," *Muppets Tonight,* ABC, 1996.

Showbiz Today, Cable News Network, 1996.

Muppets Tonight (also known as *Les muppets*), 1996, 1997.

Archie Grey Owl,"Grey Owl," *Heritage Minute,* 1998.

(Uncredited) Archie Grey Owl, "Tom, Don't Quit Your Day Job …," *The Tom Green Show,* 1999.

"The Films of Barbara Streisand," *The Directors,* 1999.

MADtv, Fox, 1999.

Voice of Ultrahouse 3000, "Treehouse of Horror XII," *The Simpsons* (animated), Fox, 2001.

Host, *Saturday Night Live* (also known as *SNL*), NBC, 2001.

Revealed with Jules Asner, E! Entertainment Television, 2002.

"Cannes Festival 2002," *Leute heute,* 2002.

"Pierce Brosnan," *Revealed with Jules Asner* (also known as *Revealed*), 2002.

Himself, "Shut It Down," *Hollywood, Inc.,* 2002.

Himself, "Lightning in a Bottle," *Hollywood, Inc.,* 2002.

Inside the Actors Studio (also known as *Inside the Actors Studio: The Craft of Theatre and Film*), Bravo, 2002.

Punk'd, MTV, 2003.

Host, "The Dreamin' with American Ballet Theatre," *Great Performances: Dance in America* (also known as *Dance in America*), PBS, 2004.

"Pierce Brosnan: Beyond Bond," *Biography,* Arts and Entertainment, 2004.

"Julianne Moore: Seeing Red," *Biography,* Arts and Entertainment, 2004.

Film 2005 (also known as *The Film Programme*), 2005.

Narrator, "Voyage to Kure," *Jean–Michel Cousteau: Ocean Adventures,* 2006.

Narrator, "The Gray Whale," *Jean–Michel Cousteau: Ocean Adventures,* 2006.

Narrator, "Sharks at Risk," *Jean–Michel Cousteau: Ocean Adventures,* 2006.

Film 2006 (also known as *The Film Programme*), 2006.

Entertainment Tonight (also known as *E.T.*), syndicated, 2008, 2009.

The Movie Loft, 2009.

Television Talk Show Guest Appearances; Episodic:

Late Night with David Letterman, NBC, 1984.

The Tonight Show Starring Johnny Carson, 1991, 1992.

The Tonight Show with Jay Leno (also known as *Jay Leno*), NBC, 1993, 1995, 1996, 1997, 1999, 2001, 2002, 2004.

"Filmen *Mama Mia/* Nyhter och vader," *Nyhetsmorgon,* 1994.

Late Show with David Letterman (also known as *Letterman* and *The Late Show*), CBS, 1995, 1997, 1999, 2004, 2006, 2008.

The Late Night with Conan O'Brien, NBC, 1995, 1997, 1999, 2004.

Die Harald Schmidt Show (also known as *Late Night Show mit Harald Schmidt*), 1995, 1998.

Corazon, corazon, 1996.

The Rosie O'Donnell Show, 1997.

Mundo VIP, 1997, 1999.

Lo+ plus, 1997, 2003.

The Big Breakfast, Channel 4, 1999.

Clive Anderson All Talk, BBC1, 1999.

The Charlie Rose Show (also known as *Charlie Rose*), PBS, 1999, 2004.

The View, ABC, 1999, 2002, 2004, 2006.

The Daily Show (also known as *A Daily Show with Jon Stewart, Jon Stewart, The Daily Show with Jon Stewart,* and *The Daily Show with Jon Stewart Global Edition*), Comedy Central, 1999, 2006, 2008.

Film 2000 (also known as *The Film Programme*), 2000.

Leute heute, 2002.

The Caroline Rhea Show, syndicated, 2002.

The Late Late Show with Craig Kilborn (also known as *The Late Late Show*), CBS, 2002.

Parkinson, 2002, 2003.

Kelly, VTV, 2003.

Morten og Peter I Dublin, 2003.

On the Record with Bob Costas, HBO, 2003.

This Morning (also known as *This Morning with Richard and Judy*), ITV, 2004.

Tavis Smiley, PBS, 2004.

T4, Channel 4, 2004.

Friday Night with Jonathan Ross, BBC, 2004.

Ant & Dec's Saturday Night Takeaway, ITV, 2004.

Film 2004 (also known as *The Film Programme*), 2004.

Richard & Judy, ITV, 2004, 2005.

Sunday Morning Shootout (also known as *Hollywood Shootout* and *Shootout*), AMC, 2004, 2005.

Ellen: The Ellen DeGenres Show (also known as *The Ellen Show*), syndicated, 2004, 2006, 2008.

Live with Regis and Kelly, 2004, 2008.

Davina, 2006.

"El Nadal," La rentadora, 2006.

Up Close with Carrie Keagan, 2007.

Breakfast, BBC, 2008.

Today (also known as *NBC News Today* and *The Today Show*), NBC, 2008.

The Late Late Show with Craig Ferguson, CBS, 2010.

Le grand journal de Canal+, 2010.

Also appeared in *Celebrity Profile.*

Stage Appearances:

(London debut) *Wait until Dark,* 1976.

McCabe, *The Red Devil Battery Sign,* Round House Theatre, then Phoenix Theatre, London, 1977.

Harry Leftwich, *Semi Monde,* Glasgow Citizen's Theatre, 1977.

Eddie Schulz, *No Orchids for Miss Blandish,* Glasgow Citizen's Theatre, 1978.

Brachiano, *Painter's Palace of Pleasure,* Glasgow Citizen's Theatre, 1978.

The Changing Room, Palace Theatre, Westcliff, England, 1978.

Ricardo, *Filumena,* Lyric Theatre, London, 1978–79.

Ken Harrison, *Whose Life Is It Anyway?,* Palace Theatre, 1980.

Also appeared in *Fuente Ovejuna, The Rats,* and *The White Devil,* all Drama Centre.

RECORDINGS

Videos:

Behind the Scenes with "Goldfinger" (short documentary; also known as *The Making of "Goldfinger"*), 1995.

Himself, *Getting Close to the Show* (documentary; also known as *Getting Close to the Show: The Making of "Dante's Peak"*), 1998.

Himself, *Die Another Day: From Script to Screen* (documentary), 2002.

Himself, *"Evelyn": The Story behind the Story* (short documentary), Metro–Goldwyn–Mayer Home Entertainment, 2003.

Himself, *"Evelyn": Behind the Scenes* (short documentary), Metro–Goldwyn–Mayer Home Entertainment, 2003.

Himself, *Inside "Die Another Day"* (short documentary), Metro–Goldwyn–Mayer Home Entertainment, 2003.

Himself, *Before, During, and "After the Sunset"* (documentary), New Line Home Video, 2005.

Himself, *"Mama Mia!": A Look inside "Mama Mia! The Movie"* (short documentary), Universal, 2008.

Himself, *"Mama Mia!": Gimme! Gimme! Gimme! Music Video* (short documentary), Universal, 2008.

Himself, *"Mama Mia!": Becoming a Singer* (short documentary), Universal, 2008.

Himself, *"Mama Mia!": Anatomy of a Musical Number—"Lay All Your Love on Me,"* Universal, 2008.

Himself, *"Mama Mia!": The Making of "Mama Mia! The Movie"* (short documentary), Universal, 2008.

Appeared in music video for song by Roy Orbison.

Video Games:

Tomorrow Never Dies (also known as *TND Game, Tomorrow Never Dies: The Game,* and *Tomorrow Never Dies: The Video Game*), 1999.

The World Is Not Enough, Electronic Arts, 2000.

Voice of James Bond, *James Bond 007: Everything or Nothing* (also known as *007: Everything or Nothing, Eon,* and *Everything or Nothing*), Electronic Arts, 2003.

OTHER SOURCES

Books:
Carrick, Peter, *Pierce Brosnan,* Citadel, 2002.
Membry, York, *Pierce Brosnan: The Biography,* Virgin Books, 2003.
Newsmakers 2000, Issue 3, Gale, 2000.

Periodicals:
Cigar Aficionado, November/December, 1997.
Cosmopolitan, September, 1996, p. 202.
Daily Mail (London), January 27, 2009, p. 7; March 2, 2009, p. 21.
Entertainment Weekly, December 1, 1995, p. 13; August 19, 2005, p. 98.
Good Housekeeping, July, 2008, p. 52.
McCall's, July, 1987.
People Weekly, April 27, 1992; May 6, 1996, p. 64; March 3, 1997, p.114; November 26, 2001, pp. 76–81; January 23, 2006, p. 95.
Redbook, May, 1989; December, 1995, p. 63; December, 1997, p. 80.
Time, December 15, 1997, p. 34; June 20, 2005, p. 75.
TV Guide, November 13, 1999, pp. 18–22; September 28, 2002, p. 32; November 9, 2002, pp. 22–26.
USA Today, December 28, 2005, p. 1D.

Electronic:
Pierce Brosnan Official Site, http://www.piercebrosnan.com, February 19, 2010.

BRYGGMAN, Larry 1938–

PERSONAL

Full name, Arvid Laurence Bryggman; born December 21, 1938, in Concord, CA; father, worked for a neon sign company; mother, a piano teacher; married Barbara Creed (divorced, 1982); married Jacqueline Schultz (an actress), 1982 (divorced, 1987); married Tracey Hanley (a director, 1999; children: (first marriage) one son; (third marriage) Ryan Hanley, Riley Claire; (with Heidi Brennan) one daughter. *Education:* City College of San Francisco, B.A.; trained for the stage at the American Theatre Wing.

Addresses: *Agent*—WME, One William Morris Pl., Beverly Hills, CA 90212.

Career: Actor. Performed with Pittsburgh Playhouse, Pittsburgh, PA, 1966–67; with Theatre Company of Boston, Boston, MA, 1967–68, 1969–71, and 1972–73;

with Long Wharf Theatre, New Haven, CT, 1968–69; with Hartford Stage Company, Hartford, CT, 1971–72, 1974–75; and with National Home Theatre, New York City, 1990.

Awards, Honors: Daytime Emmy Award nominations, outstanding actor in a daytime drama series, 1981, 1982, 1985, 1986, 1988, 1989, Daytime Emmy Awards, outstanding actor in a daytime drama series, 1984, 1987, *Soap Opera Digest* Award nominations, outstanding actor in a lead role—daytime, 1986, 1988, 1989, 1991, outstanding villain on a daytime, and outstanding contribution by an actor/actress to the form of continuing drama who is currently on a daytime serial, 1986, all for *As the World Turns;* Obie Award, *Village Voice,* 1993, for sustained excellence of work; Antoinette Perry Award, best actor in a featured role in a play, 1994, for *Picnic;* Antoinette Perry Award nomination, best actor in a featured role in a play, 2001, for *Proof;* Richard Seff Award, Obie Award, performance, Lucille Lortel Award nomination, outstanding lead actor, Drama Desk Award nomination, outstanding featured actor in a play, Outer Critics Circle Award nomination, outstanding featured actor in a play, 2005, all for *Romance.*

CREDITS

Film Appearances:
Warren Fresnell, *... And Justice for All ...,* Columbia, 1979.
Stacy, *Hanky–Panky,* Columbia, 1982.
Inspector Walter Cobb, *Die Hard: With a Vengeance* (also known as *Die Hard 3*), Buena Vista, 1995.
Lord Stanley, *Looking for Richard,* Fox Searchlight Pictures, 1996.
A man with a brief case, *The One Arm Bandit* (also known as *Crash Pad and the One Arm Bandit*), 2000.
The husband, *Crash Pad!,* 2000.
Troy Folger, *Spy Game* (also known as *Spy Game—Der finale Countdown* and *Spy game—Jeu d'espions*), Universal, 2001.
Salty, *Side by Each,* Panorama Entertainment, 2008.

Television Appearances; Series:
Dr. John Dixon, *As the World Turns,* CBS, 1969–2004.

Also appeared in *Love Is A Many Splendored Thing,* CBS.

Television Appearances; Movies:
(Uncredited) Pharmacist, *Strike Force* (also known as *Crack* and *Crackdown*), 1975.

Television Appearances; Specials:
Celebration for William Jennings Bryan, PBS, 1968.
The 8th Annual Daytime Emmy Awards, 1981.

Dr. John Dixon, *"As the World Turns"*: 30th Anniversary, CBS, 1986.

4th Annual Soap Opera Digest Awards, NBC, 1988.

The 15th Annual Daytime Emmy Awards, CBS, 1988.

Television Appearances; Episodic:

"Behind the Scenes: 'Die Hard: With a Vengeance,'" *HBO First Look,* HBO, 1995.

Rowen, "Myth of Fingerprints," *Law & Order,* NBC, 2001.

Dr. Platner's attorney, "Mercy," *Law & Order: Special Victims Unit* (also known as *Law & Order: SVU* and *Special Victims Unit*), NBC, 2003.

Stage Appearances:

(Off–Broadway debut) Tallahassee, "A Summer Ghost," *Charlatans,* in *A Pair of Pairs,* Vandam Theatre, 1962.

Armstrong's Last Goodnight, Theatre Company of Boston, Boston, 1966.

Live Like Pigs, Theatre Company of Boston, 1966.

Tiny Alice, Theatre Company of Boston, 1967.

The Duchess of Malfi, Long Wharf Theatre, New Haven, CT, 1968.

The Fun War, Theatre Company of Boston, 1968.

Jeff, *Mod Donna,* New York Shakespeare Festival, Public Theatre, New York City, 1969.

Title role, "Terrible Jim Fitch," *Stop, You're Killing Me,* Stage 73 Theatre, New York City, 1969.

Pozzo, *Waiting for Godot,* Sheridan Square Playhouse, New York City, 1971.

Play Strindberg, Theatre Company of Boston, 1972.

Buck Mulligan, Watch, Dr. Mulligan, and Bishop of Erin, *Ulysses in Nighttown,* Winter Garden Theatre, New York City, 1974.

Christian, *Dearly Beloved,* Manhattan Theatre Club, New York City, 1976.

Dr. Sheldon Henning, *Checking Out,* Longacre Theatre, New York City, 1976.

Kress, *The Basic Training of Pavlo Hummel,* Theatre Company of Boston, Longacre Theatre, 1977.

Frank Schaeffer, *Marco Polo Sings a Solo,* Joseph Papp Public Theatre, Newman Theatre, New York City, 1977.

Lieutenant Brann, *Two Small Bodies,* Playwrights Horizons Theatre, New York City, 1977.

The guard, *Museum,* New York Shakespeare Festival, Public Theatre, 1978.

Earl of Derby, *Richard III,* Cort Theatre, New York City, 1979.

Fool, *The Winter Dancers,* Marymount Manhattan Theatre, New York City, 1979.

Sir, *A Life in the Theatre,* Westchester Regional Theatre, Harrison, NY, 1980.

Tramb, major, and manager, *The Resurrection of Lady Lester,* Manhattan Theatre Club, 1981.

Arturo, *Modern Ladies of Guanabacoa,* Ensemble Studio Theatre, New York City, 1983.

Robert Ingersoll, *Royal Bob,* StageArts Theatre Company, Chernuchin Theatre, New York City, 1983.

Calvin Barkdull, *The Ballad of Soapy Smith,* New York Shakespeare Festival, Public Theatre, 1984.

Hank, "Life under Water," *Marathon '85,* Ensemble Studio Theatre, 1985.

Bijou Billins, *Walk the Dog, Willie,* The Production Company, Theatre Guinevere, New York City, 1985.

Tom Tanner and Larry Peters, *Rum and Coke,* New York Shakespeare Festival, Susan Stein Shiva Theatre, New York City, 1986.

Man shopping for television, Mr. August, newlywed couple, *Bodies, Rest and Motion,* Mitzi E. Newhouse Theatre, New York City, 1986–87.

Blood Sports, New York Theatre Workshop, Perry Street Theatre, New York City, 1987.

Andrew, *Spoils of War,* Second Stage Theatre, New York City, 1988.

Bill, "Just Horrible," *Class 1 Acts,* Manhattan Class Company, Nat Horne Theatre, New York City, 1988.

Sicinius Vellutus, *Coriolanus,* New York Shakespeare Festival, 1989 and 1990.

Banquo, *Macbeth,* New York Shakespeare Festival, Public Theatre, 1990.

Dr. Boyle, *Prelude to a Kiss,* Helen Hayes Theatre, New York City, 1990–91.

Henry, *Henry IV Parts One and Two,* New York Shakespeare Festival, 1990 and 1991.

Robert Mohr, *The White Rose,* Workshop of the Players Art (WPA) Theatre, New York City, 1991.

Pavel Petrovich Kirasanov, *Nothing Sacred,* Atlantic Theatre, New York City, 1992.

Duke Frederick, *As You Like It,* New York Shakespeare Festival, 1992.

Howard Bevans, *Picnic,* Criterion Center Stage Right, New York City, 1994.

Harry Baker and Alfred Baker, *New England,* Manhattan Theatre Club, 1995.

Alonso, *The Tempest,* New York Shakespeare Festival, 1995.

Duke of Buckingham, *Henry VIII,* New York Shakespeare Festival, Joseph Papp Public Theatre, New York City, 1997.

Once in a Lifetime, Linda Gross Theatre, New York City, 1998.

Roote, *The Hothouse,* Atlantic Theatre, 1999.

Robert, *Proof,* Manhattan Theater Club Stage II, New York City, then Walter Kerr Theatre, New York City, 2000–2001.

Emil, *A Bad Friend,* Mitzi E. Newhouse Theatre, 2003.

Graham, *Frame 312,* Linda Gross Theatre, 2003–2004.

Jon, *Roulette,* John Houseman Theatre, New York City, 2004.

Juror #11, *Twelve Angry Men,* Roundabout Theatre Company, New York City, 2004–2005.

The judge, *Romance,* Atlantic Theatre, then Mark Taper Forum, Los Angeles, 2005.

Gayev, *The Cherry Orchard,* Atlantic Theatre, 2005.

Helge, *Festen,* Music Box Theatre, New York City, 2006.

Gloucester, *King Lear,* Joseph Papp Public Theatre, 2007.

The man, *Edward Albee's "Occupant,"* Peter Norton Space, Signature Theatre Company, New York City, 2008.

John Mitchell, Chai Roberts, and Lamont Vanderhall, *Top Secret: The Battle for the Pentagon Papers,* New York Theatre Workshop, 2010.

Made stage debut as Biff, *Death of a Salesman,* San Francisco, CA; also appeared in *Ballymurphy; The Cherry Orchard; The Lincoln Mask; Irma La Douce; More Stately Mansions; Who's Afraid of Virginia Woolf?; Brecht on Brecht.*

BUNDY, Laura Bell 1981–
(Laura Bundy)

PERSONAL

Full name, Laura Ashley Bell Bundy; born April 10, 1981, in Lexington, KY; father, an electrical engineer and manufacturing company owner.

Addresses: *Agent*—WME Entertainment, One William Morris Pl., Beverly Hills, CA 90212.

Career: Actress. Laura & Amber (country music duo), member. Kreative Kids Foundation (a charity), founder. Schmancy Purses, creator and codesigner.

Awards, Honors: Drama Desk Award nomination, outstanding actress in a musical, 1993, Outer Critics Circle Award nomination, outstanding actress in a musical, both for *Ruthless!;* Antoinette Perry Award nomination, best actress in musical, Drama Desk Award nomination, outstanding actress in a musical, 2007, both for *Legally Blonde—The Musical.*

CREDITS

Film Appearances:
(As Laura Bundy) Susan Wilks, *The Adventures of Huck Finn* (also known as *The Adventures of Huckleberry Finn*), Buena Vista, 1993.
(As Laura Bundy) Courtney Aspinall, *Life with Mikey* (also known as *Give Me a Break*), Buena Vista, 1993.
Young Sarah, *Jumanji,* TriStar, 1995.
Doris, *Surf School,* Slow Hand Releasing, 2006.

Sweetheart, *Dreamgirls,* Paramount, 2006.
(As Laura Bundy) Peggy, *The Drum Beats Twice,* Vivendi Entertainment, 2008.

Television Appearances; Series:
Marah Shayne Lewis, *The Guiding Light* (also known as *Guiding Light*), CBS, 1999–2001.
"Legally Blonde the Musical": The Search for Elle Woods, MTV, 2008.

Television Appearances; Movies:
All Grown Up, 2003.

Television Appearances; Specials:
(As Laura Bundy) Kimberly Timothy, *"Stranger With Candy": Retardation, a Celebration,* Comedy Central, 1998.
Performer, *The 57th Annual Tony Awards,* CBS, 2003.
Elle Woods, *Legally Blonde: The Musical,* MTV, 2007.
New Now Next Awards, 2008.
Judge, *Miss America Pageant 2009,* The Learning Channel, 2009.

Television Appearances; Episodic:
Sharon, "Mr. Wilson's Opus," *Home Improvement,* ABC, 1996.
Julie Bloch, "Green–Eyed Monster," *Veronica Mars,* UPN, 2005.
Nora McCarthy, "Willkommen," *Cold Case,* CBS, 2006.
Tyffani, "The Homewrecker," *Modern Men,* The WB, 2006.
Alicia, "Thanksgiving," *Happy Hour,* Fox, 2008.

Stage Appearances:
Tina Denmark, *Ruthless!,* Player Theatre, New York City, 1992–93.
Dainty June, *Gypsy,* Paper Mill Playhouse, Milburn, NJ, 1998.
Amber Van Tussle, *Hair,* 5th Avenue Theatre, Seattle, WA, 2002, then Neil Simon Theatre, New York City, 2002.
Standby Galinda/Glinda, *Wicked,* George Gershwin Theatre, New York City, 2003–2004.
The Life and Times of Laura Bell Bundy (a concert), Joe's Pub, New York City, 2004.
Elle Woods, *Legally Blonde,* San Francisco, CA, 2007, then Palace Theatre, New York City, 2007–2008.
Singer, *The 24 Hour Plays 2008,* American Airlines Theatre, New York City, 2008.

Also appeared as Sherrie Christian, *Rock of Ages,* Los Angeles; Louisa, *The Sound of Music;* in *Damn Yankees; Grease!; Adventures of Huck and Finn; Pajama Game.*

RECORDINGS

Albums:

Recorded *Longing for a Place Already Gone; I'll Be Home for Christmas.*

BURKE, Brooke 1971–

PERSONAL

Full name, Brooke Lisa Burke; born September 8, 1971, in Hartford, CT; raised in Tucson, AZ; daughter of George Burke (in sales) and Donna Burke Hatounian (in sales); stepdaughter of Armen Hatounian (a mechanic); married Garth Fisher (a plastic surgeon), 2001 (some sources cite 2002; divorced, 2005 [some sources cite 2006]); children: (with Fisher) Neriah, Sierra; (with David Charvet, an actor and singer) Heaven Rain, Shaya Braven. *Education:* Studied broadcast journalism and advertising at the University of California, Los Angeles; also attended Santa Monica College. *Religion:* Jewish. *Avocational Interests:* Fitness workouts, walking, gourmet cooking.

Addresses: *Agent*—David Brady, Brady, Brannon & Rich, 5670 Wilshire Blvd., Suite 820, Los Angeles, CA 90036. *Manager*—Mark Schulman, 3 Arts Entertainment, 9460 Wilshire Blvd., 7th Floor, Beverly Hills, CA 90212. *Publicist*—Nancy Iannios, Nancy Iannios Public Relations, 8271 Melrose Ave., Suite 102, Los Angeles, CA 90046–6824.

Career: Actress and television host. Model, including work for Venus Swimwear and Frederick's of Hollywood; cover model and model for men's magazines; appeared in advertisements, infomercials, and calendars. Creator of the swimwear line Barely Brooke, 2003, and the maternity fashion line Baboosh Baby, 2007; founded the online store *BabooshBaby.com;* and co–chief executive officer of *ModernMom.com.* Involved with charities; hosted a holiday card drive and participated in benefits for hospitals.

Awards, Honors: Winner of various pageants; Spike TV Video Game Award, best performance by a human—female, 2004, for *Need for Speed: Underground 2;* champion of the celebrity dance competition *Dancing with the Stars,* 2008.

CREDITS

Television Appearances; Series:
Host, *Wild On ...,* E! Entertainment Television, 1999–2002.
Host, *Rank,* E! Entertainment Television, 2001–2003.
Host, *Life Is Great with Brooke Burke* (also known as *The Good Life with Brooke Burke*), E! Entertainment Television, 2004–2005.
Host, *Rock Star: INXS,* CBS, 2005.
Host, *Rock Star: Supernova,* CBS, 2006.
Contestant, *Dancing with the Stars* (also known as *DWTS* and *D.W.T.S.*), ABC, 2008.
Mommy correspondent, *The Doctors,* syndicated, 2009—.
Host, *She's Got the Look,* TV Land, beginning 2010.
Cohost, *Dancing with the Stars* (also known as *DWTS* and *D.W.T.S.*), ABC, 2010—.

Television Appearances; Miniseries:
Herself, *I Love the '80s Strikes Back,* VH1, 2003.

Television Appearances; Specials:
Herself, *Bathing Brooke: The Making of Brooke Burke's "2002 Special Edition Swimsuit Calendar,"* E! Entertainment Television, 2001.
Host, *Heatwave,* E! Entertainment Television, 2001.
Herself, *Barely Brooke,* E! Entertainment Television, 2002.
Herself, *Road to the Red Carpet,* E! Entertainment Television, 2002.
Herself, *The Disco Ball ... A 30–Year Celebration* (also known as *The Disco Ball*), ABC, 2003.
Herself, *Maxim Hot 100* (also known as *Maxim's "Hot 100"*), NBC, 2003.
Judge, *Miss USA 2003,* NBC, 2003.
Cohost, *Live from the Red Carpet: The 2004 Primetime Emmy Awards,* E! Entertainment Television, 2004.
Host, *Gilmore Girls Backstage Special,* ABC Family, 2004.
Host, *"Smallville" Backstage Special,* ABC Family, 2004.
Herself, *E!'s "Live Countdown to the Academy Awards,"* E! Entertainment Television, 2005.
Correspondent, *2009 Golden Globe Awards Red Carpet Special,* NBC, 2009.

Television Appearances; Awards Presentations:
Cohost of red carpet segment and presenter, *The 30th Annual People's Choice Awards,* CBS, 2004.
Presenter, *The 2004 ESPY Awards,* ESPN, 2004.
Video Game Awards 2004 (also known as *Spike TV Video Game Awards 2004, Spike TV's "The Ultimate Gamer Video Game Awards 2004,"* and *2004 Spike TV Video Game Awards*), Spike TV, 2004.
AutoRox (also known as *AutoRox Awards, First Annual AutoRox Awards, Spike TV Presents "AutoRox: The Automotive Award Show,"* and *Spike TV's "First Annual AutoRox Awards"*), Spike TV, 2005.
The 35th Annual People's Choice Awards, CBS, 2009.

Television Appearances; Episodic:
Second beautiful woman, "Solo Flight," *Pensacola: Wings of Gold* (also known as *Pensacola*), syndicated, 1998.

Herself, "Aruba (1)," *Search Party,* E! Entertainment Television, 2000.

Contestant, "Television Hosts" (also known as "TV Hosts Edition"), *Weakest Link* (also known as *The Weakest Link* and *The Weakest Link USA*), NBC, 2001.

Reporter, "All about Lydia," *That's Life,* ABC, 2002.

Herself, *The Best Damn Sports Show Period,* Fox Sports Net, 2002.

Herself, *E! News Daily* (also known as *E! News Live* and *E! News Live Weekend*), E! Entertainment Television, 2002.

Hollywood Squares (also known as *H2, H2: Hollywood Squares,* and *The Hollywood Squares*), syndicated, multiple appearances, 2002 and 2004.

Stacey, "Prior Engagement," *Rock Me, Baby,* UPN, 2003.

Herself, "CMT: 40 Sexiest Videos," *The Greatest* (also known as *CMT: The Greatest* and *CMT: The Greatest—40 Sexiest Videos*), Country Music Television, 2004.

Herself, "Need for Speed: Underground 2 Special," *Sweat,* G4techTV, 2004.

Nurse Benson, "22 Minus 1 Equals 4," *Less Than Perfect* (also known as *Office Girl*), ABC, 2004.

Park ranger, "Who's Camping Now," *It's All Relative* (also known as *Absolut relativ, En svaerfar foer mycket, Kaikki on suhteellista,* and *Todo es relativo*), ABC, 2004.

Reporter, "Being Bernie Mac," *The Bernie Mac Show* (also known as *Bernie Mac* and *Bernie Mac Show*), Fox, 2004.

Reporter, "Mr. Monk and the T.V. Star," *Monk,* USA Network, 2004.

Guest cohost, *Good Day Live,* syndicated, 2004.

Celebrity judge, *Pet Star,* Animal Planet, 2004, 2005.

Herself, "Lights, Camera, Face Crack!," *Eve* (also known as *The Opposite Sex*), UPN, 2005.

Herself, "So Jewtastic," *VH1: All Access* (also known as *All Access* and *VH1 All Access*), VH1, 2005.

(Uncredited) Herself, *The Contender,* NBC, 2005.

(In archive footage) Herself, *101 Sexiest Celebrity Bodies* (also known as *E's "101," E's "101 Sexiest Celebrity Bodies,"* and *101 Most ...*), E! Entertainment Television, 2005.

Herself, *Car Cruzin',* Men & Motors, c. 2005.

Herself, "Brooke Burke," *Payback,* Speed, 2006.

Sheryl, "Cash Springs Eternal," *Las Vegas* (also known as *Casino Eye*), NBC, 2006.

Herself, "Brooke Burke," *Who Are You Wearing,* The Learning Channel, 2008.

Herself, *The Insider,* syndicated, 2008.

Herself, *Entertainment Tonight* (also known as *Entertainment This Week, E.T., ET Weekend,* and *This Week in Entertainment*), syndicated, multiple episodes in 2008 and 2009.

Cynthia Wells, "In Plane Sight," *CSI: Miami* (also known as *CSI Miami* and *CSI: Weekends*), CBS, 2009.

(Sometimes uncredited) Herself, *Dancing with the Stars* (also known as *DWTS* and *D.W.T.S.*), ABC, multiple episodes in 2009.

Herself, *TMZ on TV* (also known as *TMZ*), syndicated, 2009.

Appeared in other programs, including *Star Search.*

Television Talk Show Guest Appearances; Episodic:

The Test, FX Network, 2001.

The Late Late Show with Craig Kilborn (also known as *The Late Late Show*), CBS, 2001, 2003, 2004.

Howard Stern (also known as *The Howard Stern Show*), E! Entertainment Television, 2002.

Last Call with Carson Daly, NBC, 2002, 2006.

The New Tom Green Show, MTV, 2003.

Jimmy Kimmel Live! (also known as *Jimmy Kimmel* and *The Jimmy Kimmel Project*), ABC, multiple episodes in 2003, 2004, 2008.

Good Day Live, syndicated, 2004.

"Celebrity Diet Secrets," *The Tyra Banks Show* (also known as *Tyra*), syndicated, 2006.

"Brooke and Alfonso," *Sidewalks Entertainment* (also known as *Sidewalks* and *Sidewalks Entertainment Hour*), syndicated, 2008.

Ellen: The Ellen DeGeneres Show (also known as *Ellen* and *The Ellen DeGeneres Show*), syndicated, 2008.

The Morning Show with Mike and Juliet (also known as *The Morning Show with Mike & Juliet*), Fox, 2008.

The Bonnie Hunt Show, syndicated, 2009.

Chelsea Lately, E! Entertainment Television, 2009.

The Wendy Williams Show, Black Entertainment Television and syndicated, 2009.

Appeared in other programs, including *Jenny Jones,* syndicated.

Film Appearances:

(Uncredited) Waitress on roller skates, *The Wraith* (also known as *Interceptor* and *Phantom*), New Century Vista Film Company, 1986.

Jill, *The Hazing* (also known as *Dead Scared*), MTI Home Video, 2004.

Katherine, *Knuckle Sandwich,* 2004, Westlake Entertainment Group, 2007.

Stage Appearances:

Pieces (of Ass) (series of monologues), Raleigh Studios Hollywood, Hollywood, CA, 2003.

RECORDINGS

Fitness Videos; as Herself:

Gunnar Peterson's "Core Secrets: Bun Battle," Guthy-Renker, 2003.

Gunnar Peterson's "Core Secrets: Fun-damentals," Guthy-Renker, 2003.

Video Games:
Host of the People and Places category, *Trivial Pursuit Unhinged,* Atari, 2004.
Voice of Rachel Teller, *Need for Speed: Underground 2,* Electronic Arts, 2004.
Voice, *Big Bumpin',* Microsoft/King Games/Burger King, 2006.
Voice, *Pocketbike Racer,* Microsoft/King Games/Burger King, 2006.

WRITINGS

Nonfiction:
(Contributor) Melanie Dunea and Nigel Parry, *Precious* (photographs and accompanying text), power-House Books, 2004.

OTHER SOURCES

Periodicals:
Chicago Tribune, November 27, 2008.
People Weekly, May 28, 2001, pp. 105–06; August 31, 2009, p. 70.
TV Guide, November 3, 2008, p. 44.
USA Today, December 9, 2008, p. 4D.

Electronic:
Brooke Burke Official Site, http://brookeburke.com, February 24, 2009.

BURKE, Marylouise
(Mary Louise Burke)

PERSONAL

Education: Studied acting at Hedgerow Theatre, Philadelphia, PA, prior to 1973.

Career: Actress. Circle Repertory Company, past member of theatre laboratory. Previously worked as a usage inspector for the Army Corps of Engineers in Philadelphia, PA.

Member: Actors' Equity Association.

Awards, Honors: Drama Desk Award, outstanding featured actress in a play, 2000, for *Fuddy Meers;* Drama Desk Award nomination, outstanding actress in a play, Outer Critics Circle Award nomination, outstanding actress in a play, 2003, Garland Award, Back Stage West, all for *Kimberly Akimbo.*

CREDITS

Stage Appearances:
Margaret, *The Broken Pitcher,* Goethe House, Martinique Theatre, New York City, 1981.
Mama, *The Return of Pinocchio,* Double Image Theatre, 47th Street Theatre, New York City, 1986.
Mother, *The Eden Cinema,* UBU Repertory Theatre, Harold Clurman Theatre, New York City, 1986.
Grandmama, sorceress, Laura, and Madame d'Urfe, *Casanova,* New York Shakespeare Festival, Martinson Hall, Public Theatre, New York City, 1991.
Mrs. Krebs, *Inherit the Wind,* National Actors Theatre, Royale Theatre, New York City, 1996.
Gertie, *Fuddy Mears,* Minetta Lane Theatre, New York City, 1999–2000.
Sheila, *Wyoming,* 78th Street Theatre Laboratory, New York City, 2000.
Karla, *Wonder of the World,* Manhattan Theatre Club Stage I, New York City, 2001–2002.
Title role, *Kimberly Akimbo,* South Coast Repertory, Costa Mesa, CA, 2001, then Manhattan Theatre Club Stage I, 2003.
Jack's mother, *Into the Woods* (musical), Ahmanson Theatre, Los Angeles, then Broadhurst Theatre, New York City, 2002.
Hilda, *Wintertime,* Second Stage Theatre, New York City, 2004.
Vera, *The Oldest Profession,* Peter Norton Space, New York City, 2004.
Madame Caron, *Is He Dead?,* Lyceum Theatre, New York City, 2007–2008.
Margaret, *The Savannah Disputation,* Playwrights Horizons Theatre, New York City, 2009.

Also appeared in *The Chairs,* Pearl Theatre Company, New York City; *Dark Ride,* New York City; *A Devil Inside,* Soho Repertory Theatre, New York City; *Dinner at Eight,* Long Wharf Theatre, New Haven, CT; *Good,* Soho Repertory Theatre; *Hot Keys,* New York City; *I Ain't Your Uncle,* Hartford Stage Company, Hartford, CT; *A Lifetime of Reasons,* All Seasons Theatre Company, New York City; *Marvin's Room,* Hartford Stage Company; *The Matchmaker,* McCarter Theatre, Princeton, NJ; *Once in a Lifetime,* La Jolla Playhouse, La Jolla, CA; *The Piano Lesson,* Broadway production; *Seven Guitars,* Broadway production; *Suddenly Last Summer,* Hartford Stage Company; and *When We Are Married,* Long Wharf Theatre.

Major Tours:
Toured as Miss Framer, *Lettice and Lovage,* U.S. cities.

Film Appearances:
Fern, *Angie,* Buena Vista, 1994.
Aunt Phyllis, *Jeffrey,* Orion, 1995.

Drena, *Hudson River Blues* (also known as *Family Blues*), Romance Classics, 1997.

Father Gladen's fan on the porch, *Celebrity*, Miramax, 1998.

Louisa, *One True Thing*, MCA/Universal, 1998.

Lillian, *Meet Joe Black*, MCA/Universal, 1998.

Neighbor woman, *Bringing Out the Dead*, Paramount, 1999.

Yvette, *Urbania*, Lions Gate Films, 2000.

Sister Grace, *Diary of a City Priest*, Heartland Film Festival, 2001.

Connie Trabucco, *Series 7: The Contenders* (also known as *Series 7*), USA Films, 2001.

Mrs. Flam, *Martin & Orloff*, Belladonna Productions/Cineblast Productions, 2002.

(Uncredited) President Jocelyn Carr's secretary, *Mona Lisa Smile*, Columbia, 2003.

Madge, *The Warrior Class*, Echo Bridge Home Entertainment, 2004.

Mom, *Something for Henry* (short film), 2004.

Miles's mother, *Sideways*, Fox Searchlight, 2004.

Delores, *The Baxter*, Lions Gate Films, 2005.

Aunt Grandma, *Pizza*, IFC Films, 2005.

Aunt Eileen, *Must Love Dogs*, Warner Bros., 2005.

Lunch lady, *A Prairie Home Companion*, Picturehouse Entertainment, 2006.

Joan Kayser, *Things That Hang from Trees*, Radio London Films, 2006.

(As Mary Louise Burke) Janice, *Ira & Abby*, Magnolia Pictures, 2006.

Herself, *"A Prairie Home Companion": Exclusive Sneak Peek* (short documentary), Picturehouse Entertainment, 2006.

Babe, *The Cake Eaters*, Screen Media Films, 2007.

Esther, *Call Your Mother* (short film), 2008.

Linda, *We Pedal Uphill*, Cinevolve Studios, 2008.

Mrs. Deakins, *Doubt*, Miramax, 2008.

(As Mary Louise Burke) Barbara Bascombe, *I Love You Phillip Morris*, Consolidated Pictures Group, 2009.

Gamma, *A Christmas Carrot* (short film), 2009.

Ms. Gelband, *An Invisible Sign of My Own*, 2010.

(Uncredited) Librarian, *Rabbit Hole*, Fox Searchlight, 2010.

Television Appearances; Series:

Jessica's mother, *Hung*, HBO, 2009.

Television Appearances; Movies:

Arlene, *Amy & Isabelle* (also known as *Oprah Winfrey Presents: "Amy and Isabelle"*), ABC, 2001.

(As Mary Louise Burke) Carol, *My Sexiest Mistake*, Oxygen, 2004.

Rosemary Finley, *The Mastersons of Manhattan*, NBC, 2007.

Television Appearances; Pilots:

Jessica's mother, *Hung*, HBO, 2009.

Television Appearances; Episodic:

Estelle, "In Memory Of," *Law & Order*, NBC, 1991.

Mrs. Collins, "Legacy," *Law & Order*, NBC, 1997.

Nurse Sally, "Summary Judgement," *Hope & Faith*, ABC, 2003.

Curious woman, "Serendipity," *Law & Order: Special Victims Unit* (also known as *Law & Order: SVU* and *Special Victims Unit*), NBC, 2003.

Sally, *As the World Turns*, CBS, 2008.

(As Mary Louise Burke) Flora Meegar, "Power Hungry," *Fringe*, Fox, 2008.

Mom, "St. Valentine's Day," *30 Rock*, NBC, 2009.

Also appeared in *All My Children*, ABC.

BURNS, Kathleen Kinmont
   See KINMONT, Kathleen

BYRNES, Darcy Rose 1998–

PERSONAL

Born November 4, 1998, in CA; daughter of C. J. Byrnes (an actor) and Cathy D'Arcy (an actress).

Addresses: *Agent*—Coast to Coast Talent, Inc., 3350 Barham Blvd., Los Angeles, CA 90068. *Manager*—Curtis Talent Management, 9607 Arby Dr., Beverly Hills, CA 90210.

Career: Actress.

Awards, Honors: Young Artist Award, best performance in a television series (comedy or drama)—young actress age ten or younger, 2005, Young Artist Award, best performance in a television series (comedy or drama)—guest starring young actress, 2006, Young Artist Award, best performance in a television series (comedy or drama)—recurring young actress, 2007, Young Artist Award nomination, best performance in a television series (comedy or drama)—recurring young actress, 2008, all for *The Young and the Restless*; Young Artist Award nomination, best performance in a television series—guest starring young actress, 2008, for *Cold Case*.

CREDITS

Film Appearances:

Daughter, *The Sparky Chronicles: The Map* (short film), Gospel Communications International, 2003.

Jennifer, *The Land of the Astronauts*, Cineville, 2010.

Television Appearances; Series:

Abby Carlton, *The Young and the Restless* (also known as *Y&R*), CBS, 2003–2008.

Abby Carlton, *The Bold and the Beautiful* (also known as *Belleza y poder*), CBS, 2007.

Lucy Zinman, *How I Met Your Mother* (also known as *H.I.M.Y.M.*), CBS, 2008.

Kiki George, *Dirty Sexy Money*, ABC, 2008–2009.

Television Appearances; Movies:

Hannah McKenzie, *The Kidnapping* (also known as *Black Friday*), 2007.

Heather, *Shark Swarm*, Hallmark Channel, 2008.

Dawn, *Healing Hands*, Hallmark Channel, 2010.

Rebecca Knepp, *Amish Grace*, Lifetime Movie Network, 2010.

Television Appearances; Episodic:

Young Melissa, "The Innocents," *Without a Trace* (also known as *W.A.T.*), CBS, 2005.

Entertainment Tonight (also known as *E.T.*), syndicated, 2005.

SoapTalk, SoapNet, 2006.

Abby Bradford in 1999, "A Dollar, a Dream," *Cold Case*, CBS, 2007.

Gwyneth, "Game Night," *Brothers & Sisters*, ABC, 2007.

Gracie Rousakis, "Homeward Bound," *Private Practice*, ABC, 2009.

Phoebe Burnes, "A Taste of Her Own Medicine," *Medium*, NBC, 2009.

Marika Greenewald, "The Social Contract," *House M.D.* (also known as *House*), NBC, 2009.

Maddy, "Witch Lady," *My Name Is Earl*, NBC, 2009.

Maddy, "Pinky," *My Name Is Earl*, NBC, 2009.

Drew Stanton, "Cursed," *Ghost Whisperer*, CBS, 2009.

Stage Appearances:

Sandy, *Annie*, 2003.

Evil Queen and Little Cinderella, *Happily Never After*, 2003.

Cockney matchstick girl, *Twas the Night*, Evergreen Music Conservatory, 2003.

Dancer, *Into the Woods*, Evergreen Music Conservatory, 2003.

The Wizard of Oz, 2004.

The Chronicles of Narnia: The Lion, the Witch & the Wardrobe, 2004.

The Music Man, 2004.

Molly, *Annie*, 2005.

Fairy godmother, *Cinderella*, Colony Theatre, Burbank, CA, 2005.

The Sound of Music, 2005.

Title role, *Annie*, Alex Theatre, Glendale, CA, 2009.

C

CAMACHO, Mark 1964–
(Marc Camacho, Mark Camocho)

PERSONAL

Born April 12, 1964, in Montreal, Quebec, Canada. *Education:* Studied theatre at Concordia University.

Addresses: *Agent*—Encore Entertainment, 403 St. Joseph W., Suite 10, Outremont, Quebec H2V 2P3, Canada.

Career: Actor and voice performer. Also worked as a real estate agent.

CREDITS

Film Appearances:
Krabel, *The Amityville Curse,* Vidmark Entertainment, 1990.
Paramedic, *Scanners II: The New Order,* Triton Pictures, 1991.
Scanning customer, *Snake Eater III: His Law* (also known as *Snake Eater III ... His Law*), Moviestore Entertainment, 1992.
Mario, *Canvas* (also known as *Canvas: The Fine Art of Crime*), Optima Productions, 1992.
Cop outside hotel, *Twin Sisters,* 1992.
(English version) Voice of Conrad, *Jungledyret* (animated; also known as *Amazon Jack, Go Hugo Go, Hugo the Movie Star, Jungle Jack,* and *Jungledyret Hugo*), 1993.
Bank manager, *The Neighbor,* Westwind, 1993.
Tim, *The Myth of the Male Orgasm,* Telescene Communications, 1993.
First writer, *Mrs. Parker and the Vicious Circle* (also known as *Mrs. Parker and the Round Table*), Fine Line, 1994.

Lawyer, *Stalked* (also known as *Traquee*), Republic, 1994.
Waiter, *Dr. Jekyll and Ms. Hyde,* Savoy Pictures, 1995.
Photo shop assistant, *Rainbow* (also known as *Les voyageurs de l'arc–en–ciel*), Allegro/Vine International, 1995.
Drunk driver, *Marked Man* (also known as *Le guet–apens*), Live Entertainment, 1995.
Police officer at diner, *Hollow Point* (also known as *Arsenal de pointe* and *Rysk Roulette*), October Films, 1995.
The lookout, *Joyeux calvaire* (also known as *Poverty and Other Delights*), Funfilm Distribution, 1996.
First reporter, *Rowing Through,* 1996.
Voice of Rascal and Rosco, *La freccia azzurra* (animated; also known as *Der blaue pfeil, How the Toys Saved Christmas, La fleche bleue,* and *The Blue Arrow*), 1996.
(English version) Voice of Conrad, *Jungledyret 2—den store filmhelt* (animated; also known as *Amazon Jack 2: The Movie Star, Djungeldjuret Hugo—den stora filmhjalten, Hugo the Movie Star,* and *Viidakkovekara Jusso elokuvasankarina*), 1996.
Ritz–Carlton bartender, *Afterglow,* Sony Pictures Classics, 1997.
Clyde, *Affliction,* 1997, Lions Gate Films, 1998.
Police sergeant, *Little Men* (also known as *Louisa May Alcott's "Little Men"*), 1997, Legacy Releasing, 1998.
Dan Albright, *The Kid,* Cinepix Film Properties, 1997.
Detective Lawlor, *For Hire,* Fries Film Group, 1997.
Presidential aide number one, *The Peacekeeper,* 1997.
Leroy, *Perpetrators of the Crime,* 1998.
Walter Rosenbaum, *Fatal Affair* (also known as *The Stalker*), 1998.
FBI Agent Dobson, *Sublet* (also known as *Codename: Jaguar*), 1998.
Department store guard, *The Sleep Room* (also known as *La pavillon de l'oubli*), 1998.
Mark Brewster, *Random Encounter* (also known as *Rencontre fortuite*), 1998.
C. J., *Snake Eyes,* Paramount, 1998.

Nick, *Out of Control,* Motion International, 1998.
Bexter, *Babel,* Motion International, 1998.
Jack Bruckner, *Going to Kansas City,* 1998.
Lieutenant Sam Waterton, *Dead Silent,* 1999.
First interrogator, *The Whole Nine Yards* (also known as *Le nouveau voisin*), Warner Bros., 2000.
Marc Cory, *Nowhere in Sight,* Blackwatch Releasing/Saban Pictures International, 2000.
Fire and Ice: The Rocket Richard Riot (documentary), Galafilm Distribution, 2000.
Eric, *The Score,* Paramount, 2001.
Jewelry store guard, *Heist* (also known as *Le vol*), Warner Bros., 2001.
Peter, *Protection,* Alliance Atlantis Communications, 2001.
Window washer, *Dead Awake,* Nu Image, 2001.
Hotel desk clerk, *Aftermath,* Christal Films, 2002.
Overseer J. Franklin, *Asbestos,* 2002.
Joseph Pagnozzi, *Federal Protection,* DEJ Productions, 2002.
Robot holding cell clerk, *The Adventures of Pluto Nash* (also known as *Pluto Nash*), Warner Bros., 2002.
Detective Rigney, *Abandon,* Paramount, 2002.
John, *Tunnel* (also known as *The Tunnel*), 2002.
Detective Costello, *Deception* (also known as *Decoy*), Hearst Entertainment Productions, 2003.
Johnny Christofaro, *Mambo italiano,* Samuel Goldwyn, 2003.
Gilbert, *Jericho Mansions* (also known as *House of Jericho*), Monarch Home Video, 2003.
(As Mark Camocho) Glass' lawyer, *Shattered Glass,* Lions Gate Films, 2003.
Bartender, *Wicker Park,* Metro–Goldwyn–Mayer, 2004.
Oliver Frensky, *Arthur's Halloween,* 2004.
Henford Phelps, *The Ecstasy Note* (short film), 2006.
Oliver Frensky, *Arthur's Missing Pal* (animated), Lions Gate Films Home Entertainment, 2006.
Sanson the executioner/Doc, *Let Them Eat,* 2006.
Norman, *I'm Not There.* (also known as *I'm Not There*), Weinstein Company, 2007.
Lawyer, *Afterwards* (also known as *Ein Engel im winter* and *Et apres*), 2008.
Pittsy, *Punisher: War Zone,* Lions Gate Films, 2008.
Stage manager, *Dead Like Me: After Death* (also known as *Dead Like Me*), Metro–Goldwyn–Mayer Home Entertainment, 2009.
Mark, *Barney's Version,* 2010.

Television Appearances; Series:
Voice of Spritz T. Cat, Bucky, and Road Runner, *Samurai Pizza Cats* (animated; also known as *Kyatto ninden teyanddee*), syndicated, 1991.
Voice of Carlos, *Around the World in Eighty Dreams* (animated; also known as *Saban's Around the World in Eighty Dreams, Au pays de Carlos,* and *Les aventures de Carlos*), 1992.
Voice of Oliver Frensky, *Arthur* (animated), PBS, 1996–2001.
Voice of Lyle, *Animal Crackers* (animated), 1997.

Voice, *Princess Sissi* (animated; also known as *Sissi*), Fox, 1997.
Voice of Dad, *Rotten Ralph* (animated), 1999.
Voice of Zosky, *Kaput and Zosky: The Ultimate Obliterators* (animated), 2002–2003.
Harry and Dragon, *Potatoes and Dragons* (animated; also known as *Patates and Dragons*), 2004.

Television Appearances; Miniseries:
Second police officer, *The Maharaja's Daughter* (also known as *Die Tochter des maharadschas*), 1994.
Chas Sweeney, *Hiroshima,* Showtime, 1995.
Willie Moretti, *Bonanno: A Godfather's Story* (also known as *Bonanno: The Youngest Godfather* and *The Youngest Godfather*), Showtime, 1999.
Levi Lyman, *P. T. Barnum,* Arts and Entertainment, 1999.
Macloud, *Dice,* 2001.
Contremaitre J. Franklin, *Asbestos,* 2002.
Rocco Perri, *Il duce canadese* (also known as *Il duce canadese: Le Mussolini canadien*), 2004.
Russ the poker player, *10.5: Apocalypse* (also known as *10.5*), NBC, 2006.

Television Appearances; Movies:
Phil, *Deadbolt* (also known as *Sequestree* and *3:15 a Time for Dying*), 1993.
Vendor, *Pretty Poison,* Fox, 1996.
First presidential aide, *The Peacekeeper* (also known as *Hellbent* and *Red Zone*), HBO, 1997.
Mark Brewster, *Random Encounter,* HBO, 1998.
Detective Levine, *The Girl Next Door,* CBS, 1998.
FBI Agent Dobson, *Sublet* (also known as *Codename: Jaguar*), Cinemax, 1998.
Leroy, *Perpetrators of the Crime,* Cinemax, 1998.
Walt Rosenbaum, *Fatal Affair* (also known as *The Stalker*), Cinemax, 1998.
(U.S. version) Voice of Walrus, *Oi! Get Off Our Train* (animated; also known as *The Animal Train*), 1998.
Coombs, *Execution of Justice,* Showtime, 1999.
Lieutenant Sam Waterton, *Dead Silent,* Lifetime, 1999.
Tiffany's cab driver, *The Audrey Hepburn Story,* ABC, 2000.
Tag Hunt, *Killing Moon,* 2000.
John, *The Tunnel,* 2000.
Rick Tucci, *Stiletto Dance,* HBO, 2001.
Sewell, *The Warden,* 2001.
Steve Lamboise, *Agent of Influence,* CTV, 2002.
Jon, *Just a Walk in the Park,* ABC, 2002.
Sam Cavallo, *Obsessed,* Lifetime, 2002.
Sammy Birch, *Gleason* (also known as *Gleason: The Jackie Gleason Story*), CBS, 2002.
Tony Carbonetti, *Rudy: The Rudy Guiliani Story* (also known as *Rudy's Wars*), USA Network, 2003.
Student Seduction, Lifetime, 2003.
Veterinarian, *The Wool Cap,* TNT, 2004.
Phil, *The Perfect Neighbor,* Lifetime, 2005.
Detective Yokum, *A Lover's Revenge,* Lifetime, 2005.

Government official number one, *One Dead Indian*, CTV, 2006.
Network director, *Time Bomb*, CBS, 2006.
Clyde, *Thrill of the Kill*, Lifetime, 2006.
Murphy, *Mind Over Murder*, 2006.
Freed, *Framed for Murder*, Lifetime, 2007.
Tim, *Too Young To Marry*, Lifetime, 2007.
Craig Perkins, *Sticks and Stones*, 2008.
Craig Braddock, *Infected* (also known as *They're Among Us*), Sci–Fi Channel, 2008.
Detective Ruiz, *My Neighbor's Secret*, 2009.

Television Appearances; Specials:
Voice of Dad, *Rotten Ralph*, The Disney Channel, 1996.
Voices of Oliver Frensky and security guard, *Arthur's Perfect Christmas* (animated), PBS, 2000.

Television Appearances; Pilots:
Sewell, *The Warden*, TNT, 2001.

Television Appearances; Episodic:
Delivery person, "The Tale of the Nightly Neighbours," *Are You Afraid of the Dark?*, Nickelodeon, 1992.
Leonard Buckley, "The Tale of the Shiny Red Bicycle," *Are You Afraid of the Dark?*, Nickelodeon, 1993.
Defense lawyer, "Crossing the Line," *Sirens*, ABC, 1994.
Myron Perryman, "The First Time," *Sirens*, ABC, 1994.
Warden Opus, "Prisoner of Luff," *Space Cases*, 1996.
Norman Emerson, "The Mystery of the Mice That Roared," *The Mystery Files of Shelby Woo*, 1998.
Macloud, *Dice*, 2001.
Commentary voice, "Missing Over New York," *Mayday* (also known as *Air Crash Investigations* and *Air Emergency*), The Discovery Channel, 2004.
Voice of the Fugitive, "I Saw Stroker Killing Santa," *Stroker and Hoop*, Carton Network, 2005.
Mr. Brewer, "One of Those Days," *Rumours*, 2006.
Bernard Linden, "Re–Entry," *The Dead Zone* (also known as *Stephen King's "The Dead Zone"*), USA Network, 2007.
Hector, "Fun," *Less Than Kind*, 2009.
Jerry Renfrew, "Springing Jett," *The Foundation*, ITV, 2009.

Also appeared as Mr. Walker, "Sweet Science," *Lassie*.

Television Additional Voices; Animated Series:
Animal Crackers, 1997.
Tripping the Rift, Sci–Fi Channel, 2004–2007.

Television Additional Voices; Animated Movies:
David Copperfield (also known as *Charles Dickens' "David Copperfield"*), NBC, 1993.

Stage Appearances:
Appeared as Romano, *Paradise by the River*, Centaur Theatre, Montreal, Quebec, Canada; also appeared in a production of *Speed Zone*.

Major Tours:
Appeared in a touring production of *Pinocchio*.

RECORDINGS

Video Games:
Voice, *Jagged Alliance*, 1994.
Voice, *Jagged Alliance: Deadly Games*, Sir–Tech, 1995.
Fruit Heart, *Yoshi Story* (also known as *Yoshi's Story*), 1997.
Voice of Kyle "Shadow" Simmons, *Jagged Alliance 2* (also known as *Jagged Alliance 2: Unfinished Business*), Sir–Tech, 1999.
Voice, *Wizardry 8*, Sir–Tech, 2001.
Voice of Bodyguards and Kashim, *Evolution Worlds*, 2002.
Voice, *Splinter Cell* (also known as *Tom Clancy's "Splinter Cell"*), 2002.
Voice, *Rainbow Six 3: Black Arrow* (also known as *Tom Clancy's "Rainbow Six 3: Black Arrow"*), 2003.
Voice of Sand Warriors, *Prince of Persia: Warrior Within*, 2004.
Voice of Jiri Skalnic, *Still Life*, The Adventure Company, 2005.
(As Marc Camacho) Doyle, *Far Cry Instincts*, Ubisoft Entertainment, 2005.
Voice of Max Winters, *Teenage Mutant Ninja Turtles*, Ubisoft Entertainment, 2007.
Dennis Cohen and Alvarez Cabrero, *Rainbow Six: Vegas 2*, Ubisoft Entertainment, 2008.

Video Games; as Additional Voices:
Splinter Cell: Chaos Theory, 2005.
(As Marc Camacho) *Prince of Persia: The Two Thrones*, 2005.
Rainbow Six: Vegas (also known as *Tom Clancy's Rainbow Six: Vegas*), Ubi Soft Entertainment, 2006.
Assassin's Creed II, 2009.

OTHER SOURCES

Periodicals:
Montreal Mirror, January 9, 2003.

***

CLOKE, Kristen 1968–
    (Kristin Cloke)

PERSONAL

Full name, Kristen Ann Cloke; born September 2, 1968, in Van Nuys, CA; married Glen Morgan (a writer and producer), June 13, 1998; children: Chelsea (stepdaughter), Winslow, Greer Autumn. *Education:* Attended California State University, Northridge.

Addresses: *Agent*—Mitchell K. Stubbs and Associates, 8675 West Washington Blvd., Suite 203, Culver City, CA 90232. *Manager*—Newlander Management, PO Box 261067, Encino, CA 91426–1067.

Career: Actress, director, and producer. Alliance Repertory Company, Burbank, CA, associate artistic director, producer, writer, and actress.

Awards, Honors: *Universe* Reader's Choice Award, best actress in a genre television series, *Sci–Fi Universe,* 1996, for *Space: Above and Beyond;* Daytime Emmy Award nomination, 1996, for "The Long Road Home," *ABC Afterschool Specials.*

CREDITS

Television Appearances; Series:
Lieutenant, then Captain Shane Autumn Vansen, *Space: Above and Beyond,* Fox, 1995–96.
Lara Means, a recurring role, *Millennium,* Fox, 1997–98.

Television Appearances; Pilots:
Lieutenant Shane Autumn Vansen, *Space: Above and Beyond,* Fox, 1995.
Gloria Kornacki, *Skip Chasers,* CBS, 1998.
Beth, *Men of a Certain Age,* TNT, 2009.

Television Appearances; Movies:
Francine, *Mother of the Bride,* CBS, 1993.
Gina, *A Part of the Family,* Lifetime, 1994.

Television Appearances; Specials:
Amanda, "The Long Road Home," *ABC Afterschool Specials,* ABC, 1995.
Herself and Leigh, *What Have You Done? The Remaking of "Black Christmas,"* HD Network, 2006.

Television Appearances; Episodic:
Suzanne, "She Loves Me," *Sydney,* CBS, 1990.
Annette, *Dear John,* 1992.
Suzanne Rogers, "Look Ma, No Pants" *Doogie Howser, M.D.,* ABC, 1992.
Annie Overstreet, "Witness," *Silk Stalkings,* USA Network, 1992.
Annie Overstreet, "Domestic Agenda," *Silk Stalkings,* USA Network, 1992.
Annie Overstreet, "Lady Luck," *Silk Stalkings,* USA Network, 1992.

Shirley Constantine, "Deliver Us from Evil—March 19, 1966," *Quantum Leap,* NBC, 1992.
Catherine Wynn, "Brother's Keeper," *Reasonable Doubts,* NBC, 1992.
Shauna, "Sunday Dinner," *Cheers,* NBC, 1993.
Josie Swanson, "Vanishing Act: Parts 1 & 2," *Diagnosis Murder,* CBS, 1993.
MayBeth Serlin, "Women in Love," *Winnetka Road,* NBC, 1994.
Wendy Cochran (some sources cite Wendy Kaufman), "Terminal Island," *One West Waikiki,* CBS, 1994.
The salesperson, "When I'm Sixty–four," *Mad about You,* NBC, 1994.
Emma Kemp, "Dear Deadly," *Murder, She Wrote,* CBS, 1994.
Lenore, *Under One Roof,* CBS, 1995.
Melissa Rydell Ephesian, "The Field Where I Died," *The X–Files,* Fox, 1996.
Tamara Simpson/Harrington, "Noir," *Vengeance Unlimited* (also known as *Mr. Chapel*), ABC, 1998.
Allison/the woman, "The Ones that Lie in Wait," *The Others,* NBC, 2000.
Allison/the woman, "Life Is for the Living," *The Others,* NBC, 2000.
Rabbi Marisa Levin, "Senioritis," *Felicity,* The WB, 2001.

Film Appearances:
Christine, *Megaville,* International Video Entertainment, 1990.
Louise, *The Marrying Man* (also known as *Too Hot to Handle*), Buena Vista, 1991.
(As Kristin Cloke) Velma, *Stay Tuned,* Warner Bros., 1992.
Kristen "Krissie" Bell, *Caged Fear* (also known as *Hotel Oklahoma, Innocent Young Female,* and *Jail Force*), Asso Film, 1992.
Kelly McCord, *The Rage,* Miramax, 1997.
Valerie "Val" Lewton, *Final Destination* (also known as *Destination ultime*), New Line Cinema, 2000.
(Uncredited) Dr. Bludworth, *Willard,* New Line Cinema, 2003.
Leigh Colvin, *Black Christmas* (also known as *Black X–mas* and *Noel noir*), Metro–Goldwyn–Mayer/Weinstein Company, 2006.
Showing Up (documentary), 2010.

Stage Work:
Producer, *The Grace to Climb with Eagles,* Alliance Repertory Theatre, Burbank, CA, 1997.
Producer, *Night and Her Stars,* 1997.

Also directed a production of *Dirty Mustard.*

RECORDINGS

Documentary Videos:
The Year of the Rat, New Line Home Video, 2003.

(In archive footage) *Turn the Tide: Making Millennium—Season Two,* Twentieth Century–Fox Home Entertainment, 2004.

May All Your Christmases Be Black, Dimension Home Video, 2007.

OTHER SOURCES

Periodicals:

Cult Times, August, 2002, p. 11.
Femme Fatales, June, 1997, pp. 13, 60.
Starburst Special, May, 2004, pp. 30–36.
Starlog, March, 1996.

Electronic:

Kristen Cloke Official Site, http://www.kristencloke. com, February 16, 2010.

CORLETT, Ian James 1962–
(Ian Corlett, Ian James Corlette, Jerry J. Todd)

PERSONAL

Born August 29, 1962, in Burnaby, British Columbia, Canada; married; wife's name, Sandra; children: Philip (an actor and voice artist), Claire (an actress and voice artist). *Avocational Interests:* Playing hockey, following professional motosport, auto racing.

Addresses: *Agent*—Cunningham, Escott, Dipene & Associates, 10635 Santa Monica Blvd., Suite 130, Los Angeles, CA 90025.

Career: Actor, voice artist, producer, director, writer, and composer. Voice performer for radio and television commercials, beginning c. 1984; provider of postproduction automated dialogue replacement voices for films, television programs, and videos. Provided the voice of Bob for the theme park attraction *ReBoot: The Ride* (also known as *Journey into Chaos*), IMAX Corporation. Wrote for advertising. Worked in a family business, selling pianos, keyboards, and professional recording equipment.

Awards, Honors: Award for most promising filmmaker, British Columbia Student Film Festival, c. 1980; Gemini Award (with Peter Sauder), best writing in a children's or youth program and series, Academy of Canadian Cinema and Television, 1999, for "Roll the Camera," *Rolie Polie Olie.*

CREDITS

Television Appearances; Animated Series:

(English version) Voice of Dr. Tofu Ono, Mikado Sanzenin, and Jusenkyo guide, *Ranma 1/2* (also known as *Ranma 1/2: The Digital Dojo* and *Ranma nibun no ichi*), originally broadcast in Japan by Fuji Television, 1989–92.

Voice of Spiff, *Spiff & Hercules* (also known as *Spiff and Hercules*), beginning c. 1989, Channel 4, beginning 1993.

Voice of Dr. Albert W. Wily, *Captain N: The Game Master* (animated with live action segments; also known as *Captain N: Game Master* and *Captain N and the Video Game Masters*), NBC, 1989–90, then known as *Captain N and the Adventures of Super Mario Bros. 3* (also known as *The Adventures of Super Mario Bros. 3* and *Super Mario Bros. 3*), NBC, 1990–91, then known as *Captain N and the New Super Mario World* (also known as *Super Mario World*), NBC, 1991–92, syndicated, 1992, PAX, 1998–2000.

Voice of Naugahide, *G.I. Joe* (also known as *Action Force, G.I. Joe: A Great American Hero,* and *Chijo saikyo no Expert Team G.I. Joe*), syndicated, 1990–92.

Voice of Blu, *Nilus the Sandman,* The Family Channel, 1991–97.

Voice of Mutter, *Captain Zed and the Zee Zone,* CITV, beginning 1991, wknd@stv, beginning 2009.

Voices, *Super Trolls,* syndicated, beginning c. 1992.

Voice of professor emeritus, *Stone Protectors,* syndicated, 1993.

Voice of Dr. Hiss and other characters, *The Bots Master* (also known as *Bots master, The Botz Master, ZZ Bots,* and *Le maitre des bots*), syndicated, 1993–94.

Voice of Vortex, Daj, and Tornado, *Double Dragon,* syndicated, 1993–94.

Voice of Coconuts and other characters, *Sonic the Hedgehog* (also known as *The Adventures of Sonic the Hedgehog, Sonic,* and *Sonic SatAM*), ABC and syndicated, 1993–95.

Voice of Jorg Beethoven, Dino Allegro, Topper the monkey, and Dribble, *Hurricanes,* syndicated, c. 1993–97.

Voice of Glitch–Bob, Bob, and others, *ReBoot,* YTV and other networks as well as ABC, 1994–96, and Cartoon Network, 1999–2001.

(As Jerry J. Todd; English version) Voice of Tataki Shuuichi, *Key: The Metal Idol* (also known as *Key the Metal Idol*), originally released in Japan, 1994, PBS, beginning c. 1996.

Voice of Victor and ship's computer, *Dark Stalkers* (also known as *Darkstalkers* and *Night Warriors: Darkstalker's Revenge*), UPN, 1995.

Voice of Damnd, *Final Flight,* beginning 1995.

(English version) Voice of Quinze Barton, Quatre Raberba winner, and others, *Mobile Suit Gundam Wing* (also known as *Gundam W, Gundam Wing, Mobile Suit Gundam 00, New Mobile Report Gundam–W, New Mobile Report Gundam Wing,* and *New Mobile War Chronicle Gundam Wing*), originally released in Japan, Bandai Channel and TV Asahi, 1995–96, Cartoon Network, 2000.

(Sometimes credited as Ian Corlett) Voice of title character, Ruff, Snake Man, Metal Man, and other characters, *Megaman* (also known as *Mega Man* and *Rockman*), ABC Family and syndicated, beginning 1995.

Voice of Elwood, *The Littlest Pet Shop,* syndicated, 1995–96.

Voice of Kidwell "Inferno" Pyre, *G.I. Joe Extreme,* syndicated, 1995–97.

Voice of Jason, Brad Logan, and Snake Oil, *Vortech: Undercover Conversion Squad* (also known as *Vortech* and *Vor–Tech*), multiple channels, including ABC, also Fox, episodes beginning c. 1996.

Voice of Cheetor, Sentinel, Silverbolt, Waspinator, and Maximal computer, *Beast Wars: Transformers* (also known as *Animutants, Beast Wars, Beasties, Beasties: Transformers,* and *Transformers: Beast Wars*), broadcast by YTV, also syndicated, 1996–98, and Cartoon Network, 1998–99.

(English version) Voice of Gohan, Goku, Kuwi, Master Roshi, and others, *Dragon Ball Z* (also known as *DBZ* and *What's My Destiny Dragonball*), originally released in Japan, Animax, Fuji Television, and BS Fuji, 1989–96, Cartoon Network, 1996–2003.

Voice of Einstone and Pompeii Pete, *The Wacky World of Tex Avery* (also known as *Tex Avery Theater*), Cartoon Network and syndicated, beginning 1997.

Voice of Addishenal, *3 Friends & Jerry* (also known as *3 Friends and Jerry*), Fox Family, Nickelodeon, and other channels, including Australian Broadcasting Corporation, 1998–2000.

Voice of Otis, Ten Cents, Zigi, and others, *Salty's Lighthouse,* The Learning Channel, c. 1998–2000.

Voice of Filbert, *Pocket Dragon Adventures,* BBC, c. 1998–2003.

Voice of Baby Chassis, Daddy–O, and Wade, *Weird–Ohs,* Fox and YTV, 1999–2000.

Voice of Cheetor, *Beast Machines: Transformers* (also known as *Beast Machines* and *Beast Machines: Battle for the Sparks*), Fox, 1999–2000.

(English version) Voice of Hare, *Monster Rancher* (also known as *Monster Farm: Enbanseki no himitsu, Monster Farmer,* and *Monsterrancher*), originally released in Japan, Tokyo Broadcasting System, also Sci–Fi Channel, 1999, and Fox, YTV, and syndicated, 2001.

Voice of Mark "Charger" McCutchen, *NASCAR Racers,* Fox, 1999–2001.

Voice of Knuckles and Cyrus, *Sonic Underground* (also known as *Sonic le rebelle*), UPN, BKN, Sci–Fi Channel, and TeleToon, 1999–2004.

Voice of Mister Pop, Mefirst Wizard, El Pie, magic crayon, and other characters, *Dragon Tales,* PBS, 1999–2005.

Voice of Martin Fenwick, *Sherlock Holmes in the 22nd Century,* Fox, 1999–2000, syndicated, 2001, 2002–2005, 2006.

Voices, *Sabrina the Animated Series* (also known as *Disney's "Sabrina"* and *Sabrina*), ABC and UPN, 1999–2000, The Disney Channel, 1999–2007.

Voice of Bart and Paully, *D'Myna Leagues,* YTV, beginning 2000.

Voice of Willy Tidwell, King Louis, and others, *Yvon of the Yukon,* YTV, 2000–2005.

(English version) Voice of Master Rochi and turtle hermit, *Dragon Ball,* originally broadcast in Japan by Fuji Television and other networks, 1986 89, Cartoon Network, 2001–2003.

Voice of Bill, *Sitting Ducks,* Cartoon Network, 2001–2004.

Voice, *Make Way for Noddy* (also known as *Noddy*), Chorion, beginning 2001, PBS Kids Sprout, beginning 2004.

Voice of Jake, *Tracey McBean,* Australian Broadcasting Corporation Kids and Discovery Kids, 2001–2006.

Voice of Andrew "Andy" Larkin, *What's with Andy?* (also known as *What's with Andy II*), TeleToon, 2001–2008, ABC Family, 2001–2002, and Toon Disney, 2005.

Voice of Taz, *Baby Looney Tunes,* Cartoon Network, 2002–2005.

Voice of Mr. Horace Cramp, *The Cramp Twins,* various networks, including YTV, Fox, and BBC, 2002–2006.

Voice of Mr. Highpants and Rondo, Jr., *Yakkity Yak,* Nickelodeon, 2003.

Voices, *Gadget and the Gadgetinis,* syndicated, 2003.

Voice of Mercury, Todd, and owl, *Silverwing,* TeleToon, beginning 2003.

Voice, *Something Else,* [Canada and United Kingdom], beginning 2003.

(English version) Voice of smooth talker, a recurring role, *Tenjho tenge* (also known as *Heaven and Earth*), originally released in Japan, Nagoya Broadcasting Network and TV Asahi, 2004, G4techTV Canada, 2007.

Voice of Odbald, *Being Ian,* YTV, beginning 2005.

Voice of Skrash and Vakkon, *Alien Racers,* TeleToon and Fox, beginning 2005.

Voice of Hugh Test, *Johnny Test,* The WB, 2005–2006, The CW, 2006–2008.

Voice of Sam L. Jackson, police officer, and others, *Where My Dogs At?,* MTV2, 2006.

Voice of Grumpy Bear, *Care Bears: Adventures in Care–a–Lot,* CBS, 2007–2008.

Voice of Mr. Smith, *Monster Buster Club* (also known as *MBC* and *MBC Monster Buster Club*), Toon Disney and Jetix, beginning 2008.

Voice of Conductor and other characters, *Dinosaur Train,* PBS Kids, beginning 2009.

Voice of uncle, *Body Powers* (interstitial series), PBS, beginning c. 2009.

Voice of Mighty Ray, Mr. No Hands, and ApeTrully, *Hero: 108,* Cartoon Network, beginning 2010.

Television Appearances; Animated Miniseries:

Voice, *G.I. Joe: Operation Dragonfire,* syndicated, 1989.

Television Appearances; as Ian Corlett; Animated Movies:

Voice of Bob, *ReBoot: Daemon Rising* (consists of episodes of the television series), Cartoon Network and YTV, 2001.

Voice of Glitch–Bob, *ReBoot: My Two Bobs* (consists of episodes of the television series; also known as *Re-Boot: The Movie II*), Cartoon Network and YTV, 2001.

Television Appearances; Animated Specials:

Voice of little kid, *Casper's Haunted Christmas* (also known as *Le noel hante de Casper*), USA Network, 2000.

Voice of Captain Candy, *Barbie in "The Nutcracker,"* CBS and YTV, 2001.

Television Appearances; Animated Episodes:

Voice of Bugsy and Waldo Winch, "Hijack," *The Adventures of T–Rex* (also known as *T–Rex*), syndicated, 1992.

Voice of yelling weight lifter, "Pumping Iron," *Beavis and Butt–Head* (also known as *The Bad Boys* and *Beavis and Butt–head*), MTV, 1994.

Voice of Presley's father, "Pack to the Future," *Mummies Alive!*, syndicated, 1997.

Voice of Ethers, "Robopop," *RoboCop: Alpha Commando* (also known as *Robocop: Alpha Commando*), syndicated, 1998.

Voice of Mr. James Brass, "A Really, Really Big Shoo," *RoboCop: Alpha Commando* (also known as *Robocop: Alpha Commando*), syndicated, 1998.

Voice of mail person and second dog, "Extra! Extra!/CatDog Squared," *CatDog*, Nickelodeon, 1999.

Voice of Robert Cursor and e–mail, "Where No Sprite Has Gone Before," *ReBoot*, YTV and Cartoon Network, 1999.

Voice of Jackie Chan, "The Last Affirmative Action Hero," *The PJs* (also known as *PJs: The Projects*), Fox, 2000.

Voice of third teacher, "Home School Dazed," *The PJs* (also known as *PJs: The Projects*), Fox, 2000.

(English version) Voice of Boss Rabbit, "Boss Rabbit's Magic Touch," *Dragon Ball,* originally broadcast in Japan, Fuji Television and other networks, c. 1980, Cartoon Network, 2001.

Voice of Dr. Zalost, "The Tower of Dr. Zalost," *Courage the Cowardly Dog,* Cartoon Network, 2001.

Voice of Freaky Fred, "Courageous Cure/Ball of Revenge," *Courage the Cowardly Dog,* Cartoon Network, 2002.

Voice of James, "Evil Boyfriend," *Totally Spies!* (also known as *Totally Spies* and *Totally Spies Undercover!*), ABC Family and TeleToon, 2002.

Voice of lifeguard, "Broken Dreams," *Home Movies* (also known as *Cine–Maniac*), Cartoon Network, 2002.

Voice of Mr. Pants, "History," *Home Movies* (also known as *Cine–Maniac*), Cartoon Network, 2002.

Voice of the people of Nearburg, "CatDog 3001/Cloud Bursting," *CatDog*, Nickelodeon, 2002.

Voice of thug, "War World: Part 1," *Justice League* (also known as *JL, JLA, Justice League of America,* and *Justice League Unlimited*), Cartoon Network, 2002.

Voice of B.O.B., "Here Comes the Sun," *Totally Spies!* (also known as *Totally Spies* and *Totally Spies Undercover!*), ABC Family and TeleToon, 2003.

Voice of Sarge, "Eclipsed: Part 1," *Justice League* (also known as *JL, JLA, Justice League of America,* and *Justice League Unlimited*), Cartoon Network, 2003.

Voice of television announcer, "Grandma's Piano/Guide Games," *The Cramp Twins,* various networks, including YTV, Fox, and BBC, 2003.

Voice of driving instructor, "Those Bitches Tried to Cheat Me," *Home Movies* (also known as *Cine–Maniac*), Cartoon Network, 2004.

Voice of female counselor, "Camp," *Home Movies* (also known as *Cine–Maniac*), Cartoon Network, 2004.

Voice of Mr. Bad Cop, "The Sidewalk Soiler," *Tripping the Rift,* Sci–Fi Channel and SPACE, 2004.

Voice of living mall, "Do the Twitch/Day of the Living Mall/Bulky Blocky/Piece of Cake," *ChalkZone* (also known as *Chalk Zone*), Nickelodeon, 2005.

(English version) Voice of Mr. Moku, "Babbo: The Legendary ARM!" (also known as "Babbo: The Legendary AERM!" and "The Legendary ARM! Babbo!!"), *MAER* (also known as *MAR, Maerchen Awakens Romance,* and *Marchen Awakens Romance*), originally broadcast in Japan, TV Tokyo, 2005, Cartoon Network and YTV, 2007.

Voice of Dave Chappelle, "Being with the Browns," *Where My Dogs At?,* MTV2, 2006.

(English version) Voice of Rondo, Jr., "Rukia's Decision, Ichigo's Feelings," *Bleach,* originally broadcast in Japan by TV Tokyo, also broadcast by Cartoon Network, 2006.

Voice of Slug and Poe, "Commander in Stripes/Ellen vs. Slug/An Egg–cellent Question," *Edgar & Ellen,* Nicktoons, 2007.

Voice, "Ethel's New Friend/Vicky Sprocket," *Ricky Sprocket, Showbiz Boy* (also known as *Ricky Sprocket*), TeleToon and Nicktoons, 2007.

Voice of pizza boy and Stephen Baldwin, "Wedding," *Lil' Bush: Resident of the United States* (also known as *Lil' Bush*), Comedy Central, 2008.

Voice of line master, "Rock–a–Bye Voltar/iDestruct," *The League of Super Evil* (also known as *LOSE* or *L.O.S.E.*), Cartoon Network and YTV, 2009.

Some sources state that Corlett provided voices for other programs.

Television Appearances; Animated Pilots:

Voice of Cliff and Morgan Ziegler/Zitz, *Battletoads* (also known as *Battle Toads*), Fox, 1991.

Voice of Mark "Charger" McCutchen, *NASCAR Racers: The Movie*, Fox, 1999.

Television Additional Voices; Animated Series:

Postproduction additional voices, *Michel Vaillant* (also known as *Heroes on Hot Wheels* and *Michael Vaillant*), 1986–89.

Madeline, The Family Channel, c. 1990.

Gadget Boy and Heather (also known as *Gadget Boy*), syndicated, beginning 1995.

Mobile Suit Gundam Wing (also known as *Gundam W, Gundam Wing, Mobile Suit Gundam 00, New Mobile Report Gundam–W, New Mobile Report Gundam Wing,* and *New Mobile War Chronicle Gundam Wing*), originally released in Japan, Bandai Channel and TV Asahi, 1995–96, Cartoon Network, 2000.

Super Duper Sumos, Nickelodeon, 2002–2003.

Also provided voices for other series.

Television Work; Other; Animated Series:

(With others) Producer, *Dragon Ball Z* (also known as *DBZ* and *What's My Destiny Dragonball*), broadcast on other networks, including YTV, originally released in Japan, Animax, Fuji Television, and BS Fuji, 1989–96, Cartoon Network, 1996–2003.

Theme song vocalist, *Salty's Lighthouse,* The Learning Channel, c. 1998–2000.

(With others) Creator, *Yvon of the Yukon,* YTV, 2000–2005.

Creator and executive producer, *Being Ian,* YTV, beginning 2005.

Some sources state that Corlett worked on other programs.

Animated Film Appearances:

(English version) Voice of Hikari Daitokuji, *Project A–Ko 2: Daitokuji zaibatsu no inbo* (also known as *Project A–Ko 2: Plot of the Daitokuji Financial Group* and *Project A–Ko 4: Final*), dubbed version released by Central Park Media Corporation, originally released in Japan by Soeishinsha Company, c. 1987.

(English version) Voice of Mikado Sanzenin, *Ranma 1/2: Chugoku Nekonron daikessen! Okite yaburi no gekito hen* (also known as *Ranma 1/2: Big Battle at Nekonron! The No–Rules All–Out Battle, Ranma 1/2: Big Trouble in Nekonron, China,* and *Ranma 1/2: The Movie, Big Trouble in Nekonron, China*), Viz Video, originally released in Japan by Argo Pictures, 1991.

Voice of mirror, *Snow White* (also known as *Sugar & Spice: Snow White*), 1991.

Voice of Scarecrow, *The Wizard of Oz* (short film; also known as *Sugar & Spice: The Wizard of Oz*), Saban Productions, 1991.

(As Ian Corlett) Voice, *Cinderella* (also known as *La cenicienta*), GoodTimes Home Video, 1994.

(As Ian Corlett) Voice, *Happy, the Littlest Bunny,* GoodTimes Home Video, 1994.

(As Ian Corlett) Voice, *Leo the Lion: King of the Jungle* (also known as *Leo Leon*), 1994.

(As Ian Corlett) Voice, *The Nutcracker,* GoodTimes Home Video, 1994.

(As Ian Corlett) Voice, *Pocahontas* (also known as *The Adventures of Pocahontas: Indian Princess*), GoodTimes Home Video, 1994.

(As Ian Corlett) Voice, *Sleeping Beauty* (also known as *La bella durmiente*), GoodTimes Home Video, 1994.

(As Ian Corlett) Voice, *Alice in Wonderland* (also known as *Alicia en el pais de las maravillas*), GoodTimes Home Video, 1995.

(As Ian Corlett) Voice, *Black Beauty* (also known as *Hermoso negro*), GoodTimes Home Video, 1995.

(As Ian Corlett) Voice, *Curly: The Littlest Puppy,* GoodTimes Home Video, 1995.

(As Ian Corlett) Voice, *Heidi,* GoodTimes Home Video, 1995.

(As Ian Corlett) Voice, *Hercules,* Goodtimes Entertainment, 1995.

(As Ian Corlett) Voice, *Jungle Book* (also known as *El libro de la selva*), GoodTimes Home Video, 1995.

(As Ian Corlett) Voice, *Little Red Riding Hood,* GoodTimes Home Video, 1995.

(As Ian Corlett) Voice, *Magic Gift of the Snowman* (also known as *El regalo magico del muneco de nieve*), GoodTimes Home Video, 1995.

(As Ian Corlett) Voice, *Snow White* (also known as *Blancanieves*), 1995.

(As Ian Corlett) Voice, *The Hunchback of Notre Dame,* GoodTimes Home Video, 1996.

(Sometimes credited as Ian Corlett; English version) Voice of Mowgli, *The Adventures of Mowgli* (also known as *Adventures of Maugli, Adventures of Mowgli, The Jungle Book,* and *Rudyard Kipling's "The Jungle Book"*), originally released as animated shorts in the former Soviet Union, between 1967 and 1971, then combined and released as a feature film, 1973, English version released, c. 1996.

(English version) Voice of Dr. Greed, assistant hunter, and other characters, *Die furchtlosen Vier* (also known as *The Fearless Four*), Warner Bros., 1997.

(English version) Voice of Lord Granion, *Slayers Great* (also known as *Slayers: Great*), originally released in Japan, Toei Animation, 1997.

(As Ian James Corlette; English version) Voice, *Cudnovate zgode segrta Hlapica* (also known as *Lapitch the Little Shoemaker, The Little Shoemaker,* and *Lapitch, der kleine Schuhmacher*), originally released in Croatia, Croatia Film, 1997, dubbed version released, Sony Wonder, 2000.

Voices, *The Mighty Kong,* Warner Home Video/Legacy Releasing Corporation, 1998.

Voices, *Mummies Alive! The Legend Begins* (consists of episodes of the television series), Buena Vista Home Video, 1998.

(As Ian Corlett) Voice of Captain Patch, *Little Witch,* 1999.

(English version) Voice of fish waiting for bus, *Hjaelp, jeg er en fisk* (also known as *A Fish Tale, Help! I'm a Fish,* and *Hilfe! Ich bin ein Fisch*), HanWay Films, 2000.

Voice, *Monster Mash,* MCA/Universal, 2000.

Voice of Hobie and palace guard, *Barbie as Rapunzel* (also known as *Barbie Rapunzel*), Artisan Entertainment, 2002.

Voice of Baby Taz, *Baby Looney Tunes: Eggs-traordinary Adventure,* Warner Bros., 2003.

Voice of Ivan, *Barbie of Swan Lake,* Artisan Entertainment, 2003.

Voice of Bumblz, *Bumblz: Clubhouse Friends,* Bumblz Media, 2004.

Voice of Wolfie and a guard, *Barbie as the Princess and the Pauper,* Universal, 2004.

Voice of Mr. Mint and Snow Beaver, *Candyland: Great Lollipop Adventure,* Hasbro, 2005.

Voice of announcer and newsperson, *Bratz: Super Babyz,* MGA Entertainment/Mike Young Productions, 2007.

(As Ian James Corlette) Voice of Pat, *Barbie as the Island Princess* (also known as *Island Princess*), Universal Studios Home Entertainment, 2007.

Voice of Paulie, *Tom and Jerry: A Nutcracker Tale,* Warner Bros., 2007.

Voice, *Care Bears: Oopsy Does It!* (also known as *The All–New Care Bears in "Oopsy Does It!"*), Twentieth Century–Fox/Kidtoon Films, 2007.

(As Ian Corlett) Voice of Gary, *Holly Hobbie and Friends: Marvelous Makeover,* Sony Wonder, 2009.

Live Action Film Appearances:

Voice of Major Keena, *Warriors of Virtue* (also known as *Creature Zone* and *Magic warriors*), Metro–Goldwyn–Mayer, 1997.

Voice of center controller, *Altitude,* Alliance Films, 2010.

Film Work:

Director and producer, *Company Man* (short film), 2005.

Worked on other films.

RECORDINGS

Video Games:

Voice of pilot, *Homeworld,* Relic Entertainment, 1999.

(English version) Voice of Cheetor, Quickstrike, and sentinel, *Transformer Beast Wars Metals: Gekitotsu! Gangan Battle,* originally released in Japan, 1999, Bay Area Multimedia, 2000.

(English version) Voice of Pichu, Mr. Game, and Watch, *Super Smash Bros. Melee* (also known as *Dai–Ranto Smash Brothers Deluxe*), Nintendo, 2001.

Voice, *Crash Twinsandity* (also known as *Crash: Twinsandity* and *Crash Bandicoot 5*), Vivendi Universal Games, 2004.

Voice of Arslan, *Devil Kings* (also known as *Sengoku basara*), Capcom Entertainment, 2005.

Provided the voice of Super Joe for *Bionic Commando.*

Albums; with Others:

Programmer of drum tracks and computer technician for sequences, *Operation: Mindcrime by Queensryche,* EMI, 1988.

Hats off to Madeline (soundtrack; also known as *Hats off to Madeline: Songs from the Hit TV Series*), Rhino Records, 1996.

(As Ian James Corlette) *Barbie as the Island Princess* (film soundtrack; also known as *Island Princess*), Koch Records, 2007.

WRITINGS

Teleplays; Animated Episodes; with Others:

Dragon Ball Z (also known as *DBZ* and *What's My Destiny Dragonball*), series originally released in Japan, Animax, Fuji Television, and BS Fuji, 1989–96, Cartoon Network, episodes 1996–2003.

(With Peter Sauder) "Roll the Camera," *Rolie Polie Olie,* The Disney Channel, 1998.

Donkey Kong Country (based on the *Donkey Kong* video games), TeleToon, Fox Family, Fox, and other networks, 1998–2000.

"Four–Alarm Fire and Brimstone," *Rescue Heroes* (also known as *Rescue Heroes: Global Response Team* and *Rescue Heroes: GRT*), CBS, The WB, and TeleToon, 2000.

Dragon Ball, originally broadcast in Japan by Fuji Television and other networks, 1986–89, Cartoon Network, 2001–2003.

The Adventures of Paddington Bear (based on the books by Michael Bond), HBO and This TV, 2004.

"Bad Day at White Rock," *Being Ian,* YTV, 2005.

"Sask–Watch," *Being Ian,* YTV, 2005.

Some sources state that Corlett wrote for other programs.

Television Music; Composer of Theme Songs for Animated Series:

Yvon of the Yukon, YTV, 2000–2005.

What's with Andy? (also known as *What's with Andy II*), TeleToon, 2001–2008, ABC Family, 2001–2002, and Toon Disney, 2005.

Screenplays:
Company Man (short film), 2005.

Nonfiction:
E Is for Ethics: How to Talk to Kids about Morals, Values, and What Matters Most, illustrated by R. A. Holt, Atria Books, 2010.

OTHER SOURCES

Electronic:
Ian James Corlett, http://www.ianjamescorlett.com, January 8, 2010.

CRAVENS, Pierce 1986–

PERSONAL

Born January 8, 1986, in Dallas, TX. *Education:* Attended the University of Pennsylvania.

Career: Actor.

CREDITS

Film Appearances:
Tim, *Larry's Visit* (short film), 1996.
(Uncredited) Singing voice, *Wide Awake,* Miramax, 1998.
Teen usher, *The Life Before Her Eyes,* Magnolia Pictures, 2007.
Jasper, *Gathering Wool* (short film), 2009.
Kevin, *Rising Stars,* 2010.

Film Work:
Automated dialogue replacement (ADR), *Dead Man Walking,* Gramercy, 1995.
Executive producer, *Pitch* (short film), 2006.

Television Appearances; Series:
Billy, *The Guiding Light* (also known as *Guiding Light*), CBS, 1993–95.

Television Appearances; Specials:
Performer, *The Walt Disney Company and McDonald's Presents the American Teacher Awards,* 1995.
Kathie Lee Gifford: We Need a Little Christmas, CBS, 1996.
Slimer number two, *Nickelodeon Kids' Choice Awards '99,* Nickelodeon, 1999.

Narrator, *School* (documentary; also known as *School: The Story of American Public Education*), PBS, 2001.
Voice of Joshua Finkel, *The Finkle Files,* Cartoon Network, 2003.

Television Appearances; Episodic:
Today (also known as *NBC News Today* and *The Today Show*), NBC, 1992.
Day One, 1993.
In Person with Maureen O'Boyle, 1996.
Terry, *The Guiding Light* (also known as *Guiding Light*), CBS, 1996.
(Uncredited) Young boy, *Late Show Backstage with David Letterman* (also known as *Letterman* and *The Late Show*), CBS, 1997.
The Chris Rock Show, HBO, 1998.
Performer, *The Rosie O'Donnell Show,* syndicated, 1999.
Late Night with Conan O'Brien, NBC, 2000, 2001, 2003.
Voice of Representative Peabody, "A Forgotten Yesterday," *Fillmore!* (animated; also known as *Disney's "Fillmore!"*), ABC, 2003.

Stage Appearances:
Boy, *All's Well That Ends Well,* Joseph Papp Public Theatre, New York Shakespeare Festival, New York City, 1993.
Chip, *Beauty and the Beast,* Palace Theatre, New York City, 1994.
Alternate, *Beauty and the Beast,* Palace Theatre, 1994–96.
Tiny Tim, *A Christmas Carol,* Madison Square Garden, New York City, 1996.
Jack Thayer, Jr., *Titanic,* Lunt–Fontanne Theatre, New York City, 1997.
Edgar, *Ragtime,* Ford Center for the Performing Arts, New York City, 1998–99.
Alfred Temple and understudy for the role of Sid Sawyer, *The Adventures of Tom Sawyer,* Minskoff Theatre, New York City, 2001.
Silver Nitrate, Blue Heron Arts Center, New York City, 2004.

Also appeared as Prince, *Prince and the Pauper;* Colin, *Secret Garden;* Oliver, *Oliver!*

RECORDINGS

Video Games:
Voice of teen male—player character, *Thrillville,* LucasArts Entertainment Company, 2006.

Albums:
Appeared on three albums.

CURTIS, Wendee Lee
   See LEE, Wendee

CUTHBERTSON, Iain 1930–2009

PERSONAL

Born January 4, 1930, in Glasgow, Scotland; died September 4, 2009, in Glasgow, Scotland. Actor and director. Cuthbertson was a familiar face in television in the United Kingdom, having gained popularity for his roles in *Budgie* and *Sutherland's Law,* both series that aired in the 1970s. His acting career began in theatre in the 1950s. In 1958 he joined the Citizens Theatre Company in Glasgow, where he appeared in productions of *Cat on a Hot Tin Roof* and *Othello.* He became the company's general manager in 1962. Three years later he moved to London and took the position of associate director at the Royal Court Theatre. There he performed in *Serjeant Musgrave's Dance* and directed *Ubu Roi.* Around this time Cuthbertson began acting in television. His first series was *The Borderers,* which aired in the late 1960s. In *Budgie,* which aired from 1971 to 1972, Cuthbertson played a Scottish gangster, and in *Sutherland's Law,* which aired from 1973 to 1976, he starred as Scottish prosecutor John Sutherland. He also acted in films, such as *The Railway Children* in 1970 and *Gorillas in the Mist* in 1988. After suffering a stroke in 1982 that affected his speech, Cuthbertson retired from the stage, turning his focus to television and film. His first television series after the stroke was *SuperGran,* a children's comedy program that aired from 1985 to 1987. He had a recurring role in *Seaforth* in 1994 and guest starred in countless shows, including *Inspector Morse, Screenplay,* and *Casualty.* His final film role was Connolly in 2001's *Strictly Sinatra.*

PERIODICALS

Guardian, September 11, 2009.
Times (London), September 8, 2009.

D–E

DAY, Linda 1938–2009
(Linda Gail Day)

PERSONAL

Original name, Linda Gail Brickner; born August 12, 1938, in Los Angeles, CA; died of complications from leukemia and breast cancer, October 23, 2009, in Georgetown, TX. Director. Day directed hundreds of television episodes in the course of her career, primarily during the 1980s and 1990s. She entered the television industry as a script supervisor; the most prominent series she worked on was *Soap* in the late 1970s. After joining *WKRP in Cincinnati* in 1978 as associate director, she took over the director's position in the early 1980s and worked on nearly a dozen installments of the show. Also in the 1980s Day directed episodes of *Who's the Boss?, Knots Landing, Dallas, Gimme a Break!, Kate & Allie,* and many more. She received an Emmy Award nomination in 1981 for one of her *Archie Bunker's Place* episodes. Day remained busy in the 1990s, directing for such series as *The 5 Mrs. Buchanans, Unhappily Ever After, Clueless,* and *Sabrina, the Teenage Witch.* Not long before her death, she was honored by the Directors Guild of America for her groundbreaking work as a female director in a predominantly male industry.

PERIODICALS

Los Angeles Times, October 31, 2009.
Variety, October 26, 2009.

DAY, Wendee
See LEE, Wendee

DENBO, Jamie 1973–

PERSONAL

Born July 24, 1973, in Boston, MA; married John Ross Bowie (an actor), June 5, 2004. *Education:* Boston University, B.S.

Addresses: *Agent*—Pakula, King and Associates, 9229 West Sunset Blvd., Suite 315, Los Angeles, CA 90069. *Manager*—Aaron Kaplan, Kapital Entertainment, 9200 Sunset Blvd., Suite 430, Los Angeles, CA 90069.

Career: Actress, producer, and writer. Upright Citizens Brigade (theatre company), New York City, member of company and acting teacher, 1998—; Ronna & Beverly (comedy duo), comedian; appeared in commercials. Walt Disney World, Orlando, FL, worked as member of ensemble of the Who What and Warehouse Improv Company and as member of "Streetmosphere" show at Disney MGM Studios (now Disney's Hollywood Studios); Chicago City Limits, former member of touring company; News in Revue, former member of ensemble.

CREDITS

Television Appearances; Series:
(Uncredited) Herself and miscellaneous characters, including Greta Denbo and Suri Cruise, *The Late Late Show with Craig Ferguson,* CBS, between 2006 and 2008.
Tina Difabio, *Happy Hour,* Fox, 2006–2008.
Raylene, *Weeds,* Showtime, 2009.
Jolene, *Brothers,* Fox, 2009.

Television Appearances; Pilots:
Fuddy's wife, *What's Up, Peter Fuddy?,* Fox, 2001.
Val, *Eddie's Father,* The WB, 2004.

Tina Difabio, *Happy Hour,* Fox, 2006.
Terriers, FX Network, 2010.

Television Appearances; Specials:
Gina, "Beep," *Jump Cuts,* Comedy Central, 2004.
Jessica, *Wiener Park,* NBC, 2005.
Beverly Kahn–Ginsberg, *Ronna & Beverly,* Showtime, 2009.

Television Appearances; Episodic:
Woman in bathroom, "The Freak Show," *Sex and the City* (also known as *S.A.T.C.*), HBO, 1999.
Hooker, "Big City," *Upright Citizens Brigade,* Comedy Central, 1999.
Late Friday, NBC, 2002.
Jane, "Walter's First Lawsuit," *A.U.S.A.,* NBC, 2003.
Karen, "Ring of Fire," *Rock Me, Baby,* UPN, 2003.
Girl at bar, "Crying, Lying, and Still Trying," *Significant Others,* Bravo, 2004.
Executive Vice President Jamie Samuels, "How Low Can You Go?," *My Big Fat Obnoxious Boss,* Fox, 2004.
Executive Vice President Jamie Samuels, "Finale: The Real Boss Is ...," *My Big Fat Obnoxious Boss,* Fox, 2005.
Erica, *Weekends at the DL,* Comedy Central, 2005.
Waitress, "The Honeymooners," *Love, Inc.,* UPN, 2005.
Pageant mom, "The Prefect of Wanganui," *Reno 911!,* Comedy Central, 2005.
Cindy, "The Big Reality Bites Episode," *Half & Half,* UPN, 2006.
Natalie Bynum, "One Wrong Move," *Without a Trace* (also known as *W.A.T.*), CBS, 2007.
Ren Faire girl, "Ex–Wife and Her New Husband," *Reno 911!,* Comedy Central, 2007.
Ren Faire Rachel, "Dangle's Wedding," *Reno 911!,* Comedy Central, 2007.
Lindsay Port in 2008, "Spiders," *Cold Case,* CBS, 2008.
Voice, "Insurmountable High Score/Tim vs. the Baby," *The Life & Times of Tim* (animated), HBO, 2008.
Voice, "Mugger/Cin City," *The Life & Times of Tim* (animated), HBO, 2008.
Voice, "Theo Strikes Back/Amy Gets Wasted," *The Life & Times of Tim* (animated), HBO, 2008.
Jennifer, "Great Moments in Human Interaction" segment, *Atom TV,* Comedy Central, 2008.
Pageant mother, "Did Garcia Steal Dangle's Husband?," *Reno 911!,* Comedy Central, 2008.
Pageant mother, "Baghdad 911," *Reno 911!,* Comedy Central, 2008.
Jamie Fowler, "Denise Handicapped," *Curb Your Enthusiasm,* HBO, 2009.

Television Work; Specials:
Executive producer, *Ronna & Beverly,* Showtime, 2009.

Film Appearances:
Allison, *Last Night at Eddie's,* Boston Pictures, 1997.

Sharon on the Leslie Grant show, *Lost Souls,* New Line Cinema, 2000.
Felicia Cummings, *Felicia and the Great Quebec,* 2003.
Cate, *Still Single,* 2004.
Jill Watson, *Blackballed: The Bobby Dukes Story* (also known as *Blackballed*), 7th Floor, 2004.
Bertha, *Must Love Dogs,* Warner Bros., 2005.
Susan Jones, *Goodnight Burbank* (short film), Evil Global Corporation, 2006.
Wet T–shirt girl, *Wild Girls Gone,* 2007.
Marv's wife, *Yes Man,* Warner Bros., 2008.
Gretchen Becky, *Love Shack,* 2010.

Stage Appearances:
Appeared in productions of *All in the Timing,* Orlando Theatre Project, Orlando, FL; *Steel Magnolias,* Marblehead Little Theatre; and *Twelfth Night,* Sterling Renaissance Festival.

Internet Appearances; Episodic:
Nurse Robin, *Childrens' Hospital,* The WB.com, 2008.

RECORDINGS

Video Games:
Voice, *Panty Raider: From Here to Immaturity,* Brady Games/MacMillan Publishing, 2000.

WRITINGS

Television Specials:
Ronna & Beverly, Showtime, 2009.

Screenplays:
Felicia and the Great Quebec, 2003.

De PABLO, Cote 1979–
(Maria Jose de Pablo)

PERSONAL

Original name, Maria Jose de Pablo Fernandez; born November 12, 1979, in Santiago, Chile; daughter of Maria Olga Fernandez (a television personality); father, a businessman; immigrated to the United States, c. 1989. *Education:* Carnegie Mellon University, B.F.A., acting and music theatre, 2000. *Avocational Interests:* Writing and performing original music.

Addresses: *Agent*—Paradigm, 360 North Crescent Dr., North Bldg., Beverly Hills, CA 90210. *Manager*—Inspire Entertainment, 1517 South Bentley Ave., Suite

202, Los Angeles, CA 90025. *Publicist*—42West, 11400 West Olympic Blvd., Suite 11400, Los Angeles, CA 90064.

Career: Actress. Appeared in television commercials, including Volkswagen autos.

Awards, Honors: Imagen Award, best supporting actress—television, 2006, ALMA Award nomination, outstanding actress in a drama television series, American Latino Media Arts Awards, 2008, Imagen Award nomination, best supporting actress—television, 2009, all for *Navy NCIS: Naval Criminal Investigative Service.*

CREDITS

Film Appearances:
Bruja, *The Last Rites of Ransom Pride,* 2009.

Television Appearances; Series:
(As Maria Jose de Pablo) Cohost, *Control,* Univision, 1994–95.
Marguerite Cisneros, *The Jury,* Fox, 2004.
Ziva David, *Navy NCIS: Naval Criminal Investigative Service* (also known as *NCIS* and *NCIS: Naval Criminal Investigative Service*), CBS, 2005—.

Television Appearances; Episodic:
Fiona, "Hostile Makeover," *The $reet,* Fox, 2000.
Gina, "Do It Yourself," *The Education with Max Bickford,* CBS, 2001.
The Late Late Show with Craig Ferguson, CBS, 2006.
Entertainment Tonight (also known as *E.T.*), syndicated, 2008, 2009.
The Early Show, CBS, 2009.

Also appeared in *All My Children,* ABC.

Stage Appearances:
Juliet, *Measure for Measure,* Public Theatre, New York City, 2001.
Dolores Fuentes, *The Mambo Kings,* Golden Gate Theatre, San Francisco, CA, then Broadway Theatre, New York City, 2005.

RECORDINGS

Video Games:
Voice of Melanie Sanchez, *ToCA Race Driver,* 2002.

DHARMA, Jake
    See SHAW, Scott

DIATCHENKO, Dimitri
(Demetri Diatchenko)

PERSONAL

Born in San Francisco, CA. *Education:* Stetson University, Deland, FL, B.A., music, 1994; Florida State University, Tallahassee, FL, M.A., music performance, 1996. *Avocational Interests:* Martial arts.

Addresses: *Agent*—Sutton, Barth & Vennari, 145 S. Fairfax Ave., Suite 310, Los Angeles, CA 90036; (voiceover work) AVO Talent, 8500 Melrose Ave., Suite 212, West Hollywood, CA 90069. *Manager*—Barry Bookin Management, 4545 San Feliciano Dr., Woodland Hills, CA 91364. *Publicist*—Charles Sherman Public Relations, 8306 Wilshire Blvd., #2017, Beverly Hills, CA 90211.

Career: Actor and voice performer. Also performs and teaches classical guitar. Appeared in television commercials, including ads for Ford trucks, Lay's potato chips, and Heineken beer.

Awards, Honors: (All for music) Concerto competition winner, Stetson University and Florida State University, 1994; quarter finalist, Oberlin International Guitar Competition, 1994; first place, Collegiate Soloist Competition, Florida MTNA, 1994; silver medalist, Wurlitzer National Collegiate Artist Competition, 1995; semifinalist, Stotsenberg International Classical Guitar Competition, 1999; grand championship finalist, instrumental original category, World Championship of Performing Arts, 2003.

CREDITS

Television Appearances; Episodic:
Thug #1/Carl, "A Mime Is a Terrible Thing to Waste," *Diagnosis Murder,* CBS, 1997.
Sergeant, "D.O.A.," *Timecop,* ABC, 1998.
Robert Jackson, "Power Angels," *Walker, Texas Ranger* (also known as *Walker*), CBS, 1999.
Anton Marisovich, "True Stories," *Pensacola: Wings of Gold,* syndicated, 1999.
"Val Point Blank," *V.I.P.* (also known as *V.I.P.—Die Bodyguards*), syndicated, 2000.
(Uncredited) Alexei, "Smuggler's Blues," *18 Wheels of Justice,* TNN, 2000.
Voice of elder beaver, "All Work and No Play," *The Wild Thornberrys* (animated), Nickelodeon, 2001.
Vilmos, "The Frame," *Alias,* ABC, 2004.
(As Demetri Diatchenko) Darsikska, "The Wild Bunch," *Wanted,* TNT, 2005.

Waiter #1, "Odd Couples," *The Suite Life of Zack and Cody* (also known as *TSL*), The Disney Channel, 2006.

Attendant, "Not So Suite 16," " *The Suite Life of Zack and Cody* (also known as *TSL*), The Disney Channel, 2006.

Sergei Kraislov, "Table for Three," *Desire*, MyNetworkTV, 2006.

Lyov Lysowsky, "Honor among Thieves," *Criminal Minds*, CBS, 2007.

Gavin Lundy, "Fall from Grace," *Shark*, CBS, 2007.

Russian #2, "The Lying King," *The Riches*, FX Network, 2008.

Gold Teeth, "Breakdown," *My Own Worst Enemy*, NBC, 2008.

Yuri Ovsenko, "Push Comes to Shove," *Without a Trace* (also known as *W.A.T*), CBS, 2008.

Andrei, "Wolfe in Sheep's Clothing," *CSI: Miami* (also known as *CSI: Weekends*), CBS, 2009.

Voice, "Spies Reminiscent of Us," *Family Guy* (animated; also known as *Padre de familia*), Fox, 2009.

Television Appearances; Pilots:
Bodyguard, *Total Security*, ABC, 1997.
Dar Sitska, *Wanted*, TNT, 2005.
Boris, *Burn Notice*, USA Network, 2007.

Film Appearances:
Richter, *Goiterboy* (short film), AtomFilms, 1997.
Trainee, *G.I. Jane*, Buena Vista, 1997.
The Settlement, Bedford, 1999.
Title role, *Norman J. Lloyd* (short film), ABCD Productions, 2001.
Poker player, *Love Made Easy*, 2006.
Claudius, *Roma Sub Rosa: The Secret under the Rose* (short film; also known as *The Secret Under the Rose*), Cobblestone Studios, 2006.
Jesse the mechanic, *The Genius Club*, Eleven Arts, 2006.
Alexi, *Miriam*, Seventh Art Releasing, 2006.
Grammy, *The Longest Yard Sale*, Reverie Pictures, 2007.
Ivan, *Remarkable Power*, Dalton Pictures, 2008.
Russian suit, *Indiana Jones and the Kingdom of the Crystal Skull*, Paramount, 2008.
Russian underling, *Get Smart*, Warner Bros., 2008.
Bob, *Burning Palms*, Films in Motion, 2010.

Also appeared in the short films *Third on a Match* and *Used Cars*; in *Reverie Extremist*.

Stage Appearances:
Appeared as Dillard Nations, *Foxfire*, Deland Cultural Arts Players, FL.

RECORDINGS

Albums; Classical Guitar:
Six String–2000, LCA Records, 2000.

Acoustic Journey: World Music for Solo Guitar, LCA Records, 2001.

Pasion, Fuego y Romanza: Latin Music for Solo Guitar, LCA Records, 2003.

Songs I Know by Heart, LCA Records, 2004.

Video Games:
Voice of Sledge, *Quake 4*, Activision, 2005.
Additional voices, *Medal of Honor: European Assault*, Electronic Arts, 2005.
Voice of paramilitary leader, *SOCOM: U.S. Navy SEALs—Combined Assault*, Sony, 2006.
SOCOM: U.S. Navy SEALs: Fireteam Bravo 2, Sony, 2006.
Voice of Boris Bullski/Titanium Man, *Iron Man*, Sega, 2008.
Voice of Commander Oleg Vodnik, *Command & Conquer: Red Alert 3*, BeachHouse, 2008.
Voice of the Commissar, *Call of Duty: World at War*, Activision, 2008.
Voice of Golden Dawn Agent/Wehrmacht officer/black market agent, *Wolfenstein*, Activision Blizzard, 2009.
Voice of Commander Oleg Vodnik, *Command & Conquer: Red Alert 3—Uprising*, Electronic Arts, 2009.
Voice of Serbian soldiers, *Uncharted 2: Among Thieves*, Naughty Dog, 2009.

Also appeared in the video games *Singularity, Aion, Rogue Warrior, Riddler 3, Resistance: Retribution, Navy SOCOM: Confrontation, Fracture, Soldier of Fortune*, and *James Bond 6: From Russia with Love*.

Music Videos:
Appeared as cop on horseback in "Addicted" by Enrique Iglesias.

WRITINGS

Film Scores:
Full Count (short film), Straight A Productions, 2006.

Film Songs:
"Tango en Paraiso," *Remarkable Power*, Dalton Pictures, 2008.

"Tango en Paraiso" was published in *Master Anthology of New Classic Guitar Solos, Volume 1*, Mel Bay Publications.

OTHER SOURCES

Electronic:
Dimitri Diatchenko Official Site, http://www.dimitrid.com, December 26, 2009.

ECKSTEIN, George 1928–2009

PERSONAL

Born May 3, 1928, in Los Angeles, CA; died of lung cancer, September 12, 2009, in Brentwood, CA. Producer and writer. Television producer and writer Eckstein is remembered for producing the 1971 television movie *Duel,* which was directed by then-fledgling director Steven Spielberg, and for cowriting the final episode of the successful television series *The Fugitive,* which aired in 1967. Eckstein began his career in the early 1960s, writing television episodes for such series as *Dr. Kildare, The Untouchables,* and *Gunsmoke.* He started work as a writer on *The Fugitive* in 1963 and in 1965 became a producer of the show. Continuing to write for television, over the next several decades he penned episodes of *The New Adventures of Huckleberry Finn* and *Jake and the Fatman* as well as scripts for television movies, including several Perry Mason movies and *Jane Doe: The Wrong Face,* his final writing effort for television. Eckstein was executive producer of the detective series *Banacek* in the 1970s and a producer of a number of movies for television, among them *Tail Gunner Joe, Where the Ladies Go,* and *When We Were Young.*

PERIODICALS

Los Angeles Times, September 13, 2009.

EDISON, Matthew 1975–

PERSONAL

Born August 22, 1975, in Canada; great–great–great grand–nephew of Thomas Edison (an inventor).

Addresses: *Agent*—Gary Goddard Agency, 10 Saint Mary St., Suite 305, Toronto, Ontario M4Y 1P9, Canada.

Career: Actor.

CREDITS

Film Appearances:
Quincy, *Interstate 60: Episodes of the Road* (also known as *I–60* and *Interstate 60*), Samuel Goldwyn, 2002.
Paramedic, *Green Door* (short film), 2008.
Nerdy student, *Flash of Genius,* 2008.
Himself, *Trust, Honour and Reputation: The Making of "Othello: The Tragedy of the Moor"* (short documentary; also known as *Trust, Honour and Reputation*), 2008.
Max, *Moving Parts* (short film), 2009.

Television Appearances; Series:
Graham Wolf, *At the Hotel,* CBC, 2006.
Darren, *House Party,* Comedy Network, 2008.

Television Appearances; Miniseries:
Embassy clerk, *Anne of Green Gables: The Continuing Story* (also known as *Anne 3* and *Anne ... La maison aux pignons verts: Les annees de tourmente*), CBC and PBS, 2000.

Television Appearances; Movies:
Albert Lassiter, *Murder in a Small Town,* Arts and Entertainment, 1999.
Kevin, *This Time Around,* ABC Family, 2003.
Billy, Young Spags' Friend, *Our Fathers,* 2005.
Ian Kohler, *Waking Up to Wally: The Walter Gretzky Story* (also known as *La longue absence*), CBC, 2005.
Paul Elliot "Kilroy" Fraser, *The Dive from Clausen's Pier,* Lifetime, 2005.
Louis Baxter, *Princess* (also known as *Princess: A Modern Fairytale*), ABC Family, 2008.
Alec, *Glitch* (also known as *Static*), 2008.
Peter Kahane, *Of Murder and Memory,* Lifetime, 2008.
Tolley Phillips, *The Wild Girl,* Hallmark Channel, 2010.

Television Appearances; Specials:
Frank Arbus, *The Dead Beat,* 2008.

Television Appearances; Episodic:
Mike Buckley, "The Tale of the Shiny Red Bicycle," *Are You Afraid of the Dark?,* YTV and Nickelodeon, 1993.
Louis Nitkin, "Death Trap," *Code Name: Eternity* (also known as *Code: Eternity*), Sci–Fi Channel, 2000.
Morton Schane, "Before I Die," *A Nero Wolfe Mystery* (also known as *Nero Wolfe*), Arts and Entertainment, 2002.
Ed Erskine Jr., "The Silent Speaker: Parts 1 & 2," *A Nero Wolfe Mystery* (also known as *Nero Wolfe*), Arts and Entertainment, 2002.
Nate the trooper, "Immune to Murder," *A Nero Wolfe Mystery* (also known as *Nero Wolfe*), Arts and Entertainment, 2002.
O'Reagan's assistant, "The Foosball," *Billable Hours,* Showcase, 2006.
Voice of Lord Byron and Jacques, "Nightmare on Joe's Street," *Time Warp Trio* (animated), NBC, 2006.
Paul Wilson, "The Green Muse," *Murdoch Mysteries,* Bravo Canada, 2009.

Stage Appearances:

Horace, *The School for Wives,* Premiere Dance Theatre, Toronto, Ontario, Canada, 2000.

Title role, *Amadeus,* 2003.

WRITINGS

Television Movies:

(With others) *Othello* (also known as *Othello: The Tragedy of the Moor*), CBC, 2008.

Stage Plays:

The Domino Heart, 2003.

ESTERMAN, Laura 1945–
  (Blanche Blackwell)

PERSONAL

Born March 12, 1945, in New York, NY; daughter of Benjamin (a doctor) and Sophie (maiden name, Milgram) Esterman. *Education:* Radcliffe College, B.A.; studied acting at London Academy of Music and Dramatic Art.

Addresses: *Agent*—Bret Adams, Ltd., 448 West 44th St., New York, NY 10036.

Career: Actress. Member of a number of theatre companies.

Awards, Honors: Jeff awards, best actress in a principal role, Joseph Jefferson Awards Committee, 1976, for *Mourning Becomes Electra,* and 1978, for *Much Ado about Nothing;* Jeff Award, best actress in a principal role, 1990, Obie Award, best performance, *Village Voice,* Drama Desk Award, outstanding actress in a play, and Outer Critics Circle Award, best actress in a play, all 1992, all for *Marvin's Room.*

CREDITS

Stage Appearances:

Elsie, *The Time of Your Life,* Lincoln Center, Vivian Beaumont Theater, New York City, 1969.

Sharon Stover, *The Pig Pen,* Theatre at St. Clement's Church, New York City, 1970.

Sissy, *The Carpenters,* American Place Theatre, New York City, 1970–71.

Sidonia, *The Waltz of the Toreadors,* Philadelphia Drama Club, Philadelphia, PA, 1972, and Circle in the Square, New York City, 1973.

Regina Engstrand, *Ghosts,* Roundabout Theatre Company, New York City, 1973.

Masha, *The Seagull,* Roundabout Theatre Company, 1973–74.

Lady Macbeth, *Macbeth,* New York Shakespeare Festival, Lincoln Center, Mitzi E. Newhouse Theater, New York City, 1974.

Sara Benjamin, *God's Favorite,* Eugene O'Neill Theatre, New York City, 1974–75.

Lorna, *Golden Boy,* Manhattan Theatre Club, New York City, 1975.

Mrs. Brimmins, *Rubbers* (produced in a double–bill with *Yanks 3 Detroit 0 Top of the Seventh*), American Place Theatre, 1975.

Shirley, *Even the Window Is Gone,* New Dramatists, New York City, 1976.

Young woman, *The Pokey,* Manhattan Theatre Club, 1976.

Giulianella, *Saturday, Sunday, Monday,* Arena Stage, Washington, DC, c. 1976.

Lavinia, *Mourning Becomes Electra,* Goodman Theatre, Chicago, IL, c. 1976.

The Bridge at Belharbour (one–act play; also known as *The Bridge at Belharbor* and *The Bridge at Bel Harbour*), Manhattan Theatre Club, 1977.

The Rivals, CENTERSTAGE, Baltimore, MD, c. 1977.

Margarita, *The Master and Margarita,* New York Shakespeare Festival, Joseph Papp Public Theater, LuEsther Hall, New York City, 1978.

Nicole, *Bonjour, la, Bonjour,* Tyrone Guthrie Theater, Minneapolis, MN, 1978.

Beatrice, *Much Ado about Nothing,* Goodman Theatre, c. 1978.

Kathleen, *Terra Nova,* Center Theatre Group, Mark Taper Forum, Los Angeles, 1979.

Mimi, *Chinchilla,* Phoenix Theatre, New York City, 1979.

Tiebele, *Tiebele and Her Demon,* Brooks Atkinson Theatre, New York City, 1979–80.

Cleopatra Maximovna, *The Suicide,* American National Theatre and Academy (ANTA) Theatre, New York City, 1980.

Dusa, *Dusa, Fish, Stas, and Vi,* Manhattan Theatre Club, 1980.

Gretchen, *Rip Van Winkle; or, The Works,* Yale Repertory Theatre, University Theatre, New Haven, CT, 1981.

Helena, *A Midsummer Nights Dream,* Brooklyn Academy of Music, Brooklyn, New York City, 1981.

Melinda, *The Recruiting Officer,* Brooklyn Academy of Music, 1981.

Peasant woman, *Oedipus the King,* Brooklyn Academy of Music, Lepercq Space, Brooklyn, 1981.

Irene Connor, *Two Fish in the Sky,* New York Shakespeare Festival, Parish Hall at Church of the Heavenly Rest, New York City, 1982.

Animal Kingdom, Berkshire Theatre Festival, Main Stage, Stockbridge, MA, 1982.

Sunrise at Campobello, Berkshire Theatre Festival, Main Stage, 1982.

Title role, *Mary Barnes,* American Musical and Dramatic Academy Theatre, New York City, 1983.

Alms for the Middle Class, Geva Theatre, Rochester, NY, c. 1983.

Donna, *Kvetch,* Odyssey Theatre, Los Angeles, 1986, and Westside Arts Theatre, New York City, 1987.

Luisa Baccara, *Tamara,* Park Avenue Armory, New York City, 1987–89.

Benefactors, Studio Arena Theatre, Buffalo, NY, c. 1988.

Mrs. Samsa, *Metamorphosis,* Ethel Barrymore Theatre, New York City, 1989.

Bessie, *Marvin's Room,* Goodman Theatre Studio, Chicago, IL, 1990, Playwrights Horizons Theatre, New York City, 1991, and Minetta Lane Theatre, New York City, 1992.

Clara Fisher Hyland, *The Show Off,* Roundabout Theatre Company, Criterion Center Stage Right Theatre, New York City, 1992.

Laurie, *Two Rooms,* Signature Theatre, New York City, 1993.

Title role, *Edith Stein,* Jewish Repertory Theatre, New York City, 1994.

Tess Brodsky, *The Yiddish Trojan Women,* American Jewish Theatre, New York City, 1996.

Jan, *Good as New,* Manhattan Class Company (MCC) Theatre, New York City, 1997.

Anne Bittenhand, *The Psychic Life of Savages,* Wilma Theatre, Philadelphia, PA, 1998.

Farmer and Rose, *The American Clock,* Roundabout Theatre Company, Peter Norton Space, Signature Theatre, 1998.

Amanda Wingfield, *The Glass Menagerie,* Yale Repertory Theatre, 1999.

Sophia Belkin, *Cranes,* Theatre at St. Clement's Church, 1999.

Maureen, *The Wax,* Playwrights Horizons Theatre, 2000–2001.

Shirley, *True Love,* Zipper Factory Theater, New York City, 2001–2002.

Sarah Bernhardt, *Duet,* Greenwich Street Theatre, New York City, 2003–2004.

Terrorism, New Group, Harold Clurman Theatre, New York City, 2005.

Rachel, *Two Thousand Years,* New Group, Acorn Theatre, New York City, 2008.

Appeared in other productions, including an appearance as Masha, *The Three Sisters,* Mummers Theater, Oklahoma City, OK; and in *Out of Our Father's House.* Performer in summer stock productions in Vermont; CENTERSTAGE, Baltimore, MD, member of company, 1968–69; Playhouse in the Park, Cincinnati, OH, member of company, 1970–71; Repertory Theatre of St. Louis, St. Louis, MO, guest artist, 1971–72; Arena Stage, Washington, DC, member of company, 1979–80.

Major Tours:

Bessie, *Marvin's Room,* U.S. cities, c. 1990.

Film Appearances:

Road Movie, 1974, Image Entertainment, 2000.

Female voyager, *Alone in the Dark,* New Line Cinema, 1982.

Nora Lawlor, *Ironweed,* TriStar, 1987.

Homeless woman, *Me and Him* (also known as *Ich und Er*), Columbia, 1990.

Lolly, *Awakenings,* Columbia, 1990.

New York journalist, *The Doors,* TriStar, 1991.

Cousin Ophelia, *Addams Family Values* (also known as *Addams Family 2, Addams Family 2.,* and *The Addams Family 2*), Paramount, 1993.

Neighbor, *Jaded,* c. 1996 (other sources cite 1997 or 1999).

Performer in play and messenger, *Chinese Coffee,* Fox Searchlight/Twentieth Century–Fox, 2000.

Vanessa Boulette, *Suspended Animation* (also known as *Mayhem*), First Run, 2001.

Psychiatrist, *From Other Worlds,* 2004.

Judit, *Arranged,* Film Movement, 2007.

Television Appearances; Series:

Felice Carpenter, *Another World* (also known as *Another World: Bay City* and *AW: Bay City*), NBC, 1980.

Television Appearances; Movies:

Arlene, *Children of the Night,* CBS, 1985.

Sarah's cousin, *The Confession,* Cinemax, 1999.

Television Appearances; Specials:

Susan Braver, "The Trial of Bernhard Goetz," *American Playhouse,* PBS, 1988.

Television Appearances; Episodic:

Miss Conover, "A Pocketful of Steele," *Remington Steele,* NBC, 1984.

Ms. Resnick, "Into the Frying Pan," *The Facts of Life,* NBC, 1985.

Psychiatrist, "Cheers," *St. Elsewhere,* NBC, 1985.

Gloria Rheinhold, "Fifty Ways to Floss Your Lover," *L.A. Law,* NBC, 1987.

Waitress, "Matchmaker," *Family Ties,* NBC, 1987.

Professor Florence Cooley, "Paranoia," *Law & Order* (also known as *Law & Order Prime*), NBC, 1995.

Eva Walcoff, "Blood Money," *Law & Order* (also known as *Law & Order Prime*), NBC, 1999.

Marge, "Alone in a Crowd," *Third Watch,* NBC, 2000.

Mrs. Sandomir, "Noncompliance," *Law & Order: Special Victims Unit* (also known as *Law & Order's Sex Crimes, Law & Order: SVU,* and *Special Victims Unit*), NBC, 2000.

Elderly landlady, "Identity Crisis," *Law & Order: Criminal Intent* (also known as *Law & Order: CI*), NBC, 2009.

Sue Moyer, "Home Is Where You Hang Your Holster," *Life on Mars*, ABC, 2009.

Radio Appearances; Series:

The Madonna Vampira, *The Fourth Tower of Inverness* (also known as *Jack Flanders: 4th Tower of Inverness*), ZBS Foundation, broadcast in various formats, beginning 1972.

Ruby, *Ruby: The Adventures of a Galactic Gumshoe* (also known as *Ruby 1: Adventures of a Galactic Gumshoe*), ZBS Foundation, broadcast in various formats, beginning 1982.

Ruby, *Ruby 2: The Further Adventures of a Galactic Gumshoe* (also known as *Ruby 2*), ZBS Foundation, broadcast in various formats, beginning 1985.

(As Blanche Blackwell) Ruby, *Ruby 3* (consists of Part One: The Underworld and Part Two: The Invisible World), ZBS Foundation, broadcast in various formats, beginning 1990.

(As Blackwell) Ruby, *Ruby 4,* (consists of "Part One: The Moon Coins of Sonto Lore," 1994, "Part Two: The Turban of El Morya," 1994, "Part Three: Dark Night of the Reptoids," 1994, and "Part Four: Mad Moon for Rubina"), ZBS Foundation, broadcast in various formats, 1995.

(As Blackwell) Ruby, *Ruby 5: Land of the Zoots*, ZBS Foundation, broadcast in various formats, beginning 1998.

The Madonna Vampira, *Return to Inverness*, ZBS Foundation, broadcast in various formats, beginning 2000.

(As Blackwell) Ruby, *Ruby 6: The Illusionati*, ZBS Foundation, broadcast in various formats, beginning 2001.

(As Blackwell) Ruby, *Ruby 6.5: Far Flung Farouk*, ZBS Foundation, broadcast in various formats, beginning 2004.

(As Blackwell) Ruby, *Ruby 7: Dream Weaver, Dream Deceiver*, ZBS Foundation, broadcast in various formats, beginning 2006.

(As Blackwell) Ruby, *Ruby 7.5: The Tookah's Tales*, ZBS Foundation, broadcast in various formats, beginning 2008.

(As Blackwell) Ruby, *Ruby 8: The Good King Kapoor*, ZBS Foundation, broadcast in various formats, beginning 2009.

Radio Appearances; Pilots:

Ruby Tuesday, *Tired of the Green Menace?*, ZBS Foundation, 1977.

Appeared as Ruby Starr, *Rebel from Utopia;* and appeared in other *Ruby* pilots and in other programs, ZBS Foundation.

RECORDINGS

Audiobooks:

Beyond the Darkness: My Death Journey to the Edge of Hell by Angie Fenimore, Random House, 1995.

Appeared in several recordings related to her appearances in the *Ruby* radio programs.

F

FEDERMAN, Wayne 1959–

PERSONAL

Born June 22, 1959, in Los Angeles, CA. *Education:* New York University Tisch School of Arts, B.F.A., acting.

Addresses: *Agent*—Ellis Talent Group, 4705 Laurel Canyon Blvd., Valley Village, CA 91607.

Career: Actor, comedian, and writer. Performed as a stand–up comedian in clubs, including Catch a Rising Star and The Comic Strip. Appeared in television commercials, including work for Hertz, U.S. Navy, McDonald's, Ford Ranger, and 7–11 stores. No Fat Guy (improvisational group), cofounder, c. 1987.

CREDITS

Film Appearances:
New Wave Comedy (documentary), 1986.
Wiseass, *Ambition,* Miramax, 1991.
Policeman Dave, *Jack Frost* (also known as *Frost*), Warner Bros., 1998.
Doc, *Dill Scallion,* The Asylum, 1999.
Tully, *Freak Talks about Sex* (also known as *Blowin' Smoke*), Lions Gate Films, 1999.
Admissions guy, *Legally Blonde,* Metro–Goldwyn–Mayer, 2001.
Allan, *Love & Support,* Hi Tide, 2001.
Glen Federman, *The Third Wheel,* Miramax, 2002.
Paramedic, *American Girl* (also known as *Confessions of an American Girl*), MGM Home Entertainment, 2002.
Ronnie the Rooster, *Waking Up in Reno,* Miramax, 2003.

Officer Dave, *Dumb and Dumberer: When Harry Met Lloyd,* New Line Cinema, 2003.
(Uncredited) Whiskey sour man, *View from the Top,* Miramax, 2003.
Bathroom guy, *Charlie's Angels: Full Throttle,* Columbia, 2003.
Patient, *50 First Dates,* Columbia, 2004.
Q–Ball Curtis, *Y.M.I.,* Vanguard, 2004.
Smart tech customer, *The 40 Year Old Virgin* (also known as *The 40 Year–Old Virgin* and *The 40–Year–Old Virgin*), Universal, 2005.
Josh, *Max and Josh* (short film), Purple Fur Coat Productions, 2006.
Stu Simmons, *Grilled,* New Line Cinema, 2006.
Airport attendant, *Unaccompanied Minors* (also known as *Grounded*), Warner Bros., 2006.
Fantasy baseball guy, *Knocked Up,* Universal, 2007.
Airport guard, *This Is Not a Test,* Image Entertainment, 2008.
Blind man, *Step Brothers,* Columbia, 2008.
Comedy & magic manager, *Funny People,* Universal, 2009.

Television Appearances; Episodic:
Paul, "Some Nights to Remember," *Dear John,* NBC, 1990.
Wayne, "Eclipse," *Baywatch* (also known as *Baywatch Hawaii*), NBC, 1990.
"TV or Not TV," *L.A. Law,* NBC, 1991.
A&M Wolf, "The Cat's in the Cradle," *A Different World,* NBC, 1992.
Desk clerk, *Black Tie Affair,* NBC, 1993.
Doctor, "It's a Tough Job ... But Why Does My Father Have to Do It?," *Doogie Howser, M.D.,* ABC, 1993.
Assistant, "You Ought to Be in Pictures," *Almost Home* (also known as *The Torkelsons: Almost Home*), ABC, 1993.
Fred Meyer, "Double Indignity," *Living Single* (also known as *My Girls*), Fox, 1994.
Fred Meyer, "Legal Briefs," *Living Single* (also known as *My Girls*), Fox, 1995.

Fred Meyer, "Mommy Not Dearest," *Living Single* (also known as *My Girls*), Fox, 1995.
Premium Blend, Comedy Central, 1997.
King Comic, "The Prey," *The New Adventures of Robin Hood* (also known as *Les novelles aventures de Robin des bois*), TNT, 1997.
Stan Sanders, "Adolf Hankler," *The Larry Sanders Show,* HBO, 1998.
Voice of sea lions, "Eliza–cology," *The Wild Thornberrys* (animated), Nickelodeon, 1998.
Randy Stark, "Freaky Friday," *NewsRadio* (also known as *The Station*), NBC, 1999.
Dean, "The Wire," *Curb Your Enthusiasm,* HBO, 2000.
"Hollywood A.D.," *The X Files* (also known as *The X–Files*), Fox, 2000.
Late Friday, NBC, 2001.
"Pete Maravich," *ESPN SportsCentury,* ESPN, 2001.
The Late Late Show with Craig Kilborn (also known as *The Late Late Show*), CBS, 2002.
Teacher, "Lord of the Bees," *Oliver Beene,* Fox, 2003.
"Wayne Federman," *Comedy Central Presents,* Comedy Central, 2003.
"Bystand Me," *King of the Hill* (animated), Fox, 2005.
Johnson, "Is She Really Going Out with Him?," *Courting Alex,* CBS, 2006.
Johnson, "Girlfriend," *Courting Alex,* CBS, 2006.
Vault company rep, "Strife," *Heist,* NBC, 2006.
Wayne Handleman, "1985 World's Strongest Man," *Cheap Seats: Without Ron Parker* (also known as *Cheap Seats*), ESPN, 2006.
Mr. Kaminsky, "First Kiss," *Wizards of Waverly Place,* The Disney Channel, 2007.
Head Case, Starz!, 2008.
"Kathy at the Apollo," *Kathy Griffin: My Life on the D–list,* Bravo, 2009.
Late Night with Jimmy Fallon, NBC, 2009.
Dean Weinstock, "Vehicular Fellatio," *Curb Your Enthusiasm,* HBO, 2009.

Television Appearances; Movies:
The messenger, *Parent Trap: Hawaiian Honeymoon* (also known as *Parent Trap IV: Hawaiian Honeymoon*), NBC, 1989.
Wayne Frommer, *Kiss My Act,* ABC, 2001.

Television Appearances; Specials:
Comedy Central Presents Behind–the–Scenes at the American Comedy Awards, Comedy Central, 1998, 1999.
Pistol Pete: The Life and Times of Pete Maravich, CBS, 2001.
Host, *Reel Comedy: White Chicks,* Comedy Central, 2004.
Wildest Court Show Moments, E! Entertainment Television, 2007.

Stage Appearances:
Snow White and the Seven Dwarfs, 13th Street Theatre, New York City, c. 1987.

Appeared in a one–man show at 13th Street Theatre, c. 1987.

RECORDINGS

Video Games:
Stand–up performance #6, *Don't Quit Your Day Job,* 1996.

Videos:
Hollywood Desperado: Rebel or Royalty (documentary), Jaime Monroy, 2008.

WRITINGS

Television Series:
(And head monologue writer) *Late Night with Jimmy Fallon,* NBC, 2009—.

Television Specials:
35th Annual Key Art Awards, Starz!, 2006.

Television Episodes:
"Wayne Federman," *Comedy Central Presents,* Comedy Central, 2003.
Cheap Seats: Without Ron Parker (also known as *Cheap Seats*), ESPN, 2006.
Head Case, Starz!, 2008.

Also contributed to *Politically Incorrect,* HBO.

Screenplays:
Max and Josh (short film), Purple Fur Coat Productions, 2006.

Nonfiction:
(With Marsha Terrill and Jackie Maravich) *The Acclaimed Authorized Biography of Pistol Pete,* 2007.

Also contributor to periodicals, including *Sports Illustrated* and *Wall Street Journal.* Contributed to the Ronald Reagan biography *Dutch* by Edmund Morris. Wrote speeches for film producer Jerry Bruckheimer and Internet tycoon Marc Andreessen. Wrote for advertising campaigns, including Blue Cross/Blue Shield, and for board games, including "Taboo."

OTHER SOURCES

Electronic:
Wayne Federman Official Site, http://www.waynefederman.com/, December 26, 2009.

FENTON, George 1950–

PERSONAL

Original name, George Richard Ian Howe; born October 19, 1950, in London, England.

Addresses: *Agent*—The Gorfaine Schwartz Agency, 4111 West Alameda Ave., Suite 509, Burbank, CA 91505.

Career: Composer, conductor, orchestrator, and actor. Also worked as a church organist and visiting professor at the Royal College of Music, London.

Member: Royal Society of Music.

Awards, Honors: Television Award nomination, best original television music, British Academy of Film and Television Arts, 1981, for *Shoestring, Bloody Kiss,* and *Fox;* Television Award, best original television music, British Academy of Film and Television Arts, 1982, for *Bergerac, Going Gently, The History Man,* and *BBC News;* Apex Award nomination, original score—drama, 1982, Film Award nomination, best score, British Academy of Film and Television Arts, Academy Award nomination (with Ravi Shankar), best original score, 1983, all for *Gandhi;* Television Award, best original television music, British Academy of Film and Television Arts, 1983, Grammy Award nomination (with Shankar), best album of original score written for a motion picture or television, 1984, all for *An Englishman Abroad, Saigon—Year of the Cat, Walter and June, The Ghost Writer, Breakfast Time, Natural World,* and *Village Earth;* Television Award nomination, best original television music, British Academy of Film and Television Arts, 1985, for *The Jewel in the Crown;* Television Award, best original television music, British Academy of Film and Television Arts, 1987, for *The Monocled Mutineer;* Golden Globe Award nomination (with Jonas Gwangwa), best original score for a motion picture, Academy Award nomination (with Gwangwa), best original score, Academy Award nomination (with Gwangwa), best song, Apex Award nomination, best original score—drama, 1987, Film Award nomination (with Gwangwa), best score, British Academy of Film and Television Arts, 1988, Grammy Award nomination (with Gwangwa), best song written specifically for a motion picture or for television, all for *Cry Freedom;* Television Award nomination, best original television music, British Academy of Film and Television Arts, 1989, for *Talking Heads;* Academy Award nomination, best original score, 1989, Film Award nomination, best original score, British Academy of Film and Television Arts, 1990, for *Dangerous Liaisons;* Academy Award nomination, best original score, Apex Award nomination, original score—comedy, 1991, both for *The Fisher King;* Television Award nomination, best original television movie, British Academy of Film and Television Arts, 1991, for *The Trials of Life;* Film Award nomination, best original film score, British Academy of Film and Television Arts, 1991, for *Memphis Belle;* Television Award nomination, best original television music, British Academy of Film and Television Arts, 1994, for *Life in the Freezer;* BMI Film Music Award, 1994, for *Groundhog Day;* Anthony Asquith Award for Film Music nomination, British Academy of Film and Television Arts, 1996, for *The Madness of King George;* Apex Award nomination, best original score—comedy, 1998, for *The Object of My Affection;* Saturn Award nomination, best music, Academy of Science Fiction, Fantasy, and Horror Films, 1999, for *Ever After;* BMI Film Music Award, 1999, for *You've Got Mail;* Golden Globe Award nominations, best original score—motion picture and best original song—motion picture, 2000, both for *Anna and the King;* Rota Soundtrack Award, Venice Film Festival, 2001, for *The Navigators;* Video Premiere Award nomination, best original score, DVD Exclusive Awards, 2001, for *Grey Owl;* Televsion Award, best original television music, British Academy of Film and Television Arts, Emmy Award, outstanding music composition for a series—dramatic underscore, 2002, both for *The Blue Planet;* BMI Film Music Award, 2003, for *Sweet Home Alabama;* Emmy Award nomination, outstanding music composition for a miniseries, movie or a special, 2005, for *Pride;* Anthony Asquith Award for Film Music nomination, British Academy of Film and Television Arts, 2006, for *Mrs. Henderson Presents;* BMI Film Music Award, 2005, for *Hitch;* Television Award nomination, best original television music, British Academy of Film and Television Arts, Emmy Award, outstanding music composition for a series—original dramatic score, 2007, both for *Planet Earth;* Academy Fellowship of Ivor Novello Award, 2007.

CREDITS

Film Work:
Music coordinator, *Adult Fun,* 1972.
Music director, *Hussy,* 1979.
Music director, conductor, and orchestrator, *Gandhi* (also known as *Richard Attenborough's "Gandhi"*), Columbia, 1982.
Music director, *Bloody Kids,* Palace/BFI, 1983.
Music director and conductor, *Runners,* Hanstall, 1983.
Music director and pianist, *Billy the Kid and the Green Baize Vampire,* 1985.
Music supervisor, *White of the Eye,* Cinema Group, 1987.
Music director and conductor, *84 Charing Cross Road,* Columbia, 1987.
Music arranger and conductor, *White Mischief,* Columbia, 1987.

Conductor and music arranger: score, *Cry Freedom*, 1987.

Conductor and orchestrator, *A Handful of Dust*, New Line Cinema, 1988.

Conductor and orchestrator, *High Spirits*, TriStar, 1988.

Orchestrator and conductor, *We're No Angels*, Paramount, 1989.

Conductor and (uncredited) orchestrator, *Memphis Belle*, 1990.

Song producer, "How about You," and (uncredited) conductor and orchestrator, *The Fisher King*, TriStar, 1991.

Song producer, "Weatherman" and "Take Me Round Again," *Groundhog Day*, Columbia, 1993.

Orchestrator, *Born Yesterday*, Buena Vista, 1993.

Conductor, *Shadowlands*, 1993.

Music adapter (from the works of G. F. Handel) and orchestrator, *The Madness of King George* (also known as *The Madness of George III* and *The Madness of King George III*), Samuel Goldwyn, 1994.

Orchestrator, *China Moon*, Orion, 1994.

Adapter and music supervisor, *Interview with the Vampire* (also known as *Interview with the Vampire: The Vampire Chronicles*), Warner Bros., 1994.

Conductor, *Mary Reilly*, TriStar, 1996.

Conductor, *The Crucible*, Twentieth Century–Fox, 1996.

Orchestrator and conductor, *August*, Samuel Goldwyn, 1996.

Music producer, *Heaven's Prisoners*, New Line Cinema, 1996.

Orchestrator, *The Woodlanders*, Miramax, 1997.

Song performer, "Low Key Lightly," *Living Out Loud* (also known as *The Kiss*), New Line Cinema, 1998.

Conductor: score, and song producer and arranger, "You Were Meant for Me," *The Object of My Affection*, Twentieth Century–Fox, 1998.

(Uncredited) Conductor and music producer, *You've Got Mail*, Warner Bros., 1998.

Conductor, *Anna and the King*, Fox 2000 Pictures, 1999.

Music conductor, *Grey Owl*, New City Releasing, 1999.

Conductor, *Lucky Numbers* (also known as *Le bon numero*), Paramount, 2000.

Music conductor, *Center Stage* (also known as *Centre Stage*), Sony Pictures Releasing, 2000.

Music performer and music producer, *Sweet 16* (also known as *Felices deicseis*), Lions Gate Films, 2002.

Music conductor and arranger, "Learning to Be Nicer," *Seabiscuit*, Universal, 2003.

Conductor, *Valiant* (animated), Buena Vista, 2005.

Music conductor, *Hitch*, Columbia, 2005.

Producer, "Isn't it Romantic," "The Nearness of You," "Auld Lang Syne," and conductor, *Last Holiday*, Paramount, 2006.

Conductor, *Earth*, Disneynature, 2009.

Film Appearances:

Guest, *The Waiters*, 1969.

Harry, *Private Road*, 1971.

Himself, *The Making of "Deep Blue"* (documentary), Miramax Home Entertainment, 2006.

Television Work; Miniseries:

Additional music arranger, *The Jewel in the Crown*, 1984.

Television Work; Movies:

Conductor and music adaptor, *102 Boulevard Haussmann*, 1990.

Television Appearances; Series:

Martin Gimbel, *Emmerdale Farm* (also known as *Emmerdale*), 1976.

Television Appearances; Movies:

First brother, *A Day Out*, 1972.

M. Roland, *Cheri*, 1973.

Television Appearances; Specials:

The 60th Annual Academy Awards Presentation, ABC, 1988.

Television Appearances; Episodic:

Appeared as himself, "Love & Seduction," *Music Behind the Scenes*.

Stage Work:

Music arranger, *Good*, Royal Shakespeare Company, Warehouse Theatre, London, 1981, then Booth Theatre, New York City, 1982.

Stage Appearances:

Butley, 1971.

The Pleasure Principle, 1973.

Twelfth Night, 1975.

WRITINGS

Film Scores:

(With Michael Feast and David Dundas) *Private Road*, Maya Films, 1971.

The Waterloo Bridge Handicap, 1978.

Hussy, 1979.

Dead End, 1980.

(With Ravi Shankar) *Gandhi*, Columbia, 1982.

Bloody Kids (also known as *One Joke Too Many*), Palace/BFI, 1983.

Runners, Hanstall, 1983.

The Company of Wolves, Cannon, 1985.

Billy the Kid and the Green Baize Vampire, 1985.

Past Caring, 1985.

Clockwise, Universal/Cannon, 1986.

Cry Freedom, Universal, 1987.
84 Charing Cross Road, Columbia, 1987.
White Mischief, Columbia, 1987.
A Handful of Dust, New Line Cinema, 1988.
The Dressmaker, Film Four, 1988.
High Spirits, TriStar, 1988.
Dangerous Liaisons, Warner Bros., 1988.
Ghoulies II, Empire, 1988.
We're No Angels, Paramount, 1989.
Memphis Belle, Warner Bros., 1990.
The Long Walk Home, Miramax, 1990.
White Palace, Universal, 1991.
The Fisher King, TriStar, 1991.
Hero (also known as *Accidental Hero*), Columbia, 1992.
Final Analysis, Warner Bros., 1992.
Shadowlands, Savoy Pictures, 1993.
Groundhog Day, Columbia, 1993.
Born Yesterday, Buena Vista, 1993.
Mixed Nuts (also known as *Lifesavers*), TriStar, 1994.
The Madness of King George (also known as *The Madness of George III*), Samuel Goldwyn, 1994.
China Moon, Orion, 1994.
Ladybird Ladybird, Samuel Goldwyn, 1994.
The Viking Sagas (also known as *The Icelandic Sagas*), New Line Home Video, 1995.
Land and Freedom (also known as *Tierra y libertad* and *Terra e liberta*), 1995.
In Love and War, New Line Cinema, 1996.
Mary Reilly, TriStar, 1996.
Heaven's Prisoners, New Line Cinema, 1996.
Multiplicity, Columbia, 1996.
Carla's Song (also known as *La cancion de Carla*), Shadow Distribution, 1996.
The Crucible, Twentieth Century–Fox, 1996.
The Woodlanders, Miramax, 1997.
My Name Is Joe (also known as *Mein Name is Joe* and *Mi nombre es Joe*), Artisan Entertainment, 1998.
Living Out Loud (also known as *The Kiss*), New Line Cinema, 1998.
Ever After (also known as *Cinderella* and *Ever After: A Cinderella Story*), Twentieth Century–Fox, 1998.
Dangerous Beauty (also known as *Courtesan, The Honest Courtesan, A Destiny of Her Own,* and *Venice*), Warner Bros., 1998.
The Object of My Affection, Twentieth Century–Fox, 1998.
You've Got Mail (also known as *You Have Mail*), Warner Bros., 1998.
Entropy (also known as *Entrophy*), 1999.
Grey Owl, New City Releasing, 1999.
Anna and the King, Fox 2000 Pictures, 1999.
Bread and Roses (also known as *Brot und Rosen* and *Pan y rosas*), Lions Gate Films, 2000.
Center Stage (also known as *Centre Stage*), Sony Pictures Entertainment, 2000.
Lucky Numbers (also known as *Le bon numero*), Paramount, 2000.
Summer Catch, Warner Bros., 2001.

The Navigators (also known as *Geschichten von den gleisen* and *La Cuadrilla*), First Look Pictures Releasing, 2001.
Sweet Sixteen (also known as *Felices dieciseis*), 2002.
Sweet Home Alabama, Buena Vista, 2002.
Too Close to the Bone, 2002.
Deep Blue (documentary), Miramax, 2003.
Imagining Argentina, Arenas Entertainment, 2003.
A Fond Kiss … (also known as *Just a Kiss, Solo un beso, Un bacio appassionato,* and *Un beso*), Castle Hill Productions, 2004.
Stage Beauty, Lions Gate Films, 2004.
Casting a Spell: Making "Bewitched" (short documentary), Sony Pictures Home Entertainment, 2005.
Why I Love "Bewitched," 2005.
"Bewitched": Star Shots (short documentary), Sony Pictures Home Entertainment, 2005.
Hitch, Columbia, 2005.
Tickets, Facets Multimedia Distribution, 2005.
Valiant (animated), Buena Vista, 2005.
Bewitched, Columbia, 2005.
Mrs. Henderson Presents (also known as *Mrs. Henderson Presents*), Weinstein Company, 2005.
The Making of "Deep Blue" (documentary), Miramax Home Entertainment, 2006.
Last Holiday, Paramount, 2006.
The Wind That Shakes the Barley (also known as *El viento que agita la cebada, Il vento che accarezza l'erba,* and *Le vent se leve*), IFC First Take, 2006.
The History Boys, Fox Searchlight, 2006.
Earth (documentary; also known as *Unsere Erde*), 2007.
It's a Free World … (also known as *En un mundo libre …, In questo mondo libero, It's a Free World,* and *Polak potrzebny od zaraz*), IFC Films, 2007.
Fool's Gold, Warner Bros., 2008.
Earth, Disneynature, 2009.
The Bounty Hunter, Columbia, 2010.

Film Title Songs:
(With Jonas Gwangwa) *Cry Freedom,* Universal, 1987.

Film Songs:
"Beyond My Control" and "A Final Request," *High Heels* (also known as *Tacones lejanos* and *Talons aiguilles*), 1991.
Groundhog Day, Columbia, 1993.
Anna and the King, Fox 2000 Pictures, 1999.
"Learning to Be Nicer," *Seabiscuit,* Universal, 2003.

Television Music; Series:
Out, 1978.
Six Plays by Allan Bennett, 1978–79.
Fox, 1980.
Bergerac, 1981–85.
Call Me Mister, 1986.
The Trials of Life (also known as *David Attenborough: "The Trials of Life"*), BBC, 1990, TNT, 1991.

The Ren & Stimpy Show (animated; also known as *VH–1 Rem and Stimpy Rocks*), 1991–96.
Life in the Freezer, 1993.
Planet Earth (also known as *Planet Earth Extremes*), BBC and The Discovery Channel, 2006.
Planet Earth: The Future, BBC, 2006.
Life, Fox Family, 2009.

Television Theme Music; Series:
Shoestring, 1980.
BBC News, BBC, 1981.
Bergerac, 1981–87.

Television Music; Miniseries:
Shoestring, 1979.
The History Man (also known as *Malcolm Bradbury's "The History Man"*), 1981.
The Jewel in the Crown, PBS, 1984.
Talking Heads, 1987.
Talking Heads 2, BBC, 1998.
Shanghai Vice, 1999.
The Blue Planet, The Discovery Channel, 2001.

Television Music; Movies:
Rain on the Roof, 1980.
No Country for Old Men, 1981.
Parole, CBS, 1982.
Walter, 1982.
Saigon: Year of the Cat, 1983.
An Englishman Abroad, 1983.
Breakfast Time, 1983.
Natural World, 1983.
Village Earth, 1983.
Walter and June (also known as *Loving Walter*), 1983.
The Monocled Mutineer, BBC, 1986, KCET, 1990.
East of Ipswich, 1987.
102 Boulevard Haussmann, Arts and Entertainment, 1991.
Pride, Arts and Entertainment, 2004.

Television Music; Specials:
The Ghost Writer, PBS, 1983.
"A Chip in the Sugar," *2 Monologues: In My Defence/A Chip in the Sugar,* PBS, 1992.
China: Beyond the Clouds (also known as *National Geographic's "China: Beyond the Clouds"*), PBS, 1994.
The Fall of Saigon, The Discovery Channel, 1995.
Great White Bear, PBS, 1998.
Telling Tales, 2000.
Talking Heads 2: Miss Fozzard Finds Her Feet, PBS, 2001.
A French Affair (documentary), 2003.
Love and Death in Shanghai (documentary), 2007.

Television Music; Episodic:
"Last Summer," *ITV Playhouse,* ITV, 1977.
"Cold Harbour," *ITV Playhouse,* ITV, 1978.

"Private Ear," *Shoestring,* 1979.
"Going Gently," *BBC2 Playhouse,* BBC2, 1981.
"Crimes," *Play for Tomorrow,* 1982.
"Bright Eyes," *Play for Tomorrow,* 1982.
"Cricket," *Play for Tomorrow,* 1982.
"The Nuclear Family," *Play for Tomorrow,* 1982.
"Shades," *Play for Tomorrow,* 1982.
"Easter 2016," *Play for Tomorrow,* 1982.
"Our Winnie," *Objects of Affection,* 1982.
"A Woman of No Importance," *Objects of Affection,* 1982.
"Say Something Happened," *Objects of Affection,* 1982.
"Her Big Chance," *Talking Heads,* 1988.
"Waiting for the Telegram," *Talking Heads 2,* 1998.
"Ocean World," *The Blue Planet,* 2001.

Stage Music:
Much Ado about Nothing, National Theatre Company, Olivier Theatre, London, 1981.
A Month in the Country, National Theatre Company, Olivier Theatre, 1981.
The Duchess of Malfi, Royal Exchange Theatre Company, Round House Theatre, London, 1981.
Don Juan, National Theatre Company, Cottesloe Theatre, London, 1981.
Good, Royal Shakespeare Company, Warehouse Theatre, London, 1981, then Booth Theatre, New York City, 1982.
Antony and Cleopatra, Royal Shakespeare Company, Pit Theatre, London, 1983.
Macbeth, Royal Shakespeare Company, Barbican Theatre, London, 1983.
Mother Courage, Royal Shakespeare Company, Barbican Theatre, 1984.
Bengal Lancer, Lyric Hammersmith Theatre, London, 1985.

Also wrote scores for *A Fair Quarrel; The Cherry Orchard; The Changeling; Measure for Measure; Julius Caesar,* Riverside Studios; *Good,* Royal Shakespeare Company; *Dick,* Royal Court Theatre, London; *Buffalo Bill Wild West Show,* Euro–Disney.

Stage Incidental Music:
Twelfth Night, Royal Shakespeare Company, Stratford–upon–Avon, England, 1974.
Racing Demon, Center Theatre Group, Ahmanson Theatre, Los Angeles, 1994–95, then Vivian Beaumont Theatre, New York City, 1995.
The Judas Kiss, Broadhurst Theatre, New York City, 1998.

OTHER SOURCES

Periodicals:
Entertainment Weekly, January 17, 1997, p. 62.

FERRY, April 1932–

PERSONAL

Original name, April Cecilia Gaskins; born October 31, 1932, in NC; married Stephen Robertson Ferry (divorced, 1968).

Addresses: *Agent*—United Talent Agency, 9560 Wilshire Blvd., Suite 500, Beverly Hills, CA 90212. *Office*—1615 Shell Ave., Venice, CA 90291–3856.

Career: Costume designer and actress. Also worked as costume supervisor and in wardrobe departments.

Member: Costume Designers Guild.

Awards, Honors: Fennecus Award nomination, best costume design for a fantasy, 1987, for *Made in Heaven;* Emmy Award nomination, outstanding costume design for a miniseries or special, 1989, for *My Name Is Bill W;* Apex Award nomination, 1994, and Academy Award nomination, 1995, both best costume design, both for *Maverick;* Fennecus Award, best contemporary costume design, 1998, for *Playing by Heart;* Costume Designers Guild Awards, 2006, 2007, and Costume Designers Guild Award nomination, 2008, all outstanding costume design for a period or fantasy television series, for *Rome;* Emmy Award (with others), outstanding costumes for a series, 2006, for the episode "Triumph," *Rome;* Emmy Award nomination (with others), outstanding costumes for a series, 2007, for "De Patre Vostro (About Your Father)," *Rome;* Cymru Award, best costume design, Welsh unit of British Academy of Film and Television Arts, 2009, for *The Edge of Love.*

CREDITS

Film Costume Designer:
The Big Chill, Columbia, 1983.
Mike's Murder, 1984.
Costumes for Cher, *Mask,* Universal, 1985.
Gotcha!, Universal, 1985.
Poltergeist II: The Other Sid (also known as *Poltergeist 2*), Metro–Goldwyn–Mayer, 1986.
Big Trouble in Little China (also known as *John Carpenter's "Big Trouble in Little China"*), Twentieth Century–Fox, 1986.
Planes, Trains & Automobiles, Paramount, 1987.
Made in Heaven, Lorimar, 1987.
She's Having a Baby, Paramount, 1988.
Child's Play, United Artists, 1988.
Three Fugitives, Buena Vista, 1989.

Leviathan, Metro–Goldwyn–Mayer, 1989.
Immediate Family, Columbia, 1989.
Almost an Angel, Paramount, 1990.
Radio Flyer, Columbia, 1992.
The Babe, Universal, 1992.
Unlawful Entry, Twentieth Century–Fox, 1992.
Free Willy (also known as *Sauvez Willy*), Warner Bros., 1993.
Beethoven's 2nd, Universal, 1993.
Maverick, Warner Bros., 1994.
Little Giants, Warner Bros., 1994.
The Associate, Buena Vista, 1996.
Shadow Conspiracy, Buena Vista, 1997.
Little Boy Blue, Castle Hill, 1997.
Flubber (also known as *Disney's "Flubber: The Absent Minded Professor"*), Buena Vista, 1997.
Claudine's Return (also known as *Fire of Love* and *Kiss of Fire*), Jazz Pictures, 1998.
Playing by Heart (also known as *Intermedia*), Miramax, 1998.
Brokedown Palace, Twentieth Century–Fox, 1999.
U–571, Universal, 2000.
Boys and Girls, Dimension Films, 2000.
Costumes for California unit, *Down to You,* Miramax, 2000.
Donnie Darko (also released as *Donnie Darko: The Director's Cut*), Pandora Cinema, 2001.
15 Minutes (also known as *15 Minuten Ruhm*), New Line Cinema, 2001.
Frailty (also known as *Daemonisch* and *Frailty—Nessuno e al sicuro*), Lions Gate Films, 2001.
National Security, Columbia, 2003.
Terminator 3: Rise of the Machines (also known as *T3* and *Terminator 3–Der aufstand der maschinen*), Warner Bros., 2003.
Los Angeles costumes, *Timeline,* Paramount, 2003.
Southland Tales, Destination Films, 2007.
The Edge of Love, Capitol Films, 2009.
The Box, Warner Bros., 2009.
Surrogates (also known as *Vicarious*), Walt Disney, 2009.
Los Angeles costumes, *My Life in Ruins,* Fox Searchlight, 2009.

Film Appearances:
Bosslady, *Mike's Murder,* 1984.

Television Costume Designer; Series:
Rome, HBO, 2005, 2007.

Television Costume Designer; Movies:
My Name Is Bill W., ABC, 1989.
Decoration Day, NBC, 1990.
The Rockford Files: I Still Love L.A., CBS, 1994.
The Rockford Files: A Blessing in Disguise, CBS, 1995.
The Rockford Files: Punishment and Crime, CBS, 1996.
The Rockford Files: If the Frame Fits, CBS, 1996.
The Rockford Files: Godfather Knows Best, CBS, 1996.

The Rockford Files: Friends and Foul Play, CBS, 1996.
Don King: Only in America, HBO, 1997.
Point of Origin, HBO, 2002.

Television Costume Designer; Miniseries:
The Sophisticated Gents, NBC, 1981.

Television Appearances; Episodic:
"Donnie Darko," *Anatomy of a Scene,* 2001.

FONDACARO, Phil 1958–
    (Phil Fondicaro, H. G. Golas)

PERSONAL

Born November 8, 1958, in New Orleans, LA; brother of Sal Fondacaro (an actor); married Elena R. Bertagnolli (a talent manager and actress), February 17, 2001.

Addresses: *Manager*—Elena Fondacaro, Fonolli Management, 11218 Osborne St., Lake View Terrace, CA 91342.

Career: Actor. Appeared in commercials, including promotions for Sega, 1990, Polaroid instant cameras, 1998, and Beyond.com, 1999. Also worked as occasional stunt performer.

CREDITS

Film Appearances:
Mortimer, *The Penny Elf,* American Film Institute, 1981.
Guest at Hotel Rainbow, *Under the Rainbow,* Warner Bros., 1981.
(Uncredited) Demon clown, *Something Wicked This Way Comes,* Buena Vista, 1983.
Ewok, *Star Wars: Episode VI—Return of the Jedi* (also known as *Return of the Jedi* and *Star Wars VI: Return of the Jedi*), Twentieth Century–Fox, 1983.
(As H. G. Golas) Mickey, *Hard Rock Zombies,* Vestron Video, 1984.
Voices of creeper and henchman, *The Black Cauldron* (animated; also known as *Taran and the Magic Cauldron*), Buena Vista, 1985.
One of the Stone Canyon cliff dwellers, *The Dungeonmaster* (also known as *Ragewar*), Empire Pictures, 1985.
(As H. G. Golas) Rocky Magellan, *American Drive–in,* Vestron Video, 1985.
(Uncredited) Drone, *Invaders from Mars,* Cannon, 1986.

Malcolm Mallory/Torok the Troll, *Troll,* Empire Pictures, 1986.
Dan the bartender, *Steele Justice,* Paramount, 1987.
Sir Nigel Penneyweight, *Ghoulies II,* Empire Pictures, 1987.
Greaser Greg, *The Garbage Pail Kids Movie,* Atlantic Releasing, 1987.
Vohnkar, *Willow,* Metro–Goldwyn–Mayer, 1988.
(Uncredited) Hooded dwarf, *Phantasm II* (also known as *Phantasm II: The Never Dead Part Two*), Universal, 1988.
Horace Bosco, *Memories of Me,* Metro–Goldwyn–Mayer, 1988.
Stinksucker, *Monster High,* Columbia, 1989.
Sammael, *Night Angel* (also known as *Hellborn*), Fries Entertainment, 1990.
Dwarf, *Meridian* (also known as *Kiss of the Beast, Meridian: Kiss of the Beast,* and *Phantoms*), Full Moon Entertainment, 1990.
Ango, *Joey Takes a Cab,* 1991.
(Uncredited) Man at birthday party, *The Doors,* 1991.
Ray Vernon, *Dollman vs. Demonic Toys* (also known as *Dollman vs. the Demonic Toys*), Paramount Home Video, 1993.
Harliss, *The Nature of the Beast* (also known as *Bad Company* and *Hatchet Man*), New Line Cinema, 1995.
Vincent Prather, *Bordello of Blood* (also known as *Tales from the Crypt Presents: Bordello of Blood*), Universal, 1996.
Dracula, *The Creeps,* Amazing Fantasy Entertainment, 1997.
Voice of Lil Wolf, *Redux Riding Hood,* 1997.
Bob, *Sweet Jane,* Phaedra Cinema, 1998.
Cousin Itt, *Addams Family Reunion,* Twentieth Century–Fox, 1998.
Hylas, *Blood Dolls,* Full Moon Entertainment, 1999.
Himself, *Hollyweird,* 1999.
Gus Wolfson, *Bit Players,* Weary World Productions, 2000.
Abbot Graves, *Sideshow,* Full Moon Entertainment, 2000.
Sleazy hotel manager, *Gentleman B.* (also known as *Criminal Mentality* and *The Gentleman Bandit*), Phaedra Cinema, 2000.
(As Phil Fondicaro) Millionaire, *The Theory of the Leisure Class,* 2001.
Elf, *The Polar Express* (also released as *The Polar Express: An IMAX 3D Experience*), Warner Bros., 2004.
Chihuahua, *Land of the Dead* (also known as *George A. Romero's "Land of the Dead," Land of the Dead—Le territoire des morts,* and *La terre des morts*), Universal, 2005.
Ivan, *Decadent Evil* (also known as *Decadent Evil Dead*), Full Moon Entertainment/Wizard Entertainment, 2005.
Club patron, *Evil Bong* (also known as *Charles Band's "Evil Bong"*), Full Moon Pictures, 2006.

Michael Bates, *Immortally Yours* (also known as *Kiss of the Vampire*), MTI Home Video, 2009.

Television Appearances; Movies:
Quaid, *Condor,* ABC, 1986.
Oscar, *Double, Double, Toil and Trouble,* ABC, 1993.
Dwarf rabbi, *The Elevator,* Cinemax, 1996.

Television Appearances; Series:
Roland the troll, a recurring role, *Sabrina, the Teenage Witch* (also known as *Sabrina* and *Sabrina Goes to College*), ABC, between 1997 and 2000.

Television Appearances; Pilots:
Bell ringer, *Star Trek: The Next Generation—Encounter at Farpoint* (also known as *Encounter at Farpoint*), 1987.
Antonio, *Brotherhood of the Gun* (also known as *Hollister*), CBS, 1991.

Television Appearances; Specials:
Title role, *Fuzz Bucket,* ABC, 1986.

Television Appearances; Episodic:
Hooded henchman, "Rapunzel," *Faerie Tale Theatre* (also known as *Shelley Duvall's "Faerie Tale Theatre"*), Showtime, 1982.
Bernard, "Snow White and the Seven Dwarves," *Faerie Tale Theatre* (also known as *Shelley Duvall's "Faerie Tale Theatre"*), Showtime, 1984.
The Yattering, "The Yattering and Jack," *Tales from the Darkside,* syndicated, 1987.
Anxiety, "Nice Work if You Can Get It," *thirtysomething,* ABC, 1987.
Alien, "Nightmare Island," *Superboy* (also known as *The Adventures of Superboy*), syndicated, 1989.
Big Moe, "Leaping In without a Net—November 18, 1958," *Quantum Leap,* NBC, 1990.
Second alien, "Married ... with Aliens," *Married ... with Children,* Fox, 1990.
Lo Dara, *Santa Barbara,* NBC, 1991.
Big Eddie, "Mama," *Tequila and Bonetti,* CBS, 1992.
Dwarf thug, "Prototype," *Mann & Machine,* NBC, 1992.
Little Tom Masion, "Payback," *Renegade,* USA Network and syndicated, 1992.
Emmet, "Food for Thought," *Tales from the Crypt* (also known as *"HBO's Tales from the Crypt"*), HBO, 1993.
Circus clown, "Big Top Bago," *Johnny Bago,* CBS, 1993.
Green man, "Heal Thyself," *Northern Exposure,* CBS, 1993.
Green man, "Grand Prix," *Northern Exposure,* CBS, 1994.
Charles Stratton, "Wizard of Bras," *Medicine Ball,* Fox, 1995.
Bounty hunter, "Into the Mystic," *Sliders,* Fox, 1996.
Mac, "Data World," *Sliders,* Sci–Fi Channel, 1999.

Doorman, "Road Trip," *The Pretender,* NBC, 1999.
Leroy, "A Clown's Prayer" (also known as "Send in the Clowns"), *Touched by an Angel,* CBS, 2000.
Gerald Soloman, "Blood Is Thicker than Death," *The War Next Door,* USA Network, 2000.
Big Hack, "Lazarus," *Walker, Texas Ranger* (also known as *Walker*), CBS, 2000.
Christmas elf, "A Christmas Quarrel," *Daddio,* NBC, 2000.
Trenchcoat munchkin, *Passions,* NBC, 2002.
Kevin Marcus, "A Little Murder," *C.S.I.: Crime Scene Investigation* (also known as *C.S.I., CSI: Las Vegas,* and *Les experts*), CBS, 2002.
Brian's father, "Let It Bleed," *10–8: Officers on Duty* (also known as *10–8* and *10–8: Police Patrol*), ABC, 2003.
Himself, "Fight Night," *The Girls Next Door* (also known as *The Girls of the Playboy Mansion*), E! Entertainment Television, 2005.

Television Work; Episodic:
Additional voice, "Rome Alone/Amusement Back," *Timon and Pumbaa* (animated; also known as *The Lion King's "Timon & Pumbaa"*), 1996.
Additional voice, "Hercules and the Owl of Athens," *Hercules* (animated; also known as *Disney's "Hercules"*), 1998.

RECORDINGS

Videos:
(From archive footage) Voice of Ewok, *Star Wars: Battlefront* (video game), LucasArts Entertainment, 2004.
Ivan, *Blood, Sweat & Fears,* Wizard Entertainment, 2005.

FRANKEL, Richard 1954–

PERSONAL

Addresses: *Contact*—Richard Frankel Productions, 729 7th Avenue, 12th Floor, New York, NY 10019.

Career: Executive, producer, and director. Circle Repertory Company, New York City, managing director, 1982–85; Baruch, Frankel, Viertel Group (stage production company; also known as Viertel, Baruch, Frankel Group, Frankel, Viertel, Baruch Group, Frankel, Baruch, Viertel, Routh Group, Baruch, Viertel, Routh, Frankel Group, and R/F/B/V Group), New York City, partner, producer, and director, 1985—. Also general manager of Richard Frankel Productions and Frankel Green Theatrical Management.

Awards, Honors: Drama Desk Award nomination, outstanding new play, and Lucille Lortel Award, outstanding play, League of Off–Broadway Theatres and Producers, both 1989, for *The Cocktail Hour;* Outer Critics Circle Awards, outstanding off–Broadway musical, 1992, for *Song of Singapore;* Drama Desk Award, outstanding new play, and Outer Critics Circle Award, best off–Broadway play, both 1992, for *Marvin's Room;* two Drama Desk Award nominations, outstanding new play, 1993, for *Jeffrey* and *Oleanna;* Antoinette Perry Award nomination, best musical, 1995, for *Smokey Joe's Cafe;* Outer Critics Circle Award nomination, outstanding off–Broadway musical, 1995, for *Das Barbecu;* Antoinette Perry Award nomination, best revival of a musical, 1998, for *The Sound of Music;* Drama Desk Award nomination, outstanding new musical, 1998, for *Forever Tango;* Lucille Lortel Award and Outer Critics Circle Award nomination, both outstanding revival, 1999, for *The Mystery of Irma Vep;* Antoinette Perry Award nomination, best musical, and Drama Desk Award nomination, best new musical, both 2000, for *Swing!;* Drama Desk Award and Lucille Lortel Award, both unique theatrical experience, 2001, for *Mnemonic;* Antoinette Perry Award nomination and Drama Desk Award, both best revival of a musical, 2006, for *Sweeney Todd;* Antoinette Perry Award and Drama Desk Award, both best revival of a musical, 2007, for *Company;* Antoinette Perry Award and Drama Desk Award, best revival of a play, both 2009, for the trilogy *The Norman Conquests.*

CREDITS

Stage Producer:
Sills & Company, Lamb's Theatre, New York City, 1986.
Penn & Teller, Ritz Theatre (now Walter Kerr Theatre), New York City, 1987–88.
Frankie and Johnny in the Clair de Lune, Manhattan Theatre Club, Westside Theatre Upstairs, 1987–89.
The Cocktail Hour, Promenade Theatre, New York City, 1988–89.
Love Letters, Promenade Theatre, then Edison Theatre, New York City, 1989–90.
Song of Singapore (musical), Song of Singapore Theatre, New York City, beginning 1991.
Penn & Teller: The Refrigerator Tour, Eugene O'Neill Theatre, New York City, 1991.
Penn & Teller Rot in Hell, John Houseman Theatre, New York City, 1991–92.
Marvin's Room, Playwrights Horizons Theatre, Minetta Lane Theatre, New York City, 1992.
Bubbe Meises, Bubbe Stories, Cherry Lane Theatre, New York City, 1992–93.
Oleanna, Orpheum Theatre, New York City, 1992–94.
Jeffrey, Workshop of the Players Art, Minetta Lane Theatre, 1993–94.
Later Life, Westside Theatre Upstairs, New York City, 1993–94.

Das Barbecu (musical), Minetta Lane Theatre, 1994.
Inside Out, Cherry Lane Theatre, 1994–95.
Smokey Joe's Cafe (musical revue), Virginia Theatre, New York City, 1995–2000.
Three–for–All, Union Square Theatre, New York City, 1997.
Associate producer, *Tap Dogs,* Union Square Theatre, 1997.
Forever Tango (dance special), Walter Kerr Theatre, 1997–98, then Marquis Theatre, 1998.
The Sound of Music (musical), Martin Beck Theatre, New York City, 1998–99.
The Mystery of Irma Vep, Westside Theatre Downstairs, 1998–99.
The Weir, Walter Kerr Theatre, 1999.
Associate producer, *If Memory Serves,* Promenade Theatre, 1999.
Swing! (musical revue), St. James Theatre, 1999–2001.
Mnemonic, Theatre de Complicite, John Jay College of Criminal Justice of the City University of New York, New York City, 2001.
My Old Lady, Promenade Theatre, 2002.
The Water Coolers, Dillon's Theatre, New York City, 2002.
Executive producer, *Surviving Grace,* Union Square Theatre, 2002.
Little Shop of Horrors (puppet musical), Virginia Theatre, 2003–2004.
Sweeney Todd (musical), Eugene O'Neill Theatre, 2005–2006.
Company (musical), Ethel Barrymore Theatre, New York City, 2006–2007.
The Fantasticks (musical), Jerry Orbach Theatre, Snapple Theatre Center, New York City, beginning 2006.
The Norman Conquests: Round and Round the Garden, Circle in the Square, New York City, 2009.
The Norman Conquests: Table Manners, Circle in the Square, 2009.
The Norman Conquests: Living Together, Circle in the Square, 2009.
Burn the Floor (dance special), Longacre Theatre, New York City, 2009–10.
A Little Night Music (musical), Walter Kerr Theatre, beginning 2009.

Frankel's production company presented numerous other stage plays, with other partners at the helm.

Television Executive Producer; Specials:
Sting in Tuscany: All This Time, Arts and Entertainment, 2001.
Sting: Sacred Love, Arts and Entertainment, 2003.

Television Appearances; Episodic:
"Penn and Teller," *Bravo Profiles,* Bravo, 2001.

RECORDINGS

Video Work:
Executive producer, *Janet Jackson: The Rhythm Nation Compilation,* A & M Records, 1990.
Executive producer, *Amy Grant: Building the House of Love,* 1994.
Producer, *Sting ... All This Time,* 2001.

ADAPTATIONS

A performance of the stage production of *Frankie and Johnny in the Clair de Lune* was filmed as *Frankie and Johnny,* released by Paramount in 1991. A performance of the stage production *Smokey Joe's Cafe* was televised by Broadway Television Network and also offered as a pay–per–view selection in 2000. A performance of the stage production *Company* was televised as *Company: A Musical Comedy,* and broadcast by PBS in 2007.

FRASER, Hugh
(Hugh Frazer)

PERSONAL

Married Belinda Lang (an actress); children: Lily. *Education:* Attended London Academy of Music and Dramatic Art and Webber Douglas Academy of Dramatic Art.

Addresses: *Agent*—Ken McReddie Associates Ltd., 11 Connaught Pl., London W2 2ET, England.

Career: Actor. Actor with Traverse Theatre Workshop and with Lindsay Kemp's theatre company. Former member of the musical group Telltale, 1970s.

CREDITS

Television Appearances; Miniseries:
Nicholas, *The Crezz,* Thames, 1976.
Des, *Out,* 1978.
Sir Anthony Eden, *Edward & Mrs. Simpson,* Thames, 1978, syndicated, 1980.
Zelek Kaydan, *The Lost Tribe,* BBC, 1980.
Terry Wilson, *The Olympian Way,* BBC, 1981.
George Hill, *Reilly: The Ace of Spies,* Thames, 1983, PBS, 1984.
Kellner, *Bird of Prey 2,* BBC, 1984.
Richard Lefray, *The Price,* 1985.
Robert Bennett, *Edge of Darkness,* BBC2, 1985, syndicated, 1986.
Reverend Saunders, *Intimate Contact,* HBO, 1987.

Dearman, *Yesterday's Dreams,* CTV, 1987.
Robert, *Lizzie's Pictures,* BBC, 1987.
Peter Jackson, *Codename: Kyril,* Showtime, 1988.
Sir Charles Warren, *Jack the Ripper,* CBS, 1988.
George Gregory, *Death in Holy Orders* (also known as *P. D. James's "Death in Holy Orders"*), PBS, 2003.
Tristan Garel–Jones, *The Alan Clark Diaries,* BBC, 2004, 2006.
McMillan, *Le grand Charles,* 2006.
(Uncredited) General Sir Arthur Wellsley, Duke of Wellington, *Sharpe's Challenge,* BBC America, 2006.

Television Appearances; Movies:
Montfleury, *The Man in the Iron Mask,* NBC, 1976.
Gordon Knightly, *The World Cup: A Captain's Tale,* Tyne Tees, 1982.
Robert Colquohoun, *Cloud Howe,* BBC Glasgow, 1982.
Dr. Stephen Daker, *Heartattack Hotel,* BBC, 1983.
Brush salesman, *Nelly's Version,* 1983.
Culick, *The Insurance Man,* BBC, 1986.
Oliver Mortimer, *The Bretts II,* PBS, 1989.
King James II, *Lorna Doone,* ITV, 1990.
Sir Arthur Wellesley, Duke of Wellington, *Sharpe's Company,* PBS, 1994.
Sir Arthur Wellesley, Duke of Wellington, *Sharpe's Enemy,* PBS, 1994.
Sir Arthur Wellesley, Duke of Wellington, *Sharpe's Gold,* syndicated, 1995.
Sir Arthur Wellesley, Duke of Wellington, *Sharpe's Battle,* syndicated, 1995.
Sir Arthur Wellesley, Duke of Wellington, *Sharpe's Siege,* PBS, 1996.
Sir Arthur Wellesley, Duke of Wellington, *Sharpe's Mission,* ITV, 1996.
Captain Arthur Hastings, *Poirot: Murder on the Links,* Arts and Entertainment, 1996.
Captain Arthur Hastings, *Poirot: Dumb Witness,* Arts and Entertainment, 1996.
Sir Arthur Wellesley, Duke of Wellington, *Sharpe's Waterloo,* syndicated, 1997.
Captain Arthur Hastings, *Poirot: Lord Edgeware Dies,* Arts and Entertainment, 2000.
Captain Arthur Hastings, *Poirot: Evil under the Sun,* Arts and Entertainment, 2001.
Captain Arthur Hastings, *Poirot: Murder in Mesopotamia,* Arts and Entertainment, 2001.
General DeCoppet, *The Lost Battalion,* Arts and Entertainment, Arts and Entertainment, 2001.
Sir Arthur Wellesley, Duke of Wellington, *Sharpe's Honour,* ITV, 2004.
Stephen Quinn, *A Very Social Secretary,* Channel 4, 2005.

Television Appearances; Series:
Singer, *Rainbow,* 1972.
Captain Arthur Hastings, "Poirot"(also known as "Agatha Christie's 'Poirot'"), *Mystery!),* PBS, 1989–93.

Some episodes of the "Poirot" series were also broadcast as segments of *Agatha Christie: Poirot, Agatha Christie's Poirot, Series II, Agatha Christie's Poirot, Series III, Agatha Christie's Poirot, Series IV, Poirot, Series V, Poirot VI, Poirot VII,* ITV; episodes were also aired on Arts and Entertainment.

Television Appearances; Specials:
Musician, "Early Struggles," *Play for Today,* BBC, 1976.
Will Langley, "Licking Hitler," *Play for Today,* BBC, 1978.
Baxter, *One Fine Day* (also known as *Six Plays by Alan Bennett: One Fine Day*), London Weekend Television, 1979.
Narrator, *Safety Tips for Kids,* 2003.

Television Appearances; Episodic:
(Uncredited) Member of militia, "The Smugglers: Episode 4," *Doctor Who,* 1966.
Sergeant Fraser, "Big Elephant," *Target,* BBC, 1977.
Paul Standing, "Clerical Error," *Tales of the Unexpected* (also known as *Roald Dahl's "Tales of the Unexpected"*), Anglia, 1979.
Geoff, "Hands," *ITV Playhouse,* ITV, 1980.
Mr. Denzil Arrow, "Straw Man: Parts 1 & 2," *Smuggler,* ITV, 1981.
Dr. Reeve, "Ignorance in the Field," *Crown Court,* Granada, 1982.
Gavin Winchell, "Longshot," *Call Me Mister,* BBC, 1986.
Sherlock Holmes, "Murder on the Bluebell Line," *Q.E.D.,* BBC, 1987.
Giles Trent, *Game, Set & Match,* Granada, 1988, PBS, 1989.
Adrian, "Events at Drimaghleen," *Screenplay,* BBC, 1991.
Detective Chief Inspector Bobby Gault, "Gingerbread," *Taggart,* Scottish Television, 1993.
Marcus Menzies, "Close to Heaven: Part 2," *Peak Practice,* CTV, 1999.
(As Hugh Frazer) Marcus Menzies, "Hearts and Minds," *Peak Practice,* CTV, 1999.
Chris Harrington, "Predators," *Badger,* BBC, 2000.
Paul Adamson, *New Tricks,* BBC, 2004.
Himself, "Agatha Christie's Poirot," *Super Sleuths,* ITV, 2006.

Television Appearances; Other:
Also appeared as Naismith, *The Advocates,* Scottish Television; the chaplain, *A Class of His Own,* BBC; winged angel, *Drummonds,* London Weekend Television; Colonel Skinner, *Ghulami;* Saunders, *Heartland,* BBC; and as counsel, *The Innocents,* Channel 4.

Film Appearances:
Deviation, 1971.
Disc jockey, *The Ritz,* Warner Bros., 1976.

Officer, *The Duellists,* Paramount, 1977.
Captain Harold Lester, *Hanover Street,* Columbia, 1979.
Louis Talmann, *The Draughtsman's Contract,* United Artists, 1982.
Police Inspector Tortyev, *Firefox,* Warner Bros., 1982.
Usher at wedding, *The Missionary,* Columbia, 1982.
Dr. Arno Stang, *Curse of the Pink Panther,* Metro–Goldwyn–Mayer, 1983.
Geoffrey Watkins, *Patriot Games,* Paramount, 1992.
Frederick, *101 Dalmatians,* Buena Vista, 1996.
Arthur Burnett, *The Baby Juice Express,* 2001, Universal Home Video, 2004.
Mr. Fraser, *Chaos and Cadavers,* High Point Film and Television, 2003.
Voice of news reader, *Jackboots on Whitehall* (animated), Cinema Four/Matador Pictures/Entertainment Motion Pictures, 2010.

Appeared as Lenny in the film *Slade in Flame.*

Stage Appearances:
Nocella, *Filumena,* Lyric Theatre, London, 1978.
Billy Wiper, Nicholas Jeal, Roger Blacklawn, and Roy Shish, *The Loud Boy's Life,* Royal Shakespeare Company, Warehouse Theatre, London, 1980.
Georgi Abashvili, delegate, Bizergan Kazbeki, Sandro Oboladze, and stableman, *The Caucasian Chalk Circle,* Royal Shakespeare Company, Warehouse Theatre, 1980.
Claudio, *Much Ado about Nothing,* Royal Shakespeare Company, Warehouse Theatre, 1980.
Howard, *Bastard Angel,* Royal Shakespeare Company, Warehouse Theatre, 1980.
Hastings, *She Stoops to Conquer,* Lyric Theatre Hammersmith, London, 1982.

Appeared as Heinrich, *Cakewalk,* Hampstead Theatre, London; Harry Bagley, *Cloud Nine,* Royal Court Theatre, London; Harcourt, *Country Wife,* Actors Company; M.D., *Gaffers,* Royal Court Theatre; Graham, *The Genius,* Royal Court Theatre; Wangel, *The Lady from the Sea,* National Theatre, Oslo, Norway; multiple roles, *Our Sunday Times,* Royal Court Theatre; Sorge, *Power of the Dog,* Hampstead Theatre; Tom, *Rough Magic,* New End Hampstead Theatre, London; David, *Scent of Flowers,* Actors Company; Peyote, *Teeth 'n Smiles,* Royal Court Theatre; Del, *Traps,* Royal Court Theatre; John, *Walking on Walter,* Liveprool Playhouse, Liverpool, England; and Petulant, *The Way of the World,* Chichester Festival Theatre, Chichester, England; also performer in repertory productions in Edinburgh, Scotland, and in Ipswich, Manchester, and Oxford, England.

Major Tours:
Georgi Abashvili, delegate, Bizergan Kazbeki, Sandro Oboladze, and stableman, *The Caucasian Chalk Circle,* Royal Shakespeare Company, 1979.

Claudio, *Much Ado about Nothing,* Royal Shakespeare Company, 1980.

Appeared as Philip, *The Philanthropist,* Mobil Touring Theatre.

RECORDINGS

Audio Books:
Spider's Web by Agatha Christie and Charles Osborne, Audio Partners, 2000.
And Then There Were None by Agatha Christie, Audio Partners, 2001.
The Adventures of the Christmas Pudding and The Mystery of the Spanish Chest by Agatha Christie, Audio Partners, 2001.
The Under Dog and Other Stories by Agatha Christie, Audio Partners, 2001.
(With Nigel Hawthorne) *Murder in the Mews: Three Perplexing Cases for Poirot* by Agatha Christie, Audio Partners, 2002.
Hallowe'en Party by Agatha Christie, 2003.

FRENCH, Ron
(Ron E. French)

PERSONAL

Education: Graduated from Wilfred Laurier University.

Addresses: *Office*—Unity Pictures Group, Inc., 2400 Boundary Rd., Burnaby, British Columbia V5M 3Z3, Canada. *Agent*—Paradigm, 360 North Crescent Dr., North Bldg., Beverly Hills, CA 90210.

Career: Producer, production manager, and director. Began career working for Stephen J. Cannell Productions as assistant director then unit production manager; then worked as freelance production manager; French-film (later known as Unity Pictures Group), founder, 2001.

Awards, Honors: DVD Premiere Award nomination, best live action DVD premiere movie, DVD Exclusive Awards, 2003, for *Slap Shot 2: Breaking the Ice.*

CREDITS

Film Work:
Second assistant director, *The Experts* (also known as *Les experts*), Paramount, 1989.

Unit production manager, *Thir13en Ghosts* (also known as *13 fantomes*), Warner Bros., 2001.
Producer, *Slap Shot 2: Breaking the Ice,* Universal Home Entertainment, 2002.
Producer, *K–9: P.I.,* Universal Home Video, 2002.
Producer, *"Stargate SG–1": Children of the Gods—The Final Cut,* Twentieth Century Fox Home Entertainment, 2009.
(As Ron E. French) *The Plan* (also known as *Battlestar Galactica: The Plan*), Universal Studios Home Entertainment, 2009.

Also worked as production assistant, *Maggie & Pierre.*

Television Work; Series:
Third assistant director, *:20 Minute Workout,* 1983.
Production manager, *The Commish,* ABC, 1991–94.
Production manager, *Strange Luck,* Fox, 1995.
Producer and production manager, *Stargate SG–1* (also known as *La porte des etoiles*), Showtime, 1997.
(As Ron E. French) Production manager, *The X–Files,* Fox, 1997–99.
Coproducer and production manager, *Strange World,* ABC, 1999.
Coproducer and production manager, *Cold Feet,* NBC, 1999.
Producer, *That Was Then,* ABC, 2002.
Unit production manager, *Peacemakers,* USA Network, 2003.
Production manager, *Battlestar Galactica* (also known as *BSG*), Sci–Fi Channel, 2004.
Line producer, *Battlestar Galactica* (also known as *BSG*), Sci–Fi Channel, 2004–2007.
(As Ron E. French) Producer, *Battlestar Galactica: Razor Flashbacks,* Sci–Fi Channel, 2007.
Producer, *Battlestar Galactica* (also known as *BSG*), Sci–Fi Channel, 2008–2009.
Producer, *Defying Gravity,* ABC, CTV, and BBC, 2009.

Television Work; Miniseries:
Production assistant: Toronto, *Kane & Abel,* CBS, 1985.
Third assistant director and trainee assistant director, *Anne of Green Gables* (also known as *Ein zauberhaftes madchen*), CBC and PBS, 1985.
Production manager, *Battlestar Galactica* (also known as *Battlestar Galactica: The Miniseries*), Sci–Fi Channel, 2003.

Television Work; Movies:
Third assistant director, *Unnatural Causes,* NBC, 1986.
Second assistant director, *As Is,* Showtime, 1986.
Second assistant director, *Really Weird Tales,* HBO, 1987.
Advisor, *The Mountain and the Molehill,* Arts and Entertainment, 1989.
First assistant director, *Home Movie,* 1992.

Associate producer and production manager, *Sherlock Holmes Returns* (also known as *1994 Baker Street: Sherlock Holmes Returns*), CBS, 1993.

Unit production manager, *A Dream Is a Wish Your Heart Makes: The Annette Funicello Story* (also known as *A Dream Is a Wish Your Heart Makes*), CBS, 1995.

Production manager, *Them,* UPN, 1996.

Production manager, *Stand Against Fear* (also known as *Moment of Truth: Stand Against Fear* and *Unlikely Suspects*), NBC, 1996.

Production manager, *Badge of Betrayal,* ABC, 1997.

Production manager, *Moment of Truth: Into the Arms of Danger* (also known as *Running Wild* and *Into the Arms of Danger*), NBC, 1997.

(As Ron E. French) Production manager, *Dodson's Journey,* CBS, 2001.

(As Ron E. French) Line producer, *Underfunded,* USA Network, 2006.

(As Ron E. French) Producer, *Battlestar Galactica: Razor* (also known as *Razor*), Sci–Fi Channel, 2007.

Executive producer, *Meteor Storm,* SyFy, 2010.

Television Work; Pilots:

Production manager, *The Wonder Cabinet,* Fox, 1999.

Coproducer and production manager, *Dark Angel* (also known as *James Cameron's "Dark Angel"*), Fox, 2000.

(As Ron E. French) Unit production manager, *Bionic Woman* (also known as *The Bionic Woman*), NBC, 2007.

Television Work; Episodic:

Third assistant director, "Blackmailers Don't Shoot," *Philip Marlowe, Private Eye,* HBO, 1986.

Third assistant director, "Spanish Blood," *Philip Marlowe, Private Eye,* HBO, 1986.

Assistant director, "Pickup on Noon Street," *Philip Marlowe, Private Eye,* HBO, 1986.

Assistant director, "Guns at Cyrano's," *Philip Marlowe, Private Eye,* HBO, 1986.

Assistant director, *Knightwatch,* ABC, 1988.

Television Appearances; Episodic:

Tourist, "Under Pressure," *Knots Landing,* CBS, 1987.

Mr. Singer, "Farewell My Lovelies," *Falcon Crest,* CBS, 1988.

(As Ron E. French) "Blinded by the Son," *Strange Luck,* Fox, 1996.

Internet Producer; Series:

(As Ron E. French) *Battlestar Galactica: The Face of the Enemy,* 2008–2009.

WRITINGS

Screenplays:

The Message (short film), Paradise Valley Media, 2010.

FREWER, Matt 1958–

PERSONAL

Born January 4, 1958, in Washington, DC; raised in Victoria, British Columbia, Canada; son of Frederick Charlesley (a Canadian naval officer) and Gillian Anne (maiden name, German) Frewer; married Amanda Hillwood (an actress and documentarian), November 10, 1984; children: one daughter. *Education:* Studied acting at Bristol Old Vic Theatre School, graduating in 1980; studied medicine at the Queens University at Kingston. *Religion:* Roman Catholic. *Avocational Interests:* Sports, reading, writing short stories and screenplays, sketching wildlife.

Addresses: *Agent*—Stone Manners Talent and Literary, 9911 West Pico Blvd., Suite 1400, Los Angeles, CA 90035. *Manager*—Gilbertson Management, 1334 Third St., Suite 201, Santa Monica, CA 90401.

Career: Actor, voice performer, producer, and writer. Best known for role as Max Headroom, commercial spokesman for New Coke soft drink, 1987. Rainforest Action Network, spokesperson.

Awards, Honors: Gemini Award nomination, best performance by an actor in a guest role, Academy of Canadian Cinema and Television, 2000, for *Da Vinci's Inquest;* Gemini Award, best performance in a children's or youth program or series, 2000, for *Mentors;* CableACE Award, best presenter/host, for role as Max Headroom.

CREDITS

Film Appearances:

(Film debut) Senior, *The Lords of Discipline,* Paramount, 1983.

Cornered executive who jumps, "The Crimson Permanent Assurance," *The Meaning of Life* (also known as *Monty Python's "The Meaning of Life"*), Universal, 1983.

Truck driver, *Supergirl* (also known as *Supergirl: The Movie*), TriStar, 1984.

Second soldier, *Spies Like Us,* Warner Bros., 1985.

Tom MacWhirter, *The Fourth Protocol,* Lorimar, 1987.

CIA agent, *Ishtar,* Columbia, 1987.

Charles Cross, *Far from Home,* Vestron, 1989.

Russell "Big Russ" Thompson, Sr., *Honey, I Shrunk the Kids,* Buena Vista, 1989.

Alec, *Speed Zone!* (also known as *Cannonball Fever*), Orion, 1989.

Ernie Dills, *Short Time,* Twentieth Century–Fox, 1990.

Ed Kelvin, *The Taking of Beverly Hills* (also known as *Boomer: The Taking of Beverly Hills*), Columbia, 1991.

Chuck (Receding Bingo winner), *Twenty Bucks,* Triton Pictures, 1993.

Principal Todd Moss, *National Lampoon's "Senior Trip"* (also known as *Senior Trip, Senior School,* and *La folle excursion de National Lampoon*), New Line Cinema, 1995.

Voice of the Pink Panther, *Driving Mr. Pink,* 1995.

(Uncredited) Cleo and Leo, *Return to Two Moon Junction,* 1995.

Jobe Smith, *Lawnmower Man II: Beyond Cyberspace* (also known as *Lawnmower Man 2: Jobe's War*), New Line Cinema, 1996.

Voice of Panic, *Hercules,* Buena Vista, 1997.

(Uncredited) Voice of Frank Burris, *Heartwood,* Porch-Light Entertainment, 1998.

Voice of Jackal, *Gargoyles: The Hunted* (animated), 1998.

Voice of Jackel, *Gargoyles: Brothers Betrayed* (animated), 1998.

Nathan, Lucy, Mom, Dad, and Son, *6ix* (short film), 1999.

Voice of Panic, *Hercules: Zero to Hero* (animated), 1999.

Voice of Frazzled, *CyberWorld,* IMAX Corp., 2000.

Voice of Panic, *Mickey's House of Villains* (animated), 2002.

Frank, *Dawn of the Dead* (also known as *L'armee des morts, L'aube des morts,* and *Zack Snyder's "Dawn of the Dead"*), Universal, 2004.

Dr. Anton Keller, *Intern Academy* (also known as *Medecin en herbe* and *White Coats*), First Look International, 2004.

Ned Glover, *A Home at the End of the World,* Warner Independent Pictures, 2004.

Farmer Joseph, *Going the Distance* (also known as *National Lampoon's "Going the Distance"*), Metro-Goldwyn-Mayer Home Entertainment, 2004.

Cameron Geary, *Geraldine's Fortune* (also known as *La fortune de Geraldine*), Seville Pictures, 2004.

Mr. Clarkson, *Riding the Bullet* (also known as *Stephen King's "Riding the Bullet"*), Lions Gate Films Home Entertainment, 2004.

Quicksilver Highway: An Interview with Matt Frewer (short documentary), Anchor Bay Entertainment, 2005.

Himself, *Working with a Master: Mick Garris* (short documentary), Anchor Bay Entertainment, 2006.

Jason Taylor, *Weirdsville,* Magnolia Pictures, 2007.

Edward Lindsey, *Wushu Warrior,* Phase 4 Films, 2008.

Edgar Jacobi/Moloch the Mystic, *Watchman* (also known as *Watchman: The IMAX Experience*), Warner Bros., 2009.

Ted Duncan, *Darfur,* 2009.

Frankie and Alice, Checkmark, 2009.

Television Appearances; Series:

Title role, *The Max Headroom Show,* Cinemax, 1985.

Max Headroom and host, *The Original Max Talking Headroom Show,* Cinemax, 1987.

Edison Carter/Max Headroom, *Max Headroom* (also known as *Max Headroom: 20 Minutes into the Future*), ABC, 1987–88.

Dr. Michael Stratford, *Doctor, Doctor,* CBS, 1989–91.

Bob Moody, *Shaky Ground,* Fox, 1992–93.

Voice of title role, *The Pink Panther* (animated), syndicated, 1993.

The exterminator, *The Itsy Bitsy Spider,* 1994.

Voice of Jackal, *Gargoyles* (animated), syndicated, 1994–96.

Voice of Lloyd, *Dumb and Dumber* (animated), ABC, 1995.

Voice of Leader, *The Incredible Hulk and Friends* (animated; also known as *The Incredible Hulk*), UPN, 1996–97.

Voice of Booby Vicious, *Bruno the Kid* (animated), 1996.

OSIR case manager Matt Praeger, *PSI Factor: Chronicles of the Paranormal,* syndicated, 1997–99.

Voice of Panic, *Disney's "Hercules"* (animated; also known as *Hercules*), ABC and syndicated, 1998–99.

Voice of Dedgar Deadman, *Toonsylvania* (animated; also known as *Steven Spielberg Presents "Toonsylvania"*), Fox, 1998.

Voice of Panic, *House of Mouse* (animated; also known as *Disney's "House of Mouse"*), ABC, 2001–2002.

Ted Altman, *Intelligence,* CBC, 2006–2007.

Jim Taggart, *Eureka* (also known as *A Town Called Eureka*), Sci-Fi Channel, 2006–2009.

Television Appearances; Miniseries:

Francis Lane, *The First Olympics—Athens 1896* (also known as *Dream One* and *The First Modern Olympics*), NBC, 1984.

American at bar, *Tender Is the Night,* BBC, 1983, then Showtime, 1985.

Trashcan man, *Stephen King's "The Stand"* (also known as *The Stand*), 1994.

Dr. Chet Wakeman, *Taken* (also known as *Steven Spielberg Presents "Taken"*), Sci-Fi Channel, 2002.

White Knight, *Alice,* Syfy, 2009.

Television Appearances; Movies:

Edison Carter/Max Headroom, *Max Headroom* (also known as *Max Headroom: 20 Minutes into the Future*), Channel Four, 1984.

Soldier, *Displace Person* (also known as *D.P.*), PBS, 1985.

Troy McKinney, *The Positively True Adventures of the Alleged Texas Cheerleader-Murdering Mom,* HBO, 1993.

Bob Miller, *The Day My Parents Ran Away* (also known as *Missing Parents*), Fox, 1993.

The Cat in the Hat, *In Search of Dr. Seuss,* TNT, 1994.

Edwin O. Reischauer, *Long Shadows,* PBS, 1994.

General Alexander Haig, *Kissinger and Nixon*, TNT, 1995.

Russell Tresh, *Generation X*, Fox, 1996.

Gene Krantz, *Apollo 11* (also known as *Apollo 11: The Movie*), The Family Channel, 1996.

Lieutenant Colonel Max Durbin, *Dead Fire* (also known as *Le vaisseau de l'enfer*), Sci–Fi Channel, 1997.

Dr. George/Charlie, *Quicksilver Highway*, Fox, 1997.

Gerald Krzemien, *Breast Men*, HBO, 1997.

Scott Wagner, *In the Doghouse*, Showtime, 1998.

Al Fisher, *Jailbait*, MTV, 2000.

Sherlock Holmes, *The Hounds of Baskervilles* (also known as *Le chien des Baskerville*), CTV and Odyssey, 2000.

Sherlock Holmes, *The Sign of Four* (also known as *Le signe des quatre*), Hallmark Channel, 2001.

Sherlock Holmes, *The Royal Scandal* (also known as *Scandal in Bohemia* and *Le chant des sirenes*), Hallmark Channel, 2001.

Sherlock Holmes, *The Case of the Whitechapel Vampire* (also known as *Sherlock Holmes and the Case of the White Chapel Vampire*), Hallmark Channel, 2002.

Ted Altman, *Intelligence*, CBC, 2005.

Ralph Carver, *Desperation* (also known as *Stephen King's "Desperation"*), ABC, 2006.

Television Appearances; Specials:

Himself, *"Supergirl": The Making of the Movie*, 1984.

Max Headroom, *The Max Headroom Christmas Special*, Cinemax, 1986.

Max Headroom, *Tina!* (also known as *Tina Turner: Break Every Rule* and *Break Every Rule*), HBO, 1987.

Max Headroom, *A Night of Comic Relief 2*, 1989.

CBS Comedy Bloopers, CBS, 1990.

CBS Comedy Bloopers II, CBS, 1990.

The 4th Annual American Comedy Awards, ABC, 1990.

The 5th Annual American Comedy Awards, ABC, 1991.

Hollywood Hockey Cup, Comedy Central, 1996.

Dr. Louis Panic, *Disney's "Hercules": From Zero to Hero*, ABC, 1997.

Greg, *Desert's Edge*, The Movie Channel, 1997.

Inside Steven Spielberg Presents: Taken, Sci–Fi Channel, 2002.

Television Appearances; Episodic:

Roger de Carnac, "The Betrayal," *Robin Of Sherwood* (also known as *Robin Hood*), HTV, 1984.

Soldier, "Displaced Person," *American Playhouse*, PBS, 1985.

Late Night with David Letterman, 1986, 1988.

Pee Wee, "No Chemo, Sabe?," *St. Elsewhere*, NBC, 1987.

Cliff King, "Hostile Takeover," *Miami Vice*, NBC, 1988.

Cliff King, "Redemption in Blood," *Miami Vice*, NBC, 1988.

The Tonight Show Starring Johnny Carson (also known as *The Tonight Show*), NBC, 1990.

Professor Berlingoff Rasmussen, "A Matter of Time," *Star Trek: The Next Generation* (also known as *Star Trek: TNG*), syndicated, 1991.

Voice of Mac Duff, "Grandma's Dead," *Tiny Toon Adventures* (animated; also known as *Steven Spielberg Presents ... "Tiny Toon Adventures"*), syndicated, 1992.

Voice of Mac Duff, "Take Elmyra Please," *Tiny Toon Adventures* (animated; also known as *Steven Spielberg Presents ... "Tiny Toon Adventures"*), syndicated, 1992.

Howard Raymer, "Tornado Days," *Eerie, Indiana*, 1992.

Voice of Sidney Debris/Sid the Squid, "The Man Who Killed Batman," *Batman: the Animated Series* (animated; also known as *Batman* and *The Adventures of Batman & Robin*), Fox, 1993.

Voice of Peter Blaine, "Trains, Toons, and Toon Trains," *Bonkers* (animated; also known as *Disney's "Bonkers"*), 1993.

Edwin O. Reischauer, "Long Shadows," *American Playhouse*, PBS, 1994.

Voice of Inspector 47, "In the Rainforest," *The Magic School Bus* (animated; also known as *Scholastic's "The Magic School Bus"*), PBS, 1994.

Harold Sawyer, "Survival of the Fittest," *Picket Fences*, CBS, 1994.

Voice of Chaos, "When Chaos Comes Calling," *Aladdin* (animated; also known as *Disney's "Aladdin"*), CBS, 1994.

Craftsworth, "Tasty Paste," *Quack Pack* (animated), 1996.

Bob, "Supernatural," *Tracey Takes On ...*, HBO, 1996.

Voice of Leader, "Hulk Buster," *Iron Man* (animated; also known as *The Marvel Action Hour: Iron Man*), 1996.

Norman Glass, "First Anniversary," *The Outer Limits* (also known as *The New Outer Limits*), 1996.

Norbert Datry, "Fool's Gold," *Dead Man's Gun*, Showtime, 1997.

Voice of Toymaker, *Mickey Mouse Works* (animated; also known as *Mickey's Laugh Factory* and *Mouseworks*), 1999.

Frederick Banting, "A Transient, Shining Trouble," *Mentors*, 1999.

Larry Williams, "Fantasy," *Da Vinci's Inquest*, CBC, 2000.

Larry Williams, "Reality," *Da Vinci's Inquest*, CBC, 2000.

Dr. Lansing, "Wonderland," *The Eleventh Hour* (also known as *Bury the Lead*), CTV, 2004.

Wally, "Chocolate," *Masters of Horror*, 2005.

Himself, *Boogie* (also known as *Boogie Arhus*, *Boogie Listen*, *Boogie Update*, and *Boogie lordag*), 2009.

Also appeared in *The Twilight Zone*, CBS.

Television Work; Series:
Associate producer, *Psi Factor: Chronicles of the Paranormal,* syndicated, 1996.

Stage Appearances:
(Stage debut) Wolf, *Bent,* Theatre Royal, York, England, 1980.
(London debut) Murph, *The Indian Wants the Bronx,* Soho Poly Theatre, London, 1981.
Lysander, *A Midsummer Night's Dream,* Round House Theatre, London, 1981.
Prince, *Romeo and Juliet,* Shaw Theatre, London, 1982.
Malcolm, *Macbeth,* Shaw Theatre, 1983.
Deathtrap, Northcott Theatre, Exeter, England, 1984.
On the Razzle, Leeds Playhouse, Leeds, England, 1984.

Major Tours:
Vladimir, *Waiting for Godot,* British cities, 1980.
The gentleman caller, *The Glass Menagerie,* British cities, 1981.
The Comedy of Errors, New Shakespeare Company, British cities, 1981.
Androcles, *A Midsummer Night's Dream,* New Shakespeare Company, British cities, 1981.
Much Ado about Nothing, New Shakespeare Company, British cities, 1981.

Internet Appearances; Episodic:
Jim Taggart, *Eureka: Hide and Seek,* 2006.

RECORDINGS

Videos:
Himself, *Inside "Taken"* (short documentary), 2002.

Appeared as Max Headroom in the music video "Paranoimia" by Art of Noise.

Video Games:
Voice of Panic, *Hercules* (also known as *Disney's "Hercules"*), 1997.

WRITINGS

Television Episodes:
"Frozen Faith," *Psi Factor: Chronicles of the Paranormal,* syndicated, 1998.

Fiction:
(With wife, Amanda Hillwood) Author of the children's book *The Fez Brothers.*

FROY, Herald
    See WATERHOUSE, Keith

G

GAINS, Courtney 1965–

PERSONAL

Born August 22, 1965, in Denver, CO (some sources cite Los Angeles, CA). *Avocational Interests:* Writing songs and playing guitar.

Addresses: *Agent*—Christopher Black, Opus Entertainment, 5225 Wilshire Blvd., Suite 905, Los Angeles, CA 90036. *Manager*—Chris Row, CR Management, 23852 Pacific Coast Highway, Suite 627, Malibu, CA 90265.

Career: Actor, producer, and writer. Appeared in commercials. Performed with bands, including the Gathering, 1990s, Ripple Street (trio), beginning 2007, and Benny Bliss and the Disciples of Greatness.

Member: Screen Actors Guild.

CREDITS

Film Appearances:
Rag, *Hardbodies,* Columbia, 1984.
Malachai, *Children of the Corn* (also known as *Stephen King's "Children of the Corn"*), New World, 1984.
Doug, *Secret Admirer* (also known as *The Letter*), Orion, 1985.
Mark Dixon, *Back to the Future,* Universal, 1985.
The Orkly Kid, 1985.
Red Dick Barker, *Lust in the Dust,* New World, 1985.
Hardbodies 2, 1986.
Goose Trammel, *Winners Take All,* Embassy Entertainment, 1986.
Kid in car, *Ratboy,* Thirteen Distributing, 1986.
Kenneth Wurman, *Can't Buy Me Love* (also known as *Boy Rents Girl*), Buena Vista, 1987.

Whitey, *Colors,* Orion, 1988.
Hans Klopek, *The 'burbs,* Universal, 1989.
Sergeant Eugene McVey, *Memphis Belle,* Warner Bros., 1990.
Vincent Reynosa, *The Killing Grounds,* A–Pix Entertainment, 1997.
Tex, *Dilemma,* Cinequanon Pictures International, 1997.
Tyson Jones, *The Landlady,* Trimark Pictures, 1998.
Dr. Joseph McConnell, *King Cobra* (also known as *Anaconda 2*), 1999.
Mike Watt, *Dreamers,* Cinema Art Entertainment, 2000.
The Making of Bret Michaels (documentary), 2002.
Sheriff Wade, *Sweet Home Alabama,* Buena Vista, 2002.
Lorenzo the Black Hand, *National Lampoon Presents "Dorm Daze"* (also known as *Dorm Daze* and *National Lampoon's "Dorm Daze"*), 120 Degree Films/Hill & Brand Entertainment, 2003.
W. Fritz Bean, *No Ordinary Hero* (short film), Absolute Pictures, 2004.
The writer, *Headshot* (short film), Dos Muchachos Productions, 2004.
Scooter the grip, *Freezerburn,* Brookturn Company, 2005.
Dr. Cecil Westlake, *The Phobic,* Alex Ryan Productions, 2006.
Clerk, *He's Such a Girl,* Kinesis Entertainment, 2009.
Benny Bliss, *Benny Bliss and the Disciples of Greatness,* Anthem Pictures, 2009.
Danny, *Raven,* GruntWorks Entertainment, 2009.
The stranger, *Sibling Rivalry,* Blank Page Entertainment, 2009.
Agent Donovan, *They Came from Outer Space,* 1066 Pictures/Dave Gist Productions, 2009.
Andrew, *The Ascent,* Regent Worldwide Sales, 2009.
Courtney, *Cinema Salvation,* Perspective Films, 2009.
Finch, *Shadowheart,* Anchor Bay Entertainment, 2009.
Tattoos: A Scarred History (documentary), Pillay–Evans Productions/TASH Films, 2009.
Tell Me About ... (documentary), David Gist Productions, 2009.

Michael's father, *The Quiet Ones* (also known as *It's Always the Quiet Ones*), Ningun Films/SaintSinner Entertainment, 2010.

Film Work:

Co–executive producer, *National Lampoon Presents "Dorm Daze"* (also known as *Dorm Daze* and *National Lampoon's "Dorm Daze"*), 120 Degree Films/Hill & Brand Entertainment, 2003.

Coproducer, *The Phobic,* Alex Ryan Productions, 2006.

Producer, *Benny Bliss and the Disciples of Greatness,* Anthem Pictures, 2009.

Executive producer, *Sibling Rivalry,* Blank Page Entertainment, 2009.

Television Appearances; Movies:

Punk who robs Brian, *The Children of Times Square* (also known as *Street Wise*), ABC, 1986.

Chips, *American Harvest* (also known as *Race Against the Harvest*), CBS, 1987.

Vietnam War Story II, HBO, 1988.

Barlow, *In the Line of Duty: The Price of Vengeance,* NBC, 1994.

First deputy, *Runaway Daughters,* Showtime, 1994.

Church, *Behind Enemy Lines,* HBO, 1996.

Cameron, *No Code of Conduct,* USA Network, 1998.

Ernie, *Shadow of Doubt* (also known as *Reasonable Doubt*), Cinemax, 1998.

Hood, *Her Married Lover* (also known as *A Clean Kill*), Lifetime, 1999.

Scotty, *Studio House,* 2005.

Jack McAllister, *Desolation Canyon,* Hallmark Channel, 2006.

Television Appearances; Series:

Roy Cantwell, a recurring role, *The Guardian,* CBS, 2003–2004.

Television Appearances; Episodic:

Mechanic, "Twin Engines," *Misfits of Science,* NBC, 1985.

Bo, "The Test," *Starman,* ABC, 1987.

"Blindsided," *21 Jump Street,* Fox, 1987.

Jeff Hilford, "The Russian Exchange Student," *Superboy* (also known as *The Adventures of Superboy*), syndicated, 1988.

Kirby Anthony, "Breakpoint," *FBI: The Untold Stories,* ABC, 1993.

Video store guy, "The Smelly Car," *Seinfeld,* NBC, 1993.

Coley Hiffern, "Hatton's Turn: Parts 1 & 2," *In the Heat of the Night,* NBC, 1993.

Doug, "The Poker Game," *Bakersfield P.D.,* Fox, 1993.

Henderson, "House of Horror," *Tales from the Crypt* (also known as *HBO's "Tales from the Crypt"*), HBO, 1993.

Ronnie, "ER Confidential," *ER,* NBC, 1994.

"Knee–High Noon," *Legend,* UPN, 1995.

Pete, "Survivors," *JAG* (also known as *JAG: Judge Advocate General*), NBC, 1996.

Norman Harrison, "Divorce, Palm Beach Style," *Silk Stalkings,* USA Network, 1996.

Jim–Joe, "Cranked Up," *Pacific Blue,* USA Network, 1996.

Eddie Dobbs, "Payback," *Nash Bridges* (also known as *Bridges*), CBS, 1997.

Dwayne, "Slam–Dunk Dead," *Diagnosis Murder,* CBS, 1997.

Joe Beldon, "Don't You Be My Valentine," *Brooklyn South,* CBS, 1998.

D.J. Marcy Steadwell, "Ms. Hellfire," *Charmed,* The WB, 2000.

Detective Guthrie, "Girls Own Juice," *Fastlane,* Fox, 2002.

Holden Gemler, "The Getaway," *Alias,* ABC, 2003.

The John Kerwin Show, syndicated, 2005.

Gary Silverstein, "Escaped," *Navy NCIS: Naval Criminal Investigative Service* (also known as *NCIS* and *NCIS: Naval Criminal Investigative Service*), CBS, 2006.

Six–fingered man, "Mr. Monk Is on the Run: Parts 1 & 2," *Monk,* USA Network, 2008.

Lloyd, "Sold a Guy a Lemon Car," *My Name Is Earl,* NBC, 2008.

Stan Gerber, "Death and the Maiden," *CSI: Crime Scene Investigation* (also known as *C.S.I., CSI: Las Vegas,* and *Les experts*), CBS, 2009.

Television Appearances; Other:

Joe, "Welcome Home, Jellybean" (special), *CBS Schoolbreak Special,* CBS, 1984.

Silas, "Shivers" (pilot), *CBS Summer Playhouse,* CBS, 1989.

30 Even Scarier Movie Moments (miniseries), Bravo, 2006.

RECORDINGS

Videos:

Voice of Lieutenant Ted "Radio" Rollins, *Wing Commander III: Heart of the Tiger* (video game), 1994.

Harvesting Horror: Children of the Corn, Anchor Bay Entertainment, 2004.

Appeared as student singer in the instructional video *Singer's Workout.*

Albums:

Gains, 2000.

WRITINGS

Screenplays:

Benny Bliss and the Disciples of Greatness, Anthem Pictures, 2009.

OTHER SOURCES

Electronic:
Courtney Gains Official Site, http://www.courtneygains. net, February 16, 2010.
Loudside, http://www.loudside.com, May 31, 2007.

GIBB, Lee
   See WATERHOUSE, Keith

GLATTER, Lesli Linka
   (Lesli Glatter)

PERSONAL

Married Clayton Campbell (an artist and art center director); children: Nick. *Education:* Attended the American Film Institute's Directing Workshop for Women.

Addresses: *Agent*—Kimberly Bialek, William Morris Endeavor Entertainment (WmEE2), One William Morris Place, Beverly Hills, CA 90212. *Manager*—David J. Kanter, Anonymous Content, 3532 Hayden Ave., Culver City, CA 90232.

Career: Director, producer, choreographer, and dancer. Also a director of commercials. Began career in modern dance; worked as a choreographer in the United States, Europe, and Asia. American Film Institute, member of the education and training board; Mediascope, member of the board of directors; Independent Features Project, mentor for Project Involve; Step Up Women's Network, member of the advisory board.

Member: Directors Guild of America (member of the national board of directors, former member of the Western Directors Council), Women in Film (Silver Circle).

Awards, Honors: Academy Award nomination (with Sharon Oreck), best short film, live action, 1985, for *Tales of Meeting and Parting;* Directors Guild of America Award nomination, outstanding directorial achievement in dramatic series—night, 1990, for *Twin Peaks;* Directors Guild of America Award, outstanding directorial achievement in dramatic series—night, 2009, for "Guy Walks into an Advertising Agency," *Mad Men.*

CREDITS

Television Director; Movies:
Into the Homeland, HBO, 1987.
"The Promise," *Vietnam War Story II,* HBO, 1988.
State of Emergency, HBO, 1994.

Television Director; Episodic:
"No Day at the Beach," *Amazing Stories* (also known as *Steven Spielberg Presents "Amazing Stories"* and *Steven Spielberg's "Amazing Stories"*), NBC, 1985, released on video as part of *Amazing Stories: Book Three,* MCA/Universal Home Video, 1992.
"One for the Books," *Amazing Stories* (also known as *Steven Spielberg Presents "Amazing Stories"* and *Steven Spielberg's "Amazing Stories"*), NBC, 1986.
"Without Diana," *Amazing Stories* (also known as *Steven Spielberg Presents "Amazing Stories"* and *Steven Spielberg's "Amazing Stories"*), NBC, 1987, released on video as part of *Amazing Stories: Book Five,* MCA/Universal Home Video, 1992.
Twin Peaks, ABC, four episodes, between 1990 and 1991.
On the Air, ABC, multiple episodes in 1992.
Black Tie Affair (also known as *The Girl in 1216* and *Smoldering Lust*), NBC, 1993.
"Lower Than the Angels," *Birdland,* ABC, 1994.
"O.C.D.P.D. Blue," *Birdland,* ABC, 1994.
"Serge the Concierge," *NYPD Blue,* ABC, 1994.
"A Sudden Fish," *NYPD Blue,* ABC, 1994.
Emergency Room (also known as *Emergency Room*), NBC, multiple episodes, between 1995 and 2008.
"Chapter Eighteen," *Murder One,* ABC, 1996.
"Don't You Be My Valentine," *Brooklyn South* (also known as *A esquadra de Brooklyn* and *Brooklyn Sud*), CBS, 1998.
"Gay Avec," *Brooklyn South* (also known as *A esquadra de Brooklyn* and *Brooklyn Sud*), CBS, 1998.
"Touched by an Amnesiac," *Buddy Faro,* CBS, 1998.
"A Single Life," *Law & Order: Special Victims Unit* (also known as *Law & Order's Sex Crimes, Law & Order: SVU,* and *Special Victims Unit*), NBC, 1999.
"Girlfriends and Boyfriends," *Freaks and Geeks* (also known as *Freaks & Geeks, Freaks og Geeks, Nollor och noerdar,* and *Voll daneben, voll im Leben*), NBC, 2000.
"Kim Kelly Is My Friend," *Freaks and Geeks* (also known as *Freaks & Geeks, Freaks og Geeks, Nollor och noerdar,* and *Voll daneben, voll im Leben*), NBC, 2000.
"Rory's Dance," *Gilmore Girls* (also known as *Gilmore Girls: Beginnings* and *The Gilmore Way*), The WB, 2000.
(And producer) "The Appraisal," *Citizen Baines* (also known as *The Second Act*), CBS, 2001.
(And producer) "Days of Confusion," *Citizen Baines* (also known as *The Second Act*), CBS, 2001.
"Sacrifice," *Law & Order: Special Victims Unit* (also known as *Law & Order's Sex Crimes, Law & Order: SVU,* and *Special Victims Unit*), NBC, 2001.
"Star-Crossed Lovers and Other Strangers," *Gilmore Girls* (also known as *Gilmore Girls: Beginnings* and *The Gilmore Way*), The WB, 2001.
"True Love," *Third Watch,* NBC, 2001.

"Do No Harm," *Presidio Med,* CBS, 2002.

"It Should've Been Lorelai," *Gilmore Girls* (also known as *Gilmore Girls: Beginnings* and *The Gilmore Way),* The WB, 2002.

"With Grace," *Presidio Med,* CBS, 2002.

The West Wing (also known as *West Wing* and *El ala oeste de la Casablanca),* NBC, multiple episodes, between 2002 and 2006.

(As Lesli Glatter) "The Family Ties," *The O.C.* (also known as *California Teens, Newport Beach, O.C., O.C., California, Orange County, A Narancsvidek, O.C.—Um estranho no paraiso,* and *Zycie na fali),* Fox, 2005.

"Hour Five," *Revelations,* NBC, 2005.

"Hour Six," *Revelations,* NBC, 2005.

"Let It Be," *Grey's Anatomy* (also known as *Complications, Procedure, Surgeons, Under the Knife,* and *Grey's Anatomy—Die jungen Aerzte),* ABC, 2005.

"Prime Suspect," *Numb3rs* (also known as *Numbers* and *Num3ers),* CBS, 2005.

"To Serve and to Protect," *Jonny Zero,* Fox, 2005.

"Nevada Day: Part 1," *Studio 60 on the Sunset Strip* (also known as *Studio 7 on the Sunset Strip* and *Studio 60),* NBC, 2006.

"The Other Woman," *The Closer* (also known as *L.A.: Enquetes prioritaires* and *Se apostasi anapnois),* TNT, 2006.

"Stringers," *The Evidence,* ABC, 2006.

(As Lesli Glatter) "Chapter Five 'Fight or Flight'" (also known as "Fight or Flight"), *Heroes* (also known as *Heroes: Villains),* NBC, 2007.

"Home by Another Way," *Journeyman,* NBC, 2007.

"Mother & Child Reunion," *Heartland,* TNT, 2007.

Mad Men, AMC, episodes beginning 2007.

(As Lesli Glatter) "Friends with Benefits," *Swingtown,* CBS, 2008.

"Her Old Man & the Sea," *The Starter Wife,* USA Network, 2008.

"Crimson Casanova," *The Mentalist* (also known as *Mentalist),* CBS, 2009.

"A Dozen Red Roses," *The Mentalist* (also known as *Mentalist),* CBS, 2009.

"Endgame," *The Unit,* CBS, 2009.

"The Greater Good," *House M.D.* (also known as *Doctor House, Dr House, Dr. House, Dr. [H]ouse, Dr. House—Medical Division, Dr. House: Medical Division,* and *House),* Fox, 2009.

"Red Scare," *The Mentalist* (also known as *Mentalist),* CBS, 2009.

"Su–Su–Sucio," *Weeds,* Showtime, 2009.

"Unchained," *Lie to Me,* Fox, 2009.

"Wilson," *House M.D.* (also known as *Doctor House, Dr House, Dr. House, Dr. [H]ouse, Dr. House—Medical Division, Dr. House: Medical Division,* and *House),* Fox, 2009.

(As Lesli Glatter) "You Don't Want to Know," *House M.D.* (also known as *Doctor House, Dr House, Dr. House, Dr. [H]ouse, Dr. House—Medical Division, Dr. House: Medical Division,* and *House),* Fox, 2009.

Some sources state that Glatter directed other programs.

Television Director; Pilots:

Gilmore Girls (also known as *Gilmore Girls: Beginnings* and *The Gilmore Way),* The WB, 2000.

The Big House (also known as *Being Brewster),* ABC, 2001.

In My Life, The WB, 2002.

Newton, UPN, 2003.

Pretty Little Liars, ABC Family, 2010.

Director of other pilots, including *Forty Deuce* (also known as *40–Deuce* and *40 Deuce);* director of the un-aired pilot for *Gilmore Girls* (also known as *Gilmore Girls: Beginnings* and *The Gilmore Way),* The WB.

Film Director:

(And producer) *Tales of Meeting and Parting* (short film), 1984.

Now and Then (also known as *Dear Friends* and *The Gaslight Addition),* New Line Cinema, 1995.

The Proposition (also known as *Tempting Fate),* Poly-Gram Filmed Entertainment, 1998.

Film Choreographer:

To Live and Die in L.A., Metro–Goldwyn–Mayer, 1985.

RECORDINGS

Videos:

Herself, *Secrets from Another Place: Creating Twin Peaks* (multipart documentary; includes Part I—Northwest Passage: Creating the Pilot, Part II—Freshly Squeezed: Creating Season One, Part III—Where We're From: Creating the Music, and Part IV—Into the Night: Creating Season Two), CBS DVD, 2007.

Video Director; with Others:

(Episode "No Day at the Beach") *Amazing Stories: Book Three,* MCA/Universal Home Video, 1992.

(Episode "Without Diana") *Amazing Stories: Book Five,* MCA/Universal Home Video, 1992.

GOLAS, H. G.
   See FONDACARO, Phil

GOODALL, Caroline 1959–

PERSONAL

Full name, Caroline Cruice Goodall; born November 13, 1959, in London, England; father, a publisher; mother, a journalist; sister of Victoria Goodall (a producer); married Derek Hoxby (an actor), February 10, 1990 (divorced, 1993); married Nicola Pecorini (a steadicam operator and cinematographer), September 17, 1994; children: (second marriage) Gemma, Leone. *Education:* University of Bristol, B.A. (with honors).

Addresses: *Agent*—Michael Lazo, Paradigm, 360 North Crescent Dr. N., Beverly Hills, CA 90210; Lindy King, United Agents, 12–26 Lexington St., London W1F 0LE, England. *Manager*—Helen Rolland, Rolland Management, 205 Beattie St., Rozelle, New South Wales 2039, Australia.

Career: Actress. Appeared with the Royal Shakespeare Company and National Theatre, London.

Awards, Honors: Australian Film Institute Award nomination, best actress, 1990, for *Cassidy;* Australian Film Institute Award, best lead actress, 1995, for *Hotel Sorrento;* Silver Logie Award nomination, best actress, *TV Week* (Australia), 1999, for *A Difficult Woman.*

CREDITS

Film Appearances:
Sally, *Every Time We Say Goodbye,* TriStar, 1986.
Moira Banning, *Hook,* TriStar, 1991.
Kristel, *Cliffhanger* (also known as *Cliffhanger–l'ultima sfida* and *Cliffhanger, traque au sommet*), TriStar, 1993.
Elyne Mitchell, *The Silver Brumby* (also known as *The Silver Stallion: King of the Wild Brumbies*), Roadshow, 1993.
Emilie Schindler, *Schindler's List,* Universal, 1993.
Susan Hendler, *Disclosure,* Warner Bros., 1994.
Meg Moynihan, *Hotel Sorrento* (also known as *Sorrento Beach*), Trimark Pictures, 1995.
Dr. Alice Sheldon, *White Squall,* Buena Vista, 1996.
Annie Summers, *Casualties,* Trimark Pictures, 1997.
Jenny Field, *The Secret Laughter of Women,* 1999.
Johanna Pollack, *Harrison's Flowers* (also known as *Les fleurs d'Harrison*), Universal, 2000.
Helen Thermopolis, Mia's mom, *The Princess Diaries,* Buena Vista, 2001.
Mrs. Duke, *Shattered Glass,* Lions Gate Films, 2003.
Sandy, *Easy,* Magic Lamp/Screen Media Ventures, 2003.
Michelle Foster, *Chasing Liberty,* Warner Bros., 2004.
Helen Thermopolis O'Donnell, *The Princess Diaries 2: Royal Engagement,* Buena Vista, 2004.
Ms. Claire, *Haven,* Freestyle Releasing, 2004.
Mrs. Parker, *The Chumscrubber* (also known as *Glueck in kleinen dosen*), Newmarket Films, 2005.
Ida, *The Thief Lord* (also known as *Herr der diebe*), Twentieth Century–Fox Home Entertainment, 2006.
Martha Dandridge, *We Fight to Be Free* (short film), Greystone Communications, 2006.
Sarah Watkins, *River's End,* American World Pictures, 2007.

Lisa Westwood, *De zeven van Darah, de strijd om Pareo Rots* (also known as *The Seven of Daran: Battle of Pareo Rock*), Walt Disney, 2008.
Dr. Tullen, *My Life in Ruins* (also known as *Driving Aphrodite* and *Mi vida en ruinas*), Fox Searchlight, 2009.
Lady Radly, *Dorian Gray,* Alliance Films/Momentum Pictures, 2009.

Also appeared as Karen, *Minutes.*

Television Appearances; Movies:
Ann Bolton, *Charles & Diana: A Royal Love Story,* ABC, 1982.
Katherine James, *The Webbers* (also known as *At Home with the Webbers* and *Webber's World*), 1993.
Liv Gustavson, *Diamond Swords* (also known as *Les epees de diamant*), 1995.
Heather Frazer, *Opernball* (also known as *Opera Ball*), 1998.
Debra Loomis, *Rhapsody in Bloom,* Starz!, 1998.
Anne Travers, *Trust,* BBC, 1999.
Sally Love, *Love and Murder* (also known as *Criminal Instincts: Love and Murder* and *Crimes et passion*), Lifetime, 2000.
Laura Bowden, *Me & Mrs. Jones,* PBS, 2002.

Television Appearances; Miniseries:
Charlie Cassidy, *Cassidy,* Australian Broadcasting Corporation, 1989.
Sally Raglan, *After the War,* Granada, 1989, PBS, 1990.
Helen Simmons, *Ring of Scorpio,* Nine Network, 1990.
Amy Johnson, *The Great Air Race* (also known as *Half a World Way*), Australian Broadcasting Corporation, 1990.
Rosalind "Roz" Leigh, *The Sculptress,* BBC, 1996, PBS, 1997.
Dr. Anne Harriman, *A Difficult Woman,* Australian Broadcasting Corporation, 1998.
Igraine, *The Mists of Avalon* (also known as *Die Nebel von Avalon*), TNT, 2001.

Television Appearances; Series:
Estelle, *The Moon Stallion,* BBC, 1978.
Anne–Marie Colman, *Gems,* 1985.

Television Appearances; Specials:
Mandy, "Royal Celebration," *Screen One,* BBC, 1993.
Bella, *Sex 'n' Death,* BBC America, 1999.

Television Appearances; Episodic:
Jenny Buchanan, "Steele Searching: Part 1," *Remington Steele,* NBC, 1985.
Holly Peverill, "Wink Three Times," *Tales of the Unexpected* (also known as *Roald Dahl's "Tales of the Unexpected"*), syndicated, 1988.

Helen Derwent, "Rumpole and the Quality of Life," *Rumpole of the Bailey,* PBS, 1988.

Lady Maud Yardly, "The Adventure of the Western Star," *Poirot* (also known as *Agatha Christie: Poirot* and *Agatha Christie's "Poirot"*), PBS, 1990.

Dr. Leslie Ashton, "The Wrong Stuff—January 24, 1961," *Quantum Leap,* NBC, 1991.

Maddie Hodges, "Eastbridge Boulevard," *The Commish,* ABC, 1993.

Voice of Vanessa Fisk, "Neogenic Nightmare: Part 11: Tablet of Time," *Spider–Man* (animated), Fox, 1995.

Voice of Vanessa Fisk, "Neogenic Nightmare: Part 12: Ravages of Time," *Spider–Man* (animated), Fox, 1995.

Rebecca, "Promised Land," *The Outer Limits* (also known as *The New Outer Limits*), Showtime and syndicated, 1998.

Joanna Liddy, "Neighbours," *Murder in Mind,* BBC America, 2001.

Dr. Emily Ryan, "Secrets & Flies," *CSI: Crime Scene Investigation* (also known as *C.S.I., CSI: Las Vegas,* and *Les experts*), CBS, 2005.

Elizabeth Powell, "Bob," *Alias,* ABC, 2005.

Grace Starkey, "Dead Letters," *Midsomer Murders,* Arts and Entertainment, 2006.

Television Appearances; Other:

Appeared as Jean, *Function Rooms.*

Stage Appearances:

Hypatia Tarleton, *Misalliance,* Royal Shakespeare Company, Barbican Theatre, London, 1986.

Cholla, *Heresies,* Royal Shakespeare Company, Pit Theatre, London, 1986.

Appeared as Rebecca, *Command or Promise,* National Theatre, London; Lou, *Erpingham Camp,* Plymouth, England; Sybil, *Private Lives,* Oxford, England; Lady Anne, *Richard III,* Royal Shakespeare Company; Juliet, *Romeo and Juliet,* Shaw Theatre; Isobel, *Secret Rapture,* South Coast Repertory, Costa Mesa, CA; Susan, *Susan's Breasts,* Royal Court Theatre; Louise, *Tons of Money,* Scarborough; in *True Dare Kiss,* National Theatre; as Viola, *Twelfth Night,* Plymouth; and Elizabeth, *While the Sun Shines,* Royal Exchange Theatre.

Major Tours:

Lady Anne, *Richard III,* Royal Shakespeare Company, Australian cities, 1986.

Also appeared as Joan, *Time and Time Again,* British cities.

GOODMAN, Robyn 1947–

PERSONAL

Born August 24, 1947, in New York, NY. *Education:* Brandeis University, graduated, 1969.

Career: Executive, producer, and actress. Second Stage Theatre, New York City, cofounder and artistic director, c. 1979–92; Manhattan Theatre Club, New York City, director of artistic development for two years; Aged in Wood (production company), cofounder, partner, and producer. Counts Media, board member; Underground Theatre, curator of speech and debate; Roundabout Theatre Company, artistic consultant.

Awards, Honors: Lucille Lortel Award, outstanding musical, League of Off–Broadway Theatres and Producers, and Drama Desk Award nomination, outstanding new musical, both 2001, for *Bat Boy: The Musical;* Lucille Lortel Award nomination, outstanding musical, and Drama Desk Award nomination, outstanding new musical, both 2002, for *tick, tick, BOOM!;* Antoinette Perry Award nomination, best play, 2002, for *Metamorphoses;* Lucille Lortel Award nomination, outstanding play, and Drama Desk Award nomination, outstanding new play, both 2003, for *Our Lady of 121st Street;* Antoinette Perry Award, best musical, 2004, for *Avenue Q;* Lucille Lortel Award nomination, outstanding musical, Drama Desk Award nomination, best new musical, both 2005, and *Broadway.com* Audience Award, favorite long–running off–Broadway show, 2009, all for *Altar Boyz;* Lucille Lortel Award nomination, outstanding play, 2006, for *Red Light Winter;* Antoinette Perry Award, best musical, 2008, for *In the Heights;* Antoinette Perry Award nomination and Drama Desk Award nomination, both best revival of a musical, 2009, for *West Side Story.*

CREDITS

Stage Producer:

Lake No Bottom, Second Stage Theatre, McGinn–Cazale Theatre, New York City, 1990.

Associate producer, *A Class Act* (musical), Ambassador Theatre, New York City, 2001.

Bat Boy, the Musical, Union Square Theatre, New York City, 2001.

tick, tock, BOOM! (musical), Jane Street Theatre, New York City, 2001–2002.

Metamorphoses, Circle in the Square, New York City, 2002–2003.

Our Lady of 121st Street, LAByrinth Theatre Company, Union Square Theatre, 2003.

Avenue Q (puppet musical), John Golden Theatre, New York City, 2003–2009, then New World Stages Stage III, Vineyard Theatre, New York City, 2009—.

Steel Magnolias, Lyceum Theatre, New York City, 2005.

Altar Boyz (musical), New World Stages Stage IV, New York City, 2005–10.

Red Light Winter, Barrow Street Theatre, New York City, 2006.

Barefoot in the Park, Cort Theatre, New York City, 2006.

High Fidelity (musical), Imperial Theatre, New York City, 2006.

In the Heights (musical), Richard Rodgers Theatre, New York City, 2008.
West Side Story (musical), Palace Theatre, New York City, 2009—.

Stage Appearances:
Clarisse, *When You Comin' Back Red Ryder?*, Circle Repertory Company, Eastside Playhouse, New York City, 1973.
Lady Anne and Mistress Shore, *Richard III*, New York Shakespeare Festival, Mitzi E. Newhouse Theatre, New York City, 1974.
The Spelling Bee, Playwrights Horizons Theatre, New York City, 1976.
Liz, Mira Zadal, and Kate Siv, *Museum*, New York Shakespeare Festival, LuEsther Hall, Public Theatre, New York City, 1978.
Bits & Pieces, Second Stage Theatre, Park Royal Theatre, New York City, 1980.
Fishing, Second Stage Theatre, Park Royal Theatre, 1981.
Flux, Second Stage Theatre, Park Royal Theatre, 1982.
Something Different, Second Stage Theatre, South Street Theatre, New York City, 1983.

Film Appearances:
ShowBusiness: The Road to Broadway (documentary), Regent Releasing, 2007.

Television Appearances; Specials:
I Knew It Was You: Rediscovering John Cazale, HBO, 2009.

Television Appearances; Episodic:
Appeared in the serial *Another World* early in her career.

Television Work; Series:
Supervising producer, *One Life to Live*, ABC, c. 1992–96.

GOSSETT, Robert 1954–

PERSONAL

Born March 3, 1954, in the Bronx, New York, NY; father, a police officer, mother, a nurse's aide, laundry worker, and peace worker; cousin of Louis "Lou" Gossett, Jr. (an actor and producer); married first wife (marriage ended); married Michele (a director and teacher); children: (first marriage) one daughter; (second marriage) two. *Education:* Graduated from the High School of Performing Arts and the American Academy of Dramatic Arts.

Addresses: *Agent*—Jeffrey Leavitt, Leavitt Talent Group, 11500 West Olympic Blvd., Suite 400, Los Angeles, CA 90064. *Publicist*—Liza Anderson, Anderson Group Public Relations, 8060 Melrose Ave., 4th Floor, Los Angeles, CA 90046.

Career: Actor. Appeared in advertisements. Worked with the Neighborhood Youth Corps at the Everyman Street Theater Company and with Har–You Act (Harlem Youth), Harlem, New York City. Speaker at various venues. Involved with charities, events for charities, and served as a mentor and as a volunteer basketball coach.

Member: Screen Actors Guild.

Awards, Honors: *Drama–Logue* Award and Theatre Award, National Association for the Advancement of Colored People (NAACP), both best actor, 1993, for *Indigo Blues*; *Drama–Logue* Award and *LA Weekly* Theatre Award, both best actor, 1995, for *Washington Square Moves*; Screen Actors Guild Award nominations (with others), outstanding performance by an ensemble in a drama series, 2006, 2008, 2009, and 2010, and Vision Award nomination, best performance—drama, National Association for Multi–Ethnicity in Communications (NAMIC), 2009, all for *The Closer*.

CREDITS

Television Appearances; Series:
Lieutenant Lou Hudson, *Silk Stalkings*, CBS and USA Network, 1992–93.
Woody Stumper, *Passions* (also known as *Harmony's Passions* and *The Passions Storm*), NBC, 2001.
Commander Taylor, *The Closer* (also known as *L.A.: Enquetes prioritaires* and *Se apostasi anapnois*), TNT, 2005—.

Television Appearances; Miniseries:
Arnold Walker, *Common Ground*, CBS, 1990.
Detective Lukes, *Menendez: A Killing in Beverly Hills*, CBS, 1994.

Television Appearances; Movies:
First corrections officer, *Locked Up: A Mother's Rage* (also known as *Other Side of Love*), CBS, 1991.
Plainclothes police officer, *Ladykiller*, USA Network, 1992.
Detective Bobbins, *Donato and Daughter* (also known as *Dead to Rights* and *Under Threat*), CBS, 1993.
(Uncredited) Dr. Feelgood, *Sex, Love and Cold Hard Cash*, USA Network, 1993.
Lieutenant Graham, *Ray Alexander: A Taste for Justice*, NBC, 1994.

Lieutenant Graham, *Ray Alexander: A Menu for Murder,* NBC, 1995.

Cummings, *Alien Nation: The Udara Legacy,* Fox, 1997.

Partner, *The Maker,* HBO, 1997.

Detective Peter Lipton, *A Crime of Passion,* CBS, 1999.

Michael, *Flying By,* Lifetime Movie Network, 2009.

Television Appearances; Episodic:

Stage manager, "Dance Mania," *The Cosby Show,* NBC, 1987.

Dr. Carlson, "A Mind Is a Terrible Thing to Waste," *Amen,* NBC, 1989.

Preston Stuart, "Sing, Sister, Sing," *Amen,* NBC, 1989.

Charles Griffin, "Pool Hall Blues—September 4, 1954," *Quantum Leap,* NBC, 1990.

Edward Manley, "Watts a Matter?," *L.A. Law,* NBC, 1990.

John Lee, "Miracle in Oaktown," *Hangin' with Mr. Cooper* (also known as *Super Mr. Cooper, Echt super, Mr. Cooper, Mr. Cooper et nous,* and *Vivir con Mr. Cooper*), ABC, 1992.

Third customer, "License to Hill," *Cheers,* NBC, 1992.

Lonnie Edwards, "Oscar, Meyer, Weiner," *NYPD Blue,* ABC, 1993.

Winston Bowman, "The Bridges of Dade Country," *Nurses,* NBC, 1993.

Russ Campbell, *Dudley,* CBS, 1993.

Security man, "Terminal Island," *One West Waikiki* (also known as *Waikiki*), CBS, 1994.

Sheriff Pyke, "Shock the Monkey," *Dead at 21,* MTV, 1994.

Detective Smith, "Two Flew over the Cuckoo's Nest," *Melrose Place* (also known as *Place Melrose*), Fox, 1995.

Dr. Max Frye, "My Baby Is Out of This World," *Diagnosis Murder* (also known as *Dr. Mark Sloan*), CBS, CBS, 1995.

Jimmy Christopher, "The Murder Trade," *Diagnosis Murder* (also known as *Dr. Mark Sloan*), CBS, 1996.

Lyle Battle, "Dreamboat," *Second Noah,* ABC, 1996.

Paul Stettling, "The Journalist," *Touched by an Angel,* CBS, 1996.

Adam Winfield, "The Bet," *Pacific Palisades* (also known as *Brentwood* and *L.A. Affairs*), Fox, 1997.

Adam Winfield, "Past & Present Danger," *Pacific Palisades* (also known as *Brentwood* and *L.A. Affairs*), Fox, 1997.

Adam Winfield, "Runaway," *Pacific Palisades* (also known as *Brentwood* and *L.A. Affairs*), Fox, 1997.

Detective Woods, "Forgive and Forget," *Beverly Hills 90210* (also known as *Beverly Hills, Beverly Hills, 90210, Beverly Hills 90210 Classic, Class of Beverly Hills,* and *L.A. Beat*), Fox, 1997.

Detective Woods, "Pride and Prejudice," *Beverly Hills 90210* (also known as *Beverly Hills, Beverly Hills, 90210, Beverly Hills 90210 Classic, Class of Beverly Hills,* and *L.A. Beat*), Fox, 1997.

Detective Woods, "The Right Thing," *Beverly Hills 90210* (also known as *Beverly Hills, Beverly Hills, 90210, Beverly Hills 90210 Classic, Class of Beverly Hills,* and *L.A. Beat*), Fox, 1997.

Detective Woods, "The Way We Weren't," *Beverly Hills 90210* (also known as *Beverly Hills, Beverly Hills, 90210, Beverly Hills 90210 Classic, Class of Beverly Hills,* and *L.A. Beat*), Fox, 1997.

Doctor, "Do Something," *7th Heaven* (also known as *Seventh Heaven* and *7th Heaven: Beginnings*), The WB, 1997.

Robert Dixon, "Stealing Home: Parts 1 & 2," *Promised Land* (also known as *Home of the Brave*), CBS, 1997.

Sergeant Stryker, "An Officer and a Homeboy or, Full Metal Jackass," *Homeboys in Outer Space,* UPN, 1997.

Eddie, "The Domino Effect," *Sister, Sister,* The WB, 1998.

Executive storyteller, "Romeo and Julie," *Working,* NBC, 1999.

Mr. Franklin, "Secrets and Guys," *Charmed,* The WB, 1999.

Colonel James "Jim" McGinnis, "Cold Comfort," *Dark Angel* (also known as *James Cameron's "Dark Angel"*), Fox, 2000.

Photography professor, "The Screw–Up," *That's Life,* ABC, 2000.

Colonel James "Jim" McGinnis, " ... And Jesus Brought a Casserole," *Dark Angel* (also known as *James Cameron's "Dark Angel"*), Fox, 2001.

Colonel James "Jim" McGinnis, "Designate This," *Dark Angel* (also known as *James Cameron's "Dark Angel"*), Fox, 2001.

Colonel James "Jim" McGinnis, "The Kidz Are Aiight," *Dark Angel* (also known as *James Cameron's "Dark Angel"*), Fox, 2001.

Dan Matson, "Everybody Falls Down," *Judging Amy,* CBS, 2001.

John, "Mr. Fix It," *Yes, Dear,* CBS, 2001.

Photography professor, "Photographs," *That's Life,* ABC, 2001.

Malik Clay, "Lies of Minelli," *Philly,* ABC, 2002.

Malik Clay, "Meat Me in Philly," *Philly,* ABC, 2002.

"Court Date," *First Monday,* CBS, 2002.

Howard Sykes, "The Big Ruckus," *Dragnet* (also known as *L.A. Dragnet*), ABC, 2003.

Ken Gross, "Only Schmucks Pay Income Tax," *NYPD Blue,* ABC, 2003.

Jack Hayes, "Most Likely," *Crossing Jordan* (also known as *Untitled Tim Kring Project*), NBC, 2004.

Mr. Taylor, "The Man in the Wall," *Bones* (also known as *Brennan, Bones—Die Knochenjaegerin, Dr. Csont,* and *Kondid*), Fox, 2005.

Incident commander, "Out of the Ashes: Parts 2–4," *The Young and the Restless* (also known as *Y&R, The Innocent Years, Atithasa niata, Les feux de l'amour, Schatten der Leidenschaft,* and *Tunteita ja tuoksuja*), CBS, 2007.

Himself, *The John Kerwin Show,* syndicated, 2007.

Himself (contestant), *Wheel of Fortune* (also known as *Shoppers' Bazaar*), syndicated, 2007.

Dr. Everett Daniels, "Believe the Unseen," *ER* (also known as *Emergency Room*), NBC, 2008.

Dr. Everett Daniels, "Status Quo," *ER* (also known as *Emergency Room*), NBC, 2008.

Judge Willie Joe Blackwell, "A Slip Slope," *The Sarah Silverman Program* (also known as *Sarah Silverman*), Comedy Central, 2010.

Provided a voice for the animated series *Dilbert*, UPN; appeared as Reverend Thomas Matthews in an episode of *Family Law*, CBS; and appeared as Joseph, *George*, ABC.

Television Appearances; Pilots:

Dixon Banks, *Heartbeat* (also known as *HeartBeat*), ABC, 1989.

Dover, *Shannon's Deal*, NBC, 1989.

Moe's World, ABC, 1992.

Adam Winfield, "Welcome to the Neighborhood," *Pacific Palisades* (also known as *Brentwood* and *L.A. Affairs*), Fox, 1997.

Jerry Marshall, *The Warden*, TNT, 2001.

Commander Taylor, *The Closer* (also known as *L.A.: Enquetes prioritaires* and *Se apostasi anapnois*), TNT, 2005.

Film Appearances:

Eddie, *Over the Brooklyn Bridge*, Metro–Goldwyn–Mayer, 1984.

Television anchor, *Batman Returns* (also known as *Batman 2*), Warner Bros., 1992.

Barker, *Phoenix*, 1995.

Ben Phillips, *The Net* (also known as *The Internet* and *System*), Columbia, 1995.

John, *White Man's Burden* (also known as *White Man*), Savoy Pictures, 1995.

FBI agent Whit Carver, *Arlington Road* (also known as *Arlington Rd.*), Screen Gems, 1999.

Horace Metcalf, *Jimmy Zip*, The Asylum, 1999.

Phil Jackson, *The Living Witness* (also known as *Wanted*), 1999.

Damone, *Devious Beings*, Signet, 2002.

Detective, *Such's Life* (short film), 2004.

Leo, *The Inner Circle* (also known as *Potluck*), Porch-Light Entertainment, 2004.

Detective Peter Farrell, *Tied to a Chair* (also known as *Spring in Her Step* and *A Spring in Her Step*), 2009.

Stage Appearances:

One Flew over the Cuckoo's Nest, Mercer Arts Center, Mercer Hansbury Theater, New York City, c. 1972–73.

The Last Minstrel Show, c. 1978.

Melvin "Mel" Walker, *Weep Not for Me*, Negro Ensemble Company, Theatre Four, New York City, 1981.

Private Louis Henson, *A Soldier's Play*, Negro Ensemble Company, Theatre Four, c. 1981.

Aaron, Riggins, and Richard, *Colored People's Time*, Negro Ensemble Company, Cherry Lane Theatre, New York City, 1982.

Bubba and Bruce Mitchell, *Sons and Fathers of Sons*, Negro Ensemble Company, Theatre Four, 1983.

Duncan, *Manhattan Made Me*, Negro Ensemble Company, Theatre Four, 1983.

Indigo Blues, Mojo Ensemble, Los Angeles, c. 1993.

Al, *Washington Square Moves*, Mojo Ensemble, c. 1993.

Appeared in other productions, including *Fences* and *A Raisin in the Sun*; also appeared in street productions of the Everyman Street Theater Company, New York City area. Also a member of the Milwaukee Repertory Company.

GRAVES, Rupert 1963–

PERSONAL

Born June 30, 1963, in Weston–super–Mare, Somerset, England; son of Richard Harding (a musician and music teacher) and Mary Lousilla (some sources spell middle name as "Louisilla"; a travel coordinator; maiden name, Roberts) Graves; married Susie Lewis (a producer and production coordinator), c. 2001; children: three, including Joseph. *Avocational Interests:* Soccer, playing guitar, running, reading.

Addresses: *Agent*—Barry McPherson, Agency for the Performing Arts, 405 South Beverly Dr., Beverly Hills, CA 90212; Lindy King, United Agents, 12–26 Lexington St., London W1F 0LE, England.

Career: Actor. Provided voice work for advertisements. Worked as a clown with a traveling circus in England and as a children's entertainer with Silly Billy Pickles and the Peanut Street Gang; worked in a shoe factory and in fish and chips shops.

Member: Pre–Raphaelite Seahorse Club (cochairperson, 1987–89).

Awards, Honors: Montreal World Film Festival Award, best actor, 1996, for *Intimate Relations;* Laurence Olivier Award nomination, best actor, Society for West End Theatre, 1998, for *Hurlyburly;* Theatre World Award, outstanding new performer, and Special Achievement Award (with others), outstanding ensemble performance, Outer Critics Circle awards, both 1999, for *Closer*.

CREDITS

Film Appearances:

Freddy Honeychurch, *A Room with a View,* Cinecom International, 1986.

Alec Scudder, *Maurice,* Cinecom International, 1987.

John Beaver, *A Handful of Dust,* New Line Cinema, 1988.

Gerald Ormerod, *The Children* (also known as *Meine liebe Rose*), Channel Four Films/Isolde Films/Maram/Arbo Fil, 1990, shortened version released by Hemdale Home Video, 1992.

Philip Herriton, *Where Angels Fear to Tread,* Fine Line, 1991.

Martyn Fleming, *Damage* (also known as *Fatale*), New Line Cinema, 1992.

Greville, *The Madness of King George* (also known as *The Madness of George III* and *The Madness of King George III*), Samuel Goldwyn, 1994.

Hermann Korn, *The Sheltering Desert,* 1994.

Paul Prentice, *Different for Girls* (also known as *Crossing the Border*), First Look Pictures Releasing, 1995.

Harold Guppy, *Intimate Relations,* Lions Gate Films, 1996, Fox Searchlight, 1997.

Alan Terry, *The Innocent Sleep,* Castle Hill, 1997.

Officer on train, *Bent,* Metro–Goldwyn–Mayer, 1997.

Septimus Warren Smith, *Mrs. Dalloway* (also known as *Virginia Woolf's "Mrs. Dalloway"*), First Look Pictures Releasing, 1997.

Christian, *The Soldier's Leap* (short film), 1998.

Joseph Lees, *Dreaming of Joseph Lees* (also known as *Obsession*), Twentieth Century–Fox, 1998.

Nicholas Winton, *Vsichni moji blizci* (also known as *All My Loved Ones* and *Wszyscy moi bliscy*), Northern Arts Entertainment, 1999.

Mark, *Room to Rent,* Pathe/United International Pictures, 2000.

Matt, *Snake* (short film), 2001.

Jeffrey, *Extreme Ops* (also known as *EX, Extremist, The Extremists,* and *The eXtremists*), Paramount, 2002.

Vinny, *A New Religion* (short film), 2004.

Dominic, *V for Vendetta* (also known as *V for Vendetta: At the IMAX, V for Vendetta: The IMAX Experience, V—V for Vendetta,* and *V wie Vendetta*), Warner Bros., 2005.

Eddy Taylor, *Rag Tale,* Becker Films, 2005.

Himself, *The King's Head: A Maverick in London* (documentary; also known as *A Maverick in London: The Story of the King's Head Theatre*), Dragonfly Films/XI Pictures, 2006.

Mark, *Intervention* (also known as *Funny Farm*), Alliance Atlantis, 2007.

Robert, *Death at a Funeral* (also known as *Funeral Party* and *Sterben fuer Anfaenger*), Metro–Goldwyn–Mayer, 2007.

George, *The Waiting Room,* Kojo Pictures, 2008.

Inconceivable (also known as *Art in Las Vegas*), 2008.

Made in Dagenham (also known as *Dagenham Girls* and *We Want Sex*), Paramount, 2010.

Some sources cite appearances in other films, including *The Day I Ran into All of My Ex–Boyfriends.*

Film Director:

Second unit assistant director, *Decadence,* 1994.

Checkout Girl (short film), 2000.

Television Appearances; Series:

Tipping, *Vice Versa,* ATV, 1980–81.

Simon Boulderstone, *Fortunes of War,* BBC, 1987, broadcast as part of *Masterpiece Theatre* (also known as *ExxonMobil Masterpiece Theatre, Masterpiece,* and *Mobil Masterpiece Theatre*), PBS, 1988.

Voice of Paul Nash and Robert Cude, *The Great War* (documentary; also known as *The Great War and the Shaping of the 20th Century* and *1914–1918*), BBC and PBS, 1996.

Jolyon Forsyte, Jr., *The Forsyte Saga,* Granada, 2002, broadcast as part of *Masterpiece Theatre* (also known as *ExxonMobil Masterpiece Theatre, Masterpiece,* and *Mobil Masterpiece Theatre*), PBS, 2002.

Television Appearances; Miniseries:

Arthur Huntingdon, *The Tenant of Wildfell Hall,* BBC and CBC, 1996, broadcast as part of *Masterpiece Theatre* (also known as *ExxonMobil Masterpiece Theatre, Masterpiece,* and *Mobil Masterpiece Theatre*), PBS, 1997.

Dennis Hamilton, *The Blonde Bombshell* (also known as *Blonde Bombshell: The Diana Dors Story*), ITV, 1999.

Octavian, *Cleopatra,* ABC, 1999.

Narrator, *Animal Minds* (documentary), BBC2 and PBS, 1999, part of program broadcast as "Inside the Animal Mind Part One: Are Animals Intelligent?," *Nature* (documentary), PBS, 2002.

Patrick Standish, *Take a Girl Like You,* BBC, 2000, broadcast as part of *Masterpiece Theatre* (also known as *ExxonMobil Masterpiece Theatre, Masterpiece,* and *Mobil Masterpiece Theatre*), PBS, 2001.

George Villiers (duke of Buckingham), *Charles II: The Power & the Passion* (also known as *Charles II, Charles II: The Power and the Passion, The Last King,* and *The Last King: The Power and the Passion of Charles II*), BBC, 2003, Arts and Entertainment, 2004.

Jolyon Forsyte, *The Forsyte Saga: To Let,* Granada, 2003, broadcast as *The Forsyte Saga, Series II* as part of *Masterpiece Theatre* (also known as *Exxon-Mobil Masterpiece Theatre, Masterpiece,* and *Mobil Masterpiece Theatre*), PBS, 2004.

(In archive footage) *Retrosexual: The 80s,* VH1, 2004.

Lord of the North, *Son of the Dragon,* Hallmark Channel, 2006.

Daniel Cosgrave, *Midnight Man,* ITV, 2008.

Sir Arthur Hill, *Garrow's Law,* BBC, 2009.

Television Appearances; Movies:

Guthrie, "Good and Bad at Games," *Film on Four,* Channel 4, 1983.

Teddy, *St. Ursula's in Danger,* BBC, 1983.
Tonio, *Puccini,* Channel 4, 1984.
Axel von dem Bussche, *The Plot to Kill Hitler,* CBS, 1990.
Milton, *Una questione privata* (also known as *A Private Affair*), Radiotelevisione Italiana (RAI), 1991.
Neil, "Royal Celebration," *Screen One,* BBC, 1993.
David Martin, *Open Fire,* ITV, 1994.
Jones, *Doomsday Gun* (also known as *Big gun*), HBO, 1994.
Voice of Linus, *Pride,* BBC and Arts and Entertainment, 2004.
Robin Cape, *Clapham Junction,* Channel 4, 2007.
Roger, *The Dinner Party* (also known as *People Like Us*), BBC, 2007.
Dr. Christiaan Barnard, *To Be First* (also known as *The First New Heart*), Channel 4 and The Discovery Channel, c. 2007.
Mordechai, *God on Trial,* BBC2, 2008, broadcast as part of *Masterpiece Theatre* (also known as *Exxon-Mobil Masterpiece Theatre, Masterpiece,* and *Mobil Masterpiece Theatre*), PBS, 2008.
Lance Fortescue, *Marple: A Pocket Full of Rye* (also known as *Agatha Christie: Marple–A Pocket Full of Rye, Agatha Christie Marple: A Pocket Full of Rye, Agatha Christie's "Marple," Marple, Miss Marple,* and *A Pocket Full of Rye*), ITV, c. 2008, broadcast as "A Pocket Full of Rye," *Miss Marple, Series IV* as part of *Masterpiece Mystery!,* PBS, 2009.
Lexy, *The Good Times Are Killing Me,* CTV, 2009.

Television Appearances; Specials:
Oliver Knightly, *The Revengers' Comedies* (also known as *Sweet Revenge* and *Amour, vengeance et trahison*), BBC, 1997.
Narrator, *Rush: 50 Years of Drugs in Britain* (documentary; also known as *A History of Street Drugs in Britain*), Channel 4, 1998.
Himself, *The Making of "Charles II"* (documentary), ITV, 2003.
Narrator, "Year of the Chimpanzee," *Survival Special* (documentary; also known as *Survival* and *Survival Special: Year of the Chimpanzee*), ITV, c. 2003.
William Shakespeare, *A Waste of Shame: The Mystery of Shakespeare and His Sonnets* (also known as *A Waste of Shame*), BBC, 2005, BBC America, 2006.

Television Appearances; Awards Presentations:
The Evening Standard Theatre Awards 2003, ITV, 2003.

Television Appearances; Episodic:
Prefect, "Yesterday's Hero," *Return of the Saint* (also known as *The Son of the Saint*), ITC, 1978.
Yan, "Five Go Down to Sea: Parts 1 & 2," *The Famous Five* (also known as *Enid Blyton's "Famous Five"*), ITV, 1979.
Starting Out, BBC Educational, c. 1981.
"Mona," *All for Love,* ITV, 1982.

John Neil, *Union Matters,* BBC Educational, c. 1982.
Billy, "Happy Families," *Inspector Morse,* CTV, 1992, known as *Inspector Morse, Series VII: Happy Families* and broadcast as part of *Mystery!,* PBS, 1994.
Himself, *One Foot in the Past* (documentary), BBC2, 1994.
Dominic Collier, *Harry,* BBC, 1995.
Narrator, "Inside the Animal Mind Part One: Are Animals Intelligent?," *Nature* (documentary), PBS, 2002, originally broadcast as part of the miniseries *Animal Minds* (documentary), BBC2 and PBS, 1999.
William Sampson, "Divided They Fall," *Spooks* (also known as *MI–5*), BBC and Arts and Entertainment, 2005.
Colonel John Garrett, "Duty and Honour: Parts 1 & 2," *Waking the Dead,* BBC, 2008.
Danny Moore, *Ashes to Ashes,* BBC and BBC America, 2008.
Alex Pickman, "Falling Darkness," *Lewis* (also known as *Inspector Lewis*), ITV, 2010.
Alfred Harderman, "The Man Who Smiled," *Wallender* (also known as *Kommissar Wallender*), BBC, 2010.
Inspector Lestrade, "A Study in Scarlet," *Sherlock,* BBC, 2010.
John Smith, "Defence," *Law & Order: UK* (also known as *Law & Order: London*), ITV and other channels, 2010.
"Fashion Victim," *New Tricks* (also known as *Team Pullman*), BBC, c. 2010.

Television Appearances; Pilots:
Inspector Lestrade, *Sherlock,* BBC, 2010, broadcast as part of *Masterpiece Theatre* (also known as *Exxon-Mobil Masterpiece Theatre, Masterpiece,* and *Mobil Masterpiece Theatre*), PBS, c. 2010.

Stage Appearances:
Alastair Grahame and Mr. Toad, *The Killing of Mr. Toad,* King's Head Theatre, London, 1983.
Clayton Vosper, *Sufficient Carbohydrate,* Hampstead Theatre, London, 1983, and Albery Theatre, London, 1984.
Alan, *Torch Song Trilogy,* Albery Theatre, 1985.
Wolfgang Amadeus Mozart (title role), *Amadeus,* Clwyd Theatr Cymru, Mold, Wales, 1986.
Algernon Moncrieff, *The Importance of Being Earnest,* Crucible Theatre, Sheffield, England, 1987.
Marchbanks, *Candida,* King's Head Theatre, 1987.
Giovanni, *'Tis Pity She's a Whore,* National Theatre, Olivier Theatre, London, 1988.
David and Barnaby Grace, "A Tale for a King," *A Madhouse in Goa,* Lyric Hammersmith Theatre, London, 1989.
Tom Jones, *The History of Tom Jones,* Palace Theatre, Watford, England, 1989.
Presley Straw, *The Pitchfork Disney,* Bush Theatre, London, 1991.

Lysander, *A Midsummer Night's Dream*, National Theatre, Olivier Theatre, 1992.

Otto, *Design for Living*, Gielgud Theatre, London, 1995.

Baptiste, *Les enfants du paradis*, Barbican Theatre, London, 1996.

Eddie, *Hurlyburly*, Peter Hall Company, Old Vic Theatre and Queen's Theatre, both London, 1997.

Don Parritt, *The Iceman Cometh*, Almeida Theatre, London, 1998.

Dan, *Closer*, Music Box Theatre, New York City, 1999.

Mick, *The Caretaker*, Yvonne Arnaud Theatre, Mill Studio, Guildford, England, and Comedy Theatre, London, both 2000.

Third voice, *Speak Truth to Power: Voices from Beyond the Dark*, Playhouse Theatre, London, 2001.

Dr. Frederick Treves, *The Elephant Man*, Royale Theatre, New York City, 2002.

Lord Illingworth, *A Woman of No Importance*, Theatre Royal Haymarket, London, 2003.

Greg, *Dumb Show*, Royal Court Theatre, London, 2004.

Kerry, *The Exonerated*, Theatre at Riverside Studios, London, 2006.

Appeared in other productions.

Major Tours:

Marchbanks, *Candida*, DAMA Academy, U.S. cities, c. 1987.

Radio Appearances:

Denis Barlow, *The Loved One*, BBC Radio 4, 1990.

Roland Leighton, *Vera Brittain: Letters from a Lost Generation*, BBC Radio Four, 1998.

Reader, *The French Ball*, BBC Radio 4, 2002.

Reader, *Poste Restante: The Mombasa Mail Flag*, BBC Radio 4, 2004.

The riding master *Embers*, BBC Radio 3, 2006.

Teddy, *The Homecoming*, BBC Radio 3, 2007.

RECORDINGS

Audiobooks:

The Picture of Dorian Gray by Oscar Wilde, CSA Tell-tapes, 1993.

Richard II by William Shakespeare, Arkangel/Penguin Audiobooks, 1998.

Letters from a Lost Generation: First World War Letters of Vera Brittain and Four Friends by Vera Brittain and others, BBC Radio Collection/BBC Audiobooks, 1999.

Videos:

Himself, *Freedom! Forever! Making "V for Vendetta"* (short documentary), Warner Home Video, 2006.

WRITINGS

Screenplays:

(With Jacqueline Swanson) *Checkout Girl* (short film), 2000.

OTHER SOURCES

Periodicals:

Telegraph (London), August 30, 2008.

Electronic:

Rupert Graves Online, http://www.rupert-graves.com, January 11, 2010.

GREENE, Graham 1952–

PERSONAL

Born June 22, 1952, in Six Nations Reserve, Ontario, Canada; son of John (an ambulance driver and maintenance worker) and Lillian Greene; married Hilary Blackmore (a stage manager), December 20, 1990; children: (with Carol Lazare; an actress) one daughter. *Education:* Attended George Brown College, Toronto, Ontario, Canada; Centre for Indigenous Theatre, graduate of Native Theatre School, 1974.

Addresses: *Agent*—Celia Chassels, Gary Goddard Agency, 10 St. Mary St., Suite 305, Toronto, Ontario M4Y 1P9, Canada. *Manager*—Susan Smith, Susan Smith and Associates, 1344 North Wetherly Dr., Beverly Hills, CA 90069.

Career: Actor, producer, director, and writer. Performed with Ne'er–Do–Well Thespians, Toronto, Ontario, Canada, and with Theatre Passe Muraille; appeared as Sitting Bull, "Sitting Bull," a series of one–minute television spots called *Heritage Minute*. Formerly owned a recording studio in Ancaster, Ontario; also worked as an audio technician for rock and roll bands. Worked at a carpet warehouse and at various other jobs, including builder of railroad cars, t–shirts seller, high–steel worker, civil technologist, drafter, landscape gardener, factory laborer, carpenter, and bartender.

Awards, Honors: Dora Mavor Moore Award, best actor, Toronto Theatre Alliance, 1989, for *Dry Lips Oughta Move to Kapuskasing*; Academy Award nomination, best supporting actor, 1991, for *Dances with Wolves*; Gemini Award nomination, best guest performance in a series by an actor or actress, Academy of Canadian

Cinema and Television, 1994, for *North of 60;* Gemini Award, best performance in a children's or youth program or series, 1994, for *The Adventures of Dudley the Dragon;* Gemini Award nomination, best supporting actor in a dramatic program, 1997, for *The Outer Limits;* Gemini Award, best performance in a preschool program or series, 1998, for "Dudley and the Tiny Raincloud," *The Adventures of Dudley the Dragon;* First Americans in the Arts Award, outstanding supporting actor in a film, and Screen Actors Guild Award nomination (with others), outstanding cast in a theatrical motion picture, both 2000, for *The Green Mile;* Gemini Award nomination (with others), best performance in a comedy program or series, 2000, for *The Red Green Show;* Grammy Award (with others), best spoken–word album for children, National Academy of Recording Arts and Sciences, 2000, for *Listen to the Storyteller;* Best Actor Award, Tokyo International Film Festival, 2002, Prism Award nomination, best performance in a theatrical feature film, Entertainment Industries Council, and Independent Spirit Award nomination, best lead actor, Independent Features Project/West, both 2003, all for *Skins;* Golden Boot Award, Motion Picture and Television Fund, 2003; Earle Grey Award, Gemini Awards, 2004; honorary law degree, Wilfrid Laurier University, 2008.

CREDITS

Film Appearances:
Mick Walsh, *Smiles,* 1981.
Looks and Smiles, Artificial Eye, 1982.
Eddie Mills, *Running Brave,* Buena Vista, 1983.
Ongwata, *Revolution,* Viking Film, 1985.
Jimmy, *Powwow Highway,* Anchor Bay Entertainment, 1988.
Kicking Bird, *Dances with Wolves,* Orion, 1990.
Arthur, *Clearcut,* Northern Arts Entertainment, 1991.
Walter Crow Horse, *Thunderheart,* TriStar, 1992.
Author on history, *Rain without Thunder,* Orion Classics, 1992.
Calhoun, *Benefit of the Doubt* (also known as *Im Bann des zweifels*), Miramax, 1993.
Alaskan dad, *North,* Columbia, 1994.
Hunt Weller, *Camilla,* Miramax, 1994.
Jim, *Huck and the King of Hearts,* Prism, 1994.
Joseph, *Maverick,* Warner Bros., 1994.
Skyano, *Savage Land,* Hemdale, 1994.
Joe Lambert, *Die Hard: With a Vengeance* (also known as *Die Hard 3*), Twentieth Century–Fox, 1995.
Narrator, *First Nation Blue,* 1996.
Willow John, *The Education of Little Tree* (also known as *L'education de Little Tree*), Paramount, 1997.
Ol' Billy, *Heart of the Sun,* Dancing Stones Film Production, 1997.
Mike and Conrad, *Shattered Image,* Lions Gate Films, 1998.
Voice of Andrew Bahr, *The Herd* (documentary), 1998.

Jim Bernard, *Grey Owl,* New City Releasing, 1999.
George Baines, *Bad Money,* Sky Entertainment, 1999.
Arlen Bitterbuck, *The Green Mile* (also known as *Stephen King's "The Green Mile"*), Warner Bros., 1999.
Burly, *Misery Harbour* (also known as *Flugten fra jante* and *Flykten fraan jante*), Europafilm/ScanBox/United International Pictures, 1999.
Albert, *Touched,* Red Sky Entertainment, 1999.
Detective Connor, *Desire* (also known as *Begierde* and *Fatale Sehnsucht*), Remstar Distribution, 2000.
Joe Menzies, *Lost and Delirious* (also known as *La rage au coeur* and *Rebelles*), Lions Gate Films, 2001.
Earl, *Christmas in the Clouds,* Random Ventures/Stockbridge Munsee Band of Mohican Indians, 2001.
Mogie Yellow Lodge, *Skins,* First Look Pictures Releasing, 2002.
Peter Yellowbear, *Snow Dogs* (also known as *Chiens des neiges*), Buena Vista, 2002.
Edgar K. B. Montrose, *Duct Tape Forever* (also known as *Red Green's "Duct Tape Forever"*), TVA International, 2002.
Charley, *Punch & Judy,* 2002.
Wolf, *Phil the Alien,* Lions Gate Films, 2004.
Calvin, *Transamerica,* IFC Films/Weinstein Company, 2005.
Copeland, *When I Find the Ocean,* Monterey Media, 2006.
Sheriff, *A Lobster Tale,* Peace Arch Entertainment Group, 2006.
Henry Sanipass, *Just Buried,* Liberation Entertainment, 2007.
Bud Wilson, *Breakfast with Scot,* Regent Releasing/here! Films, 2007.
Jim Burns, *All Hat,* Screen Media Ventures, 2008.
Voice of Grandpa, *The Legend of Secret Pass* (animated), JC2 Animated Entertainment/Lords Productions/Strategic Dreamers/310 Studios/Arkwatch Holdings, 2008.
Voices of first elder and shaman of Lost Land, *Turok: Son of Stone* (animated), Genius Products, 2008.
Harry Clearwater, *New Moon* (also known as *Twilight: New Moon, The Twilight Saga: New Moon,* and *Twilight 2*), Summit Entertainment, 2009.
Turquoise Jack, *Valley of the Sun,* Hotbed Media/Ranch House Pictures, 2010.
Dilton Harper, *Running Mates,* Boutique Films, 2010.
Gunless, Alliance Films, 2010.

Film Work:
Producer and director, *Finding Love ... Again,* 1999.

Television Appearances; Series:
The chief, *Spirit Bay,* 1984.
Dan Jackson, *9B,* 1988.
Leonard Quinhagak, a recurring role, *Northern Exposure,* CBS, 1992–93.

Edgar K. B. Montrose, *The Red Green Show* (also known as *The New Red Green Show*), Global TV, 1994–97, CBC, beginning 1997.

Mr. Crabby Tree, *The Adventures of Dudley the Dragon*, 1994–97.

Host, *Exhibit A* (also known as *Forensic Files* and *Secrets of Forensic Science*), The Learning Channel, 1997–2001.

Terminal City, CBC, 1998.

Sherman Blackstone, *Wolf Lake*, UPN, 2001, then CBS, 2001–2002.

Narrator, *Rocket Science*, 2002.

Rebroadcasts of *The Red Green Show* appeared in the United States on PBS.

Television Appearances; Movies:

Murder Sees the Light, 1986.

Mawasin, *Lost in the Barrens*, The Disney Channel, 1991.

Ishi, *The Last of His Tribe* (also known as *Ishi* and *The Last Free Indian*), HBO, 1992.

Raymond Maracle, "Cooperstown," *TNT Screenworks*, TNT, 1993.

The peacemaker, *The Broken Chain*, TNT, 1993.

Samuel Smith, *Rugged Gold* (also known as *Epreuves d'amour en Alaska*), The Family Channel, 1994.

Will, *Medicine River*, 1994.

Vern, "Spirit Rider," *WonderWorks Family Movie*, PBS, 1994.

Tollander (some sources cite Tolliver), *Sabotage*, HBO, 1996.

Chingachgook, *The Pathfinder* (also known as *La legende de Pathfinder*), Showtime, 1996.

Keith, *The Hired Heart* (also known as *Sweetwater Redemption*), Lifetime, 1997.

Nick Rollins, *Wounded*, HBO, 1997.

O Kagh, *Song of Hiawatha*, Showtime, 1997.

Detective Mike Balvalori, *Dead Innocent* (also known as *Eye*), HBO, 1998.

Eddie Lester, *Stranger in Town*, Showtime, 1998.

Sergeant Garson Longfellow, *Shadow Lake*, 1999.

Walter Pearce, *Trial by Fire*, CBC, 2000.

Colin Reid, *The New Beachcombers*, CBC, 2002.

In the Echo, 2002.

Jake Cotter, *Big Spender*, Animal Planet, 2003.

Slick Nakai, *Coyote Waits*, PBS, 2003.

Slick Nakai, *A Thief of Time*, PBS, 2004.

Colin Reid, *A Beachcombers Christmas*, CBC, 2004.

John Blackhorse, *Buffalo Dreams*, The Disney Channel, 2005.

Lloyd Blackburn, *Spirit Bear: The Simon Jackson Story*, CTV, 2005.

Bill Louis, *Luna: Spirit of the Whale*, 2007.

Joseph, *The Wild Girl*, Hallmark Channel, 2010.

Also appeared in *Unnatural Causes*.

Television Appearances; Specials:

Komi's father, "Where the Spirit Lives," *American Playhouse*, PBS, 1990.

The Making of "Dances with Wolves," 1990.

Narrator, "Wolf: Return of a Legend," *ABC's World of Discovery* (also known as *World of Discovery*), ABC, 1993.

Voice, *Earth and the American Dream*, HBO, 1993.

Voice of Black Elk, *The Wild West*, CBS, 1993.

Voice, "The Way West," *The American Experience*, PBS, 1995.

Arctic Adventure, TBS and syndicated, 1996.

Independence Day 2001, ABC, 2001.

Narrator, *Science Highway*, 2001.

Red Green Live '02, PBS, 2002.

Dream Makers, Bravo, 2006.

Television Appearances; Miniseries:

Voice, *500 Nations*, CBS, 1995.

Cohost, *Great Drives*, 1996.

Voices, *Freedom: A History of Us*, PBS, 2003.

Conquering Bear, *Into the West*, TNT, 2005.

Cohost, *CBC Winnipeg Comedy Festival* (also known as *Winnipeg Comedy Festival*), CBC, 2005.

Host, *The War that Made America*, PBS, 2006.

Television Appearances; Episodic:

"The Black Curse," *The Great Detective*, 1979.

John Norton, "Journey to Queenston," *Read All about It!*, 1983.

Pinball, "Mailman," *Adderly*, CBS, 1986.

Cherokee, "Wardogs," *Captain Power and the Soldiers of the Future*, 1987.

Paulo, "Tango Bellarosa," *Street Legal*, 1987.

Wanika, "Dances with Sharks," *L.A. Law*, NBC, 1991.

Sheriff Sam Keeyani, "Night of the Coyote," *Murder, She Wrote*, CBS, 1992.

Narrator, "Squanto and the First Thanksgiving," *American Heroes and Legends* (animated), Showtime, 1993.

Rico Nez, "The Art of the Deal," *North of 60*, CBC, 1993.

Peter Henderson, "Northern Explosion," *Murder, She Wrote*, CBS, 1994.

Native Indian, "This Day in History," *Royal Canadian Air Farce*, CBC, 1994.

Red Hawk, "O Western Wind: Part 1," *Lonesome Dove: The Series*, syndicated, 1994.

Red Hawk, "Down Come Rain: Part 2," *Lonesome Dove: The Series*, syndicated, 1994.

Red Hawk, "When Wilt Thou Blow: Part 3," *Lonesome Dove: The Series*, syndicated, 1994.

Voice of Brown Bear, "Snow White," *Happily Ever After: Fairy Tales for Every Child* (animated), HBO, 1995.

Mr. Jones, "Lies I Told My Father," *Liberty Street*, 1995.

"Behind the Scenes: 'Die Hard: With a Vengeance,'" *HBO First Look*, HBO, 1995.

Chief weapons officer, "The Light Brigade," *The Outer Limits* (also known as *The New Outer Limits*), Showtime, 1996.

Charlie, "Finding Richter," *Poltergeist: The Legacy,* 1997.

Grey Eagle, "Medicine Man," *Dead Man's Gun,* 1997.

Dr. David Lands, "Heartland," *PSI Factor: Chronicles of the Paranormal,* syndicated, 1998.

Frozen dead guy, *Royal Canadian Air Farce* (also known as *Air Farce, Air Farce Live,* and *Air Farce: Final Flight*), CBC, 1999.

Lonetree, "Prayer for the White Man," *First Wave,* Sci–Fi Channel, 1999.

Mayor, *Safe Harbor,* The WB, 1999.

Ferryman, "101 Damnations," *Big Wolf on Campus* (also known as *Le loup–garou du campus*), Fox, 2000.

Michael Nighthorse, "The Hit Parade," *Cover Me: Based on the True Life of an FBI Family* (also known as *Cover Me*), USA Network, 2000.

Michael Nighthorse, "Killing Me Softly," *Cover Me: Based on the True Life of an FBI Family* (also known as *Cover Me*), USA Network, 2000.

Michael Nighthorse, "The River," *Cover Me: Based on the True Life of an FBI Family* (also known as *Cover Me*), USA Network, 2001.

John Graves Simcoe, "Canada: A Mildly Informative, Not Overly Long People's History," *Royal Canadian Air Farce,* CBC, 2001.

Senior Senator Jackson, "Next Question," *Mister Sterling,* NBC, 2003.

George, "The Dreamer," *The Collector,* 2005.

Chief James Clearwater, "Bones of Contention," *Numb3rs* (also known as *Num3ers*), CBS, 2005.

Also appeared as Iroquois man, "Autumn and Smoke: Parts 1 & 2" and "Star Light, Star Bright," episodes of *The Campbells;* and in *Night Heat.*

Television Appearances; Awards Presentations:
The 63rd Annual Academy Awards, ABC, 1991.
The 13th Annual Call–ace Awards, TNT, 1992.
2004 Gemini Awards, CBC, 2004.

Television Appearances; Pilots:
Professor Duke Joseph, *Wolf Lake,* CBS, 2001.

Stage Appearances:
Native American alcoholic, *The Crackwalker,* 1980.
The crow, *Jessica,* 1982.
Pierre St. Pierre, *Dry Lips Oughta Move to Kapuskasing,* c. 1989.
Shylock, *The Merchant of Venice,* Stratford Festival, Stratford, Ontario, Canada, 2007.
Lenny, *Of Mice and Men,* Stratford Festival, 2007.

Narrator of *Tecumseh!,* an annual outdoor drama, Sugarloaf Mountain Amphitheatre, Chillicothe, OH; also appeared in productions of *Coming through Slaughter* and *Diary of a Crazy Boy.*

RECORDINGS

Videos:
(Uncredited) *Walking the Mile* (also known as *Walking the Mile: The Making of "The Green Mile"*), Warner Bros. Home Video, 2000.
The Highest Step in the World, 2002.
Declaration of Independence, Declaration of Independence, Inc., 2003.
Dances with Wolves: The Creation of an Epic, Metro–Goldwyn–Mayer Home Entertainment, 2003.
When I Find the Ocean: Behind the Scenes, Monterey Media, 2008.

Albums:
Narrator, *Listen to the Storyteller,* Sony Classical, c. 2000.

WRITINGS

Screenplays:
Finding Love ... Again, 1999.

OTHER SOURCES

Books:
Encyclopedia of World Biography, 2nd edition, Gale, 1998.
Newspapers '97, Gale, 1998.
Notable Native Americans, Gale, 1995.
St. James Encyclopedia of Popular Culture, St. James Press, 2000.

Periodicals:
Maclean's, October 20, 1997, p. 74.

GRIFFITH, Melanie 1957–

PERSONAL

Born August 9, 1957, in New York, NY; daughter of Peter Griffith (an advertising executive and actor) and Tippi Hedren (an actress and model); married Don Johnson (an actor), January 8, 1976 (divorced July, 1976); married Steven Bauer (an actor), September 8, 1981 (divorced, 1987); remarried Don Johnson, June 26, 1989 (divorced, 1996); married Antonio Banderas (an actor), May 14, 1996; children: (second marriage)

Alexander; (third marriage) Dakota Mayi (a model and actress); (fourth marriage) Stella del Carmen. *Education:* Attended Hollywood Professional School; studied acting with Stella Adler.

Addresses: *Agent*—WME Entertainment, One William Morris Pl., Beverly Hills, CA 90212. *Manager*—Untitled Entertainment, 1801 Century Park East, Suite 700, Los Angeles, CA 90067. *Publicist*—Slate PR 8322 Beverly Blvd., Suite 201, Los Angeles, CA 90048.

Career: Actress and producer. Green Moon (production company), partner; also worked as a model. Appeared in television commercials for Revlon cosmetics, 1996–2000, and Wyler Wetta watchers, 2000; appeared in print ads for The Gap clothing stores, 2002. Feed the Children, volunteer; Sabera Foundation, honorary president; Sahmbala Preserve (an animal refuge), fundraiser.

Awards, Honors: Miss Golden Globe, 1975; named star of tomorrow, Motion Picture Bookers Club, 1984; National Society of Film Critics Award, best supporting actress, 1984, and Golden Globe Award nomination, best performance by an actress in a supporting role in a motion picture, 1985, both for *Body Double;* Golden Globe Award nomination, best performance by an actress in a motion picture—comedy/musical, 1987, for *Something Wild;* Academy Award nomination, best actress, 1989, Golden Globe Award, best actress in a musical or comedy film, 1989, Film Award, best actress, British Academy of Film and Television Arts, 1990, all for *Working Girl;* Golden Globe Award nomination, best performance by an actress in a supporting role in a series, miniseries or motion picture, 1996, for *Buffalo Girls;* Emmy Award nomination, outstanding supporting actress in a miniseries or movie, Golden Globe Award nomination, best performance by an actress in a supporting role in a series, miniseries or motion picture made for TV, 2000, both for *RKO 281;* Santi Jordi Award, best foreign actress, 2000, for *Crazy in Alabama* and *Another Day in Paradise;* Tairnuba Arte Award, Taormina International Film Festival, 2000; Australian Film Institute Award nomination, best actress in a supporting role, 2003, for *The Night We Called It a Day.*

CREDITS

Film Appearances:
(Uncredited) Extra, *Smith!,* 1969.
(Uncredited) Extra, *The Harrad Experiment,* 1973.
Delly Grastner, *Night Moves,* Warner Bros., 1975.
Schuyler Devereaux, *The Drowning Pool,* Warner Bros., 1975.
Karen Love ("Miss Simi Valley"), *Smile,* United Artists, 1975.

Susie, *Joyride,* American International Pictures, 1977.
Hitchhiker, *One on One,* Warner Bros., 1977.
Young girl, *Ha–Gan* (also known as *The Garden*), 1977.
Lucy, *Underground Aces,* 1980.
Melanie, *Roar,* Alpha–Filmways, 1981.
Holly Body, *Body Double,* Columbia, 1984.
Loretta, *Fear City* (also known as *Border* and *Ripper*), Twentieth Century–Fox, 1985.
Audrey Hankel/Lulu, *Something Wild,* Orion, 1986.
Flossie Devine, *The Milagro Beanfield War,* Universal, 1988.
Kate, *Stormy Monday,* Atlantic Releasing, 1988.
Edith "E." Johnson, tracker, *Cherry 2000,* Orion, 1988.
Tess McGill, *Working Girl,* Twentieth Century–Fox, 1988.
Patty Palmer, *Pacific Heights,* Twentieth Century–Fox, 1990.
Maria Ruskin, *The Bonfire of the Vanities,* Warner Bros., 1990.
Lureen, *In the Spirit,* Castle Hill, 1990.
Lily Reed, *Paradise,* Buena Vista, 1991.
Linda Voss, *Shining Through,* Twentieth Century–Fox, 1992.
Emily Eden, *A Stranger Among Us* (also known as *Close to Eden*), Buena Vista, 1992.
Billie Dawn, *Born Yesterday,* Buena Vista, 1993.
V, *Milk Money,* Paramount, 1994.
Toby Roebuck, *Nobody's Fool,* Paramount, 1994.
Tina Tercell, *Now and Then,* New Line Cinema, 1995.
Betty Kerner, *Two Much* (also known as *Loco de amor*), Buena Vista, 1995.
Katherine, *Mulholland Falls,* Metro–Goldwyn–Mayer, 1996.
Herself, *On the Set of "Lolita"* (short documentary), 1997.
Charlotte Haze, *Lolita,* Samuel Goldwyn, 1998.
Nicole Olivier, *Celebrity,* Miramax, 1998.
Sid, *Another Day in Paradise,* Trimark Pictures, 1998.
Kitt Devereaux, *Shadow of Doubt* (also known as *Reasonable Doubt*), New City Releasing, 1998.
Herself, *Junket Whore* (documentary), 1998.
Aunt Lucille, *Crazy in Alabama,* TriStar, 1999.
(Unwitting cameo) Herself, *The Book That Wrote Itself,* 1999.
Herself, *Ljuset haaller mig saellskap* (documentary; also known as *Sven Nykvist: Light Keeps Me Company* and *Light Keeps Me Company*), First Run Features, 2000.
Honey Whitlock, *Cecil B. DeMented* (also known as *Cecil B. Demented*), Artisan Entertainment, 2000.
Lulu McAfee, *Forever Lulu* (also known as *Along for the Ride*), Artisan Entertainment, 2000.
Life with Big Cats (documentary), 2000.
Diane Milford, *Tart* (also known as *Naive*), 2001.
Voice of Margalo, *Stuart Little 2,* Sony Pictures Entertainment, 2002.
Sarah James, *Tempo,* Universal, 2002.
Eve, *Shade,* Dimension Films, 2003.

Barbara Marx Sinatra, *The Night We Called It a Day* (also known as *All the Way* and *All the Way: The Kidnapping of a Music Legend*), Miracle Entertainment, 2003.

Have Mercy, 2006.

Voice, *Around the World in 50 Years 3–D* (animated), 2009.

Television Appearances; Series:

Tracy Quinn, *Carter Country,* ABC, 1978–79.

Me & George, 1998.

Lee Arnold, *Twins,* The WB, 2005–2006.

Bunny, *Viva Laughlin,* CBS, 2007–2008.

Television Appearances; Miniseries:

Jinny Massengale, *Once an Eagle,* NBC, 1976.

Dawn Bennett, *The Star Maker,* NBC, 1981.

Dora DuFran, *Buffalo Girls,* CBS, 1995.

Television Appearances; Movies:

Girl in hotel room, *Daddy, I Don't Like It Like This,* CBS, 1978.

Johnnie, *Steel Cowboy,* NBC, 1978.

Hadley, "Hills Like White Elephants," *Women & Men: Stories of Seduction,* HBO, 1990.

Marion Davies, *RKO 281* (also known as *RKO 281: The Battle Over "Citizen Kane"*), HBO, 1999.

Herself, *Searching for Debra Winger* (documentary), Showtime, 2003.

Miranda Wells, *Heartless* (also known as *Lethal Seduction*), CBS, 2005.

Television Appearances; Pilots:

Private Sylvie Knoll, *She's in the Army Now* (also known as *G.I. Joans*), ABC, 1981.

Karen, *Golden Gate,* ABC, 1981.

Page Chapel, *Me & Henry,* CBS, 1998.

Bunny, *Viva Laughlin,* CBS, 2007.

Television Appearances; Specials:

Superstars and Their Moms, TBS, 1989.

The 3rd Annual Hollywood Insider Academy Awards Special, USA Network, 1989.

Host, *That's What Friends Are For,* CBS, 1990.

Victory & Valor: A Special Olympics All–Star Celebration (also known as *The International Special Olympics All–Star Gala*), ABC, 1991.

Host, *The Grand Opening of Euro Disney,* CBS, 1992.

A Night to Die For, 1995.

Telemaraton, 1995.

Life with Big Cats: Tippi Hedren and Shambala, Animal Planet, 1998.

Bravo Profiles: The Entertainment Business, 1998.

(Uncredited) Guest at entrance, *Andrew Lloyd Webber: The Royal Albert Hall Celebration,* 1998.

Canned Ham: "Cecil B. Demented," Comedy Central, 2000.

Hollywood Salutes Bruce Willis: An American Cinematheque Tribute, TNT, 2000.

Intimate Portrait: Tippi Hedren, Lifetime, 2001.

Still Cher, 2002.

Conversations from the Edge with Carrie Fisher, Oxygen, 2002.

Voice, *Happy to Be Nappy and Other Stories of Me* (documentary), HBO, 2004.

Inside the Actors Studio: 10th Anniversary Special, Bravo, 2004.

Herself, *Naked* (documentary), BBC, 2005.

Herself, *El disco del ano* (documentary), Canal+ Espana, 2006.

Ceremonia de inauguracion–56 festival internacional de cine de San Sebastian, 2008.

(Uncredited) *Premio Donostia a Antonio Banderas,* 2008.

Resumen—56 festival internacional de cine de San Sebastian, 2008.

Television Appearances; Awards Presentations:

The ... Annual Academy Awards Presentations, ABC, 1989, 1990, 1998.

Presenter, *The Walt Disney Company Presents the American Teacher Awards,* The Disney Channel, 1992, 1994.

Host, *One Child, One Dream: The Horatio Alger Awards,* NBC, 1993.

Presenter, *The 19th Annual People's Choice Awards,* CBS, 1993.

Presenter, *The ... Annual Tony Awards,* CBS, 1994, 2003.

The Horatio Alger Awards, NBC, 1994.

Presenter, *The Blockbuster Entertainment Awards,* CBS, 1995.

Presenter, *The Horatio Alger Awards,* CBS, 1995.

Presenter, *The ... Annual Golden Globe Awards,* NBC, 1997, 2004, 2006.

The 56th Annual Golden Globe Awards, NBC, 1999.

The European Film Awards, 1999.

The 5th Annual ALMA Awards, ABC, 2000.

Nickelodeon Kids' Choice Awards '02, Nickelodeon, 2002.

Television Appearances; Episodic:

Stacey Blain, "The House on Possessed Hill," *The Hardy Boys/Nancy Drew Mysteries* (also known as *The Nancy Drew Mysteries*), ABC, 1978.

Julie McDermott, "The Action," *Starsky and Hutch,* ABC, 1978.

Dawn Peters, "Red Handed," *Vega$,* ABC, 1979.

Girl, "Man from the South," *Alfred Hitchcock Presents,* NBC, 1985.

Christine von Marburg, "By Hooker, by Crook," *Miami Vice,* NBC, 1987.

Host, *Saturday Night Live* (also known as *SNL*), NBC, 1988.

(Uncredited) *Lo + plus,* 1995.

Cinema 3 (also known as *Informatiu cinema*), 1995.

La Lloll, 1995.

Inside the Actors Studio (also known as *Inside the Actors Studio: The Craft of Theatre and Film*), Bravo, 1995, 2001.

Corazon, corazon, 1995, 1996.

Inside Edition, syndicated, 1996.

Narrator, "Marilyn Monroe," *Sex and the Silver Screen,* Showtime, 1996.

Caiga quien caiga, 1998.

El informal, 1999.

Hollywood Squares (also known as *H2* and *H2: Hollywood Squares*), syndicated, 1999.

Herself, "Atame!," *La gran ilusion,* 2000.

Herself, "La blanca paloma," *La gran ilusion,* 2000.

Herself, "Beverly Pills," *Liquid News,* 2001.

(Uncredited) Herself, *Banzai,* Fox, 2003.

Herself, "Singers," *When I Was a Girl,* WE, 2003.

Biography, Arts and Entertainment, 2004, 2005, 2007.

(Uncredited) Herself, "Random Acts of Courage," *The Contender,* NBC, 2005.

(Uncredited) Herself, "Tears of Pain and Sorrow," *The Contender,* NBC, 2005.

Voice of Hermione Granger, Love–a–Lot Bear, and Wish Beart, "Password: Swordfish," *Robot Chicken,* Cartoon Network, 2006.

Voice of herself, "The Monkey Suit," *The Simpsons* (animated), Fox, 2006.

Herself, "Sitcom Stylings," *My First Time,* TV Land, 2006.

La noche de Quintero, 2007.

"Idol Gives Back: Part One," *American Idol: The Search for a Superstar* (also known as *American Idol*), Fox, 2007.

Entertainment Tonight (also known as *E.T.*), syndicated, 2008.

Exclusiv–Das Star–Magazin, 2008.

Brandie Henry, "Sheila Carlton," *Nip/Tuck,* FX Network, 2010.

Television Talk Show Guest Appearances; Episodic:

The Howard Stern Show (also known as *The Howard Stern Summer Show*), 1990.

The Tonight Show Starring Johnny Carson, NBC, 1992.

The Rosie O'Donnell Show, syndicated, 1997, 1998, 1999, 2000, 2002.

The Roseanne Show, 1998.

Clive Anderson All Talk, BBC1, 1999.

Late Show with David Letterman (also known as *Letterman* and *The Late Show*), CBS, 2001.

The Tonight Show With Jay Leno (also known as *Jay Leno*), NBC, 2001, 2005.

Conversations from the Edge with Carrie Fisher, Oxygen, 2002.

The Oprah Winfrey Show (also known as *Oprah*), syndicated, 2004, 2005.

Ellen: The Ellen DeGeneres Show, syndicated, 2005.

The View, ABC, 2005.

Corazon de ..., 2005, 2006, 2007, 2008.

Television Co–Executive Producer; Pilots:

Henry & Me, CBS, 1998.

Stage Appearances:

Roxie Hart, *Chicago,* Ambassador Theatre, New York City, 2003.

OTHER SOURCES

Books:

International Dictionary of Films and Filmmakers, Volume 3: *Actors and Actresses,* St. James Press, 1996.

Newsmakers 1989, Issue 4, Gale Research, 1989.

Periodicals:

American Film, March, 1988, pp. 49–52.

Good Housekeeping, August, 1998, p. 94.

Interview, November, 1988, p. 110; October, 1998, p. 48; August, 2000, p. 107.

Ladies' Home Journal, September, 1997, p. 136; September, 1998, p. 180.

Los Angeles, May, 1989, p. 124.

Los Angeles Magazine, February, 1999, p. 76.

Newsweek, January 2, 1989, p. 56.

Washington Post, December 29, 1988.

H

HAMMER, Jack
    See NORRIS, Daran

HAWTHORNE, Kimberly
(Kim Hawthorne)

PERSONAL

Married; husband's name, Curt; children: Julian, Bailey. *Education:* Birmingham–Southern College, B.A., musical theatre, 1990.

Career: Actress and voice performer. Julian Bailey Designs, jewelry designer, 2006—.

CREDITS

Television Appearances; Series:
Belinda Keefer, *All My Children* (also known as *All My Children: The Summer of Seduction* and *La force du destin*), ABC, c. 1994–95.
Assistant district attorney Dana Kramer, *Another World* (also known as *Another World: Bay City* and *AW: Bay City*), NBC, 1997.
Voice of Karen O'Malley, *Spider–Man Unlimited* (animated; also known as *Spiderman Unlimited*), Fox, c. 1999–2001.
(As Kim Hawthorne) Detective Rose Williams, *Da Vinci's Inquest* (also known as *Coroner Da Vinci*), CBC, between 2000 and 2005.
(As Kim Hawthorne) Voice of Bernice Shaw and Dr. Sandy, *Mary–Kate and Ashley in Action!* (animated; also known as *Mary–Kate and Ashley in Action*), ABC, 2001–2002.

(As Kim Hawthorne) Theo, *Jeremiah* (also known as *Jeremiah—Krieger des Donners*), Showtime, 2002–2003.
Voice, *Stargate: Infinity* (animated; also known as *Stargate Infinity*), Fox, 2002–2003.
(As Kim Hawthorne) Voices, *Gadget and the Gadgetinis* (animated), syndicated, 2003.
(As Kim Hawthorne) Ellen, *Lucky Louie* (also known as *American Dream*), HBO, 2006.
Jada Temple, *Whistler*, CTV and The N, 2006.

Television Appearances; Miniseries:
Sphinx, *Voyage of the Unicorn* (also known as *La merveilleuse traversee de la licorne*), Hallmark Channel, 2001.
(As Kim Hawthorne) Jill Hunter, *10.5* (also known as *Earthquake 10.5, Magnitude 10.5, 10.5: Apocalypse,* and *10.5 Richter*), NBC, 2004.

Television Appearances; Movies:
(As Kim Hawthorne) Pastor Jessie Haynes, *Behind the Mask,* CBS, 1999.
Ms. Tennyson, *Deadlocked* (also known as *Deadlocked—Die fuenfte Gewalt*), TNT, 2000.
Officer Lynda Byron, *A Vision of Murder: The Story of Donielle* (also known as *Sight Unseen* and *A Vision of Murder*), CBS, 2000.
(As Kim Hawthorne) Laura Rodericks, *The Wedding Dress,* CBS, 2001.
(As Kim Hawthorne) Voice of anchorperson, *Inspector Gadget's Last Case: Claw's Revenge* (animated; also known as *Inspector Gadget in Claw's Revenge*), 2002.
(As Kim Hawthorne) Trisha Rogers, *Lucky 7* (also known as *Lucky Seven*), ABC Family, 2003.
Lightning: Bolts of Destruction (also known as *Heaven's Fury* and *La colere du ciel*), PAX, 2003.
(As Kim Hawthorne) Barbara Owens, *Murder at the Presidio,* USA Network, 2005.
(As Kim Hawthorne) Diana, *Voodoo Moon* (also known as *Children of the Cornpone*), Sci–Fi Channel, 2005.

Television Appearances; Episodic:

Faith Todd, "The More Things Change," *In the Heat of the Night,* NBC, 1991.

Sue Howell, "Ruda's Awakening," *In the Heat of the Night,* NBC, 1991.

Young woman, "Hello and Goodbye," *I'll Fly Away,* NBC, 1992.

Daphne Gordon, "Hard Choices," *In the Heat of the Night,* NBC, 1994.

(Uncredited) "The Judge," *Millennium,* Fox, 1996.

(As Kim Hawthorne) Waitress, "A Kiss Is Just a Kiss," *Soul Man* (also known as *Father's Day*), ABC, 1998.

"The Greatest Gift," *Cosby,* CBS, 1998.

(As Kim Hawthorne) Cassandra, "Nightwoman Returns," *Night Man* (also known as *NightMan*), syndicated, 1999.

LGT receptionist, "Unsafe Sex," *Beggars and Choosers* (also known as *TV business*), Showtime, 1999.

(As Kim Hawthorne) Morgan Winters, "The Haven," *The Outer Limits* (also known as *The New Outer Limits*), Showtime, Sci–Fi Channel, and syndicated, 1999.

(As Kim Hawthorne) Nurse, "Borrowed Time," *Millennium,* Fox, 1999.

"Lost Souls," *First Wave,* Sci–Fi Channel, 1999.

(As Kim Hawthorne) Jacinda Katsuno, "Flushed," *Dark Angel* (also known as *James Cameron's "Dark Angel"*), Fox, 2000.

(As Kim Hawthorne) Kegan, "Beneath the Surface," *Stargate SG–1* (also known as *La porte des etoiles* and *Stargaate SG–1*), Showtime and syndicated, 2000.

(As Kim Hawthorne) Cheryl, "The Bokor," *Night Visions* (also known as *Night Terrors* and *Nightvisions*), Fox, 2001.

(As Kim Hawthorne) Dr. Marissa Hamilton, "Do You See What I See?," *Mysterious Ways* (also known as *One Clear Moment, Anexegeta phainomena, Les chemins de l'etrange, Mysterious ways—les chemins de l'etrange, Rajatapaus,* and *Senderos misteriosos*), PAX, 2001.

(As Kim Hawthorne) Jacinda Katsuno, "Shortie's in Love," *Dark Angel* (also known as *James Cameron's "Dark Angel"*), Fox, 2001.

(As Kim Hawthorne) Lawyer, "Forced Perspective," *Andromeda* (also known as *Gene Roddenberry's "Andromeda"*), Sci–Fi Channel, 2001.

(As Kim Hawthorne) Kelly Hayes, "Past Imperfect," *John Doe* (also known as *Der Fall John Doe!* and *Mies vailla nimeae*), Fox, 2002.

(As Kim Hawthorne) Luanne Ferris, "Above the Law," *Just Cause,* W Network and PAX, 2002.

Madeline Thomas, "Hi, Noonan," *Breaking News,* originally produced for TNT, broadcast by Bravo, 2002.

Madeline Thomas, "My Suspect Vinny," *Breaking News,* originally produced for TNT, broadcast by Bravo, 2002.

Madeline Thomas, "Rachel Glass and the No Good, Very Bad Day," *Breaking News,* originally produced for TNT, broadcast by Bravo, 2002.

(As Kim Hawthorne) Muriel, "Chosen," *The Twilight Zone* (also known as *Twilight Zone*), UPN, 2002.

Tri–Camille, "The Torment, the Release," *Andromeda* (also known as *Gene Roddenberry's "Andromeda"*), Sci–Fi Channel, 2004.

(As Kim Hawthorne) Yolanda Watkins, "Liberally," *The L Word* (also known as *Earthlings*), Showtime, 2004.

(As Kim Hawthorne) Yolanda Watkins, "Listen Up," *The L Word* (also known as *Earthlings*), Showtime, 2004.

Agent Powers, "First Disaster," *Commander in Chief* (also known as *Untitled Geena Davis Project, Welcome Mrs. President, Rouva presidentti,* and *Senora presidenta*), ABC, 2005.

Agent Powers, "First Scandal," *Commander in Chief* (also known as *Untitled Geena Davis Project, Welcome Mrs. President, Rouva presidentti,* and *Senora presidenta*), ABC, 2005.

Herself, *eTalk Daily* (also known as *eTalk* and *e–Talk Daily*), CTV, 2007.

(As Kim Hawthorne) Wendy Kramer, "Smoke Gets in Your CSIs," *CSI: Miami* (also known as *CSI Miami* and *CSI: Weekends*), CBS, 2009.

Also appeared in other programs, including *Guiding Light* (also known as *The Guiding Light*), CBS; and provided a voice for *Alienators: Evolution Continues* (animated; also known as *Evolution* and *Evolution: The Animated Series*), Fox and YTV.

Television Appearances; Pilots:

(As Kim Hawthorne) Surgeon, *The Wonder Cabinet,* Fox, 1999.

Voice, *NASCAR Racers: The Movie* (animated), Fox, 1999.

(As Kim Hawthorne) Jacinda Katsuno, *Dark Angel* (also known as *James Cameron's "Dark Angel"*), Fox, 2000.

(As Kim Hawthorne) Special agent Clara Tompkins, *HRT* (also known as *Hostage Rescue Team* and *H.R.T.*), CBS, 2001.

Madeline Thomas, *Breaking News,* originally produced for TNT, broadcast by Bravo, 2002.

Voice, "Decision," *Stargate: Infinity* (animated; also known as *Stargate Infinity*), Fox, 2002.

(As Kim Hawthorne) Ellen, *Lucky Louie* (also known as *American Dream*), HBO, 2006.

Television Additional Voices; Series:

Sonic Underground (animated; also known as *Sonic le rebelle*), UPN, BKN, Sci–Fi Channel, and TeleToon, 1999–2004.

Film Appearances:

Harriet, *Drop Squad* (also known as *The D.R.O.P. Squad*), Gramercy, 1994.

(As Kim Hawthorne) Agent Cassavettes, *See Spot Run* (also known as *Agent 11* and *Spot*), Warner Bros., 2001.

(As Kim Hawthorne) Agent Hickley, *Along Came a Spider* (also known as *Im Netz der Spinne* and *Le masque de l'araignee*), Paramount, 2001.

(As Kim Hawthorne) Panel operator, *3000 Miles to Graceland* (also known as *Crime Is King, Destination: Graceland,* and *3,000 Miles to Graceland*), Warner Bros., 2001.

Fugitives Run (also known as *Cowboys Run, Don't Call Me Tonto,* and *Ne m'appelez pas Tonto*), American World Pictures, 2003.

Lajjun, *The Chronicles of Riddick* (also released as *The Chronicles of Riddick: The Director's Cut, Pitch Black 2, Pitch Black 2: Chronicles of Riddick,* and *Riddick*), Universal, 2004.

Nina, *Broken Kingdom* (also known as *The Disposables*), c. 2009.

Some sources cite appearances in other films.

Stage Appearances:
Minnie Dove Charles, *Flyin' West,* Alliance Theatre Company, Atlanta, GA, beginning 1992, Crossroads Theatre Company, New Brunswick, NJ, beginning 1993, Indiana Repertory Theatre, Indianapolis, IN, 1994, Long Wharf Theatre, New Haven, CT, 1994, and John F. Kennedy Center for the Performing Arts, Eisenhower Theater, Washington, DC, 1994.

Understudy for the role of Queen, *The Life* (musical), Ethel Barrymore Theatre, New York City, 1997–98.

Constant Star, PlayMakers Repertory Company, University of North Carolina at Chapel Hill, Center for Dramatic Art, Paul Green Theatre, Chapel Hill, NC, 1999.

Appeared in *From the Mississippi Delta.* Appeared in productions at other venues, including the Arizona Theatre Company, Tucson, AZ; the Atlanta Shakespeare Company, Atlanta, GA; the Manhattan Theatre Club, New York City; the Milwaukee Repertory Theater, Milwaukee, WI; and Syracuse Stage, Syracuse, NY.

RECORDINGS

Videos:
(As Kim Hawthorne) Herself, *Lucky Louie: A Week in the Life* (short documentary), Home Box Office Home Video, 2007.

Albums:
(With others) *The Life* (soundtrack album), c. 2004.

Also worked on a solo album.

OTHER SOURCES

Electronic:
Julian Bailey Designs, http://www.julianbaileydesigns.com, January 12, 2010.

HILL, Walter 1942–
(Walt Hill, Thomas Lee)

PERSONAL

Full name, Walter Wesley Hill; born January 10, 1942, in Long Beach, CA; father worked as a riveter and dockyard foreman; married Hildy Gottlieb (an agent and producer); children: Joanna Wesley, Maura Joan, Miranda Ellen. *Education:* Attended University of the Americas, Mexico City, Mexico, 1959–60; Michigan State University, B.A., 1962, M.A., 1963; attended Directors Guild of America training school, c. 1966.

Addresses: *Agent*—International Creative Management, International Creative Management, 10250 Constellation Way, 9th Floor, Los Angeles, CA 90067.

Career: Director, producer, and writer. Also worked as assistant director. Phoenix Company, cofounder, c. 1981. Former construction worker and oil driller, mid–1960s.

Awards, Honors: Edgar Allan Poe Award nomination (with others), best motion picture, Mystery Writers of America, 1976, for *The Drowning Pool;* nomination for Golden Palm Award, Cannes Film Festival, 1980, for *The Long Riders;* Grand Prix, Cognac Festival du Film Policier, and Edgar Allan Poe Award nomination (with others), best motion picture, both 1983, for *48 Hrs.;* Readers' Choice Award, best foreign–language film, Kinema Junpo Awards, 1985, for *Streets of Fire;* Saturn Award nomination (with others), best writing, Academy of Science Fiction, Fantasy, and Horror Films, 1993, for *Alien3;* Bronze Wrangler (with others), best theatrical motion picture, Western Heritage Awards, 1994, for *Geronimo: An American Legend;* Golden Boot Award, Motion Picture and Television Fund, 1994; Golden Satellite Award nomination (with others), best animated or mixed media film, International Press Academy, 1998, for *Alien: Resurrection;* Emmy Award, outstanding directing of a drama series, 2004, and Directors Guild of America Award (with others), outstanding direction of a nighttime dramatic series, 2005, both for premiere episode, *Deadwood;* Emmy Award nomination and Directors Guild of America Award, both outstanding direction of a miniseries or movie for television, Emmy Award (with others), outstanding miniseries, and Bronze Wrangler Award (with others), outstanding television feature film, all 2007, for *Broken Trail;* Joseph Plateau Award, Flanders International Film Festival, 2007.

CREDITS

Film Director:
Hard Times (also known as *The Streetfighter*), Columbia, 1975.
The Driver, Twentieth Century–Fox, 1978.
The Long Riders, United Artists, 1980.
The Warriors, Paramount, 1980.
Southern Comfort, Twentieth Century–Fox, 1981.
48 Hrs. (also known as *48 Hours*), Paramount, 1982.
Streets of Fire, Universal, 1984.
Brewster's Millions, Universal, 1985.
Crossroads, Columbia, 1986.
Extreme Prejudice, TriStar, 1987.
Red Heat, TriStar, 1988.
Johnny Handsome, TriStar, 1989.
Another 48 Hrs. (also known as *Another 48 Hours*), Paramount, 1990.
Trespass (also known as *Looters*), Universal, 1992.
Geronimo: An American Legend, Columbia, 1993.
Wild Bill, Metro–Goldwyn–Mayer, 1995.
Last Man Standing (also known as *Gundown* and *Welcome to Jericho*), New Line Cinema, 1996.
(As Thomas Lee) *Supernova,* Metro–Goldwyn–Mayer, 2000.
Undisputed (also known as *Undisputed—Sieg ohne ruhm*), Miramax, 2002.

Film Producer:
Producer of ultimate director's cut, *The Warriors,* 1979.
Alien (also released as *Alien: The Director's Cut*), Twentieth Century–Fox, 1979.
Southern Comfort, Twentieth Century–Fox, 1981.
Rustler's Rhapsody (also known as *Esos locos cuatreros*), Paramount, 1985.
Blue City, Paramount, 1986.
Red Heat, TriStar, 1988.
Alien3 (also known as *Alien III*), Twentieth Century–Fox, 1992.
Geronimo: An American Legend, Columbia, 1993.
Last Man Standing (also known as *Gundown* and *Welcome to Jericho*), New Line Cinema, 1996.
Alien: Resurrection (also known as *Alien 4*), Twentieth Century–Fox, 1997.
Ritual (also known as *Tales from the Crypt Presents: Revelation* and *Tales from the Crypt Presents: Voodoo*), Miramax, 2001.
Undisputed (also known as *Undisputed—Sieg ohne ruhm*), Miramax, 2002.
AVP: Alien vs. Predator (also known as *Alien vs. Predator* and *AVP*), Twentieth Century–Fox, 2004.

AVPR: Aliens vs. Predator—Requiem (also known as *Aliens vs. Predator w, AVP: Aliens vs. Predator—Requiem, AVP: Requiem, AVPR,* and *AVP2*), Twentieth Century–Fox, 2007.

Film Executive Producer:
(With Gordon Carroll and David Giler) *Aliens,* Twentieth Century–Fox, 1986.
Tales from the Crypt: Demon Knight (also known as *Demon Keeper, Demon Knight,* and *Tales from the Crypt Presents Demon Knight*), Universal, 1995.
Tales from the Crypt Presents: Bordello of Blood (also known as *Bordello of Blood*), Universal, 1996.

Film Appearances:
Himself, *Directed by John Ford,* 1971.
Dead People (also known as *Messiah of Evil, Revenge of the Screaming Dead,* and *The Second Coming*), 1973.
(As Walt Hill) Second plainclothes officer, *Up Yours—A Rockin' Comedy* (also known as *Up Your Ladder*), 1979.
Howard Hawks: American Artist (documentary), 1997.

Television Creator; Series:
Dog and Cat, ABC, 1977.
Tales from the Cryptkeeper (animated; also known as *New Tales from the Cryptkeeper*), syndicated, 1993–95.

Television Executive Producer; Series:
Tales from the Crypt (also known as *HBO's "Tales from the Crypt"*), HBO, 1989–97, Fox, 1994–95.
Perversions of Science, HBO, 1997.

Television Work; Miniseries:
Producer and director, *Broken Trail,* AMC, 2006.

Television Work; Pilots:
Executive producer, *Two–Fisted Tales,* Fox, 1992.
Director, *Madso's War,* Spike, 2009.

Television Director; Episodic:
(With Robert Reneau) "The Man Who Was Death," *Tales from the Crypt* (also known as *HBO's "Tales from the Crypt"*), HBO, 1989.
(With others) "Cutting Cards," *Tales from the Crypt* (also known as *HBO's "Tales from the Crypt"*), HBO, 1990.
(With Mae Woods and William M. Gaines) "Deadline," *Tales from the Crypt* (also known as *HBO's "Tales from the Crypt"*), HBO, 1991.
"Dream of Doom," *Perversions of Science,* HBO, 1997.
Premiere episode, *Deadwood,* HBO, 2004.

Television Executive Producer; Episodic:
"Transylvania Express," *Tales from the Cryptkeeper* (animated; also known as *New Tales from the Cryptkeeper*), syndicated, 1994.

Television Work; Other:
Director, *Music Videos and Inside "Streets of Fire"* (special), 1984.
Executive producer, *W.E.I.R.D. World* (movie), Fox, 1995.

Television Appearances; Specials:
The 56th Annual Primetime Emmy Awards, 2004.
Broken Trail: The Making of a Legendary Western, 2006.

RECORDINGS

Videos:
(In archive footage) *East Meets West: "Red Heat" and the Kings of Carolco,* Lions Gate Films, 2004.
The Warriors: The Phenomenon, Paramount Home Video, 2005.
Commemoration: Howard Hawks' "Rio Bravo," Sparkhill Production, 2007.

Directed music videos related to the 1984 film *Streets of Fire.*

WRITINGS

Screenplays:
The Getaway (based on novel by Jim Thompson), National General, 1972.
Hickey & Boggs, United Artists, 1972.
The MacKintosh Man, Warner Bros., 1973.
The Thief Who Came to Dinner, Warner Bros., 1973.
(With Tracy Keenan Wynn and Lorenzo Semple, Jr.) *The Drowning Pool* (based on novel by Ross Macdonald), Warner Bros., 1975.
(With Bruce Henstell and Bryan Gindorff) *Hard Times* (also known as *The Streetfighter*), Columbia, 1975.
The Driver, Twentieth Century–Fox, 1978.
Alien, Twentieth Century–Fox, 1979.
(Uncredited) *The Long Riders,* United Artists, 1980.
(With David Shaber) *The Warriors* (based on novel by Sol Yurick and *Anabasis* by Xenophon), Paramount, 1980.
(With Michael Kane and David Giler) *Southern Comfort,* Twentieth Century–Fox, 1981.
(With Larry Gross, Roger Spottiswoode, and Steven E. De Souza) *48 Hrs.* (also known as *48 Hours*), Paramount, 1982.
(With Gross) *Streets of Fire,* Universal, 1984.

(With Lukas Heller) *Blue City* (based on novel by Ross Macdonald), Paramount, 1986.
(With Harry Kleiner and Troy Kennedy Martin) *Red Heat* (also based on story by Hill), TriStar, 1988.
(With Giler and Larry Ferguson) *Alien3* (also known as *Alien III;* based on story by Vincent Ward), Twentieth Century–Fox, 1992.
The Getaway (remake of his 1972 film *The Getaway*), Universal, 1994.
Wild Bill (based on the play *Fathers and Sons* by Thomas Babe), Metro–Goldwyn–Mayer, 1995.
Last Man Standing (also known as *Gundown* and *Welcome to Jericho;* based on the film *Yojimbo*), New Line Cinema, 1996.
Undisputed (also known as *Undisputed—Sieg ohne ruhm*), Miramax, 2002.

Also wrote *The Last Good Kiss* and two educational films for high schools.

Television Episodes:
(With Robert Reneau) "The Man Who Was Death," *Tales from the Crypt* (also known as *HBO's Tales from the Crypt*), HBO, 1989.
(With others) "Cutting Cards," *Tales from the Crypt* (also known as *HBO's Tales from the Crypt*), HBO, 1990.
(With Mae Woods and William M. Gaines) "Deadline" (based on the comic magazine Shock SuspenStories), *Tales from the Crypt* (also known as *HBO's Tales from the Crypt*), HBO, 1991.

Television Pilots:
Dog and Cat, ABC, 1977.

Other:
Author of magazine articles and short stories.

ADAPTATIONS

The 1986 film *Aliens* was based on a story by Hill; the 1990 film *Another 48 Hrs.* was based on characters created by Hill.

OTHER SOURCES

Books:
Contemporary Authors, Volume 140, Gale, 1993.
Dictionary of Literary Biography, Volume 44: *American Screenwriters,* Second Series, Gale, 1986.
International Dictionary of Films and Filmmakers, Volume 2: *Directors,* 4th edition, St. James Press, 2000.

Periodicals:

Atlantic Monthly, December, 1995, p. 120.
Films and Filming, October, 1984, pp. 17–19.
Film Comment, May/June, 1980; March/April, 1983, pp. 9–18.

HILTON–JACOBS, Lawrence 1953–
(Lawrence Hilton–Jacobs, Lawrence Hilton–Jacques, Lawrence–Hilton Jacobs)

PERSONAL

Born September 4, 1953, in New York, NY; son of Hilton and Clothilda Jacobs. *Education:* Studied at Al Fann's Theatrical School and with Negro Ensemble Company, New York City. *Avocational Interests:* Piano, singing.

Addresses: *Agent*—Ethan Salter, Henderson Hogan Agency, 8929 Wilshire Blvd., Suite 312, Beverly Hills, CA 90211.

Career: Actor, director, writer, and composer. Appeared in commercials for Ames, 1999, Sony Walkman, 2001, Cingular Wireless service, 2003, and other products. Also worked as delivery person, florist, messenger, stock person, and freelance artist and package designer.

Awards, Honors: Image Award nomination, outstanding lead actor in a drama series, miniseries, or television movie, National Association for the Advancement of Colored People, 1993, for *The Jacksons: An American Dream;* Anniversary Award (with others), TV Land Awards, 2007, for *Roots.*

CREDITS

Film Appearances:
(Uncredited) Mugger, *Death Wish,* Paramount, 1974.
(Uncredited) Boy playing street basketball, *The Gambler,* 1974.
(As Lawrence Hilton–Jacques) Charles, *Claudine,* Twentieth Century–Fox, 1974.
Richard "Cochise" Morris, *Cooley High,* American International Pictures, 1975.
Rommel, *Youngblood,* American International Pictures, 1978.
Garrett Floyd, *The Annihilators* (also known as *Action Force),* New World, 1985.
Blade Runner, *Paramedics,* Crow Productions, 1987, Vestron Pictures, 1988.
Detective Jon Chance, *L.A. Vice* (also known as *L.A. Heat),* PM Entertainment Group, 1989.

(As Lawrence–Hilton Jacobs) Chesare, *Guerrero del este de Los Angeles* (also known as *East L.A. Warriors),* Peliculas Cinemax, 1989.
Rubin, *Kill Crazy,* Media Home Entertainment, 1990.
(As Lawrence–Hilton Jacobs) Jon Chance, *Chance,* PM Entertainment Group, 1990.
(As Lawrence–Hilton Jacobs) Detective Jon Chance, *Angels of the City,* Raedon, 1990.
Jesse Palmer, *Quiet Fire,* 1991.
Lou Parsons, *Indecent Behavior,* WEA Video, 1993.
Druilet, *Tuesday Never Comes,* 3 Star, 1993.
(As Lawrence–Hilton Jacobs) *Mr. Right Now!,* 1999.
(As Lawrence Hilton Jacobs) Motherchild, *Southlander: Diary of a Desperate Musician* (also known as *Southlander),* Propaganda Films, 2001.
Hip, Edgy, Sexy, Cool, 2002.
The Streetsweeper, Hillcrest Entertainment, 2002.
Mr. Fly, *Killer Drag Queens on Dope,* Singa Home Entertainment, 2004.
(As Lawrence–Hilton Jacobs) Anthony, *30 Miles,* Madacy Entertainment, 2005.
(As Lawrence–Hilton Jacobs) Ross, *Don't Give Me the Finger* (short film), Vanguard International Cinema, 2005.
(As Lawrence–Hilton Jacobs) Mandingo, *Sublime,* Warner Bros., 2007.
Orderly, *Otis,* Warner Bros., 2008.
Mr. Walker, *Tamales and Gumbo,* Colored Wind Productions/Stelly Entertainment, 2008.
Chief, *Strawberries for the Homeless,* Colored Wind Productions/Stelly Entertainment, 2009.
Himself, *Directors on Directing,* 2009.

Film Work:
(As Lawrence Hilton Jacobs) Associate producer, *L.A. Heat,* PM Video, 1989.
(As Lawrence–Hilton Jacobs) Director, *Angels of the City,* Raedon, 1990.
Director, *Sweetfire,* 1991.
Director, *Quiet Fire,* 1991.
(As Lawrence Hilton Jacobs) Associate producer, *Directors on Directing,* 2009.

Television Series:
(As Lawrence–Hilton Jacobs) Frederick Percy "Boom–Boom" Washington, *Welcome Back, Kotter,* ABC, 1975–79.
Lucky Washington, *Rituals,* 1985.
Sergeant Dobbs, a recurring role, *Alien Nation,* Fox, 1989.

Television Miniseries:
Noah, *Roots* (also known as *Alex Haley's "Roots"),* ABC, 1977.
Joseph Jackson, *The Jacksons: An American Dream,* ABC, 1992.
The 100 Greatest TV Quotes and Catchphrases, TV Land, 2006.

Television Appearances; Movies:
Russell Dodd, *The Comedy Company*, CBS, 1978.
Al Leon, *For the Love of It*, ABC, 1980.
(As Lawrence Hilton Jacobs) Marlan Clark, *Tidal Wave: No Escape*, ABC, 1997.

Also appeared a film titled *The Sojourner*.

Television Appearances; Specials:
ABC team member, *Battle of the Network Stars II*, ABC, 1977.
Welcome Back Kotter: The E! True Hollywood Story, E! Entertainment Television, 2000.
TV Guide's Truth Behind the Sitcom Scandals 5, Fox, 2000.
ABC's 50th Anniversary Celebration, ABC, 2003.

Television Appearances; Pilots:
Komedy Tonite, NBC, 1978.
Sergeant Dobbs, *Alien Nation*, Fox, 1989.

Television Appearances; Episodic:
Donny and Marie (also known as *The Osmond Family Show*), 1976.
Premiere episode, *The Captain and Tennille*, 1976.
Dave Rich, "Can't Win for Losin'," *Baretta*, ABC, 1976.
Soul Train, 1978.
Bandstand (also known as *AB* and *American Bandstand*), 1978.
Thomas Sims, "Dear John," *Paris*, CBS, 1979.
(As Lawrence–Hilton Jacobs) Wes Carter, "The Price of Anger," *Barnaby Jones*, CBS, 1980.
Young man/pimp, "Needlepoint," *Darkroom*, ABC, 1981.
"The Uptight End," *Lewis & Clark*, 1981.
Theodus Nickerson, "Grace under Pressure," *Hill Street Blues*, NBC, 1984.
Contestant, *The Star Games*, 1985.
"Love and Video Dating/Love at the Bus Stop," *New Love, American Style*, ABC, 1986.
(As Lawrence–Hilton Jacobs) Gordon Tate, "The Blue Chip Stomp," *Simon & Simon*, CBS, 1986.
Lamar, "The Inheritance," *Fame*, syndicated, 1986.
Warren, "The Good Samaritan," *The Redd Foxx Show*, 1986.
Ebony/Jet Showcase, 1986.
Crumley, "The Cookie Crumbles," *Hill Street Blues*, NBC, 1987.
Rocky, "The Trial of Reno Raines," *Renegade*, USA Network and syndicated, 1994.
Rocky, "Escape," *Renegade*, USA Network and syndicated, 1994.
Joe Neal, "Take the Points," *Pointman*, syndicated, 1995.
Kevin Jones, "Swing Thing," *Martin*, Fox, 1995.
Sergeant Baker, "All–American Murder," *Diagnosis Murder*, CBS, 1995.

Charlie Grace, ABC, 1995.
Greg Harvey, "Torn between Two Brothers," *The Parent 'Hood*, The WB, 1996.
Staff, "Superbad Foxy Lady Killer or Ty and Morris Get the Shaft," *Homeboys in Outer Space*, UPN, 1996.
Phil, "Dead Man Sliding," *Sliders*, Fox, 1996.
Louis, "Roseambo," *Roseanne*, ABC, 1996.
(As Lawrence Hilton Jacobs) Himself, "A Penney Saved ...," *Ellen* (also known as *These Friends of Mine*), ABC, 1996.
(As Lawrence–Hilton Jacobs) Mr. Black, "Boys on the Hide," *Weird Science*, USA Network, 1997.
Freddy "Boom–Boom" Washington, "The Welcome Back Show," *Mr. Rhodes*, NBC, 1997.
James, "Race Relations," *Tracey Takes On ...*, HBO, 1997.
(As Lawrence–Hilton Jacobs) Rushion Brooks, "Cold Busted," *Moesha*, UPN, 1997.
(As Lawrence–Hilton Jacobs) Rushion Brooks, "Break It Down," *Moesha*, UPN, 1997.
Richie, "Help a Brother Out," *The Wayans Bros.*, The WB, 1998.
Robert Edwards, "A Prayer for the Lying," *L.A. Doctors* (also known as *L.A. Docs*), CBS, 1998.
Milton, "Rollin' in the Dough," *The Jamie Foxx Show*, The WB, 2000.
(As Lawrence–Hilton Jacobs) Principal Merton, "Teach Me Tonight," *Gilmore Girls* (also known as *Gilmore Girls: Beginnings*), The WB, 2002.
Voice of diver, "Sunspots," *Static Shock*, The WB, 2002.
Principal Merton, "Keg! Max!," *Gilmore Girls* (also known as *Gilmore Girls: Beginnings*), The WB, 2003.
Leonard James, "New York Bound," *Girlfriends*, UPN, 2004.
Mr. Carter, "There Goes the Bride," *That's So Raven!*, The Disney Channel, 2004.
Interviewee, "Oddballs & Original Characters," *TV Land Confidential* (also known as *TV Land Confidential: The Untold Stories*), TV Land, 2007.
"Finales," *TV Land Confidential* (also known as *TV Land Confidential: The Untold Stories*), TV Land, 2007.
The Singing Bee, 2007.

Television Appearances; Awards Presentations:
The 19th Annual TV Week Logie Awards, 1977.
The 5th Annual TV Land Awards, TV Land, 2007.

Stage Appearances:
Appeared in *I Love My Wife*, Broadway production; and in productions of *Cora's Second Cousin*, *The Dean*, *The Exterminator*, *Mask in Black*, and *What the Wine Sellers Buy*.

RECORDINGS

Videos:
(As Lawrence–Hilton Jacobs) *Remembering "Roots,"* Warner Home Video, 2002.

WRITINGS

Screenplays:

(As Lawrence Hilton Jacobs) Contributor of dialogue, *L.A. Heat,* PM Video, 1989.

Chance, PM Entertainment Group, 1990.

(As Lawrence–Hilton Jacobs; and music composer) *Angels of the City,* Raedon, 1990.

HOBBY, James
 See **NAPIER, James**

HOLBROOK, Hal 1925–
 (Harold Holbrook)

PERSONAL

Full name, Harold Rowe Holbrook, Jr.; born February 17, 1925, in Cleveland, OH; son of Harold Rowe, Sr., and Aileen (a vaudeville dancer; maiden name, Davenport) Holbrook; married Ruby Elaine Johnston (an actress), September 22, 1945 (divorced, 1965); married Carol Eve Rossen (an actress), December 28, 1966 (divorced, 1979); married Dixie Carter (an actress and singer), May 27, 1984; children: (first marriage) Victoria, David; (second marriage) Eve (an actress). *Education:* Denison University, B.A. (with honors), 1948; trained for the stage with Uta Hagen at Herbert Berghof Studios, 1953.

Addresses: *Agent*—Abrams Artists Agency, 9200 Sunset Blvd., Suite 1130, Los Angeles, CA 90069; Cunningham, Escott, Dipene, and Associates, 10635 Santa Monica Blvd., Suite 140, Los Angeles, CA 90025.

Career: Actor. Performed as a singer, 1956–58. Appeared in television commercials, including Allstate insurance, Real Yellow Pages, Zephyrhills bottled water, and Restore America; hosted infomercials, including Fisher Investments, 2005. National Council on Arts and Government, committee member; also member of Commission on International Cultural Exchange. *Military service:* U.S. Army, Corps of Engineers, 1943–46.

Member: International Platform Association, Actors' Equity Association, American Federation of Television and Radio Artists, Screen Actors Guild, Mark Twain Memorial Association, Players Club (New York City), Lambs Club.

Awards, Honors: Vernon Rice Drama Desk Award, Obie Award, *Village Voice,* and Outer Critics Circle Award, all c. 1959, special citation, New York Drama

Critics Circle, and Antoinette Perry Award, best dramatic actor, both 1966, and Emmy Award nomination, best actor in a single dramatic performance, 1967, all for *Mark Twain Tonight!;* Grammy Award nomination, outstanding documentary or spoken word recording, National Academy of Recording Arts and Sciences, 1959, for *Mark Twain Tonight!;* Grammy Award nomination, best documentary or spoken word recording, 1961, for *More of Hal Holbrook in Mark Twain Tonight!;* Grammy Award nomination, best spoken word, documentary, or drama recording, 1967, for *Mark Twain Tonight! Vol. 3;* Emmy Award nomination, outstanding supporting actor in a single performance, 1969, for *The Whole World Is Watching;* Emmy Award nomination, outstanding actor in a single performance, 1971, for *A Clear and Present Danger;* Emmy Award, outstanding actor in a drama series, 1971, for *The Bold Ones;* Golden Apple, male star of the year, Hollywood Women's Press Club, 1971; Torch of Liberty Award, Anti–Defamation League of B'nai B'rith, 1972, and Emmy Award nomination, outstanding actor in a single performance, 1973, both for *That Certain Summer;* Emmy awards, outstanding lead actor in comedy or drama special and actor of the year, both 1974, for "Pueblo," *ABC Theatre;* Emmy Award, outstanding lead actor in a limited series, 1976, for *Sandburg's Lincoln;* Emmy Award nomination, outstanding lead actor in a drama or comedy or special, 1978, for *Our Town;* Emmy Award nomination, outstanding lead actor in a limited series, 1978, for *The Awakening Land;* Emmy Award, outstanding performer in informational programming, 1988, for "New York City," *Portrait of America;* Emmy Award, outstanding individual achievement in informational programming, 1989, for "Alaska," *Portrait of America;* Annual CableACE Award, best informational or documentary host, National Cable Television Association, 1998, for *Portrait of America;* William Shakespeare Award for Classical Theatre, Shakespeare Theatre, Washington, DC, 1998; Theatre Hall of Fame, inductee, 2000; Academy Award nomination, best performance by an actor in a supporting role, Critics Choice Award nomination, best supporting actor, Broadcast Film Critics Association, Online Film Critics Association Award nomination, best supporting actor, Screen Actors Guild Award nomination, outstanding performance by a male actor in a supporting role, Screen Actors Guild Award nomination (with others), outstanding performance by a cast in a motion picture, 2008, all for *Into the Wild;* Special Jury Award (with others), best ensemble cast, SxSW Film Festival, 2009, for *That Evening Sun;* also received honorary degrees, including D.Arts, Kenyon College, and D.H.L., Denison University and Ohio State University, all 1979.

CREDITS

Stage Appearances:

Title role, *Mark Twain Tonight!* (solo show), Lock Haven State Teachers College, Lock Haven, PA,

1954, then (off–Broadway debut), 41st Street Theatre, 1959, later Longacre Theatre, New York City, 1966.

The Doctor in Spite of Himself, Westport Country Playhouse, Westport, CT, 1958.

(Broadway debut) Young man, *Do You Know the Milky Way?,* Billy Rose Theatre, 1961.

John of Gaunt, *Richard III,* American Shakespeare Festival, Stratford, CT, 1962.

Hotspur, *Henry IV, Part I,* American Shakespeare Festival, 1962.

Title role, *Abraham Lincoln in Illinois,* Phoenix Theatre Company, Anderson Theatre, New York City, 1963.

Reverend Harley Barnes, then Quentin, *After the Fall,* Repertory Theatre of Lincoln Center, American National Theatre and Academy, Washington Square Theatre, New York City, 1964.

Major, *Incident at Vichy,* Repertory Theatre of Lincoln Center, American National Theatre and Academy, Washington Square Theatre, 1964–65.

Marco Polo, *Marco Millions,* Repertory Theatre of Lincoln Center, American National Theatre and Academy, Washington Square Theatre, 1965.

M. Loyal and narrator of prologue, *Tartuffe,* Repertory Theatre of Lincoln Center, American National Theatre and Academy, Washington Square Theatre, 1965.

Jim O'Connor, *The Glass Menagerie,* Brooks Atkinson Theatre, New York City, 1965.

Adam, Captain Sanjar, and Prince Charming, *The Apple Tree* (musical), Shubert Theatre, New York City, 1966–67.

Gene Garrison, *I Never Sang for My Father,* Longacre Theatre, 1968.

Don Quixote (Cervantes), *Man of La Mancha* (musical), Martin Beck Theatre, New York City, 1968.

Mr. Winters, *Does a Tiger Wear a Necktie?,* Belasco Theatre, New York City, 1969.

Winnebago, *Lake of the Woods,* American Place Theatre, New York City, 1971.

Jake K. Bowsky, *Buried Inside Extra,* New York Shakespeare Festival, Martinson Hall, Public Theatre, New York City, then produced in London, both 1983.

Frank Elgin, *The Country Girl,* Chelsea Playhouse, New York City, 1984.

Title role, *King Lear,* Great Lakes Theatre Festival, Cleveland, OH, 1990, then Roundabout Theatre Company, New York City, 1990–91.

Willy Loman, *Death of a Salesman,* Orpheum Theatre, Memphis, TN, 1996.

Senator Alan Hughes, *An American Daughter,* Cort Theatre, New York City, 1997.

A Life in the Theatre, Pasadena Playhouse, Pasadena, CA, 2001.

Mark Twain Tonight, Brooks Atkinson Theatre, New York City, 2005.

Also appeared in summer stock, 1947–53; appeared in regional productions of *The Merchant of Venice, Our Town,* and *Uncle Vanya.*

Major Tours:

Title role, *Mark Twain Tonight!,* U.S. cities, 1954–59, then U.S., European, and Saudi Arabian cities, 1959–61, and U.S. cities, intermittently, 1962—.

Andrew Mackerel, *The Mackerel Plaza,* U.S. cities, 1963.

King Arthur, *Camelot,* U.S. cities, 1969.

Also performed scenes from classic plays with Ruby Johnston Holbrook, southwestern U.S. cities, between 1947 and 1953.

Film Appearances:

(Film debut) Gus Leroy, *The Group,* United Artists, 1966.

Senator John Fergus, *Wild in the Streets,* American International Pictures, 1968.

Cameron, *The Great White Hope,* Twentieth Century–Fox, 1970.

David Hoffman, *The People Next Door,* Avco Embassy, 1970.

Dr. Warren Watkins, *They Only Kill Their Masters,* Metro–Goldwyn–Mayer, 1972.

Voice of elder, *Jonathan Livingston Seagull,* Paramount, 1973.

Lieutenant Briggs, *Magnum Force,* Warner Bros., 1973.

Joe, *The Girl from Petrovka,* Universal, 1974.

Deep Throat, *All the President's Men,* Warner Bros., 1976.

Commander Joseph J. Rochefort, Jr., *Midway* (also known as *The Battle of Midway* and *Battle of Midway*), Universal, 1976.

Harry, *Rituals* (also known as *The Creeper* and *Ils etait cinq*), Coast, 1977.

Alan Campbell, *Julia,* Twentieth Century–Fox, 1977.

Dr. James Kelloway, *Capricorn One,* Warner Bros., 1978.

Paul Steward, *Natural Enemies* (also known as *Hidden Thoughts*), Cinema V, 1979.

Father Malone, *The Fog* (also known as *John Carpenter's "The Fog"*), Avco Embassy, 1980.

President Adam Scott, *The Kidnapping of the President,* Crown International, 1980.

Jim MacVey, *Girls Nite Out* (also known as *Girls Night Out* and *The Scaremaker*), Aries, 1982.

Henry Northrup, "The Crate," *Creepshow* (also known as *Cuentos de ultratumba* and *Stephen King's "Creepshow"*), Warner Bros., 1982.

Judge Benjamin Caulfield, *The Star Chamber,* Twentieth Century–Fox, 1983.

Lou Mannheim, *Wall Street,* Twentieth Century–Fox, 1987.

Archbishop Mosely, *The Unholy,* Vestron, 1988.

Hamilton "Ham" Johnson, *Fletch Lives,* Universal, 1989.

Oliver Lambert, *The Firm,* Paramount, 1993.

Narrator, *Stormchasers,* 1995.

Dr. Evans, *Carried Away* (also known as *Acts of Love*), New Line Cinema, 1996.

Voice of Cranston, *Cats Don't Dance* (animated), Warner Bros., 1997.

Voice of Amphitryon, *Hercules* (animated), Buena Vista, 1997.

Sheriff Sam Rogers, *Eye of God* (also known as *Beyond Obsessions*), Peachtree Entertainment, 1997.

Henshaw, *Operation Delta Force*, Live Entertainment, 1997.

Dr. Franklin Hill, *Hush*, TriStar, 1998.

Boyd Callahan, *Rusty: The Great Rescue* (also known as *Rusty* and *Rusty: A Dog's Tale*), 1998.

Isaac Green, *Waking the Dead*, Gramercy, 1999.

Man on the beach, *Walking to the Waterline*, Porchlight Entertainment, 1999.

Smitty, *The Florentine*, Bcb Productions, Inc., 1999.

O'Dell, *The Bachelor*, New Line Cinema, 1999.

Captain "Mr. Pappy," *Men of Honor* (also known as *Men of Honour*), Twentieth Century–Fox, 2000.

Voice of Ak, Master Woodsman of the World, *The Life & Adventures of Santa Claus* (animated), Universal Studios Home Video, 2000.

Congressman T. Johnston Doyle, *The Majestic*, Warner Bros., 2001.

Himself, *"Dirty Harry": The Original*, 2001.

Tom Walker, *Purpose*, Lakeshore Entertainment, 2002.

The professor, *Shade*, RKO Radio Pictures, 2003.

Narrator, *Our Country* (short documentary), Giant Screen Films, 2003.

Narrator, *Woodward and Bernstein: Lighting the Fire* (short documentary), Warner Home Video, 2006.

Narrator, *Telling the Truth about Lies: The Making of "All the President's Men"* (short documentary), Warner Home Video, 2006.

Narrator, *Out of the Shadows: The Man Who Was Deep Throat* (short documentary), Warner Home Video, 2006.

Ron Franz, *Into the Wild*, Paramount Vantage, 2007.

Narrator, *Silent Wings: The American Glider Pilots of World War II* (documentary), Inacom Entertainment Company, 2007.

Papa, *Killshot*, Third Rail Releasing, 2008.

Himself, *The Evolution of Clint Eastwood* (short documentary), Warner Home Video, 2008.

Himself, *The Long Shadow of "Dirty Harry"* (short documentary), 2008.

Himself, *A Moral Right: The Politics of Dirty Harry* (short documentary), Warner Home Video, 2008.

Himself, *"Into the Wild": The Experience* (short film), Paramount Home Entertainment, 2008.

Himself, *"Into the Wild": The Story, the Characters* (short film), Paramount Home Entertainment, 2008.

Abner Meecham, *That Evening Sun*, Freestyle Releasing, 2009.

Flying Lessons, 2010.

Hec, *Good Day for It*, 2010.

Also appeared in *Final Clue*.

Television Appearances; Series:

(Television debut) Grayling Dennis, *Hollywood Screen Test*, ABC, 1953.

Grayling Dennis, *The Brighter Day*, CBS, 1954–59.

Senator Hays Stowe, *The Bold Ones* (also known as *The Bold Ones: The Senator* and *The Senator*), NBC, 1970–71.

Host, *Great Performances: Theatre in America* (also known as *Theatre in America*), PBS, 1974–76.

Host, *Omnibus*, ABC, 1980–81.

Host, *Portrait of America*, TBS, 1983–88.

Reese Watson, *Designing Women*, CBS, 1986–89.

Evan Evans, *Evening Shade* (also known as *Arkansas*), CBS, 1990–94.

Voice of Amphitryon, *Hercules* (animated; also known as *Disney's "Hercules"*), syndicated, 1998.

Television Appearances; Miniseries:

Abraham Lincoln, *Sandburg's "Lincoln"* (also known as *Lincoln*), NBC, 1974.

Portius Wheeler, *The Awakening Land*, NBC, 1978.

District Attorney Calvin Sledge, *Celebrity* (also known as *Tommy Thompson's "Celebrity"*), NBC, 1984.

John Adams, *George Washington*, CBS, 1984.

Abraham Lincoln, *North and South*, ABC, 1985.

General Charles Hedges, *Dress Gray*, NBC, 1986.

Abraham Lincoln, *North and South, Book II* (also known as *North and South II*), ABC, 1986.

Jonas Coe, *Emma: Queen of the South Seas*, syndicated, 1988.

Dr. Andrew McKaig, *Mario Puzo's "The Fortunate Pilgrim"* (also known as *The Fortunate Pilgrim* and *Mamma Lucia*), NBC, 1988.

Bob Hennis, *Innocent Victims*, ABC, 1996.

Pete, *Ken Follett's "The Third Twin"* (also known as *The Third Twin*), CBS, 1997.

Host, *The Mighty Mississippi*, History Channel, 1998.

Harold L. Ickes, *Haven*, CBS, 2001.

Mark Twain, PBS, 2002.

Television Appearances; Movies:

Mitch Collins, *The Wacky Zoo of Morgan City*, NBC, 1970.

Harlan Webb, *Goodbye Raggedy Ann*, CBS, 1971.

Larry Hackett, *Suddenly Single*, ABC, 1971.

Doug Salter, *That Certain Summer*, ABC, 1972.

Commander Jeremiah A. Denton, Jr., *When Hell Was in Session*, NBC, 1979.

Arthur Sinclair, *Murder by Natural Causes*, CBS, 1979.

Budd Johansen, *Off the Minnesota Strip*, ABC, 1980.

John Webster, *The Killing of Randy Webster*, 1981.

Grandpa Grier, *The Three Wishes of Billy Grier*, ABC, 1984.

President Maxwell Monroe, *Under Siege*, NBC, 1986.

Sam Nash, "Act I," *Plaza Suite*, ABC, 1987.

Joseph Bundy, *I'll Be Home for Christmas* (also known as *A Rockport Christmas*), NBC, 1988.

General George C. Marshall, "Day One" (also known as "Hiroshima"), *AT&T Presents,* CBS, 1989.

Jim Coltrane, *Sorry, Wrong Number,* USA Network, 1989.

Dr. Beardsley, *A Killing in a Small Town* (also known as *Evidence of Love*), CBS, 1990.

Jim Smith, *Bonds of Love,* CBS, 1993.

William "Bill" McKenzie, *A Perry Mason Mystery: The Case of the Lethal Lifestyle* (also known as *A Perry Mason Mystery: The Case of the Famous Fatality*), NBC, 1994.

"Wild Bill" McKenzie, *A Perry Mason Mystery: The Case of the Grimacing Governor,* NBC, 1994.

"Wild Bill" McKenzie, *A Perry Mason Mystery: The Case of the Jealous Jokester,* NBC, 1994.

Admiral Frank Kelso, *She Stood Alone: The Tailhook Scandal,* ABC, 1995.

Uncle Ren Corvin, *All the Winters That Have Been,* CBS, 1997.

Alexander Miller, *Beauty,* CBS, 1998.

Lloyd Flanders, *My Own Country,* Showtime, 1998.

Senator Rupert Hornbeck, *Judas Kiss,* Cinemax, 1998.

Senior partner, *The Street Lawyer,* ABC, 2003.

Dean Davis Winters, *Captain Cook's Extraordinary Atlas,* 2009.

Television Appearances; Specials:

Title role, *Mark Twain Tonight!,* CBS, 1967.

Narrator, *Jane Goodall and the World of Animal Behavior: The Wild Dogs of Africa,* 1973.

Commander Lloyd M. Bucher, "Pueblo," *ABC Theatre,* ABC, 1974.

Narrator, *The Baboons of Combe* (documentary), ABC, 1974.

Narrator, "The Animals Nobody Loved," *National Geographic Specials,* PBS, 1976.

Stage Manager, *Our Town,* NBC, 1977.

(Uncredited) Host, *Secret Service,* 1977.

(Uncredited) Host, *Tartuffe,* 1978.

Narrator, *Willa Cather's America,* PBS, 1978.

Host, *Kennedy Center Tonight: A Salute to Duke* (also known as *A Salute to Duke*), 1981.

Narrator, *The Warlords: Hitler's Master Race—The Mad Dream of the S.S.,* 1981.

Narrator, *Warlords: Rommel—The Strange Death of the Desert Fox,* 1981.

Narrator, "Four Americans in China," *National Geographic Special,* PBS, 1985.

All–Star Party for Clint Eastwood, CBS, 1986.

Narrator, *Adolph Hitler: Portrait of a Tyrant,* HBO, 1987.

Narrator, *Colossus of the Golden Gate,* 1987.

Superman's 50th Anniversary: A Celebration of the Man of Steel (also known as *Superman 50th Anniversary*), CBS, 1988.

The Kennedy Center Honors: A Celebration of the Performing Arts, CBS, 1988.

Freedom Festival '89, CBS, 1989.

Host and narrator, *An American Image,* syndicated, 1989.

The "Designing Woman" Special: Their Finest Hour, CBS, 1990.

Host, *The Secrets of Dick Smith,* 1991.

Host, *Eastwood & Co. Making "Unforgiven"* (also known as *Clint Eastwood on Westerns*), ABC, 1992.

Narrator, *Sailing the World Alone,* PBS, 1996.

Narrator, *The Battle of the Alamo,* The Discovery Channel, 1996.

Narrator, *America on Wheels,* PBS, 1996.

Narrator, *Battleship,* The Discovery Channel, 1997.

Narrator, *Lewis & Clark: The Journey of the Corps of Discovery,* PBS, 1997.

Host and narrator, *Trail of Hope: The Story of the Mormon Trail,* PBS, 1997.

Presenter, *Broadway '97: Launching the Tonys,* PBS, 1997.

Narrator, *Lost in Middle America … and What Happened Next,* PBS, 1999.

Narrator, *A Place Apart,* 1999.

"Outer Limits" Farewell Tribute, Showtime, 2000.

Voice of Benjamin Franklin, *Founding Fathers,* History Channel, 2000.

"Entertainment Tonight" Presents: The Real "Designing Women," 2000.

Intimate Portrait: Dixie Carter, Lifetime, 2001.

AFI's 100 Years, 100 Thrills: America's Most Heart–Pounding Movies, CBS, 2001.

(Uncredited) Himself, *Mark Twain,* 2001.

Narrator, *The Legend of the Three Trees,* 2001.

Voice of Benjamin Franklin, *Founding Brothers,* History Channel, 2002.

CBS at 75, CBS, 2003.

The "Designing Women" Reunion, Lifetime, 2003.

Narrator, *The Cultivated Life: Thomas Jefferson and Wine,* 2005.

Voice of Harrison Grey Otis, *Inventing L.A.: The Chandlers and Their Times* (documentary), PBS, 2009.

Television Appearances; Awards Presentations:

Presenter, *The … Annual Tony Awards,* 1972, 1997, CBS, 2006.

The 11th Annual CableACE Awards, syndicated, Black Entertainment Television, TBS, CNBC, AMC, Bravo, The Family Channel, Nickelodeon, TNT, Lifetime, and CBS, 1990.

Presenter, *The Ninth Annual Soap Opera Awards,* NBC, 1993.

13th Annual Critics' Choice Awards Red Carpet Premiere, 2008.

The 80th Annual Academy Awards, ABC, 2008.

Presenter, *The 14th Annual Screen Actors Guild Awards,* TBS and TNT, 2008.

Television Appearances; Pilots:

Jonathan Murray, "The Cliff Dwellers," *Preview Tonight,* ABC, 1966.

Chancellor Graham, *The Whole World Is Watching,* NBC, 1969.

Hays Stowe, *A Clear and Present Danger,* NBC, 1970.

Matthew Sand, *Travis Logan, D.A.,* CBS, 1971.

Dr. Simon Abbott, *The Oath: 33 Hours in the Life of God* (also known as *33 Hours in the Life of God*), NBC, 1976.

Jim Hammer/J. R. Swackhamer, *The Legend of the Golden Gun,* NBC, 1979.

Colonel Calvin Turner, *Behind Enemy Lines* (also known as *92 Grosvenor Street*), NBC, 1985.

Roy, *Matthew,* CBS, 1998.

Television Appearances; Episodic:

"Late for Supper," *Mr. Citizen,* ABC, 1955.

Mark Twain, *The Tonight Show,* NBC, 1956.

Toast of the Town (also known as *The Ed Sullivan Show*), CBS, 1956.

Mark Twain, *The Sound of Laughter,* NBC, 1958.

I Remember Mama, CBS, 1958.

Abraham Lincoln, *Exploring,* NBC, 1963.

"Abe Lincoln in Illinois," *Discovery* (also known as *Discovery '62* and *Discovery '63*), 1963.

Abraham Lincoln, "Abe Lincoln from Illinois," *Toast of the Town* (also known as *The Ed Sullivan Show*), CBS, 1963.

Mark Twain, *Toast of the Town* (also known as *The Ed Sullivan Show*), CBS, 1966.

Thomas, "Faces," *Coronet Blue,* CBS, 1967.

Tom Wingfield, "The Glass Menagerie," *CBS Playhouse,* CBS, 1966.

Narrator, "Wild World," *Off to See the Wizard,* 1968.

Christopher Simes, "The Fraud," *The F.B.I.,* ABC, 1969.

Mayor John Adrian, "The Perfect Image," *The Name of the Game,* NBC, 1969.

Guest panelist, *What's My Line?,* 1969.

The Tonight Show Starring Johnny Carson (also known as *The Tonight Show*), NBC, 1970.

The Mike Douglas Show, 1970.

He Said, She Said, 1970.

Narrator, "Surrender at Appomattox," *Appointment with Destiny,* 1972.

Host, "Who's Happy Now?," *Great Performances,* PBS, 1975.

(Uncredited) *Saturday Night Live* (also known as *SNL*), NBC, 1978.

New Love American Style, ABC, 1985.

"Love and the Mountain Man," *The New Love, American Style,* ABC, 1986.

"Hugh Morgan Hill," *An American Portrait,* CBS, 1986.

Narrator, "In the Path of a Killer Volcano," *Nova,* PBS, 1992.

Narrator, "Daley, the Last Boss," *The American Experience,* PBS, 1996.

Narrator, "Super Bridge," *Nova,* PBS, 1997.

Justice Ollie Hardison, "Final Appeal: Parts 1 & 2," *The Outer Limits* (also known as *The New Outer Limits*), Showtime and syndicated, 2000.

Judge Richard Lloyd, "One Mistake," *Family Law,* CBS, 2000.

"The Making of 'Men on Honor,'" *HBO First Look,* HBO, 2000.

Himself, "'The Majestic,'" *HBO First Look,* HBO, 2001.

Assistant Secretary of State Albie Duncan, "Gone Quiet," *The West Wing,* NBC, 2001.

Assistant Secretary of State Albie Duncan, "Game On," *The West Wing,* NBC, 2002.

Mr. Humphries, "And the Heartbeat Goes On," *Becker,* CBS, 2002.

Edward Lincoln Shanowski, "A Room of One's Own," *Hope & Faith,* ABC, 2005.

John Schwinn, "The Fleshy Part of the Thigh," *The Sopranos,* HBO, 2006.

Mickey Stokes, "Escaped," *Navy NCIS: Naval Criminal Investigative Service* (also known as *NCIS* and *NCIS: Naval Criminal Investigative Service*), CBS, 2006.

Walter Perkins, "Truth Will Out," *ER,* NBC, 2008.

Walter Perkins, "The Chicago Way," *ER,* NBC, 2008.

Tavis Smiley, PBS, 2008.

Entertainment Tonight (also known as *E.T.*), syndicated, 2008.

"Oscar Nominees Special," *Sunday Morning Shootout* (also known as *Hollywood Shootout* and *Shootout*), AMC, 2008.

Also appeared as himself, "The Films of George A. Romero," *The Directors.*

Television Director; Episodic:

"Ted–Bare," *Designing Women,* CBS, 1988.

"Reservations for Eight," *Designing Women,* CBS, 1988.

"Ms. Meal Ticket," *Designing Women,* CBS, 1989.

"The Fur Lies," *Designing Women,* CBS, 1990.

Radio Appearances:

Army Engineer Show, ABC, 1946.

RECORDINGS

Albums:

Recorded soundtrack albums of his solo shows, including *Mark Twain Tonight!*, *More of Hal Holbrook in Mark Twain Tonight!*, and *Mark Twain Tonight!, Vol. 3.*

WRITINGS

Stage Shows:

Mark Twain Tonight! (solo show), first produced at Lock Haven State Teachers College, Lock Haven, PA, 1954.

Television Specials:
(Uncredited; adaptor) *Mark Twain Tonight!,* CBS, 1967.

OTHER SOURCES

Books:
St. James Encyclopedia of Popular Theatre, St. James Press, 2000.

Periodicals:
Memphis Business Journal, February 5, 1996, p. 23.

HOLLY, Lauren 1963–
  (Holly Lauren)

PERSONAL

Full name, Lauren Michael Holly; born October 28, 1963, in Bristol, PA; daughter of Grant (an English literature professor, producer, and screenwriter) and Michael Ann (an art history professor and administrator) Holly; married Daniele "Danny" Quinn (an actor and producer), 1991 (divorced, 1993); married Jim Carrey (a comedian and actor), September 23, 1996 (divorced, 1998); married Francis Greco (an investment banker), March 11, 2001; children: (third marriage) Alexander Joseph, George, Henry Charles. *Education:* Sarah Lawrence College, B.A., English literature, 1985; also attended London Academy of Music and Dramatic Art.

Addresses: *Agent*—Fortitude, 8619 Washington Blvd., Culver City, CA 90232. *Manager*—Gilbertson Management, 1334 3rd St., Suite 201, Santa Monica, CA 90401.

Career: Actress. Hollycould Productions, cofounder. Appeared in television commercials, including Wesson oil and Cabbage Patch dolls; appeared in informercial for Youthful Essence, 2008.

Awards, Honors: Daytime Emmy Award nomination, best ingenue in a daytime drama series, 1988, *Soap Opera Digest* Award nomination, outstanding daytime heroine, 1989, both for *All My Children;* Q Award, best supporting actress in a quality drama series, Viewers for Quality Television, 1994, Screen Actors Guild Award nominations (with others), outstanding performance by an ensemble in a drama series, 1995, 1996, all for *Picket Fences;* MTV Movie Award (with Jim Carrey), best kiss, 1995, for *Dumb and Dumber;* Golden Satellite Award nomination, best supporting actress in a

miniseries or television movie, International Press Academy, 2002, for *Jackie, Ethel, Joan: The Women of Camelot;* Bronze Wrangler Award (with others), television feature film, Western Heritage Awards, 2003, for *King of Texas.*

CREDITS

Film Appearances:
Lisa, *Seven Minutes in Heaven* (also known as *Deslices de joventud*), Warner Bros., 1986.

Nikki, *Band of the Hand,* TriStar, 1986.

Jazz, *The Adventures of Ford Fairlane,* Twentieth Century–Fox, 1990.

(Uncredited) Suzie Bryant, Channel 7 newsreporter, *Live Wire,* 1992.

Linda Emery Lee, *Dragon: The Bruce Lee Story,* Universal, 1993.

Mary Swanson, *Dumb & Dumber* (also known as *Dumb Happens* and *Dumb and Dumber*), New Line Cinema, 1994.

Elizabeth Tyson, *Sabrina,* Paramount, 1995.

Darian Smalls, *Beautiful Girls,* Miramax, 1996.

Lieutenant Emily Lake, *Down Periscope,* Twentieth Century–Fox, 1996.

Jennifer Robertson, *A Smile Like Yours,* Paramount, 1997.

Teri Halloran, *Turbulence,* Metro–Goldwyn–Mayer, 1997.

Claudia, *No Looking Back,* Gramercy, 1998.

Claire, *Entropy* (also known as *Entrophy*), Interlight/Phoenician Entertainment/Tribeca Productions, 1999.

Cindy Rooney, *Any Given Sunday,* Warner Bros., 1999.

Gigi, *What Women Want,* Paramount, 2000.

Frances Chadway, *The Last Producer* (also known as *The Final Hit*), 2000.

(English version) Voice of Chihiro's mother, *Sen to Chihiro no kamikakushi* (animated; also known as *Miyazaki's "Spirited Away," Sen, Sen and the Mysterious Disappearance of Chihiro, Spirited Away,* and *The Spiriting Away of Sen and Chihiro*), Buena Vista, 2002.

Amber Connors, *Changing Hearts,* Porchlight Entertainment, 2002.

Buckley Clarke, *Pavement* (also known as *Die Spur des morders*), Motion Picture Corp. of America, 2002.

Rachel Purdy, *Counting Sheep,* Oregon Creative/Rubicon Film Productions, 2002.

Ms. Travers, *In Enemy Hands* (also known as *U–Boat*), Lions Gate Films Home Entertainment, 2003.

Herself, *The Art of "Spirited Away"* (short documentary), Buena Vista Home Video, 2003.

Daphne Widesecker, *The Pleasure Drivers,* Anchor Bay Entertainment, 2005.

Boutique owner, *The Chumscrubber* (also known as *Gluck in kleinen dosen*), Newmarket Films, 2005.

Kim Davis, *Down and Derby* (also known as *Racing Ace*), Freestyle Releasing, 2005.

Molly Mahoney, *The Godfather of Green Bay*, Blue Moon Pictures, 2005.

Maggie Davidson, *Fatwa* (also known as *Days of Terror*), 2006.

Rachel Purdy, *Raising Flagg*, Cinema Libre Studio, 2006.

Marilyn, *Chasing 3000*, 2008.

Kate Allison, *The Least among You*, 2009.

(Uncredited) Psychiatrist, *Crank: High Voltage* (also known as *Crank 2*, *Crank: High Voltage—Fully Charged*, and *High Voltage*), Lions Gate Films, 2009.

Liza Genson, *The Perfect Age of Rock 'n' Roll*, 2009.

Gillian, *Final Storm*, Event Film Distribution, 2009.

Audrey Valentine, *You're So Cupid!*, SunWorld Pictures, 2010.

Television Appearances; Series:

Julie Rand Chandler, *All My Children* (also known as *AMC*), ABC, 1986–89.

Kate Ward, *The Antagonists*, CBS, 1991.

Maxine "Max" Stewart Lacos, *Picket Fences*, CBS, 1992–96.

Dr. Jeremy Hanlon, *Chicago Hope*, CBS, 1999–2000.

NCIS Director Jenny Shepard, *Navy NCIS: Naval Criminal Investigative Service* (also known as *NCIS* and *NCIS: Naval Criminal Investigative Service*), CBS, 2005–2008.

Television Appearances; Miniseries:

Ethel Skakel Kennedy, *Jackie, Ethel, Joan: The Women of Camelot* (also known as *Jackie, Ethel, Joan: The Kennedy Women*), NBC, 2001.

Television Appearances; Movies:

Tracy, *Love Lives On*, ABC, 1985.

Stacey Munger, *Blind Justice*, CBS, 1986.

Betty Copper, *Archie: To Riverdale and Back Again* (also known as *Archie: Return to Riverdale* and *Weekend Reunion*), NBC, 1990.

Suzie Bryant, *Fugitive Among Us*, CBS, 1992.

Carol, *Dangerous Heart*, USA Network, 1994.

Marybeth, *Vig* (also known as *Money Kings*), Cinemax, 1998.

Frances Chadway, *The Last Producer* (also known as *The Final Hit*), USA Network, 2000.

Mrs. Rebecca Lear Highsmith, *King of Texas* (also known as *Boss Lear*), TNT, 2002.

James' wife, *Living with the Dead* (also known as *Talking to Heaven*), 2002.

Susan, *Santa, Jr.*, Hallmark Channel, 2002.

Grace Carpenter, *Just Desserts*, Hallmark Channel, 2004.

Jodie Colter, *Caught in the Act* (also known as *Mind of the Crime*), Lifetime, 2004.

Mary, *Before You Say "I Do,"* Hallmark Channel, 2009.

Heather, *Too Late to Say Goodbye*, Lifetime, 2009.

Television Appearances; Specials:

Presenter, *The American Television Awards*, ABC, 1993.

The Golden Globe's 50th Anniversary Celebration, NBC, 1994.

Presenter, *The 22nd Annual People's Choice Awards*, CBS, 1996.

Comedy Central Spotlight: Kelsey Grammar, Comedy Central, 1996.

Presenter, *A Home for the Holidays*, CBS, 2003.

The 2005 Radio Music Awards, NBC, 2005.

Television Appearances; Pilots:

Exwife, *Fourplay*, CBS, 2000.

Wife, *Destiny*, CBS, 2001.

Title role, *Libby Montana*, Lifetime, 2003.

Tess, *Bounty Hunters*, 2005.

Television Appearances; Episodic:

(As Holly Lauren) Carla Walicki, "Ewe and Me, Babe," *Hill Street Blues*, 1984.

(As Holly Lauren) Carla Walicki, "Last Chance Salon," *Hill Street Blues*, 1984.

Emily Brown, "Home Is the Hero," *Spencer: For Hire*, ABC, 1986.

Allison Novack, "To Thine Own Elf Be True," *My Two Dads*, 1990.

Allison Novack, "See You in September?," *My Two Dads*, 1990.

Heather Finn, "The Real Thing," *Fantasy Island*, ABC, 1998.

Laura, "The Buddy System," *Becker*, CBS, 2001.

Darla Rosario, "The Heart of the Matter," *Providence*, NBC, 2002.

Hayley Wilson, "Grand Prix," *CSI: Miami*, CBS, 2003.

Cold Pizza, ESPN2, 2004.

Corazon de ..., 2007.

Loose Women, ITV, 2007.

Entertainment Tonight (also known as *ET*), syndicated, 2007.

Anime: Drawing a Revolution, Starz!, 2007.

Ms. Earnshaw, "The Juror #6 Job," *Leverage*, TNT, 2009.

Television Talk Show Guest Appearances; Episodic:

Late Show with David Letterman (also known as *Letterman* and *The Late Show*), CBS, 1993.

The Howard Stern Show, 1997.

The Rosie O'Donnell Show, syndicated, 1997, 1998, 1999, 2001, 2002.

The Tonight Show with Jay Leno (also known as *Jay Leno*), NBC, 1998, 2001.

Late Night with Conan O'Brien, NBC, 1999.

The Late Late Show with Craig Kilborn (also known as *The Late Late Show*), CBS, 2002, 2004.

The Wayne Brady Show, syndicated, 2004.

Last Call with Carson Daly, NBC, 2004.
On–Air with Ryan Seacrest, syndicated, 2004.
The Sharon Osbourne Show (also known as *Sharon*), syndicated, 2004.
Jimmy Kimmel Live! (also known as *Jimmy Kimmel*), ABC, 2005, 2006.
The Late Late Show with Craig Ferguson, CBS, 2006.
The Megan Mullally Show, syndicated, 2006.

Television Executive Producer; Movies:
Caught in the Act (also known as *Mind of the Crime*), Lifetime, 2004.

RECORDINGS

Music Videos:
Appeared in "Graduation Day" by Chris Isaak, 1996; "Earl Had to Die" by Dixie Chicks, 2000.

OTHER SOURCES

Periodicals:
Cosmopolitan, December, 1995, p. 96.
Entertainment Weekly, June 30, 1995, p. 31.
In Style, April, 2000, p. 320.
Movieline, November, 1995, pp. 46, 48–50, 85.
People Weekly, May 31, 1993; March 20, 2006, p. 185.
TV Guide, February 17, 1996, pp. 7–8; November 2, 2002, p. 8.
US, January, 1998.

Electronic:
Lauren Holly Official Site, http://www.laurenholly.com, February 9, 2010.

HOOPER, Tobe 1943–

PERSONAL

Full name, William Tobe Hooper; born January 25, 1943, in Austin, TX; son of Norman W. R. and Lois (maiden name, Crosby) Hooper; companion of Marcia Zwilling (a television executive); children: William (a sound editor), Tony. *Education:* Studied film at University of Texas at Austin.

Addresses: *Office*—TH Nightmares, PO Box 7400, Studio City, CA 91614. *Agent*—Gersh, 9465 Wilshire Blvd., 6th Floor, Beverly Hills, CA 90212. *Manager*—Evolution Entertainment, 901 North Highland Ave., Los Angeles, CA 90038.

Career: Producer, director, writer, composer, and actor. Amberson Films, partner and director; TH Nightmares, Studio City, CA, partner. Also director of music videos and television commercials. Horror Hall of Fame, member of board of directors. University of Texas at Austin, former assistant director of film program.

Awards, Honors: Critics Award, Avoriaz Fantastic Film Festival, 1976, for *The Texas Chainsaw Massacre*; Saturn Award nomination, best director, Academy of Science Fiction, Fantasy, and Horror Films, 1983, for *Poltergeist*; International Fantasy Film Award nomination, best film, Fantasporto, 1989, for *The Texas Chainsaw Massacre, Part II*; International Fantasy Film Award nomination, best film, 1991, for *Spontaneous Combustion*; Time–Machine Honorary Award, Sitges–Catalonian International Film Festival, 2003; Fearless Vision Award, San Francisco Fearless Tales Genre Fest, 2004; Phantasmagoria Award, Philadelphia Film Festival, 2004; Lifetime Achievement Award, New York City Horror Film Festival, 2004; Hall of Fame inductee, Phoenix International Horror and Sci–Fi Film Festival, 2005; International Horror and Sci–Fi Film Festival Hall of Fame, inductee, 2005; Eyegore Award, 2008; New York Film and Television Festival Award for *Down Friday Street*; Atlanta Film Festival Award for *Eggshells (an American Freak Odyssey)*.

CREDITS

Film Director:
The Abyss (short film), 1959.
Heisters (short film), 1963.
Eggshells (an American Freak Odyssey) (also known as *Eggshells*), 1970.
The Texas Chainsaw Massacre (also known as *TCM* and *Striking Leatherface*), Bryanston, 1974.
Eaten Alive (also known as *Brutes and Savages, Death Trap, Horror Hotel, Horror Hotel Massacre, Legend of the Bayou, Murder on the Bayou, Slaughter Hotel,* and *Starlight Slaughter*), Vigo International, 1976.
(Uncredited; replaced by John Cardos) *The Dark* (also known as *The Mutilator*), 1979.
The Funhouse (also known as *Carnival of Terror* and *Funhouse: Carnival of Terror*), Universal, 1981.
(Uncredited; replaced) *Venom*, 1981.
Poltergeist, Metro–Goldwyn–Mayer/United Artists, 1982.
Lifeforce, TriStar, 1985.
Invaders from Mars, Cannon, 1986.
The Texas Chainsaw Massacre, Part II (also known as *TCM 2* and *The Texas Chainsaw Massacre Part 2*), Cannon, 1986.
Spontaneous Combustion, Taurus Entertainment, 1990.
Night Terrors (also known as *Nightmare, Tobe Hooper's "Nightmare,"* and *Tobe Hooper's "Night Terrors"*), 1993.

The Mangler, New Line Cinema, 1995.
Crocodile, 2000.
Toolbox Murders, Lions Gate Films, 2003.
Mortuary, Echo Bridge Home Entertainment, 2005.

Also directed *Down Friday Street.*

Film Work; Other:

Cinematographer, camera operator, producer, and editor, *Eggshells (an American Freak Odyssey)* (also known as *Eggshells*), 1970.

Producer and additional photographer, *The Texas Chainsaw Massacre* (also known as *TCM* and *Striking Leatherface*), Bryanston, 1974.

Conductor and music arranger, *Eaten Alive* (also known as *Brutes and Savages, Death Trap, Horror Hotel, Horror Hotel Massacre, Legend of the Bayou, Murder on the Bayou, Slaughter Hotel,* and *Starlight Slaughter*), Vigo International, 1976.

Coproducer and model maker, *The Texas Chainsaw Massacre, Part II* (also known as *TCM 2* and *The Texas Chainsaw Massacre Part 2*), Cannon, 1986.

Creator (with Kim Hendel), *Leatherface: The Texas Chainsaw Massacre III* (also known as *TCM 3*), New Line Cinema, 1990.

Coproducer, *The Texas Chainsaw Massacre,* New Line Cinema, 2003.

Executive producer, *Toolbox Murders: As It Was* (documentary), 2003.

Producer, *The Texas Chainsaw Massacre: The Beginning,* New Line Cinema, 2006.

Film Appearances:

Joby, *The Windsplitter,* Pop Films, 1971.

(Uncredited) Man in hotel corridor, *The Texas Chainsaw Massacre, Part II* (also known as *TCM 2* and *The Texas Chainsaw Massacre Part 2*), Cannon, 1986.

Himself, *Fangoria's Weekend of Horrors* (documentary), 1986.

Forensic technician, *Stephen King's "Sleepwalkers"* (also known as *Sleepstalkers* and *Sleepwalkers*), Columbia, 1992.

Himself, *"Night of the Living Dead": 25th Anniversary* (documentary), 1993.

Himself, *"Toolbox Murders": As It Was* (documentary), 2003.

Himself, *Primal Screams: An Interview with Tobe Hooper* (short documentary), Anchor Bay Entertainment, 2006.

Himself, *Inside the Graveyard* (documentary), Echo Bridge Home Entertainment, 2006.

Himself, *The Gator Creator* (short documentary), Dark Sky Films, 2007.

Himself, *The Fearmakers Collection* (documentary), Elite Entertainment, 2007.

Himself, *Into the Dark: Exploring the Horror Film* (documentary), 2009.

Television Director; Miniseries:

Salem's Lot (also known as *Blood Thirst, Salem's Lot: The Miniseries,* and *Salem's Lot: The Movie*), CBS, 1979.

"The Maze," *Shadow Realm,* Sci–Fi Channel, 2002.

"Beyond the Sky," *Taken* (also known as *Steven Spielberg Presents "Taken"*), Sci–Fi Channel, 2002.

Television Director; Movies:

I'm Dangerous Tonight, USA Network, 1990.

"Eye," *John Carpenter Presents "Body Bags"* (also known as *Body Bags* and *John Carpenter Presents "Mind Games"*), 1993.

The Apartment Complex, Showtime, 1999.

Crocodile, USA Network, 2000.

"The Maze," *Shadow Realm,* 2002.

Television Work; Specials:

Director and special effects creator, *Haunted Lives … True Ghost Stories,* CBS, 1991.

Director and creator of special visual effects, *Real Ghosts II,* UPN, 1996.

Television Work; Pilots:

Director, *Freddy's Nightmares: No More Mr. Nice Guy,* 1988.

Producer, *Phone Calls from the Dead,* UPN, 1996.

Television Director; Episodic:

"Miss Stardust," *Amazing Stories* (also known as *Steven Spielberg Presents "Amazing Stories"* and *Steven Spielberg's "Amazing Stories"*), NBC, 1987.

"No Place Like Home," *The Equalizer,* CBS, 1988.

"No More Mr. Nice Guy," *Freddy's Nightmares* (also known as *Freddy's Nightmares: A Nightmare on Elm Street: The Series*), 1988.

"Dead Wait," *Tales from the Crypt* (also known as *HBO's "Tales from the Crypt"*), HBO, 1991.

"Absolute Zero," *Nowhere Man,* UPN, 1995.

"Turnabout," *Nowhere Man,* UPN, 1995.

"The Awakening: Parts 1 & 2," *Dark Skies,* NBC, 1996.

"Panic," *Nowhere Man,* UPN, 1997.

"Panic," *Perversions of Science,* HBO, 1997.

"Souls on Board," *The Others,* NBC, 2000.

"Cargo," *Night Visions,* Fox, 2002.

"Dance of the Dead," *Masters of Horror,* Showtime, 2005.

"The Damned Thing," *Masters of Horror,* Showtime, 2006.

Television Appearances; Miniseries:

A–Z of Horror (also known as *Clive Barker's "A–Z of Horror"*), 1997.

The 100 Scariest Movie Moments, Bravo, 2004.

Television Appearances; Movies:
Second morgue worker, "The Morgue," *John Carpenter Presents "Body Bags"* (also known as *Body Bags* and *John Carpenter Presents "Mind Games"*), Showtime, 1993.

Television Appearances; Specials:
The Making of "Poltergeist," 1982.
Fear—Angst, 1984.
The Horror Hall of Fame II, 1991.
Night of the Living Dead: 25th Anniversary Edition, 1993.
Anatomy of Horror, UPN, 1995.
The American Nightmare, Independent Film Channel, 2000.
Inside Steven Spielberg Presents: Taken, Sci–Fi Channel, 2001.
The 2001 IFP/West Independent Spirit Awards, 2001.
Masters of Horror (also known as *Boogeyman II: Masters of Horror*), 2002.
The 100 Scariest Movie Moments, Bravo, 2004.
Boogeyman II: Masters of Horror, Sci–Fi Channel, 2004.
The Perfect Scary Movie (documentary), Channel 4, 2005.

RECORDINGS

Videos:
Himself, *"Texas Chainsaw Massacre": The Shocking Truth* (documentary), Exploited Film, 2000.
Himself, *The American Nightmare* (documentary), 2000.
Himself, *Inside "Taken"* (short documentary), 2002.

Music Videos; as Director:
Directed "Dancing with Myself" by Billy Idol, 1983.

WRITINGS

Screenplays:
The Texas Chainsaw Massacre (also known as *TCM* and *Stalking Leatherface*), Bryanston, 1974.
(With Howard Goldberg and Stephen Brooks) *Spontaneous Combustion,* Taurus Entertainment, 1990.
(With Brooks) *The Mangler,* New Line Cinema, 1995.

Film Stories:
The Texas Chainsaw Massacre (also known as *TCM* and *Stalking Leatherface*), Bryanston, 1974.
Spontaneous Combustion, Taurus Entertainment, 1990.

Film Music:
(With Wayne Bell) *The Texas Chainsaw Massacre* (also known as *TCM* and *Stalking Leatherface*), Bryanston, 1974.

(With Jerry Lambert) *Eaten Alive* (also known as *Brutes and Savages, Death Trap, Horror Hotel, Horror Hotel Massacre, Legend of the Bayou, Murder on the Bayou, Slaughter Hotel,* and *Starlight Slaughter*), Vigo International, 1976.
The Texas Chainsaw Massacre 2 (also known as *The Texas Chainsaw Massacre Part 2*), 1986.

Film Original Theme:
The Texas Chainsaw Massacre, New Line Cinema, 2003.

OTHER SOURCES

Books:
Muir, John Kenneth, *Eaten Alive at a Chainsaw Massacre: The Films of Tobe Hooper,* McFarland and Co., 2002.

HOPKINS, Stephen 1958–

PERSONAL

Born 1958, in Jamaica. *Education:* Studied art at the London College of Printing.

Addresses: *Agent*—Creative Artists Agency, 2000 Avenue of the Stars, Los Angeles, CA 90067.

Career: Producer, director, and writer. GreenGo Productions, Rio de Janeiro, Brazil, principal. Director of music videos and commercials; also worked as art director, artist for album covers, set designer for music videos, and storyboard artist.

Member: Directors Guild of America.

Awards, Honors: Critics' Award and International Fantasy Film Award nomination, best film, Fantasporto, 1990, both for *A Nightmare on Elm Street 5: The Dream Child;* International Fantasy Film Award nomination, best film, 1991, for *Predator 2;* Golden Satellite Award (with others), best drama series, International Press Academy, 2001, Emmy Award nomination (with others), outstanding drama series, 2002, Emmy Award nomination, outstanding directing for a drama series, Directors Guild of America Award nomination, outstanding directorial achievement in a night–time dramatic series, 2002, all for *24;* Emmy Award nomination (with others), outstanding miniseries, 2004, for *Traffic;* Golden Palm Award nomination, Cannes Film Festival, 2004, Emmy Award, outstanding directing for a miniseries, movie or dramatic special, Directors Guild of America Award nomination, outstanding directorial achievement in movies for television, 2005, all for *The Life and Death of Peter Sellers;* two Annual CableACE Award nominations, National Cable Television Association, for *Tales from the Crypt;* Australian Emmy awards, including one for *Mick Jagger—Live Down Under.*

CREDITS

Film Director:
Dangerous Game, Quantum Films, 1988.
A Nightmare on Elm Street 5: The Dream Child (also known as *Nightmare on Elm Street: The Dream Child* and *Nightmare on Elm Street 5*), New Line Cinema, 1989.
Predator 2, Twentieth Century–Fox, 1990.
Judgment Night, Universal, 1993.
Blown Away, Metro–Goldwyn–Mayer/United Artists, 1994.
The Ghost and the Darkness, Paramount, 1996.
Lost in Space (also known as *LS*), New Line Cinema, 1998.
Under Suspicion (also known as *Suspicion*), Lions Gate Films, 1999.
The Reaping, Warner Bros., 2007.

Film Work; Other:
Assistant director, *Highlander,* 1986.
Executive producer, *Crossworlds,* 1997.
Producer, *Lost in Space* (also known as *LS*), New Line Cinema, 1998.
Producer, *Under Suspicion* (also known as *Suspicion*), Lions Gate Films, 1999.

Film Appearances:
Himself, *The Hunters and the Hunted: The Making of "Predator 2"* (short documentary), Twentieth Century Fox Home Entertainment, 2005.
Gutter punk kid, *Squatter,* 2009.
Himself, *Never Sleep Again: The Elm Street Legacy* (documentary), 1428 Films, 2010.

Television Work; Series:
Co–executive producer and director, *24* (series), Fox, 2001.
Creator and executive producer, *Las Vegas Garden of Love,* ABC Family, 2005.
Executive producer, *Driving Force,* Arts and Entertainment, 2006.
Consultant, *Californication,* Showtime, 2007.
Executive consultant, *Californication,* Showtime, 2008.

Television Work; Miniseries:
Producer and director, *Traffic* (also known as *Traffic: The Miniseries*), USA Network, 2003.

Television Work; Movies:
Executive producer, *Crossworlds,* HBO, 1996.
Director, "Horny," *Tube Tales,* 1999.
Director, *The Life and Death of Peter Sellers,* HBO, 2004.

Television Work; Specials:
Director, *The Life and Death of Peter Sellers,* HBO, 2003.

Television Work; Pilots:
Director, *World of Trouble,* 2005.
Executive producer and director, *Californication,* Showtime, 2007.
Executive producer and director, *The Unusuals,* ABC, 2008.
Director, *Maggie Hill,* Fox, 2009.

Television Director; Episodic:
"Abra Cadaver," *Tales from the Crypt* (also known as *HBO's "Tales from the Crypt"*), HBO, 1991.
"Beauty Rest," *Tales from the Crypt* (also known as *HBO's "Tales from the Crypt"*), HBO, 1992.
"Staired in Horror," *Tales from the Crypt* (also known as *HBO's "Tales from the Crypt"*), HBO, 1994.
24, Fox, 2001–2002.
"Gilted Lily," *In Plain Sight,* USA Network, 2009.
"Mia Culpa," *Californication,* Showtime, 2009.

Also worked on an Australian television special, *Mick Jagger—Live Down Under.*

Television Appearances; Specials:
24 Heaven, 2002.
24: The Postmortem, 2002.

Television Appearances; Episodic:
Film 2002 (also known as *The Film Programme*), BBC, 2002.
Film 2004 (also known as *The Film Programme*), BBC, 2004.

Stage Director:
Directed *Rasputin* (an Australian production).

WRITINGS

Film Additional Material:
Dangerous Game, 1987.

Television Movies:
"Horny," *Tube Tales,* 1999.

Television Episodes:
Wrote episodes of *Tales from the Crypt* (also known as *HBO's "Tales from the Crypt"*), HBO.

OTHER SOURCES

Periodicals:
Starlog, May, 1998; December, 1990.

HOWARD, Clint 1959–

PERSONAL

Full name, Clinton E. Howard; born April 20, 1959, in Burbank, CA; son of Rance (an actor and writer) and Jean (an actress; maiden name, Speegle) Howard; brother of Ron Howard (an actor, director, producer, and writer); married, 1986 (divorced, 1987); married Melanie (a sales representative), October 29, 1995. *Avocational Interests:* Golf.

Addresses: *Agent*—TalentWorks, 3500 West Olive Ave., Suite 1400, Burbank, CA 91505.

Career: Actor.

Awards, Honors: MTV Movie Award, lifetime achievement, 1998.

CREDITS

Film Appearances:
(Uncredited) Child at party in Indian headdress, *The Courtship of Eddie's Father,* 1963.
Voice of Roo, *Winnie the Pooh and the Honey Tree* (animated), 1966.
Jo–Hi, *An Eye for an Eye* (also known as *Talion*), Embassy, 1966.
Mark Wedloe, *Gentle Giant,* Paramount, 1967.
Voice of baby elephant, *The Jungle Book* (animated), Buena Vista, 1967.
Voice of Roo, *Winnie the Pooh and the Blustery Day!* (animated), 1968.
Deed of Daring–Do, 1969.
Boy, *Old Paint,* 1969.
Cards, Cads, Guns, Gore and Death, 1969.
Andrew Tanner, *The Wild Country* (also known as *The Newcomers*), Buena Vista, 1970.
Voice of Roo, *Winnie the Pooh and Tigger Too!* (animated), 1974.
Tim Reed, *Salty,* Saltwater, 1975.
Georgie, *Eat My Dust!,* New World, 1976.

Voice of Roo, *The Many Adventures of Winnie the Pooh* (animated), 1977.
Catcher, *I Never Promised You a Rose Garden,* 1977.
Ace, *Grand Theft Auto,* New World, 1977.
Corley, *Harper Valley P.T.A.,* April Fools, 1978.
Eaglebauer, *Rock 'n' Roll High School* (also known as *Girls' Gym*), New World, 1979.
Coopersmith, *Evilspeak* (also known as *Evilspeaks*), Moreno, 1981.
Jefferey, *Night Shift,* Warner Bros., 1982.
Usher, *Flip Out* (also known as *Get Crazy*), Embassy, 1983.
Wedding guest, *Splash,* Buena Vista, 1984.
John Dexter, *Cocoon,* Twentieth Century–Fox, 1985.
Paul, *Gung Ho* (also known as *Working Class Man*), Paramount, 1986.
Rughead, *The Wraith,* New Century/Vista, 1986.
Les Sullivan, *End of the Line,* Orion, 1987.
Ronnie, *Freeway,* New World, 1988.
Slinky, *Tango & Cash,* Warner Bros., 1989.
Lou, *Parenthood,* Universal, 1989.
Jerry, *B.O.R.N.* (also known as *Merchants of Death*), Movie Outfit, 1989.
Fellow prisoner, *An Innocent Man,* 1989.
Ricky, *Silent Night, Deadly Night 4: Initiation* (also known as *Bugs, Silent Night Deadly Night IV: Initiation,* and *Initiation: Silent Night, Deadly Night 4*), Silent Films, Inc., 1990.
Monk, *The Rocketeer* (also known as *Rocketeer* and *The Adventures of the Rocketeer*), Buena Vista, 1991.
Brian, *Disturbed,* Live, 1991.
Ricco, *Backdraft,* Universal, 1991.
Flynn, *Far and Away,* Universal, 1992.
John Larrabee, *Body Chemistry II: The Voice of a Stranger* (also known as *Voice of a Stranger*), 1992.
Wishman, 1992.
Ricky, *Silent Night, Deadly Night 5: The Toy Maker,* Still Silent Films, Inc., 1992.
Ray Tidrow, *Public Enemy #2,* 1993.
Jarvis Tanner, *Ticks* (also known as *Infested*), 1993.
Friar, *Carnosaur,* New Horizons, 1993.
Drifter, *Forced to Kill,* PM, 1994.
Tourist, *Leprechaun 2* (also known as *Leprechaun II* and *One Wedding and Lots of Funerals*), Trimark Pictures, 1994.
Ray Blaisch, *The Paper,* Universal, 1994.
Otto Nielsen, *Cheyenne Warrior,* New Horizons, 1994.
Gary, *Bigfoot: The Unforgettable Encounter,* Republic Pictures, 1994.
Assistant bank manager, *Baby Face Nelson,* New Horizons, 1995.
Deakins, *Digital Man,* Republic Pictures, 1995.
Bobo, *Dillinger and Capone,* New Horizons, 1995.
Sy Liebergot—EECOM White, *Apollo 13,* Universal, 1995, released as *Apollo 13: The IMAX Experience,* 2002.
Exterminator, *Forget Paris,* Columbia, 1995.
Gregory Tudor (title role), *Ice Cream Man,* A–Pix Entertainment, 1995.

Gardener, *Twisted Love,* 1995.

Stalin, *Fist of the North Star* (also known as *Hokuto no Ken*), 1995.

Schmitz, *Barb Wire,* PolyGram Filmed Entertainment, 1996.

Hutch, *Body Armor* (also known as *Conway* and *The Protector*), A–Pix Entertainment, 1996.

Hinkley, *Santa with Muscles,* Legacy Releasing, 1996.

KJZZ disc jockey, *That Thing You Do!,* Twentieth Century–Fox, 1996.

Gus, *Unhook the Stars* (also known as *Decroche les etoiles*), Miramax, 1996.

Rapist, *Street Corner Justice,* Sunset Films International, 1996.

Johnson Ritter, *Austin Powers: International Man of Mystery* (also known as *Austin Powers—Das Scharfste, was ihre majestat zu bieten hat*), New Line Cinema, 1997.

Arnold, *Sparkle and Charm,* 1997.

Clint, *Chow Bella,* 1998.

Paco, *The Waterboy,* Buena Vista, 1998.

(Uncredited) Customer, *Telling You* (also known as *Love Sucks*), Miramax, 1998.

Cheese, *Bad Lie,* Brentwood Home Video, 1998.

EMS worker, *Twilight,* Paramount, 1998.

Dogcatcher, *Addams Family Reunion,* Twentieth Century–Fox, 1998.

Hector, *Evasive Action,* Hallmark Entertainment, 1998.

Hutch, *The Protector* (also known as *Body Armor* and *Conway*), 1998.

Nursery manager, *Fortune Hunters,* 1999.

Mr. Whitney, *Arthur's Quest,* A–Pix Entertainment, 1999.

Ken, *Edtv* (also known as *Ed TV*), MCA/Universal, 1999.

Sergeant Peters, *Austin Powers: The Spy Who Shagged Me* (also known as *Austin Powers 2: The Spy Who Shagged Me*), New Line Cinema, 1999.

Harvey, *The Million Dollar Kid* (also known as *Fortune Hunters*), A–Pix Entertainment, 1999.

Himself, *"Edtv": Caught in the Camera's Eye* (also known as *Caught in the Camera's Eye*), 1999.

Nipples, *Little Nicky,* New Line Cinema, 2000.

Millard, *My Dog Skip,* Warner Bros., 2000.

Whobris, *How the Grinch Stole Christmas* (also known as *Dr. Seuss's "How the Grinch Stole Christmas,"* *Der Grinch,* and *The Grinch*), MCA/Universal, 2000.

Arnold, *Sparkle and Charm,* Independent, 2000.

Under Oath, 2000.

Stu, *Ping!,* 2000.

100 Women, 2001.

Greg/motel clerk, *Blackwoods,* THINKFilm, 2002.

Johnson, *Austin Powers in Goldmember* (also known as *Austin Powers: Goldmember*), New Line Cinema, 2002.

Janitor, *Girl Fever* (also known as *100 Women*), Dream Entertainment/Michael/Finney Productions, 2002.

Clyde Trotter, *The Sure Hand of God,* 2002.

Pastor Jablonski, *Leaving the Land,* 2002.

Artie Lynne, *Heart of America* (also known as *Homeroom*), 2002.

Himself, *You'll Never Wiez in This Town Again,* Dimension Films, 2003.

Franciscus Abbot, *Searching for Haizmann,* Centre Communications/Haizmann, 2003.

Salish, *The House of the Dead* (also known as *House of the Dead: Le jeu ne fait que commencer*), Artisan Entertainment, 2003.

Owen, *Big Paw: Beethoven 5* (also known as *Beethoven's 5th* and *Beethoven's 5th: Big Paw*), 2003.

Pauly's business manager, *Pauly Shore Is Dead,* CKrush Entertainment, 2003.

Kate the Caterer, *The Cat in the Hat* (also known as *Dr. Seuss's "Cat in the Hat"*), Universal, 2003.

Sheriff Purdy, *The Missing,* Columbia, 2003.

Himself, *It's a Dog Life: Behind the Scenes and Cast Interviews of "Beethoven's 5th"* (short film), Universal Studios Home Video, 2003.

Mr. Goss, *Raising Genius,* Polychrome Pictures, 2004.

Ira Cutter, *The Murder of Donovan Slain* (short film), 2004.

Himself, *New Frontiers: Making "The Missing"* (short documentary), Columbia TriStar Home Entertainment, 2004.

Himself, *The Making Of: "House of the Dead,"* 2004.

Himself, *I Am Stamos* (short film), Red Navel Filmworks, 2004.

Himself, *UnConventional* (documentary), 2004.

Henrik Ibsen, *Planet Ibsen,* 2005.

The mechanic, *My Big Fat Independent Movie* (also known as *My Big Fat Indy Movie*), Anchor Bay Entertainment, 2005.

Referee, *Cinderella Man,* Universal, 2005.

INS agent, *Fun with Dick and Jane* (also known as *Alternative Career* and *Fun with Dick & Jane*), Columbia, 2005.

Himself, *Back to School: A Retrospective–"Rock 'N' Roll High School"* Rock on Edition DVD (short documentary), Buena Vista Home Entertainment, 2005.

Benny, *Cut Off,* Anchor Bay Entertainment, 2006.

Voice of Balloon Man, *Curious George* (animated), Universal, 2006.

Principal Richard Skelter, *The Powder Puff Principle* (short film), 2006.

Gene Jensen, *Church Ball,* Halestone Distribution, 2006.

Danny Boy (short film), Monkey's Uncle Productions, 2006.

Uncle Ed, *How to Eat Fried Worms,* New Line Cinema, 2006.

Fulton Chaney, *Big Bad Wolf,* Screen Media Ventures, 2006.

Himself, *"Backdraft": Bringing Together the Team* (short documentary), Universal, 2006.

Clerk, *Music Within,* Metro–Goldwyn–Mayer, 2007.

Mr. Powell, *River's End,* American World Pictures, 2007.

Doctor Koplenson, *Halloween* (also known as *Rob Zombie's "Halloween"*), Metro–Goldwyn–Mayer, 2007.

Binky the Clown, *A Plumm Summer*, Freestyle Releasing, 2007.

Todd, *A Christmas Too Many*, Lions Gate Films, 2007.

Fold (short film), 2008.

Long Larry, *Foreign Exchange*, 2008.

Lloyd Davis, *Frost/Nixon* (also known as *Frost/Nixon, l'heure de verite*), Universal, 2008.

Dick, *Play the Game*, Slowhand Cinema Releasing, 2008.

Lionel Huffer, *Senior Skip Day* (also known as *High School's Day Off*), First Look International, 2008.

Himself, *King of the B's: The Independent Life of Roger Corman* (documentary), 2009.

Narrator, *London Betty*, Maverick Entertainment Group, 2009.

Mugger, *Super Capers*, Lions Gate Film Home Entertainment, 2009.

Dickens, *Redemption* (short film), Las Vegas Film Festival, 2009.

Flight Commander Johnson, *Night at the Museum: Battle of the Smithsonian* (also known as *Night at the Museum 2* and *Night at the Museum: Battle of the Smithsonian—The IMAX Experience*), Twentieth Century–Fox, 2009.

Voice of Farmer Dan, *Curious George 2: Follow That Monkey!* (animated), Universal Home Entertainment, 2009.

Voice of Joe Cthulu, *The Haunted World of El Superbeasto*, Anchor Bay Entertainment, 2009.

Constable Sanders, *Alabama Moon*, 2009.

Roy, Sr., *Holyman Undercover*, Pure Flix Entertainment, 2010.

Ricks, *Ashley's Ashes*, FKF Media Group, 2010.

Dom, *Speed–Dating*, 2010.

George, *Last Call*, Stock's Eye Productions, 2010.

Film Work:
Additional voice, *Mr. Baseball*, Universal, 1992.
Coproducer, *Planet Ibsen*, 2005.

Television Appearances; Series:
(Television debut) Leon, *The Andy Griffith Show* (also known as *Andy of Mayberry*), CBS, 1962–64.
Stanley, *The Baileys of Balboa*, CBS, 1964–65.
Mark Wedloe, *Gentle Ben*, CBS, 1967–69.
Steve, *The Cowboys*, ABC, 1974.
Salty, 1974.
Googie, *Gung Ho*, ABC, 1986–87.
Santa Barbara, NBC, 1987.
Mimmer, *Space Rangers* (also known as *Space Marines* and *Planet Busters*), CBS, 1993.

Television Appearances; Miniseries:
Paul Lucas, *From the Earth to the Moon*, HBO, 1998.

Television Appearances; Movies:
Jody Tifflin, *The Red Pony*, NBC, 1973.
Arch, *Huckleberry Finn*, ABC, 1975.
Peanuts, *The Death of Richie* (also known as *Richie*), NBC, 1977.
Corky Macpherson, *Cotton Candy* (also known as *Ron Howard's "Cotton Candy"*), NBC, 1978.
Skyward, NBC, 1980.
Limo driver, *Little White Lies* (also known as *First Impressions*), NBC, 1989.
Sephus McCoy, *Sawbones* (also known as *Prescription for Murder* and *Roger Corman Presents "Sawbones"*), 1995.
Wede, *Not Like Us*, Showtime, 1995.
Andy Parsons, *Rattled*, USA Network, 1996.
Stalin, *Fist of the North Star* (also known as *Hokuto no Ken*), HBO, 1996.
Deputy, *Roger Corman Presents "Humanoids from the Deep"* (also known as *Humanoids from the Deep*), Showtime, 1996.
Mr. Toothache, *The Dentist 2* (also known as *The Dentist 2: Brace Yourself* and *The Dentist 2: You Know the Drill*), HBO, 1998.
Stu, *Ping!*, HBO, 2000.
Artie Lynne, *Heart of America* (also known as *Homeroom*), 2002.
Fifth Street, *The Great Commission*, Showtime, 2003.
Clyde Trotter, *The Sure Hand of God* (also known as *Sinners Need Company*), Lifetime, 2004.

Television Appearances; Specials:
Voice of Roo, *Winnie the Pooh and the Blustery Day* (animated), 1964.
Voice of Roo, *Winnie the Pooh and the Honey Tree* (animated), NBC, 1970.
Himself, "But I'm Happy," *David Letterman's Holiday Film Festival*, 1985.
Ray Tidrow, *Public Enemy Number 2*, Showtime, 1991.
Hollywood's Amazing Animal Actors, TBS, 1996.
The 1998 MTV Movie Awards, MTV, 1998.
The 1999 MTV Movie Awards, MTV, 1999.
Armagedd'NSync, 1999.
Child Stars: Their Story (also known as *Child Stars*), Arts and Entertainment, 2000.
Everybody Loves Raymond: The First Six Years, CBS, 2002.
Voice of Tug, *Rapsittie Street Kids: Believe in Santa*, 2002.
The Clint Howard Variety Show, 2002.
Behind the Scenes: "The Great Commission," Showtime, 2003.
Soul Decisions, Showtime, 2003.
Hollywood Home Movies, Arts and Entertainment, 2004.
I Love the Holidays, VH1, 2005.
"Happy Days": 30th Anniversary Reunion, ABC, 2005.
Mr. Jantzen, *Fur on the Asphalt: The "Greg the Bunny" Reunion Show*, Independent Film Channel, 2005.
I Love the 80's 3–D, VH1, 2005.

I Love the '70s: Volume 2, VH1, 2006.

Balok, *Comedy Central Roast of William Shatner,* Comedy Central, 2006.

Television Appearances; Pilots:

Chick Bosson, *The Best Defense,* ABC, 1995.

Television Appearances; Episodic:

Kid at party, *The Courtship of Eddie's Father,* ABC, 1962.

Mikey, "The Gnu, Now Almost Extinct," *Breaking Point,* ABC, 1963.

"Little Drops of Water, Little Grains of Sand," *Ben Casey,* ABC, 1963.

Billy, "Home Is the Hunted," *The Fugitive,* ABC, 1964.

Little boy, "Hey, Teacher," *Vacation Playhouse,* CBS, 1964.

Johny, "Set Fire to a Straw Man," *The Fugitive,* ABC, 1965.

David, "Look Who's Talking," *Please Don't Eat the Daisies,* NBC, 1965.

Alan Ellwood, "An Elephant Is Like a Rope," *The F.B.I.,* ABC, 1965.

Michael Thorpe, "All Ye His Saints," *Bonanza* (also known as *Ponderosa* and *Ride the Wind*), NBC, 1965.

David, "Swing That Indian Club," *Please Don't Eat the Daisies,* NBC, 1965.

David "Davy," "The Purple Avenger," *Please Don't Eat the Daisies,* NBC, 1966.

Midj, "Leave It to Dixie," *Laredo,* NBC, 1966.

"Ride a Cock–Horse to Laramie Cross," *The Virginian* (also known as *The Men from Shiloh*), NBC, 1966.

Balok, "The Corbomite Maneuver," *Star Trek* (also known as *Star Trek: TOS* and *Star Trek: The Original Series*), NBC, 1966.

Ralphie, "Three Little Kittens," *The Patty Duke Show,* ABC, 1966.

Robbie Fielding, "My Client, the Rooster," *The Jean Arthur Show,* CBS, 1966.

Tim Oliver, "A Civil Case of Murder," *Judd for the Defense,* ABC, 1967.

Tommy, "Melanie," *The Virginian* (also known as *The Men from Shiloh*), NBC, 1967.

Jody Hillman, "Teaching the Tiger to Purr," *The Monroes,* ABC, 1967.

"Stone Walls Do Not a Prison Make—So They Added the Bars," *The Red Skelton Show* (also known as *The Red Skelton Hour*), CBS, 1970.

Josh Cobb, "Incident in the Desert," *The F.B.I.,* ABC, 1970.

Randy Grainger, "The Big Brother," *The Odd Couple,* ABC, 1970.

Tom Richards, "Say Uncle," *Family Affair,* CBS, 1970.

"Blue Skies for Willie Sharpe," *Lancer,* CBS, 1970.

David, "Love and the Teacher," *Love, American Style,* ABC, 1970.

Willie Stratton, "Wolf Track," *The Virginian* (also known as *The Men from Shiloh*), NBC, 1971.

Herbie Bittman, "The Boy Who Predicted Earthquakes," *Rod Sterling's "Night Gallery"* (also known as *Night Gallery*), NBC, 1971.

Lonny, "Murdoch," *Gunsmoke* (also known as *Gun Law* and *Marshal Dillon*), CBS, 1971.

"The Tender Comrade," *Marcus Welby, M.D.* (also known as *Robert Young, Family Doctor*), ABC, 1971.

Timmy McGovern, "One for the Road," *Nanny and the Professor,* ABC, 1971.

"The Wrinkle Squad," *Insight,* 1971.

"The Price of Love," *The Mod Squad,* ABC, 1971.

Dennis, "Crossfire," *The Rookies,* ABC, 1973.

Billy Rudolph, "The House on Hyde Street," *The Streets of San Francisco,* ABC, 1973.

Tommy Sanders, "Cry Help!," *The Streets of San Francisco,* ABC, 1974.

Paul Scarne, "A Small Hand of Friendship," *Doc Elliot,* ABC, 1974.

Mark, "Lifeline," *Movin' On,* NBC, 1974.

Moose, "Bringing Up Spike," *Happy Days,* ABC, 1976.

D'Annunzio, "A Living Wage," *The Fitzpatricks,* CBS, 1978.

Donald "Junior" Hedges, Jr., "Father and Son," *Happy Days,* ABC, 1980.

Jerry Kovacovich, "Recovery," *Lou Grant,* CBS, 1982.

Late Night with David Letterman, 1986.

Police Officer sieging house, "State of Sledge," *Sledge Hammer!* (also known as *Sledge Hammer: The Early Years*), ABC, 1987.

Man in the restaurant, "Kill Zone," *Hunter,* CBS, 1990.

Tobias Lehigh Nagy (Smog Strangler), "The Trip: Part I," *Seinfeld,* NBC, 1992.

Grady, "Past Tense: Part 2," *Star Trek: Deep Space Nine* (also known as *DS9, Deep Space Nine,* and *Star Trek: DS9*), syndicated, 1995.

Mullen, "And Bingo Was Her Game–O," *Married ... with Children* (also known as *Married with Children*), Fox, 1995.

Craig P. Sykes, "Kill Shot," *Silk Stalkings,* USA Network, 1995.

"First Anniversary," *The Outer Limits* (also known as *The New Outer Limits*), Showtime, 1996.

Homeless man, "The Shot," *Gun* (also known as *Robert Altman's "Gun"*), ABC, 1997.

Pontifex, "Baby Lottery," *Total Recall 2070* (also known as *Total Recall: The Series*), Showtime, 1999.

Smitty, "Qallupilluit," *The Pretender,* NBC, 1999.

Himself, "Tammy Wins Fernando," *Strip Mall,* 2001.

Muk, "Acquisition," *Enterprise* (also known as *Star Trek: Enterprise*), UPN, 2002.

Himself, "The First Six Years of Raymond," *Everybody Loves Raymond* (also known as *Raymond*), CBS, 2002.

Gil Runkis, "Dead Wives' Club," *Crossing Jordan,* NBC, 2003.

Johnny Bark, "Key Decisions," *Arrested Development,* Fox, 2003.

Himself, "Players Halloweenie Televizzie," *Player$*, Tech TV, 2003.

Himself, "Child Stars II: Growing Up in Hollywood," *Biography*, Arts and Entertainment, 2005.

Creepy Rodney, "Stole a Badge," *My Name Is Earl*, NBC, 2006.

Himself, "Scott Baio Hires a Life Coach: Part 1," *Scott Baio is 45 ... And Single* (also known as *Scott Baio is 46 ... And Single*), VH1, 2007.

Himself, "Apollo 13," *Cinemania*, 2008.

Creepy Rodney, "Quit Your Snitchin'," *My Name Is Earl*, NBC, 2008.

Tom Miller, "Chapter Eleven 'I Am Sylar,'" *Heroes*, NBC, 2009.

Michael Carlin, "The Road Not Taken," *Fringe*, Fox, 2009.

Also appeared as himself, "The Films of Ron Howard," *The Directors*.

Television Work; Specials:

Executive producer and director, *The Clint Howard Variety Show*, 2002.

RECORDINGS

Video Games:

Larry Hammond, *Tex Murphy: Overseer* (also known as *Overseer*), Access Software, 1998.

WRITINGS

Television Movies:

(With Ron Howard) *Cotton Candy* (also known as *Ron Howard's "Cotton Candy"*), NBC, 1978.

OTHER SOURCES

Periodicals:

Entertainment Weekly, November 24, 1995, p. 113; August 20, 1999, p. 131.

People Weekly, November 23, 1998, p. 85.

Star Trek Communicator, February, 1998, p. 65.

HOWARD, Scott
    See YAPHE, Scott

HUFFMAN, Cady 1965–

PERSONAL

Full name, Catherine Elizabeth Huffman; born February 2, 1965, in Santa Barbara, CA; daughter of Clifford Roy (an attorney) and Lorayne Dolores (a preschool administrator; maiden name, Rote) Huffman; brother of Linus Huffman (an actor); married William Healy (a college basketball coach), February 6, 1993 (separated). *Education:* Studied acting privately in Los Angeles and New York City.

Addresses: *Agent*—Joanne Nici, Don Buchwald and Associates, 10 East 44th St., New York, NY 10017.

Career: Actress, producer, and production designer. Appeared in more than twenty–five commercials in the 1980s, and more recently, an ad for Wellbutrin antidepressant medication, 2006. Lighthouse, New York City, volunteer recreational therapist, 1986–87.

Awards, Honors: Antoinette Perry Award nomination, best supporting actress in a musical, 1991, for *The Will Rogers Follies*; Antoinette Perry Award, Drama Desk Award, and Outer Critics Circle Award, all outstanding featured actress in a musical, 2001, for *The Producers*; President's Medal, Hunter College of the City University of New York, 2002.

CREDITS

Film Appearances:

Flight attendant Leslie Sugar, *Hero* (also known as *Accidental Hero*), Columbia, 1992.

Dar Mullins, *Space Marines*, 1996.

Gayle, *Sunday on the Rocks*, 2 Lizzies Productions, 2004.

Billy's mother, *Billy's Dad Is a Fudge–Packer* (short film), Power Up Films, 2004.

Dancer and singer, *Romance & Cigarettes*, Metro–Goldwyn–Mayer, 2005.

Betty, *Twenty Dollar Drinks* (short film), BrindStar Productions, 2006.

Lola, *Itty Bitty Titty Committee*, Power Up Films, 2007.

Divorcing mom, *The Nanny Diaries*, Metro–Goldwyn–Mayer/Weinstein Company, 2007.

Dr. Kolton, *Dare*, Image Entertainment, 2009.

Joanna, *The Company Men*, VV Films, 2010.

Alice, *Choose*, 7th Floor, 2010.

Film Work:

Song performer, "Our Favorite Son," *Ronin*, 1998.

Producer and production designer, *Sunday on the Rocks*, 2 Lizzies Productions, 2004.

Television Appearances; Series:

Herself, *Curb Your Enthusiasm*, HBO, multiple appearances, between 2004 and 2007.

Dr. Paige Miller, *One Life to Live*, ABC, 2005–2006.

Judge, *Iron Chef America: The Series*, Food Network, multiple appearances, between 2005 and 2009.

Television Appearances; Movies:
Mary Jo, *Vows of Deception* (also known as *Deadly Seduction* and *Tangled Web*), CBS, 1996.
Dor Mullins, *Space Marines,* Showtime, 1996.
Receptionist, *Columbo: A Trace of Murder,* ABC, 1997.

Television Appearances; Specials:
Recording *"The Producers": A Musical Romp with Mel Brooks,* PBS, 2001.
The ... Annual Tony Awards, 1991, CBS 2001.
Judge, *Iron Chef America: Greatest Moments,* Food Network, c. 2008.

Television Appearances; Episodic:
Blind woman, "George Goes Too Far," *The George Carlin Show,* 1994.
Rita, "Leap into an Open Grave," *Pig Sty,* UPN, 1995.
Barking woman, "Up in Smoke: Parts 1 & 2," *Mad about You,* NBC, 1995.
Pamela Winters, "Cuba Libre," *Law & Order: Criminal Intent* (also known as *Law & Order: CI*), NBC, 2003.
Amber Licious, "Detour," *Frasier,* NBC, 2004.
Penny Sterba, "The Abominable Showman," *Law & Order: Trial by Jury,* NBC, 2005.

Also appeared in *The Guiding Light,* 1986, and *Another World,* 1987.

Stage Appearances:
The Baker's Wife, 1982.
They're Playing Our Song, 1983.
Angelique, *La Cage au Folles* (musical), Palace Theatre, New York City, 1985.
Dancer and understudy for the role of Pearl, *Big Deal* (musical; also known as *Bob Fosse's "Big Deal"*), Broadway Theatre, New York City, 1986.
As You Like It, Royal Academy of Dramatic Art, London, 1989.
Jekyll and Hyde, 1989.

Italian–American Reconciliation, English Speaking Theatre Company, Rome, 1990.
Gemini, English Speaking Theatre Company, Rome, 1990.
Ziegfield's favorite, *The Will Rogers Follies* (musical), Palace Theatre, New York City, 1991–93.
Standby for Rita Racine and Shelby Stevens, *Steel Pier* (musical), Richard Rogers Theatre, New York City, 1997.
Rosemary Lebeau, *Big Rosemary,* Helen Hayes Performing Arts Centre, New York City, 1999.
The first Gorgeous Ednaette, *Dame Edna: The Royal Tour,* Booth Theatre, New York City, 1999–2000.
Ulla, *The Producers* (musical), St. James Theatre, New York City, 2001–2003.
Presenter of introduction, *Short Talks on the Universe,* Eugene O'Neill Theatre, New York City, 2002.
Cady Huffman: Live at Ars Nova (solo show), 2006.
The Cartells, 2006.
Plain and Fancy, 2006.
Surface to Air, 2007.

Appeared in *Cymbeline,* Royal Academy of Dramatic Arts; and "L'il Abner," *City Center Encores!,* New York City.

RECORDINGS

Albums:
The Producers (original cast recording), Sony Music Entertainment, 2001.
Recording *"The Producers"—A Musical Romp with Mel Brooks,* Sony Classical, 2001.

OTHER SOURCES

Periodicals:
People Weekly, April 15, 2002, p. 125.
TV Guide, July 31, 2005, p. 39.

I–J

ISEN, Tajja 1991(?)–

PERSONAL

Born c. 1991, in Ontario, Canada; daughter of Jordie (a chiropractor, manager, and in business) and Karen Isen. *Education:* Studied English at the University of Toronto; studied piano. *Avocational Interests:* Reading, shopping.

Career: Actress, voice artist, singer, pianist, and songwriter. Appeared in advertisements; performer in albums and music videos. Sang national anthems at sporting events and sang at various functions.

Member: Canadian Actors' Equity Association, Alliance of Canadian Cinema, Television and Radio Artists (ACTRA).

Awards, Honors: Nomination for Equity Emerging Artist Award, c. 2001, for *The Lion King;* Young Artist Award nomination, best performance in a voice–over role—young actress, Young Artist Foundation, 2004, for *The Berenstain Bears;* Young Artist awards, best performance in a voice–over role—young artist, 2005, and best performance in a voice–over role—young actress, 2006, nomination for the ACTRA Award of Excellence, outstanding performance—voice, Alliance of Canadian Cinema, Television and Radio Artists (ACTRA), 2007, and Gemini Award (with others), best individual or ensemble performance in an animated program or series, Academy of Canadian Cinema and Television, 2009, all for *Atomic Betty;* Young Artist Award, best performance in a voice–over role—young actress, 2007, for *Jane and the Dragon;* Young Artist Award, best performance in a voice–over role—young actress, 2008, for *Super WHY!*

CREDITS

Television Appearances; Animated Series:
Voice of Sister Bear, *The Berenstain Bears,* YTV, Treehouse TV, and PBS, beginning 2003.
Voice of Jazzi, *The Save–Ums!* (also known as *The Save–Ums*), CBC and Discovery Kids, 2003–2006.
Voice of Trina Trapezio, *JoJo's Circus,* The Disney Channel, 2003–2007.
Voice of Elizabeth "Betty" Barrett/title role, *Atomic Betty,* TeleToon and Cartoon Network, beginning 2004.
Voice of Lil Sis, *Miss Spider's Sunny Patch Friends* (also known as *Miss Spider*), TeleToon and Nickelodeon, 2004–2006, Treehouse TV, beginning 2006.
Voice of Jane Turnkey, *Jane and the Dragon,* YTV and NBC, 2006.
Voice of Nadia Dorkovitch, *Weird Years,* YTV, beginning 2006.
Voice of Pony Tail, *Bigfoot Presents: Meteor and the Mighty Monster Trucks* (also known as *Meteor the Monster Truck*), Discovery Kids and The Learning Channel, beginning 2006.
Voice of Kayce Culp, *MP4orce: Beyond Real* (also known as *MP4orce* and *MP4ORCE: Beyond Real*), beginning c. 2006.
Voice of Princess Pea and Princess Presto, *Super WHY!* (also known as *The Reading Adventures of Super Why!* and *Super Why!*), PBS, CBC, and Nick Jr., beginning 2007.

Some sources cite appearances in other programs.

Television Appearances; Live Action Series:
Appeared in *Judy & David's Boombox,* Treehouse TV.

Television Appearances; Specials:
Voice of Betty, *Atomic Betty: The No–L Nine* (animated; also known as *Atomic Betty: The No–L 9* and *No–L 9*), TeleToon and Cartoon Network, 2005.

Television Appearances; Animated Episodes:

Voice of young ballerina, "Funny Business," *Braceface* (also known as *Sourire d'enfer*), TeleToon and ABC Family, 2003.

Voice of young Etra, "Statue of Major Limitations," *Da Boom Crew,* The WB and Cartoon Network, 2004.

Voice of Bortar, "You Can't, but Genghis Khan," *Time Warp Trio,* NBC and Discovery Kids, 2005.

Voice of Katarina, "Goliath Gets a Boo Boo/Join the Club," *JoJo's Circus,* The Disney Channel, 2005.

Voice of Katrina, "Best Pet in Circus Town/Picture Perfect," *JoJo's Circus,* The Disney Channel, 2005.

Voice of Tracy, "Adventures in Cousin–Sitting," *GirlStuff/ BoyStuff* (also known as *Girlstuff/Boystuff* and *GSBS*), YTV and Nickelodeon, 2005.

Voice of Princess Josephina, "Princess for a Day," *JoJo's Circus,* The Disney Channel, 2006.

Voice of Jenny 10, "Family Business," *Dex Hamilton: Alien Entomologist,* Australian Broadcasting Corporation, 2008, CBC, 2010.

Provided voices for other animated programs, including various voices for *Franny's Feet,* CBC, The Family Channel, and PBS.

Television Appearances; Live Action Episodes:

Mindy, "Complicated," *Doc,* PAX, 2002.

Herself, *Holly & Stephen's Saturday Showdown* (also known as *Ministry of Mayhem* and *M.O.M.*), ITV, 2005.

Television Theme Song Performer; Animated Series:

The Save–Ums! (also known as *The Save–Ums*), CBC and Discovery Kids, 2003–2006.

JoJo's Circus, The Disney Channel, 2003–2007.

Atomic Betty, TeleToon and Cartoon Network, beginning 2004.

Franny's Feet, CBC, beginning 2004, Family, beginning c. 2005, PBS, beginning 2006.

Miss BG, TVOntario, beginning 2005.

Jane and the Dragon, YTV and NBC, 2006.

Bigfoot Presents: Meteor and the Mighty Monster Trucks (also known as *Meteor the Monster Truck*), Discovery Kids and The Learning Channel, beginning 2006.

Animated Film Appearances:

Voice of title role, *Heidi,* TV–Loonland/Telemagination/ Nelvana, 2005.

Voice of Samantha and young Granny for English version, *Franklin et le tresor du lac* (also known as *Franklin and Granny's Secret* and *Franklin and the Turtle Lake Treasure*), Mars Distribution, 2006.

Some sources cite appearances in other films.

Stage Appearances:

Young Nala, *The Lion King* (musical), Princess of Wales Theatre, Toronto, Ontario, Canada, c. 2001.

Appeared in other productions.

Internet Appearances:

Some sources state that Isen has provided voices for Internet sites.

RECORDINGS

Albums; with Others:

Atomic Betty (related to the television series), KOCH Records, 2005.

Singer and pianist for solo recordings, including *A Day in the Life of Tajja Isen,* Warner Bros. Appeared in recordings and music videos, including the singles and music videos for both "Atomic Betty" and "Alien Ball (Do the Betty)," both 2005.

Judy & David Albums:

(Member of children's choir) *GoldiRocks,* All Together Now Entertainment, 2000.

(Member of children's choir) *BeanStock,* All Together Now Entertainment, 2001.

(Member of children's choir) *Red's in the Hood,* All Together Now Entertainment, 2001.

(Soloist) *Rock n' Roll Matzah Ball,* All Together Now Entertainment, 2008.

Appeared in other Judy & David recordings.

WRITINGS

Albums:

Wrote songs and wrote material for albums, including *A Day in the Life of Tajja Isen,* Warner Bros.

JACOBI, Lou 1913–2009

PERSONAL

Original name, Louis Harold Jacobovitch; born December 28, 1913, in Toronto, Ontario, Canada; died October 23, 2009, in New York, NY. Actor. Character actor Jacobi's career spanned some five decades and included work in theatre, film, and television. He began acting as a child, making his stage debut in 1924 in a

Toronto production of *The Rabbi and the Priest*. In 1955 he debuted on Broadway as Mr. Van Daan in *The Diary of Anne Frank*. He reprised the role in the film version, which was released in 1959. Other stage appearances include *The Tenth Man, Come Blow Your Horn, The Sunshine Boys,* and London productions of *Guys and Dolls, Remains to Be Seen,* and *Into Thin Air.* Jacobi made his film debut in the 1953 movie *Is Your Honeymoon Really Necessary?* and appeared in dozens of films over the following forty years, among them *Irma la Douce,* the Woody Allen film *Everything You Always Wanted to Know about Sex, Arthur,* and *I.Q.,* his final film role. A frequent guest star in episodic television, his credits range from comedies, such as *Love, American Style* and *Ivan the Terrible,* to dramas, including *Alfred Hitchcock Hour* and *St. Elsewhere.*

PERIODICALS

Guardian, November 15, 2009.
Los Angeles Times, October 27, 2009.
New York Times, October 25, 2009.
Variety, October 26, 2009.

JACOBS, Lawrence–Hilton
See HILTON–JACOBS, Lawrence

JANN, Michael Patrick 1970–
(Michael Jann, Michael P. Jann)

PERSONAL

Born May 15, 1970, in Albany, NY; married Lisa LoCicero (an actress); children: Lukas. *Avocational Interests:* Films.

Addresses: *Agent*—Creative Artists Agency, 2000 Avenue of the Stars, Los Angeles, CA 90067.

Career: Director, producer, actor, and writer. Directed hundreds of television commercials for such clients as Microsoft, ESPN, Honda, Pets.com, and the British government.

Awards, Honors: FIPRESCI Prize, special mention and Crystal Globe nomination, Karlovy Vary International Film Festival, 1999, both for *Drop Dead Gorgeous.*

CREDITS

Film Work:
Producer and first assistant director, *Aisle Six* (short film), 1991.

Director, *Drop Dead Gorgeous* (also known as *Gnadenlos schon*), New Line Cinema, 1999.

Film Appearances:
Carl, *Aisle Six* (short film), 1991.
(As Michael Jann) Party attendee, *I'm Your Man,* 1992.
(As Michael P. Jann) First funeral mourner, *Orange Quarters* (short film), 1998.
Tattoo shop owner number one, *"Reno 911!": Miami* (also known as *"Reno 911!: Miami": The Movie*), Twentieth Century–Fox, 2007.

Television Work; Series:
Segment director, *You Wrote It, You Watch It,* MTV, 1992.
Creator, opening titles, and segment director, *The State,* MTV, 1993–95.
Consulting producer, *Reno 911!,* Comedy Central, 2004–2009.
Producer, *Emily's Reasons Why Not,* ABC, 2006–2008.
Executive producer, *Little Britain USA,* HBO, 2008.

Television Director; Movies:
Ghosts/Aliens, 2009.

Television Work; Specials:
Creator, supervising producer, remote segments director, open, bumpers, and editor, *The State's 43rd Annual All–Star Halloween Special,* CBS, 1995.

Television Director; Pilots:
Reno 911!, Comedy Central, 2003.
Emily's Reasons Why Not, ABC, 2006.

Television Director; Episodic:
Reno 911!, Comedy Central, 2003–2007.
Emily's Reasons Why Not, ABC, 2006–2008.
"Oleander," *Notes from the Underbelly,* ABC, 2007.
"The Actor," *The Flight of the Conchords* (also known as *Flight of the Conchords*), HBO, 2007.
Little Britain USA, HBO, 2008.
"The Good Soil," *Reaper,* The CW, 2009.

Television Appearances; Series:
Various characters, *You Wrote It, You Watch It,* MTV, 1992.
Various, *The State,* MTV, 1993–95.

Television Appearance; Specials:
The State's 43rd Annual All–Star Halloween Special, CBS, 1995.

Television Appearances; Episodic:
Camera man, "Garcia's Anniversary," *Reno 911!,* Comedy Central, 2003.

WRITINGS

Screenplays:
Let's Go to Prison, Universal, 2006.

Television Episodes:
You Wrote It, You Watch It, MTV, 1992.
The State, MTV, 1993–95.
The Tonight Show with Jay Leno (also known as *Jay Leno*), NBC, 1995–2009.
(As Michael Jann) *The Jay Leno Show,* NBC, 2009–10.

Television Specials:
The State's 43rd Annual All–Star Halloween Special, CBS. 1995.

JAYSTON, Michael 1935–

PERSONAL

Original name, Michael James; born October 29, 1935, in Nottingham, England; son of Vincent Aubrey and Edna Myfanwy (maiden name, Llewelyn) James; married Lynn Farleigh, 1965 (divorced, 1970); married Heather Mary Sneddon, 1971 (divorced, 1977); married Elizabeth Ann Smithson, 1978; children: (second marriage) Tom Robert, Ben Patrick; (third marriage) Richard John, Katharine Sarah. *Education:* Attended University of Nottingham; trained for the stage at Guildhall School of Music and Drama. *Avocational Interests:* Cricket, darts, chess.

Career: Actor. Guildhall School of Music and Drama, fellow, 1981. Previously worked as an apprentice accountant.

Member: Cricket Society, Marylebone Cricket Club, Gelding Colliery Cricket Club (vice president), Rottingdean Cricket Club (president), Cricketers' Club, Sussex Cricket Club, Lord's Taverners Club, Eccentrics Club, S.P.A.R.K.S.

Awards, Honors: Television Award nomination, best actor, British Academy of Film and Television Arts, 1971, for *Mad Jack* and other appearances.

CREDITS

Television Appearances; Series:
Lincoln Dowling, a recurring role, *The Power Game,* 1969.
Title role, *Quiller,* 1975.

Ross Brassington, *Flesh and Blood,* 1980–82.
The Valeyard, *Doctor Who,* BBC, 1986.
Neville Badger, *A Bit of a Do,* 1989.
Sir Joshua, *Haggard,* 1990.
Earl of Rufton, *The Casebook of Sherlock Holmes,* 1990.
Colonel Mustard, *Cluedo* (also known as *Clue*), 1991.
Narrator, *Timewatch* (also known as *BBC History: Timewatch*), BBC, 1992.
Bob, *Outside Edge,* 1994.
Sparrow, *Fun at the Funeral Parlour,* BBC, 2001.
Donald De Souza, *Emmerdale Farm* (also known as *Emmerdale*), YTV, 2007–2008.

Television Appearances; Miniseries:
Frederick Henry Royce, *The Edwardians,* BBC, 1972.
Edward Rochester, *Jane Eyre,* BBC, 1972, PBS, 1973.
Peter Guillam, *Tinker, Tailor, Soldier, Spy,* 1980.
Justice Craig, *A Dinner of Herbs* (also known as *Catherine Cookson's "A Dinner of Herbs"*), 2000.

Television Appearances; Movies:
Gratiano, *The Merchant of Venice,* BBC, 1973.
Roger Masters, "Ring Once for Death" (also known as "Death in Small Doses"), *Thriller,* ATV, 1973, ABC, 1974.
Mark Walker, "Coffin for the Bride" (also known as "Kiss, Kiss, Kill, Kill"), *Thriller,* ATV, 1973, ABC, 1974.
Alfred Maiberling, "Gossip from the Forest," *Screenplay,* 1979.
Narrator, *From a Far Country* (also known as *Da un paease lontano, From a Far Country: Pope John Paul II,* and *Z dalekiego kraju*), NBC, 1981.
Auston Tupp, *Dust to Dust* (also known as *Time for Murder: Dust to Dust*), 1985.
Randall Perry, *Still Crazy Like a Fox* (also known as *Crazy Like a Fox: The Movie*), CBS, 1987.
Title role, *Macbeth,* 1988.
Roger Fitzpatrick, *Somewhere to Run,* 1989.
Rear Admiral John E. Sellings, *20,000 Leagues under the Sea,* CBS, 1997.

Television Appearances; Specials:
Wilfred Owen (solo performance), BBC, 1970.
Ludwig van Beethoven, "Beethoven," *Biography,* 1970.
Title role, *Charles Dickens,* 1970.
"The Importance of Being Earnest," *Play of the Month,* BBC, 1974.
Edmund, "King Lear," *Play of the Month,* BBC, 1975.
Mansel, "She Fell among Thieves," *BBC2 Play of the Week,* BBC, 1978, PBS, 1980.
Narrator, *The Animal Family,* 1996.
Happy Birthday BBC Two, BBC2, 2004.
(Uncredited; in archive footage) James Turner, *The Comedy Christmas,* BBC, 2007.
The British Soap Awards 2008, 2008.

Television Appearances; Pilots:

Title role, *Quiller: Price of Violence,* ABC, 1975.

Title role, *Quiller: Night of the Father,* ABC, 1975.

Television Appearances; Episodic:

Intense young man, "On the Night of the Murder," *Suspense,* 1962.

Francis Ford, "Put Out the Light," *Detective,* 1969.

Russ Stone, "The Sound of Silence," *UFO* (also known as *Gerry Anderson's "UFO"*), ITV, 1970.

Mark Tedder, "God Help Your Friends," *Callan,* 1970.

Siegfried Sassoon, "Mad Jack," *The Wednesday Play,* 1970.

Jimmy, "Competition," *Armchair Theatre,* 1971.

Henry, Bishop of Norwich, "Shouts and Murmurs," *Churchill's People,* 1975.

Keith Saunders, Queen's Counsel, "An Upward Fall," *Crown Court,* 1977.

Frederick Henry Seddon, "Root of All Evil," *Lady Killers,* 1981.

G. B. Shaw, "The Best Chess Player in the World," *Tales of the Unexpected* (also known as *Roald Dahl's "Tales of the Unexpected"*), 1984.

Keith Saunders, Queen's Counsel, "There Was an Old Woman," *Crown Court,* 1984.

"What Are Friends For?," *Big Deal,* 1985.

"Popping across the Pond," *Big Deal,* 1985.

"Breakthrough," *Big Deal,* 1985.

Miles Bennett, "Crack–Up," *C.A.T.S. Eyes,* 1986.

Helmut Staalmaker, "The German Visitor," *Room at the Bottom,* 1986.

"Undying Love," *Worlds Beyond,* 1987.

Quentin Nightingale, "A Guilty Thing Surprised: Parts 1–2," *Ruth Rendell Mysteries,* ITV, 1988.

"Shake Hands Forever: Parts 1–3," *Ruth Rendell Mysteries,* ITV, 1988.

Michael, "Stand By Your Man," *About Face,* BBC, 1989.

Valentine the hitman, "The Devil Wept in Leeds," *Stay Lucky,* 1990.

Sir Joshua Foulacre, "Haggard at Bay," *Haggard,* 1990.

Sir Joshua Foulacre, "Eye of Newt," *Haggard,* 1990.

Sir Joshua Foulacre, "Affair of Honour," *Haggard,* 1990.

Ian, "Profit and Loss," *Casualty,* BBC1, 1991.

Earl of Rufton, "The Disappearance of Lady Frances Carfax," *The Casebook of Sherlock Holmes,* PBS, 1992.

John England/Colonel X, "UnXpected," *Press Gang,* 1992.

Superintendent Masters, "Verschwinden," *The Good Guys,* 1992.

Ernest Bristow, "The Happiest Days of Your Lives: Parts 1 & 2," *The Darling Buds of May,* 1993.

Ernest Bristow, "Climb the Greasy Pole: Parts 1 & 2," *The Darling Buds of May,* 1993.

Voice of yachtsman, "The Radio Ham," *Paul Merton in Galton and Simpson's ...,* 1996.

Voice of Damon, "Sealed with a Loving Kiss," *Paul Merton in Galton and Simpson's ...,* 1996.

Michael Harvey, "Frail Mortality," *Heartbeat* (also known as *Classic Heartbeat*), ITV1, 1996.

James Turner, "Time on Our Hands," *Only Fools and Horses,* BBC, 1996.

Henry Meacher, "Two of a Kind," *Noah's Ark,* 1997.

Nick, "Hassles with Castles," *Adam's Family Tree,* 1998.

Horton Quince, "Christmas Special: Bash," *Heartburn Hotel,* 1998.

Charles Arthur Cullin, "No One's That Honest," *The Bill,* ITV1, 2000.

Judge, *Coronation Street* (also known as *Corrie* and *The Street*), 2000.

"Tom Baker," *This Is Your Life,* 2000.

Judge, "Extra Time," *Holby City* (also known as *Holby*), BBC, 2001.

Alistair Wilson, *EastEnders,* BBC, 2002.

Vern Coren, "Real Tonic," *Doctors,* BBC, 2003.

Henry Appleton, "Consequences," *The Royal,* ITV, 2003.

Henry Appleton, "Home to Roost," *The Royal,* ITV, 2004.

Bradley, "Golden Oldies," *Murder in Suburbia,* BBC America, 2005.

Vince Parker, "378," *The Bill,* ITV1, 2006.

Vince Parker, "379," *The Bill,* ITV1, 2006.

Lawrence Bremmen, "Judge Not, Lest Ye Be Judged," *Holby City* (also known as *Holby*), BBC, 2006.

Gerald Hudson, "Little White Lies," *Heartbeat* (also known as *Classic Heartbeat*), ITV1, 2006.

Henry Appleton, "Can't Buy Me Love," *The Royal,* ITV, 2007.

Henry Parkins, "Casualties of War," *Foyle's War,* PBS, 2007.

Henry Parkins, "Plan of Attack," *Foyle's War,* PBS, 2008.

Film Appearances:

Demetrius, *A Midsummer Night's Dream,* 1968.

Henry Ireton, *Cromwell,* Columbia, 1970.

Nicholas, *Nicholas and Alexandra,* Columbia, 1971.

Charles, *Follow Me!* (also known as *The Public Eye*), Universal, 1972.

Lewis Carroll/Charles Dodgson, *Alice's Adventures in Wonderland* (also known as *Lewis Carroll's "Alice's Adventures in Wonderland"*), American National Enterprises, 1972.

Captain Hardy, *A Bequest to the Nation* (also known as *The Nelson Affair*), Universal, 1973.

Teddy, *The Homecoming* (also known as *Harold Pinter's "The Homecoming"*), American Film Theatre, 1973.

Brian, *Tales that Witness Madness* (also known as *Witness Madness*), Paramount, 1973.

Detective Sergeant Wall, *Craze* (also known as *Demon Master* and *The Infernal Idol*), Warner Bros., 1973.

David Baker, *The Internecine Project* (also known as *Der schwarze panther, Ein Mann stellt eine falle,* and *G*), Allied Artists, 1974.

Arnold Craven, *Dominique* (also known as *Avenging Spirit* and *Dominique Is Dead*), Prism Pictures, 1978.

Colonel Crealock, *Zulu Dawn*, Warner Bros., 1979.

Jack Donovan, *Highlander III: The Sorcerer* (also known as *Highlander 3: The Final Conflict*, *Highlander III*, *Highlander: The Final Dimension*, and *Highlander: The Magician*), Dimension Films, 1994.

Kirk, *Element of Doubt*, 1996.

Stage Appearances:

(Stage debut) Corporal Green, *The Amorous Prawn*, Salisbury Playhouse, Salisbury, England, 1962.

Macduff, *Macbeth*, Salisbury Playhouse, 1962.

Henry II, *Becket*, Salisbury Playhouse, 1962.

Various roles, *Beyond the Fringe* (comedy revue), Bristol Old Vic Theatre, Bristol, England, 1963.

All in Good Time, Bristol Old Vic Theatre, 1963.

Scent of Flowers, Bristol Old Vic Theatre, 1963.

Duke of Exeter, *Henry V*, Royal Shakespeare Company, Aldwych Theatre, London, 1965, then Royal Shakespeare Theatre, Stratford–upon–Avon, England, 1966.

Storyteller, *The Thwarting of Baron Bolligrew*, Royal Shakespeare Company, Aldwych Theatre, 1965.

Red–haired workman, *Puntila*, Royal Shakespeare Company, Aldwych Theatre, 1965.

Second witness, *The Investigation*, Royal Shakespeare Company, Aldwych Theatre, 1965, 1966.

Duke of Exeter, *Henry IV, Part 1*, Royal Shakespeare Company, Royal Shakespeare Theatre, 1966.

Duke of Exeter, *Henry IV, Part 2*, Royal Shakespeare Company, Royal Shakespeare Theatre, 1966.

Laertes, *Hamlet*, Royal Shakespeare Company, Royal Shakespeare Theatre, 1966.

Lenny and understudy for Teddy, *The Homecoming*, Music Box Theatre, New York City, 1967.

Member of chorus, *Romeo and Juliet*, Royal Shakespeare Company, Royal Shakespeare Theatre, 1967.

Oswald, *Ghosts*, Royal Shakespeare Company, Aldwych Theatre, 1967.

Reader, *The Hollow Crown*, Royal Shakespeare Company, Aldwych Theatre, 1967.

Bertram, *All's Well that Ends Well*, Royal Shakespeare Company, Aldwych Theatre, 1968, then Theatre des Nations, Theatre de France, and Odeon, all Paris, 1968.

General Custer and Senator Logan, *Indians*, Royal Shakespeare Company, Aldwych Theatre, 1968.

Young Fashion, *The Relapse*, Royal Shakespeare Company, Aldwych Theatre, 1968.

Henry II, *Becket*, Arnaud Theatre, Guildford, England, 1972.

Martin Dysart, *Equus*, National Theatre, Old Vic Theatre, London, 1974, then Royal Shakespeare Company, Albery Theatre, London, 1976–77.

Charles Appleby, *Eden End*, National Theatre, Old Vic Theatre, 1974.

Elyot Chase, *Private Lives*, Greenwich Theatre, then Duchess Theatre, both London, 1980.

Captain von Trappe, *The Sound of Music* (musical), Apollo Theatre, 1981–82.

Mirabell, *The Way of the World*, Theatre Royal Haymarket, London, 1984.

The reverend, *Woman in Mind*, Vaudeville Theatre, London, c. 1986–87.

Father Jack, *Dancing at Lughnasa*, Garrick Theatre, London, 1992.

Ratty, *The Wind in the Willows*, Royal National Theatre, London, 1996.

Reverend Charlie Allen, Chichester Festival Theatre, Chichester, England, 1998.

Colonel Whittaker, *Easy Virtue*, Chichester Festival Theatre, 1999.

Wild Orchids, Chichester Festival Theatre, 2002.

Major Tours:

The Battle of Agincourt, Royal Shakespeare Company, 1966.

Lenny, *The Homecoming*, Royal Shakespeare Company, 1966.

First shepherd, *The Second Shepherd's Play*, Royal Shakespeare Company, 1966.

Martin Dysart, *Equus*, 1976.

Amy's View, 2002.

The Rivals, 2002.

Moment of Weakness, 2003.

Radio Appearances:

Chekhov Short Stories, BBC, 1969.

Camus Stories, BBC, 1970.

Alpha Beta, BBC, 1972.

James Bond, *You Only Live Twice*, BBC, 1990.

RECORDINGS

Videos:

(In archive footage) The Valeyard, *"Doctor Who:" The Colin Baker Years*, 2 Entertain Video, 1991.

(Uncredited; in archive footage) The Valeyard, *Rogue Time Lords*, 2007.

Trial of a Time Lord Part One, 2 Entertain Video, 2007.

(In archive footage) The Valeyard, *Trials and Tribulations*, 2 Entertain Video, 2008.

Audio Books:

Reader for audio versions of *The History of World War II by Winston Churchill*; twelve works by novelist John Le Carre; and twelve books by P. D. James, as well as other audio books.

Albums:

Spoken introductions, Saint Etienne, *Finisterre*, 2002.

WRITINGS

Print Materials:
Contributor to the book *County Champions* (of cricket).
Contributor to periodicals, including *Cricketer* and *Wisden's Monthly.*

JENSEN, Ashley 1969–
 (Ashley Jenson)

PERSONAL

Full name, Ashley Samantha Jensen; born August 11, 1969, in Annan, Dumfries and Galloway, Scotland; daughter of Ivar and Margaret (a special–needs teacher) Jensen; married Terence Beesley (an actor), January 22, 2007; children: Francis Jonathan. *Education:* Studied acting at and graduated from Queen Margaret University College; studied acting at the National Youth Theatre of Great Britain.

Addresses: *Agent*—Hamilton Hodell, Ltd., 66–68 Margaret St., 5th Floor, London W1W 8SR, England; WME Entertainment, One William Morris Pl., Beverly Hills, CA 9012; Danis Panaro Nist, 90201 West Olympic Blvd., Beverly Hills, CA 90212. *Publicist*—I/D Public Relations, 8409 Santa Monica Blvd., West Hollywood, CA 90069.

Career: Actress.

Awards, Honors: British Comedy Award, best television comedy actress, British Comedy Award, best comedy newcomer, 2005, Television Award nomination, best comedy performance, British Academy of Film and Television Arts, Golden Rose Award, best sitcom actress, Rose d'Or Light Entertainment Festival, 2006, all for *Extras;* Screen Actors Guild Award nominations (with others), outstanding performance by an ensemble in a comedy series, 2007, 2008, Scotland Television Award nomination, best acting performance in television, British Academy of Film and Television Arts, 2008, all for *Ugly Betty;* British Comedy Award nomination, best television comedy actress, Emmy Award nomination, outstanding supporting actress in a miniseries or a movie, 2008, both for *Extras: The Extra Special Series Finale.*

CREDITS

Film Appearances:
Tickets for the Zoo, 1991.
Miss Tringham, *Topsy–Turvey,* October Films, 1999.

Lindsey, *A Cock and Bull Story* (also known as *Tristram Shandy: A Cock and Bull Story*), Picturehouse Entertainment, 2005.
Narrator, *Taking Liberties* (documentary), Revolver Entertainment, 2007.
Herself, *Taping Nigel II: The Gimpening* (short documentary), 2007.
Herself, *Becoming Ugly: A New Face for Television* (short film), Buena Vista Home Entertainment, 2007.
Jennifer, *Nativity!,* E1 Entertainment, 2009.

Film Work:
Producer and art director, *Sunshine* (short film), 2010.

Television Appearances; Series:
Heather, *Roughnecks,* 1994–95.
Morag, *Bad Boys,* BBC1, 1996.
Police Constable Sue Chappell, *City Central,* BBC, 1998–2000.
Babs Leach, *Clocking Off,* BBC, 2001–2003.
Breeze Block, 2002.
Angie Raeburn, *Two Thousand Acres of Sky,* BBC, 2003.
Faye Brooks, *Sweet Medicine,* ITV, 2003.
Maggie Jacobs, *Extras,* BBC2 and HBO, 2005–2007.
Christina McKinney, *Ugly Betty,* ABC, 2006–2009.
Narrator, *Cook Yourself Thin,* Channel 4, 2007.
Narrator, *Movie Connections,* 2007–2009.
Olivia, *Accidentally on Purpose,* CBS, 2009—.

Television Appearances; Miniseries:
Oliver's Travels, PBS, 1996.
Rachel Young, *Eleventh Hour,* ITV and BBC America, 2006.

Television Appearances; Movies:
Claire Donnelly, *Down among the Big Boys,* BBC, 1993.
Nessie, *The Big Picnic,* BBC, 1996.
Dawn Deacon, *Outside the Rules,* BBC1, 2002.
Isobel, *No Holds Bard,* 2009.

Television Appearances; Specials:
Amanda Cookson, *Waiting,* ITV, 1995.
Eileen, *Temp,* Carlton TV, 1995.
TV's 50 Greatest Stars, Granada, 2006.
The Comedy Christmas, BBC, 2007.
Maggie Jacobs, *Extras: The Extra Special Series Finale,* HBO, 2007.
Presenter, *The 2007 Teen Choice Awards,* Fox, 2007.
Speechless, 2008.

Television Appearances; Pilots:
Christina McKinney, *Ugly Betty,* ABC, 2006.
Olivia, *Accidentally on Purpose,* CBS, 2009.

Television Appearances; Episodic:
"The Front," *City Lights,* BBC, 1990.
Second girl, "Country," *Rab C. Nesbitt,* BBC, 1992.
Sheena, "Wean," *Rab C. Nesbitt,* BBC, 1993.
Rosie McConnachy, "Take Good Care of My Baby," *May to December,* BBC, 1994.
Catriona MacLean, "A Night Alarm," *The Tales of the Para Handy,* BBC, 1994.
Kathleen, "Hey Jude," *Takin' Over the Asylum,* BBC, 1994.
Kate Selby, "Personal Space," *The Bill,* ITV1, 1994.
Hairdresser, "Hair: Crime," *The Baldy Man,* Carlton TV and Yorkshire TV, 1995.
Eileen, "Temp," *Capital Lives,* ITV, 1995.
Jess, "Thicker Than Water," *Casualty,* BBC1, 1996.
Diane Wyre, "Mid–Life Crisis," *The Bill,* ITV1, 1997.
Michelle Thomson, "Contact," *Dangerfield,* BBC, 1997.
Naomi Childs, *Mortimer's Law,* BBC, 1998.
Herself, *Fully Booked,* 1998.
Fiona, *EastEnders,* BBC, 2000.
Mhairi Henderson, "Mortal Causes," *Rebus,* ITV, 2001.
Rachel, "Victoria," *Coming Up,* Channel 4, 2003.
Deputy Inspector Becky Metcalf, "Fatal Error: Parts 1 & 2," *Silent Witness,* BBC, 2003.
(Uncredited) Voice of interviewer, "Christmas Special: Parts 1 & 2," *The Office,* BBC and BBC America, 2003.
Stella, "Love, Honour and Betray," *Casualty,* BBC1, 2004.
Stella, "Ring of Truth," *Casualty,* BBC1, 2004.
Policewoman number one, "The Samosa Triangle," *Meet the Magoons,* Channel 4, 2005.
(As Ashley Jenson) Agatha Ferry, "A Taste of Money," *Taggart,* ITV, 2005.
Breakfast, BBC, 2005.
Friday Night with Jonathan Ross, BBC, 2005.
GMTV, ITV, 2006.
ITV Lunchtime News, ITV, 2007.
Guest host, *The Friday Night Project,* Channel 4, 2007.
Xpose, TV3, 2007.
Narrator, *Embarrassing Illnesses,* Channel 4, 2007.
This Morning (also known as *This Morning with Richard and Judy*), ITV, 2007.
Entertainment Tonight (also known as *E.T.*), syndicated, 2007.
Jimmy Kimmel Live!, ABC, 2007.
Free Radio, VH1, 2007.
The Graham Norton Show, BBC, 2007, 2009.
"The New Intern," *Free Radio,* VH1, 2008.
"Ricky Gervais," *New Heroes of Comedy,* Channel 4, 2008.

Stage Appearances:
Stevie, *Chimps,* Hampstead Theatre, London, 1997.
King Lear, Royal Exchange Theatre, Manchester, England, 1999.

JENSON, Ashley
   See JENSEN, Ashley

JOHNSON, A. J.
   (Adrienne–Joi Johnson)

PERSONAL

Born in NJ. *Education:* Spelman College, graduated (with honors).

Career: Actress. Also worked as a fitness trainer.

Member: Delta Sigma Theta.

Awards, Honors: Young Artist Award (with others), outstanding young ensemble cast, 1990, for *A Mother's Courage: The Mary Thomas Story;* Independent Spirit Award nomination, best supporting female, Independent Features Project/West, 1991, for *House Party;* special mention (with others), Locarno International Film Festival, 2001, and Black Reel Award nomination, best supporting actress, 2002, both for *Baby Boy.*

CREDITS

Film Appearances:
Cecilia, *School Daze,* Columbia, 1988.
Sharane, *House Party,* New Line Cinema, 1990.
Shauna, *Dying Young* (also known as *The Choice of Love*), Twentieth Century–Fox, 1991.
Danitra, *Double Trouble,* Motion Picture Corporation of America, 1992.
Lewanda, *Sister Act,* Buena Vista, 1992.
(As Adrienne–Joi Johnson) Heather Lee, *The Inkwell* (also known as *No Ordinary Summer*), Buena Vista, 1994.
Lisa, *Two Shades of Blue,* Cutting Edge Entertainment/ Sterling Home Entertainment, 2000.
Juanita, *Baby Boy,* Columbia, 2001.
Nina, *Tara* (also known as *Hood Rat*), Universal, 2001.
Mild Cat, *Black Listed,* York Pictures, 2003.
Sarah, *Skin Deep,* Crosstown Releasing, 2004.

Film Work:
Choreographer of dance battle, *House Party,* New Line Cinema, 1990.

Television Appearances; Series:
Officer Lynn Stanton, *Sirens,* ABC, 1993–95.
Host, *Flab to Fab,* VH1, 2004.

Television Appearances; Movies:

Cynthia, *Murder without Motive: The Edmund Perry Story* (also known as *Best Intentions*), NBC, 1992.

Elaine, *Love, Lies & Lullabies* (also known as *Sad Inheritance*), ABC, 1993.

Venom, *High Freakquency* (also known as *24/7 Radio*), Black Entertainment Television, 1998.

Television Appearances; Miniseries:

(As Adrienne–Joi Johnson) Nell Newcombe, *The Beast* (miniseries; also known as *Peter Benchley's "The Beast"*), NBC, 1996.

Television Appearances; Specials:

Ruby Thomas, *A Mother's Courage: The Mary Thomas Story,* NBC, 1989.

(In archive footage) *It's Black Entertainment,* Showtime, 2002.

Television Appearances; Pilots:

Annie, "Coming to America," *CBS Summer Playhouse,* CBS, 1989.

Renee, *Clippers,* CBS, 1991.

Television Appearances; Episodic:

Third girl, "Mr. Hillman," *A Different World,* 1988.

Shawna Hughes, "These Things Take Time," *In the Heat of the Night,* NBC, 1989.

Christina Johnson, "Def Poet's Society," *The Fresh Prince of Bel–Air,* NBC, 1990.

Courtney, "My Fair Homeboy," *Amen,* NBC, 1991.

Marilyn, *The Preston Episodes,* Fox, 1995.

Trish Cook, "Liver Let Die," *Chicago Hope,* CBS, 1996.

Between Brothers, Fox, 1996.

Janine, "I Do, I Didn't," *The Jamie Foxx Show,* The WB, 1997.

Joan, "The Vows," *For Your Love,* 1998.

Dolores, "Our Mr. Brooks," *Cover Me: Based on the True Life of an FBI Family* (also known as *Cover Me*), USA Network, 2000.

Dolores, "Turtle Soup," *Cover Me: Based on the True Life of an FBI Family* (also known as *Cover Me*), USA Network, 2000.

Yvette, "Angels Anonymous," *Touched by an Angel,* CBS, 2001.

"Obesity in America: Why Are We So Fat and What Are We Doing about It," *Baisden after Dark,* 2008.

RECORDINGS

Videos:

Herself, *Master P. Presents the Hood Stars of Comedy, Vol. 1,* Guttar Entertainment, 2006.

Appeared in the music video "Just Coolin'" by Levert.

WRITINGS

Videos:

Master P. Presents the Hood Stars of Comedy, Vol. 1, Guttar Entertainment, 2006.

JONES, Davy 1945–
(David Jones)

PERSONAL

Full name, David Thomas Jones; born December 30, 1945, in Manchester, England; married Linda Haines, October 31, 1968 (divorced, c. 1975); married Anita Pollinger, January 24, 1981 (divorced, 1996); married Jessica Pacheco (an actress), August 30, 2009; children: Anabel, Talia Lee, Sarah, Jessica. *Avocational Interests:* Riding, training, and racing horses, photography, charity athletic events.

Addresses: *Agent*—Cunningham, Escott, Slevin, and Doherty Talent Agency, 10635 Santa Monica Blvd., Suite 140, Los Angeles, CA 90025.

Career: Actor, writer, and singer. Appeared on British television in the early 1960s; member of the musical group the Monkees, 1966–69; appeared in Monkees reunion concerts in the 1970s; appeared with original Monkees members on various reunion tours, beginning 1985; performer in solo concert tour, 2003. Appeared in commercials; teacher of motivational seminars. Trained as a horse jockey; began competitive racing career late in life; official spokesperson for the Colonial Downs racetrack annual racing season, 2002. Founder of the boutiques the Street and Zilch, 1960s, and a record label.

Awards, Honors: Antoinette Perry Award nomination, 1963, for *Oliver!;* Comeback of the Year Award (with the Monkees), *Rolling Stone Magazine* Music Awards Readers' Poll, 1986; TV Land Award, favorite guest performance by a musician on a television show, 2003, for *The Brady Bunch;* received star on Hollywood Walk of Fame, with the Monkees.

CREDITS

Television Appearances; Series:

(As David Jones) Davy Jones, *The Monkees,* NBC, 1966–68.

Letters to Laugh–In (also known as *Love Letters to Laugh–In*), multiple appearances, 1969.

Television Appearances; Specials:

Miss Teen International Pageant, 1967.

33 1/3 Revolutions Per Monkee, NBC, 1969.

The Peapicker in Piccadilly (also known as *The Tennessee Ernie Ford Show*), NBC, 1969.

(In archive footage) *NBC 60th Anniversary Celebration,* NBC, 1986.

"Sir Harry Secombe," *This Is Your Life,* 1990.

(As David Jones) Record executive, "It's Only Rock & Roll," *ABC Afterschool Specials,* ABC, 1991.

Bradymania: A Very Brady Special, 1993.

(In archive footage) *American Bandstand's Teen Idol,* 1994.

Host, *TV's All–Time Favorites,* CBS, 1995.

Miss Teen USA Pageant, 1996.

(Uncredited; in archive footage) *Hide and Seek,* 1996.

(As David Jones) Davy, *Hey, Hey It's the Monkees,* ABC, 1997.

Hey, Hey, We're the Monkees, The Disney Channel, 1997.

The Monkees: The E! True Hollywood Story, E! Entertainment Television, 1999.

The Brady Bunch: The E! True Hollywood Story, E! Entertainment Television, 1999.

Life after the Street, ITV, 2001.

VH1: A Very Classic Thanksgiving, VH1, 2004.

The Kids from Coronation Street, ITV, 2004.

Making the Monkeys, Channel 4, 2007, Smithsonian Networks, 2008.

Stars on the Street, ITV, 2009.

Television Appearances; Episodic:

Boy Meets Girls, 1960.

"Summer Theatre: June Evening," *BBC Sunday–Night Play,* BBC, 1960.

(As David Jones) Colin Lomax, *Coronation Street* (also known as *Corrie* and *The Street*), 1961.

(As David Jones) Willie Thatcher, "Four of a Kind," *Z Cars,* 1962.

(As David Jones) Frankie Sale, "The Best Days," *Z Cars,* 1962.

(As David Jones) Boy football player, "On Watch—Newtown," *Z Cars,* 1962.

Talent Scouts, 1963.

(Uncredited) Guest (with cast of *Oliver!*), *Toast of the Town* (also known as *The Ed Sullivan Show*), 1964.

Himself, *Shindig!,* 1965.

Himself, *Where the Action Is,* 1965.

(As David Jones) *Thank Your Lucky Stars,* 1965.

Greg Carter, "If You Play Your Cards Right, You Too Can Be a Loser," *Ben Casey,* 1965.

Performer, *American Bandstand* (also known as *AB, American Bandstand* 1966, *Bandstand, New American Bandstand* 1965, and *VH1's Best of American Bandstand*), ABC, 1966, 1971, 1976.

(As David Jones) Roland, "Moe Hill and the Mountains," *The Farmer's Daughter,* 1966.

Top of the Pops (also known as *All New Top of the Pops* and *TOTP*), BBC, 1967, 1968.

Dee Time, 1968.

(With the Monkees) *The Hollywood Squares,* multiple appearances, 1968.

The Glen Campbell Goodtime Hour, 1969.

Rowan & Martin's Laugh–In (also known as *Laugh–In*), NBC, 1969.

This Is Tom Jones, ABC, 1969.

The Johnny Cash Show, 1969.

The Andy Williams Show, NBC, 1969.

It's Happening (also known as *Happening '68* and *Happening '69*), ABC, 1969.

(As David Jones) Guest host, *The Music Scene,* 1969.

Ronald, "Love and the Elopement," *Love, American Style,* ABC, 1970.

Get It Together, 1970.

"The Teen Idol," *Make Room for Granddaddy,* 1970.

(As David Jones) Himself, "Getting Davy Jones," *The Brady Bunch,* ABC, 1971.

Voice, "The Haunted Horseman in Hagglethorn Hall," *The New Scooby–Doo Movies* (animated; also known as *Scooby–Doo Meets the Harlem Globetrotters* and *Scooby–Doo's New Comedy Movie Pictures*), 1972.

"Love and the Model Apartment," *Love, American Style,* ABC, 1973.

Rock Concert (also known as *Don Kirshner's Rock Concert*), 1976.

Davey Sanders, "The Bluegrass Special," *The Wonderful World of Disney* (later known as *Walt Disney's Wonderful World of Color*), NBC, 1977.

Frank Tyson, "Stable Girl: Parts 1 & 2," *Horse in the House,* 1979.

(In archive footage) *Today,* 1982.

Pop Quiz, 1984.

Saturday Superstore, 1984.

"Love–a–Gram/Love and the Apartment," *New Love, American Style,* ABC, 1986.

Blue Peter, 1986.

Showbiz Today, 1986, 1994, 1996.

Entertainment Tonight (also known as *Entertainment This Week, E.T., ET Weekend,* and *This Week in Entertainment*), syndicated, 1987, 1995, 2001.

Jerry Vicuna, "Sledge, Rattle, and Roll," *Sledge Hammer!* (also known as *Sledge Hammer: The Early Years*), ABC, 1988.

The Factory, 1988.

Crook & Chase, 1988, 1989.

Malcolm O'Dell, "The Wedge," *My Two Dads,* NBC, 1988.

Malcolm O'Dell, "Fallen Idol," *My Two Dads,* NBC, 1989.

Don't Just Sit There, Nickelodeon, 1989.

My Generation, VH1, 1989.

Nashville Now, TNN, 1989, 1991.

What's Up, Dr. Ruth?, 1990.

Almost Live!, 1990.

"No Way to Treat a Lady," *Trainer,* 1991.

(In archive footage) *Auntie's Bloomers,* 1991.

Himself, "The One Where They Go on the Love Boat," *Herman's Head,* Fox, 1992.

Reginald, "Rave On," *Boy Meets World,* ABC, 1995.

"Davy Jones," *The Single Guy,* NBC, 1996.

Prime Time Country, 1996.

Himself, "Dante's Inferno," *Sabrina, the Teenage Witch* (also known as *Sabrina* and *Sabrina Goes to College*), ABC, 1997.

"It Ain't Over Till ...," *Hitz,* 1997.

The National Lottery (also known as *The National Lottery Live*), 1997.

Access Hollywood, 1997.

"The Monkees," *Behind the Music* (also known as *VH1's "Behind the Music"*), VH1, 2000.

Fox News Live, Fox, 2000.

Voice, "Gerald's Game/Fishing Trip," *Hey Arnold!* (animated), Nickelodeon, 2002.

"Idolmakers," *48 Hours* (also known as *48 Hours Investigates* and *48 Hours Mystery*), 2002.

"NBC All–Stars Edition," *Weakest Link* (also known as *The Weakest Link USA*), 2002.

"Davey [sic] Jones," *Living in TV Land,* TV Land, c. 2005.

"Finales," *TV Land Confidential* (also known as *TV Land Confidential: The Untold Stories*), TV Land, 2007.

"Music," *TV Land Confidential* (also known as *TV Land Confidential: The Untold Stories*), TV Land, 2007.

Voice, "SpongeBob vs. the Big One," *SpongeBob SquarePants* (animated), Nickelodeon, 2009.

Also appeared as guest, *The Uncle Floyd Show.*

Television Talk Show Guest Appearances; Episodic:

Today (also known as *NBC News Today* and *The Today Show*), NBC, 1966, 1986, 1996, 1997.

The Rolf Harris Show, 1967.

The Joey Bishop Show, 1969.

Dinah! (also known as *Dinah! & Friends*), 1976.

The Mike Douglas Show, 1976.

The Tomorrow Show (also known as *Tomorrow, Tomorrow Coast to Coast,* and *The Tomorrow Show with Tom Snyder*), 1977.

The Little and Large Show, 1984.

Good Morning Britain (also known as *TV–am*), 1986, 1989.

Good Morning America (also known as *G.M.A.*), ABC, 1986, 1987, 1994, 1996.

The Morning Program, 1987.

Sally Jessy Raphael (also known as *Sally*), 1987, 1993, 2002.

CBS This Morning, CBS, 1988.

Saturday Morning Live, 1988.

Midday (also known as *Midday with Kerri–Anne*), 1988, 1989, 1991.

Aspel & Company, 1989.

A.M. Los Angeles, 1989.

The Pat Sajak Show, 1989.

The Oprah Winfrey Show (also known as *Oprah*), syndicated, 1990, 1995.

Tonight Live with Steve Vizard, 1991.

Country Kitchen (also known as *Florence Henderson's "Country Kitchen"*), 1991.

The Howard Stern Show (also known as *The Howard Stern Summer Show*), 1992.

Live with Regis and Kathie Lee, syndicated, 1992.

The Tonight Show with Jay Leno (also known as *Jay Leno*), 1995, 1996, 1998.

Breakfast News, 1997.

Noel's House Party, 1997.

The Big Breakfast, 1997.

This Morning (also known as *This Morning with Richard and Judy*), 1997, 2002.

Donny & Marie (also known as *Donny and Marie Hour*), 1999.

The Roseanne Show, 2000.

Fox and Friends (also known as *Fox and Friends First* and *Fox and Friends Weekend*), Fox, 2000.

Live with Regis and Kelly, syndicated, 2001.

The Early Show, 2001.

Open House (also known as *Open House with Gloria Hunniford*), 2002.

The Tony Danza Show, syndicated, 2005.

Television Appearances; Awards Presentations:

The 17th Annual Tony Awards, 1963.

The 18th Annual Primetime Emmy Awards, 1967.

(With the Monkees) *MTV Video Music Awards,* MTV, 1986.

The 14th Annual American Music Awards, ABC, 1987.

Guest presenter, *The 1997 Billboard Music Awards,* 1997.

The 1st 13th Annual Fancy Anvil Awards Show Program Special Live in Stereo (also known as *The 1st 13th Annual Cartoon Network Fancy Anvil Awards Show Program Special Live in Stereo*), Cartoon Network, 2002.

TV Land Awards: A Celebration of Classic TV (also known as *1st Annual TV Land Awards*), TV Land, 2003.

(In archive footage) *The Award Show Awards Show,* Trio, 2003.

Television Appearances; Other:

Lubbock, *Hunter* (pilot), CBS, 1973.

(Uncredited; in archive footage) Himself, *Hendrix* (movie), Showtime, 2000.

Host, *Meet the Royals* (miniseries), Arts and Entertainment, 2003.

Television Work; Specials:

Executive Producer, *Hey, Hey, It's the Monkees,* ABC, 1997.

Film Appearances:

(As David Jones) Davey, *Shadows,* 1959.

(As David Jones; with the Monkees) Davy, *Head,* Columbia, 1973.

Voice of Jim Hawkins, *Treasure Island* (animated), 1973.

Voice of the Artful Dodger, *Oliver Twist* (animated), 1974.

Heart and Soul (also known as *The Monkees: Heart and Soul*), 1988.

Himself, *The Brady Bunch Movie*, Paramount, 1995.

Himself, *Mayor of the Sunset Strip*, 2003.

(In archive footage) *Easy Riders, Raging Bulls: How the Sex, Drugs, and Rock 'n' Roll Generation Saved Hollywood* (documentary), Shout! Factory, 2004.

Himself, *The J–K Conspiracy*, Clear Channel, 2004.

Himself, *A Year in the Life* (also known as *Beatles Stories*), 2009.

Film Work:
Song performer, "Girl," *A Very Brady Sequel*, 1996.

Stage Appearances:
The Artful Dodger, *Oliver!* (musical), West End production, London, then Imperial Theatre, New York City, 1963–65.

Pickwick, Forty–Sixth Street Theatre, New York City, 1965.

Oblio, *The Point*, Mermaid Theatre, London, 1977.

Appeared as Jesus, *Godspell;* as Fagin, *Oliver!;* and in *The Real Live Brady Bunch;* also appeared in productions of *The Boyfriend* and *The Point.*

RECORDINGS

Albums; with the Monkees:
The Monkees, Colgems/RCA, 1967.
More of the Monkees, Colgems/RCA, 1967.
Headquarters, Colgems/RCA, 1967.
Pisces, Aquarius, Capricorn & Jones, Colgems/RCA, 1967.
The Birds The Bees & The Monkees, Colgems/RCA, 1968.
Instant Replay, Colgems/RCA, 1969.
Greatest Hits, Colgems, 1969.
Head, Colgems/RCA, 1969.
The Monkees Present, Rhino, 1969.
Changes, Colgems, 1970.
Barrel Full of Monkees, Colgems, 1971, released as *A Barrelful of Monkees: Monkees Songs for Kids!*, Kid Rhino, 1996.
Golden Hits, 1972.
Refocus, 1972.
Hit Factory, Pair, 1975.
Dolenz, Jones, Boyce & Hart, E1 Records, 1976.
Monkee Business, Rhino, 1982.
Monkee Flips, Rhino, 1984.
I'm a Believer, 1985.
Then & Now ... The Best of the Monkees, Arista, 1986.
Pool It!, Rhino, 1986.

20th Anniversary Tour, Rhino, 1986.
Live 1967, Rhino, 1987.
Missing Links, Rhino, 1987.
Missing Links, Vol. 1, Rhino, 1990.
Missing Links, Vol. 3, Rhino, 1996.
Hey Hey We're the Monkees, DJ Specialist, 1996.
Concert in Japan, Varese Sarabande, 1996.
Justus, Rhino, 1996.
The Very Best of the Monkees, Bellaphon, 1997.
Here They Come: The Greatest Hits of the Monkees, WEA International, 1998.
Headquarters Sessions, 2000.
Best of the Monkees, Rhino, 2003.
Daydream Believer: The Platinum Collection, WEA International, 2005.
The Platinum Collection, Vol. 2, WEA, 2006.
Legends Collection, Madacy, 2006.
Very Best of the Monkees, Warner, 2006.
Last Train to Clarksville and Other Hits, Flashback Records, 2007.
Forever the Monkees, Madacy, 2007.
I'm a Believer: The Best of the Monkees, Music Club Records, 2007.
Best of the Monkees, Arista, 2009.

Several other "best of" anthologies were released over the years by various record labels. Singles include "Daydream Believer," "I'm a Believer," "(I'm Not Your) Steppin' Stone," "Last Train to Clarksville," "A Little Bit Me, A Little Bit You," "Pleasant Valley Sunday," and "Words," all 1967; and "D. W. Washburn" and "Valeri," both 1968.

Solo Albums:
David Jones, 1965.
Head, Rhino, 1968.
Davy Jones, 1971.
Just Me, 2001.
The Essentials, Rhino, 2002.
Davy Jones Live!!!, 2003.
King Biscuit Flower Hour, 2003.
Just Me 2, 2004.
She, 2009.

Other solo albums include *Christmas Jones, Daydream Believin', Incredible Revisited,* and *Just for the Record,* Volumes 1–4. Singles include "Your Personal Penguin" to accompany the children's book of the same title, 2006.

Videos:
The Monkees Deluxe Limited–Edition Box, Rhino, 1966.
Head, Rhino, 1986.
Monkeemania, Vol. 1, 1986.
Monkeemania, Vol. 2, 1986.
Vol. 1: Machine, 1986.

Vol. 3: Here Come the Monkees/I Was a Teenage Monster, 1986.

Vol. 4: Hitting, 1986.

Vol. 4: Monkees a la Carte/The Prince and the Pauper, 1986.

Vol. 5: Get Out, 1986.

Vol. 6: Devil, 1986.

Dance, Monkees, Dance/Hitting the High Seas, 1991.

Heart and Soul, Rhino/WEA, 1991.

Hey Hey We're the Monkees, Pickwick, 1997.

33 1/3, Rhino, 1997.

The Monkees: Live Summer Tour, 2002.

Video Games:

Voice, *Hey Hey We're the Monkees,* 1996.

Voice, *TV Land Presents Blast from the Past,* 2001.

Other:

There Is a Happy Land (dramatic reading), BBC, 1961.

WRITINGS

Screenplays:

(Uncredited) *Head,* 1968.

Other:

(With Alan Green) *They Made a Monkee Out of Me,* Dome Press, 1987.

They Made a Monkee Out of Me ... Again, 1997.

Davy Jones: Daydream Believin', Hercules Promotions, 2000.

Writer or coauthor of several songs performed with the Monkees; author of short stories and poetry.

ADAPTATIONS

Songs recorded with the Monkees have been featured in many films and television programs, particularly the song "Daydream Believer." Jones's performance in the musical *Oliver!* was recorded for radio in 1965.

OTHER SOURCES

Books:

Jones, Davy, and Alan Green, *They Made a Monkee Out of Me,* Dome Press, 1987.

Jones, Davy, *They Made a Monkee Out of Me ... Again,* 1997.

Jones, Davy, *Davy Jones: Daydream Believin',* Hercules Promotions, 2000.

Electronic:

Davy Jones Official Site, http://www.davyjones.com, February 9, 2010.

Other:

Daydream Believers: The Monkees' Story (television special), 2000.

JONES, Trevor 1949–

PERSONAL

Full name, Trevor Alfred Charles Jones; born March 23, 1949, in Cape Town, South Africa; naturalized British citizen; married; children: four. *Education:* University of York, B.A. (with honors), 1977; National Film School (now National Film and Television School), M.A., 1978; Royal Academy of Music, A.R.A.M., 1998, F.R.A.M., 2006.

Addresses: *Agent*—Soundtrack Music Associates, 2229 Cloverfield Blvd., Santa Monica, CA 90405.

Career: Composer, conductor, and musical director. British Broadcasting Corp., classical music reviewer, 1970–75; (British) National Film and Television School, professor of music, department chair, 1999; presenter of master classes at Royal College of Music, National Film and Television Museum, British Academy of Film and Television Arts, and other venues in England and elsewhere; lecturer on film music. Member of awards jury for British Academy of Film and Television Arts, Mercury Music Prize, and International Film Festival of Flanders.

Member: Authors, Publishers, and Composers (member of media music board), Performing Right Society for Music (fellow), British Academy of Film and Television Arts.

Awards, Honors: Ivor Novello Award nomination, best theme for a television production, 1985, for *The Last Place on Earth;* Film Award nomination, best original film score, British Academy of Film and Television Arts, 1990, for *Mississippi Burning;* Ivor Novello Award nomination, best film theme, 1991, for *Arachnophobia;* Golden Globe Award nomination and Film Award nomination, British Academy of Film and Television Arts Film, both best original film score (with Randy Edelman), and American Society of Composers, Authors, and Publishers Award, top box office films, 1993, for *The Last of the Mohicans;* platinum record certification, Recording Industry Association of America, for soundtrack album, *The Last of the Mohicans;* American Society of Composers, Authors, and Publishers Award, top box office films, 1993, for *In the Name of the Father;* American Society of Composers, Authors, and Publishers Award, top box office films, 1994, for *Cliffhanger;* nomination for Anthony Asquith Award for Film and Music, British Academy of Film and Television Arts, 1997, for *Brassed Off;* American Society of Composers, Authors, and Publishers Award, top box office films, 1997, for *G.I. Jane;* Emmy Award nomination, outstanding composition of dramatic underscore for a miniseries or movie, 1998, for *Merlin;* Golden Globe Award nomination (with Sting), best original song for a motion picture, 1999, for *The Mighty;* Brit Award, best soundtrack, 1999, and American Society of Composers, Authors, and Publishers Award, top box office films, 2000, both for *Notting Hill;* platinum record certification, 2000, for soundtrack album, *Notting Hill;* Ivor Novello Award nomination, best original film score, 2001, for *Thirteen Days;* American Society of Composers, Authors, and Publishers Awards, 2001, for *From Hell,* for *Dinotopia,* 2003, for *The League of Extraordinary Gentlemen,* and 2004, for *Around the World in 80 Days;* honorary Ph.D., University of the Western Cape, 2005; nomination for Award of the Japanese Academy (with Ryo Katsuji), best score, 2006, for *Bokoku no ijisu.*

CREDITS

Film Work:

Song arranger, *Life of Brian* (also known as *Monty Python's "Life of Brian"*), Warner Bros., 1979.

Song arranger, *Time Bandits,* Avco Embassy, 1980.

Musical director, *The Dollar Bottom* (short film), 1980.

Musical director and conductor, *Brothers and Sisters,* British Film Institute, 1980.

Musical director and conductor, *Excalibur,* Orion, 1981.

Music conductor, *The Appointment,* 1981.

Synthesized sound, *The Dark Crystal,* Universal, 1982.

Orchestrator, *Nate and Hayes* (also known as *Savage Islands*), Paramount, 1983.

Music conductor, *Runaway Train,* Cannon, 1985.

Musical director and conductor, *Just Ask for Diamond* (also known as *Diamond's Edge*), Kings Road, 1988.

Music conductor, *Dominick and Eugene* (also known as *Nicky and Gino*), Orion, 1988.

Orchestrator, music conductor, and synthesizer musician, *CrissCross* (also known as *Alone Together*), Metro–Goldwyn–Mayer, 1992.

Orchestrator and synthesizer musician, *Blame It on the Bellboy,* Buena Vista, 1992.

Musician, *Freejack,* Warner Bros., 1992.

Song arranger, *The Last of the Mohicans,* Twentieth Century–Fox, 1992.

Orchestrator and synthesizer musician, *In the Name of the Father,* Universal, 1993.

Orchestrator and synthesizer musician, *Cliffhanger* (also known as *Cliffhanger–l'ultima sfida* and *Cliffhanger, traque au sommet*), TriStar, 1993.

Member of string quartet, *Dallas Doll,* Artistic License, 1994.

Orchestrator and music conductor, *Loch Ness,* Gramercy, 1995.

Orchestrator and music conductor, *Hideaway,* TriStar, 1995.

Orchestrator, music conductor, and song arranger, *Kiss of Death,* Twentieth Century–Fox, 1995.

Orchestrations and song arranger, *Richard III,* Metro–Goldwyn–Mayer, 1995.

Orchestrator, music conductor, and music producer for brass band, *Brassed Off!,* Miramax, 1996.

Song arranger, *The Chamber,* 1996.

Orchestrator and song arranger, *Roseanna's Grave* (also known as *For Roseanna* and *For the Love of Roseanna*), Fine Line, 1997.

Orchestrator, *G.I. Jane* (also known as *Navy Cross, Undisclosed, In Pursuit of Honor,* and *A Matter of Honor*), Buena Vista, 1997.

Orchestrator, *Lawn Dogs,* Strand Releasing, 1997.

Orchestrator, music conductor, and synthesizer musician, *Desperate Measures,* TriStar, 1998.

Orchestrator and synthesizer musician, *Dark City,* New Line Cinema, 1998.

Orchestrator and synthesizer musician, *The Mighty,* Miramax, 1998.

Orchestrator and synthesizer musician, *Notting Hill,* Universal, 1999.

Orchestrator and synthesizer musician, *Thirteen Days* (also known as *Thirteen Days Which Shocked the World*), New Line Cinema, 2000.

Music producer, *Titanic Town,* Shooting Gallery, 2000.

Orchestrator and synthesizer musician, *From Hell,* Twentieth Century–Fox, 2001.

Orchestrations and synthesizer musician, *Crossroads,* Paramount, 2002.

Orchestrator, synthesizer musician, and song producer, *I'll Be There,* Warner Bros., 2003.

Orchestrator, *The League of Extraordinary Gentlemen* (also known as *The League, LXG, Die liga der aussergewoehnlichen gentlemen,* and *Liga vyjicnych*), Twentieth Century–Fox, 2003.

Orchestrator and synthesized musician, *Around the World in 80 Days* (also known as *In 80 Tagen um die welt*), Buena Vista, 2004.

Television Work; Miniseries:

Executive producer, *Joni Jones,* PBS, 1987.

Orchestrator, *Gulliver's Travels,* NBC, 1996.

(Uncredited) Orchestrator and synthesized musician, *Merlin,* NBC, 1998.

Orchestrator and synthesizer musician, *Cleopatra,* ABC, 1999.

Television Work; Movies:

Music arranger, *A Private Life,* 1988.

Television Work; Specials:
Music conductor, "Dr. Fischer of Geneva," *Great Performances,* PBS, 1985.

RECORDINGS

Soundtrack Albums:
The Dark Crystal, Warner Bros., 1982.
The Last Place on Earth, Island Visual Arts, 1985.
Runaway Train, Capital Milan Records, 1985.
Labyrinth, EMI America, 1986.
Angel Heart, Antilles, 1987.
Sweet Lies, Island Records, 1988.
Dominick and Eugene, Varese Sarabande, 1988.
Mississippi Burning, Antilles, 1988.
Sea of Love, Polygram, 1989.
Bad Influence, Island Records, 1990.
Arachnophobia, Hollywood Records, 1990.
Crisscross, Intrada Records, 1992.
Freejack, Morgan Creek Records, 1992.
The Last of the Mohicans, Morgan Creek Records, 1992.
Cliffhanger, Scotti Brothers, 1993.
In the Name of the Father, Island Records, 1993.
Hideaway, TVT Records, 1995.
Kiss of Death, Milan Records, 1995.
Richard III, London Records, 1995.
Gulliver's Travels, BMG, 1996.
Brassed Off!, BMG, 1996.
Roseanna's Grave, BMG, 1997.
G.I. Jane, Hollywood Records, 1997.
Dominick and Eugene, Varese Sarabande, 1988.
Dark City, TVT Records, 1998.
Merlin, Varese Sarabande, 1998.
The Mighty, ARC–21, 1998.
Titanic Town, Island Records, 1998.
Cleopatra, 1999.
Notting Hill, Island Records, 1999.
Thirteen Days, New Line Records, 2000.
From Hell, Varese Sarabande, 2001.
Dinotopia, 2002.
The League of Extraordinary Gentlemen, Varese Sarabande, 2003.
Aegis (music from *Bokoku no ijisu*), Universal, 2005.
Fields of Freedom, 2006.
We Fight to Be Free, 2006.
Three and Out, 2008.

Other:
Recorded work with Academy of St. Martin in the Fields, Alberni String Quartet, Endemion String Quarter, Gabrielli String Quartet, Medici String Quartet, London Philharmonic Orchestra, and London Symphony Orchestra.

WRITINGS

Film Composer:
Britannia: The First of the Last, 1979.
Black Angel, 1979.
Greek dance music, *Time Bandits,* Avco Embassy, 1980.
The Dollar Bottom (short film), 1980.
Brothers and Sisters, British Film Institute, 1980.
The Beneficiary, 1980.
The Appointment, 1981.
Excalibur, Orion, 1981.
The Sender, Paramount, 1982.
The Dark Crystal, Universal, 1982.
Nate and Hayes (also known as *Savage Islands*), Paramount, 1983.
Runaway Train, Cannon, 1985.
Labyrinth, TriStar, 1986.
Angel Heart (also known as *Aux portes de l'enfer*), TriStar, 1987.
Sweet Lies, Island, 1988.
Mississippi Burning, Orion, 1988.
(Including songs) *Just Ask for Diamond* (also known as *Diamond's Edge*), Kings Road Entertainment, 1988.
Dominick and Eugene (also known as *Nicky and Gino*), Orion, 1988.
Sea of Love, Universal, 1989.
Bad Influence, Triumph Releasing, 1990.
Arachnophobia, Buena Vista, 1990.
True Colors, Paramount, 1991.
Defenseless, 1991.
(And song "The Child that I Was") *CrissCross* (also known as *Alone Together*), Metro–Goldwyn–Mayer, 1992.
Blame It on the Bellboy, Buena Vista, 1992.
Freejack, Warner Bros., 1992.
(And song adaptor) *The Last of the Mohicans,* Twentieth Century–Fox, 1992.
In the Name of the Father, Universal, 1993.
Cliffhanger (also known as *Cliffhanger–l'ultima sfida* and *Cliffhanger, traque au sommet*), TriStar, 1993.
De baby huilt (also known as *The Four A.M. Feed*), 1994.
Loch Ness, Gramercy, 1995.
Hideaway, TriStar, 1995.
Kiss of Death, Twentieth Century–Fox, 1995.
Richard III, Metro–Goldwyn–Mayer, 1995.
Brassed Off!, Miramax, 1996.
Roseanna's Grave (also known as *For the Love of Roseanna* and *For Roseanna*), Fine Line, 1997.
G.I. Jane (also known as *Navy Cross, Undisclosed, In Pursuit of Honor,* and *A Matter of Honor*), Buena Vista, 1997.
Lawn Dogs, Strand Releasing, 1997.
Desperate Measures, TriStar, 1998.
Dark City (also known as *Dark World* and *Dark Empire*), New Line Cinema, 1998.
(And title song) *The Mighty,* Miramax, 1998.
Titanic Town, Shooting Gallery, 1998.
Talk of Angels, Miramax, 1998.

Frederic Wilde, 1999.
Molly, Metro–Goldwyn–Mayer, 1999.
Notting Hill, Universal, 1999.
Thirteen Days (also known as *Thirteen Days Which Shocked the World*), New Line Cinema, 2000.
The Long Run, Universal, 2000.
To End All Wars, Argyll Film Partners, 2001.
From Hell, Twentieth Century–Fox, 2001.
Crossroads, Paramount, 2002.
(And rock version of song "All My Life") *I'll Be There,* Warner Bros., 2003.
The League of Extraordinary Gentlemen (also known as *The League, LXG, Die liga der aussergewoehnlichen Gentlemen,* and *Liga vyjicnych*), Twentieth Century–Fox, 2003.
Around the World in 80 Days (also known as *In 80 Tagen um die welt*), Buena Vista, 2004.
The Unsteady Chough (animated short film), 2004.
Bokoku no ijisu (also known as *Aegis*), Herald Film/Shochiku, 2005.
Chaos (also known as *Hit & Blast*), Capitol Films, 2005.
Fields of Freedom, Greystone Communications, 2006.
We Fight to Be Free (short film), Greystone Communications, 2006.
Alex Rider: Operation Stormbreaker, 2006.
Three and Out (also known as *A Deal Is a Deal*), Worldwide Bonus Entertainment, 2008.

Television Composer; Series:
Jim Henson Presents the World of International Puppeteering, 1985.
Dinotopia (also known as *Dinotopia: The Series*), ABC, 2002.
Jozi–H (animated), CBC, 2006–2007.
The Tudors, 2007.

Television Composer; Miniseries:
The Last Days of Pompeii, ABC, 1984.
The Last Place on Earth, 1985.
Joni Jones, PBS, 1987.
Gulliver's Travels, NBC, 1996.
Merlin, NBC, 1998.
Cleopatra, ABC, 1999.
Dinotopia, ABC, 2002.

Television Composer; Movies:
Those Glory, Glory Days, 1983.
One of Ourselves, 1983.
This Office Life, 1984.
Aderyn Pauper … and Pigs Might Fly, 1984.
A Private Life, 1988.
Murder by Moonlight (also known as *Dark of the Moon, Murder in Space,* and *Murder on the Moon*), CBS, 1989.
By Dawn's Early Light (also known as *The Grand Tour* and *Red Alert*), HBO, 1990.
Chains of Gold, Showtime, 1991.

Death Train (also known as *Alistair MacLean's "Death Train"* and *Detonator*), 1993.
Blood and Oil, 2009.

Television Composer; Specials:
(Uncredited) *The World of "The Dark Crystal,"* 1983.
"Dr. Fischer of Geneva" (also known as "The Bomb Party"), *Great Performances,* PBS, 1985.
"Guns: A Day in the Death of America," *America Undercover,* HBO, 1991.

Television Composer: Episodic:
Incidental music, "Golden Gordon," *Ripping Yarns,* 1979.
Theme music, "From an Immigrant's Notebook," *Arena,* 1985.

Video Composer:
Marvel Nemesis: Rise of the Imperfects (video game), Electronic Arts, 2005.

Other:
Composer of work commissioned by London Symphony and others; composer for theatre and ballet. Collaborator with other artists such as David Bowie, Charlotte Church, Elvis Costello, Sinead O'Connor, Britney Spears, and Sting.

OTHER SOURCES

Electronic:
Trevor Jones Official Site, http://www.trevorjonesfilmmusic.com, October 5, 2009.

JUNGER, Gil 1954–
　　(Gilbert Junger)

PERSONAL

Born November 7, 1954, in New York, NY. *Education:* University of Texas at Austin, graduated (with honors). *Avocational Interests:* Photography, golf, and music.

Addresses: *Agent*—Paradigm, 360 North Crescent Dr. N., Beverly Hills, CA 90210.

Career: Director and producer. Also worked as line producer, production supervisor, editorial supervisor, and consultant. Mid–Life Crisis, band member.

Awards, Honors: Humanitas Award, Human Family Educational and Cultural Institute, 1995, for *The John*

Larroquette Show; Emmy Award nomination and Directors Guild of America Award nomination, both outstanding directing for a comedy series, 1998, for *Ellen.*

CREDITS

Television Director; Series:
It's a Living (also known as *Making a Living*), syndicated, between 1987 and 1989.
Nurses, NBC, 1993–94.
Blossom, NBC, 1994–95.
Living Single (also known as *My Girls*), Fox, 1996–97.
Ellen (also known as *These Friends of Mine*), ABC, 1996–98.
Movie Stars, The WB, 2000.
According to Jim, ABC, 2001–2002.
Hope & Faith, ABC, 2003–2006.
Rodney, ABC, 2005–2008.
10 Things I Hate about You, ABC Family, 2009.

Television Director; Movies:
(And producer) *If Only,* ABC Family, 2003.
Jessica, 2004.
My Fake Fiance, ABC Family, 2009.
The Business of Falling in Love, ABC Family, 2010.

Television Director; Pilots:
(And producer) *Blossom,* NBC, 1990.
The Hanleys, ABC, 1998.
Charmed Life, ABC, 1998.
Helmet Heads, The WB, 1999.
Odd Man Out, ABC, 1999.
8 Simple Rules for Dating My Teenage Daughter (also known as *8 Simple Rules ...*), ABC, 2002.
Earthquake, ABC, 2004.
Kyle XY, ABC Family, 2006.
Greek, ABC Family, 2007.
Happy Campers, ABC Family, 2008.
10 Things I Hate about You, ABC Family, 2009.

Television Director; Episodic:
"Lee's Bad, Bad Day," *Hardball,* Fox, 1994.
"Faith," *The John Larroquette Show* (also known as *Larroquette*), NBC, 1995.
"Wrestling Matches," *The John Larroquette Show* (also known as *Larroquette*), NBC, 1995.
"And the Heat Goes On," *The John Larroquette Show* (also known as *Larroquette*), NBC, 1995.
"Once Again, with Feeling," *In the House,* UPN, 1995.
"Dog Catchers," *In the House,* UPN, 1995.
"Daddy's Home," *In the House,* UPN, 1995.
"A Christmas Story," *Minor Adjustments,* UPN, 1996.
"Clan of the Bare Caves," *The Jeff Foxworthy Show* (also known as *Somewhere in America*), NBC, 1996.
"Before You Say 'No,' Just Hear Me Out," *The Jeff Foxworthy Show* (also known as *Somewhere in America*), NBC, 1996.

Pearl, CBS, 1996.
Hiller and Diller, ABC, 1997.
"To Have and to Hold," *Chicago Sons,* NBC, 1997.
"Love in the Time of Cicadas," *Chicago Sons,* NBC, 1997.
"The Belligerent Waitress and the Surly Fry Cook," *Chicago Sons,* NBC, 1997.
"Beauty and the Butt," *Chicago Sons,* NBC, 1997.
"Dharma and Greg's First Romantic Valentine's Day Weekend," *Dharma & Greg,* ABC, 1998.
"A Closet Full of Hell," *Dharma & Greg,* ABC, 1998.
"The Stan Plan," *Soul Man,* ABC, 1998.
"The Choir Boys," *Soul Man,* ABC, 1998.
"Todd and the Bod," *Soul Man,* ABC, 1998.
"I'm Shrinnnking," *The Hughleys,* 1998.
"A Multi–Culti Christmas," *The Hughleys,* 1998.
"Putting Two 'n Two Together," *Two of a Kind,* ABC, 1998.
"Prelude to a Kiss," *Two of a Kind,* ABC, 1998.
"First Crush," *Two of a Kind,* ABC, 1998.
"Peeping Twins," *Two of a Kind,* ABC, 1998.
The Secret Lives of Men, ABC, 1998.
The Closer, CBS, 1998.
"Twelfth Step to Hell," *Action,* Fox, 1999.
"Two Guys, a Girl, and a Proposal," *Two Guys, a Girl and a Pizza Place* (also known as *Two Guys and a Girl*), 1999.
"Two Guys, a Girl, and Valentine's Day," *Two Guys, a Girl and a Pizza Place* (also known as *Two Guys and a Girl*), 1999.
"The Home Office," *Ladies Man,* CBS, 1999.
"Jimmy's Song," *Ladies Man,* CBS, 1999.
"Park Rage," *Ladies Man,* CBS, 1999.
"The First Girlfriends Club," *Odd Man Out,* 1999.
"Good Will Hunting," *Odd Man Out,* 1999.
"The Unbelievable Truth," *Odd Man Out,* 1999.
"My Life as a Dog," *Odd Man Out,* 1999.
"Three Years Later" (also known as "No Good Dead"), *Zoe, Duncan, Jack & Jane* (also known as *Zoe ...*), The WB, 2000.
"A Midsummer Night's Nightmare," *Zoe, Duncan, Jack & Jane* (also known as *Zoe ...*), The WB, 2000.
"Party Girls," *Zoe, Duncan, Jack & Jane* (also known as *Zoe ...*), The WB, 2000.
"Three Years Later," *Zoe, Duncan, Jack & Jane* (also known as *Zoe ...*), The WB, 2000.
"Grapefruits of Wrath," *Daddio,* NBC, 2000.
"The Premium Also Rises," *Daddio,* NBC, 2000.
"Crackers and Punishment," *Daddio,* NBC, 2000.
"The Pinch Hitter," *Inside Schwartz,* NBC, 2001.
"Eve's Date with Schwartz's Destiny," *Inside Schwartz,* NBC, 2001.
"Kissing Cousin," *Inside Schwartz,* NBC, 2002.
"Denial for a While," *In Case of Emergency,* ABC, 2007.
"Oh, Henry!," *In Case of Emergency,* ABC, 2007.
"Hazed and Confused," *Greek,* ABC Family, 2007.
"The Rusty Nail," *Greek,* ABC Family, 2007.
"Pledge Allegiance," *Greek,* ABC Family, 2008.
"Dreamguys," *'Til Death,* Fox, 2008.
"The Challenge," *Rules of Engagement,* CBS, 2009.

"Thrown for a Hoop," *Sherri,* Lifetime, 2009.
"Lost Weekend," *Sherri,* Lifetime, 2009.
"Don't Leave Me," *Sherri,* Lifetime, 2009.

Television Producer; Series:
Associate producer, *Hail to the Chief,* ABC, 1985.
Coproducer, *It's a Living* (also known as *Making a Living*), ABC, between 1985 and 1987.
Associate producer, *Tough Cookies,* CBS, 1986.
Heartland, CBS, 1989.
Lenny, CBS, 1990.
Good & Evil, ABC, 1991.
Herman's Head, Fox, 1991–92.
Nurses, NBC, 1992–94.
The Office, CBS, 1995.
Minor Adjustments, NBC, 1995, then UPN, 1996.
Ellen (also known as *These Friends of Mine*), 1997–98.
Two of a Kind, ABC, c. 1998–99.
Executive producer, *Movie Stars,* The WB, 1999–2000.
Hope & Faith, ABC, 2003–2005.

Also producer of *Walter and Emily.*

Television Producer; Pilots:
Associate producer, *The Arena,* ABC, 1986.
Woops!, Fox, 1992.

Television Producer; Episodic:
Associate producer, "The Arena," *Comedy Factory,* 1986.

(As Gilbert Junger) Producer, "It Happened Two Nights, Four Costume Changes," *Empty Nest,* NBC, 1990.
(As Gilbert Junger) Producer, "All about Harry," *Empty Nest,* NBC, 1991.

Television Appearances; Specials:
Greatest Ever Romantic Movies, Channel 5, 2007.

Film Director:
10 Things I Hate about You, Buena Vista, 1999.
Black Knight, Twentieth Century–Fox, 2001.
Get Smart's Bruce and Lloyd Out of Control, Warner Bros., 2008.

Film Appearances:
(Uncredited) Teacher, *10 Things I Hate about You,* Buena Vista, 1999.

WRITINGS

Screenplays:
Black Knight, Twentieth Century–Fox, 2001.

Television Movies:
Lyricist, "Love Will Show You Everything," *If Only,* ABC Family, 2003.

Television Episodes:
"Nancy's Birthday Party," *It's a Living* (also known as *Making a Living*), ABC, 1987.

K

KAUFMAN, Charlie 1958–

PERSONAL

Full name, Charles Stewart Kaufman; born November 19, 1958, in New York, NY; son of Myron (an engineer) and Helen (a homemaker) Kaufman; married Denise; children: Anna, additional child. *Education:* Studied film at New York University; also attended Boston University. *Avocational Interests:* Reading.

Addresses: *Agent*—United Talent Agency, 9560 Wilshire Blvd., Suite 500, Beverly Hills, CA 90212.

Career: Writer and producer. Previously worked in the circulation department of *Star Tribune* (Minneapolis, MN), c. early 1980s, and at a museum.

Awards, Honors: Toronto Film Critics Association Award, best screenplay, San Diego Film Critics Society Awards, best screenplay—original, Los Angeles Film Critics Association Award, best screenplay, Boston Society of Film Critics Award, best screenplay, 1999, Academy Award nomination, best writing—screenplay written directly for the screen, Online Film Critics Association Award, best screenplay—original, Online Film Critics Association Award nomination, best debut, Screen Award nomination, best screenplay written directly for the screen, Writers Guild of America, Santa Fe Film Critics Circle Award, best original screenplay, National Society of Film Critics Award, best screenplay, Sierra Award, best screenplay—original, Las Vegas Film Critics Society, Independent Spirit Award, best first screenplay, Golden Satellite Award nomination, best screenplay—original, International Press Academy, Golden Globe Award nomination, best screenplay—motion picture, Chicago Film Critics Award, best screenplay, Film Award, best screenplay—original, British Academy of Film and Television Arts, Saturn Award, best writer, Academy of Science Fiction, Fantasy, and Horror Films, 2000, ALFS Award, screenwriter of the year, London Critics Circle Film Awards, Nebula Award nomination, best script, Science Fiction and Fantasy Writers of America, 2001, all for *Being John Malkovich;* Toronto Film Critics Association Award (with Donald Kaufman), best screenplay, Southeastern Film Critics Association Award (with Kaufman), best screenplay—adapted, New York Film Critics Circle Award (with Kaufman), best screenplay, Boston Society of Film Critics Award (with Kaufman), best screenplay, 2002, Academy Award nomination (with Kaufman), best writing—screenplay based on material previously produced or published, Screen Award nomination (with Kaufman), best screenplay based on material previously produced or published, Writers Guild of America, USC Scripter Award nomination (with Susan Orlean), University of Southern California, Online Film Critics Association Award (with Kaufman), best screenplay—adapted, Golden Satellite Award (with Kaufman), best screenplay—adapted, Golden Globe Award nomination (with Kaufman), best screenplay—motion picture, Florida Film Critics Association Award (with Kaufman), best screenplay, Chicago Film Critics Association Award (with Kaufman), best screenplay, Film Award (with Kaufman), best screenplay—adapted, British Academy of Film and Television Arts, 2003, ALFS Award nomination (with Kaufman), screenwriter of the year, London Critics Circle, 2004, all for *Adaptation;* High Hopes Award (with others), Munich Film Festival, 2002, for *Human Nature;* National Board of Review, best screenplay, 2002, for *Human Nature, Adaptation,* and *Confessions of a Dangerous Mind;* Boston Film Critics Association Award, best writer, 2003, for *Adaptation* and *Confessions of a Dangerous Mind;* Academy Award, best writing—original screenplay, Critics Choice Award nomination, best writer, Broadcast Film Critics Association, Chicago Film Critics Association Award nomination, best screenplay—original, National Board of Review, best screenplay—original, Phoenix Film Critics Society Award, best screenplay written directly for the screen, Seattle Film Critics Award, best screenplay—original, Sierra Award, best screenplay, Las Vegas Film Critics Society, Southeastern Film Critics Association

Award, best screenplay—original, Toronto Film Critics Association Award, best screenplay, Washington DC Area Film Critics Association Award, best screenplay—original, 2004, ALFS Award, screenwriter, London Critics Circle, Film Award, best screenplay—original, British Academy of Film and Television Arts, Bram Stoker Award (with others), screenplay, Golden Globe Award nomination, best screenplay—motion picture, Kansas City Film Critics Circle Award, best screenplay—original, Online Film Critics Award (with others), best screenplay—original, Saturn Award nomination, best writer, Academy of Science Fiction, Fantasy, and Horror Films, Screen Award (with others), best original screenplay, Writers Guild of America, 2005, Literary Award, screenplay, PEN Center USA, 2006, all for *Eternal Sunshine of the Spotless Mind;* Time–Machine Honorary Award, Sitges—Catalonian International Film Festival, 2008; Austin Film Critics Award, best screenplay—original, Golden Palm Award nomination, Cannes Film Festival, Gotham Award nomination, best film, 2008, Online Film Critics Society Award nominations, best screenplay—original and breakthrough filmmaker, Independent Spirit Award (with others), best first feature, Robert Altman Award (with others), Independent Spirit Awards, 2009, all for *Synecdoche, New York.*

CREDITS

Film Work:
Executive producer, *Being John Malkovich*, USA Films, 1999.
Producer, *Human Nature*, Fine Line, 2001.
Executive producer, *Adaptation*, Sony Pictures Entertainment, 2002.
Executive producer, *Eternal Sunshine of the Spotless Mind*, Focus Features, 2004.
Director and producer, *Synecdoche, New York*, Sony Pictures Classics, 2008.

Television Work; Series:
Story editor, *The Trouble with Larry*, 1993.
Coproducer, *Misery Loves Company*, Fox, 1995.
Producer, *Ned and Stacey*, Fox, 1996–99.

Television Appearances; Specials:
The 15th Annual IFP/West Independent Spirit Awards, Independent Film Channel and Bravo, 2000.
The 72nd Annual Academy Awards, ABC, 2000.
The 77th Annual Academy Awards, ABC, 2005.

Television Appearances; Episodic:
The Charlie Rose Show (also known as *Charlie Rose*), 2004, 2008.
Cartelera, 2008.
Cinema 3 (also known as *Informatiu cinema*), 2008.
Up Close with Carrie Keagan, 2008.
Silenci?, 2008.

"Kevin Bacon/Charlie Kaufman," *The Colbert Report*, Comedy Central, 2008.

WRITINGS

Screenplays:
Being John Malkovich, USA Films, 1999, published by Faber and Faber, 2000.
Human Nature, Fine Line, 2001.
Adaptation, Sony Pictures Entertainment, 2002.
Confessions of a Dangerous Mind (also known as *Gestandnisse—Confessions of a Dangerous Mind*), Artisan Entertainment, 2002.
Eternal Sunshine of the Spotless Mind, Focus Features, 2004.
Synecdoche, New York, Sony Pictures Classics, 2008.

Television Episodes:
"Prisoner of Love," *Get a Life*, Fox, 1991.
"1977 2000," *Get a Life*, Fox, 1992.
The Edge, Fox, 1992–93.
The Trouble with Larry, CBS, 1993.
"Computer Dating," *Ned and Stacey*, Fox, 1996.
"Loganberry's Run," *Ned and Stacey*, Fox, 1996.
The Dana Carvey Show, ABC, 1996.
"Where My Third Nepal Is Sheriff," *Ned and Stacey*, Fox, 1997.
"Love," *Morel Orel* (animated), Cartoon Network, 2006.

Stage Plays:
Hope Leaves the Theater, produced in Brooklyn, NY, 2005.

OTHER SOURCES

Books:
Authors and Artists for Young Adults, Vol. 68, Thomson Gale, 2006.

Periodicals:
Los Angeles Magazine, March, 2003, p. 98.
Newsweek, November 10, 2008, p. 61.
The Observer, February 9, 2003.
Time, April 29, 2002, p. 16; October 11, 2004, p. 99.
Variety, May 12, 2008, p. 10.
Wired, November, 2008, p. 230.

KEY, Keegan Michael 1971–
   (Keegan–Michael Key)

PERSONAL

Born March 22, 1971, in Southfield, MI; married Cynthia Blaise (a dialect coach and an actress). *Education:* Pennsylvania State University, master's degree, acting.

Addresses: *Agent*—United Talent Agency, 9560 Wilshire Blvd., Suite 500, Beverly Hills, CA 90212. *Manager*—Principato, Young Management, 9465 Wilshire Blvd., Suite 880, Beverly Hills, CA 90212.

Career: Actor and writer. Planet Ant Theater, Hamtramck, MI, cofounder; Second City, Chicago, IL, performer, 1997–2003.

Awards, Honors: Joseph Jefferson Award, best actor in a revue, 2002, for *Holy War, Batman! or the Yellow Cab of Courage;* Joseph Jefferson Award, best actor in a revue, 2003, for *Curious George Goes to War;* Joseph Jefferson Award nomination, best actor in a revue, 2003, for *Pants on Fire;* Joseph Jefferson Award nomination, best actor in a principal role in a musical, 2004, for *The Second's City's "Romeo & Juliet Musical."*

CREDITS

Film Appearances:
(As Keegan–Michael Key) J, *Get the Hell Out of Hamtown,* 1999.
Television studio manager, *Garage: A Rock Saga,* David E. Barker Entertainment, 2000.
Airport stranger, *Uncle Nino,* Lange Film Releasing, 2003.
Reporter, *Mr 3000,* Buena Vista, 2004.
(As Keegan–Michael Key) Curt Braunschweib, *Alleyball,* 2006.
Arch, *Grounds Zero* (short film), FilmPhobia, 2006.
Michael, *Sucker for Shelley* (short film), 2007.
Matt, *Yoga Matt* (short film), 2008.
(As Keegan–Michael Key) Duane, *Role Models* (also known as *Vorbilder?!*), Universal, 2008.
Dwayne, *Larry of Arabia* (short film), 2008.
Grape Vine, *The Wild Bunch,* 2010.

Television Appearances; Series:
(As Keegan–Michael Key) Various, *MADtv,* Fox, 2004–2009.
Host, *The Planet's Funniest Animals,* Animal Planet, 2005—.
Various, *Reno 911!,* Comedy Central, 2008–2009.
Curtis, *Gary Unmarried,* CBS, 2009–10.

Television Appearances; Specials:
"MADtv" Holiday Show '04 Special Edition, Fox, 2004.
"White & Nerdy," Al TV, VH1, 2006.
DeShawn, *Frangela,* Fox, 2007.

Television Appearances; Episodic:
Witkowski, "Quo Vadis?," *ER,* NBC, 2001.
Orderly, "Poison Ivy," *I'm With Her,* ABC, 2004.
Queer Edge with Jack E. Jett & Sandra Bernhard (also known as *Queer Edge* and *Queer Edge with Jack E. Jett*), 2005.

Himself, "Tournament 8, Game 4," *Celebrity Poker Showdown,* Bravo, 2006.
Himself, "Tournament 8 Championship," *Celebrity Poker Showdown,* Bravo, 2006.
"Kara DioGuardi," *Talkshow with Spike Feresten,* Fox, 2008.
"Dirty Little Secret," *Gaytown,* 2008.
Woodsy, *Chocolate News,* Comedy Central, 2008.
"Keegan–Michael Key," *GSN Live,* Game Show Network, 2009.
"Keegan Michael Key," *House Arrest with Andy Dick,* Comedy Central, 2009.

Stage Appearances:
Holy War, Batman! or the Yellow Cab of Courage, Second City Theatre, Chicago, IL, 2002.
Curious George Goes to War, Second City Theatre, 2003.
Pants on Fire, Second City Theatre, 2003.
he Second's City's "Romeo & Juliet Musical," Second City Theatre, 2004.

RECORDINGS

Music Videos:
Appeared in "White and Nerdy" by Weird Al Yankovic, 2006.

Video Games:
Commentary, *NFL Blitz 2004,* 2004.

WRITINGS

Television Episodes:
MADtv, Fox, 2004–2005.

OTHER SOURCES

Periodicals:
Crain's Chicago Business, November 3, 2003, p. E8.

KINMONT, Kathleen 1965–
(Kathleen Kinmont Burns)

PERSONAL

Original name, Kathleen Kinmont Smith; born February 3, 1965, in Los Angeles, CA; daughter of Jack D. Smith (in the electrical supply business) and Abby Dalton (an actress); married Lorenzo Lamas (an actor), January 20, 1989 (divorced, 1993); married Jere Burns (an actor), 1997 (divorced, 1999).

Career: Actress.

CREDITS

Film Appearances:
Pretty skater, *Hardbodies,* Columbia, 1984.
Marianne, *Fraternity Vacation,* New World, 1985.
Fifth party girl, *Winners Take All,* Apollo Pictures, 1986.
Cindy, *Nightforce* (also known as *Night Fighters* and *Night Force*), Vestron Pictures, 1987.
Kelly Meeker, *Halloween 4: The Return of Michael Myers* (also known as *Halloween 4*), Twentieth Century–Fox, 1988.
Phoenix, *Phoenix the Warrior* (also known as *She Wolves of the Wasteland*), Sony Pictures Entertainment/Highlight Video, 1988.
Julie Ann McGuffin, *Rush Week,* Columbia, 1989.
Karin Crosse, *Roller Blade Warriors: Taken by Force* (also known as *Power Blade Warrior: Taken by Force* and *Roller Blade Warriors*), Manson International, 1989.
Party, *Midnight,* 1989.
Gloria (the bride), *Bride of Re–Animator* (also known as *Re–Animator 2*), Cineplex Odeon Films, 1990, 50th Street Films, 1991.
Detective Lisa Forester, *Snake Eater II: The Drug Buster* (also known as *Snake Eater's Revenge*), Moviestore Entertainment/Starlight, 1991.
Holly, *The Art of Dying* (also known as *Perfect Killer*), PM Entertainment Group, 1991.
Katherine Pierce, *Night of the Warrior,* Trimark Pictures, 1991.
Alexa, *CIA Code Name: Alexa* (also known as *C.I.A. Codename: Alexa* and *C.I.A. Code Name: Alexa*), PM Entertainment Group, 1992.
Heather, *Sweet Justice* (also known as *Killer Instincts*), Triboro Entertainment, 1992.
Maggie, *Final Impact,* PM Entertainment Group, 1992.
Jordan, *Final Round* (also known as *Human Target* and *Round final*), 1993.
Alexa, *CIA II: Target Alexa* (also known as *C.I.A. Codename: Viper, CIA: Target Alexa, CIA II: Code Name Alexa,* and *Codename Viper*), PM Entertainment Group, 1994.
Angela, *Texas Payback,* c. 1994.
Missy, *Stormswept,* Paragon Pictures, 1995.
Brigitte, *Punctul zero* (also known as *Cry of Redemption* and *Point Zero*), G.E.L. Releasing, 1996.
Katherine, *Dead of Night* (also known as *Dark Hunger*), Playboy Entertainment, 1996.
Koss's secretary, *That Thing You Do!* (also known as *Music Graffiti* and *The Wonders*), Twentieth Century–Fox, 1996.
Dorothy Liddell, *Stranger in the House,* Live Entertainment, 1997.
Nicole Landon, *The Corporate Ladder,* Motion Picture Corporation of America, 1997.
Alexis, *Gangland* (also known as *Action—War* and *Gangland L.A.*), Dominion International, 2000.

Detective Holly McGee, *Bare Witness,* Mainline Releasing, 2001.
Natalie Montana, *Psychotic,* 2001.
Dr. Lina Baxter, *Lime Salted Love,* 2006, Indican Pictures, 2009.
Kat, *Prank,* Masimedia, 2008.
Lily Stevens, "Rottentail" segment, *Monsterpiece Theatre Volume I,* 2009.
Ruby, *Haunting Kira,* c. 2010.

Television Appearances; Series:
Marilyn Cassidy, *Santa Barbara* (also known as *California Clan*), NBC, 1992.
Cheyenne "Chy" Phillips, *Renegade,* USA Network and syndicated, 1992–96.

Television Appearances; Movies:
Newsperson, "Safety Patrol" (also known as "Disney's 'Safety Patrol'" and "Safety Patrol!"), *The Wonderful World of Disney,* ABC, 1998.

Television Appearances; Specials:
The 61st Annual Hollywood Christmas Parade, syndicated, 1992.

Television Appearances; Episodic:
"The Good, the Bad and the Priceless," *The Master* (also known as *Master* and *Master Ninja*), NBC, 1984.
Cookie, "Smooth Operator," *Dallas* (also known as *Oil*), CBS, 1991.
Stella McKay, "The Fat Lady Sings Alone," *DEA: Special Task Force* (also known as *DEA*), Fox, 1991.
Morgan Christopher, "Someone to Baywatch over You," *Baywatch* (also known as *Baywatch Hawaii* and *Baywatch Hawai'i*), syndicated, 1994.
Charlene Ballard, "The Wedge," *Silk Stalkings,* USA Network, 1997.
(As Kathleen Kinmont Burns) Charlene Ballard, "Noir: Parts 1 & 2," *Silk Stalkings,* USA Network, 1999.
(As Burns) Dion, "Stolen Lies," *Mortal Kombat: Conquest* (also known as *Mortal Kombat* and *Mortal Kombat: Krusade*), TNT and syndicated, 1999.
Agent Madison, "South by Southwest," *V.I.P.* (also known as *V.I.P.—Die Bodyguards*), syndicated, 2001.
Dr. Richards, *Days of Our Lives* (also known as *Cruise of Deception: Days of Our Lives, Days, DOOL, Tropical Temptation, Tropical Temptation: Days of Our Lives, Des jours et des vies, Horton–sagaen, I gode og onde dager, Los dias de nuestras vidas, Meres agapis, Paeivien viemaeae, Vaara baesta aar, Zeit der Sehnsucht,* and *Zile din viata noastra*), NBC, multiple episodes in 2002.

Television Appearances; Pilots:
Cheyenne "Chy" Phillips, "Renegade," *Renegade,* USA Network and syndicated, 1992.

Appeared in the unaired pilot for *Match Game* (also known as *Match Game 2* and *M.G.2*).

RECORDINGS

Videos:
Herself, *Halloween: 25 Years of Terror* (documentary), Anchor Bay Entertainment/Trancas International Films, 2006.

WRITINGS

Screenplays:
(Story) *CIA II: Target Alexa* (also known as *C.I.A. Codename: Viper, CIA: Target Alexa, CIA II: Code Name Alexa,* and *Codename Viper*), PM Entertainment Group, 1994.

OTHER SOURCES

Periodicals:
Femme Fatales, April, 2002, pp. 38–45.

KNIGHTON, Zachary 1978–
(Zach Knighton)

PERSONAL

Born October 25, 1978, in VA. *Education:* Virginia Commonwealth University, B.F.A.; also attended Oxford University. *Avocational Interests:* Surfing and sailing.

Addresses: *Agent*—WME Entertainment, One William Morris Pl., Beverly Hills, CA 90212. *Manager*—3 Arts Entertainment, 9460 Wilshire Blvd., 7th Floor, Beverly Hills, CA 90212.

Career: Actor.

Awards, Honors: Excellence in Theatre Award, Virginia Commonwealth University; Irene Ryan Award nomination, for *Equus.*

CREDITS

Film Appearances:
Mr. Rolly, *Cherry Falls,* October Films, 2000.

Seymour, *La vie nouvelle* (also known as *A New Life*), 2002.
Travis, *The Mudge Boy,* Strand Releasing, 2003.
John Morgan, *The Prince & Me* (also known as *The Prince and Me*), Paramount, 2004.
Jim Halsey, *The Hitcher,* Rogue Pictures, 2007.
(As Zach Knighton) Brillo Murphy, *Surfer, Dude,* Anchor Bay Entertainment, 2008.
Judd, *Tug,* 2010.

Television Appearances; Series:
Laz Lackerson, *Life on a Stick,* Fox, 2005.
Dr. Bryce Varley, *FlashForward,* ABC, 2009—.

Television Appearances; Miniseries:
William Alexander, *Sally Hemings: An American Scandal,* CBS, 2000.

Television Appearances; Movies:
Clyde, *Supreme Courtships,* 2007.

Television Appearances; Pilots:
Brad, *Love, Inc.,* UPN, 2005.

Television Appearances; Episodic:
Stephen, "The Music Box," *Ed,* NBC, 2001.
Paul Wyler, "Swept Away—A Very Special Episode," *Law & Order,* NBC, 2001.
Lukas Ian Croft, "Mean," *Law & Order: Special Victims Unit* (also known as *Law & Order: SVU* and *Special Victims Unit*), NBC, 2004.
Joel's friend in cafe, "London Calling," *Related,* The WB, 2006.
Gary, "His Name is Ruth," *Related,* The WB, 2006.
Up Close with Carrie Keagan, 2007.
(As Zach Knighton) Frank's neighbor, "The Gang Solves the Gas Crisis," *It's Always Sunny in Philadelphia* (also known as *It's Always Sunny*), FX Network, 2008.
Chet Newcomb, "The Bones That Foam," *Bones,* Fox, 2009.

Stage Appearances:
Al Columbato, *Birdy,* Julia Miles Theatre, New York City, 2003.

Also appeared in *Madame Melville; The Pumpkin Pie Show; Equus;* as Hamm, *Endgame;* Clifford, *Side Man;* Marchbanks, *Candida;* Matthew, *Private Eyes.*

L

LAURENTS, Arthur 1918(?)–

PERSONAL

Born July 14, 1918 (some sources cite 1917), in Brooklyn, NY; son of Irving (an attorney) and Ada (a teacher; maiden name, Robbins) Laurents; companion of Tom Hatcher (died, 2006). *Education:* Cornell University, B.A., 1937. *Religion:* Jewish.

Addresses: *Agent*—John Buzzetti, WME Entertainment, 1325 Avenue of the Americas, New York, NY 10019.

Career: Writer and director. *Military service:* U.S. Army, 1940–45; became sergeant.

Member: Dramatists Guild (member of council), Screen Writers Guild, PEN, Society of Stage Directors and Choreographers, Academy of Motion Picture Arts and Sciences.

Awards, Honors: Citation from U.S. Secretary of War and Variety Radio Award, 1945, for *Assignment Home;* National Institute of Arts and Letters grant for literature, 1946; shared Sidney Howard Memorial Award, 1946, for *Home of the Brave;* Edgar Allan Poe Award nomination (with Patrick Hamilton), best motion picture, Mystery Writers of America, 1949, for *Rope;* Antoinette Perry Award nomination, best book for a musical, 1958, for *West Side Story;* Film Award nomination, best British screenplay, British Academy of Film and Television Arts, 1958, for *Anastasia;* Antoinette Perry Award nomination, best book for musical, 1960, for *Gypsy;* Antoinette Perry Award, best book of a musical, 1968, for *Hallelujah, Baby!;* Writers Guild of America Screen Award nomination, best original screenplay, 1974, for *The Way We Were;* Antoinette Perry Award nomina-

tion and Vernon Rice Award (now Drama Desk Award), both best director of a musical, 1975, for revival of *Gypsy;* Drama Desk Award, 1978, for *My Mother Was a Fortune Teller;* Academy Award nominations, best picture (with Herbert Ross) and best original screenplay, Writers Guild of America Screen Award, best original screenplay, Golden Globe Award, and National Board of Review Award, best picture, all 1978, for *The Turning Point;* Antoinette Perry Award, best director of a musical, 1984, and Sydney Drama Critics Award for Directing, 1985, both for *La cage aux folles;* National Board of Review Award, career achievement in screenplay category, 1999; Antoinette Perry Award nomination, best direction of a musical, 2008, for revival of *Gypsy;* inducted into Theatre Hall of Fame.

CREDITS

Stage Director:
Invitation to a March, Music Box Theatre, New York City, 1960–61.
I Can Get for You Wholesale (musical), Sam S. Shubert Theatre, then Broadway Theatre, both New York City, 1962.
Anyone Can Whistle (musical), Majestic Theatre, New York City, 1964.
The Enclave, Washington Theatre Club, Washington, DC, then Theatre Four, New York City, 1973.
Gypsy (musical), Piccadilly Theatre, London, 1973, then Winter Garden Theatre, New York City, 1974.
My Mother Was a Fortune Teller, Hudson Guild Theatre, New York City, 1978.
Scream, Alley Theatre, Houston, TX, 1978.
The Madwoman of Central Park West (musical), Studio Arena Theatre, Buffalo, NY, and 22 Steps Theatre, New York City, 1979.
"So What Are We Gonna Do Now?," *Young Playwrights Festival,* Circle Repertory Theatre, New York City, 1982.
La cage aux folles (musical), Palace Theatre, New York City, 1983, then Music Hall, Dallas, TX, 1987.

Birds of Paradise, Promenade Theatre, New York City, 1987.

Gypsy (revival), St. James Theatre, 1989–91, then Marquis Theatre, New York City, 1991.

Nick and Nora (musical), Marquis Theatre, 1991.

Jolson Sings Again, 1993.

The Radical Mystique, Manhattan Theatre Club Stage II, New York City, 1995.

My Good Name, 1997.

Venecia, George Street Playhouse, New Brunswick, NJ, 2001.

Gypsy (revival), St. James Theatre, 2008–2009.

West Side Story (revival), Palace Theatre, beginning 2009.

Major Tours; Director:

The Time of the Cuckoo, U.S. cities, 1953.

Gypsy, U.S. cities, 1974 and 1989.

La cage aux folles, Australia, 1985, U.S. cities, 1986, and London, 1986.

Television Appearances; Specials:

"Broadway Sings: The Music of Jule Styne," *Great Performances,* PBS, 1987.

"Anastasia: Her True Story," *Biography,* Arts and Entertainment, 1997.

Leonard Bernstein: Reaching for the Note, PBS, 1998.

"Gypsy Rose Lee: Naked Ambition," *Biography,* Arts and Entertainment, 1999.

Reputations: Alfred Hitchcock, 1999.

Gene Kelly: Anatomy of a Dancer, 2002.

Words and Music by Jerry Herman, PBS, 2007.

Mr. Prince, Ovation TV, 2009.

"Jerome Robbins: Something to Dance About," *American Masters,* PBS, 2009.

Television Appearances; Miniseries:

Broadway: The American Musical, PBS, 2004.

Television Appearances; Episodic:

Changing Stages, PBS, 2001.

"Rose," *Character Studies,* PBS, 2005.

Film Producer:

(With Herbert Ross) *The Turning Point,* Twentieth Century–Fox, 1977.

Documentary Film Appearances:

The Celluloid Closet, (also known as *Gefangen in der traumfabrik*), Sony Pictures Classics, 1996.

Broadway: The Golden Age, by the Legends Who Were There (also known as *Broadway, Broadway: The Golden Age,* and *Broadway: The Movie*), Dada Films, 2002.

West Side Memories, Metro–Goldwyn–Mayer/United Artists Home Entertainment, 2003.

The Needs of Kim Stanley, Frozen Motion Films, 2005.

Hollywood contra franco (also known as *A War in Hollywood*), Area de Televisio, 2008.

Hollywood Renegade, 2010.

RECORDINGS

Videos:

Looking Back: The Making of "The Way We Were," 1999.

"Rope" Unleashed, Universal, 2001.

Rescued from the Closet, Columbia TriStar Home Video, 2001.

West Side Memories, Metro–Goldwyn–Mayer/United Artists Home Entertainment, 2003.

WRITINGS

Plays:

Home of the Brave, Belasco Theatre, New York City, 1945–46, produced in London as *The Way Back,* published by Random House, 1946.

Heartsong, Shubert Theatre, New Haven, CT, 1947.

The Bird Cage, Coronet Theatre, New York City, 1950, published by Dramatists Play Service, 1950.

The Time of the Cuckoo, Empire Theatre, New York City, 1952–53, published by Random House, 1953.

A Clearing in the Woods, Belasco Theatre, 1957, published by Random House, 1957, revised edition, Dramatists Play Service, 1960.

West Side Story (musical), lyrics by Stephen Sondheim, music by Leonard Bernstein, National Theatre, Washington, DC, then Winter Garden Theatre, New York City, 1957–59, and Broadway Theatre, New York City, 1959, published by Random House, 1958.

Gypsy (musical; based on the memoirs of Gypsy Rose Lee), lyrics by Sondheim, music by Jule Stune, Broadway Theatre, 1959–60, then Imperial Theatre, New York City, 1960–61, published by Random House, 1960.

Invitation to a March, Music Box Theatre, 1960–61, published by Random House, 1961.

Anyone Can Whistle (musical), Majestic Theatre, New York City, 1964, published by Random House, 1965.

Do I Hear a Waltz? (musical; based on Laurents's earlier play *The Time of the Cuckoo*), lyrics by Sondheim, music by Richard Rodgers, Forty–Sixth Street Theatre, New York City, 1965, published by Random House, 1966, revised version, 1999.

Hallelujah Baby! (musical), Martin Beck Theatre, New York City, 1967–68, published by Random House, 1967.

The Enclave, Washington Theatre Club, Washington, DC, then Theatre Four, New York City, 1973, published by Dramatists Play Service, 1974.

Scream, Alley Theatre, Houston, TX, 1978.

(With Phyllis Newman) *My Mother Was a Fortune Teller* (musical), Hudson Guild Theatre, 1978, produced as *The Madwoman of Central Park West,* 22 Steps Theatre, New York City, 1979.

A Loss of Memory (one–act), Southampton College Theatre, Long Island University, New York City, 1981, published by Chilton, 1983.

The Time of the Cuckoo, Parish Hall, Church of the Heavenly Rest, New York City, 1986.

(Contributor of new text) *Jerome Robbins' Broadway* (musical), Imperial Theatre, 1989–90.

Nick and Nora (musical), Marquis Theatre, 1991.

Jolson Sings Again, Seattle Repertory Theatre, Seattle, WA, 1995, revised version, George Street Playhouse, New Brunswick, NJ, 1999.

The Radical Mystique, Manhattan Theatre Club Stage II, New York City, 1995.

The Time of the Cuckoo, Mitzi E. Newhouse Theatre, New York City, 2000.

Big Potato, Duke Theatre on Forty–Second Street, New York City, 2000.

(Adaptor) *Venecia,* George Street Playhouse, 2001.

New Year's Eve, George Street Playhouse, 2009.

Plays also published in anthologies and periodicals.

Screenplays:

(Uncredited; with Frank Partos and Millen Brand) *The Snake Pit* (based on novel by Mary Jane Ward), Twentieth Century–Fox, 1948.

Rope (also known as *Alfred Hitchcock's "Rope,"* based on play by Patrick Hamilton), Warner Bros., 1948.

(With Philip Yordan) *Anna Lucasta* (based on play by Yordan), Columbia, 1949.

Caught, Enterprise Pictures, 1949.

(With Carl Foreman) *Home of the Brave,* United Artists, 1949.

Anastasia (based on play by Marcelle Maurette), Twentieth Century–Fox, 1956.

Bonjour Tristesse (based on novel by Francoise Sagan), Columbia, 1958.

(With Ernest Lehman) *West Side Story,* United Artists, 1961.

(With Leonard Spigelgass) *Gypsy,* Warner Bros., 1962.

(With David Lean and H. E. Bates) *Summertime* (also known as *Summer Madness;* based on Laurents's play *The Time of the Cuckoo*), United Artists, 1965.

The Way We Were, Columbia, 1973.

The Turning Point, Twentieth Century–Fox, 1977.

Television Specials:

The Light Fantastic; Or, How to Tell Your Past, Present, and Maybe Future through Social Dancing, NBC, 1967.

"Invitation to a March" (based on his stage play), *Hollywood Television Theatre,* PBS, 1972.

Radio Plays:

Now Playing Tomorrow, 1939.

Western Electric Communicade, 1944.

The Last Day of the War, 1945.

The Face, 1945.

Radio Episodes:

Writer of episodes for radio series *Dr. Christian, Hollywood Playhouse, Manhattan at Midnight,* and *The Thin Man,* 1939–40; and episodes for *Army Service Force Presents, Assignment Home, The Man behind the Gun,* and *This Is Your FBI,* 1943–45.

Novels:

The Way We Were, Harper, 1972.

The Turning Point, New American Library, 1977.

Books:

Original Story By: A Memoir of Broadway and Hollywood, Alfred A. Knopf, 2000.

Mainly on Directing: Gypsy, West Side Story, and Other Musicals, Alfred A. Knopf, 2009.

ADAPTATIONS

Laurents's play *Home of the Brave* was broadcast as a presentation of *ITV Play of the Week* by ITV in 1957. The play *Gypsy* was adapted for a television movie which aired on CBS in 1993.

OTHER SOURCES

Books:

Contemporary Dramatists, St. James Press, 1999.

International Dictionary of Theatre, Volume 2: *Playwrights,* St. James Press, 1993.

Laurents, Arthur, *Original Story By: A Memoir of Broadway and Hollywood,* Alfred A. Knopf, 2000.

LEE, Thomas
   See HILL, Walter

LEE, Wendee 1960(?)–
   (Wendee Lee Curtis, Wendee Day, Wendy Lee, Wendy Lengyel, Wendee Swan)

PERSONAL

Original name, Wendy Day; born February 20, 1960 (some sources say April 29, 1955), in Los Angeles, CA; married; husband, a musician.

Addresses: *Contact*—c/o 11684 Ventura Blvd., #502, Studio City, CA 91604.

Career: Actress, voice artist, producer, and director. Began career as a touring dancer with the Ambassador Dance Theatre; performed as a singer and worked as a stage director and choreographer; founded Planet Dancers (a dance company); also worked as a dance instructor. Dance Outreach, artist–in–residence.

CREDITS

Film Appearances:

(English version) Voice of Akuma no ko (Beezle) and Chao, *Unico* (animated; also known as *The Fantastic Adventure of Unico–1*, *The Fantastic Adventures of Unico,* and *Yuniko*), 1981.

Voice of Dominique, *Space Adventure Cobra*, Tokyo Movie Shinsha, 1982.

(English version) Voice of Shinji Nakaoka, Eiko Nakaoka, and Ryuta Kondo, *Hadashi no Gen* (animated; also known as *Barefoot Gen*), 1983.

(English version; as Wendy Lengyel) Voice, *Katy* (animated; also known as *Katy the Caterpillar* and *Katy, la Oruga*), 1984.

(English version) Voice of Iczer–One, *Tatakate! Iczer–1* (also known as *Fight! Iczer–1*), 1985.

(English version; Streamline) Voice of Yuri, *Dati pea: Norandia no nazo* (animated; also known as *Dirty Pair: Mystery of Norlandia* and *Original Dirty Pair #5: Affair of Nolandia*), 1985.

(English version) Voice of first Juliet, *Dowa meita senshi Windaria* (animated; also known as *Once Upon a Time* and *Windaria*), 1986.

(English version) Voice of Frol, *Juichi–nin iru!* (animated; also known as *11 People!*, *There Are 11!*, and *They Were 11*), 1986.

(English version) Voice of pillage victim, *Hokuto no ken* (animated; also known as *Fist of the North Star*), 1986.

(As Wendee Swan) Voice of Stacy Embry, *Robotech: The Movie*, 1986.

(English version) Voice of bar patron and news reel narrator, *Oritsu uchugun oneamisu no tsubasa* (animated; also known as *Starquest*, *Wings of Honneamise*, and *Wings of Honneamise: Royal Space Force*), 1987.

(English version; Streamline 1994) Voice of Yuri, *Dati pea Gekijo–ban* (animated; also known as *Dirty Pair*, *Dirty Pair: The Movie*, and *Original Dirty Pair: Project Eden*), 1987.

(English version) Voice of Emu, *Kuraingu furiman* (animated; also known as *Crying Freeman* and *Crying Freeman 1: Portrait of a Killer*), 1988.

(English version; Streamline 1993) Voice of Yukiko, *Teito monogatari* (animated; also known as *Tokyo: The Last Megalopolis*), 1988.

(English version; Harmony Gold version) Voice of Lena and Bluma, *Doragon boru: Makafushigi dai boken* (animated; also known as *Dragon Ball: Mystical Adventure*), 1988.

(English version) Voice of Kei, *Akira* (animated; also known as *Akira: The Special Edition*), 1988.

Voice of Emu, *Crying Freeman 2: Fusei kakurei* (animated; also known as *Crying Freeman 2: Shades of Death, Part 1* and *Crying Freeman 2: The Enemy Within*), 1989.

(English version) Voice, *Goku Midnight Eye* (animated), 1989.

(English version) Voice of Julie and Yuri, *Dirty Pair* (animated), 1989.

(As Wendee Swan) Voice, *The Adventures of Manxmouse* (animated; also known as *Manxmouse* and *The Legend of Manxmouse*), 1989.

(English version) Voice of Emu, *Crying Freeman 3: Hiyoku renri* (animated; also known as *Crying Freeman 3: Retribution* and *Crying Freeman 3: Shades of Death, Part 1*), 1990.

(English version) Voice of Emu, *Crying Freeman 4: Oshu Togoku* (animated; also known as *Crying Freeman 4: A Taste of Revenge*, *Crying Freeman 4: The Hostages,* and *Crying Freeman: Chapter 5—The Impersonator*), 1991.

(English version; 2004 Bang Zoom!) Voice of Nagisa Tezuka, *Koko wa Greenwood* (animated; also known as *Here Is Greenwood*), 1991.

(English version) Voice of Nami Yamigumo, *Silent Mobius* (animated), 1991.

(English version) Voice of Emu, *Crying Freeman 5: Senjo no kishimojin* (animated; also known as *Crying Freeman 5: Abduction in Chinatown* and *Crying Freeman 5: The Impersonator*), 1992.

(English version) Voice of Maria an Tarf, *Isu II: Tenku no shinden* (animated; also known as *Y's II: Castle in Heavens*, *Ys 2: Citadel in the Sky,* and *Ys II Temple in the Sky*), 1992.

(English version) Voice of Jun Asuka, *Tetsu no shojo Jun* (animated; also known as *Iron Virgin Jun*), 1992.

(English version) Voice of Yuka Osenji, *Babel nisei* (animated; also known as *Babel II: Perfect Collection*), 1992.

(English version) Voice of female Kagato, Kiyone Masaki—OVA 3, *Tenchi Muyo! Ryo Oki* (animated; also known as *No Need for Tenchi*, *Tenchi Muyo! Ryo–oh–ki,* and *This End Up!*), 1992.

(English version) Voice of Tia Note Yoko, *Bastard!!!* (animated), 1992.

(English version) Voice of Elizabeth (4–6), *Morudaiba* (animated; also known as *Moldiveru*), 1993.

(English version) Voice of Emu, *Crying Freeman Kanketsu hen: Mumyo Ryusha* (animated; also known as *Crying Freedom 6: The Russian Collection* and *Crying Freeman 6: The Guiding Light of Memory*), 1993.

(English version) Voice, *Yu yu hakusho: Eizo hakusho* (animated), 1993.

(English version) Voice of Torria and narrator, *Chojiku seiki Ogasu 02* (animated; *Super Dimension Century Orguss 02*), 1993.

(As Wendee Day) Voice of Kagero, *Jubei ninpucho* (animated; also known as *Jubei Ninpocho: The Wind Ninja Chronicles* and *Ninja Scroll*), 1993.

(English version; as Wendee Lee Curtis) Voice of child B, *Samurai Showdown* (animated), 1994.

(English version) Voice of flight attendant and Julie Blanshin, *Armitage III* (animated), 1994.

(English version; Animaze 1997) Voice of airplane passenger and classmate, *Tokyo Revelation* (animated), 1994.

(English version) Voice of Ayaka Kisaragi, *Yugen kaisha* (animated; also known as *Phantom Quest Corp.* and *You gen kai sya*), 1994.

(English version) Voice of reporter and hotel clerk, *Macross Plus* (animated), 1994.

(English version) Voice of Iria, *Zeiramu 2* (animated; also known as *Zeiram 2*), 1994.

(English version; Animaze 1998) Voice of Yunlyung, *Red Hawk: Weapon of Death* (animated), 1994.

(As Wendee Day) Voice of Kagero, *Jubei ninpocho* (animated; also known as *Jubei Ninpocho: The Wind Ninja Chronicles*, *Ninja Scroll*, and *Wicked City 3*), Teletoon, 1995.

(English version) Voice of Don and Sanjhiyan number two, *Sazan aizu seima densetsu* (animated; also known as *3x3 Eyes: Legend of the Divine Demon* and *Shin 3x3 Eyes*), 1995.

(As Wendy Lee) *Penyu* (animated; also known as *Turtle*), 1995.

(English version) Voice, *Yu yu hakusho: Eizo hakhusho 2* (animated), 1996.

Voice of Dominique Flower, *Space Cobra* (animated), 1996.

Voice of Yui Hongo, *Fushigi Yugi: Memories First OAV* (animated), Pioneer Entertainment, 1996.

(English version) Voice of Keiko Nakadai, *Otenki–oneesan* (animated; also known as *A Weatherwoman* and *Weather Girl*), 1996.

(English version) Voice of Marie Kim and Pandora, *Amagaedun* (animated; also known as *Armageddon*), 1996.

(English version) Voice of Betty Moore and Lisa Siegel, *Burakku jakku* (animated; also known as *Black Jack*), 1996.

(English version) Voice of Yui Hongo, *Fushigi Yugi: The Mysterious Play—Reflections OAV 2* (animated), Pioneer Entertainment, 1997.

(English version) Voice of Yui Hongo, *Fushigi Yugi: The Mysterious Play—Reflections OAV 3* (animated), Pioneer Entertainment, 1997.

(English version) Voice, *El Hazard: The Magnificent World 2* (animated; also known as *El Hazard 2*), 1997.

(English version) Voice of student of accent, Tomoe Midou, student, doctor, and newscaster, *Battle Athletes* (animated), 1997.

(English version) Voice of Umi and Emeraude, *Rayearth* (animated), 1997.

(English version) Voice of assassin and Kosugi's companion, *Kuro no tenshi Vol 1* (animated; also known as *The Black Angel*), 1997.

(English version) Voice of Ohri, *Gestalt* (animated), 1997.

Voice of Kiyone, *Tenchi Muyo! Manatsu no Eve* (animated; also known as *Tenchi Muyo: Midsummer's Eve* and *Tenchi the Movie 2: The Daughter of Darkness*), Pioneer Entertainment, 1998.

Voice, *Error in Judgement* (animated), 1998.

(English version) Voice of Rumi, *Perfect Blue* (animated; also known as *Pafekuto buru*), 1998.

(English version) Voice of Rolls, *Sun faa sau si* (animated; also known as *Bio–Zombie, Sang dut sau shut,* and *Sheng hua shou shi*), 1998.

Voice of Kiyone, *Tenchi Muyo! In Love 2: Haruka naru omoi* (animated; also known as *Tenchi Forever* and *Tenchi Muyo: Tenchi in Love 2: Distant Memories*), 1999.

Voice of April, *Sol Bianca: The Legacy* (animated), Pioneer Entertainment, 1999.

(English language version) Voice of Rumi, *Perfect Blue* (animated), 1999.

Voice of Alpha number six, *Power Rangers Lost Galaxy: Return of the Magna Defender*, 1999.

Voice of Yui Hongo and Yui's mother, *Fushigi Yugi: The Mysterious Play—Suzaku DVD Box Set* (animated), Pioneer Entertainment, 1999.

Voice of boy, Kukuru, Lia, and news anchor, *Arc the Lad* (animated), Bang Zoom! Entertainment, 1999.

Voice of Kiyone, *Tenchi Muyo! In Love 2: Haruka naru omoi* (animated; also known as *Tenchi Forever, Tenchi Muyo: Tenchi in Love 2,* and *Tenchi Muyo: Tenchi in Love 2: Distant Memories*), 1999.

Voice of Charlotte Elbourne, *Vampire Hunter D: Bloodlust* (animated), Urban Vision Entertainment, 2000.

Voice of first little girl, first party girl, little Kokomon, and young T. K. Ishida, *Digimon: The Movie* (animated; also known as *Digimon: Digital Monsters* and *Digimon: Digital Monsters; The Movie*), Twentieth Century–Fox, 2000.

(English version) Voice of Keroberos, *Kero–chan ni omakase!* (animated), 2000.

(English version) Voice of Kerberos (small) and Sonomi Daidouji, *Kadokaputa Sakura: Fuin sareta kado* (animated; also known as *Cardcaptor Sakura: The Sealed Card*), 2000.

(English version) Voice of Charlotte, *Vampire Hunter D: Bloodlust* (animated; also known as *Banpaia hanta D, Vampire Hunter D,* and *Vampire Hunter D: Bloodlust*), 2000.

Voice of Kokomon, *Digimon Adventure 02: Hurricane Touchdown! The Golden Digimentals!* (animated), 2000.

Voice of party girl number one and T. K. Takaishi, *Digimon Adventure: Our War Game* (animated), 2000.

(English version) Voice of Faye Valentine, *Kauboi bibappu: Tengoku no tobira* (animated; also known as *Cowboy Bebop: The Movie, Cowboy Bebop the Movie: Knockin' on Heaven's Door,* and *Cowboy Bebop: Knocking' on Heavens Door*), 2001.

Alice, *Twice As Dead,* 2001.

(English version) Voice of Cyberdoll Sara, *Hand Maid May* (animated), 2001.

Voice of Ruriko Ikusawa, *Gate Keepers* (animated), Animated Works, 2001.

(English version) Voice of Mari and Bijinder, *Kikaida Zero Wan: The Animation* (animated; also known as *Kikaider 01: The Animation*), 2001.

(English version) Voice of Trigger, Angela, and Lilith, *Kurogane Communication* (animated short film), 2002.

(English version) Voice of Kaolla Su and Tama, *Love Hina Again* (animated short film), Star Child Recording, 2002.

(English version) Voice of reporter and flight attendant, *Armitage: Dual Matrix* (animated), Pioneer Entertainment, 2002.

Voice of Lovebird, *Ekusu doraiba za mubi* (animated), 2002.

(English version) Voice of Dispatch, *Ekusu doraiba: Nina ando rei denja zon* (animated), Nikkatsu, 2002.

(English version) Voice of Bearmon, *Dejimon furontia—Kodai Dejimon fukkatsu!* (animated; also known as *Digimon Frontier: Revival of the Ancient Digimon* and *Digimon: Island of the Lost Digimon*), 2002.

(English version) Voice of Yurika Saegusa, *Alive* (animated), Klock Worx Company, 2002.

(English version) Voice of Rika, *Ju–on* (also known as *The Grudge, Ju–on: Gekijo–ban,* and *Ju–on: The Grudge*), Lions Gate Films, 2002.

(English version) Voice of Yoko Ashray, boy, and Yuna Itsuki, *Aquarian Age Saga II: Don't Forget Me* (animated), Broccoli International, 2003.

Voice of Dr. Hatsumi Mataki, *Cossette no shozo* (animated short film; also known as *Le portrait de petite cossette*), Geneon Entertainment, 2004.

Mother, *Death and Pancakes* (short film), 2004.

Voice of limo girl, *Kangaroo Jack: G'Day, U.S.A.!* (animated), Warner Home Video, 2004.

Voice of Benin and Jinta Hanakari, *Bleach: Memories of Nobody* (animated; also known as *Bleach: The Movie—Memories of Nobody*), Toho Company, 2006.

(English version) Voice of Mary and Ohkubo hospital director, *Karas: The Revelation* (animated), Manga Video, 2007.

Herself, *Adventures in Voice Acting,* 2008.

Also appeared as voice of Toni, *Error in Judgment;* voice of Julie, *Fist of the North Star* (animated); voice of Iczer–One, *Iczer–One* (animated); voice of Toria, *Orgus 01* (animated); voice of Ayaka, *Phantom Quest Corp.* (animated); voice of Froi, *They Were Eleven* (animated); (English version) voice, *Like Water for Chocolate;* (English version) voice of Lola, *Run Lola Run.*

Film Work:

Automated dialogue replacement (ADR), *Twin Dragons,* 1992.

(English version) Additional voices, *Yu yu hakusho: The Golden Seal* (animated; also known as *Yu yu hakusho: The Movie*), 1993.

Additional voices, *Armitage III* (animated; also known as *Armitage III: Polymatrix*), Pioneer Entertainment, 1994.

(English version; Media Blasters 1998) Additional voices, *Yu yu hakusho: Meikai shito hen—Hono no kizuna* (animated: also known as *Fight for the Netherworld* and *Yu Yu Hakusho: The Movie—Poltergeist Report*), 1994.

Additional voices, *Rusty: A Dog's Tale* (also known as *Rusty: The Great Rescue*), Saban Entertainment, 1997.

(Uncredited) ADR, *Austin Powers: International Man of Mystery* (also known as *Austin Powers—Das Scharfste, was ihre majestat zu bieten hat*), 1997.

Additional voices, *Rusty: A Dog's Tale* (animated; also known as *Rusty* and *Rusty: The Great Rescue*), 1998.

ADR, *Nice Guys Sleep Alone,* 1999.

(Los Angeles/post–production) ADR, *Twin Dragons,* Dimension Films, 1999.

ADR director, *Love Hina Again* (animated short film), Star Child Recording, 2002.

ADR director, *Cossette no shozo* (animated short film; also known as *Le portrait de petite cossette*), Geneon Entertainment, 2003.

Additional voices, *Aquarian Age Saga II: Don't Forget Me* (animated), Broccoli International, 2003.

(English version) Additional voices, *Final Fantasy VII: Advent Children* (animated), Sony Pictures Home Entertainment, 2005.

Voice director and ADR director, *Bleach: Memories of Nobody* (also known as *Bleach: The Movie—Memories of Nobody*), 2006.

Additional voice, *The Velveteen Rabbit,* Anchor Bay Entertainment, 2009.

Television Appearances; Series:

Voice of Dominique, *Space Adventure Cobra* (animated), 1982.

(English version) Amy, *Akai kodan Zillion* (animated; also known as *Red Spark Zillion* and *Zillion*), 1987.

(English version) Voice of Bruna, *La llamada de los gnomos* (animated), 1987.

(As Wendee Swan) Voice of Scorpina, elf number two, and Stag Beetle, *Mighty Morphin Power Rangers* (also known as *Day of the Dumpster, Mighty Morphin Alien Rangers, Power Rangers,* and *Power Rangers Ninja*), Fox, 1993–95.

(English version) Voice of Shara Carter, *Uchu no kishi tekkaman buredo* (animated; also known as *Starknight Tekkaman Blade* and *Teknoman*), 1994.

(English version) Voice of Rumi Koishikawa, Chigusa, school girl, girl student A, and Rumi Matasuura, *Marmalade Boy* (animated), 1994.

(English version) Voice of Penny Round, *Tonde Buurin* (animated; also known as *Ai to yuki no pig girl Tonde Buurin* and *Super Pig*), 1994.

Voice of Umi Ryuuzaki and Princess Emeraude, *Magic Knight Rayearth* (animated), 1994.

Voice of Knighttime, Lizbot, and Red Python, *V.R. Troopers* (also known as *Saban's "V.R. Troopers"*), Fox Kids, 1995–96.

Voice of Magno, *Masked Rider* (also known as *Saban's "Masked Rider"*), 1995–96.

(English version) Voice of female scientist, radio newscaster, strolling mother, flier girl, Yuka, and Kiyone, *Maho shojo Pretty Samy* (animated; also known as *Magical Project S* and *Pretty Sammy: Magical Girl*), 1996.

(English version) Voice of Kiyone, *Shin Tenchi Muyo* (animated; also known as *New Tenchi Muyo TV* and *Tenchi in Tokyo*), 1997.

(English version) Voice of Reiha, Ruru Stone, and Reiha's mother, *Kyuketsuki Miyu* (animated; also known as *Vampire Princess Miyu*), 1997–98.

Young Gilda, *El Hazard: The Alternative World* (animated), 1998.

(English version) Voice of Kei Pirate and Twilight Suzuka, *Outlaw Star* (animated), Cartoon Network, 1998.

(English version) Voice of Ichino "Itchan" Yanagida, *Battle Athletes daiundokai* (animated; also known as *Battle Athletes Victory*), 1998.

(English version) Voice of Minako Akashi, *Yume de aetara* (animated; also known as *If I See You in My Dreams*), 1998.

(English version) Voice of Faye Valentine, *Kauboi bibappu* (animated; also known as *Cowboy Bebop*), 1998–99.

Voice of Azusa Fuyutsuki and Ryoko Sakurai, *Great Teacher Onizuka* (animated), 1999.

Voice of Alpha number six, *Power Rangers Lost Galaxy*, Fox, 1999.

(English version) Voice of Mitsuki Rara and Miss Rah, *Dual! Paralle lunlun monogatari* (animated; also known as *Parallel Dual! Trouble Adventure*), 1999.

Voice of Miruru, *Tenshi ni narumon* (animated; also known as *I Want to Be an Angel* and *I'm Gonna Be an Angel*), 1999.

Voice of Luches, *Saber Marionette J Again* (animated), 1999.

Various voices, *GTO*, 1999.

Loretto Oratorio, *Wild ARMs: Twilight Venom*, 1999.

Voice of Chibomon, Minomon, Daisy, Jarryn, Wong, Mrs. Ichijouji, and others, *Digimon: Digital Monsters* (animated; also known as *Digimon 02*, *Digimon 03*, *Digital Tamers*, and *Digimon: Season 3*), Fox, 1999–2003.

Voice of female acrobat, Yahiko Myojin, and Yumi Komagata, *Rurouni Kenshin* (animated), 2000.

Voice of Emily, Kiato, and Rena, *DinoZaurs* (animated; also known as *Prehistoric Warriors* and *DinoZaurs: The Series*), Fox, 2000.

(English version) Voice of Yoko Asahina and Little Yayoi, *Mayonaka no tantei Nightwalker* (also known as *Nightwalker: Midnight Detective*), 2000.

(English version) Voice of Alice, *Pet Shop of Horrors*, 2000.

Jun Tokita, *Brigadoon: Marin to Melan* (also known as *Brigadoon* and *Brigadoon: Marin and Melan*), 2000.

(English version) Voice of Joan, *Argento Soma* (animated; also known as *Argentosoma* and *Arujento soma*), 2000.

Buzem A Calessa, *Vandread* (also known as *Vandread: The Second Stage*), 2000.

Voice of Queen Rusephine, *Mashuranbo* (also known as *Shinzo*), 2000.

(English version) Voice of Miyuki, *Jinzo ningen Kikaida: The Animation* (also known as *Android Kikaider: The Animation, Humanoid Kikaider: The Animation,* and *Kikaider*), 2000.

Sato's wife, *Kacho Oji* (also known as *Black Heaven* and *The Legend of Black Heaven*), 2000.

Hello Kitty's Paradise, Fox Family, 2000.

(English version) Voice of Patricia "Angel" Lovejoy/Casey, *The Big O* (animated), Cartoon Network, 2001.

Voice of Weda, *Janguru was itsumo hare nochi Guu* (animated; also known as *Hare nochi Guu, Hare+Guu, JungleGuu,* and *The Jungle Was Nice, Then Came Guu*), 2001.

(English version) Voice of Chitose, *Maho shojo neko Taruto* (animated; also known as *Magical Meow Meow Taruto* and *Magical Nyan Nyan Taruto*), 2001.

Maetel, *Cosmo Warrior Zero*, 2001.

Voice of Ryoko Mitsurugi, *Samurai Girl: Real Bout High School* (animated; also known as *Samurai Girl* and *Samurai Girl: Riaru bauto hai sukuru*), 2001.

Voice of casino dealer, *Kaze no yojinbo* (animated; also known as *Bodyguard of the Wind, Kaze no yojimbo,* and *Yojimbo of the Wind*), 2001.

Voice of Karen Kasumi, *X* (animated), 2001.

Voice of young Suguru Misato, teacher Saori Shikijo, shop owner, black–haired Sakura sister, child, and Yochimiland employee, *Mahoromatic* (animated; also known as *Mahoromatic: Automatic Maiden* and *Mahoromatic: Automatic Maiden "Something More Beautiful"*), 2001.

Voice of Kachiro Kato, *Tenisu no ojisama* (animated; also known as *The Prince of Tennis*), 2001.

Voice of Batch, Lovestar, and Ms. Loon, *Mon colle knights* (animated), Fox Kids, 2001.

Voice of Ruriko Ikusawa, *Gate Keepers* (animated; also known as *Gate Keepers 21*), 2001.

Voice of Daisy, Jaarin Wong, and MarineAngemon, *Digimon Tamers* (animated), 2001.

(English version) Voice of Faye Valentine, *Cowboy Bebop* (animated), 2001–2002.

Voice of Kiriko Masaki, *Tenchi Muyo! GXP* (animated), 2002.

Voice of answering machine message, Tina Foster, and bus intercom, *Ai yori aoshi* (animated; also known as *Bluer Than Indigo* and *Bluer Than Indigo: Fate*), 2002.

Voice of Takako Shimizu, *Chobits* (animated), 2002.

Voice of Gyokuyou and Kourin, *12 kokuki* (animated; also known as *The Twelve Kingdoms*), 2002.

Voice of Miho Karasuma, *Witch Hunter Robin* (animated), Cartoon Network, 2002.

(English version) Voice of Yuriko Oozora, *Rikujo Boei–tai Mao–chan* (animated; also known as *Ground Defense Force Mao–chan*), 2002.

Voice of Adett Kisler, *Overman King–Gainer* (animated), 2002.

Voice of Kuramori, *Haibane renmei* (animated), 2002.

Voice of Janis, Dr. Antonia Bellucci, and kid A, *Heat Guy J* (animated), 2002.

Voice of Phoebe, *Kokaku kidotai: Stand Alone Complex* (animated; also known as *Ghost in the Shell: Stand Alone Complex, Ghost in the Shell: Stand Alone Complex 2nd Gig*, and *Kokaku kidotai: S.A.C. 2nd Gig*), 2002.

Voice of Chiaka Katase, *Uchu no suteruvia* (animated; also known as *Cosmic Stellvia, Sora no Stellvia, Stellvia, Stellvia of the Universe*, and *Uchu no Stellvia*), 2003.

Voice of Senes, Beast Princess, and Diana, *Sukurap–pudo purinsesu* (animated; also known as *Scrapped Princess* and *Sutepri*), WoWow, 2003.

Voice of Mari, *Texhnolyze* (animated), 2003.

Voice of Wendee Lee, *Gad Guard* (animated), 2003.

Voice of Natchan, *Onegai Twins* (animated; also known as *Please Twins!*), 2003.

Voice of Goei, *Ikki tosen* (animated), 2003.

Voice of Genkimaru, *SD Gundam Force* (animated), Cartoon Network, 2003.

Voice of maid dolls, *Avenger* (animated), 2003.

Voice of Yuko Haga, female guest, and nurse, *Takahashi Rumiko gekijo: Ningyo no mori* (animated; also known as *Mermaid Forest, Ningyo no mori*, and *Rumic Theater: Mermaid Forest*), 2003.

Voice of resident, *Gungrave* (animated), 2003.

Voice of Tina Foster, *Ai yori aoshi 'enishi'* (animated), 2003.

(English version) Voice of Moegi, Princess Fortune, Tsubaki, and others, *Naruto* (animated; also known as *Naruto Shounen–hen*), Cartoon Network, 2003–2007.

(English version) Voice of Rena Honjo, *Hikari to mizu no Daphne* (animated; also known as *Daphne in the Brilliant Blue*), 2004.

(English version) Voice of Maya Natsume, *Tenjho tenage* (animated; also known as *Heaven and Earth*), 2004.

(English version) Voice of Ainy and Muchiru Saotome, *Shin getter robo* (animated; also known as *New Getter Robo*), 2004.

Voice of Hotaru, *Samurai chanpuru* (animated; also known as *Samurai Champloo*), Fuji and Cartoon Network, 2004.

Voice of Yukie Kariya, *Soukyu no fafuna* (animated; also known as *Fafner*), 2004.

Voice of Sprocket, *Viewtiful Joe* (animated), The WB, 2004.

Voice of Rushuan Tendo, *Grenadier: Hohoemi no senshi* (animated), 2004.

Voice of Mitsuka Yoshimine, *DearS* (animated), 2004.

Voice of Kiva and Evil Kiva, *Megas XLR* (animated), Cartoon Network, 2004–2005.

(English version) Voice of Ururu Tsumugiya, *Bleach* (animated), Cartoon Network, 2004–2005.

Voice of Sola, *IGPX: Immortal Grand Prix* (animated), Cartoon Network, 2005.

Voice of Mai Kirifuda, *Duel Masters* (animated), Kids Station and Cartoon Network, 2005.

(English version) Voice of Dorothy, *Meru hevun* (animated; also known as *MAR: Marchen Awakens Romance*), 2005–2006.

(English version) Voice of Haruhi Suzumiya, *Suzumiya Haruhi no yuutsu* (animated; also known as *The Melancholy of Haruhi Suzumiya*), 2006.

Voice of Sonia Sky, *MegaMan Star Force* (animated), 2007.

(English version) Voice of Konata Izumi, *Raki suta* (animated; also known as *Lucky Star*), 2007.

Also appeared as voice of puzzle girl, *Hello Kitty* (animated); voice of Nadia, *Nadia* (animated).

Television Appearances; Miniseries:

(English version) Voice of Chris, *Kido senshi Gandamu 0080 pocketto no naka no senso* (animated; also known as *Gundam 0080: A War in the Pocket* and *Mobile Suit Gundam 0080: A War in the Pocket*), 1989.

BT, *Immortal Grand Prix* (animated), Cartoon Network, 2003.

(English version) Voice of Makie Kohinata, *Koi kaze* (animated), 2004.

Television Appearances; Movies:

Voice of Vanessa Leeds, *Codename: Robotech* (animated), 1985.

Voice of Rosemary Moon, *City Hunter: Secret Service* (animated; also known as *City Hunter* and *Secret Police*), 1996.

Voice, *Gotcha*, 1998.

Voice, *Error in Judgement*, Cinemax, 1999.

Voice, *Firetrap*, HBO, 2001.

Also appeared as voice of Cathy, Sally Willis, and Viximon, *Digimon Tamers: The Movie*; voice of Jena Hida, *Digimon: The Next Generation*; voice of Christina Mackenzie, *Gundam 0080: War in the Pocket*; singing Voice of Jenna and Kiri, *Pokemon Magica 2*; voice of Ann, *Pokemon Magica 3*.

Television Appearances; Specials:

Narrator, *Celebrity Weddings: In Style,* ABC, 1999.

(English version) Voice of Kaolla Su, Tama, and Young Keitaro Urashima, *Rabu Hina kurisumasu supesharu: Sairento ivu* (animated; also known as *Love Hina Christmas Special: Silent Eye*), 2000.

(English version) Voice of Kaolla Su and Tama, *Love Hina Spring Special* (animated; also known as *Love Hina Spring Special: I Wish Your Dream* and *Rabu Hina Haru Supesharu: Kimi sakura chiru nakare!*), 2000.

Television Appearances; Episodic:

Voice of Vanessa Leeds, "Boobytrap," *Robotech* (animated), 1985.

(English version) Voice of Bobby Bear, "Ika naide! Sensei," *Maple Town monogatari* (animated; also known as *Gushi de Mapletown, Maple Town,* and *Maple Town Story*), 1986.

Voice of Linko, "Tabidachi, San Francisco kara no shotaijo," *Street Fighter II: V* (animated; also known as *Street Fighter II: Victory*), 1995.

Voice of Impersonator, "Rangers of Two Worlds: Parts 1 & 2," *Power Rangers Zeo* (also known as *ZeoRangers*), 1996.

Voice of Alpha number six, "Dark Specter's Revenge: Parts 1 & 2," *Power Rangers in Space,* Fox, 1998.

(English version) Voice of Patricia "Angel" Lovejoy, "Electric City," *The Big O* (animated; also known as *Big O* and *The Big O II*), 1999.

(English version) Voice of Patricia "Angel" Lovejoy, "Underground Terror," *The Big O* (animated; also known as *Big O* and *The Big O II*), 1999.

(English version) Voice of Motoko Aoyama and Kaolla Su, "I Love You!/Romantic Confession Inside a Cave/Tall Tale," *Rabu Hina* (animated; also known as *Love Hina*), 2000.

Voice of Kukuru, news anchor, boy and Lia, "Pale Goddess," *Arc the Lad* (animated), 2000.

Voice of Kukuru, news anchor, boy and Lia, "Beyond the Sound of Waves," *Arc the Lad* (animated), 2000.

Voice of Redeye, "Uniquely Trip," *Power Rangers Time Force,* Fox, 2001.

Voice of Redeye mutant, "Reflections of Evil," *Power Rangers Time Force,* Fox, 2001.

(English version) Voice of Ixquic, "The City of Wind," *Saibogu 009* (animated; also known as *Cyborg 009: The Cyborg Soldier* and *Cyborg 009*), Cartoon Network, 2002.

(English version) Voice of Ixquic, "Old Friends," *Saibogu 009* (animated; also known as *Cyborg 009: The Cyborg Soldier* and *Cyborg 009*), Cartoon Network, 2002.

(English version) Voice of Nacchan and Hatsuho Kazami, "Mazuiyo seinsei," *Onegai Teacher* (animated; also known as *Please Teacher!*), 2002.

(English version) Voice of Nacchan and Hatsuho Kazami, "Himitsu na futari," *Onegai Teacher* (animated; also known as *Please Teacher!*), 2002.

Voice of Swanmon, "Glean Eggs and Scram," *Digimon Frontier* (animated), 2002.

(English version) Voice of BlackRose, "Unison," *.hack// SIGN* (animated), Cartoon Network, 2003.

(English version) Voice of Fee Carmichael, "Taiki no soto de," *Planetes* (animated), 2003.

Voice of Marsoon and woman, "The Menace of Mansuit/K–9 Quarry," *Duck Dodgers* (animated; also known as *Duck Dodgers in the 24 ½ Century*), Cartoon Network, 2004.

(English version) Voice of Moegi and Shijima, "Kikyo," *Naruto: Shippunden* (animated), 2007.

Interviewee, *Anime: Drawing a Revolution,* Starz!, 2007.

Voice of sister, "C's World," *Code Geass: Lelouch of the Rebellion* (animated), 2008.

Also appeared as (English version) voice of Yuri, "Project Eden," *Dati pea* (animated; also known as *Dirty Pair*); voice of Nadine (Hot Wheels), *Weird Science;* voice, *Dave's World;* voice, *Sweet Valley High.*

Television Additional Voices; Series:

El Hazard: Wanderers (animated), 1995.

Tenshi ni narumon (animated; also known as *I Want to Be an Angel* and *I'm Gonna Be an Angel*), 1999.

Mashuranbo (also known as *Shinzo*), 2000.

.hack//Tasogare no udewa densetsu (animated; also known as *.hack//Legend of the Twilight*), 2002.

Gungrave, 2003.

Moso dairinin (animated; also known as *Paranoia Agent*), Cartoon Network, 2004.

Television Additional Voices; Specials:

Love Hina Spring Special (animated; also known as *Love Hina Spring Special: I Wish Your Dream* and *Rabu Hina Haru Supesharu: Kimi sakura chiru nakare!*), 2000.

Television Work; Series:

Producer, *Digimon: Digital Monsters* (animated; also known as *Digimon 02, Digimon 03,* and *Digimon: Season 3*), Fox, 1999.

Voice director, *DinoZaurs* (animated), Fox, 2000.

Television Work; Specials:

Automated dialogue replacement (ADR) director, *Rabu Hina kurisumasu supesharu: Sairento ivu* (animated; also known as *Love Hina Christmas Special: Silent Eve*), 2000.

ADR director, *Love Hina Spring Special* (animated; also known as *Love Hina Spring Special: I Wish Your Dream* and *Rabu Hina Haru Supesharu: Kimi sakura chiru nakare!*), 2001.

Television Work; Pilots:

Voice director, *MegaMan Star Force* (animated), Cartoon Network, 2007.

Television Work; Episodic:

Voice director, *Mighty Morphin Power Rangers* (also known as *Day of the Dumpster, Mighty Morphin Alien Rangers, Power Rangers,* and *Power Rangers Ninja*), Fox, 1993–94.

(English version) Voice director, *Outlaw Star* (animated), Cartoon Network, 1998.

Voice director, *Digimon: Digital Monsters* (animated; also known as *Digimon 02, Digimon 03,* and *Digimon: Season 3*), Fox, 1999.

Automated dialogue replacement (ADR) director, "Sleeping Dirty," *Wild ARMs: Twilight Venom,* 1999.

Director, *Digimon: Digital Monsters* (animated), 1999–2001.

Director, *Rabu Hina* (animated; also known as *Love Hina*), 2000.

Voice director, *DinoZaurs* (animated; also known as *Prehistoric Warriors* and *DinoZaurs: The Series*), Fox, 2000.

ADR director, *Rabu Hina* (animated; also known as *Love Hina*), 2000–2001.

ADR director, *Outlaw Star,* 2001.

ADR director, *Uchu no suteruvia* (animated; also known as *Cosmic Stellvia, Sora no Stellvia, Stellvia, Stellvia of the Universe,* and *Uchu no Stellvia*), 2003.

ADR director, *Avenger,* 2003.

ADR director, "Hohoemi no senshi," *Grenadier: Hohoemi no senshi* (animated), 2004.

ADR director, *Bleach,* 2004–2006.

ADR director and story editor, *Duel Masters* (animated), Kids Station and Cartoon Network, 2004–2006.

Voice director, *Bleach,* 2004–2007.

Director, *Bleach,* 2006.

Director and voice director, *MegaMan Star Force,* 2007.

Also worked as voice director, *Bubu Cha Cha;* voice director, *Masked Rider;* voice director, *Super Pig;* voice director, *The Three Friends and Jerry;* voice director, *Uchu no kishi tekkaman bureido* (animated; also known as *Teknoman*); voice director, *V.R. Trooper,* Fox Kids; voice director, *Zoe and Charlie.*

Stage Work:

Director and choreographer for a stage production of *Mary Poppins.*

RECORDINGS

Video Games; Appearances:

Voice, *Inherit the Earth: Quest for the Orb,* 1994.
Voice, *Might and Magic: World of Xeen,* 1994.
Voice, *Blood and Magic,* Interplay, 1996.
Voice, *Where in the U.S.A. Is Carmen Sandiego?,* 1996.

(English version) Voice of Jo and Mikado, *Bushido Blade 2,* 1998.

(English version) Voice of Wanda, *Brave Fencer Musashiden* (also known as *Brave Fencer Musashi*), 1998.

Voice, *Heroes of Might and Magic III: The Restoration of Erathia,* 3DO, 1999.

Voice, *Might and Magic VIII: Day of the Destroyer,* 2000.

(English version) Voice of Leanne Caldwell, "PD4", and boy, *The Bouncer,* Electronic Arts, 2000.

Voice of Hana Tsu–Vachel, *Fear Effect 2: Retro Helix* (also known as *Fear Effect 2*), Eidos Interactive, 2001.

Voice of Queen Theodora, Mary, and Fetherian queen, *Growlanser III: The Dual Darkness,* 2001.

(English version; uncredited) Voice of Mary Godwin, *Xenosaga Episode I: Chikara he no ishi* (also known as *Xenosaga, Xenosaga Episode I Reloaded, Xenosaga Episode I: Der Wille zur Macht,* and *Xenosaga Episode I: The Will to Power*), Namco Hometek, 2002.

Voice, *Might and Magic IX,* 2002.

(Uncredited) Voice of Diao Chan, *Kessen II,* 2002.

(English version) Voice of BlackRose, *.hack//Osen kakudai vol. 1* (also known as *.hack//Infection* and *.hack//Infection Part 1*), Bandai Games, 2002.

Voice of Aribeth, *Neverwinter Nights,* 2002.

(English version) Voice of BlackRose, *.hack//Akusei heni vol. 2* (also known as *.hack//Mutation* and *.hack//Mutation Part 2*), Bandai Games, 2002.

(English version) Voice of BlackRose, *.hack//Shinshoku osen vol. 3* (also known as *.hack//Outbreak* and *.hack//Outbreak Part 3*), Bandai Games, 2002.

(English version; uncredited) Voice of Nel Zelpher, *Star Ocean: Till the End of Time* (also known as *"Star Ocean: Till the End of Time"—Director's Cut*), Square Enix, 2003.

(English version; uncredited) Voice of Da Qiao, Zhen Ji, and Xiao Qiao, *Shin sangoku muso 3* (also known as *Dynasty Warriors 4, Dynasty Warriors 4: Hyper,* and *Shin sangoku musou—Hyper*), KOEI Corp., 2003.

(English version) Voice of BlackRose, *.hack//Zettai houi vol. 4* (also known as *.hack//Quarantine* and *.hack//Quarantine Part 4*), Bandai Games, 2003.

(Uncredited) Voice of Lu Ling Qi, *Sangokushi senki 2* (also known as *Dynasty Tactics 2*), KOEI Corp., 2003.

(English version; uncredited) Voice of Faerie, *Drag–On Dragoon* (also known as *Drakengard*), Square Enix, 2003.

(English version; uncredited) Voice of Da Qiao, Zhen Ji, and Xiao Qiao, *Shin sangoku muso 3 mushoden* (also known as *Dynasty Warriors 4: Xtreme Legends*), KOEI Corp., 2003.

(English version) Voice of Chai Xianghua, *Soulcalibur II,* Namco Hometek, 2003.

(English version; uncredited) Voice of Succubus, *Castlevania* (also known as *Castlevania: Lament of Innocence*), Konami of America, 2003.

Voice of announcer, *Lords of Everquest,* Sony Online Entertainment, 2003.

(English version) Voice of Toshimi Tagami, *Kokaku kidotai: Stand Alone Complex* (also known as *Ghost in the Shell: Stand Alone Complex*), Bandai America, 2004.

(English version; uncredited) Voice of Da Qiao, Zhen Ji, and Xiao Qiao, *Shin sangoku muso 3* (also known as *Dynasty Warriors 4: Empires*), KOEI Corp., 2004.

(English version; uncredited) Voice of Stephania Wojinski, *Breakdown,* Namco Hometek, 2004.

(English version; uncredited) Voice of Oichi, *Sengoku muso* (also known as *Samurai Warriors*), KOEI Corp., 2004.

(English version; uncredited) Voice of Lita Blanchimont, *Irisu no Atorie: Etanaru mana* (also known as *Atelier Iris: Eternal Mana*), NIS America, 2004.

(English version; uncredited) Voice of Natalie, *Gasha meka sutajiamu saru batore* (also known as *Ape Escape: Pumped & Primed*), Ubi Soft Entertainment, 2004.

(English version; uncredited) Voice of Sera, *Dijitaru debiru saga: Abataaru teyuunaa* (also known as *Shin Megami Tensei: Digital Devil Saga*), Atlus USA, 2004.

(English version; uncredited) Voice of Jewel and Viki, *Genso suikoden IV* (also known as *Suikoden IV*), Konami Digital Entertainment America, 2004.

(Uncredited) Voice of Rita, *Biohazard Outbreak: File 2* (also known as *Resident Evil: Outbreak—File #2*), Capcom Entertainment, 2004.

(English version; uncredited) Voice of Inahime (Ina) and Oichi, *Sengoku muso mushoden* (also known as *Samurai Warriors: Xtreme Legends*), KOEI Corp., 2004.

(English version; uncredited) Voice of Pheremone Contra and Lucia, *Neo Contra,* Konami Digital Entertainment America, 2004.

(English version; uncredited) Voice of Nastsaya Vasilievna Obertas, *Ace Combat 5: The Unsung War* (also known as *Ace Combat: Squadron Leader*), Namco Hometek, 2004.

Various voices, *EverQuest II,* Sony Online Entertainment, 2004.

(English version) Voice, *SpellForce: Shadow of the Phoenix,* 2004.

Voice, *Champions: Return to Arms,* 2005.

(English version; uncredited) Voice of Sera, *Dijitaru debiru saga: Abataaru teyuunaa 2* (also known as *Shin Megami Tensei: Digital Devil Saga 2*), Atlus USA, 2005.

(English version; uncredited) Voice of Da Qiao, Zhen Ji, and Xiao Qiao, *Shin sangoku muso 4* (also known as *Dynasty Warriors 5*), KOEI Corp., 2005.

(English version; uncredited) Voice of Valvoga and Asagi, *Phantom Kingdom* (also known as *Makai Kingdom: Chronicles of the Sacred Tome*), NIS America, 2005.

(English version; uncredited) Voice of Raquel Applegate, *Wild ARMS: The 4th Detonator* (also known as *Wild Arms 4*), Xseed Games, 2005.

(English version; uncredited) Voice of Coriander, *Ponkotsu roman daikatsugeki Banpi Torotto* (also known as *Steamboat Chronicles*), Atlus USA, 2005.

(English version; uncredited) Voice of Ruilia and Violetta, *Grandia III,* Square Enix, 2005.

(English version) Voice of Queen Freidias and Mother Rune, *Rogue Galaxy,* Sony Computer Entertainment America, 2005.

(English version; uncredited) Voice of Lola and additional members, *Beat Down* (also known as *Beat Down: Fists of Vengeance*), Capcom Entertainment, 2005.

(English version; uncredited) Voice of Isabella, *Tales of Legendia,* 2005.

Voice, *Rainbow Six: Lockdown,* Namco Hometek, 2005.

(English version; uncredited) Voice of Da Qiao, Xiao Qiao, and Zhen Ji, *Shin sangoku muso 4 mushoden* (also known as *Dynasty Warriors 5: Xtreme Legends*), KOEI Corp., 2005.

(English version; uncredited) Voice of Seneca, *Rhapsodia* (also known as *Suikoden Tactics*), Konami Digital Entertainment America, 2005.

Voice, *Dungeons & Dragons: Dragonshard,* Infogames UK, 2005.

(English version; uncredited) Voice of Chai Xianghua, *Soulcaliber III* (also known as *Soul Caliber III: Arcade Edition*), Namco Hometek, 2005.

(English version; uncredited) Voice of Nephry Osborne and Rose, *Tales of the Abyss,* Namco Bandai Games America, 2005.

(English version; uncredited) Voice of Nigredo, *Xenosaga Episode III: Also Sprach Zarathustra,* Namco Bandai Games America, 2006.

(English version; uncredited) Voice of Claire Branch, *Ar tonelico: Sekai no owari de utai tsuzukeru shojo* (also known as *Ar Tonelico: Melody of Elemia*), NIS America, 2006.

(English version; uncredited) Voice of incidental characters, *Dirge of Cerberus: Final Fantasy VII,* Square Enix, 2006.

(English version; uncredited) Voice of Rozalin and Taro, *Makai senki Deisugaia 2* (also known as *Disgaea 2: Cursed Memories*), NIS America, 2006.

(English version; uncredited) Voice of Hazuki, *Genso suikoden V* (also known as *Suikoden V*), Konami Digital Entertainment America, 2006.

(English version; uncredited) Voice of Marcela Vasquez, *Ace Combat Zero: The Belkan War* (also known as *Ace Combat: The Belkan War*), Namco Bandai Games America, 2006.

(English version; uncredited) Voice of Da Qiao, Xiao Qiao, and Zhen Ji, *Shin sangoku muso 4: Empires* (also known as *Dynasty Warriors 5: Empires*), KOEI Corp., 2006.

(English version; uncredited) Voice of Anesthesia and Dr. Anesthesia, *Rumble Roses XX,* Konami Digital Entertainment America, 2006.

(English version) Voice of Zelkova, *.hack//G.U. Vol. 1: Saitan* (also known as *.hack//G.U. Vol.1//Rebirth*), 2006.

(English version; uncredited) Voice of Yula Ellis and Ella Fulchapen, *Irisu no atorie: Guran fuantazumu* (also known as *Atelier Iris 3: Grand Phantasm* and *Iris no Atelier: Gran Fantasm*), 2006.

(English version) Voice of Zelkova and misc. voices, *.hack//G.U. Vol.2: Kimi omo koe* (also known as *.hack//G.U. Vol.2//Reminisce*), Namco Bandai Games America, 2006.

Voice of Vampire (female), *EverQuest II: Echoes of Faydwer*, 2006.

(English version) Voice of Anedia, *Culdcept SAGA*, Namco Bandai Games America, 2006.

(English version; uncredited) Voice of Rebecca Streisand, *Wild ARMs: The Vth Vanguard* (also known as *Wild ARMs 5*), Namco Bandai Games America, 2006.

(English version; uncredited) Voice of Zelkova and misc. voices, *.hack//G.U. Vol.3: Aruku you na hayasa de* (also known as *.hack//G.U. Vol.3//Redemption*), Namco Bandai Games America, 2007.

(English version; uncredited) Voice of Feinne, Tricia, and Resilience, *Soul cradle: Sekai o kurau mono* (also known as *Soul Nomad & the World Eaters*), NIS America, 2007.

(English version; uncredited) Voice of Lillet Blan, *Grim-Grimoire*, 2007.

(English version; uncredited) Voice of Elfaria, Alice, and Alice's mother, *Odin Sphere*, Atlus USA, 2007.

Voice of Cierra, *Riviera: The Promised Land*, Atlus USA, 2007.

(English version; uncredited) Voice of Da Qiao and Xing Cai, *Muso Orochi* (also known as *Warriors Orochi*), KOEI Corp., 2007.

(English version; uncredited) Voice of Zhen Ji, *Shin sangoku muso 5* (also known as *Dynasty Warriors 6*), KOEI Corp., 2007.

(English version; uncredited) Voice of Cynthia Kazakov and tutorial voice, *Kaduokenusu: Nyu burado* (also known as *Trauma Center: New Blood*), Atlus USA, 2007.

(English version; uncredited) Voice of Valentine, *Guilty Gear 2: Overture*, Aksys Games, 2007.

(English version; uncredited) Voice of the Bagged One, *Baroque*, Atlus USA, 2008.

(English version; uncredited) Voice of Da Qiao and Xing Cai, *Musou Orochi mao sairin*, 2008.

(English version; uncredited) Voice of Aqua, *Teiruzu obu Shinfuonia: Ratatosuku no Kishi* (also known as *Tales of Symphonia: Dawn of the New World*), Namco Bandai Games America, 2008.

(English version; uncredited) Voice of Chihiro Fushimi and Sayoko Uehara, *Persona 4* (also known as *Shin Megami Tensei: Persona 4*), Atlus USA, 2008.

(English version; uncredited) Voice of Chai Xianghua, *Soulcaliber IV*, Namco Bandai Games America, 2008.

(English version; uncredited) Voice of Nan and Witcher, *Teiruzu obu Vesuperia* (also known as *Tales of Vesperia*), Namco Bandai Games America, 2008.

(English version) Voice of Karal and Moon Queen, *Kaze no Kuronoa: Door to Phantomile* (also known as *Klonoa*), Namco Bandai Games America, 2008.

(English version; uncredited) Voice of Mizue Hoshino, *Katamari damashii Tribute* (also known as *Katamari Forever*), Namco Bandai Games America, 2009.

Video Games; as Additional Voices:

(English version) *Kokaku kidotai* (also known as *Ghost in the Shell*), 1997.

Brave Fencer Musashi, Square Soft, 1998.

Growlanser III: The Dual Darkness, 2001.

(English version) *Front Mission 4*, Square Enix, 2003.

Biohazard Outbreak: File 2 (also known as *Resident Evil: Outbreak—File #2*), Capcom Entertainment, 2004.

(Uncredited) *Death by Degrees* (also known as *Tekken's Nina Williams in "Death by Degrees"*), Namco Hometek, 2005.

Ponkotsu roman daikatsugeki Banpi Torotto (also known as *Steamboat Chronicles*), Atlus USA, 2005.

Tales of the Abyss, Namco Bandai Games America, 2005.

Xenosaga Episode III: Also Sprach Zarathustra, Namco Bandai Games America, 2006.

Ar tonelico: Sekai no owari de utai tsuzukeru shojo (also known as *Ar Tonelico: Melody of Elemia*), NIS America, 2006.

Culdcept SAGA, Namco Bandai Games America, 2006.

(English version; uncredited) *Seiken densetsu 4* (also known as *Dawn of Mana*), Square Enix, 2006.

(English version; uncredited) *Odin Sphere*, Atlus USA, 2007.

(English version; uncredited) *Operation Darkness*, Atlus USA, 2007.

(English version; uncredited) *Ace Combat 6: Kaiho heno senka* (also known as *Ace Combat 6: Fires of Liberation*), Namco Bandai Games America, 2007.

(English version; uncredited) *Armored Core: For Answer*, Ubisoft Entertainment, 2008.

Dragon Age: Origins, Electronic Arts, 2009.

Video Games:

Director: English voices—Cup of Tea Productions, *Wild ARMS: The 4th Detonator* (also known as *Wild Arms 4*), Xseed Games, 2005.

Voice director; English version and voiceover director: English voices—Cup of Tea Productions, Inc., *Tales of Legendia*, Namco Hometek, 2005.

Director: English voices—Cup of Tea Productions, *Tales of the Abyss*, Namco Bandai Games America, 2005.

Voiceover director: English voices—Cup of Tea Productions, Inc., *Xenosaga Episode III: Also Sprach Zarathustra*, Namco Bandai Games America, 2006.

Director: English voices—Cup of Tea Productions, *Tales of the World: Radiant Mythology,* Namco Bandai Games America, 2006.
Director: English voices—Cup of Tea Productions, *Teiruzu obu Shinfuonia: Ratatosuku no Kishi* (also known as *Tales of Symphonia: Dawn of the New World*), Namco Bandai Games America, 2008.
Director: English voices—Cup of Tea Productions, *Teiruzu obu Vesuperia* (also known as *Tales of Vesperia*), Namco Bandai Games America, 2008.
Director: English voices—Cup of Tea Productions, *Kaze no Kuronoa: Door to Phantomile* (also known as *Klonoa*), Namco Bandai Games America, 2008.
Voice director, *Doragonboru evoryushon* (also known as *Dragonball Evolution*), Namco Bandai Games America, 2009.

WRITINGS

Television Episodes:
Wild ARMs: Twilight Venom, 1999.
(English version) *Duel Masters,* Kids Station and Cartoon Network, 2004–2006.

OTHER SOURCES

Periodicals:
Animatedrica, May, 2000.

Electronic:
Wendee Lee Official Site, http://www.wendeelle.com/, January 19, 2010.

LEITCH, Christopher
(Chris Leitch)

PERSONAL

Addresses: *Agent*—Paradigm, 360 North Crescent Dr., North Bldg., Beverly Hills, CA 90210.

Career: Director and writer.

CREDITS

Film Director:
The First Paintings, 1974.
The Hitter, Peppercorn–Wormser, 1979.
The Border (also known as *The Blood Barrier, Border Patrol,* and *Border Cop*), 1979.
Teen Wolf Too, Atlantic Releasing, 1987.

Courage Mountain (also known as *Courage Mountain: Heidi's New Adventure* and *Heidi—Le sentier du courage*), Triumph Releasing, 1989.

Film Producer:
The Hitter, Peppercorn–Wormser, 1979.

Television Director; Miniseries:
"Book of the Heart: Part 2" and "Book of the Shadow: Parts 1 & 2," *Samurai Girl,* ABC Family, 2008.

Television Director; Movies:
Spy Games, ABC, 1991.
Moment of Truth: Murder or Memory? (also known as *Murder or Memory?* and *Murder or Memory?: A Moment of Truth*), NBC, 1994.
She Fought Alone (also known as *Scared by Love*), NBC, 1995.
A Friend Betrayal (also known as *Stolen Youth*), NBC, 1996.
Little Girls in Pretty Boxes, Lifetime, 1997.
A Nightmare Come True (also known as *A Dream of Murder*), CBS, 1997.
Crowned and Dangerous, ABC, 1997.
I've Been Waiting for You, NBC, 1998.
Cab to Canada, CBS, 1998.
The Patty Duke Show: Still Rockin' in Brooklyn Heights, CBS, 1999.
Satan's School for Girls, ABC, 2000.
The Wednesday Woman, CBS, 2000.
A Family in Crisis: The Elian Gonzalez Story (also known as *The Elian Gonzalez Story*), Fox Family, 2000.
Three Blind Mice (also known as *Ed McBain's "Three Blind Mice"*), CBS, 2001.
A Christmas Visitor, Hallmark Channel, 2002.
The Survivors Club, CBS, 2004.
Black Widower, Lifetime, 2006.
Mind Over Murder, Lifetime, 2006.
Housesitter (also known as *The Housesitter*), Oxygen, 2007.
Secrets in the Walls, Lifetime, 2010.

Television Work; Movies:
Coproducer, *A Christmas Visitor,* Hallmark Channel, 2002.
Producer, *The Survivors Club,* CBS, 2004.

Television Director; Pilots:
Malibu Shores, CBS, 1996.
(As Chris Leitch) *Miami Medical,* CBS, 2010.

Television Director; Episodic:
"Remembering Melody," *The Hitchhiker* (also known as *Deadly Nightmares* and *Le voyageur*), HBO, 1984.

"Petty Thieves," *The Hitchhiker* (also known as *Deadly Nightmares* and *Le voyageur*), HBO, 1985.

"Man at the Window," *The Hitchhiker* (also known as *Deadly Nightmares* and *Le voyageur*), HBO, 1985.

"Host Link," *Misfits of Science*, NBC, 1985.

"The Lady in the Iron Mask," *Moonlighting*, ABC, 1985.

"The Gloating Place," *Alfred Hitchcock Presents*, NBC, 1986.

"An Impossible Silence," *Beauty and the Beast*, CBS, 1987.

Shell Game, CBS, 1987.

"China Moon," *Beauty and the Beast*, CBS, 1988.

"Down to a Sunless Sea," *Beauty and the Beast*, CBS, 1988.

"To Reign in Hell," *Beauty and the Beast*, CBS, 1988.

"Chao Ong," *China Beach*, ABC, 1988.

"After Burner," *China Beach*, ABC, 1989.

"Nightfall," *China Beach*, ABC, 1989.

"Sugar Blues," *Equal Justice*, 1990.

"Holly's Choice," *China Beach*, ABC, 1990.

"Escape," *China Beach*, ABC, 1990.

My Life and Times, ABC, 1991.

"Sight Unseen," *The Flash*, CBS, 1991.

"Close to Home," *Undercover*, 1991.

Nightmare Cafe, NBC, 1992.

South Beach, NBC, 1993.

"Less Moonlight," *Key West*, Fox, 1993.

"The System," *Key West*, Fox, 1993.

Missing Persons, 1993–94.

Traps, CBS, 1994.

Hawkeye, syndicated, 1994.

The Commish, ABC, 1994.

Malibu Shores, NBC, 1996.

"Styx Feet Under," *Charmed*, The WB, 2004.

"Whole," *So noTORIous*, VH1, 2006.

"Drink the Cup," *Close to Home*, CBS, 2007.

(As Chris Leitch) "Fallen Idols," *CSI: Crime Scene Investigation* (also known as *CSI: Las Vegas, C.S.I.,* and *Les experts*), CBS, 2007.

"Speaky Spokey," *Da Kink in My Hair*, 2008.

"Di Heart of Di Matter," *Da Kink in My Hair*, 2008.

(As Chris Leitch) "Condor," *Jericho*, CBS, 2008.

(As Chris Leitch) "The Theory of Everything," *CSI: Crime Scene Investigation* (also known as *CSI: Las Vegas, C.S.I.,* and *Les experts*), CBS, 2008.

(As Chris Leitch) "The Descent of Man," *CSI: Crime Scene Investigation* (also known as *CSI: Las Vegas, C.S.I.,* and *Les experts*), CBS, 2009.

(As Chris Leitch) "Counterfeit," *The Beast*, Arts and Entertainment, 2009.

WRITINGS

Screenplays:

The Hitter, Peppercorn–Wormser, 1979.

Universal Soldier, TriStar, 1992.

Television Episodes:

"O.D. Feelin'," *The Hitchhiker* (also known as *Deadly Nightmares* and *Le voyageur*), HBO, 1986.

"The Curse," *The Hitchhiker* (also known as *Deadly Nightmares* and *Le voyageur*), HBO, 1986.

"Homebodies," *The Hitchhiker* (also known as *Deadly Nightmares* and *Le voyageur*), HBO, 1987.

LENGYEL, Wendy
    See LEE, Wendee

LENNEY, Dinah 1956–

PERSONAL

Born November 18, 1956, in Englewood, NJ; daughter of Nelson Gross (a business person and politician); children: more than one.

Career: Actress, educator, and author. Also worked as dialogue coach. Teacher of acting classes at University of California, Los Angeles, and Pepperdine University.

CREDITS

Film Appearances:

First reporter, *Three Fugitives*, Buena Vista, 1989.

Newscaster, *Internal Affairs*, Paramount, 1990.

Registrar, *Mr. Jones*, TriStar, 1993.

Roz, *Babyfever*, Rainbow Releasing, 1994.

Second technician, *The Puppet Masters* (also known as *Robert A. Heinlein's "The Puppet Masters"*), Buena Vista, 1994.

Television Appearances; Series:

Friday Forrester, a recurring role, *A Fine Romance* (also known as *A Ticket to Ride*), CBS, 1989.

Nurse Shirley, *ER*, NBC, 1995–2009.

Television Appearances; Episodic:

Karen Press, "Steele Blushing," *Remington Steele*, NBC, 1985.

"The Shape of Things," *Newhart*, CBS, 1985.

Francine, "The World Next Door," *The Twilight Zone*, CBS, 1986.

Woman, "Irrevocably Yours," *Knots Landing*, 1986.

Receptionist, "Sparky Brackman R.I.P.????–1987," *L.A. Law*, NBC, 1987.

Sarah, "I'll Be Home for Christmas," *thirtysomething*, ABC, 1987.

Secretary Megan Reynolds, "Devil with a Blue Dress On," *Murphy Brown,* CBS, 1988.

Laura, *The Bradys,* CBS, 1990.

Voice of Baby Lisa, "Give a Sucker an Even Break," *Baby Talk,* ABC, 1991.

Voice of Baby Lisa, "The Whiz Kid," *Baby Talk,* ABC, 1991.

Voice of Baby Lisa, "Tooth and Nail," *Baby Talk,* ABC, 1991.

Talk show host, "Kelly Does Hollywood: Part 1," *Married … with Children,* Fox, 1991.

Dr. Marks, "Hell Hath No Fury," *Cracker* (also known as *Cracker: Mind over Murder*), ABC, 1997.

Cameron's teacher, "Sexual Healing," *Get Real,* Fox, 1999.

Mrs. Vandenbosch, "History Lessons," *Get Real,* Fox, 2000.

Dr. Hoffman, "Hey, Ugly!," *Any Day Now,* Lifetime, 2000.

Mary Klein, Smithsonian curator, "The Women of Qumar," *The West Wing,* NBC, 2001.

"Penelope in Makeup," *The Amanda Show,* 2001.

(Uncredited) Sylvia Pierce, "Grounded," *Judging Amy,* CBS, 2001.

Special Agent Shannon Hodgins, "Jump," *Joan of Arcadia,* CBS, 2004.

Teacher, "Secret Truths," *South of Nowhere,* The N, 2005.

(Uncredited) Woman, "Whatever Happened to Baby Bodashka?," *Crumbs,* ABC, 2006.

Alissa Kline, "Res Ipsa," *Without a Trace* (also known as *W.A.T.*), CBS, 2007.

Mrs. Hobart, "In Which Addison Has a Very Casual Get Together," *Private Practice,* ABC, 2007.

Prison warden, "Undercover," *Law & Order: Special Victims Unit* (also known as *Law & Order: SVU* and *Special Victims Unit*), NBC, 2008.

Lotto commissioner, "Mr. Monk Gets Lotto Fever," *Monk,* USA Network, 2008.

Eileen/Alan Park, "Earthlings Welcome Here," *Terminator: The Sarah Conner Chronicles,* Fox, 2008.

Television Appearances; Other:

Shirley, *If Tomorrow Comes* (miniseries), CBS, 1986.

Friday Forrester, a recurring role, *A Fine Romance* (pilot; also known as *A Ticket to Ride*), CBS, 1989.

Stage Appearances:

Jane, *The First Picture Show,* American Conservatory Theatre, San Francisco, CA, 1999.

Rosie, *Fedunn,* Odyssey Theatre, Los Angeles, 2002.

WRITINGS

Books:

(With Mary Lou Belli) *Acting for Young Actors: The Ultimate Teen Guide,* Watson–Guptill Publications, 2006.

Bigger than Life: A Murder, a Memoir (nonfiction), University of Nebraska Press, 2007.

LERNER, Ken
(Kenneth Lerner)

PERSONAL

Born in Brooklyn, NY; son of George (an antiques dealer and fisherman) and Blanche Lerner; brother of Michael Lerner (an actor); children: Sam (an actor). *Education:* Studied acting with Stella Adler, Peggy Feury, and Roy London.

Addresses: *Agent*—Ellis Talent Group, 4705 Laurel Canyon Blvd., Valley Village, CA 91607.

Career: Actor. Also worked as an acting teacher; appeared in commercials for Snickers candy bars, Dunkin' Donuts, American's Dairy Farm, FedEx delivery service, and other products and services.

Awards, Honors: Best Actor Award, Association of Independent Commercial Directors, for work on a Snickers commercial.

CREDITS

Film Appearances:

Eagle I, *Grand Theft Auto,* New World, 1977.

Michael, *Hot Tomorrows,* 1978.

Peewee, *Gas Pump Girls,* Cannon, 1978.

Tony Paoli, Jr., *Any Which Way You Can,* Warner Bros., 1980.

Doctor, *Irreconcilable Differences,* Warner Bros., 1984.

Waiter, *Secret Admirer* (also known as *The Letter*), Orion, 1985.

Ken, *Jake Speed,* New World, 1986.

Stuart, *Miracles,* Orion, 1986.

Finley, *Project X,* Twentieth Century–Fox 1987.

(As Kenneth Lerner) Agent, *The Running Man,* TriStar, 1987.

Gravenstein, *Hit List,* New Line Cinema, 1989.

Arthur, *Relentless,* New Line Cinema, 1989.

Ray, *The Fabulous Baker Boys,* Twentieth Century–Fox, 1989.

Josh, *Immediate Family,* Columbia, 1989.

Tom Delaney, *Robocop 2,* Orion, 1990.

Dr. Freedman, *The Exorcist III* (also known as *The Exorcist III: Legion* and *William Peter Blatty's "The Exorcist III"*), Twentieth Century–Fox, 1990.

Pete, *The Doctor,* Buena Vista, 1991.

Optometrist, *Diary of a Hitman,* Vision International, 1991.

Tony, *Fast Getaway,* New Line Cinema, 1991.

(As Kenneth Lerner) *And You Thought Your Parents Were Weird!,* 1991.

Roger Graham, *Unlawful Entry,* Twentieth Century–Fox, 1992.

Jude's analyst, *Mother's Boys,* Dimension Films, 1994.

Al Rosenberg, *Relentless IV: Ashes to Ashes,* 1994.

Tony Bush, *Fast Getaway II,* Live Video, 1994.

James, *Dream a Little Dream 2,* 1994.

Saul Slobin, *Rave Review,* 1995.

Alex Shaw, *Bodily Harm,* 1995.

Sergeant Moss, *For Better or Worse,* Columbia, 1996.

Producer, *Dead Girl,* 1996.

(Uncredited) Justice of the peace, *High Voltage,* 1997.

Dean Barlow, *Senseless,* Dimension Films, 1998.

(Uncredited) Teacher, *Godzilla* (also known as *Gojira*), Sony Pictures Entertainment, 1998.

Dr. Rifkin, *The Story of Us,* Universal, 1999.

Judge Levin, "Inside Out," *Boys Life 3,* Strand Releasing, 2000.

Hotel clerk, *True Vinyl,* 2000.

Rosen, *The Woman Every Man Wants* (also known as *Perfect Lover* and *La mujer que todo hombre quiere*), 2001.

Coroner Glen, *They Crawl* (also known as *Crawlers*), Lions Gate Films, 2001.

Saulley, *Jesus, Mary and Joey* (also known as *Welcome Back Miss Mary*), 2003, Panorama Entertainment, 2006.

Hank's lawyer, *National Security,* Columbia, 2003.

Rob the production manager, *Frankie and Johnny Are Married,* IFC Films, 2003.

Sid Freeman, *Mafioso: The Father, the Son,* American Cinema International, 2004.

Himself, *Special Thanks to Roy London* (documentary), 2005.

Rosenbloom, *All In,* MTI Home Video, 2007.

Phil, *Undisputed II: Last Man Standing* (also known as *Undisputed 2*), New Line Home Video, 2007.

Jack, *The Ticket* (short film), 2007.

Television Appearances; Series:

Rocco Baruffi, a recurring role, *Happy Days* (also known as *Happy Days Again*), ABC, between 1974 and 1983.

Jonathan Saunders, *Chicago Hope,* CBS, 1994–99.

Television Appearances; Movies:

Long Island Bucks member, *Million Dollar Infield,* CBS, 1982.

Lawyer, *Best Kept Secrets,* ABC, 1984.

Aaron, *Love on the Run,* NBC, 1985.

Dr. Peter Bristol, *A Twist of the Knife,* CBS, 1993.

Earl Cleaver, *Trial by Fire,* ABC, 1995.

Bob Arum, *Don King: Only in America,* HBO, 1997.

Television Appearances; Pilots:

Desk officer, *The Two–Five,* ABC, 1978.

Gus Brown and Midnight Brewster, NBC, 1985.

Mickey, *Philby,* ABC, 1989.

Mulligan, *The Michael Richards Show,* NBC, 2000.

Peep Show, Fox, 2005.

Television Appearances; Specials:

Happy Days: 30th Anniversary Reunion, ABC, 2005.

Television Appearances; Episodic:

Frankie, "Richie Fights Back," *Happy Days* (also known as *Happy Days Again*), ABC, 1975.

Frankie, "Fonzie the Flatfoot," *Happy Days* (also known as *Happy Days Again*), ABC, 1975.

Frankie, "The Second Anniversary Show," *Happy Days* (also known as *Happy Days Again*), ABC, 1976.

Pete, "Laverne & Shirley Meet Fabian," *Laverne & Shirley* (also known as *Laverne & Shirley & Company, Laverne & Shirley & Friends,* and *Laverne DeFazio & Shirley Feeney*), ABC, 1977.

Air, "I Do," *A New Kind of Family,* ABC, 1979.

Ivan, "The Valley Strangler," *Mrs. Columbo* (also known as *Kate Columbo, Kate Loves a Mystery,* and *Kate the Detective*), NBC, 1979.

Dentist, "Girlfriends," *The Last Resort,* 1979.

Reporter, "Power Play," *Benson,* 1980.

Pool cleaner, "The Resurrection of Carlini," *The Greatest American Hero,* 1982.

Doctor, "Date Rape," *Cagney & Lacey,* 1983.

Officer Kern, "The Hardcase," *Riptide,* NBC, 1984.

Robert Silver, "Ewe and Me, Babe," *Hill Street Blues,* NBC, 1984.

"A Very Practical Joke," *Scene of the Crime,* NBC, 1984.

"Judgement Day: Parts 1 & 2," *The A–Team,* NBC, 1985.

Dr. Cutler, "Jewel Heist," *It's a Living* (also known as *Making a Living*), syndicated, 1986.

Mr. Van Cleve, "Dwight Schmindlapp Is Not a Quitter," *Newhart,* CBS, 1986.

Officer Chazin, "Leave It to Willie," *Valerie* (also known as *The Hogan Family* and *Valerie's Family*), NBC, 1986.

David, "To Live and Die on TV," *Sledge Hammer!* (also known as *Sledge Hammer: The Early Years*), 1986.

"The Runner Falls on His Kisser," *Hill Street Blues,* NBC, 1987.

Mr. Feinman, "'D' Is for Date," *Family Ties,* NBC, 1987.

Max, "Up from Down Under," *The Facts of Life,* NBC, 1987.

Salesman, "The Card," *The Twilight Zone* (also known as *The New Twilight Zone*), 1987.

Attorney Peter Duble, "The Son Also Rises," *L.A. Law,* NBC, 1988.

Dr. Walter Neff, "Sex and the Married Detective," *Columbo,* NBC, 1989.

Howard Nelson, "Unacceptable Loss," *Hunter,* NBC, 1990.

Doctor, "Blanche Delivers," *The Golden Girls,* NBC, 1990.

Leonard Marshall, "Who's Minding the Kid?," *Who's the Boss?,* ABC, 1990.

Nolan Wheeler, "The Accident," *Matlock,* NBC, 1991.

Jim Hollister, "The Poisoned Tree," *The Commish,* ABC, 1991.

Dr. Garabedian, "Love and Death," *Eddie Dodd,* 1991.

Bristol, "A Twist of the Knife," *Diagnosis Murder,* CBS, 1993.

Sid Weinberg, "Since I Don't Have You," *Fallen Angels,* Showtime, 1993.

Peter Duble, "Dead Issue," *L.A. Law,* NBC, 1994.

Dr. Rieder, "Love the One You're With," *Cafe Americain,* 1994.

Harry Stopak, "Hit and Run," *ER,* NBC, 1994.

Danforth, "A Star Is Bared," *Blossom,* NBC, 1995.

David Neiberg, "Dirty Socks," *NYPD Blue,* ABC, 1995.

Jerry Korman, "Home Is Where the Tart Is," *Beverly Hills, 90210* (also known as *Class of Beverly Hills*), Fox, 1995.

Jerry Korman, "Must Be a Guy Thing," *Beverly Hills, 90210* (also known as *Class of Beverly Hills*), Fox, 1995.

Jerry Korman, "Everything's Coming up Roses," *Beverly Hills, 90210* (also known as *Class of Beverly Hills*), Fox, 1995.

James Reid, "Pilot Error," *JAG* (also known as *JAG: Judge Advocate General*), NBC, 1995.

Ron Demerjian, "See Me," *Dangerous Minds,* ABC, 1996.

Harry Gandolphi, "Chapter Three, Year Two," *Murder One,* ABC, 1996.

Mark Haney, "Every Picture Tells a Story," *EZ Streets,* 1996.

Principal Bob Flutie, "The Harvest," *Buffy the Vampire Slayer* (also known as *BtVS, Buffy,* and *Buffy, the Vampire Slayer: The Series*), The WB, 1997.

Principal Bob Flutie, "Welcome to the Hellmouth," *Buffy the Vampire Slayer* (also known as *BtVS, Buffy,* and *Buffy, the Vampire Slayer: The Series*), The WB, 1997.

Principal Bob Flutie, "Teacher's Pet," *Buffy the Vampire Slayer* (also known as *BtVS, Buffy,* and *Buffy, the Vampire Slayer: The Series*), The WB, 1997.

Principal Bob Flutie, "The Pack," *Buffy the Vampire Slayer* (also known as *BtVS, Buffy,* and *Buffy, the Vampire Slayer: The Series*), The WB, 1997.

The criminalist, "Ricochet," *Gun* (also known as *Robert Altman's "Gun"*), ABC, 1997.

Dick Klinedorf, "Dental Men Prefer Blondes," *Total Security,* ABC, 1997.

Wally DeCarlo, "Honeymoon at Viagra Falls," *NYPD Blue,* ABC, 1998.

Cop, "Two Guys, a Girl, and a Psycho Halloween," *Two Guys, a Girl, and a Pizza Place* (also known as *Two Guys and a Girl*), ABC, 1998.

Dawson, "See Dharma Run," *Dharma & Greg,* ABC, 1999.

Rabbi Sam Benzig, "Do unto Others," *The Practice,* ABC, 1999.

Feinstein, "Drew and the Racial Tension Play," *The Drew Carey Show,* ABC, 2000.

Principal Fleiss, "Barricade," *Brutally Normal,* The WB, 2000.

Principal Fleiss, "Well Solved Sherlock," *Brutally Normal,* The WB, 2000.

Mr. Bellamy, "Human Touch," *Judging Amy,* CBS, 2000.

Saul Singer, "Two Birds with One Sloan," *Diagnosis Murder,* CBS, 2000.

Bob, "My Best Friend's Tush," *Will & Grace,* NBC, 2000.

Attorney Dick Raditz, "Sex, Lies, and Second Thoughts," *Ally McBeal,* Fox, 2000.

Sid Lumsky, "Restoration," *Touched by an Angel,* CBS, 2000.

Stan Seidel, "Orion in the Sky," *ER,* NBC, 2002.

"The Whole Truth," *Providence,* NBC, 2002.

Rick, "Dinner with Friends," *Happy Family,* NBC, 2003.

Professor Spafford, "The One with the Soap Opera Party," *Friends,* NBC, 2003.

Voice of Boris, "Tight Squeeze," *Spider–Man* (also known as *Spider–Man: The New Animated Series*), MTV, 2003.

Charles James, "My Life in Four Cameras," *Scrubs,* NBC, 2005.

Norman Hanes, "Lenny Scissorhands," *NYPD Blue,* ABC, 2005.

Howard Bridge, "Smile," *Boston Legal,* ABC, 2006.

Congressman Marino, "Requiem," *The West Wing,* NBC, 2006.

Albert Hencheck, "Bloodbath," *Navy NCIS: Naval Criminal Investigative Service* (also known as *NCIS* and *NCIS: Naval Criminal Investigative Service*), CBS, 2006.

Judge Abraham Schlichter, "Drink the Cup," *Close fo Home,* CBS, 2007.

Mr. Jerry Nivens, "A La Cart," *CSI: Crime Scene Investigation* (also known as *C.S.I., CSI: Las Vegas* and *Les experts*), CBS, 2007.

Dr. Ron Forsythe, "Where and Why," *Without a Trace* (also known as *W.A.T.*), CBS, 2007.

Police attorney, "Nanny McDead," *Castle,* ABC, 2009.

Dr. Bernstein, "The Story of Lucy and Jessie," *Desperate Housewives,* ABC, 2009.

Dr. Bernstein, "A Spark. To Pierce the Dark.," *Desperate Housewives,* ABC, 2009.

Dr. Levine, "Baseball Was Better with Steroids," *Two and a Half Men,* CBS, 2009.

"A Distinctive Horn," *Weeds,* Showtime, 2009.

Also appeared as Barry Schneider, *Civil Wars,* ABC; as Buzz Atkins, "Back in the Bottle," *The Court;* as Mr. Steinway, "Mitigating Circumstances," *Courthouse;* and in *The District,* CBS, *King of Queens,* CBS, and as Tony, *Nash Bridges,* CBS.

Stage Appearances:
Howard Fine, *The Waverly Gallery*, Pasadena Playhouse, Pasadena, CA, 2002.

Also appeared as Jonathan, *Arsenic and Old Lace*, Falcon Theatre; and in *El Salvador*.

Stage Director:
Closer, Stages, Hollywood, CA, 2004.

OTHER SOURCES

Periodicals:
Buffy the Vampire Slayer, December, 2004, pp. 54–56.

Electronic:
Ken Lerner Studio, http://www.kenlerner.com, October 20, 2009.

LITTLE, Kim

PERSONAL

Born August 27, in Stillwater, OK; married David Michael Latt (a producer, writer, director, editor), October 8, 1994; children: one daughter.

Career: Actress. Appeared in television commercials for Lee Jeans, 1998. Taught at Comedy Traffic School.

Awards, Honors: Best actress nominations, Worldfest, Bare Bones, Melbourne Underground Film Festival, Delta Film Festival, all for *Jane White Is Sick & Twisted*; best actress nominations, Fantasporto Film Festival and Valenciennes, both for *Killers*; best actress nominations at other film festivals, including Sitges International Film Festival, Columbus Film & Video Film Festival, Breckenridge Film Festival, Madrid International Film Festival, and HBO's Comedy Arts Festival; best actress award, Close Encounters Film Festival.

CREDITS

Film Appearances:
Bre, *Rock and Roll Fantasy* (also known as *Sorority House Party*), The Asylum, 1992.
Ann, *Boiler Room* (also known as *Lost in Hollywood*), Caroli Productions, 1992.
Norma, *Younger and Younger*, 1993.
Laura, *Second Cousin, Once Removed*, 1994.

Dr. Ginger, *Almighty Fred*, Around the Scenes Releasing, 1996.
Heather, *Killers* (also known as *Killer Instinct*), The Asylum, 1997.
Mary Ellen, *Social Intercourse*, The Asylum, 1998.
Audrey Hobbs, *Wildflower* (also known as *Blood Related* and *Virgin Nights*), Lions Gate Films, 1999.
Nurse Kim, *... And Call Me in the Morning*, 1999.
Marilyn Monroe, *Evil Hill* (short film), 1999.
Susan, *The Stranger* (also known as *The Deputy*), Flybolt Productions, 1999.
(English version) Voice of Nami Kikushima, *Otogiriso* (also known as *St. John's Wort*), The Asylum, 2001.
Olivia, *Hourly Rates*, Visionary Films, 2002.
The Hit (short film), 2002.
Jane White, *Jane White Is Sick & Twisted*, Artist View Entertainment, 2002.
Heather, *Killers 2: The Beast*, The Asylum, 2002.
Sheriff Deputy Rachel Lander, *Scarecrow Slayer* (also known as *Scarecrow: Resurrection*), York Entertainment, 2003.
(Uncredited) FBI agent, *Death Valley: The Revenge of Bloody Bill*, The Asylum, 2004.
Detective Lowenstein, *Jolly Roger: Massacre at Cutter's Cove*, The Asylum, 2005.
Rebecca, *War of the Worlds* (also known as *H. G. Wells' "War of the Worlds"* and *Invasion*), The Asylum, 2005.
FBI agent Jamie McEnroy, *The 9/11 Commission Report*, The Asylum, 2006.
Mary Lou, *666: The Child*, The Global Asylum, 2006.
Specialist Sustin, *30,000 Leagues Under the Sea*, The Asylum, 2007.
Dr. Leah Perrot, *Supercroc*, The Asylum, 2007.
Lynn Anderson, *The Apocalypse*, The Asylum, 2007.
Victoria, *War of the Worlds 2: The Next Wave* (also known as *War of the Worlds: The Next Wave*), The Asylum, 2008.
Allison, *Countdown: Jerusalem*, The Asylum, 2009.

Television Appearances; Series:
Nurse Susan Hilliard, *Diagnosis Murder*, CBS, 1998–99.

Television Appearances; Episodic:
Blonde Shill, "Dutch Schultz's Treasure," *Unsolved Mysteries*, NBC, 1992.
Angelina Erikson, "Dog Day Afternoon," *Martial Law*, CBS, 2000.
Carol, "Charmed Again: Part 2," *Charmed*, The WB, 2001.
Laurie Brooks, "Precautions," *Strong Medicine*, Lifetime, 2002.

Also appeared as guest, *New Attitudes*, Lifetime.

Television Appearances; Movies:
Receptionist, *Emma's Wish*, CBS, 1998.

(Uncredited) Betty Mae, *Assignment Berlin* (also known as *Babyhandel Berlin—Jenseits aller Skrupel*), Showtime, 1998.

Stage Appearances:
Appeared as Julie, *Jake's Women,* and Mary Bailey, *It's a Wonderful Life,* both SPTC/Simi Cultural Arts Center; Yvonne, *Art,* SPTC; Marvel Ann, *Psycho Beach Party,* The Improv, Luna Park, CA; Susy, *Wait until Dark,* and Mademoiselle de Tourvel, *Les Liaison Dangereuses,* both Conejo Players Theatre; Sandra, *A Thousand Clowns,* Ottavios; Monroe, *Senseless Violence & Things to Annoy You,* Senseless Theatre Group, the Complex; Vicki, *The Well of Horniness,* Artists Confronting AIDS, St. Genesius; and Kaye, *Stage Door,* Woodland Hills Theatre, CA.

RECORDINGS

Videos:
H. G. Wells' "War of the Worlds": Behind the Scenes, The Asylum, 2005.
Jolly Roger: Massacre at Cutter's Cove—Behind the Scenes, The Asylum, 2005.

OTHER SOURCES

Periodicals:
Cinescape, October, 2003, p. 27.
Femmes Fatales Magazine, August, 1998.
G.C. Magazine, January, 2002, pp. 28–30.
Sirens of the Cinema, January, 2002, p. 5.

Electronic:
Kim Little Official Site, http://www.kimlittle.tv/, November 22, 2009.

LOGUE, Donal 1966–
(Donal F. Logue)

PERSONAL

Full name, Donal Francis Logue; born February 27, 1966, in Ottawa, Ontario, Canada; father a teacher and Carmelite missionary; mother's name, Elizabeth Logue (a Carmelite missionary); married Casey Walker; children: Finn. *Education:* Attended Harvard University; studied at British–American Drama Academy, London.

Addresses: *Agent*—Creative Artists Agency, 2000 Avenue of the Stars, Los Angeles, CA 90067. *Manager*—Perri Kipperman, Kipperman Management, 420 West End Ave., Suite 1G, New York, NY 10024.

Career: Actor, producer, director, and writer. Music Television Network (MTV), writer and actor for promotional spots featuring cabdriver Jimmy McBride, beginning 1994; also appeared in other commercials. Worked with theatre groups and as member of road crew for musical groups.

Awards, Honors: Special Jury Prize, outstanding performance in dramatic category, Sundance Film Festival, 2000, for *The Tao of Steve;* Ashland Independent Film Festival Award, best acting, 2005, for *Tennis, Anyone …?*.

CREDITS

Film Appearances:
Dr. Gunter Janek, *Sneakers,* Universal, 1992.
Captain Ellis Spear, *Gettysburg,* New Line Cinema, 1993.
Bill Pierce, *The Crew,* Cineville, 1994.
Chance Geer, *Disclosure,* Warner Bros., 1994.
Jacob Mayer, *Little Women,* Columbia, 1994.
Derek, *Miami Rhapsody,* Buena Vista, 1995.
Jimmy, *3 Ninjas Knuckle Up,* Columbia/TriStar, 1995.
Alex, *Baja,* 1996.
First video photographer, *Diabolique,* Warner Bros., 1996.
Gnome, *The Size of Watermelons,* Norstar Entertainment, 1996.
Rick, *Jerry Maguire,* TriStar, 1996.
Tony, *Eye for an Eye,* Paramount, 1996.
Webster, *Dear God,* Paramount, 1996.
Earl, *Metro,* Buena Vista, 1997.
Goldman, *Men with Guns,* Norstar Entertainment, 1997.
Red, *First Love, Last Rites,* Strand Releasing, 1997.
Tom Stone, *Glam,* 1997.
(Uncredited) Marl, *The Thin Red Line,* Twentieth Century–Fox, 1998.
Quinn, *Blade,* New Line Cinema, 1998.
Die Wholesale, Storm Entertainment, 1998.
Father Brian Norris, *Runaway Bride,* Paramount, 1999.
Alex Lowe, *Takedown* (also known as *Hackers 2: Takedown* and *Track Down*), Dimension Films, 2000.
Dan Scott, *The Patriot* (also known as *Der Patriot*), Columbia, 2000.
Dex, *The Tao of Steve,* Sony Pictures Classics, 2000.
Eamon McGarvey, *The Big Tease* (also known as *Je m'appelle Crawford*), Warner Bros., 2000.
Pat Duffy, *The Opportunists,* First Look Pictures Releasing, 2000.
Pug, *Reindeer Games* (also known as *Deception*), Dimension Films, 2000.
Stew Albert, *Steal This Movie* (also known as *Abbie!*), Lions Gate Films, 2000.
Charley Best, *The Million Dollar Hotel,* Lions Gate Films, 2001.
Sonny, *The Chateau,* Pretty Pictures, 2001, IFC Films, 2002.

Raymond McGillicudy, *Comic Book Villains,* Lions Gate Films, 2002.

Lloyd Whitworth, *Confidence* (also known as *Confidence: After Dark* and *En toute confiance*), Lions Gate Films, 2003.

Stage actor Harvey, *American Splendor,* Fine Line, 2003.

Ray O'Connor, *Two Days,* American World Pictures, 2003.

Jack, *Just like Heaven,* DreamWorks, 2005.

Danny Macklin, *Tennis, Anyone ...?,* Fireside Releasing, 2006.

(Uncredited) Buzz, *Jack's Law,* 11 Pictures/Dr. October, 2006.

Jimbo, *The Groomsmen,* Bauer Martinez Studios, 2006.

Uncle Bingo, *Citizen Duane,* THINKFilm, 2006.

Mark Brady, *Almost Heaven,* Norstar Releasing/Odeon Films, 2006.

Voice of Troy, *Shark Bait* (animated; also known as *Pi's Story* and *The Reef*), Weinstein Company, 2007.

Don Wollebin, *Fast Track* (also known as *The Ex*), Metro–Goldwyn–Mayer/Weinstein Company, 2007.

Daryll, *The Good Life,* Epic Pictures, 2007.

Mack, *Ghost Rider* (also known as *Spirited Racer*), Sony Pictures Entertainment, 2007.

Captain Ken Narlow, *Zodiac,* Paramount, 2007.

Chazz Coleman, *Purple Violets,* iTunes, 2007.

Uncle Eddie, *No Place Like Home,* Multiple Productions, 2008.

Detective Alex Balder, *Max Payne,* Twentieth Century–Fox, 2008.

One Fast Move or I'm Gone: Kerouac's Big Sur (documentary), Kerouac Films, 2008.

Bunting, *The Lodger,* Stage 6 Films, 2009.

Film Work:

Co–executive producer, *Men with Guns,* Norstar Entertainment, 1997.

Coproducer, *Comic Book Villains,* Studio Home Entertainment, 2002.

Producer and director, *Tennis, Anyone ...?,* Fireside Releasing, 2006.

Television Appearances; Series:

Ken Schuler, *Public Morals,* CBS, 1996.

Assistant District Attorney Dick Flood, a recurring role, *The Practice,* ABC, between 1997 and 1999.

Sean Finnerty, *Grounded for Life,* Fox, 2001–2005.

Chuck Martin, a recurring role, *ER,* NBC, between 2003 and 2005.

Eugene Gurkin, *The Knights of Prosperity,* ABC, 2007.

Captain Kevin Tidwell, *Life,* NBC, 2008–2009.

Television Appearances; Movies:

(As Donal F. Logue) Brian, *Getting Up and Going Home* (also known as *Unfaithful*), Lifetime, 1992.

Shane Pencil, *Medusa: Dare to Be Truthful* (also known as *Dare to Be Truthful*), 1992.

Bobbi Campbell, *And the Band Played On,* HBO, 1993.

Kevin Uchytil, *Labor of Love: The Arlette Schweitzer Story,* CBS, 1993.

Bob Mathews, *The Yarn Princess* (also known as *More than a Miracle*), 1994.

Cletus, *The Grave,* HBO, 1996.

Steven Burnett, *A Bright Shining Lie,* HBO, 1998.

Television Appearances; Pilots:

Tucci, *The Next Big Thing,* CBS, 1999.

Eugene Gurkin, *The Knights of Prosperity,* ABC, 2007.

Oliver Hackett, *Hackett,* Fox, 2008.

Television Appearances; Specials:

James McNamara, "Darrow," *American Playhouse,* PBS, 1991.

"Steve McQueen: Life in the Fast Lane," *Biography,* Arts and Entertainment, 2004.

Television Appearances; Miniseries:

Danny McGoff, Sr., *Common Ground,* CBS, 1990.

I Love the '80s, VH1, 2002.

I Love the '70s, VH1, 2003.

I Love the '80s Strikes Back, VH1, 2003.

Television Appearances; Episodic:

Dr. Havlock, "Video Vigilante," *The Commish,* ABC, 1992.

Agent Tom Colton, "Squeeze," *The X–Files,* Fox, 1993.

Tommy Tom, "Hot Ticket," *Almost Home* (also known as *The Torkelsons: Almost Home*), ABC, 1993.

Judd Bromell, "Baby Blues," *Northern Exposure,* CBS, 1994.

"Broken Ties," *Sweet Justice,* NBC, 1995.

Danny Macklin, "Wizard of Bras," *Medicine Ball,* Fox, 1995.

Billy, "Lovenest," *The Single Guy,* NBC, 1996.

Billy, "Wedding," *The Single Guy,* NBC, 1996.

Luke, "The Hole," *Gun* (also known as *Robert Altman's "Gun"*), ABC, 1997.

Eddie, "Friends," *Felicity,* The WB, 1999.

"Just Like Heaven," *HBO First Look,* HBO, 2005.

Square Off, TV Guide Channel, 2006.

Tom's friend, "A Regular Earl Anthony," *Damages,* FX Network, 2007.

(Uncredited) Fully, "Mr. Monk Is Up All Night," *Monk,* USA Network, 2007.

Television Talk Show Guest Appearances; Episodic:

Late Night with Conan O'Brien, NBC, between 2000 and 2007.

The Tonight Show with Jay Leno (also known as *Jay Leno*), NBC, 2001.

The Rosie O'Donnell Show, syndicated, 2001.

Howard Stern, E! Entertainment Television, 2002.

Jimmy Kimmel Live! (also known as *Jimmy Kimmel*), ABC, between 2003 and 2007.

The Late Late Show with Craig Kilborn (also known as *The Late Late Show*), CBS, 2004.
The Late Late Show with Craig Ferguson, CBS, 2006.
The View, ABC, 2006, 2007.
The Late Show with David Letterman (also known as *The Late Show* and *Letterman*), CBS, 2007.

Television Appearances; Award Presentations:
Host, *2001 Sundance Film Festival Awards,* Sundance Channel, 2001.
Presenter, *The 16th Annual IFP/West Independent Spirit Awards,* Independent Film Channel, 2001.
The 2001 Billboard Music Awards, Fox, 2001.

Television Appearances; Other:
Cooter Kincaid, *Wiener Park,* 2005.
Misfit, *1%,* HBO, 2008.

Television Producer; Episodic:
"Operation: Fighting Shape," *The Knights of Prosperity,* ABC, 2007.

Stage Appearances:
Appeared in productions of *Be Bop a Lula, The Comedy of Errors,* and *Curse of the Starving Class.*

RECORDINGS

Videos:
Jimmy McBride (Jimmy the cabdriver), *I Want My MTV,* 1996.
Reflections on "The X–Files," Twentieth Century–Fox Home Entertainment, 2004.

WRITINGS

Screenplays:
Tennis, Anyone ...?, Fireside Releasing, 2006.

Songs Featured in Films:
"Hey Jules," *The Groomsmen,* Bauer Martinez Studios, 2006.

Other:
Contributor to magazines, including *National Lampoon.*

OTHER SOURCES

Periodicals:
Entertainment Weekly, April 7, 1995, p. 75; September 1, 2000, p. 52.
TV Guide, September 10, 2007, p. 113.

LUCKEY, Ray

PERSONAL

Born in Washington, DC.

Career: Actor, production designer, art director, and producer. Happy–Go–Luckey Productions, owner. Worked as an art director for television commercials, including the Honey Association and a public service announcement for Healthy Heart, and infomercials. Previously worked as in architecture and construction management.

CREDITS

Film Production Designer:
10:30 Check Out (short film), Pure Profit Records, 2002.
Jolly Roger: Massacre at Cutter's Cove, The Asylum, 2005.
War of the Worlds (also known as *H. G. Wells' "War of the Worlds"* and *Invasion*), The Asylum, 2005.
The Marionette (short film), Rudderpost Films, 2006.
Holla, Lions Gate Films, 2006.
Kill the Habit, 2010.

Also production designer for *The 5th String* (short film), *Just Desserts* (short film), *The Sound of a Voice* (short film), *Umbakka* (short film), *Catching Kelly* (short film), *White Men in Seminole Flats* (short film), and *Bedmates.*

Film Executive Producer:
The Marionette (short film), Rudderpost Films, 2006.
Last Call before Sunset, 2007.
Pretty Twisted (short film), 2009.
Kill the Habit, 2010.

Film Art Director:
G.I. Jesus, 2006.

Film Appearances:
Townsperson, *War of the Worlds* (also known as *H. G. Wells' "War of the Worlds"* and *Invasion*), The Asylum, 2005.
Pizza delivery guy, *Last Call before Sunset,* 2007.
Guy exiting bar, *Pretty Twisted* (short film), 2009.

RECORDINGS

Music Videos:
Producer for music video by Jennifer Harris.

LUPONE, Patti 1949–

PERSONAL

Full name, Patti Ann LuPone; born April 21, 1949, in Northport, NY; daughter of Orlando Joseph (a school administrator) and Angela Louise (a college library administrator; maiden name, Patti) LuPone; sister of Robert LuPone (an actor); married Matt Johnston (a camera operator), December 12, 1988; children: Joshua Luke. *Education:* Juilliard School, B.F.A., 1972.

Addresses: *Agent*—(theatre) International Creative Management, International Creative Management, 10250 Constellation Way, 9th Floor, Los Angeles, CA 90067; (commercials and voice work) Innovative Artists Talent and Literary Agency, 1505 10th St., Santa Monica, CA 90401.

Career: Actress and singer. Acting Company, New York City, member of company, 1972–76. Columbia Broadcasting System, appeared in the public service announcement campaign *CBS Cares,* 2009; Craft and Folk Art Museum, Los Angeles, volunteer, 1999–2000. Performed with her brothers as the LuPone Trio, mid–1960s. Once worked as a chicken farmer.

Member: Actors' Equity Association, Screen Actors Guild, American Federation of Television and Radio Artists.

Awards, Honors: Antoinette Perry Award nomination, best actress in a featured role in a musical, 1976, and Drama Desk Award nomination, both for *The Robber Bridegroom;* Antoinette Perry Award and Drama Desk Award, both best actress in a musical, 1980, for *Evita;* Laurence Olivier Award, best actress in a musical or entertainment, Society of West End Theatre, 1985, for *Les miserables* and *The Cradle Will Rock;* Drama Desk Award and Antoinette Perry Award nomination, both best actress in a musical, 1988, for *Anything Goes;* Laurence Olivier Award nomination, c. 1993, for *Sunset Boulevard;* Outer Critics Circle Award, outstanding solo performance, 1996, for *Patti LuPone on Broadway;* Daytime Emmy Award nomination, outstanding performer in a children's special, 1996, for *The Song Spinner;* Drama Desk Award nomination, outstanding featured actress in a play, 1998, for *The Old Neighborhood;* Emmy Award nomination, outstanding guest actress in a comedy series, 1998, for "Beware of Greeks," *Frasier;* National Board of Review Award and Online Film Critics Society Award, both best ensemble (with others), 2000, and Florida Film Critics Award (with others), best ensemble cast, 2001, all for *State and Main;* Antoinette Perry Award nomination, Drama Desk Award nomination, and Outer Critics Circle

Award nomination, all best actress in a musical, and Drama League Award, outstanding contribution to musical theatre, all 2006, for *Sweeney Todd;* Antoinette Perry Award, Drama Desk Award, and Outer Critics Circle Award, all best actress in a musical, and Drama League Award, distinguished performance, all 2008, for *Gypsy;* Grammy Awards, best classical album and best opera recording, National Academy of Recording Arts and Sciences, 2009, for *Weill: Rise and Fall of the City of Mahagonny.*

CREDITS

Stage Appearances:
(Stage debut) Title role, *Iphigenia,* Young Vic Theatre, London, 1970.
(Off–Broadway debut) Lady Teazle, *The School for Scandal,* The Acting Company, Good Shepherd–Faith Church Theatre, New York City, 1972.
Kathleen, *The Hostage,* The Acting Company, Good Shepherd–Faith Church Theatre, 1972.
Natasha, *The Lower Depths,* The Acting Company, Good Shepherd–Faith Church Theatre, 1972.
Bianca and member of ensemble, *Women Beware Women,* Good Shepherd–Faith Church Theatre, 1972.
Hyacinthe, *Scapin,* City Center Theatre, New York City, 1972.
The Diary of Adam and Eve from the Apple Tree, City Center Theatre, 1972.
Lizzie, *Next Time I'll Sing to You,* Acting Company, Good Shepherd–Faith Church Theatre, 1972, then Billy Rose Theatre, 1973–74.
(Broadway debut) Irina, *The Three Sisters,* Acting Company, Billy Rose Theatre, 1973–74, then Harkness Theatre, New York City, 1975.
Lucy Lockit, *The Beggar's Opera* (musical), Acting Company, Billy Rose Theatre, 1973–74.
Boy, *Measure for Measure,* Acting Company, Billy Rose Theatre, 1973–74.
Rosamund, *The Robber Bridegroom* (musical), Acting Company, Harkness Theatre, 1975.
Prince Edward, *Edward II,* Acting Company, Harkness Theatre, 1975.
Kitty Duval, *The Time of Your Life,* Acting Company, Harkness Theatre, 1975.
Genevieve (title role), *The Baker's Wife* (musical), John F. Kennedy Center for the Performing Arts, Washington, DC, 1976.
Ruth, *The Woods,* St. Nicholas Theatre Company, Chicago, IL, 1977.
All Men Are Whores, Yale Cabaret, New Haven, CT, 1977.
Rita and Lily La Pon, *The Water Engine,* New York Shakespeare Festival, Martinson Hall, Public Theatre, New York City, 1977–78, then Plymouth Theatre, New York City, 1978.
Call girl, *Working* (musical), Forth–Sixth Street Theatre, New York City, 1978.
The Blue Hour, Public Theatre, New York City, 1978.

Stage Directions, Public Theatre, 1978.

Monagh, *Catchpenny Twist,* Hartford Stage Company, Hartford, CT, 1978.

Eva Peron (title role), *Evita* (musical), Dorothy Chandler Pavilion, Los Angeles, then Orpheum Theatre, San Francisco, CA, later Broadway Theatre, New York City, 1979–81.

Ruth, *The Woods,* Second Stage Theatre, Park Royal Theatre, New York City, 1981.

Rosalind, *As You Like It,* Tyrone Guthrie Theatre, Minneapolis, MN, 1982.

Moll and Sister Mister, *The Cradle Will Rock,* Acting Company, Vivian Beaumont Theatre, Lincoln Center, New York City, 1982, then American Place Theatre, New York City, 1983, and Old Vic Theatre, London, 1985.

Edmond's wife, *Edmond,* Provincetown Playhouse, New York City, 1982–83.

Cleo, *America Kicks Up Its Heels,* Playwrights Horizons Theatre, New York City, 1983.

Stars of Broadway, Colonie Coliseum, Albany, NY, 1983.

Nancy, *Oliver!* (musical), Mark Hellinger Theatre, New York City, 1984.

Reporter, *Accidental Death of an Anarchist,* Belasco Theatre, New York City, 1984.

Fantine, *Les miserables,* Royal Shakespeare Company, Barbican Theatre, then Palace Theatre, both London, 1985.

Henry IV, Part I, John F. Kennedy Center for the Performing Arts, 1985.

The Count of Monte Cristo, American National Theatre, John F. Kennedy Center for the Performing Arts, 1985.

Reno Sweeney, *Anything Goes!* (musical), Vivian Beaumont Theatre, Lincoln Center, 1987–89.

Patti LuPone Live, Westwood Playhouse, Los Angeles, 1992.

Sondheim—A Celebration at Carnegie Hall, Carnegie Hall, New York City, 1992.

Host, *Company: The Original Cast in Concert,* Vivian Beaumont Theatre, Lincoln Center, 1993.

Norma Desmond, *Sunset Boulevard* (musical), Adelphi Theatre, London, 1993.

Vera Simpson, "Pal Joey" (concert), *Encores! Great American Musicals,* City Center Theatre, New York City, 1995.

Patty LuPone on Broadway (solo concert), Walter Kerr Theatre, New York City, 1995.

Maria Callas, *Master Class,* John Golden Theatre, New York City, between 1996 and 1997, then Queen's Theatre, London, 1997.

Jolly, *The Old Neighborhood,* Booth Theatre, New York City, 1997–98.

Annie Get Your Gun (benefit performance), Lincoln Center, 1998.

Doin' What Comes Natur'lly (tribute to Ethel Merman), 1998.

Mrs. Nellie Lovett, *Sweeney Todd* (benefit concert), Avery Fisher Hall, Lincoln Center, New York City, 2000.

Matters of the Heart (solo concert), Vivian Beaumont Theatre, Lincoln Center, 2000.

Dottie Otley, *Noises Off,* Brooks Atkinson Theatre, New York City, 2001–2002.

Reno Sweeney, *Anything Goes!* (musical; revival), Vivian Beaumont Theatre, Lincoln Center, 2002.

Coulda, Woulda, Shoulda (solo concert), Carnegie Hall, 2002.

Performer of national anthem, *Runt of the Litter,* Manhattan Class Company Theatre, New York City, 2002.

Desiree, *A Little Night Music,* Ravinia Festival, Highland Park, IL, 2002.

Fosca, *Passion,* Ravinia Festival, 2003.

The Lady with the Torch (solo cabaret concert), Feinstein's at the Regency, New York City, 2004.

The old lady, *Candide* (concert), Avery Fisher Hall, Lincoln Center, 2004.

La Mome Pistache, "Can–Can" (musical), *City Center Encores!,* City Center Theatre, 2004.

Sunday in the Park with George, Ravinia Festival, 2004.

Cora Hoover Hooper, *Anyone Can Whistle,* Ravinia Festival, 2005.

Children and Art (benefit performance), Young Playwrights, New Amsterdam Theatre, New York City, 2005.

Fosca, *Passion* (concert), Billy Rose Theatre, 2005.

Regina (opera), John F. Kennedy Center for the Performing Arts, 2005.

Mrs. Nellie Lovett, *Sweeney Todd* (musical; revival), Eugene O'Neill Theatre, New York City, 2005–2006.

Rose, *Gypsy,* Ravinia Festival, 2006.

To Hell and Back (opera), Baroque Philharmonia Orchestra, Mountain View Center for the Performing Arts, Mountain View, CA, 2006.

The Rise and Fall of the City of Mahagonny (opera), Los Angeles Opera, 2007.

Mama Rose, *Gypsy* (musical; revival), City Center Theatre, 2007, then St. James Theatre, New York City, 2008–2009.

Annie Oakley, *Annie Get Your Gun* (concert), Ravinia Festival, 2009.

Appeared as Raina, *Arms and the Man,* Harkness Theatre; as Mrs. Lovett, *Sweeney Todd,* Ravinia Festival, Highland Park, IL; also appeared in productions of *Arms and the Man, Love's Labour's Lost, The Orchestra,* and *The Way of the World.*

Major Tours:

The Baker's Wife (musical), U.S. cities, 1976.

Eva Peron, *Evita* (musical), U.S. cities, 1979.

Matters of the Heart (solo concert), U.S. and international cities, 1999, 2003.

Mrs. Nellie Lovett, *Sweeney Todd* (musical), 2001.

Coulda, Woulda, Shoulda (solo concert), U.S. cities, 2003.

Also toured in the concert *An Evening with Patti LuPone and Mandy Patinkin.*

Television Appearances; Series:
Elizabeth "Libby" Thatcher, *Life Goes On* (also known as *Glenbrook*), ABC, 1989–93.
District Attorney Francesca Gold, a recurring role, *Falcone*, CBS, 2000.
Stella Coffa, a recurring role, *Oz*, HBO, 2003.

Television Appearances; Miniseries:
Vincenzina, *Un siciliano in Sicilia*, RAI, 1987.
Miss C. Canzinarra, *Bonanno: A Godfather's Story* (also known as *Bonanno: The Youngest Godfather* and *The Youngest Godfather*), Showtime, 1999.
(In archive footage) Eva Peron, "Tradition: 1957–1979," *Broadway: The American Musical*, PBS, 2004.

Television Appearances; Movies:
Narrator, *Piaf*, 1984.
Claudia Alta "Lady Bird" Taylor Johnson, *LBJ: The Early Years*, NBC, 1987.
Rita Lang, "The Water Engine," *TNT Screenworks*, TNT, 1992.
Joanna Saxen, *Her Last Chance* (also known as *The Morning After* and *A Daughter's Courage*), NBC, 1996.
Emmy Cosell, *Monday Night Mayhem*, TNT, 2002.

Television Appearances; Specials:
Kitty Duval, "The Time of Your Life" (broadcast of stage performance), *American Playhouse*, PBS, 1976.
Command Performance: The Stars Salute the President, 1981.
Starfest: The Stars Salute Public Television, 1983.
Moll, "The Cradle Will Rock" (broadcast of stage performance), *American Playhouse*, PBS, 1983, then broadcast by *America's Musical Theatre*, PBS, 1985.
Grammy Living Legends, CBS, 1989.
ABC Fall Preview, ABC, 1989.
The House I Live In (also known as *In Performance at the White House*), PBS, 1990.
The 14th Annual Kennedy Center Honors: A Celebration of the Performing Arts, CBS, 1991.
In a New Light (also known as *In a New Light: A Call to Action in the War against AIDS*), ABC, 1992.
A Capitol Fourth, PBS, 1992.
"Sondheim: A Celebration at Carnegie Hall," *Great Performances*, PBS, 1993.
Zantalalia, *The Song Spinner*, Showtime, 1995.
An Evening with Patti LuPone (broadcast of stage performance), PBS, 1997.
Colm Wilkinson Sings Music from Les Miz, Phantom, Evita, and Much More with Special Guest Patti LuPone, PBS, 1997.
"Gloria Swanson: The Greatest Star," *Biography*, Arts and Entertainment, 1997.
The Singer and the Song: In Performance at the White House, PBS, 1999.
John Williams, Yo–Yo Ma, Frank McCourt and Patti LuPone, PBS, 2000.
Mrs. Lovett, *Sweeney Todd: The Demon Barber of Fleet Street in Concert* (broadcast of stage performance), PBS, 2001.
Intimate Portrait: Kellie Martin, Lifetime, 2002.
(In archive footage) "Broadway's Lost Treasures," *Great Performances*, PBS, 2003.
(In archive footage) "Broadway's Lost Treasures II," *Great Performances*, PBS, 2004.
Strip Search, HBO, 2004.
The old lady, "Candide," *Great Performances*, PBS, 2005.
Fosca, "Passion," *Live from Lincoln Center* (also known as *Great Performances: Live from Lincoln Center*), PBS, 2005.
"American Songbook: Audra McDonald & Friends—Build a Bridge," *Live from Lincoln Center* (also known as *Great Performances: Live from Lincoln Center*), PBS, 2006.
"The Rise and Fall of the City of Mahagonny," *Great Performances*, PBS, 2007.

Television Appearances; Pilots:
Linda Tidmunk, *Cowboy Joe*, ABC, 1988.
Elizabeth "Libby" Thatcher, *Life Goes On* (also known as *Glenbrook*), ABC, 1989.
The Family Brood, CBS, 1998.
Good Guys, Bad Guys, NBC, 2000.
Vera, *Life at Five Feet*, NBC, 2002.

Television Appearances; Episodic:
"Requiem for a Stolen Child: Parts 1 & 2," *The Andros Targets*, 1977.
Gabby Giordano, "Dueling Divas," *Life Goes On*, ABC, 1991.
Voice of Pam, "Dinner at Eight," *Frasier*, NBC, 1993.
Grace Cavendish, "There But for the Grace," *Remember WENN*, AMC, 1996.
Ruth Miller, "Homesick," *Law & Order*, NBC, 1996.
Ruth Miller, "Navy Blues," *Law & Order*, NBC, 1997.
Aunt Zora Crane, "Beware of Greeks," *Frasier*, NBC, 1998.
"A Review to Remember," *Encore! Encore!*, NBC, 1998.
(Uncredited) *Saturday Night Live* (also known as *SNL*), NBC, 1998.
Alice Dupree, "Thief of Hearts," *Touched by an Angel*, CBS, 2001.
Herself, "Bully Woolley," *Will & Grace*, NBC, 2005.
Mrs. Weiner, "Don't Ask, Don't Tell," *Ugly Betty*, ABC, 2007.
Herself, "The Homecoming Opening/Sweeney Todd from Stage to Screen," *Broadway Beat*, 2008.
Sylvia Rossitano, "Goodbye, My Friend," *30 Rock*, NBC, 2009.

Television Talk Show Guest Appearances; Episodic:
CBS Sunday Morning, CBS, 1995.

The Rosie O'Donnell Show, syndicated, multiple appearances, 1996–2001.
The Tony Danza Show, syndicated, 2004.
Breakfast with the Arts, Arts and Entertainment, 2005, 2006.
The View, ABC, 2008.

Television Appearances; Awards Presentations:
The ... Annual Tony Awards, 1980, then CBS, 1998, 2006.
Presenter, *The ... Annual Tony Awards,* 1981, then CBS, 1992, 2007.
The 47th Annual Golden Globe Awards, TBS, 1990.
Presenter, *50th Annual Drama Desk Awards,* 2005.

Television Work; Series:
Song performer (with other cast members), "Ob–la–Di, Ob–la–Da" (theme song), *Life Goes On* (also known as *Glenbrook*), ABC, 1989–93.

Film Appearances:
(Uncredited) *King of the Gypsies,* Paramount, 1978.
Lydia Hedberg, *1941,* Universal, 1979.
Lisa D'Angelo, *Fighting Back* (also known as *Death Vengeance*), Paramount, 1982.
Cat's Eye, Metro–Goldwyn–Mayer, 1985.
Elaine, *Witness,* Paramount, 1985.
Wanda Valentini, *Wise Guys,* Metro–Goldwyn–Mayer, 1986.
Florine Werthan, *Driving Miss Daisy,* Warner Bros., 1989.
Aunt Nan, *Family Prayers* (also known as *A Family Divided*), Arrow Releasing, 1993.
Joan Marshall, *The 24–Hour Woman,* Artisan Entertainment, 1998.
Sylvia Levine Polinsky, *Just Looking* (also known as *Cherry Pink*), Sony Pictures Classics, 1999.
Van Klerk, *Bad Faith* (also known as *Cold Blooded* and *Le delateur*), Bedford, 1999.
Helen, *Summer of Sam,* Buena Vista, 1999.
Sherry Bailey, *State and Main* (also known as *Sequences et consequences*), Fine Line, 2000.
Betty Croft, *Heist* (also known as *Le vol*), Warner Bros., 2001.
Sandy, *The Victim,* Reel Lies, 2001.
Maggie, *City by the Sea* (also known as *The Suspect*), Warner Bros., 2002.
Jack Mitchell: My Life Is Black and White (documentary), Highberger Media, 2006.
Broadway: Beyond the Golden Age (documentary), Second Act Productions, 2010.

Film Work:
Song performer, "Love Cannot Stay" and "A Piece of Pie," *Love Streams,* Metro–Goldwyn–Mayer, 1984.

RECORDINGS

Albums:
Forbidden Broadway, Volume 2, DRG, 1991.
Patti LuPone Live!, RCA Victor, 1993.
Heat Wave: Patti LuPone Sings Irving Berlin, Philips, 1995.
The Best of Broadway, Rhino, 1995.
Matters of the Heart, Varese Sarabande, 1999.
Contributor, *Divas Collection,* First Night, 2003.
The Lady with the Torch, Ghostlight, 2006.
The Lady with the Torch ... Still Burning, Sh–K–Boom, 2006.
Patti LuPone at Les Mouches, Ghostlight, 2008.

Also recorded *Grateful* and *Sondheim: A Celebration at Carnegie Hall,* RCA Victor. Contributor to the albums *Blue Moon, Family Guy: Live in Vegas, Philadelphia Chickens,* and *To Hell and Back.*

Cast Recordings:
The Baker's Wife, Take Home Tunes, 1978.
Working, Columbia, c. 1978.
Evita (original Broadway cast recording), MCA, 1979.
The Cradle Will Rock, Polydor, 1985.
Les miserables, David Geffen, 1987.
Anything Goes!, RCA Victor, 1988.
Sunset Boulevard (London cast recording), Polydor, 1994.
Pal Joey, DRG, 1995.
Sweeney Todd (live performance), New York Philharmonic Special Editions, 2000.
Sweeney Todd (Broadway cast recording), New York Philharmonic Special Editions, 2006.
Weill: Rise and Fall of the City of Mahagonny, 2008.
Gypsy, Time–Life, 2008.

According to some sources, also performed for a cast recording of *Hey! Mr. Producer.*

Videos:
Between Two Worlds: The Making of "Witness," Paramount Home Video, 2005.

OTHER SOURCES

Periodicals:
New York Times, January 24, 1988; July 8, 2007; March 28, 2008, p. E1.
Opera News, November, 1999, p. 46.
Time, February 24, 1998, p. 69.
Variety, November 24, 1997, p. 72.

Electronic:
Patti LuPone Official Site, http://www.pattilupone.net, February 16, 2010.

M

MACHADO, Eduardo 1953–

PERSONAL

Born June 11, 1953, in Havana, Cuba; immigrated to the United States, 1961 (some sources say 1956); son of Othon Eduardo and Gilda (maiden name, Hernandez) Machado; married Harriett Marilyn Bradlin, June 19, 1972 (divorced). *Education:* Graduated from the New Dramatists. *Religion:* Roman Catholic.

Addresses: *Office*—INTAR Theatre, PO Box 756, New York, NY 101087.

Career: Artist director, director, playwright, and actor. INTAR Hispanic American Theatre, New York City, artistic director; formerly served as an artistic associate at the Public Theatre, New York City, the Flea Theatre/Bat Theatre Company, and the Cherry Lane Alternative. Columbia University, head of graduate playwriting department; also taught playwriting at the Public Theatre, Mark Taper Forum, Sarah Lawrence College, the Playwrights Center, and New York University. Served as playwright–in–residence at the Mark Taper Forum, Los Angeles, CA, 1993; National Endowment for the Arts and Theater Communications Group playwrights–in–residence fellowship at Theater for the New City, 1999.

Member: Actors Studio, Ensemble Studio Theater, New Dramatists.

Awards, Honors: National Endowment for the Arts Youth Grant, 1978; National Endowment for the Arts Playwriting Grant, 1981, 1983, 1986; Rockefeller Foundation Playwriting Award, 1985; *L.A. Weekly* Awards, 1990, 1993, 1994; Dramalogue Awards, best play, 1991, 1994; Ford Foundation Grant, 1993; Viva Los Artistas Award, City of Los Angeles, 1993; Bernice and Barry Stavis Playwright Award, National Theatre Conference, 1995; Berrilla Kerr Grant, 2001.

CREDITS

Stage Work:
Director, *Related Retreats,* New York City, 1990.
Dramaturg, *Young Playwrights Festival (1993),* Playwrights Horizons Theatre, New York City, 1993.

Stage Appearances:
A Visit, New York City, 1981.

Film Director:
Directed *Exiles in New York.*

Film Appearances:
Alfonso Ossorio, *Pollock,* Sony Pictures Classics, 2000.

Also appeared in *The Champ.*

Television Appearances; Episodic:
Appeared in *Maude; The Nancy Walker Show; All in the Family; The Dancing Beater; Mary Hartman; What's Happening.*

RECORDINGS

Taped Readings:
Broken Eggs, 1996.

WRITINGS

Stage Plays:
Rosario and the Gypsies, Ensemble Studio Theatre, New York City, 1982.

The Modern Ladies of Guanabacoa, Ensemble Studio Theatre, 1983.

Broken Eggs, Ensemble Studio Theatre, 1984.

Fabiola, Ensemble Studio Theatre, 1985.

(With Geraldine Sherman) *When It's Over,* Long Wharf Theatre, New Haven, CT, 1987.

Why to Refuse, Theatre for a New City, New York City, 1987.

Wishing You Well, New York City, 1987.

A Burning Beach, American Place Theatre, New York City, 1988.

Don Juan in New York City, Theatre for a New City, 1988.

Once Removed, NM, 1988.

Garded (opera libretto), Philadelphia, PA, 1988.

Cabaret Bambu, New York City, 1989.

Stevie Wants to Play the Blues, Los Angeles Theatre Center, Los Angeles, 1990.

(Adapter) *The Day You Love Me,* Mark Taper Forum, Los Angeles, 1990.

Pericones, New York City, 1990.

Related Retreats, New York City, 1990.

In the Eye of the Hurricane, Louisville, KY, 1991.

When the Sea Drowns in Sand, Actors Theatre of Louisville, Louisville, KY, 2000, then produced as *Havana Is Waiting,* Cherry Lane Theatre, New York City, 2001.

The Cook, Intar Hispanic American Theatre, New York City, 2003.

Kissing Fidel, Kirk Theatre, New York City, 2005.

Also wrote *Crocodile Eyes,* Theatre for a New City, New York City; *Across a Crowded Room.*

Screenplays:
Wrote *Exiles in New York.*

Television Specials:
Death Squad, 1989.

China Rios, HBO, 1989.

In the Heat of Saturday Night, 1990.

Nonfiction:
(With Michael Domitrovich) *Tastes Like Cuba: An Exile's Hunger for Home* (a food memoir), Penguin Group, 2007.

OTHER SOURCES

Books:
Contemporary Dramatists, 6th edition, St. James Press, 1999.

Contemporary Hispanic Biography, Volume 2, Gale Group, 2002.

Periodicals:
American Theatre, January, 1995, p. 14.

MADDALENA, Marianne

PERSONAL

Born in Lansing, MI. *Education:* Attended Michigan State University.

Addresses: *Agent*—Mike Simpson, WME Entertainment, 1 William Morris Pl., Beverly Hills, CA 90212.

Career: Producer and writer. Worked as a secretary, then an assistant to filmmaker Wes Craven; Wes Craven Productions, producer and artistic partner, c. 1990; Craven/Maddalena Films, founder and president.

Awards, Honors: Independent Spirit Award nomination, best feature, Independent Features Project/West, 1995, for *New Nightmare.*

CREDITS

Film Producer:
Shocker (also known as *Shocker: No More Mr. Nice Guy*), Universal, 1989.

The People under the Stairs (also known as *Wes Craven's "The People under the Stairs"*), Universal, 1991.

New Nightmare (also known as *A Nightmare on Elm Street 7* and *Wes Craven's "New Nightmare"*), New Line Cinema, 1994.

Scream 2, Miramax/Dimension Films, 1997.

Music of the Heart, Miramax, 1999.

Scream 3, Miramax/Dimension Films, 2000.

Cursed (also known as *Wes Craven's "Cursed"* and *Verflucht*), Miramax/Dimension Films, 2005.

Red Eye, DreamWorks, 2005.

The Hills Have Eyes, Fox Searchlight, 2006.

The Breed, First Look International, 2006.

The Hills Have Eyes II, Fox Atomic, 2007.

The Last House on the Left, Rogue Pictures, 2009.

Film Executive Producer:
Vampire in Brooklyn (also known as *Wes Craven's "Vampire in Brooklyn"*), Paramount, 1995.

Scream, Miramax/Dimension Films, 1996.

Dracula (also known as *Dracula 2001* and *Wes Craven Presents "Dracula 2000"*), Miramax/Dimension Films, 2000.

New York, I Love You (also known as *New York, je t'aime*), Vivendi Entertainment, 2009.

Film Appearances:
Herself, *New Nightmare* (also known as *A Nightmare on Elm Street 7* and *Wes Craven's "New Nightmare"*), New Line Cinema, 1994.
(Uncredited) Flight passenger, *Red Eye*, DreamWorks, 2005.

Television Work; Series:
Senior producer, *Nightmare Cafe*, NBC, 1992.
Coproducer, *Orion*, 2006.

Television Work; Movies:
Producer, *Night Visions* (also known as *Chameleon Blue*), NBC, 1990.
Executive producer, *Don't Look Down* (also known as *Wes Craven Presents "Don't Look Down"*), ABC, 1998.
Executive producer, *They Shoot Divas, Don't They?*, VH1, 2002.

Television Work; Pilots:
Co–executive producer, *Hollyweird*, Fox, 1998.

RECORDINGS

Videos:
Behind the "Scream," 2000.
Surviving the Hills: Making of "The Hills Have Eyes," Twentieth Century–Fox Home Entertainment, 2006.
The Hills Have Eyes 2: Mutant Attacks (also known as *Mutant Attacks*), Twentieth Century–Fox Home Entertainment, 2007.
Exploring the Hills: The Making of "The Hills Have Eyes 2," Twentieth Century–Fox Home Entertainment, 2007.

MADSEN, Michael 1958–

PERSONAL

Full name, Michael Soren Madsen; born September 25, 1958, in Chicago, IL; son of Calvin (a firefighter) and Elaine (a writer and producer) Madsen; brother of Virginia Madsen (an actress); married Georganne LaPierre (an actress; some sources spell the name Georgia LaPier), c. 1980s (divorced); married Jeannine Bisignano (an actress; divorced); married De Anna Morgan (a model and actress), April 15, 1996; children: (second marriage) Christian, Max; (third marriage) Cody

(stepson), Hudson Lee, Calvin Michael, Luke Ray. *Avocational Interests:* Boxing, building motorcycles, auto racing.

Addresses: *Agent*—Alix Gucovsky, Special Artists Agency, 9465 Wilshire Blvd., Suite 470, Beverly Hills, CA 90212. *Manager*—Chuck Binder, Binder and Associates, 1465 Lindacrest Dr., Beverly Hills, CA 90210. *Publicist*—Liza Anderson, Anderson Group Public Relations, 8060 Melrose Ave., 4th Floor, Los Angeles, CA 90046.

Career: Actor, producer, and poet. Steppenwolf Theatre, Chicago, IL, apprentice actor for two years. Appeared in commercial for Toyota Verso, 2005; voice for radio public service announcements. Also worked as an auto mechanic, gas station attendant, hospital orderly, house painter, and cook.

Awards, Honors: Independent Firecracker Award for Poetry, 1998, for *Burning in Paradise*; Rebel Award, Rebelfest, 2005; Career Achievement Award, Temecula Valley International Film Festival, 2007; Will Rogers Pioneer Award, 2007; Maverick Award, Methodfest, 2007; Festival Prize, Boston Film Festival, 2007, Feature Film Award, New York International Independent Film and Video Festival, 2008, and Jury Award, Mount Shasta International Film Festival, 2008, all best actor, for *Strength and Honour.*

CREDITS

Film Appearances:
Cecil Moe, *Against All Hope* (also known as *One for the Road*), 1982.
Steve, *WarGames*, Metro–Goldwyn–Mayer, 1983.
Bartholomew "Bump" Bailey, *The Natural*, TriStar, 1984.
Frank, *Racing with the Moon*, Paramount, 1984.
Stu, *The Killing Time*, New World, 1987.
Earl, *Shadows in the Storm*, Vidmark International, 1988.
Sebastian, *Iguana* (also known as *La iguana*), Enterprise Iguana, 1988.
Enzio, *Blood Red*, Hemdale Releasing, 1989.
Vince Miller, *Kill Me Again*, Metro–Goldwyn–Mayer, 1990.
Earl, *The End of Innocence*, Skouras, 1991.
James "Jimmy" Lennox, *Thelma & Louise*, Metro–Goldwyn–Mayer, 1991.
Tom Baker, *The Doors*, TriStar, 1991.
Cliff Burden, *Fatal Instinct* (also known as *To Kill For*), New Line Home Video, 1992.
Mr. Blonde/Vic Vega, *Reservoir Dogs*, Miramax, 1992.
Morris Poole, *Almost Blue*, Live Home Video, 1992.
Richard Montana, *Inside Edge*, Atlantic Home Video, 1992.
Steve, *Straight Talk*, Buena Vista, 1992.

Detective Pat Laurenzi, *Money for Nothing,* Buena Vista, 1993.

Glen Greenwood, *Free Willy* (also known as *Sauvez Willy),* Warner Bros., 1993.

Harry Talbot, *Trouble Bound,* ITC, 1993.

Mickey, *A House in the Hills,* Live Home Video, 1993.

Detective Matt Dixon, *Dead Connection* (also known as *Final Combination* and *Lights Out),* Gramercy, 1994.

(Uncredited) Gun seller, *Blue Tiger* (also known as *Irezumi),* 1994.

(Uncredited; in archive footage) Mr. Blonde/Vic Vega, *Who Do You Think You're Fooling?,* 1994.

Randy Parker, *Season of Change,* Monarch Home Video, 1994.

Rudy Travis, *The Getaway,* Universal, 1994.

Virgil Earp, *Wyatt Earp,* Warner Bros., 1994.

Glen Greenwood, *Free Willy 2: The Adventure Home* (also known as *Sauvez Willy 2),* Warner Bros., 1995.

Preston "Press" Lennox, *Species,* Metro–Goldwyn–Mayer, 1995.

Eddie Hall, *Mulholland Falls,* Metro–Goldwyn–Mayer, 1996.

Larry (Mr. Lawrence), *Red Line,* Orion Home Video, 1996.

Dominick "Sonny Black" Napolitano, *Donnie Brasco,* TriStar, 1997.

Gunnery Sergeant Zach Massin, *Surface to Air,* 1997.

Uncle Joseph "Joe" Mason, *Catherine's Grove,* 1997.

Brad Abraham, *Trail of a Serial Killer* (also known as *Papertrail* and *Serial Cops),* Avalanche Home Entertainment, 1998.

Burl Rogers, *Detour* (also known as *Too Hard to Die),* October Films/Shoreline Entertainment, 1998.

Frank Barlow, *Fait Accompli* (also known as *VooDoo Dawn),* Cutting Edge Entertainment, 1998.

Gene, *Flat Out,* Artist View Entertainment, 1998.

Haynes, *Rough Draft* (also known as *Diary of a Serial Killer),* Goldbar International, 1998.

Jimmie D., *The Thief & the Stripper* (also known as *Final Reckoning* and *Strip 'n Run),* Bruder Releasing/Ground Zero, 1998.

Preston "Press" Lennox, *Species II,* Metro–Goldwyn–Mayer, 1998.

Ballad of the Nightingale, August Entertainment, 1998.

Whitey, *The Florentine,* BCB Productions, 1999.

Ben, *The Stray,* PM Entertainment Group, 2000.

Agent Briggs, *The Alternate* (also known as *Agent of Death),* Replacement Productions, 2000.

Dan Olinghouse, *The Ghost* (also known as *Code of the Dragon),* Regent Entertainment, 2000.

Jeremy Banes, *Fall* (also known as *Fall: The Price of Silence),* Annex Entertainment, 2000.

Mr. Ball, *The Price of Air,* Artistic License, 2000.

Will, *Choke,* Artist View Entertainment, 2000.

Jay Peters, *Bad Guys,* Giants Entertainment, 2000.

Uncle, *Ides of March* (also known as *Ultimate Target),* Giants Entertainment, 2000.

Conner, *Outlaw,* 2001.

Jed Griffin, *Pressure Point* (also known as *Backroad Justice),* Velocity Pictures, 2001.

Sparks, *Extreme Honor* (also known as *Last Line of Defence 2),* MTI Home Video, 2001.

James Alexander, *LAPD: To Protect and to Serve,* Fries Film Group/Trinity Home Entertainment, 2001.

(Uncredited) Narrator, *42K,* 2001.

Russ, *Love.com* (also known as *Primal Instinct),* Cinemavault Releasing, 2002.

Baker Jacks, *The Real Deal,* MC–One, 2002.

Damian Falco, *Die Another Day* (also known as *D.A.D.),* Metro–Goldwyn–Mayer, 2002.

The producer, *Where's Angelo?* (short film), Evolving Pictures Entertainment, 2002.

Special Agent Leon Fogel, *Welcome to America,* Risk Entertainment, 2002.

T. J., *My Boss's Daughter,* Dimension Films, 2003.

Budd (Sidewinder), *Kill Bill: Vol. 1* (also known as *Kill Bill, Kill Bill Part 1,* and *Quentin Tarantino's "Kill Bill: Volume One"),* Miramax, 2003.

Geno, *Vampires Anonymous,* Lantern Lane Entertainment, 2003.

Wallace Sebastian "Wally" Blount, *Blueberry* (also known as *The Adventures of Mike S. Blueberry, Renegade,* and *Blueberry: L'experience secrete),* Columbus TriStar Home Entertainment, 2004.

Budd (Sidewinder), *Kill Bill: Vol. 2* (also known as *Kill Bill, Kill Bill Part 2,* and *Vol. 2),* Miramax, 2004.

Himself, *Pauly Shore Is Dead,* CKrush Entertainment, 2004.

Boss, *Smatyvay udochki* (also known as *Jacked$),* Gelvars, 2005.

Bob, *Sin City* (also known as *Frank Miller's "Sin City"),* Dimension Films, 2005.

Steven Miller, *L.A. Dicks,* Melee Entertainment, 2005.

The American, *Muzhskoy sezon. Barkhatnaya revolyutsiya* (also known as *Law of Corruption, The Velvet Revolution,* and *Muzhskoy sezon),* Karo Premiere, 2005, Tavix Pictures, 2009.

(Uncredited) Maugrim, *The Chronicles of Narnia: The Lion, the Witch, and the Wardrobe* (also known as *The Chronicles of Narnia),* Buena Vista, 2006.

Kevin Harrision, *Chasing Ghosts,* Sony Pictures Home Entertainment, 2006.

Seal, *All In,* MTI Home Video, 2006.

Oliver, *Scary Movie 4,* Dimension Films, 2006.

Guillermo List, *Canes* (also known as *The Covenant: Brotherhood of Evil),* Fries Film Group/Insight Film Studios, 2006.

Major Blevins, *UKM: The Ultimate Killing Machine,* Archetype Films/Genius Products, 2006.

Colonel J. T. Colt, *The Last Drop,* First Look International, 2006.

J. T. Goldman, *Hoboken Hollow,* Pumpjack Entertainment, 2006.

The Distance (documentary), 2006.

Funny Money, THINKFilm, 2007.

Senator Atwood, *Cosmic Radio,* Velocity Pictures, 2007.

Ray, *Machine,* Artist View Entertainment, 2007.

Sean Kelleher, *Strength and Honour,* Eclipse Pictures, 2007.

Cooper, *Afghan Knights,* Curb Entertainment, 2007.

Jackal, *Tooth & Nail,* After Dark Films, 2007.

Being Michael Madsen, Mean Time Productions, 2007.

Making of the 15th Raindance Film Festival (short film), Raindance Film Festival, 2007.

Detective Max Walker, *Vice,* 41 Inc., 2008.

Officer Lawdale (Tin Man), *House,* Roadside Attractions, 2008.

The gent, *Hell Ride,* Dimension Films/Third Rail Releasing, 2008.

Monk, *Last Hour,* 2008.

Dean, *Deep Winter,* Sony Pictures Home Entertainment, 2008.

Lester, *No Bad Days,* MTI Home Video, 2008.

Major Baxter, *45 R.P.M.,* Alliance Atlantis, 2008.

Leo Ibiza, *Killer's Freedom,* Lava Production/Starway Film, 2008.

Mr. Ball, *Los Angeles,* Westlake Entertainment Group, 2008.

Miles Rennberg, *Boarding Gate,* Magnolia Pictures, 2008.

So You Want Michael Madsen? (documentary), Xristos Productions, 2008.

Narrator, *Through Your Eyes* (documentary), KOAN, 2008.

Clinton Manitoba, *You Might as Well Live,* E1 Entertainment, 2009.

Stuart Bunka, *Lost in the Woods,* New Horizons Home Video, 2009.

J. Marcone, *Road of No Return,* Shoreline Entertainment, 2009.

The reverend, *Clear Lake, WI,* Arsenal Pictures, 2009.

Dr. Azirra, *The Portal,* Birch Tree Entertainment, 2009.

Dreq, *Serbian Scars,* VPR Studios, 2009.

Vick Donovan, *A Way with Murder,* PFG Entertainment, 2009.

Dan Moeller, *Hired Gun,* Tavix Pictures, 2009.

Dave, *Shannon's Rainbow,* Supernova Media/Summit Works, 2009.

The associate, *Break,* Cinema Epoch, 2009.

George, *Ligeia* (also known as *Edgar Allan Poe's "Ligeia"*), Poe Vision, 2009.

Commander, *Put* (also known as *The Way*), Way Film, 2009.

Farragute, *Outrage,* Spirit Films, 2009.

Willie, *Chamaco,* 2009.

Doe, *The Killing Jar,* 2009.

Martell, *The Big I Am,* 2009.

Dr. Turner, *Let the Game Begin,* 2009.

Bed and Breakfast, 2009.

Rich McShane, *Six Days in Paradise,* 2009.

Lester Storm, *Not Another Not Another Movie,* 2009.

John Lawson, *Money to Burn,* 2009.

Father Roy, *The Bleeding,* 2009.

Road Raiders, 2009.

Leblanc, *Now Here,* 2009.

The man, *The Brazen Bull,* 2009.

Film Producer:

The Price of Air, Artistic License, 2000.

Coproducer, *Being Michael Madsen,* Mean Time Productions, 2007.

Los Angeles, Westlake Entertainment Group, 2008.

Road of No Return, Shoreline Entertainment, 2009.

A Way with Murder, PFG Entertainment, 2009.

Now Here, 2009.

The Brazen Bull, 2009.

Joseph Johnson, *Christmas Crash,* 2009.

Voice of Kilowog, *Green Lantern: First Flight* (animated), Warner Premiere, 2009.

Film Executive Producer:

Tooth & Nail, After Dark Films, 2007.

Vice, 41 Inc., 2008.

Television Appearances; Series:

August "Augie" Danzig, *Our Family Honor,* ABC, 1985–86.

Mick Jenkins, *The Outsiders,* Fox, 1990.

Mr. Chapel, *Vengeance Unlimited* (also known as *Mr. Chapel*), ABC, 1998–99.

Terry Maddock, *Big Apple,* CBS, 2001.

Narrator, *Animal Precinct,* Animal Planet, 2001.

Don Everest (The Matador), *Tilt,* ESPN, 2005.

Television Appearances; Movies:

Jimmy Lenox, *Special Bulletin,* NBC, 1983.

Pierce, *Montana,* TNT, 1990.

Cal Hudson, *Baby Snatcher,* CBS, 1992.

Blood, *Beyond the Law* (also known as *Fixing the Shadow*), HBO, 1994.

John Wilbur Hardin, *Man with a Gun* (also known as *Gun for Hire* and *Hired for Killing*), HBO, 1995.

Johnny (Wolf), *The Winner,* The Movie Channel, 1996.

Nick, *Executive Target,* HBO, 1996.

Sal, *The Last Days of Frankie the Fly* (also known as *Frankie the Fly*), HBO, 1996.

Skarney, *The Maker,* HBO, 1997.

Dallas Greyson, *The Sender,* HBO, 1998.

Donnelly, *The Girl Gets Moe* (also known as *Love to Kill*), HBO, 1998.

Dalton, *Supreme Sanction,* HBO, 1999.

Frank Miller, *High Noon,* TBS, 2000.

Joe, *The Inspectors 2: A Shred of Evidence,* Showtime, 2000.

Tyler Pierce, *Sacrifice,* HBO, 2000.

Zippo, *Luck of the Draw,* Cinemax, 2000.

Frank McGregor, *44 Minutes: The North Hollywood Shoot–out,* FX Network, 2003.

Detective Harker, *Frankenstein,* USA Network, 2004.

Croc Hawkins, *Croc,* 2007.

Agent Lind, *Living & Dying,* HBO, 2007.

Vincent Scaillo, *Crash and Burn,* Spike TV, 2008.

Television Appearances; Specials:

Steve McQueen: King of Cool, AMC, 1998.
Presenter, *The Brit Awards*, ITV, 2002.
The 100 Greatest Movie Stars, Channel 4, 2003.
Sam Peckinpah's West: Legacy of a Hollywood Renegade, Starz!, 2004.
"Steve McQueen: Life in the Fast Lane," *Biography*, Arts and Entertainment, 2004.
Michael Jackson: The One, CBS, 2004.
Sin City: The Premiere, ITV2, 2005.
Bullets over Hollywood, Starz!, 2005.
Host, *A Very Quentin Christmas*, Starz!, 2005.

Also appeared in *Maxim Hot 100*, NBC.

Television Appearances; Pilots:

Boogie, *Diner*, CBS, 1983.
August "Augie" Danzig, *Our Family Honor*, ABC, 1985.

Television Appearances; Miniseries:

Lieutenant "Foof" Turkell (Devilfish), *War and Remembrance*, ABC, 1988.
I Love the '70s, VH1, 2003.

Television Appearances; Episodic:

Mike O'Connor, "Monday, Tuesday, Sven's Day," *St. Elsewhere*, NBC, 1983.
Mike O'Connor, "Remission," *St. Elsewhere*, NBC, 1983.
Boyd Evans Strout, "Heat," *Cagney & Lacey*, CBS, 1984.
Sally Alvarado, "Give a Little, Take a Little," *Miami Vice*, NBC, 1984.
John Hampton, "Man at the Window," *The Hitchhiker* (also known as *Deadly Nightmares* and *Le voyageur*), HBO, 1985.
Johnny Fosse, "The St. Louis Book of Blues," *Crime Story*, NBC, 1986.
Johnny Fosse, "The War," *Crime Story*, NBC, 1986.
(Uncredited) Johnny Fosse, "Crime Pays," *Crime Story*, NBC, 1986.
Blue, "Jimmy—October 14, 1964," *Quantum Leap*, NBC, 1989.
Sergeant Greg Block, "Sleeping Dogs," *Tour of Duty*, CBS, 1989.
"Snowfall," *Jake and the Fatman*, CBS, 1989.
Stan Frankel, "Finger on the Trigger," *Gabriel's Fire*, 1991.
"Heist," *Film Genre* (also known as *Hollywood History*), 2002.
MADtv, Fox, 2002.
"Tarantino Special," *Tracks*, 2004.
Comme au cinema, 2004.
Seitenblicke, 2004.
25—Das Magazin, 2004.
(In archive footage) *Cinema mil*, 2005.

Interviewee for an episode of *Anime: Drawing a Revolution*, Starz!.

Television Talk Show Guest Appearances; Episodic:

The Late Show with David Letterman (also known as *The Late Show* and *Letterman*), CBS, 1994.
Late Night with Conan O'Brien, NBC, 2000.
Friday Night with Jonathan Ross, BBC, 2003.
The Bronx Bunny Show, Starz!, 2003.
The Sharon Osbourne Show (also known as *Sharon*), syndicated, 2003, 2004.
On–Air with Ryan Seacrest, 2004.
Jimmy Kimmel Live! (also known as *Jimmy Kimmel*), ABC, 2004.
Dinner for Five, Independent Film Channel, 2004.
Henry's Film Corner, Independent Film Channel, 2005.
Cribs (also known as *MTV Cribs*), MTV, 2005.
Tubridy Tonight, 2006.
Up Close with Carrie Keagan, 2008.

Television Associate Producer; Movies:

Executive Target, HBO, 1996.
The Sender, HBO, 1998.
Living & Dying, HBO, 2007.

Stage Appearances:

Appeared in productions of *Carnal Knowledge*, *Of Mice and Men*, and *A Streetcar Named Desire*, all Steppenwolf Theatre, Chicago, IL.

RECORDINGS

Videos:

Thelma & Louise: The Last Journey, Metro–Goldwyn–Mayer Home Entertainment, 2003.
It Happened That Way, Warner Home Video, 2004.
The Making of "Kill Bill: Volume 2," Miramax Home Video, 2004.
Zen & Now: A Dinner with David Carradine and Friends, Warner Home Video, 2004.
Les nouveaux refus, 2004.
The Origin: Making "Species," Metro–Goldwyn–Mayer Home Entertainment, 2005.
Prohibition Opens the Floodgates, Warner Home Video, 2006.
Morality and the Code: A How–to Manual for Hollywood, Warner Home Video, 2006.
Molls and Dolls: The Women of Gangster Films, Warner Home Video, 2006.
Stool Pigeons and Pine Overcoats: The Language of Gangster Films, Warner Home Video, 2006.
Welcome to the Big House, Warner Home Video, 2006.
Gangsters: The Immigrant's Hero, Warner Home Video, 2006.
The Maltese Falcon: One Magnificent Bird, Warner Home Video, 2006.

The Business End: Violence in Cinema, Leva Film-Works, 2008.

The Evolution of Clint Eastwood, Warner Home Video, 2008.

The Long Shadow of Dirty Harry, Warner Home Video, 2008.

The Craft of Dirty Harry, Warner Home Video, 2008.

Visiting Uwe (also known as *Visiting Uwe—The Uwe Boll Homestory*), Computec Media, 2008.

Appeared in the music videos "U Rock My World" by Michael Jackson, 2001; and "Kill the Music."

Video Games:

Voice of Toni Cipriani, *Grand Theft Auto III* (also known as *GTA3*), Rockstar Games, 2001.

Voices of Rafferty and others, *True Crime: Streets of LA,* Activision, 2003.

Voice of Tanner, *Driv3r,* Infogrames Entertainment, 2004.

Voice of Detective Jack Frozenski, *Narc,* Midway Games, 2005.

(English version) Voice of Shimano, *Yakuza* (also known as *Ryu ga gotoku*), Sega of America, 2006.

Voice of Mr. Blonde, *Reservoir Dogs,* Sci Games, 2006.

Audio Books:

Narrator of *Burning in Paradise* by Michael Madsen.

WRITINGS

Poetry Collections:

Eat the Worm, Vantage Press, 1994.

Beer, Blood, and Ashes, Holiday, 1995.

Burning in Paradise, foreword by Dennis Hopper, Incommunicado Press, 1998.

A Blessing of the Hounds (also includes short stories), introduction by Quentin Tarantino, 12 Gauge Press, 2002.

46 Down: A Book of Dreams and Other Ramblings, 12 Gauge Press, 2004.

The Complete Poetic Works of Michael Madsen, Volume 1: *1995–2005,* 13 Hands Publications, 2005.

American Badass, 13 Hands Publications, 2009.

Other:

Signs of Life (autobiography), 13 Hands Publications, 2006.

OTHER SOURCES

Books:

Madsen, Michael, *Signs of Life,* 13 Hands Publications, 2006.

Periodicals:

Cosmopolitan, March, 1993.

Entertainment Weekly, September 4, 1998, p. 88; April 23, 2004, p. 761.

Film Threat, February, 1993, pp. 52–53; December 21, 2004.

Interview, July, 1987, p. 87.

Los Angeles Times, February 6, 1994.

Maxim, September, 2002, p. 121; February, 2007, pp. 82–83.

Orange Coast, October, 1998, pp. 39–42.

Playboy, April, 1996, pp. 144–48; September, 2002, p. 28; March, 2004, p. 46.

Premiere, January, 1994, p. 24; September 1, 2003, p. 20; February 1, 2006, p. 20.

Razor, June/July, 2001, pp. 56–61.

Rolling Stone, May 13, 1993.

Spin, April, 2004, p. 46.

Venice, March, 1997, pp. 40–45.

Electronic:

Michael Madsen Official Site, http://www.michaelmadsen.com, October 5, 2009.

MANGANIELLO, Joe 1976–

PERSONAL

Full name, Joseph Michael Manganiello; born December 28, 1976, in Pittsburgh, PA. *Education:* Carnegie Mellon University, undergraduate degree, drama.

Addresses: *Agent*—Bauman, Redanty, and Shaul Agency, 5757 Wilshire Blvd., Suite 473, Los Angeles, CA 90036. *Manager*—Holly Lebed Personal Management, 10535 Wilshire Blvd., Suite 808, Los Angeles, CA 90024.

Career: Actor, stunt fighter, and stunt performer. Previously worked as a roadie for Goldfinger (a rock band) and shoveling sand and gravel as well as doing demolitions for a construction company.

CREDITS

Film Appearances:

Ruslan Zmeyev, *Out of Courage 2: Out for Vengeance* (short film; also known as *OC2: Out for Vengeance*), 1999.

Black Dildo, *The Ketchup King,* 2002.

Flash Thompson, *Spider-Man,* Columbia, 2002.

Flash Thompson, *Spider-Man 3* (also known as *Spider-Man 3: The IMAX Experience*), Columbia, 2007.

Matt Cooper, *Impact Point,* Sony Pictures Home Entertainment, 2008.
Patient, *Wounded* (short film), 2008.
Ryan, *Not Evelyn Cho* (short film), 2009.
Charlie, *Irene in Time,* Rainbow Releasing, 2009.
Lieutenant Sean Macklin, *Behind Enemy Lines: Colombia,* Twentieth Century Fox Home Entertainment, 2009.

Film Work:
Executive producer and (uncredited) stunt fighter, *Out of Courage 2: Out for Vengeance* (short film; also known as *OC2: Out for Vengeance*), 1999.
(Uncredited) Stunts, *Spider–Man,* Columbia, 2002.

Television Appearances; Series:
Brad, *How I Met Your Mother* (also known as *H.I.M.Y.M.*), CBS, 2006–2009.
Solomon Cortez, *American Heiress,* MyNetworkTV, 2007.
Officer Litchman, *ER,* NBC, 2007.
Owen Morello, *One Tree Hill,* The CW, 2008–10.
Rick, *100 Questions,* NBC, 2009.

Television Appearances; Pilots:
Scott, "Plucky," *So noTORIous,* VH1, 2006.

Television Appearances; Episodic:
Rick Cavanaugh, "Notting Hell," *Jake in Progress,* ABC, 2006.
Tom Harper, "Daddy's Little Girl," *CSI: Crime Scene Investigation* (also known as *CSI: Las Vegas, C.S.I.,* and *Les experts*), CBS, 2006.
Carson Stuart, "Urban Legend," *Las Vegas,* NBC, 2006.
James Miller, "Escape," *Close to Home,* CBS, 2006.
Scott, "Whole," *So noTORIous,* VH1, 2006.
Chad Miller, "My No Good Reason," *Scrubs,* NBC, 2007.
I Love the New Millennium, VH1, 2008.
Stu, "Joy Ride," *'Til Death,* Fox, 2008.
Tony Ramirez, "Target Specific," *CSI: Miami,* CBS, 2009.
Angelo Filipelli, "Once in a Lifetime," *Medium,* CBS, 2009.
Rob Meyers, "Criminal Justice," *CSI: NY* (also known as *CSI: New York*), CBS, 2010.
Alcide Herveaux, "It Hurts Me Too," *True Blood,* HBO, 2010.
Alcide Herveaux, "9 Crimes," *True Blood,* HBO, 2010.

Television Work; Episodic:
(Uncredited) Stunt fighter, "Daddy's Little Girl," *CSI: Crime Scene Investigation* (also known as *CSI: Las Vegas, C.S.I.,* and *Les experts*), CBS, 2006.
Stunts, "Escape," *Close to Home,* CBS, 2006.
Stunt fighter, "Family Business," *ER,* NBC, 2007.
(Uncredited) Stunt fighter, "Running to Stand Still," *One Tree Hill,* The CW, 2008.

(Uncredited) Stunt fighter, "Our Life Is not a Movie or Maybe," *One Tree Hill,* The CW, 2008.
(Uncredited) Stunt fighter, "Sympathy for the Devil," *One Tree Hill,* The CW, 2008.
(Uncredited) Stunts, "Criminal Justice," *CSI: NY* (also known as *CSI: New York*), CBS, 2010.

WRITINGS

Screenplays:
Out of Courage 2: Out for Vengeance (short film; also known as *OC2: Out for Vengeance*), 1999.

MANN, Danny
(Daniel Mann)

PERSONAL

Addresses: *Agent*—Danis Panaro Nist, 9201 West Olympic Blvd., Beverly Hills, CA 90212.

Career: Actor and voice performer.

CREDITS

Film Appearances:
Voice of Hector and Fish Market proprietor, *Heathcliff, The Movie* (animated), Clubhouse Pictures, 1986.
Voice, *Mad Scientist,* 1988.
Voice of Icarus, the squirrel, *Little Nemo: Adventures in Slumberland* (animated; also known as *Little Nemo*), Hemdale Film Corp., 1989.
Voice of Wolf, *Rover Dangerfield,* 1991.
Voices of Ash and voice dispatch, *FernGully: The Last Rainforest* (animated; also known as *FernGully 1*), Twentieth Century–Fox, 1992.
Voice of Mozo, *Thumbelina* (animated; also known as *Hans Christian Andersen "Thumbelina"*), 1994.
Voice of Percy, *Pocahontas* (animated), Buena Vista, 1995.
Voice of Ferdinand the Duck, *Babe* (also known as *Babe, the Gallant Pig*), Universal, 1995.
Voice of Kaltag, *Balto* (animated), Universal, 1995.
Voice of Skippy, *Alien Encounter,* 1995.
Voices of Ferdinand the Duck and Tug, *Babe: Pig in the City,* MCA/Universal, 1998.
Voice of Allosaurus, *The Land before Time VI: The Secret of Saurus Rock* (animated), Universal Studio Home Video, 1998.
Voice of Head Cossack, *Bartok the Magnificent,* 1999.
Voice, *Aladdin and the Adventure of All Time* (animated), 2000.
Voice of Ninja Cat, *Cats & Dogs,* Warner Bros., 2001.

Additional character voice, *Osmosis Jones* (animated), Warner Bros., 2001.

Voice of Robo Dog & Spy Car, *Looney Tunes: Back in Action* (animated; also known as *Looney Tunes Back in Action: The Movie*), Warner Bros., 2003.

(English version) Voice of Cook and Sultan, *The Nutcracker and the Mouseking* (animated; also known as *Nussknacker und Masuekonig*), Anchor Bay Entertainment, 2004.

Voice of Jean–Paul Bidet and B–M Man, *Disaster!* (animated; also known as *Disaster—The Movie*), Dream Entertainment, 2005.

Voice of Serge, *Open Season* (animated), Columbia, 2006.

Voice Dino and Zoo Penguin, *Happy Feet* (animated; also known as *Happy Feet: The IMAX Experience*), Warner Bros., 2006.

Voice of Serge, *Open Season 2* (animated), Sony Pictures Home Entertainment, 2008.

Voice of Construction Worker Steve, *Up* (animated; also known as *Helium*), Walt Disney Studios Motion Pictures, 2009.

Film Work:

Additional voices, *My Little Pony and Friends* (animated), 1986.

Special vocal effects, *Born to Be Wild* (also known as *Katie*), Warner Bros., 1995.

Additional voices, *Babe: Pig in the City*, MCA/Universal, 1998.

Additional voices, *The Emperor's New Groove* (animated), Buena Vista, 2000.

Additional voices, *Monsters, Inc.* (animated), Buena Vista, 2001.

Additional voices, *Finding Nemo* (animated), Buena Vista, 2003.

Automated dialogue replacement (ADR), *Shrek 2* (animated), DreamWorks, 2004.

ADR, *Dawn of the Dead*, 2004.

Additional voices, *Ice Age: The Meltdown* (animated; also known as *Ice Age 2* and *Ice Age: The Meltdown*), Twentieth Century–Fox, 2006.

Additional voices, *Cars* (animated), Buena Vista, 2006.

Additional voice, *The Wild* (animated; also known as *La vie sauvage*), Walt Disney Pictures, 2006.

Additional voices, *Surf's Up* (animated), Columbia, 2007.

Additional voices, *Horton Hears a Who!* (animated; also known as *Dr. Seuss' "Horton Hears a Who!,"* *Horton,* and *Horton Hears a Who!*), Twentieth Century–Fox, 2008.

(English version) Additional voices, *Gake no ue no Ponyo* (animated; also known as *Ponyo, Ponyo on the Cliff by the Sea,* and *Ponyo on the Cliff*), Walt Disney Studios Motion Pictures, 2008.

Additional voices, *Tokyo Mater* (animated short film), Walt Disney Motion Pictures Group, 2008.

Additional voices, *Cloudy with a Chance of Meatballs* (animated; also known as *Cloudy with a Chance of Meatballs: An IMAX 3D Experience*), Columbia, 2009.

Television Appearances; Series:

Voice of Hector and fish market proprietor, *Heathcliff & the Catillac Cats* (animated; also known as *Heathcliff, Cats & Co., The Heathcliff and Dingbat Show, Les entrechats,* and *The Heathcliff and Marmaduke Show*), ABC, 1984–87.

Voice of Cloudraker, Freeway, Lightspeed–Spoilsport, *Transformers* (animated; also known as *Super God Robot Force, Tatakae! Cho robot seimeitai Transformers, The Transformers, Transformers: 2010,* and *Transformers: Generation 1*), syndicated, 1984.

Voice of Creep, *Galaxy High School* (animated), CBS, 1986.

Voice of Punkster, Putter, and PC, *Popples* (animated; also known as *Poporuzu*), syndicated, 1986.

Voice of various characters, *Little Wizards* (animated), ABC, 1987.

Voice of Strongheart, *Lady Lovelylocks and the Pixietails* (animated), syndicated, 1987.

Voice of Luigi and Bud, *Slimer! And the Real Ghostbusters* (animated), syndicated, 1988–89.

Voice of Control, *Hard Time on Planet Earth* (animated), CBS, 1989.

Voice of Chester, *Camp Candy* (animated), syndicated, 1989.

Voice of Rarf, *Zazoo U* (animated), Fox, 1990.

Voice of Super Snooper, *Wake, Rattle & Roll* (also known as *Jump, Rattle & Roll*), 1990.

Voice, *Kid's Play* (animated), 1990.

Voice of Einstein, *Back to the Future* (animated; also known as *Back to the Future: The Animated Series*), CBS, 1991.

Voices of No Eyes and Twin–Beaks, *Little Dracula* (animated), 1991.

Voice of Tasha, *Land of the Lost* (animated), ABC, 1991.

Voice of Dog, *Fievel's American Tails* (animated), CBS, 1991.

Voice of J. Gander Hooter, *Darkwing Duck* (animated), 1991.

Voice, *Yo! Yogi* (animated), NBC, 1991–92.

Voice of Boothill Buzzard, *Wild West C.O.W. Boys of Moo Mesa* (animated), ABC, 1992.

Voice, *Madeline* (animated), Fox Family, 1993.

Voice of Family Dog, *Family Dog* (animated), CBS, 1993.

Voice of Dinosaur Neil, Dr. Mung Mung, and Tongue Tongue, *The Tick* (animated), Fox, 1994.

Voice of Daggar, *Skeleton Warriors* (animated), CBS, 1994.

Voice, *Duckman: Private Dick/Family Man* (animated), USA Network, 1994–97.

Voice, *The Twisted Tales of Felix the Cat* (animated), CBS, 1995.

Voice of the announcer, *Hudson Street*, ABC, 1995.

Voice of Monkey, *Jumanji* (animated), UPN, 1996.

Voice, *Space Goofs* (animated), Fox, 1997.

Voice, *Channel Umptee–3* (animated), The WB, 1997.

(English version) Voice of Gorgious Klaatu, *Les zinzins de l'espace* (also known as *Space Goofs* and *Home to Rent*), 1997.

Voice of Raijcan, *Psi–Kix* (animated), 2008.

Television Appearances; Specials:

Voice of Phil Silverfish, *Twas the Night before Bumpy,* ABC, 1995.

Voice of Dr. Toothinstein, *Elise: Mere Mortal,* 2002.

Voice of Three–Eyed Jack and Wall–Eyed Tom, *Party Wagon* (animated), Cartoon Network, 2004.

Voice, *Party Wagon,* Cartoon Network, 2004.

Television Appearances; Specials:

Voice, "Liberty and the Littles," *ABC Weekend Specials,* ABC, 1986.

Voice, *Here Comes the Bride ... There Goes the Groom,* CBS, 1995.

Voice, *Totally Animals II,* CBS, 1996.

Comedy voice–over, *Here Comes the Bride ... There Goes the Groom 2,* CBS, 1996.

Narrator, *The Greatest Shows You Never Saw,* CBS, 1996.

Television Appearances; Pilots:

Voice of announcer and editor, *The Tony Danza Show,* NBC, 1997.

Television Appearances; Episodic:

Voice of Banana 9000, "Adventures in Slime and Space," *The Real Ghostbusters* (animated), 1987.

Voice of Backwoods Beagle, "Ducky Mountain High," *DuckTales* (animated), 1987.

Oscar's voice, "Read My Lips," *Friday the 13th* (also known as *Friday the 13th: The Series* and *Friday's Curse*), 1988.

Voice of bus passenger, "Not in Our Stars," *Hard Time on Planet Earth* (animated), 1989.

Voice of additional cast, "Partners in Slime," *The Real Ghostbusters* (animated), 1989.

Voice, "Beach Blanket Bobby," *Bobby's World,* 1990.

Voice of radio D.J., "Bat Scratch Fever," *Batman: The Animated Series* (animated), Fox, 1992.

Dog, "The Gift," *Fievel's American Tails,* 1992.

Voice of Ursak Steele/The Guardian, "Long Live the King," *Skeleton Warriors* (animated), CBS, 1995.

Voice, "The Germinator," *Quack Pack,* 1996.

Voice of Dinosaur Neil, "That Mustache Feeling," *The Tick* (animated), 1996.

Voice of Dinosaur Neil, "The Tick vs. Dot and Neil's Wedding," *The Tick* (animated), 1996.

Voice of Bellbot, "The Tick vs. Prehistory," *The Tick* (animated), 1996.

Voice, *C–Bear and Jamal* (animated), Fox, 1996.

Big Duck, "Halloween," *Cybill,* CBS, 1997.

Voice, "The Big Bad Bug Syndrome," *Men in Black: The Series* (animated), The WB, 1998.

Voice of Dr. Don't, "Pete Patrick Private Investigator," *Oh Yeah! Cartoons* (animated), Nickelodeon, 1998.

Voice of Colonel/Sergeant, "Veterans Day," *Hey Arnold!* (animated), Nickelodeon, 1999.

Voices of Whaler and Pirate 2, "Dishonest Abe/ Blackbeard, Warm Heart," *Time Squad* (animated), 2001.

Voice of Elder, "Jack and the Warrior Women," *Samurai Jack* (animated), Cartoon Network, 2001.

Voice of townspersons ten and eleven, "Big Al's Big Secret," *Time Squad* (animated), 2001.

Voice of Harry Houdini and employee, "Houdini Whodunit?!/Feud for Thought," *Time Squad* (animated), 2002.

Voice of Kartok and soldier, "Jack and the Spartans," *Samurai Jack* (animated), 2002.

Voice, "Enter the Cat," *Jackie Chan Adventures* (animated), 2002.

Voice of Amorpho, "Forever Phantom," *Danny Phantom* (animated), Nickelodeon, 2003.

Flip and Radio Ad, "C.A.R.R. Trouble," *Stroker and Hoop* (animated), Cartoon Network, 2004.

Voice of Cerebrus number three, person number one, and priest, "House of Pain/A Grim Prophecy/Mandy Bites Dog," *Grim & Evil* (animated; also known as *The Grim Adventures of Billy & Mandy*), Cartoon Network, 2004.

Voice of Cat, Frog, and Parrot, "M Is for Mercy," *W.I.T.C.H.* (animated), ABC Family, 2006.

Voice of Cerebrus number two and bicycle guy, "Waking Nightmare/Beware of the Undertoad," *Grim & Evil* (animated; also known as *The Grim Adventures of Billy & Mandy*), Cartoon Network, 2007.

Also appeared as voice, *The Jetsons* (animated); voice of old player numbers one and two, adman number two, poll tax broker, customer, *Rugrats,* Nickelodeon; in *Family,* ABC; *The Pink Panther.*

Television Additional Voices; Series:

Scooby and Scrappy–Doo (animated), ABC, 1979.

Scooby and Scrappy–Doo/Puppy Hour (animated), 1982.

The Jetsons (animated), 1987.

Fantastic Max (animated), 1988.

Captain Planet and Planeteers (animated; also known as *The New Adventures of Captain Planet*), TBS and syndicated, 1990.

Tale Spin (animated), syndicated, 1990.

Rugrats (animated), Nickelodeon, 1991.

Yo, Yogi! (animated), 1991.

Darkwing Duck (animated), ABC and syndicated, 1991.

Problem Child (animated), USA Network, 1993.

The Pink Panther (animated), 1993.

Aladdin (animated; also known as *Disney's Aladdin*), CBS and syndicated, 1993.

The Shnookums and Meat Funny Cartoon Show (animated), 1993.

Sonic the Hedgehog (animated; also known as *Sonic SatAM*), ABC and syndicated, 1993–95.

Where on Earth Is Carmen Sandiego? (animated), PBS and syndicated, 1994.

The Mask: The Animated Series (animated), 1995.
Earthworm Jim, The WB, 1995.
Jumanji (animated), UPN, 1996.
All Dogs Go to Heaven: The Series (animated), 1996.
Men in Black: The Series (animated), 1997.

Television Work; Movies:
Loop group voice, *It's a Very Merry Muppet Christmas Movie,* 2002.

Television Additional Voices; Episodic:
"The Time Bandit," *TaleSpin* (animated), 1990.
"While the City Snoozes," *Aladdin* (animated; also known as *Disney's "Aladdin"*), CBS and syndicated, 1995.
"Raven's Revenge," *Spicy City,* 1997.
"Starstruck/Who's Taffy?," *Rugrats* (animated), Nickelodeon, 2002.

RECORDINGS

Video Games; Appearances:
Voice, *Pocahontas* (also known as *Disney's "Pocahontas"*), 1996.
Voice of Gorgious, *Stupid Invaders,* Ubi–Soft, 2001.
Voice, *GoldenEye: Rogue Agent,* Electronic Arts, 2004.
Voice of Ebenezer Von Clutch, *Crash Tag Team Racing,* Vivendi Universal Games, 2005.
Tony, *True Crime: New York City,* Activision, 2005.
Voice of Abe Hunter and Charlie Hazelgrove, *The Darkness,* 2007.
Voice of Pirate number three, *Ratchet & Clank Future: Tools of Destruction,* Sony Computer Entertainment America, 2007.
Voice of Gyptian, lab technician, and steward, *The Golden Compass,* Sega of America, 2007.
Voice, *Ratchet & Clank Future: Quest for Booty,* 2008.
(As Daniel Mann) Voice, *Marvel: Ultimate Alliance 2,* 2009.

Video Games; as Additional Voices:
Ultimate Spider–Man, Activision, 2005.
(English version) *Gothic 3,* 2006.
Spider–Man 3, Activision, 2007.
Crash of the Titans, 2007.

MARCIANO, David 1960–

PERSONAL

Born January 7, 1960, in Newark, NJ; son of Pasquale and Grace Delta Rose (maiden name, Caprio) Marciano; married Katayoun Amini (an actress and writer),

October 20, 1991; children: Ariana Grace, Mina Chiara, Marcello. *Education:* Attended Northeastern University; studied acting at Drama Studio of London, Berkeley, CA.

Addresses: *Agent*—Tim Angle, Don Buchwald and Associates, 6500 Wilshire Blvd., Suite 2200, Los Angeles, CA 90048.

Career: Actor. Appeared in commercials for Sprite and Pepsi soft drinks, Denny's and Howard Johnson's restaurants, Michelob beer, V–8 juice, Sudafed cold medication, and other products. Previously worked as a bartender.

Member: Screen Actors Guild.

Awards, Honors: Gemini Award nominations, best leading actor in a continuing dramatic role, Academy of Canadian Cinema and Television, 1995, 1996, both for *Due South.*

CREDITS

Television Appearances; Series:
Jeffrey Lassick, *Civil Wars,* ABC, 1991–93.
Ray Vecchio, *Due South* (also known as *Direction: Sud*), CBS, 1994–96.
Len Mildmay, a recurring role, *Judging Amy,* CBS, 2000–2001.
Detective Steve Billings, *The Shield,* FX Network, 2005–2008.

Television Appearances; Movies:
Franklin "Frankie" Bando, *Street of Dreams,* CBS, 1988.
Monte Fontaine, *Police Story: Gladiator School,* ABC, 1988.
Calvin, "The Fragging," *Vietnam War Story II,* HBO, 1988.
Rick Powell, *Kiss Shot,* CBS, 1989.
Kenneth Burch, *Eyes of Terror* (also known as *Visions of Terror*), NBC, 1994.

Television Appearances; Miniseries:
Pastey, *Gypsy,* CBS, 1993.
Giorgio, *The Last Don* (also known as *Mario Puzo's "The Last Don"*), CBS, 1997.
Giorgio Clericuzio, *The Last Don II* (also known as *Mario Puzo's "The Last Don II"*), CBS, 1998.

Television Appearances; Pilots:
Sal Bernadini, "Tickets, Please," *CBS Summer Playhouse,* CBS, 1988.
Sal, *Maverick Square,* ABC, 1991.

Jeffrey Lassick, *Civil Wars,* ABC, 1991.
Detective Ray Vecchio, *Due South* (also known as *Direction: Sud*), CBS, 1994.
Carl, *Kilroy,* HBO, 1999.
Terry Laguna, *Eyes,* ABC, 2005.

Television Appearances; Specials:
Himself, *Speechless,* 2008.

Television Appearances; Episodic:
Lorenzo Steelgrave, "The Loose Cannon," *Wiseguy,* CBS, 1987.
Dee Jay, "Somewhere over the Radio," *China Beach,* ABC, 1988.
Hugo Stone/Superboy impersonator, "The Beast and Beauty," *Superboy* (also known as *The Adventures of Superboy*), syndicated, 1988.
Insane Wayne Bataglia, "Wizard of Odds," *Sonny Spoon,* 1988.
Jerry "Bones" Bonaventure, "Three for the Money," *Midnight Caller,* 1990.
Hancock, "A Day in the Life of Logan Murphy," *Disney Presents "The 100 Lives of Black Jack Savage"* (also known as *Black Jack Savage*), 1991.
Billy Gordon, "Trust Me on This: Parts 1 & 2," *Reasonable Doubts,* NBC, 1993.
Max Stumpp, "Greed for a Pirate Dream," *SeaQuest DSV* (also known as *SeaQuest 2032*), NBC, 1994.
James Block, "Into the Light," *Touched by an Angel,* CBS, 1996.
Ray Vecchio, "Burning Down the House," *Due South* (also known as *Un tandem du choc*), CTV, 1997.
Ray Vecchio, "Call of the Wild: Parts 1 & 2," *Due South* (also known as *Un tandem du choc*), CTV, 1999.
Eddie Michaels, "Gangland: Parts 1 & 2," *Diagnosis: Murder,* CBS, 1999.
Jimmy Bangs, "Rock and a Hard Place," *Nash Bridges* (also known as *Bridges*), CBS, 2000.
"Kids" (also known as "Worshipping at Shirley's Temple"), *The Lot,* AMC, 2001.
George, "The Honeymoon's Over," *Providence,* NBC, 2001.
George, "Rocky Road," *Providence,* NBC, 2001.
Dr. Paul Gianni, "The Perfect Babysitter," *The Mind of the Married Man,* HBO, 2002.
Dr. Paul Gianni, "The Corvette," *The Mind of the Married Man,* HBO, 2002.
Dr. Paul Gianni, "The Pony Ride," *The Mind of the Married Man,* HBO, 2002.
Dr. Paul Gianni, "A Hard Pill to Swallow," *The Mind of the Married Man,* HBO, 2002.
Senior Chief Sinclair, "In Thin Air," *JAG* (also known as *JAG: Judge Advocate General*), CBS, 2002.
"Murder.com," *The Division* (also known as *Heart of the City*), 2003.
Detective Raymond Gerson, "And the Wenner Is ...," *NYPD Blue,* ABC, 2003.

Frank Samuels, "XX," *CSI: Crime Scene Investigation* (also known as *C.S.I., CSI: Las Vegas,* and *Les experts*), CBS, 2004.
Karl Drewdetski, "Creatures of the Night," *CSI: NY,* CBS, 2004.
Bartender, "Lt. Jane Doe," *Navy NCIS: Naval Criminal Investigative Service* (also known as *NCIS* and *NCIS: Naval Criminal Investigative Service*), CBS, 2004.
Edmond Dobbs, "Common Thread," *Joan of Arcadia,* CBS, 2005.
Murphy, "The Tyrant," *House M.D.* (also known as *House*), Fox, 2009.
Jason Wilkie, *Lie to Me,* Fox, c. 2009.

Also appeared as a thug in *The Bold & the Beautiful,* ABC, and in *Duet,* Fox.

Film Appearances:
Hellbent, Raedon Video, 1988.
First police officer, *Lethal Weapon 2,* Warner Bros., 1989.
Tony, *Harlem Nights,* Paramount, 1989.
Kreig, *Come See the Paradise,* 1990.
A. D., *Dark Spiral,* 1999.
Detective, *Around the Bend,* Warner Independent Pictures, 2004.
Man, *Chicken Man* (short film), Macedon Media, 2006.
Announcer, *Intellectual Property* (also known as *Dark Mind*), Strategic Film Partners, 2007.
District Attorney Henry Giles, *Caught in the Middle* (short film), 2009.
Detective Brown, *Caught on Tape,* Fluid Entertainment, 2009.

Stage Appearances:
Appeared as Schlosser, *Awake and Sing;* Putnam, *The Crucible;* Taledo, *Exit 188;* blind man, *The Machine Stops;* sergeant, *Mother Courage;* Diggory, *She Stoops to Conquer;* Martin/Hinson, *Streamers;* a cop, *Street Scene;* a man, *Talk to Me;* and Morton Gross, *The Water Engine.*

RECORDINGS

Videos:
Ride Forever, Network Video, 2006.

MARSDEN, Kristie 1982–

PERSONAL

Full name, Kristie Nichole Marsden; born February 2, 1982, in Burnaby, British Columbia, Canada.

Addresses: *Manager*—Carrier Talent Management, #705–1080 Howe St., Vancouver, British Columbia V6Z 2T1, Canada.

Career: Actress and voice performer. Appeared in television commercials for Hasbro's Taco Bell Playdough, 2000, and Mattel's Princess Bride Barbie, 2000.

CREDITS

Television Appearances; Series:
(English version) Voice of Sayu Yagami, *Desu Noto* (animated; also known as *Death Note*), Nippon Television, 2006–2007.
Erin, *About a Girl,* The N, 2007–2008.
Voice of Whitney Stane/Madame Masque, *Iron Man: Armored Adventure* (animated), NickToons, 2008–2009.

Television Appearances; Episodic:
Lucy, "Flushed," *Dark Angel* (also known as *James Cameron's "Dark Angel"*), Fox, 2000.
Teenage girl, "Dead," *2gether: The Series,* MTV, 2000.
Rose, "Lonewolf," *Freedom,* UPN, 2000.
Rachel, "The Witness," *Beyond Belief: Fact or Fiction* (also known as *Beyond Belief*), Fox, 2001.
Drama student, "My So–Called Episode," *These Arms of Mine,* 2001.
Drama student, "To Sir, with Live," *These Arms of Mine,* 2001.
Latina girl, "T&A," *The Chris Isaak Show,* Showtime, 2001.
Cleo, "The Changing," *Wolf Lake,* CBS, 2001.
Goth girl, "Don't Fear the Reaper," *Strange Frequency,* VH1, 2001.
Voice of Holly, "Puppy Love," *Mary–Kate and Ashley in Action!* (animated), ABC, 2001.
Voice of Flee, "Rave Reviews," *Mary–Kate and Ashley in Action!* (animated), ABC, 2002.
Erin, "Yearbook," *Just Deal,* NBC, 2002.
Donna Shoemaker, "Bloody Mary," *Supernatural,* The WB, 2005.
Marie, "Pick Me Up," *Masters of Horror,* Showtime, 2006.
Tracey, "Living Dead," *Saved,* TNT, 2006.
Gloria, "Daddy's Little Girl," *The 4400,* USA Network, 2007.
Student #1, "Zero to Murder in Sixty Seconds," *Psych,* USA Network, 2007.
Skye, "Lights, Camera … Homicidio," *Psych,* USA Network, 2008.

Also appeared as (English version) voice of Frau Bow, *Kido senshi Gandamu* (animated; also known as *First Gundam, Mobile Soldier Gundam,* and *Mobile Suit Gundam*), Cartoon Network; Ester at 18, "Griz Tracks," *Animal Miracles* (also known as *Miracle Pets*), PAX;

voice of Italian girl, "Roman Holiday," *Alienators: Evolution Continues* (animated; also known as *Evolution: The Animated Series*), Fox.

Television Apperances; Movies:
Blair, *I Was a Teenage Faust,* Showtime, 2002.
Female dancer, *Reefer Madness* (also known as *Reefer Madness: The Movie Musical* and *Kifferwahn*), Showtime, 2004.

Television Appearances; Pilots:
Stephanie, *Maybe It's Me,* The WB, 2001.

Film Appearances:
Soccer pal Olivia, *The Sisterhood of the Traveling Pants* (also known as *The Sisterhood of the Travelling Pants*), Warner Bros., 2005.
(English version) Voice of Yuri Hayakawa, *Toki o kakeru shojo* (animated; also known as *The Girl Who Leapt through Time*), Bandai Entertainment, 2006.
Dream woman, *Brain Fart* (short film), Skycorner Productions, 2007.

Stage Appearances:
Zaneeta Shinn, *The Music Man,* Vancouver Playhouse, Vancouver, British Columbia, Canada, 2001.

Appeared as fall down girl, *Oklahoma!,* and Shprintze, *Fiddler on the Roof,* both Theatre under the Stars; Tuptim, *The King & I,* Chava, *Fiddler on the Roof,* and Agnus, *Oliver!,* all Royal City Musical Theatre, New Westminster, British Columbia; dream Emma, *A Time to Remember,* Footlight Theatre; Dorothy, *The Wizard of Oz,* and Diana Barry, *Anne of Green Gables,* both Gateway Theatre; Rain, *Somewhere in the World,* Jeanne Aucoin, *Pelagie,* and Harold, *Caledonia,* all Charlottetown Festival, Charlottetown, Prince Edward Island, Canada; Marta, *Company,* Arts Club.

Stage Appearances; Major Tours:
Sophie Sheridan, *Mamma Mia!,* U.S. cities, 2002–2004.

Toured as member of children's choir, *Joseph and the Amazing Technicolor Dreamcoat,* U.S. cities.

RECORDINGS

Video Games:
Voice of Fraw Bow, *Kido senshi Gandamu* (also known as *Mobile Suit Gundam: Journey to Jaburo*), 2000.

Albums:
Appeared as contributor, *Somewhere in the World* (original cast recording), Charlottetown Festival, Charlottetown, Prince Edward Island, Canada.

OTHER SOURCES

Electronic:

Kristie Marsden Official Site, http://www.kristiemarsden.com/, November 22, 2009.

MATHERS, James 1936–

PERSONAL

Born October 31, 1936, in Seattle, WA.

Addresses: *Agent*—Michael Zanuck Agency, 28035 Dorothy Dr., Suite 120, Agoura Hills, CA 91301.

Career: Actor. Began career as a playwright and actor at the Magic Theatre, Eureka Theatre, San Francisco Repertory, and Bay Area Playwright's Festival, all San Francisco, CA; spent ten years with the Manhattan Class Company, Nat Horne Theatre; worked as a writer, director, editor, and producer of industrial films, education, films, and audio/visual productions.

CREDITS

Film Appearances:

Dr. Henry Jekyll, *Dr. Jekyll's Dungeon of Death* (also known as *Dr. Jekyll's Dungeon of Darkness, The Dungeon,* and *The Jekyll Experiment*), New American Films, 1979.

(Uncredited) Captain Mills, *The Right Stuff,* Warner Bros., 1983.

Director, *Guilty by Suspicion* (also known as *La liste noire*), Warner Bros., 1991.

Pilot, *Homo Faber* (also known as *O taxidiotis, The Voyager,* and *Voyager*), Castle Hill Productions, 1991.

Pilot, *True Identity,* Buena Vista, 1991.

Brian, *Improper Conduct,* Monarch Home Video, 1995.

Jerry Montegna, *Mean Guns,* New City Releasing, 1997.

Marshall Adams, *Fire Down Below,* Warner Bros., 1997.

Old man, *Mosaic* (short film), Atom Bomb Productions, 1998.

Man at carnival, *Rusty: A Dog's Tale* (also known as *Rusty* and *Rusty: The Great Rescue*), Twentieth Century–Fox Home Entertainment, 1998.

Teacher, *Me and You and Everyone We Know,* IFC Films, 2005.

Gary, *Gone Postal* (short film), 2005.

Smudging Shaman, *Full Moon* (short film), 2005.

Bernard Golinko, *The Poughkeepsie Tapes,* Metro–Goldwyn–Mayer, 2007.

Arthur Frain, *SpaceDisco One,* 2007.

Mr. Stevens, *Acts of Mercy,* Ambrosia Films, 2009.

Harold, *Kiss the Abyss,* Silverline Entertainment, 2010.

Television Appearances; Movies:

Internal affairs officer number two, *In the Line of Duty: A Cop for the Killing* (also known as *A Cop for the Killing* and *In the Line of Duty: Blood Brothers*), NBC, 1990.

Goodrich, *None So Blind,* ABC, 1990.

Man on street, *The Heart of Justice,* TNT, 1992.

Detective McRanney, *"Murder, She Wrote": South by Southwest,* CBS, 1997.

Television Appearances; Specials:

Benjamin, "A Town's Revenge," *ABC Afterschool Special,* ABC, 1989.

Television Appearances; Episodic:

Parole board chairman, "Louis' Date," *Gabriel's Fire,* ABC, 1990.

Officer Mullins, "Gunz 'n Boyz," *MacGyver,* ABC, 1991.

Mr. Keough, "Say Goodnight Gracie," *L.A. Law,* NBC, 1992.

Warden, "Trial by Fire," *Bodies of Evidence,* CBS, 1993.

Verachek, "Good Soldiers," *SeaQuest DSV* (also known as *SeaQuest 2032*), NBC, 1995.

Sheriff number three, "The Big Bang Theory," *Melrose Place,* Fox, 1995.

Sheriff, "Dead Sisters Walking," *Melrose Place,* Fox, 1996.

Guard, "Living with Disaster," *Melrose Place,* Fox, 1996.

Deputy number one, "Over Dick's Dead Body," *Melrose Place,* Fox, 1996.

Deputy, "Moving Violations," *Melrose Place,* Fox, 1996.

Judge Nash, "A Mate for Life," *Beverly Hills 90210* (also known as *Class of Beverly Hills*), Fox, 1996.

General Manager Ferren, "Jaroldo!," *The Pretender,* NBC, 1997.

Dr. Carpenter, "The Promise," *Ally McBeal,* Fox, 1997.

Judge Allen Stephenson, "The Promise," *Ally,* Fox, 1997.

"Capital Crime," *JAG* (also known as *JAG: Judge Advocate General*), CBS, 2002.

Marvin Dobie, "Late Returns," *Cold Case,* CBS, 2004.

Patient, "X–Mas," *7th Heaven* (also known as *Seventh Heaven*), The WB, 2005.

Roth, "Lost in America," *ER,* NBC, 2006.

Security guard, "300 Patients," *ER,* NBC, 2007.

Also appeared as guest, *Spike Feresten Talk Show,* Fox; in *One Life to Live,* ABC; *All My Children,* ABC; *America's Most Wanted.*

Stage Appearances:
Appeared as Jay Henry, *Dylan,* Skylight Theatre; Maurice, *Swampland,* Sacred Fools; Cabot, *Desire Under the Elms,* San Francisco Repertory, San Francisco, CA; Editor Webb, *Our Town,* Santa Rosa Repertory, Santa Rosa, CA; Henry II, *The Lion in Winter,* Florida Shakespeare; Lee, *True West,* Theatre Virginia; Sergeant Phillips, *Sister Gloria's Pentecostal Baby,* Manhattan Class Company; Hal, *Happy Birthday Wanda June,* New York City; Weston, *Curse of the Starving Class,* Douglas Fairbanks Theatre, New York City; Svidrigaylov, *Crime and Punishment,* Harold Clurman Theatre, New York City.

RECORDINGS

Video Games:
Voice of Captain Edward "Eddie" Shrote, *The Darkness,* 2007.

WRITINGS

Screenplays:
Dr. Jekyll's Dungeon of Death (also known as *Dr. Jekyll's Dungeon of Darkness, The Dungeon,* and *The Jekyll Experiment*), 1979.

Also wrote *Flight of the Raven; Red Tom; Late Hit; Ten Days in a Madhouse; The Crossing; L.A. Nightmares; The Raven* (educational film).

Television Movies:
Wrote *Everyman.*

Television Episodes:
Wrote episodes of *Straight from Heaven; The Miracle.*

Stage Plays:
Wrote *Spiral,* Two Roads Theatre, Los Angeles; *Henry & Dad,* Whitmore–Lyndley Theatre, Los Angeles.

Short Story Collections:
Published *The Pied Piper of Larrabee Gulch & Other Stories.*

MATHERS, James 1955–
    (Jim Mathers, Jimmy Mathers, Sheamus James Mathers, James Michaels)

PERSONAL

Born May 5, 1955, in Los Angeles, CA; brother of Jerry Mathers (an actor) and Susie Mathers (an actress); married Charlene Richards (a writer and nonprofit executive), August 15, 1998; children: three. *Education:* Attended the Film School at California State University, Northridge.

Addresses: *Office*—Migrant FilmWorkers, PO Box 1973, Studio City, CA 91614.

Career: Cinematographer, director, and actor. Worked as a director for music videos, television commercials, and public service announcements. The Migrant FilmWorkers, founder; The Digital Cinema Society (a nonprofit educational cooperative), cofounder and president. Regular contributor to a number of industry trade journals, including *Studio Monthly, Definitions—The HiDef Source Book,* and *Digital Cinema Magazine.*

CREDITS

Film Cinematographer:
(Assistant) *50 Years of Action!,* 1985.
Take Two, 1988.
Memorial Valley Massacre (also known as *Valley of Death*), Nelson Entertainment, 1988.
Outlaw Force, Trans World Entertainment, 1988.
Zadar! Cow from Hell, 1989.
(As Jim Mathers) *The Forgotten One,* Academy Home Entertainment, 1989.
(As Jim Mathers) *Down the Drain,* Ascot Video, 1990.
Night Eyes (also known as *Hidden View* and *Hidden Vision*), 1990.
Syngenor (also known as *Syngenor: Synthesized Genetic Organism*), 1990.
Last Call, Prism Entertainment, 1991.
Legal Tender (also known as *Ladies Game*), Prism Entertainment, 1991.
(As Jim Mathers) *Rock 'n' Roll High School Forever,* Avid Home Video, 1991.
(Additional; as Jim Mathers) *The Terror Within II,* Concorde Productions, 1991.
The Search for Signs of Intelligent Life in the Universe, Orion Classics, 1991.
(As James Michaels) *The Other Woman,* 1991.
Silent Night, Deadly Night 5: The Toy Maker, Lions Gate Films Home Entertainment, 1991.
(As Jim Mathers) *House IV* (also known as *House 4: The Repossession* and *House IV: Home Deadly Home*), Ascot Video, 1992.
Play Nice, 1992.
(As Jim Mathers) *Round Trip to Heaven,* Prism Entertainment, 1992.
Snapdragon, Prism Entertainment, 1993.
Wild Cactus, 1993.
(As Jim Mathers) *Night Eyes Three* (also known as *Night Eyes III: On Guard*), Turner Home Entertainment, 1993.
L.A. Goddess, Prism Entertainment, 1993.
(As James Michaels) *Snapdragon,* 1993.

(As James Michaels) *Improper Conduct,* 1994.
Sexual Malice, A–Pix Entertainment, 1994.
Young at Hearts, Outsider Pictures, 1995.
Turbo: A Power Rangers Movie, 1996.
Beetleborgs: Vampire Files (short film), Twentieth Century–Fox Home Entertainment, 1996.
Curse of the ShadowBorg, 1997.
(As James Michaels) *Sex: The Annabel Chong Story* (documentary), 1998.
Intrepid (also known as *Deep Water*), Starlight, 2000.
XCU: Extreme Close–Up, Ardustry Home Entertainment, 2001.
Last Night with Angel (short film), 2003.
American Crude, 2004.
(As James Michaels) *Tranced,* 2005.
Getting Around: Alternatives for Seniors Who No Longer Drive (documentary), 2005.
Forest Lawn: The First Hundred Years (documentary), 2005.
Who Is Harry Nilsson (And Why Is Everybody Talkin' About Him?) (documentary), 2006.
The U.S. vs. John Lennon (documentary), Lions Gate Films, 2006.
Dystopia (short film), 2007.
Dummy Hoy: A Deaf Hero, 2007.
For the Bible Tells Me So (documentary), First Run Features, 2007.
Balancing the Books (also known as *Fatal Secrets*), Artist View Entertainment, 2008.
American Crude, Sony Pictures Home Entertainment, 2008.
Waiting for Yvette (short film), Wolfe Releasing, 2008.
(Second unit) *Manure,* 2009.
Aussie and Ted's Great Adventures (also known as *Aussie & Ted*), Cinetel Films, 2009.
(Additional) *It Might Get Loud,* Sony Pictures Classics, 2009.
The Chicago 8, 2010.
Montana Amazon, 2010.

Also worked as cinematographer on *The Game; Tainted Love.*

Film Work; Other:

Director, *Beetleborgs Metallix: The Movie,* 1997.
Producer and director, *Digital Cinema Solutions* (short film), Jim Mathers Video/Films, 2003.
Interview camera operator, *The 11th Hour,* Warner Independent Pictures, 2007.

Film Appearances:

Peter Carey, *Summer Magic,* 1963.
Matt Boley, *Mail Order Bride,* 1963.
Freddie, *The New Interns,* 1964.
Mike, *The Dirty Mind of Young Sally* (also known as *Innocent Sally*), 1970.

(As Sheamus James Mathers) Homeless man, *Aussie and Ted's Great Adventures* (also known as *Aussie & Ted*), Cinetel Films, 2009.

Television Cinematographer; Movies:

Honor Thy Father and Mother: The True Story of the Menendez Murders (also known as *Honor Thy Father & Mother: The Menendez Killings*), Fox, 1994.
St. Patrick: The Irish Legend (also known as *Saint Patrick, the Irish Legend*), Fox Family, 2000.
Trapped: Buried Alive, PAX, 2002.
Ghost Dog: A Detective Tail, PAX, 2003.

Television Cinematographer; Specials:

Hey, Hey It's the Monkees, ABC, 1997.
Gilda Radner's Greatest Moments, ABC, 2002.
When I Fall in Love: The One & Only Nat King Cole, 2003.
(As Jim Mathers) *The 100 Greatest TV Characters of All Time,* Bravo, 2004.
Beautiful Dreamer: Brian Wilson and the Story of "Smile," Showtime, 2004.
Ricky Nelson Sings, 2005.
Getting Around: Alternatives for Seniors Who No Longer Drive, 2006.
The Electric Company's Greatest Hits & Bits, PBS, 2006.
How Bruce Lee Changed the World, History Chanel, 2009.

Also worked as cinematographer on *In the Name of Heaven.*

Television Director; Specials:

What You Are Doing Tonight?, 1998.
Bail Agent, 2005.

Television Camera Operator; Specials:

(As Jim Mathers) *Child Stars: Their Story,* Arts and Entertainment, 2000.
Intimate Portrait: Sarah Ferguson, Lifetime, 2001.
Intimate Portrait: Patty Duke, Lifetime, 2001.
Beautiful Dreamer: Brian Wilson and the Story of "Smile," Showtime, 2004.

Television Field Producer; Specials:

The States, History Channel, 2006.

Television Cinematographer; Episodic:

Hypernauts, ABC, 1996.
Mystic Knights of Tir Na Nog (also known as *Saban's "Mystic Knights of Tir Na Nog"*), Fox, 1998.
Black Tie, 1995.

Television Director; Episodic:
Big Bad Beetleborgs (also known as *Saban's "Big Bad Beetleborgs"*), Fox, 1996.
Beetleborgs Metallix (also known as *Saban's "Beetleborgs Metallix"*), Fox, 1997–98.
"Memories of Mirinoi," *Power Rangers Lost Galaxy*, Fox, 1999.
Extreme Courage, 2002.
The Great Adventure, Fine Living Network, 2005.

Television Camera Operator; Episodic:
Hunter, 1984.
(As Jim Mathers) *Sciography*, Sci–Fi Channel, 2000.
Scariest Places on Earth, 2000–2002.
Oblivious, 2001.

Television Second Camera; Episodic:
(As Jim Mathers) *How Clean Is Your House*, Lifetime, 2005.

Television Appearances; Series:
Benji Major, *Ichabod and Me*, 1961.

Television Appearances; Episodic:
Marshall Burns, "Little Pitchers Have Big Fears," *Bewitched*, 1964.
Boy number two, "Bats of a Feather," *The Munsters*, 1965.
Norman, "The State vs. Chip Douglas," *My Three Sons*, 1966.
"Log 161: And You Want Me To Get Married?," *Adam–12*, 1968.
"Log 61," *Adam–12*, 1968.
The Smith Family, 1971.

OTHER SOURCES

Electronic:
James Mathers Official Site, http://www.migrantfilmworkers.com, February 11, 2010.

MATHESON, Hans 1975–

PERSONAL

Born 1975, in the Outer Hebrides, Scotland.

Addresses: *Agent*—Lou Coulson, Lou Coulson Associates, 37 Berwick St., London W1V 3RF, England.

Career: Actor.

CREDITS

Film Appearances:
Eddie, *Stella Does Tricks*, British Film Institute, 1996, Strand Releasing, 2000.
Jimmy Dolen, *The Future Lasts a Long Time*, 1996.
Silver Johnny, *Mojo*, Channel Four Films, 1997.
Marius, *Les Miserables*, Columbia, 1998.
Luke Shand, *Still Crazy*, Columbia, 1998.
Virgil Guppy, *Bodywork*, New City Releasing, 1999.
Jeno Varga, *Canone inverso–Making Love*, Cecchi Gori Distribuzione, 2000.
Tomas, *I Am Dina* (also known as *Dina*, *Dina—Meine Geschichte*, *Ich bin Dina*, *Jeg aar Dina*, and *Jeg er Dina*), Columbia TriStar, 2002.
Private Jack Hawkstone, *Deathwatch*, Lions Gate Films, 2002.
Angus McCulloch, *Half Light* (also known as *Half Light—Gefangen zwischen licht und schatten*), First Look International, 2006.
Merisi Caravaggio, *Bathory*, Tantrafilm, 2008.
Lord Coward, *Sherlock Holmes*, Warner Bros., 2009.
Ixas, *Clash of the Titans*, Warner Bros., 2010.

Television Appearances; Series:
Thomas Cranmer, *The Tudors*, Showtime, 2008.

Television Appearances; Miniseries:
Jake, *Family Money*, Channel 4, 1997.
Frederick Hackett, *Bramwell IV*, PBS, 1999.
Mordred, *The Mists of Avalon* (also known as *Die Nebel von Avalon*), TNT, 2001.
Yuri Zhivago, *Doctor Zhivago* (also known as *Doktor Schiwago*), PBS, 2002.
Nero, *Imperium: Nerone* (also known as *Imperium: Nero* and *Neron*), 2004.
Robert Devereux, Earl of Essex, *The Virgin Queen* (also known as *Elizabeth I: The Virgin Queen*), PBS, 2006.
Alex D'Urberville, *Tess of the D'Urbervilles*, PBS, 2008.
Himself, *The Story of the Costume Drama*, ITV3, 2008.

Television Appearances: Movies:
Ben Carter, *Poldark*, BBC, 1996.
Manny, *Christmas*, 1996.
Boy, "Steal Away," *Tube Tales*, British Sky, 1999.
Jake, *Comfortably Numb*, 2004.

Television Appearances; Specials:
Himself, *Venice Report*, 1997.

Television Appearances; Episodic:
Lee, "Still Waters," *The Bill*, 1995.
Gary Creed, "Old Habits," *Wycliffe*, 1996.
Frederick Hackett, *Bramwell III*, 1996.

Stage Appearances:

Appeared as Silver Johnny in a production of *Mojo*, Royal Court Theatre, London.

OTHER SOURCES

Periodicals:

Empire, November, 1998, p. 28.
Flicks, December, 1998, p. 50.

MATTHEWS, Erin 1973–

PERSONAL

Born February 6, 1973, in Portland, OR; married Christian Campbell, May 12, 2001 (divorced, 2003).

Addresses: *Agent*—Sovereign Talent Group, 10474 Santa Monica Blvd., Suite 301, Los Angeles, CA 90025.

Career: Actress.

CREDITS

Television Appearances; Episodic:

P. A., *Leaving L.A.*, ABC, 1997.
Gerri DelaPena, "The Ultimatum," *The $treet*, Fox, 2000.
Lily, "Here Comes the Bride," *All of Us*, UPN, 2003.
Lily, "Kindergarten Confidential," *All of Us*, UPN, 2003.
Lily, "A Family Affair," *All of Us*, UPN, 2004.
Lily, "Thirty Candles," *All of Us*, UPN, 2004.
Lily, "Handle Your Business," *All of Us*, UPN, 2005.
Lauren, "Every Day a Little Death," *Desperate Housewives*, ABC, 2005.
Martha Krell, "Compulsion," *CSI: Crime Scene Investigation* (also known as *CSI: Las Vegas, C.S.I.* and *Les experts*), CBS, 2005.
Karen, "Waiting for Oprah," *Hot Properties*, ABC, 2005.
Janice Burke, "The Bitch Is Back," *Las Vegas*, NBC, 2005.
Karen Kunkle, "People Who Use People," *Hannah Montana*, The Disney Channel, 2006.
Karen Kunkle, "Get Down, Study–udy–udy," *Hannah Montana*, The Disney Channel, 2007.
Karen Kunkle, "Sleepwalk This Way," *Hannah Montana*, The Disney Channel, 2007.
Guest, *The 1/2 Hour News Hour*, multiple episodes, Fox News Channel, 2007.
Elizabeth, "A Chill Goes through Her Veins," *Castle*, ABC, 2009.

Television Apperances; Movies:

Liz Ortega, "Private File," *Weapons of Mass Distraction*, HBO, 1997.
Jessie Springer, TV show host, *The Last Man on Planet Earth*, UPN, 1999.

Television Apperances; Pilots:

Handsome guy's girlfriend, *Lie to Me*, Fox, 2009.

Film Appearances:

(English version) Voice of Mei–Shin, *Sazan aizu* (animated; also known as *3x3 Eyes* and *Sazan Eyes*), Bandai Entertainment, 1991.
(English version) Voice of Yohko Yamamoto, *Soreyuke! Uchu senkan Yamamoto Yoko* (animated; also known as *Starship Girl Yamamoto Yohko*), 1996.
Connie, *Cement*, Cargo Films, 1999.
Sarah, *Shattered!*, 2008.
Stewardess, *Valentine's Day*, Warner Bros., 2010.

Also appeared as Samantha, *Drinking Games*.

Stage Appearances:

Sally and understudy for the role of Mae, *Reefer Madness*, Variety Arts Theatre, New York City, 2001.
Various roles, *Louis & Keely Live at the Sahara* (musical), Audrey Skirball Kenis Theatre, Geffen Playhouse, Westwood, CA, 2009.

Also appeared as the understudy for the roles of Debbie, Roberta, and Donna, *Debbie Does Dallas*, Jane Street Theatre.

RECORDINGS

Video Games:

Voice of Rogue, *X–Men Legends*, Activision, 2004.
Ridge Racer 7, Namco Bandai Games, 2006.
Voice of Sleeping Beauty, witch 4, and Dronkey, *Shrek the Third*, Activision, 2007.
Voice of Susan Storm and Invisible Woman, *Fantastic Four: Rise of the Silver Surfer*, Take Two Interactive Software, 2007.
Voice of Dr. Lizbeth Baynham, *Mass Effect*, Microsoft Game Studios, 2007.
Voice of Merrill, Valora, and others, *Dragon Age: Origins*, Electronic Arts, 2009.

McCONNOHIE, Michael 1951–
(Michael McConnahie, Michael McConnihie, Mike McConnohie, Mike McConohie, Jeffrey Platt, Jeremy Platt)

PERSONAL

Full name, Michael D. McConnohie; born July 23, 1951, in Mansfield, OH. *Education:* Phoenix College, A.A., 1975; California State University, Northridge,

B.A., 1981; attended University of California, Los Angeles, 1983–84. *Avocational Interests:* Computing, travel, scuba diving.

Addresses: *Office*—Voxworks Ltd., 5348 Vegas Dr., Suite 14, Las Vegas, NV 89108. *Agent*—Kristene Wallis, Wallis Agency, 210 Pass Ave., Suite 205, Burbank, CA 91505.

Career: Actor, voice artist, director, and writer. Voxworks (voice talent agency), Las Vegas, NV, president; worked as a foreign dubbing supervisor, voice director, and post–production voice for automated dialog replacement and loop groups. Worked in radio in Des Moines, IA, Phoenix, AZ, and Los Angeles; appeared in radio and television commercials; appeared in reenactments for museum and film studio tours and for Renaissance Pleasure Faire; also appeared in industrial films. *Military service:* U.S. Marine Corps.

Member: Screen Actors Guild, American Federation of Radio and Television Artists, Actors' Equity Association.

CREDITS

Television Appearances; Animated Series:
Voice of Rolf Emerson, *Robotech,* syndicated, 1985.

Voice of Cosmos, Tracks, and other voices, *Transformers* (also known as *Super God Robot Force, Tatakae! Cho robot seimeitai Transformers, Transformers: Generation 1,* and *Transformers: 2010*), syndicated, 1985–86.

(As Mike McConnohie) Voice of Cross Country and E5 Robert M. Blais, *G.I. Joe* (also known as *Action Force* and *Chijo saikyo no Expert Team G.I. Joe*), syndicated, 1986.

Voice of Ectar and Lexor, *Visionaries: Knights of the Magical Light* (also known as *Visionaries*), syndicated, 1987.

Voice of Gork, *Masked Rider* (also known as *Saban's "Masked Rider"*), 1995–96.

Voice of Norris Packard, *Mobile Suit Gundam: The 08th MS Team* (also known as *Kido senshi gundam: Dai 08 MS shotai*), Cartoon Network, 1996.

Voice of Ben Packer, *Bureau of Alien Detectors,* UPN, 1996.

Voice of Fred Lou, Harry MacDougal, and Fred's bodyguard, *Outlaw Star,* Cartoon Network, 1998.

Voice of Sneero, *Walter Melon,* Fox, 1998.

Voice of Soushi Okina, *Rurouni Kenshin,* 2000.

Voice of funeral unit commander, Dignitary A, and general, *Argentosoma* (also known as *Arujento soma*), 2000.

Voice of Hibiki's grandfather, Doyen, and others, *Vandread* (also known as *Vandread: The Second Stage*), 2000, 2001.

Voice of Azulongmon, Candlemon, and Vajramon (Henry's sensei), *Digimon: Digital Monsters* (also known as *Digimon 02, Digimon 03, Digimon: Season 3,* and *Digimon Tamers*), Fox, 2000–2002, then ABC Family, 2002–2003.

Voice of Ironhide and Hotshot, *Transformers: Robots in Disguise,* Fox, 2001–2002.

Voice of teacher and Count Akuma, *Gate Keepers* (also known as *Gate Keepers 21*), 2002.

Voice of Cummings, *Geneshaft,* G4 Tech TV, 2003.

Voice of Alec, *Scrapped Princess* (also known as *Sukurappudo purinsesu* and *Sutepri*), Cartoon Network, 2004.

Voice of Rikie, *Samurai Champloo* (also known as *Samurai chanpuru*), Cartoon Network, 2004.

Voice of Lance of the Beast Sword, *Rave Master,* Cartoon Network, 2004.

Voice of Takekawa and commander, *Ghost in the Shell: Stand Alone Complex* (also known as *Ghost in the Shell: Stand Alone Complex 2nd Gig, Kokaku kidotai: S.A.C. 2nd Gig,* and *Kokaku kidotai: Stand Alone Complex*), Cartoon Network, 2004–2005.

Voice of Keiichi Ikari, *Paranoia Agent* (also known as *Moso dairinin*), Cartoon Network, 2005.

Voice of Mousou and Hoki, *Naruto* (also known as *Naruto Shounen–hen*), Cartoon Network, 2005.

Narrator, *Bobobo–bo Bo–bobo,* Cartoon Network, 2005–2007.

Voice of Husserl, *Ergo Proxy,* 2006.

Voice of golden bat, *Android Kikaider: The Animation* (also known as *Humanoid Kikaider: The Animation, Kikaider,* and *Jinzo ningen Kikaida: The Animation*); voice of Chojiro Sasakibe, *Bleach,* Cartoon Network; voices of hospital guard, male television show host, and Gate Company chairman, *Cowboy Bebop* (also known as *Kauboi bibappu*); voices, *Daigunder* (also known as *Bakuto sengen daigunda* and *Daigunda*); voices of Candlemon leader, Golemon, Sepikmon, and Vademon, *Digimon Frontier*; voices of VESPER leader, Uncle Sakuta, and ship captain, *Mahoromatic* (also known as *Mahoromatic: Automatic Maiden* and *Mahoromatic: Automatic Maiden "Something More Beautiful"*); voice of Kinue, *Mirage of Blaze* (also known as *Hono no miraju*); (as Michael McConnahie) voice of Minoru Edajima, *Please Teacher!* (also known as *Onegai Teacher!*); voices of Teknoman Lance and Ringo Richards, *Teknoman* (also known as *Starknight Tekkaman Blade* and *Uchu no kishi tekkaman bureido*).

Television Appearances; Live Action Series:
Member of the Amazing Dolphin Brothers, *The Gong Show,* NBC, 1978.

Little Michael McConnohie, *The Gong Show,* syndicated, 1988.

Television Appearances; Movies:
Voice of detective, *8–Man After* (animated), Sci–Fi Channel, 1995.

Harbormaster Bill, *Long Lost Son,* Lifetime, 2006.

Also appeared in the television movie *What Should You Do?*, Lifetime.

Television Appearances; Miniseries:
Voice, *Chasing the Sun*, PBS, 2001.
Voice of Timmer, *Immortal Grand Prix* (animated), Cartoon Network, 2003.

Television Appearances; Live Action Episodes:
Voice of Gork, "A Friend in Needs: Parts 1 & 3," *Mighty Morphin' Power Rangers* (also known as *Mighty Morphin Alien Rangers*, *Mighty Morph'n Power Rangers*, and *Power Rangers Ninja*), 1995.
Voice of Strike Out, "The Curve Ball," *Power Rangers Turbo*, 1997.
Voice of Motor Mantis, "Mean Wheels Mantis," *Power Rangers Lost Galaxy* (also known as *Operation Lightspeed*), Fox, 1999.
Voice of Mantevil, "Yesterday Again," *Power Rangers Lightspeed Rescue*, Fox, 2000.
Narrator, "Lionheart," *Power Rangers Wild Force*, Fox, 2002.
Max Cartwright, "The Greenhouse Effect," *The District*, CBS, 2002.

Also appeared in episodes of *Arrest and Trial*, *General Hospital*, ABC, *Jimmy Kimmel Live!*, ABC, and *Passions*, NBC.

Television Appearances; Animated Episodes:
Voice of mole monster, "The Poe and the Pendulum," *Beetleborgs Metallix* (also known as *Saban's "Beetleborgs Metallix"*), 1997.
Voice of Schwarzwald and Michael Seebach, "Underground Terror," *The Big O* (also known as *The Big O II*), 1999.
Voice of Schwarzwald and Michael Seebach, "Enemy Is Another Big!," *The Big O* (also known as *The Big O II*), 2000.
Voice of Cynthia's father, "Polarization War," *Cyborg 009* (also known as *Cyborg 009: The Cyborg Soldier* and *Saibogu 009*), 2001.
Voice of Captain Jurgens, "Blue Monday," *Kokyo shihen Eureka Sebun* (also known as *Eureka 7* and *Psalms of Planets Eureka Seven*), Cartoon Network, c. 2006.
Voice of Captain Jurgens, "Acperiance 1," *Kokyo shihen Eureka Sebun* (also known as *Eureka 7* and *Psalms of Planets Eureka Seven*), Cartoon Network, c. 2006.
Voice of Captain Jurgens, "The Beginning," *Kokyo shihen Eureka Sebun* (also known as *Eureka 7* and *Psalms of Planets Eureka Seven*), Cartoon Network, c. 2006.
Voice of Cherrymon, "Digivice Meltdown!," *Digimon Data Squad* (also known as *Digimon Savers*), The Disney Channel, 2008.

Voice of Cherrymon, "The Wild Boy of the Digital World," *Digimon Data Squad* (also known as *Digimon Savers*), The Disney Channel, 2008.
Voice of sand ninja, "Noruma kuria," *Naruto: Shippuden*, The Disney Channel, 2009.

Television Work; Episodic:
(As Michael McConnihie) Additional voices, "The Deserter," *Avatar: The Last Airbender*, Nickelodeon, 2005.

Directed episodes of several animated series, including *Swiss Family Robinson*, The Family Channel.

Animated Film Appearances:
(As Jeffrey Platt) Voice of Rolf Emerson, *Robotech: The Movie*, 1986.
Voice of Rolf Emerson, *Robotech II: The Sentinels*, 1986.
Voice of Cross Country, *G.I. Joe: The Movie* (also known as *Action Force: The Movie*), 1987.
(As Platt) Narrator, *The Adventures of Manxmouse* (also known as *The Legend of Manxmouse* and *Manxmouse*), 1989.
Voice of Van Buskirk, *Lensman* (also known as *Lensman: Secret of the Lens* and *SF Shinseiki Lensman*), 1990.
Voice of Shin, *Fist of the North Star* (also known as *Hokuto no ken*), Streamline, 1991.
Voice of Etiquette Master, *Little Nemo: Adventures in Slumberland* (also known as *Little Nemo*), Hemdale Releasing, 1992.
Voice of Leonard Dawson, *The Professional*, Streamline, 1992.
Voice of Hiakowa, *Tokyo: The Last Megalopolis* (also known as *Teito monogatari*), Streamline, 1993.
(Uncredited) Voice of police chief, *Lethal Panther 2* (also known as *Partners in Law* and *Magkasangga sa batas*), 1993.
Voice of Mughi, *Dirty Pair* (also known as *Dirty Pair: The Movie*, *Original Dirty Pair: Project Eden*, and *Dati pea gekijo–ban*), Streamline, 1994.
Voice of Demitrio Mardini, *Armitage: Dual–Matrix*, 2002.
Voice of captain, *Deadly Cargo* (also known as *Camara oscura*), Manga Films, 2003.
Voice of forensics people, security people, and member of Section 9, *Innocence* (also known as *Ghost in the Shell 2: Innocence*, *Innocence: Ghost in the Shell*, and *Innocence—Inosensu*), DreamWorks, 2004.
Voice of Huntley Grimes, *Frog–g–g!*, End of All Cinema, 2004.
Voice, *Appleseed* (also known as *Appurushida*), Allied Artists, 2006.
Narrator and voice of Shinichi Mechazawa, *Cromartie High School* (also known as *Chromartie High–The Movie*, *Cromartie High: The Movie*, and *Sakigake!! Kuromati Koko: The Movie*), Tokyo Shock, 2006.

Voice of George Sternberg, *Sea Monsters: A Prehistoric Adventure* (short film), National Geographic Giant Screen Films, 2007.

Voice of WilPharma chief executive, *Resident Evil: Degeneration* (also known as *Biohazard CG, Biohazard: Degeneration,* and *Resident Evil CG*), Sony Pictures Home Entertainment, 2008.

Voice of American newscaster, *Fly Me to the Moon,* 2008.

(Uncredited) Voices of The Foreheads, *Trail of the Screaming Forehead,* IPA Asia Pacific, 2009.

Also provided voices for English–language versions of many other anime films, including voice of Cagliostro, *Arsene Lupin and the Castle of Cagliostro* (also known as *The Castle of Cagliostro, Lupin III: Castle of Cagliostro, Lupin the Third: The Castle of Cagliostro,* and *Rupan sansei: Kariosutoro no shiro*); voice of Loose Cannon (Mad Dog), *Attack the Gas Station!* (also known as *Kayuso seubgyuksageun*); (as Mike McConnohie) voices, *Barefoot Gen* (also known as *Hadashi no Gen*); voice of Fujitaka Kinomoto, *Cardcaptor Sakura: The Sealed Card* (also known as *Kadokaputa Sakura: Fuin sareta kado*); voice of Inspector Nitta, *Crying Freeman* (also known as *Crying Freeman 1: Portrait of a Killer,* and *Kuraingu furiman*) and *Crying Freeman 4: A Taste of Revenge* (also known as *Crying Freeman: Chapter 5—The Impersonator, Crying Freeman 4: The Hostages,* and *Crying Freeman 4: Oshu Tokoku*); voices of General Pei and Tao Pai Pai, *Dragon Ball: Mystical Adventure* (also known as *Doragon boru: Makafushigi dai boken*); voice, *Ekusu doraiba: Nina ando rei denja zon;* voice of Rico Ganbino, *Ekusu doraiba za mubi;* voices of Goman and secretary, *Gundress;* (as Mike McConnohie) voice of Mika, *The Little Polar Bear* (also known as *Der kleine eisbaer* and *Der kleine eisbaer–Der Kinofilm*); voice of Gordon, *Lupin III: The Mystery of Mamo, Lupin the 3rd: The Movie—The Secret of Mamo, Secret of Mamo,* and *Rupan Sansei: Mamo karano chousen*); voice of Ramba Ral, *Mobile Suit Gundam I* (also known as *Kido senshi Gundami I*) and *Mobile Suit Gundam II: Soldiers of Sorrow* (also known as *Kido senshi Gandamu II: Ai senshihen*); voice of Director Makino, *Naruto the Movie: Ninja Clash in the Land of Snow* (also known as *Gekijo–ban Naruto: Daikatsugeki! Yukihime ninpocho dattebayo!!*); voice of reporter, *Neo Tokyo* (also known as *Labyrinth Tales, Manie–Manie,* and *Meikyu monogatari*); voice of Leonard Dawson, *The Professional: Golgo 13* (also known as *Golgo 13*); (as Jeremy Platt) voice of King Drako, *Windaria* (also known as *Once upon a Time* and *Dowa meita senshi Windaria*); voice of Kamiya, *Zeiram 2* (also known as *Zeiramu 2*).

Live Action Film Appearances:
Voice of Master Tatsu, *Teenage Mutant Ninja Turtles* (also known as *Teenage Mutant Ninja Turtles: The Movie* and *Teenage Mutant Ninja Turtles: The Original Movie*), New Line Cinema, 1990.

Voice of Tatsu, *Teenage Mutant Ninja Turtles II: The Secret of the Ooze,* New Line Cinema, 1991.
Stan, *The Bike Squad,* Mainline Releasing, 2002.

Film Work; Additional Voices:
Akira (also known as *Akira: The Special Edition*), Animaze, 2001.

Stage Appearances:
Appeared as Lancelot in the musical *Camelot,* Hawthorne Showcase Theatre; Lieutenant Practice, *Little Murders,* Drake Theatre, Des Moines, IA; Don Quixote (title role), *Man of la Mancha* (musical), Burbank Little Theatre, Burbank, CA; and Tom Paine's Reputation, *Tom Paine,* Drake Theatre.

RECORDINGS

Live Action Videos:
Narrator and Dr. Mario Ezekiel Chang–Goldstein, *How to Do the Asian Squat,* 2002.
Himself, *Adventures in Voice Acting,* 2008.

Animated Videos:
Voice of man, *Robot Carnival,* 1991.
Voice of D, *Vampire Hunter D* (also known as *Kyuketsuki Hunter D*), 1992.
Voices, *Saint Tail* (also known as *Mysterious Thief Saint Tail* and *Kaitou Saint Tail*), 1995.
Voice, *Trigun* (also known as *Trigun #1: The $60,000,000,000 Man* and *Toraigan*), 1998.
(As Mike McConnohie) Voice of Captain Harlock, *Kasei ryodan danasight four–nine* (also known as *DNA Sights 999.9* and *Fire Force DNA Sight 999.9*), 1998.
Voice, *The Prince of Light: The Legend of Ramayana,* 2001.
Voice of Minami Kuramitsu and Mr. Kaunaq, *Tenchi Muyo! GXP,* 2002.
Voice of Gale, Prime Minister Marius, Worsley, Duke Nowels, and several other characters, *Last Exile,* Geneon Entertainment, 2003.
Voice of Principal Burden, *Scream Bloody Murder,* York Entertainment, 2003.
Voice of Kimata, shop owner, and Izaki, *Texhnolyze,* Pioneer Entertainment, 2004.
Voice of Don Pirulo, *Gad Guard,* ADV Films, 2004.
Voice of old gentleman and coworker, *Mermaid Forest* (also known as *Rumic Theatre: Mermaid Forest, Ningyo no mori,* and *Takahashi Rumiko gekijo: Ningyo no mori*), Geneon Entertainment, 2004.
Voice of Doug, *Licensed by Royalty,* Pioneer Entertainment, 2004.
Voice of Big Daddy, Deed, Scott, and others, *Gungrave,* Geneon Entertainment, 2004.
Voice of Yamazaki and Shibata, *Ghost Talker's Daydream,* Bandai, 2004.

Voice of Dr. Rem and Dr. Steiner, *Galerians: Rion,* Image Entertainment, 2004.

Voice of Hannibal army commander, announcer, Guan Yu, and others, *Aquarian Age Saga II: Don't Forget Me ...,* Broccoli International, 2005.

Voice of bodyguard, *Phantom: The Animation,* Anime Works, 2005.

Voice of Goutetsu, *Street Fighter Alpha: Generations,* Manga Video, 2005.

Voice of Babbo, *MAER: Maerchen Awakens Romance* (also known as *Meru hevun*), Viz Media, 2006.

Voice of God of Select–o–Vision, *Kamichu!,* Geneon Entertainment, 2006.

Voice of police chief, *Karas: The Prophecy,* Manga Video, 2006.

Voice of Wild Geese member, *Hellsing Ultimate,* 2006.

Voice of police chief, *Karas: The Revelation,* Manga Video, 2007.

Voice of Seth, *Street Fighter IV: The Ties that Bind* (also known as *Sutorito faita IV—Aratanaru kizuna*), Capcom Entertainment, 2009.

Voice of master, *Babel II: Perfect Collection* (also known as *Babel nisei*); voice, *Casshan* (also known as *Casshan: Robot Hunter*); voices of Zess Voder and Edge, *Cosmo Warrior Zero;* voices of driver and cell guard, *Crimson Wolf* and *Hon ran*); voice of Oran Garcia, *Dirty Pair: Mystery of Norlandia* (also known as *Original Dirty Pair #5: Affair of Norlandia* and *Dati pea: Norandia no nazo*); voice of Shinichi Ibaragi, *Figure 17* (also known as *Figyua 17 Tsubasa & Hikaru*); voice of Cross–Country, *G.I. Joe: Arise, Serpentor, Arise!* (also known as *Action Force: Arise, Serpentor, Arise!*); voice of Rikushiro Onigawara, *Ground Defense Force Mao–chan* (also known as *Rikujo Boei-tai Mao–chan*); voices of Follower Deputy A and Joe, *Gun Frontier;* voices of communicator and Baker, *Haibane renmei;* voice of Ider, *Hare+Guu,* (also known as *The Jungle Was Nice, Then Came Guu, Hare nochi Guu, Janguru wa itsumo hare nochi Guu,* and *JungleGuu*); voices of policeman and Celestial, *Heat Guy J;* narrator, *Ikki tosen;* voice of Yuichi Boss Tachibana, *Initial D* (also known as *Inisharu D* and *Initial D: Second Stage*); voice, *Jin Jin;* voice of Dr. Kozaburo Nambu, *Kagaku ninja tai Gatchaman*); voice of the emperor of Britannia, *Kodo giasu: Hangyaku no rurushu* (also known as *Code Gaess: Lelouch of the Rebellion*); voices of Hakura's father, flier, and Honi, *Kurogane Communication;* (as Mike McConohie) B. D., *Megazone 23 II* (also known as *Megazone 23 Part 2: Project Card* and *Megazone 23 Part 2: Himitsu Kudasai*); voice of Axis general, *Mobile Suit Gundam 0083: Stardust Memory* (also known as *Kido senshi gundam 0083: Stardust Memory*); voice of Benkei Musashibou, *New Getter Robo* (also known as *Shin getter robo*); voice of operator, *Noein—To Your Other Self;* voice of Minamoto no Mitsunaka, *Otogi zoshi;* voice of Yassaba Jim, *Overman King–Gainer;* voice of Tatsu, *PokeMadness 3000;* voice of Chou, *Sazan Eyes* (also known as *3x3 Eyes* and *Sa-*

zan aizu); voice of Tadanori Kiryu, *Scryed* (also known as *Sukuraido* and *s–CRY–ed*); voice of Kozo Minashiro, *Soukyu no fafuna* (also known as *Fafner*), Xebec; voices of Ilita's subordinate, Dr. Hassan, pirate corpse, and several other characters, *Space Pirate Captain Harlock: The Endless Odyssey* (also known as *Space Pirate Captain Herlock: The Endless Odyssey—Outside Legend*); voice of Gordon, *Spirit of Wonder: Miss China's Ring* (also known as *Spirit of Wonder: Miss China's Melancholy* and *Spirit of Wonder: China–san no yuutsu*); voices of D3, Minami Kuramitsu, and others, *Tenchi Muyo! Ryo Oki* (also known as *No Need for Tenchi, Tenchi Muyo! Ryo–oh–ki,* and *This End Up!*); voice of Hehachiro, *Tsukikage Ran: Carried by the Wind;* voice of Gekkei, *The Twelve Kingdoms* (also known as *12 kokuki*); voice of Umihito Katase, *Uchu no suteruvia* (also known as *Cosmic Stellvia, Stellvia, Stellvia of the Universe, Sora no Stellvia,* and *Uchu no Stellvia*); voices of Kouichi and Yuko's father, *Vampire Princess Miyu;* voices of anchorman and Issei Sagawa, *Weather Girl* (also known as *A Weatherwoman* and *Otenki–oneesan*); voice of Durban, *Wild ARMs: Twilight Venom;* voices of Yuji Higashi, Kazuma Kurata, Twuneo Tazawa, and several other characters, *Witch Hunter Robin;* voice of Kyogou Monou, *X;* voice of Kanahara, *Yojimbo of the Wind* (also known as *Bodyguard of the Wind* and *Kaze no yojimbo*); voice of Sada, *Y's II: Castle in the Heavens* (also known as *Ys 2: Citadel in the Sky, Ys II Temple in the Sky,* and *Isu II: Tenku no shinden*); and voice of Li–Akron, *Zatch Bell!* Some of these videos were originally broadcast as Japanese–language television series.

Video Games:

(Also director) Voices of Lieutenant Christensen and Commander Taraz, *Star Trek: 25th Anniversary Enhanced,* 1992.

Voices of Gellman, Savant, and first soldier, *Star Trek: Judgment Rites,* 1993.

Voice, *Might and Magic: World of Xeen,* 1994.

Voices of Stump Ettin, Scourge, and whispering voice, *Stonekeep,* 1995.

Voice, *Descent 2,* 1996.

Voice, *Might and Magic VII: For Blood and Honor,* 1999.

Voices of Necromancer and Warriv, *Diablo II,* Blizzard Entertainment, 2000.

Voice of Necromancer, *Diablo II: Lord of Destruction,* Blizzard Entertainment, 2001.

Voice of Gerhart Orvelle, *Growlander III: The Dual Darkness,* 2001.

(Uncredited) Voice of Commander Margulis, *Xenosaga Episode I: The Will to Power* (also known as *Xenosaga, Xenosaga I: Reloaded, Xenosaga Episode I: Chikara he no ishi, Xenosaga Episode I: Der Wille zur macht,* and *Xenosaga Episode I Reloaded*), 2002.

(Uncredited) Voice of Xu Huang, *Kessen II,* 2002.

Voice of Lance, *Groove Adventure Rave: Fighting Live* (also known as *Rave Master*), 2002.

Voices of Lord Uther and Kel Thuzad, *WarCraft III: Reign of Chaos,* Blizzard Entertainment, 2002.

(Uncredited) Voices of Captain Gordon and Maderas, *Disgaea: Hour of Darkness* (also known as *Makai senki deisugaia*), Atlus USA, 2003.

(Uncredited) Voices of Zhang Liao and Zhou Tai, *Dynasty Warriors 4* (also known as *Dynasty Warriors 4: Hyper, Shin sangoku musou–Hyper,* and *Shin sangoku muso 3*), KOEI, 2003.

(Uncredited) Narrator, *Dynasty Tactics 2* (also known as *Sankokushi senki 2*), KOEI, 2003.

(Uncredited) Voices of Kel'thuzad and the recycled Uther, *Warcraft III: The Frozen Throne,* Blizzard Entertainment/Sierra, 2003.

(Uncredited) Voices of Zhang Liao and Zhou Tai, *Dynasty Warriors 4: Xtreme Legends* (also known as *Shin sangoku muso 3 mushoden*), KOEI, 2003.

(Uncredited) Narrator and voice of Rinaldi Gandolfi, *Castlevanis* (also known as *Castlevania: Lament of Innocence*), Konami of America, 2003.

(Uncredited) Voices, *Front Mission 4,* Square Enix, 2004.

(Uncredited) Voices of Vox and other characters, *Star Ocean: Till the End of Time* (also released as *Star Ocean: Till the End of Time—Director's Cut*), Square Enix, 2004.

(Uncredited) Voice of Botos, *Rockman X Command Mission* (also known as *Mega Man Command Mission*), Capcom Entertainment, 2004.

(Uncredited) Voices of Zhang Liao and Zhou Tai, *Dynasty Warriors 4: Empires* (also known as *Shin sangoku muso 3: Empires*), KOEI, 2004.

(Uncredited) Voice of Glen Ogawa, *Breakdown,* Namco Hometek, 2004.

Voice of X, *Cool Girl* (also known as *Cy Girls*), Konami Digital Entertainment America, 2004.

Voice of Minister Ishimura, *Shadow Hearts II* (also known as *Shadow Hearts: Covenant*), Midway Home Entertainment, 2004.

Voice of Margulis, *Xenosaga Episode II: Jenseits von gut und boese*), Namco Hometek, 2004.

(Uncredited) Voice of Glen, *Suikoden IV* (also known as *Genso suikoden IV*), Konami Digital Entertainment America, 2004.

(Uncredited) Voices, *Biohazard Outbreak: File 2* (also known as *Resident Evil: Outbreak—File #2*), Capcom Entertainment, 2004.

Voices of Slumlord Valthun, Plordo Blotterdook, and Steward Sal, *EverQuest II,* Sony Online Entertainment, 2004.

Voice of Kel'thuzad, *World of Warcraft,* Blizzard Entertainment, 2004.

Voice, *Ghost Recon Advanced Warfighter* (also known as *Tom Clancy's "Advanced Warfighter"*), 2005.

(Uncredited) Voices of Zhang Liao and Zhou Tai, *Dynasty Warriors 5* (also known as *Shin sangoku muso 4*), KOEI, 2005.

Voice of ogre, *Rave Master: Special Attach Force,* Konami Computer Entertainment, 2005.

(Uncredited) Voices, *Grandia III,* Square Enix, 2005.

(Uncredited) Voices of gang members, *Beat Down* (also known as *Beat Down: Fists of Vengeance*), Capcom Entertainment, 2005.

(Uncredited) Voices of gang members, *Urban Reign,* Namco Hometek, 2005.

(Uncredited) Voices of Zhang Liao and Zhou Tai, *Dynasty Warriors 5: Xtreme Legends* (also known as *Shin sangoku muso 4 mushoden*), KOEI, 2005.

(Uncredited) Voice of Astaroth, *Soul Calibur III: Ardace Edition* (also known as *Soulcalibur III*), Namco Hometek, 2005.

(Uncredited) Voice of Pete Saville, *Eureka Seven Vol. 1: The New Wave* (also known as *Eureka sebun TR1: New Wave*), Namco Bandai Games America, 2005.

(Uncredited) Narrator, *Castlevania: Curse of Darkness* (also known as *Akumajo Dorakiyura: Yami no juin*), Konami Digital Entertainment America, 2005.

(Uncredited) Voice of Vandesdelca Musto Fende/Van Grants, *Tales of the Abyss,* Namco Bandai Games America, 2005.

(Uncredited) Voices of Sir John and others, *Steambot Chronicles* (also known as *Ponkotsu roman daikatsugeki banpi torotto*), Atlus USA, 2006.

Voice of Margulis, *Xenosaga Episode III: Also Sprach Zarathustra,* Namco Bandai Games America, 2006.

Voice, *EverQuest II: Kingdom of Sky,* Sony Online Entertainment, 2006.

Voice of Manzo the Saw, *Samurai Champloo* (also known as *Samurai Champloo: Sidetracked*), Namco Bandai Games America, 2006.

(Uncredited) Voice of Captain Gordon, *Disgaea 2: Cursed Memories* (also known as *Makai senki seidugaia 2*), NIS America, 2006.

(Uncredited) Voices of Marscal Godwin, Skald Egan, ship captain, and a Godwin soldier, *Genso suikoden V* (also known as *Suikoden V*), Konami Digital Entertainment America, 2006.

(Uncredited) Voices of Zhang Liao and Zhou Tai, *Dynasty Warriors 5: Empires* (also known as *Shin sangoku muso 4: Empires*), KOEI, 2006.

(Uncredited) Voices, *Ace Combat Zero: The Belkan War* (also known as *Ace Combat: The Belkan War*), Namco Bandai Games America, 2006.

Voice of Sirius, *.hack//G.U. Vol. 1//Rebirth* (also known as *.hack//G.U. Vol. 1: Saitan*), Namco Bandai Games America, 2006.

(Uncredited) Voice of Walther, *Valkyrie Profile 2: Silmeria,* Square Enix, 2006.

First narrator and voice of head of VSSE, *Time Crisis 4,* Namco Bandai Games America, 2006.

Voice of Leighton, *Paraworld,* SEK Games, 2006.

Voice of Sirius, *.hack//G.U. Vol. 2//Reminisce* (also known as *.hack//G.U. Vol. 2: Kimi omo koe*), Namco Bandai Games America, 2006.

Voices of Gottlieb and others, *Culdcept SAGA,* Namco Bandai Games America, 2006.

Voices of Jiro's father, Marumaro's father, and Yasato, *Blue Dragon,* Microsoft, 2006.

Voice from EDF headquarters, *Earth Defense Force 2017* (also known as *Earth Defence Force 2017* and *Chikyu boeigun 3*), D3 Publisher of America, 2006.

Voice of Sirius, *.hack//G.U. Vol. 3//Redemption* (also known as *.hack//G.U. Vol. 3: Aruku you na hayasa de*), Namco Bandai Games America, 2007.

Voice, *Supreme Commander*, THQ, 2007.

Voice from agency, *Crackdown*, Microsoft, 2007.

Voice, *Tom Clancy's Ghost Recon: Advanced Warfighter 2*, Ubi Soft Entertainment, 2007.

(Uncredited) Voices of Zhang Liao and Zhou Tai, *Warriors Orochi* (also known as *Muso Orochi*), KOEI, 2007.

(Uncredited) Voices, *Ace Combat 6: Fires of Liberation* (also known as *Ace Combat 6: Kaiho heno senka*), Namco Bandai Games America, 2007.

Voices, *Jericho* (also known as *Clive Barker's "Jericho"*), Codemasters, 2007.

(Uncredited) Voice of Astaroth Alpha, *Soulcalibur Legends,* Namco Bandai Games America, 2007.

(Uncredited) Narrator and voice of Professor Wilkens, *Trauma Center: New Blood* (also known as *Kadoukeusu: Nyu burado*), Atlus USA, 2007.

(Uncredited) Voice of Dr. Paradigm, *Guilty Gear 2: Overture*, Aksys Games, 2007.

(Uncredited) Voices, *Operation Darkness*, Atlus USA, 2008.

Voice of Seth, *Street Fighter IV,* Capcom Entertainment, 2008.

(Uncredited) Voice of Astaroth, *Soulcalibur IV,* Namco Bandai Games America, 2008.

(Uncredited) Voices, *Tales of Vesperia* (also known as *Teiruzu obu Vesuperia*), Namco Bandai Games America, 2008.

(Uncredited) Voice of Balbagan, *Infinite Undiscovery,* Square Enix, 2008.

Voices of the Lich king, King Ymiron, and Commander Kolurg, *World of Warcraft: Wrath of the Lich King,* Blizzard Entertainment, 2008.

Voices of Kano, Ganthet, and newscaster, *Mortal Kombat vs. DC Universe,* Midway, 2008.

Voice of Ludope, *The Last Remnant,* Square Enix, 2008.

Voice of Raki, *Eternal Poison,* 2008.

(Uncredited) Voice of Stephen D. Kenny, *Star Ocean: The Last Hope,* Square Enix, 2009.

Voice of Red Faction commander, *Red Faction Guerrilla,* THQ, 2009.

Voice of Jegran, *Final Fantasy Crystal Chronicles: The Crystal Bearers* (also known as *Fainaru fantaji kurisutaru kuronikuru: Kurisutaru beara*), Square Enix, 2009.

(Uncredited) Voice of Dr. Michael Kaufmann, *Silent Hill: Shattered Memories,* Konami Digital Entertainment America, 2009.

Also voices of Nana Man and Dr. Peelgood, *Clayfighter.*

Audio Books; Reader:

The Tao of Physics by Fritjof Capra, Audio Renaissance, 1990.

If You Meet the Buddha on the Road, Kill Him by Sheldon B. Kopp, Audio Renaissance, 1990.

Pilgrimage: A Memoir of Poland and Rome by James A. Michener, Audio Renaissance, 1990.

Sudden Fury by Leslie Walker, Audio Renaissance, 1990.

Two of a Kind: The Hillside Stranglers by Darcy O'Brien, Audio Renaissance, 1990.

The Book of Qualities, Audio Renaissance, 1991.

A Faint Cold Fear by Robert Daley, Audio Renaissance, 1991.

The Executioner's Song by Norman Mailer, Audio Renaissance, 1991.

In Cold Blood, Audio Renaissance, 1991.

Deadly Medicine, Audio Renaissance, 1991.

Perot: An Unauthorized Biography by Todd Mason, Audio Renaissance, 1992.

18mm Blues by Gerald A. Browne, Audio Renaissance, 1993.

Zero Coupon by Paul Erdman, Audio Renaissance, 1993, unabridged edition, Books on Tape, 1996.

The Juicy Truth about Johnny Appleseed, Soundlines Entertainment, 1994.

Zero Coupon: Library Edition, Audio Renaissance, 1994.

Fatal Cure by Robin Cook, Audio Renaissance, unabridged edition, Books on Tape, both 1994.

Liz: An Intimate Biography of Elizabeth Taylor, Audio Renaissance, 1995.

A Lifetime of Riches: The Biography of Napoleon Hill by Michael J. Ritt, Jr. and C. David Heyman, Audio Renaissance, 1995.

Eighteen Millimeter Blues, Books on Tape, 1998.

High Tech High Touch: Technology and Our Search for Meaning by John Naisbitt, Nana Naisbitt, and Douglas Philips, Soundelux Audio, 1999.

Bill and Hillary: The Marriage by Christopher P. Andersen, Soundelux Audio, 1999.

Forbes Greatest Technology Stories: Inspiring Tales of the Entrepreneurs and Inventors Who Revolutionized Modern Business by Jeffrey S. Young, Audio Scholar, 2000.

Deus Lo Volt! A Chronicle of the Crusades by Evan S. Connell, Soundelux Audio, 2000.

The Double Helix by James D. Watson, Soundelux Audio, 2000.

The Informant: A True Story by Kurt Eichenwald, Soundelux Audio, 2000.

WRITINGS

Animated Television Episodes:

Samurai Pizza Cats (also known as *Kyatto ninden teyandee*), 1991.

Digimon: Digital Monsters (also known as *Digimon 02, Digimon 03, Digimon: Season 3,* and *Digimon Tamers*), Fox, between 1999 and 2001.

Flint the Time Detective, Fox Family, 2000.

"The Two Faces of Ultra Magnus," *Transformers: Robots in Disguise,* Fox, 2001.

"Peril from the Past," *Transformers: Robots in Disguise,* Fox, 2001.

"Mistaken Identity," *Transformers: Robots in Disguise,* Fox, 2002.

Automated dialog replacement scriptwriter, *Scrapped Princess* (also known as *Sukurappudo purinsesu* and *Sutepri*), Cartoon Network, 2004.

Writer for various other English–language television series, including *Funky Fables,* syndicated; *Grimm's Fairy Tales,* Nickelodeon; *Gulliver's Travels,* syndicated; *Honeybee Hutch,* syndicated; *The Little Mermaid,* HBO; *Ollie's Oxtails,* BBC Australia; *Pinocchio,* HBO; and *Swiss Family Robinson,* The Family Channel.

OTHER SOURCES

Electronic:

Michael McConnohie Official Site, http://www.michaelmcconnohie.com, February 8, 2010.

McDONELL, Ryan 1983–

PERSONAL

Full name, Ryan Christopher McDonell; born July 13, 1983, in Berwick, Nova Scotia, Canada; son of Hughie (a folk musician) and Colleen McDonell.

Addresses: *Agent*—Red Management, 415 W. Esplanade, Vancouver, British Columbia V7M 1A6, Canada.

Career: Actor. Member of the rock band TV Heart Attack. Previously a member of the rock band Fifth Penny Back.

CREDITS

Television Appearances; Series:
Lieutenant Eammon "Gonzo" Pike, a recurring role, *Battlestar Galactica* (also known as *BSG*), Sci–Fi Channel, 2006–2008.

Television Appearances; Episodic:
Street punk #1, "Azoth the Avenger Is a Friend of Mine," *The Twilight Zone,* UPN, 2002.

"Machinery of the Mind," *Andromeda* (also known as *Gene Roddenberry's "Andromeda"*), syndicated, 2004.

Dealer, "The Yogi," *The Collector,* City TV, 2004.

Phillip Murch, "Homecoming," *Masters of Horror,* Showtime, 2005.

With band TV Heart Attack, "Crossroads," *Whistler,* CTV and The N, 2007.

Stuart Campbell, "Metallo," *Smallville* (also known as *Smallville Beginnings* and *Smallville: Superman the Early Years*), The WB, 2009.

Stuart Campbell, "Crossfire," *Smallville* (also known as *Smallville Beginnings* and *Smallville: Superman the Early Years*), The WB, 2009.

Stuart Campbell, "Pandora," *Smallville* (also known as *Smallville Beginnings* and *Smallville: Superman the Early Years*), The WB, 2009.

Stuart Campbell, "Sacrifice," *Smallville* (also known as *Smallville Beginnings* and *Smallville: Superman the Early Years*), The WB, 2010.

Also appeared as a musical guest star in an episode of *Kaya,* MTV.

Television Appearances; Movies:
Anderson, *A Very Cool Christmas* (also known as *Too Cool for Christmas*), Lifetime, 2004.

C. J., *Meltdown* (also known as *Meltdown: Days of Destruction*), Sci–Fi Channel, 2006.

Jonathan Gillis, *Final Days of Planet Earth,* Hallmark Channel, 2006.

Will Spring (some sources cite Will Doyle), *Eight Days to Live,* CTV and Lifetime, 2006.

Paulie, *Destination: Infestation* (also known as *Swarm* and *Ants on a Plane*), 2007.

Patrick Hughes, *The Secret Lives of Second Wives,* Lifetime, 2008.

Film Appearances:
Russian officer, *K–19: The Widowmaker* (also known as *K*19: The Widowmaker, K–19—Showdown in der Tiefe* and *K–19: Terreur sous la mer*), Paramount, 2002.

Luke, *Snakehead Terror,* Image Entertainment, 2004.

Chip, *When Jesse Was Born* (short film), Ginger Pants Productions, 2005.

Constable #2, *Vancouver* (short film), Big Ben Pictures, 2005.

Derek, *Eighteen,* Allumination Filmworks, 2005.

Skip, *Dr. Dolittle 3* (also known as *Docteur Dolittle 3*), Twentieth Century–Fox, 2006.

Kaine Fraizer, *Slap Shot 3: The Junior League,* Universal, 2008.

(Uncredited) Student, *Elegy,* Sony Pictures Home Entertainment, 2008.

Also appeared in *Purgatory,* Ginger Pants Productions; *My Entropy,* Entropy INC; *Boys Night In,* Merge; *Temptations,* Lifetime; *Bent Cigarettes,* PMP; *Connie and*

Carla Do L.A., Universal; *The Soft Revolution,* Stampede Breakfast; *Stars Wait for Us,* NYU Films; *The Wilderness Within,* Trinity.

Stage Appearances:
Appeared as Ponyboy, *The Outsiders,* WKNS Theatre & Company; appeared in a number of productions in eastern Canada.

RECORDINGS

Video Games:
Appeared with TV Heart Attack, *NHL 09,* EA Sports; as various characters, *Skate 2,* EA Sports.

McKELLAR, Danica 1975–
(Danica McKeller)

PERSONAL

Full name, Danica Mae McKellar; born January 3, 1975, in La Jolla (some sources cite San Diego), CA; daughter of Christopher (a real estate developer) and Mahalia (a homemaker) McKellar; sister of Crystal McKellar (an actress); married Mike Verta (a composer and visual effects artist), March 22, 2009. *Education:* University of California, Los Angeles, B.S. (summa cum laude), 1998. *Avocational Interests:* Mathematics, ballroom dancing, yoga.

Addresses: *Agent*—Laura Nolan, Creative Culture, 47 East 19th St., 3rd Floor, New York, NY 10003; (voice work) CESD Voices, 10635 Santa Monica Blvd., Suite 130, Los Angeles, CA 90025. *Manager*—Matt Sherman, Matt Sherman Management, 9107 Wilshire Blvd., Suite 225, Beverly Hills, CA 90210. *Publicist*—Michelle Beta, Rogers and Cowan Public Relations, Pacific Design Center, 8687 Melrose Ave., 7th Floor, Los Angeles, CA 90069.

Career: Actress, producer, director, and writer. Morning Starlight Productions, principal; creator of the Internet advice site *DanicaMcKellar.com,* another Internet site, *MathDoesntSuck.com,* and an Internet column at the Web site *Celebrity Sightings.* Appeared in television commercials, beginning c. 1984. Cocreator of the mathematical physics theorem named the Chayes–McKellar–Winn Theorem.

Awards, Honors: Young Artist Award, best young actress in a featured, costarring, supporting, or recurring role in a comedy or drama series or special, 1989,

Young Artist Award nominations, best young actress costarring in a television series, 1990, 1992, and 1993, and TV Land Award nomination, "character you'd pay to do your homework for you," 2008, all for *The Wonder Years;* California Independent Film Festival Award (with John Milton Branton), best short film, 2002, for *Speechless.*

CREDITS

Television Appearances; Series:
Gwendolyne "Winnie" Cooper, *The Wonder Years,* ABC, 1988–93.
Elsie Snuffin, a recurring role, *The West Wing,* NBC, 2002–2003.
Voice of Freida Goren, *Static Shock!* (animated), The WB, 2003–2004.
Voices of Elsa and Renee, *Game Over,* UPN, 2004.
Maddie Monroe, *Inspector Mom,* Lifetime (also, according to some sources, an Internet series), 2006–2007.

Television Appearances; Movies:
Lindsey Scott, *Camp Cucamonga* (also known as *How I Spent My Summer* and *Lights Out*), NBC, 1990.
Kristin Guthrie, *Moment of Truth: Cradle of Conspiracy* (also known as *Cradle of Conspiracy*), NBC, 1994.
Annie Mills Carman, *Justice for Annie: A Moment of Truth Movie* (also known as *Search for Justice*), NBC, 1996.
Katherine Stern, *Path of Destruction,* Sci–Fi Channel, 2005.
Caroline, *Heatstroke,* Sci–Fi Channel, 2008.

Television Appearances; Specials:
A Busch Gardens/Sea World Summer Celebration, CBS, 1994.
TVography: The Wonder Years: Comedy Coming of Age, 2002.
The ... Annual Family Television Awards, 2004, presenter, The WB, 2005.
"Child Stars II: Growing Up in Hollywood," *Biography,* Arts and Entertainment, 2005.
Maddie Monroe, *Inspector Mom: Kidnapped in Ten Easy Steps,* 2007.

Television Appearances; Pilots:
Gwendolyne "Winnie" Cooper, *The Wonder Years,* ABC, 1988.
Maddie Monroe, *Inspector Mom,* Lifetime, 2006.

Television Appearances; Miniseries:
I Love the New Millennium, VH1, 2008.

Television Appearances; Episodic:
Nola, "Her Pilgrim Soul," *The Twilight Zone* (also known as *The New Twilight Zone*), CBS, 1985.

Deidre Dobbs, "Shelter Skelter," *The Twilight Zone* (also known as *The New Twilight Zone*), CBS, 1987.

Patty, "Day of the Orphan," *The Super Mario Bros. Super Show!*, NBC, 1989.

Voice of Lisa, "A Formula for Hate," *Captain Planet and the Planeteers* (animated; also known as *The New Adventures of Captain Planet*), TBS, 1992.

Aria Tensus, "The War Prayer," *Babylon 5* (also known as *B5*), TNT, 1994.

Laurie Maston, "Stolen Lullaby," *Walker, Texas Ranger* (also known as *Walker*), CBS, 1994.

Alison Trent, "Victims," *Sirens*, 1994.

Jolie, "As Bad as It Gets," *Working*, NBC, 1998.

Mary Dutton, "How Long Has This Been Going On?," *The Love Boat: The Next Wave*, UPN, 1998.

Loveline, 1998.

Jolie, "She Loves Me Yeah, Yeah, Yeah," *Working*, NBC, 1999.

Daughter, *Random Play*, 1999.

Happy Hour, 1999.

Wendy, "Don't Ask," *The Division* (also known as *Heart of the City*), Lifetime, 2001.

Sandrine, "Sibling Rivalry," *Even Stevens*, The Disney Channel, 2001.

"TV Child Stars Edition," *The Weakest Link* (also known as *The Weakest Link USA*), NBC, 2001.

Voice of Sapphire Stagg, "Metamorphosis: Parts 1 & 2," *Justice League* (animated; also known as *JL* and *Justice League Unlimited*), Cartoon Network, 2002.

Celebrity judge, *Pet Star*, Animal Planet, 2003.

Voice of Sharona, "My Hair Lady," *King of the Hill* (animated), Fox, 2004.

Voice of Misty, "Cheer Factor," *King of the Hill* (animated), Fox, 2004.

Sally, "Without a Tracer," *Century City*, CBS, 2004.

Claudia, "Friend or Foe?," *Eve*, UPN, 2004.

Erin Kendall, "Witness," *Navy NCIS: Naval Criminal Investigative Service* (also known as *NCIS* and *NCIS: Naval Criminal Investigative Service*), CBS, 2005.

Keirsten, "And Justice for All," *Jack & Bobby*, The WB, 2005.

Rosemary Wyatt, "Moving Day," *NYPD Blue*, ABC, 2005.

Natalie Pascal, "Feeling No Pain," *Strong Medicine*, Lifetime, 2005.

Trudy, "The Pineapple Incident," *How I Met Your Mother* (also known as *H.I.M.Y.M.*), CBS, 2005.

Herself, *Attack of the Show!*, G4, 2005.

Wanda, "Designing Mr. Perfect," *Cyberchase*, PBS, 2006.

"Life After ...," *20/20* (also known as *ABC News 20/20*), ABC, 2006.

"Person of the Week: Danica McKellar," *ABC Evening News* (also known as *ABC World News*), ABC, 2007.

Voice of Katerina "Kat" Metropoulos, "Girls on the Go!," *Random! Cartoons*, Nickelodeon, 2007.

Trudy, "Third Wheel," *How I Met Your Mother* (also known as *H.I.M.Y.M.*), CBS, 2007.

"Freddy and Danica," *Sidewalks Entertainment* (also known as *Sidewalks* and *Sidewalks Entertainment Hour*), 2007.

Current TV, 2008.

Herself, "The One with the Robot Braces," *Brink*, 2009.

Herself, "The One with the Nano Water," *Brink*, 2009.

Herself, "The One with Cellphone Microscopes," *Brink*, 2009.

Herself, "Anna's Date," *Free Radio*, Comedy Central, 2009.

Abby, "The Psychic Vortex," *The Big Bang Theory*, CBS, 2010.

Television Talk Show Guest Appearances; Episodic:

The Wayne Brady Show, syndicated, 2002.

Tavis Smiley, PBS, 2007.

Today (also known as *NBC News Today* and *The Today Show*), NBC, 2007, 2008, 2009.

Good Morning America (also known as *G.M.A.*), ABC, 2008.

Jimmy Kimmel Live! (also known as *Jimmy Kimmel*), ABC, 2008.

The Morning Show with Mike & Juliet, Fox and syndicated, 2009.

Glenn Beck, Fox News Channel, 2009.

Television Producer; Specials:

Inspector Mom: Kidnapped in Ten Easy Steps, 2007.

Television Producer; Episodic:

"The Mystery of Mrs. Plumlee," *Inspector Mom*, Lifetime, 2006.

Film Appearances:

Lauren, *Sidekicks*, Triumph Releasing, 1992.

Sarah, *XCU: Extreme Close Up* (also known as *Extreme Close–up*), Crystal Lake Entertainment, 2001.

Dana Woodman, *Speechless*, Morning Starlight Productions, 2001.

Tiffany, *Jane White Is Sick & Twisted*, Artist View Entertainment, 2001.

Molly Wright, *The Good Neighbor* (also known as *The Killer Next Door*), Creative Light Worldwide, 2001.

Sexy Sally, *Reality School*, Hypnotic Films, 2002.

Pam Hatch, *The Year that Trembled*, Novel City Pictures, 2002.

Sissie, *Hip, Edgy, Sexy, Cool*, 2002.

Debbie, *Sex and the Teenage Mind*, Goldade Productions, 2002.

Herself, *Naked Movie*, Seven Arts Entertainment, 2002.

Rachael, *Black Hole*, Hollywood Star Entertainment, 2002.

Herself, *Four Fingers of the Dragon*, Dragon Films, 2003.

Lacy Baldwin, *Raising Genius*, Allumination Filmworks, 2004.

Sleepwalker, *Intermission* (short film), 2004.

Pet shop girl, *Quiet Kill* (also known as *Nightmare Boulevard*), I.Q. Entertainment, 2004.

Emily, *Hack!,* Allumination Filmworks, 2007.

Jenny Valentine, *21 and a Wake–Up,* DMZ Productions, 2009.

Film Producer and Director:

Speechless, Morning Starlight Productions, 2001.

Broken (short film), Morning Starlight Productions, 2005.

Stage Appearances:

Rizzo, *Grease* (musical), Grove Theatre, Upland, CA, 1999.

Catherine, *Proof,* San Diego Repertory Theatre, San Diego, CA, 2003.

RECORDINGS

Videos:

Voice, *Canceled Lives: Letters from the Inside,* 1993.

Appeared in the music video "No More Rhyme" by Debbie Gibson.

Video Games:

Voice of Jubilee, *X–Men Legends,* Activision, 2004.

Voices of Lolla Cotgrove and Pona, *EverQuest II,* Sony Online Entertainment, 2004.

(As Danica McKeller) Voices, *Onimusha: Dawn of Dreams* (also known as *Shin Onimusha: Dawn of Dreams*), Capcom Entertainment, 2006.

Voice of invisible woman, *Marvel: Ultimate Alliance,* Activision, 2006.

Voice of invisible woman, *Marvel: Ultimate Alliance 2,* Savage Entertainment/Vicarious Visions/n–Space, 2009.

WRITINGS

Screenplays:

Speechless, Morning Starlight Productions, 2001.

Broken (short film), Morning Starlight Productions, 2005.

Television Episodes:

(Contributor) "The Mystery of Mrs. Plumlee," *Inspector Mom,* Lifetime, 2006.

(Additional dialogue) "The Corpse's Costume," *Inspector Mom,* Lifetime, 2006.

"Casualty Friday," *Inspector Mom,* Lifetime, 2006.

Television Writing; Other:

Inspector Mom (pilot), Lifetime, 2006.

Inspector Mom: Kidnapped in Ten Easy Steps (special), 2007.

Other:

Math Doesn't Suck: How to Survive Middle–School Math without Losing Your Mind or Breaking a Nail, Hudson Street Press, 2007.

Kiss My Math: Showing Pre–Algebra Who's Boss, Hudson Street Press, 2008.

Former columnist for the magazine *Teen Beat.* Contributor to *British Journal of Physics* and other journals.

OTHER SOURCES

Periodicals:

Chicago Tribune, March 24, 2009.

Newsweek, August 6, 2007, p. 43.

New York Times, July 19, 2005, p. 2.

People Weekly, September 21, 1998, pp. 149–51; March 15, 1999, p. 332; January 24, 2000, p. 27; June 26, 2000, p. 91.

TV Guide, March 14, 1998, p. 6; October 26, 2002, p. 12; December 21, 2009, p. 15.

USA Today, August 14, 2007.

Electronic:

Danica McKellar Official Site, http://www.danicamckellar.com, February 16, 2010.

MathDoesntSuck Web site, http://www.mathdoesntsuck.com, March 3, 2010.

McKENZIE, Julia 1941–
(Julie N. McKenzie)

PERSONAL

Full name, Julia Kathleen McKenzie; born February 17, 1941, in Enfield, Middlesex, England; daughter of Albion McKenzie and Kathleen Rowe; married Jerry Harte (an actor), 1972. *Education:* Trained for the theatre at Guildhall School of Music, London, England. *Avocational Interests:* Cooking, gardening.

Addresses: *Contact*—Ken McReddie Associates, 36–40 Glasshouse St., London W1B 4DL, England.

Career: Actress and director.

Awards, Honors: Antoinette Perry Award nomination, best actress in featured role—musical, 1977, for *Side by Side by Sondheim; London Evening Standard*

Theatre Award, best actress, 1987, for *Woman in Mind;* Laurence Olivier Award, actress of the year, Society of West End Theatre, 1982, for *Guys and Dolls;* Television Award nomination, best light entertainment performance, British Academy of Film and Television Arts, 1985, for *Fresh Fields;* Laurence Olivier Award, best actress in a musical or entertainment, Society of West End Theatre, 1994, for *Sweeney Todd.*

CREDITS

Stage Appearances:
(London debut) *Maggie May,* Adelphi Theatre, 1966.
Gloria, *Mame,* Drury Lane Theatre, London, 1969.
Girl in owl coat, *Promises, Promises,* Prince of Wales Theatre, London, 1970.
April, *Company,* Her Majesty's Theatre, London, 1971.
Cowardly Custard, Mermaid Theatre, London, 1973.
Cole, Mermaid Theatre, 1974.
The Norman Conquests, Globe Theatre, London, 1975.
(New York debut; as Julie N. McKenzie) *Side by Side by Sondheim,* Music Box Theatre, 1977.
Ten Times Table, Globe Theatre, 1978.
Outside Edge, Queen's Theatre, London, 1979.
The Play's the Thing, Greenwich Theatre, London, 1979.
Lily, *On the Twentieth Century,* Her Majesty's Theatre, 1980.
Maggie Hobson, *Hobson's Choice,* Lyric Hammersmith Theatre, London, 1981.
Anna Kopecka, *Schweyk in the Second World War,* Olivier Theatre, London, 1982.
Miss Adelaide, *Guys and Dolls,* Olivier Theatre, 1982.
Susan, *Woman in Mind,* Vaudeville Theatre, London, 1987.
Sally Plummer, *Follies,* Shaftesbury Theatre, London, then West End Theatre, New York City, 1987.
Witch, *Into the Woods,* Phoenix Theatre, London, 1990.
Sweeney Todd, Royal National Theatre, London, 1993.
Communicating Doors, Gielgud Theatre, London, 1995.
Margaret Lord, *The Philadelphia Story,* Old Vic Theatre, London, 2005.

Stage Director:
Stepping Out, Duke of York's Theatre, London, 1985.
Just So, Watermill Theatre, Bagnor, Berkshire, England, 1989.
Steel Magnolias, Lyric Theatre, London, 1989.
Putting It Together, Manhattan Theatre Club Stage I, New York City, 1993.
(With Bob Avian) *Hey Mr. Producer! The Musical World of Cameron Mackintosh,* Lyceum Theatre, 1998.

Film Appearances:
Voice of Rose Maybud, *Dick Deadeye, or Duty Done,* 1975.

Miss Dolly Dormancott, *The Wildcats of St. Trinians,* 1980.
Mrs. Herrick, *Those Glory Glory Days,* Cinecom International, 1983.
Gillian, *Shirley Valentine,* Paramount, 1989.
Voice of the Old Lady and Freda, *The Snow Queen,* 1995.
Audrey, *Vol-au-vent,* Winchester Films, 1996.
Lottie Crump, *Bright Young Things,* THINKFilm, 2003.
Miss Abernathy, *These Foolish Things,* Outsider Pictures, 2006.
Marjorie, *Notes on a Scandal,* Twentieth Century–Fox, 2006.

Television Appearances; Series:
Maggie, *Maggie and Her,* 1976–79.
Georgie Bodley, *That Beryl Marston …!,* 1981.
Hester Fields, *Fresh Fields,* 1984–86.
Sharing Time, 1984.
Hester Fields, *French Fields,* 1989–91.

Television Appearances; Miniseries:
Maureen Rafferty, *The Best of Families,* 1977.
Sybil Bryan, *Ike,* ABC, 1979.
Pen Muff, *Fame Is the Spur,* BBC, 1982.
Mrs. Forthby, *Blott on the Landscape,* Arts and Entertainment, 1986.
Mrs. Poyser, "Adam Bede," *Masterpiece Theatre* PBS, 1992.
Mrs. Jarley, *The Old Curiosity Shop,* The Disney Channel, 1995.
Jack mum, *Jack and the Beanstalk: The Real Story* (also known as *Jim Henson's "Jack and the Beanstalk: The Real Story"*), CBS, 2001.
Mrs. Forrester, *Cranford* (also known as *Cranford Christmas Special* and *Elizabeth Gaskell's "Cranford"*), BBC1 and PBS, 2007–2008.
Return to Cranford, PBS, 2010.

Television Appearances; Movies:
Laurie Hamilton, *For Richer, for Poorer,* NBC, 1977.
Betty Wilson, *Dear Box Number,* 1983.
Jennifer Pusey, *Hotel du Lac,* Arts and Entertainment, 1986.
Voice of Mavis, *Jack and the Beanstalk,* HBO, 2000.
Margaret Munroe, *Death in Holy Orders* (also known as *P. D. James' "Death in Holy Orders"*), BBC and PBS, 2003.
Prue, *Celebration,* 2006.
Margaret Snell, *You Can Choose Your Friends,* 2007.
Miss Marple, *Marple: A Pocket Full of Rye* (also known as *Agatha Christie Marple: "A Pocket Full of Rye"* and *Agatha Christie: Marple—"A Pocket Full of Rye"*), BBC and PBS, 2008.
Miss Marple, *Marple: Murder Is Easy* (also known as *Agatha Christa Marple: "Murder Is Easy"*), BBC and PBS, 2008.

Miss Marple, *Marple: Why Didn't They Ask Evans?* (also known as *Agatha Christie: Marple—"Why Didn't They Ask Evans?"*), 2009.

Miss Marple, *Marple: They Do It With Mirrors* (also known as *Agatha Christie: Marple—"They Do It With Mirrors"*), Arts and Entertainment, 2009.

Miss Marple, *Marple: The Secret of Chimneys*, 2010.

Miss Marple, *Marple: The Mirror Crack'd from Side to Side*, BBC and Arts and Entertainment, 2010.

Miss Marple, *Marple: The Blue Geranium*, 2010.

Television Appearances; Specials:

The Royal Variety Performance 1979, 1979.

An Audience with Dame Edna Everage, 1980.

Julia and Company, 1986.

Mrs. Amberson, *The Shadowy Third* (also known as *Ghosts: The Shadowy Third*), 1995.

Hey, Mr. Producer! The Musical World of Cameron Mackintosh (also known as *Great Performances: "Hey, Mr. Producer! The Musical World of Cameron Mackintosh"* and *Hey, Mr. Producer!*), PBS, 1998.

The Evening Standard Theatre Awards, ITV, 2003.

Musicality (documentary), Channel 4, 2004.

Herself and Miss Marple, *Top of the Cops* (documentary), ITV, 2009.

Also appeared in *Song by Song*, PBS.

Television Appearances; Episodic:

Various, *Frost's Weekly*, 1973.

Clinic nurse, *The Two Ronnies*, PBS, 1973.

Phyllis Barnes, "During the Ball" segment, *The Two Ronnies*, PBS, 1973.

Party hostess, *The Two Ronnies*, PBS, 1973.

Various characters, *The Two Ronnies*, PBS, 1975.

Battle of the Sexes, 1976.

Panelist, *The Sweepstakes Game*, 1976.

Performer, *The Good Old Days*, 1977.

Herself, *Blankety Blank* (also known as *Lily Savage's "Blankety Blank"*), 1980.

Panelist, *The Theatre Quiz*, 1981.

"Julia McKenzie," *This Is Your Life*, 1981.

The Bob Monkhouse Show, 1983.

Looks Familiar, 1984, 1985.

Diana and introduction, "Absent Friends," *Theatre Night*, 1985.

Wogan (also known as *The Wogan Years*), 1990.

Masterchef, 1992.

Call My Bluff, 1997.

Presenter, *Showtime Wales*, 2002.

Sheila Harthog, "Moonlight," *The Last Detective*, ITV, 2003.

This Morning (also known as *This Morning with Richard and Judy*), ITV, 2004, 2005.

Countdown, Channel 4, 2005.

Ruby Wilmott, "Down among the Dead Men," *Midsomer Murders*, ITV and Arts and Entertainment, 2006.

Sylvia Landridge, "And on the Way I Dropped It," *Where the Heart Is*, ITV, 2006.

"Hereford Cathedral Christmas Carols," *Songs of Praise*, 2007.

The Alan Titchmarsh Show, ITV, 2009.

Television Work; Specials:

Director, deviser, production staging, and stage producer, *Hey, Mr. Producer! The Musical World of Cameron Mackintosh* (also known as *Great Performances: "Hey, Mr. Producer! The Musical World of Cameron Mackintosh"* and *Hey, Mr. Producer!*), PBS, 1998.

Radio Appearances:

Voice of Mrs. Flittersnoop, *The Incredible Adventures of Professor Braneswam*, BBC Radio 4, 2001.

OTHER SOURCES

Periodicals:

American Theatre, May/June, 1993, p. 39.

McKORKINDALE, A. B.
   See SCOTT, Leigh

McLANE, Derek 1958–

PERSONAL

Born in 1958, in London, England; father, a history educator; mother, a professor; married Wendy Ettinger (a film producer), 1991; children: Cooper, Hudson, Kathryn. *Education:* Harvard College, B.A., 1981; Yale School of Drama, M.F.A., 1984.

Addresses: *Agent*—Abrams Artists Agency, 275 7th Ave., New York, NY 10001.

Career: Set designer. Began career as an apprentice and assistant to Robin Wagner and Michael Bennett; designed sets for three large shows for Toyota autos. New Group, member of board of directors, 1999.

Awards, Honors: Drama Desk Award nomination, outstanding set design for a play, 1996, for *The Monogamist*; Obie Award, sustained excellence in scenic design, *Village Voice,* 1997; Drama Logue Award, 1997, for *Harmony;* Drama Desk Award nomination, outstanding set design of a play, 1997, for *Present Laughter;* Drama Desk Award nomination, outstanding set design of a play, 1998, for *Misalliance;* Drama Desk Award nomination, outstanding set design of a play, 2000, for *East Is East;* Joseph Jefferson Award nomination, scenic design, 2002, for *Glengarry Glen Ross;* Drama Desk Award nomination, outstanding set design of a play, 2002, for *The Women;* Michael Merritt Award, excellence and collaboration in design, 2003; Drama Desk Award nomination, outstanding set design of a play, Lucille Lortel Award, outstanding scenic design, League of Off–Broadway Theatres and Producers, Obie Award, scenic design, 2004, all for *I Am My Own Wife;* Lucille Lortel Award, outstanding scenic design, Drama–Logue Award, 2005, both for *Intimate Apparel;* Drama Desk Award nomination, outstanding set design of a play, Lucille Lortel Award nomination, outstanding scenic design, 2006, both for *Abigail's Party;* Antoinette Perry Award nomination, best scenic design of a musical, 2006, for *The Pajama Game;* Lucille Lortel Award, outstanding scenic design, Henry Hewes Design Award nomination, scenic design, Outer Critics Circle Award nomination, outstanding scenic design, 2007, all for *The Voysey Inheritance;* Drama Desk Award nomination, outstanding set design of a musical, Lucille Lortel Award nomination, outstanding scenic design, 2008, both for *10 Million Miles;* Henry Hewes Design Award nomination, scenic design, 2008, for *Rafta, Rafta ...;* Henry Hewes Design Award nomination, scenic design, 2009, for *Ruined;* Antoinette Perry Award, best scenic design of a play, Drama Desk Award nomination, outstanding set design of a play, Outer Critics Circle Award nomination, 2009, all for *33 Variations;* American Theatre Wing Award.

CREDITS

Stage Set Designer:
Ten by Tennessee, Lucille Lortel Theatre, New York City, 1986.
The Concept, Circle in the Square Downtown, New York City, 1986.
Three Postcards, Playwrights Horizons Theatre, New York City, 1987.
Young Playwrights Festival (1987), Playwrights Horizons Theatre, 1987.
Four Short Operas, Playwrights Horizons Theatre, 1991.
Traps, New York Theatre Workshop, New York City, 1993.
Owners, New York Theatre Workshop, 1993.
And Baby Makes Seven, Lucille Lortel Theatre, 1993.
Desdemona, Circle Repertory Theatre, New York City, 1993.
First Lady Suite, Joseph Papp Public Theatre, New York City, 1993.

Hello Again, Mitzi E. Newhouse Theatre, New York City, 1993–94.
What's Wrong With This Picture?, Brooks Atkinson Theatre, New York City, 1994.
Titus Andronicus, Theatre at St. Clement's Church, New York City, 1994.
Suburbia, Mitzi E. Newhouse Theatre, 1994.
The Family of Mann, McGinn–Cazale Theatre, New York City, 1994.
Durang/Durang, Manhattan Theatre Club Stage II, New York City, 1994.
Silence, Cunning, Exile, Joseph Papp Public Theatre, New York City, 1995.
Henry VI, Theatre at St. Clement's Church, 1995.
Luck, Pluck and Virtue, Linda Gross Theatre, New York City, 1995.
Night and Her Stars, Manhattan Theatre Club Stage II, New York City, 1995.
Troilus and Cressida, Delacorte Theatre, New York City, 1995.
The Monogamist, Playwrights Horizons Theatre, 1995.
Holiday, Circle in the Square Theatre, 1995–96.
The Springhill Singing Disaster, 47th Street Theatre, New York City, 1996.
Summer and Smoke, Criterion Center Stage Right Theatre, New York City, 1996.
Present Laughter, Walter Kerr Theatre, New York City, 1996–97.
Three Sisters, Criterion Center Stage Right Theatre, 1997.
London Assurance, Roundabout Theatre, New York City, then Criterion Center Stage Right, 1997.
Minutes from the Blue Route, Linda Gross Theatre, 1997.
Psychopathia Sexualis, Manhattan Theatre Club Stage I, New York City, 1997.
Violet, Playwrights Horizons Theatre, 1997.
Misalliance, Laura Pels Theatre, New York City, 1997.
Honour, Belasco Theatre, New York City, 1998.
The Maiden's Prayer, Vineyard Theatre, New York City, 1998.
From Above, Playwrights Horizons Theatre, 1998.
The Uneasy Chair, Playwrights Horizons Theatre, 1998.
The Primary English Class, Minetta Lane Theatre, New York City, 1998.
Captains Courageous: The Musical, Manhattan Theatre Club Stage I, 1999.
East Is East, Manhattan Theatre Club Stage I, 1999.
Saturday Night, Second Stage Theatre, New York City, 2000.
The Waverly Gallery, Promenade Theatre, New York City, 2000.
Naked, Classic Stage Company (CSC) Theatre, New York City, 2000.
What the Butler Saw, Theatre at St. Clement's Church, 2000.
More Lies About Jerzy, Vineyard Theatre, 2001.
Time and Again, Manhattan Theatre Club Stage II, 2001.
Newyorkers, Manhattan Theatre Club Stage II, 2001.

Serviceman, Theatre at St. Clement's Church, 2001.
The Credeaux Canvas, Playwrights Horizons Theatre, 2001.
The Women, American Airlines Theatre, New York City, 2001–2002.
Hobson's Choice, Linda Gross Theatre, 2002.
Sweeney Todd, Kennedy Center for the Performing Arts, Washington, DC, 2002.
Merrily We Roll Along, Kennedy Center for the Performing Arts, 2002.
Company, Kennedy Center for the Performing Arts, 2002.
Sunday in the Park with George, Kennedy Center for the Performing Arts, 2002.
Passion, Kennedy Center for the Performing Arts, 2002.
A Little Night Music, Kennedy Center for the Performing Arts, 2002.
Glengarry Glen Ross, Steppenwolf Theatre Company, Chicago, IL, 2002.
Comedians, Samuel Beckett Theatre, New York City, 2003.
The Women of Lockerbie, Theatre at St. Clement's Church, 2003.
Berkshire Village Idiot, Zipper Theatre, New York City, 2003.
Rounding Third, John Houseman Theatre, New York City, 2003.
The Look of Love, Brooks Atkinson Theatre, 2003.
I Am My Own Wife, Playwrights Horizons Theatre, 2003, then Lyceum Theatre, New York City, 2003–2004.
Aunt Dan and Lemon, Acorn Theatre, New York City, 2003–2004.
Intimate Apparel, Laura Pels Theatre, 2004.
Modern Orthodox, New World Stages, New York City, 2004–2005.
Lone Star Love, John Houseman Theatre, 2004–2005.
Hurlyburly, Acorn Theatre, 2005.
Fran's Bed, Playwrights Horizons Theatre, 2005.
Little Women, Virginia Theatre, New York City, 2005.
Abigail's Party, 2005.
The Great American Trailer Park Musical, New World Stages, New York City, 2005.
Abigail's Party, Acorn Theatre, 2005–2006.
Macbeth, Delacorte Theatre, 2006.
Barefoot in the Park, Cort Theatre, New York City, 2006.
The Pajama Game, American Airlines Theatre, 2006.
The Threepenny Opera, Studio 54, New York City, 2006.
Lestat, Palace Theatre, New York City, 2006.
The Prime of Miss Jean Brodie, Acorn Theatre, 2006.
The American Pilot, Manhattan Theatre Club Stage II, 2006.
Two Trains Running, Peter Norton Space, New York City, 2006–2007.
The Voysey Inheritance, Linda Gross Theatre, 2006–2007.
The Scene, Second Stage Theatre, New York City, 2007.
The Fever, Acorn Theatre, 2007.
10 Million Miles, Linda Gross Theatre, 2007.
Things We Want, Acorn Theatre, 2007.
The Piano Teacher, Vineyard Theatre, 2007.
Grease, Brooks Atkinson Theatre, 2007–2009.
Two Thousand Years, Acorn Theatre, 2008.
Rafta, Rafta ..., Acorn Theatre, 2008.
Good Boys and True, Second Stage Theatre, 2008.
Becky Shaw, Second Stage Theatre, 2009.
Ruined, Manhattan Theatre Club Stage I, 2009.
Mourning Becomes Electra, Acorn Theatre, 2009.
Groundswell, Acorn Theatre, 2009.
Our House, Playwrights Horizons Theatre, 2009.
The Retributionists, Playwrights Horizons Theatre, 2009.
The Starry Messenger, Acorn Theatre, 2009.
33 Variations, Eugene O'Neill Theatre, New York City, 2009.
Ragtime, Neil Simon Theatre, New York City, 2009–10.

Also worked as set designer for *A Touch of the Poet, Griller,* and *The Visit,* all Goodman Theatre, Chicago, IL; *The Libertine,* Steppenwolf Theatre Company, Chicago; *The Rose Tattoo,* Chicago; *I Am My Own Wife,* Chicago; *A Winter's Tale,* Chicago; *Harmony,* La Jolla Playhouse, La Jolla, CA; *Drowning Crow; Waiting for Godot; The Caretaker; Heartbreak Hotel; Hedda Gabler; Misalliance; The Homecoming; Twelfth Night; The Father; Griller; The Visit; Jenufa; Salome; Lysistrata; Elektra.*

Major Tours; as Set Designer:
Designed sets for *South Pacific,* U.S. cities; *Tallulah,* U.S. cities; *Sunset Boulevard,* U.S. cities.

Film Work:
Art direction assistant, *Sticky Fingers,* Spectrafilm, 1988.

Television Work; Specials:
Scenic designer, *2 Years ... Later,* NBC, 1990.
Set designer, *The Women,* PBS, 2002.

Television Scenic Designer; Episodic:
Later with Bob Costas, NBC, 1988.

Also designed sets for *Late Night with David Letterman,* CBS.

Television Appearances; Episodic:
Himself, "Design," *Working in the Theatre,* 2006.

OTHER SOURCES

Electronic:
Derek McLane Official Site, http://derekmclane.org, February 1, 2010.

McNEELY, Joel 1959–

PERSONAL

Born 1959, in Madison, WI; married Margaret Batjer (a concert violinist and educator); children: Joshua, Claire. *Education:* Attended Interlochen Center for the Arts; University of Miami, Coral Gables, FL, B.Mus.; University of Rochester, M.Mus.

Addresses: *Agent*—First Artists Management, 4764 Park Granada, Suite 210, Calabasas, CA 91302.

Career: Composer, orchestrator, conductor, music producer, and musician. Counterpoint Music Studio, Los Angeles, owner and composer; conductor of symphony orchestras in the United States and abroad, including Royal Scottish National Orchestra, BBC Concert Orchestra, London Philharmonic Orchestra and London Symphony Orchestra, Munich Philharmonic Orchestra, Western Australian Symphony Orchestra, Seattle Symphony Orchestra, and Los Angeles Chamber Orchestra; worked as song arranger and producer for recording artists, including Jonatha Brooke, Rosemary Clooney, Crosby, Stills, and Nash, Linda Ronstadt, and Carly Simon; worked as a studio musician in the film industry; performer on flute, saxophone, piano, and bass. University of Southern California, faculty member at Thornton School of Music; teacher of private classes and master classes in composition; lecturer at American Film Market, University of Miami, Coral Gables, FL, James Madison University, and other institutions; Interlochen Center for the Arts, faculty member and member of board of trustees, also advisor to DeRoy Motion Picture Arts Program.

Member: American Society of Composers, Authors, and Publishers.

Awards, Honors: Emmy Award, outstanding musical composition of a dramatic underscore for a series, 1993, for "Young Indiana Jones and the Scandal of 1920," and Emmy Award nomination, outstanding music direction, 1993, for "Young Indiana Jones and the Mystery of the Blues," both *The Young Indiana Jones Chronicles;* Film Music Award, *Gramophone,* c. 1996, for the recording *Vertigo;* Film and Television Music Award, top box office film, American Society of Composers, Authors, and Publishers, 1998, for *Air Force One;* Annie Award nomination, outstanding music in an animated feature production (with songwriter Jonatha Brooke), International Animated Film Society, 2003, for "I'll Try," *Return to Never Land;* Grammy Award, outstanding classical crossover album, National Academy of Recording Arts and Sciences, for

The Day the Earth Stood Still; Path of Inspiration Award, Interlochen Center for the Arts; Distinguished Alumni Award, University of Miami, Coral Gables, FL.

CREDITS

Film Orchestrator and Music Conductor:
The Avengers, Warner Bros., 1998.
Virus (also known as *Virus—Schiff ohne wiederkehr*), Universal, 1999.
Ghosts of the Abyss (short documentary; also known as *Titanic3D: Ghosts of the Abyss*), Buena Vista/Walt Disney, 2003.
(And song arranger) *Pooh's Heffalump Movie* (animated), Buena Vista, 2005.
(And song producer) *Tinker Bell* (animated), Walt Disney, 2008.

Film Music Conductor:
Flipper, Universal, 1996.
Wild America, Warner Bros., 1997.
Return to Never Land (animated; also known as *Peter Pan: Return to Never Land*), Buena Vista, 2002.
(And song arranger) *The Jungle Book 2,* Buena Vista, 2003.

Film Orchestrator:
Short Circuit, 1986.
Iron Will, Buena Vista, 1994.
Additional orchestrations, *Gold Diggers: The Secret of Bear Mountain,* Universal, 1995.
(And score producer) *Holes,* Buena Vista, 2003.

Film Work; Other:
Musician, *Supercop,* Dimension Films, 1996.
Musician, "Duo," *Drive Me Crazy,* Twentieth Century–Fox, 1999.

Television Work; Movies:
Theme music performer, *Return to the Batcave: The Misadventures of Adam and Burt,* CBS, 2003.

Television Work; Episodic:
Music director, "Young Indiana Jones and the Mystery of the Blues," *The Young Indiana Jones Chronicles,* ABC, 1992.

Television Appearances; Specials:
Musica de cine, 2008.

RECORDINGS

Albums:
Saxophonist, Matt Harris, *Hit and Run,* 1986.
Samantha (soundtrack recording), Intrada, 1991.

Conductor, *Psycho: The Complete Original Motion Picture Score,* Varese Records, 1992.

Composer, Sedona, *Natural Colours,* 1992.

The Young Indiana Jones Chronicles (television soundtrack), four volumes, Varese Sarabande, 1992–94.

Radioland Murders: Music from the Motion Picture (soundtrack recording), Varese Sarabande, 1994.

Iron Will, Varese Sarabande, 1994.

Terminal Velocity (soundtrack recording), Varese Sarabande, 1994.

(With Seattle Symphony Orchestra) *Hollywood '94,* Varese Sarabande, 1994.

(With Seattle Symphony Orchestra) *Fahrenheit 451,* Varese Sarabande, 1995.

Conductor, Alan Silvestri, *Voyages,* 1995.

(With Royal Scottish National Orchestra) *Hollywood '95,* 1995.

Orchestrator, *Ghost,* Volume 2: *Classic Fantasy Film Music* (original soundtrack), 1995.

(With Royal Scottish National Orchestra) *Hollywood '96,* Varese Sarabande, 1996.

(With London Symphony Orchestra) *Flipper* (soundtrack recording), UNI/MCA, 1996.

Composer and orchestrator, *Star Wars: Shadows of the Empire* (original soundtrack), Varese Sarabande, 1996.

Supercop (original soundtrack), 1996.

(With Royal Scottish National Orchestra) *Vertigo,* Varese Sarabande, 1996.

Batmania: Songs Inspired by Batman TV Series (original soundtrack), 1997.

Conductor, *Batman Trilogy,* 1997.

Conductor, *Out of Africa* (original soundtrack), Varese Sarabande, 1997.

Arranger, Rosemary Clooney, *70: Seventieth Birthday Celebration,* 1998.

(With National Philharmonic Orchestra) *Torn Curtain: The Unused Score,* Varese Sarabande, 1998.

Conductor, John Barry, *Body Heat,* Varese Sarabande, 1998.

Titanic: Film Scores of James Horner, 1998.

Towering Inferno and Other Disaster Classics, Varese Sarabande, 1998.

The Trouble with Harry (original soundtrack recording), Varese Sarabande, 1998.

Amazing Stories (original soundtrack recording), Varese Sarabande, 1999.

Orchestrator, *Star Wars Collection* (original soundtrack recording), 1999.

Conductor, *Citizen Kane,* Varese Sarabande, 1999.

Conductor, *Twilight Zone* (original soundtrack recording), Varese Sarabande, 1999.

Sally Hemings: An American Scandal, Varese Sarabande, 2000.

Marnie, Varese Sarabande, 2000.

Orchestrator, *Lover's Prayer,* Varese Sarabande, 2000.

Conductor, *Jaws,* Varese Sarabande, 2000.

Conductor, *Last of the Mohicans,* Varese Sarabande, 2000.

Conductor, *In Session: A Film Music Celebration,* 2001.

Conductor, *The Three Worlds of Gulliver,* Varese Sarabande, 2001.

Composer and conductor, *Return to Never Land* (original soundtrack recording), Walt Disney, 2002.

Conductor, *Paramount 90th Anniversary Collections: Scores,* 2002.

Other albums include *The Avengers,* Gold Circle; *The Day the Earth Stood Still,* Varese Sarabande; *Ghosts of the Abyss,* Touchstone; *The Jungle Book 2,* Walt Disney; *Mulan II,* Walt Disney; *Rebecca,* Varese Sarabande; *Soldier,* Varese Sarabande; *Sunset Boulevard,* Varese Sarabande; and *Virus,* Hippo/MCA.

Videos:

Music conductor, *Virus: Ghost in the Machine,* Universal Studios Home Video, 1999.

WRITINGS

Film Music:

Additional music, *The Pick–up Artist,* Twentieth Century–Fox, 1987.

You Talkin' to Me?, Metro–Goldwyn–Mayer, 1987.

Samantha, Planet Productions, 1991, Academy Entertainment, 1992.

Terminal Velocity, Buena Vista, 1994.

Radioland Murders, Universal, 1994.

Squanto: A Warrior's Tale (also known as *The Last Great Warrior*), Buena Vista, 1994.

(And songs "Kaiser Bill" and "Hard to Bid Farewell") *Iron Will,* Buena Vista, 1994.

Gold Diggers: The Secret of Bear Mountain (also known as *Le secret de Bear Mountain*), Universal, 1995.

Flipper, Universal, 1996.

Supercop, Dimension Films, 1996.

Jing cha gu shi III: Chao ji jink cha (dubbed version; also known as *Police Story 3* and *Supercop*), Miramax, 1996.

Vegas Vacation (also known as *National Lampoon's "Vegas Vacation"*), Warner Bros., 1997.

Wild America, Warner Bros., 1997.

Additional music, *Air Force One* (also known as *AFO*), Columbia, 1997.

The Avengers, Warner Bros., 1998.

Zack and Reba, Live International/Victory Multimedia, 1998.

Soldier, Warner Bros., 1998.

Virus (also known as *Virus—Schiff ohne wiederkehr*), Universal, 1999.

The Adventures of Young Indiana Jones: The Phantom Train of Doom, 1999.

The Adventures of Young Indiana Jones: Oganga, the Giver and Taker of Life, 1999.

All Forgotten (also known as *Lover's Prayer*), Seven Hills Productions, 2000.

Return to Never Land (animated; also known as *Peter Pan in Return to Never Land*), Buena Vista, 2002.

Ghosts of the Abyss (short documentary; also known as *Titanic3D: Ghosts of the Abyss*), Buena Vista/Walt Disney, 2003.

Holes, Buena Vista, 2003.

Uptown Girls, Metro–Goldwyn–Mayer, 2003.

Song "Right Where I Belong," *The Jungle Book 2* (animated), Buena Vista, 2003.

Stateside (also known as *Sinners*), Samuel Goldwyn Films, 2004.

America's Heart and Soul (documentary), Walt Disney, 2004.

Mulan II (animated), Buena Vista Home Entertainment, 2004.

Additional music, *The Stepford Wives,* Paramount, 2004.

Pooh's Heffalump Movie (animated), Buena Vista, 2005.

Lilo & Stitch 2: Stitch Has a Glitch (animated; also known as *Lilo & Stitch 2*), Buena Vista Home Entertainment, 2005.

The Fox and the Found 2 (animated), Buena Vista, 2006.

Cinderella III: A Twist in Time (animated), Buena Vista, 2007.

I Know Who Killed Me, TriStar, 2007.

The Adventures of Young Indiana Jones: Passion for Life, Paramount, 2007.

The Adventures of Young Indiana Jones: Love's Sweet Song, Universal, 2007.

The Adventures of Young Indiana Jones: Demons of Deception, Universal, 2008.

The Adventures of Young Indiana Jones: Scandal of 1920, Universal, 2008.

The Adventures of Young Indiana Jones: Winds of Change, Paramount, 2008.

Tinker Bell (animated), Walt Disney, 2008.

Tinker Bell and the Lost Treasure (animated), Walt Disney, 2009.

Television Music; Series:

Our House, NBC, 1986.

The Young Indiana Jones Chronicles, ABC, 1992–93.

The Boys of Twilight, CBS, 1992.

(Including theme music) *Buddy Faro,* CBS, 1998.

Dark Angel (also known as *James Cameron's "Dark Angel"*), Fox, 2000–2002.

(Including theme music) *All Souls,* UPN, 2001.

The Court, ABC, 2002.

American Dad (animated), Fox, 2009.

Television Music; Movies:

Davy Crockett (also known as *Davy Crockett: Rainbow in the Thunder*), NBC, 1988.

Splash, Too, ABC, 1988.

Parent Trap III, NBC, 1989.

Parent Trap Hawaiian Honeymoon (also known as *Parent Trap IV: Hawaiian Honeymoon*), NBC, 1989.

Polly, NBC, 1989.

Polly: Comin' Home!, NBC, 1990.

Hitler's Daughter, USA Network, 1990.

Frankenstein: The College Years, Fox, 1991.

Lady Against the Odds, NBC, 1992.

Young Indiana Jones: The Attack of the Hawkmen, The Family Channel, 1995.

Buffalo Soldiers, TNT, 1997.

Road Rage (also known as *Death Driver*), NBC, 1999.

Santa Who?, ABC, 2000.

Television Music; Miniseries:

Sally Hemings: An American Scandal, CBS, 2000.

Television Music; Pilots:

(Including theme music) *Appearances,* NBC, 1990.

Dark Angel (also known as *James Cameron's "Dark Angel"*), Fox, 2000.

Television Music; Episodic:

"Looking Out for the Little Guy," *Tiny Toon Adventures* (animated; also known as *Steven Spielberg Presents … Tiny Toon Adventures*), Fox and syndicated, 1990.

"Mr. Popular's Rules of Cool," *Tiny Toon Adventures* (animated; also known as *Steven Spielberg Presents … Tiny Toon Adventures*), Fox and syndicated, 1990.

"Beauty and the Beet," *Darkwing Duck* (animated), 1991.

Video Music:

Star Wars: Shadows of the Empire (video game), LucasArts Entertainment, 1996.

Virus: Ghost in the Machine, Universal Studios Home Video, 1999.

Other:

Composer of classical pieces commissioned by Los Angeles Chamber Orchestra, Pacific Serenades, and Palisades Chamber Music.

OTHER SOURCES

Electronic:

Joel McNeely Official Site, http://www.joelmcneely.com, October 6, 2009.

Soundtrack, http://www.soundtrackmag.com, October 1, 2002.

MEDLIN, Lex

PERSONAL

Full name, Lex Michael Medlin; married Lori Bell, 2004. *Education:* Attended American Academy of Dramatic Arts, Pasadena, CA, 1990–91.

Addresses: *Manager*—Pop Art Management, PO Box 55363, Sherman Oaks, CA 91413.

Career: Actor and producer.

Awards, Honors: Gold Award, animated short (with others), WorldFest Houston, 2006, for *The Hot Sand.*

CREDITS

Television Appearances; Series:
Kevin McBrokelman, *Rock Me, Baby,* UPN, 2003–2004.
Larry Cone, *Happy Hour,* Fox, 2006–2008.
Detective Andy Williams, *Southland,* NBC, 2009, then TNT, beginning 2010.

Television Appearances; Episodic:
Frat big shot, "Radio Daze," *Beverly Hills, 90210* (also known as *Class of Beverly Hills*), Fox, 1993.
"Sudden Death," *Silk Stalkings,* USA Network, 1996.
Bud, "The Return of Megaman," *Team Knight Rider,* syndicated, 1998.
Gary Gala, "Ben's Brother," *One World,* NBC, 1998.
Inspector Smith, "She's a Man, Baby, a Man!," *Charmed,* The WB, 1999.
The tall guy, "The One with the Routine," *Friends,* NBC, 1999.
"The Big Bounce," *Jack & Jill,* The WB, 2001.
Derek, "Tommy's Not Gay," *Titus,* Fox, 2001.
Jerry Bergner, "Still in School," *Still Standing,* CBS, 2002.
Jerry Bergner, "Still Family," *Still Standing,* CBS, 2002.
Jerry Bergner, "Still Hairdressing," *Still Standing,* CBS, 2003.
Jerry Bergner, "Still Mom," *Still Standing,* CBS, 2003.
Jerry Bergner, "Still Flirting," *Still Standing,* CBS, 2004.
"Tropical Housewarming/Latin Birthday Lounge," *Party Starters,* Food Network, 2004.
Mike Evans, "The Contractor," *Married to the Kellys,* ABC, 2004.
Dowd, "The Hook Up," *Cuts,* UPN, 2005.
Assistant director, "Mac and Charlie Write a Movie," *It's Always Sunny in Philadelphia* (also known as *It's Always Sunny*), FX Network, 2009.
Pastor Paul Hicks, "Good Faith," *The Closer,* TNT, 2009.
Thom Hygard, "Book of Judges," *Mental,* Fox, 2009.
Thom Hygard, "Obsessively Yours," *Mental,* Fox, 2009.
Thom Hygard, "Bad Moon Rising," *Mental,* Fox, 2009.
Richard Meckler, "Happy Birthday, Mr. Monk," *Monk,* USA Network, 2009.
Chet, "Let It Go," *Men of a Certain Age,* TNT, 2009.
Cupid, "My Bloody Valentine," *Supernatural,* The WB, 2010.

Television Appearances; Pilots:
Dad, *Bad Haircut,* The WB, 2001.
Mike, *The Middle,* ABC, 2007.

Film Appearances:
Tyler Vinterberg, *Film Club* (short film), Mediatrip.com, 2000.
Tom, *A Couple on the Side* (short film), Mojotooth Productions, 2003.
Mating Rituals, Go Long Productions, 2004.
Jake, *Releaf* (short film), Hail Mountain Films, 2004.
Captain Miller, *The Hot Sand* (short film), Propelled Productions, 2005.
Taco Bell customer, *The Man Who Ate Too Much* (short film), Plan B Productions, 2007.
Housing official #7, *Quality Time* (also known as *My Apocalypse*), Valley Films, 2008.

Film Producer:
The Hot Sand (short film), Propelled Productions, 2005.

RECORDINGS

Video Games:
The Sopranos: Road to Respect, THQ, 2006.

MELNICK, Daniel 1932–2009

PERSONAL

Born April 21, 1932, in New York, NY; died of lung cancer, October 13, 2009, in Los Angeles, CA. Producer. Film and television producer and studio head Melnick was the man behind such films as *All That Jazz* and *Network* and such television series as *Get Smart.* His career began in television in the 1960s, when he served as executive producer for *East Side/West Side* and *Get Smart.* He moved into film production in the 1970s. *Straw Dogs,* his first film, generated controversy because of its violence and dark theme. In 1972 Melnick joined Metro-Goldwyn-Mayer, where he oversaw the production of *That's Entertainment* and *The Sunshine Boys,* among others films. In the mid-1970s he moved to Columbia Pictures, becoming its president in 1978 for a brief period. At Columbia he produced a number of successful films, including *Kramer vs. Kramer* and *The China Syndrome.* His other credits include *Footloose,* the Steve Martin comedy *Roxanne,* and *Altered States.* Melnick's final work was *Blue Streak,* which was released in 1999.

PERIODICALS

Guardian, October 21, 2009.
Los Angeles Times, October 15, 2009.

New York Times, October 17, 2009.
Variety, October 13, 2009.
Washington Post, October 19, 2009.

MICHAELS, James
  See MATHERS, James

MILANO, Alyssa 1972–

PERSONAL

Full name, Alyssa Jayne Milano; born December 19, 1972, in Brooklyn, NY; daughter of Thomas M. (a film music editor) and Lin (a fashion designer and talent manager) Milano; married Cinjun August Tate (a musician), January 1, 1999 (divorced November 20, 1999); married Dave Bugliari (an agent), August 15, 2009. *Avocational Interests:* Disneyland, hockey, baseball, piano, flute.

Addresses: *Agent*—Creative Artists Agency, 2000 Avenue of the Stars, Los Angeles, CA 90067. *Publicist*—True Public Relations, 6725 Sunset Blvd., Suite 570, Los Angeles, CA 90028.

Career: Actress and producer. Appeared in television and print commercials, including promotions for Candies perfume, 1999, 2000, and 1–800–COLLECT telephone service, 2000.

Member: Actors' Equity Association, Screen Actors Guild, American Federation of Television and Radio Artists.

Awards, Honors: Young Artist Award, best young supporting actress in a television series, 1986, Young Artist Award, exceptional performance by a young actress starring in a television comedy or drama series, 1987, Young Artist Award, best young female superstar in television, 1988, Kids' Choice Awards, favorite television actress, 1988, 1989, 1990, three Youth in Film awards, best supporting actress in a television series, all for *Who's The Boss?;* Young Artist Award nomination, exceptional performance by a young actress starring in a feature film comedy or drama, 1987, for *Commando;* Young Artist Award nomination, best young actress in a special, pilot, movie of the week, or miniseries, 1989, for *Dance 'til Dawn;* Silver Prize, Tokyo Music Festival, 1989; Annie Award nomination, outstanding individual achievement for voice acting by a female performer in an animated feature production,

International Animated Film Society, 2001, for *Lady and the Tramp II: Scamp's Adventure;* Peace Mediation Award, Peace Mediation Association, 2002; Kids' Choice Award, favorite television actress, 2005, Teen Choice Award nomination, television—choice actress, 2006, both for *Charmed.*

CREDITS

Film Appearances:
(Film debut) Diane Sloan, *Old Enough,* Orion, 1982.
Jenny Matrix, *Commando,* Twentieth Century–Fox, 1985.
Lurleen, *Speed Zone!* (also known as *Cannonball Fever),* Orion, 1989.
Kimmy, *Where the Day Takes You,* New Line Cinema, 1992.
Diana, *Little Sister* (also known as *Mister Sister),* Live Home Video, 1992.
Marian Delario, *Double Dragon* (also known as *Double Dragon: The Movie),* Gramercy, 1993.
Fan, *The Webbers* (also known as *At Home with the Webbers* and *Webber's World),* 1993.
Herself, *Canceled Lives: Letters from the Inside,* 1993.
Marian Delario, Power Corps Chief, *Double Dragon* (also known as *Double Dragon: The Movie),* 1994.
Charlotte, *Embrace of the Vampire* (also known as *The Nosferatu Diaries: Embrace of the Vampire),* 1994.
Lily, *Poison Ivy II* (also known as *Poison Ivy 2* and *Poison Ivy II: Lily),* New Line Cinema, 1995.
Cristina, *Deadly Sins,* 1995.
Katie, *Jimmy Zip,* 1996.
Margo Masse, *Fear* (also known as *No Fear* and *Obsession mortelle),* 1996.
Chelsea, *Glory Daze,* 1996.
Amaryllis, *Public Enemies* (also known as *Public Enemy #1* and *Public Enemy No. 1),* 1996.
Hugo Dugay, *Hugo Pool* (also known as *Pool Girl),* 1997.
Herself, *Buckle Up,* 1998.
Jimmy Zip, Asylum/Highland Crest Pictures, 1999.
Speaking voice of Angel, *Lady and the Tramp II: Scamp's Adventure* (animated), Buena Vista Home Video/Walt Disney Home Video, 2001.
Herself and Angel, *The Making of "Lady and the Tramp II: From Tramp to Scamp"* (short documentary), 2001.
Amy, *Buying the Cow,* Destination Films, 2002.
Amy Kayne, *Kiss the Bride,* Imageworks Entertainment International, 2002.
Cyndi, *Dickie Roberts: Former Child Star* (also known as *Dickie Roberts: (Former) Child Star),* Paramount, 2003.
Voice of 26, *Dinotopia: Quest for the Ruby Sunstone* (animated), Goodtimes Entertainment, 2005.
Herself, *Rockin' the Corps: An American Thank You,* National CineMedia, 2005.
Allegra, *The Blue Hour,* 2007.

Gwen Williamson, *Pathology*, Metro–Goldwyn–Mayer, 2008.

Herself, *Interview with Rose McGowan* (short film), Paramount Home Entertainment, 2008.

Herself, *Interview with Alyssa Milano* (short film), Paramount Home Entertainment, 2008.

Voice of Aimee Brenner, *"Justice League": Crisis on Two Earths* (animated), Warner Home Video, 2010.

Jesse Young, *My Girlfriend's Boyfriend*, 2010.

Film Work:

Producer, *My Girlfriend's Boyfriend*, 2010.

Television Appearances; Series:

(Television debut) Samantha "Sam" Micelli, *Who's the Boss?*, ABC, 1984–92.

Recurring role, *American Treasury*, CBS, 1988–89.

Jennifer Mancini Campbell, *Melrose Place*, Fox, 1997–98.

Phoebe Halliwell Turner, *Charmed*, The WB, 1998–2006.

Billie Cunningham, *My Name Is Earl*, NBC, 2007–2008.

Television Appearances; Miniseries:

Tracey Van der Byl, *Diamond Hunters*, syndicated, 2001.

Television Appearances; Movies:

Jennifer, *The Canterville Ghost*, syndicated and HTV, 1986.

Vanessa Crawford, *Crash Course* (also known as *Driver's Ed*, *Driving Academy*, and *Driving School*), NBC, 1988.

Shelley Sheridan, *Dance 'Til Dawn* (also known as *Senior Prom*), NBC, 1988.

Eve, *Conflict of Interest*, HBO, 1992.

Sylvia Velliste, *Candles in the Dark*, syndicated, 1993.

Amy Fisher, *Casualties of Love: The "Long Island Lolita" Story* (also known as *The Buttafuoco Story* and *Casualty of Love*), CBS, 1993.

Rita Summers, *Confessions of a Sorority Girl* (also known as *Rebel Highway*, *Confessions of a Sorority Girl*, and *Rebel Highway: Confessions of a Sorority Girl*), Showtime, 1994.

Amy Winslow, *The Surrogate*, ABC, 1995.

Denise Harris, *To Brave Alaska*, ABC, 1996.

Cristina Herrera, *Deadly Sins*, HBO, 1996.

Amaryllis, *Public Enemies* (also known as *Public Enemy #1*), HBO, 1996.

Hugo Dugay, *Hugo Pool*, The Movie Channel, 1997.

Suzanne, *Below Utopia* (also known as *Body Count*), HBO, 1997.

Frances Ella "Fizzy" Fitz, *Goldrush: A Real Life Alaskan Adventure* (also known as *Gold Rush!*), ABC, 1998.

Annie Stevens, *Reinventing the Wheelers*, ABC, 2007.

Louisa, *Single with Parents*, 2008.

Patty Montanari, *Wisegal*, Lifetime, 2008.

Rebecca Thomas, *Romantically Challenged*, ABC, 2009.

Television Appearances; Specials:

Tim McCarver Kids Around, ABC, 1987.

Videopolis StarTracks II, The Disney Channel, 1989.

Cohost, *Ice Capades with Jason Bateman and Alyssa Milano*, ABC, 1989.

Laura, *AFI Presents "TV or Not TV?,"* NBC, 1990.

Host, *The Making of "The Little Mermaid,"* The Disney Channel, 1990.

The 47th Annual Golden Globe Awards, TBS, 1990.

The 17th Annual People's Choice Awards, CBS, 1991.

Voices That Care, Fox, 1991.

Celebrity Profile: Alyssa Milano, E! Entertainment Television, 1999.

Herself and Phoebe Halliwell Turner, *The Women of "Charmed,"* E! Entertainment Television, 2000.

Intimate Portrait: Alyssa Milano, Lifetime, 2003.

"Charmed": Behind the Magic (documentary), LivingTV, 2003.

The 2003 Teen Choice Awards, Fox, 2003.

Playboy's 50th Anniversary Celebration, Arts and Entertainment, 2003.

"Melrose Place": The E! True Hollywood Story, E! Entertainment Television, 2003.

Shannen Doherty: The E! True Hollywood Story, E! Entertainment Television, 2003.

Voice of April, *Jimmy Neutron: Win, Lose and Kaboom* (animated; also known as *The Adventures of Jimmy Neutron, Boy Genius: Win, Lose and Kaboom!*), Nickelodeon, 2004.

"Who's the Boss": The E! True Hollywood Story, E! Entertainment Television, 2005.

Presenter, *Nickelodeon's 18th Annual Kids' Choice Awards*, Nickelodeon, 2005.

"Charmed": Access All Areas (documentary), 2005.

The Greatest: The 40 Hottest Rock Star Girlfriends and Wives, VH1, 2005.

Nickelodeon Kids' Choice Awards '05, Nickelodeon, 2005.

Hope for Haiti Now: A Global Benefit for Earthquake Relief, 2010.

Television Appearances; Pilots:

Animal Crack–Ups, ABC, 1987.

Malibu Beach Party (also known as *Alyssa Milano Week*), syndicated, 1989.

Television Appearances; Episodic:

Jessica Sharp, "Frame Up," *Jem* (also known as *Jem and the Holograms* and *Jem: The Movie*), 1985.

The New Hollywood Squares, 1987.

Body by Jake, syndicated, 1988.

"Halloween," *Steampipe Alley*, syndicated, 1988.

Laura, "Softly from Paris," *Serie rose* (also known as *Erotisches zur nacht* and *Softly from Paris*), 1990.

Hannah Valesic, "Caught in the Act," *The Outer Limits* (also known as *The New Outer Limits*), 1995.
Hannah Valesic, "The New Breed," *The Outer Limits* (also known as *The New Outer Limits*), 1995.
Showbiz Today, Cable News Network, 1995.
(Uncredited) Herself, "The Velveteen Touch of a Dandy Fop," *Mr. Show with Bob and David* (also known as *Mr. Show*), 1996.
Meg Winston, "They Shoot Horses, Don't They?," *Spin City,* ABC, 1997.
Gina Williams, "Superfriends," *Fantasy Island,* ABC, 1998.
"Time Square," *MTV Live,* MTV, 1998.
Entertainment Tonight (also known as *E.T.*), syndicated, 2000, 2001, 2002, 2005, 2008, 2010.
Meg Winston, "Rain on My Charades," *Spin City,* ABC, 2001.
Voice, "Mr. Griffin Goes to Washington," *Family Guy* (animated; also known as *Padre de familia*), Fox, 2001.
Access Hollywood, syndicated, 2001.
"Alyssa Milano Revealed," *Revealed with Jules Asner* (also known as *Revealed*), E! Entertainment Television, 2002.
"Who's the Boss?," *TV Tales,* 2002.
"Alyssa Milano," *Love Chain,* 2003.
E! News Daily (also known as *E! News Live* and *E! New Live Weekend*), E! Entertainment Television, 2003.
Tinseltown TV, International Channel, 2003.
The Insider, syndicated, 2004, 2005.
Corazon de ..., 2005.
Kyra Blaine, "A Rose for Everafter," *Castle,* ABC, 2010.

Television Talk Show Guest Appearances; Episodic:
The Tonight Show Starring Johnny Carson, NBC, 1986.
The Arsenio Hall Show, syndicated, 1989.
The Rosie O'Donnell Show, 1996, 1998.
The Tonight Show with Jay Leno (also known as *Jay Leno*), 1997, 1998, 2001, 2003.
Late Night with Conan O'Brien, NBC, 1998, 2002.
The Wayne Brady Show, syndicated, 2003.
Good Day Live, syndicated, 2004.
On–Air with Ryan Seacrest, syndicated, 2004.
Ellen: The Ellen DeGeneres Show (also known as *The Ellen Show*), syndicated, 2004.
Tavis Smiley, PBS, 2004.
The Tony Danza Show, syndicated, 2004, 2005.
The View, ABC, 2004, 2009.
The Tyra Banks Show, syndicated, 2007.
Live with Regis and Kelly, syndicated, 2007, 2008.
The Late Late Show with Craig Ferguson, CBS, 2008.
Jimmy Kimmel Live!, ABC, 2008.
The Morning Show with Mike & Juliet, Fox and syndicated, 2009.
Rachael Ray, syndicated, 2009.
The Bonnie Hunt Show, NBC, 2009.

Television Work; Series:
Producer, *Charmed,* The WB, 2002–2006.

Television Work; Movies:
Executive producer, *Below Utopia* (also known as *Body Count*), HBO, 1997.
Producer, *Wisegal,* Lifetime, 2008.

Stage Appearances:
Terry, *All Night Long,* Second Stage Theatre Company, McGinn–Cazale Theatre, New York City, 1984.
Butterflies Are Free, Los Angeles, 1991.

Also appeared as Adele, *Jane Eyre* (musical), Theatre Opera Music Institute, New York City; Lisa, *Tender Offer,* New York Ensemble Theatre, New York City; in *Warning Signals,* Manhattan Theatre Club, New York City.

Major Tours:
(Stage debut) July, *Annie,* U.S. cities, 1980–81.

Internet Appearances:
Alyssa Milano's Evolution: Jersey Shore (short film), www.funnyordie.com, 2010.

RECORDINGS

Exercise Videos:
Alyssa Milano's "Teen Steam" (also known as *Teen Steam*), 1988.

Video Games:
Voice of Dr. Ilyssa Selwyn, *Ghost Busters* (also known as *Ghostbusters: The Video Game*), Atari, 2009.

Music Videos:
Appeared as Josie in the music videos "Josie" and "The Urethra Chronicles" by Blink 182; in the "Voices That Care" music video.

Albums:
Alyssa, 1999.
Locked inside a Dream, 1999.
Look in My Heart, 1999.
Do You See Me, 1999.
The Best in the World, 1999.

WRITINGS

Nonfiction:
Safe at Home: Confessions of a Baseball Fanatic, William Morrow, 2009.

OTHER SOURCES

Books:
Bankston, John, *Alyssa Milano: A Real–Life Reader Biography,* Mitchell Lane Publishers, 2001.
Newsmakers, Issue 3, Gale, 2002.

Periodicals:

Details, April, 1999, pp. 132–39.
Detour, November, 1997, pp. 64–66.
Entertainment Weekly, December 25, 1998, pp. 21–24; November 21, 2008, p. 12.
Esquire, January, 2006, p. 86.
FHM, November, 2002, pp. 136, 140, 142.
In Style, November, 1997, pp. 242–47.
Ocean Drive, November, 1999.
People Weekly, March 28, 1994, p. 59; January 18, 1999, p. 54.
Premiere, April, 1996, p. 50.
Sirens of Cinema, winter, 2001, pp. 18–24.
Stuff, September, 1999; December, 2001, pp. 66–74.
TV Guide, December 12, 1998, pp. 22–29; August 7, 1999, p. 11; September 28, 2002, p. 51.

Electronic:

Alyssa Milano, http://www.alyssa.com, January 2, 2003.

MILLER, Paul 1949(?)–

PERSONAL

Full name, Paul D. Miller; born c. 1949; son of Walter C. Miller (a director and producer); married; wife's name, Shirley; children: Trevor, Tess. *Education:* Ohio University, B.A. and B.S.C.

Addresses: *Office*—Rickmill Productions, 860 North Las Palmas Ave., Hollywood, CA 90038. *Manager*—Mark Schulman, 3 Arts Entertainment, 9460 Wilshire Blvd., 7th Floor, Beverly Hills, CA 90212.

Career: Director and producer. Rickmill Productions, Hollywood, CA, partner. Worked as a stage manager and associate director for television networks in Los Angeles, and as a consultant.

Awards, Honors: Directors Guild of America Award nomination, outstanding directorial achievement in a musical or variety program, 1991, for the premiere episode of *In Living Color;* Directors Guild of America Award (with others), outstanding directorial achievement in a musical or variety program, 1999, for *The 52nd Annual Tony Awards;* Emmy Award nomination, outstanding directing for a variety or music program, 2001, for *The 54th Annual Tony Awards;* Emmy Award nomination (with others), outstanding variety, music, or comedy special, 2007, for *Lewis Black: Red, White, and Screwed;* Emmy Award nomination (with others), outstanding variety, music, or comedy special, 2009, for *Kathy Griffin: She'll Cut a Birch.*

CREDITS

Television Executive Producer and Director; Series:
Viva Variety, Comedy Central, 1997.
(Producer only) *Premium Blend* (also known as *Comedy Central's "Premium Blend"*), Comedy Central, 1997–98.
Comedy Central Presents (series of specials), Comedy Central, 1998–2009.
Celebrity Rap Star, MTV, 2007.

Television Producer and Director; Series:
House of Buggin', Fox, 1995.

Television Director; Series:
Madame's Place, syndicated, 1982.
Saturday Night Live (also known as *SNL*), NBC, 1986–89.
ALF, NBC, 1989–90.
In Living Color, Fox, 1990–93.
The Carol Burnett Show, CBS, 1991.
The Parent 'Hood, The WB, between 1995 and 1997.
MADtv, Fox, 1997.
Blue Collar TV, The WB, 2004–2006.

Also segment director of sketches for other television series.

Television Executive Producer and Director; Specials:
Disney's Christmas Fantasy on Ice (also known as *Christmas Fantasy on Ice*), CBS, 1992.
Disney's Nancy Kerrigan Special: Dreams on Ice, CBS, 1995.
Disney's Champions on Ice, ABC, 1996.
Kevin James: Sweat the Small Stuff, Comedy Central, 2001.
Jim Breuer: Hardcore, 2002.
Patton Oswalt: No Reason to Complain, Comedy Central, 2004.
George Lopez: Why You Crying?, Showtime, 2004.
Lewis Black: Black on Broadway, HBO, 2004.
Mario Cantone: Laugh Whore, Showtime, 2005.
Lewis Black: Red, White, and Screwed, HBO, 2006.
Amazing Johnathan: Wrong on Every Level, Comedy Central, 2006.
Christopher Titus: The 5th Annual End of the World Tour, Comedy Central, 2007.
My Buddy Bill (also known as *Rick Cleveland's "My Buddy Bill"*), Comedy Central, 2008.
Kathy Griffin: She'll Cut a Bitch, 2009.
Kathy Griffin: Balls of Steel, Bravo, 2009.
Jo Koy: Don't Make Him Angry, Comedy Central, 2009.

Television Producer and Director; Specials:
Norman's Corner, Cinemax, 1988.
Def Comedy Jam: Prime Time, Fox, 1995.
The Wizard of Oz on Ice, CBS, 1996.

Wanda Sykes: Tongue Untied, Comedy Central, 2003.
Out on the Edge, Comedy Central, 2004.
The Word According to Whoopi, Bravo, 2007.

Television Producer; Specials:
Placido Domingo ... Stepping Out with the Ladies, CBS, 1990.
Coproducer, *Def Comedy Jam: Primetime,* 1995.
Executive producer, *Secrets of the NY Friars Club Roast,* 2000.
Associate producer, *40 Hottest Hotties of the 90's,* 2008.

Television Director; Specials:
The Wolfman Jack Radio Show, 1980.
A Christmas Carol, The Entertainment Channel, 1982.
Welcome to the Fun Zone, 1984.
Walt Disney World's Happy Easter Parade, ABC, 1985, 1992.
The Magic of David Copperfield (also known as *The Magic of David Copperfield VII: Familares*), CBS, 1985.
The Joe Piscopo New Jersey Special, ABC, 1986.
From Hawaii with Love, syndicated, 1986.
Stuart Pankin, Cinemax, 1987.
Martin Mull Live! from North Ridgeville, HBO, 1987.
Joe Piscopo Live from UCLA, HBO, 1987.
Emmanuel Lewis: My Very Own Show, ABC, 1987.
Super Model Search: Look of the Year (also known as *Look of the Year*), ABC, 1988.
Sally Field & Tom Hanks' Punchline Party, HBO, 1988.
The Montreal International Comedy Festival, HBO, 1988.
Harry Shearer ... The Magic of Live, HBO, 1988.
Dennis Miller: Mr. Miller Goes to Washington (also known as *Live from Washington It's Dennis Miller* and *Mr. Miller Goes to Washington Starring Dennis Miller*), HBO, 1988.
The Comedy Store 15th Year Class Reunion, NBC, 1988.
Be Careful What You Ask For, NBC, 1990.
Spy Magazine Presents How to Be Famous, NBC, 1990.
The Montreal International Comedy Festival (also known as *Just for Laughs* and *The Annual Montreal Comedy Festival*), Showtime, 1990, 1991, 1992, 1993, 1994.
The Dave Thomas Comedy Show, CBS, four specials, 1990.
A Comedy Salute to Michael Jordan, NBC, 1991.
The Spy Magazine's Hit List: The 100 Most Annoying and Alarming People and Events of 1992, NBC, 1992.
Martin Mull: Talent Takes a Holiday, Showtime, 1992.
Laughing Back: Comedy Takes a Stand, Lifetime, 1992.
Hurricane Relief, Showtime, 1992.
The 15th Annual Young Comedians Show—Hosted by Dana Carvey, HBO, 1992.
Legend to Legend Night, NBC, 1993.

David Foster's Christmas Album, NBC, 1993.
Count on Me, PBS, 1993.
Baseball Relief: An All–Star Comedy Salute (also known as *Comic Relief: Baseball Relief '93*), Fox, 1993.
Men, Movies & Carol, CBS, 1994.
Carol Burnett: The Special Years, CBS, 1994.
National Memorial Day Concert, PBS, 1995, then annually, 1998–2001, 2007–2009.
A Capitol Fourth, PBS, annually, 1995–2001, 2005–2009.
Howie Mandel on Ice, HBO, 1997.
U.S. Comedy Arts Festival Tribute to Monty Python (also known as *Monty Python's Flying Circus: Live at Aspen*), HBO, 1998.
CMA 40th: A Celebration, CBS, 1998.
Saturday Night Live: The Best of Phil Hartman, NBC, 1998.
Vikki Carr: Memories, Memorias, PBS, 1999.
Sunday at the Oscars, ABC, 1999.
NFL All–Star Comedy Blitz, CBS, 1999.
An American Celebration at Ford's Theatre, ABC, annually, 1999–2004, and (also known as *An American Celebration at Ford's Theatre: Salute to the Troops*), 2005.
Director of half–time show, *Super Bowl XXXIII,* 1999.
Director of film clips, *Saturday Night Live's Presidential Bash 2000,* NBC, 2000.
Grand Ole Opry 75th—A Celebration, CBS, 2000.
The Carol Burnett Show: Show Stoppers, CBS, 2001.
Saturday Night Live Christmas Special, NBC, 2002, 2007.
Countdown to the Emmys, 2002.
Rockin' for the U.S.A.: A National Tribute to the U.S. Military, CBS, 2002.
Greatest Moments 2003 (also known as *TV Guide's Greatest Moments 2003*), ABC, 2003.
Tough Crowd Stands Up with Colin Quinn, Comedy Central, 2003.
The Book of David: The Cult Figure's Manifesto, Comedy Central, 2003.
Oscar Countdown 2003, ABC, 2003.
Jay Mohr: My Turn, Comedy Central, 2003.
American Idol: The Final Two, 2003.
Saturday Night Live: The Best of Tom Hanks, NBC, 2004.
Director of film clips, *Saturday Night Live's Presidential Bash 2004: The Great Debates,* NBC, 2004.
Boyz in the Woods, The WB, 2004.
Funniest Commercials of the Year, TBS, annually, 2004–2005, then 2007–09.
D. L. Hughley: Shocked & Appalled, Comedy Central, 2005.
A Holiday Celebration at Ford's Theatre, ABC, 2007.
The World's Funniest Commercials: Hilarious Liaisons, TBS, 2008.
The World's Funniest Commercials, 2008, 2009.
Funniest Movies of the Year: 2008, TBS, 2008.
Super Bowl's Greatest Commercials, CBS, 2009, 2010.
Director of film clips from archive footage, *SNL Presents: A Very Gilly Christmas,* NBC, 2009.

Television Director; Awards Presentations:
The Stuntman Awards, syndicated, 1986.
The 10th Annual Ace Awards, USA Network and other cable networks, 1989.
The ... Annual Tony Awards, CBS, (segment director) 1991, 1998, (and producer), 1999, 2000–2001.
The ... Annual Country Music Association Awards, CBS, annually, 1994–2007, then ABC, 2006–2009.
The 35th Annual Academy of Country Music Awards, 2000.
2004 Taurus World Stunt Awards, 2004.
Segment director, *The 50th Annual Grammy Awards,* CBS, 2008.

Television Director; Episodic:
The Best of Sullivan, syndicated, 1980.
Fridays, 1981.
The Love Connection, syndicated, 1983.
Anything for Money, syndicated, 1984.
America, syndicated, 1985.
FTV, syndicated, 1985.
"Inside Entertainment," *Not Necessarily the News,* HBO, 1987.
"Not Necessarily the Media," *Not Necessarily the News,* HBO, 1987.
"Chester Gets a Show," *It's Garry Shandling's Show,* Fox, 1990.
"Mad at Brad," *It's Garry Shandling's Show,* Fox, 1990.
Sunday Best, NBC, 1991.
The Carol Burnett Show, CBS, 1991.
"Up All Night," *Dream On,* HBO, 1992.
Down the Shore, Fox, c. 1992.
"With Bobcat Goldthwait," *The Ben Stiller Show,* Fox, 1992.
"With James Doohan," *The Ben Stiller Show,* Fox, 1992.
"On Melrose Avenue," *The Ben Stiller Show,* Fox, 1992.
"At the Beach," *The Ben Stiller Show,* Fox, 1992.
Segment director, *Townsend Television,* Fox, 1993.
"The Nanny–in–Law," *The Nanny,* CBS, 1994.
"A Plot for Nanny, *The Nanny,* CBS, 1994.
"Frannie's Choice," *The Nanny,* CBS, 1994.
"I Don't Remember Mama," *The Nanny,* CBS, 1994.
"Boyz II Men II Women," *In the House,* NBC, 1995.
"Come Back, Kid," *In the House,* NBC, 1996.
"A Star Is Almost Born," *The Jamie Foxx Show,* The WB, 1996.
"I Do, I Didn't," *The Jamie Foxx Show,* The WB, 1997.
"Family Affair," *Between Brothers,* Fox, 1997.
"Dusty's in Love," *Between Brothers,* Fox, 1997.
"Skin Deep," *Brotherly Love,* NBC, 1997.
"You Can Almost Go Home Again," *Hitz,* 1997.
"Give the Drummer Some," *Hitz,* 1997.
"Veronica's Construction Worker," *Veronica's Closet,* NBC, 1999.
"Veronica's Record," *Veronica's Closet,* NBC, 2000.
Hype, The WB, three episodes, 2000.
Premium Blend (also known as *Comedy Central's "Premium Blend"*), Comedy Central, 2001.

According to some sources, also directed episodes of *Extreme Makeover,* ABC.

Television Producer; Episodic:
Stand–up Nation with Greg Giraldo (also known as *Friday Night Stand–up with Greg Giraldo*), Comedy Central, 2005.

Television Director; Pilots:
Buckshot, ABC, 1980.
Be Careful What You Ask For, NBC, 1990.
The Ben Stiller Show, Fox, 1992.
Director of Steve Martin segments, *Toonces, the Cat Who Could Drive a Car,* NBC, 1992.
(And producer) *House of Buggin',* Fox, 1995.

Television Work; Miniseries:
Segment producer, *1988 Summer Olympic Games,* NBC, 1988.
Director, *The Dave Thomas Comedy Show* (also known as *Dave Thomas*), 1990.

Film Work:
Director, *The Pest,* TriStar, 1997.
Producer, *A Love Song for Bobby Long,* Lions Gate Films, 2004.

RECORDINGS

Video Director:
Saturday Night Live: The Best of Robin Williams, 1991.
Saturday Night Live Christmas (also known as *Saturday Night Live Christmas Past*), 1999.
Monty Python Live, 2001.

WRITINGS

Television Series:
Diff'rent Strokes, 1978.

MORGAN, Piers 1965–

PERSONAL

Full name, Piers Stefan Morgan; born March 30, 1965, in Newick, East Sussex, England; son of Anthony Glynne Pughe–Morgan and Gabrielle Georgina Sybille (maiden name, Oliver) Morgan; married Marion Elizabeth Shalloe, July 13, 1991 (divorced, 2008); children: Spencer William, Stanley Christopher, Albert

"Bertie." *Education:* Studied journalism at Harlow College. *Avocational Interests:* Cricket, Arsenal football club.

Addresses: *Manager*—James Grant Media, Ltd., 94 Strand on the Green, Chiswick, London W4 3NN, England.

Career: Television personality. Worked as a reporter for Surrey and South London newspapers, 1987–89; *The Sun* (a newspaper), show business editor, 1989–94; *News of the World* (a newspaper), 1994–95; *The Mirror* (a newspaper, previously *The Daily Mirror*), London, England, editor, 1995–2004; Press Gazette, coproprietor, 2005–06. Won *Celebrity Apprentice,* 2008.

CREDITS

Television Appearances; Series:
Presenter, *Morgan and Platell,* Channel 4, 2004–2005.
Presenter, *You Can't Fire Me, I'm Famous,* BBC1, 2006–2007.
Judge, *America's Got Talent,* 2006—.
Judge, *Britain's Got Talent,* ITV, 2007–2009.
Himself, *Britain's Got More Talent,* ITV, 2007–2009.
Presenter, *The Dark Side of Fame with Piers Morgan,* BBC, 2008.
Himself, *The Apprentice* (also known as *Celebrity Apprentice* and *The Celebrity Apprentice*), NBC, 2008–2009.
Host, *Piers Morgan On ...,* ITV, 2008—.
Host, *Piers Morgan's Life Stories,* ITV, 2009—.

Television Appearances; Specials:
Victoria's Secrets, Channel 4, 2000.
Fredrik Ljungberg: Up Close, Sky Television, 2003.
Presenter, *The Importance of Being Famous,* Channel 4, 2003.
Test the Nation: The 2004 Test, BBC, 2004.
Test the Nation: The Big Entertainment Test, BBC, 2005.
Death of Celebrity, Channel 4, 2005.
How TV Changed Football Forever, Sky Television, 2007.
Comic Relief: The Apprentice (also known as *Comic Relief Does "The Apprentice"*), BBC, 2007.
Comic Relief 2007: The Big One, BBC, 2007.
The Real Cherie, BBC, 2007.
The Royal Variety Performance, ITV, 2007.
The National Television Awards 2008, ITV, 2008.
Ant & Dec's Christmas Show, ITV, 2009.
Host, *I Dreamed a Dream: The Susan Boyle Story,* TV Guide Network, 2009.
Host (Today Show), *Stud Finder,* DIY Network, 2009.

Television Appearances; Episodic:
The Word, Channel 4, 1992.

Have I Got News For You (also known as *HIGNFY, Have I Got Old News for You, Have I Got a Little Bit More News for You,* and *Have I Got the 90s for You*), BBC, 1996.
Question Time, 1998, 1999, 2000, 2001, 2002, 2003, 2005, 2006, 2007, 2008, 2009.
Clarkson, BBC2, 1999.
Richard & Judy, Channel 4, 2001, 2003, 2005.
Breakfast with Frost, BBC1, 2002, 2003, 2004.
"Tabloid Tales," *Tabloid Tales,* BBC, 2003.
Guest presenter, *The Wright Stuff,* Five Network, 2003, 2005.
This Week, BBC, 2003, 2005, 2006.
GMTV, ITV, 2003, 2006.
This Morning (also known as *This Morning with Richard and Judy*), ITV, 2003, 2004, 2006, 2007, 2008, 2009.
In the Know, BBC, 2004.
Presenter, *Morgan and Platell,* Channel 4, 2004.
"Piers Morgan," *HARDtalk Extra,* BBC, 2005.
What's the Problem? With Anne Robinson, BBC, 2005.
"Presenters Edition," *The Weakest Link* (also known as *Weakest Link Champions' League*), BBC, 2005.
Breakfast, BBC, 2005, 2006, 2008.
The Paul O'Grady Show (also known as *The New Paul O'Grady Show*), ITV, 2005, 2009.
Loose Women, ITV, 2005, 2007, 2009.
The Daily Politics, BBC, 2006.
Davina, BBC, 2006.
Who Wants to Be a Millionaire, syndicated, 2006.
8 Out of 10 Cats, Channel 4, 2006.
The Sharon Osbourne Show, ITV, 2006.
The Tonight Show with Jay Leno (also known as *Jay Leno*), NBC, 2006, 2007.
The Dame Edna Treatment, ITV, 2007.
Parkinson, BBC, 2007.
Entertainment Tonight (also known as *E.T.*), syndicated, 2007, 2009.
Hell's Kitchen, ITV, 2007, 2009.
Happy Hour (also known as *Al Murray's "Happy Hour"*), ITV, 2008.
Ant & Dec's Saturday Night Takeaway, ITV, 2008.
Live with Regis and Kelly, syndicated, 2008.
Chopping Block, NBC, 2008.
The Alan Titchmarsh Show, ITV, 2009.
"Ashton Kutcher," *Larry King Live,* Cable News Network, 2009.
The ONE Show, BBC, 2009.
"Piers Morgan: Writer and Broadcaster," *HARDtalk,* BBC, 2009.
The Tonight Show with Conan O'Brien, NBC, 2009.
Peter Andre: The Next Chapter, ITV, 2009.

WRITINGS

Books:
Private Lives of the Stars, 1990.
Secret Lives of the Stars, 1991.
Phillip Schofield—To Dream a Dream, 1992.

Take That—Our Story, 1993.
Take That—On the Road, 1994.
The Insider, 2005.
Don't You Know Who I Am?: Insider Diaries of Fame, Power and Naked Ambition, 2007.
God Bless America, 2009.

Also writes a column for *Mail on Sunday* on sports; writes occasional columns for *GQ.*

OTHER SOURCES

Periodicals:
New Statesman, February 25, 2002.

Electronic:
Piers Morgan Official Site, http://www.officialpiersmorgan.com/, February 10, 2010.

MULKEY, Chris 1948–
(Vic Mulkey)

PERSONAL

Full name, Christian H. Mulkey; born May 3, 1948, in Viroqua, WI; father in business; mother, a university registrar; married Karen Landry (an actress and writer); children: Amelia, Elizabeth. *Education:* Attended University of Minnesota. *Avocational Interests:* Playing basketball, running marathons.

Addresses: *Agent*—Julia Buchwald, Don Buchwald and Associates, 6500 Wilshire Blvd., Suite 2200, Los Angeles, CA 90048. *Manager*—Verve Entertainment, 6140 West Washington Blvd., Culver City, CA 90232.

Career: Actor, producer, musician, composer, and writer. Children's Theatre Company of Minnesota, past member of ensemble; Vic Mulkey and the Blue Veins, bandleader and musician; Out Among 'Em, member of trio.

Awards, Honors: Independent Spirit Award nominations, best male lead and best screenplay (with others), Independent Features Project/West, both 1989, for *Patti Rocks;* Los Angeles Drama Critics Award, for *Blue Widow;* Copper Wing Award (with others), best ensemble acting, Phoenix Film Festival, 2007, for *Little Chenier.*

CREDITS

Film Appearances:
Billy Regis, *Loose Ends,* University of California, Los Angeles, 1976.

Cullen Garret, *Deadbeat* (also known as *Avenged, Getting Even,* and *Tomcats*), Dimension Films, 1976.
Fred, *The Boss' Son,* 1978.
Reggie Flynn, *Sunnyside,* American International Pictures, 1979.
Vernon Biggs, *The Long Riders,* United Artists, 1980.
Russell Monk, *All Night Long,* Universal, 1981.
Deputy Ward, *First Blood* (also known as *Rambo* and *Rambo: First Blood*), Orion, 1982.
Second cop, *48 Hrs.,* Paramount, 1982.
Daniels, *Timerider: The Adventure of Lyle Swann* (also known as *Timerider*), Jensen Farley, 1983.
Finch, *Dreamscape,* Twentieth Century–Fox, 1984.
David Johnson, *Runaway,* TriStar, 1984.
Torch runner, *Auto–Olympia,* 1984.
Red, *Quiet Cool,* New Line Cinema, 1986.
Jack DeVries, *The Hidden,* New Line Cinema, 1987.
Steve Ayres, *Heartbreak Hotel,* Buena Vista, 1988.
Voice, *Rain Man,* United Artists, 1988.
Billy Regis, *Patti Rocks,* FilmDallas, 1988.
Scott Morofsky, *Jack's Back,* Palisades Entertainment Group, 1988.
Chris, *In Dangerous Company,* Sandstar Releasing, 1988.
Larry, *Under the Gun,* 1988.
Nick Detroit, *From Hollywood to Deadwood,* Island Pictures, 1989.
Jamie Sanford, *Write to Kill,* RCA, 1990.
Man in bookstore, *Ambition,* Miramax, 1991.
Chad, *Denial* (also known as *Loon*), Martina Ritt–Tom Walsh, 1991.
Raymond, *Gas Food Lodging,* IRS Media, 1992.
George, *The Silencer,* Academy, 1992.
Steve, *Bound and Gagged: A Love Story,* Triboro Releasing, 1992, Northern Arts Entertainment, 1993.
Bram Walker, *Ghost in the Machine* (also known as *Deadly Terror*), Twentieth Century–Fox, 1993.
Eric, *Dead Cold,* Live Entertainment, 1995.
Major Hunt, *Broken Arrow,* Twentieth Century–Fox, 1996.
Tim, *The Fan,* TriStar, 1996.
Dan Goldman, *Foxfire,* Samuel Goldwyn Films, 1996.
Caleb Farnsworth, *Amanda* (also known as *Amanda–18 Hands*), Sony Pictures Entertainment, 1996.
Dirk Jaspers, *Full Moon Rising,* Moondog Productions, 1996.
Vic Bolsha, *Big Business,* 1997.
Second cop, *Bulworth,* Twentieth Century–Fox, 1998.
Dad, *The Last Tzaddik,* American Film Institute, 1998.
Aaron, *Sugar Town,* October Films/USA Films, 1999.
Rick Conesco, *Jimmy Zip,* Asylum, 1999.
Jacob McTeague, *Slow Burn,* Artisan Entertainment, 2000.
Things Left Unsaid, 2000.
The agent, *Universal Groove,* 2001, OM Entertainment, 2007.
John Grubb, *American Girl* (also known as *Confessions of an American Girl*), Metro–Goldwyn–Mayer Home Entertainment, 2002.
Frank Clay, *Radio,* Columbia, 2003.

Mr. Lackey, *Mysterious Skin,* Tartan/TLA Releasing, 2004.

Earl Slangley, *North Country,* Warner Bros., 2005.

Carlson, *Dirty,* Silver Nitrate Releasing, 2005.

Herb, *Dreamland,* Sony Pictures Home Entertainment, 2006.

Austin, *Thanks to Gravity* (also known as *Love and Debate*), Virgil Films and Entertainment, 2006.

Detective Brown, *One Night with You,* 2006, KHP Releasing, 2008.

Father Collins, *Wasted,* Weinstein Company, 2007.

Sheriff Kline Lebauve, *Little Chenier* (also known as *Little Chenier: A Cajun Story*), Radio London Films, 2007.

Sir, *The Curiosity of Chance,* TLA Releasing, 2007.

Agent Frank Pinsky, *D–War* (also known as *Dragon Wars, Dragon Wars: D–War,* and *War of the Dragons*), Freestyle Releasing, 2007.

Strank, *I Tried,* Codeblack Entertainment, 2007.

Charles, *Luck of the Draw* (short film), Tica Productions/Cinespire Entertainment/Madigan Productions, 2007.

Mills McCallum, *Nanking* (documentary), ThinkFilm, 2007.

Paul Gunderson, *Older than America,* Older than America, 2008.

Dennis, *Shattered!,* Americana Films/FireRock Entertainment, 2008.

Lieutenant Colonel Graff, *Cloverfield* (also known as *Monstrous* and *1–18–08*), Paramount, 2008.

Reverend Dobbins, *The Sacrifice* (short film), 2008.

Irate man, *Mr. Vinegar and the Curse* (short film), E & J Productions, 2008.

Hollis, *Dead*Line,* Secret Hideout Films, 2008.

Lieutenant Bossville Jones, *Breathe* (short film), Wayfinder Films, 2009.

Al, *Bare Knuckles,* Etebari Enterprises, 2009.

Bernie Rampart–Pillage, *(818),* 2009.

John, *Dark Moon Rising,* 2009.

Whiskey Beginnings: The Junior Johnson Story, 2009.

Film Work:

Associate producer and musiciar , *The Block* (short film), Pecan Street Productions, 2008.

Coproducer, *Dark Moon Rising,* 2009.

Producer, *Whiskey Beginnings: The Junior Johnson Story,* 2009.

Television Appearances; Series:

Hank Jennings, *Twin Peaks,* ABC, 1990–91.

Officer Pete Walsh, *Arresting Behavior,* ABC, 1992.

Denny Boyer, *Bakersfield P.D.,* Fox, 1993–94.

Colliar Sims, a recurring role, *Any Day Now,* Lifetime, 1998–2002.

Doug Norman, a recurring role, *Saving Grace,* TNT, between 2007 and 2009.

Television Appearances; Miniseries:

Radio man, *A Rumor of War,* CBS, 1980.

Charlie White, *Drug Wars: The Cocaine Cartel,* NBC, 1992.

Lanny Shelton, *Texas Justice* (also known as *Blood Will Tell*), ABC, 1995.

James, *Naomi & Wynonna: Love Can Build a Bridge* (also known as *Love Can Build a Bridge*), NBC, 1995.

Big Ears Bywaters, *Broken Trail,* AMC, 2006.

Television Appearances; Movies:

Nurse Watkins, *Act of Love,* NBC, 1980.

Sonny Manse, *The Killing of Randy Webster,* CBS, 1981.

Jeremy Blake, "Dangerous Company," *CBS Afternoon Playhouse,* CBS, 1982.

Burn's Chicago lawyer, *The Man Who Broke 1,000 Chains* (also known as *Unchained*), HBO, 1987.

Richard Halloran, *Deadly Care,* CBS, 1987.

Detective Stryker, *Tricks of the Trade,* CBS, 1988.

Ron Weddington, *Roe vs. Wade,* NBC, 1989.

Ira Rosenberg, *Rainbow Drive,* Showtime, 1990.

Matthew "Matt" Hendricks, *Angel of Death* (also known as *Intimate Terror: Angel of Death*), CBS, 1990.

Richard Froeming, *Runaway Father,* CBS, 1991.

Bill, *The Switch,* CBS, 1993.

Jordan, *Deadbolt* (also known as *3:15 a Time for Dying* and *Sequestree*), 1993.

Jonathan "Jon" Blake, *Nowhere to Hide,* ABC, 1994.

Jones, *Behind Enemy Lines,* HBO, 1996.

Jerry Pascoe, *Weapons of Mass Distraction,* HBO, 1997.

Commander John Kirsch, *Sub Down* (also known as *Sub Down: Take the Dive*), USA Network, 1997.

Lennox, *Twist of Fate* (also known as *Psychopath*), Cinemax, 1997.

Sheriff, *The Cowboy and the Movie Star* (also known as *Love on the Edge*), Fox Family Channel, 1998.

Richard Poe, *Requiem for Murder* (also known as *Classy Kill* and *Muertre en bemol*), Cinemax, 1999.

Travel agent, *Manhood,* Showtime, 2003.

Sheriff Ramsey, *Knight Rider,* NBC, 2008.

Bill Rander, *A Teacher's Crime,* Lifetime, 2008.

Television Appearances; Specials:

Griffin, "Dirty Work," *Vietnam War Story: The Last Days,* HBO, 1989.

Al Swearinger, *Hometown Boy Makes Good,* HBO, 1989.

Hank Jennings (in archive footage), *Twin Peaks/Cop Rock: Behind the Scenes,* 1990.

Broken Trail: The Making of a Legendary Western, AMC, 2006.

Television Appearances; Pilots:

Eddie Monroe, *K–9000,* Fox, 1991.

Denny Boyer, *Bakersfield P.D.,* Fox, 1993.

Television Appearances; Episodic:

Dealer, "Playin' Police," *Baretta*, ABC, 1976.

Joshua, "The Reunion," *Baretta*, ABC, 1977.

Curt Davis, "Terror on a Quiet Afternoon," *Barnaby Jones*, 1978.

Soldier, "Tea and Empathy," *M*A*S*H*, CBS, 1978.

"The Yearning Point," *Eight Is Enough*, ABC, 1978.

Reggie Martin, "Angels on Skates," *Charlie's Angels*, ABC, 1979.

Roller, "The Prodigals," *The Waltons*, CBS, 1980.

"The Russians Are Coming," *The White Shadow*, CBS, 1980.

Dave, "Forty Tons of Trouble," *CHiPs* (also known as *CHiPs Patrol*), NBC, 1981.

Glickman, "Jungle Swamp Survival," *Private Benjamin*, 1981.

Thomas, "The Survival Syndrome," *T. J. Hooker*, ABC, 1982.

Billy Ray, "Lulu's Gone Away," *The Dukes of Hazzard*, CBS, 1983.

Sharp, "The Haunting of J. D. Hogg," *The Dukes of Hazzard*, CBS, 1985.

Rhodes, "Steele Blushing," *Remington Steele*, NBC, 1985.

Tony, "Blood and Honor," *Magnum, P.I.*, CBS, 1985.

Ray Dobson, "The Junction," *The Twilight Zone* (also known as *The New Twilight Zone*), CBS, 1987.

Sylvia's ex–boyfriend, "Dial L for Laundry," *It's Garry Shandling's Show*, Showtime, 1987.

Danny Yates, "An Impossible Silence," *Beauty and the Beast*, CBS, 1987.

Bones Jennings, "The Country Boy," *Matlock*, NBC, 1987.

Joey Freeman, "Always a Thief," *Murder, She Wrote*, CBS, 1990.

George Spahn, "The Difference between Men and Women," *thirtysomething*, ABC, 1991.

Richard Foley, "Honi Soit Qui Mal y Pense," *Civil Wars*, ABC, 1992.

Kurt Ross, "Pitch and Woo," *Grace under Fire*, ABC, 1994.

Al Wallace, "Murder by Twos," *Murder, She Wrote*, CBS, 1994.

Dan, "It Happened One Night," *Blossom*, NBC, 1995.

Bobby Gallante, "Give Them Names," *Leaving L.A.*, ABC, 1997.

Foreman Cox, "A Woman's Place," *Walker, Texas Ranger* (also known as *Walker*), CBS, 1997.

Erskine, "Doodlebugs," *Touched by an Angel*, CBS, 1998.

Special Agent Becker, "Imagine: Parts 1 & 2," *Michael Hayes*, CBS, 1998.

Mike, "Black Box," *The Outer Limits* (also known as *The New Outer Limits*), Showtime and syndicated, 1998.

Voices of Walter Shreeve and Shriek, "Shriek," *Batman Beyond* (animated; also known as *Batman of the Future*), The WB, 1999.

Voice of Shreik, "Babel," *Batman Beyond* (animated; also known as *Batman of the Future*), The WB, 2000.

Voice of Shreik, "Where's Terry?," *Batman Beyond* (animated; also known as *Batman of the Future*), The WB, 2000.

Kevin Van Horn, "Reelin' In the Years," *Boomtown*, NBC, 2002.

Leonard Murphy, "Forced Entry," *CSI: Miami*, CBS, 2003.

Mr. Young, "Feeling the Heat," *CSI: Crime Scene Investigation* (also known as *C.S.I.*, *CSI: Las Vegas*, and *Les experts*), CBS, 2003.

Major Phelps, "The Boast," *JAG* (also known as *JAG: Judge Advocate General*), CBS, 2003.

Martin Akins, "Love Lies Bleeding," *Touching Evil*, USA Network, 2004.

Mike, "Further Instructions," *Lost*, ABC, 2006.

Bob, "Al–Baqara," *Sleeper Cell* (also known as *Sleeper Cell: American Terror*), Showtime, 2006.

Bob, "Torture," *Sleeper Cell* (also known as *Sleeper Cell: American Terror*), Showtime, 2006.

Pat Hall, "Shuffle, Ball Change," *Cold Case*, CBS, 2007.

Danny, "Four," *Smith*, CBS, 2007.

Coach, "Last Days of Summer," *Friday Night Lights*, NBC, 2007.

Coach, "Bad Ideas," *Friday Night Lights*, NBC, 2007.

Coach, "Are You Ready for Friday Night?," *Friday Night Lights*, NBC, 2007.

Coach, "Backfire," *Friday Night Lights*, NBC, 2007.

Guest, *The John Kerwin Show*, 2007.

Sheriff Britt Hallum, "Elephant's Memory," *Criminal Minds*, CBS, 2008.

Sheriff Griffin, "Wayne's World 3: Killer Shark," *Shark*, CBS, 2008.

Navy Captain Richard Owens, "Agent Afloat," *Navy NCIS: Naval Criminal Investigative Service* (also known as *NCIS* and *NCIS: Naval Criminal Investigative Service*), CBS, 2008.

Bernie Benton, "The Triangle," *CSI: NY*, CBS, 2008.

Doug Knowles, "Day 7: 10:00 p.m.–11:00 p.m.," *24*, Fox, 2009.

Doug Knowles, "Day 7: 12:00 a.m.–1:00 a.m.," *24*, Fox, 2009.

Karl Hogeland, "Duplicate Bridge," *In Plain Sight*, USA Network, 2009.

Willis, "Kindergarten Dominatrix," *Solly's Wisdom*, 2009.

"Just a Girl in the World," *Law & Order*, NBC, 2009.

Also appeared as Pete, *If Not for You*, CBS; and in *On Screen*, Total Living Network.

Stage Appearances:

Eddie Desmopoulis, *Flags*, Odyssey Theatre Ensemble, Los Angeles, 2005.

Appeared in *Blue Widow*, South Coast Repertory, Costa Mesa, CA.

RECORDINGS

Videos:
Voice of Colonel Jacob "Hawk" Manley, *Wing Commander IV: The Price of Freedom* (video game), Electronic Arts, 1995.
Voice of Colonel Jacob "Hawk" Manley, *Wing Commander: Prophecy* (video game; also known as *Wing Commander V*), Origin Systems, 1997.
Journey into the Unknown, Weinstein Company, 2007.

Albums:
(With Vic Mulkey and the Blue Veins) *Vic's Christmas Cruise,* 2000.
(With Vic Mulkey and the Blue Veins) *Voodoo Walking,* 2003.
(With Vic Mulkey and the Blue Veins) *Live and Naked at the Club Lingerie,* 2005.

Recorded the albums *A Blue Vein Noel; Christmas in a Blue Vein; It Is about the Heart* and *Out Among 'Em.*

WRITINGS

Screenplays:
(With David Burton Morris, John Jenkins, and Karen Landry) *Patti Rocks* (also based on a story by Mulkey), FilmDallas Pictures, 1988.
(With Murray Mintz) *Big Business,* 1997.
(And composer) *The Block* (short film), Pecan Street Productions, 2008.
Whiskey Beginnings: The Junior Johnson Story, 2009.

OTHER SOURCES

Electronic:
Chris Mulkey Official Site, http://www.chrismulkey.com, October 6, 2009.

MULKEY, Vic
See MULKEY, Chris

MULLIGAN, Carey 1985–

PERSONAL

Full name, Carey Hannah Mulligan; born May 28, 1985, in England; daughter of Stephen (a hotel group executive) and Nano (a lecturer; maiden name, Booth) Mulligan. *Education:* Attended Woldingham School.

Addresses: *Agent*—Chris Andrews, Creative Artists Agency, 2000 Avenue of the Stars, Los Angeles, CA 90067; Ness Evans, Julian Belfrage & Associates, 14 New Burlington St., London W1S 3BQ, England. *Publicist*—WKT Public Relations, 335 North Maple Dr., Suite 351, Beverly Hills, CA 90210.

Career: Actress. Worked as a runner at a studio and worked at a pub.

Member: Screen Actors Guild.

Awards, Honors: Television Award, best supporting actress in a motion picture or miniseries, Online Film & Television Association, 2006, for *Bleak House;* named best guest actress, readers of *Doctor Who* magazine, 2007, and Constellation Award, best actress in a science fiction television episode or best female performance in a 2007 science fiction television episode, TCON Promotional Society, 2008, both for "Blink," *Doctor Who;* Shooting Star Award, Berlinale European Film Promotion, 2009; Drama Desk Award nomination, outstanding featured actress in a play, 2009, for *The Seagull;* National Board of Review Award, Toronto Film Critics Circle Association Award, Dallas–Fort Worth Film Critics Association Award, and British Independent Film Award, all best actress, Chicago Film Critics Association awards, best actress and most promising newcomer, Washington, DC, Area Film Critics Award, best breakthrough performance, Hollywood Breakthrough Award, actress of the year, Hollywood Film Festival, Satellite Award nomination, best actress in a motion picture, drama, International Press Academy, and Washington, DC Area Film Critics Award nomination, best actress, all 2009, Film Award, best leading actress, British Academy of Film and Television Arts, ALFS Award, British actress of the year, London Critics Circle Film awards, Vancouver Film Critics Circle Award, best actress, Virtuoso Award, Santa Barbara International Film Festival, Central Ohio Film Critics Association awards, best actress and breakthrough film artist (for acting), Chlotrudis Award nomination, best actress, Academy Award nomination, best performance by an actress in a leading role, Golden Globe Award nomination, best performance by an actress in a motion picture—drama, Screen Actors Guild Award nomination, outstanding performance by a female actor in a leading role, nomination for Rising Star Award, British Academy of Film and Television Arts, ALFS Award nomination, actress of the year, London Critics Circle Film awards, Critics Choice Award nomination, best actress, Broadcast Film Critics Association awards, Online Film Critics Society Award nomination, best actress, and Screen Actors Guild Award nomination (with others), outstanding performance by a cast in a motion picture, all 2010, all for *An Education.*

CREDITS

Film Appearances:
Kitty Bennet, *Pride & Prejudice* (also known as *Orgueil et prejuges*), Focus Features, 2005.
Rachel, *And When Did You Last See Your Father?* (also known as *When Did You Last See Your Father?*), Sony Pictures Classics, 2007.
Emma, *Blood on Benefits* (short film), Keychain Productions, c. 2007.
Carol Slayman, *Public Enemies*, Universal, 2009.
Cassie Willis, *Brothers*, Lionsgate, 2009.
Jenny, *An Education*, Sony Pictures Classics, 2009.
Rose, *The Greatest*, Paladin/High Fliers Distribution, 2009.
Kathy, *Never Let Me Go*, Fox Searchlight, 2010.
Winnie Gekko, *Wall Street 2: Money Never Sleeps* (also known as *Money Never Sleeps* and *Wall Street 2*), Twentieth Century–Fox, 2010.

Television Appearances; Series:
Ada Clare, *Bleak House*, BBC, 2005, broadcast as part of *Masterpiece Theatre* (also known as *ExxonMobil Masterpiece Theatre, Masterpiece, Masterpiece Theatre: Bleak House,* and *Mobil Masterpiece Theatre*), PBS, 2006.
Emily Pritchard, *The Amazing Mrs. Pritchard*, BBC, 2006, broadcast as part of *Masterpiece Theatre* (also known as *ExxonMobil Masterpiece Theatre, Masterpiece,* and *Mobil Masterpiece Theatre*), PBS, 2007.

Television Appearances; Movies:
Violet Willett, *Agatha Christie: The Sittaford Mystery* (also known as *Agatha Christie—Marple: The Sittaford Mystery, Agatha Christie's "Marple," Marple, Miss Marple, Miss Marple, Series II,* and *The Sittaford Mystery*), ITV, 2006, broadcast on *Mystery!*, PBS, 2006.
Elsie Kipling, *My Boy Jack*, ITV, 2007, broadcast as a *Masterpiece Classic* on *Masterpiece Theatre* (also known as *ExxonMobil Masterpiece Theatre, Masterpiece,* and *Mobil Masterpiece Theatre*), PBS, 2008.
Isabella Thorpe, *Northanger Abbey*, ITV, 2007, broadcast as part of The Complete Jane Austen, *Masterpiece Theatre* (also known as *ExxonMobil Masterpiece Theatre, Masterpiece,* and *Mobil Masterpiece Theatre*), PBS, 2008.

Television Appearances; Specials:
(Uncredited; in archive footage) Kitty Bennet, *Pride and Prejudice Revisited*, BBC, 2005.
Herself, *The 50 Greatest Television Dramas* (also known as *The 50 Greatest TV Dramas*), Channel 4, 2007.
Herself, *Golden Globes Red Carpet Live*, Sky Television, 2010.

(And in archive footage) Herself, *Guion busca estrella*, Canal+ Espana, 2010.
Herself, *Live from the Red Carpet: 82nd Annual Academy Awards* (also known as *Live from the Red Carpet* and *Oscars 2010 Live from the Red Carpet*), E! Entertainment Television, 2010.
Herself, *Live from the Red Carpet: 67th Annual Golden Globe Awards* (also known as *Live from the Red Carpet* and *Golden Globes 2010 Live from the Red Carpet*), E! Entertainment Television, 2010.

Appeared in other programs.

Television Appearances; Awards Presentations:
Critics' Choice Movie Awards (also known as *15th Annual Critics' Choice Movie Awards*), VH1, 2010.
The 82nd Annual Academy Awards, ABC, 2010.
Orange British Academy Film Awards, BBC and BBC America, 2010.
16th Annual Screen Actors Guild Awards (also known as *Screen Actors Guild 16th Annual Awards*), TNT and TBS, 2010.
The 67th Annual Golden Globe Awards, NBC, 2010.

Television Appearances; Episodic:
Herself, "'Pride & Prejudice': A Classic in the Making," *HBO First Look*, HBO, 2005.
Emily Harrogate, "Sins of the Father: Part 1," *Trial & Retribution* (also known as *Lynda La Plante's "Trial & Retribution"* and *Trial & Retribution X*), ITV, 2006.
Herself, "Do You Remember the First Time?," *Doctor Who Confidential* (also known as *Doctor Who Confidential: Cut Down*), BBC, 2007.
Sally Sparrow, "Blink," *Doctor Who* (also known as *Dr. Who*), BBC, CBC, Sci–Fi Channel, and other channels, 2007.
Sister Bridgid, "Wren Boys: Parts 1 & 2," *Waking the Dead*, BBC, 2007.
Herself, *Entertainment Tonight* (also known as *Entertainment This Week, E.T., ET Weekend,* and *This Week in Entertainment*), syndicated, 2009, multiple episodes in 2010.
Herself, *Cinema 3* (also known as *Cinema tres* and *Informatiu cinema*), Televisio de Catalunya, 2010.

Television Talk Show Guest Appearances; Episodic:
The Charlie Rose Show (also known as *Charlie Rose*), PBS, 2009.
Late Night with Jimmy Fallon, NBC, 2009.
Late Show with David Letterman (also known as *The Late Show, Late Show Backstage,* and *Letterman*), CBS, 2009.
Made in Hollywood, syndicated, 2009.
Up Close with Carrie Keagan, 2009.
(In archive footage) *Breakfast*, BBC, multiple episodes in 2010.

The Late Late Show with Craig Ferguson (also known as *The Late Late Show*), CBS, multiple episodes in 2010.
Live from Studio Five (also known as *Studio Five*), Channel Five, multiple episodes in 2010.
The View, ABC, 2010.

Stage Appearances:
Return to the Forbidden Planet, Woldingham School, Surrey, England, c. 2001.
Nickie, *Sweet Charity* (musical), Woldingham School, c. 2002.
Fran, *Towerblock Dreams*, Theatre at Riverside Studios, London, 2004.
Hermia and Celia, *Forty Winks*, Royal Court Theatre, London, 2004.
Angelique, *The Hypochondriac*, Almeida Theatre, London, 2005–2006.
Nina, *The Seagull*, Royal Court Theatre, 2007, Walter Kerr Theatre, New York City, 2008.

Radio Appearances; Specials:
Chloe, "Arcadia," *Saturday Play*, BBC Radio 4, 2007.
Elinor Brooke, *Life Class*, BBC Radio 4, 2007.

RECORDINGS

Videos; as Herself; Short Documentaries:
The Bennets, Universal, 2006.
On Set Diaries, Universal, 2006.

OTHER SOURCES

Periodicals:
Interview, October, 2008, p. 44.
Telegraph (London), November 10, 2007; February 20, 2010.

MURDOCH, Rupert 1931–

PERSONAL

Full name, Keith Rupert Murdoch; born March 11, 1931, in Melbourne, Victoria, Australia; immigrated to the United States, 1974, naturalized citizen, 1985; son of Sir Keith (a journalist and newspaper owner) and Dame Elisabeth Joy (a welfare activist; maiden name, Greene) Murdoch; married Patricia Booker, 1956 (divorced, 1960); married Anna Maria Tory (a novelist), April 28, 1967 (divorced, 1999); married Wendi Deng (an executive), June 25, 1999; children: (first marriage) Prudence; (second marriage) Elisabeth, James, Lachlan;

(third marriage) Grace Helen, Chloe. *Education:* Worcester College, Oxford, B.A., B.S. *Avocational Interests:* Swimming, playing tennis, skiing.

Addresses: *Office*—News Corp. Ltd., 1211 Avenue of the Americas, 8th Floor, New York, NY 10036; Sky Italia, Viale Europe 59 Cologno Monzese, Milan 20090, Italy. *Publicist*—Rubenstein Associates, 1345 Avenue of the Americas, 30th Floor, New York, NY 10105.

Career: Publisher and chief executive officer. *Adelaide News*, Adelaide, Australia, owner and publisher, 1952—; News America Publishing, Inc., chairperson, 1974—; *Times* Newspaper Holdings, vice president, 1981—; Reuters Holdings PLC, director, 1984; Twentieth Century–Fox Film Corp., co–owner and chairperson, 1985—; William Collins PLC, Glasgow, Scotland, chairperson, 1989—; News Corp. Ltd., Sydney, Australia, chairperson and chief executive officer, 1991—; STAR Group, Ltd., chairman, 1993–98; Fox Entertainment Group, chief executive officer, 1995—; British Sky Broadcasting, chairman, 1999–2007; DirecTV Group, chairperson, 2003–07. Cruden Investments, co–owner; News Ltd. Group and Associated Companies, Australia, managing director; News International Group Ltd., London, past managing director; City Post Publishing Corp., chairperson; Bemrose Publishing Co., owner; Bay Books, owner; Townsend Hook Paper Co., owner; United Technologies (United States), director. Media properties include the television network Fox Broadcasting Co., the television studio Twentieth Century–Fox TV, the film studio Fox Filmed Entertainment, more than twenty Fox–owned television stations, the cable television networks FX, Fox Sports Net, Fox Family Channel, Fox News Channel, and more than twenty regional sports networks, Channel 10 in Sydney and Channel 10 in Melbourne, both in Australia, News Group Productions and Skyband in the United States, and Satellite Television PLC in England; other cable and satellite properties include Star TV, Japan's JSkyB, and SkyLatin America, Telepiu; part owner of London Weekend Television. Newspaper holdings include *New York Post, Village Voice, San Antonio Express, San Antonio News, Boston Herald,* and *Chicago Sun–Times* in the United States; *Times, Sunday Times, Times Literary Supplement, Times Educational Supplement,* and *Times Higher Education Supplement* in London; *Australian, Daily Telegraph, Sunday Telegraph, Daily Mirror, Sunday Sun, News and Sunday Mail,* and *Sunday Times* in Australia. Magazine holdings include *Antique Collector's Guide, Licensed Bookmaker, New Idea, New York, Star, Trader, TV Guide,* and *TV Week.* Ansett Transport Industries, England, chief executive officer; Santos Energy Co., owner; Convoys Transport Co., owner; New York State Lotto, director. Other holdings, past and present, include the Los Angeles Dodgers, 1998–2004, Los Angeles Kings, and Los Angeles Lakers, and partial ownership of the New York Knicks, the New York Rangers, and Madison Square Garden.

Awards, Honors: Decorated Companion of the Order of Australia), 1984; Commander, first class, White Rose Award, 1985; Ellis Island Medal of Honor, National Ethnic Coalition of Organizations, 1986, 1990; Knight Order of St. Gregory the Great, 1998; Australian Centenary Medal, Queen's New Years Honours List, 2001.

CREDITS

Film Work:
Presenter, *Gallipoli,* 1981.

Television Appearances; Specials:
Bullish on America, PBS, 1993.
Barbara Walters Presents "The 10 Most Fascinating People of 1994," ABC, 1994.
Gateway to the Future, 1996.
Dame Edna, Arts and Entertainment, 2001.
THS Investigates: Online Nightmares, E! Entertainment Television, 2006.
How TV Changed Football Forever, Sky One, 2007.
New York 360 Degrees Presents: The 2007 Matrix Awards, 2007.

Television Appearances; Episodic:
"Barbara Taylor Bradford," *This Is Your Life,* 1990.
Voice of himself, "Sunday, Cruddy, Sunday," *The Simpsons* (animated), Fox, 1999.

"Media Revolution: Stop Press?," *The Money Programme,* BBC, 2009.

OTHER SOURCES

Books:
Business Leader Profiles for Students, Gale Research, 1999.
Encyclopedia of World Biography, Gale Research, 1998.
Chenoweth, Neil, *Rupert Murdoch: The Untold Story of the World's Greatest Media Wizard,* Crown Publishers, 2002.
Wolff, Michael, *The Man Who Owns the News: Inside the Secret World of Rupert Murdoch,* Broadway Books, 2008.

Periodicals:
AdAgeGlobal, January, 2002, p. 6.
Crain's New York Business, June 15, 2009, p. 1.
Economist, September 12, 1998, p. 20.
Esquire, October, 2008, p. 155.
Fortune, October 26, 1998, p. 92.
New Statesman, August 6, 2001, p. 8; July 27, 2009, p. 14.
Newsweek, July 12, 1999, p. 36.
New York Times, August 10, 2009, p. B1; August 19, 2009, p. B2.
Time, May 4, 1998, p. 87.
Variety, February 2, 1998, pp. 17–19; June 28, 1999, p. 4.

N

NAPIER, James 1982–
(James Hobby, James Robertson)

PERSONAL

Full name, James William Robertson Napier; born March 24, 1982, in Wellington, New Zealand; nephew of Marshall Napier (an actor); cousin of Jessica Napier (an actress).

Career: Actor, producer, director, and writer. Lead singer and guitarist with the punk rock band the Pistol Whips.

Awards, Honors: Film Award nomination (with others), best feature film under a million dollars, New Zealand Film and Television Awards, 2009, for *I'm Not Harry Jenson*.

CREDITS

Television Appearances; Series:
Glen McNulty, *Shortland Street*, TV New Zealand, 2001.
(As James Robertson; credited as James Hobby for one early episode) Jared Preston, *Being Eve*, Nickelodeon, 2001–2002.
Jay, *The Tribe*, WAM, 2002–2003.
Conner McKnight/Red Dino Thunder Ranger, *Power Rangers Dino Thunder*, ABC Family, 2004.

Television Appearances; Episodic:
Luke Bertram, "Pride and Prejudice," *Mercy Peak*, TV New Zealand, 2003.
Luke Bertram, "Light My Fire," *Mercy Peak*, TV New Zealand, 2003.

Eric McKnight, "Storm before the Calm: Parts 1 & 2," *Power Rangers Ninja Storm*, ABC, 2003.
Conner McKnight/Red Dino Thunder Ranger, "Wormhole," *Power Rangers S.P.D.* (also known as *Power Rangers Space Patrol Delta*), The Disney Channel, 2005.
Conner McKnight/Red Dino Thunder Ranger, "History," *Power Rangers S.P.D.* (also known as *Power Rangers Space Patrol Delta*), The Disney Channel, 2005.
Mark, "I Should Be So Lucky," *Go Girls*, TV New Zealand, 2009.
Mark, "Faking It," *Go Girls*, TV New Zealand, 2009.
Mark, "Sex, Lies, and Home Renovations," *Go Girls*, TV New Zealand, 2009.
Mark, "Dream Believers," *Go Girls*, TV New Zealand, 2009.

Film Appearances:
(Uncredited) Little One, *Mad Max beyond Thunderdome* (also known as *Mad Max III*), Warner Bros., 1985.
Interviewer, *I'm Not Harry Jenson*, 2009.

Film Work:
Coproducer and director, *I'm Not Harry Jenson*, 2009.

WRITINGS

Screenplays:
I'm Not Harry Jenson, 2009.

NAPIER, Jessica 1979–
(Jess Napier)

PERSONAL

Born April 4, 1979, in Wellington, New Zealand; immigrated to Australia, c. 1988; daughter of Marshall

Napier (an actor); cousin of James Napier (an actor); married David Adler (divorced, 2009).

Addresses: *Manager*—New Wave Entertainment, 2660 West Olive Ave., Burbank, CA 91505.

Career: Actress. An animal liberationist.

CREDITS

Film Appearances:

Deborah/Debbie, *Love Serenade,* Miramax, 1996.
Rachel, *Blackrock,* 1997.
Princess, *War Story* (short film), 1998.
Raffy Carruthers, *Cut* (also known as *The Curse*), Lions Gate Films Home Entertainment, 2000.
Sophie, *City Loop* (also known as *Bored Olives*), Beyond Films, 2000.
Jane, *Twitch* (short film), Shorts International, 2000.
Jade, *Angst,* Beyond Films, 2000.
Jet Set, 2001.
Georgia, *Lawless Heart,* First Look International, 2001.
Sweet Dreams, 2002.
Lyra, *New Skin,* 2002.
German girlfriend, *Stuffed Bunny* (short film), 2002.
Jessica, *Post* (short film), 2004.
Christine, *The Illustrated Family Doctor,* 2005.
Jen, *Safety in Numbers,* Image Entertainment, 2005.
Broken Spoke waitress, *Ghost Rider* (also known as *Spirited Racer*), Sony Pictures Home Entertainment, 2007.
Kimberly, *Don't Panic* (short film), 2007.
Kate, *Savages Crossing,* 2009.

Television Appearances; Series:

Edwina Amadio, *Echo Point,* Ten Network, 1995.
Gerry Davis, *Wildside,* Australian Broadcasting Corporation, 1997–99.
Kaye Kelso, *Stingers,* Nine Network, 1998.
Becky Howard, *McLeod's Daughter,* Nine Network and Hallmark Channel, 2001–2003.
Jess Daily, *The Alice,* Nine Network, 2005–2006.
Simone Robsen, *Sea Patrol* (also known as *Sea Patrol II: The Coup* and *Sea Patrol III: Red Gold*), Nine Network and Hallmark Channel, 2009.
Nicole, *Rescue Special Ops,* Nine Network, 2009.

Television Appearances; Movies:

Klammie, *Child Star: The Shirley Temple Story,* ABC, 2001.
Jess Daily, *The Alice,* 2004.

Television Appearances; Episodic:

(As Jess Napier) Tracey, "One for Dad," *Police Rescue,* Australian Broadcasting Corporation, 1991.

Zoe, "The Only Constant," *Police Rescue,* Australian Broadcasting Corporation, 1996.
Michelle, "Night of the Monster," *Twisted Tales* (also known as *Twisted*), Nine Network, 1996.
Vanessa, "The Witness," *Water Rats,* Nine Network, 1997.
Brodie Cochrane, "Who Killed Cock Robin?," *Murder Call,* Nine Network, 1997.
Gladice, "London Calling," *The Lost World* (also known as *Sir Arthur Conan Doyle's "The Lost World"*), DirecTV and syndicated, 2000.
Amy, "Making Music," *Head Start,* 2001.
Herself, "Celebrity All in the Family," *Who Wants to Be a Millionaire,* syndicated, 2002.
Annabelle, "Private Dick," *Chandon Pictures,* The Movie Network, 2007.
Pam Elton, "Life's Little Miracles," *All Saints* (also known as *"All Saints": Medical Response Unit*), Seven Network, 2007.
Elyse Leine, "Out of Control 2," *All Saints* (also known as *"All Saints": Medical Response Unit*), Seven Network, 2009.

NAPIER, Marshall
(Marshall James Napier)

PERSONAL

Born in New Zealand; uncle of James Napier (an actor); children: Jessica Napier (an actress).

Addresses: *Manager*—Shanahan Management, Berman House, 91 Campbell St., Sydney 2010, Australia.

Career: Actor.

CREDITS

Film Appearances:

Constable Wyllie, *Beyond Reasonable Doubt,* 1980, Satori, 1983.
Trev Bond, *Bad Blood,* Hoyts Distribution, 1981.
Police driver, *Goodbye Pork Pie,* Greg Lynch Film Distributors, 1981.
Air force security guard, *Carry Me Back,* Kiwi Films, 1982.
Driver, *Warlords of the 21st Century* (also known as *Battle Truck*), New World, 1982.
Andy, *Wild Horses,* Satori, 1984.
Joe Voot, *Pallet on the Floor,* Mirage, 1984.
Hobbes, *Dangerous Orphans,* Cinepro/New Zealand Film Commission, 1985.
Major Hudson, *Lie of the Land,* 1985.
Sel Bishop, *Came a Hot Friday,* Orion Classics, 1985.

Voice of Hunk Murphy, *Footrot Flats: The Dog's Tale* (animated; also known as *Footrot Flats: The Dog's Tail Tale*), Magpie Productions, 1987.

Detective Wallace, *Starlight Hotel*, Republic, 1988.

Frank Le Mat, *Georgia*, Jethro Films Production, 1988.

Searle, *The Navigator: A Mediaeval Odyssey* (also known as *The Navigator* and *The Navigator: An Odyssey across Time*), Circle Films, 1988.

Detective Inspector Cross, *The Grasscutter*, Central, 1990.

Captain Johnson, *The Phantom Horsemen* (also known as *South Pacific Adventures*), Grundy, 1990.

Desmond Clark, *The Big Steal*, Hoyts Distribution, 1990.

Mr. Rupert Elloitt, *Flirting*, Samuel Goldwyn, 1992.

Detective Dave Green, *Shotgun Wedding*, Beyond Films/David Hannay Productions, 1993.

George LePine, *Lucky Break* (also known as *Paperback Romance*), United International Pictures, 1994.

Henderson, *Spider & Rose*, Dendy Films, 1994.

Chair of the judges, *Babe* (also known as *Babe, the Gallant Pig*), Universal, 1995.

Mr. Cronin, *Race the Sun*, TriStar, 1996.

Brendan Shaw, *Children of the Revolution*, Miramax, 1997.

Sergeant Oakes, *Dead Heart*, Fox Lorber, 1997.

Bank manager, *Diana & Me*, Roadshow Entertainment, 1997.

Mr. Berne, *The Sugar Factory*, Imagine Films Entertainment, 1998.

Robert, *Strange Planet*, New Vision Films, 1999.

Sir Geoffrey Hallerton, *In a Savage Land*, Universal, 1999.

Mike Hughes, *The Shirt*, Cult Classic Pictures, 2000.

Professor Charles Lawrence, *Muggers*, REP Distribution, 2000.

Jet Set, Black Frame, 2001.

Captain Jip, *New Skin*, Rogue Star Productions, 2002.

Prison warder, *Black and White*, New Vision Films, 2002.

Priest, *Stuffed Bunny* (short film), 2002.

Doug Gillespie, *Bad Eggs*, Roadshow Entertainment, 2003.

Don Ferric, *Travelling Light*, Dendy Films, 2003.

Sold Out (short film), 2004.

Turf O'Keefe, *Get Rich Quick*, Vivo Films, 2004.

Sergeant Strunk, *The Water Horse* (also known as *The Water Horse: Legend of the Deep*), Columbia, 2007.

Tom, *I'm Not Harry Jenson*, 2009.

Officer Underwood, *The Clinic*, Polyphony Entertainment, 2009.

Benson, *Griff the Invisible*, Transmission, 2010.

Television Appearances; Series:

Sergeant Fred "Frog" Catteau, *Police Rescue*, Australian Broadcasting Corporation, 1991–92.

Gary O'Leary, *Secrets*, Australian Broadcasting Corporation, 1993–94.

Joe DaSilva, a recurring role, *Water Rats*, Nine Network, between 1996 and 1999.

Harry Ryan, *McLeod's Daughters*, Nine Network, 2001–2006.

Wilton Sparkes, *City Homicide*, Seven Network, 2007–2008.

Also appeared as Bill Kennon in the series *Always Afternoon*.

Television Appearances; Miniseries:

Brodie, *Seven Deadly Sins*, Australian Broadcasting Corporation, 1993.

Dixon, *Stark* (also known as *Ben Elton's "Stark"*), Australian Broadcasting Corporation, 1993.

Draco, *The Girl from Tomorrow Part Two: Tomorrow's End*, 1993.

Tony Eustace, *Blue Murder*, Australian Broadcasting Corporation, 1995.

Commander Wallingford, *The Beast* (also known as *Peter Benchley's "The Beast"*), NBC, 1996.

Peter Collins, *The Farm*, Australian Broadcasting Corporation, 2001.

Television Appearances; Movies:

Keith Reid, *The Clean Machine*, Ten Network, 1988.

Dale Counahan, *Halifax f.p.: Lies of the Mind*, 1994.

Blake, *13 Gantry Row*, 1998.

Mayor Cass Cassidy, *Meteorites!*, USA Network, 1998.

Norscrum, *Airtight*, UPN, 1999.

John Radij, *My Husband My Killer*, Ten Network, 2001.

Television Appearances; Specials:

Narrator, *Eyes of the Tiger: Diary of a Dirty War*, Nine Network, 2006.

Television Appearances; Episodic:

Detective Sergeant Wright, "A Party! That's What We Need," *Seekers*, TV New Zealand, 1986.

Talbot, "Reprisal," *Mission: Impossible*, ABC, 1989.

Stan Brodie, "A Weekend in the Country," *G.P.*, Australian Broadcasting Corporation, 1991.

Stan Brodie, "The Good and Faithful Servant," *G.P.*, Australian Broadcasting Corporation, 1992.

"Death Takes a Holiday," *Time Trax*, syndicated, 1993.

Charlie Dunn, "The Search," *Snowy River: The McGregor Saga* (also known as *Banjo Paterson's "The Man from Snowy River"*), The Family Channel, 1995.

Tom, "Third Party," *Twisted Tales* (also known as *Twisted*), Nine Network, 1996.

Jim Jamieson, "Possession," *Blue Heelers*, Seven Network, 1997.

John Scanlan, "Oil and Water," *Blue Heelers*, Seven Network, 1999.

Mick Mason, "Shoot the Messenger," *All Saints* (also known as *All Saints: Medical Response Unit*), Seven Network, 1999.

(As Marshall James Napier) Drakul, "Barbarians at the Gate," *The Lost World* (also known as *Sir Arthur Conan Doyle's "The Lost World"*), syndicated, 2000.

Ian Hanrahan, "Secrets and Lies," *All Saints* (also known as *All Saints: Medical Response Unit*), Seven Network, 2001.

Ian Hanrahan, "Changing Places," *All Saints* (also known as *All Saints: Medical Response Unit*), Seven Network, 2001.

General Grynes, " ... Different Destinations," *Farscape*, Sci–Fi Channel, 2001.

John Allott, "Make or Break," *Head Start*, 2001.

John Allott, "Dischord," *Head Start*, 2001.

John Allott, "Business or Pleasure," *Head Start*, 2001.

John Allott, "Crash and Burn," *Head Start*, 2001.

Eddie Thomas, "Feud," *Stingers*, Nine Network, 2001.

"Celebrity All in the Family," *Who Wants to Be a Millionaire*, ABC, 2002.

Basil, "The Man with the Dancing Fi," *Chandon Pictures*, The Movie Network, 2009.

Appeared as Mason in an episode of *Adventurer*, TV New Zealand; and in *The Neville Purvis Family Show*.

RECORDINGS

Videos:

Over Easy: On Location with "Bad Eggs," Roadshow Entertainment, 2003.

NEMIRSKY, Michael

PERSONAL

Career: Production designer. Also worked as art director, assistant art director, associate producer, second unit director, dresser, and drafter.

Member: Art Directors Guild.

CREDITS

Television Production Designer; Movies:
Firefighter (also known as *Greater Alarm*), CBS, 1986.
Exile, NBC, 1990.
Sky High, NBC, 1990.
Silent Motive, Lifetime, 1991.
Home Movie, 1992.
Diagnosis Murder (also known as *A Diagnosis of Murder*), CBS, 1992.
Nowhere to Hide, ABC, 1994.

The Other Mother: A Moment of Truth Movie, NBC, 1995.
The Surrogate, ABC, 1995.
For Hope, ABC, 1996.
Silent Cradle (also known as *Le berceau muet*), Lifetime, 1997.
Tricks, Showtime, 1997.
Loyal Opposition: Terror in the White House, The Family Channel, 1998.
Evolution's Child, USA Network, 1999.
Resurrection, ABC, 1999.
My Mother, the Spy, Lifetime, 2000.
Becoming Dick, E! Entertainment Television, 2000.
Love Lessons (also known as *A Time to Decide*), CBS, 2000.
Wasted, MTV, 2003.
Thanksgiving Family Reunion (also known as *Holiday Reunion; National Lampoon's Holiday Reunion, National Lampoon's Thanksgiving Family Reunion,* and *National Lampoon's Thanksgiving Reunion*), TBS, 2003.
Bob the Butler, The Disney Channel, 2005.
Best Friends, Lifetime, 2005.
Disaster Zone: Volcano in New York, Sci–Fi Channel, 2006.
Meltdown (also known as *Meltdown: Days of Destruction*), Sci–Fi Channel, 2006.
Murder on Pleasant Drive, Lifetime, 2006.
Past Tense, Lifetime, 2006.
Ace of Hearts (also known as *L'as de coeur*), FoxFaith, 2008.
Yeti: Curse of the Snow Demon, Sci–Fi Channel, 2008.
NYC: Tornado Terror, Sci–Fi Channel, 2008.
Desperate Hours: An Amber Alert, 2008.
Meteor Storm, Syfy, 2010.

Television Production Designer; Series:
21 Jump Street, Fox, 1987.
Glory Days, Fox, 1990.
The Commish, ABC, 1992–93.
The X–Files, Fox, 1993.
Sliders, Fox, 1994–95.
The Adventures of Shirley Holmes, Fox Family, 1996.
(And associate producer) *Welcome to Paradox*, Sci–Fi Channel, 1998.
Cold Feet, NBC, 1999.
Freedom, UPN, 2000.
The Chris Isaak Show, Showtime, 2001.
All the Comforts, 2008.

Television Production Designer; Miniseries:
Samurai Girl, ABC Family, 2008.

Television Production Designer; Pilots:
21 Jump Street, Fox, 1987.
The X–Files, Fox, 1993.
Alaska, ABC, 2003.

Television Appearances; Episodic:
Sheldon Kruger, "Into the Shop," *Welcome to Paradox,* Sci–Fi Channel, 1998.

Film Production Designer:
Spacehunter: Adventures in the Forbidden Zone (also known as *Adventures in the Creep Zone, Road Gangs,* and *Spacehunter*), Columbia, 1983.
Kingsgate, Exile Productions, 1989.
The Portrait, 1992.
Portraits of a Killer (also known as *Portraits of Innocence* and *Portraits de l'innocence*), 1996.
Vice, 41, 2008.
Impulse, Sony Pictures Entertainment, 2008.
Dancing Trees, 2009.
Christmas Crash. NGN Productions, 2009.
Paradox, Bron Management/Arcana Studio/Legacy Filmworks, 2009.
Circle of Pain, Lions Gate Films/Grindstone Entertainment Group, 2010.

NESBITT, James 1965–

PERSONAL

Born January 15, 1965, in Coleraine, Ireland; father, a French teacher and headmaster; married Sonia Forbes–Adam, 1993; children: Peggy, Mary. *Education:* Studied philosophy at the University of Ulster; studied acting at the Central School of Speech and Drama, London. *Religion:* Protestant. *Avocational Interests:* Football (soccer).

Addresses: *Agent*—United Talent Agency, 9560 Wilshire Blvd., Suite 500, Beverly Hills, CA 90212; Artists Rights Group, Ltd., 4 Great Portland St., London W1W 8 PA, England.

Career: Actor. Appeared in television commercials, including Persil dishwashing liquid, Sky Sports Premiership Plus, Birds Eye Steam Fresh Vegetables, Yellow Pages telephone directories, and BBC America. Riverside Theatre, Coleraine, Northern Ireland, intern.

Awards, Honors: Screen Actors Guild Award nomination (with others), outstanding performance by a cast, 1999, for *Waking Ned;* British Comedy Award nominations, best television comedy actor, 1999, 2001, British Comedy Award, best television comedy actor, 2000, National Television Award, most popular comedy performance, 2003, all for *Cold Feet;* Television and Radio Industries Club Award, television drama performer of the year, 2002; British Independent Film Award, best actor, Stockholm Film Festival Award, best

actor, 2002, Television Award nomination, best actor, British Academy of Film and Television, Irish Film and Television Award nomination, best actor in a feature film, 2003, all for *Bloody Sunday;* Irish Film and Television Award, best actor in a television drama, 2003, Irish Film and Television Award nomination, best actor in television, 2005, Irish Film and Television Award nomination, best actor in a lead role in television, 2006, all for *Murphy's Law;* National Television Award nomination, most popular actor, 2004, for *Canterbury Tales;* Irish Film and Television Award nomination best actor in a television drama, 2004, for *Wall of Silence;* Golden Globe Award nomination, best performance by an actor in a miniseries or motion picture made for television, for *Jekyll,* 2008.

CREDITS

Film Appearances:
Policeman, *The End of the World Man* (also known as *The Bulldozer Brigade*), Family Home Entertainment, 1985.
Fintan O'Donnell, *Hear My Song,* Miramax, 1991.
Tony, *Go Now,* Gramercy, 1995.
Uncle Joe, *Jude,* Gramercy, 1996.
Greggy, *Welcome to Sarajevo,* Miramax, 1997.
Constable Hubert Porter, *This Is the Sea,* Paramount Home Video, 1997.
Graham Armstrong, *The James Gang,* HandMade Films, 1997.
Gerald Clarke, *Jumpers* (short film), 1997.
Ryan, *Resurrection Man,* Polygram, 1998.
Pig Finn, *Waking Ned* (also known as *A la sante de Ned, Vielles canailles,* and *Waking Ned Devine*), Fox Searchlight, 1998.
"Mad Dog" Billy Wilson, *The Most Fertile Man in Ireland,* Alibi Films International, 1999.
Stanley, *Women Talking Dirty,* Jef Films International, 1999.
Voice of dad, *Furry Story* (animated short film), Northern Lights Short Film Scheme, 2000.
Walter Adair, *Wild About Harry,* ContentFilm International, 2000.
James "Jimmy" Hands and Lord Nelson in show, *Lucky Break* (also known as *Lucky Break—Rein oder raus*), Paramount, 2001.
Ivan Cooper, *Bloody Sunday* (also known as *Sunday*), Paramount Classics, 2002.
(Uncredited) *The Boys from County Clare* (also known as *The Boys & Girl from County Clare*), Samuel Goldwyn, 2003.
Himself, *Bloody Sunday: History Retold,* (short documentary), Paramount Home Video, 2003.
Himself, *Ivan Cooper Remembers* (short documentary; also known as *Bloody Sunday: Ivan Cooper Remembers*), Paramount Home Video, 2003.
Ronnie, *Millions,* Fox Searchlight, 2004.
Detective Banner, *Match Point,* DreamWorks, 2005.

Peter, *Blessed,* G2 Pictures, 2008.
Joe Griffen, *Five Minutes of Heaven,* IFC Films, 2009.
Crilly, *Cherrybomb,* Little Film Company, 2009.
Cathal, *Outcast,* 2009.
Narrator, *George Best: The Legacy* (documentary), Creation Film and Television, 2009.
Connor, *Matching Jack,* 2010.
The Way, Icon Entertainment International, 2010.

Television Appearances; Series:
Duncan, *Searching,* ITV, 1995.
Leo McGarvey, *Ballykissangel,* BBC1, 1996–98.
Adam Williams, *Cold Feet* (also known as *Life, Love & Everything Else*), ITV, 1998–2003.
John Dolan, *Playing the Field,* BBC, 1998–2000.
Matt, *Tractor Tom,* ITV, 2003.
Tommy Murphy, *Murphy's Law,* BBC1 and BBC America, 2003–2007.
Dr. Tom Jackman/Mr. Hyde/Dr. Jekyll, *Jekyll,* BBC and BBC America, 2007.
Pilate, *The Passion,* BBC1, 2008.
Max Raban, *Midnight Man,* 2008.
Himself, *Northern Ireland's Greatest Haunts,* BBC Northern Ireland, 2009.
Clem Donnelly, *The Deep,* 2010.

Television Appearances; Miniseries:
David Laney, *Touching Evil,* PBS, 1997.
David Laney, *Touching Evil II* (also known as *Mystery!: "Touching Evil II"*), ITV, 1998, PBS, 2000.
Thomas Murphy, *Murphy's Law,* BBC1 and BBC America, 2001.
Nick Zakian, "The Miller's Tale," *The Canterbury Tales,* BBC and BBC America, 2003.
Mike Swift, *Occupation,* BBC1 and BBC America, 2009.

Television Appearances; Movies:
Young man, *Virtuoso,* Arts and Entertainment, 1991.
Stuart Robe, *Wall of Silence,* ITV, 2004.
Joe Keyes, *Passer By,* BBC, 2004.
Jack Parlabane, *Quite Ugly One Morning,* ITV, 2004.
Ray, *Big Dippers,* ITV, 2005.

Television Appearances; Specials:
Comic Relief: The Record Breaker, BBC, 1999.
Narrator, *Body Story,* Channel 4, 1998, The Discovery Channel, 2001.
Cold Feet: The Final Call, ITV, 2003.
Comic Relief 2003: The Big Hair Do, BBC, 2003.
The National Television Awards, ITV, 2003.
Host, *Irish Film and Television Awards,* 2003.
The Importance of Being Famous, Channel 4, 2003.
The British Comedy Awards 2003, ITV, 2003.
2003 TV Moments, BBC, 2004.
The Variety Club Showbusiness Awards 2004, 2004.

Host and presenter, *2nd Irish Film and Television Awards,* IFTN, 2004.
Host and presenter, *3rd Irish Film and Television Awards,* 2005.
Team Europe member, *All*Star Cup 2006,* ITV, 2006.
The 50 Greatest Television Dramas (also known as *The 50 Greatest TV Dramas*), Channel 4, 2007.
4th Irish Film and Television Awards, 2007.
The British Academy Television Awards, BBC, 2007.
The Graham Norton Show: "Doctor Who" Special, BBC America, 2008.
Presenter, *2008 Brit Awards,* BBC America, 2008.

Television Appearances; Pilots:
Adam Williams, *Cold Feet* (also known as *Life, Love & Everything Else*), ITV, 1997.

Television Appearances; Episodic:
(Uncredited) B Special, "The Cry," *Play for Today,* BBC1, 1984.
Martin Mulholland, "Stamp Duty," *Boon,* ITV, 1991.
Yuri, "Germany—Mid–August 1916," *The Young Indiana Jones Chronicles,* ABC, 1992.
Humphrey, "The Hero," *Covington Cross* (also known as *Charring Cross*), ABC, 1992.
Skeeball, "Sailortown," *Comedy Playhouse,* ITV, 1993.
Niall, "Love Lies Bleeding," *Screenplay,* Granada TV, 1993.
Jerry Boyle, "The Kakiemon Tiger," *Lovejoy,* BBC and Arts and Entertainment, 1993.
Sean Phelan, "Unknown Soldier," *Between the Lines* (also known as *Inside the Line*), BBC, 1994.
Corporal Bryan Casey, "Sweet Revenge," *Solider Soldier,* ITV, 1995.
Priest, *Common As Muck,* BBC, 1997.
"Oblivious Popstars," *Oblivious,* The Nashville Network, 2003.
"Television Drama: Part 2," *The South Bank Show,* ITV, 2004.
"Richard Harris," *The Hollywood Greats* (also known as *Hollywood Greats*), BBC1, 2004.
Top Gear, BBC, 2005.
All–Star Cup 2005, Sky Television, 2005.
OFI Sunday, ITV, 2005.
Tubridy Tonight, 2006.
(Uncredited) *The Play's the Thing,* Channel 4, 2006.
Guest host, *The Friday Night Project,* Channel 4, 2007.
The Podge and Rodge Show, 2007.
"Dame Edna's 50th Anniversary Special," *The Dame Edna Treatment,* ITV, 2007.
A Question of Sport, BBC, 2007.
Never Mind the Buzzcocks, BBC, 2008.
Narrator, "Footballers' Wives to Brideshead Revisited," *Drama Trails,* ITV, 2008.
Hans M. Prince, "Cinderella," *Fairy Tales,* BBC, 2008.
The ONE Show, BBC, 2009.
Xpose, TV3, 2009.

Also appeared as himself, *The Johnny Vaughn Film Show.*

Television Talk Show Guest Appearances; Episodic:
The Brian Conley Show, ITV, 2001.
Breakfast, BBC, 2001, 2007.
Kelly, UTV, 2001, 2002, 2003, 2004.
Parkinson, BBC, 2002, 2004, 2007.
Richard & Judy, Channel 4, 2002, 2004, 2006.
Patrick Kielty ... Almost Live! (also known as *Patrick Kielty ... Live!*), BBC, 2003.
The Terry and Gaby Show, Channel 5, 2003.
This Morning (also known as *This Morning with Richard and Judy*), ITV, 2003, 2004, 2005.
Friday Night with Jonathan Ross, BBC, 2003, 2005.
The Late Late Show, 2004.
The Graham Norton Show, BBC, 2008.
The Friday Show, BBC, 2009.

Television Work; Series:
Creative consultant, *Murphy's Law*, BBC1 and BBC America, 2004–2007.

Stage Appearances:
(Professional debut) *Up on the Roof*, Theatre Royal, Plymouth, England, Donmar Warehouse, London, and Apollo Theatre, London, 1987.
Hamlet, Leicester Haymarket Theatre, Leicester, England, 1989.
Una Poka, Tricycle Theatre, London, 1992.
Jesus, *Darwin's Flood*, Bush Theatre, London, 1994.
Damien, *Paddywack*, Cockpit Theatre, London, and Long Wharf Theatre, New Haven, CT, 1994.
Shoot the Crow, Trafalgar Studios, London, 2005.

Also appeared in *Can't Pay? Won't Pay!*; *Philadelphia Here I Come*; *As You Like It*; *Translations*, Birmingham Repertory, Birmingham, England; *As You Like It.*

Major Tours:
Guildenstern, *Hamlet*, international cities, 1989.

RECORDINGS

Music Videos:
Appeared in "The Day I Died" by Just Jack.

NEVINS, Claudette

PERSONAL

Original name, Claudette Weintraub; born April 10, in Wilkes–Barre, PA; daughter of Joseph (a fur salesman) and Anna (a garment worker; maiden name, Lander)

Weintraub; married Elliot Nevins (divorced); married Benjamin L. Pick (a real estate investor); children: (second marriage) Jessica, Sabrina. *Education:* New York University, B.A.; studied acting with Michael Howard. *Religion:* Jewish. *Avocational Interests:* Reading, tennis, travel, walking.

Addresses: *Agent*—TalentWorks, 3500 West Olive Ave., Suite 1400, Burbank, CA 91505.

Career: Actress.

Member: Screen Actors Guild, Actors' Equity Association, American Federation of Television and Radio Artists, Phi Beta Kappa.

CREDITS

Television Appearances; Series:
(Television debut) *Love of Life*, 1965–68.
Margaret Thompson, *The Headmaster*, CBS, 1970.
Courtney Fielding, *Husbands, Wives & Lovers*, CBS, 1978.
Barbara Huffman, *Married: The First Year*, CBS, 1979.
Angela Aries, *Behind the Screen*, CBS, 1981.
Constance Fielding, a recurring role, *Melrose Place*, Fox, 1993–98.
Mrs. Porter Webb, a recurring role, *JAG* (also known as *JAG: Judge Advocate General*), CBS, 1997.

Television Appearances; Movies:
Mary Lant, *Mrs. Sundance*, ABC, 1974.
Marilyn Sheppard, *Guilty or Innocent: The Sam Sheppard Murder Case*, NBC, 1975.
Maggie Hancock, *The Dark Side of Innocence* (also known as *The Hancocks*), NBC, 1976.
Ellen Sumner, *The Possessed*, NBC, 1977.
Frances Harrington, *More than Friends* (also known as *Love Me and I'll Be Your Best Friend*), ABC, 1978.
Janet Bouvier Auchincloss, *Jacqueline Bouvier Kennedy*, ABC, 1981.
Dr. Robin Samuel, *Don't Go to Sleep*, ABC, 1982.
Andrea, *Take Your Best Shot*, CBS, 1982.
Lenore Beavier, *Child of Darkness, Child of Light*, USA Network, 1991.
Mrs. Stillman, *Dead Silence* (also known as *Crash*), Fox, 1991.
Margaret Silverstein, *Widow's Kiss*, HBO, 1994.
Clarice, *Abandoned and Deceived*, ABC, 1995.

Television Appearances; Pilots:
Courtney Fielding, *Husbands and Wives*, CBS, 1977.
Sigourney Tompkins, *Jake's M.O.*, NBC, 1987.
Captain Bea Landry, "Silent Whisper," *CBS Summer Playhouse*, CBS, 1988.

Television Appearances; Specials:
Carrie Mason, *There Were Times, Dear,* PBS, 1987.

Television Appearances; Episodic:
Grace Kearney, "Once Bitten," *The Nurses* (also known as *The Doctors and the Nurses*), CBS, 1964.
Ruth Parker, "The Prosecutor," *The Defenders,* CBS, 1965.
"The Engineer," *The F.B.I.,* ABC, 1972.
"Ear to the Ground," *Police Story,* NBC, 1973.
"Backlash," *The Bob Newhart Show,* CBS, 1973.
Ellen Calabrese, "Requiem for an Informer," *Police Story,* NBC, 1973.
Hostess, "Mister Emily Hartley," *The Bob Newhart Show,* CBS, 1973.
Ellen Calabrese, "The Hunters (aka Big Jim Morrison)," *Police Story,* NBC, 1974.
Lisa Howard, "Image in a Cracked Mirror," *Barnaby Jones,* CBS, 1974.
Suzanne Kelly, "Illusion of the Cat's Eye," *The Magician,* NBC, 1974.
Ellen Calabrese, "Glamour Boy," *Police Story,* NBC, 1974.
Francis Yeager, "Mystery Cycle," *Barnaby Jones,* CBS, 1974.
Annette James, "An Act of Love," *Petrocelli,* NBC, 1974.
Ellen Calabrese, "Explosion," *Police Story,* NBC, 1974.
Voices of Judy Franklin and Nova, "Flames of Doom," *Return to the Planet of the Apes,* NBC, 1975.
Helene Garland, "The Arsonist," *Archer,* NBC, 1975.
Marge Wayne, "Street Games," *Harry O,* ABC, 1975.
Jessica Shannon, "Reflections," *Harry O,* ABC, 1975.
Claudia Elwood, "Beware the Dog," *Barnaby Jones,* CBS, 1975.
Mrs. Martindale, "Chapter I," *Rich Man, Poor Man—Book II,* ABC, 1976.
Empress of Evil, "Empress of Evil: Parts 1 & 2," *Electra Woman and Dyna Girl,* ABC, 1976.
Alice, "The Lady from Liechtenstein: Part 1," *Switch,* CBS, 1976.
Ann Louise Clement, "Trouble in Chapter 17," *The Rockford Files* (also known as *Jim Rockford, Private Investigator*), NBC, 1977.
Irene Mott, "Henhouse," *Lou Grant,* CBS, 1977.
Dee Grogan, "The Will to Live," *Rafferty,* CBS, 1977.
Paula, "A Love Story," *The Fitzpatricks,* CBS, 1977.
"Child of Danger," *Barnaby Jones,* CBS, 1977.
Pat Runkle, "Memory of a Nightmare," *Barnaby Jones,* CBS, 1978.
Genevieve, "Formula for Murder," *Switch,* CBS, 1978.
"Mechanic," *The Lazarus Syndrome,* ABC, 1979.
Madeleine, "The One that Got Away," *Shirley,* NBC, 1979.
Barbara, "The Older Woman," *Three's Company,* ABC, 1979.
Sybil, "Caviar with Everything," *Mrs. Columbo* (also known as *Kate Columbo, Kate Loves a Mystery,* and *Kate the Detective*), NBC, 1979.

Donna Marie Parker, "Mr. and Mrs. Who?," *M*A*S*H,* CBS, 1979.
Anita Parks, "Run to Death," *Barnaby Jones,* CBS, 1980.
Susan Philby, "Civil Wives," *Knots Landing,* CBS, 1980.
Claire Hopkins, "The Ties that Bind," *Family,* ABC, 1980.
Senora Piranda, "A Couple of Harts," *Hart to Hart,* ABC, 1981.
Hannah Chadway, "Concours d'Elegance," *CHiPs* (also known as *CHiPs Patrol*), NBC, 1981.
Madame's Place (puppet talk show), syndicated, 1982.
Veronica, "Testimony of Evil (Dead Men Don't Laugh)," *Police Squad!,* CBS, 1982.
Marge Royer, "The Perfect Wedding: Parts 1 & 2," *One Day at a Time,* CBS, 1982.
Phyllis Reardon, "Mixed Doubles," *Magnum, P.I.,* CBS, 1982.
"Informed Consent," *The Mississippi,* CBS, 1983.
Marge Royer, "Take My Ex," *One Day at a Time,* CBS, 1983.
Cynthia Kingston, "How the Other Half Dies," *Legmen,* NBC, 1984.
"The Three Million Dollar Spirit," *Lime Street,* ABC, 1985.
"Love and the First Date," *New Love, American Style,* ABC, 1986.
Judge Sheila Mooney, "Brother Can You Spare a Crime?," *Hardcastle and McCormick,* ABC, 1986.
"Masquerade," *Brothers,* Showtime, 1987.
"Customer's Always Right," *The Tortellis,* NBC, 1987.
Myrna Dawson, "Prized Possessions," *Hotel* (also known as *Arthur Hailey's "Hotel"*), ABC, 1987.
Mrs. Samuels, "On the Road Again," *Head of the Class,* ABC, 1988.
Sarah Schindler, "Romancing the Drone," *L.A. Law,* NBC, 1988.
Margo Silver, "The Incredible Hunk," *Out of This World,* syndicated, 1988.
Mrs. Kittle, "Bon Appetit," *Trial and Error,* 1988.
Cherry, "The Boys in the Board Room," *Just in Time,* 1988.
"Big Brass Cookie Jar," *Snoops,* CBS, 1989.
Sheila, "Conflict of Interest," *Mancuso, FBI,* NBC, 1989.
Mildred Crater, "Not with My Sister You Don't," *Free Spirit,* NBC, 1989.
Mildred Crater, "Radio Nights," *Free Spirit,* NBC, 1989.
"Wes, Laurie, Georgia," *Lifestories,* NBC, 1990.
Lizzie Burns, "Will Power," *Dallas,* CBS, 1990.
"Life's Little Lessons," *Teech,* CBS, 1991.
"Naked Hearts," *Veronica Clare,* Lifetime, 1991.
Roseland Price, "This Is Art?," *Designing Women,* CBS, 1991.
"Variations on a Theme," *The Antagonists,* CBS, 1991.
"Love, Amanda," *Veronica Clare,* Lifetime, 1991.
"A Tiger's Tale," *The Young Riders,* ABC, 1991.
Monica Schlossberg, "Whippet 'til It Breaks," *Civil Wars,* ABC, 1992.
Monica Schlossberg, "Das Boat House," *Civil Wars,* ABC, 1992.

Claudia Graham, "The Body Politic," *Picket Fences,* CBS, 1993.

Vivian Carson, "Moving Targets," *Beverly Hills, 90210* (also known as *Class of Beverly Hills*), Fox, 1993.

Vivian Carson, "And Did It ... My Way," *Beverly Hills, 90210* (also known as *Class of Beverly Hills*), Fox, 1993.

Barbara Trevino, "Witness," *Lois & Clark: The New Adventures of Superman* (also known as *Lois & Clark* and *The New Adventures of Superman*), ABC, 1994.

Ellen Porter, "Chore Patrol," *Thunder Alley,* ABC, 1994.

Mrs. DiMateo, "She's Having Our Baby: Part 1," *Coach,* ABC, 1995.

Judge, "Fire in the Belly," *ER,* NBC, 1996.

Mrs. Rainy, "See You in September," *7th Heaven* (also known as *Seventh Heaven* and *7th Heaven: Beginnings*), The WB, 1997.

Mrs. Rainy, "Breaking Up Is Hard to Do," *7th Heaven* (also known as *Seventh Heaven* and *7th Heaven: Beginnings*), The WB, 1997.

Ms. Hollings, "It's My Party," *Ally McBeal,* Fox, 1998.

Karen Cassidy, "Culture Clash," *Judging Amy,* CBS, 2000.

Judge Arlene Stanton, "Imperfect Victims," *The District,* CBS, 2000.

Joyce Sidwell, "Magician," *Providence,* NBC, 2001.

Audrey Simmons, "God's Work," *The Agency,* CBS, 2001.

Audrey Simmons, "First Born," *The Agency,* CBS, 2002.

Joyce Sidwell, "Shadow Play," *Providence,* NBC, 2002.

Cathy Payton, "Doppelganger: Part 2," *Without a Trace* (also known as *W.A.T.*), CBS, 2004.

Ava Rey, "The Y Factor," *Strong Medicine,* Lifetime, 2005.

Ava Rey, "Gunshot Wedding," *Strong Medicine,* Lifetime, 2005.

Also appeared in *Cassie and Co.*

Stage Appearances:

Middle of the Night, Woodstock Playhouse, Woodstock, NY, 1958.

Waltz of the Toreadors, Woodstock Playhouse, 1958.

Sara, *Major Barbara,* Arena Stage, Washington, DC, 1959.

Dunyasha, *The Cherry Orchard,* Arena Stage, 1959.

Diana, *Ring Around the Moon,* Arena Stage, 1960.

Pearl, *The Iceman Cometh,* Arena Stage, 1960.

Halinka Apt, *The Wall,* Billy Rose Theatre, New York City, 1960–61.

Acte, *The Emperor,* Maidman Playhouse, New York City, 1963.

In White America, Sheridan Square Playhouse, New York City, 1963–65.

Julie Danton, *Danton's Death,* Vivian Beaumont Theatre, Lincoln Center, New York City, 1965–66.

Standby for role of Susy Hendrix, *Wait until Dark,* Music Box Theatre, New York City, 1966.

Jean McCormack and Mimsey Hubley, *Plaza Suite* (three one–acts), Plymouth Theatre, New York City, between 1968 and 1970.

Emmeline, *King Arthur,* Atlanta Repertory Theatre, Atlanta, GA, 1968.

Teresa, *The Hostage,* Atlanta Repertory Theatre, 1968.

Ruth, *The Homecoming,* Atlanta Repertory Theatre, 1968.

Olivia, *Twelfth Night,* Atlanta Repertory Theatre, 1968.

Olga, *You Can't Take It with You,* Atlanta Repertory Theatre, 1969.

Regina, *The Little Foxes,* Atlanta Repertory Theatre, 1969.

Barbara, *Major Barbara,* Atlanta Repertory Theatre, 1969.

Ellie, *The Great White Hope,* Ahmanson Theatre, Los Angeles, 1969–70.

Standby for the role of Anna, *Old Times,* Mark Taper Forum, Los Angeles, 1972.

Olive, *Caesarean Operations,* Theatre West, Los Angeles, 1972.

Adriana, *A Comedy of Errors,* Los Angeles Shakespeare Festival, John Anson Ford Theatre, Los Angeles, 1974.

Mrs. James, *The Death and Life of Jesse James,* Mark Taper Forum, 1975.

Kate, *P.S. Your Cat Is Dead,* Westwood Playhouse, Los Angeles, 1976.

Jane Merryweather, *The Journalists,* Back Alley Theatre, Los Angeles, 1978.

Rita, *First Love, Best Love,* Strasberg Theatre Center, Los Angeles, 1983–84.

Nell, *Passion Play,* Mark Taper Forum, 1984.

Dona Ana, *Don Juan in Hell,* Room for Theatre, Los Angeles, 1986–87.

Interviewer, *Larkin,* Mark Taper Forum, 1988.

Myra, *Deathtrap,* California Theatre, San Bernardino, CA, 1990.

Lillian Cornwall, *Isn't It Romantic,* Pasadena Playhouse, Pasadena, CA, 1993.

Lady Rumpers, *Habeas Corpus,* Matrix Theatre, Los Angeles, 1994.

Mad Forest, Matrix Theatre, 1996.

Freda, *Dangerous Corner,* Matrix Theatre, 1997.

An American Daughter, Los Angeles TheatreWorks, Matrix Theatre (also recorded for future radio broadcasts), 1998.

Kit, Mom, and Cat, *The Water Children,* Matrix Theatre, 1998.

After the Fall, Los Angeles TheatreWorks (recorded for future radio broadcasts), 1999.

Cakewalk, Los Angeles TheatreWorks, Skirball Theatre, Los Angeles (recorded for future radio broadcasts), 2000.

Margaret Lord, *The Philadelphia Story,* Court Theatre, Los Angeles, 2000.

Major Tours:

Norma Brown, *Invitation to a March,* East Coast cities, 1961–62.

A Shot in the Dark, 1962.

Ellie, *The Great White Hope,* U.S. cities, 1969–70.

Ruth, *Blithe Spirit,* California cities, 1982–83.

Film Appearances:

Pam Albright, *The Mask* (also known as *Eyes from Hell, Eyes of Hell, Face of Fire,* and *The Spooky Movie Show*), Warner Bros., 1961.

Solly, *... All the Marbles* (also known as *The California Dolls*), Metro–Goldwyn–Mayer, 1981.

Over Here Mr. President, 1983.

Page Hiller, *Tuff Turf,* New World, 1985.

Dr. Rissner, *Sleeping with the Enemy,* Twentieth Century–Fox, 1991.

Dr. Lisa Farrow, *Final Vendetta* (also known as *Surrogate Mother* and *Sweet Evil*), A–Pix Entertainment, 1996.

The Doyles, 1997.

Second Son'a officer, *Star Trek: Insurrection* (also known as *Star Trek 9*), Paramount, 1998.

Voice, *Aladdin and the Adventures of All Time* (animated), 2000.

Barbara Collins, *Eulogy,* Lions Gate Films, 2004.

NEWMAN, David 1954–

PERSONAL

Full name, David Louis Newman; born March 11, 1954, in Los Angeles, CA; son of Alfred (a composer and conductor) and Martha Montgomery Newman; brother of Thomas Montgomery Newman (a composer) and Maria Newman (a composer and musician); cousin of Randy Newman (a composer, conductor, singer, pianist, and songwriter), Carroll Newman (a producer), and Joey Newman (a composer, orchestrator, music arranger, and conductor); married; wife's name, Krystyna; children: Brianne (stepdaughter), Diana. *Education:* University of Southern California, B.A., M.A.; classically trained violinist and conductor.

Addresses: *Agent*—First Artists Management, 4764 Park Granada, Suite 210, Calabasas, CA 91302.

Career: Composer, conductor, orchestrator, and actor. Sundance Institute, music director and workshop presenter, 1987–91; Los Angeles Pops (orchestra), music director and conductor, c. 1990; previously worked as a studio musician and member of community orchestras; guest conductor of international orchestras; composer of scores for industrial films.

Awards, Honors: BMI Film Music Awards, 1988, for *Throw Momma from the Train,* 1990, for *The War of the Roses,* 1995, for *The Flintstones,* and 1997, for *The Nutty Professor;* Academy Award nomination (with others), best original score for a musical or comedy film, Golden Satellite Award nomination, outstanding original score, International Press Academy, and Annie Award nomination (with others), outstanding music in an animated feature production, International Animated Film Society, 1998, all for *Anastasia;* Saturn Award nomination, best music, Academy of Science Fiction, Fantasy and Horror Films, 2000, for *Galaxy Quest;* BMI Film Music Awards, 2001, for *Nutty Professor II: The Klumps,* and 2002, for *Dr. Dolittle 2;* BMI Film Music Award, 2002, and Annie Award nomination, outstanding music in an animated feature production, 2003, both for *Ice Age;* BMI Film Music Awards, 2003, for *How to Lose a Guy in 10 Days* and *Scooby–Doo;* BMI Film Music Award, 2004, for *Daddy Day Care;* BMI Film Music Award, 2005, for *Are We There Yet?.*

CREDITS

Film Orchestrator and Music Conductor:

(Uncredited) *Hoffa,* 1992.

Coneheads, Paramount, 1993.

Tommy Boy, Paramount, 1995.

Jingle All the Way, Twentieth Century–Fox, 1996.

Out to Sea, Twentieth Century–Fox, 1997.

Anastasia (animated), Twentieth Century–Fox, 1997.

Scooby–Doo, Warner Bros., 2002.

Ice Age (animated), Twentieth Century–Fox, 2002.

Life or Something Like It, Twentieth Century–Fox, 2002.

Film Orchestrator:

Wise Guys, Metro–Goldwyn–Mayer, 1986.

Dragnet, Universal, 1987.

Mr. Destiny, Buena Vista, 1990.

The Marrying Man (also known as *Too Hot to Handle*), Buena Vista, 1991.

Paradise, Buena Vista, 1991.

Talent for the Game, Paramount, 1991.

Honeymoon in Vegas, Columbia, 1992.

The Mighty Ducks (also known as *Champions* and *The Mighty Ducks Are the Champions*), Buena Vista, 1992.

The Air Up There, Buena Vista, 1994.

(And vocal arranger) *My Father the Hero* (also known as *My father, ce heros*), Buena Vista, 1994.

The Cowboy Way, Universal, 1994.

Boys on the Side (also known as *Avec ou sans hommes*), Warner Bros., 1995.

Operation Dumbo Drop (also known as *Dumbo Drop*), Buena Vista, 1995.

The Phantom, Paramount, 1996.

The Nutty Professor, Universal, 1996.

Galaxy Quest, DreamWorks, 1999.

The Affair of the Necklace, Warner Bros., 2001.

Death to Smoochy (also known as *Toetet Smoochy*), Warner Bros., 2002.

Duplex (also known as *Our House* and *Der Appartement—Schreck*), Miramax, 2003.

Film Music Conductor:

(Uncredited) *Battle beyond the Stars,* New World, 1980.

Big Bully, Warner Bros., 1996.

Never Been Kissed, Fox 2000, 1999.

Brokedown Palace, Twentieth Century–Fox, 1999.

Bedazzled (also known as *Teuflisch*), Twentieth Century–Fox, 2000.

102 Dalmatians, Buena Vista, 2000.

Dr. Doolittle 2 (also known as *DR.2* and *DR2*), Twentieth Century–Fox, 2001.

How to Lose a Guy in 10 Days (also known as *Wie werde ich ihn los in 10 tagen*), Paramount, 2003.

Daddy Day Care, Columbia, 2003.

The Cat in the Hat (also known as *Dr. Seuss' "The Cat in the Hat"*), Universal, 2003.

Scooby Doo 2: Monsters Unleashed (also known as *Scooby–Doo 2: Monstres en liberte*), Warner Bros., 2004.

(Uncredited) *Are We There Yet?,* Columbia, 2005.

Monster–in–Law (also known as *Das Schwiegermonster*), New Line Cinema, 2005.

Serenity, Universal, 2005.

Film Work; Other:

(Uncredited) Violinist, *E.T. the Extra–Terrestrial* (also known as *E.T.* and *E.T. the Extra–Terrestrial: The 20th Anniversary*), Universal, 1982.

Song arranger and music director, *The Brave Little Toaster* (animated short film), Hyperion, 1987.

Film Appearances:

Graves, *The Runestone,* 1990.

Television Music Conductor; Specials:

"Twentieth Century–Fox Fanfare," *20th Century–Fox: The Blockbuster Years,* AMC, 2000.

WRITINGS

Film Music:

Frankenweenie, Buena Vista, 1984.

Critters, New Line Cinema, 1986.

Vendetta (also known as *Angels behind Bars* and *Never Surrender … Fight to the Last*), Concorde, 1986.

The Kindred, FM Home Video, 1986.

Malone, Orion, 1987.

Throw Mama from the Train, Orion, 1987.

My Demon Lover, New Line Cinema, 1987.

The Brave Little Toaster (animated short film), Hyperion, 1987.

Additional music, *Dragnet,* Universal, 1987.

Bill & Ted's Excellent Adventure, Orion, 1989.

Heathers, New World, 1989.

Disorganized Crime (also known as *Disorganised Crime*), Buena Vista, 1989.

Little Monsters (also known as *Little Ghost Fighters*), Metro–Goldwyn–Mayer, 1989.

Gross Anatomy (also known as *A Cut Above*), Buena Vista, 1989.

The War of the Roses, Twentieth Century–Fox,1989.

R.O.T.O.R., Imperial Entertainment, 1989.

Cranium Command, 1989.

Back to Neverland, 1990.

Madhouse, Orion, 1990.

Meet the Applegates (also known as *The Applegators*), Triton Pictures, 1990.

Fire Birds (also known as *Wings of the Apache*), Buena Vista, 1990.

The Freshman, TriStar, 1990.

DuckTales: The Movie—Treasure of the Lost Lamp (animated; also known as *Duck Tales, Duck Tales: The Movie, Treasure of the Lost Lamp,* and *La bande a picsou: le tresor de la lampe perdue*), Buena Vista, 1990.

Mr. Destiny, Buena Vista, 1990.

The Runestone, Hyperion, 1990.

The Marrying Man (also known as *Too Hot to Handle*), Buena Vista, 1991.

Talent for the Game, Paramount, 1991.

Don't Tell Mom the Babysitter's Dead, Warner Bros., 1991.

Bill & Ted's Bogus Journey, Orion, 1991.

Rover Dangerfield, Warner Bros., 1991.

Paradise, Buena Vista, 1991.

Other People's Money (also known as *Riqueza ajena*), Warner Bros., 1991.

Michael & Mickey, 1991.

Honeymoon in Vegas, Columbia, 1992.

(And theme song) *The Mighty Ducks* (also known as *Champions* and *The Mighty Ducks Are the Champions*), Buena Vista, 1992.

That Night (also known as *One Hot Summer*), Warner Bros., 1992.

Hoffa, Twentieth Century–Fox, 1992.

The Itsy Bitsy Spider, 1992.

The Sandlot (also known as *The Sandlot Kids*), Twentieth Century–Fox, 1993.

Coneheads, Paramount, 1993.

Undercover Blues, Universal, 1993.

The Air Up There, Buena Vista, 1994.

My Father, the Hero (also known as *My father, ce heros*), Buena Vista, 1994.

The Flintstones, Universal, 1994.

The Cowboy Way, Universal, 1994.

I Love Trouble, Buena Vista, 1994.

(Uncredited) Additional music, *Corrina, Corrina,* 1994.

Boys on the Side (also known as *Avec ou sans hommes*), Warner Bros., 1995.

Tommy Boy, Paramount, 1995.

Operation Dumbo Drop (also known as *Dumbo Drop*), Buena Vista, 1995.
Big Bully, Warner Bros., 1996.
The Phantom, Paramount, 1996.
The Nutty Professor, Universal, 1996.
Matilda (also known as *Roald Dahl's "Matilda"*), Sony Pictures Entertainment, 1996.
(And "Turbo Man Theme") *Jingle All the Way,* Twentieth Century–Fox, 1996.
Out to Sea, Twentieth Century–Fox, 1997.
Anastasia (animated), Twentieth Century–Fox, 1997.
1001 Nights, 1998.
Never Been Kissed, Fox, 1999.
Brokedown Palace, Twentieth Century–Fox, 1999.
Bowfinger, Universal, 1999.
Galaxy Quest, DreamWorks, 1999.
The Flintstones in Viva Rock Vegas, Universal, 2000.
Nutty Professor II: The Klumps (also known as *The Klumps*), Universal, 2000.
Duets, Buena Vista, 2000.
Bedazzled (also known as *Teuflisch*), Twentieth Century–Fox, 2000.
102 Dalmatians (animated), Buena Vista, 2000.
Dr. Doolittle 2 (also known as *DR.2* and *DR2*), Twentieth Century–Fox, 2001.
The Affair of the Necklace, Warner Bros., 2001.
(And songs "The Cookie Chant," "Friends Come in All Sizes," and "Smoochy's Magic Jungle Theme") *Death to Smoochy* (also known as *Toetet Smoochy*), Warner Bros., 2002.
Ice Age (animated), Twentieth Century–Fox, 2002.
Life or Something like It, Twentieth Century–Fox, 2002.
Scooby–Doo, Warner Bros., 2002.
How to Lose a Guy in 10 Days (also known as *Wie werde ich ihn los in 10 tagen*), Paramount, 2003.
Daddy Day Care, Columbia, 2003.
Duplex (also known as *Our House* and *Der Appartement—Schreck*), Miramax, 2003.
The Cat in the Hat (also known as *Dr. Seuss' "The Cat in the Hat"*), Universal, 2003.
Scooby Doo 2: Monsters Unleashed (also known as *Scooby–Doo 2: Monstres en liberte*), Warner Bros., 2004.
Are We There Yet?, Columbia, 2005.
Man of the House, Columbia, 2005.
Monster–in–Law (also known as *Das Schwiegermonster*), New Line Cinema, 2005.
Serenity, Universal, 2005.
Norbit, Paramount, 2007.
Welcome Home, Roscoe Jenkins, Universal, 2008.
The Spirit (also known as *Will Eisner's "The Spirit"*), Lions Gate Films, 2008.
My Life in Ruins (also known as *Driving Aphrodite*), Fox Searchlight, 2009.
Crazy on the Outside, Boxing Cat Films, 2009.

Songs Featured in Films:
"You'll End up Eating Worms," *The Worm Eaters,* New American Films, 1977.

"Samson and Delilah" and "You're in Paradise Now," *Pass the Ammo,* New Century/Vista, 1987.

Television Music; Movies:
The Flamingo Rising, CBS, 2001.
Scooby–Doo! The Mystery Begins (animated), Cartoon Network, 2009.

Television Music; Specials:
It's a Bird, It's a Plane, It's Superman, ABC, 1975.
Spotlight on Location—Nutty Professor II: The Klumps, 2000.

Television Music; Series:
Ripley's Believe It or Not, ABC, 1982.

Television Music; Episodic:
"Aladdin and His Wonderful Lamp," *Faerie Tale Theatre* (also known as *Shelley Duvall's "Faerie Tale Theatre"*), Showtime, 1984.
"Such Interesting Neighbors," *Amazing Stories* (also known as *Steven Spielberg Presents "Amazing Stories"* and *Steven Spielberg's "Amazing Stories"*), NBC, 1987.
"The Thing from the Grave," *Tales from the Crypt* (also known as *"HBO's Tales from the Crypt"*), HBO, 1990.

Video Music:
The Making of "Anastasia," Twentieth Century–Fox Home Entertainment, 2006.

ADAPTATIONS

The "Original Mighty Ducks Theme" was also featured in the sequels *D2: The Mighty Ducks,* 1994, and *D3: The Mighty Ducks,* 1996.

NORRIE, Daran
    See NORRIS, Daran

NORRIS, Brian R.
    (Brian Norris)

PERSONAL

Brother of Graham Norris (an actor). *Education:* University of California, Los Angeles, B.A.; trained with Lesly Kahn in Los Angeles.

Addresses: *Agent*—Meredith Fine, Coast to Coast Talent, Inc., 3350 Barham Blvd., Los Angeles, CA 90068. *Manager*—Mimi Ditrani, Peter Schiff Co., 9465 Wilshire Blvd., Suite 480, Beverly Hills, CA 90212.

Career: Actor. Los Angeles Theatre Ensemble, Los Angeles, founding member. Appeared in commercial for TurboTax computer software; appeared as Candygram delivery boy in commercial for Swiffer cleaning products.

Member: American Federation of Television and Radio Artists, Screen Actors Guild.

CREDITS

Television Appearances; Episodic:
Kenny Moore, "Gimme Shelter," *Nash Bridges* (also known as *Bridges*), CBS, 1999.
Teen in compound, "For Better or for Worse," *Big Love*, HBO, 2009.
Pizza delivery guy, "Three's Not Company," *Sonny with a Change*, The Disney Channel, 2009.
Cop, *General Hospital*, ABC, 2009.
Brandon, "Attack of the No–Men," *Kamen Rider: Dragon Knight*, The CW, 2009.
Brandon, "A Dragon Caged," *Kamen Rider: Dragon Knight*, The CW, 2009.

Television Appearances; as Brian Norris; Episodic:
First lout, "The Bitch Is Back," *Veronica Mars*, The CW, 2007.
Mailroom boy, "Indian Summer," *Mad Men*, AMC, 2007.
Todd, "The Benefactor," *Mad Men*, AMC, 2008.
Young Jerry, "Stole an RV," *My Name Is Earl*, NBC, 2008.
Scared soldier, "Into Hell: Parts 1 & 2," *The Unit*, CBS, 2008.
Lucas, "Road Kill," *Navy NCIS: Naval Criminal Investigative Service* (also known as *NCIS* and *NCIS: Naval Criminal Investigative Service*), CBS, 2008.
Marcus Braden (some sources cite role of Marcus Holmes), "The Best Policy," *Lie to Me*, Fox, 2009.

Television Work; Series:
(English version) Voice of Albert, *Vipo the Flying Dog* (animated), 2007.

Internet Appearances; Episodic:
Jonas, "The Mother of All Days," *In the Motherhood*, Inthemotherhood.com, 2007.

Film Appearances:
Student dancer, *Lloyd* (also known as *Lloyd: The Ugly Kid* and *The Ugly Kid*), SoHo Entertainment, 2001.

Henry, *Nourishment* (short film), Out of the Park Productions/Line 9 Productions, 2007.

Stage Appearances:
Appeared in productions of *Bingo with the Indians*, Rogue Machine Theatre; *Much Ado about Nothing*, Actors Crew; *Richard III*, California Shakespeare Festival; *Stone Cold Dead Serious*, Los Angeles Theatre Ensemble, Los Angeles; *Treefall*, Rogue Machine Theatre; and *Wounded*, Los Angeles Theatre Ensemble.

OTHER SOURCES

Electronic:
Brian R. Norris Official Site, http://www.briannorrisonline.com, February 18, 2010.

NORRIS, Daran 1964–
(Jack Hammer, Daran Norrie, Daran W. Norris, Darin Norris, Darran Norris, Darren Norris, James Penrod, Justin Shyder, Bob Thomas, Rob Thomas)

PERSONAL

Original name, Daran Morrison Nordland; born November 1, 1964, in Ferndale, WA; married Mary McGlynn, June 17, 1988.

Addresses: *Agent*—Defining Artists, 100 Universal City Plaza, Suite 2000, Universal City, CA 91608.

Career: Actor and voice artist.

CREDITS

Film Appearances:
(English version; as Justin Shyder) Voice of second instructor, *Juichi–nin iru!* (animated; also known as *11 People!*, *There Are 11!*, and *They Were 11*), 1986.
Club Scum M.C., *Hobgoblins*, American Cinema Marketing, 1987.
(English version) Voice of astronomy teacher, *Teito monogatari* (animated; also known as *Tokyo: The Last Megalopolis*), 1988.
Laundromat John, *Vice Academy* (also known as *Vicebusters*), 1989.
(English version; as Justin Shyder) Voice of Zangetsu the Mid–day, *Jaianto robo: Animeshon* (animated; also known as *Gaint Robo: The Animation*, *Giant*

Robo: The Day the Earth Stood Still, Giant Robo: The Night Earth Stood Still, and Jaianto Robo—Chikyu ga seishi suru hi) 1991.

(As James Penrod) Dark Schneider, Bastard!!, 1992.

(English version; as James Penrod) Voice of Detective Todo, Rakusho! Hyper Doll (animated), 1995.

(English version; as Rob Thomas) Burakku jakku (animated; also known as Black Jack), 1996.

(As Jack Hammer) Voice of Tasuki, Fushigi Yugi: Memories First OAV (animated), 1996.

(As James Penrod) Voice of Tasuki, Fushigi Yugi: The Mysterious Play—Reflections OAV 2 (animated), 1997.

Andrew Baily, Invisible Dad, A–Pix Entertainment, 1997.

Young man, The Souler Opposite, Curb Entertainment, 1998.

(As Daran W. Norris) George, Billy Frankenstein, 1998.

Stamper, The Kid with the X–Ray Eyes, New Horizons Home Video, 1999.

Inviati speciali, 2000.

Voice, Adventures in Odyssey: The Last Days of Eugene Meltsner (animated), 2000.

Red Sox replay, In the Bedroom, Miramax, 2001.

(English version) Voice of Vincent Volaju, Kauboi bibappu: Tengoku no tobira (animated; also known as Cowboy Bebop: Tengoku no tobira, Cowboy Bebop: Knockin' on Heavens Door, Cowboy Bebop the Movie: Knockin' on Heaven's Door, and Cowboy Bebop: The Movie), Sony Pictures Entertainment, 2001.

(English version) Voice of Brutus, Der kleine Eisbar (animated; also known as Der kleine eisbar—Der Kinofilm and The Little Polar Bear), 2001.

Voiceover, Aunt Luisa, 2002.

(English version; as Bob Thomas) Voice of Kiichi Goto, WXIII: Patlabor the Movie 3 (animated), 2002.

Voice of Cosmo, Jimmy Neutron's Nicktoon Blast (animated short film; also known as Jimmy Neutron Adventures), Universal, 2003.

Announcer, The Cat in the Hat (also known as Dr. Seuss' "The Cat in the Hat"), Universal, 2003.

Voice, Aero–Troopers: The Nemeclous Crusade (animated), Creative Light Worldwide, 2003.

Voice of Commander Courage and Bruce Easly, Comic Book: The Movie (animated), Miramax Home Entertainment, 2004.

(As Daran Norrie) Director, The Greatest Short Film Ever!!! (short film), 2004.

(English version) Voice of Sandayu Asama, Gekijo–ban Naruto: Daikatsugeki! Yukihime ninpocho dattebayo!! (animated; also known as Naruto the Movie: Ninja Clash in the Land of Snow), Toho Company, 2004.

Voice of Spottswoode, Team America: World Police (also known as Team America), Paramount, 2004.

(English version) Voice of Vitalstatistix, Asterix et les Vikings (animated; also known as Asterix and the Vikings and Asterix og vikingerne), 2006.

Voice of Louie, Bolt (animated), Walt Disney Studios Motion Pictures, 2008.

Voice of 1940s newscaster, Beyond All Boundaries (short film), 2009.

Himself, "Spider–Man": Re–Animated (short documentary), Sony Pictures Home Entertainment, 2009.

Himself, "Hobgoblins": The Making of a Disaster Piece (short documentary), Shout! Factory, 2009.

Film Additional Voices:

Die Abenteuer von Pico und Columbus (animated; also known as Pico und Columbus and The Magic Voyage), 1992.

(English version; as Rob Thomas) El Hazard: The Magnificent World 2 (animated; also known as El Hazard 2), 1997.

Dinosaur (animated), Buena Vista, 2000.

The Adventures of Tom Thumbs & Thumbelina (animated), 2002.

(English version) Gekijo–ban Naruto: Daikatsugeki! Yukihime ninpocho dattebayo!! (animated; also known as Naruto the Movie: Ninja Clash in the Land of Snow), 2004.

(Uncredited; English version) Hauru no ugoku shiro (animated; also known as Howl's Moving Castle), Buena Vista International, 2004.

Also appeared as (English version; as Jack Hammer) additional voices, Rupan sansei: Kariosutoro no shiro (animated; also known as Arsene Lupin and the Castle of Cagliostro, Lupin III: Castle of Cagliostro, Lupin the Third: The Castle of Cagliostro, and The Castle of Cagliostro).

Television Appearances; Series:

(English version; as Jack Hammer) Voice of narrator and Chap, Kido senshi Gundam 0083: Stardust Memory (animated; also known as Mobile Suit Gundam 0083: Stardust Memory), 1991.

Voice of narrator, Guile's friend, vice cope, bellhop, and doctor, Street Fighter II: V (animated; also known as Street Fighter II: Victory), 1995.

(Uncredited) Series announcer/narrator, V.I.P., syndicated, 1998.

Voice of tax collector, El Hazard: The Alternative World (animated), 1998.

(English version; as Jack Hammer) Voice of Lahrrl's coach, Battle Athletes daiundokai (animated; also known as Battle Athletes Victory), 1998.

(English version; as Jack Hammer) Voice of Morgan, Cowboy Andy, and bartender, Kauboi bibappu (animated; also known as Cowboy Bebop), 1998–99.

Voice of Brock Hammand and announcer, The Chimp Channel, TBS, 1999.

(English version; as James Penrod) Voice of fiance, Gate Keepers (animated; also known as Gate Keepers 21), 2001.

Voice of Sinon, soldier, and various characters, *Time Squad* (animated), Cartoon Network, 2001–2002.

Voice of Gabriolis and Redda, *Mon Colle Knights* (animated), 2001.

Voice of Cosmo, Mr. Turner, and other characters, *The Fairly OddParents* (animated), Nickelodeon, 2001–2008.

Voice of Egbert and Gingerbread Man, *Oswald* (animated), CBS, 2001–2002.

Voice of Heavy Load, *Transformers: Robots in Disguise* (animated), Fox Kids, 2001.

Voice of narrator, Colonel Stank, and Galactic Ranger number one, *Commander Cork* (animated), Cartoon Network, 2002.

Voice of Nanao, *Kokaku kidotai: Stand Alone Complex* (animated; also known as *Ghost in the Shell: Stand Alone Complex, Ghost in the Shell: Stand Alone Complex 2nd Gig*, and *Kokaku kiotari: S.A.C. 2nd Gig*), 2002.

Voice of Mercurymon, *Digimon: Digital Monsters* (animated), ABC, 2002–2003.

Voice of various characters, *Samurai Jack* (animated), Cartoon Network, 2002–2004.

Various voices, *The Powerpuff Girls* (animated; also known as *PPG* and *Youlide–Chui nu*), 2002–2005.

Voice of Nanobot number one, *The Adventures of Jimmy Neutron: Boy Genius* (animated), Nickelodeon, 2002–2005.

Various voices, *Codename: Kids Next Door* (animated), 2002–2007.

Voice of announcer and other characters, *Dexter's Laboratory* (animated; also known as *Dexter de Shiyanshi* and *Dexter's Lab*), Cartoon Network, 2003.

Various voices, *Star Wars: Clone Wars* (animated), Cartoon Network, 2003–2005.

Cliff McCormack, *Veronica Mars*, UPN then The CW, 2004–2007.

Gordy, *Ned's Declassified School Survival Guide* (also known as *Neds ultimativer schulwahnsinn*), Nickelodeon, 2004–2007.

Dr. Electric, *The Buzz on Maggie* (also known as *Disney's "The Buzz on Maggie"*), The Disney Channel, 2005.

(English version) Voice of Sangorou, *Naruto* (animated; also known as *Naruto Shounen–hen*), Cartoon Network, 2005.

Various voices, *The Life and Times of Juniper Lee*, Cartoon Network, 2005–2006.

Voice of Jack Smith, *American Dad!* (animated), Fox, 2005–2009.

Voice of Dick Daring, Slone Stone, and others, *The Replacements* (animated), The Disney Channel, 2006–2009.

Voice of Emilano Suarez, *El Tigre: The Adventures of Manny Rivera* (animated), Nickelodeon, 2007.

Voice of J. Jonah Jameson, *The Spectacular Spider–Man* (animated), The CW, 2008–2009.

Various voices, *The Marvelous Misadventures of Flapjack*, Cartoon Network, 2008–2009.

Also appeared as Marcel Daran, George Marshall, and H. Von Myer, *Rupan sansei: Part II* (animated; also known as *Lupin the 3rd* and *The New Lupin III*).

Television Appearances; Movies:

Flat top, *Earth Angel*, ABC, 1991.

Voice of Diamondhead, *Ben 10: Race Against Time* (animated), Cartoon Network, 2007.

Announcer, *Gym Teacher: The Movie*, Nickelodeon, 2008.

Television Appearances; Specials:

Voice of Alien official and clerk, *Bagboy!*, 2002.

Voice of Cosmo and Dad Turner, "*The Fairly OddParents*" in: "*Abra Catastrophe!*" (animated; also known as *Abra–Catastrophe, The Fairly OddParents Movie*, and *The Fairy OddParents in Abra Catastrophe!*), Nickelodeon, 2003.

Announcer, *Nickelodeon's 16th Annual Kids' Choice Awards*, Nickelodeon, 2003.

Voice of Mr. Reed, Sheriff, and cowardly lion, *A Scooby–Doo Halloween* (animated), The WB, 2003.

Voice of Cosmo, Mr. Turner, and Jorgen Von Strangle, "*The Fairly OddParents*" in "*School's Out! The Musical*" (animated), Nickelodeon, 2004.

Voice of Cosmo, Mr. Turner, and Jorgen, *The Jimmy Timmy Power Hour* (animated), Nickelodeon, 2004.

Voice of Mr. Turner, Como, and others, "*The Fairly OddParents*" in: "*Channel Chasers* (animated), Nickelodeon, 2004.

Announcer, *Penn & Teller: Off the Deep End*, NBC, 2005.

Voice of Cosmo, Mr. Turner, Jorgen von Strangle, and Anti–Cosmo, *The Jimmy Timmy Power Hour 2: When Nerds Collide* (animated), Nickelodeon, 2006.

Voice of Cosmo, Jorgen Von Strangle, Mr. Turner, and the April Fool, "*The Fairly OddParents*" in "*Fairy Idol*" (animated), Nickelodeon, 2006.

Voice of Cosmo and Mr. Turner, *The Jimmy Timmy Power Hour 3: The Jerkinators!* (animated), Nickelodeon, 2006.

Voice of Count Spankulot and janitor, *Codename: Kids Next Door—Operation Z.E.R.O.* (also known as *Operation: Z.E.R.O.*), Cartoon Network, 2006.

Television Appearances; Pilots:

Voice of Chief, *T.U.F.F. Puppy*, Nickelodeon, 2010.

Television Appearances; Episodic:

Voice of Santa Claus, "Jingle Bells, Something Smells," *Shnookums and Meat Funny Cartoon Show* (animated), 1993.

Voice of Smart Animals, "Smarten Up," *Street Sharks*, 1994.

Voice of Porkey Pine, "Ow. Hey!," *Shnookums and Meat Funny Cartoon Show* (animated), 1995.

Waiter, *Mad TV*, Fox, 1995.

Passerby, *Mad TV*, Fox, 1996.

Voice of Dad Turner, Cosmo, and others, "What Is Funny?," *Oh Yeah! Cartoons* (animated), Nickelodeon, 1998.

Voice of Mr. Turner and Cosmo, "The Fairly Odd Parents," *Oh Yeah! Cartoons* (animated), Nickelodeon, 1998.

Man, "Choose Me," *Becker*, CBS, 1999.

Counselor, "Heroes," *The Jersey*, 1999.

Voice of karaoke emcee, "Empty the Dragon," *Son of Beach* (animated), 2002.

Voice of man number two, man number three, Hunch Bishop, and Prince, "Jack Is Naked", *Samurai Jack* (animated), 2002.

Voice of Spartok, "Jack and the Spartans", *Samurai Jack* (animated), 2002.

Voice of narrator, taxman, and penguin, "Super Santa: South Pole Joe," *Oh Yeah! Cartoons* (animated), Nickelodeon, 2002.

Voice of narrator, reindeer, and corn, "Super Santa: Vegetation," *Oh Yeah! Cartoons* (animated), Nickelodeon, 2002.

Voice of Cowardly Lion, Mr. Reed, and Sheriff, "A Scooby Doo Halloween," *What's New, Scooby–Doo?* (animated), The WB, 2002.

Voice of Ugo DiRinaldi and shopkeeper, "Pompeii and Circumstance," *What's New, Scooby–Doo?* (animated), The WB, 2003.

Voice of Camel Sam and tourist dad, "Mummy Scares Best," *What's New, Scooby–Doo?* (animated), The WB, 2003.

Voice of Dr. Destiny, "Only a Dream: Parts 1 & 2," *Justice League* (animated), 2003.

Voice of shop teacher, mopey, and old lady number two, "Attack of the 5 1/2 Ft. Geek/Doom with a View," *My Life as a Teenage Robot* (animated), Nickelodeon, 2003.

Voice, "Kim Jong II Must Die," *Kid Notorious*, Comedy Central, 2003.

Voice of Gynok, Brock, and VJ announcer, "Thanksgiving Throwdown," *Megas XLR* (animated), Cartoon Network, 2004.

Glamorous man, *Grounded for Life*, 2004.

Voice of bullet and newscaster number two, "Public Enemies," *Danny Phantom* (animated), Nickelodeon, 2005.

Voice of Brent, "Meltdown," *The Batman* (animated), The WB, 2005.

Voice of fox bounty hunter, cyborg number one, and hungortus, "Good Duck Hunting/Consumption Overruled," *Duck Dodgers* (animated; also known as *Duck Dodgers in the 24 1/2 Century*), Cartoon Network, 2005.

Voice of Santa, elf, and mall cop, "I Saw Stroker Killing Santa Claus," *Stroker and Hoop* (animated), Cartoon Network, 2005.

Voice of Santa, "Putting the 'Ass' in Assassin," *Stroker and Hoop* (animated), Cartoon Network, 2005.

Voice of imaginary man, "Challenge of the Superfriends," *Foster's Home for Imaginary Friends* (animated), Cartoon Network, 2006.

Voice of Tynar, "B Is for Betrayal," *W.I.T.C.H.* (animated), ABC Family, 2006.

Voice of Ralph Runtner and Alien dad, "The Family Business," *Loonatics Unleashed* (animated), The WB, 2006.

Voice, *Kim Possible* (animated), The Disney Channel, 2006.

Voice of Conrad Conrad, "SamSquatch," *Random! Cartoons* (animated), Nickelodeon, 2007.

Voice of Ranger Stu and students, "Kamen no gundan to yabumen," *Bleach* (animated), Cartoon Network, 2007.

Voice of bubble gum vendor and screaming vendor, "Grubble Gum/The Cinnamini Monster," *Chowder* (animated), Cartoon Network, 2007.

Captain Terrific, "Captain Terrific," *Imagination Movers*, 2009.

Tony Carolla, "Investors Dinner," *Party Down*, 2009.

Larry King, *State of the Union* (also known as *Tracey Ullman's "State of the Union"*), Showtime, 2009.

Voice of Seymour Smooth, "I Think I'm a Clone Now/Answer All My Questions and Win Stuff," *WordGirl*, PBS, 2009.

Also appeared as voice of Cosmo, Jorgan and dog number two, "'The Fairly OddParents': The Really Bad Day," *Oh Yeah! Cartoons* (animated), Nickelodeon.

Television Additional Voices; Series:

El Hazard: Wanderers (animated), 1995.

(English version; as Jack Hammer) *Battle Athletes daiundokai* (animated; also known as *Battle Athletes Victory*), 1998.

ChalkZone (animated), Nickelodeon, 2002.

Television Additional Voices; Episodic:

"Documentary/Girls Gone Mild," *The Powerpuff Girls* (animated; also known as *PPG* and *Youlide–Chui nu*), 2004.

"The King of Omashu," *Avatar: The Last Airbender* (animated), Nickelodeon, 2005.

RECORDINGS

Video Games:

Voice of Ice Lord, King Graham, and Weapon Seller Gnome, *King's Quest VIII: Mask of Eternity* (also known as *King's Quest: Mask of Eternity*), 1998.

Voice of Venom/Eddie Brock, Myterio/Quentin Beck, Scorpion/Mac Gargan, Human Torch of the Fantastic Four/Johnny Storm, *Spider–Man*, Activision, 2000.

(As Darren Norris) Voice, *Civilizations: Call to Power 2,* 2000.

(As Darren Norris) Voice of squad voice and dropship voice number thirteen, *Ground Control,* 2000.

(Uncredited; English version) Voice of Ventre, *SkyGunner,* 2001.

Voice of Sandman, Beetle, public address, Shocker, Professor X, and Professor Charles Xavier, *Spider-Man 2 Enter: Electro,* Activision, 2001.

(As Darran Norris) Voice of Dark Acolyte, Engineer, and Old Obi–Wan, *Star Wars: The Clone Wars,* 2002.

Voice of Roy Verhaegan and others, *Minority Report,* Activision, 2002.

Voice of Hammet and Set, *The Scorpion King: Rise of the Akkadian* (also known as *The Scorpion King*), Universal Interactive Studios, 2002.

(As Darren Norris) Voice of Aragon and Tom Bombadil, *The Lord of the Rings: The Fellowship of the Ring,* 2002.

(English version) Voice of Piros, *.hack//Osen kakudai* (also known as *.hack//Infection* and *.hack//Infection Part I*), 2002.

Voice of Rongo, *The Mark of Kri,* 2002.

(English version) Voice of Piros, *.hack//Shinshoku osen vol. 3* (also known as *.hack//Mutation* and *.hack//Mutation Part 2*), 2002.

Voice of Roy Verhaegan, *Minority Report,* 2002.

(English version) Voice of Piros, *.hack//Shinshoku osen vol. 3* (also known as *.hack//Outbreak* and *.hack//Outbreak Part 3*), 2002.

(English version) Voice of Osric, *Onimusha buraiden* (also known as *Onimusha Blade Warriors*), Capcom Entertainment, 2003.

(English version; uncredited) Voice of Biwig and Crosell, *Star Ocean: Till the End of Time* (also known as *"Star Ocean: Till the End of Time"—Director's Cut*), Square Enix, 2003.

(English version) Voice of Piros, *.hack//Zettai houi vol. 4* (also known as *.hack//Quarantine* and *.hack//Quaratine Part 4*), Bandai Games, 2003.

(English version) Voice of Rodyle and Shadow, *Tales of the Symphonia,* 2003.

(English version; uncredited) Voice of Manah (Evil Voice), *Drag–On Dragoon* (also known as *Drakengard*), Square Enix, 2003.

(As Darren Norris) Voice, *Command & Conquer: Generals Zero Hour,* Electronic Arts, 2003.

(English version) Voice of Gato and Kaji, *Naruto: Nautimetto hiro* (also known as *Naruto: Ultimate Ninja*), Namco Bandai Games America, 2003.

(As Darren Norris) Voice of Gollum, *The Hobbit,* Sierra Entertainment, 2003.

(As Darren Norris) Voice of Henry, 01–12, and Shrub Patrol 1, *Armed & Dangerous,* LucasArts Entertainment Company, 2003.

Voice of Cosmo, *Fairly Odd Parents: Breakin da Rules,* THQ, 2004.

(English version) Voice of soldier, *Onimusha 3* (also known as *Onimusha 3: Demon Siege*), Capcom Entertainment, 2004.

(As Darren Norris) Voice of Red Alert and Cyclonus, *Transformers,* Atari, 2004.

Voice of Cosmo, *Nicktoons Movin' Eye Toy,* THQ, 2004.

Voice of Cosmo, dad, and Jorgen, *The Fairly Odd Parents: Shadow Showdown,* THQ, 2004.

(As Darren Norris) Voice of Generic Amygdalan, Generic Centaur Enemy, and Generic Dragon Enemy, *EverQuest III,* Sony Online Entertainment, 2004.

Voice of Chuck, Milligan, Cal, and Bum, *Vampire: The Masquerade—Bloodlines,* Activision, 2004.

Voice of G0–T0, *Star Wars: Knights of the Old Republic II—The Sith Lords* (also known as *Star Wars: KOTOR II*), LucasArts Entertainment Company, 2004.

Voice of Cosmo, *Nicktoons Unite,* 2005.

(English version; uncredited) Voice of Genius Weissheit, *Radiata Stories,* Square Enix, 2005.

(Uncredited) Voice of soldiers, *Death by Degrees* (also known as *Tekken's Nina Williams in "Death by Degrees"*), Namco Hometek, 2005.

(English version; uncredited) Voice of Lu Meng and Pang De, *Shin sangoku muso 4* (also known as *Dynasty Warriors 5*), KOEI Corp., 2005.

(As Darren Norris) Voice of announcer, sop, sailor, and construction worker, *Madagascar,* Activision, 2005.

(English version; uncredited) Voice of Comfrey, Commander Ferguson, Dino, and Mayor Marlow, *Ponkotsu roman daikatsugeki Banpi Torotto* (also known as *Steamboat Chronicles*), Atlus USA, 2005.

(English version) Voice of Uzo, *Tenchi no Mon* (also known as *Key of Heaven* and *Kingdom of Paradise*), Sony Computer Entertainment America, 2005.

(English version; uncredited) Voice of La–Ilim, *Grandia III,* Square Enix, 2005.

(English version; uncredited) Commander Vaclav Bloud, *Tales of Legendia,* Namco Hometek, 2005.

(English version; uncredited) Various gang members, *Urban Reign,* Manco Hometek, 2005.

(English version; uncredited) Voice of Lu Meng and Pang De, *Shin sangoku muso 4: Empires* (also known as *Dynasty Warriors 5: Xtreme Legends*), KOEI Corp., 2005.

Voice of Dallas, *Ratchet: Deadlocked,* Sony Computer Entertainment America, 2005.

(English version; uncredited) Voice of AWACS Eagle Eye, *Ace Combat Zero: The Belkan War* (also known as *Ace Combat: The Belkan War*), Namco Bandai Games America, 2006.

(English version; uncredited) Voice of Lu Meng and Pang De, *Shin sangoku muso 4: Empires* (also known as *Dynasty Warriors 5: Empires*), KOEI Corp., 2006.

(English version; uncredited) Voice of Piros the 3rd, Grein, and Salvador Aihara, *.hack//G.U. Vol. 1: Saitan* (also known as *.hack//G.U. Vol. 1//Rebirth*), 2006.

(English version) Voice of Belze, Great SenseiVillains, and narrator, *God Hand,* 2006.

(English version) Voice of Piros the 3rd, Grein, Salvador Aihara, and misc. voices, *.hack//G.U. Vol. 2: Kimi omo koe* (also known as *.hack//G.U. Vol.2// Reminisce*), Namco Bandai Games America, 2006.

Voice of Cosmo, *Nicktoons: Battle for Volcano Island,* THQ, 2006.

Voice, *Resistance: Fall of Man,* Sony Computer Entertainment America, 2006.

(English version) Voice of Piros the 3rd, Grein, Salvador Aihara, and misc. voices, *.hack//G.U. Vol. 3: Aruku you na hayasa de* (also known as *.hack//G.U. Vol. 3//Redemption*), Namco Bandai Games America, 2007.

(English version; uncredited) Voice of Lu Meng, *Muso Orochi* (also known as *Warriors Orochi*), KOEI Corp., 2007.

Voice of Cosmo, *Nicktoons: Attack of the Toybots,* THQ, 2007.

Voice of narrator, *Ratchet & Clank Future: Tools of Destruction,* Sony Computer Entertainment America, 2007.

Voice of Honex, *Bee Movie Game,* Activision, 2007.

(English version; uncredited) Voice of Lu Meng, *Shin sangoku muso 5* (also known as *Dynasty Warriors 6*), KOEI Corp., 2007.

(English version) Voice of Volf, *Ninja Garden II,* Microsoft Game Studios, 2008.

Voice of J. Jonah Jameson, *Spider–Man: Web of Shadows,* Activision, 2008.

(English version) Voice of Volf, *Ninja Gaiden Sigma 2,* Tecmo, 2009.

Video Games; as Additional Voices:

(English version; as James Penrod) *Bushido Blade 2,* 1998.

The Scorpion King: Rise of the Akkadian (also known as *The Scorpion King*), Universal Interactive Studios, 2002.

(English version; uncredited) *Xenosaga Episode 1: Chikara he no ishi* (also known as *Xenosaga, Xenosaga Episode I Reloaded, Xenosaga Episode I: Der Wille zur macht,* and *Xenosaga Episode I: The Will to Power*), 2002.

The Mark of Kri, 2002.

Minority Report, 2002.

Star Wars: Knights of the Old Republic (also known as *Star Wars: KOTOR*), LucasArts Entertainment Company, 2003.

True Crime: Streets of LA, Activision, 2003.

(As Darren Norris) *The Hobbit,* Sierra Entertainment, 2003.

Metal Arms: Glitch in the System, Vivendi Universal Games, 2003.

(English version; uncredited) *Front Mission 4,* Square Enix, 2003.

(English version; uncredited) *Breakdown,* Namco Hometek, 2004.

Doom 3 (also known as *Doom III*), Activision, 2004.

(Uncredited) *Biohazard Outbreak: File 2* (also known as *Resident Evil: Outbreak—File #2*), Capcom Entertainment, 2004.

(English version; uncredited) *Ace Combat 5: The Unsung War* (also known as *Ace Combat: Squadron Leader*), Namco Hometek, 2004.

Star Wars: Knights of the Old Republic II—The Sith Lords (also known as *Star Wars: KOTOR II*), LucasArts Entertainment Company, 2004.

(As Darran Norris) *Doom 3: Resurrection of Evil,* Activision, 2005.

Rise of the Kasai, Sony Computer Entertainment America, 2005.

Grandia III, Square Enix, 2005.

(English version; uncredited) *Project Sylpheed* (also known as *Project Sylpheed: Arc of Deception*), Microsoft Games Studios, 2006.

(English version; uncredited) *Operation Darkness,* Altus USA, 2007.

(English version; uncredited) *Ace Combat 6: Kaiho heno senka* (also known as *Ace Combat 6: Fires of Liberation*), Namco Bandai Games America, 2007.

Monsters vs. Aliens, Activision, 2009.

NORRIS, Graham 1981–

PERSONAL

Born March 13, 1981; brother of Brian R. Norris (an actor). *Education:* Yale University, theatre degree (magna cum laude).

Addresses: *Manager*—Kritzer, Levine, Wilkins, and Griffin Entertainment, 11872 La Grange Ave., 1st Floor, Los Angeles, CA 90025.

Career: Actor. Appeared in television commercials, including McDonald's restaurants.

CREDITS

Film Appearances:

Miles, *Swordswallowers and Thin Men,* Warner Home Video, 2003.

John Spurlick, *All In,* 2005.

Cop, *The Black Dahlia* (also known as *Black Dahlia* and *Die schwarze Dahlie*), Universal, 2006.

Editor, *The Jane Austen Book Club,* Sony Pictures Classics, 2007.

Danny Hansen, *No Pink* (short film), 2007.

Kyle, *Man Overboard,* 2008.

Jared, *Rest Stop: Don't Look Back,* 2008.

Einstein, *Kill Speed,* Epic Pictures Group, 2010.
Einstein, *Fast Glass,* 2010.

Also appeared as Jared, *Rest Stop 2.*

Television Appearances; Specials:
Mike Quin, *Bloody Thursday,* 2009.

Television Appearances; Episodic:
Dereck, "Raincoats and Recipes," *Gilmore Girls,* The WB, 2004.

Dereck, "Norman Mailer, I'm Pregnant!," *Gilmore Girls,* The WB, 2004.
Timid waiter, "The UnGraduate," *Gilmore Girls,* The WB, 2005.
The fan, "Stage Fright," *Dollhouse,* Fox, 2009.
Johnny, "Beating a Dead Workforce," *Better Off Ted,* ABC, 2010.

Stage Appearances:
Gosling, *Photograph 51,* Fountain Theatre, Los Angeles, 2009.

O

O'BANNON, Dan 1946–2009
(Daniel Thomas O'Bannon)

PERSONAL

Full name, Daniel Thomas O'Bannon; born September 30, 1946, in St. Louis, MO; died of complications from Crohn's Disease, December 17, 2009, in Santa Monica, CA. Writer, actor, director, and editor. O'Bannon spent most of his career working in the genres of science fiction and horror. He is best known as the author of the screenplay for the popular film *Alien*. O'Bannon attended film school at the University of Southern California. With classmate John Carpenter he cowrote, edited, and acted in the science fiction film *Dark Star*, which was released in 1974. He then wrote the 1979 blockbuster *Alien*. In 1985 O'Bannon wrote and directed *The Return of the Living Dead,* and he also directed *The Resurrected*. Among O'Bannon's other screenplays are *Total Recall,* which starred Arnold Schwarzenegger; *Blue Thunder; Lifeforce;* and *Screamers.*

PERIODICALS

Los Angeles Times, December 19, 2009.
New York Times, December 21, 2009.
Variety, December 18, 2009.

O'BRIEN, Skip

PERSONAL

Addresses: *Agent*—The Culbertson Group, 8430 Santa Monica Blvd., Suite 210, West Hollywood, CA 90069.

Career: Actor. Appeared in television commercials, including Six Flags amusement parks.

CREDITS

Film Appearances:
Bartender, *Prizzi's Honor,* Twentieth Century–Fox, 1985.
Prisoner, *Echo Park,* Metro–Goldwyn–Mayer, 1986.
Policeman, *Side Out,* TriStar, 1990.
Security guard, *Higher Learning,* Columbia, 1995.
State trooper, *Black Sheep,* Paramount, 1996.
Johnny, construction worker, *A Very Brady Sequel,* Paramount, 1996.
Court guard, *Liar Liar,* Universal, 1997.
Lou Warren, *A Perfect Pitch* (short film), 1998.
Universal Studio guard, *The Muse,* October Films, 1999.
Customs agent, *Blow,* New Line Cinema, 2001.
Sheriff Harlan Bremmer Sr., *The Hitcher,* Rogue Pictures, 2007.

Television Appearances; Series:
Detective Ray O'Riley, *CSI: Crime Scene Investigation* (also known as *CSI: Las Vegas, C.S.I.,* and *Les experts*), CBS, 2000–2003.

Television Appearances; Movies:
Foreman, *Spooner,* The Disney Channel, 1989.
Guard, *Perfect Prey* (also known as *When the Bough Breaks II: Perfect Prey*), HBO, 1998.
Paul, *Audrey's Rain,* Hallmark Channel, 2003.

Television Appearances; Pilots:
Detective Ray O'Riley, *CSI: Crime Scene Investigation* (also known as *CSI: Las Vegas, C.S.I.,* and *Les experts*), CBS, 2000.
Ray/bartender, *Protect and Serve,* CBS, 2007.

Television Appearances; Episodic:

Guard, "Change of Life," *Highway to Heaven*, NBC, 1986.

Bodyguard, "Allegra," *Hunter*, NBC, 1987.

Bus driver, "Nemesis," *The Wonder Years*, ABC, 1989.

Cop, "Dad and Buried," *Over My Dead Body*, CBS, 1990.

Burly guy, "Fence Neighbors," *The Torkelsons*, NBC, 1991.

Policeman, "They Shoot Guns, Don't They?," *Double Rush* (also known as *Lickety Split*), CBS, 1995.

Live Shot, UPN, 1995.

Cop on the street, "Columbus Day," *Gun* (also known as *Robert Altman's "Gun"*), ABC, 1997.

"Sacraments," *Nash Bridges* (also known as *Bridges*), CBS, 1998.

Any Day Now, Lifetime, 1998.

"Judgment," *Vengeance Unlimited* (also known as *Mr. Chapel*), ABC, 1999.

Ed Garrett, "The Apartment," *Providence*, NBC, 2000.

Police officer number two, "Prime Suspect," *Ally McBeal*, Fox, 2000.

Worker, "Traffic Jam," *Malcolm in the Middle*, Fox, 2000.

Captain Tanner, "Foreign Affair," *The District*, CBS, 2001.

Captain Tanner, "The Project," *The District*, CBS, 2001.

Correction Officer Saunders, "Pro Se," *The Practice*, ABC, 2002.

Toby, "It's a Dog Eat Drew World," *The Drew Carey Show*, ABC, 2002.

Blue Jays head coach, "Bringing the Heat," *The Jersey*, The Disney Channel, 2002.

Coach Staley, "Extreme Action Figures," *The Division* (also known as *Heart of the City*), Lifetime, 2003.

Sergeant Chitwood, "Mr. Monk Goes to the Ballgame," *Monk*, USA Network, 2003.

Larry Brody, "Touch & Go," *ER*, NBC, 2004.

Garrett Palmer, "Party Girl," *Without a Trace* (also known as *W.A.T*), CBS, 2005.

Terry Lucas, "Revolution," *Cold Case*, CBS, 2005.

Sheriff Nicol, "The Best Little Pie Shop in Tulsa," *Rodney*, ABC, 2006.

O'CONNELL, Deirdre
(Deidre O'Connell, Dierdre O'Connell)

PERSONAL

Addresses: *Agent*—Innovative Artists, 1505 10th St., Santa Monica, CA 90401. *Manager*—Precision Entertainment, 5820 Wilshire Blvd., Suite 200, Los Angeles, CA 90036.

Career: Actress.

Awards, Honors: Drama Desk Award nomination, outstanding featured actress in a play, 1991, for *Love and Anger*; Independent Spirit Award nomination, best supporting female, 1992, for *Pastime*; DramaLogue Award, for *Jenks*; DramaLogue Award and Los Angeles Critics Award, for *Stars in the Morning Sky*.

CREDITS

Film Appearances:

Nellie, *Tin Men*, Buena Vista, 1987.

Second assistant, *Anna*, Vestron Pictures, 1987.

Shanda, *Stars and Bars*, Columbia, 1988.

Ella, *Misplaced*, Original Cinema, 1989.

Mrs. Halsey, *Brain Dead* (also known as *Paranoia*), Concorde, 1990.

Irene, *State of Grace*, Orion, 1990.

Inez Brice, *Pastime* (also known as *One Cup of Coffee*), Miramax, 1991.

Diary of a Madman, 1991.

Sally Cutler, *Falling from Grace*, Columbia, 1992.

Lily, *Straight Talk*, Buena Vista, 1992.

(As Dierdre O'Connell) Ellen, *Leaving Normal*, Universal, 1992.

Shelly, *CrissCross* (also known as *Criss Cross* and *Alone Together*), 1992.

Isabelle Malley, *Cool World*, Paramount, 1992.

Nan Gordon, *Fearless*, Warner Bros., 1993.

Waitress, *Smoke* (also known as *Smoke—Raucher unter sich*), Miramax, 1995.

Dr. Garcia Scott, NASA Space biologist, *Invader* (also known as *Lifeform*), Live Entertainment, 1996.

Mrs. Balford, *City of Angels* (also known as *Stadt der engel*), Warner Bros., 1998.

Lenny's teacher, *Just Looking*, Sony Pictures Classics, 1999.

Mrs. Gerber, *Hearts in Atlantis*, Warner Bros., 2001.

Phyllis, *Ball in the House* (also known as *Relative Evil*), 2001.

Gwyn, *Dragonfly* (also known as *Im Zeichen der libelle*), Universal, 2002.

Helen, *Second Hand Lions*, New Line Cinema, 2003.

Hollis, *Eternal Sunshine of the Spotless Mind*, Focus Features, 2004.

Marge Dwyer, *Imaginary Heroes*, Sony Pictures Classics, 2004.

Deirdre, *Winter Passing*, Focus Features, 2005.

Cosmo, *A Couple of Days and Nights*, Westlake Entertainment, 2005.

Jane, *Stephanie Daley* (also known as *What She Knew*), Regent Releasing, 2006.

Cynthia, *Trainwreck: My Life as an Idiot*, 2007.

Mrs. Fuller, *What Happens in Vegas*, Twentieth Century–Fox, 2008.

Voice of Deb, *Wendy and Lucy*, Oscillocope Pictures, 2008.

Ellen's mother, *Synecdoche, New York*, Sony Pictures Classics, 2008.

Television Appearances; Series:
Sherri Rescott Watley, *Loving*, ABC, 1985–86.
Heidi Schiller, *Sirens*, ABC, 1993.
Shirley Crockmeyer, *Second Noah*, ABC, 1996.
Susan Blum, *L.A. Doctors* (also known as *L.A. Docs*), CBS, 1998–99.

Television Appearances; Miniseries:
(As Deidre O'Connell) Barbara Young, "The Original Wives Club," *From the Earth to the Moon*, HBO, 1998.

Television Appearances; Movies:
Mom, *Daybreak* (also known as *Bloodstream*), HBO, 1993.
Peggy, *Fighting for My Daughter*, ABC, 1995.
Holly, *Kansas*, ABC, 1995.
Roberta, *Trial by Fire*, ABC, 1995.
Winona, *Our Son, the Matchmaker*, CBS, 1996.
Doris, *Chasing the Dragon*, Lifetime, 1996.
Marilyn Middleton, *A Deadly Vision* (also known as *Murder in Mind*), ABC, 1997.
Lacey, *Breast Men*, HBO, 1997.
Kate Faxton, *Murder in a Small Town*, Arts and Entertainment, 1999.
Landry, *Just Ask My Children*, Lifetime, 2001.
Donna Brady, *A Dog Year*, HBO, 2009.
Linda, *You Don't Know Jack*, 2010.

Television Appearances; Specials:
Kitty McKay, *Journey into Genius*, PBS, 1988.

Television Appearances; Pilots:
Shirley Crockmeyer, *Second Noah*, ABC, 1996.

Television Appearances; Episodic:
Lisa Martin, "Hearing Ear Dogs for the Deaf," *Fernwood 2 Night* (also known as *Fernwood Tonight*), 1977.
Catherine, "Louis in Love," *Kate & Allie*, CBS, 1987.
Nancy Carlson, "Gunplay: The Last Day in the Life of Brian Darling," *Lifestories: Families in Crisis*, HBO, 1992.
Jane Schuman, "Breeder," *Law & Order*, NBC, 1994.
Ellen Wheeler, "You Gotta Have Heart," *Chicago Hope*, CBS, 1994.
Ellen Wheeler, "Genevieve and Fat Boy," *Chicago Hope*, CBS, 1994.
Joanna Wilder, "All My Children," *Law & Order*, NBC, 2001.
Jenny Baldwin, "Vanished: Parts 1 & 2," *The Practice*, ABC, 2001.
LAC Arts interviewer, "The Last Time," *Six Feet Under*, HBO, 2002.
Nina Lipton, "The Good Child," *Law & Order: Criminal Intent* (also known as *Law & Order: CI*), NBC, 2005.

Dr. Valerie Knight, "Just a Girl in the World," *Law & Order*, NBC, 2009.
Dr. Valerie Knight, "Dignity," *Law & Order*, NBC, 2001.

Also appeared as Terrance, "Fire Down Below," *H.E.L.P.*, ABC.

Stage Appearances:
Willy the space freak, *The Unseen Hand*, Provincetown Playhouse, New York City, 1982.
Molly Malloy, *The Front Page*, Lincoln Center, New York City, 1986–87.
The Tempest, La Jolla Playhouse, La Jolla, CA, 1987.
Putana, *'Tis a Pity She's a Whore*, Public Theatre, New York City, 1992.
Samantha, *House Arrest: First Edition*, Arena Stage, Kreeger Theatre, Washington, DC, 1997.
Amanda Gringa, *In the Blood*, Public Theatre, 1999.
Lavinia, *Two–Headed*, Women's Project Theatre, New York City, 2000.
Buffer Starr, *World of Mirth*, Theatre Four, New York City, 2001.
Linda Ledbetter, *Stone Cold Dead Serious*, Loeb Drama Center, Cambridge, MA, 2002.
Denise, *The Mystery of Attraction*, Tribeca Playhouse, New York City, 2003.
Manic Flight Reaction, Playwrights Horizons Theatre, New York City, 2005.
Marty, *Circle Mirror Transformation*, Playwrights Horizons Theatre, 2009–10.
A Life of the Mind, Acorn Theatre, New York City, 2010.

Also appeared in *The Dream Express* (lounge act), Joe's Pub; *Moe's Lucky Seven*, Playwrights Horizons Theatre; *Approximating Mother*, Women's Project Theatre; *Etta Jenks*, Women's Project Theatre; *Tales of the Lost Formicians*, Women's Project Theatre; *A Lie of the Mind*, Promenade Theatre; *Love and Anger*, NYTW; *Stars in the Morning Sky*, Los Angeles Theatre Center, Los Angeles; *Three Ways Home*, Los Angeles Theatre Center; *The Geography of Luck*, Los Angeles Theatre Center; *Revelers*; *Fool for Love*, Trinity Repertory Company; *Agnes of God*, Westport and Cape Playhouse, Westport, CT; *As You Like It*; *The Seagull*; *Mud*, Signature Theatre.

ORTH, David 1965–

PERSONAL

Born March 13, 1965, in Kitchener, Ontario, Canada. *Education:* Trained with Second City improvisational comedy group and with Anthony Cheetam, Susan Bristow, and Ron Leach. *Avocational Interests:* Fitness workouts, riding motorcycles.

Career: Actor. Appeared in commercials.

CREDITS

Television Appearances; Series:
Ned Malone, *The Lost World* (also known as *Sir Arthur Conan Doyle's "The Lost World"*), syndicated, 1999–2002.

Television Appearances; Movies:
Mike, *Double Standard*, NBC, 1988.
Arthur Jr., *The Last Best Year*, ABC, 1990.
Private Mazur, *Le peloton d'execution* (also known as *Firing Squad*), CTV, 1991.
Mail carrier, *Star Command* (also known as *In the Fold* and *Star Command—Gefecht im wltall*), UPN, 1996.
Rick, *Melanie Darrow*, USA Network, 1997.
Tim, *Labor of Love*, Lifetime, 1998.
Bobby Nolan, *In Her Mother's Footsteps* (also known as *Deadly Inheritance*), Lifetime Movie Network, 2006.
Marcia, *Past Lies*, 2008.
Pilot, *NYC: Tornado Terror*, Sci–Fi Channel, 2008.

Television Appearances; Miniseries:
Beefsteak, "The Lawrenceville Stories," *American Playhouse*, PBS, 1986.
Coach Chaney, *Fallen*, ABC Family, 2006.

Television Appearances; Episodic:
"Tell Me a Story," *Night Heat*, CBS, 1987.
Scott Thomas, "Vanity's Mirror," *Friday the 13th* (also known as *Friday's Curse* and *Friday the 13th: The Series*), syndicated, 1988.
Vance Cassidy, "Demon Hunter," *Friday the 13th* (also known as *Friday's Curse* and *Friday the 13th: The Series*), syndicated, 1989.
Brian, "The Dying Generation," *The Hitchhiker* (also known as *Deadly Nightmares* and *Le voyageur*), USA Network, 1989.
(In archive footage) Scott Thomas, "Face of Evil," *Friday the 13th* (also known as *Friday's Curse* and *Friday the 13th: The Series*), syndicated, 1989.
Tommy Betz, "Midnight Riders," *Friday the 13th* (also known as *Friday's Curse* and *Friday the 13th: The Series*), syndicated, 1990.
"Trial by Peers," *My Secret Identity*, syndicated, 1991.
Young Nolan Randolph, "The Dying of the Light," *Beyond Reality*, USA Network, 1992.
Benjy, "Great Wide World Over There," *The Ray Bradbury Theatre* (also known as *The Bradbury Trilogy, Mystery Theatre, Le monde fantastique de Ray Bradbury,* and *Ray Bradbury presente*), USA Network, 1992.
Prep school friend, "Midterm Madness," *Class of '96,* Fox, 1993.
Chuckie, "While She Was Out," *The Hidden Room,* Lifetime, 1993.
Billy Sullvan, "Midnight Minus One," *RoboCop* (also known as *RoboCop: The Series*), syndicated, 1994.
Chris, "Medea," *F/X: The Series,* syndicated, 1997.
M.B.A. student Fred, "Blood on the Floor," *Traders,* Global TV, 1998.
M.B.A. student Fred, "Little Monsters," *Traders,* Global TV, 1998.
Jason, "Jason and the Argonauts," *Mythic Warriors: Guardians of the Legend,* CBS, 1998.
Jason, "Jason and Medea," *Mythic Warriors: Guardians of the Legend,* CBS, 1999.
Jason, "Castor and Pollux," *Mythic Warriors: Guardians of the Legend,* CBS, 1999.
Air safety representative, "Astral Projections," *Total Recall 2070* (also known as *Total Recall: The Series*), Showtime, 1999.
Celebrity contestant, *Search Party,* E! Entertainment Television, 2000.
Johnny Ringo, "Dead Man's Hill," *The Lost World* (also known as *Sir Arthur Conan Doyle's "The Lost World"*), syndicated, 2001.
Christopher, "Anywhere I Lay My Head," *Degrassi: The Next Generation* (also known as *Degrassi, nouvelle generation*), The N, 2004.
Christopher, "Voices Carry: Parts 1 & 2," *Degrassi: The Next Generation* (also known as *Degrassi, nouvelle generation*), The N, 2004.
Tom Bell, Togo, and Buddy's owner, "Bad Hair Day," *Sue Thomas: F.B.Eye* (also known as *Sue Thomas, l'oeil du FBI*), PAX, 2004.
William Dennett, "No Exit," *Mutant X,* syndicated, 2004.
Darren Carlyle, "Upstairs Downstairs," *Blue Murder* (also known as *En quete de preuves*), Global TV, 2004.
Captain Radner, "The Siege: Part 2," *Stargate: Atlantis* (also known as *La porte d'Atlantis*), Sci–Fi Channel, 2005.
Soldier with megaphone, "Commencement," *Smallville* (also known as *Smallville Beginnings* and *Smallville: Superman the Early Years*), 2005.
Sheriff, "Scarecrow," *Supernatural,* The WB, 2006.
Uncle Steve Tanner, "Papa Was a Rolling Stone," *Falcon Beach,* ABC Family, 2006.
Mr. Tanner, "And the Envelope Please," *The Evidence,* ABC, 2006.
Mr. Wincorn, "Lesson Number One," *The L Word,* Showtime, 2007.
Jonah, "Post Partum," *Blood Ties,* Lifetime, 2007.
Doctor, "Fracture," *Smallville* (also known as *Smallville Beginnings* and *Smallville: Superman the Early Years*), The CW, 2008.

Voices of Blizzard and Donnie Gill, "Cold War," *Iron Man: Armored Adventures* (animated), Nicktoons, 2009.
Trooper Pekarski, "Johari Window," *Fringe,* Fox, 2010.

Film Appearances:
Voices of Todd and Carnie, *Boom Boom Sabotage* (animated short film), FUNimation Entertainment, 2006.
Dr. Serling, *White Noise 2: The Light* (also known as *White Noise: The Light, White Noise 2,* and *Interferences 2*), Rogue Pictures/Universal, 2007.
Peter Garrity, *On the Other Hand, Death* (also known as *On the Other Hand, Death: A Donald Strachey Mystery*), here! Films, 2008.
Jeremy Potter, *Messages Deleted,* Waterfront Entertainment, 2009.
AF1 lieutenant, *2012,* Columbia, 2009.

RECORDINGS

Videos:
The Lost World: Underground, ILC Prime, 2002.
Voice of Talon, *Devil Kings* (video game), Capcom Entertainment, 2005.

OTHER SOURCES

Periodicals:
Cult Times, March, 2005, p. 12.
Xpose, July, 2002, pp. 34–37.

ORTIZ, Valery M. 1984–
(Valery Ortiz)

PERSONAL

Full name, Valery Milagros Ortiz; born August 1, 1984, in San Juan, Puerto Rico; engaged to Jesse Carrion (an actor and singer). *Education:* Attended the University of Central Florida, 2002–04; studied ballet at the Southern Ballet Theatre Performing Arts Centre, Orlando, FL. *Avocational Interests:* Decorating, hiking, reading, and writing.

Addresses: *Agent*—Abrams Artists Agency, 9200 Sunset Blvd., Suite 1130, Los Angeles, CA 90069. *Manager*—Spectrum Productions, PO Box 933, Agoura Hills, CA 91301. *Publicist*—Bridge and Tunnel Communications, 8019 Melrose Ave., Suite 3, Los Angeles, CA 90046.

Career: Actress and television personality.

CREDITS

Film Appearances:
(As Valery Ortiz) Jell–O, *Date Movie,* Twentieth Century–Fox, 2006.
Rosa, *From a Place of Darkness,* Lono Entertainment, 2008.

Television Appearances; Series:
LATV Live, 2005–2006.
(As Valery Ortiz) Madison Duarte, *South of Nowhere,* The N, 2005–2008.
(As Valery Ortiz) Roxanne, *What about Brian,* ABC, 2006–2007.
LATV Does Hollywood, 2006–2007.
On the Up, 2007.

Also appeared as host, *Splat!,* Nickelodeon.

Television Appearances; Pilots:
Waitress, *Emily's Reasons Why Not,* ABC, 2006.

Television Appearances; Episodic:
(As Valery Ortiz) Buck's friend number two, "Forever Young," *10 Items or Less,* TBS, 2008.
Marisol Acosta, "Stealing Home," *Cold Case,* CBS, 2009.
"Black and White and Red All Over," *Gigantic,* Nickelodeon, 2010.

Stage Appearances:
Appeared in *Latins Anonymous* and *The Vagina Monologues,* both Orlando Premiere, Orlando, FL; as Maria, *West Side Story;* Helena, *A Midsummer Night's Dream.*

Internet Appearances; Web Series:
Lupe, *Diary of a Single Mom,* www.pic.tv, 2009–10.

OTHER SOURCES

Electronic:
Valery M. Ortiz Official Site, http://www.valeryortiz.com, February 9, 2010.

OWEN, Clive 1964–

PERSONAL

Born October 3, 1964, in Coventry, Warwickshire, England; son of Jess (a singer) and Pamela Owen; married Sarah–Jane Fenton (an actress), March 6, 1995; children: Hannah, Eve. *Education:* Royal Academy of Dramatic Arts, graduated, 1987.

Addresses: *Agent*—Creative Artists Agency, 2000 Avenue of the Stars, Los Angeles, CA 90067. *Publicist*—42 West, 220 West 42nd St., 12th Floor, New York, NY 10026.

Career: Actor. Young Vic Theatre Company, actor. Suspense Festival (adult puppet festival), founder; Electric Palace Cinema, Harwich, England, patron, 2006. Lancome, spokesperson for the men's fragrance Hypnose Homme and various men's skin care products; BMW Automobiles, starred as the driver in the promotional ad campaign *The Hire,* 2001–02. Once worked as a house cleaner.

Member: Academy of Motion Picture Arts and Sciences.

Awards, Honors: Screen Actors Guild Award, Broadcast Film Critics Association Award, Florida Film Critics Circle Award, Phoenix Film Critics Society Award nomination, Online Film Critics Society Award, and Special Achievement Award, Satellite Awards, International Press Academy, all best ensemble (with others), 2002, for *Gosford Park;* New York Film Critics Award and Toronto Film Critics Association Award, best supporting actor, and National Board of Review Award (with others), best ensemble, all 2004, Academy Award nomination, best supporting actor, Golden Globe Award, best supporting actor in a motion picture, Film Award, best supporting actor, British Academy of Film and Television Arts, Sierra Award, best supporting actor, Las Vegas Film Critics Society, London Film Circle Film Award nomination, British actor of the year, Golden Satellite Award nomination, best supporting actor in a dramatic role, International Press Academy, Critics Choice Award nominations, best supporting actor and best acting ensemble (with others), Broadcast Film Critics Association, and Online Film Critics Society Award nomination, best supporting actor, all 2005, for *Closer;* MTV Movie Award nomination (with Rosario Dawson), best kiss, 2006, for *Sin City;* Saturn Award nomination, best actor, Academy of Science Fiction, Fantasy, and Horror Films, 2007, for *Children of Men;* Central Ohio Film Critics Association Award, actor of the year, 2007, for *Children of Men* and *Inside Man;* Satellite Award nomination, best actor in a motion picture comedy or musical, 2007, for *Shoot 'em Up.*

CREDITS

Film Appearances:
Jake, *Vroom,* 1988.
Richard Gillespie, *Close My Eyes,* Castle Hill, 1991.
Paul Reisner, *Century,* IRS Releasing, 1993.
Nick Sharman, *The Turnaround,* 1994.
Jake Golden, *The Rich Man's Wife,* Buena Vista, 1996.
Max, *Bent,* Goldwyn Entertainment/Metromedia, 1997.
Jack Manfred (title role), *Croupier* (also known as *Der Croupier*), British Film Institute, 1998.
Colin Briggs, *Greenfingers* (also known as *Jailbuds*), Metro–Goldwyn–Mayer, 2000.
Robert Parks, *Gosford Park,* USA Films, 2001.
Nick Callahan, *Beyond Borders* (also known as *Jenseits aller grenzen*), Paramount, 2002.
The professor, *The Bourne Identity* (also known as *Die Bourne identitaet*), Universal, 2002.
Will Graham, *I'll Sleep When I'm Dead,* Paramount, 2003.
Title role, *King Arthur* (also released as *King Arthur: Director's Cut*), Buena Vista, 2004.
Larry, *Closer,* Columbia, 2004.
Dwight, *Sin City* (also known as *Frank Miller's "Sin City"*), Buena Vista, 2005.
Charles Schine, *Derailed,* Weinstein Company, 2005.
(Uncredited) Nigel Boswell/Agent 006, *The Pink Panther,* Metro–Goldwyn–Mayer/Columbia, 2006.
Dalton Russell, *Inside Man,* Universal, 2006.
Theo Faron, *Children of Men,* Universal, 2006.
Smith, *Shoot 'em Up,* New Line Cinema, 2007.
Sir Walter Raleigh, *Elizabeth: The Golden Age* (also known as *Elizabeth—L'age d'or* and *Elizabeth—Das goldene koenigreich*), Universal, 2007.
Louis Salinger, *The International,* Columbia, 2009.
Ray Koval, *Duplicity* (also known as *Duplicity—Gemeinsame Geheimsache*), Universal, 2009.
Joe Warr, *The Boys Are Back,* Miramax, 2009.

Film Executive Producer:
The Boys Are Back, Miramax, 2009.

Television Appearances; Movies:
Gideon Sarn, "Precious Bane," *Masterpiece Theatre,* PBS, 1989.
John Ridd, *Lorna Doone,* Thames, 1990.
Devin O'Neil, *Class of '61,* ABC, 1993.
Detective Constable George Byrne, *The Magician,* 1993.
Bill, *An Evening with Gary Lineker,* 1994.
Corneliu Bratu, *Nobody's Children,* USA Network, 1994.
Damon Wildeve, *The Return of the Native* (also known as *Thomas Hardy's "The Return of the Native"*), CBS, 1994.
Dov, *Doomsday Gun,* HBO, 1994.
Paul, *Bad Boy Blues,* BBC, 1995.
Michael Deacon, *The Echo,* BBC, 1998.
Michael Anderson, *Split Second* (also known as *The Cyclist*), BBC, 1999.
Detective Chief Inspector Ross Tanner, "Second Sight," *Mystery!,* PBS, 1999.

Detective Chief Inspector Ross Tanner, *Second Sight: Hide and Seek,* BBC, 2000, then broadcast as an episode of *Mystery!,* PBS, 2001.
Detective Chief Inspector Ross Tanner, *Second Sight: Kingdom of the Blind,* BBC, 2000, then broadcast as an episode of *Mystery!,* PBS, 2001.
Detective Chief Inspector Ross Tanner, *Second Sight: Parasomnia,* BBC, 2000, then broadcast as an episode of *Mystery!,* PBS, 2001.

Television Appearances; Specials:
The Making of "Gosford Park," 2001.
Starz Special: On the Set of "King Arthur," Starz!, 2004.
The Making of "King Arthur," 2004.
Starz on the Set: Sin City, Starz!, 2005.
Sin City: The Premiere, ITV2, 2005.
The Ultimate Heist: Making "Inside Man," 2006.
San Sebastian 2006: Cronica de Carlos Boyero, Canal+ Espana, 2006.
Children of Men: Visions of the Future, Sci–Fi Channel, 2007.
(In archive footage) *Maquillando entre monstruos,* Canal+ Espana, 2007.
(Uncredited; in archive footage) *Ceremonia de inauguracion–56 festival internacional de cine de San Sebastian,* 2008.
(Uncredited; in archive footage) Max, *Premio Donostia a Ian McKellen,* 2009.

Television Appearances; Miniseries:
Nick Sharman, *Sharman,* Carlton, 1996.
Narrator, *Walk On By: The Story of Popular Song* (also known as *Popular Song: Soundtrack of the Century* and *The Story of Pop*), BBC, 2001, ABC, 2002.

Television Appearances; Series:
Stephen Crane and Derek Love, *Chancer,* PBS, 1990–91.

Television Appearances; Episodic:
Police Constable Parslew, "Up the Down Escalator," *Rockliffe's Babies,* 1987.
Geoff, "Peacemaker," *Boon,* Central, 1988.
"Derailed," *E! Behind the Scenes,* E! Entertainment Television, 2005.
Corazon de ..., 2005, 2006.
Le grand journal de Canal, 2005, 2009.
(In archive footage) *Headline News,* 2006.
Film '72 (also known as *Film 2006, Film of the Year,* and *The Film Programme*), BBC, 2006.
"The Extra Special Series Finale," *Extras,* HBO, 2007.
Entertainment Tonight (also known as *Entertainment This Week, E.T., ET Weekend,* and *This Week in Entertainment*), syndicated, several appearances, 2007–2009.
At the Movies (also known as *Margaret & David at the Movies*), Australian Broadcasting Corporation, 2009.

Dias de cine, 2009.
Cinema 3 (also known as *Informatiu cinema*), 2009.
Xpose, TV3, 2009.
Live from Studio Five (also known as *Studio Five*), 2010.

Television Talk Show Guest Appearances; Episodic:
Friday Night with Jonathan Ross, BBC, 2004, 2009.
Good Morning America (also known as *G.M.A.*), ABC, 2005.
The Early Show, CBS, 2005.
Larry King Live, Cable News Network, 2005.
Late Night with Conan O'Brien, NBC, 2005, 2007.
The Daily Show (also known as *A Daily Show with Jon Stewart, The Daily Show with Jon Stewart Global Edition,* and *Jon Stewart*), Comedy Central, 2006.
Live with Regis and Kelly, syndicated, 2006, 2009.
Today (also known as *NBC News Today* and *The Today Show*), NBC, 2007.
Up Close with Carrie Keagan, ABC, 2007, 2009.
The Charlie Rose Show (also known as *Charlie Rose*), PBS, 2009.
Late Night with Jimmy Fallon, NBC, 2009.

Television Appearances; Awards Presentations:
The 10th Annual Critics' Choice Awards, The WB, 2005.
The 77th Annual Academy Awards, ABC, 2005.
The 62nd Annual Golden Globe Awards, NBC, 2005.
The Brit Awards 2005, BBC America, 2005.
3rd Irish Film and Television Awards, 2005.
The Orange British Academy Film Awards, 2005.
Presenter, *The 79th Annual Academy Awards,* ABC, 2007.

Stage Appearances:
Leonard Chateris, *The Philanderer,* Hampstead Theatre, London, 1992.
Dan, *Closer,* London, 1997.
Bri, *A Day in the Death of Joe Egg,* New Ambassadors Theatre, London, 2001.

Appeared as Claudio, *Measure for Measure,* and Romeo, *Romeo and Juliet,* both Young Vic Theatre, London; in *The Cat and the Canary,* Watford, England, and *Design for the Living,* Donmar Warehouse Theatre, London; as Louis Dubedat, *The Doctor's Dilemma,* Royal Exchange Theatre; and in *Twelfth Night,* Crucible Theatre, Sheffield, England.

RECORDINGS

Video Games:
Voice of Lev Arris, *Privateer 2: The Darkening,* Electronic Arts, 1996.

OTHER SOURCES

Periodicals:
Entertainment Weekly, November 11, 2005, p. 8.
Esquire, March, 2009, pp. 98–105.
Fade In, Volume 10, number 2, 2007, pp. 52–62.
Los Angeles Times, July 4, 2004.
Movieline's Hollywood Life, December, 2004, pp. 82–83, 109.
Playboy, September, 2007, pp. 49–50, 53–54, 142–43.
Premiere, September 1, 2003, pp. 56–57.
Scottish Daily Record, September 2, 2000.
She, November, 1999.
Sports Illustrated, November 14, 2005, p. 24.
USA Today, February 10, 2009, pp. 1D, 3D.
USA Weekend, December 8, 2006, pp. 8–9.
Venice, August, 2000.
Washington Post, September 7, 2007, pp. 32, 34.

OYELOWO, David 1976–

PERSONAL

Born April 1, 1976, in Oxford, England; married, 1998; wife's name, Jessica (an actress); children: three sons. *Education:* Attended London Academy of Music and Dramatic Art.

Addresses: *Agent*—International Creative Management, 10250 Constellation Way, 9th Floor, Los Angeles, CA 90067; Christian Hodell, Hamilton Hodell Ltd., 66–68 Margaret St., 5th Floor, London W1W 8SR, England. *Manager*—Rigberg Entertainment Group, 1180 South Beverly Dr., Suite 601, Los Angeles, CA 90035.

Career: Actor, producer, director, and writer.

Awards, Honors: Ian Charleson Award, outstanding young actor in a classical theatre role, National Theatre and *Sunday Times,* 2001, for *Henry VI;* Screen Nation Award nomination and *Evening Standard* Award nomination, both best newcomer, 2002; Satellite Award, best actor in a miniseries or television movie, International Press Academy, 2007, for *Five Days;* Screen Nation Award nomination, best actor in a film, 2007, for *The Last King of Scotland;* Screen Nation Award nomination, best actor in a television series, 2007, for *Born Equal, Five Days,* and *Shoot the Messenger.*

CREDITS

Film Appearances:
C. J., *Dog Eat Dog,* FilmFour, 2001.
Charlie, *Tomorrow La Scala!,* Film Council, 2002.

Commuter, *End of the Line* (short film), Screen East, 2004.
Payne, *A Sound of Thunder,* Warner Bros., 2005.
Patrol officer, *Derailed,* Weinstein Company, 2005.
Mercury, *American Blend,* White Stripes Entertainment, 2006.
Dr. Junju, *The Last King of Scotland,* Fox Searchlight, 2006.
Muddy Waters, *Who Do You Love,* 2008, International Film Circuit, 2010.
Homer, *Rage,* Adventure Pictures/Vox3 Films, 2009.
Joe "Lightning" Little, *Red Tails,* Partnership Pictures, 2010.

Also appeared as Earl, *Circles,* APT Films.

Film Work:
Producer and director, *Big Guy* (short film), 2009.

Television Appearances; Miniseries:
Eddie Barton the sexy member of Parliament, *Mayo* (also known as *The Gil Mayo Mysteries*), BBC America, 2006.
Matt Wellings, *Five Days,* HBO, 2007.
Himself, *British Film Forever,* BBC, 2007.
Joseph of Arimethea, *The Passion,* BBC, 2008.
Gilbert, *Small Island,* PBS, 2009.
Keme Tobodo, *Blood and Oil,* BBC, 2009.

Television Appearances; Movies:
Graham, *The Best Man* (also known as *Best Man, Worst Friend, Unhitched,* and *Ein trauzeuge zum verlieben*), ABC Family, 2005.
Orlando de Boys, *As You Like It,* HBO, 2006.
Yemi, *Born Equal,* BBC, 2006.
Joseph Pascale, *Shoot the Messenger,* BBC, 2006.
Joseph Asagai, *A Raisin in the Sun,* ABC, 2009.

Television Appearances; Series:
(Uncredited) Danny Hunter, *Spooks* (also known as *MI–5*), Arts and Entertainment, 2002–2004.

Also appeared as Lester Peters in *Brothers and Sisters,* BBC.

Television Appearances; Episodic:
Breakfast, BBC, 2002.
Richard & Judy, Channel 4, 2003.
RI:SE, Channel 4, 2003.
Patrick, "Reunion Special: Parts 1 & 2," *As Time Goes By,* PBS, 2005.
Kremlin Busang, premiere episode, *The No. 1 Ladies' Detective Agency,* HBO, 2008.
Leonard Grisham, *Sweet Nothing in My Ear,* CBS, 2008.

Television Appearances; Other:
Appeared as Trev, *King of Hearts,* Channel 4; and as Sonny MacDonald, *Maisie Raine,* BBC.

Stage Appearances:
King Palasgus, *The Suppliants,* Gate Theatre, London, 1998.
Aboan, *Oroonoko,* Royal Shakespeare Company, Stratford–upon–Avon, England, 1999.
Bonario, *Volpone,* Royal Shakespeare Company, 1999.
Dercetus, *Antony and Cleopatra,* Royal Shakespeare Company, 1999.
Title role, *Henry VI Part I,* Royal Shakespeare Company, 2000.
Title role, *Henry VI Part II,* Royal Shakespeare Company, 2000.
Title role, *Henry VI Part III,* Royal Shakespeare Company, 2000.
Ghost of Henry VI, *Richard III,* Royal Shakespeare Company, 2000.
Monday, *The God Botherers,* Bush Theatre, London, 2003.
Title role, *Prometheus Bound,* Sound Theatre, London, 2005, then Classic Stage Company, East Thirteenth Street Theatre, New York City, 2007.

Also appeared as Ralph, *Bouncers;* Aufidius, *Coriolanus;* Congrio, *Los Escombros;* as Tereus, *The Love of the Nightingale;* in title role, *Mirad;* as sailor boy, *A Taste of Honey;* and Tiger Brown, *The Threepenny Opera.*

Stage Director:
The White Devil, Pavillion Theatre, Brighton, England, 2006.

WRITINGS

Television Specials:
Graham & Alice, BBC, 2006.

Books:
Henry VI Part 1, Faber, 2003.

OTHER SOURCES

Periodicals:
Radio Times, August 26, 2006, p. 138.

OYELOWO, Jessica 1978–

PERSONAL

Original name, Jessica Watson; born 1978; married David Oyelowo (an actor), 1998; children: three sons.

Addresses: *Manager*—Rigberg Entertainment Group, 1180 South Beverly Blvd., Suite 601, Los Angeles, CA 90035.

Career: Actress, producer, and composer. National Youth Music Theatre, former member of company. Appeared in commercials, including ads for Nicorette smoking–cessation chewing gum, 2002.

CREDITS

Television Appearances; Movies:
First handmaiden, *Don Quixote,* TNT, 2000.
Isobel, *The Sight,* FX Network, 2000.
Makeup artist, *The Deal,* HBO, 2003.

Television Appearances; Miniseries:
Felicite, *Madame Bovary,* PBS, 2000.
Alex Jones, *Mayo* (also known as *The Gil Mayo Mysteries*), BBC America, 2006.

Television Appearances; Episodic:
Flora, *Unfinished Business,* BBC, 1999.
Emma the lodger, "The Photographer," *People Like Us,* BBC, 1999.
Claire Jones, "This Means Nothing to Me," *Reach for the Moon,* 2000.
"Swinger," *Lee Evans: So What Now?,* BBC America, 2001.
Rose Darvey, "Deep Sleep," *Helen West,* Arts and Entertainment, 2002.
Rose Darvey, "Shadow Play," *Helen West,* Arts and Entertainment, 2002.
Jackie Cole, *Murphy's Law,* BBC America, 2007.

Television Appearances; Other:
Rachel McBain, "Pilot: The Story Begins" (pilot), *Hex,* Sky Television, 2004.
(Uncredited; in archive footage) Princess Margaret, *Hitler: The Comedy Years,* Channel 4, 2007.

Film Appearances:
Sarah, *Sleepy Hollow* (also known as *Sleepy Hollow— Koepfe werden rollen*), Paramount, 1999.
Princess Margaret, *Churchill: The Hollywood Years,* Pathe, 2004.
Bear vendor, *Big Guy* (short film), 2009.
Lady Poirtine, *Alice in Wonderland,* Walt Disney, 2010.

Film Executive Producer:
Big Guy (short film), 2009.

Stage Appearances:

Rosalind, *As You Like It,* Jermyn Street Theatre, London, 1997.

Hurly Burly, Old Vic Theatre Company, Queen's Theatre, London, 1997.

Angela, *Up on the Roof* (musical), Chichester Festival Theatre, Chichester, England, 2002.

Title character, *Ana in Love,* Hackney Empire Theatre, London, 2006.

Roxane, *Cyrano de Bergerac,* Royal Exchange Theatre, Manchester, England, 2006–2007.

Radio Appearances:

Maria, *In the End,* BBC4, 1999.

Mrs. Equiano, *Grace Unshackled—The Olaudah Equiano Story,* BBC7, 2007.

WRITINGS

Film Music Composer:

Big Guy (short film), 2009.

P

PACAR, Johnny 1981–

PERSONAL

Original name, John Edward Pacuraru; born June 6, 1981, in Dearborn, MI; son of John and Judith Pacuraru. *Avocational Interests:* Snowboarding, muscle cars, animals, cooking.

Addresses: *Agent*—Ken Kaplan, Gersh Agency, 9465 Wilshire Blvd., 6th Floor, Beverly Hills, CA 90212.

Career: Actor. Appeared in a commercial for Sprite soda, 2001. Fairlene (band), singer and guitarist; also solo vocalist.

Awards, Honors: Orlando Film Festival Award, best supporting actor, 2009, for *Love Hurts.*

CREDITS

Television Appearances; Series:
Jimmy Francis, a recurring role, *American Dreams* (also known as *Our Generation*), NBC, 2003–2004.
Jackson, *Flight 29 Down,* Discovery Kids, 2005–2007.
Damon Young, *Make It or Break It,* ABC Family, 2009–10.

Television Appearances; Movies:
Jesse Harper, *Combustion* (also known as *Silent Killer*), Lifetime, 2004.
Danny Sinclair, *Now You See It …,* The Disney Channel, 2005.
Jeff, "Front of the Class," *Hallmark Hall of Fame* (also known as *Hallmark Television Playhouse*), CBS, 2008.

Television Appearances; Pilots:
Jackson, *Flight 29 Down: The Hotel Tango,* NBC, 2007.
Eli at age nineteen, *Eli Stone,* ABC, 2008.

Television Appearances; Episodic:
Jason Christopher, "Can They Do That with Vegetables?," *Judging Amy,* CBS, 2002.
Boone, "Chapter Forty–Nine," *Boston Public,* Fox, 2002.
Boone, "Chapter Fifty–Five," *Boston Public,* Fox, 2003.
Boone, "Chapter Fifty–Seven," *Boston Public,* Fox, 2003.
Rush Bauer, "Moving On Up," *The Brothers Garcia,* Nickelodeon, 2003.
Adam Whitman, "Star Crossed," *Tru Calling,* Fox, 2003.
Noah, "What George Doesn't Noah …," *George Lopez,* ABC, 2004.
Intoxicated boy, "When Push Comes to Shove: Part 2," *Medium,* NBC, 2005.
Dayton in 1995, "Rampage," *Cold Case,* CBS, 2006.
Nathan Atherton, "Just Murdered," *CSI: Miami,* CBS, 2007.
(Uncredited) "Crazy Little Thing Called Love," *Crossing Jordan,* NBC, 2007.
Ben Kensith, "In Sickness & in Health," *Crossing Jordan,* NBC, 2007.
Miles Maitland, "Stage Fright," *Ghost Whisperer,* CBS, 2009.

Film Appearances:
Sam, *Purgatory House,* Image Entertainment, 2004.
(Uncredited) Jamal, *Little Black Book,* Columbia, 2004.
Spike, *Detroit* (also known as *Corrupted Minds* and *Panic in Detroit*), Radio London Films, 2007.
Roddy, *Wild Child,* Universal, 2008.
Travis, *The Dead Undead,* 2009.
Justin Bingham, *Love Hurts,* Lantern Lane Entertainment, 2009.
Damon, *Cryptic,* R–Squared Films, 2010.
Texas Slim, *Fort McCoy,* Marzipan Entertainment, 2010.

Appeared as Disco in a short film titled *The Bitch Room.*

RECORDINGS

Videos:
The Making of "Purgatory House," Free Dream Pictures, 2005.

Appeared in the music video "Perfect" by Simple Plan.

PAGE, Michelle 1987–

PERSONAL

Full name, Michelle Laone Page; born January 19, 1987, in Fort Worth, TX. *Education:* Trained at Royal Academy of Dramatic Arts, London, 2009. *Avocational Interests:* Sports.

Addresses: *Agent*—Arlene Gluckman–Jones, AKA Talent Agency, 6310 San Vicente Blvd., Suite 200, Los Angeles, CA 90048. *Manager*—Stephanie Nese, Framework Entertainment, 9057 Nemo St., Suite C, West Hollywood, CA 90069.

Career: Actress. Appeared in commercials, including ads for AT&T phone service, 2001, Cedar Point amusement park, Taco Bell restaurants, and Radio Shack; appeared in public service announcements for Partnership for a Drug Free America and White House Office of National Drug Control Policy.

Member: Screen Actors Guild.

Awards, Honors: Bonehead Award, best actress, Bare Bones International Film Festival, 2009, for *Dog.*

CREDITS

Film Appearances:
Punk rocker girl, *Single White Female 2: The Psycho,* Sony Pictures Entertainment, 2005.
Punk girl in bank, *Miss Congeniality 2: Armed & Fabulous,* Warner Bros., 2005.
Carrie, *Spaceboy* (short film), 2006.
Kat, *Kush,* Endurance Pictures, 2007.
Ravyn, *Sublime,* Warner Home Video, 2007.
Girl with boyfriend, *Burying the Ex* (short film), American Cinema, 2008.
Kaye Frobisher, *Together Again for the First Time,* Asgaard Entertainment/Ocean Park, 2008.
Elizabeth "Lizzie" Hansen, *Dog,* Dead Mouse Productions, 2009.

Tara, *Sensored,* Hannover House, 2010.
Mara, *Rogue River,* Vision Entertainment Group/Kejo Productions/Rogue River Productions, 2010.
Lacy, *American Disciples,* Toeknee Films, 2010.

Also appeared in the independent short films *The Forest* and *Seamus and Magellan;* in *Ground Truth,* produced by U.S. Department of Homeland Security; and another film for the Bullying Project, produced by the Museum of Tolerance.

Film Associate Producer:
Rogue River, Vision Entertainment Group/Kejo Productions/Rogue River Productions, 2010.
American Disciples, Toeknee Films, 2010.

Television Appearances; Episodic:
Natasha, "All the News Fit to Print," *Crossing Jordan,* NBC, 2004.
Kimberly Beaudreux, "Felony Flight," *CSI: Miami,* CBS, 2005.
Karen Watson in 1964, "The Good–bye Room," *Cold Case,* CBS, 2007.
Darah Keegan, "Road Trip," *Standoff,* Fox, 2007.
Justine Berry, "Player under Pressure," *Bones,* Fox, 2008.
Hope, "Red Tide," *The Mentalist,* CBS, 2008.
Amanda, "Hedge Fund Homeboys," *Castle,* ABC, 2009.
Emma Silber, "Cursed," *Ghost Whisperer,* CBS, 2009.
Emily, "We're Already Here," *Saving Grace,* TNT, 2009.
Entertainment Tonight (also known as *Entertainment This Week, E.T., ET Weekend,* and *This Week in Entertainment*), syndicated, 2009.

Stage Appearances:
Rebecca Gibbs, *Our Town,* Fort Worth, TX, 1999.

Also appeared in the musical *The Unsinkable Molly Brown,* Casa Manana Theatre, Fort Worth, TX.

PANJABI, Archie 1972–
(Archie Panabi)

PERSONAL

Full name, Archana Panjabi; born May 31, 1972, in Edgeware, Middlesex, England. *Education:* Brunel University, B.Sc, management studies.

Career: Actress. Regularly provided voiceovers for radio, especially Indian voices. Appeared in television commercials, including AA car breakdown service, 2000.

Awards, Honors: Shooting Star Award, Berlin International Film Festival, 2005; Prix Cine Femme, best actress, Mons International Festival of Love Films, 2005, Reims Film Festival, best actress, 2006, both for *Yasmin;* Chopard Trophy, female revelation, Cannes Film Festival, 2007; Screen Actors Guild Award nomination (with others), outstanding performance by an ensemble in a drama series, 2010, for *The Good Wife.*

CREDITS

Film Appearances:

Joyoti, *Bideshi* (short film), British Film Institute, 1995.
Meenah Khan, *East Is East,* Miramax, 1999.
Adult Pim, *Delilah* (short film), South West Screen, 2001.
Pinky Bhamra, *Bend It Like Beckham* (also known as *Kick It Like Beckham*), Fox Searchlight, 2002.
Shashi, *Arranged Marriage* (short film), 2002.
Sumi, *Cross My Heart,* 2003.
Check In, *Code 46,* Metro–Goldwyn–Mayer, 2003.
Yasmin Husseini, *Yasmin,* 2004.
Sarita, *Chromophobia,* Momentum Pictures, 2005.
Ghita Pearson, *The Constant Gardener* (also known as *Der ewige gartner*), Focus Features, 2005.
Gemma, *A Good Year,* Fox 2000, 2006.
Sharmila, *Lezioni di volo* (also known as *Flying Lessons*), TF1 International, 2007.
Casting girl, *I Could Never Be Your Woman,* Weinstein Company, 2007.
Asra, *A Mighty Heart,* Paramount Vantage, 2007.
Chandra Dawkin, *Traitor,* Overture Films, 2008.
Teacher, *My World* (short film), 2008.
Karen, *The Happiness Salesman* (short film), 2009.
Animal adoption officer, *Be Good* (short film), 2009.
Anna, *Espion(s)* (also known as *Espions* and *Spy(ies)*), 2009.
Saamiya Nasir, *The Infidel,* 2010.

Television Appearances; Series:

Various roles, *Brand Spanking New Show* (also known as *Harry Enfield's "Brand Spanking New Show"*), Sky Television, 2000.
Rita Dhillon, *Grease Monkeys,* BBC, 2003–2004.
Megan Sharma, *Sea of Souls,* BBC, 2004.
Jane Lesser, *Personal Affairs* (also known as *Pas*), BBC, 2009.
Kalinda Sharma, *The Good Wife,* CBS, 2009—.

Also appeared as Meera Baines, *Postman Pat,* BBC.

Television Appearances; Miniseries:

Basya, Pharaoh's daughter, *In the Beginning,* NBC, 2000.
Farida, *Final Demand,* BBC, 2003.
Alsana, *White Teeth,* PBS, 2003.

Clare, "The Man of Law's Tale," *Canterbury Tales,* BBC and BBC America, 2003.

Television Appearances; Movies:

Chandra (Mr. Jones), *Tough Love,* Granada, 2000.
Nadia's probation officer, *The Secret,* BBC, 2002.
Niala, *This Little Life,* BBC, 2003.
Ashley, *A Very Social Secretary,* Channel 4, 2005.

Television Appearances; Specials:

(As Archie Panabi) Heena, *Under the Moon,* BBC, 1995.
Voice of Leila, *Ivor the Invisible,* Channel 4, 2001.
Tahira Tabassum, *Britain's First Suicide Bombers,* BBC, 2006.
Voice, *Love Triangle,* Channel 4, 2007.

Television Appearances; Pilots:

Kalinda Sharma, *The Good Wife,* CBS, 2009.

Television Appearances; Episodic:

"Alternative Culture," *The Thin Blue Line,* BBC and BBC America, 1996.
Lamisa Khan, "Colour Blind," *A Mind to Kill* (also known as *Yr Heliwr*), Channel 5 and Channel 3, 2001.
WPC Jill Evans, "Vigilante," *Murder in Mind,* BBC and BBC America, 2001.
Shanaz Arad, "A Pound of Flesh," *The Bill,* ITV1, 2001.
Shanaz Arad, "Home Run," *The Bill,* ITV1, 2001.
"Little Englander," *Single Voices,* ITV, 2002.
Ali Saffron, "From This Moment On," *Holby City* (also known as *Holby*), BBC, 2002.
Dental assistant, "Of Mice and Ben," *My Family,* BBC1 and BBC America, 2002.
Maya, *Life on Mars,* BBC1 and BBC America, 2006, 2007.
Amita Joshi, "Peripheral Vision: Parts 1 & 2," *Silent Witness,* 2007.

Radio Appearances:

Appeared as Blaze, *Westway,* BBC World Service.

PARSONS, Jim 1973–

PERSONAL

Full name, James Joseph Parsons; born March 24, 1973, in Houston, TX; father, a president of a plumbing company; mother, a first grade teacher. *Education:* University of Houston, B.A., theatre; University of San

Diego, M.A., theatre. *Avocational Interests:* Playing piano, and watching sports, especially tennis, baseball, and basketball.

Addresses: *Agent*—Innovative Artists, 1505 10th St., Santa Monica, CA 90401.

Career: Actor. Appeared in television commercials, including Quiznos restaurants, DiGiorno frozen pizza, Stride Gum, and FedEx shipping; appeared in public service announcements CBS Cares, 2009. Infernal Bridegroom Productions (a theater company), Houston, TX, cofounder; appeared in stage productions at the Old Globe Theatre, San Diego, CA. Previously worked as an assistant at Microsoft Sidewalk, Houston, TX.

Awards, Honors: Emmy Award nomination, outstanding lead actor in a comedy series, Satellite Award nomination, best actor in a series—comedy or musical, International Press Academy, Television Critics Association Award, individual achievement in comedy, 2009, all for *The Big Bang Theory.*

CREDITS

Film Appearances:
Casting assistant, *Nowhere to Go But Up* (also known as *Happy End* and *I Want to be Famous*), 2003.
Tim, *Garden State,* Fox Searchlight, 2004.
Oliver, *Heights,* 2005.
Justin, "Emme's Story," *The Great New Wonderful,* Vivendi Entertainment, 2005.
Sidney, *The King's Inn* (short film), Finneran Films, 2005.
Receptionist, *10 Items or Less,* THINKFilm, 2006.
Classmate, *School for Scoundrels,* Metro–Goldwyn–Mayer, 2006.
Jimmy Pea, *On the Road with Judas,* 2007.
Spim, *Gardener of Eden,* 2007.

Television Appearances; Series:
Rob Holbrook, *Judging Amy,* CBS, 2004–2005.
Sheldon Cooper, *The Big Bang Theory,* CBS, 2007—.

Television Appearances; Movies:
Why Blitt?, 2004.
Kris, *Taste,* 2004.

Television Appearances; Specials:
Presenter, *The 61st Primetime Emmy Awards,* CBS, 2009.
Screams Awards 2009 (also known as *Scream 2009*), Spike TV, 2009.
The 36th Annual People's Choice Awards, CBS, 2010.

Presenter, *The 67th Annual Golden Globe Awards,* 2010.

Television Appearances; Pilots:
Sheldon Cooper, *The Big Bang Theory,* CBS, 2007.

Television Appearances; Episodic:
Chet, "The Road," *Ed,* NBC, 2002.
Entertainment Tonight (also known as *E.T.*), syndicated, 2007, 2008, 2009.
The Late Late Show with Craig Ferguson, CBS, 2008, 2009.
"KDOG," *Free Radio,* VH1, 2009.
The View, ABC, 2009.
Late Show with David Letterman (also known as *Letterman* and *The Late Show*), CBS, 2009.
The Bonnie Hunt Show, NBC, 2009.
Rachael Ray, syndicated, 2009.
The Tonight Show with Conan O'Brien, NBC, 2009.
Voice of Sheldon Cooper, "Business Guy," *Family Guy* (animated; also known as *Padre de familia*), Fox, 2009.

Stage Appearances:
Appeared in *Endgame; Guys and Dolls; What Happened Was; The Balcony.*

PATTON, Mike 1968–

PERSONAL

Full name, Michael Allen Patton; born January 27, 1968, in Eureka, CA; married Titi Zuccatosta, 1994 (marriage ended, 2001). *Education:* Attended Humboldt State University.

Career: Actor, voice performer, singer, writer, and composer. Ipecac Records, cofounder and co–owner. Founder and member of the band Mr. Bungle, 1985–2004; songwriter and vocalist with Faith No More, 1989–98, then 2009—; performed with the Fantomas, Maldoror, Tomahawk, Lovage, Peeping Tom, and Moonraker, and as a soloist; former member of Weird Little Boy project.

CREDITS

Film Appearances:
Concert Film Ozzy Osbourne, Faith No More, Young M.C. (concert film), 1993.
A Bookshelf on Top of the Sky: 12 Stories about John Zorn (documentary), 2002.

Frank/David, *Firecracker* (also known as *Steve Balderson's "Firecracker"*), 7 Arts, 2005.
Wamego Strikes Back (documentary), Dikenga Films, 2007.

Film Work:
(With Faith No More) Song "The Perfect Crime," *Bill and Ted's Bogus Journey,* Warner Bros., 1991.
Song performer, "Procura o Cara," *No coracao dos deuses,* Riofilmes, 1999.
Song performer, "Lifeboat," *29 Palms,* Artisan Entertainment, 2002.
Creature vocalist, *I Am Legend* (also known as *I Am Legend: The IMAX Experience*), Warner Bros., 2007.
Song performer, "Bird's Eye," *Body of Lies,* Warner Bros., 2008.
Song performer, "Kickin'" and "Sweet Cream," *Crank: High Voltage* (also known as *Crank: High Voltage—Fully Charged, Crank 2,* and *High Voltage*), Lions Gate Films, 2009.

Television Appearances; Specials:
The 1990 MTV Video Music Awards, MTV, 1990.
Freaks, Nerds & Weirdos, MTV, 1994.

Television Appearances; Episodic:
(With Faith No More) *MTV's Most Wanted,* MTV Europe, 1995.
(With Peeping Tom) *The Henry Rollins Show,* Independent Film Channel, 2007.
Voice of Rikki Kixx, "Snakes N Barrels II: Parts 1 & 2," *Metalocalypse,* Comedy Central, 2008.
(Uncredited) Himself, "Kings of Leon," *Reading and Leeds 2009,* BBC3, 2009.

RECORDINGS

Videos:
Faith No More: Live at the Brixton Academy (also known as *You Fat B**tards: Live at the Brixton Academy*), Warner Reprise, 1990.
Hard 'n Heavy Volume 12, WEA International, 1991.
Faith No More: Video Croissant, Warner Reprise, 1993.
Bjork: Inner or Deep Part of an Animal or Plant Structure, Elektra, 2004.
Wamego: Making Movies Anywhere, Dikenga Films, 2004.
Kaada Patton: Romances, 2007.
Making "Crank 2," Lions Gate Films Home Entertainment, 2009.

Video Games:
Voice of "the darkness," *The Darkness,* 2k Games/Starbreeze Studios/Union Entertainment, 2007.
Voice of the Anger Sphere, *Portal,* Electronic Arts, 2007.

Voices for "infected sounds," *Left 4 Dead,* Steam, 2008.
Voice of Nathan Spencer, *Bionic Commando,* Capcom Entertainment, 2009.
Voices for "infected sounds," *Left 4 Dead 2,* Steam, 2009.
Voice of the outsider, *Edge of Twilight,* Fuzzyeyes Studio, 2009.

Albums:
(With Mr. Bungle) *Goddammit I Love America!,* 1988.
(With Faith No More) *The Real Thing,* Slash/Reprise, 1989.
Mr. Bungle, Warner Bros., 1991.
(With Faith No More) *Bill and Ted's Bogus Journey* (film soundtrack recording), Warner Bros., 1991.
(With Faith No More) *Angel Dust,* 1992.
(With Mr. Bungle) *Disco Volante,* Warner Bros., 1995.
Adult Themes for Voice, 1996.
Pranzo Oltranzista, 1997.
(With Faith No More) *Who Cares a Lot* (retrospective compilation), 1998.
(With Mr. Bungle) *California,* Warner Bros., 1999.

Also recorded demonstration tales with Mr. Bungle, including "Bowl of Chiley" and "OU818."

WRITINGS

Film Music Composer:
A Perfect Place (short film), Fantoma Films, 2008.
(Including songs "Kickin'" and "Sweet Cream") *Crank: High Voltage* (also known as *Crank: High Voltage—Fully Charged, Crank 2,* and *High Voltage*), Lions Gate Films, 2009.

Songs Featured in Films:
"Another Body Murdered," *Judgment Night,* Universal, 1993.
"Digging the Grave," *Jack Frusciante e uscito dal gruppo* (also known as *Jack Frusciante Left the Band*), Brosfilm/Medusa Produzione, 1996.
"Ricochet," *Fox Hunt,* Capcom Entertainment, 1996.
"Falling to Pieces," *Black Hawk Down,* Columbia, 2001.
"Bird's Eye," *Body of Lies,* Warner Bros., 2008.
"I'm Gonna Getcha," *Obsessed,* Screen Gems, 2009.

Television Songwriter; Pilots:
"Mojo," *Californication,* Showtime, 2007.

Video Music Composer:
Faith No More: Live at the Brixton Academy (also known as *You Fat B**tards: Live at the Brixton Academy*), Warner Reprise, 1990.
Faith No More: Video Croissant, Warner Reprise, 1993.

(And scriptwriter) *Kaada Patton: Romances,* 2007.
Making "Crank 2," Lions Gate Films Home Entertainment, 2009.

OTHER SOURCES

Books:
Contemporary Musicians, Gale, Volume 7, 1992, Volume 58, 2006.

Electronic:
Ipecac Web site, http://www.ipecac.com, February 20, 2010.

PENROD, James
    See NORRIS, Daran

PERCY, Lee 1953–

PERSONAL

Full name, Lee Edward Percy; born February 10, 1953, in Kalamazoo, MI; son of Richard Noyes and Helen Louise (maiden name, Sheffield) Percy. *Education:* Attended Goodman School of Drama, at Chicago Art Institute, 1971, and Juilliard School, 1972; University of California, Santa Cruz, B.A., 1977.

Addresses: *Agent*—International Creative Management, 10250 Constellation Way, 9th Floor, Los Angeles, CA 90067.

Career: Film editor. VisArt Ltd., San Francisco, CA, director, 1977. Worked as radio news reporter for the political campaign of George McGovern, 1972; consultant to Kjos Publishing Company, 1973–74, and others.

Member: American Cinema Editors, Academy of Motion Picture Arts and Sciences, Motion Picture Editors Guild.

Awards, Honors: Eddie Award, best edited motion picture for non–commercial television, American Cinema Editors, 1995, for *Against the Wall;* Eddie Award nomination (with Curtiss Clayton), best edited miniseries or motion picture for non–commercial television, 2007, for *Mrs. Harris;* Emmy Award, outstanding single–camera picture editing for a miniseries or movie,

2009, and Eddie Award nomination, best edited miniseries or motion picture for television, 2010, both (with Brian A. Kates) for *Taking Chance;* Emmy Award nomination, outstanding single–camera picture editing for a miniseries or movie, 2009, and Eddie Award nomination, best edited miniseries or motion picture for television, 2010, both (with Alan Heim) for *Grey Gardens.*

CREDITS

Film Editor:
Shogun Assassin, New World, 1980.
(With Mauro Alice) *The Killing of America* (documentary; also known as *Violence*), Embassy, 1982.
They Call Me Bruce? (also known as *A Fistful of Chopsticks*), Artists Releasing, 1982.
Re–animator, Empire Pictures, 1985.
Additional film editing, *Kiss of the Spider Woman* (also known as *O beijo da mulher aranha*), Island, 1985.
Troll, Empire Pictures, 1986.
From Beyond (also known as *H. P. Lovecraft's "From Beyond"*), Empire Pictures, 1986.
Dolls (also known as *The Doll*), Empire Pictures, 1987.
Slam Dance, Island, 1987.
Checking Out, Warner Bros., 1989.
Blue Steel, Metro–Goldwyn–Mayer, 1990.
Reversal of Fortune, Warner Bros., 1990.
Year of the Gun, Triumph Releasing, 1991.
Single White Female, Columbia, 1992.
Corrina, Corrina, New Line Cinema, 1994.
Kiss of Death, Twentieth Century–Fox, 1995.
Before and After, Buena Vista, 1996.
Desperate Measures, TriStar, 1998.
54 (also known as *Fifty–Four*), Miramax, 1998.
Boys Don't Cry, Fox Searchlight, 1999.
Bill's Gun Shop, Polychrome Pictures, 2001.
The Center of the World (also known as *The Centre of the World*), Artisan Entertainment, 2001.
The Believer, Fireworks Pictures, 2002.
Murder by Numbers (also known as *Murd3r 8y Num8ers*), Warner Bros., 2002.
Maria Full of Grace (also known as *Maria, llena eres de gracia*), Fine Line, 2004.
At Home at the End of the World, Warner Independent Pictures, 2004.
A Love Song for Bobby Long, Lions Gate Films, 2004.
The Ice Harvest, Focus Features, 2005.
Wind Chill, TriStar, 2007.
Noise, THINKFilm, 2008.
Daylight, Parts and Labor/White Buffalo Entertainment, 2009.
As Good as Dead, VVS Films, 2009.
Amelia, Fox Searchlight, 2009.
Frank the Rat, Frank the Rat Productions, 2009.

Television Film Editor; Movies:
Against the Wall, HBO, 1994.
Left, Showtime, 2001.

Just Another Story, HBO, 2004.
Mrs. Harris, HBO, 2005.
Additional film editing, *Bernard and Doris,* HBO, 2008.
Taking Chance, HBO, 2009.
Grey Gardens, ABC, 2009.
Additional film editing, *Into the Storm,* HBO, 2009.

Television Appearances; Episodic:
Appeared in an episode of *Anatomy of a Scene,* Sundance Channel.

OTHER SOURCES

Electronic:
Lee Percy Official Site, http://www.lpercy.com, February 20, 2010.

PERRY, Ward

PERSONAL

Addresses: *Agent*—The Characters Talent Agency, 1505 Second Ave., 2nd Floor, Vancouver, British Columbia V6H 3Y4, Canada.

Career: Actor and voice performer.

CREDITS

Film Appearances:
(English version) Voice of Governor Proud, *The Humanoid,* 1986.
(English version) Voice of Kami, *Doragon boru Z 1: Ora no gohan wo kaese* (animated; also known as *Dead Zone, Dead Zone: The Movie, Dragon Ball Z 1: Return My Gohan!,* and *Dragon Ball Z: Dead Zone*), 1989.
(English version) Voice of Rowen of Strata, *Yoroiden Samurai Trooper: Kikotei densetsu* (animated; also known as *Ronin Warriors: New Adventures OVA—Legend of the Inferno Armor*), 1989.
(English version) Voice of Rowen of Strata, *Yoroiden Samurai Trooper Gaiden* (animated; also known as *Ronin Warriors: New Adventures OVA—Gaiden*), 1989.
(English version) Voice of Kishimei and Dr. Kochin, *Doragon boru Z 2: Kono yo de ichiban tsuyoi yatsu* (animated; also known as *Dragon Ball Z: The Movie—World's Strongest* and *The World's Strongest*), 1990.

Voice of Turtles, *Doragon boru Z 3: Chikyu marugoto cho kessen* (animated; also known as *Dragon Ball Z 3: The Ultimate Decisive Battle for Earth, Dragon Ball Z: The Movie—The Tree of Might, Dragon Ball Z: The Super Battle in the World, Dragon Ball Z: The Tree of Might,* and *The Tree of Might*), 1990.
(English version) Voice of Rowen of Strata, *Yoroiden Samurai Trooper: Message* (animated; also known as *Ronin Warriors: Message OVA*), 1991.
Voice of Geese Howard, *Fatal Fury: Legend of the Hungry Wolf* (animated), 1992.
Voice of Genpachi Inukai, *Hakkenden shin sho* (animated; also known as *Hakkenden* and *The Legend of the Dog Warriors: The Hakkenden*), 1993.
Voice of Geese Howard, *Fatal Fury 2: The New Battle* (animated), 1993.
Voices of Lawrence Blood and Geese Howard, *Garou densetu* (animated; also known as *Fatal Fury: The Motion Picture*), 1994.
Voice of Geese Howard, *Fatal Fury I* (animated), 1995.
Voice of Geese Howard, *Fatal Fury 2,* 1996.
Voice of Yakushimaru, *Please Save My Earth* (animated), Viz Video, 1996.
Voice of Staffer A, *Key: The Metal Idol,* 1996.
Voice of villager, *Warriors of Virtue,* Metro–Goldwyn–Mayer, 1997.
Voice of Huitzil and other voices, *Vampire Hunter: The Animated Series* (animated; also known as *Night Warriors: Darkstalkers' Revenge*), 1997.
(English version) Voice of councilmember number three and scientist, *Merutiransa* (animated; also known as *Melty Lancer*), 1999.
(English version) Voice of Gaddes, *Escaflowne* (animated; also known as *Escaflowne: The Movie*), Bandai Entertainment, 2000.
(English version) Voice of Sounga, *Inuyasha—Tenka hadou no ken* (animated; also known as *Inuyasha the Movie 3: Swords of an Honorable Ruler* and *Swords of an Honorable Ruler*), 2003.
(English version) Voice of Gora, *Inuyasha–Guren no houraijima* (animated; also known as *Inuyasha the Movie 4: Fire on the Mystic Island*), 2004.

Film Additional Voices:
Ginga tetsudo Three–Nine (animated; also known as *Galaxy Express 999, Galaxy Express 999: The Signature Edition,* and *Ginga tetsudo 999*), 1979.
Sayonara, ginga tetsudo Suri–Nain: Andromeda shuchakueki (animated; also known as *Adieu, Galaxy Express 999: Last Stop Andromeda* and *Adieu, Galaxy Express 999: The Signature Edition*), 1981.
(English version) *Kyofun no byoningen saishu kyoshi* (animated; also known as *The Scary Bionic Man: The Ultimate Teacher* and *The Ultimate Teacher*), 1988.
Galaxy Express 999 (animated), Viz Video, 1996.

Adieu, Galaxy Express 999 (animated), Viz Video, 1997.

Television Appearances; Series:
Voice of Ryu Jose, *Kido senshi Gandamu* (animated; also known as *Mobile Suit Gundam*) 1979.

(English version) Voice of Hiroshi, professor, and Chachamaru Regular 2, *Mezon Ikkoku* (animated; also known as *Maison Ikkoku*), 1986–88.

Voice of Badamon, Rowen, and Sekhemet, *Yoroiden Samurai Troopers* (animated; also known as *Ronin Warriors* and *Legendary Armor Samurai Troopers*), 1988.

Voice of Brad Loser Wright, *Skysurfer Strike Force* (animated), 1995.

Voice of Dodoria and Rezun, *Dragon Ball Z* (animated; also known as *DBZ*), Showtime and syndicated, 1996.

(English version) Voice of board member number two, *Silent Mobius* (animated), 1998.

Voice of Commander Geibridge, *Brain Powerd* (animated; *Buren pawado*), 1998.

(English version) Voice of Jade Emperor and East General, *Monkey Magic* (animated), 1998.

Voice of Big Blue and others, *Monster Farm: Enbanseki no himitsu* (animated; also known as *Monster Rancher*), 1999–2001.

Voice of Dryden Fassa, *Escaflowne* (animated; also known as *FoxKids "Escaflowne"* and *The Vision of Escaflowne*), Fox, 2000.

Voice of Howard, *Mobile Suit Gundam Wing* (animated; also known as *Gundam Wing* and *Mobile Suit Gundam 00*), Cartoon Network, 2000.

Voice of servant number two, *Inuyasha* (animated), 2000.

Keith, *Project ARMS*, 2001.

(English version) *Chikyu boei kazoku* (animated; also known as *The Daichis: Earth's Defense Family*), 2001.

Kirihara group employee, *The SoulTaker*, 2001.

Voice of DesertMan, *Rockman.exe* (also known as *MegaMan: NT Warrior*, *MegaMan: NT Warrior*, and *Rockman.exe*), 2001.

Voice of Scavenger and frustrated guy, *Transformers: Armada* (animated; also known as *Transufoma: Maikuron densetsu*), Cartoon Network, 2002.

Voice of Kojiro Murdock, *Kido senshi Gundam Seed* (animated; also known as *Gundam Seed* and *Mobile Suit Gundam Seed*), Cartoon Network, 2002–2003.

Voice of Mr. Shinjo, *Master Keaton*, 2003.

(English version) Voice of Gilbert the Impaler and Watts, *Zoids Fuzors* (animated), Cartoon Network, 2003–2004.

Television Appearances; Miniseries:
(English version) Voice of Matsusaki, *D* (animated; also known as *Dark Soldier D*), 1998.

(English version) Voice of Sayuri's father, seed solider number three, and man at shelter, *Chikyu shojo Arjuna* (animated; also known as *Earth Girl Arjuna*), 1999.

Television Appearances; Movies:
Voice of Geese Howard, *Fatal Fury: Legend of the Hungry Wolf* (animated), 1992.

Voice of Kishimei and Dr. Kochin, *Dragon Ball Z: The Movie—The World Strongest* (animated), Cartoon Network, 2000.

Voice of Rezzun, *Dragon Ball Z: The Movie—The Tree of Might* (animated), Cartoon Network, 2000.

Voice of Nikki, *Dragon Ball Z: The Movie—Dead Zone* (animated), Cartoon Network, 2000.

Voice of Agent Faces, *G.I. Joe: Spy Troops the Movie* (animated), 2003.

Television Appearances; Episodic:
Voice of Hokuto Yakushimaru, "Feelings," *Please Save My Earth* (animated), 1996.

Voice of helicopter pilot, "Adrift," *X–Men Evolution* (animated), 2001.

(English version) Voice of Ryu Jose, "Lalah's Dilemma," *Kido senshi Gandamu* (animated; also known as *First Gundam, Mobile Soldier,* and *Mobile Suit Gundam*), Cartoon Network, 2004.

Voice of Landmine, "The Sun," *Transformer: Super Link* (animated; also known as *Transformers: Energon*), TV Tokyo, 2004.

Television Additional Voices; Series:
(English version) *Saber Marionette J* (animated), 1996.

Mobile Suit Gundam Wing (animated; also known as *Gundam Wing*), Cartoon Network, 2000.

Also appeared as additional voices, *Ranma 1/2*.

Television Additional Voices; Movies:
Mobile Suit Gundam Wing: The Movie–Endless Waltz (animated; also known as *Endless Waltz* and *Gundam Wing: The Movie–Endless Waltz*), Cartoon Network, 2000.

RECORDINGS

Video Games:
(English version) Voice of Ryu Jose, *Kido senshi Gandamu* (also known as *Mobile Suit Gundam: Journey to Jaburo*), 2000.

(Uncredited; English version) Voice of Ryu Jose, *Kido senshi Gandamu: Renpou vs. Zeon DX* (also known as *Mobile Suit Gundam: Federation vs. Zeon*), 2001.

(English version) Voice of Ryu Jose, *Kido senshi Gandamu: Meguriai sora* (also known as *Mobile Suit Gundam: Encounters in Space*), Bandai Games, 2003.

WRITINGS

Television Episodes:
Tranufoma: Maikuron densetsu (animated; also known as *Transformers: Armada*), 2002.
Bakugan Battle Brawlers, 2007.

Television Automated Dialogue Replacement (ADR) Script: English; Episodic:
Saber Marionette J (animated), 1996.
Dragon Ball Z (animated; also known as *DBZ*), Showtime and syndicated, 1996.
Monkey Magic (animated), syndicated, 1998.

Television Script Confirmation (English adaptation); Episodic:
Ronin Warriors, Cartoon Network, 1999.

PHILIPS, Nathan
    See PHILLIPS, Nathan

PHILLIPS, Graham 1993–

PERSONAL

Born April 14, 1993.

Addresses: *Agent*—Abrams Artist Agency, 9200 Sunset Blvd., Suite 1130, Los Angeles, CA 90069. *Manager*—Untitled Entertainment, 1801 Century Park East, Suite 700, Los Angeles, CA 90067.

Career: Actor. Sang national anthem at Los Angeles Dodgers baseball game.

Awards, Honors: Young Artist Award nomination, best performance in a television movie, miniseries or special—leading young actor, 2008, for *Ben 10: Race against Time;* Young Artist Award nomination, best performance in a feature film—supporting young actor—comedy or musical, 2008, for *Evan Almighty;* Screen Actors Guild Award nomination (with others), outstanding performance by an ensemble in a drama series, 2010, for *The Good Wife.*

CREDITS

Film Appearances:
Boy soprano, *Noel,* Screen Media Films, 2004.
Ensemble, *The Ten Commandments: The Musical,* Seventh Art Releasing, 2006.
Jordan Baxter, *Evan Almighty,* Universal, 2007.
Himself, *"Evan Almighty": The Building of Noah's Ark* (short documentary), Universal Home Entertainment, 2007.
Himself, *"Evan Almighty": The Ark–Itects of Noah's Ark* (short documentary), Universal Home Entertainment, 2007.
Mark Wakefield, *Stolen Live* (also known as *Stolen*), IFC Films, 2009.

Television Appearances; Series:
Zach Florrick, *The Good Wife,* CBS, 2009—.

Television Appearances; Movies:
Jeff Huff, *Love's Long Journey,* Hallmark Channel, 2005.
Voice of Ben Tennyson, *Ben 10: Race Against Time* (animated), Cartoon Network, 2007.

Television Appearances; Episodic:
Winthrop, "Mentalo Case," *The King Of Queens,* CBS, 2002.
Toby Carroll, "Legacy," *Judging Amy,* CBS, 2004.
Kyle/Jonah Wheeler, "Mace vs. Scalpel," *Crossing Jordan,* NBC, 2006.
"The Ark, the Animals, and *Evan Almighty*," *HBO First Look,* HBO, 2007.
"Evan Allmachtig," *Das grobe RTL special zum film,* 2007.

Also appeared in *Today,* NBC.

Stage Appearances:
Evan, *13—The Musical,* Bernard B. Jacobs Theatre, New York City, 2008–2009.

Also appeared as title role, *The Little Prince,* New York City Opera, Lincoln Center, New York City; Young Clyde, *An American Tragedy,* Metropolitan Opera; Tiny Tim, *A Christmas Carol—The Musical,* Broadway production; in *The Ten Commandments—The Musical,* Kodak Theatre, Los Angeles.

PHILLIPS, Nathan 1980–
    (Nathan Philips)

PERSONAL

Born 1980, in Sunbury, Victoria, Australia.

Addresses: *Agent*—WME Entertainment, One William Morris Place, Beverly Hills, CA 90212. *Manager*—Principato/Young Management, 9465 Wilshire Blvd., Suite 880, Beverly Hills, CA 90212. *Publicist*—Baker/Winokur/Ryder, 825 Eighth Ave., Worldwide Plaza, New York, NY 10019.

Career: Actor, producer, and director.

Awards, Honors: IF Award nomination, best actor, and Film Critics Circle of Australia Award nomination, best actor, 2002, both for *Australian Rules.*

CREDITS

Film Appearances:
Ryan Jeffers, *Warriors of Virtue: The Return to Tao* (also known as *Warriors of Virtue 2, Warriors of Virtue 2: Return to Tao,* and *Warriors of Virtue 2: The Return to Tao),* Miramax, 2002.
Gary "Blacky" Black, *Australian Rules,* Beyond Films, 2002.
Dave, *Take Away,* Mondayitis Productions, 2003.
Trig, *One Perfect Day,* Terra Entertainment, 2004.
Brandon, *Under the Radar,* Hoyts Distribution, 2004.
Ben Mitchell, *Wolf Creek,* Dimension Films, 2005.
Philip, *You and Your Stupid Mate,* Lightning Entertainment, 2005.
The Opposite of Velocity (short film), 2005.
Sean Jones, *Snakes on a Plane* (also known as *Serpents a bord* and *SoaP),* New Line Cinema, 2006.
Jerry, *West,* Lightning Entertainment, 2007.
Carlo, *Redline,* Chicago Releasing, 2007.
Jack, *Dying Breed,* Omnilab Media, 2008.
(As Nathan Philips) Baker Smith, *Surfer, Dude,* Anchor Bay Entertainment, 2008.
Eric, *Message from the CEO* (short film), 2009.
Malcolm Rennie, *Balibo* (also known as *The Balibo Conspiracy),* Footprint Films, 2009.
Benji, *Quit,* Rebel's Wood, 2009.

Film Work:
Executive producer, *The Opposite of Velocity* (short film), 2005.
Director, *Message from the CEO* (short film), 2009.

Television Appearances; Series:
John "Teabag" Teasdale, *Neighbours,* Ten Network, 1999.
Red O'Malley, *The Saddle Club,* Australian Broadcasting Corporation, 2001–2002.
Angus Moore, *Something in the Air,* Australian Broadcasting Corporation, 2002.

Television Appearances; Movies:
Hugh, *Child Star: The Shirley Temple Story,* ABC, 2001.

Television Appearances; Episodic:
Phoenix, "Hackers" (also known as "In the Realm of Hackers"), *Frontline,* PBS, 2001.
Cameron Sharp, "Dragged," *Blue Heelers,* Seven Network, 2001.
Charlie Sanderson, "The Object of My Affection," *Stingers,* 2004.
Rove Live, Ten Network, 2005.
The 7PM Project, Ten Network, 2009.

RECORDINGS

Videos:
The Snake Pit: On the Set of "Snakes on a Plane" (short documentary), New Line Home Video, 2006.
The Making of "Wolf Creek" (documentary), Weinstein Company, 2006.
(And in archive footage) *Pure Venom: The Making of "Snakes on a Plane"* (short documentary), New Line Home Video, 2006.
(And in archive footage) *Snakes on a Blog* (short documentary), New Line Cinema, 2006.

PICATTO, Alexandra 1983–

PERSONAL

Full name, Alexandra Melina Picatto; born March 6, 1983, in Collinsville, IL; sister of Antoinette Picatto (an actress); married Chris Olivero (an actor), August 12, 2006.

Career: Actress.

CREDITS

Television Appearances; Series:
Amy Shepherd, *Get Real,* Fox, 1999–2000.

Television Apperances; Movies:
Elizabeth, *Not Like Us,* Showtime, 1995.
Danielle Knowlton, *The Colony,* USA Network, 1995.
Blair Robbins, *Blackout,* CBS, 2001.

Television Appearances; Episodic:
Rita, "Breaking up Is Hard to Do," *7th Heaven* (also known as *7th Heaven: Beginnings* and *Seventh Heaven),* The WB, 1997.
Tina Hitchens, "The Devil's Music," *Charmed,* The WB, 1999.
Bridget, "Lois vs. Evil," *Malcolm in the Middle,* Fox, 2000.

Carol Williams, "Jackson," *Kate Brasher,* CBS, 2001.
Whitney, "Space Between Us," *Summerland,* The WB, 2005.

Also appeared in *Kidsongs,* PBS; *Teen Angel,* ABC.

Television Appearances; Specials:
Celia, *Blackbird Hall,* 1995.

Film Appearances:
Charley Simms, *Getting There* (also known as *Getting There: Sweet 16 and Licensed to Drive*), Warner Home Video, 2002.

RECORDINGS

Videos:
Herself, *Kidsongs: If We Could Talk to Animals* (short film), Together Again Productions, 1993.
Herself, *Kidsongs: Boppin' with the Biggles* (short film), Together Again Productions, 1995.
Herself, *Kidsongs: Country Sing Along* (short film), Together Again Productions, 1995.

PLATT, Jeffrey
    See MCCONNOHIE, Michael

PLATT, Jeremy
    See MCCONNOHIE, Michael

POLLAN, Tracy 1960–

PERSONAL

Full name, Tracy Jo Pollan; born June 22, 1960, in New York, NY; daughter of Stephen M. (a financial consultant, attorney, and writer) and Corky (a journalist and magazine editor) Pollan; sister of Michael Pollen (an author and university professor); married Michael J. Fox (an actor), July 17, 1988; children: Sam, Schuyler Frances and Aquinnah Kathleen (twins), Esme Annabelle. *Education:* Trained for the stage with Lee Strasberg and at Herbert Berghof Studios; studied dance at Alvin Ailey School and Martha Meredith School. *Religion:* Jewish.

Addresses: *Manager*—Anonymous Content, 3532 Hayden Ave., Culver City, CA 90232.

Career: Actress and producer. Former member of Actors Studio, New York City. Appeared in television commercials, including work for AT&T phone services.

Awards, Honors: Emmy Award nomination, outstanding guest actress in a drama series, 2000, for *Law & Order: Special Victims Unit.*

CREDITS

Television Appearances; Movies:
Leslie Churchill, *Sessions,* ABC, 1983.
Eileen Grafton, *Trackdown: Finding the Goodbar Killer* (also known as *Trackdown*), CBS, 1983.
Mary Beth Phillips, *The Baron and the Kid,* CBS, 1984.
Suzanne Tenney, *A Good Sport,* CBS, 1984.
Title role, *The Abduction of Kari Swenson,* NBC, 1987.
Elizabeth Van Lew, *A Special Friendship,* CBS, 1987.
Liz O'Reilly, *Fine Things* (also known as *Danielle Steel's "Fine Things"*), NBC, 1990.
Lisa Ann Rohn, *Dying to Love You* (also known as *Lethal White Female*), CBS, 1993.
Kim Harrison, *Children of the Dark,* CBS, 1994.
Beth Twitty, *Natalee Holloway,* Lifetime, 2009.

Television Appearances; Specials:
Jen Robbins, "The Great Love Experiment," *ABC Afterschool Specials,* ABC, 1984.
Nicki Davis, "The Little Sister" (also known as "Forbidden" and "The Tender Age"), *American Playhouse,* PBS, 1985.
I Am Your Child, ABC, 1997.
Golden Hanger Awards, E! Entertainment Television, 1999.
Ladies' Home Journal's Most Fascinating Women to Watch, CBS, 2001.
(In archive footage) *Michael J. Fox: The E! True Hollywood Story,* E! Entertainment Television, 2006.
Michael J. Fox: Adventures of an Incurable Optimist, ABC, 2009.

Television Appearances; Miniseries:
Kathleen Kennedy, *The Kennedys of Massachusetts,* ABC, 1990.
Lindsay Boxer, *1st to Die* (also known as *James Patterson's "1st to Die"*), NBC, 2003.

Television Appearances; Series:
Ellen Reed, *Family Ties,* NBC, 1985–86.

Television Appearances; Pilots:
For Lovers Only, ABC, 1982.
Title role, *Anna Says,* ABC, 1999.
Kay Hench, *Hench at Home,* ABC, 2003.

Television Appearances; Episodic:
Renee Miller, "The Thirty Year Itch," *Spin City,* ABC, 1997.
Renee Miller, "It Happened One Night," *Spin City,* ABC, 1998.
Harper Anderson, "Closure: Parts 1 & 2," *Law & Order: Special Victims Unit* (also known as *Law & Order: SVU* and *Special Victims Unit*), NBC, 2000.
Inside the Actors Studio (also known as *Inside the Actors Studio: The Craft of Theatre and Film*), Bravo, 2005.
Caitlyn Lynch, "How to Make a Killing in Big Business: Parts 1–3," *Medium,* NBC, 2009.
Rachael Ray, syndicated, 2009.
Entertainment Tonight (also known as *Entertainment This Week, E.T., ET Weekend,* and *This Week in Entertainment*), syndicated, 2009.

Television Executive Producer; Pilots:
Anna Says, ABC, 1999.

Film Appearances:
Leslie, *Baby, It's You,* Paramount, 1983.
Mary, *Promised Land* (also known as *Young Hearts*), Vestron, 1988.
Vicky, *Bright Lights, Big City,* United Artists, 1988.
Mara, *A Stranger Among Us* (also known as *Close to Eden*), Buena Vista, 1992.

Stage Appearances:
Peggy, *Album,* Workshop of the Players Art, Cherry Lane Theatre, New York City, 1980–81.
Julie Jackson, *Pack of Lies,* Royale Theatre, New York City, 1985.
Lucy, *Women in Mind,* Manhattan Theatre Club Stage I, City Center Theatre, New York City, 1988.
Molly at age twenty–one, *Jake's Women,* Neil Simon Theatre, New York City, 1992.

OTHER SOURCES

Periodicals:
Parade, February 2, 2003, p. 13.
People Weekly, May 8, 2000, p. 128; June 18, 2001, p. 61.
TV Guide, February 22, 2003, pp. 36–37; April 13, 2009, p. 43.

PRATT, Deborah
(Deborah M. Pratt)

PERSONAL

Born in Chicago, IL; married Donald P. Bellisario (a producer, director, and writer), June 30, 1984 (divorced,

1991); children: Nickolas, Troian Avery (an actress). *Education:* Webster University, bachelor's degree.

Addresses: *Manager*—Epidemic Pictures and Management, Inc., 1635 North Cahuenga Blvd., 5th Floor, Hollywood, CA 90028.

Career: Actress, voice performer, producer, director, and writer.

Member: Actors' Equity Association, Screen Actors Guild, Producers Guild of America, Directors Guild of America, Writers Guild of America.

Awards, Honors: Lillian Gish Award, Women in Film, 1990, for an episode of *Quantum Leap;* Emmy Award nominations (with others), outstanding drama series, 1990, 1991, and 1992, all for *Quantum Leap;* Emmy Award nomination (with others), outstanding animated program of more than one hour, 1999, for *Out Friend, Martin.*

CREDITS

Film Appearances:
Meagan, *Spacehunter: Adventures in the Forbidden Zone* (also known as *Adventures in the Creep Zone, Road Gangs,* and *Spacehunter*), Columbia, 1983.
Robin Dwyer, *Last Rites,* Metro–Goldwyn–Mayer, 1988.
Dr. Allison Williams, *Exit to Eden,* Savoy Pictures, 1994.
Madison, *Unspoken* (short film), Alluvial Filmworks, 2007.
Rachel, *Chinaman's Chance* (also known as *I Am Somebody*), Plus Entertainment, 2008.
Voice of Ziggy, *Quantum Leap: A Leap to Di For,* RASCO Motion Pictures, 2009.
Cassandra Williamson, *Peep World,* Occupant Films, 2010.

Television Appearances; Series:
Marella, *Airwolf* (also known as *Lobo del aire*), CBS, 1984–85.
(Uncredited) Voice of Ziggy, *Quantum Leap,* NBC, 1989–93.

Television Appearances; Pilots:
Katmandu, 1980.
Bonnie Madison, *She's with Me,* NBC, 1982.
Marella, *Airwolf,* CBS, 1984.

Television Appearances; Movies:
Susan, *Love Is Not Enough,* NBC, 1978.
Jennifer, *Grambling's White Tiger,* NBC, 1981.
Sissy, *Three on a Match,* NBC 1987.

Television Appearances; Specials:
Prime Times, NBC, 1983.

Television Appearances; Episodic:
Kate, "Pattern for Evil," *Police Woman,* NBC, 1975.
Carol, "Crash Diet," *CHiPs* (also known as *ChiPs Patrol*), NBC, 1978.
Kat Mandu, "Fonzie Meets Kat," *Happy Days,* ABC, 1979.
Connie, "Phyl's Wedding," *Phyl & Mikhy,* CBS, 1980.
"Humiliation," *Strike Force,* ABC, 1982.
Sandra, "The Odd Triangle," *The New Odd Couple,* ABC, 1982.
Jill, "Who's Arnold?," *Benson,* ABC, 1983.
Vanessa, "The Way to a Man's Heart," *Gimme a Break!,* NBC, 1983.
Gloria, "Rembrandt's Girl," *Magnum, P.I.,* CBS, 1984.
Gloria, "Echoes of the Mind: Parts 1 & 2," *Magnum, P.I.,* CBS, 1984.
Gloria, "Tran Quoc Jones," *Magnum, P.I.,* CBS, 1984.
Sandra Browning, "Flashpoint," *Hunter,* NBC, 1987.
Nicole, "A Perfect Match," *Tequila and Bonetti,* CBS, 1992.

Television Work; Series:
Coproducer, *Quantum Leap,* NBC, 1989.
Supervising producer, *Quantum Leap,* NBC, 1989–90.
Co–executive producer, *Quantum Leap,* NBC, 1990–93.
Executive producer, *The Net,* USA Network, 1998–99.

Television Co–executive Producer; Episodic:
"Runt of the Litter," *Tequila and Bonetti,* CBS, 1992.
"Tale of the Dragon," *Tequila and Bonetti,* CBS, 1992.

Television Work; Other:
Producer and director, *Girlfriends* (special), Showtime, 1997.
(As Deborah M. Pratt) Director, *Cora Unashamed* (movie), PBS, 2000.

RECORDINGS

Videos:
Player, *Elephant Parts* (also known as *Michael Nesmith in "Elephant Parts"*), Pacific Arts, 1981.

WRITINGS

Television Series:
Quantum Leap, NBC, 1989–93.
The Net, USA Network, 1998–99.

Television Specials:
Girlfriends, Showtime, 1997.
Our Friend, Martin (animated), Starz!, 1999.

Television Episodes:
(As Deborah M. Pratt) "Fallen Angel," *Airwolf* (also known as *Lobo del aire*), CBS, 1984.
(As Deborah M. Pratt) "Little Games," *Magnum, P.I.,* CBS, 1985.
(As Deborah M. Pratt) "Little Girl Who," *Magnum, P.I.,* CBS, 1986.
Songwriter, "Alphabet Rap," "Shock Theatre—October 3, 1954, *Quantum Leap,* NBC, 1991.

Songs Featured in Films:
Lyricist, "All of My Life," *Last Rites,* Metro–Goldwyn–Mayer, 1988.

PROBST, Jeff 1962–

PERSONAL

Full name, Jeffrey Lee Probst; born October 26, 1962 (some sources cite November 4, 1961), in Wichita, KS; son of Jerry (a business executive) and Barbara Probst; married Shelley Wright (a producer of auto shows and psychotherapist), 1996 (divorced, 2001). *Education:* Attended Seattle Pacific University.

Addresses: *Agent*—Sean Perry, WME Entertainment, 1 William Morris Pl., Beverly Hills, CA 90212.

Career: Television host, director, and writer. Columbia Broadcasting System, appeared several times in the public service announcement campaign *CBS Cares,* between 2001 and 2009; appeared in a commercial for Marriott Fairfield Inn, 2001. Serpentine Project (non-profit foundation for older children exiting foster care), founder, 2007. KIRO–TV, Seattle, WA, hosted garden and car shows; also worked as a producer and narrator of sales and marketing videos for airplane manufacturer Boeing.

Awards, Honors: Teen Choice Award nomination, choice television personality, 2001, Emmy Award, 2001, and Emmy Award nomination, 2002, both outstanding special class program (with others), Emmy Award nominations (with others), outstanding reality–competition program, 2003, 2004, 2005, 2006, Teen Choice Award nomination, choice host of a television reality or variety show, 2003, and Emmy Awards, outstanding host of a reality or reality–competition program, 2008, 2009, all for *Survivor;* Method Fest

Award, best screenplay for a feature film, and Seattle International Film Festival Award, best director, both 2001, Sonoma Film Festival Award, breakout director, and DVD Exclusive Award nomination, best screenplay for a DVD premiere movie, 2003, all for *Finder's Fee.*

CREDITS

Television Appearances; Series:
Himself, *Sound fX,* FX Network, 1994.
Host, *Backchat,* FX Network, 1995.
Correspondent, *Access Hollywood,* syndicated, 1996.
Host, *Rock & Roll Jeopardy!,* VH1, 1998.
Host, *Hollywood on Trial,* Court TV, 1999.
Host, *Dave Barlia: Extreme Stuntman,* NBC, 1999.
Host and announcer, *Survivor,* CBS, 2000—.

Television Appearances; Specials:
Host, *Family Business,* FX Network, 1996.
Host, *Dave Barlia: Extreme Stuntman,* NBC, 1999.
Survivor: The E! True Hollywood Story, E! Entertainment Television, 2001.
Playboy's 50th Anniversary Celebration, Arts and Entertainment, 2003.
VH1 Goes inside Live with Regis and Kelly, VH1, 2004.
Maxim Hot 100, VH1, 2004.
Commentator, *101 Most Unforgettable SNL Moments,* E! Entertainment Television, 2004.
Unforgettable Moments in Television Entertainment: A Museum of Television & Radio Special, NBC, 2005.
AutoRox, Spike TV, 2005.
MLB vs. Survivor, CBS, 2007.
Live from the Red Carpet: The 2008 Emmy Awards, E! Entertainment Television, 2008.
TV Guide Live at the Emmy Awards, TV Guide Channel, 2008.
Big Night of Stars (also known as *Jimmy Kimmel's Big Night of Stars*), ABC, 2008.
Host, *Live for the Moment,* CBS, 2010.

Also host of various reunion shows and other specials related to the series *Survivor,* CBS.

Television Appearances; Episodic:
"Best Desert Island Disc," *The List,* 2000.
Entertainment Tonight (also known as *Entertainment This Week, E.T., ET Weekend,* and *This Week in Entertainment*), syndicated, multiple appearances, beginning 2003.
"Survivor," *VH1 Goes Inside,* VH1, 2003.
Interviewee, "Idlewild South," *Space Ghost Coast to Coast* (also known as *SGC2C*), Cartoon Network, 2003.
MADtv, Fox, 2003, 2004, 2005, guest host, 2006, 2007.
Contestant, *Celebrity Blackjack,* Game Show Network, 2004.

Det sista oeraadet, 2004.
(Uncredited) "One Punch Away," *The Contender,* NBC, 2005.
Jeopardy!, syndicated, 2005.
(In archive footage) "Hoaxes, Cheats, and Liars," *20 to 1,* Nine Network, 2006.
Wheel of Fortune, syndicated, 2007.
Dancing with the Stars (also known as *D.W.T.S.*), ABC, 2008.
"Jeff Probst," *Close–Up,* TV Guide Channel, 2008.
"Tying the Not," *Head Case,* Starz!, 2009.
"Survivor," *Infanity,* TV Guide Channel, 2009.

According to some sources, also voice of Vice Principal Raycliff for the animated series *Fillmore!* (also known as *Disney's "Fillmore!*), ABC.

Television Talk Show Guest Appearances; Episodic:
The Daily Show (also known as *A Daily Show with Jon Stewart, The Daily Show with Jon Stewart Global Edition,* and *Jon Stewart*), 2000.
Howard Stern, 2001.
The Oprah Winfrey Show (also known as *Oprah*), syndicated, 2001.
The Rosie O'Donnell Show, syndicated, 2002.
The View, ABC, 2004, 2006.
The Wayne Brady Show, syndicated, 2004.
The Late Late Show with Craig Kilborn (also known as *The Late Late Show*), CBS, 2004.
The Tony Danza Show, syndicated, 2004, 2005.
Live with Regis and Kelly, syndicated, multiple appearances, beginning 2004.
Jimmy Kimmel Live! (also known as *Jimmy Kimmel*), ABC, 2005.
Dennis Miller, CNBC, 2005.
The Late Late Show with Craig Ferguson, CBS, 2005, 2006, 2007.
Late Night with Conan O'Brien, NBC, 2006.
Ellen: The Ellen DeGeneres Show (also known as *The Ellen Show*), syndicated, 2006, 2009.
Rachael Ray, syndicated, multiple appearances, beginning 2006.
The Morning Show with Mike & Juliet, Fox and syndicated, 2007.
The Tyra Banks Show, CW Network, 2007.
Larry King Live, Cable News Network, 2008.
The Bonnie Hunt Show, NBC, 2009.
Late Night with Jimmy Fallon, NBC, 2009.

Television Appearances; Awards Presentations:
The 52nd Annual Primetime Emmy Awards, ABC, 2000.
Presenter, *The 55th Annual Primetime Emmy Awards,* Fox, 2003.
Presenter, *The 2003 Primetime Creative Arts Emmy Awards,* E! Entertainment Television, 2003.
3rd Annual DVD Exclusive Awards, FX Network, 2003.
Host, *8th Annual Prism Awards,* FX Network, 2004.
Host, *The 60th Primetime Emmy Awards,* ABC, 2008.

The 7th Annual TV Land Awards, TV Land, 2009.
The 36th Annual People's Choice Awards, 2010.

Television Appearances; Other:
Kevin Leeds, *Face of a Stranger* (movie), CBS, 1991.
I Love the '90s: Part Deux (miniseries), VH1, 2005.
Himself, *I Get That a Lot,* CBS, 2009.

Television Work; Specials:
Producer, *MLB vs. Survivor,* CBS, 2007.
Creator, *Live for the Moment,* CBS, 2010.

Television Producer; Episodic:
"The Final Showdown," *Survivor,* CBS, 2006.
"This Game Ain't Over," *Survivor,* CBS, 2006.

Film Appearances:
The A–List, 2001.

Film Director:
Finders' Fee, Silverline Pictures, 2001.

Radio Appearances; Series:
Host of *Howard Stern Celebrity Fan Roundtable,* Sirius/XM.

Internet Appearances; Episodic:
Tom Green Live!, TomGreen.com, 2007.

RECORDINGS

Compilation Videos:
Survivor–Season One: The Great and Most Outrageous Moments, 2000.
Survivor–Season Two: The Great and Most Outrageous Moments, 2000.

WRITINGS

Television Series:
Survivor, CBS, 2000—.

Television Episodes:
According to some sources, also writer for the series *Head Case,* Starz!.

Screenplays:
Finder's Fee, Silverline Pictures, 2001.

OTHER SOURCES

Periodicals:
Broadcasting & Cable, February 13, 2006, p. 3.
Entertainment Weekly, February 11, 2005, p. 37; December 23, 2005, p. 27.
Good Housekeeping, January, 2003, p. 184.
People Weekly, August 14, 2000, p. 133; May 14, 2001, p. 146; October 17, 2005, p. 105.
TV Guide, August 9, 2003, p. 27; December 12, 2005, p. 25; September 15, 2008, pp. 18–19.
USA Today, April 28, 2008, p. 4D.

R

REDFORD, J. C. A. 1953–
(Jac Redford, Jack Redford)

PERSONAL

Full name, Jonathan Alfred Clawson Redford; born July 14, 1953, in Los Angeles, CA.

Addresses: *Agent*—Cheryl Taino, Gorfaine, Schwartz Agency, 4111 West Alameda Ave., Suite 509, Burbank, CA 91505.

Career: Composer, orchestrator, and conductor. Los Angeles Master Chorale, producer; Sundance Film Institute, music consultant; University of Southern California and University of California, Los Angeles, guest lecturer.

Member: Academy of Motion Picture Arts and Sciences (member of music branch executive committee), Academy of Television Arts and Sciences (member of music branch executive committee).

Awards, Honors: Emmy Award nominations, outstanding dramatic underscore for a television series, 1984, for "In Sickness and in Health," and 1985, for "Fade to White," two episodes of *St. Elsewhere;* awards from American Society of Composers, Authors, and Publishers, top television series, 1992, 1993, 1994, 1995, 1996, all for *Coach.*

CREDITS

Film Music Orchestrator:

(And song producer and music conductor) *Bye, Bye Love,* Twentieth Century–Fox, 1995.

Contributor of additional orchestration, *Deep Impact,* 1998.
Mighty Joe Young (also known as *Mighty Joe*), Buena Vista, 1998.
Deep Impact, Paramount, 1998.
Bicentennial Man (also known as *Der 200—Jahre Mann*), Buena Vista, 1999.
The Perfect Storm, Warner Bros., 2000.
How the Grinch Stole Christmas (also known as *Dr. Seuss' "How the Grinch Stole Christmas," The Grinch,* and *Der Grinch*), Universal, 2000.
(And conductor) *Cirque du Soleil: Journey of Man,* Sony Pictures, 2000.
Enemy at the Gates (also known as *Duell—Enemy at the Gates*), Paramount, 2001.
Iris, Miramax, 2001.
Windtalkers, Metro–Goldwyn–Mayer, 2002.
The Missing, Columbia, 2003.
The Spiderwick Chronicles (also known as *The Spiderwick Chronicles: The IMAX Experience*), Paramount, 2008.
(As Jac Redford) *Leatherheads* (also known as *Ein verlockendes spiel*), Universal, 2008.
WALL–E (animated), Walt Disney, 2008.
Revolutionary Road, DreamWorks, 2008.
Tigger & Pooh and a Musical Too (animated; also known as *My Friends Tigger & Pooh: Tigger & Pooh and a Musical Too*), Walt Disney Studios Home Entertainment, 2009.

Film Music Conductor:

The Little Mermaid (animated), Buena Vista, 1989.
Billy Bathgate, Buena Vista, 1991.
Benny & Joon, Metro–Goldwyn–Mayer, 1993.
Heart and Souls, Universal, 1993.
The Joy Luck Club, Buena Vista, 1993.
The Nightmare before Christmas (also known as *Tim Burton's "The Nightmare before Christmas"* and *Tim Burton's "The Nightmare before Christmas"* in Disney Digital 3–D), Buena Vista, 1993.
(As Jack Redford) *Black Beauty,* Warner Bros., 1994.

A Pyromaniac's Love Story (also known as *Burning Love*), Buena Vista, 1995.
The Other Sister, Buena Vista, 1999.
One Night with the King, Gener8Xion Entertainment/ FoxFaith, 2006.

Film Work; Other:

Song arranger, title song, *The Trip to Bountiful,* Island Pictures, 1985.
Song producer, "Good Company," *Oliver & Company* (animated), Buena Vista, 1988.
Vocal arranger, *XXX* (also known as *Triple X*), Sony Pictures Releasing, 2002.
Music arranged, "The Blue Danube Waltz, Opus 314," *Bobby Jones: Stroke of Genius,* Film Foundry Releasing, 2004.

RECORDINGS

Albums:

Is This the Way to Carnegie Hall?, Crystal Records, 1988.
Oliver & Company (soundtrack recording), Walt Disney Music, 1988.
Disney's "D2, the Mighty Ducks" (soundtrack recording), Hollywood Records, 1994.
Bye, Bye Love (soundtrack recording), Giant Records, 1995.
D3, the Mighty Ducks (soundtrack recording), Hollywood Records, 1996.

Other albums include *The Astronomers* (soundtrack); *A Choir of Angels II: Mission Music; Eternity Shut in a Span* and *Evening Wind,* both choral music for Clarion Records; and *The Trip to Bountiful* and *What the Deaf Man Heard,* both soundtrack recordings.

WRITINGS

Television Music Composer; Series:

Starsky and Hutch (also known as *Starsky & Hutch*), ABC, 1977, 1979.
James at 15 (also known as *James at 16*), NBC, 1977.
240–Robert, ABC, 1979.
American Dream, ABC, 1981.
Bret Maverick, NBC, 1981–82.
Knots Landing, CBS, 1982.
Tucker's Witch, CBS, 1982.
King's Crossing, ABC, 1982.
St. Elsewhere, NBC, between 1982 and 1888.
Fame, NBC, 1982–83, then syndicated, 1983–87.
Trauma Center, ABC, 1983.
Cutter to Houston, CBS, 1983.
Voyagers!, NBC, 1983.
Whiz Kids, CBS, 1984.
Automan, ABC, 1984.

Hawaiian Heat, ABC, 1984.
Cover Up, CBS, 1984.
The Best Times, NBC, 1985.
The Twilight Zone (also known as *The New Twilight Zone*), CBS, 1986.
(Including theme music) *Coming of Age,* CBS, 1988–89.
Annie McGuire, CBS, 1988–89.
Coach, ABC, between 1989 and 1994.
Capital News, ABC, 1989–90.
Additional music, *Princesses,* CBS, 1991.
The Astronomers, PBS, 1991.
Home Fires, NBC, 1992.
Delta, ABC, 1992.
(Including theme music) *The Road Home,* CBS, 1994.
Composer and lyricist, *Adventures from the Book of Virtues* (also known as *The Book of Virtues*), PBS, between 1996 and 1998.

Television Music Composer; Movies:

The Long Summer of George Adams, NBC, 1982.
Honeyboy, NBC, 1982.
Happy Endings, NBC, 1983.
Helen Keller: The Miracle Continues, syndicated, 1984.
Going for the Gold: The Bill Johnson Story, CBS, 1985.
Alex: The Life of a Child, ABC, 1986.
Easy Prey, ABC, 1986.
Independence, NBC, 1987.
Stamp of a Killer (also known as *Dangerous Affection*), NBC, 1987.
The Long Journey Home, CBS, 1987.
Save the Dog! (also known as *Go for Broke!*), The Disney Channel, 1988.
Breaking Point, TNT, 1989.
A Son's Promise, ABC, 1990.
Web of Deceit (also known as *Conspiracy to Kill*), USA Network, 1990.
Stop at Nothing, Lifetime, 1991.
Conagher (also known as *Louis L'Amour's "Conagher"*), TNT, 1991.
Locked Up: A Mother's Rage (also known as *Other Side of Love*), CBS, 1991.
Kiss of a Killer, ABC, 1993.
For Their Own Good, ABC, 1993.
One More Mountain, ABC, 1994.
And Then There Was One, Lifetime, 1994.
Is There Life Out There?, CBS, 1994.
For the Future: The Irvine Fertility Scandal (also known as *For the Children: The Irvine Fertility Scandal*), Lifetime, 1996.
Two Voices (also known as *Two Small Voices*), Lifetime, 1997.
What the Deaf Man Heard, CBS, 1997.
Chance of a Lifetime, CBS, 1998.
Grace & Glorie, CBS, 1998.
My Last Love (also known as *To Live For*), ABC, 1999.
The Promise, NBC, 1999.
The Color of Love: Jacey's Story, CBS, 2000.
Leroy & Stitch, 2006.

Television Music Composer; Miniseries:

The Key to Rebecca (also known as *Ken Follett's "The Key to Rebecca"*), syndicated, 1985.

Naomi & Wynonna: Love Can Build a Bridge (also known as *Love Can Build a Bridge*), NBC, 1995.

Mama Flora's Family, CBS, 1998.

Television Music Composer; Pilots:

(Including theme music) *Young Guy Christian,* ABC, 1978.

The Dooley Brothers, CBS, 1979.

Bret Maverick (also known as *Bret Maverick: The Lazy Ace*), 1981.

Bliss, ABC, 1984.

(Including theme music) *The City,* ABC, 1986.

Camp California, ABC, 1989.

Capital News, ABC, 1990.

Dad's a Dog, ABC, 1990.

Coconut Downs, ABC, 1991.

Television Music Composer; Specials:

The Diaries of Adam and Eve, PBS, 1989.

Television Music Composer; Episodic:

Final episode, *Family Ties,* NBC, 1989.

"The Rat to Bear Arms," *Capitol Critters,* ABC, 1992.

"A Little Romance," *Capitol Critters,* ABC, 1992.

"To Kill a Legend," *Murder, She Wrote,* CBS, 1994.

"Anything You Want," *7th Heaven* (also known as *Seventh Heaven* and *7th Heaven: Beginnings*), The WB, 1996.

Composer of music for more than 500 television episodes throughout his career.

Film Music Composer:

Christmas Snows, Christmas Winds, 1978.

Stingray (also known as *Abigail Wanted*), Nelson Entertainment, 1978.

The Trip to Bountiful, Island Pictures, 1985.

Extremities, Atlantic Releasing, 1986.

Cry from the Mountain, 1986.

Oliver & Company (animated), Buena Vista, 1988.

Newsies (also known as *Newsboys*), Buena Vista, 1992.

D2: The Mighty Ducks (also known as *The Mighty Ducks 2*), Buena Vista, 1994.

Heavyweights, Buena Vista, 1995.

Bye, Bye Love, Twentieth Century–Fox, 1995.

A Kid in King Arthur's Court, Buena Vista, 1995.

D3: The Mighty Ducks, Buena Vista, 1996.

The Joyriders, Trident Releasing, 1999.

George of the Jungle 2, Walt Disney, 2003.

(Including song "Kingdom of Love") *One Night with the King,* Gener8Xion Entertainment/FoxFaith, 2006.

Magdalena: Released from Shame, Nardine Productions, 2007.

BURN–E (animated short film), Buena Vista Home Entertainment, 2008.

Stage Music:

Don't Count Your Chickens until They Cry Wolf (musical), book by Carol Lynn Wright Pearson, produced at Sundance Summer Theatre, Provo Canyon, UT, 1976, published by Anchorage Press, 1979.

I Believe in Make Believe (musical), book by Pearson, produced at Sundance Summer Theatre, 1977, published by Anchorage Press, c. 1979.

Clementina's Cactus (ballet for children), 1983.

subVersions (dance work), produced at Collage Dance Theatre, Los Angeles, 2000.

Also composer of music to accompany presentations of non–musical stage plays.

Video Music Composer:

Winnie the Pooh ABC's: Discovering Letters and Words, Disney Learning Adventures, 2004.

Winnie the Pooh 123's: Discovering Numbers and Counting, Disney Learning Adventures, 2004.

Concert Music:

Five Sonnets, 1976.

Valse Triste, 1980.

October Overtures, 1980.

Dream Dances, 1982.

Five Songs for Flute and French Horn, 1982.

Clementia's Cactus, 1983.

Inside Passage, 1984.

Christ Is Alive!, 1986.

Diminutiae, 1986.

The Growing Season, 1987.

The Key to Rebecca, 1988.

A Paschal Feast, Plough Down Sillion Music, 1988.

St. Elsewhere, 1990.

It Is Well with My Soul, 1990, AnderKamp Music Publishing, 2000.

Water Walker, 1993.

The Ancient of Days, 1993.

Welcome All Wonders: A Christmas Celebration, 1993.

In Dulci Jubilo, 1994.

Shepherd Story, 1995.

He Is Risen Indeed!, 1997.

At Cana's Feast, 1998.

A Connoisseur's Confession: For Jazz Chorus, Plough Down Sillion Music, 1998.

Love Never Fails, 1998.

Thy Kingdom Come, 1999.

Wine Thou Blessing, 1999.

Waltzing with Shadows: For 'Cello and Piano, Plough Down Sillion Music, 2000.

The Story the Skin Tells, 2000.

The Dance of Forgetting, 2000.

Easy to Digest, 2000.

Waltzing with Shadows, 2000.
A Psalm Triptych, 2001.
Great Is the Lord, 2001.
Love is the every only god, 2001.
Arkexit: A Divertimento for Orchestra, Plough Down Sillion Music, 2002.
The Alphabet of Revelation, 2002.
Napili Bay, 2PM, 2002.
Down to the River to Pray, 2003.
Night Pieces: SATB with Cor Anglais, French Horn, Harp, Viola, and Cello, with poems by William Wordsworth, Plough Down Sillion Music, 2004.
The Martyrdom of St. Polycarp, 2004.
Night Pieces, 2004.
Evening Wind, 2005.
Of Mercy and Judgment: SATB with Piano, Plough Down Sillion Music, 2005.
Tidestar Pulling: An Elegy for Orchestra, 2006.
Time and a Summer's Day, 2006.
Via Gioiosa, 2006.
Glory, 2008.
In the Beauty of Holiness, 2008.
Phantastes, 2008.
What the Bird Said Early in the Year, 2008.

Composer of music for symphony, chorale, and ballet, as well as art songs and chamber music, with works performed by orchestras and musical groups around the world; composer of vocal music and liturgical works.

Other:

Welcome All Wonders: A Composer's Journey (memoir), Baker Books, 1997.

Songwriter for recording artists, "Stand Up to the Night," 1986; "Love and Desire," 1989; "Prologue: The Great Adventure," 1992; "Prelude: The Ancient Faith," 1993; "The Conscience of the Kind," 1995; "Reprise" and "Prelude," 1997; and "The Journey," 1999.

OTHER SOURCES

Books:

Redford, J. A. C., *Welcome All Wonders: A Composer's Journey,* Baker Books, 1997.

Electronic:

J. A. C. Redford Official Site, http://www.jacredford. com, October 6, 2009.

REED HALL, Alaina 1946–2009
(Alaina Reed, Alaina Reed-Amini)

PERSONAL

Original name, Bernice Ruth Reed; born November 10, 1946, in Springfield, OH; died of breast cancer, December 17, 2009, in Santa Monica, CA. Actress. Reed Hall's claim to fame was the long-running children's television series *Sesame Street,* in which she played Olivia Robinson from 1976 to 1988. Audiences may also recognize her from the television comedy series *227,* which aired from 1985 to 1990. It was on the set of *227* that Reed Hall met her first husband, Kevin Peter Hall. Though best known for her television work, Reed Hall began her career on the stage and in nightclubs in the 1970s. She appeared in Broadway musical theatre productions of such plays as *Sgt. Pepper's Lonely Hearts Club Band on the Road, Chicago,* and *Hair* and was a singer in clubs. A frequent guest star in episodic television, Reed Hall acted in episodes of the animated children's series *Sonic the Hedgehog,* the comedy-drama series *Ally McBeal,* and, in 2007, the medical drama *ER,* her final television appearance. She also acted in several films, including *Death Becomes Her* and *Cruel Intentions.* In 2008 she married Tamim Amini and changed her name to Alaina Reed-Amini.

PERIODICALS

Los Angeles Times, December 22, 2009.
New York Times, December 23, 2009.
Playbill, December 23, 2009.
Variety, December 22, 2009.

REEDUS, Norman 1969–

PERSONAL

Full name, Norman Mark Reedus; born January 6, 1969, in Hollywood, FL; children: (with Helena Christensen) Mingus Lucien.

Addresses: *Agent*—Julia Buchwald, Don Buchwald and Associates, 6500 Wilshire Blvd., Suite 2200, Los Angeles, CA 90048. *Manager*—ROAR, 9701 Wilshire Blvd., 8th Floor, Beverly Hills, CA 90212.

Career: Actor. Previously worked as a fashion model for Prada and in a motorcycle shop in Venice, CA; has exhibited work as a painter, photographer, sculptor, and video artist.

Awards, Honors: Special Jury Award, best acting performance, New England Film and Video Festival, 1999, for *Floating.*

CREDITS

Film Appearances:

Jeremy, *Mimic*, Miramax, 1997.

Harry Odum, *Six Ways to Sunday*, Stratosphere Entertainment, 1998.

Toby, *I'm Losing You*, Strand Releasing, 1998.

Danny, *Reach the Rock*, Gramercy, 1998.

Larry, *Davis Is Dead*, 1998.

Van, *Floating*, Phaedra Cinema, 1999.

Warren Anderson, *8MM* (also known as *8mm–Acht Millimeter*), Columbia, 1999.

Murphy MacManus, *The Boondock Saints* (also known as *Mission des dieux*), Indican Pictures, 1999.

Brautigan, *Let the Devil Wear Black*, Trimark Pictures, 1999.

Young man, *Dark Harbor*, New City Releasing, 1999.

Lucien Carr, *Beat*, 2000.

Travis, *Gossip*, Warner Bros., 2000.

Jonathan Casey, *Preston Tylk* (also known as *Bad Seed*), New City Releasing, 2000.

Jack, *Sand* (also known as *Sandstorm*), 2000.

Nick Nero, *The Beat Nicks*, 2000.

Josh "Scud" Frohmeyer, *Blade II*, New Line Cinema, 2002.

Marco, *Deuces Wild* (also known as *Deuces Wild—Wild in den strassen*), Metro–Goldwyn–Mayer, 2002.

Sex tools delivery boy, *Luster* (also known as *Muse*), TLA Releasing, 2002.

Kurt, *Nobody Needs to Know*, Kick It Over Productions, 2003.

Recovery man, *Octane* (also known as *Pulse*), Overseas Film Group, 2003.

Archie, *Tough Luck*, Curb Entertainment, 2003.

Robert, *Until the Night*, American World Pictures, 2004.

Osama no kampo (also known as *Han fang dao*, *Wang dao zhi zhong yao*, and *Zhong yao*), Asmik Ace Entertainment, 2004.

Himself, *Overnight*, ThinkFilm, 2004.

Polizist Schmitz, *Antikoerper* (also known as *Antibodies* and *Antimatter*), 2005, subtitled version, Dark Sky Films, 2007.

Billy Neal, *The Notorious Betty Page*, Picturehouse Entertainment, 2006.

Henry Flesh, *Walls* (short film), Tsunami Films, 2006.

Vincent Harris, *A Crime* (also known as *Un crime*), ARP Selection, 2006.

Detective in morgue, *American Gangster*, Universal, 2007.

Ray Perso, *Moscow Chill* (also known as *Moroz po kozhe*), MTI Home Video, 2007.

Swain, *Hero Wanted*, Sony Pictures Entertainment, 2008.

Seth, *Dead*Line* (short film), Secret Hideout Films, 2008.

Lucien, *Clown* (short film), Boost Mobile, 2008.

Chess, *Cadillac Records*, TriStar, 2008.

Mac, *Red Canyon*, Fireside Releasing, 2009.

Shepard, *Pandorum*, Overture Films, 2009.

Murphy MacManus, *The Boondock Saints II: All Saints Day*, Apparition, 2009.

Henry, *Night of the Templar*, 2009.

John Rollins, *Messengers 2: The Scarecrow*, Sony Pictures Entertainment, 2009.

Film Work:

Director, *I Thought of You* (short film), No. 5, 2006.

Coproducer of a film titled *Whitey*.

Television Appearances; Pilots:

Norman, *13 Graves*, Fox, 2006.

Television Appearances; Episodic:

Nate Parks, "Sense and Sense Ability," *Charmed*, The WB, 2003.

Nate Parks, "Necromancing the Stone," *Charmed*, The WB, 2003.

(In archive footage) *Celebrities Uncensored*, 2004.

Kirby Sweetman, "John Carpenter's Cigarette Burns," *Masters of Horror*, Showtime, 2005.

"The Notorious Bettie Page," *HBO First Look*, HBO, 2006.

Derek Lord, "Influence," *Law & Order: Special Victims Unit* (also known as *Law & Order: SVU* and *Special Victims Unit*), NBC, 2006.

Stage Appearances:

Maps for Drowners, Tiffany Theatre, Hollywood, CA, c. 1997.

WRITINGS

Film Scripts:

I Thought of You (short film), No. 5, 2006.

OTHER SOURCES

Electronic:

Norman Reedus Official Site, http://www. normanreedusonline.com, October 6, 2009.

RICH, Christopher 1953–
(Chris Rich)

PERSONAL

Full name, Christopher Rich Wilson; born September 16, 1953, in Dallas, TX; married Nancy Frangione (an actress), 1982 (divorced, 1996); married Eva Halina (a gymnast); children: (second marriage) Lily Hanna and Daisy Grace (twins). *Education:* University of Texas, graduated; Cornell University, master's degree. *Avocational Interests:* Collecting books and fine wines, golf, reading.

Career: Actor, producer, and director. Appeared in numerous commercials.

CREDITS

Television Appearances; Series:
Alexander "Sandy" Cory, *Another World* (also known as *Another World: Bay City*), NBC, 1981–85, 1999.
Eric Charming, *The Charmings,* ABC, 1987—.
Miller Redfield, *Murphy Brown,* CBS, 1989–1997.
Dr. Neil Beck, *The George Carlin Show,* Fox, 1994.
Brock Hart, *Reba,* The WB, 2001–2006, then The CW, 2006–2007.
Attorney Melvin Palmer, a recurring role, *Boston Legal,* ABC, between 2005 and 2008.

Television Appearances; Movies:
Third IA officer, *In the Line of Duty: A Cop for the Killing* (also known as *A Cop for the Killing* and *In the Line of Duty: Blood Brothers*), NBC, 1990.
Scott Faul, *In the Line of Duty: Manhunt in the Dakotas* (also known as *In the Line of Duty: The Twilight Murders* and *Midnight Murders*), NBC, 1991.
Jack Ehrlich, *Going Home,* CBS, 2000.

Television Appearances; Miniseries:
Lute Cantrell, *The Gambler Returns: The Luck of the Draw* (also known as *The Gambler IV*), NBC, 1991.

Television Appearances; Pilots:
Dr. Russell Sears, *The Recovery Room,* CBS, 1985.
Cubby Lyons, *She's with Me,* NBC, 1986.
Eric Charming, *The Charmings,* ABC, 1987.
Ned, *Smart Guys,* NBC, 1988.
Voice of Napoleon, *Hound Town* (animated), NBC, 1989.
Bob, *A Girl's Life,* ABC, 1989.
Archie Andrews, *Archie: To Riverdale and Back Again* (also known as *Archie: Return to Riverdale* and *Weekend Reunion*), NBC, 1990.
Brock Hart, *Reba,* The WB, 2001.

Television Appearances; Specials:
"Testing Dirty," *ABC Afterschool Specials,* ABC, 1990.
P. J. Murphy, *R. L. Stine's "Ghosts of Fear Street,"* ABC, 1998.
(In archive footage) Alexander "Sandy" Cory, *The 16th Annual Soap Opera Awards,* 2000.
Host, *The WB's Outrageous Outtakes,* The WB, 2003.

CMT: The Greatest—Sexiest Southern Women, Country Music Television, 2006.
CMT: The Greatest—20 Greatest Country Comedy Shows, Country Music Television, 2006.

Television Appearances; Episodic:
Vaughn Parker, "Where There's a Will ...," *Sweet Surrender,* NBC, 1987.
Derrick Benton, "The Drowning Pool," *Baywatch,* NBC, 1989.
Ned, "To Live and Drive in LA," *Married People,* 1990.
John, "Complainin' in the Rain," *Empty Nest,* NBC, 1990.
Steven Tate, *Likely Suspects,* Fox, 1992.
"Audie's Great Guy," *Sibs,* 1992.
Jim Morgan, "Winner Take Millicent," *Almost Home* (also known as *The Torkelsons: Almost Home*), ABC, 1993.
Mark, "A Midsummer Night's Dream On," *Dream On,* HBO, 1993.
Doc McCoy, "A.K.A. Kansas," *The Adventures of Brisco County Jr.* (also known as *Brisco County Jr.*), Fox, 1993.
(Uncredited) Crew member, "Born to the Purple," *Babylon 5* (also known as *B5*), 1994.
Kurt Jacobs, "A Fine Friendship," *The Nanny,* CBS, 1995.
Dan Goodwin, "The Way Things Never Were," *The Client* (also known as *John Grisham's "The Client"*), CBS, 1995.
Mr. Jones, "The Impossible Mission Episode," *Mr. & Mrs. Smith,* CBS, 1996.
Ted Fisher, "No Place like Home," *Renegade,* USA Network and syndicated, 1996.
Dr. Ben Shipley, "Tainted Love," *Hope & Gloria,* NBC, 1996.
"A Brush with Bob," *The Louie Show,* 1996.
Special Agent David Katz, "Till Death Do Us Part," *Nash Bridges* (also known as *Bridges*), CBS, 1996.
Special Agent Katz, "Lost and Found," *Nash Bridges* (also known as *Bridges*), CBS, 1997.
Chuck Metcalf, "Life ... and Fisticuffs," *Life ... and Stuff,* CBS, 1997.
Lowell, "Again with the Astronaut," *Alright Already,* The WB, 1998.
Representative Francis Shafer, "A Tale of Two Pants: Parts 1 & 2," *Suddenly Susan,* NBC, 1998.
Lowell, "Again with the White House," *Alright Already,* The WB, 1998.
Kyle Wentworth, "Sue You," *The Tony Danza Show,* NBC, 1998.
Agent David Katz, "The Tourist," *Nash Bridges* (also known as *Bridges*), CBS, 1998.
Matt, "Divorce, Downbeat, and Distemper," *The Love Boat: The Next Wave,* UPN, 1999.
John, "Love Means Never Having to Say You're Sorry," *Sabrina, the Teenage Witch* (also known as *Sabrina* and *Sabrina Goes to College*), ABC, 1999.
Ron Perth, "Be Patient," *ER,* NBC, 2000.

Senator Jefferson, "Three Men and a Smoking Diaper," *The Lone Gunmen,* Fox, 2001.

(As Chris Rich) Guest, *Hollywood Squares* (also known as *H2* and *H2: Hollywood Squares*), syndicated, 2002, 2003.

"Los Angeles: Canyon Valley Drive," *Trading Spaces,* The Learning Channel, 2004.

Judge, *Pet Star,* Animal Planet, 2004, 2005.

"Reba," *CMT Giants,* Country Music Television, 2006.

Johnny Kad, "Fools in Love," *The Wedding Bells,* Fox, 2007.

"Reba McEntire," *Project Mom,* 2007.

Bruce, "Crime Doesn't Pay," *Desperate Housewives,* ABC, 2009.

Television Director; Series:

Reba, The WB, multiple episodes, between 2003 and 2006.

Television Associate Producer:

In the Line of Duty: Manhunt in the Dakotas (movie; also known as *In the Line of Duty: The Twilight Murders* and *Midnight Murders*), NBC, 1991.

The Gambler Returns: The Luck of the Draw (miniseries; also known as *The Gambler IV*), 1991.

Film Appearances:

Stud with sports car, *The First Time* (also known as *Doin' It* and *First Lesson*), 1982, New Line Cinema, 1983.

Dave, *Prisoners of Inertia,* 1989.

Morgan "Morg" McPherson, *Flight of the Intruder,* 1990, Paramount, 1991.

Rich, *The Joy Luck Club,* Buena Vista, 1993.

Sandy, *Critics and Other Freaks,* 1997.

Seventh Veil, Film Artists Network, 2003.

Stage Appearances:

Dionysus, *The Bacchae* (also known as *Bacchus and Bromius*), Circle in the Square, New York City, 1980.

OTHER SOURCES

Periodicals:

TV Guide, November 30, 2002, p. 12.

RICKS, Tijuana 1978–

PERSONAL

Born September 19, 1978, in Metairie, LA. *Education:* Washington University, undergraduate degree, performing arts and psychology; Yale University School of Drama, M.F.A., acting.

Career: Actress.

CREDITS

Film Appearances:

Bernice, *The Architect,* Magnolia Pictures, 2006.

Valley View nurse, *The Savages,* Fox Searchlight, 2007.

Narissa, *The Girl in the Park* (also known as *Girl in the Park*), Weinstein Company, 2007.

Television Appearances; Series:

Nurse Maggie, *The Guiding Light* (also known as *Guiding Light*), CBS, 2006–2009.

Sergeant Royce, *Law & Order,* NBC, 2009.

Television Appearances; Episodic:

Dr. Marnie Aiken, "Haunted," *Law & Order: Special Victims Unit* (also known as *Law & Order: SVU* and *Special Victims Unit*), NBC, 2004.

Detective Carol Clay, "Publish and Perish," *Law & Order,* NBC, 2005.

Dr. Marnie Aiken, "Taboo," *Law & Order: Special Victims Unit* (also known as *Law & Order: SVU* and *Special Victims Unit*), NBC, 2006.

Mrs. Mosely, "Downhill," *Conviction,* NBC, 2006.

Narrator, "Silencer," *Law & Order: Criminal Intent* (also known as *Law & Order: CI*), NBC, 2007.

(Uncredited) Brenda, "Sedgewick's," *Six Degrees,* ABC, 2007.

Flight attendant, "Believe in the Stars," *30 Rock,* NBC, 2008.

Carrie, "If I Were a Sick Man," *Royal Pains,* USA Network, 2009.

Carrie, "Crazy Love," *Royal Pains,* USA Network, 2009.

Stage Appearances:

Cora Lee, *The Women of Brewster Place,* Arena Stage, Washington, DC, 2006.

RIEDINGER, Juan 1981–

PERSONAL

Born February 27, 1981, in Banff, Alberta, Canada. *Education:* University of Calgary, B.A., c. 2005, and B.Sc.

Addresses: *Agent*—Jason Ainslie, Principals Talent, 2323 Boundary Rd., Suite 117, Vancouver, British Columbia V5M 4V8, Canada.

Career: Actor, producer, director, and writer. Commercials include work for Verizon wireless services, 2005; also worked on public service announcements.

Member: Alliance of Canadian Cinema, Television, and Radio Artists, Union of British Columbia Performers.

Awards, Honors: Jury Prize, Las Vegas International Film Festival, and Hollywood MiniDV Festival Prize, both best actor, 2007, for *Zero Hour;* Leo Award nominations, best short drama (with others) and best direction in a short drama, Motion Picture Arts and Sciences Foundation of British Columbia, both 2009, for *Shark Out of Water.*

CREDITS

Film Appearances:

Haro, *Do You Mind if I Tell You a Story?* (short film), Cinemanovel Films, 2006.

Skater Yellow, *Balloon and the Beast* (short film), VFS Productions, 2006.

Derek, *Queen for a Day* (short film), Captured Films, 2006.

Jacob, *Future Language of Slaves* (short film), Captured Films, 2006.

Marty, *I, Stalker* (short film), VFS Productions, 2006.

First drug addict, *The Entrance,* Entrance Productions/ Horizon Entertainment, 2006.

Morgue attendant, *Black Christmas* (also known as *Black X–Mas* and *Noel noir*), Metro–Goldwyn– Mayer/Weinstein Company, 2006.

Tate, *Integrity of the Amish* (short film), 2007.

Jay, *Zero Hour,* Indiepix, 2007.

Wealthy patron, *Trans Neptune: or The Fall of Pandora, Drag Queen Cosmonaut* (short film), Frameline Distributors, 2007.

Rat, *The Wheel and the Wound* (short film), 2007.

Scotty, *AVPR: Aliens vs Predator—Requiem* (also known as *Aliens vs. Predator 2, AVP: Requiem, AVP: Aliens vs. Predator—Requiem, AvPR,* and *AvP2*), Twentieth Century–Fox, 2007.

Brock, *A Great Day for Death* (short film), VFS Productions, 2008.

Darby, *The Year without Hockey* (short film), Quarter– Life Productions, 2008.

Tony Franklin, *Educated Guess* (short film; also known as *E.G* and *Suposition instruite*), Hatchway Entertainment, 2008.

William Kwan, *The Day the Earth Stood Still* (also known as *The Day the Earth Stood Still: The IMAX Experience* and *D.T.E.S.S.*), Twentieth Century–Fox, 2008.

Thief Frankford, Jr., *Bollywood Beckons* (short film), 2008.

Jesse, *Without Light,* York Entertainment, 2008.

K–Dog, *Shred,* Peace Arch Home Entertainment, 2008.

K–Dog, *Revenge of the Boarding School Dropouts* (also known as *Shred 2: Revenge of the Boarding School Dropouts*), Peace Arch Home Entertainment, 2009.

Carl, *Don't Call Me Zombie* (short film), Ouroboros Productions, 2009.

Dirk, *Jennifer's Body,* Twentieth Century–Fox, 2009.

Punk Blue, *Hardwired,* Sony Pictures Entertainment, 2009.

Harry Kent, *Monbella and the Curse of 1809,* 2009.

Daniel Pulver, *The Gig* (short film), VFS Productions, 2009.

Gray, *On a Dark and Stormy Night,* Bullet Proof Pictures/Made in the Shade Productions/ KarmaCritic Films, 2009.

Corporal Darren Stark, *The Duty of Living,* Panopticon Films/Meredith Films/RetelasFilm/Shindig Pictures, 2010.

Appeared in numerous other short films and unreleased films.

Short Film Director:

(And producer) *Shark Out of Water,* Made in the Shade Productions/Strangeways Productions, 2008.

Our Son Is a ..., 2009.

The Boys Club, 2009.

Pigmalion, 2009.

Naked, 2009.

Television Appearances; Movies:

Deckhand, *Luna: Spirit of the Whale,* 2007.

Thief, *Ace of Hearts* (also known as *L'as de coeur*), Fox- Faith, 2007.

Bones, *Held Hostage,* Lifetime, 2009.

Television Appearances; Miniseries:

Anane, *Fallen,* ABC Family, 2007.

Television Appearances; Episodic:

Detective Brett Longoria, "The Fifth Taste," *Godiva's,* Bravo, 2006.

Detective Brett Longoria, "Exit Strategies," *Godiva's,* Bravo, 2006.

Guy, "Pressure Drop," *Intelligence,* CBC, 2006.

Ian Reddick, "Blood Price: Parts 1 & 2," *Blood Ties,* Lifetime, 2007.

Rocker dude, "Literary License to Kill," *The L Word,* Showtime, 2007.

Student Sean, "The Education of Jaime Sommers," *The Bionic Woman,* NBC, 2007.

Lowell Wilson, "Progeny," *Smallville* (also known as *Smallville Beginnings* and *Smallville: Superman the Early Years*), The CW, 2007.

Delivery man, "Lights, Camera ... Homicidio," *Psych,* USA Network, 2008.

A. J., "Stiletto," *Smallville* (also known as *Smallville Beginnings* and *Smallville: Superman the Early Years*), The CW, 2009.

Miles, "Out of the Woods," *The Guard* (also known as *Search and Rescue*), Global TV, 2009.

Urban Rush, 2010.

Ted, "Sam, Interrupted," *Supernatural,* The CW, 2010.
Frakface, *Caprica,* Syfy, 2010.

Stage Appearances:
Appeared as Pearce, *Jack of Hearts,* Nickel and Dime Theatre; and as De Recha, *Virtual Reality,* Aumentare Theatre.

Internet Work; Pilots:
Associate producer and director, *These Charming Men,* TheseCharmingMen.ca, 2008.

WRITINGS

Screenplays:
Shark Out of Water (short film), Made in the Shade Productions/Strangeways Productions, 2008.

OTHER SOURCES

Electronic:
Juan Riedinger Official Site, http://juanriedinger.workbooklive.com, February 21, 2010.

ROBEK, Kirsten

PERSONAL

Born in Canada. *Education:* York University, Toronto, Ontario, Canada, B.F.A.; attended the American Academy of Dramatic Arts Los Angeles.

Career: Actress.

Awards, Honors: Leo Award nomination, best performance by a female in a short drama, Motion Picture Arts and Sciences Foundation of British Columbia, 2001, for *Evirati;* Leo Award, short drama: best performance by a female, 2004, for *The Watchers.*

CREDITS

Television Appearances; Series:
Nurse Davies, *Mercy Point* (also known as *Space Hospital*), UPN, 1998–99.

Television Appearances; Movies:
Production assistant, *Susie Q,* The Disney Channel, c. 1996.
Attendant, *The Advocate's Devil,* ABC, 1997.

Hannah, *Love in Another Town* (also known as *Barbara Taylor Bradford's "Love in Another Town"*), CBS, 1997.
Susan Evslin, *Quarantine,* ABC, 2000.
Dove (Tim's sister), *Beer Money,* USA Network, 2001.
Jeanette, *Mindstorm* (also known as *Le projet Mindstorm*), Sci–Fi Channel, 2001.
Lauren, *Avalanche Alley* (also known as *SOS avalanche*), 2001.
Mary Jensen, *Devil Winds,* PAX, 2003.
Cindy Williams, *Behind the Camera: The Unauthorized Story of "Mork & Mindy,"* NBC, 2005.
Nurse Lily, *14 Hours,* TNT, 2005.
Miriam Mak, *Anna's Storm* (also known as *Hell's Rain*), Lifetime Movie Network, 2007.

Television Appearances; Episodic:
Georgia, "Hidden Agenda," *Viper,* syndicated, 1997.
(Uncredited) Nurse, "Sleeping Beauty," *The Sentinel* (also known as *Sentinel*), UPN, 1997.
Lydia, "The Internment," *Poltergeist: The Legacy* (also known as *Poltergeist, El legado, Poltergeist—Die unheimliche Macht, Poltergeist: El legado,* and *Poltergeist, les aventuriers du surnaturel*), Showtime and syndicated, 1998.
Stacy, "Motel California," *First Wave,* Sci–Fi Channel, 1998.
Clare, "The Womanizer," *Dead Man's Gun,* Showtime, 1999.
Lizzy, "Lurch, Man of Leisure," *The New Addams Family,* Fox Family, 1999.
Lieutenant Astor, "Divide and Conquer," *Stargate SG–1* (also known as *La porte des etoiles* and *Stargaate SG–1*), Showtime and syndicated, 2000.
Suzy, "Camp Sanopi," *Mysterious Ways* (also known as *One Clear Moment, Anexegeta phainomena, Les chemins de l'etrange, Mysterious ways—les chemins de l'etrange, Rajatapaus,* and *Senderos misteriosos*), NBC, 2000.
Arriane, "Renovation," *Night Visions* (also known as *Night Terrors* and *Nightvisions*), Fox, 2001.
Josie, "Love's Divine," *Mysterious Ways* (also known as *One Clear Moment, Anexegeta phainomena, Les chemins de l'etrange, Mysterious ways—les chemins de l'etrange, Rajatapaus,* and *Senderos misteriosos*), PAX, 2001.
Karen, "The Unsinkable Iwa Gudang," *Cold Squad* (also known as *Files from the Past, Cold Squad, brigade speciale,* and *Halott uegyek*), CTV, 2001.
Gretchen Rania, "Cui Bono," *Andromeda* (also known as *Gene Roddenberry's "Andromeda"*), syndicated, 2002.
Julie, "And the Ground, Sown with Salt," *Jeremiah* (also known as *Jeremiah—Krieger des Donners*), Showtime, 2002.
Marie Donner, "Four Feet Under," *Wolf Lake,* UPN, 2002.
Miriam Williams, "The Love," *Special Unit 2* (also known as *SU2*), UPN, 2002.

Candace, "Let the Games Begin," *The Chris Isaak Show,* Showtime, 2004.

(In archive footage) Julie, "Tripwire," *Jeremiah* (also known as *Jeremiah—Krieger des Donners*), Showtime, 2004.

Stephanie Cope, "Ghost Story," *Dead Like Me* (also known as *Dead Girl, Mitt liv som doed,* and *Tan muertos como yo*), Showtime, 2004.

Emily Keriakis, "The Farmer," *The Collector,* CityTV and SPACE, 2006.

Selena Dupree, "The Fifth Taste," *Godiva's,* Bravo, 2006.

Medical examiner, "Audrey Parker's Come and Gone," *The 4400* (also known as *4400* and *Los 4400*), USA Network and Sky Television, 2007.

Mina, "Bad to the Drone," *Eureka* (also known as *EUReKA* and *A Town Called Eureka*), Sci–Fi Channel, 2008.

Mrs. Wallace, "It's the Great Pumpkin, Sam Winchester," *Supernatural* (also known as *Sobrenatural*), The CW, 2008.

Will's mother, "Kush," *Sanctuary,* Sci–Fi Channel, 2008.

Will's mother, "Sanctuary for All: Parts 1 & 2," *Sanctuary,* Sci–Fi Channel, 2008.

Susan Gillespie, "Fracture," *Fringe,* Fox, 2009.

Television Appearances; Pilots:
Other Shelley, *Cold Feet,* NBC, 1999.

Film Appearances:
Alison, *Middlemen,* The Asylum, 2000.
Evirati (short film), 2000.
Christine Marshall, *The Void,* Lions Gate Films Home Entertainment/Avalanche Home Entertainment/Trimark Video, 2001.
Pie mom, *Cats & Dogs* (also known as *Cats and Dogs, Felines and Canines, Fighting Like Cats and Dogs,* and *Like Cats & Dogs*), Warner Bros., 2001.
Judy, *The Watchers* (short film), Painting Pictures, 2003.
Sherry, *Pursued,* First Independent Pictures, 2004.
Say Yes (short film), Hybrid Productions, 2005.
Alicia Devlin, *Till Death Do You Part* (short film), Vancouver Film School, 2006.
Barbara Higgins, *The Saddest Boy in the World* (short film), 2006.
Tempbot (short film), Spy Films/W K Entertainment, 2006.
Jenny, *Smokin' Aces 2: Assassins' Ball* (also known as *Smokin' Aces: Blowback, Smokin' Aces 2, Smokin' Aces 2: Blowback,* and *Untitled Smokin' Aces Prequel*), Universal Studios Home Entertainment, 2009.

RECORDINGS

Video Games:
(English version) Postproduction voice, *Meiwaku seijin: Panic Maker* (also known as *Under the Skin*), Capcom Entertainment, 2004.

ROBERTSON, James
See **NAPIER, James**

RODRIGUEZ, Elizabeth

PERSONAL

Education: Trained with Maggie Flanagan.

Addresses: *Agent*—Stone Manners Talent and Literary Agency, 9911 West Pico Blvd., Suite 1400, Los Angeles, CA 90035. *Publicist*—Carri McClure, McClure and Associates Public Relations, 5225 Wilshire Blvd., Suite 909, Los Angeles, CA 90036.

Career: Actress. LAByrinth Theatre Company, New York City, member of company.

CREDITS

Film Appearances:
Consuela, *Fresh,* Miramax, 1994.
Marisol, *Dead Presidents,* Buena Vista, 1995.
Celia Gonzalez, *I Think I Do,* Strand Releasing, 1998.
Gaby, *Return to Paradise* (also known as *All for One*), MCA/Universal, 1998.
Fifth Bentwood girl, *Golfballs!* (also released as *Golf Balls!*), Key East Entertainment/Prism Leisure, 1999.
Jan, *Acts of Worship,* 2001, Manifesto Films, 2003.
Martha Oliveras, *Blow,* New Line Cinema, 2001.
Sasha, *Four Lane Highway,* 2005, Sky Island Films, 2007.
Carmen, *Sueno* (also known as *Dream*), Destination Films, 2005.
Gina Calabrese, *Miami Vice,* Universal, 2006.
Sonia Martinez, *Tracks of Color* (short film), CCS Entertainment/Fraternal Artists, 2007.
Older Isabelle, *On Bloody Sunday,* Polychrome Pictures, 2007.
Martel, *A Line in the Sand,* Entertainment 7, 2008.
Event coordinator, *Jack Goes Boating,* Overture Films, 2010.
Beck, *Pound of Flesh,* Park Entertainment/Rock 'n Read Productions, 2010.
Sarah, *Tonight at Noon,* Unison Films, 2010.

Television Appearances; Series:
Carmen Morales, *All My Children* (also known as *AMC*), ABC, 2008–2009.

Television Appearances; Movies:
Tanya Santos, *Inflammable,* CBS, 1995.

Selena Sanchez, *Without Warning* (also known as *Diagnosis Murder: Without Warning*), CBS, 2002.

Television Appearances; Specials:
Erika, "POWER: The Eddie Matos Story," *Lifestories: Families in Crisis*, HBO, 1994.
Jan, "My Summer as a Girl," *CBS Schoolbreak Special*, CBS, 1994.
Miami Vice: Undercover, NBC, 2006.

Television Appearances; Pilots:
Gina, *New York Undercover* (also known as *Uptown Undercover*), Fox, 1994.

Television Appearances; Episodic:
Elvira Juarez, "Old Friends," *Law & Order*, NBC, 1994.
Caridad Montero, "Rebels," *Law & Order*, NBC, 1995.
Gina, "Innocent Bystanders," *New York Undercover* (also known as *Uptown Undercover*), Fox, 1995.
Gina, "Downtown Girl," *New York Undercover* (also known as *Uptown Undercover*), Fox, 1995.
Gina, "Old Tyme Religion," *New York Undercover* (also known as *Uptown Undercover*), Fox, 1995.
Tanya, "Thin Line," *New York News*, CBS, 1995.
"Broadway Joe," *New York News*, CBS, 1995.
Amalia Lopez, "UnAmerican Graffiti," *NYPD Blue*, ABC, 1995.
Maritza Alvarez, "God's Chillin'," *Oz*, HBO, 1997.
Maritza Alvarez, "Capital P," *Oz*, HBO, 1997.
Del Bianco, "In Loco Parentis," *Trinity*, NBC, 1998.
Del Bianco, "Hang Man Down," *Trinity*, NBC, 1998.
Nurse Sandra, "Great Expectations," *ER*, NBC, 1999.
Christina Flores, "Unhand Me," *City of Angels*, CBS, 2000.
Nurse Sandra, "The Greatest of Gifts," *ER*, NBC, 2000.
Anita Rios, "Bats Off to Larry," *NYPD Blue*, ABC, 2000.
Maria, "Finch and the Fighter," *Just Shoot Me!*, NBC, 2001.
Sylvie, "Familia," *Six Feet Under*, HBO, 2001.
Nurse Sandra, "I'll Be Home for Christmas," *ER*, NBC, 2001.
Sergeant Chris Reyes, "The Chosen Few," *Third Watch*, NBC, 2002.
Lita Valverde, "Cherrypoppers," *The Shield*, FX Network, 2002.
Lita Valverde, "The Quick Fix," *The Shield*, FX Network, 2003.
Angel "Angie" Martinez, "Old," *Kath & Kim* (also known as *Kath & Kim: The American Series*), NBC, 2008.
Isabel Alvarez, "Boy Gone Astray," *Law & Order*, NBC, 2009.
Ingrid Alvarez, "Playing Cards with Coyote," *FlashForward*, ABC, 2009.
Gina Lopresi in 2010, "Bombers," *Cold Case*, CBS, 2010.

Stage Appearances:
Cleo, *Robbers*, American Place Theatre, New York City, 1997.

Saint Monica and a soldier, *The Last Days of Judas Iscariot*, LAByrinth Theatre Company, Martinson Hall, Public Theatre, New York City, 2005.
Marina, *Beauty of the Father*, Manhattan Theatre Club Stage II, New York City, 2006.
Irene, *A View from 151st Street*, LAByrinth Theatre Company, LuEsther Hall, Public Theatre, 2007.
Jessica, *Unconditional*, LAByrinth Theatre Company, LuEsther Hall, Public Theatre, 2008.

Also appeared in *Den of Thieves*, Black Dahlia Theatre, Los Angeles; as understudy for the roles of Inez, Norca, and Sonja, *Our Lady of 121st Street*, Union Square Theatre; in *Roger and Vanessa*, Actors' Gang Theatre; and in *No Time for Comedy*, *The Odd Couple*, and *Reservations for Two*.

ROERIG, Zach 1985–
(Zachary Roerig)

PERSONAL

Full name cited variously as Zachary George Roerig or Zachary Daniel Roerig; born February 22, 1985, in Montpelier, OH; son of Daniel and Andrea Roerig. *Avocational Interests:* Sports, working outdoors.

Addresses: *Agent*—Marnie Sparer, Innovative Artists Talent and Literary Agency, 1505 10th St., Santa Monica, CA 90401.

Career: Actor. Worked as a model; appeared in advertisements and catalogues. Fackler Monuments (tombstone manufacturers), employee of family business.

CREDITS

Television Appearances; Series:
Casey Hughes, *As the World Turns*, CBS, 2005–2007.
Hunter, *One Life to Live* (also known as *Between Heaven and Hell* and *One Life to Live: The Summer of Seduction*), ABC, 2007.
Cash, *Friday Night Lights*, NBC, 2008–2009.
Matt Donovan, *The Vampire Diaries*, The CW, beginning 2009.

Television Appearances; Episodic:
Messenger, "All in the Family," *Law & Order* (also known as *Law & Order Prime*), NBC, 2004.
Himself, "Meet the Soap Stars," *Party Planner with David Tutera*, The Discovery Channel, 2005.

Himself, "What America Eats," *Martha*, syndicated, 2005.

Man at wedding, "Two Weddings and a Funeral," *Reba* (also known as *Deep in the Heart, Family Planning,* and *Sally*), The WB, 2006.

Himself, "I'm Getting My Big Break," *MTV's "True Life"* (also known as *True Life* and *True Life: I'm Getting My Big Break*), MTV, 2006.

Alex, *Guiding Light* (also known as *The Guiding Light*), CBS, 2007.

Television Appearances; Pilots:

Grady Love, *Split Decision*, The CW, 2006.
Taft, *The Prince*, The WB, 2006.
Matt Donovan, *The Vampire Diaries*, The CW, 2009.

Film Appearances:

(As Zachary Roerig) Jason Matthews, *Flutter Kick* (short film), 2005.

Joe as a teenager, *Tie a Yellow Ribbon*, 2007.

Adam, *Dear Me* (also known as *Dear Me: A Blogger's Tale*), Shutter Star Pictures, 2008.

The American soldier, *Official Selection* (short film), 2008.

Matt Mullen, *Assassination of a High School President* (also known as *The Sophomore*), Freestyle Releasing, 2008.

Jason, *Strawberry Wine*, Glass Ceiling Productions/ Swirl Films, 2009.

Film Work:

Producer, *Strawberry Wine*, Glass Ceiling Productions/ Swirl Films, 2009.

OTHER SOURCES

Electronic:

Teen Vogue, http://www.teenvogue.com, February 25, 2010.

ROGERS, Trenton 2000–

PERSONAL

Born August 19, 2000, in NC. *Education:* Trained with Nora Eckstein at Young Actors Space. *Avocational Interests:* Karate, swimming, soccer, gymnastics, skateboarding, biking, reading, singing, music, writing and filmmaking as a hobby.

Addresses: Agent—Savage Agency, 6212 Banner Ave., Los Angeles, CA 90038; (voice work) Arlene Thornton and Associates, Inc., 12711 Ventura Blvd., Suite 490, Studio City, CA 91604–2477; Youth Division, Coast to Coast Talent Group, Inc., 3350 Barham Blvd., Los Angeles, CA 90068. *Manager*—Curtis Talent Management, 9607 Arby Dr., Beverly Hills, CA 90210.

Career: Actor and voice performer. Appeared in many television and radio commercials and print ads, including work for Oscar Meyer "Lunchables" processed foods, Toyota autos, CocaCola soft drinks, Toys R Us toy stores, and Radio Shack electronics stores; voice of Leo for toys and video games related to the "Little Einsteins" franchise.

Member: Screen Actors Guild, American Federation of Television and Radio Artists.

CREDITS

Film Appearances:

(English version) Voice of Toshio and other characters, *Hohokekyo tonari no Yamada–kun* (animated; also known as *My Neighbors the Yamadas*), Walt Disney, 2005.

Robby Greene, *The Magnificent Charlie Greene* (short film), 2008.

Six–year–old boy, *He's Just Not That into You* (also known as *Er steht einfach nicht auf dich!*), New Line Cinema, 2009.

Kid crossing guard and paperboy, *Opposite Day*, TVA Films, 2009.

Chad Taylor, *Buried Treasure* (short film), 2009.

Danny Parker, *The No Sit List*, Phase 4 Films, 2009.

Mickie, *Boston Girls*, Cinema Epoch, 2010.

Television Appearances; Series:

Voice of Leo, *Little Einsteins* (animated), The Disney Channel, 2005–2007.

Television Appearances; Pilots:

Jack, *Women in Law*, 2006.
First fantasy kid, *Fugly*, CBS, 2007.

Television Appearances; Episodic:

Brian, "Jimmy the Teacher," *Yes, Dear*, CBS, 2005.

Jack, "High Bar," *Women in Law*, 2006.

Four–year–old Clark, "Super Men," *CSI: NY*, CBS, 2006.

Four–year–old Danny, "Leaving Las Vegas," *CSI: Crime Scene Investigation* (also known as *C.S.I., CSI: Las Vegas,* and *Les experts*), CBS, 2007.

Nancy Pelosi's grandson, *Jimmy Kimmel Live!* (also known as *Jimmy Kimmel*), ABC, 2007.

"Chad Kimball," *The 1/2 Hour News Hour*, Fox News Channel, 2007.

Himself, *YourLA*, 2007.

Cooper, "The Forty–Year–Old Virgin Queen," *The Starter Wife,* USA Network, 2008.

Cooper, "The Diary of a Mad Ex–Housewife," *The Starter Wife,* USA Network, 2008.

Young boy, "Henry and the Terrible Day," *My Own Worst Enemy,* NBC, 2008.

Duke Weston, "AK–51," *Sons of Anarchy,* FX Network, 2008.

Duke Weston, "The Culling," *Sons of Anarchy,* FX Network, 2009.

Duke Weston, "Na Triobloidi," *Sons of Anarchy,* FX Network, 2009.

RECORDINGS

Videos:

Voice of boy, *Einstein Pals,* Walt Disney, 2010.

Voice of Russian boy for the video game *Metro 2033.* Appeared as a boy in the music video "Empty Walls" by Serj Tankian, and as a baseball kid in the music video "Little Wonders" by Rob Thomas.

ROSE, Anika Noni 1972–

PERSONAL

Born September 6, 1972, in Bloomfield, CT; daughter of John, Jr. (a corporate attorney) and Claudia Rose; married. *Education:* Florida A & M University, B.A., 1994; American Conservatory Theatre, M.F.A., 1998.

Addresses: *Agent*—Ashley Josephson, United Talent Agency, 9560 Wilshire Blvd., Suite 500, Beverly Hills, CA 90212; Kenny Goodman, WME Entertainment, 1 William Morris Pl., Beverly Hills, CA 90212. *Manager*—David Williams, David Williams Management, 9614 Olympic Blvd., Suite F, Beverly Hills, CA 90212. *Publicist*—Rogers and Cowan Public Relations, Pacific Design Center, 8687 Melrose Ave., 7th Floor, Los Angeles, CA 90069.

Career: Actress, singer, and voice performer.

Member: Actors' Equity Association.

Awards, Honors: Dean Goodman Choice Award, 1998, for *Valley Song;* Upstage–Downstage Award, *San Francisco Bay Guardian,* 1999, for *Insurrection: Holding History;* Obie Award (with others), outstanding performance, *Village Voice,* 2001, for *Eli's Comin';* Antoinette Perry Award, best featured actress in a musi-

cal, Clarence Derwent Award, Actors' Equity Association, *Theatre World* Award, and Lucille Lortel Award, outstanding featured actress, League of Off–Broadway Theatres and Producers, and Drama Desk Award nomination, outstanding featured actress in a musical, all 2004, and Los Angeles Ovation Award and Los Angeles Critics Circle Award, 2005, all for *Caroline, or Change;* Image Award nomination, outstanding supporting actress in a motion picture, National Association for the Advancement of Colored People, Screen Actors Guild Award nomination (with others), outstanding cast in a motion picture, all 2007, for *Dreamgirls;* Grammy Award nomination (with others), best compilation soundtrack album for film, television, or other visual media, National Academy of Recording Arts and Sciences, 2008, for *Dreamgirls;* Image Award nomination, best actress in a television movie, miniseries, or dramatic special, 2008, for *The Starter Wife;* Satellite Award nomination, best supporting actress in a series, miniseries, or movie made for television, International Press Academy, 2009, and Image Award nomination, best supporting actress in a drama series, 2010, both for *The No. 1 Ladies' Detective Agency;* Image Award nomination, best actress in a motion picture, Black Reel Award, best voice performance, and Black Reel Award nomination (with others), best ensemble, all 2010, for *The Princess and the Frog;* Black Reel Award, best song, 2010, for "Almost There," and Black Reel Award nomination, best song, 2010, for "Down in New Orleans," both from *The Princess and the Frog;* also received Bay Area Theatre Critics Circle Award (with others), best ensemble, for *Insurrection: Holding History,* and Garland Award and DramaLogue Award, both for *Valley Song.*

CREDITS

Film Appearances:

Kaya, *From Justin to Kelly* (also known as *From Justin to Kelly: With Love*), Twentieth Century–Fox, 2003.

Fog, *Temptation,* 2004.

Choir member, *Surviving Christmas,* DreamWorks, 2004.

Black Theatre Today: 2005 (documentary), 2005.

Lorrell Robinson, *Dreamgirls,* DreamWorks/Paramount, 2006.

Herself, *Wrestling with Angels,* Balcony Releasing, 2006.

R'ch'lle, *Just Add Water,* Sony Pictures Home Entertainment, 2008.

Voice of Princess Tiana, *The Princess and the Frog* (animated), Walt Disney, 2009.

Therapist, *Skyler,* Fountain House Entertainment/Green Rose Pictures, 2009.

Television Appearances; Series:

Grace Makutsi, *The No. 1 Ladies' Detective Agency,* HBO, 2008–2009.

Television Appearances; Miniseries:
Lavender Caraway, *The Starter Wife,* USA Network, 2007.

Television Appearances; Movies:
Film noir female, *King of the Bingo Game* (also known as *Ralph Ellison's "King of the Bingo Game"*), PBS, 1999.

Television Appearances; Specials:
Broadway under the Stars, CBS, 2006.
Dreamgirls: Divas Drama and Destiny, VH1, 2007.
Dreamgirls: T4 Movie Special, Channel 4, 2007.
Dreams Come True: A Celebration of Disney Animation, 2009.
An Evening of Stars: Tribute to Lionel Richie, 2010.

Television Appearances; Episodic:
"Domestic Abuses," *100 Centre Street,* Arts and Entertainment, 2001.
Monay, "Thicker than Water," *Third Watch,* NBC, 2002.
"The Making of 'Dreamgirls,'" *HBO First Look,* HBO, 2006.
Made in Hollywood, 2009.

Television Talk Show Guest Appearances; Episodic:
The Oprah Winfrey Show (also known as *Oprah*), syndicated, 2006.
Up Close with Carrie Keagan, ABC, 2007.
The View, ABC, 2007, 2009.
Tavis Smiley, PBS, 2007, 2009.
Rachael Ray, syndicated, 2007, 2009.
The Brian McKnight Show, 2009.
Jimmy Kimmel Live! (also known as *Jimmy Kimmel*), ABC, 2009.
Breakfast, BBC, 2010.
Live from Studio Five (also known as *Studio Five*), Channel 5, 2010.

Also appeared in an episode of *Hack,* CBS.

Television Appearances; Awards Presentations:
The 58th Annual Tony Awards (also known as *The 2004 Tony Awards*), CBS, 2004.
The 79th Annual Academy Awards, ABC, 2007.
Presenter, *38th NAACP Image Awards,* Fox, 2007.
Presenter, *The 61st Annual Tony Awards,* CBS, 2007.

Stage Appearances:
His Soul, *Hyriotaphia, or the Death of Dr. Browne,* Berkeley Repertory Theatre, Berkeley, CA, 1998.
Veronica Jonkers, *Valley Song,* Berkeley Repertory Theatre, c. 1998.
Rusty, *Footloose* (musical), Richard Rodgers Theatre, New York City, between 1998 and 2000.

Insurrection: Holding History, Geary Theatre, San Francisco, CA, c. 1999.
Mariane, *Tartuffe,* American Conservatory Theatre, Geary Theatre, 1999.
Eli's Comin' (revue), Vineyard Theatre, New York City, 2001.
Me and Mrs. Jones (musical), Prince Music Theatre, Philadelphia, PA, 2001.
Carmen Jones, 2001.
Emmie Thibodeaux, *Caroline, or Change* (musical), New York Shakespeare Festival, Estelle R. Newman Theatre, Public Theatre, New York City, 2003–2004, then Eugene O'Neill Theatre, New York City, 2004, and Los Angeles production, 2005.
Maggie, *Cat on a Hot Tin Roof,* Broadhurst Theatre, New York City, 2008.

Appeared in productions of *Leonard Bernstein's Mass,* performed at the Vatican; as Lutiebelle, *Purlie,* City Center Encores series, New York City; and as Polly Peachum, *The Threepenny Opera,* Geary Theatre, San Francisco, CA.

RECORDINGS

Videos:
Building the Dream, 2007.
Three Days in Cannes, 2009.
Barack Obama: Road to the White House, 2009.

Appeared in a motivational video series "Dr. Mike."

OTHER SOURCES

Books:
Contemporary Black Biography, Volume 70, Gale, 2009.

Periodicals:
American Theatre, April, 2009, p. 36.
Black Enterprise, February, 2010, p. 120.
Entertainment Weekly, August 18, 2006, p. 99.
Jet, June 4, 2007, p. 40.

Electronic:
Anika Noni Rose Official Site, http://www.anikanonirose.com, February 21, 2010.

ROSSI, George 1961–

PERSONAL

Born September 28, 1961, in Scotland; married; wife's name, Catrin, 1988 (separated); children: Matilda, Santino.

Career: Actor.

CREDITS

Television Appearances; Series:
Deputy Constable Duncan Lennox, *The Bill,* ITV1, 1993–2003.
Kevin, *Roughnecks,* 1994–95.

Television Appearances; Miniseries:
The Monocled Mutineer, BBC, 1986.
Second mysterious man, *The Singing Detective,* BBC, 1986, then PBS, 1988.
Media photographer, *A Very British Coup,* PBS, 1988.
Eddie, *Respectable,* Channel 5, 2006.
Deputy Constable McCormack, *Whitechapel,* ITV1, 2009.

Television Appearances; Movies:
Mahler, *Max Headroom* (also known as *Max Headroom: 20 Minutes into the Future*), ABC, 1985.
McBrayne, *Pickles: The Dog Who Won the World Cup,* ITV, 2006.

Television Appearances; Episodic:
Danny Salmon, "Extras," *First Sight,* Channel 4, 1987.
Des, "Texas Rangers," *Boon,* ITV, 1987.
Rodrigo, "Throbbing and Waiting," *Small World,* Granada, 1988.
(Uncredited) Pathologist, "A Sleeping Life: Part One," *Ruth Rendell Mysteries,* PBS, 1989.
Dilkes, "Tales from the River Bank," *Boon,* ITV, 1990.
Grizzly McMoose, "The Yukon," *T–Bag and the Rings of Olympus,* 1991.
Zeropoulos, "Death in the Clouds," *Agatha Christie: Poirot* (also known as *Agatha Christie's "Poirot"* and *Poirot*), PBS and Arts and Entertainment, 1992.
Ewan Robb, "Double Exposure," *Taggart,* ITV, 1992.
Alkmaar, "Newton's Run," *Bugs,* BBC, 1996.
D. S. Donaldson, premiere episode, *Trial & Retribution* (also known as *Lynda La Plante's "Trial & Retribution"*), ITV, 1997.
Deputy Inspector Pete Skinner, "Berserker," *Taggart,* ITV, 1998.
Jeff Francis, "Holding On," *Holby City* (also known as *Holby*), BBC, 2004.
Lenny, *Hotel Babylon,* BBC America, 2006.

Film Appearances:
Bruno, *Comfort and Joy,* Universal, 1984.
Third removal man, *The Chain,* Norstar Releasing, 1985.
Billy the Kid and the Green Baize Vampire (also known as *Billy and the Vampire*), VTI Home Video, 1987.
Chopper, *I Bought a Vampire Motorcycle,* Hobo Film Enterprises, 1990.

Eddie, *The Big Man* (also known as *The Big Man: Crossing the Line* and *Crossing the Line*), Miramax, 1991.
Waiter, *Staggered* (also known as *Mad Wedding*), 1994, Entertainment in Video, 2001.
Triage medic, *In Love and War,* New Line Cinema/Warner Bros., 1996.
Sergeant Baggio, *Roseanna's Grave* (also known as *For Roseanna* and *For the Love of Roseanna*), Fine Line, 1997.
Zantos, *RPM,* New City Releasing, 1998.
Husband, *Call Me* (short film), Starfish Films, 2004.
Control room producer, *The Number One Girl,* Visual Entertainment, 2005.
Bruce McFadden, *Wild Romance,* Independent Films, 2006.

RECORDINGS

Videos:
(In archive footage) Eddie, *Ultimate Fights from the Movies,* Flixmix, 2002.

ROVEN, Charles 1949–
    (Chuck Roven)

PERSONAL

Born August 2, 1949; married Dawn Steel (a producer), May 30, 1985 (died December 20, 1997); married Stephanie Haymes; children: (first marriage) Rebecca Steel; (second married; stepchildren) Zoe, Hayley. *Education:* Attended University of Southern California and University of California, Los Angeles.

Addresses: *Office*—Atlas Entertainment, 9200 Sunset Blvd., 10th Floor, Los Angeles, CA 90069. *Agent*—Creative Artists Agency, 2000 Avenue of the Stars, Los Angeles, CA 90067. *Publicist*—Mara Buxbaum, I/D Public Relations, 8409 Santa Monica Blvd., West Hollywood, CA 90069.

Career: Producer. Worked as personal manager for race car driver Shirley Muldowney; Roven–Cavallo Entertainment, cofounder, c. 1989, and talent manager for music groups; Mosaic Media Group, Los Angeles, cofounder, 1994; Atlas Entertainment, Los Angeles, principal, 1994—. Sometimes credited as Chuck Roven.

Awards, Honors: Boston Society of Film Critics Award (with others), best picture, 1999, for *Three Kings;* ShoWest Award, producer of the year, National Association of Theatre Owners, 2008; Motion Picture Producer of the Year Award (with others), theatrical motion picture category, Producers Guild of America, 2009, for *The Dark Knight*.

CREDITS

Film Producer:
(Assistant producer) *Some Call It Loving* (also known as *Dream Castle* and *Sleeping Beauty*), 1973.
Heart Like a Wheel, Twentieth Century–Fox, 1983.
Made in U.S.A., Dino de Laurentiis, 1987.
The Blood of Heroes (also known as *Salute of the Jugger*), HBO Home Video, 1988.
Johnny Handsome, TriStar, 1989.
Cadillac Man, Orion, 1990.
Final Analysis, Warner Bros., 1992.
Angus (also known as *Angus—Voll Cool*), New Line Cinema, 1995.
Twelve Monkeys, Universal, 1995.
City of Angels (also known as *Stadt der engel*), Warner Bros., 1998.
(With Dawn Steel) *Fallen,* Warner Bros., 1998.
Three Kings, Warner Bros., 1999.
Rollerball, Metro–Goldwyn–Mayer, 2002.
Scooby–Doo, Warner Bros., 2002.
Bulletproof Monk, Metro–Goldwyn–Mayer, 2003.
Scooby Doo–2: Monsters Unleashed (also known as *Scooby–Doo 2: Monstres en liberte*), Warner Bros., 2004.
Executive producer, *Kicking & Screaming,* Universal, 2005.
Batman Begins (also known as *Batman Begins: The IMAX Experience*), Warner Bros., 2005.
The Brothers Grimm, Miramax/Dimension Films, 2005.
Idlewild, Universal, 2006.
Live!, Weinstein Company, 2007.
The Bank Job, Lions Gate Films, 2008.
Get Smart, Warner Bros., 2008.
Get Smart's Bruce and Lloyd Out of Control, Warner Bros., 2008.
The Dark Knight (also known as *Batman: The Dark Knight* and *The Dark Knight: The IMAX Experience*), Warner Bros., 2008.
The International, Columbia, 2009.

Television Appearances; Episodic:
"Inside 'Scooby Doo 2: Monsters Unleashed,'" *HBO First Look,* HBO, 2004.
"Batman Begins: An Origin Story," *HBO First Look,* HBO, 2005.
"The Dark Knight: Escalation," *HBO First Look,* HBO, 2008.

RECORDINGS

Videos:
The Hamster Factor and Other Tales of Twelve Monkeys, 1997.

Making Angels, 1998.
Under the Bunker: On the Set of "Three Kings," 2000.
David O. Russell's "Three Kings" Video Journal, 2000.
Scooby Doo: Unmasking the Mystery, Warner Home Video, 2002.
Gotham City Rises, Warner Home Video, 2005.
Batman: The Journey Begins, Warner Home Video, 2005.

OTHER SOURCES

Periodicals:
House & Garden, February, 1993, pp. 58–68.

ROWE, Mike 1962–

PERSONAL

Full name, Michael Gregory Rowe; born March 18, 1962, in Baltimore, MD; father, a teacher. *Education:* Attended Towson State University, MD.

Addresses: *Agent*—Agency for the Performing Arts, 405 S. Beverly Dr., Beverly Hills, CA 90212.

Career: Actor, producer, and writer. Appeared in television commercials for Tylenol, 1999, and Ford F150 Trucks, 2007. Host of a segment selling diamonds on QVC, 1990–93. Previously sang with the Baltimore Opera.

Awards, Honors: Emmy Award nominations (with others), outstanding reality program, 2008 and 2009, for *Dirty Jobs.*

CREDITS

Television Appearances; Series:
Host, *Prevention's Bodysense,* 1996.
Host, *Worst Case Scenario,* TBS, 2002.
Narrator, *The Most,* History Channel, 2002.
Announcer, *American Chopper: The Series* (also known as *American Chopper*), The Discovery Channel, 2003–2007.
Announcer, *Kevin & Drew Unleashed,* The Discovery Channel, 2004.
Announcer, *American Casino,* The Discovery Channel, 2004.
Announcer, *American Hot Rod,* The Discovery Channel, 2004.
Announcer, *Ghost Hunters,* Sci–Fi Channel, 2004–2007.

Host, *Dirty Jobs,* The Discovery Channel, beginning 2005.
Narrator, *Deadliest Catch: Crab Fishing in Alaska* (also known as *Deadliest Catch*), The Discovery Channel, 2005–2009.
Narrator, *The Ultimate Fighter,* Spike TV, 2005–2009.
Announcer, *Bounty Girls Miami,* truTV, 2007.
Announcer, *UFO Hunters,* Sci–Fi Network, 2007–2008.
Host, *After the Catch* (also known as *After the Catch II* and *After the Catch III*), The Discovery Channel, 2007–2008.
Narrator, *Ghost Hunters International* (also known as *G.H.I.*), Sci–Fi Channel, beginning 2008.
Narrator, *Ghost Lab,* The Discovery Channel, 2009.
(Uncredited) Narrator, *Ghost Hunters Academy* (also known as *G.H.A.*), SyFy, beginning 2009.

Television Appearances; Specials:
Just What I Wanted, 1995.
Narrator, *Glass Jungle,* The Learning Channel, 1996.
Narrator, *Borneo Burning,* Animal Planet, 1999.
101 Craziest TV Moments, E! Entertainment Television, 2005.
Host, *Dirty Jobs: Dirtiest Water Jobs,* The Discovery Channel, 2005.
Host, *Dirty Jobs: Dirtiest Tools & Machines,* The Discovery Channel, 2005.
Host, *Dirty Jobs: Super Dirty,* The Discovery Channel, 2006.
Host, *Dirty Jobs: Jobs That Bite,* The Discovery Channel, 2006.
Host, *Dirty Jobs: 100th Dirty Job Special,* The Discovery Channel, 2006.
Host, *Dirty Jobs: Viewer's Choice,* The Discovery Channel, 2006.
Announcer, *Ghost Hunters Halloween Special,* Sci–Fi Channel, 2007.
Narrator, *Deadliest Catch: Behind the Scenes,* The Discovery Channel, 2007.
40 Greatest Reality TV Moments, 2007.
Host, *You Spoof Discovery* (also known as *You Spoof Disovery: The Ultimate Viewer–submitted Low-cost High–quality Extremely Entertaining Discovery Parody Special Hosted by Mike Rowe of Dirty Jobs, Who Also Narrates the Series "American Chopper," "American Hot Rod," and "Deadliest Catch"*), The Discovery Channel, 2007.
Narrator, *Deadliest Catch: Best of Season 2,* The Discovery Channel, 2007.
Narrator, *Deadliest Catch: Best of Season 3,* The Discovery Channel, 2007.
Host, *Dirty Jobs: Dirty Innovators,* The Discovery Channel, 2007.
Host, *Dirty Jobs: Dirtiest Machines on the Planet,* The Discovery Channel, 2007.
Host, *Dirty Jobs: Crew's Cruise,* The Discovery Channel, 2007.
Host, *Dirty Jobs: Creepy, Slimy, and Just Plain Weird,* The Discovery Channel, 2007.

Host, *Dirty Jobs: 150th Dirty Job Extravaganza,* The Discovery Channel, 2007.
Announcer, *Ghost Hunters: Return to St. Augustine Lighthouse,* Sci–Fi Channel, 2008.
Announcer, *Ghost Hunters Live Halloween Special,* Sci–Fi Channel, 2008.
Host, *Dirty Jobs: Tight Spaces,* The Discovery Channel, 2008.
Host, *Dirty Jobs: Greenland Shark Quest,* The Discovery Channel, 2008.
Host, *Dirty Jobs: Brown Plate Special,* The Discovery Channel, 2008.
Host, *Dirty Jobs: Brown before Green II,* The Discovery Channel, 2009.
Host, *Dirty Jobs: 200th Look Back Special,* The Discovery Channel, 2009.
Narrator, *Deadliest Catch: Behind the Scenes—Season 5,* The Discovery Channel, 2009.

Television Appearances; Episodic:
Voice of Mike, "Closets," *Dr. Katz, Professional Therapist* (animated), Comedy Central, 1997.
Host, *Evening Magazine,* CBS, 2005.
Voice of meter maid, "Meter Made," *American Dad!* (animated), Fox, 2007.
"Howe Caverns," *American Chopper: The Series* (also known as *American Chopper*), The Learning Channel, 2009.
Narrator, "Survivors," *Wild Pacific,* The Discovery Channel, 2009.
Narrator, "Eat or Be Eaten," *Wild Pacific,* The Discovery Channel, 2009.
Narrator, "A Fiery Birth," *Wild Pacific,* The Discovery Channel, 2009.

Television Talk Show Guest Appearances; Episodic:
The View, ABC, 2005 and 2006.
The Tony Danza Show, syndicated, 2006.
"Oprah's Most Burning Questions," *The Oprah Winfrey Show* (also known as *Oprah*), syndicated, 2006.
Voice, *The Daily Show* (also known as *A Daily Show with Jon Stewart, Jon Stewart, The Daily Show With Jon Stewart,* and *The Daily show with Jon Stewart Global Edition*), Comedy Central, 2007.
The Late Late Show with Craig Ferguson, CBS, 2007.
Larry King Live, Cable News Network, 2007 and 2009.
Guest, *The Big Story,* Fox News Channel, 2007.
The Tonight Show with Jay Leno (also known as *Jay Leno*), NBC, 2007 and 2008.
The O'Reilly Factor, Fox News Channel, 2008.
Rachael Ray, syndicated, 2008.
Jimmy Kimmel Live! (also known as *Jimmy Kimmel*), ABC, 2008.
The Bonnie Hunt Show, NBC, 2009.

Television Appearances; Pilots:
Host, "Bat Cave Scavenger," "Worm Dung Farmer," and "Roadkill Cleaner," *Dirty Jobs,* The Discovery Channel, 2003.

Television Appearances; Miniseries:
Host, *The Most,* History Channel, 2001.

Television Work; Series:
Coproducer, *Dirty Jobs,* The Discovery Channel, 2005–2007.
Producer, *Dirty Jobs,* The Discovery Channel, 2007–2009.
Executive producer, *Dirty Jobs,* The Discovery Channel, beginning 2008.

Television Work; Specials:
Coproducer, *Dirty Jobs: Dirtiest Water Jobs,* The Discovery Channel, 2005.
Coproducer, *Dirty Jobs: Dirtiest Tools & Machines,* The Discovery Channel, 2005.
Coproducer, *Dirty Jobs: Super Dirty,* The Discovery Channel, 2006.
Coproducer, *Dirty Jobs: Jobs That Bite,* The Discovery Channel, 2006.
Coproducer, *Dirty Jobs: 100th Dirty Job Special,* The Discovery Channel, 2006.
Coproducer, *Dirty Jobs: Viewer's Choice,* The Discovery Channel, 2006.
Coproducer, *You Spoof Discovery* (also known as *You Spoof Disovery: The Ultimate Viewer–submitted Low–cost High–quality Extremely Entertaining Discovery Parody Special Hosted by Mike Rowe of Dirty Jobs, Who Also Narrates the Series "American Chopper," "American Hot Rod," and "Deadliest Catch"*), The Discovery Channel, 2007.
Producer, *Dirty Jobs: Dirty Innovators,* The Discovery Channel, 2007.
Producer, *Dirty Jobs: Dirtiest Machines on the Planet,* The Discovery Channel, 2007.
Producer, *Dirty Jobs: Crew's Cruise,* The Discovery Channel, 2007.
Producer, *Dirty Jobs: Creepy, Slimy, and Just Plain Weird,* The Discovery Channel, 2007.
Producer, *Dirty Jobs: 150th Dirty Job Extravaganza,* The Discovery Channel, 2007.
Producer, *Dirty Jobs: Tight Spaces,* The Discovery Channel, 2008.
Coproducer, *Dirty Jobs: Really Dirty Animals,* The Discovery Channel, 2008.
Producer, *Dirty Jobs: Greenland Shark Quest,* The Discovery Channel, 2008.
Producer, *Dirty Jobs: Brown Plate Special,* The Discovery Channel, 2008.
Producer, *Dirty Jobs: Brown before Green II,* The Discovery Channel, 2009.

Television Work; Pilots:
Co–executive producer, "Bat Cave Scavenger," "Worm Dung Farmer," and "Roadkill Cleaner," *Dirty Jobs,* The Discovery Channel, 2003.

Film Appearances:
Narrator, *Lost in the Fog* (short documentary), 2008.

WRITINGS

Television Series:
Contributor and creator, *Dirty Jobs,* The Discovery Channel, beginning 2005.

OTHER SOURCES

Periodicals:
TV Guide, July 16, 2007, p. 55.
U.S. News & World Report, July 1, 2009, p. 43.

RUNTE, Kurt Max
(Kurt Runte)

PERSONAL

Canadian. *Education:* University of Victoria, B.F.A.

Addresses: *Agent*—Russ Mortensen, Pacific Artists Management, 685–1285 West Broadway, Vancouver, British Columbia V6H 3X8, Canada.

Career: Actor.

Awards, Honors: Leo Award nomination, best supporting actor in a feature–length drama, Motion Picture Arts and Sciences Foundation of British Columbia, 2004, for *Little Brother of War.*

CREDITS

Television Appearances; Miniseries:
Road block soldier, *Taken* (also known as *Steven Spielberg Presents "Taken"*), Sci–Fi Channel, 2002.
Sheriff Martin Willis, *The Andromeda Strain,* Arts and Entertainment, 2008.
Gunther Lutz, *Impact* (also known as *Last Impact—Der Einschlag*), ABC, 2008–2009.

Television Appearances; Movies:
Pete Collins, *The Commish: Redemption,* ABC, 1996.
Lumberyard manager, *The Perfect Mother* (also known as *The Mother–in–Law*), CBS, 1997.
First police officer, *Dirty Little Secret,* USA Network, 1998.
Alex Del Zoppo as a young man, *Sweetwater* (also known as *Sweetwater: A True Rock Story*), VH1, 1999.

Member of *Richard III* troupe, *The Goodbye Girl* (also known as *Neil Simon's "The Goodbye Girl"*), TNT, 2004.

Jack Meldon, *The Last Trimester,* Lifetime, 2006.

(As Kurt Runte) Brooks, *Lost behind Bars,* Lifetime, 2006.

Copilot, *NYC: Tornado Terror,* Sci–Fi Channel, 2008.

Allan Stone, *Fatal Kiss* (also known as *Love to Kill*), 2008.

Captain Yolenkov, *Polar Storm,* Sci–Fi Channel, 2009.

Television Appearances; Series:

Detective Jason Breen, a recurring role, *Kyle XY,* ABC Family, 2006.

Television Appearances; Pilots:

Unit Commander Forsch, *Harsh Realm,* Fox, 1999.

Lawyer, *The Virgin of Akron, Ohio,* Lifetime, 2007.

Television Appearances; Episodic:

Jack Beaumont, "Holy Matrimony," *Viper,* syndicated, 1996.

Federal marshal, "Lamentation," *Millennium,* Fox, 1997.

Devlin, "Sleeping Beauty," *The Sentinel,* UPN, 1997.

(Uncredited) First man and military man, "Tempus Fugit," *The X–Files,* Fox, 1997.

Ranger, "Patient X," *The X–Files,* Fox, 1998.

"Stanley Caron," *Cold Squad,* CTV, 1998.

Taylor, "Chem Lab," *The Net,* USA Network, 1999.

Officer Lyle Rooke, "The Looking Glass," *Da Vinci's Inquest* (also known as *Coroner Da Vinci*), CBC, 1999.

Major Boyd, "A Matter of Time," *Stargate SG–1* (also known as *La porte des etoiles*), Showtime, 1999.

"Death by Gossip," *Hollywood Off–Ramp,* E! Entertainment Television, 2000.

Finn, "Still at Large," *First Wave,* Sci–Fi Channel, 2000.

Clyde, "Haven," *Dark Angel* (also known as *James Cameron's "Dark Angel"*), Fox, 2001.

Mike Roberts/John Doe number twenty–eight, "John Doe No. 28," *Mysterious Ways,* NBC, 2001.

Father, "My So–Called Life and Death," *Night Visions,* Fox, 2001.

Senior resident, "One Night at Mercy," *The Twilight Zone,* UPN, 2002.

Anthony, "Cold Comfort," *Tom Stone* (also known as *Stone Undercover*), CBC, 2002.

Colonel Kirkland, "Lost City: Part 2," *Stargate SG–1* (also known as *La porte des etoiles*), Sci–Fi Channel, 2004.

Anton Plotchnik, "In Escrow," *Dead like Me,* Showtime, 2004.

Stargate SG–1 (also known as *La porte des etoiles*), Sci–Fi Channel, 2004.

Dr. Rothstein, "1988," *Reunion,* Fox, 2005.

Dr. Rothstein, "1997," *Reunion,* Fox, 2006.

Ensign Charles Bellamy, "The Captain's Hand," *Battlestar Galactica* (also known as *BSG*), Sci–Fi Channel, 2006.

Mysterious man, "Lead, Follow, or Get Out of the Way," *The L Word,* Showtime, 2006.

Filip, "Down for the Count," *The Evidence,* ABC, 2006.

Tony, "Dead Flowers," *Godiva's,* Bravo, 2006.

Tony, "Inked," *Godiva's,* Bravo, 2006.

Uniformed police officer, "Nightshifter," *Supernatural,* The CW, 2007.

Judge, "The Amazing Howie," *Painkiller Jane,* Sci–Fi Channel, 2007.

Mercenary leader, "Paradise Lost," *The Bionic Woman,* NBC, 2007.

Agent Turner, "Welcome Back, Carter," *Eureka* (also known as *A Town Called Eureka*), Syfy, 2009.

Police officer, "Echo," *Smallville* (also known as *Smallville Beginnings* and *Smallville: Superman the Early Years*), The CW, 2009.

S

SACKHEIM, Daniel
(Dan Sackheim)

PERSONAL

Son of William Sackheim (a producer).

Addresses: *Agent*—WME Entertainment, One William Morris Pl., Beverly Hills, CA 90212.

Career: Director, producer, and editor. Sometimes credited as Dan Sackheim.

Awards, Honors: Emmy Award nomination (with others), outstanding drama series, 1992, for *Law & Order;* Emmy Award, outstanding individual achievement in directing in a dramatic series, 1994, for *NYPD Blue;* Emmy Award nomination (with others), outstanding drama series, 2007, Television Producer of the Year Award nomination (with others), episodic–drama, Producers Guild of America, 2008, both for *House M.D.*

CREDITS

Film Work:
(As Dan Sackheim) Apprentice editor, *Seems Like Old Times* (also known as *Neil Simon's "Seems Like Old Times"*), 1980.
Editor, *Stripes*, Columbia, 1981.
(As Dan Sackheim) Second assistant editor, *Annie*, Columbia, 1982.
Assistant editor, *The Toy*, 1982.
Assistant editor, *Love Streams*, 1984.
Assistant film editor, *No Small Affair*, 1984.

Producer, *The X–Files* (also known as *Blackwood, Fight the Future, The X–Files: Fight the Future, X–Files: Blackwood, Aux frontieres du reel, The X Files Movie,* and *X–Files: The Movie*), Twentieth Century–Fox, 1998.
Director, *The Glass House*, 2001.

Film Appearances:
Himself, *The Making of "The X Files: Fight the Future,"* 1998.
Himself, *Inside "Harsh Realm"* (short documentary), Twentieth Century–Fox Home Entertainment, 2004.

Television Work; Series:
Associate producer, *Alfred Hitchcock Presents*, NBC and syndicated, 1985–86.
Associate producer and music supervisor, *Miami Vice*, NBC, 1986–88.
Coproducer, *Gideon Oliver* (also known as *By the Rivers of Babylon*), 1989.
Coproducer, *Nasty Boys*, NBC, 1990.
Coproducer, *H.E.L.P.*, ABC, 1990.
Coproducer, *Law & Order*, NBC, 1990.
Producer, *Law & Order*, NBC, 1990–92.
Producer, *The Human Factor*, CBS, 1992.
Producer, *Crime & Punishment*, NBC, 1993.
Consulting producer, *Millennium*, Fox, 1998.
Consulting producer, *The X–Files*, Fox, 1998–2000.
Executive producer, *Harsh Realm*, Fox, 1999–2000.
Co–executive producer, *Judging Amy*, CBS, 2001–2002.
Executive producer and showrunner, *The Lyon's Den*, NBC, 2003.
Consulting producer, *Las Vegas*, NBC, 2004.
Consulting producer, *Hawaii*, NBC, 2004–2005.
Consulting producer, *House M.D.* (also known as *House*), Fox, 2004–2005.
Executive producer, *Night Stalker*, ABC, 2005–2006.
Co–executive producer, *House M.D.* (also known as *House*), Fox, 2006.

Executive producer, *House M.D.* (also known as *House*), Fox, 2006–2007.
Executive producer, *Life*, NBC, 2007–2009.
(As Dan Sackheim) Executive producer, *Lie to Me*, Fox, 2009—.

Television Work; Miniseries:
Director, *Grand Avenue*, HBO, 1996.
Director and co–executive producer, *Kingpin*, NBC, 2003.

Television Coproducer; Movies:
Tongs, ABC, 1989.
Things That Go Bump in the Night, ABC, 1989.
Sleep Well, Professor Oliver, ABC, 1989.
Nasty Boys, NBC, 1989.
The Last Plane from Coramaya, ABC, 1989.
Kennonite, ABC, 1989.
Easy Come, Easy Go, ABC, 1989.
Only the Good Die Young, ABC, 1990.
Kill or Be Killed, NBC, 1990.
In Vino Veritas, ABC, 1990.

Television Co–Executive Producer; Movies:
Homeland Security, NBC, 2004.

Television Director; Movies:
Midnight Run for Your Life, syndicated, 1994.
In the Shadow of Evil, CBS, 1995.
The Lottery, NBC, 1996.
Homeland Security, NBC, 2004.

Television Work; Pilots:
Co–producer, *Law & Order*, NBC, 1990.
Supervising producer, *The X–Files*, Fox, 1993.
Director and executive producer, *Harsh Realm*, Fox, 1999.
Director and executive producer, *Mayor of Baltimore*, CBS, 2003.
(As Dan Sackheim) Director, *Night Stalker*, ABC, 2005.

Television Director; Episodic:
"Mushrooms," *Law & Order*, NBC, 1991.
"Misconception," *Law & Order*, NBC, 1991.
"Trust," *Law & Order*, NBC, 1992.
"Vengeance," *Law & Order*, NBC, 1992.
"The Working Stiff," *Law & Order*, NBC, 1992.
"Skin Deep," *Law & Order*, NBC, 1992.
"Mother Love," *Law & Order*, NBC, 1993.
"Deep Throat," *The X–Files*, Fox, 1993.
"Tempest in a C–Cup," *NYPD Blue*, ABC, 1993.
"Conduit," *The X–Files*, Fox, 1993.
"Our Denial," *Crime & Punishment*, NBC, 1993.
"Dead and Gone," *NYPD Blue*, ABC, 1994.
"Life Lessons," *Earth 2*, NBC, 1994.
"The Host," *The X–Files*, Fox, 1994.

"ER Confidential," *ER* (also known as *Emergency Room*), NBC, 1994.
"Ted and Carey's Bogus Adventure," *NYPD Blue*, ABC, 1996.
"Closure," *Millennium*, Fox, 1998.
"Kitsunegari," *The X–Files*, Fox, 1998.
"S.R. 819," *The X–Files*, Fox, 1999.
"Leviathan," *Harsh Realm*, Fox, 1999.
"Three Percenters," *Harsh Realm*, Fox, 2000.
"The Last Word," *Judging Amy*, CBS, 2001.
"Imbroglio," *Judging Amy*, CBS, 2002.
"Come Back Soon," *Judging Amy*, CBS, 2002.
(As Dan Sackheim) "Blood," *The Lyon's Den*, NBC, 2003.
"Hawaiian Justice," *Hawaii*, NBC, 2004.
"The Count of Montecito," *Las Vegas*, NBC, 2004.
"Scavenger," *Law & Order: Special Victims Unit* (also known as *Law & Order: SVU* and *Special Victims Unit*), NBC, 2004.
"Three," *Night Stalker*, ABC, 2005.
House, M.D. (also known as *House*), Fox, 2005–2007.
Life, NBC, 2007–2009.
(As Dan Sackheim) "The Core of It," *Lie to Me*, Fox, 2009.
(As Dan Sackheim) "Black Friday," *Lie to Me*, Fox, 2009.
"Sweet Sixteen," *Lie to Me*, Fox, 2010.

WRITINGS

Television Episodes:
"Mirror Image," *Miami Vice*, 1988.

St. GERMAIN, Tabitha
(Kit St. Germain, Kitanou St. Germain)

PERSONAL

Born in Boston, MA; raised in Canada, Lesotho, and Swaziland. *Avocational Interests:* Reading.

Addresses: *Agent*—Elena Kirschner, Red Management, 415 West Esplanade, Box 3, North Vancouver, British Columbia V7M 1A6, Canada.

Career: Actress, voice artist, and writer. Affiliated with Helix (a writing group) and Ink Oink Art, Inc. (a publisher).

Member: Union of British Columbia Performers/ Alliance of Canadian Cinema, Television and Radio Artists (ACTRA).

Awards, Honors: Dora Mavor Moore awards, best actress in a musical, Toronto Alliance for the Performing Arts, 1995, for *Assassins,* and 1996, for *The Barber of Seville;* Jessie Richardson Theatre Award (Vancouver theatre award), best actress, 1997, for *The Anger in Ernest and Ernestine;* Leo Award nomination, short drama: best performance by a female, Motion Picture Arts and Sciences Foundation of British Columbia, 2004, for *The Watchers;* Elan Award, best female voice–over in an animated feature or television production, Canadian Awards for the Electronic and the Animated Arts, 2008, for *Ricky Sprocket, Showbiz Boy.*

CREDITS

Television Appearances; Animated Series:

(English version) Voice of Kozue's friend, *Mezon Ikkoku* (also known as *Maison Ikkoku*), originally released in Japan, Fuji Television, 1986–88, in the United States, c. 1996.

(English version) Voice of Gotenks, *Dragon Ball Z* (also known as *DBZ* and *What's My Destiny Dragonball*), broadcast on other networks, including YTV, originally released in Japan, Animax, Fuji Television, and BS Fuji, 1989–96, Cartoon Network, 1996–2003.

(English version) Voice of Yuki Matsuoka, *Hana yori dango* (also known as *Boys before Flowers, Boys over Flowers,* and *Meteor Garden*), originally broadcast by TV Tokyo, 1996–97.

(English version) Voice of Criff Gray, *Infinite Ryvius* (also known as *Mugen no rivaiasu*), originally released in Japan, Bandai Channel and TV Tokyo, 1999–2000.

Voice of Portia, *Weird–Ohs,* Fox and YTV, 1999–2000.

Voice of Nazz, *Ed, Edd n' Eddy,* Cartoon Network, beginning 1999.

Voice of Nikki Tinker, *D'Myna Leagues,* YTV, beginning 2000.

Voice of Eddie, *Generation O!* (also known as *Molly O*), YTV and The WB, 2000–2001.

(English version) Voice of Cappy and Pashmina, *Tottoko Hamutaro* (also known as *Hamtaro* and *Trotting Hamtaro*), originally released in Japan, TV Tokyo, 2000–2006, then Cartoon Network, YTV, and Jetix, beginning 2002.

Voice of Fidget Wilson, *Action Man,* Fox, 2000–2001.

(English version) Voice of Alice, *Project ARMS* (also known as *Project Arms*), originally released in Japan, TV Tokyo, 2001.

(English version) Voice of Maddy, *Rockman.exe* (also known as *Megaman, MegaMan NT Warrior, MegaMan NT Warrior Axess,* and *Rockman.exe Axess*), originally released in Japan, beginning 2001, then The WB and TeleToon, 2003–2005.

(English version) Voice of Pokemaru, artist, and voice on television, *Chikyu boei kazoku* (also known as *The Daichis: Earth's Defense Family, Earth Defence Family,* and *The Family Defensive Alliance*), Animax Asia, originally released in Japan, WoWow, 2001.

(English version) Voice of Precis F. Newman, *Star Ocean EX,* originally released in Japan, TV Tokyo, 2001, in the United States, c. 2001.

(English version) Voice of Sayuri Shirakawa, *Arjuna* (also known as *Earth Girl Arjuna, Earth Maiden Arjuna, Chikyu shojo Arjuna,* and *Chikyuu shoujo Arjuna*), originally released in Japan, TV Tokyo, 2001, Animax Asia and Animax South Africa, 2001.

(English version) Voice of Kasumi Shiina, *SoulTaker* (also known as *The SoulTaker*), originally released in Japan, WoWow, 2001, TechTV, beginning 2001.

Voice of Serge and other characters, *Aaagh! It's the Mr. Hell Show!* (also known as *The Mr. Hell Show*), BBC2 and Showtime, between 2001 and 2002.

Voice of Dinah Doll, Miss Pink Cat, and others, *Make Way for Noddy* (also known as *Noddy*), Chorion, beginning 2001, PBS Kids Sprout, beginning 2004.

(English version) Voice of Krystal, *Go! Go! Itsutsugo Land* (also known as *Go! Go! Quintuplets Land* and *Quintuplets*), originally released in Japan, Tokyo Broadcasting System, 2001–2002, Fox, c. 2002.

(English version) Voice of Alexis, *Transformers: Armada* (also known as *Super Living–Robot Transformer The Legend of Micron Transformers: Micron Legend, Cho robotto seimeitai transformer micron densetsu, Toransufoma: Arumada,* and *Transufoma: Maikuron densetsu*), originally broadcast by TV Tokyo and YTV, then Cartoon Network, 2002–2003.

Voice of Mari Phelps, *The Cramp Twins,* various networks, including YTV, Fox, and BBC, 2002–2006.

(English version) Voice of Birdy, Pink Haro, and Flay Allster, *Kido senshi Gundam Seed* (also known as *Gundam Seed* and *Mobile Suit Gundam Seed*), originally broadcast in Japan, Bandai Channel, KIDS STATION, Mainichi Broadcasting, and Tokyo Broadcasting System, 2002–2003, then Cartoon Network and YTV, 2004–2005.

(English version) Voice of Shiel Messiah, *Tokyo Andaguraundo* (also known as *Tokyo Underground*), beginning c. 2002.

Voice of Penelope, *Yakkity Yak,* Nickelodeon, 2003.

(English version) Voice of Sandra, Ciao, Julia, and other characters, *Zoids Fuzors* (also known as *Zoids: Fuzors*), released in Japan, Tokyo Broadcasting System, 2003 and 2004–2005, Cartoon Network, 2003.

(English version) Voice of Mimi and other characters, *Astro Boy* (also known as *Astro Boy tetsuwan atomu*), The WB, c. 2003–2004.

(English version) Voice of Alexis, *Transformers: Energon* (also known as *Transformer: SuperLink* and *Transformer: Super Link*), released in Japan, TV Tokyo, broadcast on other channels, including Cartoon Network, 2004–2005.

Voice of Ethel, *ToddWorld,* TVO (TVOntario), Discovery Kids, and other channels, including CBeebies and Australian Broadcasting Corporation, beginning c. 2004.

(English version) Voice of Shana, Domino, and others, *Shakugan no Shana* (also known as *Shana of the Burning Eyes*), originally released by different channels, Japan, 2005.

Voice of Brett and others, *Team Galaxy,* YTV, beginning 2005.

Voice of Sandra "Sandi" Crocker, *Being Ian,* YTV, beginning 2005.

(English version) Voice of Professor Lucy Suzuki and others, *Transformers: Cybertron* (also known as *Transformers Cybertron: Robots in Disguise* and *Transformers: Galaxy Force*), released in Japan, TV Aichi, broadcast on other channels, including The WB, 2005, and Cartoon Network and YTV, 2005–2006.

(English version) Voice of Sting Raid A and Chaos Choir member, *Elemental gelade* (also known as *Erementar Gerad* and *Tenku to mirai no uta*), originally released in Japan, 2005, iaTV, 2007.

Voice of Andrea and Melanie, *Krypto the Superdog,* Cartoon Network, 2005–2006, The CW, 2006.

Voice of Portia, *Bratz,* Fox, 2005–2007.

Voice of Milo Powell (title role), *Captain Flamingo,* YTV, beginning 2006.

(English version) Voice of Miss Keen and others, *Demashita! Powerpuff Girls Z* (also known as *Powerpuff Girls Z*), Cartoon Network, TV Tokyo, and AT–X, beginning 2006.

Voice of title role and other characters, *Pucca,* Toon Disney and Jetix, beginning 2006.

(English version) Voice of Naomi Misura, *Death Note* (also known as *Desu noto*), originally broadcast in Japan by Nippon Television, 2006–2007.

Voice of Ethel, Vanessa, Benny, and others, *Ricky Sprocket, Showbiz Boy* (also known as *Ricky Sprocket*), TeleToon and Nicktoons, beginning 2007.

Voice of Cheer Bear, *Care Bears: Adventures in Care–a–Lot,* CBS, 2007–2008.

Voice of Tookie, Magnolia, and old ladybug, *George of the Jungle,* Cartoon Network and TeleToon, 2007–2008.

Voice of Ida Palmer, Maxine Marx, and Chester, *Zeke's Pad,* YTV, beginning 2008.

Voice of Martha, Mom, and Baby Jake, *Martha Speaks,* PBS, beginning 2008.

Voice of Wendy and John, *Monster Buster Club* (also known as *MBC* and *MBC Monster Buster Club*), Toon Disney and Jetix, beginning 2008.

(English version) Voice of Soma Peries, *Mobile Suit Gundam 00* (also known as *Gundam 00* and *Kidou senshi Gundam Double O*), originally released in Japan, 2007–2008, Sci–Fi Channel, 2008–2009.

Voice of Phoebe and others, *Kid vs Kat* (also known as *Kid vs. Kat* and *Look What My Sister Dragged In*), YTV, beginning 2008, Disney XD and Jetix, beginning 2009.

Voice of Heloise and others, *Jimmy Two–Shoes* (also known as *Jimmy Cool*), TeleToon, beginning 2009.

Voice of Lightning Liz, Suzie Scouts, and other characters, *The League of Super Evil* (also known as *LOSE* or *L.O.S.E.*), Cartoon Network and YTV, beginning 2009.

Voice of Mrs. Conductor and member of the ensemble, *Dinosaur Train,* PBS Kids, beginning 2009.

Voice of title role, *Shelldon,* qubo (NBC, ION Television, and Telemundo), beginning 2009.

Voice of Tinny, *RollBots,* The CW and YTV, beginning 2009.

Provided voices for other animated programs, including the voices of Pazzi and Bookworm for the English version of *Mix Master* (also known as *Mix Master King of Cards* and *Kadeu Wang Mikseu Maseuteo*), Nicktoons, originally broadcast in South Korea on KBS; and provided the voice of a monkey for *Team Awesome.*

Television Appearances; Animated Movies:

Voice of Noel, *Timothy Tweedle* (also known as *Timothy Tweedle the First Christmas Elf*), The Disney Channel, 2000.

Voice of Olive Oyl and Swee' Pea, *Popeye's Voyage: The Quest for Pappy,* Fox, 2004.

Television Appearances; Live Action Movies:

Dominique, *Eve's Christmas,* Lifetime, 2004.

Some sources cite an appearance in *Salem Witch Trials,* CBS, 2002.

Television Appearances; Animated Specials:

Voice of Poil, *Casper's Haunted Christmas* (also known as *Le Noel hante de Casper*), USA Network, 2000.

Voice of Noelle, Gigi, and elf kid, *Donner,* ABC Family, 2001.

Voice of Liana, *Dennis the Menace in Cruise Control* (also known as *Dennis the Menace: Cruise Control*), Nickelodeon, 2002.

Voice of Scary Godmother and Ruby, *Scary Godmother Halloween Spooktakular,* various channels, including Cartoon Network, 2003.

Voice of Scary Godmother and Ruby, *Scary Godmother: The Revenge of Jimmy* (also known as *Scary Godmother 2: The Revenge of Jimmy*), Cartoon Network, 2005.

Voice of Shaily, *A Very Fairy Christmas,* 2006.

Television Appearances; Animated Episodes:

Voices, *The Legend of Zelda,* broadcast as part of *The Super Mario Bros. Super Show!* (live action and animated; also known as *Club Mario* and *Super Mario*), NBC, episodes c. 1989–91.

Voices, *Beetlejuice,* ABC, episodes c. 1989–91, Fox, 1991.

Voices, *Hurricanes,* syndicated, episodes c. 1993–97.

Voices, *Vortech: Undercover Conversion Squad* (also known as *Vortech* and *Vor–Tech*), multiple channels, including ABC, also Fox, episodes beginning c. 1996.

Voice, "Bleepin' Beauty," *Blazing Dragons,* TeleToon, c. 1997.

Voice of Binky, "Scribmallion," *Pocket Dragon Adventures,* BBC and syndicated, 1998.

Voice of Eve, "Eve's Night," *Monster Rancher* (also known as *Monster Farm: Enbanseki no himitsu* and *Monster Farmer*), originally released in Japan, Tokyo Broadcasting System, broadcast by Sci–Fi Channel, 1999, and Fox, YTV, and syndicated, 2001.

Voices, *Sabrina the Animated Series* (also known as *Disney's "Sabrina"* and *Sabrina*), ABC and UPN, episodes c. 1999–2000, The Disney Channel, episodes c. 1999–2007.

(English version) Voice of Koume, "The Suspicious Faith Healer and the Black Kirara," *InuYasha* (also known as *Inuyasha*), originally released in Japan, Nippon Television and Yomiuri TV, dubbed version broadcast by YTV, c. 2000, dubbed version also broadcast by Cartoon Network, c. 2002.

(English version) Voice of Nazuna and Sayo, "The Mystery of the New Moon and the Black–Haired Inuyasha," *InuYasha* (also known as *Inuyasha*), originally released in Japan, Nippon Television and Yomiuri TV, dubbed version broadcast by YTV, c. 2000, dubbed version also broadcast by Cartoon Network, c. 2002.

Voice, *What about Mimi?* (also known as *Mimis Plan*), TeleToon, 2001.

Voice of chorus member, "Broken Dreams," *Home Movies* (also known as *Cine–Maniac*), Cartoon Network, 2002.

Voices for English version, *Kokaku kidotai: Stand Alone Complex* (also known as *Ghost in the Shell: Stand Alone Complex* and *Kokaku kidotai: Stand Alone Complex 2nd Gig*), originally broadcast by Nippon Television Network, 2002, Cartoon Network, episodes c. 2004–2005, also broadcast by other networks, including YTV, beginning 2005, and Cuatro, beginning 2005.

Voice of Danielle Moonstar, "Ghost of a Chance," *X–Men: Evolution,* The WB, 2003.

Voice of dentist, "Fruit Canal/Lemon Overboard," *Coconut Fred's Fruit Salad Island!,* The WB, 2005.

Voice of Spratt, "Broken Bonds," *Dragon Booster,* ABC Family, Toon Disney, and CBC, 2005.

Voices, *Martin Mystery,* YTV and Nickelodeon, 2005.

Voices, *Firehouse Tales,* Cartoon Network, episodes beginning c. 2005.

Voice of Aphrodite, "Chaos 101," *Class of the Titans,* TeleToon, 2006.

Voice of Asta and Nazy Grunty for English version, "Join," *.hack//Roots,* Cartoon Network and channels in Japan, 2006.

Voice of Dove, "Gale Force Winds," *Storm Hawks,* YTV and Cartoon Network, 2007.

Voices for English version, *Burakku ragun* (also known as *Black Lagoon* and *Black Lagoon: The Second Barrage*), originally broadcast in Japan by multiple channels, 2006, G4techTV Canada, different episodes, c. 2007–2008, Starz! Edge, 2008.

Voice of Maria Hill, "Technovore," *Iron Man: Armored Adventures,* various channels, including TeleToon, Nicktoons, Disney XD, Australian Broadcasting Corporation, 2009.

Provided voices for other programs, including *Free Willy,* ABC; *Madeline,* Fox Family; and *Tales from the Cryptkeeper* (also known as *New Tales from the Cryptkeeper*), ABC. Some sources state that St. Germain has provided voices for other animated programs, including *The Adventures of Super Mario Bros. 3* (also known as *Captain N & The Adventures of Super Mario Bros. 3* and *Super Mario Bros. 3*), broadcast as part of *The Super Mario Bros. Super Show!* (live action and animated; also known as *Club Mario* and *Super Mario*), NBC; *ALF,* NBC; *Billy the Cat,* The Family Channel; *C.O.P.S.* (also known as *C.O.P.S. (Central Organization of Police Specialists)* and *Cyber C.O.P.S.*), syndicated; *Fantastic Four* (also known as *Fantastic Four: World's Greatest Heroes*), Cartoon Network; *Fat Dog Mendoza,* Cartoon Network; *RoboCop: Alpha Commando* (also known as *Robocop: Alpha Commando*), syndicated; *Rupert Bear* (also known as *Rupert*), YTV; *Swamp Thing,* Fox and USA Network; and *The Wacky World of Tex Avery* (also known as *Tex Avery Theater*), Cartoon Network and syndicated.

Television Appearances; Live Action Episodes:

Melancholia, "Melancholia Finds Romance," *The New Addams Family,* YTV and Fox Family, 1998.

Melancholia, "Morticia the Matchmaker," *The New Addams Family,* YTV and Fox Family, 1998.

"Mr. IQ," *Police Academy: The Series* (also known as *Police Academy*), syndicated, 1998.

Catastrophia, "Catastrophia's Career," *The New Addams Family,* YTV and Fox Family, 1999.

Delia Pendergast, "What Will the Neighbors Think?," *The Outer Limits* (also known as *The New Outer Limits*), Showtime and syndicated, 1999.

Dr. Corso, "Clean," *Cold Squad* (also known as *Files from the Past, Cold Squad, brigade speciale,* and *Halott uegyek*), CTV, 2001.

Dr. Kensington, "Dead Dog Walking," *Mysterious Ways* (also known as *One Clear Moment, Anexegeta phainomena, Les chemins de l'etrange, Mysterious ways—les chemins de l'etrange, Rajatapaus,* and *Senderos misteriosos*), PAX, 2001.

Melissa Jorgensen, "Banging on the Wall," *Da Vinci's Inquest* (also known as *Coroner Da Vinci*), CBC, 2001.

"When I Was Big; Seven Hours of Bad Luck," *Beyond Belief: Fact or Fiction* (also known as *Beyond Belief* and *Strange Truth: Fact or Fiction*), Fox, 2002.

Ms. Randal, "Blackboard Jungle," *Just Cause,* W Network and PAX, 2003.

Corrine, "Working Stiff," *Alice, I Think,* CTV, 2006.

Some sources cite appearances in other programs, including *Due South* (also known as *Due South: The Series, Direction: Sud,* and *Un tandem de choc*), CTV, CBS, and TNT; *Katts and Dog* (also known as *Rin Tin Tin: K–9 Cop*), CTV and The Family Channel; *The Kids in the Hall* (also known as *KITH* and *Kith*), CBC, HBO, CBS, and Comedy Central; *Stargate SG–1* (also known as *La porte des etoiles* and *Stargaate SG–1*), Showtime, Sci–Fi Channel, and syndicated; *Strange Luck* (also known as *Drole de chance, Strange Luck—Dem Zufall auf der Spur,* and *Um homem de sorte*), Fox; and *Street Legal,* CBC.

Television Work; Additional Voices for Animated Series:

Sabrina's Secret Life, Toon Disney and syndicated, 2003–2004.

(English version) *Astro Boy* (also known as *Astro Boy tetsuwan atomu*), The WB, c. 2003–2004.

Animated Film Appearances:

Voice of La Rue, *The Adventures of Snowden* (also known as *Snowden*), c. 1997.

Voice, *Madeline: Lost in Paris,* The Walt Disney Company, 1999.

(English version) Voice of fish waiting for bus, *Hjaelp, jeg er en fisk* (also known as *A Fish Tale, Help! I'm a Fish,* and *Hilfe! Ich bin ein Fisch*), HanWay Films, 2000.

Voice, *Monster Mash,* MCA/Universal, 2000.

Voice of Miriam, *Ben Hur,* Goodtimes Entertainment, 2003.

Voice of Baby Lucinda, *In Search of Santa,* Buena Vista Home Video/Miramax Home Entertainment, 2004.

Voice of Empress Cathebel, *Ark,* Creative Light Worldwide, 2004.

Voice of Nokama, *Bionicle 2: Legends of Metru Nui* (also known as *Bionicle: The Mask Maker, Bionicle: Metru Nui, City of Legends,* and *Untitled Bionicle Project*), Buena Vista/Miramax, 2004.

(As Kitanou St. Germain) Voice of Beth, *2 Cool at the Pocket Plaza* (animated short film), Mattel, 2005.

Voice of Minty and Thistle Whistle, *My Little Pony: A Very Minty Christmas,* Paramount Home Entertainment, 2005.

Voice of Nokama, *Bionicle 3: Web of Shadows,* Buena Vista Home Video/Miramax Home Entertainment, 2005.

(English version) Voice of Tachikoma, *Kokaku kidotai: Stand alone complex—The laughing man* (also known as *Ghost in the Shell: Stand Alone Complex—The Laughing Man*), originally released in Japan, Bandai, 2005.

Voice, *Mucha Lucha! The Return of El Malefico,* Warner Bros., 2005.

Voice of Beth, *Pollyworld* (also known as *PollyWorld*), 2006.

Voice of the dancing mistress, *Barbie in the 12 Dancing Princesses* (also known as *12 Dancing Princesses*), Universal Studios Home Entertainment, 2006.

Voice of Dandelion, Topaz, Teeny Mermaid, and first mermaid, *Barbie: Mermaidia* (also known as *Barbie Fairytopia: Mermaidia*), Family Home Entertainment/Lions Gate Films Home Entertainment, 2006.

Voice of Minty, *My Little Pony: The Runaway Rainbow,* SD Entertainment, 2006.

Voice of Minty and Wysteria, *My Little Pony: The Princess Promenade,* Paramount Home Entertainment, 2006.

(As Kitanou St. Germain) Voice of Minty and Wysteria, *My Little Pony: A Very Pony Place,* Paramount Home Entertainment, 2006.

Voice of salesclerk, *Barbie Diaries* (also known as *The Barbie Diaries*), Lions Gate Films Home Entertainment/Family Home Entertainment, 2006.

Voice of Dandelion and Topaz, *Barbie Fairytopia: Magic of the Rainbow* (also known as *Magic of the Rainbow*), Universal Studios Home Video, 2007.

(As Kitanou St. Germain) Voice of princess, *The Ten Commandments,* Promenade Pictures, 2007.

Voice, *Care Bears: Oopsy Does It!* (also known as *The All–New Care Bears in "Oopsy Does It!"*), Twentieth Century–Fox/Kidtoon Films, 2007.

Voice of Minty, Thistle Whistle, and Wysteria, *My Little Pony Live! The World's Biggest Tea Party,* Paramount Home Video, 2008.

Voice of Robin, *The Nutty Professor* (also known as *The Nutty Professor 2: Facing the Fear*), Genius Products, 2008.

Voice of the Spirit of Christmas Past, seamstress, and baby, *Barbie in a Christmas Carol* (also known as *Barbie: A Christmas Carol*), Universal Studios Home Entertainment, 2008.

Voice of Willa, Coral, and Flutterpixie, *Barbie Mariposa and Her Butterfly Fairy Friends* (also known as *Barbie Mariposa, Barbie: Mariposa,* and *Mariposa*), Universal Studios Home Entertainment, 2008.

Voice of Chrysella and others, *Barbie Presents: Thumbelina* (also known as *Barbie Presents Thumbelina* and *Thumbelina*), Universal Studios Home Entertainment, 2009.

Voice of Miette Walla, *Barbie and the Three Musketeers,* Universal Studios Home Entertainment, 2009.

Voice of Zuma, *Barbie in a Mermaid Tale,* Universal Studios Home Entertainment, 2010.

Appeared in other productions.

Live Action Film Appearances:

Brenda, *The Watchers* (short film), Painting Pictures, 2003.

Receptionist, *Neverwas,* 2005.

Film Additional Voices:

In Search of Santa (animated), Buena Vista Home Video/Miramax Home Entertainment, 2004.

Stage Appearances:

Assassins (musical), produced in the Toronto, Ontario, Canada area, c. 1995.

The Barber of Seville (musical), produced in the Toronto area, c. 1996.

The Anger in Ernest and Ernestine, produced in the Vancouver, British Columbia, Canada area, c. 1997.

Appeared in other productions, including productions in the Toronto area, including *Agnes of God, Flowers, The Importance of Being Earnest,* and *Le malade imaginaire.*

Major Tours:

Appeared in tours, including a tour of a Lillian Hellman play in New Brunswick, Canada, 1980s.

Radio Appearances:

Reader, "Open Arms," *Between the Covers,* CBC Radio, c. 2009.

Internet Appearances; Episodic:

Herself, "Episode 12," *Voiceprint with Trevor Devall & Guests* (also known as *Trevor Devall*), http://www.trevordevall.com, March 8, 2008.

RECORDINGS

Video Games:

Voice of soldiers, *Kido senshi Gundamu: Meguriai sora* (also known as *Mobile Suit Gundam: Encounters in Space*), Bandai, 2003.

Voice of Cosmi, Annie Campbell, Princess Cleo, and little girls, *Meiwaku seijin: Panic Maker* (also known as *Under the Skin*), Capcom Entertainment, 2004.

(Uncredited) Voice of Flay Allster, *Battle Assault 3 Featuring Gundam Seed,* 2004.

Voice of Bramble, *Devil Kings* (also known as *Sengoku basara*), Capcom Entertainment, 2005.

Voice, *SSX on Tour,* Electronic Arts, 2005.

Voices, *Crash: Mind over Mutant,* Sierra Entertainment, 2008.

Videos:

Appeared in videos.

WRITINGS

Fiction; as Kit St. Germain:

The Thirteenth Fairy (novel), c. 2002, Trafford, 2003.

The Tinker's Dam (novella), published in *Neverlands and Otherwheres,* edited by Adicus Ryan Garton and Reverend Brian Worely, Susurrus Press, 2008.

"Sure of Charlie" (short fiction), published in *Escape Clause* (also known as *Escape Clause: Canadian Speculative Fiction and Art* and *Escape Clause: A Speculative Fiction Annual*), edited by Clelie Rich, illustrated by Lee Tockar, Ink Oink Art, Inc., 2009.

Author of short fiction, including "Estrangement" (2006), "Fortune's Food" (2006), and "As He Was" (2009), all published in *Strange Horizons,* as well as other works of fiction, including "The Man Who Was Loved" and *Just until Martile.*

Writings for the Internet:

As Kit Germain, author of a blog at *Tabitha St. Germain,* http://www.tabithastgermain.com.

OTHER SOURCES

Electronic:

Tabitha St. Germain, http://www.tabithastgermain.com, March 11, 2010.

St. JAMES, Rebecca 1977–

PERSONAL

Original name, Rebecca Jean Smallbone; born July 26, 1977, in Sydney, New South Wales, Australia; daughter of David and Helen Smallbone.

Career: Actress, singer, songwriter, recording artist, and author. Also motivational speaker; Compassion International, spokesperson.

Awards, Honors: Named favorite female artist in contemporary Christian music by readers of the magazine *CCM,* annually, 2002–08; gold album certification, Recording Industry Association of America, for *God* and *Pray,* 2006; Grammy Award, National Academy of Recording Arts and Sciences, also for *Pray;* Dove Award.

CREDITS

Film Appearances:

Buck's assistant, *Left Behind* (also known as *Left Behind: The Movie*), 2000.

Voice of Mary Magdalene, *The First Easter* (animated short film), CRC–TV, 2001.

Maggie/Mary Magdalene, *Hero: The Rock Opera,* EMI CMG Distribution, 2004.

Voice of Hope the music box angel, *An Easter Carol* (animated; also known as *VeggieTales: An Easter Carol*), Word Entertainment, 2004.

Colleen, *Unidentified,* Five & Two Pictures, 2006.

Annie, *To the Wall,* Oakwater Films, 2009.

Sarah Collins, *Sarah's Choice,* Pure Flix Entertainment, 2009.

Kari, *Rising Stars,* Doberman Entertainment, 2010.

Film Work; Song Performer:

"Lamb of God," *Left Behind II: Tribulation Force* (also known as *Tribulation Force*), Cloud Ten Pictures, 2002.

"My Hope," *Left Behind: World at War,* Columbia, 2005.

Television Appearances; Specials:

The 26th Annual Dove Awards, The Family Channel, 1995.

Host, *Gospel's Greatest Performances: 30 Years of the Dove Awards,* PAX, 1998.

Host, *The 35th Annual GMA Music Awards,* UPN, 2004.

Television Appearances; Episodic:

Praise the Lord (also known as *TBN's "Praise the Lord"*), Trinity Broadcasting Network, 2002.

Fox and Friends (also known as *Fox and Friends First* and *Fox and Friends Weekend*), Fox News Channel, 2004.

Panelist, *Hannity,* Fox News Channel, 2010.

Also appeared in *Life Today with James Robison.*

Stage Appearances; Major Tours:

Appeared as Maggie/Mary Magdalene in the national touring production of *Hero: The Rock Opera.*

RECORDINGS

Albums:

Refresh My Heart, c. 1990.

Rebecca St. James, ForeFront, 1994.

God, ForeFront, 1996.

Christmas, ForeFront, 1997.

Pray, ForeFront, 1998.

Heaven and Earth: A Tapestry of Worship, Sparrow, 1999.

Transform, ForeFront, 2000.

Yes, I Believe in God, Word Music, 2000.

Narrator, *The Jabez Prayer Collection: 30 Life–Changing Prayers from the Bible for Children,* by Stephen Elkins, with book, Broadman & Holman, 2001.

Song of Love, Word Music, 2002.

Wait for Me, the Best from Rebecca St. James, Fore-Front, 2003.

Live Worship: Blessed Be Your Name, ForeFront, 2004.

WOW #1's: 31 of the Greatest Christian Music Hits Ever, Provident Label Group, 2005.

Worship Together, with video, EMI, 2005.

Nineties: The Ultimate Collection, two volumes, EMI CMG Distribution, 2007.

Alive in Florida, ForeFront, 2007.

Other albums include *Here I Am; If I Had One Chance to Tell You Something Special;* and *No Secrets.*

Videos:

The Making of "Left Behind: The Movie," 2000.

The Making of "Unidentified," Five & Two Pictures, 2006.

WRITINGS

Books:

40 Days with God: A Devotional Journey, Standard Publishing, 1996.

(With Dale Reeves) *Wait for Me: Rediscovering the Joy of Purity in Romance,* Thomas Nelson Publishers, 2002.

(With Lynda Hunter Bjorklund) *SHE: Safe Healthy Empowered; The Woman You're Made to Be,* Tyndale House Publishers, 2004.

(With Bjorklund) *SHE Teen: Becoming a Safe, Healthy, and Empowered Woman—God's Way,* Tyndale House Publishers, 2005.

(General editor) *Sister Freaks: Stories of Women Who Gave Up Everything for God,* Warner Faith, 2005.

Pure: A 90–Day Devotional for the Mind, Body, and Spirit, Faith Words, 2008.

(General editor) *Loved: Stories of Forgiveness,* Faith-Words, 2009.

Songs Featured in Films:

"My Hope," *Left Behind: World at War,* Columbia, 2005.

Other:

Vocal scores include "Song of Love," Hal Leonard, 2002.

OTHER SOURCES

Electronic:

Rebecca St. James Official Site, http://www.rsjames. com, March 11, 2010.

SAJAK, Pat 1946(?)–

PERSONAL

Original name, Patrick Leonard Sajdak; born October 26, 1946 (some sources cite 1947), in Chicago, IL; father a trucking industry foreman; married, wife's name Sherrill, 1979 (divorced, c. 1985); married Lesly Brown (a fashion model and photographer), December 31, 1989; children: Patrick Michael James, Maggie Marie. *Education:* Attended Columbia College, Chicago, IL. *Avocational Interests:* Travel, playing tennis and racquetball, the Chicago Cubs.

Addresses: *Office*—P.A.T. Productions, 10202 West Washington Blvd., David Lean Suite 230, Culver City, CA 90232–3195.

Career: Game and talk show host and producer. WEDC–Radio, Chicago, IL, worked as a newscaster; WNBS–Radio, Murray, KY, disc jockey, 1971–72; WSM–TV, Nashville, TN, staff announcer, host of a public affairs program, and weatherman, between 1972 and 1977; KNBC–TV, Los Angeles, weather reporter and host of local talk show, 1977–81; P.A.T. Productions, Culver City, CA, founder and principal. Previously worked as a hotel and motel desk clerk. *Military service:* U.S. Army, disc jockey for Armed Forces Radio, 1968–72; served in Vietnam.

Awards, Honors: Daytime Emmy Award nominations, best game show host, annually, 1985–87, 1989, 1993,1997–2000, 2002–03, 2007–08, all for *Wheel of Fortune;* Daytime Emmy Award nomination, special program achievement, 1985, for *The Macy's Thanksgiving Day Parade;* People's Choice Award, favorite television game show host, television, Proctor & Gamble Productions, 1987; received star on Hollywood Walk of Fame, 1994.

CREDITS

Television Appearances; Series:
Los Angeles anchor, *The NewsCenter* (also known as *NewsCenter 4*), 1974.
Cohost, *The Sunday Show,* KNBC, 1976.
Host, *Wheel of Fortune,* NBC, 1981–89, syndicated, 1983—.
Guest panelist, *The Match Game/Hollywood Square Hour,* 1984.
Host, *College Bowl,* 1984.
Kevin Hathaway, *Days of Our Lives* (also known as *Days* and *DOOL*), NBC, 1983.
Super Password, 1984–88.

Host, *The Pat Sajak Show,* CBS, 1989–90.
Host, *Pat Sajak Weekend,* Fox News Channel, 2003.

Television Appearances; Specials:
Host, *Macy's Thanksgiving Day Parade,* NBC, 1984, 1985, 1986.
NBC 60th Anniversary Celebration, NBC, 1986.
Presenter, *The 13th Annual Daytime Emmy Awards,* NBC, 1986, 2001, ABC, 2003.
Host, *The ... Tournament of Roses Parade,* NBC, 1986, 1987.
Jack Paar Is Alive and Well!, NBC, 1987.
The 15th Annual Daytime Emmy Awards, CBS, 1988.
Happy Birthday, Bugs! 50 Looney Years (also known as *Hollywood Celebrates Bugs Bunny's 50th Birthday*), CBS, 1990.
American Bandstand 40th Anniversary Special, ABC, 1992.
Host, *Variety Reviews '92,* syndicated, 1993.
Host, *This Is Your Life,* NBC, 1993.
The 29th Annual Academy of Country Music Awards, NBC, 1994.
Disney's Most Unlikely Heroes, ABC, 1996.
Plugged In: A Parents' Guide to TV, The Family Channel, 1997.
Intimate Portrait: Vanna White, Lifetime, 1998.
"Vanna White: Game Show Goddess," *Biography,* Arts and Entertainment, 1999.
It's Only Talk: The Real Story of America's Talk Shows, Arts and Entertainment, 1999.
The Great American History Quiz: 50 States, History Channel, 2001.
(In archive footage) Himself, *The Most Outrageous Game Show Moments,* NBC, 2002.
Rated "R": Republicans in Hollywood, AMC, 2004.
(In archive footage) *101 Biggest Celebrity Oops,* E! Entertainment Television, 2004.
(In archive footage) *101 Most Unforgettable SNL Moments,* E! Entertainment Television, 2004.
Wheel of Fortune: The E! True Hollywood Story, E! Entertainment Television, 2005.
ABC Boscov's Thanksgiving Day Parade, ABC, 2006.

Television Appearances; Episodic:
Password Plus, 1981.
Just Men!, 1983.
"The Big Apple: Part 1," *Gimme a Break!,* ABC, 1984.
Announcer, *Washingtoon,* 1985.
"Wheel of Fortune," *The A–Team,* 1986.
"The Wheel of Misfortune," *227,* 1986.
Santa Barbara, NBC, 1988.
Lou Rawls Parade of Stars, 1989.
Dr. Brian Brandon, "The Two Faces of Ed," *The Commish,* ABC, 1992.
Voice, "Under Chuckie's Kid/Chuckie Is Rich," *Rugrats* (animated), Nickelodeon, 1994.
"End of the Season," *The Larry Sanders Show,* HBO, 1994.

Guest host, *Jeopardy!,* syndicated, 1997.
"As My Career Lay Dying," *The Larry Sanders Show,* HBO, 1998.
Interviewee on "A&E Biography: Nina Van Horn," *Just Shoot Me!,* NBC, 2000.
Guest host, *Larry King Live,* Cable News Network, 2000.
"Inner Tube," *The King of Queens,* CBS, 2001.
Entertainment Tonight (also known as *Entertainment This Week, E.T., ET Weekend,* and *This Week in Entertainment*), syndicated, 2007.
Contestant, "Million Dollar Celebrity Invitational Quarterfinal 5," *Jeopardy!,* syndicated, 2010.

Television Talk Show Guest Appearances; Episodic:
Late Night with David Letterman, 1988, 1991, 1993.
The Tonight Show with Jay Leno (also known as *Jay Leno*), NBC, 1993.
Guest or guest host, *Live with Regis and Kelly,* syndicated, numerous appearances, between 2003 and 2008.
The Bonnie Hunt Show, NBC, 2008.
(In archive footage) *The Tonight Show with Conan O'Brien,* NBC, 2009.

Appeared in episodes of *Hour Magazine* and *The Merv Griffin Show.*

Television Executive Producer; Series:
The Pat Sajak Show, CBS, 1989–90.

Film Appearances:
Buffalo news anchor, *Airplane II—The Sequel* (also known as *Flying High II* and *Flying High II: The Sequel*), Paramount, 1982.
Season of the Samurai (documentary), Brain Science/mod3productions, 2006.

Film Executive Producer:
Leo the Late Bloomer, 1999.
Space Case, 2001.
Merry Christmas Space Case (animated short film), Weston Woods Studios, 2003.

Radio Appearances; Series:
Host of the syndicated *Pat Sajak Baseball Hour.*

RECORDINGS

Videos:
Playboy: The Best of Pamela Anderson, 1995.
Voice, *Mission of Mercy,* 2003.

OTHER SOURCES

Books:
Contemporary Newsmakers 1985: Issue Cumulation, Gale, 1986.

Periodicals:
New York Times, December 11, 1988.
Sports Illustrated, August 5, 2002, p. 22.
TV Guide, November 19, 2007, p. 114.
USA Today, May 16, 2005, p. 3B.

SALES, Soupy 1926–2009
(Milton Supman)

PERSONAL

Original name, Milton Supman; born January 26, 1926, in Franklinton, NC; died October 22, 2009, in the Bronx, New York, New York. Comedian and actor. Known for his slapstick comedy, Sales is credited with making the pie-in-the-face gag a staple of the genre. He began his entertainment career in the early 1950s in radio. Soon, he made the transition to television with a live children's show, *Soupy Sales Comics,* in Detroit. The show quickly gained viewers, and Sales found himself in demand. Renamed *The Soupy Sales Show* in 1955, the program began airing on ABC. Sales moved to Los Angeles and continued hosting his television show, which went into syndication in 1964. It was canceled in 1966 but was resurrected in 1976 and again from 1979 to 1980 as *The New Soupy Sales Show.* Sales also appeared as a frequent panelist on such television game shows as *What's My Line?* and *The $10,000 Pyramid.* In the late 1970s he was a regular on the variety program *Sha Na Na.* Sales acted in a number of motion pictures, including *The Two Little Bears, Birds Do It,* and *Angels and Angles.* His autobiography, *Soupy Sez! My Life and Zany Times,* was published in 2001.

PERIODICALS

Los Angeles Times, October 23, 2009.
New York Times, October 23, 2009.

SAVAGE, Ben 1980–

PERSONAL

Full name, Bennett Joseph Savage; born September 13, 1980, in Chicago, IL; son of Lew (a real estate executive) and Joanne (a homemaker) Savage; brother of Fred Savage (an actor) and Kala Savage (an actress). *Education:* Stanford University, graduated, 2004.

Addresses: *Agent*—Joseph Rice, Abrams Artists Agency, 9200 Sunset Blvd., Suite 1130, Los Angeles, CA 90069.

Career: Actor. Appeared in television commercials for Sunbeam bread, 1989, Frosted Cheerios breakfast cereal, 1996, and other products. Office of U.S. Senator Arlen Specter, intern, 2003. Elizabeth Glazer Pediatric AIDS Foundation, volunteer.

Awards, Honors: Young Artist Award nomination, best young actor starring in a motion picture, 1990, for *Little Monsters;* Young Artist Award nomination, best youth actor in a leading role in a television series, 1994, Young Artist Award nominations, best leading young performer in a television comedy series, 1997 and 1998, YoungStar Award nomination, best young actor in a television comedy series, *Hollywood Reporter,* 1998, Blimp Award (with Rider Strong), favorite television friends, Kids' Choice Awards, 2000, all for *Boy Meets World;* L.A. Ovation Award, best actor, 1998, for *Unexpected Tenderness.*

CREDITS

Television Appearances; Series:
Matthew Lacey, a recurring role, *Dear John* (also known as *Dear John USA*), NBC, 1988–90.
Chris Bankston, a recurring role, *A Family for Joe,* NBC, 1990.
Cornelius "Cory" A. Matthews, *Boy Meets World,* ABC, 1993–2000.

Television Appearances; Movies:
Andy, *She Woke Up,* ABC, 1992.
Voice of Jack, *Jack & the Beanstalk,* HBO, 2000.
Todd, *Making It Legal,* ABC, 2007.

Television Appearances; Miniseries:
Coty Wyckoff, *Wild Palms,* ABC, 1993.

Television Appearances; Specials:
How I Spent My Summer Vacation, ABC, 1993.
ABC Saturday Morning Preview Special, ABC, 1994.
The Walt Disney World Very Merry Christmas Parade, ABC, 1995.
Richard Bickerstaff, *Aliens for Breakfast,* ABC, 1995.
Earth Day at Walt Disney World, The Disney Channel, 1996.
Host, *Walt Disney World Happy Easter Parade,* ABC, 1997.
Host, *A Magical Walt Disney World Christmas,* ABC, 1997.
All–Star TGIF Magic, ABC, 1997.
67th Annual Hollywood Christmas Parade, UPN, 1998.

(In archive footage) *50 Cutest Child Stars: All Grown Up,* E! Entertainment Television, 2005.

Television Appearances; Pilots:
Sam Kelvin, *Hurricane Sam,* CBS, 1990.
Cornelius "Cory" A. Matthews, *Boy Meets World,* ABC, 1993.

Television Appearances; Awards Presentations:
Presenter, *8th Annual Kids' Choice Awards,* Nickelodeon, 1995.
The 3rd Annual Family Television Awards, CBS, 2001.

Television Appearances; Episodic:
Curtis Hartsell, "The St. Valentine's Day Massacre," *The Wonder Years,* 1990.
Cornelius "Cory" Matthews, "Acting Out," *Maybe This Time,* ABC, 1996.
Stuart, "Close to You," *Party of Five,* Fox, 1996.
Stuart, "Christmas," *Party of Five,* Fox, 1996.
Cornelius "Cory" Matthews, "One Dog Night," *Teen Angel,* ABC, 1997.
The Martin Short Show, 1999.
Late Night with Conan O'Brien, NBC, 1999, 2000.
Himself, "Time Release Capsule," *Phil of the Future,* The Disney Channel, 2005.
Seth Cosella, "Still the Boss," *Still Standing,* CBS, 2005.
Mark Ratner, "Chuck versus the Cougars," *Chuck,* NBC, 2008.
Kirby Morris, "Cloudy with a Chance of Gettysburg," *Without a Trace* (also known as *W.A.T.*), CBS, 2008.

Film Appearances:
Eric Stevenson, *Little Monsters* (also known as *Little Ghost Fighters*), Metro–Goldwyn–Mayer, 1989.
Sam, *Big Girls Don't Cry ... They Get Even* (also known as *Stepkids*), New Line Cinema, 1992.
Roger, *Clifford,* Orion, 1994.
Teddy Benevides, *Swimming Upstream,* Media Entertainment, 2004.
Ford Davis, *Car Babes,* Radio London Films, 2007.
Patrick, *Palo Alto, CA* (also known as *Palo Alto*), Anchange Productions, 2007.
John, *Doesn't Texas Ever End,* Inner ViZion Productions/Mpire Films, 2009.
American Dream: Illusion or Reality? (documentary), 2009.
Jared, *Closing Time* (short film), 2010.

Stage Appearances:
Roddy Stern, *Unexpected Tenderness,* Marilyn Monroe Theatre, Los Angeles, 1998.

SCHOFIELD, Phillip 1962–
(Philip Schofield)

PERSONAL

Born April 1, 1962, in Oldham, Lancashire, England; married Stephanie Lowe, 1993; children: Molly, Ruby.

Addresses: *Manager*—George Ashton, James Grant Media Ltd., 94 Strand on the Green, Chiswick, London W4 3NN, England.

Career: Television and radio personality, program host, and actor. Hospital Radio Plymouth, broadcaster, beginning c. 1977; British Broadcasting Corp. (BBC), Broadcasting House, London, bookings clerk for Radio Outside Broadcasts, 1979–81; Radio Hauraki, Auckland, New Zealand, Sunday morning program host, c. 1982; BBC, continuity announced, 1985–93; ITV, program host, 1993–95; Carlton Television, staff presenter, beginning 1996. Appeared in commercials and print ads.

Awards, Honors: Named show business personality of the year, Variety Club of Great Britain, 1993; National Television Award, best daytime program, 2004, for *This Morning;* International Golden Rose Award, best game show, Rose d'Or Festival, 2005, for *Test the Nation;* voted all–time favorite children's presenter in readers' poll, *Radio Times,* 2005, 2006; named BBC/SOS top man on television, three times; four *TV Times* Awards.

CREDITS

Television Appearances; Series:
Presenter, *Shazam,* TV New Zealand, c. 1981.
Going Live!, BBC, 1987–90.
Host, *The Movie Game,* BBC, 1988–90.
Television's Greatest Hits (also known as *TV's Greatest Hits*), BBC, 1992–95.
Presenter, *The National Lottery* (also known as *The National Lottery Live*), BBC, 1994.
Presenter, *Talking Telephone Numbers,* ITV, 1994–97.
Presenter, *Schofield's Quest,* London Weekend Television, 1995.
Presenter, *Tenball,* 1996.
Presenter, *One in a Million,* 1996–97.
Presenter, *Schofield's TV Gold,* 1996.
Host, *City Hospital,* BBC1, 1999.
Host, *The National Lottery: Winning Lines,* BBC, 2001–2004.
Presenter, *This Morning* (also known as *This Morning with Richard and Judy*), ITV, 2002—.
Presenter, *Have I Been Here Before?,* ITV, 2005–2007.

Host, *I'm a Celebrity Exclusive,* ITV1, 2006.
Host, *Dancing on Ice* (also known as *Dancing on Ice: Christmas Special* and *Dancing on Ice: The Skate–Off*), ITV, 2006—.
The Xtra Factor, ITV2, 2006–2009.
Presenter, *All Star Mr & Mrs,* ITV, 2008—.
Host, *The Cube,* 2009.

Also host of *Schofield's Europe* and *Take Two,* both BBC.

Television Appearances; Specials:
Comic Relief, BBC, 1988.
A Night of Comic Relief 2, BBC, 1989.
Phil Scratchit, *Scrooge: A Christmas Sarah,* BBC, 1990.
Comic Relief (also known as *Comic Relief 3: The Stonker*), BBC, 1991.
(In archive footage) *Comic Relief: Behind the Nose,* BBC, 1992.
Host, *Schofield's Christmas TV Gold,* Carlton, 1993.
Schofield's Adventures in Hawaii, Carlton, 1996.
Schofield's Gold, 1996.
Six Little Angels, 1996.
Presenter, *Now We're Talking,* ITV, 1996.
An Audience with Bruce Forsyth, ITV, 1997.
(Uncredited) *An Audience with Elton John,* ITV, 1997.
Schofield's Animal Odyssey, BBC, 1999.
Predictions, ITV, 2000.
(In archive footage) *I Love Christmas,* BBC, 2001.
Presenter, *Test the Nation: The [Annual] Test,* BBC, 2002, 2003, 2004, 2005.
Presenter, *Test the Nation: The National IQ Test ...,* BBC, 2002, 2003, 2004.
Presenter, *Test the Nation: The National Relationship Test,* BBC, 2003.
Presenter, *Test the Nation: The National Quiz,* BBC, 2003.
The 100 Greatest Musicals, Channel 4, 2003.
Hogmanay Live, BBC, 2003.
Best Ever Magic Tricks, ITV1, 2003.
Best Ever Hidden Camera Stunts, ITV1, 2003.
Presenter, *Test the Nation: The Great British Test,* BBC, 2004.
Presenter, *Test the Nation: The Popular Music Test,* BBC, 2004.
Presenter, *Test the Nation: The Big Entertainment Test,* BBC, 2005.
Narrator, *When Ken Met Deirdre,* ITV, 2005.
Narrator, *Emmerdale: The Dingle Family Album,* ITV, 2005.
Narrator, *Emmerdale: The Sugden Family Album,* ITV, 2005.
(Uncredited) *Harry Potter at the Castle: Magic at Midnight,* ITV, 2005.
Presenter, *ITV 50 Greatest Shows,* ITV, 2005.
Presenter, *Best Ever Ads,* ITV, 2005.
Presenter, *Test the Nation: Know Your English Test,* BBC, 2005.

Presenter, *Best Ever Family Films,* 2005.
Presenter, *Best Ever Christmas Films,* 2005.
(Uncredited) *The Big Fat Quiz of the Year,* Channel 4, 2005.
(In archive footage) *Greatest Before They Were Stars TV Moments,* Channel 5, 2005.
Narrator, *Best Ever Muppet Moments,* ITV, 2006.
The Prince's Trust 30th Birthday: Live, ITV, 2006.
(Uncredited) Audience member, *An Audience with Take That: Live!,* ITV, 2006.
It Started with ... Swap Shop, BBC, 2006.
Viewer of the Year 2006, ITV, 2006.
Presenter, *Best Ever Ads 2,* ITV1, 2006.
Presenter, *It's Now or Never,* ITV, 2006.
Phillip Schofield's Night before Christmas, ITV1, 2006.
The British Soap Awards ...: The Party, ITV, 2006, 2008.
Narrator, *Corrie in the Dock,* ITV, 2007.
Host, *The Royal Variety Performance,* ITV, 2007.
Star Traders: The Christmas Challenge, ITV, 2007.
(Uncredited; in archive footage) *The Big Fat Quiz of the Year,* Channel 4, 2007.
(Uncredited) *Emmerdale 5000,* 2008.
Narrator, *Dancing on Ice: The Story of Bolero with Torvill and Dean,* ITV, 2009.
(In archive footage) *Almost Famous II,* BBC3, 2009.

Television Appearances; Awards Presentations:
The National Television Awards, ITV, 2006, audience member, 2007.
Host, *The British Soap Awards,* ITV, 2006, 2007, 2008, 2009.

Television Appearances; Miniseries:
I Love 1980's, BBC2, 2001.
The Impressionable Jon Culshaw, ITV, 2004.
The Story of Light Entertainment, BBC2, 2006.
Dancing on Ice Friday, ITV, 2010.

Television Appearances; Episodic:
Television reviewer, *Saturday Superstore,* 1987.
Noel's House Party, BBC, 1992.
The All New Alexei Sayle Show, BBC, 1994.
"1998 Celebrity Special," *Stars in Their Eyes,* ITV, 1998.
Live Talk, ITV, 2001.
Celebrity Ready, Steady, Cook, BBC, 2001.
TV Nightmares, ITV, 2002.
"Children's TV Presenters Special," *The Weakest Link* (also known as *Weakest Link Champions' League*), BBC, 2003.
Who Wants to Be a Millionaire, syndicated, 2003.
SM:TV Live (also known as *Saturday Morning Television Live, SM:TV,* and *SM:TV Gold*), ITV1, 2003.
Astounding Celebrities, ITV, 2003.
The Frank Skinner Show, ITV, 2003.
Ant & Dec's Saturday Night Takeaway, ITV, multiple appearances, 2003–2009.
Celebrity Fit Club, VH1, 2004.

I'm a Celebrity, Get Me Out of Here! (also known as *I'm a Celebrity*), ITV, 2004.
The X Factor, ITV, 2004.
Bo' Selecta! (also known as *Bo' Selecta! Vol. 3*), Channel 4, 2004.
Brainiac: Science Abuse, The Discovery Channel, 2004.
The Kumars at No. 42, BBC America, 2004.
"Live Final 2004," *Stars in Their Eyes Kids,* ITV, 2004.
The Paul O'Grady Show (also known as *The New Paul O'Grady Show*), ITV, 2004, 2005.
Room 101, BBC, 2005.
Emmerdale Farm (also known as *Emmerdale*), YTV, 2005.
"Live Grand Final 2005," *Stars in Their Eyes,* ITV, 2005.
"The Nation's Favourite," *Absolute Power,* BBC, 2005.
(As Philip Schofield) "Zippy and George's Puppet Legends," *Favouritism,* Channel 4, 2005.
Loose Women, ITV, 2005, 2009.
Bad Girls, BBC America, 2006.
"Daniel Radcliffe," *Extras,* HBO, 2006.
The Sharon Osbourne Show, ITV, 2006.
Soapstar Superstar, ITV, 2007.
Premiere episode, *Coronation Street: Confidential,* ITV, 2007.
Dancing on Ice: Defroster, ITV, 2007.
Friday Night with Jonathan Ross, BBC, 2007.
The Apprentice: You're Fired! (also known as *The Apprentice: You're Hired!*), BBC, 2007.
The Friday Night Project, Channel 4, 2008.
Happy Hour (also known as *Al Murray's Happy Hour*), ITV, 2008.
TV Burp (also known as *Harry Hill's TV Burp*), ITV, 2008.
"Plasticine," *James May's Toy Stories,* BBC, 2009.
(In archive footage) "The Truth about Eternal Youth," *The Truth about Beauty,* ITV, 2009.
"The Final: Part 1," *Celebrity Big Brother* (also known as *Comic Relief Big Brother*), 2010.

Film Appearances:
Television announcer, *Cheeky,* 2003, Guerilla Films, 2006.
Television presenter, *Are You Ready for Love?,* 2006, Sony Pictures Home Entertainment, 2009.
Himself, *An Jowl yn Agas Kegin* (short film), O–Region, 2007.

Stage Appearances:
Title role, *Joseph and the Amazing Technicolor Dreamcoat* (musical), Palladium, London, 1993, then Oxford Apollo Theatre, 1995–96, and Labatt's Apollo Theatre Hammersmith, London, 1996.
Title role, *Doctor Dolittle,* Labatt's Apollo Theatre Hammersmith, 1998–99.
Jack the Ripper, *The Lodger,* Windsor, England, 2000.

Major Tours:
Title role, *Joseph and the Amazing Technicolor Dream-coat,* British and Irish cities, 1993–95.
Title role, *Doctor Dolittle,* British cities, 1999–2001.

RECORDINGS

Videos:
Andrew Lloyd Webber: The Premiere Collection Encore, Really Useful Group, 1992.

OTHER SOURCES

Electronic:
Phillip Schofield Official Site, http://www.officialphillipschofield.com, February 21, 2010.

SCOTT, Leigh 1972–
(A. B. McKorkindale, Leigh Slawner)

PERSONAL

Full name, Leigh Scott Andrew Slawner; born February 18, 1972, in Milwaukee, WI; son of Ben and Laura Slawner; married Shaley (an actress), 2001 (marriage ended, 2007). *Education:* University of Southern California, graduated, c. 1994.

Career: Actor, director, producer, film editor, cinematographer, and writer. Worked as an assistant director, second unit director, line producer, and digital artist. Concorde Pictures, intern in production, development, and marketing; The Asylum, film director, 2004–07; Bullet Films, Lafayette, LA, chief executive officer, 2007–09; Blackthorn Industries, president, chief executive officer, and producer. Also owned a college bar in the Los Angeles area.

Member: Pi Kappa Alpha.

CREDITS

Film Appearances:
"Not My Baby" man, *Between the Sheets,* Stoneface Entertainment, 1998.
Dr. Armstrong, *King of the Lost World,* The Asylum, 2005.
Dr. Cadaverella, *Frankenstein Reborn* (also known as *Frankenstein*), The Asylum, 2005.
Guard, *Dead Men Walking,* The Asylum Home Entertainment/Breakout Entertainment, 2005.

Harry Ellis, *Shapeshifter,* The Asylum, 2005.
Ray, *Jolly Roger: Massacre at Cutter's Cove,* The Asylum, 2005.
Sean, *War of the Worlds* (also known as *H. G. Wells' "War of the Worlds," Invasion,* and *The Worlds in War*), The Asylum, 2005.
Ben Gunn, *Pirates of Treasure Island,* The Asylum, 2006.
Jeff, *The 9/11 Commission Report,* The Asylum, 2006.
The Old One, *Dracula's Curse* (also known as *Bram Stoker's "Dracula's Curse"*), Eagle Entertainment, 2006.
Sawney Bean and David, *Hillside Cannibals* (also known as *Hillside Cannibals: The Legend of Sawney Bean*), The Asylum, 2006.
Doug, *The Hitchhiker,* The Asylum, 2007.
Fontaine, *Koreatown* (also known as *Bury Me in L.A.*), David E. Baker Entertainment, 2007.
General Sabir, *Transmorphers* (also known as *Robot Wars*), The Asylum, 2007.
(As Leigh Slawner) Nick, *The Apocalypse,* The Asylum, 2007.
Zach, *Invasion of the Pod People* (also known as *Invasion: The Beginning*), The Asylum, 2007.

Film Director:
Beach House (also known as *The Freshman* and *Venice Beach Girls*), Cinequanon Pictures/Sullivan Park Pictures International, 1995.
(As Leigh Slawner) *Art House,* The Asylum, 1998.
First assistant director, *The Quarry,* 2002.
Second unit director, *Scarecrow Slayer* (also known as *Scarecrow: Resurrection* and *Scarecrow 2*), York Entertainment, 2003.
The Beast of Bray Road, The Asylum Home Entertainment, 2005.
Frankenstein Reborn (also known as *Frankenstein*), The Asylum, 2005.
King of the Lost World, The Asylum, 2005.
Dracula's Curse (also known as *Bram Stoker's "Dracula's Curse"*), Eagle Entertainment, 2006.
Dragon, The Asylum, 2006.
Exorcism: The Possession of Gail Bowers, The Asylum Home Entertainment, 2006.
Hillside Cannibals (also known as *Hillside Cannibals: The Legend of Sawney Bean*), The Asylum, 2006.
The 9/11 Commission Report, The Asylum, 2006.
Pirates of Treasure Island, The Asylum, 2006.
The Hitchhiker, The Asylum, 2007.
Transmorphers (also known as *Robot Wars*), The Asylum, 2007.
Chrome Angels, 2009.
The Witches of Oz, 2010.

Film Producer:
(As Leigh Slawner) *Art House,* The Asylum, 1998.
Jane White Is Sick & Twisted, Artist View Entertainment/D & K Enterprises, 2002.

Coproducer, *The Quarry,* 2002.
Chrome Angels, 2009.
The Witches of Oz, 2010.

Film Line Producer:
Hitters, Fries Film Group, 2002.
Dead Men Walking, The Asylum Home Entertainment/
   Breakout Entertainment, 2005.
Jolly Roger: Massacre at Cutter's Cove, The Asylum,
   2005.
War of the Worlds (also known as *H. G. Wells' "War of
   the Worlds," Invasion,* and *The Worlds in War*), The
   Asylum, 2005.

Film Editor:
(As A. B. McKorkindale) *Art House,* The Asylum, 1998.
Death Valley: The Revenge of Bloody Bill (also known
   as *Bloody Bill* and *Death Valley*), The Asylum,
   2004.
The Beast of Bray Road, The Asylum Home Entertain-
   ment, 2005.
Frankenstein Reborn (also known as *Frankenstein*), The
   Asylum, 2005.
Dracula's Curse (also known as *Bram Stoker's "Dracu-
   la's Curse"*), Eagle Entertainment, 2006.
Dragon, The Asylum, 2006.
Exorcism: The Possession of Gail Bowers, The Asylum
   Home Entertainment, 2006.
The 9/11 Commission Report, The Asylum, 2006.
Pirates of Treasure Island, The Asylum, 2006.
The Hitchhiker, The Asylum, 2007.
Transmorphers (also known as *Robot Wars*), The
   Asylum, 2007.

Film Cinematographer:
Invasion of the Pod People (also known as *Invasion:
   The Beginning*), The Asylum, 2007.
The Witches of Oz, 2010.

Film Digital Artist:
Jolly Roger: Massacre at Cutter's Cove, The Asylum,
   2005.

Television Appearances; Movies:
The Old One, *Wolvesbayne,* Syfy, 2009.

Television Director; Movies:
Flu Bird Horror (also known as *Flu Birds*), Sci–Fi Chan-
   nel, 2008.
The Dunwich Horror (also known as *H. P. Lovecraft's
   "The Darkest Evil"* and *H. P. Lovecraft's "The Dun-
   wich Horror"*), Syfy, 2009.

Television Producer; Movies:
The Dunwich Horror (also known as *H. P. Lovecraft's
   "The Darkest Evil"* and *H. P. Lovecraft's "The Dun-
   wich Horror"*), Syfy, 2009.

Wolvesbayne, Syfy, 2009.
House of Bones, Syfy, c. 2010.

RECORDINGS

Videos; as Himself; Short Documentaries:
Frankenstein Reborn: Behind the Scenes, The Asylum
   Home Entertainment, 2005.
H. G. Wells' "War of the Worlds": Behind the Scenes,
   The Asylum Home Entertainment, 2005.
King of the Lost World: Behind the Scenes, The Asylum
   Home Entertainment, 2005.
Dracula's Curse: Behind the Scenes, The Asylum Home
   Entertainment, 2006.
*Exorcism: The Possession of Gail Bowers—Behind the
   Scenes,* The Asylum Home Entertainment, 2006.
When a Killer Calls: Behind the Scenes, The Asylum
   Home Entertainment, 2006.

WRITINGS

Screenplays:
(As Leigh Slawner; with Dan O'Donahue) *Art House,*
   The Asylum, 1998.
The Beast of Bray Road, The Asylum Home Entertain-
   ment, 2005.
Frankenstein Reborn (based on the writings of Mary
   Shelley and other films; also known as *Franken-
   stein*), The Asylum, 2005.
(With Carlos De Los Rios and David Michael Latt) *King
   of the Lost World* (based on the novel *The Lost
   World,* by Arthur Conan Doyle, and other work),
   The Asylum, 2005.
Dracula's Curse (based on the writings of Bram Stoker
   and other films; also known as *Bram Stoker's
   "Dracula's Curse"*), Eagle Entertainment, 2006.
(With Eliza Swenson) *Dragon,* The Asylum, 2006.
Exorcism: The Possession of Gail Bowers, The Asylum
   Home Entertainment, 2006.
The 9/11 Commission Report, The Asylum, 2006.
(With De Los Rios; and story with Latt) *Pirates of
   Treasure Island* (based on the novel *Treasure Island,*
   by Robert Louis Stevenson), The Asylum, 2006.
(With Jeshua De Horta) *The Hitchhiker* (based on other
   films), The Asylum, 2007.
Invasion of the Pod People (story by Ron Magid and
   Jay Marks; also known as *Invasion: The Beginning*),
   The Asylum, 2007.
Transmorphers (also known as *Robot Wars*), The
   Asylum, 2007.
Chrome Angels, 2009.
The Witches of Oz (based on the writings of L. Frank
   Baum and other films), 2010.

Teleplays; Movies:
The Dunwich Horror (based on the work of H. P. Love-
   craft; also known as *H. P. Lovecraft's "The Darkest
   Evil"* and *H. P. Lovecraft's "The Dunwich Horror"*),
   Syfy, 2009.

Wolvesbayne, Syfy, 2009.

(Story) *Quantum Apocalypse* (also known as *Judgment Day*), Syfy, 2010.

SHAH, Pooja 1979–
(Poojah Shah)

PERSONAL

Born August 8, 1979, in London, England. *Education:* University of Brighton, B.A. (with honors), 2001; trained in Indian classical dance.

Addresses: *Manager*—A & J Management, 242a Ridgeway, Botany Bay, Enfield EN2 8AP, England.

Career: Actress. Performed with Finchley Youth Theatre. Appeared in commercials and corporate films; also worked as a model.

CREDITS

Film Appearances:

Mary Magdalene, *Jesus the Curry King,* Aylesbury Film, 2002.

(As Poojah Shah) Meena, *Bend It Like Beckham* (also known as *Kick It like Beckham*), Fox Searchlight, 2002.

Ian's wife, *Suzie Gold,* Pathe, 2004.

Sonya, *CryBaby* (short film), 2005.

Mindi, *Weekend Lovers,* Little Kiran Productions, 2006.

Gauri, *Cash and Curry,* Tavix Pictures, 2008.

Amy, *Ten Dead Men,* MTI Home Video, 2009.

Meena, *The Story of _____,* Magnet Films/Abadi Films, 2009.

Television Appearances; Series:

Sinjata Kapoor, *Is Harry on the Boat?,* Sky Television, 2002.

Kareena Ferreira, *EastEnders,* BBC, 2003–2005.

Sara Anderson, *Raw,* 2008.

Television Appearances; Miniseries:

Comic Relief in da Bungalow, BBC, 2005.

Strictly Dance Fever, BBC, 2005.

The All Star Talent Show, Channel 5, 2007.

Amy Garnett, *Missing,* 2009.

Television Appearances; Specials:

EastEnders: Christmas Party, BBC, 2004.

The Big Fat Quiz of the Year, Channel 4, 2004.

Conversations with Dead Men, 2008.

Also appeared in *Sex, Lies, and Soaps,* Channel 4.

Television Appearances; Episodic:

Mira Ashar, "Ladies' Night," *Holby City* (also known as *Holby*), BBC, 2002.

Nanda, "The Man Who Wouldn't Be King," *Adventure Inc.* (also known as *Aventure et associes*), syndicated, 2003.

RI:SE, Channel 4, 2003.

Reshna Dewan, "Blood Money," *The Bill,* ITV1, 2007.

Reshna Dewan, "To Honour and Obey," *The Bill,* ITV1, 2007.

Soapstar Superchef, ITV, 2007.

I'm a Celebrity, Get Me Out of Here! NOW!, ITV, 2008.

Saaya Lunn, "Leaving God," *Doctors,* BBC, 2009.

Also appeared in *Lovebites,* Channel 4, and *Talkback,* Thames.

Stage Appearances:

Father, *The Proposal,* London Arts Festival, London, 1993.

Helen, *Breaking the Six Minute Scream,* 1994.

Deb, Mrs. Finch, and Angela, *Fen,* Finchley Theatre, London, 1995.

Nanny Ogg, *Wyrd Sisters,* Finchley Theatre, 1996.

Tribe member, *Song for a Dark Queen,* Finchley Theatre, 1997.

Wise woman, *Light in the Village,* Finchley Theatre, 1997.

Titania, *A Midsummer Night's Dream,* Finchley Theatre, 1997.

Inspire Me, Finchley Youth Theatre, Pattichion Theatre, Limassol, Cyprus, 1997.

Manni, *The Untouchable,* Bush Theatre, London, 2002.

Sona, *The Deranged Marriage,* Rifco Arts Theatre, 2005.

Alaska (reading), Royal Court Theatre, London, 2005.

Understudy for Vina and Milly, *Rafta Rafta,* National Theatre, London, 2007.

Also performed in many public readings.

Major Tours:

Toured British cities in *The Deranged Marriage.*

Radio Appearances:

Nalini, *Silver Street,* BBC, 2007.

Meena, *Barry in Watford,* BBC, 2007.

RECORDINGS

Videos:

Jess, *Italian Learning Video,* Education Learning, 1997.

Voice of Detective McGeachy, *iD3* (video game), Upset Media, 2009.

OTHER SOURCES

Electronic:

Pooja Shah Official Site, http://www.poojashah.com, February 22, 2010.

SHANKLIN, James 1957–
(Jim Shanklin)

PERSONAL

Born October 31, 1957, in Baltimore, MD; son of James, Sr. and Margaret K. Shanklin. *Education:* Yale University, M.F.A., 1997.

Addresses: *Agent*—Mitch Shankman, Kazarian, Spencer, Ruskin, and Associates, 11969 Ventura Blvd., 3rd Floor, Box 7409, Studio City, CA 91604.

Career: Actor. Appeared in commercials for Folgers coffee, American Airlines, Spring soft drinks, Wrigley's chewing gum, United Parcel Service, and several other products.

Member: Screen Actors Guild, American Federation of Television and Radio Artists, Actors' Equity Association.

CREDITS

Film Appearances:
Frank Jansen, *Fare Well Miss Fortune,* FSS Creative/VE Productions, 1999.
Valet, *The Emperor's Club,* Universal, 2002.
Hal, *Winter Excursion* (short film), Revelation Films, 2002.
Hospital chaplain, *Mission: Impossible III* (also known as *M:i:III*), Paramount, 2006.
Bill, *Disappearing* (short film), 2006.
Unseen figure, *First.* (short film), One Dream, 2007.
Congress person, *Evan Almighty,* Universal, 2007.
Dr. Cooper, *Jonna's Body, Please Hold,* Mad Lively/Always Alice, 2007.

Television Appearances; Series:
(Sometimes credited as Jim Shanklin) *Literary Visions,* 1992.
Doug Holliwell, *As the World Turns,* CBS, 2000–2001.

Television Appearances; Episodic:
Frank Olson, *Unsolved Mysteries,* NBC, 1994.
Ken Bradley, "The Last of the Watermen," *Homicide: Life on the Street* (also known as *Homicide* and *H: LOTS*), NBC, 1994.
Dr. Hale, *Another World* (also known as *Another World: Bay City*), NBC, 1998.
Matt Vasco, "Stalker," *Law & Order,* NBC, 1998.
Waiter, "History of the World," *Third Watch,* NBC, 1999.
Secret Service agent, "Ohio," *Third Watch,* NBC, 2000.
Judge Mark McDow, "Narcosis," *Law & Order,* NBC, 2000.
Anesthesiologist, "Second Opinion," *The Sopranos,* HBO, 2001.
Attorney John Davis, "All My Children," *Law & Order,* NBC, 2001.
Man in suit, "Sacrilege," *The Job,* ABC, 2002.
"The Towers," *It's a Miracle,* PAX, 2002.
Second tourist, "Don't Hide Your Bag," *Whoopi,* NBC, 2003.
Dr. Heinrick Schmidt, "Pre–trial Blues," *The Practice,* ABC, 2004.
Physicist, "Vector," *Numb3rs* (also known as *Num3ers*), CBS, 2005.
Judge Heuson, "The Paper War," *Judging Amy,* CBS, 2005.
Les Molineaux, "In Your Face," *Blind Justice,* ABC, 2005.
Judge W. Mosley, "The Runner," *Just Legal,* The WB, 2005.
Detective Morgan, "They Asked Me Why I Believe in You," *Desperate Housewives,* ABC, 2005.
Gerry Levitt, "State of the Unions," *Commander in Chief,* ABC, 2006.
Detective Fallon, "Remember: Parts 1 & 2," *Desperate Housewives,* ABC, 2006.
(Uncredited; in archive footage) Detective Morgan, "All the Juicy Details," *Desperate Housewives,* ABC, 2006.
Bob Spurlock, "Field of Dreams," *The Riches,* FX Network, 2008.
Gerald Hirsh, "A Dollar and a Dream," *Without a Trace* (also known as *W.A.T.*), CBS, 2008.
Jack Spyer, "To Catch a Fed," *The Cleaner,* Arts and Entertainment, 2008.
Frank Wilson in 2008, "The Dealer," *Cold Case,* CBS, 2008.
Doctor, "Empire," *Big Love,* HBO, 2009.
Navy Captain Martin Armstrong, "The Inside Man," *Navy NCIS: Naval Criminal Investigative Service* (also known as *NCIS* and *NCIS: Naval Criminal Investigative Service*), CBS, 2009.
Dr. Stanley, *The Young and the Restless* (also known as *Y&R*), CBS, 2010.

Television Appearances; Specials:
Appeared in the title role, *Hamlet,* PBS.

Stage Appearances:
Durwood Peach, *Landscape of the Body,* Yale Repertory Theatre, New Haven CT, 1996.

Antrobus, *Skin of Our Teeth,* Yale Repertory Theatre, 1997.

Understudy for the roles of Dr. Harvey Kelekian, Mr. Bearing, and lab technician, *Wit,* Union Square Theatre, New York City, 1998–2000.

Prosecutor, store owner, white citizen, and person in suit, *Everybody's Ruby,* New York Shakespeare Festival, Anspacher Theatre, Public Theatre, New York City, 1999.

Cinna and Lucilius, *Julius Caesar,* New York Shakespeare Festival, Delacorte Theatre, Public Theatre, 2000.

Gil and Harlow the drifter, *Thief River,* Guthrie Theatre, Minneapolis, MN, 2002.

Also appeared in a production of *As You Like It,* New York Shakespeare Festival, Public Theatre; as Giles and Gavin, *House and Garden,* Manhattan Theatre Club, New York City; in *Map of the World* and *Paradise Lost,* Center Stage, Baltimore, MD; *Richard III,* Shakespeare Theatre, Washington, DC; *Rosencrantz and Guildenstern Are Dead,* Studio Theatre; and *Time of Your Life,* Arena Stage, Washington, DC.

Major Tours:
James Carville, Chuck Colson, and more than a dozen other characters, *The Presidents,* U.S. cities, 2003.

RECORDINGS

Videos:
(As Jim Shanklin) Commentator and voice of James, *The Amistad Revolt: All We Want Is Make Us Free,* Amistad Committee, 1995.

OTHER SOURCES

Electronic:
James Shanklin Official Site, http://jamesshanklin.com, February 22, 2010.

SHAW, Ming–Hu
  See SHAW, Scott

SHAW, Scott 1958–
  (Jake Blade, Jake Dharma, Ming–Hu Shaw, DJ Acid X)

PERSONAL

Born September 23, 1958, in Los Angeles, CA. *Education:* Pierce College, A.A., 1979; California State University, Northridge, B.A., 1982; California State University, Los Angeles, M.A., geography, 1983; Emerson College of Herbology, M.Herbology, 1983; Northwestern University, Ph.D., 1987; California State University, Dominguez Hills, M.A., humanities, 1996.

Career: Actor, martial artist, producer, director, cinematographer, film editor, and writer. No Mercy Productions, president, 1991–96; Light Source Films, Los Angeles, president, beginning 1996. University of California, Los Angeles, teacher of filmmaking classes. Certified master instructor in tae kwon do and hapkido; Shaw's Taekwondo, chief instructor, 1976–85; founder of Kawa Do International, 1982, and Ki Sul Kwan Hapkido. Asian Studies Ltd., president, 1987–93; Buddha Rose International, chief executive officer and published, beginning 1988. Certified meditation and yoga instructor. Also worked as a bodyguard.

Member: American Federation of Television and Radio Artists, Screen Actors Guild, Hapkido Taekwondo International (president), World Tae Kwon Do Federation, U.S. National Karate Association, Hapkido Moo Hak Kwan Association, Tae Kwon Do Jido Kwan, Korea Hapkido Federation, Korea Martial Arts Association, Korea Tae Kwon Do Association, American College of Herbology (fellow).

Awards, Honors: Tokyo Experimental Film Festival Award, best director of a feature–length film, 1993, for *Samurai Vampire Bikers from Hell.*

CREDITS

Film Appearances:
(As Ming–Hu Shaw) Ah Ling, *Lung Feng cha lou* (also known as *Lung Fung Restaurant* and *Lung Fung Tea House*), 1990.

Elliot MacKinzie, *Just a Moment that Passes in Time,* 1990.

Ace, *The Divine Enforcer* (also known as *Deadly Avenger*), Prism Entertainment, 1991.

(Uncredited) Cyberdine technician, *Terminator 2: Judgment Day* (also known as *T2, T2: Extreme Edition, T2—Terminator 2: Judgment Day, T2: Ultimate Edition, El exterminator 2,* and *Terminator 2—Le jugement dernier*), TriStar, 1991.

Hawk, *The Roller Blade Seven,* 1991.

(As Ming–Hu Shaw) Lion, *Zhi zai chu wei* (also known as *Today's Hero*), 1991.

Mr. Cool, *Capital Punishment* (also known as *Kickbox Terminator*), Screen Pix Home Video, 1991.

Long mao shao xu (also known as *Lethal Contact*), 1991.

Alexander Hell, *Samurai Vampire Bikers from Hell* (also known as *Alexander Hell* and *Hellzone Rangers*), 1992.

(As Ming–Hu Shaw) Dao li, *Jing ling bian* (also known as *Banana Spirit*), 1992.

(As Ming–Hu Shaw) Fighter, *Nu hei xia huang ying* (also known as *Deadly Dream Woman*), 1992.

Hawk, *The Legend of the Rollerblade Seven,* 1992.

Sam Hemmingway, "Some Guys Have All the Luck," *Inside Out II* (also known as *Double Vision*), 1992.

Copilot, *The Naked Truth,* 1992.

Himself, *The Player,* Fine Line, 1992.

Hawk, *Return of the Roller Blade Seven,* 1993.

Sam Rockmore, *Atomic Samurai* (also known as *Samurai Johnny Frankenstein*), 1993.

(Uncredited) *Pocket Ninjas* (also known as *Triple Dragon*), 1993.

Alexander Hell, *Samurai Ballet,* 1994.

Max, *Exploding Angel,* 1995.

Daredevil Dan Donovan, *Ghost Taxi* (also known as *Ride with the Devil*), 1996.

Jack B. Quick, *Shotgun Boulevard,* 1996.

Max Hell, *Toad Warrior* (also known as *Hell Comes to Frogtown III*), 1996.

Detective Jake Blade, *Hollywood Cops* (also known as *Rock 'n Roll Cops*), Light Source Films/No Rules Cinema, 1997.

Notti di paura (also known as *Across Red Nights* and *Mosca*), 1997.

Jack B. Quick, *Guns of El Chupacabra* (also known as *El Chupacabra*), 1997.

Jack B. Quick, *Guns of El Chupacabra II,* 1998.

Jack B. Quick, *Armageddon Boulevard,* H.V. Films, 1998.

Himself, *Strange Universe: Aliens Are Proof,* 1998.

Daredevil Dan Donovan, *Ride with the Devil,* 1999.

Johnny Wasteland, *Quest of the Invisible Ninja,* 2000.

Poppuguruupu koroshiya (also known as *Pop Beat Killers*), 2000.

Truck Baker, *Undercover* (also known as *No Boundaries* and *Slip into Oblivion*), Light Source Films/No Rules Cinema, 2001.

Liquid Tokyo, Light Source Films, 2001.

Sedona, 2001.

Himself, *Kung Fu Choreography,* 2001.

Detective Jake Blade, *Rock n' Roll Cops* (also known as *Hollywood P.D. Undercover*), Asia Filmworks/Light Source Films/No Rules Cinema, 2002.

Max Hell, *Max Hell Frog Warrior* (also known as *Max Hell Comes to Frogtown*), Light Source Films/Tag Entertainment, 2002.

Jericho Rider, *Shadows of Hong Kong,* 2002.

Big Action, *Hitman City,* Asia Filmworks/Light Source Films/No Rules Cinema, 2003.

Jake Blade, *Rock n' Roll Cops 2: The Adventure Begins* (also known as *The Rock n' Roll Cops*), Light Source Films, 2003.

Elijah Starr, *Vampire Blvd.,* Light Source Films/No Rules Cinema, 2004.

Ace X, *Super Hero Central* (also known as *The Adventures of Ace X and Kid Velvet*), Light Source Films, 2004.

Nick Cross, *The Final Kiss* (also known as *Blood on the Guitar*), Light Source Films, 2005.

Interview (short documentary), Light Source Films, 2005.

Himself, *Dinner and Drinks,* Light Source Films, 2005.

Michael Black, *Killer: Dead or Alive,* Light Source Films, 2006.

Jack B. Quick, *9mm Sunrise,* Light Source Films, 2006.

Jedediah Diesel, *Vampire Noir,* Light Source Films, 2007.

Professor Andre DuVena', *Witch's Brew,* Light Source Films, 2007.

Ace X, *The Adventures of Ace X and Kid Velvet,* Light Source Films, 2008.

Sealed with a Bullet, Light Source Films, 2008.

Jazz Drake, *The Hard Edge of Hollywood,* Light Source Films, 2008.

Vampire Black: Trail of the Dead, Light Source Films, 2008.

Himself, *Frogtown News,* Light Source Films, 2008.

Film Producer and Director:

(And stunt coordinator and, as Jake Blade, film editor; also contributor of additional cinematography) *Samurai Vampire Bikers from Hell* (also known as *Alexander Hell* and *Hellzone Rangers*), 1992.

(And stunt coordinator) *Atomic Samurai* (also known as *Samurai Johnny Frankenstein*), 1993.

(And, as Blade, cinematographer, and film editor) *Samurai Ballet,* 1994.

(And martial arts choreographer) *Toad Warrior* (also known as *Hell Comes to Frogtown III*), 1996.

(And, as Blade, film editor) *Hollywood Cops* (also known as *Rock 'n Roll Cops,* Light Source Films/No Rules Cinema, 1997.

Guns of El Chupacabra II, 1998.

(And film editor; also contributor of additional cinematography) *Lingerie Kickboxer,* 1998.

(And cinematographer) *Blade Sisters,* 1999.

Big Sister, 2000.

Quest of the Invisible Ninja, 2000.

(And cinematographer and, as Jake Dharma, film editor) *Sedona,* 2001.

(And cinematographer, and, as Blade, film editor) *Undercover* (also known as *Slip into Oblivion*), Light Source Films/No Rules Cinema, 2001.

(As Ming–Hu Shaw) *Shadows of Hong Kong,* 2002.

(And film editor, music supervisor, and stunt coordinator) *Max Hell Frog Warrior* (also known as *Max Hell Comes to Frogtown*), Light Source Films/Tag Entertainment, 2002.

(And, as Blade, film editor; also contributor of additional cinematography) *Rock n' Roll Cops* (also known as *Hollywood P.D. Undercover*), Asia Filmworks/Light Source Films/No Rules Cinema, 2002.

(And, as Blade, cinematographer and film editor) *Hitman City,* Asia Filmworks/Light Source Films/No Rules Cinema, 2003.

(And stunt coordinator and, as Blade, film editor) *Rock n' Roll Cops 2: The Adventure Begins* (also known as *The Rock n' Roll Cops*), Light Source Films, 2003.

(And cinematographer and, as Blade, film editor) *Vampire Blvd.*, Light Source Films/No Rules Cinema, 2004.

(And, as Blade, cinematographer and film editor) *Super Hero Central* (also known as *The Adventures of Ace X and Kid Velvet*), Light Source Films, 2004.

Legend of the Dead Boyz, Light Source Films, 2004.

(And, as Jake Dharma, cinematographer and film editor) *The Final Kiss* (also known as *Blood on the Guitar*), Light Source Films, 2005.

(And, as Dharma, film editor) *Interview* (short documentary), Light Source Films, 2005.

Dinner and Drinks, Light Source Films, 2005.

(And, as Dharma, film editor) *9mm Sunrise*, Light Source Films, 2006.

(And cinematographer and film editor) *One Shot Sam*, Light Source Films, 2006.

(And, as Dharma, cinematographer and film editor) *Vampire Noir*, Light Source Films, 2007.

(And, as Dharma, film editor) *Witch's Brew*, Light Source Films, 2007.

(And, as Dharma, film editor) *Yin Yang Insane*, Light Sources Films, 2007.

(And, as Dharma, film editor) *The Adventures of Ace X and Kid Velvet*, Light Source Films, 2008.

Sealed with a Bullet, Light Source Films, 2008.

Producer only (and, as Dharma, film editor) *The Hard Edge of Hollywood*, Light Source Films, 2008.

(And, as Dharma, cinematographer and film editor) *Vampire Black: Trail of the Dead*, Light Source Films, 2008.

(And film editor) *Naked Avenger*, Light Source Films, 2008.

(And film editor) *Frogtown News*, Light Source Films, 2008.

(And film editor) *Angel Blade*, Light Source Films, 2008.

(And film editor) *A Drive with Linnea and Donald* (short film), Light Source Films, 2008.

(And cinematographer) *A Little Bit about What Is Going On* (documentary), 2008.

(And, as Dharma, film editor) *The Cancelled Movie*, Light Source Films, 2009.

(And, as Dharma, cinematographer and film editor) *Bluegrass Christmas Party* (documentary), Light Source Films, 2009.

Film Producer:

Supervising producer, *UFO: Secret Video*, 1986.

(And stunt coordinator and film editor) *The Roller Blade Seven*, 1991.

(And film editor) *The Legend of the Rollerblade Seven*, 1992.

(And stunt coordinator, martial arts choreography, and film editor) *Return of the Roller Blade Seven*, 1993.

The Devil's Pet (also known as *Queen of Lost Island*), 1994.

Little Lost Sea Serpent, 1995.

Baby Ghost, 1995.

Ghost Taxi (also known as *Ride with the Devil*), 1996.

Shotgun Boulevard, 1996.

Rollergator, 1996.

(And film editor) *Guns of El Chupacabra* (also known as *El Chupacabra*), 1997.

(And film editor) *Armageddon Boulevard*, H.V. Films, 1998.

Vampire Child, 1999.

Ride with the Devil, 1999.

Film Executive Producer and Director:

Just a Moment that Passes in Time, 1990.

(And, as Jake Dharma, cinematographer and film editor) *Killer: Dead or Alive*, Light Source Films, 2006.

Film Director:

(And cinematographer) *Guongdong Province, China: Poverty and Promise*, 1990.

Cambodia: Living in the Killing Fields, 1996.

(And cinematographer) *Liquid Tokyo*, Light Source Films, 2001.

Film Work; Other:

Sword choreographer, *Samurai Cop*, 1989.

Additional cinematography, *Venomous*, Phoenician Entertainment, 2001.

Television Appearances; Episodic:

Steve Jennings, "Little Girl Lost," *Wolf*, CBS, 1990.

(Uncredited) Shoplifter, "The Robbery," *Seinfeld*, 1990.

Tony, "The Unknown," *Knots Landing*, CBS, 1991.

Bobby, "Getting Personal," *Head of the Class*, ABC, 1991.

James Andrews, premiere episode, *Eddie Dodd*, 1991.

Buck, "Between a Rock and a Hard Place," *Who's the Boss?*, ABC, 1991.

Cowboy, "Truth and Consequences," *Gabriel's Fire*, ABC, 1991.

Robbie, "Leonard Kraleman: All–American," *Coach*, ABC, 1991.

Sir Galumet, "Good Knight MacGyver: Parts 1 & 2," *MacGyver*, ABC, 1991.

Man of the People, NBC, 1991.

(Uncredited) Axe, "Glitter Rock—April 12, 1974," *Quantum Leap*, 1991.

Stevie Marks, *General Hospital*, 1991.

Skater, "Beach Blanket Brandon," *Beverly Hills, 90210* (also known as *Class of Beverly Hills*), Fox, 1991.

Jay Stinton, "The Pool Hall," *Man of the People*, 1991.

Surfer Craig, "Boss Lady," *Saved by the Bell*, 1991.

James, "Teufelsnacht," *The Visitor*, 1997.

"Lost Boys and Gothic Girls," *413 Hope St.*, 1997.

The producer, *Strange Universe*, 1997.

Dr. Salabaster, "Last Resort," *Mercy Point,* 1998.

The wind monster, "Dolomite in Space," *MADtv,* Fox, 2000.

Thor, premiere episode, *The John Henson Project,* Spike TV, 2004.

Alec, "B.C.," *Moonlight,* CBS, 2007.

Jason Mack, "Everyone Knows It's Windy," *Life on Mars,* ABC, 2009.

Television Appearances; Other:

Jimmy T., *Blade in Hong Kong,* 1985.

Jimmy Baines, *Sunset Beat,* 1990.

Rock star manager, *Palomino* (movie; also known as *Danielle Steel's "Palomino"*), 1991.

Vigilante, *... And Then She Was Gone* (also known as *In a Stranger's Hand*), 1991.

RECORDINGS

Videos:

Hapkido (instructional videotape), four volumes, CFW Enterprises/Unique Publications, 1994.

Music Albums:

Themes from the Zen Movies, 2007.

Just Zen, 2007.

Nights of Gothic Horror, 2007.

Ambient Light, 2007.

Sanskrit, 2009.

Beggar's Grave, 2009.

Vampire, 2009.

WRITINGS

Screenplays:

Just a Moment that Passes in Time, 1990.

The Roller Blade Seven, 1991.

The Legend of the Rollerblade Seven, 1992.

Samurai Vampire Bikers from Hell (also known as *Alexander Hell* and *Hellzone Rangers;* also based on story by Shaw), 1992.

Atomic Samurai (also known as *Samurai Johnny Frankenstein;* also based on story by Shaw), 1993.

Return of the Roller Blade Seven, 1993.

Samurai Ballet, 1994.

Ghost Taxi (also known as *Ride with the Devil*), 1996.

Shotgun Boulevard, 1996.

Toad Warrior (also known as *Hell Comes to Frogtown III*), 1996.

Hollywood Cops (also known as *Rock 'n Roll Cops;* also based on story by Shaw), Light Source Films/No Rules Cinema, 1997.

Guns of El Chupacabra (also known as *El Chupacabra;* also based on story by Shaw), 1997.

Armageddon Boulevard, H.V. Films, 1998.

Lingerie Kickboxer, 1998.

Vampire Child, 1999.

Ride with the Devil, 1999.

Blade Sisters, 1999.

Quest of the Invisible Ninja, 2000.

Undercover (also known as *No Boundaries* and *Slip into Oblivion;* also based on story by Shaw), Light Source Films/No Rules Cinema, 2001.

Shadows of Hong Kong, 2002.

Rock n' Roll Cops (also known as *Hollywood P.D. Undercover*), Asia Filmworks/Light Source Films/No Rules Cinema, 2002.

Max Hell Frog Warrior (also known as *Max Hell Comes to Frogtown*), Light Source Films/Tag Entertainment, 2002.

Hitman City, Asia Filmworks/Light Source Films/No Rules Cinema, 2003.

Rock n' Roll Cops 2: The Adventure Begins (also known as *The Rock n' Roll Cops;* also based on story by Shaw), Light Source Films, 2003.

Vampire Blvd., Light Source Films/No Rules Cinema, 2004.

Super Hero Central (also known as *The Adventures of Ace X and Kid Velvet*), Light Source Films, 2004.

Legend of the Dead Boyz, Light Source Films, 2004.

The Final Kiss (also known as *Blood on the Guitar*), Light Source Films, 2005.

Killer: Dead or Alive (also based on story by Shaw), Light Source Films, 2006.

9mm Sunrise (also based on story by Shaw), Light Source Films, 2006.

Vampire Noir (also based on story by Shaw), Light Source Films, 2007.

Witch's Brew, Light Source Films, 2007.

The Adventures of Ace X and Kid Velvet (also based on story by Shaw), Light Source Films, 2008.

Vampire Black: Trail of the Dead, Light Source Films, 2008.

Naked Avenger, Light Source Films, 2008.

Film Music:

(And composer of songs "Dry Bones Wheelzone" and "Them Roller Blades") *The Roller Blade Seven,* 1991.

The Legend of the Rollerblade Seven, 1992.

Samurai Vampire Bikers from Hell (also known as *Alexander Hell* and *Hellzone Rangers*), 1992.

Return of the Roller Blade Seven, 1993.

Samurai Ballet, 1994.

Rock 'n Roll Cops, Light Source Films/No Rules Cinema, 1997.

Armageddon Boulevard, H.V. Films, 1998.

Sedona, 2001.

Undercover (also known as *Slip into Oblivion*), Light Source Films/No Rules Cinema, 2001.

Rock n' Roll Cops (also known as *Hollywood P.D. Undercover*), Asia Filmworks/Light Source Films/No Rules Cinema, 2002.

(As DJ Acid X) *Hitman City,* Asia Filmworks/Light Source Films/No Rules Cinema, 2003.

(As DJ Acid X) *Interview* (short documentary), Light Source Films, 2005.

(As DJ Acid X) *The Final Kiss* (also known as *Blood on the Guitar*), Light Source Films, 2005.

(As DJ Acid X) *Killer: Dead or Alive*, Light Source Films, 2006.

Vampire Noir, Light Source Films, 2007.

(As DJ Acid X) *Yin Yang Insane*, Light Source Films, 2007.

(As DJ Acid X) *Witch's Brew*, Light Source Films, 2007.

Vampire Black: Trail of the Dead, Light Source Films, 2008.

(As DJ Acid X) *The Cancelled Movie*, Light Source Films, 2009.

Books:

Bangkok and the Nights of Drunken Stupor, Buddha Rose Publications, 1988.

Cambodian Refugees in Long Beach, California: The Definitive Study, Buddha Rose Publications, 1989.

TKO: A Drunken Night in Tokyo, Buddha Rose Publications, 1989.

The Passionate Kiss of Illusion, Buddha Rose Publications, 1990.

Time, Buddha Rose Publications, 2990.

Hapkido: The Korean Art of Self Defense, Charles E. Tuttle, 1997.

The Ki Process: Korean Secrets for Cultivating Dynamic Energy, Samuel Weiser, 1997.

The Warrior Is Silent: Martial Arts and the Spiritual Path, Inner Traditions, 1998.

Samurai Zen, Samuel Weiser, 1999.

Zen O'Clock: Time to Be, Samuel Weiser, 1999.

Simple Bliss, Element Books, c. 2000.

The Tao of Self Defense, Samuel Weiser, 2000.

About Peace, Red Wheel Publications, 2001.

Yoga: The Inner Journey, iUniverse.com, 2001.

Nirvana in a Nutshell: 157 Zen Meditations, Red Wheel Publications, 2002.

Taekwondo Basics, photographs by Hae Won Shin, Charles E. Tuttle, 2003.

The Little Book of Yoga Breathing: Pranayama Made Easy, Samuel Weiser, 2004.

Chi Kung for Beginners: Master the Flow of Chi for Good Health, Stress Reduction, and Increased Energy, Llewellyn Publications, 2004.

Advanced Taekwondo, Charles E. Tuttle, 2005.

Hapkido: Essays on Self-Defense, Buddha Rose Publications, 2008.

Zen Buddhism: The Pathway to Nirvana, Buddha Rose Publications, 2008.

Zen Filmmaking, Buddha Rose Publications, 2008.

Zen: Tales from the Journey, Buddha Rose Publications, 2008.

Yoga: A Spiritual Guidebook, Buddha Rose Publications, 2009.

Shattered Thoughts, Buddha Rose Publications, 2009.

China Deep, Buddha Rose Publications, 2009.

Independent Filmmaking: Secrets of the Craft, Buddha Rose Publications, 2009.

Marguerite Duras and Charles Bukowski: The Yin and Yang of Modern Erotic Literature, Buddha Rose Publications, 2009.

The Screenplays, Buddha Rose Publications, 2009.

Zen in the Blink of an Eye, Buddha Rose Publications, 2009.

Other books include *The Tao of Chi*, Llewellyn Publications. Contributor to books, including *The Ultimate Guide to Tae Kwon Do* (*Inside Kung Fu* Magazine Series 3), edited by John R. Little and Curtis F. Wong, McGraw–Hill, 1999.

Other:

Hapkido (instructional videotapes), four volumes, CFW Enterprises/Unique Publications, 1994.

Contributor to magazines, including *Black Belt*, *Inner Self*, *Inside Karate*, *Inside Kung Fu*, *Inside Taekwondo*, *Kick*, *Kung Fu Illustrated*, *Martial Art History*, *Martial Art Masters*, *Martial Art Movies*, *Martial Arts Combat & Sports*, *Martial Arts Illustrated*, *Martial Arts Legends*, *Masters and Styles*, *Secrets of the Masters*, and *Taekwondo Times*. Contributor of articles to online sources. Editor in chief, *Scream of the Buddha*, 1988–95; contributing editor, *Tae Kwon Do*, 1989–96.

ADAPTATIONS

Shaw also created stories for other films that he produced and directed, including *Angel Blade*, *The Hard Edge of Hollywood*, *Sealed with a Bullet*, and *Vampire Black: Trail of the Dead*, all 2008, and *The Cancelled Movie*, 2009.

OTHER SOURCES

Periodicals:

Draculina, Issue 18, 1994, pp. 26–31; February, 1998, pp. 36–39.

Femme Fatales, July, 1998, pp. 56–60.

Independent Video, Issue 7, 1993, pp. 18–23.

Inside Taekwondo, Volume 3, number 6, 1994, pp. 58–65.

Publishers Weekly, May 11, 1998, p. 64; April 30, 1999, pp. 22–26.

Taekwondo Times, November, 1998, pp. 56–61.

Electronic:

Scott Shaw Official Site, http://scottshaw.com, October 7, 2009.

SHEPHERD, Elizabeth 1936–
(Elizabeth Shephard)

PERSONAL

Born August 12, 1936, in London, England; daughter of a Methodist missionary. *Education:* Attended University of Bristol.

Career: Actress. Performed at Stratford Festival, Stratford, Ontario, Canada, and Shaw Festival, Niagara–on–the–Lake, Ontario.

Awards, Honors: Gemini Award nomination, best lead actress in a single dramatic program or miniseries, Academy of Canadian Cinema and Television, 1986, for *The Cuckoo Bird.*

CREDITS

Television Appearances; Miniseries:
Ada Clare, *Bleak House,* BBC, 1959.
Frances Le Roy, *The Citadel,* 1960–61.
Sally Louth, *They Met in a City,* BBC, 1961.
Toni Buddenbrooks, *Buddenbrooks,* BBC, 1965.
Syrie Van Epp, *The Corridor People,* Granada, 1966.
Emma Sholto, *The Bastard* (also known as *The Kent Chronicles*), syndicated, 1978.
Tania, *The Birds Fall Down,* BBC, 1978.
Isobel Batchelor, *Frost in May,* BBC, 1982.
Cleopatra the mother, *The Cleopatras,* BBC, 1983.
Lady Sutton, *By the Sword Divided,* BBC, 1983.

Television Appearances; Movies:
Joan Brandon, "The Cathedral," *Saturday Playhouse,* 1959.
Isabel Robson, "Doctor Everyman's Hour," *ITV Play of the Week* (also known as *Play of the Week*), ITV, 1961.
"The Tin Whistle Man," *ITV Play of the Week* (also known as *Play of the Week*), ITV, 1963.
Joanna Howarth, "Spoiled," *The Wednesday Play,* BBC, 1968.
Ellen, "Park People," *ITV Saturday Night Theatre* (also known as *ITV Sunday Night Theatre*), ITV, 1969.
Kate, *The Cuckoo Bird,* 1985.
Kingsley, *Spenser: Pale Kings and Princes,* Lifetime, 1994.
Vera, *End of Summer,* Showtime, 1997.
Grace Hoover, *Let Me Call You Sweetheart* (also known as *Mary Higgins Clark's "Let Me Call You Sweetheart"*), The Family Channel, 1997.
Teresa Rodriguez, *Time to Say Goodbye?,* Lifetime, 1997.

Hannah Rothschild, *The White Raven,* HBO, 1998.
Hilda McCourt, *Love and Murder* (also known as *Criminal Instincts: Love and Murder* and *Crimes et passion*), Lifetime, 2000.
Betty Timmons, *Love and Treason,* CBS, 2001.
Dr. Hilda McCourt, *Verdict in Blood* (also known as *Les liens du sang*), CTV, 2002.
Miss Richter, *The Piano Man's Daughter* (also known as *La fille de l'homme au piano*), CBC, 2003.
NTSB: The Crash of Flight 323, CBC, 2004.
Margaret Thatcher, *Shades of Black: The Conrad Black Story,* CTV, 2006.

Television Appearances; Series:
Title role, *Amelia,* BBC, 1961.
Valerie Koester, *The Phoenix Team,* CBC, 1980.
Registered Nurse Judy Owens, *Side Effects,* CBC, 1994–96.
Peggy Holmes, *The Adventures of Shirley Holmes,* Fox Family, 1996.
Voice of Infinity, *Silver Surfer,* Fox, 1998.

Television Appearances; Specials:
First witch, *Macbeth,* 1968.
Dawn, *Joy,* 1972.
Hegai, *The Thirteenth Day: The Story of Esther,* ABC, 1979.

Television Appearances; Episodic:
Jean Hambridge, "The Burning Question," *No Hiding Place,* ITV, 1960.
Grace, "A Two–to–One Chance," *It Happened like This,* 1962.
"The Long Voyage," *Jezebel ex UK,* ITV, 1963.
Wendy, "Personal and Private," *Suspense,* BBC, 1963.
"Drama '63: The Perfect Friday," *Drama 61–67,* ITV, 1963.
Martha Blake, "Time Out of Mind," *Armchair Mystery Theatre,* 1964.
Frau Lenz, "The Schloss Belt," *The Troubleshooters* (also known as *Mogul*), BBC, 1965.
Jocasta Sinclair, "Someone's Head Has to Roll," *The Troubleshooters* (also known as *Mogul*), BBC, 1966.
Louise Carron, "Dangerous Secret," *Danger Man* (also known as *Secret Agent* and *Secret Agent aka Danger Man*), ITV, 1966.
Valerie Ross, "Towpath," *Dixon of Dock Green,* BBC, 1967.
"S for Sugar, A for Apple, M for Missing," *Love Story,* ITV, 1968.
Joan Fortune, "The German Song," *Detective,* BBC, 1968.
Jennifer Davis, "Deaths on the Champs Elysees," *Detective,* BBC, 1968.
Fiona Cowley, "With All My Worldly Goods," *The Main Chance,* YTV, 1969.

(As Elizabeth Shephard) Diana Strickland, "A Lady of Virtue," *The Duchess of Duke Street*, PBS, 1976.

Queen Draga of Serbia, "Three Weeks," *Romance*, Thames, 1977.

Lady Potts, "The 4:10 to Zurich," *Q.E.D.* (also known as *Mastermind*), CBS, 1982.

"A Sword in the Hand of David," *Crown Court*, ITV, 1983.

(As Elizabeth Shephard) Isis, "Sara's Homecoming," *Road to Avonlea* (also known as *Avonlea* and *Tales from Avonlea*), The Disney Channel, 1990.

Madeline Novak, "Keeping Secrets," *Street Legal*, CBC, 1991.

Professor Hauser, "Midterm Madness," *Class of '96*, Fox, 1993.

Professor Hauser, "The Best Little Frat House at Havenhurst," *Class of '96*, Fox, 1993.

Eileen Mahern, "The Faithful Follower," *The Hidden Room*, Lifetime, 1993.

Dr. Morton, "Done to a Crisp," *The Mighty Jungle*, The Family Channel, 1994.

Marian Smithy (some sources cite Marian Smithwick), "The Creeping Darkness/Power," *PSI Factor: Chronicles of the Paranormal*, syndicated, 1996.

Martha Haskell, "Another Country," *Black Harbour*, CBC, 1997.

Jane Witherspoon, "The Traitor," *Poltergeist: The Legacy*, Sci–Fi Channel, 1999.

Jane Witherspoon, "Double Cross," *Poltergeist: The Legacy*, Sci–Fi Channel, 1999.

Jane Witherspoon, "Unholy Congress," *Poltergeist: The Legacy*, Sci–Fi Channel, 1999.

Voice of Agatha Harkness, "The Sorceress' Apprentice," *Avengers*, Fox, 2000.

Mrs. Partridge, "Crusader in the Crypt," *The Secret Adventures of Jules Verne*, Sci–Fi Channel and syndicated, 2000.

Anna, "Expose," *Twice in a Lifetime*, PAX, 2000.

Paulina Kundera, *All My Children* (also known as *AMC*), ABC, 2003.

Mrs. Donovan, "Solitary," *Law & Order: Special Victims Unit* (also known as *Law & Order: SVU* and *Special Victims Unit*), NBC, 2009.

Film Appearances:

Susan, *The Queen's Guards*, Twentieth Century–Fox, 1961.

Sue Goodwin, *What Every Woman Wants*, United Artists, 1962.

Joan Marshall, *Blind Corner* (also known as *Man in the Dark*), Planet Film Productions, 1963.

Lady Rowena Trevanion/Lady Ligeia Fell, *The Tomb of Ligeia* (also known as *Edgar Allan Poe's "The Tomb of Ligeia,"* *Last Tomb of Ligeia*, *Ligeia*, and *Tomb of the Cat*), American International Pictures, 1964.

Alison Ashurst, *Hell Boats* (also known as *MTB Malta World War 2*), United Artists, 1970.

Joan Hart, *Damien: Omen II* (also known as *Omen II* and *Omen II: Damien*), Twentieth Century–Fox, 1978.

Frances, *Double Negative* (also known as *Deadly Companion*), Quadrant Films, 1980.

Joan Scott, *The Kidnapping of the President*, Crown International, 1980.

Mrs. Wiseman, "Julia," *Love*, Coup Films/Velvet Film Productions, 1982.

Lady Caroline Braunceston, *Invitation to the Wedding*, Chancery Lane, 1985.

Mrs. Issel, *Head Office*, TriStar, 1986.

Dr. Sybil Thiel, *Criminal Law*, Hemdale, 1989.

Matthew's mother, *Mustard Bath* (also known as *Bain de moutarde*), 9Y6S Film, 1993.

Title role, *Felicity's View* (short film), Extra Sensory Productions, 1999.

Mayor Hackett, *The Spreading Ground*, Smooth Pictures, 2000.

Mrs. Waterson, *Desire* (also known as *Begierde* and *Fatale Sehnsucht*), Advanced, 2000.

Frances Putnam, *Amelia*, Fox Searchlight, 2009.

Stage Appearances:

War and Peace, Bristol Old Vic Theatre Company, Phoenix Theatre, 1962.

Mrs. Marjorie Hasseltine, *Conduct Unbecoming*, Ethel Barrymore Theatre, New York City, 1970.

The Breakdown, Carpe Diem Theatre, Toronto, Ontario, Canada, 1998.

The Water Crawlers, Buddies in Bad Times, 2000.

Footfalls [and] *Krapp's Last Tape* (double–bill), duMaurier World Stage Festival, Toronto, 2000.

The Coronation Voyage, Vancouver Playhouse, Vancouver, British Columbia, Canada, 2000.

Frau Schneider, *Cabaret* (musical), Citadel Theatre, Edmonton, Alberta, Canada, 2001.

Miss Havisham, *Great Expectations*, Derby Theatre, Derby, England, then Walnut Street Theatre, Philadelphia, PA, 2002.

Lily, *Walk Right Up*, Stratford Studio Theatre, 2002.

Flora Humble, *Humble Boy*, Theatre Calgary, Calgary, Alberta, 2005.

December Fools, Abington Theatre Company, New York City, 2006.

Appeared in *Kennedy's Children*, *Old Times*, *The Seagull*, and *A Streetcar Named Desire*, all Centaur Theatre, Montreal, Quebec, Canada; in *Passion Play*, Saidye Bronfman Centre, Montreal; also appeared in productions of *The Cherry Orchard*, *Immediate Family* (solo show), and *Tartuffe*.

SHORTER, Clinton 1971–

PERSONAL

Born March 18, 1971, in North Vancouver, British Columbia, Canada.

Career: Composer, music editor, recording engineer, and music arranger. Also worked as assistant composer for film music. Composer for hundreds of commercials, including work for Panasonic and Yamaha. Once worked at a music store.

Awards, Honors: Leo Award nomination, best musical score for a short drama, Motion Picture Arts and Sciences Foundation of British Columbia, 2007, for *Nostalgia Boy;* Hollywood Music in Media Award, best original score for a film.

CREDITS

Television Work; Series:
Music editor, *Crash Test Mommy,* Life Network, between 2005 and 2006.

Music editor for the series *Beggars and Choosers,* Showtime; *The Fearing Mind,* Fox Family; *Making the Cut; Mysterious Ways; Peacemakers,* USA Network; and *So Weird,* The Disney Channel.

Television Work; Movies:
Music performer, "Method," *The Inspectors 2: A Shred of Evidence,* Showtime, 2000.

Film Work:
Music editor, *The Last Stop* (also known as *Dernier arret*), Lions Gate Films, 2000.
Music arranger, *Saving Silverman* (also known as *Evil Woman*), Columbia, 2001.
Music editor, *Water's Edge,* Lions Gate Films, 2004.

WRITINGS

Television Composer; Movies:
Songwriter, "Method," *The Inspectors 2: A Shred of Evidence,* Showtime, 2000.
Secret Lives, Lifetime, 2005.
Deck the Halls, Lifetime, 2005.
A Decent Proposal, Lifetime, 2006.
Ties that Bind, Lifetime, 2006.
Presumed Dead, Lifetime, 2006.
12 Hours to Live, Lifetime, 2006.
Her Fatal Flaw, Lifetime, 2006.
Under the Mistletoe, Lifetime, 2006.
Secrets of an Undercover Wife, Lifetime, 2007.
Judicial Indiscretion, Lifetime, 2007.
I Know What I Saw (also known as *Post Mortem*), Lifetime, 2007.
Nightmare at the End of the Hall, Lifetime, 2008.
The Secret Lives of Second Wives, Lifetime, 2008.
NYC: Tornado Terror, Sci–Fi Channel, 2008.

Television Composer; Episodic:
"Stain'd," *This Space for Rent,* CBC, 2007.
"Elvis Kwan Blows," *This Space for Rent,* CBC, 2007.

Television Composer; Series:
Urban Rush, 2001.

Also composer of additional music for the series *The Adventures of Shirley Holmes,* Fox Family; *Beggars and Choosers,* Showtime; *The Dead Zone* (also known as *Stephen King's "Dead Zone"*), USA Network; *The Fearing Mind,* Fox Family; *Mysterious Ways;* and *So Weird,* The Disney Channel.

Film Music Composer:
(Additional music) *Legends: The Story of Siwash Rock* (short film), National Film Board of Canada, 2000.
Come Together, Rocket Chicken International, 2001.
Canadian Zombie (short film), 2002.
Something Fishy (short film), IFILM, 2002.
Human Trials: Testing the AIDS Vaccine (documentary), Avanti Pictures, 2003.
Just Smile and Nod (short film), CineClix Distribution, 2004.
A Clown's Gift (short film), Centurion Pictures, 2004.
Blinded (short film), Centurion Pictures, 2004.
Alive in Joburg (short film), Spy Films, 2005.
The Cabin Movie, 2005, Panorama Entertainment, 2007.
Severed (also known as *Severed: Forest of the Dead*), Screen Media 7, 2005.
Nostalgia Boy (short film), Nostalgic Pictures, 2006.
Unnatural & Accidental, Odeon Films, 2006.
Normal, Porchlight Home Entertainment, 2007.
Terminus (short film), Spy Films, 2007.
Spoon, Distant Horizon, 2008.
District 9, TriStar, 2009.
Cole, Rampart Films/Titlecard Pictures, 2009.

OTHER SOURCES

Electronic:
Clinton Shorter Official Site, http://www.clintonshorter.com, February 22, 2010.

SHYDER, Justin
    See NORRIS, Daran

SINCLAIR, Kim 1954–

PERSONAL

Born July 10, 1954, in Auckland, New Zealand.

Career: Production designer, art director, and set designer. Also worked as set decorator.

Awards, Honors: Film Award, best design, New Zealand Film and Television Awards, 2001, for *Her Majesty;* Art Directors Guild Award nomination (with others), excellence in production design for a period or fantasy film, 2004, for *The Last Samurai;* Academy Award, best art direction, and Film Award, best production design, British Academy of Film and Television Arts, both (with others), 2010, for *Avatar.*

CREDITS

Film Production Designer:
(Uncredited) *Constance,* 1984.
Willow, Metro–Goldwyn–Mayer, 1988.
My Grandpa Is a Vampire (also known as *Grampire* and *Moonrise*), New Zealand Film Commission, 1991.
Alex (also known as *Alex: The Spirit of a Champion*), Cineplex–Odeon, 1993.
The Climb (also known as *Le defi*), Ellipse Programme/ Spellbound Pictures, 1998.
Nightmare Man, Isambard Productions/Telescene Film Group, 1999.
Vertical Limit (also known as *Vertical Limit—In grosser gefahr*), Columbia, 2000.
Her Majesty, Panorama Entertainment, 2001.
The Last Samurai (also known as *The Last Samurai: Bushidou*), Warner Bros., 2003.
Black Sheep, IFC Films, 2006.
Under the Mountain, Walt Disney, 2009.

Film Work; Other:
Set designer, *The Quiet Earth,* Skouras, 1985.
Art director for Fiji, *Cast Away,* Twentieth Century–Fox, 2000.
Art director for Thailand, *Beyond Borders* (also known as *Jenseits aller grenzen*), Paramount, 2003.
Supervising art director, *The Legend of Zorro* (also known as *Z*), Columbia, 2005.
Lead supervising art director, *Avatar* (animated; also known as *Avatar: An IMAX 3D Experience* and *James Cameron's "Avatar"*), Twentieth Century–Fox, 2009.

Television Production Designer; Movies:
Every Woman's Dream, CBS, 1996.
Atomic Twister, TBS, 2002.

Television Production Designer; Other:
The Adventures of the Black Stallion (series), The Family Channel, 1990.
The Tommyknockers (miniseries; also known as *Stephen King's "The Tommyknockers"*), ABC, 1993.

Worked as production designer for the series *High Tide,* syndicated, and *One West Waikiki.*

SINCLAIR, Malcolm 1950–

PERSONAL

Born June 5, 1950, in London, England. *Education:* Attended University of Hull; trained at Bristol Old Vic Theatre School.

Addresses: *Agent*—Caroline Dawson and Associates, 125 Gloucester Rd., 2nd Floor, London SW7 4TE, England.

Career: Actor.

Member: British Actors' Equity Association.

Awards, Honors: Laurence Olivier Award nomination, best supporting actor, Society of West End Theatre, 2002, for *Privates on Parade.*

CREDITS

Television Appearances; Miniseries:
Tom Truelove, *Victorian Scandals,* 1976.
Rudolf Rassendyll/King Rudolf V, *The Prisoner of Zenda,* BBC, 1984.
Alan Sturridge, *The Big Battalions,* Channel 4, 1991.
Abbe Castanede, *The Scarlet and Black* (also known as *Scarlet and Black*), BBC, 1993.
London doctor, *Scarlett,* CBS, 1994.
Richard Rampton, *McLibel!,* BBC, 1997.
Prince Shcherbatsky, *Anna Karenina,* PBS, 2000.
Conyngham, *Victoria & Albert,* Arts and Entertainment, 2001.
Commander Alistair Denville, *Making Waves,* ITV, 2004.
Sir Andrew McNeil, *The Amazing Mrs. Pritchard,* PBS, 2006.

Television Appearances; Movies:
Arthur, *Esther Waters,* BBC, 1977.
Charles Frayling, *God on the Rocks,* Channel 4, 1990.
Estate agent, "Sweet Nothing,: *Screen One,* BBC, 1990.
John Le Mesurier, "Hancock," *Screen One,* BBC, 1991.
Now That It's Morning, Channel 4, 1991.
Quinn, *A Question of Guilt,* BBC, 1993.
Frobisher, *The Writing on the Wall* (also known as *Operation Schmetterling*), BBC, 1994.
Hugo Tripp, *Under the Moon,* 1995.

Nicholas Purnell, *Anybody's Nightmare,* 2001.
Anthony, *Falling,* ITV, 2005.
Noel Coward, *Daphne,* Logo, 2007.

Television Appearances; Series:
Assistant Chief Constable Freddy Fisher, *Pie in the Sky,* BBC, 1994–97.
Multiple characters, *The Last Machine,* BBC2, 1995.

Television Appearances; Episodic:
Peter Lambert, "Rumpole and the Age of Miracles," *Rumpole of the Bailey,* PBS, 1988.
Patric Duvalais, "Inside Story," *French Fields,* 1990.
Mr. Pollock/Sinton, "Undercover," *Boon,* Central, 1990.
Edward Clayton, "The Mystery of the Spanish Chest," *Agatha Christie: Poirot* (also known as *Agatha Christie's Poirot* and *Poirot*), London Weekend Television, 1991.
Philip Langley, "The Best You Can Buy," *The Bill,* ITV1, 1991.
Pommier, "SOS from a Gemini," *Moon and Son,* 1992.
Tom Kenyon, "High Drivers," *The Bill,* ITV1, 1994.
Chief constable, "Quarry," *A Touch of Frost,* 1995.
Brig Henry Devonshire, "No Pain, No Gain," *Soldier Soldier,* 1997.
Mike Price, "Toys and Boys," *Casualty,* BBC1, 1998.
Geoffrey Levinson, "Tinderbox," *The Bill,* ITV1, 1999.
Giles Luckhurst, "The More Loving One," *Kavanagh QC,* ITV, 1999.
Alan Bradford, "Beyond the Grave," *Midsomer Murders,* Arts and Entertainment, 2000.
Julian, "The Executioner's Mask," *Relic Hunter* (also known as *Relic Hunter—Die Schatzjaegerin* and *Sydney Fox l'aventuriere*), syndicated, 2001.
Blythe, "The Patient's Eyes," *Murder Rooms: Mysteries of the Real Sherlock Holmes,* 2001.
Cecil Greenaway, "So Long, Samantha," *The Brief,* ITV, 2004.
Quentin Glazer, "They Understand Me in Paris," *Rosemary & Thyme,* ITV, 2004.
Bank chief, "Jobless," *My Dad's the Prime Minister,* BBC, 2004.
Sir Peter Dulford, "My Daughter, Right or Wrong," *Judge John Deed,* BBC, 2006.
Sir Peter Dulford, "Evidence of Harm: Parts 1 & 2," *Judge John Deed,* BBC, 2007.
Reece, "A Designers Paradise," *Hustle* (also known as *Hu$tle*), AMC, 2007.
Johnny Hammond, "Shot at Dawn," *Midsomer Murders,* Arts and Entertainment, 2008.
Father Martin Keppler, "Plan of Attack," *Foyle's War,* PBS, 2008.
Mitchell Crompton, *Material Girl,* BBC, 2010.

Television Appearances; Other:
Ronnie, "Me and the Girls" (special; also known as "Noel Coward Stories" and "Noel Coward Stories: Me and the Girls"; broadcast in England as an episode of *Star Quality*), *Masterpiece Theatre,* PBS, 1987.

Appeared in *Auntie's Bloomers;* in the title role, *Byron—A Personal Tour,* BBC; and in *Everyone a Winner,* BBC.

Film Appearances:
Deputy stage manager, *Success Is the Best Revenge* (also known as *Le succes a tout prix*), Gaumont, 1984.
Dr. Triefus, *The Young Poisoner's Handbook* (also known as *Das Handbuch des jungen giftmischers*), Astra Film, 1995.
Paul Doring, *Keep the Aspidistra Flying* (also known as *Comstock and Rosemary* and *A Merry War*), Lions Gate Films, 1997.
Cardinal of Lyon, *The Statement* (also known as *Crimes contre l'humanite*), Sony Pictures Classics, 2003.
Spanish priest, *Secret Passage,* 2004, Starmedia Home Entertainment, 2006.
Major Wilson, *V for Vendetta* (also known as *V for Vendetta: At the IMAX, V for Vendetta: The IMAX Experience,* and *V wie Vendetta*), Warner Bros., 2005.
Monsignor Francis Hughes, *Rabbit Fever,* Maiden Voyage Pictures, 2006.
Dryden, *Casino Royale* (also known as *James Bond 007—Casino Royale*), Columbia, 2006.
Charles Kemble, *The Young Victoria,* Apparition, 2009.

Stage Appearances:
Romeo and Juliet, Bristol Old Vic Theatre Company, Bristol Little Theatre, Bristol, England, 1975.
Serebryakov, *Uncle Vanya,* Royal Shakespeare Company, Young Vic Theatre, London, 1988.
The Three Musketeers, Bristol Old Vic Theatre Company, Theatre Royal, Bristol, 1988.
George, Duke of Clarence, *Richard III,* Royal National Theatre, London, then Brooklyn Academy of Music Theatre, New York City, 1992.
The Case of Rebellious Susan, Orange Tree Theatre, London, 1994.
Cressida, Albery Theatre, London, 2000.
Privates on Parade, Donmar Warehouse Theatre, London, 2001.
Buckingham, *Richard III,* Royal Shakespeare Company, Royal Shakespeare Theatre, Stratford–upon–Avon, England, 2003.
Headmaster, *The History Boys,* Broadhurst Theatre, New York City, 2006.
Stephen, *Dealer's Choice,* Menier Chocolate Factory Theatre, London, 2007.

Also appeared in *Anatole,* Gate Theatre, London; in title role, *By Jeeves,* Duke of York's Theatre, London; in *Dark River,* Orange Tree Theatre, London; *Facades,*

Lyric Hammersmith Theatre, London; as Mazzini Dunn, *Heartbreak House,* Almeida Theatre, London; as Osborne, *Journey's End,* West End production; in *Little Lies,* Wyndham's Theatre, London; *London's Cuckolds,* Lyric Hammersmith Theatre; *The Millionairess,* Greenwich Theatre, London; as Kingston, *Racing Demon,* National Theatre, London; in *The Misanthrope,* National Theatre; *Splendids,* Lyric Hammersmith Theatre; and Malvolio, *Twelfth Night,* Crucible Theatre, Sheffield, England.

Concert appearances include *Midsummer Night's Dream,* Boston Symphony Orchestra, Boston, MA, and Carnegie Hall, New York City; *Morning Heroes,* Royal Liverpool Philharmonic Orchestra, Liverpool, England; *Peter and the Wolf,* East of England Orchestra, Nottingham; *A Soldier's Tale,* Nash Ensemble; and *A Survivor in Warsaw,* Boston Symphony Orchestra, then with London Philharmonic Orchestra, Royal Festival Hall, London.

Major Tours:
Solinus, *Comedy of Errors,* Royal Shakespeare Company, British cities, 1987.
Horatio, *Hamlet,* Royal Shakespeare Company, British cities, 1987.

SLAWNER, Leigh
    See SCOTT, Leigh

SMITH, Wyatt 1994–

PERSONAL

Born November 29, 1994, in Lake Arrowhead, CA. *Avocational Interests:* Skiing, swimming, kayaking, golf, ceramics.

Addresses: *Agent*—Meredith Fine, Coast to Coast Talent, Inc., 3350 Barham Blvd., Los Angeles, CA 90068. *Manager*—Leslie Allan–Rice, Leslie Allan–Rice Management, 1007 Maybrook Dr., Beverly Hills, CA 90210.

Career: Actor. Appeared in more than seventy–five commercials, beginning at age five.

CREDITS

Television Appearances; Series:
Brian Kmetko, *Make It or Break It,* ABC Family, 2009–10.

Television Appearances; Pilots:
Young Eddie, *Lost at Home,* 2003.
(Uncredited) Boy in airplane terminal, *Joey,* NBC, 2004.
Brian Kmetko, *Make It or Break It,* ABC Family, 2009.

Television Appearances; Miniseries:
Roadside boy, *Meteor,* NBC, 2009.

Television Appearances; Movies:
Billy, *A Gunfighter's Pledge,* Hallmark Channel, 2008.

Television Appearances; Episodic:
Young Ethan, *Passions,* NBC, 2001, 2002.
Boy in 1953, "Red Glare," *Cold Case,* CBS, 2004.
Travis Stewart, "Conditional Surrender," *Judging Amy,* CBS, 2004.
Alden, "Girl Power," *Drake & Josh,* Nickelodeon, 2005.
Owen, "The Headmaster," *Stacked,* Fox, 2006.
Owen, "Poker," *Stacked,* Fox, 2006.
Ryan Bynum, "One Wrong Move," *Without a Trace* (also known as *W.A.T.*), CBS, 2007.
Frankie, "Judgment Day," *Navy NCIS: Naval Criminal Investigative Service* (also known as *NCIS* and *NCIS: Naval Criminal Investigative Service*), CBS, 2008.
Josh Bancroft, "Life on the Line," *Ghost Whisperer,* CBS, 2009.

Film Appearances:
Boy in crowd, *Dickie Roberts: Former Child Star* (also known as *Dickie Robert: (Former) Child Star*), Paramount, 2003.
Voice of Kid Rat, *Garfield* (also known as *Garfield: The Movie*), Twentieth Century–Fox, 2004.
(Uncredited) Boy at wedding, *The 40 Year Old Virgin,* Universal, 2005.
Street vendor, *Fight It* (short film), Ghostwater Films, 2007.
Charlie Tyler, *Never Back Down,* Summit Entertainment, 2008.
Jarrett, *The Perfect Game,* IndustryWorks Pictures, 2009.

STOLTE, Christian 1962–
    (Chris Stolte, Christian Stolti)

PERSONAL

Full name, Christian Joseph Stolte; born October 16, 1962, in St. Louis, MO.

Addresses: *Agent*—Bob Schroeder, Aria Talent, 1017 West Washington Blvd., Suite 2C, Chicago, IL 60607.

Career: Actor and writer. Worked as an acting instructor.

Member: Screen Actors Guild, American Federation of Television and Radio Artists, Actors' Equity Association.

Awards, Honors: Jeff Award, best new work, and Jeff Award nomination (with others), best ensemble, both Joseph Jefferson Awards Committee, 1998, for *Canus Lunis Balloonis;* Midwest Independent Film Festival Award, best actor, 2007, for *Crime Fiction.*

CREDITS

Film Appearances:
(As Christian Stolti) Ambulance attendant, *The Public Eye,* Universal, 1992.

Rocky Scanlon, *Bruised Orange,* 1999.

Second police officer at train station, *Stir of Echoes* (also known as *The Secret Sense*), Twentieth Century–Fox, 1999.

(As Chris Stolte) *Time to Pay,* 1999, Singa Home Entertainment, 2005.

Police officer in Ukrainian village, *Brat 2* (also known as *Brother II, The Brother 2,* and *On the Way Home*), 2000, Palisades Tartan, 2009.

Court guard, *Novocaine,* Artisan Entertainment/Eagle Pictures/Momentum Pictures, 2001.

Miami police officer, *Ali* (also known as *Muhammad Ali*), Columbia, 2001.

Ernest Caldwell, *Legwork* (short film), Digital Film Project/Saga Studios, 2002.

Joe, *Last Day* (short film), Spoke Film, 2002.

Rooney's business associate, *Road to Perdition,* Dream-Works, 2002.

Father, *What Are You Having?* (short film), Bucktown Pictures, 2003.

Reporter, *Mr. 3000* (also known as *Mr 3000*), Buena Vista, 2004.

Inmate JZX773412, *Asylum* (short film), c. 2004.

John Rucinski, *Death of a President* (also known as *D.O.A.P.*), Newmarket Films, 2006.

Young boy's father, *Stranger Than Fiction* (also known as *Killing Harold Crick*), Columbia, 2006.

(As Christian Stolti; in archive footage) Val's thug, *Payback: Straight Up—The Director's Cut,* 2006, Paramount, 2007.

Don Lee Boone, *Crime Fiction,* Crime Fiction Pictures, c. 2006, Anthem Pictures, 2008.

Second voice, *Already Dead,* Arclight Films, 2007.

Charlie, *The Man in the Silo,* Rhythm and Light, 2008.

Coach Driskill, *Were the World Mine* (musical; also known as *Fairies: A Musical Dream Come True* and *Were the World Mine: A Musical Dream Come True*), SPEAKproductions, 2008.

Dan Boyle, *The Express* (also known as *The Express: The Ernie Davis Story*), Universal, 2008.

Nick Dinotto, *Osso Bucco,* River West Films, 2008.

Pete, *Leatherheads* (also known as *Ein verlockendes Spiel*), Universal, 2008.

Professor VanOver, *Fraternity House,* 2008.

Sergeant Sayles, *The Lucky Ones* (also known as *The Return*), Lionsgate/Roadside Attractions, 2008.

Voice of second banjo player, *The Promotion* (also known as *Quebec*), Third Rail Releasing, 2008.

Charles Makley, *Public Enemies,* Universal, 2009.

Clarence Darby, *Law Abiding Citizen,* Overture Films, 2009.

Hank Bailey, *Under New Management,* The Good Film/OGO Films/The Cutaia Group/ZAM Entertainment, 2009.

(Uncredited) Jesse's father, *A Nightmare on Elm Street* (also known as *Nightmare*), Warner Bros., 2010.

Sales manager, *Ca$h* (also known as *The Cache, Ca$h!,* and *The Root of All Evil*), Roadside Attractions, 2010.

Television Appearances; Series:
Inmate JZX773412, *Asylum* (short film), produced as part of *Project Greenlight 2* (also known as *Project Greenlight*), HBO, c. 2004.

Corrections officer Keith Stolte, *Prison Break* (also known as *The Break, Prison Break: Manhunt, Prison Break: On the Run, Grande evasion, I apodrasi, Pako, Pogenemine,* and *Prison Break—Em busca da verdade*), Fox, 2005–2007.

Television Appearances; Episodic:
Elvis McCutcheon, "Pick–Up Schticks," *Cupid* (also known as *Love Therapy*), ABC, 1998.

Bradley, "Take Me out to the Ballgame," *Early Edition,* CBS, 1999.

Vincent, "Friends & Strangers," *Turks,* CBS, 1999.

Vincent, "Hearts of Fire," *Turks,* CBS, 1999.

(As Chris Stolte) Driver, "Tell Me No Secrets ...," *ER* (also known as *Emergency Room*), NBC, 2006.

Sullivan, "Hothead," *The Beast,* Arts and Entertainment, 2009.

Television Appearances; Pilots:
Setup man, *Turks,* CBS, 1999.

Corrections officer Keith Stolte, *Prison Break* (also known as *The Break, Prison Break: Manhunt, Prison Break: On the Run, Grande evasion, I apodrasi, Pako, Pogenemine,* and *Prison Break—Em busca da verdade*), Fox, 2005.

Stage Appearances:
Rudolph, Johannes, and member of ensemble, *Born Guilty,* A Red Orchid Theatre, Chicago, IL, c. 1994.

Colin, *Canus Lunis Balloonis,* A Red Orchid Theatre, 1997.

Patrick, *A Mislaid Heaven,* Famous Door Theatre Company, Chicago, 1998.

Laurent, *Therese Raquin,* Greasy Joan & Co., American Theater Company (ATC), Chicago, c. 1999.

Charlie Doyle, *And Neither Have I Wings to Fly,* Fox Theatricals, Victory Gardens Theater, Chicago, 2000.

Ham Peggotty, *David Copperfield,* Steppenwolf Theatre, Mainstage Theatre, Chicago, 2001.

Bobby Gould, *Speed–the–Plow,* Piven Theatre Workshop, Evanston, IL, 2002.

Yvan, *Art,* Indiana Repertory Theatre, Indianapolis, IN, 2002.

Brad, *Orange Flower Water,* Steppenwolf Theatre, Garage Theatre, Chicago, 2003.

Jessie, bellhop, and waiter, *Plaza Suite,* Indiana Repertory Theatre, 2004.

A, *No One Will Be Immune* (one–act play), David Mamet Festival, produced as part of the program One–Acts Evening C: Ghost Stories (also known as Ghost Stories), Goodman Theatre, Owen Theatre, Chicago, 2006.

Defense attorney, *Romance,* David Mamet Festival, Goodman Theatre, Owen Theatre, 2006.

Appeared in other productions, including appearances as Walter, *Dirty Work,* Oxford Festival, Oxford, MS; and as Emperor Justinian, *Theodora.*

Major Tours:

Mr. Baker, radio technician, and Express man, *The Man Who Came to Dinner,* Steppenwolf Theatre, Mainstage Theatre, Chicago, IL, and Inventing America Festival, Barbican Centre, London, both 1998.

Al Paradiso, *Side Man,* Steppenwolf Theatre, Mainstage Theatre, 1999, Galway Arts Festival, Galway, Ireland, 2000, Melbourne International Arts Festival, Melbourne, Victoria, Australia, 2001, and Vail, CO, production, 2002.

Understudy for the roles of Randle Patrick "R. P." McMurphy and Billy Bibbitt, *One Flew over the Cuckoo's Nest,* Steppenwolf Theatre, Mainstage Theatre, 2000, BITE:oo, Barbican Centre, 2000, and Royale Theatre (later known as the Bernard B. Jacobs Theatre), New York City, 2001.

RECORDINGS

Albums; with Others:

Were the World Mine (soundtrack), P.S. Classics, 2008.

WRITINGS

Writings for the Stage:

Canus Lunis Balloonis, A Red Orchid Theatre, Chicago, IL, 1997.

SULLIVAN, Daniel 1940–

PERSONAL

Full name, Daniel J. Sullivan; born June 11, 1940, in Wray, CO; son of John Martin and Mary Catherine (maiden name, Hutton) Sullivan; married third wife, Shelley Plimpton (an actress; divorced); children: (first marriage) Megan Anne; (second marriage) John, Rachel. *Education:* San Francisco State College (now University), B.A.

Career: Director, actor, and writer. Actor's Workshop, San Francisco, CA, actor, 1963–65; Lincoln Center Repertory Company, New York City, actor and director, 1965–73; director of regional theatre productions, 1973–79; Seattle Repertory Theatre, Seattle, WA, resident director, 1979–81, artistic director, 1981–97; Manhattan Theatre Club, New York City, acting artistic director, 2007–08; Lincoln Center Theatre, associate director. California Institute of Arts, Valencia, instructor, 1973–74; University of Illinois at Urbana–Champaign, Swanlund Professor of Theatre. National Endowment for the Arts, member of board of directors of Theatre Panel, Communications Group, beginning 1982; Commonwealth Award Panel, member.

Awards, Honors: Drama Desk Award, most promising director, New York Theatre Critics, 1972, for *Suggs;* Antoinette Perry Award nomination and Drama Desk Award nomination, both best director of a play, 1989, for *The Heidi Chronicles;* Lucille Lortel Award, outstanding director, League of Off–Broadway Theatres and Producers, 1992, for *Substance of Fire;* Antoinette Perry Award nomination, best director of a play, 1992, for *Conversations with My Father;* Antoinette Perry Award nomination and Drama Desk Award nomination, both best director of a play, 1993, for *The Sisters Rosensweig;* Drama Desk Award nomination, outstanding director of a play, 2000, for *Dinner with Friends;* Outer Critics Circle Award nomination, outstanding director of a play, 2000, for *Dinner with Friends* and *A Moon for the Misbegotten;* Julia Hansen Award for Excellence in Directing, Drama League, 2000; Antoinette Perry Award, best direction of a play, and Lucille Lortel Award, outstanding director, both 2001, for *Proof;* Antoinette Perry Award nomination, best direction of a play, 2002, for *Morning's at Seven;* Outer Critics Circle Award nomination, 2004, and Lucille Lortel Award nomination, 2005, both outstanding director of a play, for *Intimate Apparel;* Antoinette Perry Award nomination, best direction of a play, 2006, for *Rabbit Hole;* Obie Award, *Village Voice,* and Drama Desk Award nomination, both outstanding direction of a play, 2006, Lucille Lortel Award, outstanding director, 2007, and nomination for Joe A. Callaway Award, Actors' Equity

Association, all for *Stuff Happens;* Mr. Abbot Award, lifetime achievement, Stage Directors and Choreographers Foundation, 2007; nomination for Joe A. Callaway Award, outstanding director, 2009, for *Twelfth Night.*

CREDITS

Stage Director:

In White America, Repertory Theatre of Lincoln Center, Theatre–in–the–Schools Program, New York City, 1967–68.

Scenes from American Life, Forum Theatre (now Mitzi E. Newhouse Theatre), New York City, 1971.

Play Strindberg, Forum Theatre, 1971.

Narrow Road to the Deep North, Vivian Beaumont Theatre, Lincoln Center, New York City, 1971–72.

Suggs, Forum Theatre, 1972.

The Plough and the Stars, Vivian Beaumont Theatre, Lincoln Center, 1972–73.

The Matchmaker, Hartford Stage Company, Hartford, CT, 1978–79.

The American Clock, Harold Clurman Theatre, New York City, 1980.

Two Gentlemen of Verona, Seattle Repertory Theatre, Seattle, WA, 1981–82.

Bedroom Farce, Seattle Repertory Theatre, 1981–82.

Major Barbara, Seattle Repertory Theatre, 1981–82.

Romeo and Juliet, Seattle Repertory Theatre, 1982–83.

The Front Page, Seattle Repertory Theatre, 1982–83.

Taking Steps, Seattle Repertory Theatre, 1982–83.

The Vinegar Tree, Seattle Repertory Theatre, 1982–83.

Shivaree, Long Wharf Theatre, New Haven, CT, then Seattle Repertory Theatre, 1983–84.

Make and Break, Seattle Repertory Theatre, 1983–84.

As You Like It, Seattle Repertory Theatre, 1983–84.

Our Town, Seattle Repertory Theatre, 1984–85.

The Mandrake and *The Wedding* (double–bill), Seattle Repertory Theatre, 1984–85.

The Merry Wives of Windsor, Old Globe Theatre, San Diego, CA, 1984–85.

I'm Not Rappaport, Seattle Repertory Theatre, 1984–85, then American Place Theatre, New York City, 1985, later Booth Theatre, New York City, 1985–88.

Girl Crazy, Seattle Repertory Theatre, 1985–86.

The Merry Wives of Windsor, Seattle Repertory Theatre, 1985–86.

Cat's–Paw, Seattle Repertory Theatre, 1986.

Red Square, Seattle Repertory Theatre, 1987.

The Heidi Chronicles, Playwrights Horizons Theatre, New York City, 1988–89, then Plymouth Theatre, New York City, 1989–90.

The Cherry Orchard, Seattle Repertory Theatre, 1989–90.

Robbers, Seattle Repertory Theatre, 1989–90.

Inspecting Carol, Seattle Repertory Company, 1991.

Conversations with My Father, Seattle Repertory Theatre, 1991, then Royale Theatre, New York City, 1992–93, later Center Theatre Group, Ahmanson Theatre, Los Angeles, 1993.

The Substance of Fire, Playwrights Horizons Theatre, 1991, then Mitzi E. Newhouse Theatre, New York City, 1992, later Center Theatre Group, Music Center of Los Angeles County, Los Angeles, 1993.

The Sisters Rosensweig, Mitzi E. Newhouse Theatre, 1992–93, then Ethel Barrymore Theatre, New York City, 1993–94.

The Merry Wives of Windsor, New York Shakespeare Festival, Delacorte Theatre, Public Theatre, New York City, 1994.

London Suite, Union Square Theatre, New York City, 1995.

A Fair Country, Mitzi E. Newhouse Theatre, 1996.

An American Daughter, Cort Theatre, New York City, 1997.

Psychopathia Sexualis, City Center Stage, New York City, then Manhattan Theatre Club Stage I, New York City, 1997.

Ah, Wilderness!, Lincoln Auditorium, Vivian Beaumont Theatre, Lincoln Center, 1998.

Far East, Mitzi E. Newhouse Theatre, 1998–99.

Dinner with Friends, Variety Arts Theatre, New York City, 1999–2001.

A Moon for the Misbegotten, Walter Kerr Theatre, New York City, 2000.

Proof, Manhattan Theatre Club Stage II, then Walter Kerr Theatre, beginning 2000.

Spinning into Butter, Mitzi E. Newhouse Theatre, 2000.

Major Barbara, Roundabout Theatre Company, American Airlines Theatre, New York City, 2001.

Ten Unknowns, Lincoln Center Theatre, 2001.

In Real Life, Manhattan Theatre Club Stage II, 2002.

I'm Not Rappaport, Booth Theatre, 2002.

Morning's at Seven, Lyceum Theatre, New York City, 2002.

Short Talks on the Universe (collection of short plays), Eugene O'Neill Theatre, New York City, 2002.

The Retreat from Moscow, Booth Theatre, 2003–2004.

Sight Unseen, Manhattan Theatre Club, Biltmore Theatre, New York City, 2004.

Intimate Apparel, Roundabout Theatre Company, Laura Pels Theatre, New York City, 2004.

Third, Mitzi E. Newhouse Theatre, 2005.

Brooklyn Boy, Manhattan Theatre Club, Biltmore Theatre, 2005.

Julius Caesar, Belasco Theatre, New York City, 2005.

After the Night and the Music, Manhattan Theatre Club, Biltmore Theatre, 2005.

Stuff Happens, Estelle R. Newman Theatre, Public Theatre, New York City, 2006.

Rabbit Hole, Manhattan Theatre Club, Biltmore Theatre, 2006.

Prelude to a Kiss, Roundabout Theatre Company, American Airlines Theatre, 2007.

The Homecoming, Cort Theatre, 2007–2008.

A Midsummer Night's Dream, Delacorte Theatre, Public Theatre, 2009.

The Night Watcher, Primary Stages, 59E59 Theatre A, New York City, 2009.

Accent on Youth, Samuel J. Friedman Theatre, New York City, 2009.

Time Stands Still, Samuel J. Friedman Theatre, 2010.

Major Tours; Director:

I'm Not Rappaport, U.S. cities, 1986–87.

The Heidi Chronicles, U.S. cities, 1990.

The Sisters Rosensweig, U.S. cities, 1994.

Stage Appearances:

Trojan and understudy for the roles of Anchises, Topman, and Olpides, *Tiger at the Gates,* Vivian Beaumont Theatre, Lincoln Center, New York City, 1968.

Harry, *The Time of Your Life,* Vivian Beaumont Theatre, Lincoln Center, 1969.

Navigator, *Camino Real,* Vivian Beaumont Theatre, Lincoln Center, 1970.

Night, *Amphitryon,* Repertory Theatre of Lincoln Center, Forum Theatre (now Mitzi E. Newhouse Theatre), New York City, 1970.

Brother, *The Good Woman of Setzuan,* Vivian Beaumont Theatre, Lincoln Center, 1970.

Understudy for the role of Jimmy Farrell, *The Playboy of the Western World,* Vivian Beaumont Theatre, Lincoln Center, 1971.

Understudy for the role of Stanley, *The Birthday Party,* Forum Theatre, 1971.

Bates, *Landscape and Silence,* Forum Theatre, 1971.

Yakima, *Enemies,* Vivian Beaumont Theatre, Lincoln Center, 1972.

Launcelot Gobbo, *The Merchant of Venice,* Vivian Beaumont Theatre, Lincoln Center, 1973.

Pablo Gonzalez and understudy for the role of Stanley Kowalski, *A Streetcar Named Desire,* Vivian Beaumont Theatre, Lincoln Center, 1973.

Savages, Center Theatre Group, Mark Taper Forum, Los Angeles, 1974–75.

Prologue and Timoteo, *The Mandrake,* and Her Husband, *The Wedding* (double–bill), Seattle Repertory Theatre, Seattle, WA, 1984–85.

Dr. Caius, *The Merry Wives of Windsor,* Seattle Repertory Theatre, 1985–86.

Mr. Feathers, *Robbers,* Seattle Repertory Theatre, 1989–90.

Film Director:

The Substance of Fire, Miramax, 1996.

Television Appearances; Episodic:

"Directors on Directing," *Working in the Theatre,* 2008.

Broadway Beat, 2007, 2008.

WRITINGS

Plays:

The Mandrake (adaptation of work by Niccolo Machiavelli; double–bill with *The Wedding*), Seattle Repertory Theatre, Seattle, WA, 1984–85.

Girl Crazy (adaptation of original play by Guy Bolton and John McGowan), music by George Gershwin, lyrics by Ira Gershwin, Seattle Repertory Theatre, 1985–86.

Truffles in the Soup, 1988.

Inspecting Carol, Seattle Repertory Theatre, 1991.

Songs Featured in Films:

Lyricist, *The Substance of Fire,* Miramax, 1996.

ADAPTATIONS

The stage production of *Far East,* as directed by Sullivan, was later broadcast as a television special by PBS, 2001.

OTHER SOURCES

Periodicals:

American Theatre, March, 2007, p. 26.

SUPMAN, Milton
      See SALES, Soupy

SWAN, Wendee
      See LEE, Wendee

T

THOMAS, Bob
  See NORRIS, Daran

THOMAS, Rob
  See NORRIS, Daran

THOMSON, Erik 1967–

PERSONAL

Born April 27, 1967, in Inverness, Scotland; raised in New Zealand; married Caitlin McDougall (an actress), April 7, 1999. *Education:* Victoria University, Wellington, New Zealand, B.A.; New Zealand Drama School, B.F.A.

Addresses: *Agent*—RGM Associates, 64–76 Kippax St., Suites 202, 206 Level 2, Surry Hills, New South Wales 2010, Australia.

Career: Actor.

Awards, Honors: Silver Logie Award, 2003, and Silver Logie Award nomination, 2004, both most popular actor, *TV Week* (Australia), for *All Saints;* Australian Film Institute Award and Film Critics Circle of Australia Award nomination, both best supporting actor, 2004, for *Somersault;* Australian Film Institute Award nomination, best supporting actor, 2008, for *The Black Balloon;* Film Award nomination, best leading actor, New Zealand Film and Television Awards, 2008, for *We're Here to Help;* Silver Logie Award nomination, most popular actor, 2009, for *Packed to the Rafters.*

Film Appearances:
Title role, *Justin Brown,* Forever and a Day Filmworks, 2001.
Richard, *Somersault,* 2004, Magnolia Pictures, 2006.
Rob, *Tackle* (short film), Australian Film, Television, and Radio School, 2004.
Chas, *Man Janson* (short film), 2005.
Dave Henderson, *We're Here to Help,* South Pacific Pictures, 2007.
Simon Mollison, *The Black Balloon,* NeoClassics Films, 2008.
Mr. Thomson, *Beautiful,* Jump Street Films, 2009.
Digby, *The Boys Are Back,* Miramax, 2009.
Bob, *Accidents Happen,* Image Entertainment, 2010.

Television Appearances; Series:
James Rose, *Plainclothes,* TV New Zealand, 1995.
Brett Barrett, *Pacific Drive,* c. 1996.
Mitch Stevens, *All Saints* (also known as *All Saints: Medical Response Unit*), Seven Network, 1999–2003.
Presenter, *Getaway* (also known as *United Travel Getaway*), Nine Network, 2004–2007.
Jack Jaffers, *The Alice,* Nine Network, 2005–2006.
Dave Rafter, *Packed to the Rafters,* Nine Network, 2008–2009.

Television Appearances; Movies:
Kieron, *13 Gantry Row,* 1998.
Jack Jaffers, *The Alice,* 2004.
Rob, *BlackJack: Dead Memory,* Ten Network, 2006.

Television Appearances; Miniseries:
Professor James Cameron, *Through My Eyes* (also known as *Through My Eyes: The Lindy Chamberlain Story*), Seven Network, 2004.

Television Appearances; Specials:
The Best of Aussie Cop Shows, 2002.
The 2008 Australian Film Institute Awards, 2008.

Television Appearances; Episodic:
Young man, "By the Numbers," *The Ray Bradbury Theatre* (also known as *The Bradbury Trilogy, Mystery Theatre, The Ray Bradbury Theatre, Le monde fantastique de Ray Bradbury,* and *Ray Bradbury presente*), USA Network, 1992.
Wilcox, "Cash Crop," *High Tide,* syndicated, 1995.
Charles Hart, "Stalked," *High Tide,* syndicated, 1995.
King Daulin, "The Vanishing Dead," *Hercules: The Legendary Journeys,* syndicated, 1995.
Hades, "Death in Chains," *Xena: Warrior Princess* (also known as *Xena*), syndicated, 1995.
Hades, "The Other Side," *Hercules: The Legendary Journeys,* syndicated, 1995.
Hades, "Highway to Hades," *Hercules: The Legendary Journeys,* syndicated, 1995.
Hades, "Not Fade Away," *Hercules: The Legendary Journeys,* syndicated, 1996.
Hades, "Mortal Beloved," *Xena: Warrior Princess* (also known as *Xena*), syndicated, 1996.
Hades, "Intimate Stranger," *Xena: Warrior Princess* (also known as *Xena*), syndicated, 1996.
Hades, "Adventures in the Sin Trade: Part 1," *Xena: Warrior Princess* (also known as *Xena*), syndicated, 1996.
Joe, "Island of Adventure," *The Enid Blyton Adventure Series,* 1996.
Lloyd Menzies, "The Gingerbread Man," *Water Rats,* Nine Network, 1998.
Hades, "A Lady in Hades," *Young Hercules,* Fox, 1998.
Paul Duncan, *Wildside,* ABC (Australia), 1999.
"All Saints Special," *The Weakest Link,* BBC, 2001.
Fantasy Greg, "Here We Go Again," *Always Greener,* Seven Network, 2002.
Micallef Tonight, Nine Network, 2003.
David Simpson, "A Human Cost: Parts 1–4," *MDA,* Australian Broadcasting Corporation, 2005.
Sunrise, Seven Network, 2009.
The 7PM Project, Ten Network, 2009.

Stage Appearances:
Performed in several Shakespearean plays, including *Julius Caesar,* and in *Angels in America* and *Twelve Angry Men.*

TOCHI, Brian 1959–
     (Brian Keith Tochi, Brian Toshi)

PERSONAL

Full name, Brian Keith Tochi; born May 2, 1959, in Los Angeles, CA. *Education:* Attended the University of Southern California, University of California at Los Angeles, and University of California at Irvine.

Addresses: *Contact*—Abrams Artists Agency, CA.

Career: Actor and voice artist. Involved with such causes as Famous Phone Friends, Make–A–Wish Foundation, Special Olympics, and Young Artists United.

CREDITS

Film Appearances:
Tommy, *The Omega Man,* Warner Bros., 1971.
Seikura at age eighteen, *The Octagon* (also known as *The Man without Mercy*), Danton Films, 1980.
Toshiro Takashi, Tri–Lam, *Revenge of the Nerds,* Twentieth Century–Fox, 1984.
Sam Boon Tong, *Stitches,* International Film Marketing, 1985.
Cadet Nogata, *Police Academy 3: Back in Training,* Warner Bros., 1986.
Nogata, *Police Academy 4: Citizens on Patrol* (also known as *Citizens on Patrol: Police Academy 4*), Warner Bros., 1987.
Stockbroker, *One Man Force,* Shapiro–Glickenhaus Entertainment, 1989.
Voice of Leonardo, *Teenage Mutant Ninja Turtles* (also known as *Teenage Mutant Ninja Turtles: The Movie* and *Teenage Mutant Ninja Turtles: The Original Movie*), New Line Cinema, 1990.
Voice of Leonardo, *Teenage Mutant Ninja Turtles II: The Secret of the Ooze,* New Line Cinema, 1991.
Himself, *The Player,* Fine Line, 1992.
Voice of Leonardo, *Teenage Mutant Ninja Turtles III,* New Line Cinema, 1993.
(Uncredited) Voice of the fighting hyena, *The Lion King* (animated; also known as *El rey leon*), 1994.
Asian boy, *Critics and Other Freaks,* 1997.
(Uncredited) Concert security chief, *Fathers' Day,* 1997.
(Uncredited) Male trooper, *Starship Trooper,* 1997.
(Uncredited) Fight bully, *Fight Club,* 1999.
Kim Pao, *The Silent Force,* Vision Films, 2001.
Charlie Watanabe at age thirty–three, *The Boys of Sunset Ridge,* PorchLight Entertainment, 2001.
Voice of Mighty Steel Leg Sing, *Siu lam juk kau* (animated; also known as *Shaolin Soccer* and *Shao lin zu qiu*), 2001.
(Uncredited) Voice of Makani, *Forgetting Sarah Marshall,* Universal, 2008.
Preacher, *I Do* (short film), The Pond Productions, 2009.

Film Additional Voices:
(Uncredited) *The Prince of Egypt* (animated), 1998.
The Iron Giant, Warner Bros., 1999.
Mulan II (animated), Buena Vista Home Video, 2004.

Television Appearances; Series:
Voice of Alan Chan, *The Amazing Chan and the Chan Clan* (animated), CBS, 1972.

Crown Prince Chulalongkorn, *Anna and the King,* CBS, 1972.

Tee Gar "Teegar" Soom, *Space Academy,* CBS, 1977–81.

Host, *Razzmatazz,* 1979–82.

Dragon, *The Renegades,* ABC, 1983.

Kai, *Santa Barbara,* NBC, 1988–90.

Chief foreign correspondent, *Channel One News,* 1990–93.

Voice of Liu Kang, *Mortal Kombat: The Animated Series* (animated; also known as *Mortal Kombat: Defenders of the Realm*), USA Network, 1995.

Voice of Master Hama and others, *Johnny Bravo* (animated), 1999–2001.

Voice of Shiv, *Static Shock* (animated), The WB, 2000–2004.

Television Appearances; Movies:

Ling, *We're Fighting Back,* CBS, 1981.

Toshiro Takashi, *Revenge of the Nerds III: The Next Generation,* Fox, 1992.

Takashi, *Revenge of the Nerds IV: Nerds in Love,* Fox, 1994.

Television Appearances; Specials:

Voice of guard, "Yeh–Shen: A Cinderella Story from China," *CBS Storybreak,* CBS, 1985.

Television Appearances; Pilots:

Dragon, *Renegades,* ABC, 1982.

Television Appearances; Episodic:

Kim, "Along Came Kim," *He & She,* 1968.

Ray Tsingtao, "And the Children Shall Lead," *Star Trek* (also known as *Star Trek: TOS* and *Star Trek: The Original Series*), NBC, 1968.

Tommy, "What Goes Up …," *The Brady Bunch,* ABC, 1970.

Young boy, "A Tale of Two Hamsters," *The Partridge Family,* ABC, 1971.

Jimmy Okura, "One for the Road," *Nanny and the Professor,* ABC, 1971.

Chin, "One Lonely Step," *The Bold Ones: The New Doctors* (also known as *The New Doctors*), 1971.

Flower boy, "Assassination," *Adam–12,* 1971.

Max Redding, "This Is Max," *Marcus Welby, M.D.* (also known as *Robert Young, Family Doctor*), ABC, 1971.

Ho Fong, "The Tide," *Kung Fu,* ABC, 1973.

Davie Simms, "Trail of the Serpent," *The Streets of San Francisco,* 1973.

Shen Ung, "The Demon God," *Kung Fu,* ABC, 1974.

Davey, "Year of the Dragon: Parts 1 & 2," *Police Story,* 1975.

Larry, "Strike II," *Marcus Welby, M.D.* (also known as *Robert Young, Family Doctor*), ABC, 1976.

Joey Lee, "The Pagoda Factor," *Hawaii Five–O* (also known as *McGarrett*), CBS, 1978.

Darrell, "The Deadly Dolphin," *Wonder Woman* (also known as *The New Adventures of Wonder Woman* and *The New Original Wonder Woman*), CBS, 1978.

Joey Lee, "Number One with a Bullet: Parts 1 & 2," *Hawaii Five–O* (also known as *McGarrett*), CBS, 1978–79.

Jonathan Chan, "Out–of–Time Step," *The Master* (also known as *Master Ninja*), NBC, 1984.

Dr. Alan Poe, "Playing God: Part 1," *St. Elsewhere,* NBC, 1984.

David Wong, "Wong's Lost and Found Emporium," *The Twilight Zone* (also known as *The New Twilight Zone*), CBS, 1985.

Voice of Bunjiro "Bunji" Bennet, Karate–1, and Rivet Rick, "The Glitch," *Bionic Six* (animated), 1987.

Ensign Peter Lin, "Night Terrors," *Star Trek: The Next Generation* (also known as *Star Trek: TNG*), syndicated, 1991.

Eddie Lok, "Murder in the Courthouse," *Diagnosis Murder,* CBS, 1995.

Voice of the tailor, "Little Red Riding Hood," *Happily Ever After: Fairy Tales for Every Child* (animated), HBO, 1995.

Voice, "The Emperor's New Clothes," *Happily Ever After: Fairy Tales for Every Child* (animated), HBO, 1995.

Ricky, "Lock and Load, Babe," *Vanishing Son,* 1995.

Voice of Sushi Master, "Something Fishy Around Here," *The Sylvester & Tweety Mysteries* (animated), 1995.

Voice of first technician and terrorist pilot, "Nemesis," *The Real Adventures of Jonny Quest* (animated; also known as *Jonny Quest: The Real Adventures*), Cartoon Network and syndicated, 1996.

Voice of Ken Otsuki, "Other Space," *The Real Adventures of Jonny Quest* (animated; also known as *Jonny Quest: The Real Adventures*), Cartoon Network and syndicated, 1997.

Voice of Turtle photographer and Tsui, "The Little Mermaid, *Happily Ever After: Fairy Tales for Every Child* (animated), HBO, 1997.

(As Brian Toshi) Voice of Toshi, Japanese dad, Japanese boy number one, and Japanese boy number three, "Last But Not Beast," *Dexter's Laboratory* (animated; also known as *Dexter de Shinyanshi* and *Dexter's Lab*), Cartoon Network, 1998.

Voice of Albino, "Mind Games," *Batman Beyond* (animated; also known as *Batman of the Future*), The WB, 1999.

Voice of Hiro, "Sense and Sensitivity," *The Weekenders* (animated; also known as *Disney's "The Weekenders"*), 2000.

Voice of boy and Kid B, "Jack and the Shoes," *Samurai Jack* (animated), Cartoon Network, 2001.

Chef, "Billy's Growth Spurt/The Time Hole Incident/Billy and the Bully," *Grim & Evil* (animated; also known as *The Grim Adventures of Billy and Mandy*), Cartoon Network, 2002.

Announcer and television chef, "Little Rock of Horror/The Pie Who Loved Me/Dream a Little Dream,"

Grim & Evil (animated; also known as *The Grim Adventures of Billy and Mandy*), Cartoon Network, 2002.

Voice of Hakimoto, "3–D Struction," *What's New Scooby–Doo?* (animated), The WB, 2002.

Voice of J. J. Hakimoto, "The Vampire Strikes Back," *What's New Scooby–Doo?* (animated), The WB, 2003.

Voice, "Exchange," *Kim Possible* (also known as *Disney's "Kim Possible"*), The Disney Channel, 2003.

Voice of Cheese Ninja leader, "Operation: T.H.E.–S.H.O.G.U.N./Operation: C.O.L.L.E.G.E.," *Codename: Kids Next Door* (animated), Cartoon Network, 2003.

Voice of Asian police pilot, "Breaking Out Is Hard to Do," *Family Guy* (animated; also known as *Padre de familia*), Fox, 2005.

Voice of the Whoosh, "Master & Disaster/All in the Crime Family," *Duck Dodgers* (animated; also known as *Duck Dodgers in the 24 1/2th Century*), Cartoon Network, 2005.

Voice of Than, "The Serpent's Pass," *Avatar: The Last Airbender* (animated), Nickelodeon, 2006.

Voice of Ham Ghao, "The Firebending Masters," *Avatar: The Last Airbender* (animated), Nickelodeon, 2008.

Also appeared as voice of Mr. Briggs, "Stuff'll Kill Ya," *As Told by Ginger* (animated), Nickelodeon; voice of the tourist kid number two, "R.V. Having Fun Yet?," *All Grown Up* (animated; also known as *Rugrats All Grown Up*), Nickelodeon.

Television Additional Voices; Series:
Scooby and Scrappy–Doo (animated), ABC, 1979.
Challenge of the GoBots (animated), syndicated, 1984.
The Karate Kid (animated), NBC, 1989.

Also provided additional voices for *Captain Planet and the Planeteers* (animated).

Television Work; Movies:
(As Brian Keith Tochi) Producer, supervising producer, director, and production supervisor, *Tales of a Fly on the Wall*, 2004.

Television Additional Voices; Episodic:
(Uncredited) "City of Walls and Secrets," *Avatar: The Last Airbender* (animated), 2006.

RECORDINGS

Video Games:
(Uncredited) Voice of Fei Fong Wong, *Xenogears*, 1998.
(English version) Voice of Wisdom Official Venom and Wisdom Official Raven, *EOE: Eve of Extinction* (also known as *EOE: Hokai no zenya*), Eidos Interactive, 2002.

(English version) *Tenchu san* (also known as *Tenchu: Wrath of Heaven*), Activision, 2003.

Voice of Kang Brother, *True Crime: Streets of LA*, Activision, 2003.

Voice of Paladin, Guard number one, and Soldier number one, *Jumper* (also known as *Jumper: Griffin's Story*), RedTribe and Collision Studios, 2008.

(Uncredited) Voice of Imperial Ore collector and Imperial Nanocore, *Command & Conquer: Red Alert 3*, 2008.

Video Games; as Additional Voices:
Bruce Lee: Quest of the Dragon, 2002.
True Crime: Streets of LA, Activision, 2003.
Area 51, Midway Manufacturing Company, 2005.

WRITINGS

Television Movies:
Tales of a Fly on the Wall, 2004.

OTHER SOURCES

Periodicals:
Star Trek Communicator, February, 1998, pp. 68–69.

TODD, Hallie 1962–

PERSONAL

Birth name, Hallie Eckstein; born January 7, 1962, in Los Angeles, CA; daughter of George Eckstein (a writer and producer) and Ann Morgan Guilbert (an actress); married Glenn Withrow (an actor), 1991; children: Ivy. *Education:* Attended Idyllwild School of Music and Arts, University of Southern California.

Addresses: *Office*—Hallie Todd Studios, 13636 Ventura Blvd., Suite 298, Sherman Oaks, CA 91423.

Career: Actress. In House Media, Inc. (a production facility and acting conservatory), Burbank then Sherman Oaks, CA, cofounder; Hallie Todd Studios (an acting conservatory), Sherman Oaks, CA, acting teacher.

Awards, Honors: CableACE Award nomination, actress in a comedy series, National Cable Television Association, 1987, for *Brothers*.

CREDITS

Film Appearances:
(Uncredited) Linda's friend, *Fast Times at Ridgemont High* (also known as *Fast Times*), 1982.

Cathy Stanton, *Sam's Son*, Invictus, 1984.
Robin Jackson, *The Check Is in the Mail …* (also known as *The Cheque Is in the Post*), Ascot Films, 1986.
Mrs. "Jo" McGuire, *The Lizzie McGuire Movie*, Buena Vista, 2003.
Herself, *Hilary's Roman Adventure* (short documentary), 2004.
Nancy, *The Mooring*, 2010.

Film Work:
Executive producer, *The Mooring*, 2010.

Television Appearances; Series:
Patti Eubanks, *The Best of Times* (also known as *Changing Times*), CBS, 1983.
Penny Waters, *Brothers*, Showtime, 1984–89.
Rhoda Markowitz, *Murder, She Wrote*, CBS, 1990–91.
Kate Griffith, *Going Places*, ABC, 1990–91.
Lanie Clark, *Life with Roger*, The WB, 1996–97.
Mrs. "Jo" McGuire, *Lizzie McGuire*, The Disney Channel, 2001–2004.

Television Appearances; Movies:
Joann Fray, *Who Will Love My Children?*, ABC, 1983.
Michelle Thompson, *The Ultimate Christmas Present*, The Disney Channel, 2000.
Jill Snider, *Thanksgiving Family Reunion* (also known as *National Lampoon's "Holiday Reunion," Holiday Reunion, National Lampoon's "Thanksgiving Family Reunion,"* and *National Lampoon's "Thanksgiving Reunion"*), TBS, 2003.

Television Appearances; Specials:
Brenda, "Have You Ever Been Ashamed of Your Parents?," *ABC Afterschool Specials*, ABC, 1983.
Express Yourself, 2001.

Television Appearances; Pilots:
Patti Eubanks, *The Best of Times* (also known as *Changing Times*), CBS, 1983.

Television Appearances; Episodic:
Marci Murdock, "Daylight Serenade," *Family*, 1980.
Cindy DeGeralimo, "Cindy," *Highway to Heaven*, NBC, 1985.
Lucy, "Nice and Easy," *The Golden Girls*, NBC, 1986.
Denise, "The Kid," *Growing Pains*, ABC, 1986.
Alison, *Heartbeat*, ABC, 1988.
Moira McShane, "Class Act," *Murder, She Wrote*, CBS, 1989.
Lal, "The Offspring," *Star Trek: The Next Generation* (also known as *Star Trek: TNG*), syndicated, 1990.
Ellen Maddox, "The Birds and the Elephants," *Laurie Hill*, ABC, 1992.
Miss Chapin, "In the Still of the Night," *Brooklyn Bridge*, CBS, 1992.

Monica Reese, "Chapter Eighteen," *Murder One*, ABC, 1996.
Susan Stimpson, "Left–Handed Murder," *Diagnosis Murder*, CBS, 1996.
Julie, *Fast Forward*, ABC, 1997.
Marci, "Breaking Them Up Is Hard to Do," *Two of a Kind*, ABC, 1998.
Marigold, "Sabrina the Matchmaker," *Sabrina, the Teenage Witch* (also known as *Sabrina*), ABC, 1999.
Hollywood Squares (also known as *H2* and *H2: Hollywood Squares*), syndicated, 2003.
Voice of Summer Gale, "Day of the Snowmen," *Kim Possible* (animated; also known as *Disney's "Kim Possible"*), The Disney Channel, 2003.
Miss Shaw, "Dirty Magazine," *Malcolm in the Middle*, Fox, 2004.
Voice of Dr. Phyliss, "Freaky Tuesday," *Brandy & Mr. Whiskers* (animated; also known as *Disney's "Brandy & Mr. Whiskers"*), The Disney Channel, 2005.

WRITINGS

Screenplays:
The Mooring, 2010.

OTHER SOURCES

Electronic:
Hallie Todd Official Site, http://www.hallietoddstudios.com, February 10, 2010.

TODD, Jerry J.
 See CORLETT, Ian James

TODD, Richard 1919–2009
 (Richard Andrew Palethorpe Todd)

PERSONAL

Full name, Richard Andrew Palethorpe Todd; born June 11, 1919, in Dublin, Ireland; died of cancer, December 3, 2009, in Little Humby, Lincolnshire, England. Actor. Todd's fame reached its peak early in his career with leading roles in the 1950s. He debuted as an actor in a 1936 London stage production of *Twelfth Night*. In 1945 he played Corporal Lachlan "Lachie" MacLachlan in a New York production of *The Hasty Heart*. He reprised the role in the 1949 film version, and his performance garnered him an Academy Award nomination. In the following decades he was a character actor known for his military roles: he appeared in the 1954 film *The Dam Busters,* which chronicles the deeds of the Royal Air Force during World War II, and the 1962 film *The Longest Day,* about D-Day. Todd also acted in Alfred Hitchcock's *Stage Fright* and in film versions of *Saint Joan* and *Dorian Gray.* His final film performance was in *Murder One* in 1988. In television Todd guest starred in episodes of such British series as *Midsomer Murders, Heartbeat,* and *Doctor Who,* and he was a regular on *Boy Dominic,* which aired in the mid-1970s. In 1993 Todd was awarded the Order of the British Empire.

PERIODICALS

Daily Mail, December 5, 2009.
Guardian, December 4, 2009.
New York Times, December 5, 2009.
Times (London), December 5, 2009.

TRAMMELL, Sam 1971–

PERSONAL

Born May 15, 1971, in New Orleans, LA. *Education:* Brown University, B.A., semiotics; also studied philosophy at the University of Paris.

Addresses: *Agent*—Innovative Artists, 1505 10th St., Santa Monica, CA 90401. *Publicist*—Marleah Leslie and Associates, 1645 North Vine St., Suite 712, Los Angeles, CA 90028.

Career: Actor. Appeared in productions at Barrington Stage Festival, Delaware Theatre Company, Wilmington, DE, Hartford Stage Company, Hartford, CT, Manitoba Theatre Center, New York Stage and Film Theatre, New York City, Rushmore Festival, and Williamstown Theatre Festival, Williamstown, MA.

Awards, Honors: *Theatre World* Award, outstanding new performer, Antoinette Perry Award nomination, best featured actor in a play, Clarence Derwent Award, outstanding Broadway debut, Drama League Award, 1998, all for *Ah, Wilderness!;* Special Achievement Award (with others), Satellite Awards best ensemble—television, International Press Academy, 2009, Screen Actors Guild Award nomination (with others), outstanding performance by an ensemble in a drama series, 2010, both for *True Blood.*

CREDITS

Stage Appearances:
Tommy, *The Cover of Life,* Hartford, CT, 1992–93.

Understudy for Jack, *The Rose Tattoo,* Circle in the Square Uptown, New York City, 1995.
Frankie, *A Lie of the Mind,* One Dream Theatre, 1995.
Carl, *Dealer's Choice,* Manhattan Theatre Club Stage II, New York City, 1997.
Eric, *My Night with Reg,* New Group, Intar Hispanic American Theatre, New York City, 1997.
Richard, *Ah, Wilderness!,* Vivian Beaumont Theatre, Lincoln Center, New York City, 1998.
Russel Burke and Adam Burke, *If Memory Serves,* Promenade Theatre, New York City, 1999.
Kit Marlowe, Joseph Papp Public Theatre, Newman Theatre, New York City, 2000.
Brandon, *Rope,* Zipper Theatre, New York City, 2005.

Also appeared in *Ancestral Voices,* Lincoln Center Theatre, New York City.

Film Appearances:
Nolan, *The Hotel Manor Inn,* 1994.
Greg Chute, *Childhood's End,* 1996.
Will, *Wrestling with Alligators,* Homegrown Pictures/ Portman Productions, 1998.
Lee, *Beat,* 2000.
Red Hopkins and Tom Hopkins, *Fear of Fiction,* 2000.
Simon, *Autumn in New York,* Metro–Goldwyn–Mayer, 2000.
John Dietrich, *Followers,* Castle Hill, 2000.
Derrick Hall/Zane Waye, *Undermind,* Double A Films/ Vertical Pictures, 2002.
The Last Full Measure (short film), American Film Institute, 2004.
Tim, *AVPR: Aliens vs Predator—Requiem* (also known as *AVP: Aliens vs. Predator—Requiem, AVP: Requiem, Aliens vs. Predator 2, AvP2,* and *AvPR*), Twentieth Century–Fox, 2007.
Taylor, *Miracle of Phil* (short film), 2008.
The Details, 2010.

Television Appearances; Series:
Liam McCallister, *Trinity,* NBC, 1998.
Kevin "Space" Lauglin, *Going to California,* Showtime, 2001–2002.
Sam Merlotte, *True Blood,* HBO, 2008—.

Television Appearances; Movies:
Simon Troyer, "Harvest of Fire," *Hallmark Hall of Fame,* CBS, 1996.
Vincent Rubio, *Anonymous Rex,* Sci–Fi Channel, 2004.
Jeff, *What If God Were the Sun?,* Lifetime, 2007.

Television Appearances; Specials:
VH1 Divas Live 2009, VH1, 2009.
Scream Awards (also known as *Scream 2009*), Spike TV, 2009.

Television Appearances; Pilots:

Sonny Dupree, *Maximum Bob,* ABC, 1998.

Sullivan Street, The WB, 2000.

Ken Thompson, *Bones,* Fox, 2005.

Kevin O'Neil, *Justice,* Fox, 2006.

Television Appearances; Episodic:

Sonny Dupree, "Once Bitten …," *Maximum Bob,* ABC, 1998.

Ethan Hartig, "Maternity," *House M.D.* (also known as *House*), Fox, 2004.

Kiko Ellsworth, "First Response," *Strong Medicine,* Lifetime, 2005.

Marty Levine, "The Paper War," *Judging Amy,* CBS, 2005.

Marty Levine, "Revolutions Per Minute," *Judging Amy,* CBS, 2005.

Marty Levine, "My Name Is Amy Gray …," *Judging Amy,* CBS, 2005.

Charles Wright, "Heroes," *CSI: NY* (also known as *CSI: New York*), CBS, 2006.

Thomas Gill, "Hot Shot," *Numb3rs* (also known as *Num3ers*), CBS, 2006.

Matt Chambers, "Crocodile," *Dexter,* Showtime, 2006.

Porter Rawley in 1981, "Blood on the Tracks," *Cold Case,* CBS, 2007.

The Bonnie Hunt Show, CBS, 2008.

"Kia," *Free Radio,* VH1, 2009.

Chelsea Lately, E! Entertainment Television, 2009.

Dr. Brian Seward, "Things to Do in Phoenix When You're Dead," *Medium,* NBC, 2009.

Gray Vanderhoven, "Identity Crisis," *Law & Order: Criminal Intent* (also known as *Law & Order: CI*), NBC, 2009.

Also appeared in *As the World Turns; One Life to Live.*

OTHER SOURCES

Periodicals:

Back Stage, July 18, 1997, pp. 33–35.

Variety, March 23, 1998, p. 98.

TRAVANTI, Daniel J. 1940–

(Dan Travanti, Dan Travanty, Daniel Travanty, Don Travanty)

PERSONAL

Full name, Danielo Giovanni Travanti; born March 7, 1940, in Kenosha, WI; son of John (an auto worker) and Elvira (maiden name, DeAngelis) Travanti. *Education:* University of Wisconsin, B.A.; Loyola Marymount University, Los Angeles, M.A., English literature, 1978; studied drama at Yale University, 1961–62.

Addresses: *Agent*—TGMD Talent Agency, 6767 Forest Lawn Dr., Suite 101, Los Angeles, CA 90068.

Career: Actor. *Military service:* U.S. Army, c. 1963.

Member: Phi Beta Kappa.

Awards, Honors: Woodrow Wilson fellowship, 1961–62; Emmy Awards, outstanding lead actor in a drama series, 1981, 1982, Golden Globe Award, best actor in a television series, 1982, Golden Globe Award nominations, best actor in a television series, 1983, 1984, 1985, 1986, Emmy Award nominations, outstanding lead actor in a drama series, 1983, 1984, 1985, Q Award, best actor in a quality drama series, Viewers for Quality Television, 1985, TV Land Award nomination, favorite crimestopper in a drama, 2003, all for *Hill Street Blues;* CableACE Award nomination, actor in a dramatic or theatrical program, National Cable Television Association, 1984, for *A Case of Libel;* CableACE Award nomination, actor in a movie or miniseries, 1987, for *Murrow;* Wisconsin Performing Arts Hall of Fame, inductee, 1994; Joseph Jefferson Award nomination, best actor in a principal role in a play, 1999, for *Old Wicked Songs.*

CREDITS

Film Appearances:

(As Dan Travanty) Carlo, *Who Killed Teddy Bear,* 1965.

(As Dan Travanty) Sergeant Chassman, *The Organization,* Twentieth Century–Fox, 1971.

Johnny Parisi, *St. Ives,* Warner Bros., 1976.

Interviewer, *It's My Turn* (also known as *A Perfect Circle*), 1980.

Morely Barton, *Midnight Crossing,* Vestron, 1988.

Dr. Arnold Mayer, *Millennium,* Twentieth Century–Fox, 1989.

Jerry Leavy, *Fellow Traveller,* Paramount, 1989.

Duprell, *Megaville,* 1991.

Hello Stranger, 1992.

Skin, 1992.

Warden, *Just Cause,* Warner Bros., 1995.

Mario Moretti, *Shao Nu xiao yu* (also known as *Siao Yu* and *Shao nyu siao yu*), EDKO Film, 1995.

Harrison, *Something Sweet,* Cineblast Productions/Gel Films, 2000.

Peter Mallow, *Design,* Traveller Jones Productions, 2002.

Dr. Wayne, *For Earth Below,* 2002.

Interviewee, *Wisconsin Born & Bred: The Entertainers* (documentary), 2004.

Television Appearances; Series:
Spence Andrews, *General Hospital,* ABC, 1979.
Captain Frank Furillo, *Hill Street Blues,* NBC, 1981–87.
Lieutenant Ray McAuliffe, *Missing Persons,* ABC, 1993–94.
William Sloan, *Poltergeist: The Legacy,* Showtime and Sci–Fi Channel, 1997.

Television Appearances; Movies:
(As Dan Travanty) Tod, *The Love War,* ABC, 1970.
John Walsh, *Adam,* NBC, 1983.
David Ackermann, *Aurora* (also known as *Aurora by Night, Encounter,* and *Qualcosa di biondo*), NBC, 1984.
John Walsh, *Adam: His Song Continues,* NBC, 1986.
Edward R. Murrow (title role), *Murrow,* HBO, 1986.
Charles "Joe" Hynes, *Howard Beach: Making the Case for Murder* (also known as *In the Line of Duty: Howard Beach, Making a Case for Murder* and *Skin*), NBC, 1989.
John Tagget, *Tagget* (also known as *Dragonfire*), USA Network, 1991.
Roy Baxter, *Eyes of a Witness* (also known as *Circumstantial Evidence*), CBS, 1991.
Ted, *Weep No More My Lady* (also known as *Pleure pas ma belle* and *Mary Higgins Clark: Ne pleure pas ma belle*), syndicated, 1992.
Alan Davies, *The Christmas Stallion* (also known as *The Winter Stallion*), syndicated, 1992.
Detective Drum London, *In the Shadows, Someone's Watching* (also known as *With Harmful Intent*), NBC, 1993.
Hal Bannister, *My Name Is Kate,* ABC, 1994.
Dr. Zinthorp, *The Wasp Woman* (also known as *Forbidden Beauty* and *Roger Corman Presents "The Wasp Woman"*), Showtime, 1995.
Principal Horace Weaver, *To Sir with Love II,* CBS, 1996.
Stan Douglas, *Murder in My House* (also known as *Blood Stains* and *Meurtre a domicile*), Lifetime, 2006.

Television Appearances; Specials:
The 33rd Annual Primetime Emmy Awards, 1981.
Night of 100 Stars, 1982.
NBC team captain, *Battle of the Network Stars XII,* ABC, 1982.
NBC team captain, *Battle of the Network Stars XIII,* ABC, 1982.
Parade of Stars, ABC, 1983.
Host and narrator, *To Protect the Children,* TBS, 1986.
NBC's 60th Anniversary Celebration, NBC, 1986.
Host and narrator, *How to Raise a Street Smart Child,* HBO, 1987.
Host, *The Prince's Trust Gala,* TBS, 1989.

Host, *Trial and Error,* Fox, 1992.
Presenter, *The 45th Annual Primetime Emmy Awards,* ABC, 1993.
Narrator, *Enrico Caruso: Voice of the Century,* 1998.
John Walsh: Fighting Back, 2002.
NBC 75th Anniversary Special (also known as *NBC 75th Anniversary Celebration*), NBC, 2002.

Television Appearances; Pilots:
John Henderson, *Call to Danger,* CBS, 1968.
Lieutenant Ray McAuliffe, *Missing Persons,* ABC, 1993.

Television Appearances; Episodic:
British soldier, "Little Moon of Alban," *Hallmark Hall of Fame* (also known as *Hallmark Television Playhouse*), 1958.
(As Dan Travanty) Marty Johnson, "Child of a Night," *Route 66,* CBS, 1964.
(As Dan Travanty) Paul Jerome, "The Name of the Game," *East Side/West Side,* CBS, 1964.
"Park Runs into Vreeland," *The Nurses,* CBS, 1964.
(As Dan Travanty) Moose, "Block That Statue," *Patty Duke Show,* ABC, 1964.
(As Dan Travanty) Detective Russo, "The Siege," *The Defenders,* CBS, 1964.
(As Dan Travanty) Cutler, "Murder by Scandal," *The Reporter,* 1964.
(As Dan Travanty) Dr. Van Houten, "Where the Park Runs into Vreeland," *Doctors and the Nurses* (also known as *The Nurses*), CBS, 1964.
(As Dan Travanty) Patrolman Sanders, "The Witnesses," *Doctors and the Nurses* (also known as *The Nurses*), CBS, 1965.
Tom Brighton, "Now There's a Face," *Gidget,* ABC, 1965.
(As Dan Travanty) Barney Austin, "The Case of the Midnight Howler," *Perry Mason,* CBS, 1966.
"One Picture Is Worth ...," *Love on a Rooftop,* ABC, 1966.
(As Dan Travanty) Luca, "The Deadly Goddess Affair," *The Man from U.N.C.L.E.,* 1966.
Commander Willard, "Flipper Joins the Navy: Parts 1 & 2," *Flipper,* 1966.
(As Daniel Travanty) "A Civil Case of Murder," *Judd, for the Defense,* ABC, 1967.
(As Dan Travanty) Space hippie, "Collision of the Planets," *Lost in Space,* CBS, 1967.
"The Man with Three Blue Eyes," *Captain Nice,* 1967.
Sears, "The House That Needed a Carpenter," *The Second Hundred Years,* ABC, 1968.
(As Dan Travanty) Roy Donald Blake, "Death of a Fixer," *The FBI,* ABC, 1968.
Sullivan, "A Jew Named Sullivan," *Here Come the Brides,* ABC, 1968.
(As Dan Travanty) "The Escape," *Lancer,* CBS, 1968.
(As Dan Travanty) Milo, "Child of Sorrow, Child of Light," *The Mod Squad,* ABC, 1969.

(As Don Travanty) George, "Willie Poor Boy," *The Mod Squad,* ABC, 1969.

(As Dan Travanty) Billy Jack Lyle, "The Diamond Millstone," *The FBI,* ABC, 1970.

(As Dan Travanty) "The Savage Image," *Medical Center,* CBS, 1970.

(As Dan Travanty) Strangler, "A Perfect Piece of Casting," *Bracken's World,* 1970.

(As Dan Travanty) Roland King, "War Games," *The Most Deadly Game,* 1970.

(As Dan Travanty) Joe Burland, "The Climate of Doubt," *Men at Law* (also known as *Storefront Lawyers*), CBS, 1971.

"A Bummer for R. J.," *The Mod Squad,* ABC, 1971.

(As Dan Travanty) Harry Random, "The Choice," *The Interns,* CBS, 1971.

Tom Stabler, "Murder Times Three," *Mannix,* CBS, 1971.

(As Dan Travanty) L. K. Ferris, "Devil's Playground," *Cannon,* CBS, 1972.

"Diagnosis: Corruption," *The Man and the City,* ABC, 1972.

(As Dan Travanty) Tony Gadsen, "Image," *Mission: Impossible,* CBS, 1972.

(As Dan Travanty) "The Franklin Papers," *The FBI,* ABC, 1972.

Lon Stevens, "Echo of a Murder, *Barnaby Jones,* CBS, 1973.

(As Dan Travanty) Frank, "Joie," *Love Story,* 1973.

(As Dan Travanty) Mr. Gianelli, "The Battle of the Groups," *The Bob Newhart Show,* CBS, 1974.

(As Dan Travanty) Aaron Barker, "Like Old Times," *Gunsmoke* (also known as *Gun Law* and *Marshal Dillon*), CBS, 1974.

Lieutenant Charles "Chuck" Danena, "A Souvenir from Atlantic City," *Kojak,* CBS, 1974.

(As Dan Travanty) Carl, "The Colonel," *Gunsmoke* (also known as *Gun Law* and *Marshal Dillon*), CBS, 1974.

Lloyd Kilgore, "Theatre of Fear," *Barnaby Jones,* CBS, 1975.

"Date Fright," *Phyllis,* CBS, 1975.

"The Frame," *Kojak,* CBS, 1976.

Fred Bender, "Sins of Thy Father," *Barnaby Jones,* CBS, 1976.

Captain Badaduchi, "A Grave Too Soon," *Kojak,* CBS, 1976.

Benjamin Maxwell, "More Things in Heaven and Earth," *Family,* ABC, 1977.

Shammah, "David & Goliath," *Greatest Heroes of the Bible,* 1978.

(As Dan Travanti) Edgar, "Max in Love," *Hart to Hart,* ABC, 1979.

Lieutenant Steinmetz, "The Constant Companion," *Knots Landing,* CBS, 1980.

Himself, "The Great 5K Star Race and Boulder Wrap Party: Part 2," *CHiPs* (also known as *CHiPs Patrol*), 1980.

Host, *Saturday Night Live* (also known as *SNL*), NBC, 1982.

Himself, "A View from the Bench," *Newhart,* CBS, 1983.

Boyd Bendix, "A Case of Libel," *American Playhouse,* PBS, 1985.

Gene Garrison, "I Never Sang for My Father," *American Playhouse,* PBS, 1988.

Aspel & Company, 1989.

Paul, "I Remember You," *General Motors Playwrights Theatre,* Arts and Entertainment, 1992.

Chairman Thornwell, "The Voice of Reason," *The Outer Limits* (also known as *The New Outer Limits*), Showtime and syndicated, 1995.

President Richard Mills, "Riots, Drills and the Devil: Part 1," *Prison Break* (also known as *Prison Break: On the Run*), Fox, 2005.

President Richard Mills, "Tonight," *Prison Break* (also known as *Prison Break: On the Run*), Fox, 2006.

Barry Patmore, "Here Comes the Flood," *Grey's Anatomy,* ABC, 2008.

Also appeared in "Flipper Joins the Navy," *Flipper.*

Stage Appearances:

Othello, New York Shakespeare Festival, New York City, 1965.

Twigs, Broadway production, 1973.

Old Wicked Songs, Old Globe Theatre, Apple Tree Theatre, Chicago, IL, 1999, then San Diego, CA, 2000.

Major Barbara, Pittsburgh Irish and Classical Theatre, Pittsburgh, PA, 2003.

Henry Grunwald, *The Last Word,* Theatre at St. Clement's, New York City, 2007.

Also appeared in productions of *Only Kidding; Les liaisons dangereuses; The Taming of the Shrew; A Touch of the Poet; Who's Afraid of Virginia Woolf?.*

Major Tours:

Who's Afraid of Virginia Woolf?, 1965.

Gene Garrison, *I Never Sang for My Father,* U.S. cities, 1988.

OTHER SOURCES

Periodicals:

USA Today, May 1, 2006, p. 4D.

TURNER, Kathleen 1954–

PERSONAL

Full name, Mary Kathleen Turner; born June 19, 1954, in Springfield, MO; daughter of Allen Richard (a foreign service officer) and Patsy Turner; married Jay Weiss (a real estate developer), 1984 (marriage ended, 2007); children: Rachel Ann. *Education:* Attended Southwest Missouri State University; University of Maryland at College Park, M.F.A., 1977; trained for the stage at Central School of Speech and Drama, London.

Addresses: *Agent*—International Creative Management, 10250 Constellation Way, 9th Floor, Los Angeles, CA 90067; (voice work) Danis Panaro Nist, 9201 West Olympic Blvd., Beverly Hills, CA 90212. *Publicist*—Alan Nierob, Rogers and Cowan Public Relations, Pacific Design Center, 8687 Melrose Ave., 7th Floor, Los Angeles, CA 90069.

Career: Actress, producer, and director. Appeared in commercials, including voice work for Burger King restaurants. New York University, acting teacher. Cannes Film Festival, member of jury, 2004; Ghent Film Festival, chair of jury, 2007. Planned Parenthood, spokesperson, 1995, and longtime member of board of directors and chair of board of advocates; appeared in Safe Motherhood campaign, UNICEF; also affiliated with charitable programs of Amnesty International, Childhelp USA, Citymeals on Wheels, People for the American Way.

Member: Actors' Equity Association.

Awards, Honors: Golden Globe Award nomination, new star of the year in a motion picture, 1982, and Film Award nomination, outstanding newcomer, British Academy of Film and Television Arts, 1983, both for *Body Heat;* Los Angeles Film Critics Association Award, best actress, 1984, and Golden Globe Award, best actress in a musical or comedy film, 1985, both for *Crimes of Passion* and *Romancing the Stone;* named star of the year, National Association of Theatre Owners, 1985; Golden Globe Award, best actress in a comedy film, 1986, for *Prizzi's Honor;* Sant Jordi Award, best foreign actress, 1986, for *Crimes of Passion* and *Prizzi's Honor;* New York Film Critics Circle Award nomination, best actress, c. 1985, D. W. Griffith Award and National Board of Review Award, both best actress, 1986, Academy Award nomination, best actress, Golden Globe Award nomination, best actress in a motion picture comedy or musical, and Saturn Award nomination, best actress, Academy of Science Fiction, Fantasy, and Horror Films, all 1987, all for *Peggy Sue Got Married;* Sant Jordi Award nomination, best foreign actress, 1988, for *Peggy Sue Got Married* and *Giula e Giula;* named woman of the year, Hasty Pudding Theatricals, 1989; Antoinette Perry Award nomination, leading actress in a play, and *Theatre World* Award, both 1990, for *Cat on a Hot Tin Roof;* Golden Globe Award nomination, best actress in a motion picture comedy or musical, 1990, for *The War of the Roses;* Gold Award, best actress, WorldFest Houston, 1993, for *House of Cards;* Chlotrudis Award

nomination, best actress, 1995, for *Serial Mom;* Margaret Sanger Award, Planned Parenthood Federation of America, 2000; Woman of the World Award, Childhelp USA, 2001; Video Premiere Award nomination, best supporting actress, DVD Exclusive Awards, 2001, for *Love and Action in Chicago;* lifetime achievement award, Savannah Film and Video Festival, 2004; Antoinette Perry Award nomination and Drama Desk Award nomination, both best actress in a play, 2005, and *Evening Standard* Theatre Award, best actress, 2006, all for *Who's Afraid of Virginia Woolf?;* lifetime achievement award, Provincetown International Film Festival, 2007; Grammy Award nomination, best spoken-word recording, National Academy of Recording Arts and Sciences, for *The Complete Shakespeare Sonnets.*

CREDITS

Film Appearances:
(Film debut) Matty Walker, *Body Heat,* Warner Bros., 1981.
Dolores Benedict, *The Man with Two Brains,* Warner Bros., 1983.
Joan Wilder, *Romancing the Stone* (also known as *2 bribones tras la esmeralda perdida*), Twentieth Century–Fox, 1984.
Joanna Crane/China Blue, *Crimes of Passion* (also known as *China Blue* and *Ken Russell's "Crimes of Passion"*), New World, 1984.
Stella Clayton, *A Breed Apart,* Orion, 1984.
Irene Walker, *Prizzi's Honor,* Twentieth Century–Fox, 1985.
Joan Wilder, *The Jewel of the Nile,* Twentieth Century–Fox, 1985.
Title role, *Peggy Sue Got Married,* TriStar, 1986.
Julia, *Julia and Julia* (also known as *Giulia e Giulia*), Cinecom International, 1988.
Christy Colleran, *Switching Channels,* TriStar, 1988.
(Uncredited) Voice of Jessica Rabbit, *Who Framed Roger Rabbit* (animated), Buena Vista, 1988.
Sarah Leary, *The Accidental Tourist,* Warner Bros., 1988.
Barbara Rose, *The War of the Roses,* Twentieth Century–Fox, 1989.
Voice of Jessica Rabbit, *Tummy Trouble* (animated), Buena Vista, 1989.
Voice of Jessica Rabbit, *Rollercoaster Rabbit* (animated), Buena Vista, 1990.
Victoria Warshawski (title role), *V. I. Warshawski* (also known as *V. I. Warshawski, Detective in High Heels*), Buena Vista, 1991.
Ruth Matthews, *House of Cards,* Miramax, 1992.
Voice, *A Day at a Time,* 1992.
Voice of Jessica Rabbit, *Trail Mix–Up* (animated), Buena Vista, 1993.
Jane Blue, *Undercover Blues* (also known as *Cloak and Diaper*), Metro–Goldwyn–Mayer, 1993.

Dana Coles, *Naked in New York,* Fine Line, 1994.

Beverly Sutphin, *Serial Mom,* Savoy Pictures, 1994.

Alberta Trager, *Moonlight and Valentino,* Gramercy, 1995.

Voice of Jessica Rabbit, *The Best of Roger Rabbit* (animated; also known as *Disney and Steven Spielberg Present "The Best of Roger Rabbit"*), 1996.

Dee Dee Taylor, *The Real Blonde,* Paramount, 1997.

Voice of Mom, *Bad Baby* (also known as *Disney's "Bad Baby"*), Buena Vista, 1997.

Claudia, *A Simple Wish* (also known as *The Fairy Godmother*), Universal, 1997.

Mrs. Lisbon, *The Virgin Suicides* (also known as *Sophia Coppola's "The Virgin Suicides"*), Paramount, 1999.

Dr. Elena Kinder, *Baby Geniuses,* TriStar, 1999.

Middleman, *Love and Action in Chicago,* 1999.

Rebecca Cairn, *Prince of Central Park,* Keystone Entertainment, 2000.

Verna Chickle, *Beautiful,* Destination Films, 2000.

(Uncredited) Herself, *The Kid Stays in the Picture,* 2002.

Narrator, *Answering the Call: Ground Zero's Volunteers* (documentary), Behr Entertainment, 2005.

Voice of Constance, *Monster House* (animated; also known as *Neighbourhood Crimes & Peepers*), Columbia, 2006.

The Lady in Question is Charles Busch (documentary), Lions in Limbo, 2006.

Ms. Kornblut, *Marley & Me,* Twentieth Century–Fox, 2008.

Narrator, *Life Is a Banquet* (documentary), Total Media Group, 2009.

Television Appearances; Series:

Nola Dancy Aldrich, *The Doctors,* NBC, 1978–79.

Sue Collini, *Californication,* Showtime, 2009.

Television Appearances; Movies:

Voice of First Lieutenant Lynda Van Devanter, *Dear America: Letters Home from Vietnam* (also known as *Dear America*), 1987.

Fanny Connelyn, *Friends at Last,* CBS, 1995.

Brenda Whitlass, *Legalese,* TNT, 1998.

Claudette, *Cinderella,* Bravo, 2000.

Television Appearances; Specials:

An American Portrait, CBS, 1985.

Roger Rabbit and the Secrets of Toontown (also known as *Roger Rabbit: In Search of Toontown*), CBS, 1988.

The Kennedy Center Honors: A Celebration of the Performing Arts, CBS, 1988.

The Barbara Walters Special, ABC, 1989.

(Uncredited) Audience member, *Saturday Night Live: 15th Anniversary,* NBC, 1989.

The Siskel and Ebert Special, CBS, 1990.

Night of 100 Stars III, NBC, 1990.

American Tribute to Vaclav Havel and a Celebration of Democracy in Czechoslovakia, PBS, 1990.

Host and narrator, *Hollywood Remembers: Myrna Loy–So Nice to Come Home To,* TNT, 1990.

Narrator, "Three Dances by Martha Graham," *Dance in America* (also known as *Great Performances*), PBS, 1992.

John Barry: Moviola, PBS, 1993.

The American Film Institute Salute to Jack Nicholson, CBS, 1994.

(In archive footage) *All–Star 25th Birthday: Stars and Street Forever!* (also known as *Sesame Street's All–Star 25th Birthday: Stars and Street Forever!*), 1994.

Narrator, *Love in the Ancient World* (also known as *Liebe in der antike*), Arts and Entertainment, 1997.

Narrator, *Castles of the Sea,* The Learning Channel, 1997.

(Uncredited) *An Audience with Elton John,* 1997.

Narrator, *The Science of Sex,* The Learning Channel, 1998.

In Bad Taste: The John Waters Story, Independent Film Channel, 1999.

Narrator, "Dashiell Hammett: Detective, Writer," *American Masters,* PBS, 1999.

(In archive footage) Peggy Sue, *Coppola: un hombre y sus suenos,* 1999.

Herself, *24 Hours,* 2000.

(In archive footage) Joan Wilder and Barbara Rose, *Twentieth Century–Fox: The Blockbuster Years,* 2000.

AFI's 100 Years ... 100 Passions: America's Greatest Love Stories, 2002.

Women on Top: Hollywood and Power, AMC, 2003.

TV's Most Memorable Weddings, NBC, 2003.

Narrator, *Sexiest Moments in Film: The Seducers,* Bravo, 2004.

"Julianne Moore: Seeing Red," *Biography,* Arts and Entertainment, 2004.

"Jack Nicholson: The Joker Is Wild," *Biography,* Arts and Entertainment, 2004.

"John Waters," *Biography,* Arts and Entertainment, 2004.

Narrator, *Last of the Wild Chimps,* MSNBC, 2004.

... A Father, ... a Son, ... Once upon a Time in Hollywood, HBO, 2005.

(Uncredited; in archive footage) *Saturday Night Live: The Best of Jon Lovitz,* NBC, 2005.

(In archive footage) *Bienvenue a Cannes,* TCM, 2007.

(Uncredited; in archive footage) Christy Colleran, *Nit vint–i–cinc,* 2008.

AFI Life Achievement Award: A Tribute to Michael Douglas, TV Land, 2009.

Television Appearances; Miniseries:

The Story of Hollywood (also known as *Talking Pictures*), TBS, 1988.

Narrator, *American Cinema,* PBS, 1995.

(In archive footage) *Retrosexual: The 80's,* VH1, 2004.

Television Appearances; Episodic:
The Odd Couple, ABC, 1972.
Host, *Saturday Night Live* (also known as *SNL*), NBC, 1985, 1989.
(In archive footage) *Cinema 3,* multiple appearances, between 1986 and 2009.
De pelicula, 1987.
ABC News Nightline, ABC, 1989.
Entertainment Tonight (also known as *Entertainment This Week, E.T., ET Weekend,* and *This Week in Entertainment*), syndicated, (in archive footage) 1990, 1995, 2007, 2009.
Cinema 3 (also known as *Informatiu cinema*), 1990, 1992, 1994.
Narrator, "Rumpelstiltskin," *We All Have Tales,* Showtime, 1992.
(In archive footage) *Dias de cine,* 1992, 2007, 2009.
Primer plano, 1993.
Voice of Stacy Lavelle, "Lisa vs. Malibu Stacy," *The Simpsons* (animated), Fox, 1994.
Nurse, "Leslie's Folly," *Directed By,* Showtime, 1994.
"The Making of 'Serial Mom'," *HBO First Look,* HBO, 1994.
Host and narrator, "The Hidden City of Petra," *Ancient Mysteries* (also known as *Ancient Mysteries: New Investigations of the Unsolved*), Arts and Entertainment, 1995.
Host, "The Odyssey of Troy," *Ancient Mysteries* (also known as *Ancient Mysteries: New Investigations of the Unsolved*), Arts and Entertainment, 1995.
Narrator and host, "Pompeii: Buried Alive," *Ancient Mysteries* (also known as *Ancient Mysteries: New Investigations of the Unsolved*), Arts and Entertainment, 1995.
Host and narrator, "Camelot," *Ancient Mysteries* (also known as *Ancient Mysteries: New Investigations of the Unsolved*), Arts and Entertainment, 1995.
The Good, the Bad & the Beautiful (also known as *Popcorn Venus*), TBS, 1996.
Voice of the magic woman, "The Last Petal," *Stories from My Childhood* (animated; also known as *Mikhail Baryshnikov's "Stories from My Childhood"*), PBS, 1998.
Voice of the snow queen, "The Snow Queen," *Stories from My Childhood* (animated; also known as *Mikhail Baryshnikov's "Stories from My Childhood"*), PBS, 1998.
Corazon, corazon, 1998, (in archive footage) 2008.
(In archive footage) *... y otras mujeres de armas tomar,* 1998.
Vertigo, 1999.
Caiga quien caiga, 1999.
Voice of Miss Liz Strickland, "Rodeo Days," *King of the Hill* (animated), Fox, 2000.
Voice of Miss Liz Strickland, "Hanky Panky: Parts 1 & 2," *King of the Hill* (animated), Fox, 2000.
Charles Bing/Helena Handbasket, "The One with Chandler's Dad," *Friends,* NBC, 2001.

Charles Bing/Helena Handbasket, "The One with Monica and Chandler's Wedding: Parts 1 & 2," *Friends,* NBC, 2001.
Celebrity Charades, AMC, 2005.
"Found," *Getaway* (also known as *United Travel Getaway*), Nine Network, 2005.
Character Studies, PBS, 2005.
(Uncredited; in archive footage) China Blue, *Dos rombos,* 2005.
(In archive footage) *Cinema mil,* Televisio de Catalunya, 2005.
(In archive footage) China Blue, "Fantasies," *Sexes,* Televisio de Catalunya, 2005.
(In archive footage) Barbara Rose, "Guerra de sexes," *Sexes,* Televisio de Catalunya, 2005.
(Uncredited; in archive footage) "Barbara Rose, *Silenci?,* 2005.
Rebecca Shine, "Magnet," *Law & Order,* NBC, 2006.
Cindy Plumb, "Cindy Plumb," *Nip/Tuck,* FX Network, 2006.
(Uncredited; in archive footage) Voice of Jessica Rabbit, "Roger Rabbit," *The Angry Video Game Nerd,* 2006.
(In archive footage) Joan Wilder, "Magnificent Movies," *20 to 1,* Nine Network, 2006.
Corazon de ..., 2006, (in archive footage) 2008.
(Uncredited; in archive footage) Voice of Jessica Rabbit, "Sexiest Movie Moments," *20 to 1,* Nine Network, 2007.
(In archive footage) Mrs. Lison and Peggy Sue, *Silenci?,* 2007.
(In archive footage) Christy Colleran, *Silenci?,* 2008.
Shrink Rap, Channel 4, 2008.
(In archive footage) Alberta Trager, *Loops!,* Televisio de Catalunya, 2008.

Television Talk Show Guest Appearances; Episodic:
Late Night with David Letterman, NBC, 1985, 1988.
The Tonight Show with Jay Leno (also known as *Jay Leno*), NBC, 1993.
Wetten, dass ...?, 1994.
"Kathleen Turner," *Lauren Hutton and ...,* 1995.
Howard Stern, 1996.
The Rosie O'Donnell Show, syndicated, 1997, 1998, 1999, 2002.
Late Night with Conan O'Brien, 1998, 2002.
The Howard Stern Radio Show, 1999.
The View, ABC, 2002, 2003, 2005, 2008.
NY Graham Norton, Channel 4, 2004.
Hardball with Chris Matthews, CNBC, 2004.
Live with Regis and Kelly, syndicated, 2005.
The Daily Show (also known as *A Daily Show with Jon Stewart, The Daily Show with Jon Stewart Global Edition,* and *Jon Stewart*), Comedy Central, 2005.
The Charlie Rose Show (also known as *Charlie Rose*), PBS, 2005.
Richard & Judy, Channel 4, 2005, 2006, 2008.
Sunday AM (also known as *The Andrew Marr Show*), BBC, 2006.

This Morning (also known as *This Morning with Richard and Judy*), ITV, 2006.
Parkinson, BBC, 2006.
The Paul O'Grady Show (also known as *The New Paul O'Grady Show*), ITV, 2006.
Today with Des and Mel, ITV, 2006.
Larry King Live, Cable News Network, 2008.
GMTV, ITV, 2008.
Today (also known as *NBC News Today* and *The Today Show*), NBC, 2008, 2009.

Television Appearances; Awards Presentations:
Presenter, *The ... Annual Academy Awards*, 1982, 1985, ABC, 1992.
The ... Annual Academy Awards, 1986, 1987, (in archive footage) 1989, (in archive footage), ABC, 2003.
The ... Annual Tony Awards, CBS, 1987, 1988.
Host, *The 44th Annual Tony Awards*, CBS, 1990.
Presenter, *The ... Annual Tony Awards*, 1995, CBS, 2005.
Presenter, *The 50th Annual Drama Desk Awards*, 2005.

Television Director; Specials:
"Leslie's Follies," *Directed By*, Showtime, 1994.

Television Producer; Movies:
Friends at Last, CBS, 1995.

Stage Appearances:
Mr. T, Soho Repertory Theatre, New York City, 1977.
Judith Hastings, *Gemini*, Little Theatre, New York City, 1978.
Travesties, Manitoba Theatre Centre, Winnipeg, Manitoba, Canada, 1980.
Nina, *The Seagull*, Manitoba Theatre Centre, 1980.
Titania and Hippolita, *A Midsummer Night's Dream*, Arena Stage, Washington, DC, 1985.
Toyer!, New York City, 1985.
Title role, *Camille*, Long Wharf Theatre, New Haven, CT, 1987.
Melissa Gardner, *Love Letters*, Promenade Theatre, New York City, 1989.
Maggie, *Cat on a Hot Tin Roof*, Eugene O'Neill Theatre, New York City, 1990.
Night of 100 Stars III, Radio City Music Hall, New York City, 1990.
Yvonne (some sources cite role as Madeline), *Indiscretions*, Ethel Barrymore Theatre, New York City, 1995.
Lady Graystone, *Our Betters*, Chichester Theatre Festival, Chichester, England, 1997.
Title role, *Tallulah!* (solo show), Chichester Theatre Festival, 1997.
Mrs. Robinson, *The Graduate*, Gielgud Theatre, London, 2000, and Canon Theatre, Toronto, Ontario, Canada, 2001, then Plymouth Theatre, New York City, 2002.
Nothing Like a Dame, St. James Theatre, New York City, 2002.
Stars in the Alley, New York City, 2002.
Broadway on Broadway, New York City, 2002.
Sunny Jacobs, *The Exonerated*, Fort Worth, TX, 2004, then Bleecker Street Theatre, New York City, 2006.
Imelda, *On the Twentieth Century* (benefit concert), New Amsterdam Theatre, New York City, 2005.
Martha, *Who's Afraid of Virginia Woolf?*, Longacre Theatre, New York City, 2005, then Apollo Theatre, London, 2006.
Special guest, *Martin Short: Fame Becomes Me*, Bernard B. Jacobs Theatre, New York City, 2006.
Peg and Dr. Rutenspitz, *The Third Story*, Manhattan Class Company, Lucille Lortel Theatre, New York City, 2009.

Appeared in *Letter to the World*. Also participates in various staged readings, usually in New York City.

Major Tours:
Title role, *Tallulah!* (solo show), U.S. cities, 2000–2001.
Martha, *Who's Afraid of Virginia Woolf?*, U.S. cities, 2007.

Stage Director:
Crimes of the Heart, Williamstown Theatre Festival, Williamstown, MA, 2007, then Roundabout Theatre Company, Laura Pels Theatre, New York City, 2008.

Radio Appearances:
Deadlock, BBC, 1991.

Appeared in other British radio presentations.

RECORDINGS

Videos:
Narrator, *The Conspiracy of Silence*, 1995.
Voice of Clawdette the black cat, *National Geographic Kids: Creepy Creatures*, 2000.
(Uncredited; in archive footage) Matty Walker, *Sex at 24 Frames per Second*, Image Entertainment, 2003.
(In archive footage) *It's like Life*, Warner Home Video, 2004.

Appeared in the music video "When the Going Gets Tough, the Tough Get Going" by Billy Ocean.

Albums:
Contributor to the spoken–word recording of *The Complete Shakespeare Sonnets*.

WRITINGS

(With Gloria Feldt) *Send Yourself Roses: Thoughts on My Life, Love, and Leading Roles,* Springboard, 2008.

OTHER SOURCES

Books:

Turner, Kathleen, and Gloria Feldt, *Send Yourself Roses: Thoughts on My Life, Love, and Leading Roles,* Springboard, 2008.

Periodicals:

American Film, November, 1984.
Entertainment Weekly, May 27, 2005, pp. 56–57; June 3, 2005, p. 56.
Evening Standard (London), February 1, 2006, p. 20.
Film Comment, September/October, 1981; April, 1985.
Harper's Bazaar, April, 1995, p. 93.
Interview, August, 1995, p. 66.
New Statesman, March 13, 2006, p. 40.
Newsweek, February 25, 2008, p. 63.
New York Post, February 27, 2008.
New York Times, January 5, 1986; March 18, 1990, p. H5; February 3, 2008, p. AR8; April 5, 2008, p. B8.
People Weekly, December 24, 1984; April 25, 1994, p. 112.
Premiere, August, 1991, p. 70.

Electronic:

Kathleen Turner Official Site, http://www.kathleenturner.com, February 17, 2010.

TURTURRO, Aida 1962–

PERSONAL

Born September 25, 1962, in New York, NY (some sources say Brooklyn, NY); daughter of Domenick (an artist) and Dorothy (a homemaker) Turturro; cousin of Nicholas Turturro (an actor) and John Turturro (an actor and director). *Education:* State University of New York College at New Paltz, B.F.A., theatre, 1984. *Religion:* Roman Catholic.

Addresses: *Manager*—Framework Entertainment, 129 West 27th St., 12th Floor, Penthouse, New York, NY 10001.

Career: Actress. Also worked as a cleaning person.

Awards, Honors: Emmy Award nominations, outstanding supporting actress in a drama series, 2001, 2007, Screen Actors Guild Award nominations (with others), outstanding performance by an ensemble in a drama series, 2001, 2002, 2003, 2005, 2006, Screen Actors Guild Award (with others), outstanding performance by an ensemble in a drama series, 2008, all for *The Sopranos.*

CREDITS

Film Appearances:

Grace, *True Love,* United Artists, 1989.
Prostitute, *What about Bob?,* Buena Vista, 1991.
Angie, *Jersey Girl,* Triumph Releasing, 1992.
Wife, *Mac,* Samuel Goldwyn Company, 1993.
Officer Moran, *Life with Mikey* (also known as *Give Me a Break*), Buena Vista, 1993.
Hotel day clerk, *Manhattan Murder Mystery,* TriStar, 1993.
State employee, *The Saint of Fort Washington,* Warner Bros., 1993.
Tina, *Angie,* Buena Vista, 1994.
Men Lie, 1994.
Louise, *Junior,* Universal, 1994.
Multiple roles, *Twelve Deadly Cyns ... and Then Some,* Sony Pictures Entertainment, 1994.
Madame Esther, *The Search for One–eye Jimmy,* Cabin Fever Entertainment, 1994.
Bar waitress, *Stonewall,* 1995.
Woman on platform, *Money Train,* Columbia, 1995.
Kim, "The Dutch Master" (also known as "Der Flaemische Meister"), *Tales of Erotica* (also known as *Erotic Tales*), Trimark Pictures, 1996.
Linda, *Denise Calls Up,* Sony Pictures Classics, 1996.
Mrs. Salina, *Sleepers,* Warner Bros., 1996.
Helen Norwich, *Jaded,* Vision Films, 1996.
Angie, *Made Men,* Close Encounters Productions/Pool Party Productions, 1997.
Susan, *Fool's Paradise,* Trident Releasing, 1997.
Tiffany, *Fallen,* Warner Bros., 1998.
Fortune tellers, *Too Tired to Die,* 1998, Phaedra Cinema, 2000.
Mary, *O.K. Garage* (also known as *All Revved Up*), New City Releasing, 1998.
Tookie, *Woo,* New Line Cinema, 1998.
Psychic, *Celebrity,* Miramax, 1998.
Glory, *Freak Weather,* HKM Films, 1998.
Miss Pasquantonio, *Crossfire,* Scorpio Production, 1998.
Marta, *Illuminata,* Artisan Entertainment, 1999.
Brenda, *The 24 Hour Woman,* Artisan Entertainment/ Shooting Gallery, 1999.
Marie, *24 Nights,* Cynical Boy Productions, 1999.
Brenda Kerns, *Deep Blue Sea,* Warner Bros., 1999.
Waitress, *Mickey Blue Eyes,* Warner Bros., 1999.
Nurse Crupp, *Bringing Out the Dead,* Paramount, 1999.

Mad Greek waitress, *Play It to the Bone* (also known as *Play It*), Buena Vista, 1999.

Waitress, *Joe Gould's Secret*, USA Films, 2000.

Home Sweet Hoboken, Allied Entertainment Group, 2000.

Jean Ferraro, *Crocodile Dundee in Los Angeles,* Paramount, 2001.

Shari, *Sidewalks of New York,* Paramount Classics, 2001.

Emily and Gina, *2BPerfectlyHonest,* Monarch Home Video, 2004.

Attorney Dellasandro, *Survival of the Fittest* (short film), 2005.

Rosebud, *Romance & Cigarettes* (also known as *Romance and Cigarettes*), Metro–Goldwyn–Mayer, 2005.

Nancy Feldman, *A Little Help,* 2010.

Television Appearances; Series:

Lydia, *The Wright Verdicts,* CBS, 1995.

Fran, *As the World Turns,* CBS, 1998.

Janice Soprano, *The Sopranos,* HBO, 2000–2007.

Television Appearances; Specials:

Presenter, *VH1 Divas Live: The One and Only Aretha Franklin—A Benefit Concert for VH1 Save the Music Foundation,* VH1, 2001.

Intimate Portrait: Young Hollywood, Lifetime, 2002.

"The Sopranos": A Sitdown, HBO, 2007.

Television Appearances; Episodic:

Carmen, "Happily Ever After," *Law & Order,* NBC, 1990.

Manicurist, *Tribeca,* Fox, 1993.

Cocktail waitress, "Blue Bamboo," *Law & Order,* NBC, 1994.

Gina, "A Question of Truth," *New York News,* CBS, 1995.

Rox, "The Big Easy Episode," *Mr. & Mrs. Smith,* CBS, 1996.

Receptionist, "I.D.," *Law & Order,* NBC, 1996.

Rox, "The Poor Pitiful Put–upon Singer Episode," *Mr. & Mrs. Smith,* CBS, 1996.

Gloria, *Dellaventura,* CBS, 1997.

Caren Payne, "Race with the Devil," *The Practice,* 1997.

Wanda, *Cosby,* CBS, 1997.

(Uncredited) *Late Show with David Letterman* (also known as *Letterman* and *The Late Show*), CBS, 2004.

Maddy, "Premonition Mission," *Wild Card* (also known as *Zoe Busiek: Wild Card*), Lifetime, 2004.

"Sexiest Men," *TV Land's Top Ten,* TV Land, 2005.

(Uncredited) *Corazon de ...,* 2005.

Jimmy Kimmel Live! (also known as *Jimmy Kimmel*), ABC, 2007.

Sheryl Hawkins, " ... As the Day She Was Born," *ER,* NBC, 2008.

Sheryl Hawkins, "Truth Will Out," *ER,* NBC, 2008.

Sheryl Hawkins, "Tandem Repeats," *ER,* NBC, 2008.

Bobbi Catalano, "Bite Me," *Medium,* 2009.

Stage Appearances:

(Broadway debut) Eunice Hubbell, *A Streetcar Named Desire,* Ethel Barrymore Theatre, 1992.

Armida, *Souls of Naples,* Duke on 42nd Street, New York City, 2005.

Matron, *Cabaret* (musical), Ambassador Theatre, New York City, 2005, 2007–2008.

Also appeared in *Cavalleria Rusticana,* Westbeth Theatre, New York City; *Tony 'n' Tina's Wedding,* New York City; *The Threepenny Opera.*

RECORDINGS

Music Videos:

"Cyndi at Coney Island" and "Hey Now [Girls Just Want to Have Fun]," *Cyndi Lauper: 12 Deadly Cyns ... and Then Some,* 1994.

OTHER SOURCES

Periodicals:

Maclean's, March 12, 2001, p. 52.

People Weekly, April 17, 2000, p. 71.

Rosie, September, 2002, p. 120.

Saturday Evening Post, January/February, 2006, p. 88.

TV Guide, December 7, 2002, pp. 58–60.

V–W

Van DIEN, Casper 1968–
(Casper Robert Van, Jr. Dien, Caspar Van Dien, Robb Van Dien)

PERSONAL

Full name, Casper Robert Van Dien, Jr.; born December 18, 1968, in Ridgefield, NJ (some sources cite birthplace as Milton, FL); son of Casper Robert (a naval commander and fighter pilot) and Diane (a minister and teacher) Van Dien; married Carrie Mitchum (an actress), 1993, (divorced, 1997); married Catherine Oxenberg (an actress), May 8, 1999; children: (first marriage) Casper Robert Mitchum, Grace; (second marriage) Maya, Celeste. *Education:* Attended Florida State University, 1986–88.

Addresses: *Agent*—Barry McPherson, Agency for the Performing Arts, 405 South Beverly Dr., Beverly Hills, CA 90212.

Career: Actor and producer. Holy Cow Entertainment, founder and partner; appeared in commercials; voice for a pinball machine featuring characters from the film *Starship Troopers*. Previously worked as a bartender and lifeguard trainer.

Awards, Honors: Blockbuster Entertainment Award nomination, favorite male newcomer, 1998, for *Starship Troopers*; inducted into hall of fame, Phoenix International Horror and Sci–Fi Film Festival, 2009.

CREDITS

Television Appearances; Series:
Brad Morris, *Dangerous Women*, syndicated, 1991.
Tyler "Ty" Moody, *One Life to Live*, ABC, 1993–94.
Griffin Stone, a recurring role, *Beverly Hills, 90210* (also known as *Class of Beverly Hills*), Fox, 1994.
Chandler Williams, *Titans*, NBC, 2000–2001.
Himself, *I Married a Princess*, Lifetime, 2005.
Andre Forester, *Watch Over Me*, My Network, 2006–2007.

Television Appearances; Movies:
Lifeguard, *Menu for Murder* (also known as *Murder at the P.T.A. Luncheon*), 1990.
(As Casper Robert Van Dien, Jr.) The guy Miranda brings home, *The Webbers* (also known as *At Home with the Webbers* and *Webber's World*), 1993.
Randy, *P.C.H.* (also known as *Kill Shot*), 1995.
Roy, *Night Eyes 4* (also known as *Midnight Hour* and *Night Eyes ... Fatal Passion*), 1995.
King Tal, *Beastmaster III: The Eye of Braxus* (also known as *Beastmaster III*), 1995.
Orbit (also known as *Lethal Orbit, Countdown to Disaster, Vital Contact,* and *Vital Orbit*), 1996.
Adam, *Backroads to Vegas* (also known as *Love Notes*), 1996.
The Colony (also known as *Malibu Beach*), ABC, 1996.
Teddie Johnson and Ray Ordwell, Jr., *NightScream*, NBC, 1997.
Bystander, *Casper: A Spirited Beginning* (also known as *Casper: The Beginning* and *Casper II: Ghost Central Station*), 1997.
Title role, *James Dean: Race with Destiny* (also known as *James Dean: Live Fast Die Young*), 1997.
Crewcut hunk, *Casper Meets Wendy*, 1998.
Dallas, *Revenant* (also known as *Modern Vampires* and *Vamps*), 1998.
Jake Barnes, *On the Border*, 1998.
Tom Merrick, *The Time Shifters* (also known as *Thrill Seekers*), TBS, 1999.
Steven McKray, *Shark Attack*, HBO, 1999.
A. K., *The Collectors*, 1999.
Bart Parker, *Python*, 2000.
Connor Spears, *The Tracker*, 2000.
Sergeant Delmira, *Cutaway*, USA Network, 2000.

Tom Gerrick, *Sanctimony,* Cinemax, 2000.

Axel, *Partners* (also known as *Trust Nobody*), 2000.

Jim Travis, *A Friday Night Date* (also known as *Road Rage* and *La rage au volant*), Cinemax, 2000.

Commander Miles Sheffield, *Danger beneath the Sea,* 2001.

Bobby Moritz, *Chasing Destiny,* 2001.

Captain Ramsey, *Going Back* (also known as *Under Heavy Fire* and *Freres de guerre*), HBO, 2001.

Ace Logan, *Windfall,* 2001.

Gerry, *The Vector File,* 2002.

Eddie Burton, *Big Spender,* Animal Planet, 2003.

Kyle Considine, *Maiden Voyage* (also known as *Maiden Voyage: Ocean Hijack*), 2004.

Jack Barnes, *Premonition* (also known as *The Psychic*), 2004.

Staff Sergeant Oberron, *Skeleton Man,* Sci–Fi Channel, 2004.

Captain Abraham Van Helsing, *Dracula 3000,* 2004.

Chris Locke, *Personal Effects,* Lifetime, 2005.

Matt Fletcher, *The Fallen Ones,* Sci–Fi Channel, 2005.

Officer Philip Hallows, *Officer Down* (also known as *Assassin in Blue*), Lifetime, 2005.

Tom, *Meltdown* (also known as *Meltdown: Days of Destruction*), Sci–Fi Channel, 2006.

Danny Freemont, *The Curse of King Tut's Tomb,* Hallmark Channel, 2006.

Hawk, *Slayer,* Sci–Fi Channel, 2006.

Luke Rivers, *Aces 'n' Eights,* ION, 2008.

Jack Barrett, *Mask of the Ninja,* Spike TV, 2008.

Luther Simmonds, *One Hot Summer,* Lifetime, 2009.

Tom, *Turbulent Skies,* 2010.

Television Appearances; Episodic:

Zack Taylor, "Sex, Truth, and Theatre," *Freshman Dorm,* CBS, 1992.

Zack Taylor, "The Last Sonnet," *Freshman Dorm,* CBS, 1992.

Zack Taylor, "The Scarlett Letter," *Freshman Dorm,* CBS, 1992.

Ted, "Udder Madness," *Life Goes On,* ABC, 1992.

Jesse, "Cattle Drive: Parts 1 & 2," *Dr. Quinn, Medicine Woman,* CBS, 1994.

Roger Barrows, "I Know What Scares You," *Silk Stalkings,* USA Network, 1995.

Eric, "Blonde and Blonder," *Married ... with Children,* Fox, 1995.

(As Caspar Van Dien) Jake Miller, "Heart's Desire," *The Outer Limits* (also known as *The New Outer Limits*), Showtime, 1997.

Vibe, 1997.

Showbiz Today, 1997.

Michael, "Love at First Flight," *Rock Me, Baby,* UPN, 2004.

Corazon de ..., 2005.

Lieutenant Steven Albright, "Mr. Monk Is Underwater," *Monk,* USA Network, 2008.

Lieutenant Steven Albright, "Mr. Monk and the End: Parts 1 & 2," *Monk,* USA Network, 2009.

Television Appearances; Pilots:

Zack Taylor, *Freshman Dorm,* CBS, 1992.

Chandler Williams, *Titans,* NBC, 2000.

Television Appearances; Specials:

(As Casper Robert Van Dien, Jr.) *Shirtless: Hollywood's Sexiest Men,* 2002.

(Uncredited; in archive footage) Captain Ramsey, *The Veteran,* 2006.

Scream Awards 2007, Spike TV, 2007.

Television Talk Show Guest Appearances:

The Tonight Show with Jay Leno (also known as *Jay Leno*), NBC, 1997.

The Rosie O'Donnell Show, syndicated, 1998, 1999, 2000.

The Late Late Show with Craig Kilborn (also known as *The Late Late Show*), CBS, 1999.

Ricki Lake, 1999.

The Tony Danza Show, syndicated, 2005.

Larry King Live, Cable News Network, 2006.

The Late Late Show with Craig Ferguson, CBS, 2006.

Up Close with Carrie Keagan, ABC, 2008.

Television Work; Series:

Producer, *I Married a Princess,* Lifetime, 2005.

Television Work; Movies:

Co–executive producer, *Revenant* (also known as *Modern Vampires* and *Vamps*), 1998.

Film Appearances:

Johnny Rico, *Starship Troopers,* Sony Pictures Entertainment, TriStar, 1997.

Tarzan/John Clayton, *Tarzan and the Lost City* (also known as *Tarzan and Jane, Tarzan Jungle Warrior,* and *Tarzan und die verlorene stadt*), Warner Bros., 1998.

Brom Van Brunt, *Sleepy Hollow* (also known as *Sleepy Hollow—Koepfe werden rollen*), Paramount, 1999.

Dr. Gillen Lane, *The Omega Code,* Providence Entertainment, 1999.

Himself, *In Action,* 2000.

(Uncredited) Romantic Moritz, *What the #$*! Do We (K)now!?* (documentary; also known as *What the Bleep Do We Know!?*), Samuel Goldwyn/Roadside Attractions, 2004.

Zach, *Hollywood Flies,* Monarch Home Video, 2005.

Colonel Johnny Rico, *Starship Troopers 3: Marauder* (also known as *SST 3: Marauder*), Sony Pictures Entertainment, 2008.

Dr. John Jeffries, *Through the Air to Calais or the Wonderful Cruise of Blanchard's Balloon,* American Film Institute, 2009.

Film Work:

Executive producer, *Through the Air to Calais or the Wonderful Cruise of Blanchard's Balloon,* American Film Institute, 2009.

RECORDINGS

Videos:

(As Robb Van Dien) *Learning to Sail with ASA,* 1989.

Brom Van Brunt, *Sleepy Hollow: Behind the Legend,* Paramount, 2000.

Death from Above: The Making of "Starship Troopers," Columbia TriStar Home Video, 2002.

Giants in the Earth: The Making of "The Fallen Ones," Anchor Bay Entertainment, 2005.

Shooting "Egypt" in India, Echo Bridge Home Entertainment, 2006.

The 21st Annual Genesis Awards, Iron Image/Mersey Masala, 2007.

Fednet Mode, Sony Pictures Home Entertainment, 2008.

Appeared in a music video by Crosby, Stills, and Nash, 1990.

Video Games:

(As Robb Van Dien) Voice of third Confederation pilot, *Wing Commander IV: The Price of Freedom,* Electronic Arts, 1995.

Voice of General John Rico, *Starship Troopers,* Empire Interactive, 2005.

WRITINGS

Poetry:

Poetry (as Robb Van Dien) is included in the anthologies *On the Threshold of a Dream,* Watermark Pres, 1990; and *Quiet Moments,* Watermark Press, 1990.

OTHER SOURCES

Periodicals:

Cosmopolitan, November, 1997, p. 212.

Entertainment Weekly, May 15, 1998, p. 16.

Interview, December, 1997, p. 73.

People Weekly, December 1, 1997, p. 81.

Time, March 23, 1998, p. 93.

Electronic:

Casper Van Dien Official Site, http://caspervandien.nowcasting.com, March 4, 2010.

WALKER, Jackson 1968(?)–

PERSONAL

Born c. 1968, in Dublin, GA; married Buffy Burns (a coffee shop proprietor and active in charity work); children: Evan, Wade, Nash Jackson (deceased). *Education:* Auburn University, degree in architecture, 1992; trained at Actors Workshop, Atlanta, GA, Carter Thor Studio, Los Angeles, and with Milton Katselas and Jeffrey Tambor at Beverly Hills Playhouse.

Addresses: *Agent*—The Culbertson Group, 8430 Santa Monica Blvd., Suite 210, West Hollywood, CA 90069.

Career: Actor, producer, director, and writer. Appeared in advertisements. Worked in set and production design. Affiliated with The Dash Project, Inc. and The Unthinkable Project. Blackbird Coffee, Dublin, GA, proprietor with others. Worked as an architect in Atlanta, GA. Supporter of charities relating to Sudden Infant Death Syndrome (SIDS); Big Brothers Big Sisters, member of the advisory board.

Member: Screen Actors Guild, American Federation of Television and Radio Artists.

Awards, Honors: Award from God on Film Festival, best film category, 2005, for *Tin Man;* prize from 36 Hour Film Festival, best use of genre, 2006.

CREDITS

Film Appearances:

Fraternity brother, *Getting In* (also known as *Kamikaze College, Kill Me Tender,* and *Student Body*), 1994.

Dr. Mitchell, *Toxic Remedy* (short film), 1997.

Lee Singer, *Trouble in the Fields* (short film), 1997.

Young actor, *Bartender,* Bridge Pictures/Cutting Edge Entertainment/Danehip Entertainment, 1997.

Yeah Vous! (also known as *Yeah Vous*), c. 1998.

Harry C. Devening, *The Rising Place,* Warner Bros., 2001.

Johnny, *Tin Man* (short film), Cell/7 Films, c. 2004.

Pig owner, *The Great Debaters,* Metro–Goldwyn–Mayer, 2007.

Hero, *Awake O'Sleeper* (short film), Whiteston Motion Pictures, 2008.

Magician, *That's Magic!* (short film), Whiteston Motion Pictures, 2008.

Jonathan Grove, *The Final Destination* (also known as *Final Dead Circuit 3D, Final Destination: Death Trip, Final Destination: Death Trip 3, Final Destina-*

tion: *Death Trip 3D*, *Final Destination 4*, *The Final Destination in 3–D*, *The Final Destination 3D*, and *The Final Destination 3d*), Warner Bros., 2009.
Jude, *The Rift* (short film), Cyclone Films, 2009.
Mr. Brackman, *Madea Goes to Jail* (also known as *Tyler Perry's "Madea Goes to Jail"*), Lions Gate Films, 2009.
Rusty Rozier, *12 FL OZ* (also known as *12 Fl OZ*), Standoff Studios, 2009.
Terry Walker, *The Way Home* (also known as *Our Child Is Missing*), Freestyle Releasing, 2009.
Freedom Riders (documentary), c. 2009, broadcast as part of *The American Experience*, PBS, c. 2011.
Reverend Shadrach, *Georgia Sky*, The Tyler Perry Company/34th Street Films, 2010.

Appeared as Detective Rooke, *The Commandments*, Cell/7 Films. Appeared in other films, including *Margot Moodey's Life*.

Film Work:
Codirector, *Tin Man* (short film), Cell/7 Films, c. 2004.
Executive producer, *My Concrete Mattress* (documentary), The Dash Project, Inc./The Unthinkable Project, c. 2008, new version, c. 2009.
Producer, *12 FL OZ* (also known as *12 Fl OZ*), Standoff Studios, 2009.

Also served as the director of *A Great Deal Far Away*, 36 Hour Film Project. Worked in set and production design.

Television Appearances; Miniseries:
Daniel Ross, *We Shall Remain* (documentary), broadcast as part of *The American Experience*, PBS, 2009.

Television Appearances; Movies:
John Black, *The People v. Leo Frank*, PBS, 2009.

Television Appearances; Episodic:
"Impact," *JAG* (also known as *JAG: Judge Advocate General*), CBS, 1997.
Lifeguard, "A Long Way to Tip–a–Rory," *Melrose Place* (also known as *Place Melrose*), Fox, 1998.
(Uncredited) Best man, "Kate's Wedding," *The Drew Carey Show*, ABC, 2002.
The John Henson Project, Spike TV, c. 2004.
Franklin Fell, "You're Undead to Me," *The Vampire Diaries*, The CW, 2009.
Freedom Riders (documentary), c. 2009, broadcast as part of *The American Experience*, PBS, c. 2011.

Appeared as Detective Garrett in "Running on Empty," an episode of *Past Life* (also known as *The Reincarnationist*), Fox; some sources cite an appearance in *Navy*

NCIS: Naval Criminal Investigative Service (also known as *Naval CIS*, *Navy CIS*, *Navy NCIS*, *NCIS*, and *NCIS: Naval Criminal Investigative Service*), CBS.

Television Appearances; Pilots:
Then Came Jones, ABC, 2003.

Stage Appearances:
Otto Frank, *The Diary of Anne Frank*, Bohemian Theatrical Society, Dublin, GA, 2008.

Appeared as Brick, *Cat on a Hot Tin Roof*, as Eddie, *Fool for Love*, as the gentleman caller, *The Glass Menagerie*, as Stanley Kowalski, *A Streetcar Named Desire*, and as Nick, *Who's Afraid of Virginia Woolf?*, all Ventura Court Theatre, Studio City, CA; and appeared as Bobby, *American Buffalo*, Skylight Theatre.

RECORDINGS

Videos:
Himself, *Body Count: The Deaths of "The Final Destination"* (short documentary), Warner Bros. Home Entertainment Group, 2010.

WRITINGS

Screenplays:
Tin Man (short film), Cell/7 Films, c. 2004.

Wrote *A Great Deal Far Away*, 36 Hour Film Project.

WARD, Megan 1969–

PERSONAL

Full name, Megan Marie Ward; born September 24, 1969, in Los Angeles, CA; father an actor and drama teacher; mother an actress and drama teacher; married Michael Shore (a toy company executive), 1995; children: Oliver, Audrey. *Education:* Attended high school in Hawaii; attended junior college in Los Angeles; studied acting at Loft Studio, Los Angeles.

Addresses: *Agent*—Scott Harris, Innovative Artists, 1505 10th St., Santa Monica, CA 90401. *Manager*—Ellen Meyer, Ellen Meyer Management, 8899 Beverly Blvd, Suite 612, Los Angeles, CA 90048.

Career: Actress. Worked as a model in Japan; appeared in commercials for J. C. Penney department stores, 2002, Circuit City electronics stores, 2005, and others.

Member: Screen Actors Guild.

Awards, Honors: Saturn Award nomination, best genre television actress, Academy of Science Fiction, Fantasy, and Horror Films, 1997, for *Dark Skies.*

CREDITS

Film Appearances:

Arren Hooks, *Crash and Burn,* Paramount, 1990.

Little Sharon, *Goodbye Paradise* (also known as *Moon over Paradise*), 1991.

Alice Stilwell, *Trancers II* (also known as *Future Cop II, Trancers II: The Return of Jack Deth,* and *Trancers II: The Two Faces of Death*), Paramount Home Video, 1991.

Alice Stilwell, *Trancers III* (also known as *Death Lives, Future Cop III,* and *Trancers 3: Death Lives*), Paramount Home Video, 1992.

Lisa Sterling, *Amityville 1992: It's about Time* (also known as *Amityville V: It's about Time*), Republic, 1992.

Robyn Sweeney, *Encino Man* (also known as *California Man*), Buena Vista, 1992.

Julie, *Freaked* (also known as *Freak Show* and *Hideous Mutant Freekz*), Twentieth Century–Fox, 1993.

Alex Manning, *Arcade,* Paramount, 1993.

Katy, *PCU* (also known as *PCU Pit Party*), Twentieth Century–Fox, 1994.

Donna Leonard (some sources cite Donna Dittmeyer), *The Brady Bunch Movie,* Paramount, 1995.

Lily Dougherty, *Joe's Apartment,* Warner Bros., 1996.

Joanie, *Glory Daze* (also known as *Last Call*), Seventh Art Releasing, 1996.

Melanie, *Say You'll Be Mine* (also known as *Strangers in Transit*), Eagle Beach, 1999.

Rachel Avery, *Tick Tock* (also known as *Clockwork* and *A Friendship to Die For*), Avalanche Home Entertainment, 2000.

Cheryl Parker, *Mirror Man,* Film Movement, 2002.

Kelly, *Complete Guide to Guys* (also known as *Dave Barry's Complete Guide to Guys*), Monarch Home Video, 2005.

Rebecca, *Waking Dreams,* WonderPhil Productions, 2007.

Michelle, *The Invited,* Dark Portal/Relativity Media, 2010.

Appeared in the Japanese film *Basho's Journey.*

Television Appearances; Series:

Patty Horvath, *Class of '96,* Fox, 1993.

Nicole Manning, *Winnetka Road,* NBC, 1994.

Jill Holbrook, a recurring role, *Party of Five,* Fox, 1994–95.

Kimberly Sayers, *Dark Skies,* NBC, 1996–97.

Connie Rexroth, a recurring role, *Melrose Place,* Fox, 1997–98.

Kate Wyatt, *Four Corners,* CBS, 1998.

Kelly Stevens, *Boomtown,* NBC, 2002–2003.

Kate Howard, *General Hospital,* ABC, 2007–2009.

Host of a Japanese series, *Science Q.*

Television Appearances; Movies:

Narrator and Ashley Judd, *Naomi and Wynonna: Love Can Build a Bridge* (also known as *Love Can Build a Bridge* and *Love Can Build a Bridge: The Story of the Judds*), NBC, 1995.

Renee Perkins, *Crimes of Passion: Voice from the Grave* (also known as *From the Files of "Unsolved Mysteries": Voice from the Grave, Unsolved Mysteries: Voice from the Grave,* and *Voice from the Grave*), NBC, 1996.

Carla Engel, *Don't Look Down* (also known as *Wes Craven's "Don't Look Down"*), ABC, 1998.

Meredith, *Rated X,* Showtime, 2000.

Amy, *Mr. Ambassador,* NBC, 2003.

Christine Bennett, *Murder without Conviction,* Hallmark Channel, 2004.

Television Appearances; Pilots:

Patty Horvath, *Class of '96,* Fox, 1993.

Dr. Alix Brightland, *All Souls,* UPN, 2001.

Karen Westerly, *Summerland,* The WB, 2004.

Television Appearances; Episodic:

Tracy, "The Substitute," *What a Dummy,* 1990.

Kimberly, "Evie's High Anxiety," *Out of This World,* 1990.

DiDi, "Dating Game," *Sons and Daughters,* 1991.

Dedra Mapoles, "One Good Woman," *Sweet Justice,* NBC, 1994.

Monica, "Gift," *The Single Guy,* NBC, 1995.

Ashley Gable, "Wishboned," *Fantasy Island,* ABC, 1998.

April, "My Casual Friend's Wedding," *Jesse,* NBC, 1999.

Nancy, "The One Where Rachel Smokes," *Friends,* NBC, 1999.

Pixley Robinson, "A Girl Named Pixley," *Sports Night,* ABC, 1999.

Pixley Robinson, "The Giants Win the Pennant, the Giants Win the Pennant," *Sports Night,* ABC, 2000.

Jane, "Guns Not Butter," *The West Wing,* NBC, 2003.

Audrey Hilden, "A Night at the Movies," *CSI: Crime Scene Investigation* (also known as *C.S.I., CSI: Las Vegas,* and *Les experts*), CBS, 2003.

Hillary Sterling, "Life Rules," *Without a Trace* (also known as *W.A.T.*), CBS, 2004.

Heather Valerio, "House Arrest," *Kevin Hill,* UPN, 2004.

Laura Rowens, "Forced Entry," *Navy NCIS: Naval Criminal Investigative Service* (also known as *NCIS* and *NCIS: Naval Criminal Investigative Service*), CBS, 2004.

Susan May, "Hired Guns," *Boston Legal,* ABC, 2004.
Jennie Hale, "Vengeance," *CSI: Miami,* CBS, 2005.
Judy Anderson, "Blame It on the Rain," *ER,* NBC, 2005.
Sally, "Chicken Noodle Heads," *7th Heaven* (also known as *Seventh Heaven* and *7th Heaven: Beginnings*), The WB, 2005.
Angela Fuller, "Target," *Sleeper Cell* (also known as *Sleeper Cell: American Terror*), Showtime, 2005.
Angela Fuller, "Money," *Sleeper Cell* (also known as *Sleeper Cell: American Terror*), Showtime, 2005.
Angela Fuller, "Immigrant," *Sleeper Cell* (also known as *Sleeper Cell: American Terror*), Showtime, 2005.
Angela Fuller, "Intramural," *Sleeper Cell* (also known as *Sleeper Cell: American Terror*), Showtime, 2005.

Also appeared in *Charles in Charge.*

Stage Appearances:
Pease Blossom, *A Midsummer Night's Dream,* Talent Development Center, Honolulu, HI, c. 1973.

RECORDINGS

Videos:
Building Boomtown, Artisan Entertainment, 2004.

WATERHOUSE, Keith 1929–2009
(Herald Froy, Lee Gibb, Keith Spencer Waterhouse)

PERSONAL

Full name, Keith Spencer Waterhouse; born February 6, 1929, in Leeds, Yorkshire, England; died September 4, 2009, in London, England. Writer. Waterhouse was a prolific author who wrote stage plays, teleplays, screenplays, books, and newspaper articles. With childhood friend and longtime collaborator Willis Hall, he adapted his best-known work, the 1959 novel *Billy Liar,* for the stage and film. The movie version was released in 1963. A television series based on the novel was produced by London Weekend Television in the early 1970s. Waterhouse began his writing career as a newspaper reporter in the early 1950s and became a full-time fiction writer after the publication of his first novel, *There Is a Happy Land,* in 1957. He composed a great number of plays, many with Hall, including *All Things Bright and Beautiful, They Called the Bastard Stephen,* and *Worzel Gummidge,* a play for children. The pair also wrote screenplays, such as *Whistle Down the Wind* and *A Kind of Loving;* television series, including *Inside George Webley* and *The Upper Crusts;* and books, among them *The Television Adventures of*

Worzel Gummidge and *Worzel Gummidge at the Fair.* Waterhouse also collaborated with other writers, including Paul Cave and Guy Deghy, with whom he wrote under the joint pseudonyms Herald Froy and Lee Gibb. Additional works include the successful play *Jeffrey Bernard Is Unwell,* which was first produced in 1989; a number of novels; and memoirs, including *City Lights: A Street Life.* In the 1970s and 1980s he contributed a column to the London newspaper the *Daily Mirror,* and from 1986 until his death, he was a columnist for the London *Daily Mail.*

PERIODICALS

Daily Mail, September 7, 2009.
Evening Standard, September 4, 2009.
New York Times, September 5, 2009.

WHEDON, Joss 1964(?)–

PERSONAL

Full name, Joseph Hill Whedon; born June 23, 1964 (some sources cite 1965), in New York, NY; son of Tom (a television producer and writer) and Lee (a high school teacher; maiden name, Stearns) Whedon; grandson of John Whedon (a playwright, librettist, and television writer); married Kai Cole (a textile and interior designer); children: Arden (son), Squire (daughter). *Education:* Attended a secondary boarding school in Winchester, England; Wesleyan University, Middletown, CT, B.A., 1987.

Addresses: *Office*—Mutant Enemy, Inc., PO Box 900, Beverly Hills, CA 90213. *Agent*—Creative Artists Agency, 2000 Avenue of the Stars, Los Angeles, CA 90067.

Career: Executive, producer, director, writer, composer, and lyricist. Also rewriter of films originated by other screenwriters. Mutant Enemy, Inc. (production company), Beverly Hills, CA, founder, 1998, and chief executive officer. Once worked at a video store.

Awards, Honors: Academy Award nomination, best original screenplay, Annie Award, best writing, International Animated Film Society, and Saturn Award, best writing, Academy of Science Fiction, Horror, and Fantasy Films, all (with others), 1996, for *Toy Story;* Annie Award nomination (with composer Scott Warrender), outstanding individual achievement for music in an animated feature production, 1999, for "My Lullaby," *The Lion King II: Simba's Pride;* Eyegore Award, 2000;

Bram Stoker Award nomination, best screenplay, Horror Writers Association, 2000, for *Buffy the Vampire Slayer;* Emmy Award nomination, outstanding writing for a drama series, 2000, for "Hush," *Buffy the Vampire Slayer;* Nebula Award nomination, best script, Science Fiction and Fantasy Writers of America, 2002, for "The Body," *Buffy the Vampire Slayer;* Nebula Award nomination, best script, 2003, for "Once More, with Feeling," *Buffy the Vampire Slayer;* Nebula Award, best script, and Hugo Award, best long–form dramatic presentation, World Science Fiction Society, 2006, for *Serenity;* Outstanding Lifetime Achievement Award in Cultural Humanism, Humanist Chaplaincy, Harvard University, 2009; Emmy Award (with others), outstanding short–format live–action entertainment program, and Hugo Award, best short–form dramatic presentation, both 2009, for *Dr. Horrible's Sing–Along Blog;* Bradbury Award, excellence in screenwriting, Science Fiction Writers of America, 2009; Vanguard Award, Producers Guild of America, 2010.

CREDITS

Television Work; Series:

Story editor, *Roseanne,* ABC, 1989–90.
Coproducer, *Parenthood,* NBC, 1990.
Creator, executive producer, and director of multiple episodes, *Buffy the Vampire Slayer* (also known as *BtVS, Buffy,* and *Buffy the Vampire Slayer: The Series*), The WB, 1997–2001, then UPN, 2001–2003.
Creator, executive producer, and director of multiple episodes, *Angel* (also known as *Angel: The Series*), The WB, 1999–2004.
Creator and executive producer, *Firefly* (also known as *Firefly: The Series* and *Joss Whedon's "Firefly"*), Fox, 2002–2003.
Creator and executive producer, *Dollhouse,* Fox, 2009–10.

Television Executive Producer; Pilots:

Buffy the Vampire Slayer, Fox, 1997.
Buffy the Vampire Slayer: The Animated Series, 2004.
(And creator and director) *Dollhouse,* Fox, 2009.

Television Director; Episodic:

"Serenity," *Firefly* (also known as *Firefly: The Series* and *Joss Whedon's "Firefly"*), Fox, 2002.
"The Train Job," *Firefly* (also known as *Firefly: The Series* and *Joss Whedon's "Firefly"*), Fox, 2002.
"Objects in Space," *Firefly* (also known as *Firefly: The Series* and *Joss Whedon's "Firefly"*), Fox, 2002.
"Business School," *The Office* (also known as *The Office: US Version*), NBC, 2007.
"Branch Wars," *The Office* (also known as *The Office: US Version*), NBC, 2007.
"Ghost," *Dollhouse,* Fox, 2009.

"Echo," *Dollhouse,* Fox, 2009.
"Vows," *Dollhouse,* Fox, 2009.
Glee, Fox, 2010.

Television Appearances; Episodic:

Voice of newscaster, "I, Robot—You, Jane," *Buffy the Vampire Slayer* (also known as *BtVS, Buffy,* and *Buffy the Vampire Slayer: The Series*), The WB, 1997.
Numfar, "Through the Looking Glass," *Angel* (also known as *Angel: The Series*), The WB, 2001.
(Uncredited) Man at funeral, "The Message," *Firefly* (also known as *Firefly: The Series* and *Joss Whedon's "Firefly"*), Fox, 2003.
Douglas, "Rat Saw God," *Veronica Mars,* UPN, 2005.
Sunday Morning Shootout (also known as *Hollywood Shootout* and *Shootout*), AMC, 2005.
Rove Live, Ten Network, 2005.
Magacine, 2005.
Film '72 (also known as *Film 2005, Film of the Year,* and *The Film Programme*), BBC, 2005.
HypaSpace (also known as *HypaSpace Daily* and *HypaSpace Weekly*), SPACE, 2006.
Voice, "Rabbits on a Roller Coaster," *Robot Chicken* (animated), Cartoon Network, 2007.
Voices of cowboy and scientist, "Help Me," *Robot Chicken* (animated), Cartoon Network, 2008.
Late Night with Jimmy Fallon, NBC, 2009.

Television Appearances; Specials:

Buffy's Back, E! Entertainment Television, 2001.
The "Alien" Saga, 2002.
"Buffy the Vampire Slayer: Television with a Bite," *Biography,* Arts and Entertainment, 2003.
The 100 Greatest Scary Moments, Channel 4, 2003.
Sci Fi Inside: "Serenity," Sci–Fi Channel, 2005.
06 Spaceys, 2006.
Star Wars: The Legacy Revealed, History Channel, 2007.
Battlestar Galactica: The Phenomenon, Sci–Fi Channel, 2008.
The Write Environment, 2008.
This American Life Live! (talk show), 2009.

Television Appearances; Miniseries:

Commentator, *TV Revolution,* Bravo, 2004.

Film Director:

Serenity, Universal, 2005.
Commentary! the Musical, Mutant Enemy Productions, 2008.

Film Appearances:

Himself, *Bandwagon,* 2004.
Voice, *Commentary! the Musical,* Mutant Enemy Productions, 2008.

Internet Appearances; Miniseries:
R. Tam Sessions (short spots), 2005.

Internet Work; Miniseries:
Executive producer and director, *Dr. Horrible's Sing–along Blog*, Drhorrible.com, 2008.

RECORDINGS

Video Appearances:
"Buffy": Season 2 Overview, Fox Box, 2002.
Voice, *Buffy the Vampire Slayer: Chaos Bleeds*, Fox Interactive/Vivendi Universal Games, 2003.
"Buffy": Season 3 Overview, Fox Box, 2003.
"Buffy": Season 4 Overview, Fox Box, 2003.
"Buffy": Season 5 Overview, Fox Box, 2003.
One Step Beyond: The Making of "Alien: Resurrection," Twentieth Century–Fox Home Entertainment, 2003.
Here's How It Was: The Making of "Firefly," Twentieth Century–Fox Home Entertainment, 2003.
Serenity: The 10th Character, 2003.
"Buffy": Season 6 Overview, Fox Box, 2004.
"Buffy": Season 7 Overview, Fox Box, 2004.
"Angel": Season 4 Overview (also known as *Prophecies: Season 4 Overview*), Fox Box, 2004.
Fatal Beauty and the Beast, Fox Box, 2004.
Last Looks: The Hyperion Hotel, Fox Box, 2004.
Malice in Wonderland: Wolfram & Hart, Fox Box, 2004.
Halos & Horns: Recurring Villainy, Fox Box, 2005.
"Angel": The Final Season, Fox Box, 2005.
Re–Lighting the Firefly, 2005.
What's in a Firefly, 2005.
Future History: The Story of Earth that Was, 2005.
Joss Whedon: The Master at Play, Creative Screenwriting Magazine, 2006.
A Filmmaker's Journey, Universal Pictures Finland, 2006.
Done the Impossible: The Fans' Tale of "Firefly" and "Serenity," Done the Impossible, 2006.
(And executive producer) *The Making of Dr. Horrible's Sing–along Blog*, Easy Action, 2008.

WRITINGS

Television Series:
Buffy the Vampire Slayer (also known as *BtVS*, *Buffy*, and *Buffy the Vampire Slayer: The Series*), multiple episodes, The WB, 1997–2001, then UPN, 2001–2003.
Angel (also known as *Angel: The Series*), The WB, multiple episodes, between 1999 and 2004.
Firefly (also known as *Firefly: The Series* and *Joss Whedon's "Firefly"*), Fox, multiple episodes, 2002, 2003.

Television Episodes:
"Little Sister," *Roseanne*, ABC, 1989–90.
"House of Grown–ups," *Roseanne*, ABC, 1989–90.
"Brain–Dead Poets Society," *Roseanne*, ABC, 1989–90.
"Chicken Hearts—Chicken Hearts," *Roseanne*, ABC, 1989–90.
"The Plague," *Parenthood*, NBC, 1990.
"Small Surprises," *Parenthood*, NBC, 1990.
(With David Tyron King) "Fun for Kids," *Parenthood*, NBC, 1991.
"Ghost," *Dollhouse*, Fox, 2009.
"Man on the Street," *Dollhouse*, Fox, 2009.
"Echo," *Dollhouse*, Fox, 2009.
"Vows," *Dollhouse*, Fox, 2009.

Television Pilots:
Buffy the Vampire Slayer, Fox, 1997.
Dollhouse, Fox, 2009.

Television Specials:
This American Life Live! (talk show), 2009.

Television Music; Series:
Composer of main title theme music, "Ballad of Serenity," *Firefly* (also known as *Firefly: The Series* and *Joss Whedon's "Firefly"*), Fox, 2002.

Television Songwriter; Episodic:
"The Exposition Song," "Restless," *Buffy the Vampire Slayer* (also known as *BtVS*, *Buffy*, and *Buffy the Vampire Slayer: The Series*), UPN, 2000.
Song composer and lyricist, "Once More, with Feeling," *Buffy the Vampire Slayer* (also known as *BtVS*, *Buffy*, and *Buffy the Vampire Slayer: The Series*), UPN, 2001.
"I'll Be Mrs.," "Selfless," *Buffy the Vampire Slayer* (also known as *BtVS*, *Buffy*, and *Buffy the Vampire Slayer: The Series*), UPN, 2002.

Screenplays:
Buffy the Vampire Slayer, Twentieth Century–Fox, 1992.
Rewriter, *Speed*, Twentieth Century–Fox, 1994.
(With others) *Toy Story* (also known as *Toy Story in 3–D*), Buena Vista, 1995.
Alien: Resurrection (also known as *Alien 4*), Twentieth Century–Fox, 1997.
Titan A.E. (animated; also known as *Titan: After Earth*), Twentieth Century–Fox, 2000.
Serenity, Universal, 2005.
Commentary! the Musical, Mutant Enemy Productions, 2008.

Film Music:
Lyricist, "My Lullaby," *The Lion King II: Simba's Pride* (animated), 1998.
"Burn Me Down," *Chance*, 2003.

Internet Miniseries:

Writer and songwriter, *Dr. Horrible's Sing–along Blog*, Drhorrible.com, 2008.

Other:

Author of the graphic novels *Dangerous, Gifted,* and *Torn.* Creator of the Internet comic *Sugarshock!,* Dark Horse, 2007. Creator and writer of the comic books *Astonishing X–Men,* Marvel, beginning 2005; *Runaways,* Marvel, 2007; *Buffy the Vampire Slayer—Season 8,* Dark Horse, 2007–08; *Fray; Angel: Long Night's Journey,* Dark Horse; *Angel: After the Fall* (also known as *Angel: Season 6*), IDW Publishing; and *Serenity: Those Left Behind,* Dark Horse. author of introduction to the graphic novel *Earth X,* by Kim Krugeer and Alex Ross, Marvel; contributor to the comic book anthologies *Tales of the Slayers* and *Tales of the Vampire,* Dark Horse. Also contributor to national periodicals, including *TV Guide.* Songwriter, including "Last Time" for recording artist Anthony Head, 2002.

ADAPTATIONS

The animated film *Atlantis: The Lost Empire,* released by Buena Vista in 2001, was based on a story by Whedon.

OTHER SOURCES

Periodicals:

Buffy the Vampire Slayer, fall, 2000, p. 66; summer, 2001, pp. 58–61; March, 2002, pp. 38–41; June, 2002, p. 6; December, 2002, pp. 12–15, 26–30.
Cinefantastique, May, 1997; March, 1999, pp. 16–17, 19.
Entertainment Weekly, April 25, 1997, pp. 23–24; June 14, 2002, p. 75; May 21, 2004, pp. 46–48; August 19, 2005, p. 56.
Forbes, August 24, 2009, p. 96.
Los Angeles Times, September 11, 2005.
Mediaweek, February 17, 1997, pp. 9–10.
New Yorker, March 2, 2009, p. 76.
New York Times, September 25, 2005.
Starlog, April, 1997.
TV Guide, January 31, 2004, pp. 22–24; June 19, 2005, p. 12; November 7, 2005, p. 44; December 4, 2006, p. 31; February 12, 2007, p. 12.
USA Today, June 23, 2005.
Variety, July 21, 2008, p. 1.
Washington Post, September 30, 2005.
Wizard, July, 2005, pp. 68–72.

WILLIAMS, Davida 1986–

PERSONAL

Full name, Davida Brittany Williams; born September 5, 1986, in Los Angeles, CA; daughter of David Williams (a guitarist). *Education:* Attended Mount St. Mary's College, Los Angeles.

Addresses: *Agent*—TalentWorks, 3500 West Olive Ave., Suite 1400, Burbank, CA 91505.

Career: Actress. Appeared in more than thirty commercials as a child; appeared on book covers, including covers of the "Cheetah Girls" series. Background vocalist, including appearances on tour with the Michael Jackson entourage in Hawaii, 1994; performer with the female musical group TG4.

Awards, Honors: Young Artist Award nomination, best actress under ten in a television series or show, 1994, for *Hangin' with Mr. Cooper.*

CREDITS

Television Appearances; Series:

Claire Miller, a recurring role, *Lizzie McGuire,* ABC, 2001–2003.
Vlad, *Jonas,* The Disney Channel, 2007.
Jade Taylor, *As the World Turns,* CBS, 2008–2009.

Television Appearances; Movies:

Cry Baby Lane, Nickelodeon, 2000.

Television Appearances; Pilots:

Suzie, *Do Over,* The WB, 2002.
Claire, *Triple Play,* 2004.

Television Appearances; Episodic:

"Slumber Party," *Hangin' with Mr. Cooper,* ABC, 1993.
Girl, "Talent Show," *Me and the Boys,* ABC, 1994.
Angela, *Happily Ever After: Fairy Tales for Every Child,* HBO, 1995.
Andrea Potter, "Broken Ties," *Sweet Justice,* NBC, 1995.
Cleghorne!, The WB, 1995.
First Blue Bird, "I, Bowl Buster," *The Fresh Prince of Bel–Air,* NBC, 1996.
Discovery Scout, "The Audition," *Sister, Sister,* The WB, 1996.
Elizabeth, "The Wedding," *Cybill,* CBS, 1997.
Lisa, "Children of Time," *Star Trek: Deep Space Nine* (also known as *Deep Space Nine, DS9,* and *Star Trek: DS9*), syndicated, 1997.
(Uncredited) Girl, "Take My Breath Away," *Degrassi: The Next Generation* (also known as *Degrassi, nouvelle generation*), The N, 2002.
(Uncredited) Girl, "Don't Believe the Hype," *Degrassi: The Next Generation* (also known as *Degrassi, nouvelle generation*), The N, 2002.

(Uncredited) Girl, "Careless Whisper," *Degrassi: The Next Generation* (also known as *Degrassi, nouvelle generation*), The N, 2003.
Grace, "Coach Tracy," *The Tracy Morgan Show*, NBC, 2004.
Eliza, "Date Night," *Quintuplets*, Fox, 2004.
Girl, *Nick Cannon Presents: Short Circuitz*, MTV, 2007.

Film Appearances:
Sonja, *Younger and Younger*, Kushner–Locke, 1993.
Lauren, *Raise Your Voice*, New Line Cinema, 2004.
Zoe, *Twisted Fortune*, Warner Home Video, 2007.
Trixie, *American High School*, Anchor Bay Films, 2009.

Stage Appearances:
Appeared as Raynell in a production of *Fences*.

RECORDINGS

Videos:
Appeared with TG4 in the music video "Ain't No Need" by IMx.

WILSON, Roxane
(Roxanna Wilson, Roxanne Wilson)

PERSONAL

Full name, Roxane A. Wilson; stepdaughter of Ian Wilson (a vocalist); married Grant Bowler (an actor), January 21, 2001; children: Edie, Zeke. *Education:* Edith Cowan University, diploma, 1993.

Addresses: *Agent*—Sue Barnett, Sue Barnett and Associates, 1/96 Albion St., Surry Hills, New South Wales 2010, Australia.

Career: Actress. Also works as drama coach.

CREDITS

Television Appearances; Series:
(As Roxanne Wilson) Jennifer Chandler, *Family and Friends*, Nine Network, 1990.
(As Roxanne Wilson) Coral O'Connor, *Echo Point*, Ten Network, 1995.
Robbie Manning, *Big Sky*, 1997.
Suzi Abromavich, a recurring role, *Water Rats*, Nine Network, 1998–99.
Daniella Mayo, *Stingers*, Nine Network, 2000–2002.
Ellie Delaney, *The Alice*, Nine Network, 2005–2006.

Angela Mulroney, *Out of the Blue*, Ten Network, 2008.

Television Appearances; Movies:
Ellie Delaney, *The Alice*, 2004.

Television Appearances; Episodic:
Tessa, "The Only Constant," *Police Rescue*, Australian Broadcasting Corporation, 1996.
Marilyn O'Connor, *Wildside*, Australian Broadcasting Corporation, 1998.
Kristen Charlton, "Deadfall," *Murder Call*, Nine Network, 1998.
(As Roxanna Wilson) Atlanta, "A Devil's Deal," *Beast-Master*, syndicated, 2000.
Candy, "Guilty Creatures," *Outrageous Fortune*, TV 3 New Zealand, 2008.
Chantelle Gregory, *Rescue Special Ops*, Nine Network, 2009.

Appeared as Karen in the program *Common Law*.

Film Appearances:
Helen, *Spare Tyres* (short film), 1994.
Carmen, *Five Months in Her Bathroom* (short film), 1996.
The girlfriend, *The Final Squeak*, 1997.
Helen Stacey, *Reflections*, Combridge International, 1998.
Anne, *Change of Heart*, 1999.
(As Roxanne Wilson) *The Day Neil Armstrong Walked on the Moon*, Talking Heads Productions, 1999.
True Colours (short film), Biglove Productions, 1999.
Lady, *Erskineville Kings*, Southern Star Entertainment, 1999.
Girl in shop, *A Once Smiling Woman* (short film), Australian Film Television Radio School, 2000.
Angel, *Lucky Blue*, 2001.
Marie Rogen, *Punishment*, Glover Productions, 2008.

Appeared in the short films *The Heroes* and *Loose Ends*.

Stage Appearances:
Genevieve, *Territorial Rites*, 1988.
Mother Metz and other roles, *Red Nose*, 1992.
Hortensio, *The Taming of the Shrew*, 1993.
Amanda Prynne, *Private Lives*, 1994.
Cordelia, *Finding the Sun*, 1999.
Myra, *Freak Winds*, 2000.

Appeared as Blanche, *Bumpy Angels*; multiple roles, *The Dining Room*; keeper and Alice, *A Dream Play*; Helen of Troy, *The Greeks*; Lady Plymdale, *Lady Windermere's Fan*; Natalia Petrovna, *A Month in the Country*; Gertrude, *Rosencrantz and Guildenstern Are Dead*; and Mrs. Holly, *Suddenly Last Summer*.

WOODS, James 1947–

PERSONAL

Full name, James Howard Woods; born April 18, 1947, in Vernal, UT; son of Gail Peyton (an army intelligence officer) and Martha Ann (a schoolteacher and preschool operator; maiden name, Dixon) Woods; brother of Michael Jeffrey Woods (an actor); married Kathryn Morrison–Pahoa (a costume designer; some sources cite name as Kathryn Greko), 1980 (divorced, 1983); married Sarah Marie Owen (a horse trainer), June 2, 1989 (divorced, 1990). *Education:* Attended Massachusetts Institute of Technology, 1965–69. *Politics:* Democrat. *Religion:* Roman Catholic. *Avocational Interests:* Cooking, golf, photography.

Addresses: *Agent*—Ken Kaplan, Gersh Agency, 9465 Wilshire Blvd., 6th Floor, Beverly Hills, CA 90212.

Career: Actor. Theatre Company of Boston, actor, 1960s; voice for commercials. Director of promotional films and television public service announcements. Former reserve police officer for Los Angeles County, CA.

Member: Academy of Motion Picture Arts and Sciences, Players Club, International Platform Association, Mountaingate Country Club, Theta Delta Chi.

Awards, Honors: Obie Award, *Village Voice,* and Clarence Derwent Award, both c. 1970, for *Saved;* Theatre World Award, 1972, for *Moonchildren;* Obie Award, 1972, for *Conduct Unbecoming;* Golden Globe Award nomination, best actor in a motion picture drama, and Kansas City Film Critics Award, best supporting actor, both 1980, for *The Onion Field;* Academy Award nomination and Independent Spirit Award, Independent Features Project/West, both best actor, 1987, for *Salvador;* Emmy Award and Golden Globe Award, both best actor in a television miniseries or movie, 1987, for "Promise," *Hallmark Hall of Fame;* Golden Apple Award, male star of the year, Hollywood Women's Press Association, 1987; Emmy Award, outstanding performance in informational programming, 1988, for *Crimes of Passion;* Golden Globe Award nomination, best actor in a television miniseries or movie, 1988, for *In Love and War;* Independent Spirit Award nomination, best male lead, 1988, for *Best Seller;* Independent Spirit Award nomination, best male lead, 1989, for *The Boost;* Emmy Award, outstanding lead actor in a miniseries or special, 1989, Golden Globe Award nomination, best actor in a television miniseries or movie, 1990, and Magnolia Award, best actor, Shanghai International Television Festival, 1990, all for "My Name Is Bill W.," *Hallmark Hall of Fame;* Golden Globe Award nomination and Emmy Award nomination, both outstanding actor in a television miniseries or movie, 1993, for *Citizen Cohn;* Annual CableACE Award nomination, best actor in a dramatic series, National Cable Television Association, 1993, for "Since I Don't Have You," *Fallen Angels;* Emmy Award nomination, outstanding lead actor in a limited series or special, 1995, and Golden Globe Award nomination, best performance by an actor in a television miniseries or movie, 1996, both for *Indictment: The McMartin Trial;* Screen Actors Guild Award nomination (with others), outstanding cast performance, 1996, for *Nixon;* Catalonian International Film Festival Award, best actor, 1996, and Golden Satellite Award, best actor in a motion picture drama, International Press Academy, 1997, both for *Killer: A Journal of Murder;* Golden Globe Award nomination and Golden Satellite Award nomination, both best performance by an actor in a television miniseries or movie, 1997, for *The Summer of Ben Tyler;* Academy Award nomination and Golden Globe Award nomination, both best supporting actor, 1997, for *Ghosts of Mississippi;* received star on the Hollywood Walk of Fame, 1998; Saturn Award, best actor, Academy of Science Fiction, Fantasy, and Horror Films, 1999, for *Vampires;* Sierra Award nomination, best supporting actor, Las Vegas Film Critics Society, 2000, for *The Virgin Suicides;* Daytime Emmy Award, outstanding performer in an animated program, 2000, for *Hercules;* Role Model Award, Young Hollywood Awards, 2000; Golden Satellite Award, Golden Globe Award nomination, and Screen Actors Guild Award nomination, all outstanding actor in a television miniseries or movie, 2001, for *Dirty Pictures;* San Diego Film Festival Award, achievement in acting, 2002; Emmy Award nomination, outstanding lead actor in a miniseries or movie, 2003, and Golden Satellite Award, best actor in a television miniseries or movie, 2004, both for *Rudy: The Rudy Giuliani Story;* Maverick Tribute Award, Cinequest San Jose Film Festival, 2003; Emmy Award nomination, outstanding guest actor in a drama series, 2006, for "Body & Soul," *ER;* Satellite Award nomination, best actor in a drama series, 2007, for *Shark.*

CREDITS

Film Appearances:
Bill Schmidt, *The Visitors,* United Artists, 1972.
Lieutenant Wyatt, *Hickey & Boggs,* United Artists, 1972.
Frankie McVeigh, *The Way We Were,* Columbia, 1973.
Bank officer, *The Gambler,* Paramount, 1974.
Larry, *Distance,* Coe, 1975.
Quentin, *Night Moves,* Warner Bros., 1975.
Crainpool, *Alex & the Gypsy* (also known as *Love and Other Crimes*), Twentieth Century–Fox, 1976.
Art Lewis, *The Billion Dollar Bubble,* 1976.
Harold Bloomguard, *The Choirboys* (also known as *Aenglarna*), Universal, 1977.

Gregory Ulas Powell, *The Onion Field,* Avco Embassy, 1979.

The fiddler, *The Black Marble,* Avco Embassy, 1980.

Aldo Mercer, *Eyewitness* (also known as *The Janitor*), Twentieth Century–Fox, 1981.

Charles Pratt, *Split Image* (also known as *Captured* and *L'envoutement*), Orion, 1982.

Fast–Walking Miniver, *Fast–Walking,* Lorimar, 1982.

Max Renn, *Videodrome* (also known as *Zonekiller*), Universal, 1983.

Jake Wise, *Against All Odds,* Columbia, 1984.

Maximilian "Max" Bercovicz/Secretary Christopher Bailey, *Once upon a Time in America* (also known as *C'era una volta in America*), Warner Bros., 1984.

(In archive footage) Max Renn, *Terror in the Aisles* (also known as *Time for Terror*), 1984.

Joshua Shapiro, *Joshua Then and Now,* Twentieth Century–Fox, 1985.

Richard "Dick" Morrison, "Quitters, Inc.," *Cat's Eye* (also known as *Stephen King's "Cat's Eye"*), Metro–Goldwyn–Mayer, 1985.

Richard Boyle, *Salvador,* Hemdale Releasing, 1986.

Cleve, *Best Seller,* Orion, 1987.

Lenny Brown, *The Boost,* Hemdale Releasing, 1988.

Lloyd Hopkins, *Cop,* Atlantic Releasing, 1988.

Edward "Eddie" Dodd, *True Believer* (also known as *Fighting Justice*), Columbia, 1989.

Michael Spector, *Immediate Family* (also known as *Parental Guidance*), Columbia, 1989.

Detective Lieutenant John Moss, *The Hard Way,* Universal, 1992.

Gabriel Caine, *Diggstown* (also known as *Midnight Sting*), Metro–Goldwyn–Mayer, 1992.

Jack Russell, *Straight Talk,* Buena Vista, 1992.

Joseph Scott, *Chaplin* (also known as *Charlot*), TriStar, 1993.

Jack Benyon, *The Getaway,* Twentieth Century–Fox, 1994.

Ned Trent, *The Specialist* (also known as *El especialista*), Warner Bros., 1994.

Carl Panzram, *Killer: A Journal of Murder* (also known as *The Killer*), First Independent, 1995.

H. R. Haldeman, *Nixon,* Buena Vista, 1995.

Lester Diamond, *Casino,* Universal, 1995.

Byron de la Beckwith, *Ghosts of Mississippi* (also known as *Ghosts from the Past*), Columbia, 1996.

Reggie Makeshift, *For Better or Worse,* Columbia, 1996.

Michael Kitz, *Contact,* Warner Bros., 1997.

Uncle Sam, *Kicked in the Head,* Imperial Entertainment, 1997.

Voice of Hades, *Hercules* (animated), Buena Vista, 1997.

(Uncredited) *I Think I Cannes* (documentary; also known as *All Access*), 1997.

Alan Mann, *True Crime,* Warner Bros., 1998.

Jack Crow, *Vampires* (also known as *John Carpenter's "Vampires"* and *Vampire$*), Columbia, 1998.

Mel, *Another Day in Paradise,* Trimark Pictures, 1998.

Colonel Robert Moore, *The General's Daughter* (also known as *Wehrlos—Die Tochter des generals*), Paramount, 1999.

Dr. Harvey Mandrake (some sources cite Dr. Powers), *Any Given Sunday* (also known as *Gridiron* and *The League*), Warner Bros., 1999.

Ringside fan, *Play It to the Bone* (also known as *Play It*), Buena Vista, 1999.

Voice of Hades, *Hercules: Zero to Hero,* Buena Vista, 1999.

Mr. Lisbon, *The Virgin Suicides* (also known as *Sophia Coppola's "The Virgin Suicides"*), Paramount, 2000.

Dr. Wilhelm Von Huber, *Race to Space* (also known as *Race to Space—Mission ins unbekannte*), Columbia/TriStar Home Video, 2001.

Father McFeely, *Scary Movie 2* (also known as *Scarier Movie* and *Film de peur*), Miramax/Dimension Films, 2001.

Mr. Leonard D'Onofrio, *Riding in Cars with Boys,* Columbia, 2001.

Voice of General Hein, *Final Fantasy: The Spirits Within* (animated; also known as *Final Fantasy: The Movie* and *Fainaru fantaji*), Columbia/TriStar, 2001.

Voice of Dr. Phillium "Phil" Benedict, *Recess: School's Out* (animated), Buena Vista, 2001.

Dr. Raymond Turner, *John Q,* New Line Cinema, 2002.

Voice of evil falcon, *Stuart Little 2* (animated), Columbia, 2002.

Voice of Gloomius Maximus, *Rolie Polie Olie: The Great Defender of Fun* (animated; also known as *William Joyce's "Rolie Polie Olie: The Great Defender of Fun"*), Walt Disney Home Video, 2002.

Voice of Hades, *Mickey's House of Villains* (animated), 2002.

Narrator, *Little Warriors* (documentary), 2002.

Walter O'Brien, *Northfork* (also known as *North Fork*), Paramount, 2003.

Voice of Jallak, *Ark* (animated), Creative Light Worldwide, 2004.

(In archive footage) *Imaginary Witness: Hollywood and the Holocaust* (documentary), 2004, Shadow Distribution, 2007.

Voice of Grab Takit, *The Easter Egg Adventure* (animated), First Look International, 2005.

Hank Joyce, *Pretty Persuasion,* Samuel Goldwyn Films/Roadside Attractions/Renaissance films, 2005.

Tommy Athens, *Be Cool,* Metro–Goldwyn–Mayer, 2005.

Narrator, *Buddy* (documentary), Big Orange Films, 2005.

Vaughn Stevens, *End Game,* Metro–Goldwyn–Mayer, 2006.

Voice of Reggie Belafonte, *Surf's Up!* (animated), Columbia, 2007.

Michael's agent, *An American Carol* (also known as *Big Fat Important Movie*), Vivendi Entertainment, 2008.

Himself, *Journey to Sundance* (documentary), Hollywood Filmmakers, 2009.

Film Work:

Producer, *Cop*, Atlantic, 1988.

Producer, *Another Day in Paradise*, Trimark Pictures, 1998.

Director, *Falling in Love in Pongo Ponga* (promotional film), SKYY Vodka, 2002.

Executive producer, *Northfork* (also known as *North Fork*), Paramount, 2003.

Television Appearances; Series:

Voice of Hades, *Hercules* (animated; also known as *Disney's "Hercules"*), ABC and syndicated, 1998–99.

Voice of Hades, *House of Mouse* (animated), ABC, 2001–2002.

Sebastian Stark, *Shark*, CBS, 2006–2008.

Television Appearances; Movies:

Reporter, *Footsteps* (also known as *Footsteps: Nice Guys Finish Last* and *Nice Guys Finish Last*), CBS, 1972.

Rick, *A Great American Tragedy*, ABC, 1972.

Bank officer, *The Gambler*, ABC, 1974.

Walter, *Foster and Laurie*, CBS, 1975.

Leonard "Lenny" Schoenfeld, *F. Scott Fitzgerald in Hollywood*, ABC, 1976.

Captain Sammy Berg, "Raid on Entebbe," *The Big Event*, NBC, 1977.

Alfred Browning, *The Gift of Love*, ABC, 1978.

Danny Corelli, ... *And Your Name Is Jonah*, CBS, 1979.

Sin Eater, *The Incredible Journey of Doctor Meg Laurel*, CBS, 1979.

Robert K. Tannenbaum, *Badge of the Assassin*, CBS, 1985.

James B. "Jim" Stockdale, *In Love and War*, NBC, 1987.

Robert, "Hills like White Elephants," *Women and Men: Stories of Seduction*, HBO, 1990.

Walter Farmer, *The Boys* (also known as *The Guys*), ABC, 1991.

Roy Marcus Cohn, *Citizen Cohn* (also known as *Rules of Misconduct: The Roy Cohn Story*), HBO, 1992.

Matt Coler, *Next Door*, Showtime, 1994.

Paul Clark (some sources cite Paul Moore or Tom), *Jane's House*, CBS, 1994.

Danny Davis, *Indictment: The McMartin Trial*, HBO, 1995.

Weston Tate, *Curse of the Starving Class*, Showtime, 1995.

Temple Rayburn, *The Summer of Ben Tyler*, CBS, 1996.

Dennis Barrie, *Dirty Pictures*, Showtime, 2000.

Voice, *Daria: Is It Fall Yet?* (animated), MTV, 2000.

Rudolph "Rudy" Giuliani, *Rudy: The Rudy Giuliani Story* (also known as *Rudy's Wars*), USA Network, 2003.

Pops, *This Girl's Life*, Cinemax, 2003.

Television Appearances; Miniseries:

Karl Weiss, *Holocaust* (also known as *Holocaust—The Story of the Family Weiss*), NBC, 1978.

Bravo Profiles: The Entertainment Business, Bravo, 1998.

Voice of John Adams, *Founding Fathers*, History Channel, 2000.

Voice of John Adams, *Founding Brothers*, History Channel, 2002.

Host and narrator, *Moments in Time*, The Discovery Channel, 2003.

Captain of James Woods Gang, *Poker Royale: The James Woods Gang vs. The Unabombers*, Game Show Network, 2005.

National Heads–Up Poker Championship, 2006.

Television Appearances; Specials:

Andrew Lynch, "All the Way Home," *Hallmark Hall of Fame* (also known as *Hallmark Television Playhouse*), NBC, 1971.

Assistant District Attorney Joseph Ryan, "The Disappearance of Aimee," *Hallmark Hall of Fame* (also known as *Hallmark Television Playhouse*), NBC, 1976.

CBS' Happy New Year America 1986 (also known as *Happy New Year America*), CBS, 1985.

D. J., "Promise," *Hallmark Hall of Fame*, CBS, 1986.

Funny, You Don't Look 200: A Constitutional Vaudeville (also known as *Funny, You Don't Look 200*), ABC, 1987.

Host, *Crimes of Passion*, ABC, 1988.

Bill Wilson, "My Name Is Bill W." (also known as "The Bill Wilson Story"), *Hallmark Hall of Fame*, CBS, 1989.

Host and narrator, *Wildfire*, TBS and PBS, 1990.

Host and performer, *Voices That Care*, Fox, 1991.

Larry King TNT Extra (also known as *The Larry King Special ... Inside Hollywood*), TNT, 1991.

Welcome Home America! A USO Salute to America's Sons and Daughters, ABC, 1991.

Host and narrator, *Mobs and Mobsters*, ABC, 1992.

HBO's 20th Anniversary—We Hardly Believe It Ourselves, HBO and CBS, 1992.

Host, *Great Television Moments: What We Watched*, ABC, 1993.

Inside the Academy Awards, TNT, 1997.

A Salute to Martin Scorsese (also known as *The American Film Institute Salute to Martin Scorsese* and *25th American Film Institute Life Achievement Award: A Salute to Martin Scorsese*), CBS, 1997.

Movie Surfers: Go Inside Disney's "Hercules," The Disney Channel, 1997.

Narrator, *AFI's 100 Years ... 100 Movies* (also known as *AFI's 100 Years ... 100 Movies: The Wilder Shores of Love*), CBS, 1998.

Narrator, *America's Endangered Species: Don't Say Good–bye*, NBC, 1998.

Hollywood & Vinyl: Disney's 101 Greatest Musical Moments, VH1, 1998.

Masters of Fantasy: John Carpenter, Sci–Fi Channel, 1998.

AFI's 100 Years ... 100 Movies: The Antiheroes, 1998.

(Uncredited; in archive footage) *Sharon Stone—Una mujer de 100 caras,* 1998.

(Uncredited; in archive footage) *Femmes Fatales: Sharon Stone,* 1998.

Hollywood Salutes Jodie Foster: An American Cinematheque Tribute, TNT, 1999.

Host and narrator, *World's Deadliest Earthquakes,* ABC, 1999.

Narrator, *The Road to Rapture,* Arts and Entertainment, 1999.

AFI's 100 Years ... 100 Stars, CBS, 1999.

The Triumph of Evil, PBS, 1999.

Narrator, *Cheating Las Vegas,* The Learning Channel, 2000.

Narrator, *Palm Beach: Money, Power, and Privilege,* Arts and Entertainment, 2000.

Narrator, *Sensational Cities: New York,* The Learning Channel, 2000.

America: A Tribute to Heroes, multiple networks, 2001.

Narrator, *Digging for the Truth: Archaeology and the Bible,* History Channel, 2001.

Narrator, *The Real Untouchables,* 2001.

Narrator and voices of a Viking and prison guard, *Legend of the Lost Tribe* (animated; also known as *Robbie the Reindeer in "Legend of the Lost Tribe"*), CBS, 2002.

AFI Life Achievement Award: A Tribute to Robert De Niro, USA Network, 2003.

Intimate Portrait: Penny Marshall, Lifetime, 2003.

"Sharon Stone: Fearless," *Biography,* Arts and Entertainment, 2003.

(In archive footage) *101 Most Shocking Moments in Entertainment,* E! Entertainment Television, 2003.

"Alec Baldwin," *Biography,* Arts and Entertainment, 2004.

"Melanie Griffith," *Biography,* Arts and Entertainment, 2004.

Z Channel: A Magnificent Obsession, Independent Film Channel, 2004.

Presenter, *AFI Life Achievement Award: A Tribute to Meryl Streep,* USA Network, 2004.

Tsunami Aid: A Concert of Hope, multiple networks, 2005.

"Jodie Foster," *Biography,* Arts and Entertainment, 2005.

Stardust: The Bette Davis Story, TCM, 2006.

"James Woods," *Biography,* Arts and Entertainment, 2007.

"Anthony Hopkins," *Biography,* Arts and Entertainment, 2007.

AFI's 10 Top 10 (also known as *AFI's 100 Years ... AFI's 10 Top 10*), CBS, 2008.

Reinventando Hollywood, 2008.

Television Appearances; Pilots:

Himself, *Naked,* Bravo, 2005.

Sebastian Stark, *Shark,* CBS, 2006.

Television Appearances; Episodic:

Caz Mayer, "Death Is Not a Passing Grade," *Kojak,* CBS, 1974.

Larry Kirkoff, "The Kirkoff Case," *The Rockford Files* (also known as *Jim Rockford, Private Investigator*), NBC, 1974.

Alex Welles, "The Great Debate," *Welcome Back, Kotter,* ABC, 1975.

Doug, "Trail of Terror," *The Streets of San Francisco,* ABC, 1975.

Ted Ayres, "A Time to Mourn," *The Rookies,* ABC, 1975.

"Cops Who Sleep Together," *Bert D'Angelo/Superstar,* 1976.

Danny Reeves, "Sins of Thy Father," *Barnaby Jones,* CBS, 1976.

Lewis Packer, "Thanksgiving," *Police Story,* NBC, 1976.

Dr. Robert Styles, "An Eye to the Future," *Family,* 1977.

"Dead Man's Hand: Parts 1 & 2," *Young Maverick,* CBS, 1979.

Guest host, *Saturday Night Live* (also known as *SNL*), NBC, 1989.

Dennis Youngblood, "Oral Sex, Lies, and Videotape," *Dream On,* HBO, 1993.

Mickey Cohen, "Since I Don't Have You," *Fallen Angels,* Showtime, c. 1993.

Guest voice, "Homer and Apu," *The Simpsons* (animated), Fox, 1994.

Saturday Night Special, Fox, 1996.

"The Films of Rob Reiner," *The Directors,* 1999.

"Full Contact: The Making of 'Any Given Sunday,'" *HBO First Look,* HBO, 1999.

Voice of Major Baklava, "Leonardo Is Caught in the Grip of an Outbreak of Randal's Imagination and Patrick Swayze Either Does or Doesn't Work in the New Pet Store," *Clerks* (animated; also known as *Clerks: The Cartoon* and *Clerks: Uncensored*), ABC, 2000.

Inside the Actors Studio (also known as *Inside the Actors Studio: The Craft of Theatre and Film*), Bravo, 2000.

Rotten TV, 2000.

"Riding in Cars with Boys," *HBO First Look,* HBO, 2001.

Contestant, "Hollywood Home Game III," *World Poker Tour,* Travel Channel, 2004.

Contestant, *Celebrity Poker Showdown,* Bravo, 2004, 2005.

Manny Kowalski, "Orgy: The Musical," *Odd Job Jack,* Comedy Network, 2005.

Voice, "Peter's Got Woods," *Family Guy* (animated; also known as *Padre de familia*), Fox, 2005.

Dr. Nate Lennox, "Body & Soul," *ER,* NBC, 2006.

Himself, "Aquamom," *Entourage,* HBO, 2006.

Headline News, Cable News Network, 2006.

Entertainment Tonight (also known as *Entertainment This Week, E.T., ET Weekend,* and *This Week in Entertainment*), syndicated, 2006, 2008.

(Uncredited; in archive footage) Dr. Nate Lennox, "300 Patients," *ER,* NBC, 2007.

Voice, "Back to the Woods," *Family Guy* (animated; also known as *Padre de familia*), Fox, 2008.

(Uncredited; in archive footage) Dr. Nate Lennox, "Previously on ER," *ER,* NBC, 2009.

Provided voice of Hades for an episode of *Toon Jam* (animated); appeared in *Shark Bay,* Comedy Channel.

Television Talk Show Guest Appearances; Episodic:
The Tonight Show Starring Johnny Carson, NBC, 1979.
Late Night with David Letterman, NBC, multiple appearances, between 1989 and 1992.
Live with Regis and Kathie Lee, syndicated, 1992.
The Rosie O'Donnell Show, syndicated, 1996.
Late Night with Conan O'Brien, NBC, 1996, 2001, 2005.
Howard Stern, 1999.
The Howard Stern Show, E! Entertainment Television, 1999.
The Howard Stern Radio Show, 1999, 2000.
The Tonight Show with Jay Leno (also known as *Jay Leno*), NBC, multiple appearances, between 2001 and 2007.
Jimmy Kimmel Live! (also known as *Jimmy Kimmel*), ABC, 2004, 2005.
The Late Late Show with Craig Ferguson, CBS, 2005, 2006, 2007.

Television Appearances; Awards Presentations:
The ... Annual Academy Awards, 1987, ABC, (in archive footage) 1996, 1997.
The 41st Annual Emmy Awards, Fox, 1989.
The 7th Annual American Cinema Awards, 1990.
Presenter, *The Second International Rock Awards,* ABC, 1990.
Host, *Grammy Legends Show* (also known as *Grammy Living Legends Awards*), CBS, 1990.
Host, *The 12th Annual ACE Awards* (also known as *The Golden ACE Awards*), multiple networks, 1991.
Presenter, *The 44th Annual Primetime Emmy Awards,* Fox, 1992.
Presenter, *The American Television Awards,* ABC, 1993.
Presenter, *The 3rd Annual Screen Actors Guild Awards,* NBC, 1997.
Presenter, *The ... Annual People's Choice Awards,* CBS, 1997, 1999, 2000.
Presenter, *AFI Awards 2001,* CBS, 2001.
Presenter, *The 2001 ESPY Awards,* ESPN, 2001.
(Uncredited) *The 2001 IFP/West Independent Spirit Awards,* 2001.
The Award Show Awards Show, Trio, 2003.
7th Annual Prism Awards, FX Network, 2003.
Presenter, *The 56th Annual Writers Guild Awards,* Starz, 2004.
The 58th Annual Primetime Emmy Awards, NBC, 2006.
Presenter, *The 64th Annual Golden Globe Awards,* NBC, 2007.

Television Work; Series:
Producer, *Shark,* CBS, 2007–2008.

Stage Appearances:
Len, *Saved,* Chelsea Theatre Center of Brooklyn, Brooklyn Academy of Music, New York City, 1970.

Dale and Tom Meadows, *Borstal Boy,* Lyceum Theatre, New York City, 1970.
Conduct Unbecoming, Ethel Barrymore Theatre, New York City, 1970.
David Darst, *Trial of the Catonsville Nine,* Theatre at Good Shepherd–Faith Church, New York City, then Lyceum Theatre, both 1971.
Bob Rettie, *Moonchildren,* Royale Theatre, New York City, 1972.
Jacob "Carruthers" Perew, *Green Julia,* Sheridan Square Playhouse, New York City, 1972.
Finishing Touches, Plymouth Theatre, New York City, 1973.
Paul, "Vivien," Number Three, "In Fireworks Lie Secret Codes," and understudy for the role of Larry, "Stops along the Way," *The One Act Play Festival,* Mitzi E. Newhouse Theatre, New York City, 1981.
Dan Grady, *Gardenia,* Manhattan Theatre Club, Stage 73, New York City, 1982.

Radio Appearances; Episodic:
The Howard Stern Show, 1999.

RECORDINGS

Videos:
Hollywood on Horses, 1989.
Alan Mann, *True Crime: The Scene of the Crime,* 1999.
The General's Daughter: Behind the Secrets, 1999.
Narrator, *Cheating Las Vegas,* 2000.
The Making of "Hercules," 2000.
Once upon a Time: Sergio Leone, 2001.
Playboy Exposed: Playboy Mansion Parties Uncensored, 2001.
Into the Valley of Death, 2001.
Breaking the Silence: The Making of "Hannibal," 2001.
Behind the Scenes of "John Q," New Line Home Video, 2002.
The Return to the Onion Field, Kinowelt Home Entertainment, 2002.
Bareknuckle Film Making: The Making of Northfork, Paramount, 2003.
(In archive footage) Lester Diamond, *Casino: The Cast and Characters,* Universal, 2005.

Appeared (in archive footage) in the music video "Against All Odds (Take a Look at Me Now)" by Phil Collins, c. 1984; and in the music video "Voices that Care," 1991.

Video Games:
Voice of Hades Lord of the Dead, *Hercules* (also known as *Disney's "Hercules"*), 1997.
Voice of Gar Hob, *Of Light and Darkness,* Interplay Productions, 1998.

Voice of Hades, *Kingdom Hearts* (also known as *Kingdom Hearts: Final Mix* and *Kingudamu hatsu*), Square Enix/Square Electronic Arts, 2002.

Voice of Mike Toreno, *Grand Theft Auto: San Andreas* (also known as *GTA: San Andreas* and *San Andreas*), Rockstar Games, 2004.

(From archive footage) Voice of Hades, *Kingdom Hearts: Chain of Memories,* Square Enix, 2004.

Voice of Hades, *Kingdom Hearts II* (also known as *Kingudamu hatsu II*), Square Enix, 2005.

Voice of George Sheffield, *Scarface: The World Is Yours,* Vivendi Universal Games, 2006.

(From archive footage) Voice of Hades, *Kingdom Hearts Re: Chain of Memories,* Square Enix, 2007.

Voice of Hades, *Kingdom Hearts II: Final Mix+,* Square Enix, 2007.

Audio Books; Reader:

Koko, Simon & Schuster, 1988.

Mystery, Simon & Schuster, 1990.

Two Past Midnight: Secret Garden, Secret Window, Penguin/Highbridge, 1991.

WRITINGS

Film Scripts:

Falling in Love in Pongo Ponga (promotional film), SKYY Vodka, 2002.

OTHER SOURCES

Books:

International Dictionary of Films and Filmmakers, Volume 3: *Actors and Actresses,* 4th edition, St. James Press, 2000.

Newsmakers, Issue Cumulation, Gale, 1988.

Periodicals:

American Film, May, 1987, p. 38; May, 1990, p. 18.

Cosmpolitan, October, 1994, pp. 188–92.

Empire, Issue 1996, 1997, pp. 70–71.

Entertainment Weekly, February 7, 1997, p. 78; July 18, 1997, pp. 87–90; March 28, 2003, p. 57.

Film Comment, January/February, 1997, pp. 49–60.

Maclean's, July 21, 1997, p. 54.

Madison, February, 1999, pp. 84–91.

Maxim, October, 2006, pp. 110–11.

Movieline, February, 2000, pp. 66–69, 115.

Newsweek, June 23, 1997, p. 68.

Parade, May 23, 1999, pp. 4–6; September 24, 2006, p. 34.

People Weekly, June 26, 1995, p. 114; November 3, 1997, p. 115.

Premiere, March, 1997, pp. 51–55; September, 2005, p. 140.

Radio Times, September 14, 2002, p. 61.

Starlog, August, 1997.

Time Out New York, July 10, 2003, p. 160.

TV Guide, March 29, 2003, pp. 26–27; January 30, 2006, p. 44.

USA Today. May 3, 2007, p. 10D.

Variety, May 4, 1998, pp. 83–84.

Vogue, January, 1989, pp. 76–78.

Other:

"James Woods" (television special), *Biography,* Arts and Entertainment, 2007.

WOOLARD, David C.
(David Woolard)

PERSONAL

Career: Costume designer. Career Gear (a non–profit), cofounder (with Gary Field).

Awards, Honors: Antoinette Perry Award, best costume design, Outer Critics Circle Award (with others), design, 1993, both for *The Who's Tommy;* Antoinette Perry Award nomination, best costume design, 2001, for *The Rocky Horror Show;* Lucille Lortel nomination, outstanding costume design, League of Off–Broadway Theatres and Producers, 2001, for *The Bubbly Black Girl Sheds Her Chameleon Skin;* Henry Hewes Design Award nomination, best costume design, 2009, for *The Toxic Avenger.*

CREDITS

Stage Costume Designer:

Buck, American Place Theatre, New York City, 1983.

Great Days, American Place Theatre, 1983.

Rap Master Ronnie, Village Gate (Upstairs), New York City, 1984.

Life and Limb, Playwrights Horizon Theatre, New York City, 1985.

Hannah Senesh, Cherry Lane Theatre, New York City, 1985.

Paradise!, Playwrights Horizons Theatre, 1985.

Highest Standard of Living, Playwrights Horizons Theatre, 1986.

Frankie and Johnny in the Clair de Lune, Manhattan Theatre Club Stage I, New York City, 1987, then Westside Theatre (Upstairs), New York City, 1987–89.

American Notes, Joseph Papp Public Theatre, Susan Stein Shiva Theatre, New York City, 1988.

Godspell, Lamb's Theatre, New York City, 1988.

Just Say No, Workshop of the Players Art (WPA) Theatre, New York City, 1988.

A Few Good Men, Music Box Theatre, New York City, 1989.

Gus and Al, Playwrights Horizons Theatre, 1989.

Romance in Hard Times, Joseph Papp Public Theatre, Anspacher Theatre, then Joseph Papp Public Theatre, Newman Theatre, New York City, 1989.

Mountain, Lucille Lortel Theatre, New York City, 1990.

Mi Vida Loca, Manhattan Theatre Club Stage II, New York City, 1990.

The Colorado Catechism, Circle Repertory Theatre, New York City, 1990.

Life During Wartime, Manhattan Theatre Club Stage II, 1991.

Selling Off, John Houseman Theatre, New York City, 1991.

Breaking Legs, Promenade Theatre, New York City, 1991–92.

A ... My Name Is Alice, McGinn–Cazale Theatre, New York City, 1992–93.

Jeffrey, WPA Theatre, 1992–93, then Minetta Lane Theatre, New York City, 1993–94.

The Swan, Joseph Papp Public Theatre, Martinson Hall, New York City, 1993.

The Who's "Tommy," St. James Theatre, New York City, 1993–95.

The Naked Truth, WPA Theatre, 1994.

Durang/Durang, Manhattan Theatre Club Stage II, 1994.

Sally Marr ... and Her Escorts, Helen Hayes Theatre, New York City, 1994.

Damn Yankees, Marquis Theatre, New York City, 1994–95.

The Red Address, McGinn–Cazale Theatre, 1997.

The Young Man from Atlanta, Longacre Theatre, New York City, 1997.

Bunny Bunny, Lucille Lortel Theatre, 1997.

Defying Gravity, American Place Theatre, 1997–98.

Waiting Until Dark, Brooks Atkinson Theatre, New York City, 1998.

The Eros Trilogy, Vineyard Theatre, New York City, 1999.

Voices of the Dark, Longacre Theatre, New York City, 1999.

Marlene, Cort Theatre, New York City, 1999.

Do Re Mi, City Center Theatre, New York City, 1999.

The Bomb–itty of Errors, Bleecker Street Theatre, New York City, 1999–2000.

An Empty Plate in the Cafe du Grand Boeuf, Primary Stages, New York City, 2000.

The Bubbly Black Girl Shreds Her Chameleon Skin, Playwrights Horizons Theatre, 2000.

Boys Don't Wear Lipstick, Players Theatre, New York City, 2000.

The Rocky Horror Show, Circle in the Square, New York City, 2000–2002.

Newyorkers, Manhattan Theatre Club Stage II, 2001.

Belling Are Ringing, Plymouth Theatre, New York City, 2001.

Wonder of the World, Manhattan Theatre Club Stage I, New York City, 2001–2002.

The Carpetbagger's Children, Mitzi E. Newhouse Theatre, New York City, 2002.

What Didn't Happen, Duke on 42nd Street, New York City, 2002.

The Smell of the Kill, Helen Hayes Theatre, New York City, 2002.

It Just Catches, Cherry Lane Theatre, 2003.

Barbara's Wedding, Westside Theatre, 2003.

Polish Joke, Manhattan Theatre Club Stage II, 2003.

Dream a Little Dream, Village Theatre, New York City, 2003.

The Stendhal Syndrome, 59E59 Theatre A, New York City, 2004.

Bare: A Pop Opera, American Theatre of Actors, Chernuchin Theatre, New York City, 2004.

The Joys of Sex, Variety Arts Theatre, New York City, 2004.

Fiction, Laura Pels Theatre, New York City, 2004.

The Day Emily Married, 59E59 Theatre A, 2005.

All Shook Up, Palace Theatre, New York City, 2005.

A Mother, a Daughter, and a Gun, New World Stages Stage III, New York City, 2005.

Ring of Fire, Ethel Barrymore Theatre, New York City, 2006.

(As David Woolard) *Beyond Glory,* Laura Pels Theatre, 2007.

Old Acquaintance, American Airlines Theatre, New York City, 2007.

Dividing the Estate, 59E59 Theatre A, 2007, then Booth Theatre, New York City, 2008–2009.

The Farnsworth Invention, Music Box Theatre, New York City, 2007–2008.

The Savannah Disputation, Playwrights Horizons Theatre, 2009.

The Toxic Avenger, New World Stages, 2009–10.

West Side Story, Palace Theatre, 2009—.

(As David Woolard) *The Orphan Home Cycle Part I,* Peter Norton Space, New York City, 2009—.

Also designed costumes for *The Donkey Show,* off-Broadway production; *One Touch of Venus,* Encore; *Merrily We Roll Along,* Kennedy Center for the Performing Arts, Washington, DC.

Stage Work; Other:
Clothing stylist, *700 Sundays,* Broadhurst Theatre, New York City, 2004–2005.

Additional costumes, *33 Variations,* Eugene O'Neill Theatre, New York City, 2009.

Film Costume Designer:
Jeffrey, Orion Classics, 1995.

WOZNIAK, Stephen 1971–

PERSONAL

Full name, Stephen Joseph Wozniak; born January 22, 1971, in Dover, NH; son of John Wozniak (an inventor and aeronautical engineer). *Education:* Attended Johns Hopkins University; Maryland Institute, B.F.A. *Avocational Interests:* Fine artist, sculptor, furniture designer and crafter.

Addresses: *Office*—Inevitable Film Group, 8484 Wilshire Blvd., Suite 465, Beverly Hills, CA 90211. *Agent*—Hugh Leon, Coast to Coast Talent Group, 3350 Barham Blvd., Los Angeles, CA 90068. *Manager*—Millennium Talent Management, PO Box 480470, Los Angeles, CA 90048.

Career: Actor, producer, director, and writer. Inevitable Film Group, Beverly Hills, CA, founder, executive, and producer, 2007—; Hazmat Pictures (media production company), principal. Appeared in commercials; also appeared in music videos, industrial films, radio programs, and public television presentations. Director of music videos and commercials.

Member: Screen Actors Guild, American Federation of Television and Radio Artists.

CREDITS

Film Appearances:
One of the Corny Collins dancers, *Hairspray,* New Line Cinema, 1988.
Officer Babbage, *The Art of a Bullet,* Creative Light Worldwide, 1999.
(Uncredited) Johnny, *Psycho Beach Party,* Cinemavault Releasing/Strand Releasing, 2000.
Jack, *Exorcism,* York Entertainment, 2003.
Pastor Tompkins, *Cold Harbor,* Redfield Arts, 2003.
Ken, *Scarecrow,* York Home Video, 2003.
Paco, *Down the Barrel* (also known as *Luxury of Love*), York Entertainment, 2003.
Rocker, *The Eliminator,* Artist View Entertainment, 2004.
Jesus skater, *The Dry Spell,* Brothers Dowdle Films/Group W Films, 2005.
The Yankee merchant, *Lincoln's Eyes* (short film), BRC Imagination Arts, 2005.
Frankie, *Chaos,* Dinsdale Releasing/Dominion Entertainment, 2005.
Steve Varner, *Statistics,* 2006, Anthem Pictures, 2008.
Avraham, *Color of the Cross,* Rocky Mountain Pictures, 2006.

Also appeared in several small independent films.

Television Appearances; Movies:
Waxy, *Hope Ranch,* Animal Planet, 2004.

Television Appearances; Specials:
Casting coucher, *Sex, Warts and All,* BBC, 2002.

Jesus Christ, *Time Machine: Beyond the Da Vinci Code,* History Channel, 2005.

Television Appearances; Episodic:
Parking lot savior, "Street Smarts," *America's Most Wanted* (also known as *America's Most Wanted: America Fights Back* and *A.M.W.*), Fox, 1997.
Latia male, "Two Days and Two Nights," *Enterprise* (also known as *Star Trek: Enterprise*), UPN, 2002.
Stan Montrose, "Back in the Saddle," *The District,* CBS, 2003.
Mitch Ryder, "City on Fire," *American Dreams* (also known as *Our Generation*), NBC, 2003.
Russ, "Laura and Bridget," *My First Time,* Showtime, 2003.
Candy, "Nelda and Patrina," *My First Time,* Showtime, 2003.
Jesus, *Jimmy Kimmel Live!* (also known as *Jimmy Kimmel*), ABC, 2005.

Television Work; Episodic:
Producer and director, *NewNowNextPopLab,* Logo, 2009, 2010.

Stage Appearances:
Appeared as David Bowie, *And Ziggy Played Guitar,* Stardust Productions; Baron II, *Becket,* Vagabond Players; Hawkins, *Corpse!,* Ironclad Theatre Company; the tramp, *In the Shadow of the Glen,* Silver Spring Stage, Silver Spring, MD; Asher, *Noon,* Studio Theatre; bailiff, *Nothing Sacred,* Fells Point Theatre; Hansel and mouse prince, *The Nutcracker, a Play,* Baltimore Museum of Art, Baltimore, MD; the man, *Re–Visions,* Theatre Project; Monk, *Tour,* Studio Theatre; ticket man, *The Trip to Bountiful,* Spotlighters Theatre; and Eddie, *What the Rabbi Saw,* Stella Adler Theatre.

RECORDINGS

Videos:
Himself, *Phone Sex* (documentary), Dikenga Films, 2006.

WRITINGS

Films:
(Contributor) *Scarecrow,* York Home Video, 2003.

Television Episodes:
NewNowNextPopLab, Logo, 2009, 2010.

OTHER SOURCES

Electronic:
Stephen Wozniak Official Site, http://www.stephenwozniak.com, February 23, 2010.

Y

YANNAI, Michal 1972–
(Michal Yanai, Michal Yani)

PERSONAL

Born June 18, 1972, in Israel; daughter of Moshe Yanai (an actor); married Ofer Resles (in business), 2003 (divorced, 2005).

Career: Actress.

CREDITS

Film Appearances:
Natalie, *Neshika Bametzach* (also known as *The Day We Met*), Motion Picture Corporation of Australia, 1990.
(As Michal Yani) First English woman, *Pour Sacha* (also known as *For Sasha*), subtitled version, MK2 Diffusion, 1992.
(As Michal Yanai) Marcie, *Prison Heat*, Cannon Home Video, 1993.
Dorothy, *Hakosem!* (also known as *The Wizard!*), 1994.
Irit, *Tmuna kvutzatit im isha* (also known as *A Group Portrait with a Woman*), 2003.
Tamara, *Muchrachim lehiyot same'ach* (also known as *Joy*), Lama Productions/Metro Communications, 2005.
Leeza Pearson, *88 Minutes* (also known as *88* and *88:88 Minutes*), Columbia, 2007.
Jamie, *White Air*, Monarch Home Entertainment, 2007.
(As Yanai) Jessica, *Until Death*, Sony Pictures Home Entertainment, 2007.
Bertha, *When Nietzsche Wept*, First Look International, 2007.

Matok Ve'mar (also known as *Bittersweet*), NovoGrinza Productions, 2007.
Monique, *Finding Rin Tin Tin*, Haze Productions, 2007.
Smadar, *Pink Subaru*, Compact, 2009.

Television Appearances; Movies:
(As Michal Yanai) Sally, *Kraken: Tentacles of the Deep*, Sci–Fi Channel, 2006.
(As Yanai) Fay, *Mega Snake*, Sci–Fi Channel, 2007.

Television Appearances; Series:
Tamar Zehavi, *Ha–Shminiya* (also known as *The Eight*), 2005–2006.
Dafna Gur, *Ulai Hapa'am*, 2006–2008.

Appeared as host, *Mazal Tov;* as Mika, *Michmoret;* in *Hakita Hameofefet;* and as Dr. Yaara Dvash, *Tipul Nimratz.*

Television Appearances; Episodic:
"Ha–Dira," *Bat Yam—New York*, 1997.
Miri Shilon, *Ha–Shir Shelanu* (also known as *Our Song*), 2006.
Shnaim, 2006.
"The Broadcast," *Tom Avni 24/7*, 2007.
"Bonus: The Truth of Tom Avni," *Tom Avni 24/7*, 2007.

Television Appearances; Other:
Michael, *Behazot Halayla* (also known as *At Midnight*), 1997.
(As Michal Yanai) *What Not to Wear on the Red Carpet* (special), BBC, 2003.

Stage Appearances:
Appeared in the Israeli version of the stage play *Avenue Q*, 2007.

YAPHE, Scott 1970–
(Scott Howard)

PERSONAL

Born February 16, 1970, in Montreal, Quebec, Canada; married Jessica Holmes (an actress), 2002; children: Alexa, Jordan. *Education:* Attended Dalhousie University; Ryerson University, graduated. *Avocational Interests:* Usui ryoho reiki master.

Addresses: *Agent*—Edna Talent Management Ltd., 318 Dundas St. W., Toronto, Ontario M5T 1G5, Canada.

Career: Actor. Sketch artist and writer for the improvisational group the Puppet Bunnies. Appeared in commercials; radio performer and voice actor.

Member: Alliance of Canadian Cinema, Television, and Radio Artists.

CREDITS

Television Appearances; Series:
Host Wink Yahoo, *Uh–Oh!* (game show), YTV, 1997.
Joe Swihan, *Medabots,* Fox, 2001.
The Holmes Show, CTV, 2002.
Frankenstein, *The Bobroom,* CTV and Comedy Network, 2004.
Howie Do It, NBC, 2009.
Copper, ABC, 2010.

Also appeared in *Aaron Stone;* host of *Breakfast Zone,* YTV; as a clerk, *Riverdale,* CBC; and in *Who Rules?,* YTV.

Television Appearances; Miniseries:
(Uncredited) First journalist, *I Was a Rat* (also known as *Un bon petit rat*), BBC, 2001.
Mr. Sanger, *Bloodletting & Miraculous Cures,* Movie Central, 2010.

Television Appearances; Movies:
Law clerk, *The Girl Next Door* (also known as *Fatale innocence*), CTV, 1999.
Tim, *This Time Around,* ABC Family, 2003.

Television Appearances; Specials:
The 2nd Annual Canadian Comedy Awards, Comedy Network, 2001.
Partners and Crime, 2003.

Television Appearances; Pilots:
My Lovely Bank, c. 1983.
Voice of Mr. Griffin, *Unnatural History,* Cartoon Network, 2010.

Appeared in the pilot for *MVP,* CBC.

Television Appearances; Episodic:
Wink Yahoo, *It's Alive!,* YTV, 1993.
Harvey Moon, "Politics of Love," *Once a Thief* (also known as *John Woo's "Once a Thief"*), syndicated, 1998.
Malcolm Fortis, "Intensive Care," *Blue Murder* (also known as *En quete de preuves*), Global, 2001.
Sound man, *Leap Years,* Showtime, 2001.
Synth, "Vanishing Point," *Odyssey 5,* Showtime, 2003.
Sergei, "2005: Year of the Farce," *Royal Canadian Air Farce* (also known as *Air Farce, Air Farce Live,* and *Air Farce: Final Flight*), CBC, 2005.
Himself, *Off the Record,* HBO, 2006.

Also appeared as a reporter for *NBC Dunk St.,* YTV.

Film Appearances:
(As Scott Howard) Thin boy, *The Amityville Curse,* Vidmark Entertainment, 1990.
Agent Gabe, *The Tuxedo,* DreamWorks, 2002.
Paul, *Ham & Cheese,* Decade Distribution, 2004.
William Dalten, *Amelia,* Fox Searchlight, 2009.

Host of a training film on workplace harassment and violence for the Canadian grocery store chain No Frills.

Stage Appearances:
Appeared in title role, *The Invisible Man;* as bellhop, *Lend Me a Tenor;* Fagan, *Oliver* (musical); Gepetto, *Pinocchio;* and as Officer Krupke, *West Side Story* (musical).

Internet Appearances; Episodic:
Borse, "Beware of the Realm Raiders," *Magi–Nation,* Magi–nation.com, 2008.

RECORDINGS

Videos:
The 3rd Annual Canadian Comedy Awards, Higher Ground Productions, 2002.

YORK, Kathleen
(Bird York, Kathleen "Bird" York)

PERSONAL

Addresses: *Agent*—Nethercott Agency, 10956 Weyburn Ave., Suite 200, Los Angeles, CA 90024; Bauman, Redanty, and Shaul Agency, 5757 Wilshire Blvd., Suite 473, Los Angeles, CA 90036. *Manager*—Code Entertainment, 9229 Sunset Blvd., Suite 615, Los Angeles, CA 90069.

Career: Actress, singer, and songwriter. Also performs as a guitarist; signed to Blissed Out Records.

Awards, Honors: Academy Award nomination (with Michael Becker), best achievement in music written for motion pictures—original song, 2006, for *Crash*.

CREDITS

Film Appearances:
Charmaine, *Protocol,* Warner Bros., 1984.
Judy McCormick, *Winners Take All,* Apollo Pictures/Embassy Entertainment, 1986.
The mother, *Astronomy,* 1988.
Laura Latham, *Cold Feet,* Avenue Pictures, 1989.
Diana, *Checking Out,* Warner Bros., 1989.
Sparkle, *Flashback,* Paramount, 1990.
Dewey Brown, *I Love You to Death,* 1990.
Marie, *Wild Hearts Can't Be Broken,* Buena Vista, 1991.
Bowl of Bone: Tale of the Syuwe, 1992.
Dorrie Walsh, *Cries of Silence* (also known as *Sister Island*), 1993.
Martha, *Dream Lover,* PolyGram Filmed Entertainment, 1994.
Captain Victoria Ellis, *Dead Men Can't Dance* (also known as *DMZ* and *Rangers*), Imperial Entertainment/Live Entertainment, 1997.
Pam, *The Big Day,* Monarch Films, 1999.
Pamela Kendrick, *We Met on the Vineyard,* 1999.
Officer Johnson, *Crash* (also known as *L.A. Crash*), Lions Gate Films, 2004.
Jenny, *Sublime,* Warner Home Video, 2007.
Mrs. Smith, *Ball Don't Lie,* 2008.

Film Song Performer:
Happy Campers, 2001.
Never Get Outta the Boat, 2002.
Crash (also known as *L.A. Crash*), Lions Gate Films, 2004.
Bound by Lies (also known as *Betrayed* and *The Long Dark Kiss*), 2005.
Sublime, Warner Home Video, 2007.
In the Valley of Elah, Warner Independent Pictures, 2007.
Seven Pounds, Columbia, 2008.

Television Appearances; Series:
Little Betty, *Dallas,* CBS, 1984–85.
Susannah Lo Verde, *Aaron's Way,* NBC, 1988.

K. C. Griffin, *Vengeance Unlimited* (also known as *Mr. Chapel*), ABC, 1998–99.
Representative Andrea Wyatt, *The West Wing,* NBC, 2000–2006.
Renee Wheeler, *The O.C.,* Fox, 2004–2005.

Television Appearances; Miniseries:
Naomi Judd, *Naomi and Wynonna: Love Can Build a Bridge* (also known as *Love Can Build a Bridge*), NBC, 1995.
Claire, *A Season in Purgatory,* CBS, 1996.

Television Appearances; Movies:
Janet Resnick, *This Child Is Mine,* NBC, 1985.
Linda, *Not My Kid,* CBS, 1985.
Darlene, *Chase,* CBS, 1985.
Louise, *Thompson's Last Run,* CBS, 1986.
Susanna Dickinson, *The Alamo: Thirteen Days to Glory,* NBC, 1987.
Jenny, *Darkman,* 1992.
Rachel Kingsley, *Gregory K* (also known as *Gregory K.: A Place to Be* and *Switching Parents*), ABC, 1993.
Terry, *Love, Lies, and Lullabies* (also known as *Sad Inheritance*), ABC, 1993.
Callie Waller, *Nightjohn,* The Disney Channel, 1996.
Aurora Watling, *To Dance with Olivia,* CBS, 1997.
Daphne, *Northern Lights* (also known as *L'etoile du nord*), The Disney Channel, 1997.
First Lady Susan Russell, *A House Divided,* ABC, 2006.
Paula, *Fatal Desire* (also known as *Fatal Error*), Lifetime, 2006.
Diane, *Front of the Class,* CBS, 2009.

Television Appearances; Pilots:
K. C. Conklin, *I Gave at the Office,* NBC, 1984.
Susannah Lo Verde, *Aaron's Way: The Harvest* (also known as *Aaron's Way* and *Circle of Love*), 1988.
Veronica Clare, 1991.
Beth, *Sweet Justice,* 1994.
Wendy Wyler, *The Player,* ABC, 1997.
Soccer Moms, 2005.

Television Appearances; Specials:
Mother, *The Astronomer,* PBS, 1991.
Mother, *Astronomy,* Showtime, 1993.
Amanda, *Icebergs: The Secret Life of a Refrigerator,* Lifetime, 1998.
(As Kathleen "Bird" York) *The 78th Academy Awards,* ABC, 2006.
Park City: Where Music Meets Film, 2007.

Television Appearances; Episodic:
Terri, "In the Line of Duty," *Our Family Honor,* 1985.
Alison Baker, "A Significant Obsession," *Simon & Simon,* 1986.

Coralee, "Dig That Cat ... He's Real Gone," *Tales from the Crypt* (also known as *HBO's "Tales from the Crypt"*), HBO, 1989.

Lisa, "Celibate!," *The John Larroquette Show* (also known as *Larroquette*), NBC, 1993.

Starr, *Key West,* Fox, 1993.

Beth, *Sweet Justice,* NBC, 1994.

Deputy District Attorney Cheryl Dreyfuss, "Chapter Six," *Murder One,* ABC, 1995.

Deputy District Attorney Cheryl Dreyfuss, "Chapter Nine," *Murder One,* ABC, 1995.

Deputy District Attorney Cheryl Dreyfuss, "Chapter Thirteen," *Murder One,* ABC, 1996.

Sharon, "Pursuit of Dignity," *The Practice,* ABC, 1998.

Representative Andrea Wyatt, "Mandatory Minimums," *The West Wing,* NBC, 2000.

Representative Andrea Wyatt, "Ellie," *The West Wing,* NBC, 2001.

Anna Antenelli, "Separation," *Family Law,* CBS, 2001.

Masseuse, "The Massage," *Curb Your Enthusiasm,* HBO, 2001.

Paula, "Ripley, Believe It or Not," *Philly,* ABC, 2002.

"Lonely Hearts," *For the People* (also known as *Para la gente*), Lifetime, 2002.

Janine Crane, "Assuming the Position," *The Guardian,* CBS, 2002.

Dr. Jenna Fuller, "The Love Bandit," *Miss Match,* NBC, 2003.

Susan, "A Whisper from Zoe's Sister," *Wild Card* (also known as *Zoe Busiek: Wild Card*), Lifetime, 2005.

The Tonight Show with Jay Leno (also known as *Jay Leno*), NBC, 2006.

Jordana Locallo, "The Ten Percenter," *In Justice,* ABC, 2006.

Ellie, "Mono," *Malcolm in the Middle,* Fox, 2006.

Monique Polier, "Sweetheart, I Have to Confess," *Desperate Housewives,* ABC, 2006.

Monique Polier, "I Remember That," *Desperate Housewives,* ABC, 2007.

Monique Polier, "The Little Things You Do Together," *Desperate Housewives,* ABC, 2007.

Herself, "Providence," *After Hours with Daniel Boulud,* 2007.

Dr. Schaffer, "97 Seconds," *House M.D.* (also known as *House*), Fox, 2007.

Stephanie Flynn, "The Ex–File," *Navy NCIS: Naval Criminal Investigative Service* (also known as *NCIS* and *NCIS: Naval Criminal Investigative Service*), CBS, 2007.

Vivian Sembrook, "Bad Blood," *Ghost Whisperer,* CBS, 2007.

Jillian Parks, "Shaun of the Dead," *Shark,* CBS, 2007.

Diane, "Front of the Class," *Hallmark Hall of Fame* (also known as *Hallmark Television Playhouse*), CBS, 2008.

Assistant District Attorney Hardt, "Miscarriage of Justice," *CSI: Crime Scene Investigation* (also known as *CSI: Las Vegas, C.S.I.,* and *Les experts*), CBS, 2009.

Paula Olsen, "Count Me Out," *CSI: Miami,* CBS, 2009.

Television Song Performer; Movies:
Shelter Island, Showtime, 2003.

Television Song Performer; Pilots:
"The Ten Percenter," *In Justice,* 2006.
"Ex–Factor," *Standoff,* 2007.

Television Song Performer; Episodic:
Family Law, CBS, 2001.
"The Unveiling," *Everwood* (also known as *Our New Life in Everwood*), The WB, 2003.
"Nanette Babcock," *Nip/Tuck,* FX Network, 2003.
"Arms and the Girl," *Jake 2.0,* UPN, 2003.
"Autopsy," *House M.D.* (also known as *House*), Fox, 2005.
"Stealing Home," *CSI: NY* (also known as *CSI: New York*), CBS, 2006.

RECORDINGS

Albums; as Bird York:
Bird, Blissed Out, 1999.
Passion Junkie, 2003.
Wicked Little High, Narada, 2006.
Have No Fear (EP), 2008.

Contributor to *Cries of Silence* (soundtrack recording), and Peter Buffet's *Sugarbaby.*

WRITINGS

Screenplays:
Incest: A Family Tragedy, 2007.

Film Songs:
Happy Campers, 2001.
Never Get Outta the Boat, 2002.
Shelter Island, 2003.
Crash (also known as *L.A. Crash*), Lions Gate Films, 2004.
Bound by Lies (also known as *Betrayed* and *The Long Dark Kiss*), 2005.
Sublime, Warner Home Video, 2007.
In the Valley of Elah, Warner Independent Pictures, 2007.
Seven Pounds, Columbia, 2008.

Television Songs; Movies:
Shelter Island, Showtime, 2003.

Television Songs; Pilots:
"The Ten Percenter," *In Justice,* 2006.
"Ex–Factor," *Standoff,* 2007.

Television Songs; Episodic:
Family Law, CBS, 2001.
"The Unveiling," *Everwood* (also known as *Our New Life in Everwood*), The WB, 2003.
"Nanette Babcock," *Nip/Tuck,* FX Network, 2003.
"Arms and the Girl," *Jake 2.0,* UPN, 2003.
"Autopsy," *House M.D.* (also known as *House*), Fox, 2005.
"Stealing Home," *CSI: NY* (also known as *CSI: New York*), CBS, 2006.

OTHER SOURCES

Periodicals:
Entertainment Weekly, May 12, 1995, p. 48.
People Weekly, May 15, 1995, p. 16.
Variety, April 20, 2009, p. 12.

Electronic:
Kathleen York Official Site, http://www.york.com, February 23, 2010.

YOUNG, Sean 1959–

PERSONAL

Full name, Mary Sean Young; born November 20, 1959, in Louisville, KY; daughter of Donald Young (a journalist and television news producer) and Lee Guthrie (a journalist and screenwriter); sister of Cathleen Young (a screenwriter); married Robert Lujan (an actor and musician), November 20, 1990 (divorced, 2002); children: Rio Kelly, Quinn Lee. *Education:* Trained at School of the American Ballet, New York City.

Addresses: *Agent*—Tom Harrison, Diverse Talent Group, 9911 West Pico Blvd., Suite 350W, Los Angeles, CA 90035. *Manager*—Greg Edwards, Gem Entertainment Group, 10701 Wilshire Blvd., Suite 1202, Los Angeles, CA 90035.

Career: Actress. Shonderosa Productions, Sedona, AZ, founder and owner, 1997. National Lung Program, New York City, research assistant, 1978; also worked as a model and a secretary. American Tap Dance Orchestra, member of board of directors.

Awards, Honors: Scarlett Award, Marco Island Film Festival, and Sarasota Film Festival Award, best actress, c. 2001, for *The Amati Girls;* Cleveland Film Festival Award, best actress, c. 2001, for *Poor White Trash.*

CREDITS

Film Appearances:
(Film debut) Ariadne Charlton, *Jane Austen in Manhattan,* New Yorker, 1980.
Louise, *Stripes,* Columbia, 1981.
Rachael, *Blade Runner* (also known as *Blade Runner: The Final Cut*), Warner Bros., 1982.
Dr. Stephanie Brody, *Young Doctors in Love,* Twentieth Century–Fox, 1982.
Chani, *Dune,* Universal, 1984.
Susan Matthews–Loomis, *Baby: Secret of the Lost Legend* (also known as *Dinosaur ... Secret of the Lost Legend*), Buena Vista, 1985.
Susan Atwell, *No Way Out,* Orion, 1987.
Artist at party, *Arena Brains* (short film), 1987.
Kate Gekko, *Wall Street,* Twentieth Century–Fox, 1987.
Linda Brown, *The Boost,* Hemdale, 1989.
Tish, *Cousins* (also known as *A Touch of Infidelity*), Paramount, 1989.
Billie Lee Guthrie, *Fire Birds* (also known as *Wings of the Apache*), Buena Vista, 1990.
Ellen Carlsson and Dorothy Carlsson, *A Kiss before Dying,* Universal, 1991.
Dana Greenway, *Love Crimes,* Millimeter Films, 1992.
Phoebe, *Once upon a Crime* (also known as *7 Gauner und ein dackel* and *Es war einmal ein mord*), Metro–Goldwyn–Mayer, 1992.
Mary Miles Winter, *Forever,* Crystal Vision, 1992.
Lola Cain, *Fatal Instinct,* Metro–Goldwyn–Mayer, 1993.
Twinkle, *Hold Me, Thrill Me, Kiss Me,* Mad Dog Pictures, 1993.
Marie Barth, *Even Cowgirls Get the Blues,* Fine Line, 1994.
Lieutenant Lois Einhorn, *Ace Ventura: Pet Detective,* Warner Bros., 1994.
Jennifer Gale, *Mirage,* MCA/Universal Home Video, 1994.
Patty Dearhart (some sources spell the name "Deerheart"), *Bolt* (also known as *Rebel Run*), Avalanche Home Entertainment, 1994.
Ms. Helen Hyde, *Dr. Jekyll and Ms. Hyde,* Savoy, 1995.
Virginia Kelly/Sally, *The Proprietor* (also known as *Le proprietaire*), Warner Bros., 1996.
Lana Hawking, *Motel Blue,* AMCO Entertainment, 1997.
Stella James, *Men,* A–Pix Entertainment, 1998.
Special Delivery, Mark II Productions, 1999.
Linda Bronco, *Poor White Trash,* Hollywood Independents, 2000.
Mrs. Hill, *Sugar & Spice,* New Line Cinema, 2001.
Dr. Judy Bingham, *Mockingbird Don't Sing,* Mainline Releasing, 2001.
Rachel Anderson, *Aftermath,* Christal Films, 2002.
Monica, *The House Next Door,* Trinity Home Entertainment, 2002.
Dr. Daryl Sheleigh, *Threat of Exposure* (also known as *Control*), Waldo West Productions, 2002.

Samantha, *In the Shadow of the Cobra,* Showcase Entertainment, 2003.

Rebecca "Becky" Terrill, *A Killer Within,* Showcase Entertainment, 2004.

Cosma, *Until the Night,* Pathfinder Pictures, 2004.

Rebecca, *Ghosts Never Sleep,* Allumination Filmworks, 2005.

Mother, *Headspace,* Curb Entertainment, 2005.

Herself, *Sledge: The Untold Story* (also known as *Confessions of an Action Star*), 2005, Lightyear Entertainment, 2009.

Ivy, *The Drop,* MTI Home Video, 2006.

Miss Grace Chapman, *The Garden,* Anchor Bay Entertainment, 2006.

Brenda, *Living the Dream,* Gabriel Film Group, 2006.

Brenda, *Dating in LA* (short film), Rover Films, 2007.

Heckler (documentary), Echo Bridge Home Entertainment, 2007.

Kate, *The Man Who Came Back,* Grindstone Entertainment Group, 2008.

Madeline Volpe, *Parasomnia,* E1 Entertainment, 2008.

Laura, *Haunted Echoes,* Lightning Media, 2008.

Linda Wright, *Signal Lost* (short film), Ouat Media, 2009.

Film Work:

Costume designer, *Hold Me, Thrill Me, Kiss Me,* Mad Dog Pictures, 1992.

Director, *Dating in LA* (short film), Rover Films, 2007.

Television Appearances; Miniseries:

Rosemary Hoyt, *Tender Is the Night,* Showtime, 1986.

Leonore Bergman, *Blood & Orchids,* CBS, 1986.

Lorelei Klein, *Kingpin,* NBC, 2003.

Isadora Duncan, *Esenin,* 2005.

Television Appearances; Movies:

Rayanne Whitfield, *The Sketch Artist* (also known as *Drawing Fire*), Showtime, 1992.

Stacy Mansdorf, *Blue Ice,* HBO, 1993.

Mercedes, *Model by Day,* Fox, 1994.

Jessica Traynor, *Witness to the Execution,* NBC, 1994.

Gwen McGarrel, *Evil Has a Face,* USA Network, 1996.

Mallory Ashton Jordan Keswick, *Everything to Gain* (also known as *Barbara Taylor Bradford Trilogy: Everything to Gain*), CBS, 1996.

Angela Bayer, *Exception to the Rule* (also known as *Nach gefaehrlichen regeln*), HBO, 1997.

Annie Nielsen, *The Invader,* HBO, 1997.

Sean Livingston, *The Cowboy and the Movie Star* (also known as *Love on the Edge*), Fox Family, 1998.

Lena, *Out of Control,* Showtime, 1998.

Joyce Cottrell, *Secret Cutting* (also known as *Painful Secrets* and *Le secret de Dawn*), USA Network, 2000.

Christine, *The Amati Girls,* Fox, 2000.

Claire Sherwood, *Night Class* (also known as *Seduced by a Thief*), Lifetime, 2001.

Joanna Wade, *1st to Die* (also known as *F1rst to Die* and *James Patteron's "1st to Die"*), NBC, 2003.

Sandy Bateman, *The King and Queen of Moonlight Bay,* Hallmark Channel, 2003.

Nell MacDermott Cauliff, *Before I Say Goodbye* (also known as *Mary Higgins Clark's "Before I Say Goodbye"* and *Mary Higgins Clark: Avant de te dire adieu*), PAX, 2003.

Ann Rutka, *Third Man Out,* 2005.

Martha McCarthy, *Home for the Holidays,* Lifetime, 2005.

Jennifer Kamplan, *A Job to Kill For* (also known as *The Protege*), Lifetime, 2006.

Sybil Martin, *Jesse Stone: Sea Change,* CBS, 2007.

Martha Alden, *The Republic,* 2010.

Television Appearances; Specials:

(Uncredited; in archive footage) *The Wandering Company,* 1984.

Myra Harper, "Under the Biltmore Clock," *American Playhouse,* PBS, 1985.

Oliver Stone: Inside Out, 1992.

Seven Deadly Sins: An MTV News Special Report, MTV, 1993.

Dame Edna's Hollywood, NBC, 1993.

Host, *Marlene Dietrich: Shadow and Light,* AMC, 1996.

Politically Incorrect with Bill Maher After Party, ABC, 2001.

"Kevin Costner," *Biography,* Arts and Entertainment, 2003.

(In archive footage) *101 Most Shocking Moments in Entertainment,* E! Entertainment Television, 2003.

(In archive footage) Ellen and Dorothy Carlsson, *Premio Donostia a Matt Dillon,* 2006.

Greatest Ever Blockbuster Movies, Channel 5, 2006.

Greatest Ever 80s Movies, Channel 5, 2007.

Television Appearances; Series:

Rachael Somov, *Russians in the City of Angels,* 2003.

Gone Country (also known as *Gone Country 2* and *Gone Country 3*), Country Music Television, 2008.

Television Appearances; Episodic:

Late Night with David Letterman, NBC, 1987.

Cinema 3 (also known as *Informatiu cinema*), 1988.

Late Show with David Letterman (also known as *The Late Show* and *Letterman*), CBS, 1993.

"Glitz and Glamour," *Hollywood Women,* 1993.

(In archive footage) Ellen and Dorothy Carlsson, "Femme Fatale Month: Part 3," *Joe Bob's Drive-in Theatre,* 1993.

Paula, "All the President's Women," *Gun* (also known as *Robert Altman's "Gun"*), ABC, 1997.

Howard Stern, 1997, 2001.

Pajama Party, Oxygen, 2000.

The Test, FX Network, 2001.

The Howard Stern Radio Show, 2001.

"Kiss First, Ask Questions Later," *Rendez-Vous,* 2001.

Nancy Drummond, "Lights Up," *Third Watch*, NBC, 2002.

Nancy Drummond, "Crime and Punishment: Part 2," *Third Watch*, NBC, 2002.

Candy Sobell, "Chapter Sixty–Eight," *Boston Public*, Fox, 2003.

Deputy Wendy Kelton, "Department Investigation: Part 2," *Reno 911!*, Comedy Central, 2004.

Dusty, "Built to Kill: Part 2," *CSI: Crime Scene Investigation* (also known as *C.S.I.*, *CSI: Las Vegas*, and *Les experts*), CBS, 2006.

Anna Hayes, "Crisis of Conscience," *ER*, NBC, 2007.

Hope Brown, "The Runaway Found," *One Tree Hill*, The CW, 2007.

The John Kerwin Show, syndicated, 2007, 2009.

(In archive footage) *Entertainment Tonight* (also known as *Entertainment This Week*, *E.T.*, *ET Weekend*, and *This Week in Entertainment*), syndicated, 2008.

(In archive footage) Rachael, *Banda sonora*, 2009.

Television Appearances; Awards Presentations:

Presenter, *The 60th Annual Academy Awards*, ABC, 1988.

Presenter, *The 51st Annual Golden Globe Awards*, TBS, 1994.

(Uncredited) Audience member, *The 70th Annual Academy Awards*, ABC, 1998.

Stage Appearances:

Stardust (musical), Wilshire Theatre, Beverly Hills, CA, 1992.

RECORDINGS

Videos:

Voice of Rachael, *Blade Runner* (video game), Warner Home Video, 1997.

Stars and Stripes 1, Columbia TriStar Home Video, 2004.

Stars and Stripes 2, Columbia TriStar Home Video, 2004.

Shadows of the Bat: The Cinematic Saga of the Dark Knight—Dark Side of the Knight, Warner Home Video, 2005.

Shadows of the Bat: The Cinematic Saga of the Dark Knight—The Gathering Storm, Warner Home Video, 2005.

(Uncredited) Chani, *Deleted "Dune,"* Universal Studios Home Video, 2006.

Living the Dream: Behind the Scenes, Rover Films, 2006.

Dangerous Days: Making Blade Runner (also known as *Dangerous Days*), Warner Home Video, 2007.

(In archive footage) Rachael, *Blade Runner: Deleted and Alternate Scenes*, Warner Home Video, 2007.

Fashion Forward: Wardrobe and Styling, Warner Home Video, 2007.

OTHER SOURCES

Periodicals:

Empire, Issue 63, 1994, pp. 50–51; October, 1997, pp. 84–85.

Entertainment Weekly, February 7, 1992, pp. 14, 17–19, 21; September 21, 2007, p. 50.

Movieline, June, 1990, pp. 36–40, 86–88.

People Weekly, March 24, 1997, p. 47.

Electronic:

Mary Sean Young Official Site, http://www.maryseanyoung.com, February 17, 2010.

Z

ZAHN, Steve 1968–

PERSONAL

Full name, Steven James Zahn; born November 13, 1968, in Marshall, MN; son of Carleton Edward (a Lutheran minister) and Zelda Clair Zahn; married Robyn Peterman (a dancer and actress), July 16, 1994; children: Henry James, Audrey Clair. *Education:* Briefly attended Gustavus–Adolphus College; trained for the stage at American Repertory Theatre, Cambridge, MA, 1989–91. *Avocational Interests:* Fly fishing, gardening.

Addresses: *Agent*—WME Entertainment, 1 William Morris Pl., Beverly Hills, CA 90212; (commercials and voice work) Marcia Hurwitz, Innovative Artists Talent and Literary Agency, 1505 10th St., Santa Monica, CA 90401. *Manager*—Marsha McManus, Principal Entertainment, 1964 Westwood Blvd., Suite 400, Los Angeles, CA 90025. *Publicist*—Dominique Appel, Baker, Winokur, Ryder, 5700 Wilshire Blvd., Suite 550, Los Angeles, CA 90036.

Career: Actor. Malaparte Theatre Company, New York City, cofounder. Previously worked in a machine shop, as a corn "detassler", and at a Hardees restaurant.

Awards, Honors: Sundance Film Festival Special Jury Award, 1999, Independent Spirit Award, best supporting actor, Independent Features Project/West, and Golden Satellite Award nomination, best actor in a motion picture comedy or musical, International Press Academy, 2000, both for *Happy, Texas;* Blockbuster Entertainment Award nomination, favorite supporting actor in a comedy or romance, 2000, for *Forces of Nature;* honorary Ph.D., Northern Kentucky University, 2007; Independent Spirit Award nomination and Chlotrudis Award nomination, both best supporting actor, 2008, for *Rescue Dawn.*

CREDITS

Film Appearances:
Jeremy Tanner, *Rain without Thunder,* Orion, 1992.
Sammy Gray, *Reality Bites,* Universal, 1994.
William Barnes, *Crimson Tide,* Buena Vista, 1995.
Lenny Haise, *That Thing You Do!,* Twentieth Century–Fox, 1996.
Hans Kooiman, *Race the Sun,* TriStar, 1996.
Buff, *SubUrbia* (also known as *subUrbi@*), Sony Pictures Classics, 1997.
Running with Scissors, 1998.
Frank Hanson, *The Object of My Affection,* Twentieth Century–Fox, 1998.
Glenn Michaels, *Out of Sight,* Universal, 1998.
Eddie, *Safe Men,* October Films, 1998.
George Pappas, *You've Got Mail* (also known as *You Have Mail*), Warner Bros., 1998.
Wayne Wayne Wayne, Jr. and David, *Happy, Texas,* Miramax, 1999.
Alan, *Forces of Nature,* DreamWorks, 1999.
Voice of Monty the Mouth, *Stuart Little* (animated), Sony Pictures Entertainment, 1999.
Kresk, *Chain of Fools,* Warner Bros., 2000.
Rosencrantz, *Hamlet,* Miramax, 2000.
Wayne Lefessier, *Saving Silverman* (also known as *Evil Woman*), Sony Pictures Entertainment, 2001.
Voice of Archie, *Dr. Dolittle 2* (also known as *DR.2* and *DR2*), Twentieth Century–Fox, 2001.
Fuller Thomas, *Joy Ride* (also known as *Road Kill*), Twentieth Century–Fox, 2001.
Ross, *Chelsea Walls* (also known as *Chelsea Hotel*), Lions Gate Films, 2001.
Ray Hasek, *Riding in Cars with Boys,* Sony Pictures Entertainment, 2001.
Voice of Monty, *Stuart Little 2* (animated), Sony Pictures Entertainment, 2002.
Hank Rafferty, *National Security,* Columbia, 2003.
Marvin, *Daddy Day Care,* Columbia, 2003.
Adam L. Penenberg, *Shattered Glass,* Lions Gate Films, 2003.

Al Giordino, *Sahara* (also known as *Sahara—Abenteuer in der queste*), Paramount, 2005.

Voice of runt of the litter, *Chicken Little* (animated), Buena Vista, 2005.

Quentin, *Bandidas*, Twentieth Century–Fox, 2006.

Duane, *Rescue Dawn*, Metro–Goldwyn–Mayer, 2007.

Kenny, *The Great Buck Howard*, Magnolia Pictures, 2008.

Peter Gaulke, *Strange Wilderness*, Paramount, 2008.

Voice of Sandy Pig, *Unstable Fables: 3 Pigs & a Baby* (animated), Weinstein Company, 2008.

Mike, *Management*, Samuel Goldwyn, 2008.

Mac, *Sunshine Cleaning*, Overture Films, 2009.

Peter Dobbs, *Night Train*, E1 Entertainment, 2009.

Cliff Anderson, *A Perfect Getaway*, Rogue Pictures/Universal, 2009.

Frank, *Diary of a Wimpy Kid*, Twentieth Century–Fox, 2010.

Coach Doug Little, *Calvin Marshall*, Broken Sky Films, 2010.

Television Appearances; Miniseries:

American sergeant, *Liberty! The American Revolution*, PBS, 1997.

Elliott See, *From the Earth to the Moon*, HBO, 1998.

Augustus "Gus" McCrae, *Comanche Moon*, CBS, 2008.

Nolen Marbrey, *WWII in HD*, History Channel, 2009.

Television Appearances; Movies:

First Love, Fatal Love, 1991.

Tucker, "The 5:24," *Subway Stories: Tales from the Underground*, HBO, 1997.

Freak, *Freak Talks about Sex* (also known as *Blowin' Smoke* and *Syracuse Muse*), Cinemax, 1998.

Jack, *Employee of the Month*, Showtime, 2004.

Mr. Freeman, *Speak*, Showtime, 2004.

Television Appearances; Episodic:

(Uncredited) Spence, *All My Children* (also known as *AMC*), ABC, 1990.

Lane Bailey, "Pirates of the Caribbean," *South Beach*, NBC, 1993.

Party of Five, Fox, 1994.

Duncan, "The One with Phoebe's Husband," *Friends*, NBC, 1995.

Allan, "Armed Response," *Picture Windows* (also known as *Picture Windows: Language of the Heart*), Showtime, 1995.

"The Making of 'That Thing You Do,'" *HBO First Look*, HBO, 1996.

"The Forces of Nature," *HBO First Look*, HBO, 1999.

"The Making of 'Dr. Dolittle 2,'" *HBO First Look*, HBO, 2001.

"Saving Silverman," *Reel Comedy* (also known as *Comedy Central Canned Ham*), Comedy Central, 2001.

"Strange Wilderness," *Reel Comedy* (also known as *Comedy Central Canned Ham*), Comedy Central, 2008.

Voice of Swampy, "Dude, We're Gettin' the Band Back Together!," *Phineas and Ferb* (animated), The Disney Channel, 2008.

(In archive footage) Sammy Gray, *60/90*, 2008.

Jack Monk, Jr., "Mr. Monk's Other Brother," *Monk*, USA Network, 2009.

(In archive footage) Jack Monk, Jr., "Mr. Monk and the End: Part 2," *Monk*, USA Network, 2009.

Entertainment Tonight (also known as *Entertainment This Week*, *E.T.*, *ET Weekend*, and *This Week in Entertainment*), syndicated, 2009.

David McAlary, "Do You Know What It Means," *Treme*, HBO, 2010.

David McAlary, "Meet De Boys on the Battlefront," *Treme*, HBO, 2010.

Also appeared in *As the World Turns*, CBS.

Television Talk Show Guest Appearances; Episodic:

The Rosie O'Donnell Show, syndicated, 1996, 1999, 2001.

The Daily Show (also known as *A Daily Show with Jon Stewart*, *The Daily Show with Jon Stewart Global Edition*, and *Jon Stewart*), 1999.

The Tonight Show with Jay Leno (also known as *Jay Leno*), NBC, 2001, 2005.

Late Night with Conan O'Brien, NBC, 2005, 2007.

Live with Regis and Kelly, syndicated, 2005.

Ellen: The Ellen DeGeneres Show (also known as *The Ellen Show*), syndicated, 2005.

Tavis Smiley, PBS, 2005, 2009.

Up Close with Carrie Keagan, ABC, 2007, 2008.

Sunday Morning Shootout (also known as *Hollywood Shootout* and *Shootout*), AMC, 2008.

The Tonight Show with Conan O'Brien, NBC, 2009.

Nyhetsmorgon, 2009.

Television Appearances; Specials:

15th Annual IFP/West Independent Spirit Awards, Bravo and Independent Film Channel, 2000.

13th Annual Critics' Choice Awards, 2008.

(In archive footage) *Buscando a Penelope*, 2009.

Stage Appearances:

Willy, *Sophistry*, Playwrights Horizons Theatre, New York City, 1993.

Ringo, *Wild Dogs!*, Malaparte Theatre Company, Theatre Row Theatre, New York City, 1993.

Buff, *SubUrbia*, Mitzi E. Newhouse Theatre, New York City, 1994.

Also appeared in a production of *Biloxi Blues*, MN.

Major Tours:

Hugo Peabody, *Bye Bye Birdie* (musical), U.S. cities, 1991–92.

RECORDINGS

Videos:
Inside "Out of Sight," 1998.
Across the Sands of Sahara, Paramount Home Video, 2005.
Making "Sahara," Paramount Home Video, 2005.
Visualizing "Sahara," Paramount Home Video, 2005.
Voice of runt of the litter, *Chicken Little* (video game), Buena Vista Games, 2005.
Hatching "Chicken Little," Buena Vista Home Video, 2006.
Making of a True Story: Rescue Dawn, Metro–Goldwyn–Mayer Home Entertainment, 2007.

OTHER SOURCES

Periodicals:
Cosmopolitan, February, 1997, p. 182.
Esquire, July, 2007, p. 26.
Interview, September, 1999, p. 144.
People Weekly, May 2, 2005, p. 33.
Premiere, March, 2005, p. 30.
Variety, April 4, 2005, p. S32.
Washington Post, July 13, 2007, p. WE33; May 15, 2009, pp. WE24, WE26.

ZEMECKIS, Robert 1952–

PERSONAL

Full name, Robert Lee Zemeckis; born May 14, 1952, in Chicago, IL; married Mary Ellen Trainor (an actress), July 26, 1980 (divorced, 2000); married Leslie Harter (an actress), December 4, 2001; children: (first marriage) Alexander Francis. *Education:* Attended Northern Illinois University; University of Southern California, graduated, 1973.

Addresses: *Office*—Imagemovers, 100 University City Plaza, Bldg. 484, Universal City, CA 91608; and Dark Castle Entertainment, 4000 Warner Blvd., Bldg. 90, Burbank, CA 91522.

Career: Producer, director, writer, and editor. Partner of Imagemovers, Universal City, CA, and Dark Castle Entertainment, Burbank, CA; formerly worked as a film editor for television commercials and for NBC News, Chicago, IL. University of Southern California, member of board of counselors, School of Cinema–Television, and creator of Robert Zemeckis Center for Digital Arts, 2001.

Member: Directors Guild of America.

Awards, Honors: Special jury award, Second Annual Student Film Awards, Academy of Motion Picture Arts and Sciences, 1975, and fifteen international honors, all for *A Field of Honor;* special mention for Young Venice Award, Venice Film Festival, 1985, Academy Award nomination, Film Award nomination, British Academy of Film and Television Arts, and Screen Award nomination, Writers Guild of America, all best original screenplay, Golden Globe Award nomination, best screenplay for a motion picture, David di Donatello Award, best screenplay for a foreign film (all with Bob Gale), and Film Award nomination (with others), best film, British Academy of Film and Television Arts, and Saturn Award nomination, best director, Academy of Science Fiction, Fantasy, and Horror Films, all 1986, all for *Back to the Future;* Special Award, Los Angeles Film Critics Association, 1988, special mention for Children and Cinema Award, Venice Film Festival, 1988, Chicago Film Critics Association Award, Saturn Award, and Directors Guild of America Award nomination, all best director, 1989, Cesar Award nomination, best foreign film, Academie des Arts et Techniques du Cinema, 1989, and Audience Award, best foreign film, Sant Jordi Awards, 1989, all for *Who Framed Roger Rabbit?;* Saturn Award nomination, best director, 1991, for *Back to the Future Part III;* Saturn Award nomination, best director, 1993, for *Death Becomes Her;* Mary Pickford Alumni Award, University of Southern California, 1995; Academy Award, Golden Globe Award, Saturn Award nomination, and Directors Guild of America Award, all best director, ShoWest Award, director of the year, National Association of Theatre Owners, Film Award nomination, best film (with others) and nomination for David Lean Award, both British Academy of Film and Television Arts, Czech Lion, best foreign language film, and Amanda Award, best foreign feature film, all 1995, for *Forrest Gump;* George Pal Memorial Award, Academy of Science Fiction, Fantasy, and Horror Films, 1995; Daytime Emmy Award nomination (with others), outstanding audience participation show or game show, 1997, for *Secrets of the Cryptkeeper's Haunted House;* Saturn Award nomination, best director, 1998, for *Contact;* Sierra Award nomination, best director, Las Vegas Film Critics Society, 2000, and Chicago Film Critics Association Award nomination, best director, 2001, both for *Cast Away;* Saturn Award nomination, best director, 2001, for *What Lies Beneath;* Golden Eddie Award, filmmaker of the year, American Cinema Editors, 2001; DVD Premiere Award nomination (with others), best audio commentary for a library release, 2003, for *Used Cars;* received star on Hollywood Walk of Fame, 2004; Children's Award nomination (with Steve Starkey), best feature film, British Academy of Film and Television Arts, 2005, for *The Polar Express;* Lifetime Achievement Award, Visual Effects Society, 2005.

CREDITS

Film Executive Producer:

Trespass (also known as *Looters*), Universal, 1992.

The Public Eye, Universal, 1992.

Tales from the Crypt Presents: Demon Knight (also known as *Demon Keeper, Demon Knight,* and *Tales from the Crypt: Demon Knight*), Universal, 1995.

The Frighteners (also known as *Robert Zemeckis Presents: The Frighteners*), Universal, 1996.

Bordello of Blood (also known as *Tales from the Crypt Presents: Bordello of Blood*), Universal, 1996.

Matchstick Men, Warner Bros., 2003.

Last Holiday, Paramount, 2006.

Monster House (animated; also known as *Neighbourhood Crimes & Peepers*), Columbia, 2006.

Behind the Burly Q (documentary), First Run Features, 2010.

Film Producer:

The House on Haunted Hill, Warner Bros., 1999.

Thir13en Ghosts (also known as *Thirteen Ghosts* and *13 fantomes*), Warner Bros., 2001.

Ritual (also known as *Tales from the Crypt Presents: Revelation* and *Tales from the Crypt Presents: Voodoo*), Dimension Films, 2001.

Ghost Ship, Warner Bros., 2002.

Gothika, Warner Bros., 2003.

Clink Inc., DreamWorks, 2003.

House of Wax, Warner Bros., 2005.

The Prize Winner of Defiance, Ohio, DreamWorks/ Revolution Studios, 2005.

The Reaping, Warner Bros., 2007.

Film Producer and Director:

A Field of Honor (short film), 1973.

Death Becomes Her (also known as *La muerte le sienta bien*), Universal, 1992.

Contact, Warner Bros., 1997.

Cast Away, Twentieth Century–Fox, 2000.

What Lies Beneath, DreamWorks, 2000.

The Polar Express (animated; also known as *The Polar Express: An IMAX 3D Experience*), Warner Bros., 2004.

Beowulf (animated; also known as *Beowulf: An IMAX 3D Experience* and *Beowulf: The IMAX Experience*), Paramount, 2007.

A Christmas Carol (animated; also known as *A Christmas Carol: An IMAX 3D Experience* and *Disney's "A Christmas Carol"*), Walt Disney, 2009.

Film Director:

The Lift (student film), 1972.

I Wanna Hold Your Hand, Universal, 1978.

Used Cars, Columbia, 1980.

Romancing the Stone (also known as *2 bribones tras la esmeralda perdida*), Twentieth Century–Fox, 1984.

Back to the Future, Universal, 1985.

Who Framed Roger Rabbit? (live–action and animated), Buena Vista, 1988.

Back to the Future Part II, Universal, 1989.

Back to the Future Part III, Universal, 1990.

Forrest Gump, Paramount, 1994.

Film Appearances:

Looking Back at the Future, Agenda Films, 2006.

Television Work; Series:

Co–executive producer, *Tales from the Crypt* (series of specials; also known as *HBO's Tales from the Crypt*), HBO, 1989–96.

Creator, *Back to the Future* (also known as *Back to the Future: The Animated Series*), CBS, 1991.

Creator and producer, *Johnny Bago,* CBS, 1993.

Executive producer, *Perversions of Science,* HBO, 1997.

Also affiliated with the series *Secrets of the Cryptkeeper's Haunted House,* CBS, 1997.

Television Director; Specials:

"And All through the House," *Tales from the Crypt* (also known as *HBO's Tales from the Crypt*), HBO, 1989.

"The Ventriloquist's Dummy," *Tales from the Crypt* (also known as *HBO's Tales from the Crypt*), HBO, 1990.

"Yellow," *Two–Fisted Tales,* Fox, 1991.

"You, Murderer," *Tales from the Crypt* (also known as *HBO's Tales from the Crypt*), HBO, 1995.

The 20th Century: The Pursuit of Happiness (also known as *The Pursuit of Happiness*), Showtime, 1999.

Television Director; Episodic:

"Go to the Head of the Class," *Amazing Stories,* 1986.

"Johnny Bago Free at Last," *Johnny Bago,* CBS, 1993.

Television Executive Producer; Episodic:

"Transylvania Express," *Tales from the Cryptkeeper* (animated), ABC, 1994.

Television Work; Other:

Producer, *W.E.I.R.D. World* (movie), 1995.

Executive producer, *Ticket to Ride* (pilot), The WB, 2002.

Television Appearances: Specials:

The Making of "Back to the Future," 1985.

Roger Rabbit and the Secrets of Toontown, CBS, 1988.

Premiere Presents: Christmas Movies '89, Fox, 1989.

Back to the Future Part II Behind–the–Scenes Special Presentation, 1989.

The Secrets of the Back to the Future Trilogy, syndicated, 1990.

Masters of Illusion: The Wizards of Special Effects, 1994.

Through the Eyes of Forrest Gump, 1994.

Inside the Academy Awards, TNT, 1995.

MST3K Little Gold Statue Preview Special, 1995.

The 67th Annual Academy Awards, ABC, 1996.

Presenter, *The 68th Annual Academy Awards,* ABC, 1996.

Steven Spielberg: An Empire of Dreams, Arts and Entertainment, 1998.

The Warner Bros. Story: No Guts, No Glory—75 Years of Blockbusters, TNT, 1998.

The Warner Bros. Story: No Guts, No Glory: 75 Years of Stars, TNT, 1998.

From Star Wars to Star Wars: The Story of Industrial Light & Magic, 1999.

The Inside Reel: Digital Filmmaking, PBS, 2001.

AFI Life Achievement Award: A Tribute to Tom Hanks, USA Network, 2002.

(In archive footage) *The Cutting Edge: The Magic of Movie Editing,* Starz!, 2004.

"Bruce Willis," *Biography,* Arts and Entertainment, 2005.

(Uncredited; in archive footage) *Boffo! Tinseltown's Bombs and Blockbusters,* HBO, 2006.

Television Appearances; Episodic:

First Works, The Movie Channel, 1988.

Himself, "Rock 'n Roles," *Parker Lewis Can't Lose* (also known as *Parker Lewis*), Fox, 1991.

Nyhetsmorgon, 1994, 2001.

American Cinema, PBS, 1995.

Late Show with David Letterman (also known as *The Late Show* and *Letterman*), CBS, 1997.

Bl!tz (also known as *Blitz*), 1997.

Mundo VIP, 1997.

"Contact," *HBO First Look,* HBO, 1997.

"The Films of Robert Zemeckis," *The Directors,* Encore, 1999.

"The Making of 'Cast Away'," *HBO First Look,* HBO, 2000.

"'What Lies Beneath': Constructing the Perfect Thriller," *HBO First Look,* HBO, 2000.

MADtv, Fox, 2001.

Sunday Morning Shootout (also known as *Hollywood Shootout* and *Shootout*), AMC, 2004.

The Charlie Rose Show (also known as *Charlie Rose*), PBS, 2004.

"The Polar Express," *HBO First Look,* HBO, 2004.

4Pop, 2004.

Xpose, TV3, 2009.

RECORDINGS

Videos:

Make It Happen, 1991.

The Making of "1941," 1996.

The Making of "The Frighteners," 1998.

Behind the Scenes: Cast Away, 2000.

The Making of "Cast Away," 2001.

Wilson: The Life and Death of a Hollywood Extra, 2001.

The Island, 2001.

Back to the Future: Making the Trilogy, 2002.

Behind the Ears: The True Story of Roger Rabbit, Buena Vista Home Entertainment, 2003.

(In archive footage) *Who Made Roger Rabbit,* Buena Vista Home Entertainment, 2003.

The Art of Beowulf, Paramount, 2008.

The Origins of Beowulf, Paramount, 2008.

Creating the Ultimate Beowulf, Paramount, 2008.

A Hero's Journey: The Making of Beowulf, Paramount, 2008.

Beasts of Burden: Designing the Creatures of Beowulf, Paramount, 2008.

(Uncredited) *Beowulf: Mapping the Journey,* Paramount, 2008.

Looking Back to the Future, Universal Studios Home Entertainment, 2009.

WRITINGS

Screenplays:

The Lift (student film), 1972.

A Field of Honor (short film), 1973.

(With Bob Gale) *I Wanna Hold Your Hand,* Universal, 1978.

(With Gale) *1941* (also based on a story by Zemeckis), Universal, 1979.

(With Gale) *Used Cars,* Columbia, 1980.

(With Gale) *Back to the Future,* Universal, 1985.

(With Gale) *Trespass* (also known as *Looters*), Universal, 1992.

The Polar Express (animated; also known as *The Polar Express: An IMAX 3D Experience*), Warner Bros., 2004.

A Christmas Carol (animated; also known as *A Christmas Carol: An IMAX 3D Experience* and *Disney's "A Christmas Carol"*), Walt Disney, 2009.

Television Episodes:

(With Bob Gale and David Chase) "Chopper," *Kolchak: The Night Stalker,* ABC, 1995.

ADAPTATIONS

The screenplays *Back to the Future Part II, Back to the Future III,* and *Back to the Future ... the Ride* were based on characters created by Zemeckis and Bob Gale; the screenplay *Bordello of Blood* was based on a story by Zemeckis. The 1984 television special *Used Cars* was based on the 1980 screenplay by Zemeckis and Gale. The television episode "Go to the Head of the Class," directed by Zemeckis and first broadcast in the series *Amazing Stories,* was included in the video *Amazing Stories: Book Two,* 1992.

OTHER SOURCES

Books:

International Dictionary of Films and Filmmakers, Volume 2: *Directors,* St. James Press, 1996.

Kagan, Norman, *The Cinema of Robert Zemeckis,* Taylor Publishing, 2003.

Newsmakers, Issue 1, Gale, 2002.

Periodicals:

American Film, July/August, 1988, pp. 32–35.

Forbes, December 1, 1997, p. S121.

Hollywood Reporter, Robert Zemeckis Tribute Issue, March 9, 1995.

New Statesman and Society, December 2, 1992, p. 33.

Newsweek, December 4, 1989, p. 78.

New York, July 18, 1994, pp. 50–51.

New Yorker, June 18, 1990, pp. 91–92; August 24, 1992, p. 80; July 25, 1994.

People Weekly, January 11, 1993, pp. 17–18; June 28, 1993, pp. 10–11.

Rolling Stone, June 28, 1990, p. 31; August 20, 1992, p. 57; February 4, 1993, p. 37.

Starlog, January, 1990, pp. 37–40, 73; December, 1992; October, 1997.

Time, June 27, 1988, p. 72.

Cumulative Index

To provide continuity with *Who's Who in the Theatre*, this index interfiles references to *Who's Who in the Theatre*, 1st–17th Editions, and *Who Was Who in the Theatre* (Gale, 1978) with references to *Contemporary Theatre, Film and Television*, Volumes 1–104.

References in the index are identified as follows:

CTFT and volume number—*Contemporary Theatre, Film and Television*, Volumes 1–104
WWT and edition number—*Who's Who in the Theatre*, 1st–17th Editions
WWasWT—*Who Was Who in the Theatre*

Arell, Sherry H. 1950– CTFT–3
Arenal, Julie.. CTFT–43
  Earlier sketch in CTFT–2
Arenberg, Lee 1962– CTFT–90
  Earlier sketch in CTFT–42
Arend, Geoffrey 1978– CTFT–97
Arens, Cody 1993– CTFT–80
Aresco, Joey CTFT–60
Argarno, Michael
  See .... Angarano, Michael
Argent, Edward 1931– .... WWasWT
Argentina .... WWasWT
Argento, Asia 1975– CTFT–68
Argento, Dario 1940– CTFT–33
  Earlier sketch in CTFT–8
Argenziano, Carmen 1943–.................... CTFT–51
  Earlier sketches in CTFT–8, 15, 25
Argo, Victor 1934– CTFT–34
Argyle, Pearl 1910– .... WWasWT
Arias, Moises 1994– CTFT–96
Arias, Silvana 1977– CTFT–75
Arias, Yancey 1971– CTFT–74
Ariel, Tessa
  See .... Hoffman, Bridget
Ariola, Julie CTFT–56
Aris, Ben 1937– CTFT–19
  Earlier sketch in CTFT–3
Arkell, Elizabeth .... WWasWT
Arkell, Reginald 1882–1959 .... WWasWT
Arkin, Adam 1957– CTFT–100
  Earlier sketches in CTFT–7, 14, 24, 48
Arkin, Alan 1934– CTFT–85
  Earlier sketches in CTFT–2, 11, 18, 39;
  WWT–17
Arkin, Anthony 1967– CTFT–48
Arkin, Matthew 1960– CTFT–82
Arkoff, Lou CTFT–37
Arkoff, Samuel Z. 1918– CTFT–3
Arkush, Allan 1948–.............................. CTFT–93
  Earlier sketches in CTFT–13, 22, 43
Arledge, Roone 1931– CTFT–43
  Earlier sketch in CTFT–4
Arlen, Harold 1905–1986 .... WWT–17
Arlen, Michael 1895–1956 .... WWasWT
Arlen, Stephen 1913– .... WWasWT
Arling, Joyce 1911– .... WWasWT
Arlington, Billy 1873–? .... WWasWT
Arliss, George 1868–1946 .... WWasWT
Arm, Allisyn Ashley 1996–..................... CTFT–99
Armen, Rebecca 1957– CTFT–2
Armenante, Jillian 1968– CTFT–44
Armendariz, Pedro, Jr. 1940– CTFT–42
Armin, Robert 1952– CTFT–44
Armitage, Frank
  See .... Carpenter, John
Armitage, Richard ?–1986 .... CTFT–4
Armstrong, Alun 1946– CTFT–104
  Earlier sketch in CTFT–45
Armstrong, Anthony 1897– .... WWasWT
Armstrong, Barney 1870–? .... WWasWT
Armstrong, Bess 1953– CTFT–77
  Earlier sketches in CTFT–6, 35
Armstrong, Craig 1959– CTFT–91
Armstrong, Curtis 1953–........................ CTFT–51
  Earlier sketches in CTFT–8, 15, 25
Armstrong, Gillian 1950–....................... CTFT–18
  Earlier sketch in CTFT–7
Armstrong, Jack 1964– CTFT–52
Armstrong, Paul 1869–1915 .... WWasWT
Armstrong, R. G. 1917– CTFT–44
  Earlier sketch in CTFT–8
Armstrong, Robert 1896–....................... WWasWT
Armstrong, Samaire 1980– CTFT–66

Armstrong, Su CTFT–60
  Earlier sketch in CTFT–28
Armstrong, Vaughn 1950– CTFT–88
  Earlier sketch in CTFT–40
Armstrong, Vic 1946–............................ CTFT–60
  Earlier sketch in CTFT–28
Armstrong, Will Steven 1930–1969 .... WWasWT
Armstrong, William CTFT–77
  Earlier sketch in CTFT–34
Armstrong, William 1882–1952............. WWasWT
Arnatt, John 1917– WWT–17
Arnaud, Yvonne 1892–1958 .... WWasWT
Arnaz, Desi 1917–1986 .... CTFT–4
  Earlier sketch in CTFT–3
Arnaz, Desi, Jr. 1953– CTFT–1
Arnaz, Lucie 1951– CTFT–93
  Earlier sketches in CTFT–1, 43; WWT–17
Arndt, Denis 1939– CTFT–52
Arness, James 1923– CTFT–18
  Earlier sketch in CTFT–3
Arnett, Peter 1934– CTFT–48
  Earlier sketch in CTFT–11
Arnett, Will 1970–................................ CTFT–71
Arnette, Jeanetta 1954– CTFT–77
  Earlier sketch in CTFT–34
Arney, Randall CTFT–76
  Earlier sketch in CTFT–32
Arngrim, Alison 1962– CTFT–102
Arngrim, Stefan 1955–........................... CTFT–65
Arnold, Bill
  See .... Arnold, William
Arnold, Bonnie CTFT–29
Arnold, Danny 1925–1995 .... CTFT–3
  Obituary in CTFT–15
Arnold, David 1962–............................. CTFT–64
  Earlier sketch in CTFT–28
Arnold, Edward 1890–1956 .... WWasWT
Arnold, Franz 1878–1960...................... WWasWT

  See .... Taylor, James Arnold
Arnold, Jeanne 1931– CTFT–8
Arnold, Phyl ?–1941 .... WWasWT
Arnold, Roseanne
  See .... Roseanne
Arnold, Tichina 1971–........................... CTFT–66
  Earlier sketch in CTFT–17
Arnold, Tom ?–1969 .... WWasWT
Arnold, Tom 1947– CTFT–4
  Earlier sketch in WWT–17
Arnold, Tom 1959– CTFT–71
  Earlier sketches in CTFT–13, 22, 32
Arnold, Victor 1936–............................ CTFT–38
Arnold, William CTFT–64
  Earlier sketch in CTFT–29
Arnott, James Fullarton 1914–1982 .... CTFT–4
  Earlier sketch in WWT–17
Arnott, Mark 1950– CTFT–44
  Earlier sketch in CTFT–5
Arnott, Peter 1936– CTFT–3
Aron, Matthew
  See .... Wofe, Matthew
Aronofsky, Darren 1969–....................... CTFT–59
  Earlier sketch in CTFT–27
Aronson, Boris 1900–1980 .... WWT–17
Aronson, John B. CTFT–95
Aronstein, Martin 1936–........................ CTFT–4
  Earlier sketch in WWT–17
Arquette, Alexis 1969– CTFT–48
  Earlier sketch in CTFT–23
Arquette, Courteney Cox
  See .... Cox, Courteney
Arquette, David 1971– CTFT–49
  Earlier sketch in CTFT–23

Arquette, Lewis 1935–........................... CTFT–28
Arquette, Patricia 1968– CTFT–71
  Earlier sketches in CTFT–13, 22, 32
Arquette, Richmond 1963–..................... CTFT–97
  Earlier sketch in CTFT–46
Arquette, Rosanna 1959– CTFT–57
  Earlier sketches in CTFT–2, 6, 14, 27
Arrabal, Fernando 1932–....................... WWT–17
Arrambide, Mario 1953– CTFT–3
Arrika, Saidah
  See......................... Ekulona, Saidah Arrika
Arrley, Richmond
  See.. Noonan, Tom
Arrowsmith, William 1924– CTFT–1
Arroyave, Karina 1969–......................... CTFT–44
Arroyo, Danny CTFT–70
Arsenio
  See .... Hall, Arsenio
Arterton, Gemma 1986–......................... CTFT–92
Arthur, Bea 1922–2009 .... CTFT–72
  Earlier sketches in CTFT–4, 20, 32; WWT–17
  Obituary in CTFT–97
Arthur, Carol
  See..................................... DeLuise, Carol
Arthur, Daphne 1925–........................... WWasWT
Arthur, Jean 1905(?)–1991 .... CTFT–10
  Earlier sketch in WWasWT
Arthur, Julia 1869–1950........................ WWasWT
Arthur, Karen 1941–............................. CTFT–36
  Earlier sketch in CTFT–10
Arthur, Paul 1859–1928........................ WWasWT
Arthur, Robert ?–1929 .... WWasWT
Arthur, Robert 1909–1986 .... CTFT–4
Arthur, Syd
  See..................................... Kapelos, John
Arthur–Jones, Winifred WWT–6
Arthurs, George 1875–1944 .... WWasWT
Artus, Louis 1870–? .... WWasWT
Arundale, Grace (Kelly) .... WWasWT
Arundale, Sybil 1882–1965 .... WWasWT
Arundell, Dennis 1898–1936 .... WWasWT
Asade, Jim 1936– CTFT–2
Asano, Tadanobu 1973–......................... CTFT–77
  Earlier sketch in CTFT–34
Asara, Mike
  See..................................... Ansara, Michael
Asbury, Kelly 1960– CTFT–86
Ash, Gordon ?–1929 .... WWasWT
Ash, Leslie 1960– CTFT–77
  Earlier sketch in CTFT–34
Ash, Maie 1888–? .... WWasWT
Ash, William 1977–............................... CTFT–77
  Earlier sketch in CTFT–34
Ashanti 1980–...................................... CTFT–67
Ashbrook, Dana 1967– CTFT–72
Ashbrook, Daphne 1966– CTFT–95
  Earlier sketch in CTFT–44
Ashby, Hal 1936–1988........................... CTFT–6
Ashby, Harvey CTFT–22
  Earlier sketch in CTFT–4
Ashby, Linden 1960– CTFT–64
  Earlier sketches in CTFT–19, 29
Ashcroft, Peggy 1907–1991 .... CTFT–4
  Obituary in CTFT–10
  Earlier sketch in WWT–17
Ashe, Eve Brent
  See .... Brent, Eve
Asher, Jane 1946–................................. CTFT–8
  Earlier sketches in CTFT–2; WWT–17
Asher, William 1919–............................ CTFT–9
Asherson, Renee 1920–......................... CTFT–44
  Earlier sketch in WWT–17

Cumulative Index

Dylan, Bob 1941– CTFT–31
  Earlier sketch in CTFT–20
Dynamite, Napoleon
  See .... Costello, Elvis
Dyrenforth, James .... WWasWT
Dysart, Richard A. 1929– CTFT–51
  Earlier sketches in CTFT–4, 24; WWT–17
Dziena, Alexis 1984– CTFT–68
Dzundza, George 1945– CTFT–54
  Earlier sketches in CTFT–6, 16, 26

E

Eadie, Dennis 1869–1928 .... WWasWT
Eads, George 1967– CTFT–80
  Earlier sketch in CTFT–36
Eagan, Daisy 1979– CTFT–93
Eagels, Jeanne 1894–1929 .... WWasWT
Eagles, Greg 1970 .... CTFT–100
  Earlier sketch in CTFT–47
Eaker, Ira 1922– CTFT–1
Eakes, Bobbie 1961– CTFT–62
Eames, Clare 1896–1930 .... WWasWT
Earle, Virginia 1875–1937 .... WWasWT
Earles, Jason 1977– CTFT–82
Eason, Mules 1915–1977 .... WWT–16
Easterbrook, Leslie CTFT–7
Eastin, Steve CTFT–100
  Earlier sketch in CTFT–47
Eastman, Allan CTFT–36
Eastman, Frederick 1859–1920 ...... WWasWT
Eastman, Rodney 1967– CTFT–80
Easton, Michael 1967– CTFT–58
Easton, Richard 1933– CTFT–87
  Earlier sketches in CTFT–5, 39; WWT–17
Easton, Robert 1930– CTFT–63
Easton, Sheena 1959– CTFT–76
  Earlier sketches in CTFT–21, 32
Eastwood, Alison 1972– CTFT–96
  Earlier sketch in CTFT–46
Eastwood, Clint 1930– CTFT–95
  Earlier sketches in CTFT–1, 6, 13, 23, 45
Eastwood, Jayne CTFT–62
Eastwood, Kyle 1968– CTFT–96
Eastwood, Scott 1986– CTFT–96
Eaton, Mary 1902–1948 .... WWasWT
Eaton, Wallas 1917– WWT–17
Eaton, Walter Prichard 1878–1957 .... WWasWT
Eaves, Hilary 1914– .... WWasWT
Eaves, Obadiah CTFT–99
Ebb, Fred 1936(?)– CTFT–39
  Earlier sketches in CTFT–5, 13; WWT–17
Ebersol, Dick CTFT–14
Ebersole, Christine 1953– CTFT–83
  Earlier sketches in CTFT–2, 5, 14, 38
Ebert, Joyce 1933–1997 .... CTFT–5
  Obituary in CTFT–18
  Earlier sketch in WWT–17
Ebert, Roger 1942– CTFT–81
  Earlier sketches in CTFT–9, 35
Ebrel, Luke
  See .... Elliott, Lucas
Ebsen, Buddy 1908–2003 .... CTFT–3
  Obituary in CTFT–51
Eccles, Donald 1908–1986 .... WWT–17
Eccles, Janet 1895–1966 .... WWasWT
Eccleston, Christopher 1964– CTFT–67
  Earlier sketch in CTFT–30
Echegaray, Miguel 1848–1927 .... WWasWT

Echevarria, Rene CTFT–103
  Earlier sketch in CTFT–49
Echevarria, Rocky
  See .... Bauer, Steven
Echikunwoke, Megalyn 1983– CTFT–70
Eck, Scott 1957– CTFT–6
Eckart, Jean 1921– CTFT–3
  Earlier sketch in WWT–17
Eckart, William J. 1920– CTFT–4
  Earlier sketch in WWT–17
Eckhart, Aaaron 1968(?)– CTFT–66
  Earlier sketch in CTFT–30
Eckholdt, Steven 1961– CTFT–83
  Earlier sketch in CTFT–38
Eckhouse, James 1955– CTFT–59
  Earlier sketch in CTFT–27
Eckland, Michael
  See .... Eklund, Michael
Eckstein, Ashley 1981– CTFT–91
Eckstein, George 1928–2009 .... CTFT–2
  Obituary in CTFT–104
Eda-Young, Barbara 1945– CTFT–5
  Earlier sketch in WWT–17
Eddinger, Wallace 1881–1929 .... WWasWT
Eddington, Paul 1927–1995 .... CTFT–14
  Obituary in CTFT–15
  Earlier sketches in CTFT–6; WWT–17
Eddison, Robert 1908– WWT–17
Eddy, Nelson 1901–1967 .... WWasWT
Eddy, Teddy Jack
  See .... Busey, Gary
Ede, George 1931– CTFT–1
Edel, Uli 1947– CTFT–61
Edelman, Gregg 1958– CTFT–89
  Earlier sketches in CTFT–9, 41
Edelman, Herbert 1933–1996 .... CTFT–6
  Obituary in CTFT–16
  Earlier sketch in CTFT–1
Edelman, Randy 1947(?)– CTFT–70
  Earlier sketches in CTFT–12, 21, 31
Edelson, Kenneth CTFT–70
  Earlier sketch in CTFT–31
Edelstein, Gordon CTFT–94
Edelstein, Lisa 1967– CTFT–60
  Earlier sketches in CTFT–17, 28
Eden, Barbara 1934– CTFT–84
  Earlier sketches in CTFT–3, 9, 36
Eden, Diana CTFT–62
Eden, Richard 1956– CTFT–42
Eden, Sidney 1936– CTFT–2
Eder, Linda 1961– CTFT–81
  Earlier sketch in CTFT–37
Edeson, Arthur 1891–1970 .... CTFT–26
Edeson, Robert 1868–1931 .... WWasWT
Edgar, David 1948– CTFT–6
  Earlier sketch in WWT–17
Edgar, Marriott 1880–1951 .... WWasWT
Edgar-Bruce, Tonie
  See .... Bruce, Tonie Edgar
Edgerton, Joel 1974– CTFT–103
  Earlier sketch in CTFT–49
Edgett, Edwin Francis 1867–1946 .... WWasWT
Edgeworth, Jane 1922– WWT–17
Edginton, May ?–1957 .... WWasWT
Edgley, Gigi 1977– CTFT–86
Edgley, Michael 1943– CTFT–5
  Earlier sketch in WWT–17
Edison, Matthew 1975– CTFT–104
Ediss, Connie 1871–1934 .... WWasWT
Edlin, Tubby (Henry) 1882–? .... WWasWT
Edlund, Richard 1940– CTFT–89
  Earlier sketches in CTFT–9, 41
Edmead, Wendy CTFT–1

Edmiston, Walker 1925–2007– CTFT–53
  Obituary in CTFT–101
Edmondson, Adrian 1957– CTFT–59
  Earlier sketch in CTFT–27
Edmondson, Wallace
  See .... Ellison, Harlan
Edner, Ashley 1990– CTFT–67
  Earlier sketch in CTFT–30
Edner, Bobby 1988– CTFT–59
Edney, Florence 1879–1950 .... WWasWT
Edouin, Rose 1844–1925 .... WWasWT
Edson, Richard 1954– CTFT–67
  Earlier sketch in CTFT–30
Edwardes, Felix ?–1954 .... WWasWT
Edwardes, George 1852–1915 .... WWasWT
Edwardes, Olga 1917– .... WWasWT
Edwardes, Paula .... WWasWT
Edwards, Anthony 1962– CTFT–100
  Earlier sketches in CTFT–6, 14, 23, 47
Edwards, Ben 1916– CTFT–9
  Earlier sketch in WWT–17
Edwards, Blake 1922– CTFT–49
  Earlier sketches in CTFT–1, 6, 15
Edwards, Burt 1928– CTFT–2
Edwards, Edward CTFT–58
Edwards, Eric Alan 1953– CTFT–54
  Earlier sketches in CTFT–15, 26
Edwards, G. Spencer ?–1916 .... WWasWT
Edwards, Henry 1883–1952 .... WWasWT
Edwards, Hilton 1903– WWT–17
Edwards, Julie
  See .... Andrews, Julie
Edwards, Maurice 1922– CTFT–1
Edwards, Monique CTFT–59
Edwards, Osman 1864–1936 .... WWasWT
Edwards, Ralph CTFT–3
Edwards, Rob 1963– CTFT–11
Edwards, Sherman 1919–1981 .... WWT–17
Edwards, Stacy 1965– CTFT–70
  Earlier sketches in CTFT–20, 31
Edwards, Stephen CTFT–58
Edwards, Tom 1880–? .... WWasWT
Edwards, Vince 1928–1996 .... CTFT–7
  Obituary in CTFT–16
Efremova, Svetlana CTFT–87
Efron, Zac 1987– CTFT–74
Egan, Christopher 1984– CTFT–86
Egan, Kim CTFT–48
Egan, Maggie CTFT–53
Egan, Melissa Claire 1981– CTFT–96
Egan, Michael 1895–1956 .... WWasWT
Egan, Michael 1926– CTFT–19
  Earlier sketch in CTFT–2
Egan, Peter 1946– CTFT–73
  Earlier sketches in CTFT–5, 33; WWT–17
Egan, Sam CTFT–97
Egan, Susan 1970– CTFT–72
  Earlier sketches in CTFT–20, 32
Egbert, Brothers (Seth and Albert) .... WWasWT
Egerton, George 1860–1945 .... WWasWT
Eggar, Jack 1904– .... WWasWT
Eggar, Samantha 1939– CTFT–73
  Earlier sketches in CTFT–1, 8, 33
Eggby, David 1950– CTFT–55
Eggert, Nicole 1972– CTFT–101
  Earlier sketches in CTFT–4, 14, 23, 47
Eggerth, Marta 1916– CTFT–1
  Earlier sketch in WWasWT
Egglesfield, Colin 1973– CTFT–100
Eggold, Ryan 1984– CTFT–96
Eggolf, Gretchen 1973– CTFT–96
Egoyan, Atom 1960– CTFT–103
  Earlier sketches in CTFT–15, 24, 48

F

G

Cumulative Index

H

M

Cumulative Index

Q

R

T